21st Century

MONEY, BANKING & COMMERCE

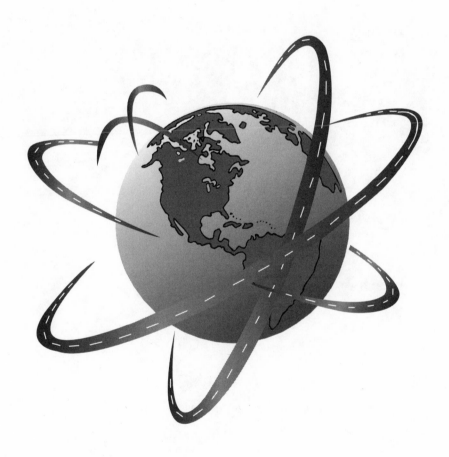

Thomas P. Vartanian

Robert H. Ledig

Lynn Bruneau

10   9   8   7   6   5   4   3   2   1

ONLINE UPDATES ON NEW DEVELOPMENTS

AN INVITATION TO OUR READERS

Timely analysis of current developments affecting electronic banking and commerce is available to keep you up to date. E-BankFutures™, a password protected web page service is available by subscription from Fried, Frank, Harris, Shriver & Jacobson. For information on obtaining a subscription, call 1-800-559-1187 or visit the 21st Century Money, Banking & Commerce website at www.ffhsj.com/21stbook.

Our goal is to make 21st Century Money, Banking & Commerce as useful and informative as possible. We welcome your comments and suggestions. You can reach Tom and Bob at Fried, Frank, Harris, Shriver & Jacobson by e-mail to 21stbook@ffhsj.com, or by phone at (202) 639-7016. Lynn can be reached at Arthur Andersen LLP by phone at (212) 708-5478.

NOTICE

This book provides only a general overview of electronic banking and commerce. The issues faced by banks and other electronic banking and commerce participants are necessarily specific to the circumstances of each particular party. This book is not intended to, nor does it purport to, provide legal or consulting advice. Such advice can only be provided by counsel or consultants that are familiar with a party's specific situation.

Fried, Frank, Harris, Shriver & Jacobson and Arthur Andersen, LLP represent clients in electronic banking and commerce matters, including matters discussed in this book.

DEDICATIONS

To my wife Karen, my daughters Alana and Mackenzie, and my mom Terry, who inspire me with their love and support, and to Paul Vartanian, Richard Pratt, Harvey Pitt, Dan Schechter, and the late Fr. Gerry Minogue for the wisdom that they have so generously shared with me.

Thomas P. Vartanian
McLean, Virginia
February 1998

To Kathy, Amy, Jenny and Meg: It's a great big beautiful tomorrow shining at the end of every day.

The Carousel of Progress
The New York World's Fair
1964-1965

To my parents, thanks for taking me there and so much more.

In remembrance of Tom O'Toole and Kit Bolle, whose understanding of banking and whose character lives on as an inspiration.

Robert H. Ledig
Oakton, Virginia
February 1998

CONTRIBUTORS

James P. Baetzhold	Joel Lanz
Nick Benvenuto	Charles W. Lockyer, Jr.
Dan Carson	Eugene E. Mueller
Beth H. Colleye	Richard E. Salisbury
Alison C. Conover	Peter H. Schwartz
Paul H. Falon	Jeffrey D. Sullivan
Robert M. Fisher	Jennifer Tipsord
Kevin Foley	Leila A. Tredemeyer
Harry M. Gruber	Maxim H. Waldbaum
Anthony S. Higgins	Peter Wayner
Jay R. Kraemer	Edward B. Whittemore

*Author And Contributor Biographies Are Included At Page 647.

ACKNOWLEDGEMENTS

Special thanks to the following individuals, who provided the assistance that made this book possible: Diane Rose, Caryl Wheeler, Debbie Rizzo, Lydia Fraser, Kimberly Denton, Hugh Jaramillo, Scott Wiesenberger, Su Kim, C. Todd Conover, Brian Kinnear, Jim McCarthy, Ed Neumann, Todd Eyler, Chris Williamson, Samantha Secrest, Kristin Allen, Coral Ramos, Lisa Henry, Richard Spencer, Holly Mueller, Jack Griem, Lawrence Scott, Scott Bevier, Joshua K. Carter, Scott M. Donaldson, Grace A. Garcia, Helena C. Lau, Robert L. Mecca, Kathleen H. Mitterway, Brendan Molloy, Michael K. Nam, Jody L. Panoff, Sergey V. Perfiliev, Teresa L. Salvato, David M. Skinner, Serena Yam, Andrew Skowronek, Scott Lang, Bill Nelson, Elliott McEntee, Deb Evans-Doyle, Mike DuBois, Kawika Daguio, Tim Jones, Bob Lehmann, Ian Macoy and Jane Larimer.

TABLE OF CONTENTS

PART I

CHAPTER 3   MONEY AS INFORMATION

PART II

CHAPTER 5 INTERAGENCY ACTIONS ADDRESSING ELECTRONIC FINANCIAL PRODUCTS AND SERVICES

CHAPTER 6 OFFICE OF THE COMPTROLLER OF THE CURRENCY'S PERSPECTIVE ON ELECTRONIC FINANCIAL PRODUCTS AND SERVICES

CHAPTER 7   FEDERAL RESERVE BOARD'S PERSPECTIVE ON ELECTRONIC FINANCIAL PRODUCTS AND SERVICES

CHAPTER 8 FEDERAL DEPOSIT INSURANCE CORPORATION'S PERSPECTIVE ON ELECTRONIC FINANCIAL PRODUCTS AND SERVICES

CHAPTER 9 THE OFFICE OF THRIFT SUPERVISION'S PERSPECTIVE ON ELECTRONIC FINANCIAL PRODUCTS AND SERVICES

CHAPTER 10 OTHER GOVERNMENTAL AND NONGOVERNMENTAL ENTITIES INFLUENCING ELECTRONIC FINANCIAL PRODUCTS AND SERVICES

PART III

CHAPTER 13 SECURITY

PART IV

CHAPTER 14   REMOTE BANKING AND FINANCIAL SERVICES

CHAPTER 15 INTERNET VALUE TRANSFER SYSTEMS

CHAPTER 16   A NEW PAYMENT SYSTEM: STORED VALUE/ELECTRONIC MONEY

CHAPTER 17   ELECTRONIC BENEFITS TRANSFER

PART V

CHAPTER 18 INTELLECTUAL PROPERTY CONSIDERATIONS

§ 18.02 Copyrights 566

   [1] The Scope of Copyright Protection 566

   [2] Obtaining Copyright 567

   [3] Protecting a Bank's Copyright Rights 568

   [4] Avoiding Copyright Infringement 569

§ 18.03 Trademarks 570

   [1] Trademark Regulation in Cyberspace 570

      [a] Domestic Federal Trademark Law 571

      [b] Federal Trademark Dilution Act 572

      [c] State Trademark Law 573

   [2] Domain Names 573

   [3] Maintaining and Strengthening Rights Through Online Trademark Use 574

   [4] Avoiding Lanham Act Liability 575

§ 18.04 Patents 576

   [1] Patentable Subject Matter 576

      [a] Generally 576

         [i]   Novelty 577

         [ii]   Utility 577

         [iii] Non-obviousness 577

      [b] Special Problems 577

         [i] Statutory Subject Matter and Computer Inventions 577

   [2] Value of Patents in Electronic Banking 578

      [a] A Patent is a Valuable Property 578

      [b] Trends in Patenting of Electronic Banking Technology 579

   [3] Acquiring and Preserving Patent Rights 582

      [a] Patent Applications and Corporate Invention Disclosure Programs 582

      [b] Role of the Patent Attorney 582

         [i] Role of the Inventor and the Financial Institution 583

      [c] The Statutory Bars 584

      [d] Cost and Timing 585

      [e] Maintaining Patent Rights 586

      [f] Enforcement 587

CHAPTER 19 THE CONFLUENCE OF INTERNATIONAL, FEDERAL, AND STATE JURISDICTION OVER INTERNET COMMERCE

APPENDICES

APPENDICES

PART I

"Cause we know where we're going, but we don't know where we been."

Road to Nowhere
—The Talking Heads

The greatest threat to understanding the present and to predicting the future is ignoring the past. The origins of modern electronic banking and commerce lie in a range of venerable financial institutions, banking products, and mediums of exchange. An understanding of how they developed can offer important insights into today's electronic banking and commerce pioneers. For example, many fields of enterprise have passed through periods of quiescence and of great upheaval. Understanding why, during those latter periods of change, certain companies and products faltered while others succeeded, can provide insights for prospering in today's marketplace. In addition, early technological innovations ultimately spawned valuable and, in retrospect, astounding offspring. The ability to predict that one day the descendants of party line telephones would carry digital images across the globe in fractions of a second and that the financial obligations represented by seashells would evolve into pulses of electricity was beyond the comprehension of any ancestral users of these early products.

Part I provides a foundation for our journey into electronic banking and commerce. Chapter 1 sets the stage with a discussion of the impact of technology on the provision of financial services. Chapter 2 traces the evolution of banking in the United States. Chapter 3 briefly reviews the history of money and extracts a number of truths about this fundamental medium of exchange. Chapter 4 recounts the story of the development of credit cards and debit cards, automated clearing houses, and automated teller machines.

Unlike the Talking Heads, most individuals and companies do not claim to see what lies ahead. Whether electronic commerce will be an express lane on the "information superhighway" or an electronic road to nowhere, only time will tell. But the road begins here.

CHAPTER 1

A REVOLUTIONARY ERA FOR THE BANKING INDUSTRY

§ 1.01   INTRODUCTION

Electronic technology is likely to have a dramatic affect on banking, finance, and commerce. Opinions vary as to whether the banking industry will be able to take advantage of new significant opportunities resulting from these developments, or whether it will have to struggle to maintain its current principal role in the economy. One prominent commentator in this regard is Bill Gates, CEO of Microsoft, the master of the new technologies that banks will be challenged to employ in the coming years. In 1994, Gates pronounced that banks were dinosaurs, at the risk of obsolescence.[1] Some in the banking industry were offended by this perceived impertinence. Some took Gates' comments as a warning that software and technology developers should now be considered competitors rather than partners. Others viewed his comments as a timely wake up call, challenging the banking industry to either take the lead in shaping and developing the technology that will be used

---

[1]   *See* Michael Meyer, *Culture Club*, NEWSWEEK, July 11, 1994, at 38 ("Banks are dinosaurs, says Gates. We can 'bypass' them.").

Bill Gates has since retreated from this competitive stance. In 1995, during an address at the Bank Administration Institute's annual conference, Mr. Gates amended his 'dinosaur' comment, stating "[w]hat I really said was that many banking systems are dinosaurs." Also during that address, Mr. Gates claimed that Microsoft is not in competition with banks. *See* Sterett Pope, *Gates Talks to the Dinosaurs*, RETAIL BANKER INT'L, Dec. 15, 1995, at 4; Karyn Spellman, *Gates Jokes with Bankers Over 'Dinosaur' Remark*, ASSOCIATED PRESS, Dec. 5, 1995.

Recently, Mr. Gates and Microsoft have attempted to create partnerships with banks. Microsoft entered into a joint venture with First Data Corporation, known as MSFDC, to supply a system for electronic bill payment to banks. So far, KeyCorp and Wells Fargo have signed onto the new system. *See* Joseph A. Giannone, *KeyCorp Exec: Fears of Microsoft 'Overhyped,'* SEATTLE TIMES, Dec. 4, 1997, at D3; Theodore Iacobuzio, *Marriage Made in Cyberspace*, ELEC. PAYMENTS INT'L, July 1, 1997, at 9.

Many bankers, however, continue to harbor suspicions about Microsoft's intentions. *See* Jeffrey Kutler, *Bankers Can Find Comfort in Microsoft's Woes*, AM. BANKER, Dec. 30, 1997, at 1.

Mr. Gates wrote an article for the New York Times in July 1997, in which he discussed the effect of the Internet on, among other things, retail banking. In that column, he stated:

These changes won't come at the expense of the banking industry. On the contrary, the future is bright . . . for institutions that evolve . . . . Technology will let banks get closer to customers, deliver a wider range of services at lower costs and streamline internal systems so that all customer data is integrated and can be used to spot trends that can lead to new products. A variety of companies, including mine, want to help banks make the transition. The Web will offer banks great opportunities . . . . It will be interesting to see which banks step up to this opportunity.

Bill Gates, *No one is Really Living a Web Lifestyle — Yet*, N.Y. TIMES, July 29, 1997, *available at* (visited Dec. 29, 1997) <http://www.htimes.com/today/access/columns/0729bill.html>.

to deliver financial services and electronic commerce in the 21st Century, or be relegated to serving as a passive conduit for information traveling through technology developed and designed by others, which might not even utilize historic banking industry channels.

As banks begin a full-fledged move to utilize the new opportunities presented by emerging technologies, they do so in the context of a number of important factors that affect the competitive position of banks as financial service providers.

§ 1.02   COMPETITION BETWEEN BANKS AND NONBANKS

Banks and savings associations were the dominant providers of financial services to both individuals and businesses until the late 1970s, when the combination of unprecedented double-digit inflation and interest rates, product innovations of non-depository institution competitors, and deregulatory government policies began to loosen the grip that banks had on the financial services sector. During the past two decades, these factors have led to a dramatic shift in the relative market positions of depository institutions and non-depository institutions across a wide range of financial services.[2]

Probably the most significant single factor leading to the aforementioned shift was the movement of funds from bank deposits to non-insured money market mutual funds during the late 1970s and early 1980s.[3] Money market mutual funds gained popularity during that time because of superior returns and the perception of a low level of risk. Many individuals began choosing to place their savings in these funds instead of traditional savings accounts at insured depository institutions. The trend toward investment in assets other than bank accounts ultimately went far beyond money market mutual funds, and eventually extended to mutual funds investing in a wide range of equity and debt instruments, as well as to direct investments in such instruments. Between 1980 and 1995, the portion of consumer assets entrusted to banks dropped from 34% to 17%.[4] Banks,

---

[2]   For an excellent discussion of how the options for obtaining financial services, particularly for consumers, have changed and expanded over the past three decades, see JOSEPH NOCERA, A PIECE OF THE ACTION: HOW THE MIDDLE CLASS JOINED THE MONEY CLASS (1994). For a discussion of the evolution of Citibank, a leading institution in terms of serving businesses and consumers, as well as in developing technology for banking and financial services applications, see PHILLIP L. ZWEIG, WRISTON (1995).

 In recent years banks have increasingly argued that because of their heavily regulated status they are often placed at a competitive disadvantage with non-depository entities. For example, banks have cited the obligations imposed on them under the Community Reinvestment Act that do not apply to non-depository entities that directly compete with banks, such as money market mutual funds. *Community Reinvestment Act: Hearings Before the Subcomm. on Financial Institutions and Consumer Credit of the House Comm. on Banking and Financial Services*, 104th Cong. 62 (1995) (statement of James M. Culberson, Jr., American Bankers Association). Banks have also argued that the prohibition on paying interest on demand accounts held by most commercial organizations places them at a significant disadvantage in attracting and retaining such customers as compared to competitors who are not subject to such limitations on the transaction capable instruments that they offer. *See ABA May Ask Congress to Expand MMDAs*, BANKING POL'Y REP., Aug. 4, 1997, at 4; Jaret Seiberg, *Fed Rebuffs ABA on NOW Accounts for Business*, AM. BANKER, July 17, 1997, at 11. Some members of Congress are beginning to agree. In 1997 bills were introduced in the Senate and House that would do away with the prohibition on interest-bearing commercial demand accounts. *See* S. 1249, 105th Cong. (1997); H.R. 2323, 105th Cong. (1997).

[3]   Money market mutual funds experienced a significant growth in both asset size and in the number of shareholders. The asset size of money market funds increased to approximately $50 billion in 1980, an increase of almost five times the asset size in 1978. *See Hearing Before the Subcomm. on Financial Institutions of the House Comm. on Banking, Housing, and Urban Affairs*, 96th Cong. (1980) (statement of J. Charles Partee, Member, Board of Governors of the Federal Reserve System). *See also Competition and Conditions in the Financial System: Hearing Before the Senate Comm. on Banking, Housing, and Urban Affairs*, 97th Cong. (1981).

[4]   *See* Terence P. Pare, *Clueless Bankers*, FORTUNE, Nov. 27, 1995, at 150.

recognizing this shift in investment preference, responded by mounting aggressive efforts to market mutual funds and other securities products to their customers.

Banks also began to face intense competition from nonbank entities for all facets of the consumer lending business. In particular, developments in the mortgage industry opened the way for nonbank entities to become major originators and holders of mortgage loans. Furthermore, nonbank entities gained substantial market shares in areas such as credit cards, consumer loans, and vehicle financing. Banks also saw their dominance in commercial lending eroded, particularly by the increasing role played by investment banking firms in making various types of equity or debt financing available to companies.

Banks have lost much of the advantage they once enjoyed in regard to obtaining and retaining the financial services business of both individuals and businesses. Changes in transaction costs represent one of the major factors influencing this loss. Transaction costs, especially search costs, have traditionally attracted customers to use one financial institution, typically a depository institution, for multiple financial products and services, thereby allowing banks to cross-subsidize these activities in an attempt to maximize overall profits. The Internet and other non-geographically limited marketing and distribution methods have the potential to significantly reduce the search costs for an individual or business interested in comparing the costs or returns associated with a single activity, such as obtaining a loan or establishing an investment relationship, offered by a variety of financial institutions. To capture these benefits, individuals and businesses will be tempted to unbundle their relationships with a particular institution and seek out the most cost effective provider of each portion of their investment and loan relationships.

The principal exception to this significant erosion of bank dominance in the provision of financial services products is in the payments system arena. If electronic banking and commerce develop in a way that ultimately erodes the banking industry's dominance in this arena, it could pose the most fundamental threat to the future of the banking industry.

The introduction of new electronic banking and commerce technology presents the threat that banks will face new forms of competition from nonbanks. Payments systems are one example of competition flowing from new technology. Although there are exceptions, such as traveler's checks and money orders, to an overwhelming degree, the movement of funds through the economy and the payments system is dominated by banks and other depository institutions. Some new electronic banking and commerce applications, such as stored value cards and electronic money, create the potential for nonbanks to gain entry to the payments system in ways not previously envisioned, either by current payment systems participants or by existing laws and regulations. For example, nonbank entities, such as transit systems and universities, are already serving as stored value issuers.

In a report issued in September 1996, the Payments System Task Force of the American Bankers Association considered the potential for new technological advances to translate into major changes in the existing payments system.[5] The report stressed the benefits to the nation of a stable, well-functioning payments

---

5   PAYMENTS SYSTEM TASK FORCE, AM. BANKERS ASS'N, THE ROLE OF BANKS IN THE PAYMENTS SYSTEM OF THE FUTURE (1996).

system. It generally recommended, among other things, that only regulated depository institutions have direct access to the Federal Reserve System's payments services and have authority to issue third-party payment instruments.[6]

Notwithstanding the report's recommendations, some nonbanks are likely to view the introduction of electronic banking and commerce as an opportunity to break into an emerging new market that should not automatically be off-limits to nonbanks. The questions regarding the types of entities that should be permitted to issue stored value instruments and the requirements that should be imposed on various types of issuers will be debated at both the federal and state level.[7]

§ 1.03   COMPETITION AMONG BANKS

At the same time that banks are facing intense competition from nonbank entities, the nature of their competition with other banks is changing substantially. Changes in laws and developments in technology are making it far more likely that a particular bank will be competing with a wide range of banks and other depository institutions without the geographic restrictions that formerly limited competition.

[1]   GEOGRAPHIC WALLS COME DOWN

Historically, the conduct of the business of banking has been subject to substantial geographic barriers. A combination of factors have limited the formation of banking organizations that operate across a wide geographic area, primarily by virtue of federal and state policies regarding interstate branching and interstate expansion by bank holding companies.

As a general matter, state law historically did not provide for the operation of interstate branches by state banks. Federal law, in turn, generally tied the branching authority of national banks to the authority available to state banks.[8] As a result, geographic expansion was generally accomplished through the use of bank holding companies that could acquire banks in other states. Even this vehicle was of limited utility because federal law required express state authorization for an out-of-state bank holding company to acquire a bank located in that state.[9] Using their authority under this provision, many states acted to limit acquisitions to out-of-state bank holding companies located within certain regions.[10]

---

[6]   *Id.* at iii, 17-21.

[7]   *See* Thomas P. Vartanian & Robert H. Ledig, *The Business of Banking in the Age of the Internet: Fortress or Prison,* BANKING POL'Y REP., Mar. 4-18, 1996, at 6.

[8]   12 U.S.C. § 36.

[9]   12 U.S.C. § 1842(d) (1988), *amended by* the Riegle-Neal Interstate Banking and Branching Efficiency Act of 1994, *infra* note 11.

[10]   For example, Massachusetts and Connecticut statutes only permitted acquisition of in-state banks by bank holding companies that were located in New England. *See Northeast Bancorp v. Board of Governors of the Fed. Reserve Sys.,* 472 U.S. 159, 165 (1985); Mark D. Rollinger, *Interstate Banking and Branching Under the Riegle-Neal Act of 1994,* 33 HARV. J. ON LEGIS. 183, 194 (1996).

The Riegle-Neal Interstate Banking and Branching Efficiency Act of 1994 resulted in the virtual elimination of the barriers to interstate expansion by banks and bank holding companies.[11] As of September 29, 1995, bank holding companies may acquire banks in any state.[12] Moreover, effective July 1, 1997, banks may engage in interstate mergers, unless a state has elected to prohibit such transactions.[13] National banks may also establish *de novo* branches in any state that has elected to allow interstate *de novo* branching by out-of-state banks.[14]

As a result of these changes, the ability of bank holding companies to expand their operations on a geographic basis through holding company acquisitions of banks, *de novo* bank formations, through mergers, or *de novo* branching, has been greatly expanded. These changes enable banks to pursue business strategies based on their natural strengths, rather than on the vagaries of geography and state legislative preferences. By expanding the pool of potential acquirers, the broad elimination of long-standing geographic barriers is spurring an industry trend towards consolidation. These changes also hold the possibility that the United States will ultimately join other major industrialized countries that have a banking system characterized by a smaller number of large nationwide banking franchises.

[2]   BANKING INDUSTRY CONSOLIDATION

Many industry analysts have argued that there are too many banks in the United States and, in any event, have predicted that a combination of business and regulatory features will lead to a major consolidation in the industry. As discussed above, to a significant extent, the large number of institutions in the United States can be attributed to the substantial historic geographic barriers to bank expansion. During the last several years, there has been a pronounced trend toward consolidation particularly among the largest institutions in the country. Among the major transactions announced or completed since January 1995 are the following:

ACQUIRING INSTITUTION (asset size)	SELLING INSTITUTION (asset size)
Chemical Banking $178 billion	Chase Manhattan $118 billion
Wells Fargo $50 billion	First Interstate $58 billion
First Union Corp. $86 billion	First Fidelity Bancorp $35 billion
NationsBank Corp. $240 billion	Barnett Banks, Inc. $44 billion

---

[11]   Riegle-Neal Interstate Banking and Branching Efficiency Act of 1994, Pub. L. No. 103-328, 1994 U.S.C.C.A.N. (108 Stat.) 2338 (codified in scattered sections of 12 U.S.C.).

[12]   *Id.* § 101 (codified at 12 U.S.C. § 1842(d)).

[13]   *Id.* § 102(a) (codified at 12 U.S.C. § 1831u(a)(2)). Only Texas and Montana elected to exercise the opt-out option.

[14]   *Id.* § 103(a) (codified at 12 U.S.C. § 36(g)).

As a result of these and similar transactions, as indicated by the following chart, the asset size of the largest 100 banking organizations has been steadily increasing during the course of this decade.

ASSET CUTOFF SIZE FOR THE
100 LARGEST BANKING ORGANIZATIONS[15]

Year	Assets
1995	$7.1 billion
1993	$5.8 billion
1990	$5.5 billion

A standard analysis would suggest that the combination of acquisition hunger on the part of large banks and the costs and personnel resources associated with developing and implementing new technologies will increasingly make small- and medium-sized banks an endangered species.

[3] THE IMPLICATIONS OF TECHNOLOGY FOR COMPETITION WITHIN THE BANKING INDUSTRY

[a] **Impact of Size on Technological Innovation.** One emerging debate in the banking industry is whether technology will favor large-, medium-, or small-sized banks, or whether it will have a relatively size neutral impact. One view is that large institutions will have a great advantage. Some large institutions, such as a Citicorp, have traditionally been leaders in the development of financial services technology and are currently focusing a great deal of effort on developing new electronic banking and commerce technology. Three large Southeastern banking organizations pioneered the first major United States stored value card trial at the Atlanta Olympics in the summer of 1996.[16] Large institutions are likely to have greater financial and managerial resources available to evaluate and implement new technologies. Moreover, they are more likely to be able to absorb the impact when resources are invested in products and services that do not prove to be successful. Large institutions can also be expected to have significant advantages in bargaining power in dealing with software vendors and other third party technology providers, both in terms of designing system specifications and in negotiating licensing terms.

Small institutions are likely to have fewer resources, both in terms of managerial and technical expertise and capital, to devote to electronic banking and commerce applications. Individually they may have difficulty attracting the attention and interest of software vendors and other technology providers. They may also find themselves in relatively weak negotiating positions with such parties. In order to overcome these

---

[15] AM. BANKER, RANKING THE BANKS 10 (1996); AM. BANKER, RANKING THE BANKS 10 (1994); AM. BANKER, RANKING THE BANKS 20 (1991).

[16] NationsBank, Wachovia Bank, and First Union Bank offered Visa Cash cards, the stored value product that was accepted at the Atlanta Summer Olympic Games.

disadvantages, small institutions may decide to act collectively to sponsor their own joint technology development initiatives and to enhance their negotiating power with third party technology providers.

On the other hand, smaller banks may have some advantages over larger institutions in deploying new technology. They may have fewer existing systems and more streamlined operations that could make the process of selecting and developing new systems easier. In some instances, technology may, in fact, work better on a smaller scale (*e.g.*, check imaging).

[b] A New Model: the "Internet Bank." Those arguing that technology will have a relatively size neutral impact contend that focusing on asset size misses the true implications of interactive financial technology. The question they pose is whether new technology offers the opportunity to design a new type of bank, an Internet bank, that, regardless of size, could attain the level of success of current brick and mortar banks. Utilizing the Internet as its advertising vehicle and as its principal method of serving customers, an Internet bank is fundamentally different from the *de novo* model that starts with a main office and seeks customers from its local community. In the new model, size and geography may become incidental rather than critical. Marketing efforts will be nationwide in scope, perhaps targeting special niche markets that the bank intends to serve. Such an institution would avoid the substantial costs associated with establishing and growing a branch network.

Banks have traditionally relied on customer confidence and trust in their reputation and local presence to attract business. In the electronic environment, however, a geographically remote bank can operate a website that is as impressive and as user-friendly as a site maintained by a local bank. Banks' use of the Internet may, therefore, result in a dramatic change in the manner in which financial institutions compete for customers, with traditional methods becoming less significant.

Several start up institutions have embarked upon an Internet bank strategy. Most prominent among these is Security First Network Bank, fsb ("SFNB"). This institution, which began serving customers on the World Wide Web on October 18, 1995, includes a description in its website of the positive features of the small town in Kentucky where it is "located," for it acknowledges that few, if any, of its customers are likely to ever visit the bank in person.[17]

Some of the questions that will be faced by new bank organizers, or existing small banks that are considering this strategy, will include the following:

- Will customers be willing to establish a full service relationship with a bank that does not have an office within driving distance?

---

[17] Security First Network Bank, fsb ("SFNB"), a federal savings bank wholly-owned by Cardinal Bancshares, Inc., ("Cardinal") a Lexington, Kentucky based bank holding company, is often cited as the first Internet-only banking institution. *See* Kelley Holland & Amy Cortese, *The Future of Money*, BUS. WEEK, June 12, 1995, at 74. Since the opening of the bank in 1995, Cardinal has expanded its activities to providing software and data processing services to other banking institutions through its Five Paces Software, Inc. subsidiary. *See Cardinal Bancshares, Inc.*, 82 Fed. Reserve Bull. 674 (July 1996) (FRB order approving Cardinal's application to permit SFNB to acquire Five Paces' software business). Cardinal recently announced its plans to sell SFNB. *See* Tim Clark, *First Online Bank's Final Withdrawal*, NEWS.COM, Nov. 6, 1997, *available at* <http://www.news.com>.

- Can an Internet-based bank be successful if it only attracts customers for specific individual products or services rather than a full service relationship?

- Will such an institution lose customers to locally-based institutions as they begin to offer the same types of online services as the Internet-based bank?

- What is the likely demographic profile of the individuals and businesses that will become customers of the bank?

- How will the cost and revenue structures of a start up Internet-based bank compare with those of a locally-oriented small institution, a medium size institution, or a large institution?

At this point it is not clear whether a *de novo* Internet bank strategy will prove a viable means of operating. Pioneer institutions will be closely watched by other banks and industry analysts. Their impact could far outweigh their size. If, for example, a large institution concludes that it can reach the customers that it wants to serve in neighboring states, or more distant regions of the United States, it may be able to do so using electronic financial technology for a fraction of the cost associated with the interstate acquisition of an existing institution. Moreover, organizations that once were inclined toward a nationwide strategy of operating banks or branches throughout the United States must reconsider the relative costs and benefits associated with such an approach. The possibility of a viable online banking strategy not dependent on in-person contact with the bank accentuates the importance of critically analyzing the viability of a branch-based strategy.

Another significant aspect of emerging interactive financial services is the potential to accelerate the commoditization of financial services products. By giving individuals and businesses the ability to conveniently access and compare information on the product offerings of a wide range of institutions (either by visiting individual websites or by visiting sites that compile offerings from multiple institutions), the focus naturally moves to a decision based on rate and terms rather than on existing relationships.

If potential borrowers routinely begin to shop for loans on the Internet rather than going to the bank where they maintain their deposits, banks lose much of the value associated with their customer relationships; value that was previously taken for granted. As financial services providers are increasingly selected based on the competition between websites, or by comparison of rates offered by local institutions and Internet banks, factors such as market recognition or reputational advantage may become less significant. A growing recognition of the potential benefits of using the World Wide Web to search for and enter into attractive transactional opportunities may increase the likelihood that individuals and businesses will unbundle their relationships with a particular institution and use the Web to shop for the best deal. Accordingly, banks will have to be alert to changes in the effectiveness of their distribution channels. Banks will also have to be creative in utilizing their natural advantages to capitalize on the new opportunities created by electronic banking and commerce.

§ 1.04   AN ACTION PLAN FOR BANKS

For most banks, the most visible manifestation of changes in their competitive environment due to innovations in electronic banking and commerce will come from the activities of other banks, not from the actions taken by nonbanks. Competitive challenges may come in a wide range of forms, including: a competitor's introduction of online banking; an announcement that a competitor plans to act as a certifying authority of its customers' digital signatures; and news that a competitor will be the lead institution on a new metropolitan area smart card.

Any of these actions by a competitor may prompt a call from an outside director to the CEO asking, "Are we doing anything on this?" For a business that has been able to adapt to change at a relatively comfortable pace, the pace may be about to change dramatically. Suddenly one of the fastest moving sectors of the economy — the interactive technology business — has become a critical part of the environment in which banks operate. A bank that does not respond to this change by developing its own capacity to analyze and integrate new opportunities into its strategy may find itself losing market share to its bank and nonbank competitors, thus reducing the value of its franchise and ultimately threatening its viability.

A bank should develop an electronic banking and commerce strategic plan that is fully integrated with its overall business plan. Electronic banking and commerce strategic plans should address the following areas:

- What are the bank's natural strengths in regard to electronic commerce and banking applications?

- What are the likely areas of present and potential customer interest in electronic banking and commerce applications?

- What electronic banking and commerce products, services, or activities should the bank consider undertaking in the short-, medium-, and long-terms?

- What additional resources, both internal and external, does the bank need in order to be able to implement this program?

- Should the bank attempt to design and develop its own technological applications or should it join with other banks, software providers, or other businesses to explore possible new products, services or activities?

Was Bill Gates' initial prophecy for banks correct? We will not know for some time. What we do know is that, as a matter of prudent management, each bank must take steps to enable it to adapt to the evolution of banking and commerce technology. An institution must commit the resources necessary to provide a capacity to monitor and evaluate the full range of developments in electronic banking and commerce. This effort to remain current in the face of advancing technologies may require reliance upon outside consultants, as well as bank personnel.

A bank should also be prepared to carefully analyze the particular products, services, or activities that are proposed for implementation. This analysis should include the following factors:

- If a third party is involved in the implementation of the product, service, or activity, do the terms of any arrangement with the third party adequately protect the interests of the bank?

- Does the bank have sufficient capacity to fully identify, analyze, and address the risks associated with the product, service, or activity?

- What are the risks associated with the product, service, or activity?

- What is the track record for the product, service, or activity?

- What is the likelihood that other developments will cause the proposed product, service, or activity to become significantly less marketable?

Dramatic changes in the ways that banks market their services, structure their operations, and deliver products and services to their customers will occur during the next decade. Furthermore, major shifts will occur in the competitive environment confronting institutions. This process will most likely be a confusing one for both individuals and businesses. Banks, however, possess a critical advantage in retaining and attracting customers: the reservoir of trust and confidence that they bring to their dealings with present and potential customers. It remains to be seen whether banks will capitalize on this advantage and continue to play a central role in 21st Century commerce.

CHAPTER 2

THE BUSINESS OF BANKING
IN THE UNITED STATES

§ 2.01   INTRODUCTION

Today's evolving technologies offer the possibility of changing radically *how* and *with whom* consumers execute financial transactions. Moreover, these evolving technologies, in many instances, will require either the adaptation of old legal principles to a new environment or the creation of new legal principles to address previously uncontemplated transactions and relationships. Changes in technology may affect how a consumer views financial transactions completed using the new technology. The perceived reliability of banks — as regulated entities insured by the Federal Deposit Insurance Corporation ("FDIC") — could prove to be an advantage (because of the value of trust to consumer confidence in the faceless world of cyberspace) or a disadvantage (because of institutional and/or regulatory constraints that limit the ability to adapt to and implement new technologies) to banks as they strive to take advantage of these new technological advances.

As a legal matter, the business of banking historically has been distinguished from general forms of commerce. This has been done by virtue of laws that circumscribe the activities in which a bank may engage and that prohibit nonbanks from engaging in the business of banking. Despite limitations on allowable activities, the banking industry has repeatedly demonstrated a vitality and adaptability that has enabled it to evolve and meet the financial needs of customers in new ways.

Throughout history, banking has been affected by several extraneous factors: the ups and downs of the economy and changes in the manner in which information is communicated and value transferred. The introduction of new financial technologies is likely to dramatically reshape the legal and commercial boundaries that define the business of banking. In that context, it is useful to review the origins and development of the banking system and the business of banking in the United States. The past should be of particular interest to those who envision a world of electronic money issued by private banks and other private entities. Such a development, if it occurs, will be a case of *Back to the Future*, because it will return us, at least partially, to the era of free banking, when much of the nation's currency took the form of notes issued by state chartered private banks rather than by the federal government. This Chapter begins with a history of the development of the dual banking system. Section 2.03 provides an overview of the federal bank regulatory structure. Finally, Section 2.04 discusses the evolution of the business of banking.

§ 2.02   THE DEVELOPMENT OF A DUAL BANKING SYSTEM IN THE UNITED STATES

[1]   EARLY DEVELOPMENTS

During the colonial period in the United States, there were no banks in the modern sense.[1] The country was largely agrarian and farmers saw little need for a monetary system beyond gold and silver coinage and stamps. They harbored suspicions of monied businesses. Merchants and traders met the farmers' financing needs with trade credit or access to the commercial markets of London and Glasgow. Rudimentary banks provided paper currency in the form of IOUs. Coins in circulation included British pounds and Spanish reals.

In an effort to provide financing for the revolution, the Continental Congress, in 1781, authorized the creation of the Bank of North America. Modeled after the state-chartered Pennsylvania Bank that had been in operation for eighteen months, the Bank of North America received its charter from Congress on December 31, 1781. In reaction to concerns regarding the validity of the first charter, the Pennsylvania Assembly re-chartered the Bank of North America in 1782.[2] The bank had authority to issue notes with interest, accept deposits, make loans, and to act as the government's fiscal agent.[3] Though it struggled as a result of public hostility toward central government, and thus toward centrally controlled banking, the Bank of North America served as a model for state banking actions.[4]

In 1787, when the Constitution was being debated, only a handful of banks had charters. Agrarian interests opposed centralized banking because they believed it would create a restrictive credit system, one favorable to New England manufacturing interests.[5] Perhaps due to the political sensitivity surrounding the issue, the Constitution contains only the following sections regarding money and banking:

> Article 1, Section 8. "The Congress shall have the power to . . . regulate Commerce with foreign Nations, and among the several States. . . ; To establish . . . uniform Laws on the subject of Bankruptcies throughout the United States; To coin Money . . . ; To provide for the Punishment of counterfeiting the Securities and current Coin of the United States. . . ."

---

[1]   *See* BENJAMIN J. KLEBANER, AMERICAN COMMERCIAL BANKING: A HISTORY 3 (1990).

[2]   *See* BRAY HAMMOND, BANKS AND POLITICS IN AMERICA 51 (1985). Massachusetts and New York also granted charters to the Bank of North America and Connecticut and Rhode Island recognized its validity.

[3]   *See id.* at 47-48.

[4]   *See* ALFRED M. POLLARD, ET AL., BANKING LAW IN THE UNITED STATES 8 (1988).

[5]   *See id.* at 9.

Article 1, Section 10. "No State shall . . . coin Money; . . . make any Thing but gold and silver Coin A Tender In payment of Debts. . . ."[6]

Following the Constitution's ratification, the need for a centralized banking system again became a topic of debate. Early efforts at creating a banking system occurred at both the state and federal levels, thus establishing the foundation for a dual banking system wherein banks may be chartered by either a state or the federal government. Following the Revolution, the states enjoyed a degree of autonomy in conducting their banking operations and, as a result, a wide array of financial practices and operations evolved.[7]

The First Bank of the United States ("First Bank") received a 20-year charter from Congress in 1791. It received the charter despite opposition from forces concerned about the government's constitutional authority to grant such a charter. Secretary of the Treasury Alexander Hamilton, who had proposed the establishment of First Bank to Congress, patterned the bank's charter after that of the Bank of England.[8] The Bank of England's experience suggested that separation of banking and commerce promoted safety and soundness.[9] Though a financial success, First Bank failed to achieve broad political support. States resented the competition that their banks encountered from First Bank.[10] Further, the issue of state taxation of First Bank's branches remained unresolved.[11] In 1811, at the end of its 20-year charter, First Bank closed its doors. During the period of the First Bank's charter, from 1791 to 1811, state banks grew at a rapid pace, from three to ninety. By 1816, the number reached 250.[12]

The effects of War of 1812 renewed the public's interest in a stable and uniform banking system that could supply credit to government and business.[13] Despite political unpopularity, based on the perception that there had been too much foreign involvement with the First Bank, President James Madison proposed the Second Bank of the United States ("Second Bank") in 1815.[14] In April 1816, the Second Bank received a 20-year charter. It served as the fiscal agent for the United States.[15] The Second Bank exerted control over the nation's banking system by purchasing state bank notes and tightening or loosening its redemption policy.

---

[6]   U.S. CONST. art. I, §§ 8, 10. *See* POLLARD, *supra* note 4, at 9.

[7]   *See* POLLARD, *supra* note 4, at 8.

[8]   *See* HAMMOND, *supra* note 2, at 128.

[9]   *See id.* at 129.

[10]   *See id.* at 199.

[11]   *See id.* at 127-128.

[12]   *See id.* at 145.

[13]   *See* POLLARD, *supra* note 4, at 10.

[14]   *See* HAMMOND, *supra* note 2, at 240.

[15]   The United States owned 20% of the bank, which was capitalized at $35,000,000. *See id.* at 244.

[2]   FEDERAL GOVERNMENT AUTHORITY TO CHARTER A BANK UPHELD

In 1818, Maryland passed a tax on notes issued by banks or branches not chartered in Maryland. The Second Bank branch in Baltimore did not pay its taxes, which led Maryland to sue the branch in the name of its cashier, James McCulloch, who Maryland also accused of improper operations. Though successful at the state level, Maryland's challenge to Second Bank was rejected by the Supreme Court. The Court's decision in *McCulloch v. Maryland*[16] is important because it found that the "necessary and proper" clause of the Constitution authorized Congress to charter a bank;[17] and that any state law that directly conflicts with federal law, such as state tax law as applied to the Second Bank, is superseded.[18] Though it had survived the constitutional challenge, Second Bank could not survive the impact of bad business practices and political considerations.[19] When rechartering came up for consideration in 1832, Secretary of Treasury Roger Taney argued that state banks were adequate to ensure stability and transferability of currency, which prompted President Andrew Jackson's veto of the charter's renewal.[20]

[3]   FREE BANKING

The late 1830s saw a rise of state banks and the concept of free banking. Under the free banking system, banking was open to anyone who could comply with state statutory requirements,[21] and state banks were free to issue bank notes.[22] In 1837, Michigan became the first state to enact a free banking statute, permitting banks to be chartered without legislative action. The existing practice of requiring legislative action for each charter raised questions of favoritism and corruption. Within a year, more than 40 banks were established in Michigan, the majority of which were placed in receivership within two years.[23]

In 1838, the New York legislature passed the New York Free Banking Act, which granted to banks the following powers:

> Such association shall have power to carry on the business of banking by discounting
> bills, notes and other evidences of debt; by receiving deposits; by buying and selling the
> gold and silver bullion, foreign coins and bills of exchange, in the manner specified in

---

[16] *See* HAMMOND, *supra* note 2, at 412-414.

[17] *McCulloch v. Maryland*, 17 U.S. (4 Wheat) 316 (1819).

[18] *See* HAMMOND, *supra* note 2, at 428-429.

[19] *See* POLLARD, *supra* note 4, at 16.

[20] "President Andrew Jackson, in his message accompanying his veto of the extension of the Second Bank of the United States, took the position that the Bank was unconstitutional, notwithstanding the Supreme Court's decision in *McCulloch v. Maryland* to the contrary." Thomas W. Merrill, *Judicial Opinions as Binding Law and as Explanations For Judgments*, 15 CARDOZO L. REV. 43, 47 (1993) (Andrew Jackson, Veto Message (July 10, 1832), *in* 2 A COMPILATION OF THE MESSAGES AND PAPERS OF THE PRESIDENTS, at 576, 586-88 (James D. Richardson ed., 1896)).

[21] *See* ANN GRAHAM, BANKING LAW § 2.03[4], at 2-11 (1997).

[22] *See* POLLARD, *supra* note 4, at 16-17. *See also Briscoe v. Bank of the Commonwealth of Kentucky*, 11 Peters 326 (1837) (wherein the Supreme Court held that a note issued by a state and backed by its full faith and credit was an impermissible bill of credit but a note issued by a state chartered bank was not).

[23] *See* HAMMOND, *supra* note 2, at 601.

their articles of association for the purposes authorized by this act; by loaning money on real and personal security and by exercising such incidental powers as shall be necessary to carry on such business; . . .[24]

Though similar to the Michigan approach, New York achieved greater success. The New York law also had a lasting effect in shaping the business of banking, for other states followed New York's example. The number of banks increased from 713 in 1838, to 1,466 in 1863.[25] The banking powers language of the New York law ultimately found its way into federal law and has remained there for more than a century.[26]

Lack of regulation and control, along with widespread speculation, resulted in an unstable banking system and produced hardship to the public. In 1857, the failure of Ohio Life Insurance and Trust Company's New York office caused a national crisis.[27] During the ensuing panic, several banks failed and interest rates rose dramatically. By the start of the Civil War, the need for stricter bank regulation was clear.

§ 2.03   THE FEDERAL BANK REGULATORY FRAMEWORK

The federal government, concerned with the state of the nation's currency and the ability to finance the Civil War, ended a quarter century of unchallenged state control of banking policy[28] by enacting the National Currency Act on February 25, 1863.[29] The National Currency Act created a new national banking system. The administration of that system was vested in the currency bureau and its chief administrator, the Comptroller of the Currency. The law was rewritten and reenacted in 1864 as the National Bank Act.[30] The new law authorized the Comptroller of the Currency to establish a staff of national bank examiners to supervise and periodically examine the national banks and to regulate the lending and investment activities of national banks. Further, the National Bank Act included provisions, such as the imposition of a punitive tax on state bank notes, that were intended to promote the growth of a national bank system and a national currency by making the issue and use of state bank notes less attractive.[31]

---

[24]   Ch. 260 §18, 1838 N.Y. Laws 245, 249.

[25]   *See* GRAHAM, *supra* note 21, § 2.03[4], at 2-11 (citing Board of Governors of the Federal Reserve System, Banking Statutes "Introduction" (1941) at 418).

[26]   12 U.S.C. § 24(Seventh).

[27]   *See* POLLARD, *supra* note 4, at 17.

[28]   *See* KLEBANER, *supra* note 1, at 64.

[29]   Act of February 25, 1863, c. 58, 12 Stat. 665 (repealed by Act of June 3, 1864, *infra* note 30).

[30]   Act of June 3, 1864, c. 106, 13 Stat. 99 (codified as amended at 12 U.S.C. §§ 1-216d). The National Bank Act's constitutionality was upheld in *Farmers' and Mechanics' Nat'l Bank v. Diarz*, 91 U.S. 29 (1875). The supremacy of federal law over state action aimed at limiting federally-chartered banks was recognized in *Davis v. Elmira Sav. Bank*, 161 U.S. 275 (1896).

[31]   *See* KLEBANER, *supra* note 1, at 64-66.

Contrary to expectations, state banks did not rush to convert and join the national bank system.[32] The number of state banks declined in the 1870s, but then enjoyed rapid growth when checking accounts gained in popularity and provided a means to circumvent the adverse tax on state bank notes.[33] State banks increased from 704 to 5,000 between 1882 and 1900 and national banks increased from 2,239 to 3,731 during the same period.[34] State banks benefited from less stringent chartering, capital, and reserve requirements than national banks. The dual banking system experienced its next major change in 1913.

[1] THE FEDERAL RESERVE SYSTEM BECOMES PART OF THE FEDERAL BANK REGULATORY FRAMEWORK

Throughout the 1800s and early 1900s, the country experienced a series of panics that highlighted the weakness of the banking system. The Panic of 1907, a result of economic downturn worldwide and imperfections in the U.S. banking system, severely tested the banking system and threatened the nation's economy.[35] It led President Theodore Roosevelt to call on his frequent adversary J. Pierpont Morgan to use Morgan's influence and economic power to head off a full-fledged crisis.[36]

Fearing that it was no longer feasible to count on a single private individual to handle future turmoil in the banking industry, Congress decided that federal action was necessary to bring greater stability to the banking system and set about drafting legislation. The Federal Reserve Act, enacted in 1913, resulted from those efforts.[37] The Federal Reserve Act created the Federal Reserve System to serve as a source of liquidity for member institutions. All national banks were required to become members of the Federal Reserve System. The Federal Reserve System also represented the federal government's first effort to exercise ongoing regulatory jurisdiction over state banks, by virtue of the ability to impose restrictions on state banks that become members of the Federal Reserve System.

Though intended to promote stability in the banking system, the Board of Governors of the Federal Reserve System could not stem the wave of bank failures that occurred in the late 1920s and early 1930s. Approximately 20,000 banks failed between 1920 and 1935.[38] The Reconstruction Finance Corporation, established by Congress in 1932, provided loans to banks in an effort to keep them open. Banks throughout the country, however, were forced to place moritoria on their obligations to pay deposits on demand. On March 5, 1933, newly inaugurated President Franklin Roosevelt suspended all bank activities. He assured the

---

[32] *See* KLEBANER, *supra* note 1, at 65.

[33] *See* POLLARD, *supra* note 4, at 20.

[34] *See* KLEBANER, *supra* note 1, at 68.

[35] *See id.* at 95-96.

[36] *See* RON CHERNOW, HOUSE OF MORGAN, c. 7 (1991).

[37] Act of December 23, 1913, ch. 6, 38 Stat. 251 (codified as amended at 12 U.S.C. §§ 221-552).

[38] *See* POLLARD, *supra* note 4, at 21 n.10. During this period, Great Britain's abandonment of the gold standard further contributed to instability in the world economy. *See* KLEBANER, *supra* note 1, at 138.

public that only sound banks would reopen and urged the American people to do their part by returning the currency that they had hoarded to the banks.[39]

In the face of mounting depositor losses, Congress recognized the need for additional federal action to diminish the chances for future widespread panics and to restore public confidence in the safety of the banking system.[40]

[2]   FEDERAL DEPOSIT INSURANCE PROVIDES A FINANCIAL SAFETY NET

In 1933, Congress passed the Banking Act of 1933, amending the Federal Reserve Act to establish the Federal Deposit Insurance Corporation ("FDIC").[41] The law made federal deposit insurance mandatory for national banks and available to state chartered banks.[42] In August 1935, when permanent insurance arrangements went into effect, 93% of commercial banks with 98.6% of deposits were federally insured.[43] Congress removed the amendment from the Federal Reserve Act in 1950 and enacted a separate Federal Deposit Insurance Act ("FDIA").[44]

[3]   CONGRESS ESTABLISHES OTHER FEDERAL DEPOSITORY INSTITUTION REGULATORS

Savings associations ("thrifts") developed in the early 1800s and evolved alongside the commercial banking system.[45] Thrifts focused on home financing and consumer savings deposits. As the thrift industry grew, it faced several problems including inadequate means of transferring funds between geographic regions as credit needs changed, lack of access to national capital markets, and absence of a central credit mechanism.[46] With the onset of the Depression, and the widespread illiquidity experienced by thrift institutions, a need for significant change in the industry was clear.

---

[39] *See* KLEBANER, *supra* note 1, at 141.

[40] *See id.* at 148.

[41] Act of June 16, 1933, Pub. L. No. 73-66, ch. 89, 48 Stat. 162 (codified as amended at 12 U.S.C. §§ 1811-1835a) [hereinafter Banking Act of 1933]. Another aspect of the Banking Act of 1933, also know as the Glass-Steagall Act, mandated the separation of commercial banking and investment banking entities. *Id.* § 13, 48 Stat. at 183. The Glass-Steagall Act was based on the premise, now widely challenged, that the banking crisis was largely attributable to bank involvement in securities underwriting and dealing activities. For an extensive discussion of the enactment of the Glass-Steagall Act and its subsequent implementation and interpretation, see HARVEY L. PITT, DAVID M. MILES, ANTHONY AIN, DAVID B. HARDISON & SUSAN WHITE HAAG, THE LAW OF FINANCIAL SERVICES 102-13 (1994 Supp.). *See also* CHERNOW, *supra* note 32, at chapters 18 and 19 (describing the Pecora hearings and the split up of J. P. Morgan and Company into J. P. Morgan and Company, a commercial bank, and Morgan Stanley and Company, an investment banking firm).

[42] Banking Act of 1933, § 8, 48 Stat. at 168 (codified at 12 U.S.C. § 264 (1946) (repealed by the Federal Deposit Insurance Act, *infra* note 44)).

[43] *See* KLEBANER, *supra* note 1, at 142.

[44] Federal Deposit Insurance Act, Pub. L. No. 81-797, 1950 U.S.C.C.A.N. (64 Stat. 783) 931 (codified as amended at 12 U.S.C. §§ 1811-1835a).

[45] *See* Dirk S. Adams & Rodney R. Peck, *The Federal Home Loan Banks and the Home Finance System*, 43 BUS. LAW. 833 (1988).

[46] *See id.* at 835.

Congress, as part of its effort to stem the financial crisis plaguing the United States in the early 1930s, decided to create a federal role in the thrift institution industry. The Federal Home Loan Bank System was therefore established by the Federal Home Loan Bank Act of 1932 to provide a credit reserve for savings and home finance institutions.[47] It consisted of the Federal Home Loan Bank Board ("FHLBB"), regional Federal Home Loan Banks, as well as member thrift institutions. These moves failed to restore liquidity to the thrift industry.[48] In 1933, Congress expanded the mission of the FHLBB by enacting the Home Owners' Loan Act of 1933 ("HOLA").[49] The HOLA authorized the FHLBB to issue federal savings and loan association charters, established the powers of such associations, and directed the FHLBB to regulate these institutions. Finally, in 1934, Congress enacted the National Housing Act of 1934 ("NHA"), establishing the Federal Savings and Loan Insurance Corporation ("FSLIC") under the direction of the FHLBB to provide federal and state thrifts with federal deposit insurance coverage similar to that provided to banks by the FDIC.[50]

Until 1989, this regulatory scheme applied to all federally chartered savings and loans, as well as to state chartered savings and loans whose deposits were FSLIC-insured. On August 9, 1989, Congress passed the Financial Institutions Reform, Recovery and Enforcement Act of 1989 ("FIRREA") abolishing the FSLIC and the FHLBB;[51] creating the Office of Thrift Supervision ("OTS"), a bureau of the Treasury Department with primary regulatory responsibility for savings associations and savings and loan holding companies; and transferring deposit insurance responsibilities for federally insured savings institutions to the FDIC.

In 1934, Congress created yet another regulatory body to oversee financial institutions. The National Credit Union Administration ("NCUA"), created by the Federal Credit Union Act of 1934,[52] presides over a system of federally chartered and state chartered credit unions, the shares or deposits of which are federally insured. The NCUA is responsible for the chartering, supervising, examining, insuring, and liquidating functions of a central bank.

[4] THE FEDERAL BANK REGULATORY AGENCIES TODAY

Over the past several decades, Congress has established a statutory framework for the consistent regulation and supervision of federally insured banks and savings associations. Under this approach, Congress enacted laws that apply to all FDIC-insured institutions and divided the authority for ensuring compliance with these

---

[47] Federal Home Loan Bank Act, Pub. L. No. 72-304, 47 Stat. 725 (codified as amended at 12 U.S.C. §§ 1421-1449).

[48] A memorable portrait of how thrifts, which had a large percentage of their assets invested in long term mortgage loans, were highly vulnerable to paralyzing runs by panicked depositors, is offered by the now classic film, IT'S A WONDERFUL LIFE.

[49] Home Owners' Loan Act of 1933, c. 64, 49 Stat. 128 (codified as amended at 12 U.S.C. §§ 1461-70).

[50] National Housing Act of 1934, c. 847, 49 Stat. 1246 (codified at 12 U.S.C. §§ 1724-30i (1988)) (repealed by the Financial Institutions Reform, Recovery, and Enforcement Act of 1989, *infra* note 51).

[51] Financial Institutions Reform, Recovery, and Enforcement Act of 1989, Pub. L. No. 101-73, 1989 U.S.C.C.A.N. (103 Stat.) 183 (codified as amended in scattered sections of 12, 15 & 18 U.S.C.).

[52] Federal Credit Union Act of 1934, ch. 750, 48 Stat. 1216 (codified as amended at 12 U.S.C. §§ 1751-95k).

laws among the four federal bank regulatory agencies — the OCC, the FRB, the FDIC, and the OTS. Each agency serves as the applicable federal bank regulatory agency for a category of insured depository institutions. The OCC serves as the applicable federal bank regulatory agency for national banks, the FRB for state chartered banks that are members of the Federal Reserve System ("state member banks"), the FDIC for state chartered banks that are not members of the Federal Reserve System ("state nonmember banks") and the OTS for federal and state savings associations.

Among the laws that are administered in this fashion are the following:

- **Enforcement Provisions of the FDIA.** These authorize the applicable federal bank regulatory agency to protect insured institutions through enforcement measures, including: issuing cease and desist orders; imposing civil money penalties; and suspending and removing individuals from participating in the affairs of insured institutions.[53]

- **Bank Merger Act.** This law requires the federal bank regulatory agency that regulates the resulting institution to approve any merger among insured institutions or any transfer of deposits from one insured institution to another.[54]

- **Change in Bank Control Act.** This law requires a party to provide prior notification to the applicable federal bank regulatory agency of certain transactions through which the notifying party would be deemed to acquire control of a depository institution.[55]

- **Prompt Corrective Action Requirements of the FDIA.** These provisions specify certain actions that a federal bank regulatory agency may or must take in regard to a depository institution that does not meet minimum capital requirements.[56]

- **Depository Institutions Management Interlocks Act.** This law prohibits certain management officials of a depository organization from serving as management officials of another depository organization, subject to determinations and enforcement by the applicable federal bank regulatory agency or agencies.[57]

- **Community Reinvestment Act.** This law encourages depository institutions to serve their local communities and establishes a system for examination and evaluation of depository institutions by the applicable federal bank regulatory agency.[58]

---

[53]   12 U.S.C. § 1818.

[54]   12 U.S.C. § 1828(c).

[55]   12 U.S.C. § 1817(j).

[56]   12 U.S.C. § 1831o.

[57]   12 U.S.C. §§ 3201-08.

[58]   12 U.S.C. §§ 2901-07.

• **Securities Exchange Act of 1934.** This law vests jurisdiction over depository institutions with publicly traded securities with the applicable federal bank regulatory agency rather than with the Securities and Exchange Commission.

In addition to their responsibilities for laws that apply to insured institutions, the federal bank regulatory agencies each have individual responsibilities with respect to institutions subject to their jurisdiction. A federal bank regulatory agency may occasionally exercise authority over institutions other than those for which it is the applicable federal bank regulatory agency.

[5] THE CURRENT FEDERAL BANK REGULATORY STRUCTURE

The following diagram illustrates the multifaceted bank regulatory regime discussed throughout this Section.

Current Federal Regulation and Supervision of Banks and Thrifts and their Holding Companies

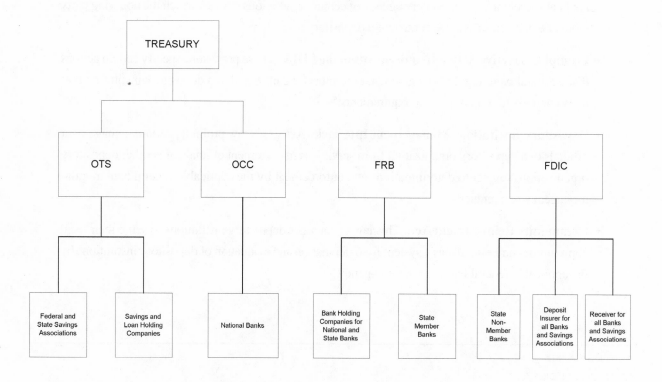

[a] Office of the Comptroller of the Currency. The OCC is an independent bureau of the Treasury. It operates under the direction of a single individual who serves as the Comptroller of the Currency. The Comptroller also serves as a member of the Board of Directors of the FDIC. The OCC is responsible for examining and supervising federally chartered national banks and federally licensed branches and agencies of foreign banks. It also serves as the appropriate federal bank regulatory agency for these entities. The OCC is authorized to approve charters for new national banks. It determines what types of activities national banks and their subsidiaries and affiliates can engage in under the National Bank Act and other applicable laws. The OCC is responsible for ruling on requests by national banks to establish new branches. The OCC also issues determinations as to whether the application of a particular state law to national banks is preempted by federal law.

[b] Board of Governors of the Federal Reserve System. The Federal Reserve System is comprised of the Board of Governors of the Federal Reserve System ("FRB") and its staff, together with the twelve Federal Reserve Banks, the Federal Open Market Committee,[59] and certain other entities. The FRB has responsibility for implementing monetary and credit policy, maintaining monetary and credit growth, and establishing reserve requirements for insured institutions.

The FRB, as the appropriate federal bank regulatory agency for state member banks, examines for compliance with, and enforces a wide range of, laws applicable to insured institutions generally. Because the FRB is not a chartering agency, it does not have a primary role in determining the powers available to state member banks; it does, however, have significant authority over these institutions by virtue of their subjecting themselves to the requirements applicable to member banks.[60]

Congress has also assigned the FRB responsibility for adopting regulations under laws applicable to insured institutions generally, or to other specifically defined groups or entities. Such regulations relevant to electronic banking and commerce include: Regulation E, which implements the Electronic Fund Transfer Act; Regulation B, which implements the Equal Credit Opportunity Act; Regulation Z, which implements the Truth In Lending Act; and Regulation DD, which implements the Truth in Savings Act.

The FRB administers and enforces the Bank Holding Company Act ("BHCA"), under which it must approve the formation of a bank holding company, the acquisition or merger of a bank holding company, and the acquisition of a bank by a bank holding company. The FRB also determines permissible activities of bank holding companies and nonbank subsidiaries of bank holding companies, examines bank holding companies and their nonbank subsidiaries, and exercises enforcement authority over these entities.

[c] Federal Deposit Insurance Corporation. The FDIC acts as the appropriate federal bank regulatory agency for state nonmember banks and thus examines for compliance with, and enforces a wide range of,

---

[59]   The Federal Open Market Committee directs FRB purchases and sales of U.S. government securities and other obligations on the open market.

[60]   *See* 12 C.F.R. pt. 208.

laws applicable to insured institutions generally. The FDIC is not a chartering agency, and therefore it does not have a primary role in determining the powers available to state nonmember banks. Under a 1991 amendment to the FDIA, the FDIC is authorized, however, to determine whether state banks, both member and nonmember, may engage, as a principal, in activities in which a national bank may not engage. The FDIC also regulates certain aspects of the operations of state nonmember banks, such as the securities activities of subsidiaries of state nonmember banks.

The FDIC's regulatory authority also encompasses activities conducted by institutions subject to the jurisdiction of other banking regulatory agencies. For example, it adopts regulations restricting golden parachutes and indemnification payments to persons associated with insured institutions and determines whether a state savings association may engage, as a principal, in activities in which a federal savings bank may not engage. The FDIC may take enforcement action against savings associations under certain circumstances if the OTS does not take such action.

The FDIC also operates two deposit insurance funds, the Bank Insurance Fund, which insures deposits held by commercial banks and some state chartered savings banks, and the Savings Association Insurance Fund, which insures deposits held by savings associations and certain savings banks. It establishes the premium level for deposit insurance coverage and determines when and how the insurance funds will be used to assist in the resolution of a failing insured institution. In almost all instances, the FDIC serves as the conservator or receiver for a troubled or failing insured institution. In its capacity as receiver, the FDIC is responsible for protecting the interests of insured depositors either through a direct payout of insurance or by arranging for the assumption of insured deposits by another insured institution. The agency, as receiver, also resolves claims against the failed institution and pursues claims on behalf of the institution.

[d] Office of Thrift Supervision. The OTS, an independent office of the United States Department of Treasury, operates under the supervision of the Director of the OTS. The Director also sits on the Board of Directors of the FDIC. The OTS serves as the chartering agency for federal savings associations and federal savings banks. It determines the activities that federal savings associations and their subsidiaries and affiliates can perform under the HOLA and other applicable laws. The OTS also serves as the applicable federal bank regulatory agency for both federal and state savings associations, and examines and enforces laws and regulations applicable to these institutions. It rules on requests by savings associations to establish new branches and issues determinations as to whether the application of a particular state law to federal savings associations is preempted by federal law.

The OTS administers the savings and loan holding company provisions of the HOLA and must approve the formation of a savings and loan holding company, the acquisition or merger of a savings and loan holding company, and the acquisition of a savings association by a savings and loan holding company. The OTS also examines savings and loan holding companies and their nonsavings association subsidiaries, and has authority to exercise enforcement authority with respect to such entities.

[6]   OVERLAPPING LEGISLATIVE AND REGULATORY REGIMES

Depository institutions in the United States are subject to the overlapping jurisdiction of federal and state laws, to varying degrees depending on the institution's charter. In their operations, they must be cognizant of these and of relevant federal preemption principles. Depending on whether the depository institutions are chartered as federal or state institutions, state corporate law principles may be fully or partially applicable to an institution's corporate governance. Federal and state banking regulators oversee banking activities of these organizations and related matters. The federal bank regulatory agencies formally act in concert issuing joint policy statements through the Federal Financial Institutions Examination Council, an organization through which they coordinate matters relating to examination policy.

§ 2.04   PERMISSIBLE BANK AND BANK HOLDING COMPANY ACTIVITIES

As the previous Sections have shown, the banking industry is heavily regulated. The separation of banking and commerce has long been a fundamental principle of the federal and state regulatory schemes. Banks generally may only conduct those activities deemed a part of, or incidental to, the business of banking. The general parameters of the business of banking can be found in the National Bank Act, as interpreted over time by the OCC and the courts.[61] Under federal law, the activities of FDIC insured state banks acting as principal are generally restricted to activities permitted for national banks as principals.[62] Separately, the Bank Holding Company Act defines the circumstances under which an entity will be deemed to be a bank for purposes of that statute and sets limitations on bank holding company activities based on whether such activities are closely related to banking.[63] An understanding of the development of limitations on both banks and bank holding companies is essential to understanding the current boundaries for these entities as they seek to expand into electronic banking and commerce.

[1]   THE SCOPE OF THE AUTHORITY TO ENGAGE IN THE BUSINESS OF BANKING UNDER THE NATIONAL BANK ACT

The basic powers of national banks are set forth in the National Bank Act.[64] The Act authorizes a national bank to:

> [E]xercise by its board of directors or duly authorized officers or agents, subject to law, all such incidental powers as shall be necessary to carry on the business of banking; by discounting and negotiating promissory notes, drafts, bills of exchange, and other

---

61   12 U.S.C. § 24(Seventh).

62   12 U.S.C. § 1831a.

63   12 U.S.C. §§ 1841(c), 1843(c)(8).

64   12 U.S.C. § 24(Seventh).

evidences of debt; by receiving deposits; by buying and selling exchange, coin and bullion; by loaning money on personal security; and by obtaining, issuing, and circulating notes according to the provisions of title 62 of the Revised Statutes.[65]

Courts and commentators have long considered whether this grant of power should be read broadly, with the enumerated powers being merely illustrative, or narrowly, with those powers providing an all-inclusive definition of the business of banking.[66] A recent Supreme Court decision, discussed below, adopted the position that the enumerated powers are illustrative.[67] In the absence of contrary congressional action, the OCC and the Court's broad reading of "incidental powers as shall be necessary to carry on the business of banking" (the "incidental powers provision") will have a considerable influence on banks' ability to evolve as new technologies and payments systems develop.

In 1864, the drafters of the National Bank Act could not have contemplated a time when a microprocessor chip would carry value and provide the ability to transfer such value to another party. Yet the statute they drafted still provides the governing authority for determining whether national banks may move into new or existing areas of financial and related activities.

[2] INCIDENTAL POWERS: BROADLY OR NARROWLY CONSTRUED

The contemporary debate over the interpretation of the incidental powers provision grew largely out of the First Circuit Court of Appeals 1972 decision in *Arnold Tours, Inc. v. Camp*.[68] Prior to *Arnold Tours*, courts had generally given the business of banking a relatively expansive reading. In 1873, the Supreme Court recognized that banks' functions, or the business of banking, fell into several broad categories, finding that "Banks, in the commercial sense are of three kinds, to wit: 1, of deposit; 2, of discount; 3, of circulation."[69] Following this decision, courts found a variety of activities incidental to these functions, including the power to: borrow money;[70] collect judgments;[71] pay taxes on behalf of depositors;[72] provide mortgages;[73] and conduct safe deposit business.[74]

---

[65] *Id.*

[66] *See* Edward L. Symons, Jr., *The "Business of Banking" in Historical Perspective*, 51 GEO. WASH. L. REV. 676 (1983); Julie L. Williams & Mark P. Jacobson, *The Business of Banking: Looking to the Future*, 50 BUS. LAW. 783 (1995) [hereinafter *The Business of Banking I*].

[67] *NationsBank v. Variable Annuity Life Ins. Co.*, 513 U.S. 251 (1995).

[68] *Arnold Tours, Inc. v. Camp*, 472 F.2d 427 (1st Cir. 1972).

[69] *Oulton v. German Savings & Loan Society*, 84 U.S. (17 Wall.) 109, 118 (1873).

[70] *Wyman v. Wallace*, 201 U.S. 230, 243 (1906).

[71] *Miller v. King*, 223 U.S. 505, 511 (1912).

[72] *Clement Nat'l Bank v. Vermont*, 231 U.S. 120, 140-141 (1913).

[73] *First Nat'l Bank v. Hartford*, 273 U.S. 548, 559-560 (1927).

[74] *Colorado Nat'l Bank v. Bedford*, 310 U.S. 41, 48-50 (1940).

In *Arnold Tours,* travel agents sued the OCC over a 1963 interpretive letter permitting national banks to offer travel agency services to customers as an incidental activity. The First Circuit, after reviewing past decisions interpreting the business of banking and the incidental powers clause, set forth a test based on those decisions:

> In our opinion . . . a national bank's activity is authorized as an incidental power, "necessary to carry on the business of banking," within the meaning of 12 U.S.C. § 24, Seventh, if it is convenient or useful in connection with the performance of one of the bank's established activities pursuant to its express powers under the National Bank Act. If this connection between an incidental activity and an express power does not exist, the activity is not authorized as an incidental power.[75]

In applying that test, the First Circuit upheld the district court's ruling that operating a travel business is not an exercise of the incidental powers referred to in 12 U.S.C. Section 24(Seventh). This decision was seen as a significant departure from prior court rulings.[76]

In subsequent cases and OCC rulings, the incidental powers provision was construed broadly to permit banks to continue a natural expansion of their activities to reflect changes in how banking and financial services were being offered to the public. For example, the Ninth Circuit found that leasing motor vehicles was incidental to the business of banking under the National Bank Act because it is the "functional equivalent" of a secured loan.[77] The D.C. Circuit, finding a direct nexus test to be "a narrow and artificially rigid view of both the business of banking and the [banking statutes]," decided that issuing stand-by letters of credit to guarantee municipal bonds was within the business of banking.[78] The OCC, criticizing the narrow approach taken in *Arnold Tours,* took a more expansive approach to the incidental powers clause in deciding, among other things, to allow national banks to provide clearing services in connection with commodities futures[79] and to act as a principal in commodity price index swaps.[80]

[a] The Supreme Court's Decision in *VALIC*. In 1995, the Supreme Court examined the incidental powers clause in *NationsBank v. Variable Annuity Life Insurance Co.* ("*VALIC*").[81] In *VALIC*, the Supreme Court firmly established the legal authority for a broad reading of the incidental powers clause when it made

---

[75]   *Arnold Tours*, 472 F.2d at 432.

[76]   *Arnold Tours* can be distinguished from prior decisions by the fact that in the court's view, the tour business was a totally separate business. *Id.* at 430.

[77]   *M&M Leasing Corp. v. Seattle First Nat'l Bank*, 563 F.2d 1377, 1380 (9th Cir. 1977), *cert. denied*, 436 U.S. 956 (1978). The court, however, did find that providing operational services such as vehicle maintenance would not fall under the business of banking. *Id.* at 1383.

[78]   *American Ins. Ass'n v. Clarke*, 865 F.2d 278, 281 (D.C. Cir. 1988).

[79]   OCC Interpretive Letter No. 494, [1989-1990 Transfer Binder] Fed. Banking L. Rep. (CCH) ¶ 83,083, at 71,191 (Dec. 20, 1989).

[80]   OCC No Objection Letter No. 87-5, [1988-1989 Transfer Binder] Fed. Banking L. Rep. (CCH) ¶ 84,034, at 76,638 (July 20, 1987).

[81]   *NationsBank v. Variable Annuity Life Ins. Co.*, 513 U.S. 251 (1995) [hereinafter *VALIC*].

clear that, within certain limits, the incidental powers clause allows for a range of new services to be offered by banks:

> We expressly hold that the "business of banking" is not limited to the enumerated powers in § 24 Seventh and that the Comptroller therefore has discretion to authorize activities beyond those specifically enumerated.[82]

In *VALIC,* the plaintiffs challenged the OCC's decision authorizing a national bank to sell annuities.[83] The OCC, in permitting the sales, determined that the annuity sales were incidental to banking within the meaning of the incidental powers provision. Further, the OCC determined that annuities were not insurance and, thus, the sale of annuities by banks should not be constrained by 12 U.S.C. Section 92, the National Bank Act provision that limits insurance sales to banks operating in towns with a population no greater than 5,000. The insurance industry opposed both determinations.

The Court in *VALIC* based its decision on its ruling in *Chevron U.S.A. Inc. v. Natural Resources Defense Council, Inc.,*[84] regarding the scope of an administrative agency's authority. In *Chevron,* the Court established the principle that where an administrative agency was filling a gap in the legislative scheme, its interpretation, as the agency charged with interpreting the statute, should be given "controlling weight," provided the interpretation is a reasonable one.[85] The Court found that the OCC's interpretation of the incidental powers clause, and its determination in accordance with such powers that the sale of annuities is incidental to the business of banking, was reasonable.[86] The Court did note, however, that the discretion allowed to the OCC must be "kept within reasonable bounds."[87]

On the question of whether annuities were insurance for purposes of 12 U.S.C. Section 92, the Court also deferred to the OCC's determination that 12 U.S.C. Section 92 was not implicated because "annuities are not insurance within the meaning of that section."[88] The Court specifically took judicial notice of the fact that modern annuities are essentially financial investment instruments.[89]

---

[82] *Id.* at 258 n.2.

[83] Letter from J. Michael Shepherd, Senior Deputy Comptroller, to Robert M. Kurueza (Mar. 21, 1990) (unpublished).

[84] *Chevron U.S.A. v. National Res. Def. Council,* 467 U.S. 837, 842 (1984).

[85] *Id.* at 844.

[86] *VALIC,* 513 U.S. at 259.

[87] *Id.* at 258 n.2. The Court specifically referred to the operation of a travel agency (an allusion to *Arnold Tours*) as an example of an activity that may exceed the reasonable bounds of the OCC's authority. *Id.*

[88] *Id.* at 264.

[89] *Id.* at 260.

The OCC has identified three factors, although not applied directly in *VALIC*, that have generally been used by courts in deciding whether a given activity or service falls within the business of banking, as articulated in the National Bank Act;[90] specifically whether the activity:

- is the functional equivalent to or a logical outgrowth of a recognized banking activity;

- benefits customers or is convenient or useful to banks; and

- presents the kind of risks banks already assume.[91]

The OCC appears to believe that this formulation gives it considerable leeway to allow national banks to expand their activities to keep pace with developments in the financial services industry and in technology. Moreover, the Court's decision in *VALIC* is likely to cause lower courts to give a good deal of deference to the OCC in cases involving challenges to the OCC's decisions regarding the scope of national bank powers.

[b] OCC Construes the National Bank Act Broadly. In its interpretive rulings and other actions,[92] the OCC has construed the incidental powers of national banks broadly. National banks are authorized, for example, to provide postal services,[93] prepare income tax returns,[94] act as a payroll issuer,[95] provide messenger services,[96] and furnish products and services by electronic means and facilities.[97] In the area of emerging electronic services, the OCC, in applying a broad construction of the powers of national banks, has authorized them to provide Internet access services, to dispense electronic media through ATMs, and to operate electronic systems for toll collections and other services. In a major expansion of the possible scope of national bank activities, the OCC in November 1996 amended its corporate activities regulations, including its regulation regarding operating subsidiary activities.[98] Historically, the OCC had taken the position that operating subsidiaries were functionally a division of the bank and were therefore limited to engaging in activities in which the national

---

[90] *See M&M Leasing Corp. v. Seattle First Nat'l Bank*, 563 F.2d 1377 (9th Cir. 1977), *cert. denied*, 436 U.S. 956 (1978) (leasing is equivalent to a loan and represents a risk banks traditionally take); *American Ins. Ass'n v. Clarke*, 865 F.2d 278 (D.C. Cir. 1988) (bank's standby credit to insure municipal bonds is the "functional equivalent" of a letter of credit); *Securities Industry Ass'n v. Clarke*, 885 F.2d 1034 (2d Cir. 1989) (selling pass-through certificate was "convenient and useful" in connection with the bank's sale of mortgages). *See also* OCC Interpretive Letter No. 649, [1994 Transfer Binder] Fed. Banking L. Rep. (CCH) ¶ 83,556, at 71,714 (May 12, 1994). (No Objection Letter to Blackfeet National Bank regarding its intention to market a new "retirement CD" annuity).

[91] OCC Interpretive Letter No. 718, [1995-1996 Transfer Binder] Fed. Banking L. Rep. (CCH) ¶ 81,033, at 90,299 (Mar. 18, 1996). For a further discussion of these factors, see *The Business of Banking I, supra* note 66, at 784-814.

[92] The OCC recently finalized a comprehensive review and recodification of its Interpretive Rulings, which includes its interpretations regarding national bank powers. Interpretive Rulings, 61 Fed. Reg. 4849 (1996).

[93] 12 C.F.R. § 7.1010.

[94] 12 C.F.R. § 7.1008.

[95] 12 C.F.R. § 7.1011.

[96] 12 C.F.R. § 7.1012.

[97] 12 C.F.R. § 7.1019.

[98] Rules, Policies, and Procedures for Corporate Activities, 61 Fed. Reg. 60,342 (1996).

bank itself could engage. As part of the amended operating subsidiary regulation, the OCC expressly authorized national banks to seek approval to engage, through an operating subsidiary, in activities that are part of or incidental to banking but which are prohibited for national banks.[99]

[c] Incidental Powers as a Separate Grant of Authority Under 12 U.S.C. § 24(Seventh). In an August 1997 article co-authored by the Chief Counsel of the OCC, the authors analyzed the nature of national banks' "incidental powers."[100] The authors adopted a framework for determining whether proposed activities fall within the incidental powers of national banks, concluding that an activity is permissible if it: "(i) facilitates the operations of the bank as a business enterprise; (ii) enhances the efficiency and quality of the content or delivery of banking services or products; or (iii) optimizes the use and value of a bank's facilities and competencies, or enables the bank to avoid economic waste in its banking franchise."[101] The authors' analysis of incidental powers is particularly useful in discussing banks' use of evolving technology because these powers form the basis for many of the bank activities that involve technological innovations. The authors' analytical framework for discussing banks' incidental powers is described in the following three subsections.

[i] *Activities that Facilitate the Operations of a Bank as a Business Enterprise.* There is general agreement that a bank, like all other business enterprises, may engage in activities that are necessary for the bank to carry on its business. A bank must be able, for example, to hire employees, issue stock, own and rent equipment, purchase the assets and assume the liabilities of other financial institutions, and optimize its own corporate structure through the use of operating subsidiaries. These powers are incidental to banks' general power to conduct a "business" under 12 U.S.C. § 24(Seventh), and do not require a separate express grant.[102]

[ii] *Activities that Enhance the Efficiency and Quality of the Content or Delivery of Banking Services or Products.* In order to remain competitive, banks must have the ability to "package and promote" their products efficiently and profitably, and to meet consumer demands. Courts have recognized this need, and have allowed banks to advertise, hire individuals to solicit business, and, subject to certain limitations, offer services that will attract the public to the banks' premises.[103] In addition, national banks may provide ancillary non-banking products and services if, as part of a mix with permissible banking products and services, the ancillary products or services are needed to successfully market the entire package.[104] For example, a bank may sell a limited amount of general purpose computer hardware in connection with the sale of banking or financial data

---

[99] 12 C.F.R. § 5.34(f).

[100] Julie L. Williams & James F.E. Gillespie, Jr., *The Business of Banking: Looking to the Future — Part II*, 52 BUS. LAW. 1279 (1997) [hereinafter *The Business of Banking II*]. In a 1995 article, *The Business of Banking I, supra* note 66, the authors presented a framework for defining the "business of banking" under 12 U.S.C. § 24(Seventh) in a contemporary context. They concluded that the definition, and national bank charters themselves, can and should accommodate developments in the financial marketplace and consumer demands.

[101] *The Business of Banking II, supra* note 100, at 1286.

[102] *Id.* at 1287.

[103] *Id.* at 1288 (citing *Franklin Nat'l Bank v. New York*, 347 U.S. 373 (1954); *Case v. First Nat'l Bank of Brooklyn*, 109 N.Y.S. 1119 (1908); *Corbett v. Devon Bank*, 299 N.E.2d 521 (Ill. 1973)).

[104] *Id.* at 1289.

processing software if the hardware is necessary for the successful marketing of the permissible software.[105] Any ancillary nonbanking products and services must be incidental to either the use or marketing of permissible banking products or services.

[*iii*] *Activities that Optimize the Use and Value of a Bank's Facilities and Competencies, or Enable the Bank to Avoid Economic Waste in its Banking Franchise.* Banks sometimes need to engage in activities that are not within the definition of the "business of banking" in order to operate in an economically rational manner. Activities that allow a bank to realize a gain or avoid loss from banking activities are considered incidental to the banking business. For example, a bank may acquire, hold, or improve otherwise impermissible property in order to mitigate losses or expenses resulting from a defaulted bank loan.[106] A bank may optimize the economic value of property and other assets to the extent that any activity is based upon a good faith effort by the bank to avoid economic waste within the business of banking. This does not empower a bank to engage in real estate development that is unrelated to its banking business.[107] Banks also may conduct litigation on behalf of third parties when that litigation is necessary to reduce the bank's own losses or costs.[108]

The article's authors note that categories (ii) and (iii) are particularly relevant in analyzing banks' use of emerging technology. According to the authors, banks are generally utilizing advances in technology to meet customer demands for improved service and to realize potential cost efficiencies. Banks that choose to take advantage of technological advances will most likely justify new activities as either enhancing "packaging and promotion" of products and services (category (ii)) or optimizing use and value of banking facilities (category (iii)). The authors point out that, in evaluating the use of technology by banks, courts and the OCC have generally adopted a broad view of the incidental powers doctrine and attempted to look through the use of technology to examine the underlying service or function provided.[109]

[3] PERMISSIBLE NONBANKING ACTIVITIES UNDER THE BANK HOLDING COMPANY ACT

As compared to limitations on the scope of bank powers, statutory restrictions on the activities of bank holding companies are a relatively recent phenomenon. They trace back to the passage of the Bank Holding

---

[105] *Id.* at 1292 (citing *Association of Data Processing Service Org. v. Board of Governors*, 745 F.2d 677 (D.C. Cir. 1984) ("*ADAPSO*")). The court in *ADAPSO* recognized that the linked sale of permissible banking products with incidental products has its limits, stating that, "[a]t some point the tail begins to wag the dog . . . if the banks' profits from the [hardware] should exceed their profits from the [banking software] surely the provision of data processing services would be incidental to hardware manufacture rather than vice-versa." *ADAPSO*, 745 F.2d at 695. The *ADAPSO* case is also discussed in Chapter 7, Section 7.03[4].

[106] *Id.* at 1294 (citing *Atherton v. Anderson*, 86 F.2d 518 (6th Cir. 1936), *rev'd on other grounds*, 302 U.S. 643 (1937); *Birdsell Mfg. Co. v. Anderson*, 104 F.2d 340 (6th Cir. 1939); *Cooper v. Hill*, 94 F. 582 (8th Cir. 1899)).

[107] *Id.* at 1295-96 ("The underlying principle is that when a bank, in good faith, acquires an asset that is necessary to conduct the banking business, the bank may, under its incidental powers, make full economic utilization of the property if using the property for purely banking purposes would leave the property underutilized.").

[108] *Id.* at 1298-99 (citing *Wylie v. Northampton Bank*, 119 U.S. 361 (1886)).

[109] *Id.* at 1302-03 ("[W]hat matters is the 'what' of the activity, not the 'how.'").

Company Act of 1956 ("BHCA").[110] The goals of that legislation were to eliminate the risks associated with: (1) geographic expansion of commonly controlled banks in a given area; and (2) the combination, under common control, of both banking and nonbanking enterprises.[111] The law originally encompassed within its definition of a bank holding company only entities that owned two or more banks.[112] While the restrictions on interstate banking in the BHCA received greater attention, Congress was equally intent on maintaining a line between banking and commerce. Under the BHCA, unless specifically authorized, bank holding companies could not own or control any company that was not a bank. They also could not engage in any business other than banking, managing or controlling banks, or providing services for banks that they controlled.[113] The underlying philosophy was that bank holding companies should confine their activities to the management and control of banks.[114] The BHCA, therefore, sought to regulate bank holding companies by providing that, with certain exceptions, bank holding companies could not manage or control nonbanking assets unrelated to the business of banking.[115] The exceptions, which related to bank premises, safe deposit businesses, bank servicing organizations, collection of debts, involuntary acquisition of shares, acquisition of shares in a fiduciary capacity, or permissible investments for national banks, were intended to ensure that bank holding companies were able to conduct operations closely related to banking.[116]

An exemption for one-bank holding companies was reconsidered but retained in 1966, because Congress concluded such entities encompassed mainly small banks.[117] Just four years later, concerns over the rapid expansion of one-bank holding companies led to the repeal of this exemption.[118] While Congress noted that no abuses had occurred, it felt prophylactic legislation was necessary in light of the rapid expansion of one-bank holding companies.[119] At the same time, Congress granted the FRB greater flexibility in administering the statute. Congress found that the "business of banking" was construed too narrowly to refer to the business of the individual bank applying for approval of a related activity rather than to the broader business of banking.[120] Congress therefore changed "business of banking" to "banking" and added a second prong to the test, namely, that the activity must "reasonably be expected to produce benefits to the public, such as greater convenience,

---

[110] Bank Holding Company Act of 1956, Pub. L. No. 84-511, c. 240, 1956 U.S.C.C.A.N. (70 Stat. 133) 169 (codified as amended at 12 U.S.C. §§ 1841-1850) ("BHCA").

[111] S. REP. No. 1095 (1955), *reprinted in* 1956 U.S.C.C.A.N. 2482, 2483.

[112] BHCA § 2(a) (codified at 12 U.S.C. § 1841(a) (1964) (amended by the Bank Holding Company Act Amendments of 1970, *infra* note 118).

[113] *Id.* § 4(a).

[114] S. REP. No. 1095, *reprinted in* 1956 U.S.C.C.A.N. at 2482.

[115] *Id.* at 2484.

[116] *Id.* at 2494.

[117] S. REP. No. 1179, *reprinted in* 1966 U.S.C.C.A.N. at 2389.

[118] Bank Holding Company Act Amendments of 1970, Pub. L. No. 91-607, § 101(a), 84 Stat. 1760, 1970 U.S.C.C.A.N. 2057 (codified as amended at 12 U.S.C. § 1841(a)) ("BHCA Amendments").

[119] S. REP. No. 91-1084 (1970), *reprinted in* 1970 U.S.C.C.A.N. 5519, 5520-22.

[120] S. CONF. REP. No. 91-1747, *reprinted in* 1970 U.S.C.C.A.N. 5561, 5564.

increased competition, or gains in efficiency, that outweigh possible adverse effects, such as undue concentration of resources, decreased or unfair competition, conflicts of interest, or unsound banking practices."[121]

After subsequent changes,[122] the current BHCA establishes a two-part test to evaluate whether a given activity falls within the parameters of the business of banking. First, the FRB must find, by order or regulation, the proposed activity "to be so closely related to banking or managing or controlling banks as to be a proper incident thereto."[123] Second, it must find there exist benefits to the public that outweigh possible adverse effects.[124]

A nonbanking entity's business generally may qualify as a permissible activity for a bank holding company either by falling within the test of permissible activities authorized by the FRB in Regulation Y,[125] or by virtue of a specific order from the FRB.[126] Regulation Y's list of permissible activities includes a variety of activities, such as making loans, engaging in certain securities activities, providing data processing services, and providing management consulting.[127]

Under Regulation Y, in order to grant an exception to the prohibition on a bank holding company engaging directly or through nonbank subsidiaries in nonbank activities, the FRB must find the activity is "so closely related to banking, or managing or controlling banks as to be a proper incident thereto."[128] Further, under Regulation Y the FRB must determine whether the performance of the activities by a particular bank holding company can reasonably be expected to produce benefits to the public — such as greater convenience, increased competition, and gains in efficiency — that outweigh possible adverse effects — such as undue concentration of resources, decreased or unfair competition, conflicts of interest, and unsound banking practices.[129]

In substantially upholding the FRB's finding that a bank holding company subsidiary could provide courier services, including courier services for financially related data, the Court of Appeals for the District of Columbia Circuit in *National Courier Association v. Board of Governors of the Federal Reserve System* rec-

---

[121] BHCA Amendments § 103(4) (codified at 12 U.S.C. § 1843(c)(8)). *See also* S. REP. NO. 91-1084 (1970), *reprinted in* 1970 U.S.C.C.A.N. at 5567.

[122] Most notable of these changes was the Competitive Equality Banking Act of 1987 ("CEBA"), which eliminated the nonbank bank loophole, that had allowed depository institutions to avoid bank status by either not making commercial loans or not accepting demand deposits. CEBA, Pub. L. No. 100-86, § 101(a), 1987 U.S.C.C.A.N. (101 Stat.) 552, at 554 (codified at 12 U.S.C. § 1841(a)). Under CEBA, non-grandfathered FDIC-insured banks, subject to certain limited exceptions, are deemed to be banks for purposes of the BHCA. CEBA § 101(c) (codified at 12 U.S.C. § 1843(f)).

[123] 12 U.S.C. § 1843(c)(8).

[124] 12 U.S.C. §§1843(a)(8), (j)(2)(A).

[125] The FRB proposed significant amendments to Regulation Y in September 1996. Bank Holding Companies and Change in Bank Control (Regulation Y), 61 Fed. Reg. 47,242 (proposed Sept. 6, 1996). These changes were adopted substantially as proposed in February 1997. See Bank Holding Companies and Change in Bank Control (Regulation Y), 62 Fed. Reg. 9290 (1997) (to be codified at 12 C.F.R. pt. 225)[hereinafter Regulation Y].

[126] There are also a number of other specific activities authorized by the BHCA for bank holding companies and their nonbank subsidiaries. 12 U.S.C. § 1843(c)(1)-(7).

[127] Regulation Y, 62 Fed. Reg. at 9301, 9335 (to be codified at 12 C.F.R. § 225.28). The activities authorized under Regulation Y are discussed further in Chapter 7, Section 7.02[2][a].

[128] *Id.* at 9329 (to be codified at 12 C.F.R. § 225.21(a)).

[129] *Id.* at 9334 (to be codified at 12 C.F.R. § 225.26(a)). As part of this determination, the FRB will evaluate the financial and managerial resources of the bank holding company.

ognized that the activity was permissible not because the transportation of interbank "cash letters" was related to banking *per se,* but rather because it was closely related to financial data processing, an activity in which banks were already permitted to engage.[130] The court indicated that the FRB should use three criteria in examining the appropriateness of a proposed service, any one of which could meet the "closely related to banking" test that Congress imposed: (1) banks have, in fact, generally provided the service; (2) banks provide operationally or functionally equivalent services; or (3) banks provide services so integrally related as to require them to provide the proposed service in specialized form.[131] The court, however, cautioned that the FRB could not be allowed to "tack one close relation on to another indefinitely."[132] In that regard, the FRB had argued that the transportation of non-financially related data on behalf of unsolicited customers was permissible as an "incidental" activity that was to be distinguished from the "closely related" test, which Congress meant to apply only to banks' principal or ordinary activities.[133] The court disagreed and reversed the FRB's order to the extent it allowed non-financially related courier services to be conducted on the ground that they were incidental to a permissible activity.[134]

---

[130] *National Courier Ass'n v. Board of Governors of the Fed. Reserve Sys.*, 516 F.2d 1229, 1239 (D.C. Cir. 1975).

[131] *Id*. at 1237.

[132] *Id*. at 1239.

[133] *Id*. at 1239-40. Such an argument was consistent with the FRB's then-existing Regulation Y (12 C.F.R. § 225.4(a) (1974)) allowing bank holding companies and their nonbank subsidiaries to engage in specified activities closely related to banking, including incidental activities necessary to carry on the permitted closely related activities. The FRB had specified certain permissible incidental activities in connection with financially related data processing (12 C.F.R. § 225.123(g) (1974)).

[134] *National Courier*, 516 F.2d at 1241.

CHAPTER 3
MONEY AS INFORMATION

"Your lovin' give me a thrill,

But your lovin' don't pay my bills,

Now give me money,

That's what I want."

Money

by Berry Gordy, Jr. and Janie Bradford

§ 3.01   INTRODUCTION

Vast amounts of money zip around the globe at the speed of light as electronically stored data. This makes some people nervous. In a recent book, the editor of the *Harvard Business Review*, Joel Kurtzman, writes:

> Money . . . has become nothing more than an assemblage of ones and zeros, the fundamental units of computing . . . that are piped through miles of wire, pumped over fiber-optic highways, bounced off satellites, and beamed from one microwave relay station to another. This new money is like a shadow. Its cool-gray shape can be seen but not touched. It has no tactile dimension, no height or weight. . . . Money is now an image.[1]

Kurtzman laments money's loss of tangibility. He sees its new shadowy form as fundamentally destabilizing, heightening the volatility and speculative uncertainty already associated with financial markets and creating a "community where neighbors, colleagues, and competitors are accessible only through electronics."[2]

---

[1]   JOEL KURTZMAN, THE DEATH OF MONEY 15-16 (1993).

[2]   *Id.* at 16.

Such brouhaha over money shedding its physical skin and slithering into cyberspace is probably unwarranted. For one thing, if money is truly dead, or at least dangerously disembodied as Kurtzman suggests, its demise is not recent. Money does not depend on palpability *per se*, and never has. In fact, most modern money has not had a palpable form for some time. While a checking account balance is money, it has no tangibility beyond the record of that fact. Indeed, at any given point in time, palpable money — that is, bills and coins — constitutes only a small fraction of the money supply. Money's most typical form is as recorded information.[3] Moreover, value has been transmitted electronically since the first days of the telegraph. So what's the big deal with electronic money? What difference does this latest transmogrification of money make?

In the past, money has taken on a myriad of forms, including whiskey, postage stamps, cigarettes, salt, tobacco, grain, fishhooks, woodpecker scalps, shells, animal skins, cocoa beans, furs, beads, limestone disks, and cattle as well as a wide variety of metals, including gold, silver, copper, bronze, nickel, aluminum, and iron. This wild array shouts one loud message — that money's form is *not* important. What is important (and what has always been important) is the social relationship that defines money *as* money and the efficacy with which any particular form of money, or what we might call a "money technology," fulfills money's multiple functions as medium of exchange, unit of account, and store of value.

Money itself is essentially a kind of information. Indeed, all of its functions involve the resolution of informational problems. As a medium of exchange, money assists in the resolution of the recurrent informational problem of matching traders. As a unit of account, money eliminates vast pricing complexity by providing a universal measuring rod that enables the conveyance of price signals. As a store of value, money acts as a general clearing house for value placed in and removed from the stream of commerce.

We are in the midst of an information revolution, the key feature of which is that technology makes information dramatically cheaper. This revolution is resulting in an exponential growth in the efficiency with which money can be generated, stored, and transmitted. How will money be affected in its various roles? What are the likely costs and benefits? To whom? Are there systemic dangers? Great opportunities? To fully grasp the implications of the latest technology in the unfolding saga of money, a brief foray into money's nature and history is warranted. Section 3.02 provides an allegorical history of money, tracing its development from barter origins to paper currency, reserve banking, and fiat money, and drawing a few lessons along the way. Section 3.03 concludes with a discussion of the future of money.

---

[3] *See* James Gleick, *Dead as a Dollar*, N.Y. TIMES (Magazine), June 16, 1996, at 28 ("of the broad American money supply, only a fraction — less than one-tenth — exists in the form of currency").

§ 3.02   AN ALLEGORICAL PERSPECTIVE ON MONEY

[1]   THE QUEST FOR THE CHICKEN-BEARING KNIGHT

Perhaps the best way to understand money is to imagine what the world was like before money existed. Prior to the development of money as a social institution — that is, in a state of society known as "barter" — for a trade of goods or services to occur, a "mutual coincidence of wants" had to be established between trading parties.

What does that mean? As an analogy, consider the institution of marriage. To achieve connubial bliss, each participant in a marriage must find a mate who not only *is* desired, but who also *desires* such a bond. Hence, for a happy marriage, there is a necessity of establishing a mutual coincidence of wants (how much simpler it would be if unrequited love sufficed!). The informational difficulties inherent in finding and establishing such a blissful equilibrium, though not insurmountable, are well known and provide the stuff of romance.

And so it was with barter. A blacksmith who specializes in armor but who wants a chicken, let's call her "Smith," was compelled to find a trading partner who not only wants armor, but has a chicken. Like finding the right partner in life, finding a chicken-bearing knight on demand can prove difficult.

Money evolved through efforts to solve this kind of informational problem. Returning to our questing blacksmith, suppose Smith found a potential trading partner who wanted the armor, but lacked the desired chicken (haven't we all felt that at one time or another?). Suppose a bucket of fishhooks was offered instead. Even though Smith had no desire for fishhooks, she might have traded anyway, *if* she calculated that fishhooks are more generally desired than armor.

Such a mediating trade allowed Smith to improve her chances of ultimately obtaining the desired chicken. For Smith, the fishhooks acquired a purpose that transcends fishing; they were employed not as fishhooks *per se*, but as a "go-between" item of exchange, the purpose of which was to facilitate a hoped-for final trade for the ultimately desired object. In other words, the fishhooks became money. Indeed, it is this "go-between" status to which we refer when we speak of money as a "medium of exchange."

Individuals, not governments, developed money. They did so for a specific private purpose: to make their own transactions more efficient. Incentive, not mandate, was the mother of invention. Indeed, this explains how the many odd things mentioned above — ranging from whiskey to shells to gold — came to be money. Money does not require the authority of the state standing behind it. It does not need a government to create it, or even bless it. If people need money, they will invent it. This remains true even in cyberspace.

There are many obvious characteristics that might prove valuable in such a money commodity, including: (1) stability of value; (2) durability; (3) recognizability; (4) transportability; (5) divisibility; (6) fungibility; and (7) intrinsic utility or desirability that supports confidence in employing it as a medium of exchange. Once a particular money form evolves — that is, once a population begins to embrace a particular commodity *as money* — its status is self-reinforcing. It becomes generally accepted *precisely because* it is generally accepted. This is perfectly rational from an individual perspective; each person is willing to accept a particular money form precisely because everyone else is. Our blacksmith would be more likely to accept fishhooks for armor if she knew fishhooks were widely employed as money.

Contemplation of money's origin reveals its most essential component — *confidence*. The key question confronting our questing blacksmith was whether this particular mediating good, the fishhooks, would be more generally accepted than her armor. In deciding that this was the case, she displayed *confidence* that she could find others who would accept the fishhooks as payment for goods. That confidence is probably induced by the fact that many people were apt to find fishhooks useful, and it is not surprising that the first monies developed on such a basis. But make no mistake about it: money's value *as money* does not derive from its intrinsic usefulness *per se*, but rather *from the confidence among those accepting it that others will accept it*. The blacksmith does not care *why* the fishhooks will prove to be generally accepted, just that they will be.

While confidence in a money commodity may be associated initially with its intrinsic value or usefulness, that is only a sufficient, not necessary, quality. What is necessary is confidence. Once achieved, a money form no longer needs to be backed by "intrinsic usefulness," governmental imprimatur, or anything else. In this sense, money as a social institution involves a particular social relationship, the status of which ultimately transcends individual choices. While money is a form of information, it is also something more than that. Its special social status and recognition makes it so.

A look at barter also unveils the manner in which money massively simplifies the price system. In barter, all goods are exchanged directly for one another. Each good is therefore priced in terms *of every other,* that is, a chicken is not priced in terms of dollars, but rather in terms of other commodities, and expressed as ratios of exchange, such as four oranges per chicken, or two bottles of wine per chicken. As a consequence, in a barter system there are many more prices to keep track of than in a money system, indeed, almost an unfathomable number. For any one good, there is not just one price as in a money system, but as many prices as there are other goods for which it might be traded.

Money replaces the confusing array of ratios with a single uniform price system. In this capacity, money becomes a universal rod for measuring value.[4] Although we take it for granted, this aspect of money results in enormous social benefits through the drastic simplification of commercial relations and information it yields. Imagine having to write annual reports in a world of barter. How would one measure a company's net worth? In chickens? In oranges? Imagine how unstable any one such commodity-measure would be; it would change anytime the relative value of that one good changed.

Money's origin in barter also exposes its social role as a general clearing house for value. In contrast to barter, money expands market possibilities across time and space by allowing trading parties to separate the point at which they contribute value to the stream of commerce from the point at which they withdraw it. Thus, money breaks the simultaneity of contribution and consumption imposed by barter, and in doing so,

---

[4]   Its value, of course, is determined by the array of goods and services you can buy with it.

takes on another role — that is, as a store of value. Money, as a store of value, "accounts" for value added and value removed from the stream of commerce.

With all social progress, there is always some irretrievable loss. And so it is with the introduction of money. Money, by its nature, simplifies transactions. Like all simplifications, it therefore also hides some things — specifically, the social relationships inherent in barter. Because the informational complexities of barter can be overwhelming, in a barter economy long-lasting human relationships become an important means of economic stabilization. In contrast, in a money economy, a cash nexus replaces what otherwise might be closer human relationships. Indeed, reduced dependence on particular human relationships is part and parcel of the freedom and efficiency that the institution of money introduces. The worker who produces a chair gets his cash and then seeks to fulfill his needs with that cash, but perhaps with a less immediate sense that his production was *for* others, as opposed to *for cash*, and that the production by others was *for* him. This may seem a rather fine point, and we do not mean to suggest that the efficiencies that money brings are not worth their weight, well, in gold, but there may be some emotional or psychological loss in disconnecting the ultimate buyer from the ultimate seller that is worthy of recognition, or, at least, a nod.

[2]   MONEY AS NEURONAL NETWORK

In its capacity as a unit of account, money provides the dynamic *informational* network by which decentralized systems of production and consumption maintain coherence; that is, a high degree of predictability, reliability, and efficiency. The capability of a decentralized economic system to attain such coherence was dubbed the "Invisible Hand" by Adam Smith precisely because such a result from an open, unplanned system was shocking — as if the Deity had planned it. Indeed, how is it possible? The answer lies in the behavior of money prices, which essentially constitute the economy's nervous system. Basically, and briefly, this works as follows:

> **Excess Supply Eliminated Through Price Signals:** An excess supply of a good puts downward pressure on its price, as it is difficult to sell in this context. As price falls, producers are signaled that it may not be worthwhile to continue to produce so many units of the good, and consumers are signaled that, at the now lowered price, they may want to buy more. Both responses together eliminate the excess supply.

> **Excess Demand Eliminated Through Price Signals:** An excess demand for a good puts upward pressure on its price, as consumers try to ensure that they can obtain the hotly sought after good. As a price rises, producers are signaled that it may be profitable to produce more of the good, and consumers are signaled that, given its now higher price, they may want to ration the good, or substitute another for it. Both responses together eliminate the excess demand.

This is, of course, nothing other than the laws of supply and demand, with which most readers are probably familiar. The point, however, is that the interplay of these forces constitutes an informational system that coherently coordinates the allocation of resources. This homeostatic mechanism ensures that, in general, about the right quantity of a good tends to get produced to meet the demand for that good, even though no central authority coordinates either consumption or production. Indeed, history has demonstrated that price signals do a much better job than would a planning authority. This testifies to the efficacy of this informational network.[5]

The monetary system thus serves as a kind of giant social computer — providing the mechanism by which the economy's array of input and output allocational puzzles are resolved. Money's great advantage, and fundamental link to liberty itself, is precisely that it provides this mechanism *without* the need for anyone to coordinate the information. The economic vibrancy displayed by free societies historically would not have been possible without the decentralization inherent in the institution of money.

[3] PRIVATE MONEY

Now suppose that a money commodity has been established through general usage as an accepted means of payment, and that it is gold. Because money acts as a store of value, individuals accumulate gold over time. People look for a safe place to store their gold. One place to turn is the goldsmith, since she is apt to have a large vault. Let's say that "Smith," the blacksmith previously introduced, plays this role as well. When Smith accepts gold from a depositor, she gives the depositor a note, "Good for so-much-gold at Smith's." Smith begins to make a little income on the side by storing gold for a fee.

Because gold is the money commodity, people use it to facilitate exchange. When an exchange is to be consummated, the buyer of a good stops by Smith's shop, redeems his note for gold, and pays the seller with that gold. The seller is then apt to redeposit the gold in Smith's shop, for safekeeping, and receive one of Smith's notes in return, as evidence of the deposit.

One day, to save themselves a trip to Smith's, someone comes up with the bright idea of substituting the note issued by Smith for the actual gold as a method of payment. That is, the buyer of a good simply gives the seller one of Smith's notes that represents a claim to gold directly. So long as Smith is trusted — and presumably she is, as people are leaving their gold with her — the note is "as good as gold." The trouble of transporting the gold or traveling to and from Smith's shop is thereby avoided.

In this manner, the paper notes issued by Smith begin to circulate as money. It is a money form based on the *confidence* that the community places in Smith and on the *information* captured by possession of the note. This is a critical turning point in the history of money — for it is at this point that money is transformed into pure information. It has become *a claim* to a part of Smith's store of gold.

---

[5] As a decentralized, interactive informational system, the pricing framework is really very much like the Internet itself. The Internet — the global computer network currently used by millions of people — appears to thrive despite the fact that "no central authority oversees it and few rules govern it." *See* Rebecca Quick, *Online Internet Addresses Spark Storm in Cyberspace*, WALL ST. J., Apr. 29, 1997, at B1. While this is not to deny that governments played a key role in the development of the Internet, or may play an important role in its governance, it stands, nonetheless, as further testimony to the powers of decentralization as applied to complex informational systems. Over time, one of the more important economic contributions of the Internet will be the extent to which it reinforces the prowess of the global pricing "network" by expediting the flow of pricing information.

[4]   THE DISCOVERY OF RESERVE BANKING

Over time, Smith notices that very little of the stored gold is ever redeemed, since most people facilitate exchange using her issued notes. As a consequence, she finds that she does not have to maintain a store of gold equivalent to the notes issued. Rather, circumstances only require her to maintain sufficient gold to meet the occasional demand for redemption. This allows Smith to earn additional income by loaning some of the gold in the vault. Alternatively, she may choose not to loan the gold itself, but rather simply to print up and loan out additional notes, since the notes themselves are money.

For example, if she determines from experience that holding gold reserves of 20% is sufficient to meet any fluctuation in the demand for redemption, she can issue notes that lay claim to up to five times the amount of gold actually in the vault. She distributes these newly issued notes in the form of loans to customers, and thereby earns interest on this money that she has just created. Borrowers are willing to take the notes precisely because others find them acceptable. While there may be sporadic demand for redemption of Smith's notes for gold, Smith can meet that demand from her gold reserves as it arises, and confidence in the notes is maintained.

This discovery is momentous, and not just for Smith. Although the notes constitute a claim to gold, there are now more claims *in the aggregate* than gold to back them up. This represents another critical step in the dematerialization of money. The money supply has been expanded, in the form of paper currency, beyond the physical supply of the money commodity. Thus, in a sense, many of the notes represent a claim to something that does not exist. But, of course, it is not the gold *per se* that supports the value of the notes, it is the community's confidence in Smith. In turn, this confidence in the money form as a viable medium of exchange renders it "backed" by the goods and services one can buy with it.

An interesting question is raised by this scenario: what limits the amount of money Smith is apt to print? The answer is the quantity of gold held in reserve. It must be sufficient to cover the expected demand for redemption.

[5]   COMPETITION IN THE CREATION OF MONEY

At this point, Smith is taking deposits and making loans as well as issuing money. She has become not only a banker, but indeed a central banker.[6] Eventually, others are apt to see that Smith has a good thing going. They may decide to buy a safe for themselves, put up a building with ionic pillars and enter into this business of reserve banking. They too will issue money backed by a gold reserve. Competition in the market for creating money will prevail. Will the money supply grow without limit? No. Like Smith, each banker will have an incentive to limit his or her creation of money as some multiple of the gold held in reserve to cover the expected demand for redemption.

---

[6]   This is essentially how the business of banking actually began. *See* VERA C. SMITH, THE RATIONALE OF CENTRAL BANKING 11 (1936). For example, there was a period of time in the United States, known as the "free banking" era, when much of the money supply was comprised of notes issued by private banks in a process very similar to this. For a description of the free banking era, see *id*. 42-56. *See also* LEWIS D. SOLOMON, RETHINKING OUR CENTRALIZED MONETARY SYSTEM: THE CASE FOR A SYSTEM OF LOCAL CURRENCIES 7-9 (1996).

[6]   DEFLATION

Now, suppose that one day a nasty rumor is spread about Smith's bank — perhaps that it has made a number of bad loans to ship owners, whose ships have just sunk in a bad storm. As a consequence, confidence in Smith's ability to meet a demand for redemption comes into question. There is a "run" on her bank to redeem notes for gold. Smith cannot meet the demand, because her gold reserves do not match the number of notes issued. As a consequence, the value of her notes collapses. Her money making days are over.

The crisis soon spreads to other money-issuing banks. The holders of Smith's previously issued but now worthless notes have trouble repaying their own debts, some of which may be to other banks. This induces a general panic with runs on other banks and the failure of other private currencies. There is thus a contraction in the money supply, which results in a falling price level, otherwise known as "deflation." Because deflation tends to leave debt payment schedules unchanged, while rendering it more difficult to meet them from current revenues, it serves to push more debt-leveraged businesses into bankruptcy. A general collapse in asset values results as individuals and businesses engage in a sell-off to try to increase their liquidity. This snowballs into more bankruptcies. The end result of these financial disruptions is a reduction in the aggregate level of economic activity and massive unemployment.

[7]   GOVERNMENT MONOPOLY

The deflation crisis discussed above presents an ideal opportunity for a government to monopolize the monetary function. Governments know a good thing when they see it, and being able to print your own money is a good thing. Governments did, in fact, take control of the lucrative business of creating money. They issued "gold certificates" and "silver certificates," redeemable in precious metals. And this operated pretty much the same as Smith's bank. As long as people remained confident that one *could* demand delivery of the precious metal from the government, there was no reason to actually do so. But like the private sector, governments also quickly realized that they could issue notes far in excess of their stock of precious metals and still meet the normal demand for redemption.[7]

[8]   FIAT MONEY

Over time people became so accustomed to employing the government's notes to facilitate exchange that the existence of a precious metal supporting the currency ceased to matter. *Once the general acceptability of a currency is established, it becomes "backed" — not by some underlying commodity — but directly by whatever one can buy with it.* Perhaps paradoxically, while commodity backing may be necessary to generate initial confidence in a money form, once that confidence is established, it is no longer needed. The acceptability of the money by others provides sufficient grounds for accepting it oneself.

---

[7]   Further, by issuing currency, the government realizes a profit called seignorage. Seignorage is discussed in further detail in Chapter 16.

Money had become a claim to nothing — that is, to nothing but the goods and services one can buy with it. In that sense, money's dematerialization was complete. It was simply declared as legal tender (an instrument that by statute is required to be accepted as payment for public and private debts), and it was so. As governments went off precious metal standards, there was no sudden collapse in the value of money. Money continued to play its multiple roles as a medium of exchange, store of value, and unit of account, despite the fact that it was backed by nothing other than the fact of general acceptability.

[9]   INFLATION

But the story does not end "happily ever after." Once governments abandoned the gold standard, they no longer faced any immediate constraint in the creation of money. Many of them did, in fact, begin to print ever larger amounts of money. This acted, in effect, as a hidden tax. By printing money and spending it, governments caused inflation — *i.e.,* a general and persistent rise in the price level — from "too much money chasing too few goods." Inflation results in a loss of spending power for many citizens, for example, those on fixed incomes or holding money balances. Thus, it acts as a tax on those individuals, but not one that the government has to collect directly. Some governments became so addicted to printing money that they induced "hyperinfla-tions," a complete collapse of confidence in their currency, and even a return to barter.

Some have argued that this persistent display of governmental irresponsibility with respect to the money supply calls for a return by governments to the gold standard. There are a number of problems with this solu-tion. First, and most importantly, tying money to gold, or any commodity of relatively fixed supply, could cause deflation, because, as an economy grows, the fixed money supply would not grow at a rate sufficient to meet the rising transactional demand for money. As we saw above, given a legacy of debt in the economy, deflation has the potential to cause serious economic turmoil. Second, even if a government pretended to be on the gold standard, it is hard to see politically how it could be maintained in the midst of an economic contraction, in which many would perceive an increase in the money supply as potentially beneficial.

[10]   THE ECONOMY AS A SAILING SHIP

While a full discussion of the macroeconomic role of money is beyond the scope of this book, two guid-ing metaphors that capture something of the big debates over the role of money in the economy may prove useful in pondering the impact of any new money technology. In one camp, there are those who see a capital-ist economy as like a large sailing ship with a deep, heavy keel. Though it be hit by a great swell, the ship nonetheless has a propensity to right itself rapidly. In the real world, the mechanisms that provide for this self-righting propensity in the economy are flexible prices, wages, and interest rates.[8]

---

[8]   For example, if aggregate investment in plant and equipment is flagging, a concurrent reduction in the demand for loanable funds will cause a drop in the interest rate (which, in essence, is the price of loanable funds.) In turn, this reduction in interest rate will help to stimulate renewed investment. Or, if workers are unemployed, a drop in wages will lift the demand for labor. Or, if there is a lack of demand for production in particular markets, a fall in price will help raise the quantity demanded.

The sailing ship camp tends to see money as a "neutral veil" over "real" economic relations. That is, aside from money's role in directly increasing the transactional efficiencies discussed above, "money does not matter." What they mean by this expression is that governmental efforts to influence the level of economic activity and unemployment through a change in the money supply are both fruitless and unnecessary. In this view, the only impact of a change in the money supply is on the general price level, but it tends to have no impact on the real allocation of resources or the level of economic activity.

[11] THE ECONOMY AS A BARGE

The other camp sees a capitalist economy as more like a barge. The cargo is business confidence. If this barge is hit by an unexpected swell, it will tip and its cargo will slide to one side, rendering it stuck in an unfortunate tilted position. In the real world, when trouble strikes the economy, it undermines business confidence and the economy can become mired in the doldrums. In the aggregate, business confidence, or a lack thereof, tends to be a self-fulfilling prophecy. That is, if all businesses are simultaneously confident, they will all be investing, employment will be high, and there will be demand for what they produce. On the other hand, if business confidence is down, businesses will all stop investing simultaneously; this will lead to lay-offs, a drop in aggregate income, a general lack of demand, and a downward spiral.

This does not imply that businesses can simply will themselves out of an economic recession or depression, because each is a victim to the general mood. It is irrational to invest when there is a general lack of investment, precisely because there is apt to be no demand for any extra production that that investment might support.

The "Barge" camp tends to see an active role for government in stimulating an economy out of its doldrums. Someone has to drag the cargo of business confidence back to the middle of the barge. Members of the barge camp view monetary policy as one means by which such stimulation might be accomplished. They argue that by increasing the money supply, the government can induce a reduction in interest rates, stimulate aggregate investment, enhance business confidence, and induce a return to prosperity.[9]

[12] MONEY AND THE BUSINESS CYCLE

Because money serves as a store of value, it promotes saving. Saving, in turn, promotes capital accumulation and economic growth. But there is a downside to the role of money as a store of value. In the world of barter, supply creates its own demand. Value contributed to the market is necessarily exactly offset by value consumed in each time period.[10] In the world of money, however, this is not necessarily so. Precisely because money breaks the simultaneity of contribution and consumption, it renders possible an excess aggregate supply of goods and services in any given time period, that is, more goods and services may be produced in the

---

[9] For a detailed history of the various schools of thought on monetary economics, see JOSEPH A. SCHUMPETER, HISTORY OF ECONOMIC ANALYSIS (1954). *See also* HENRY WILLIAM SPIEGEL, THE GROWTH OF ECONOMIC THOUGHT (1971).

[10] This is known among economists as "Say's Law."

aggregate than people want to consume. This can result in a cutback in production, economic recession, and a lowering of income for many people. The institution of money not only facilitates such good things as trade, investment, and economic growth, it also facilitates business cycles.

The exact nature of the relationship between money and business cycles is complex and controversial, and beyond the scope of this discussion. It is ironic, however, that money not only provides a means of signaling and reinforcing productive behavior (*i.e., by individuals purchasing what they deem valuable*), but *also* provides the means by which those signals can occasionally break down. When large numbers of people retreat to money holdings instead of purchasing the goods and services produced in a given time period, a recession may be generated. Through a breakdown in the signaling that normally occurs in money prices, an economy can become trapped in a vicious circle. Unemployed workers cannot signal what goods and services they would buy if they had a job, simply because they do not have the income to spend that is associated with a job. If they could signal what they *would* buy *if* they had income, this would induce business plans for greater production to meet that demand, which means that the workers might well get a job and the income to spend on those goods. But precisely because the unemployed do not have the income, the signal can never be sent, and the jobs are never offered. As a consequence, the economy may stay in the doldrums. It presents an odd scenario of: (1) excess productive capacity; (2) unemployed workers; and (3) human needs going unfulfilled. Because the signals for *potential* demand cannot be sent through money prices, the system breaks down, and the capacity for extra production — both in terms of labor and capital — is wasted.

As discussed briefly above, whether money can be effectively employed by governments to smooth out the business cycle remains a topic of debate. There are many problems with such an approach. First and fore-most is the difficulty of timing changes in the money supply so that they operate counter-cyclically. To do this one would have to know precisely when economic downturns are coming, and no one has ever been able to determine that with great accuracy. Second is the difficulty of determining the money supply itself. With changes in technology and regulation, moneys and near-moneys multiply. The decision of precisely what con-stitutes money for policy-measurement purposes is not an easy question to answer. Third, and closely related to the second point, is the difficulty of controlling the money supply. Although monetary authorities can act to increase or decrease the money supply, private actions also effect the various magnitudes one might define as money, and not always in ways that may be predicted with accuracy. Finally, in a rapidly changing world, monetary authorities have a very difficult time distinguishing the impact of their own policies from other economic influences. Thus, the hand at the economy's tiller may not know whether and when to ease up or pull harder.

§ 3.03   THE FUTURE OF MONEY

One lesson from history is that money forms and money technologies are anything but stagnant. Money evolves with changes in the economy and with emerging technological possibilities. What drives this evolution?

[1] THE COSTS AND BENEFITS OF NEW MONEY TECHNOLOGIES

If a new form of money is to prove successful, it must provide convenience, fulfill some need, or function in a manner superior to alternative payment methods. Technological feasibility is not enough. For a money form to be adopted, it must also be *economically* feasible. That is, the benefits and conveniences of the money form must outweigh the burdens as compared to other money forms.

This does *not* imply that a new payment form must be "consumer driven." If sellers find a new money form convenient,[11] they can transfer some of that benefit to the consumer in some form — such as reduced product price — to encourage consumers to employ that more convenient form. Thus, while a new money form must be embraced by consumers, its ultimate economic benefit may only accrue to them indirectly.

Another lesson from history is that a flaw in some new money form does *not* imply that it will not be adopted and successful. All money forms have flaws. The appropriate question, as indicated above, is one of trade-offs between costs and benefits. For example, while almost all money forms are insecure to some extent, it is clear that lack of security does not render a money form useless. Someone can easily steal a person's wallet and take the cash; yet, despite this risk, that person may nonetheless continue to find cash more convenient for some purposes. Adoption turns on whether the convenience of using the money form outweighs the risks and other burdens it entails. A good example is the use of credit cards as a means of online payment well before this could have been thought secure. Clearly, the calculation was made by informed users that the conveniences outweighed the risks.

[2] HOW TO INTRODUCE A NEW MONEY FORM

From an individual perspective, a money form only proves to be a convenience if it is *generally* acceptable. But how then does a money form become generally acceptable if no one is willing to use it until that precondition has been met? This really is a way of restating the necessity of confidence. No one will be willing to employ a money form as a medium of exchange if there is a serious danger he or she will end up stuck holding undesired quantities of it.

Thus, the trick to creating the confidence necessary to introduce a new money form is to provide an easy exit strategy — that is, a means by which a person using the money form as a means of exchange feels sure she will not get stuck with a valueless token. Historically, that is the role that the precious metals played in supporting the value of paper currency. But one can imagine other means of generating and maintaining such confidence. For example, momentarily setting aside legal issues, a software manufacturer, or other entrepreneur, might choose to introduce an online money form by backing it with dollars. Like Smith's bank, it would only have to maintain sufficient reserves to meet the demand for redemption. Also, like Smith's bank, this would serve to increase the money supply. Would such money creation result in a limitless expansion of the money

---

[11] *See* Brian Nixon, *E-Cash,* AMERICA'S COMMUNITY BANKER, June 1996, at 34 ("[t]ransporting physical currency among merchants and their depository institutions costs between 2 and 6 percent of the currency's face value, according to industry benchmarks").

supply? No. Like Smith's bank, the money supply would be limited by some multiple of the reserves that each online money creator felt necessary to maintain confidence in its money form. We may, indeed, return to an era of competition in the creation of money.

Software companies, or other money creators, might also back money with online goods and services. Of course, once confidence in a new money form is established, it would be accepted simply because it is generally accepted. At this point it would be transformed from a means of transferring the existing underlying dollar currency to a true private currency. A condition of generating and maintaining such confidence, however, is a public expectation that the value of the money form will not be subject to collapse, due, for example, to over-issuance. Assuring the public that the value of a money form will remain stable has not always proved to be an easy task, even for governments.

Another interesting possibility is that online "commodity" monies may evolve. That is, valuable software that can be sent online could itself be employed as a medium of exchange. Confidence in its general acceptability would be supported by its intrinsic value as a commodity. Similarly, as cyberspace evolves — and again momentarily setting aside legal issues — highly liquid and secure securities markets may develop online that allow easy and efficient transference of financial assets. In this manner, securities such as U.S. treasury bonds may come themselves to play some of the roles of money, and become very difficult to distinguish in terms of monetary policy. Finally, given that the main problem with barter was informational complexity, it may be that the information revolution allows for an occasional return to barter in some form. That is, with a wide enough online market, establishing a mutual coincidence of wants may become substantially easier than in the past.

[3] POLICY ISSUES RAISED BY THE PRIVATE ISSUANCE OF MONEY FORMS

What are the policy dangers in an online competitive creation of new money forms? From a macro-economic perspective, as long as these money forms remain a relatively small part of the overall money supply, there is very little danger to the public at large. As the use of the money form or forms grows, however, there are at least two possible dangers. One is that a crisis in confidence in these money forms could cause a sudden and dangerous collapse in the money supply, much like we saw with Smith's bank. Thus, if use of such a money form grew to be substantial in scale, it may be advisable to regulate it in a fashion designed to reinforce confidence. This might include reserve requirements, for example, and independent audits. The second, and related, danger is that monetary authorities might find it yet more difficult to measure and control monetary aggregates in a counter-cyclical fashion — assuming one thinks that they can do this at all.

[4] THE DEMAND FOR NEW MONEY FORMS

There is clearly a demand for a convenient and secure means of online payment. Whether this will come simply through the more secure employment of credit and debit cards, or through some form of electronic token, or through other means, is difficult to predict at this point.

One arena in which some form of cyber money may come to play an especially important role is in the realm of micropayments. Given a world wide market on the Web, an efficient mechanism for online micro-payments could stimulate *whole new industries* and market niches in information. For example, someone could sell poetry for a penny a poem, and, with a world wide market, make a good living, whereas otherwise they would have gone into a different profession. One can imagine many informational services that are *not* now economically feasible, but which might be rendered so by such a money form.

Where next? What new money forms will people find genuinely convenient, given the evolving needs and opportunities presented by the information revolution? No one knows for certain. The real test will be in the marketplace.

CHAPTER 4

FOUNDATIONS OF ELECTRONIC COMMERCE AND BANKING

§ 4.01   INTRODUCTION

Over the past century, the payments system in the United States has repeatedly developed new approaches to facilitating the movement of money through the economy. In its current form the payments system is recognized as a major asset for the U.S. economy.[1] A payments system must be fast, reliable, and secure.[2] This Chapter discusses the highlights of the development of the payments system during the 20th Century.

Checks, originally used for settlement between regional merchants, evolved into the dominant form of noncash payment for businesses and consumers. A complex infrastructure of processing mechanisms and procedures gradually developed to meet check settlement demands. Merchants, who in the early part of the century developed charge plates and cards for the convenience of their repeat customers, inspired issuers to develop multi-purpose charge cards in the late 1940s and credit cards in the 1950s. In the 1970s, when credit cards finally had achieved widespread use and acceptance, a national processing infrastructure was established. The computerization of the check and credit card settlement processing infrastructures in the late 1960s and early 1970s and the evolution of automated clearing house association ("ACH") transactions inspired vendors to develop automated teller machines ("ATMs") and point-of-sale ("POS") terminals linked through private networks.

The credit card, check clearing, ACH, and ATM/POS infrastructures comprise the retail electronic payments system, which will provide the backbone for electronic banking and commerce.[3] This Chapter, therefore, explores the development of these products and their supporting infrastructures; in doing so it provides the foundation for the developments in electronic financial products and services ("EFS") discussed in Part IV. It also discusses regulatory and legislative provisions, as well as industry standards that impact on the use and development of the aforementioned products and services.

---

[1]   *See* PAYMENTS SYSTEM TASK FORCE, AMERICAN BANKERS ASS'N, THE ROLE OF BANKS IN THE PAYMENTS SYSTEM OF THE FUTURE (1996).

[2]   *See* BILL BURNHAM, PIPER JAFFRAY RESEARCH, THE ELECTRONIC COMMERCE REPORT 91 (1997).

[3]   *See id.* at 105.

§ 4.02   CHECKS AND THE AUTOMATED CLEARING HOUSE ALTERNATIVE

The largest volume of noncash payments made in the United States today are made using paper checks.[4] Currently banks process and settle checks drawn on other banks through one or a combination of the following four methods: (1) direct presentment to the paying bank; (2) presentment to correspondent banks that settle the accounts either on their books or through FedWire® fund transfers;[5] (3) net settlement through FEDNET®, a nationwide system linking the Federal Reserve Banks and branches with depository institutions;[6] or (4) clearing and settlement services provided by check clearing houses. The last method and the infrastructure that supports it is likely to play an important role in the development of new electronic financial products and services.

In order to provide background for the new products and services discussed in Part IV, this Section will review: the evolution of checks; the use of electronic fund transfers ("EFTs"), both as a method of settling checks and as a substitution for checks; and the infrastructure supporting those transactions.

[1]   THE EVOLUTION OF CHECKS AS A METHOD OF PAYMENT

Checks were used as a payment method as early as the late 18th Century. Initially used by merchants for local settlement, checks had gained acceptance as a method of local exchange by the early 19th Century. By 1840, almost all payments in cities, except for small retail transactions, were made by check.[7] The popularity of checks led to a twentyfold increase in the number of bank accounts by the 1850s.[8]

The first clearing house association, established for the purpose of daily settlement of net balances among its banks, opened in New York City in 1853. Banks in other cities, encouraged by the effectiveness of that first association, established their own clearing house associations.[9] Rural America joined in the national check usage trend after 1900 when banks serving farmers expanded into rural areas.[10] Nearly 85% of the nation's business-to-business transactions were conducted by check by 1909.[11] Household checking accounts became

---

[4] *See* UNITED STATES GENERAL ACCOUNTING OFFICE: PAYMENTS, CLEARANCE, AND SETTLEMENT 93 (June 1997) [hereinafter GAO STUDY]. *See also* COMMITTEE ON THE FEDERAL RESERVE IN THE PAYMENTS MECHANISM, FEDERAL RESERVE SYSTEM, THE FEDERAL RESERVE IN THE PAYMENTS MECHANISM 6 (Jan. 1998) (stating that paper checks accounted for about 75% of all noncash transactions in 1996) [hereinafter THE FEDERAL RESERVE IN THE PAYMENTS MECHANISM].

[5] The FedWire® fund transfer system is a large-dollar real-time gross settlement system. It essentially consists of two components: (1) FEDNET®, a nationwide communications network that electronically links all Federal Reserve Banks and branches with depository institutions, and (2) a computerized system for processing and recording individual funds and transfers as they occur. Banks send messages over FedWire® authorizing the Federal Reserve to debit the sending bank's account and credit the receiving bank's account with the Federal Reserve. *See* GAO STUDY, *supra* note 4, at 17-19.

[6] *See* GAO STUDY, *supra* note 4, at 18.

[7] *See* BENJAMIN J. KLEBANER, AMERICAN COMMERCIAL BANKING: A HISTORY 27 (1990).

[8] The 1859 annual report of the New York Superintendent of Banks provides the twentyfold estimate. *See id.* at 27 (citing JOHN A. FERRIS, THE FINANCIAL ECONOMY OF THE UNITED STATES . . . (1867)), 231.

[9] *See* KLEBANER, *supra* note 7, at 27.

[10] *See id.*

[11] *See id.*

popular as the 20th Century progressed.[12] The volume of checks processed increased from 3.5 billion per year in 1939 to 13.0 billion per year in 1960,[13] and to 63.4 billion per year by 1996.[14] As check usage increased, the nation's clearing houses and the American Bankers Association responded by developing elaborate check settlement procedures.

[2]   CHECK SETTLEMENT AND THE INTRODUCTION OF ELECTRONIC FUND TRANSFERS

Initially, banks and clearing house associations settled checks through a paper-based system. The system operated using information included on the checks, such as the payor's name and account number, and the name and identifier of the payor's bank. Automated check processing equipment, which increased the efficiency of the paper-based system, was introduced in the 1950s.[15] For a time these systems made the number of checks flowing through the collection channels manageable. The development of EFT technology in the 1960s presented an opportunity to bypass or replace the check clearing process. The electronic movement of data to accomplish fund transfers did not begin, however, until the early 1970s. By 1978, over thirty check clearing houses, providing check settlement, were in place throughout the country and an interregional exchange had been established.[16] Banks clear checks through Federal Reserve Banks by batching checks at a central location, according to the banks on which they are drawn and submitting the appropriate information to the clearing house or Federal Reserve Bank, where net settlement then occurs.

As electronic fund transfers mechanisms evolved, different systems were established to meet different needs. For international wholesale payments, members of the New York Clearing House Association created the Clearing House Interbank Payments System ("CHIPS") to facilitate foreign transactions, such as the dollar leg of foreign exchange and Eurodollar placements,[17] and the Federal Reserve System's FedWire® enables financial institutions to settle large value transfers through reserve and clearing accounts held at their Federal Reserve Banks.[18] On the retail level, the ACH Network and Federal Reserve System provide a cost-efficient

---

[12]   In 1946, 34 percent of all households had checking accounts. That percentage reached 50 percent by 1956, 75 percent by 1970, and 84 percent by 1984. *See id.* at 214.

[13]   *See* BAKER & BRANDEL, THE LAW OF ELECTRONIC FUND TRANSFER SYSTEMS ¶ 1.02 (3d ed. 1996).

[14]   GAO STUDY, *supra* note 4, at 93.

[15]   In 1954, the American Bankers Association ("ABA(Bankers)") appointed a Technical Subcommittee on the Mechanization of Check Handling to establish guidelines for automated check processing equipment. In 1956, the subcommittee, after studying two proposed systems, recommended the adoption of Magnetic Ink Character Recognition ("MICR") as the machine language to be employed in check processing. Over the next few years the ABA(Bankers) developed standards for using MICR. *See* BAKER & BRANDEL, *supra* note 13, ¶ 1.01.

[16]   *See* KLEBANER, *supra* note 7, at 215.

[17]   CHIPS is an online, real-time system that transfers and settles wholesale, large dollar volume transactions. It is owned and operated by the New York Clearing House Association and makes net settlements through the Federal Reserve Bank of New York. *See* THE BANKERS ROUNDTABLE, 2 BANKING'S ROLE IN TOMORROW'S PAYMENTS SYSTEM 61 (1994) [hereinafter BANKERS ROUNDTABLE].

[18]   FedWire® had been available in telex form since the early 20th Century. *See id.* at 45.

means of settling large volumes of regularly recurring, small dollar consumer payments.[19] The ACH system will likely play a significant role in many of the new electronic payments models, and therefore will be the focus of the remainder of this Section.

[a] ACH. The ACH Network facilitates wholesale and retail electronic fund transfers in a batched environment. In 1997, the ACH Network handled 4.4 billion payments, whose dollar volume represents ten times the dollar volume flowing through the credit card and ATM/POS components combined,[20] or approximately $13 trillion.

[i] *ACH Participants.* The ACH Network consists of the Federal Reserve and three private ACH Operators: (1) New York Automated Clearing House; (2) American Clearing House; and (3) Visa.[21] No ACH involvement is required when a bank receives a payment drawn on one of its own accounts. In that case, the bank settles the transaction in what is called an "on-us" transaction, processing the payment on its internal software. When both the originating depository financial institution ("ODFI") and receiving depository financial institution ("RDFI") use the same ACH Operator, that Operator, alone, will process the transaction. The steps taken when the ODFI and RDFI do not share the same ACH Operator are described in subsection [*ii*], below. The National Automated Clearing House Association ("NACHA") maintains and develops the rules and standards for exchange of electronic payments among the participants.[22]

[ii] *Payment Flow Through ACH.* The participants in the ACH Network include: an Originator, an ODFI, an ACH Operator, a RDFI, and a Receiver. The Originator is the party who transmits the payment instructions to the ODFI. The ODFI transmits its payment entries to the ACH Operator, which, in turn, transmits or makes available the ACH entries to the RDFI. The RDFI posts the entry to the Receiver's account and notes the transaction in a statement to the Receiver. Settlement occurs later, at a pre-established time/date, through the Federal Reserve.

The two basic types of ACH entries are credit and debit. The primary distinctions between them are direction of the flow of funds and the applicable legal requirements. The legal requirements, which are discussed in Section 4.07, depend on many factors, including whether the transaction is: (1) directed to a consumer or nonconsumer depository account;[23] (2) a debit or a credit; (3) initiated by the government or private sector; and (4) an original issuance or a replacement of a previously issued payment. The status of the party through

---

[19] *See* BAKER & BRANDEL, *supra* note 13, ¶ 3.01. *See generally* THE FEDERAL RESERVE IN THE PAYMENTS MECHANISM *supra* note 4, at 38. "The Federal Reserve Banks are currently the only check collection intermediaries that provide national check collection services available to depository institutions of all sizes and locations." *Id.* at 13.

[20] Interview with Scott Lang, Director of Network Products, NACHA, in Washington, D.C. (Feb. 26, 1998). *See also* BURNHAM, *supra* note 2, at 105. In 1996, ACH volume was 750 million transactions (not including non-Federal Reserve ACH payments). The Federal Reserve processes approximately 80% of all ACH entries. *See* BURNHAM, *supra* note 2, at 105.

[21] *See id.* at 103 (including a table describing the ACH system).

[22] NATIONAL AUTOMATED CLEARING HOUSE ASSOCIATION, THE ACH RULES (1997) [hereinafter NACHA RULES].

[23] For example, transactions involving consumer accounts are subject to the Federal Reserve Board's Regulation E, discussed in greater detail in Chapter 7.

whom the consumer initiated the transaction also factors into the determination of legal requirements.[24] The direction of the flow of funds will either be inherent to the type of transaction or established through authorization. In a debit transaction, the payment data flow from ODFI to RDFI, and funds flow in the opposite direction, from RDFI to ODFI. Preauthorized bill payments, where the payee pulls the funds from the payor's account, and check truncation entries[25] are examples of debit transactions accomplished through the ACH Network. In a credit transaction, the payment data flow from ODFI to the RDFI and funds flow in the same direction. Credit transactions include preauthorized payments that are initiated by the consumer's financial institution, for example, pre-authorized direct deposit of payroll payments by employers to employees.[26] The following diagrams illustrate basic credit and debit ACH transactions.

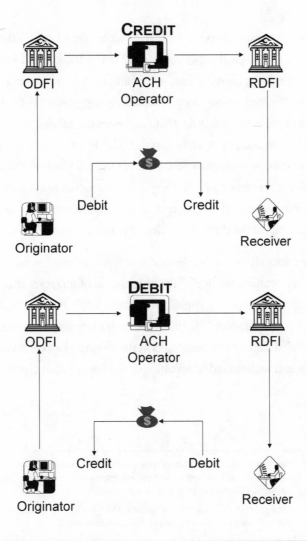

---

[24] *See* BAKER & BRANDEL, *supra* note 13, ¶ 3.04; NACHA RULES, *supra* note 22.

[25] Check truncation entries refer to the process where the bank of first deposit retains the physical check and creates a debit entry that it then transmits to the deposit account of the check issuer. For a more detailed discussion of check truncation, see BANKERS ROUNDTABLE, *supra* note 17, at 14-16.

[26] Credit transactions are covered by Article 4A of the U.C.C. *See* U.C.C. § 4A-104(a) (definition of "funds transfer"); U.C.C. art. 4A prefatory note (describing the types of transactions that fall within Article 4A).

[b] Interbank Check Imaging. In 1995, the Financial Services Technology Consortium ("FSTC")[27] established the Interbank Check Imaging ("ICI®") project to design and build a national check image interchange system.[28] Its interoperable, open system design allows for communication between several distinct imaging systems. Banks using different systems and software may thus transmit digital images of checks via the existing bank infrastructure with the knowledge that any recipient will be able to read and print a paper copy of the digitized check. The digitization of paper checks provides flexible, economical services for the financial industry by reducing paper flow, increasing transmission speed, and eliminating losses that result from manual handling of paper checks.[29] As described below, ICI® contemplates the continued use of paper checks, however, its appeal to the banking industry lies in its ability to discard or truncate paper checks at earlier points in the clearing process.

When a bank of first deposit receives a paper check, ICI® technology enables the bank to create a digital image of the check with a scanner. The original paper check need not be transported any further in the payments system, because the bank can transmit the digital check image and attendant payment information for clearing and settlement purposes. ICI® technology integrates disparate imaging platforms to allow the transmission of digitized check images. Thus, a depository institution that receives a digital check from a bank of first deposit that scanned the paper with a different imaging system can use ICI® technology to read the check image. The bank of first deposit can immediately provide provisional funds to its depositor and then transmit the image into the check clearing system for settlement with the depository institution upon which the check was drawn. Following settlement, the depositor receives final payment and the drawer receives an account statement with the truncated check data included and, at the drawer's option, a paper version of the check's image.

Though digitization of the paper checks at the depositing bank will provide enormous cost savings to the banking industry, by limiting transportation of checks, the elimination of all paper checks is the banking industry's and Federal Reserve's ultimate goal.[30] The Committee on the Federal Reserve in the Payments Mechanisms has stated that the Federal Reserve "should work with other retail payment system participants to identify areas where new or amended standards would support the growth of an electronic payments system that replicates the ease, convenience, and widespread acceptance of the paper-based check system."[31]

---

[27] Founded in September 1993, the FSTC is a not-for-profit organization of banks, financial service firms, industry partners, national laboratories, universities, and government agencies. The FSTC sponsors collaborative research and development on technical projects affecting the entire financial services industry. For more information, visit the FSTC's website at <http://www.ftsc.org>.

[28] *See FSTC Demonstrates Interbank Check Image Pilot; Multi-Vendor System Speeds Check Clearing, Cuts Fraud*, FSTC Press Release, Dec. 12, 1995, *available at* (visited Nov. 17, 1997) <http://www.fstc.org/projects/imaging/public/information.shtml>.

[29] *See FSTC Check Imaging Project Provides Path to Big Savings For Banks*, BUS. WIRE, May 13, 1997 (quoting ICI project chair Dan Vermeire of Huntington Bancshares).

[30] One estimate projects a 33% reduction in costs associated with check processing. *FSTC Demonstrates Interbank Check Image Pilot; Multi-Vendor System Speeds Check Clearing, Cuts Fraud*, *supra* note 29 (quoting Cary M. Serif of Huntington Bank).

[31] THE FEDERAL RESERVE IN THE PAYMENTS MECHANISM, *supra* note 4, at 38. The development of electronic checks may be the electronic replica sought by the FRB. See Chapter 15 for a discussion of electronic checks.

§ 4.03   THE EVOLUTION OF CREDIT CARDS

The charge card and credit card industry has evolved over the past century. In the early 1900s, department stores issued charge plates as a means of identifying their repeat customers and of keeping records of customer purchases.[32] Charge plates were small pieces of metal that were typically imprinted with the customer's name, address, and account number. At the time of purchase, the customer would present the metal plate to the salesperson to be inserted into a machine that would transfer an imprint of the plate onto a sales slip. The charge plate eventually led to the idea of stores extending credit to increase the sale of higher ticket items and to create a bonding and loyalty vehicle.[33]

The oil companies, aware of the success retailers were having with credit cards and promoting their brands, began issuing paper cards in the 1920s to their most valued customers.[34] These cards were referred to as "courtesy cards" and could be used by customers at any of the issuing company's affiliates. This effort was so successful that oil companies began issuing cards to virtually every driver they could find.[35] Originally, station managers issued each card personally. Standard Oil caught the attention of the oil industry in 1939 with a new marketing scheme in which it mailed unsolicited cards to hundreds of thousands of new prospective customers.[36] The allure of a captive set of credit card customers assisted the oil companies in signing up new franchise stations. It also allowed station owners to effectively withdraw from the financing business by transferring responsibility to the oil company. Despite the expense, oil industry members continued to invest in credit operations to capture market share. Credit restrictions, a slowdown in consumer spending, and regulations governing installment purchases during World War II effectively placed a hold on credit card operations.[37] They recommended during the post-war economic expansion.

In 1949, three New York businessmen introduced the first multi-establishment charge card, Diners Club®. Their company served as a middleman between consumers and merchants, charging both for its services.[38] The founders of Diners Club initially signed up approximately a dozen New York restaurants to accept the card and they issued the card, initially free of charge, to business travelers, who appreciated the convenience of charging their meals while in New York. Diners Club® offered convenience, not credit, for it required payment in full at the end of each month.[39] Diners Club® gradually expanded to include merchants other than restaurants and established a presence throughout the U.S., as well as internationally. Diners Club's® acceptance and popularity attracted others, such as American Express and Carte Blanche®, to enter the charge card market.[40]

---

[32] *See* LOUIS MANDELL, THE CREDIT CARD INDUSTRY, A HISTORY 17 (1990).

[34] *See id.* at 19.

[34] *See id.* at 18.

[35] *See id.* at 19.

[36] *See id.*

[37] *See id.* at 21.

[38] The accepting restaurants paid a 7% fee to fund the acceptance of the cards, which was more than offset by increased restaurant traffic. *See id.* at 3.

[39] *See* JOSEPH NOCERA, A PIECE OF THE ACTION 24 (1994).

[40] *See* MANDELL, *supra* note 32, at 7.

In addition to the travel and entertainment ("T&E") cards, a number of commercial banks established credit card programs in the 1950s. Franklin National Bank in New York formalized the practice by introducing the first modern credit card in 1951.[41] On the west coast, Bank of America in 1958 launched an enormous credit card operation. It started with a pilot operation in Fresno, California, which became known as the "Fresno Drop," where it gave credit cards, known as BankAmericards®, to every Bank of America customer in the market.[42] Merchants who accepted the card agreed to a 6% merchant discount.[43] Cardholders had the option of either paying in full at the end of the one-month grace period or incurring a monthly 11/2% interest fee.[44] By October 1959, approximately two million BankAmericards® were circulating throughout California, with acceptance from over 20,000 merchants.[45] Despite initial stumbling blocks involving the level of delinquent accounts, customer creditworthiness, and fraud, Bank of America's credit card operation was profitable by the spring of 1961.[46] In 1966, Bank of America extended its product throughout the United States by franchising a bank in each major city as its local affiliate to issue the BankAmericard®.[47] These licensee banks had the responsibility for contracting merchants to accept the card and enrolling cardmembers in their market area. They had sole responsibility for profits and losses, paying a royalty to Bank of America that was used primarily to support national advertising efforts.[48]

In 1966, a group of banks not affiliated with the BankAmericard® program joined together and created their own credit card network — Interbank Card Association.[49] It differed from BankAmericard® in that it was not dominated by a single bank. Member committees governed the association. In addition to establishing rules for authorization, clearing, and settlement, Interbank assumed marketing, security, and legal functions in order to protect the integrity of the brand. In 1969, because Interbank had not achieved satisfactory name recognition, it purchased the rights to the name "Master Charge[SM]" from the Western States Bank Card Association.[50] In 1979, Master Charge[SM] became MasterCard®.

Consumers and merchants generally did not receive credit cards with the same enthusiasm issuers experienced in sending them. Some resented banks for encouraging them to spend beyond their means.[51] Others worried about who would bear the responsibility for theft and fraud.[52]

---

[41] *See* BANKERS ROUNDTABLE, *supra* note 17, at 83.

[42] *See* NOCERA, *supra* note 39, at 26.

[43] *See id.* at 25.

[44] *See id.*

[45] *See id.* at 30.

[46] *See id.* at 32-33.

[47] The licensee banks paid a $25,000 entry fee to Bank of America, who, in turn, gave the licensee bank credit card software and guidance in running a credit card operation. *See id.* at 56.

[48] *See id.*

[49] *See* MANDELL, *supra* note 32, at 31.

[50] *See id.*

[51] *See* NOCERA, *supra* note 39, at 58.

[52] *See id.*

Issuers, eager to get their cards into the market, often sent cards without verifying the information bearing on creditworthiness. Despite these and other problems, credit cards gained a foothold in American life. Banks, including those who had tried issuing independent cards since the late 1950s, either became a BankAmericard® issuer or Master Charge^{SM} issuer. In 1970, Master Charge had operations in forty-nine states, BankAmericard in forty-four.[53] Banks challenged the rules that had prevented an issuer of one card from issuing the other and obtained the right to join both associations and issue both brands.[54]

Market segmentation began to play a bigger role in the 1980s when MasterCard and Visa issued gold cards and business cards. In 1986, Sears, Roebuck & Co. surprised the industry with the introduction of the Discover Card®, a universal card designed to compete directly with MasterCard® and Visa®.[55] Affinity and "co-branded" cards further altered the competitive landscape by offering more than just a credit card.[56] These changed consumer's perception of cards and the benefits associated with being a cardholder. In 1988, there were approximately 1.25 billion credit cards in circulation throughout the world.[57]

§ 4.04   THE CREDIT CARD TRANSACTION

When a consumer presents a credit card to a merchant, that act indicates to the merchant that the consumer has a satisfactory credit rating, that the issuer will pay or insure payment by the consumer, and that the consumer intends to pay the issuer.[58] The merchant's acceptance of the card starts the authorization, processing, and settlement cycle. This seemingly simple transaction between a consumer and a merchant is actually a complex process involving a variety of behind-the-scenes participants. This Section will identify the various participants and then explain the transaction process.[59]

[1]   PARTICIPANTS

Participants, other than the merchant and consumer, play one of four basic roles: (a) card association; (b) central processor; (c) end processor; and (d) payment support provider.

[a]   Card Associations. These are the entities that establish the standards for participation in the credit card system. They authorize financial institutions and other firms to issue their specific card brand. They also arbitrate disputes between system participants. VISA and MasterCard are card associations.

---

[53]   *See id.* at 62.

[54]   *See* MANDELL, *supra* note 32, at 98.

[55]   *See id.* at 83-84.

[56]   *See id.* at 80-81. These are cards on which names of organizations other than banks appear. *See id.*

[57]   *See id.* at xi.

[58]   *See Williams v. United States*, 192 F. Supp. 97, 99-100 (S.D. Cal. 1961).

[59]   *See generally* BURNHAM, *supra* note 2, at 95-96.

[b] Central Processors. Central processors, also referred to as regional and national switches, provide net settlement service by relaying authorization and settlement requests between end processors, defined below. Central processors are often, though not always, divisions of the card association. VISA, MasterCard, Deluxe Data, and EDS are examples of central processors.

[c] End Processors. This category includes issuers, acquirers, and third-party processors.

[i] Issuers. Issuers grant credit lines, issue credit cards, authorize purchases, and later bill their cardholders. Credit card issuers rely on the information supplied in a credit application, which they have a duty to investigate with reasonable care and diligence.[60] Financial institutions and credit card companies serve as issuers.

[ii] Acquirers. Acquirers sign up merchants to accept credit cards, provide authorization relay service, and process payments. They accept enrolled merchant drafts at a negotiated discount, which covers the acquirer's expenses. Acquirers are ultimately responsible for merchant fraud and failure, as well as for any legitimate disputes between the merchant and cardholder. Financial institutions and credit card companies serve as acquirers.

[iii] Third-Party Processors. Third-party processors serve as intermediaries between the merchant and the issuer and/or the acquirer. They may relay messages, maintain cardholder files, and even issue monthly statements. They may be an outsourcer of the merchant, issuer, or acquirer.

[d] Payment Support Providers. These are the technology companies that design, produce, and support the software, hardware, and network services that make the entire system function.[61]

[2] PROCEDURES

[a] Authorization. After the merchant runs the customer's credit card through a payment terminal, that terminal contacts the merchant's processor which, in turn, initializes the authorization request. The authorization request is transmitted to the national switch. The national switch routes the authorization request to the issuing bank's processor. When the issuing bank's processor receives the information through the network switch, it checks its computer files and transmits its authorization or rejection back through the aforementioned channels to the merchant. It also memo posts the authorized transactions, a process that produces available credit. The process usually takes about thirty seconds and occurs as part of the transaction.[62]

---

[60] *See Beard v. Goodyear Tire & Rubber Co.*, 587 A.2d 195, 200-201 (D.C. App. 1991); *TransAmerica Ins. Co. v. Standard Oil Co.*, 25 N.W.2d 210, 214 (N.D. 1982).

[61] *See* BURNHAM, *supra* note 2, at 95. First Data Corp, National Processing, and SPS Transaction Systems are current examples of third-party processors. Verifone and Transaction Netware Services are current examples of payment support providers. *Id.*

[62] *See* BANKERS ROUNDTABLE, *supra* note 17, at 90.

[b] Processing. Merchants either send the physical sales draft or electronically captured versions thereof to their acquirer's processor for processing on a regular basis. The processor separates the "on-us" transactions and electronically transmits the remainder to the national switches run by VISA and MasterCard.[63] The national switches edit and balance transmissions, verify fees, and generate reports that are sent to the cardholder banks' processors. The authorization and processing cycle is illustrated below.

[c] Settlement. Settlement takes place in two phases. First, the processor settles transactions between the financial institutions it services on a net basis. Net settlement entries are then sent through the Federal Reserve System. Second, the national switches conduct settlement, on a net basis, between the processors via FedWire®. Processors then settle with their financial institutions using the ACH system.[64]

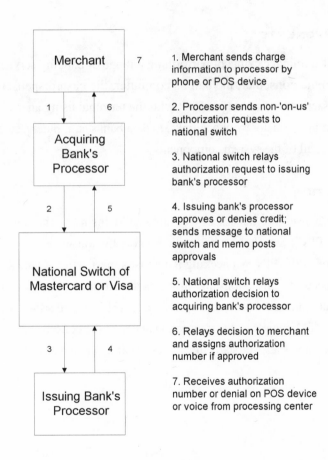

1. Merchant sends charge information to processor by phone or POS device

2. Processor sends non-'on-us' authorization requests to national switch

3. National switch relays authorization request to issuing bank's processor

4. Issuing bank's processor approves or denies credit; sends message to national switch and memo posts approvals

5. National switch relays authorization decision to acquiring bank's processor

6. Relays decision to merchant and assigns authorization number if approved

7. Receives authorization number or denial on POS device or voice from processing center

Source: The Bankers Roundtable, Banking's Role in Tomorrow's Payment Systems, (Vol. II) 90 (Furash & Co., June 1994).

---

[63]   Physical documents are truncated at the acquiring bank's processing center, they do not go to national switches. *See id*. at 91.

[64]   *See generally* BURNHAM, *supra* note 2, at 95-96.

§ 4.05   AUTOMATED TELLER MACHINE TERMINAL SYSTEMS

At the same time that credit cards had established a firm foothold in the marketplace, financial institutions in the late 1960s began to explore other ways of servicing their retail banking customers. Their efforts resulted in the development of automated teller machines ("ATMs") and point-of-sale ("POS") systems, the latter of which will be discussed in Section 4.06. The first ATM was installed in 1969.[65] By 1979 there were 13,800.[66] That number reached 64,000 in 1986.[67] In July 1997, there were approximately 150,000 ATM terminals in the United States.[68] Initially viewed as an added feature that could attract new accounts, meet customer needs, reduce transaction costs, and generate fee income, ATMs and participation in ATM networks are now an essential component of any depository institution's operating strategy.[69] ATM systems, and the networks that support them, will likely play a role in the development of new electronic financial products and services.

[1]   ATM COMPONENTS

An ATM is an EFT terminal capable of performing a range of banking services for customers. It serves as an interface between the consumer, the bank's computer, the cash dispenser, and the depository box. Consumers initiate transactions by making contact with the terminal using an access device. A communication system links the terminal, usually by phone links, to data banks, computers, authorization systems, and the controller that coordinates all of the system components.

[2]   TRANSACTION

Once the consumer uses the access device, the ATM instructs the consumer to enter a Personal Identification Number ("PIN"), which must be verified before the transaction is processed. In an online ATM system, the terminal verifies the PIN by checking it against a master file. Once the PIN is verified, the ATM offers the consumer a menu of transactions and instructs the consumer to choose one. After a transaction is requested, and an amount entered where appropriate, the ATM displays the entry and requests consumer verification. Finally, the ATM completes the transaction and asks the consumer if she wants to conduct another transaction, at which point a yes answer starts the process over again and a no answer results in termination of the session.

---

[65] *See* MANDELL, *supra* note 32, at 121.

[66] *See* BAKER & BRANDEL, *supra* note 13, ¶ 1.03[4].

[67] *See id.*

[68] *See ATM Network Charge: Hearing Before the Senate Comm. on Banking, Housing and Urban Affairs*, 105th Cong. (1997) (testimony of Anthony N. McEwen, Executive Vice President, Visa USA).

[69] *See* BAKER & BRANDEL, *supra* note 13, ¶ 6.04[2][a].

[3] PARTICIPANTS

In addition to the ATM cardholder, a number of other parties play a role in the ATM system.

[a] Issuers. Issuers provide their customers with ATM access devices, maintain customer accounts, and provide customer service. They also authorize and process account transactions. Financial institutions serve as issuers.

[b] Acquirers. Acquirers may operate ATM terminals or sponsor non-financial institutions that deploy and operate the terminals. Acquirers warrant the transaction requests and transmissions through the network. Financial institutions play the role of acquirers.

[c] Third-Party Processors. Third-party processors assist issuers and acquirers and may also own the ATM terminal. Third-party processors may also provide gateway services to networks, enabling issuers and acquirers to accept various network brand access devices and to conduct transactions with a broader customer base while maintaining only one communication link to the gateway. Third-party processors also perform transaction authorization and front end transaction processing.

[d] Networks. Communication networks ("networks") provide the link between the ATM terminal and the financial institution(s) supporting that terminal. Networks also provide switching services so that neither the issuer nor the acquirer has to connect to more than one network directly. They transmit transaction requests and approval/denial messages between participants. Networks may also provide settlement services to the issuer and acquirer. The issuer or acquirer will typically join a regional network that has access to a national network, reciprocal relations with other regional networks, or both. Network users pay for services through a combination of initiation, annual membership, monthly service, and transaction fees.

There are two primary types of networks, proprietary and shared. In a proprietary system, one institution, perhaps through a contractor, owns the terminals, communications network, data banks, and other system components. In such a system, only the customers of the proprietary bank can access the system. Shared systems fall into three categories: (i) true shared; (ii) gateway; and (iii) piggyback.

[i] True Shared System. In a true shared system, a group of financial institutions share interests in an ATM switch network accessible to each participating financial institution's customers. The sharing financial institutions display a common logo or service mark to alert consumers to their participation in the network. Network financial institutions usually operate under common technical and operating standards.[70]

[ii] Gateway. Financial institutions that do not participate in shared systems can still provide their customers with access to the shared system through what is known as a gateway, an agreement between the shared system and the financial institution. A gateway arrangement does not require the financial institution to display the network mark or adhere to network standards.[71]

---

[70] *See id.* ¶ 6.04[3].

[71] *See id.*

[*iii*] *Piggyback.* A piggyback system is where a financial institution's customers can access an ATM despite the fact that there is no agreement between the ATM operator or network. ATM operators that allow piggyback transactions must maintain their own authorization databases and bear all the risks of fraud.[72]

§ 4.06 POINT-OF-SALE SYSTEMS

Point-of-sale ("POS") terminals are EFT terminals present at merchant locations that permit payment from a customer's bank account to the merchant's account. POS systems were first introduced in 1966 by the Bank of Delaware.[73] A POS system connected three Wilmington shoe stores. Sales clerks at the stores transmitted the transaction information, including the information taken from the customer's debit card, using a touch-tone telephone. The bank then debited the customer's account and credited the shoe store's account. This initial experiment was not well received by customers.[74]

POS systems again entered the market in the early 1970s. POS systems offer merchants the opportunity to reduce administrative costs and accounts receivable. For consumers, POS systems provide an alternative to payment by cash, check, or credit card. POS systems enable financial institutions to offer an additional payment option to customers.[75] Despite these benefits, POS systems did not gain widespread acceptance until the mid-1990s.[76]

POS systems will play an important role in the payments system of the future. This Section describes a typical POS transaction, the components of the POS system, and its participants.

[1] POS TRANSACTION

A consumer takes a debit card, which she received from her financial institution, to a POS terminal at the merchant's store. At the time of purchase, the consumer inserts her card in, or otherwise makes appropriate contact with, the terminal card reader. The POS terminal then sends the consumer and merchant information, either directly or through a network, to the consumer's financial institution. The financial institution's computer will either authorize or reject the transaction and send the corresponding message back to the merchant. If the financial institution authorizes the transaction, it debits the consumer's account for the transaction amount and causes the merchant's account to be credited with the same amount. The merchant provides the consumer with a receipt verifying the transaction.

---

[72] *See id.*

[73] *See id.* ¶ 7.02[1][a].

[74] *See id.*

[75] *See id.* ¶ 7.02[2].

[76] *See* BURNHAM, *supra* note 2, at 100-102 (discussing POS growth). For a discussion of recent issues relating to unauthorized debit card transactions, see Chapter 11, Section 11.04[1].

[2] COMPONENTS

There are several components involved in the POS system other than the POS terminals. Terminals may be connected to a concentrator or a controller, devices that enable several terminals to share a communication line. Communication lines connect the terminals to either the merchant's bank or to an intermediary, called a switch, and ultimately to the merchant's bank computers. The computers exchange data with bank account servers and transmit the appropriate authorization or rejection message back to the merchant.

[3] PARTICIPANTS

POS systems may be proprietary or shared. A proprietary system serves the merchant and customer who have accounts at the same financial institution, the institution that deployed the POS terminals and conducts all communications and settlement processes. The far more common POS system arrangement is the shared or network system. In a network system, several financial institutions share the costs and communication systems and switches involved in the transaction in the transaction process. Networks will settle balances between participating financial institutions.

§ 4.07 LAWS, REGULATIONS, AND RULES IMPACTING THE DEVELOPMENT OF ELECTRONIC FUND TRANSFER SERVICES

The retail electronic payments systems described in this Chapter are governed in various ways and to some extent by: the Electronic Fund Transfer Act ("EFTA") and Regulation E; state Electronic Fund Transfer laws; the Uniform Commercial Code; Regulation CC, as promulgated under the Expedited Funds Availability Act; the National Automated Clearing House Association Operating Rules; and Regulation J. To the extent that the transaction involves a credit transaction, the following laws and regulations may also be implicated: the Truth-in-Lending Act; the Fair Credit Reporting Act, which is discussed in detail in Chapter 12; and the Equal Credit Opportunity Act, as implemented by Regulation B.[77] Beyond the scope of this Chapter is a body of private contract and case law that may also affect the rights and obligations of electronic financial products and services ("EFS") participants.[78] Because the EFTA, Regulation E, and state EFT laws have been at the forefront of the legal discussions surrounding the development of emerging electronic financial products and services, this Section will focus on those provisions. Before embarking on that discussion, however, a brief introduction of selected laws, regulations, and rules impacting on EFS is provided.

---

[77] A discussion of the Equal Credit Opportunity Act ("ECOA") is beyond the scope of this book. Interested readers should refer to THOMAS P. VARTANIAN, ROBERT H. LEDIG, ALISA BABITZ, GREG PITZER & WILLIAM L. BROWNING, THE FAIR LENDING GUIDE (1995 & supp. 1997).

[78] *See generally* BERNARD D. REAMS, JR., ELECTRONIC CONTRACTING LAW (1996); KENT D. STUCKEY, INTERNET AND ONLINE LAW, ch. 1 (1996); BENJAMIN WRIGHT, THE LAW OF ELECTRONIC COMMERCE, chs. 15-17 (Release #2 1996).

[1] THE EXPEDITED FUNDS AVAILABILITY ACT AND REGULATION CC

The Expedited Funds Availability Act ("EFAA")[79] and Regulation CC[80] require depository institutions to make funds deposited into transaction accounts available according to specified time schedules. For example, funds received for deposit through an ACH credit transfer must be made available for withdrawal no later than the business day following the banking day on which the bank received the payment.[81] Depository institutions are required to disclose their funds availability policies to their customers.

[2] REGULATION J

Regulation J[82] governs the relationship between the Federal Reserve System and the senders and recipients of checks and wire transfers. As originally adopted, Regulation J simply provided a framework for check collection by depository institutions.[83] Regulation J also controlled settlement of balances within the Federal Reserve System and, in conjunction with Regulation CC, created procedures by which banks may return unpaid checks through Federal Reserve Banks. In 1977, Regulation J was amended to provide rules and procedures for fund transfers through FedWire®.[84] ACH transfers are not subject to Regulation J's wire transfer provisions because the ACH rules proposed by the FRB have not been adopted.[85]

[3] THE NATIONAL AUTOMATED CLEARING HOUSE ASSOCIATION OPERATING RULES

The National Automated Clearing House Association ("NACHA") maintains and develops ACH Operating Rules for its member automated clearing house associations. Though federal government automated clearing houses are not association members, the Federal Reserve's Uniform ACH Operating Circular ("Operating Circular"), adopted in 1981 in substantially identical form by each Federal Reserve Bank, makes the NACHA Rules binding on the federal government automated clearing houses, and on depository institutions that are not clearing house association members.[86] The Operating Rules govern the entry format, processing, timing, and other ACH operating requirements. They also set forth the rights and duties of the originating and receiving institutions. The Operating Circular, in addition to other matters beyond the scope of the NACHA Operating Rules, sets forth the rights and obligations of the Reserve Banks and those using the Federal Reserve's ACH services.

---

[79] 12 U.S.C. §§ 4001-10.

[80] 12 C.F.R. pt. 229.

[81] 12 C.F.R. § 229.10(b).

[82] *Id.*

[83] *Id. See also* BAKER & BRANDEL, *supra* note 13, ¶ 19.03, at 19-13.

[84] 12 C.F.R. § 210.25-.32. *See also* BAKER & BRANDEL, *supra* note 13, ¶ 19.03[1], at 19-14 to 19-16.

[85] *See* BAKER & BRANDEL, *supra* note 13, ¶ 19.03, at 19-14 (noting that the wire transfer provisions were deemed inapplicable to ACH due to variations in the volume and dollar value of the two types of transactions, and that proposed Subpart C of Regulation J was never adopted).

[86] *See, e.g.*, Federal Reserve Bank of San Francisco Operating Circular 74, ACH Items (1990).

[4]   THE TRUTH IN LENDING ACT AND REGULATION Z

The Truth in Lending Act[87] ("TILA") and Regulation Z[88] require credit providers to disclose credit terms in a uniform manner. Periodic statements furnished to consumers regarding their credit accounts must disclose the date of the transaction and identification of the purchase so that consumers can review and verify each transaction.[89] TILA is intended to protect against inaccurate and unfair billing practices. TILA also provides consumers with certain protections when fraud or unauthorized use of the consumer's credit cards occurs.[90]

[5]   EQUAL CREDIT OPPORTUNITY ACT AND REGULATION B

The requirements set forth in the Equal Credit Opportunity Act ("ECOA"), as implemented by Regulation B, to protect against discrimination in any aspect of a credit transaction, will apply to any EFT service that involves an overdraft line.[91]

[6]   THE UNIFORM COMMERCIAL CODE

The National Conference of Commissioners on Uniform State Laws ("NCCUSL") and the American Law Institute ("ALI") sponsor the creation and revision of a model commercial code in an effort to promote uniformity in commercial law throughout the United States. Individual states adopt, and occasionally amend or adapt, the articles of this Uniform Commercial Code ("U.C.C.") as part of their state law. Several articles of the U.C.C. apply to the existing retail payments system and may apply to new electronic financial products and services as well. Though a full treatment of the U.C.C. and its relevant articles is beyond the scope of this work, this Section will highlight the relevant articles and their applicability.[92]

[a] U.C.C. Article 3. Article 3 of the U.C.C. generally concerns commercial paper, the rights and liabilities of parties to a commercial paper transaction, and the procedures for transferring and negotiating commercial paper. The specific commercial paper to which Article 3 applies is a "negotiable instrument," a special form of contract for the payment of money. A negotiable instrument is a signed, written document, payable to order or bearer, containing an unconditional promise or order to pay a fixed amount.[93] A paper check is currently the most common form of negotiable instrument.

U.C.C. Article 3 governs authorization. It addresses such matters as agency, forgery, material alteration, and allocation of risk of fraud and mistake. Though Article 3 has generally been found inapplicable to electronic

---

87   Consumer Credit Protection Act, Pub. L. No. 90-321, tit. I, 1969 U.S.C.C.A.N. 176 (codified as amended at 15 U.S.C. §§ 1601-67(e)).

88   12 C.F.R. pt. 226.

89   12 C.F.R. § 226.7.

90   *Martin v. American Express, Inc.*, 361 S.2d 597, 600 (Ala. Civ. App. 1978). *See* 15 U.S.C. §§ 1602(o), 1643(a).

91   *See* BAKER & BRANDEL, *supra* note 13, ¶ 12.05[1].

92   See HAROLD WEISBLATT, BANKING LAW (ed. 1997) for a complete discussion of U.C.C. Articles 3 and 4.

93   U.C.C. § 3-104(a).

payment messages that are not evidenced by a writing,[94] it may apply to electronic systems that involve traditional paper-based components.[95]

[b] U.C.C. Article 4. Article 4 addresses bank collection and deposit items and the relationship between the payor bank and its customers. An Article 4 "item" includes "any instrument for the payment of money" other than money itself.[96] Because Article 4 applies to a broader range of instruments than does Article 3, it may play a greater role in developing products and services.[97] Sections 4-103 and 4-401 supply the rules pertaining to the authorization necessary before a bank may pay funds out of a customer's account.[98] Section 4-103 gives clearing house rules, as well as Federal Reserve regulations and operating letters, the effect of agreements between system participants. In addition, 4-103 permits banks, clearing houses, and the Federal Reserve to adapt Article 4, as needed, to address developments in banking procedures and technologies.[99] Part 1 of Article 4 generally addresses delay. Part 2 details, among other things, the duty of care a bank owes to its customers and the rules governing presentment,[100] settlement,[101] and finality.[102] Part 3 focuses on the time to honor and reject payments.[103] Part 4 of Article 4 concerns bank-customer relationships and addresses such issues as wrongful dishonor liability,[104] limitations on honoring payments by the deceased or incompetent,[105] and setting time limits on the validity of a payment.[106]

[c] U.C.C. Article 4A. The sponsors of the U.C.C. created Article 4A to provide a governing body of law for wholesale, business-to-business, credit wire transfers, such as CHIPS and FedWire®. Article 4A also applies to certain consumer ACH transactions that are excepted from Regulation E and Electronic Fund Transfer Act ("EFTA") coverage.[107] It does not apply to ACH credits that are subject to the EFTA, an area that is discussed below in subsection [7]. The focus of Article 4A is on the rights and obligations of the Federal Reserve Banks, not private sector processors. The Federal Reserve Operating Circular, however, supersedes any inconsistent provisions of the article.

---

[94]   *See* BAKER & BRANDEL, *supra* note 13, ¶ 12.02[1].

[95]   *Id.*

[96]   U.C.C. § 4-104(g).

[97]   *See* BAKER & BRANDEL, *supra* note 13, ¶ 12.02[1], at 12-3 (contrasting the definition of "negotiable instrument" in Article 3 with that of "item" in Article 4). Despite the use of different terms, however, Article 4, like Article 3, has generally been found to be inapplicable to electronic payments messages that are not evidenced by a writing. *See, e.g., Evra Corp. v. Swiss Bank Corp.*, 673 F.2d 951, 955 (7th Cir. 1982); *Delbrueck & Co. v. Manufacturers Hanover Trust Co.*, 609 F.2d 1047, 1051 (2d Cir. 1979); *Walker v. Texas Commerce Bank, N.A.*, 635 F. Supp. 678, 681 (S.D. Tex. 1986).

[98]   U.C.C. §§ 4-103, 4-401.

[99]   *See* BAKER & BRANDEL, *supra* note 13, ¶ 12.02[2][a].

[100]   U.C.C. § 4-207.

[101]   *Id.* §§ 4-212, 4-213.

[102]   *Id.* § 4-213.

[103]   *Id.* §§ 4-301, 4-302, 4-304.

[104]   *Id.* § 4-402.

[105]   *Id.* § 4-405.

[106]   *Id.* § 4-404.

[107]   12 C.F.R. § 205.3(c). *See* BAKER & BRANDEL, *supra* note 13, ¶ 13.03[3][a], at 13-8.

[7]   THE ELECTRONIC FUND TRANSFER ACT AND REGULATION E

Congress enacted the EFTA[108] in 1978 to provide a basic framework for consumer protections in retail electronic fund transfers ("EFT") systems. The statute is designed to "provide a basic framework establishing the rights, liabilities, and responsibilities of participants in electronic fund transfers systems."[109] Under the EFTA, the Board of Governors of the Federal Reserve System ("FRB") may prescribe regulations governing electronically initiated debits and credits to consumer accounts, such as those typically associated with automated teller machines, point-of-sale terminals, telephone bill payment systems, computer-based home banking transactions, and automated clearing house transactions.

As financial institutions and technology, providers are developing new products and services that take advantage of advanced new technologies, they will need to be aware of the impact of the EFTA and Regulation E on those products and services. The following discussion highlights the terms and requirements of the EFTA and Regulation E.

[a] Terms. The EFTA and Regulation E provide a series of definitions that determine their applicability in various situations, a number of which are discussed below.

[i] Financial Institution. In order for the EFTA to apply, a financial institution must be involved in the relevant transaction. Under the EFTA, a "financial institution" is defined as a state chartered or national bank, a state or federally chartered savings and loan association, a mutual savings bank, a state or federal credit union, or "any other person who, directly or indirectly, holds an account belonging to a consumer."[110] Under Regulation E, the definition of "financial institution" is refined to include a "bank, savings association, credit union, or any other person that directly or indirectly holds an account belonging to a consumer, or that issues an access device and agrees with a consumer to provide electronic fund transfers services."[111] Under these definitions, entities that do not hold consumer asset accounts, but instead issue some type of card to consumers for making purchases of goods and services would also fall within the definition. Thus, there may be multiple financial institutions in a single EFT transaction.[112]

[ii] Electronic Fund Transfers. The application of the EFTA and Regulation E also depends on whether the transaction in question qualifies as an electronic fund transfer. Regulation E defines an "electronic fund transfer" as:

> any transfer of funds that is initiated through an electronic terminal, telephone, computer, or magnetic tape for the purpose of ordering, instructing, or authorizing a financial

---

[108] Financial Institutions Regulatory and Interest Rate Control Act of 1978, Pub. L. No. 95-630, tit. IX, 1978 U.S.C.C.A.N. (92 Stat.) 3728 (codified as amended at 15 U.S.C. §§ 1693-93r) (amending the Consumer Credit Protection Act, Pub. L. No. 90-321, codified as amended at 15 U.S.C. §§ 1601-93r).

[109] 15 U.S.C. § 1693(b).

[110] *Id.* § 1693a(8).

[111] 12 C.F.R. § 205.2(i).

[112] *See* BAKER & BRANDEL ¶ 12.04[2]. *See also* 12 C.F.R. § 205.14 (electronic fund transfers service provider not holding consumer's account).

institution to debit or credit an account. The term includes, but is not limited to: (1) Point-of-sale transfers; (2) Automated teller machine transfers; (3) Direct deposits or with-drawals of funds; (4) Transfers initiated by telephone; and (5) Transfers resulting from debit card transactions, whether or not initiated through an electronic terminal.[113]

Thus, to be an EFT subject to Regulation E, a transaction must have three components. There must be (i) a transfer of funds, (ii) that is initiated by electronic means, and (iii) that either debits or credits a consumer account held directly or indirectly by a financial institution. Regulation E specifically excludes transactions that are accomplished by checks, drafts, or other paper-based authorizations as well as any payments made by such means at an electronic terminal.[114] Other exclusions from the definition of "electronic fund transfer" under Regulation E include:

- check guarantees or authorizations that do not result directly in a debit or credit to a consumer account;[115]

- transfers of funds through FedWire®, or through a similar wire transfer system that is used primarily for transfers between financial institutions or between businesses;[116]

- transfers of funds involving certain purchases or sales of securities or commodities;[117]

- automatic transfers of funds under agreements between a consumer and a financial institution;[118]

- transfers of funds initiated by telephone that do not take place under a written agreement or plan, such as a telephone bill payment plan;[119] and

- preauthorized transfers to or from accounts at small institutions (holding assets of $100 million or less).[120]

[iii] *Electronic Terminals.* Both the EFTA and Regulation E define "electronic terminal" as a device, other than a telephone, that the consumer uses to initiate an electronic fund transfers, including but not limited to, point-of-sale terminals ("POS" terminals), automated teller machines ("ATMs"), and cash-dispensing machines.[121] The Official Staff Commentary to Regulation E also provides an important distinction concerning

---

[113] 12 C.F.R. § 205.3(b). The Regulation E definition closely parallels the definition set forth in the EFTA at 15 U.S.C. § 1693a(6).

[114] 12 C.F.R. § 205.3(c)(1).

[115] *Id.* § 205.3(c)(2).

[116] *Id.* § 205.3(c)(3).

[117] The exclusion applies provided that the security or commodity is regulated by the SEC or CFTC, purchased or sold through regulated broker-dealers or futures commission merchants or held in book-entry form by a Federal Reserve Bank or federal agency. *Id.* § 205.3(c)(4).

[118] *Id.* § 205.3(c)(5).

[119] *Id.* § 205.3(c)(6).

[120] *Id.* § 205.3(c)(7).

[121] 15 U.S.C. § 1693a(7); 12 C.F.R. § 205.2(h).

POS systems that make use of telephones. Because the term electronic terminal excludes a consumer's use of a telephone, a financial institution need not provide a receipt if a consumer uses a debit card at a public telephone or "initiates a transfer by a means analogous in function to a telephone, such as by home banking equipment or a facsimile machine."[122]

[iv] *Stored Value Cards.* In seeking to carry out the objectives of the EFTA and Regulation E, the FRB might view stored value cards as within the scope of the meaning of "debit instruments" that utilize "electronic terminals," and thus regulate the development and use of stored value cards on this statutory basis. Stored value cards can interface with a financial institution, a vendor, or a third party in a variety of ways that may trigger the applicability of Regulation E at different times and in different ways. Thus, when a customer downloads stored value from an ATM to a smart card, the policy considerations underlying Regulation E may apply differently than when the consumer uses that stored value at an off-line vending machine or transfers a portion of it in a "peer-to-peer" transaction. The FRB has proposed to distinguish among various types of stored value card technology and structure for purposes of the general applicability of Regulation E. It has also proposed to tailor Regulation E application to stored value products based on their maximum value capacity.[123] The FRB's proposal regarding the application of Regulation E to stored value products is discussed in detail in Chapter 7, Section 7.06[3].

[v] *Account.* The EFTA and Regulation E only apply to EFTs involving consumer "accounts." Specifically, as defined by Regulation E, an account is a demand deposit account, savings account, or other consumer asset account held directly or indirectly by a financial institution and established primarily for personal, family, or household purposes.[124] The EFTA is not limited to financial institutions holding traditional consumer accounts. For example, in 1994, the FRB interpreted "account" to include government electronic benefits transfer ("EBT").[125] In August 1997, however, the FRB exempted certain EBT accounts from Regulation E requirements.[126] The FRB acted in response to legislation enacted in 1996 that amended the EFTA to exempt state or local "needs-tested" EBT programs.[127] Federal EBT programs and state and local employment-related programs, such as pension programs, remain subject to Regulation E.

---

[122] 12 C.F.R. pt. 205, supp. I § 205.2(h).

[123] Electronic Fund Transfers, 61 Fed. Reg. 19,696, 19,699 (1996) (to be codified at 12 C.F.R. pt. 205) (proposed May 2, 1996) [hereinafter FRB Stored Value Proposal].

[124] 12 C.F.R. § 205.2(b)(1). The definition expressly excludes an account held by a financial institution under a bona fide trust agreement as well as occasional or incidental credit balances in a credit plan. *Id.* § 205.2(b)(2).

[125] Electronic Fund Transfers, 59 Fed. Reg. 10,678 (1994) (codified at 12 C.F.R. § 205.15) (adding electronic benefits transfer ("EBT") systems to Regulation E's coverage).

[126] Electronic Fund Transfers, 62 Fed. Reg. 43,467 (1997) (to be codified at 12 C.F.R. § 205.15(a)). EBT is discussed in detail in Chapter 17.

[127] Personal Responsibility and Work Opportunity Act of 1996, Pub. L. No. 104-193, §§ 891, 907, 1996 U.S.C.C.A.N. (110 Stat.) 2105, 2346 (codified at 15 U.S.C. § 1693b(d)).

[*vi*] *Access Device.* Under Regulation E an "access device" is a card, code, or other means of access that customers can use to access their accounts and initiate electronic transfers.[128] Debit cards, PINs, telephone transfer codes, and bill payment codes are examples of access devices.[129]

[b] Substantive Requirements of Regulation E. As more fully described below, Regulation E has six major substantive requirements: (1) it restricts the unsolicited issuance of account access devices; (2) it requires certain initial disclosures of the terms and conditions of the electronic fund transfer service; (3) it requires notice of certain changes in the terms or conditions initially disclosed; (4) it requires transaction receipts and periodic account statements; (5) it establishes error resolution procedures; and (6) it generally limits consumer liability for unauthorized transfers to $50.[130]

[*i*] *Issuing Access Devices.* Regulation E generally prohibits a financial institution from issuing an access device to a consumer unless either the consumer, orally or in writing, has requested the device,[131] or it is a renewal or substitute device.[132] Where a financial institution issues a renewal or substitute device, it may not issue additional devices.[133] For example, a single new card and PIN may replace a previously issued card and PIN. If a replacement device permits either additional or fewer types of electronic fund transfer services than the original device, a change in terms notice or new disclosures are required.

A financial institution may provide a consumer with an unsolicited access device only if it complies with three requirements:[134] (1) the device must not be validated;[135] (2) the device must be accompanied by an explanation that it is not validated and that the customer is free to dispose of the device if they do not wish to use it;[136] and (3) the device must be accompanied by the initial disclosures required under Regulation E.[137] The unsolicited access device may only be validated at the consumer's request and after the institution has verified the consumer's identity by reasonable means.[138] Acceptable means of identity verification may include a photograph, fingerprint, personal visit, signature comparison, or other identifying personal information.[139] The FRB has taken the position that even if reasonable means are used, if the institution fails to verify the consumer's

---

[128] 12 C.F.R. § 205.2(a)(1).

[129] *Id.* pt. 205, supp. I § 205.2(a)(1). The term does not include, however, magnetic tape or other devices used internally by a financial institution to initiate EFTs. *Id.*

[130] *Id.* §§ 205.4-.9, .11.

[131] *Id.* § 205.5(a)(1).

[132] *Id.* § 205.5(a)(2).

[133] *Id.* pt. 205, supp. I § 205.5(a)(2)(1).

[134] The FRB has published model disclosures for the unsolicited issuance of access devices. *Id.* pt. 205, app. A-1.

[135] This means that the institution has not yet performed all the procedures that would enable a consumer to initiate an electronic fund transfer using the access device. *Id.* § 205.5(b)(1).

[136] *Id.* § 205.5(b)(2).

[137] *Id.* § 205.5(b)(3).

[138] *Id.* § 205.5(b)(4).

[139] *Id.* pt. 205, supp. I § 205.5(b)(4).

identity correctly and an impostor succeeds in having the device validated, the consumer is not liable for any unauthorized transfers from the account.[140]

[*ii*] *Disclosure Statements.* A financial institution offering EFT services must provide the consumer with a readily understandable written disclosure statement of the terms and conditions of the EFT service. This may be done either at the time a customer contracts for EFT services or before the first EFT is made involving the consumer's account.[141] The disclosure statement must contain each of the following:[142]

- a summary of the consumer's liability for unauthorized EFTs under governing agreements, Regulation E, state, or other applicable law;

- the telephone number and address of the person or office to be notified when the consumer believes that an unauthorized transfer has been (or may be) made;

- the financial institution's business days;

- the types of EFTs that the consumer may make and any applicable frequency or dollar amount limitations on such EFTs;[143]

- a description of any fees imposed by the financial institution for EFTs or the right to make EFTs;[144]

- a summary of the consumer's right to receipts and periodic statements;

- a summary of the consumer's right to stop payment of preauthorized EFTs under Regulation E;

- a summary of the financial institution's liability to the consumer under the EFTA for failure to make or to stop certain transfers;

- the circumstances under which, in the ordinary course of business, the financial institution may provide information concerning the customer's account to third parties; and

- a notice setting forth the procedures and associated timing in regard to error resolution.

---

[140] *Id.*

[141] *Id.* §§ 205.4(a), 205.7(a). The FRB's Official Staff Interpretations provide additional guidance in regard to the timing of disclosures in particular circumstances, including the prior delivery of disclosures, the addition of new accounts and the addition of EFT services. *Id.* pt. 205, supp. I §§ 205.7(a)(1), (3), (4), and (6).

[142] *Id.* § 205.7(b)(1)-(10).

[143] Such limitations include, for example, daily limits on cash withdrawals from ATMs. In addition, a limit on account activity that restricts a consumer's ability to make EFTs must be disclosed even if the restriction applies to transfers made by non-electronic means, such as the restrictions imposed by Regulation D on the number of payments to third parties that can be made from a money market account. *Id.* pt. 205, supp. I §§ 205.7(b)(4)(1), (2).

[144] A financial institution is required to disclose all fees for EFTs or the right to make them. Other fees, such as minimum balance fees, stop payment fees, or overdraft fees may, but need not, be disclosed. Per-item fees for EFTs must be disclosed even if the same fee is imposed on non-electronic transfers. Itemization of the institution's various fees may be provided on the disclosure statement or an accompanying document that is referenced in the statement. *Id.* at § 205.7(b)(5)(1), (2).

The FRB has issued a set of model clauses for the required initial disclosures.[145] The FRB takes the position that the use of appropriate clauses in making disclosures will protect a financial institution from liability under sections 915 and 916 of the EFTA, provided that the clauses accurately reflect the institution's EFT services.[146]

Under the current version of Regulation E, initial disclosures must be in writing. The FRB has determined that electronic communications do not meet the writing requirement presently found in Regulation E.[147] This can have the effect of constraining the ability of financial institutions to utilize electronic means to fully deploy EFT services, including various home banking services. As a result, the FRB has proposed to allow financial institutions and their customers to agree to use electronic communications as a means of providing each other with any information that Regulation E requires be provided either orally or in writing.[148] Under the proposal, electronically communicated information would have to be clear, comprehensible, and provided in a manner that would allow a consumer to retain the information. Furthermore, a customer would be entitled to a request a paper copy of the information for up to one year after receiving the electronic communication.

[*iii*] *Changes in Terms and Conditions.* At least twenty-one days prior to changing certain terms or conditions, a financial institution must mail or deliver a written notice regarding the changes to consumers.[149] This requirement applies if the change would result in increased consumer fees, increased consumer liability, fewer types of available EFTs, or stricter limits on the transfer frequency or dollar amount.[150] The financial institution does not have to give prior notice if an immediate change in terms and conditions is needed in order to maintain or restore the security of an account or of an EFT system.[151]

[*iv*] *Receipts.* When a consumer uses an electronic terminal, including an ATM or POS machine, for an EFT, Regulation E requires that the financial institution make a receipt available.[152] A financial institution may, however, program its electronic terminal to provide the receipt only to those consumers who elect to receive the receipt.[153] The transaction receipt must show the amount, date, type of transaction and account, card

---

[145] *Id.* pt. 205, app. A-2.

[146] Official Staff Interpretations, 12 C.F.R. pt. 205, app A-2. Financial institutions may use clauses of their own design in conjunction with the FRB's model clauses. 12 C.F.R. pt. 205, app. A-3.

[147] FRB Stored Value Proposal, 61 Fed. Reg. at 19,697-98.

[148] *Id.* at 19,704 (to be codified at 12 C.F.R. § 205.4(c)).

[149] 12 C.F.R. § 205.8(a)(1).

[150] *Id.* § 205.8(a)(1)(i)-(iv). Changes involving the closing of some of an institution's ATMs or the cancellation of an access device do not require prior notice. *Id.* pt. 205, supp. I § 205.8(a)(2).

[151] *Id.* § 205.8(a)(2).

[152] *Id.* § 205.9(a). A receipt is not required if the consumer initiates, but chooses not complete, the transaction of if the consumer is unable to complete the transaction because of a "bona fide unintentional error" (*i.e.*, such as when a machine jams or runs out of paper) if the institution has taken reasonable steps to prevent such occurrences. *Id.* pt. 205, supp. I § 205.9(a)(5).

[153] *Id.* pt. 205, Supp. I § 205.9(a)(1).

or account number, terminal location, and the name of any third party (such as a merchant) involved in the EFT.[154] Financial institutions must also send periodic account statements that reflect the EFT transactions.[155] The periodic statement must provide the following information on each EFT occurring during the cycle: the amount of transfer; the date the transfer was debited or credited to the consumer's account; the type of transfer; the type of account to or from which the funds were transferred; the location of the electronic terminal at which the EFT was initiated; and the name of any third party to or from whom funds were transferred.[156] The statement must also include opening and closing account balances and the fees, if any, assessed against the account for making the EFTs, the right to make transfers, or account maintenance during the statement period.[157]

[v] *Error Resolution.* Consumers have certain rights under Regulation E regarding the resolution of errors.[158] A consumer must comply with Regulation E's error resolution requirements with respect to any oral or written notice of an error. Specifically the notice must: (1) be received by the institution no later than sixty days after the institution sends the periodic statement on which the alleged error is reflected; (2) enable the institution to identify the consumer's name and account number; and (3) indicate why the consumer believes an error exists.[159]

A financial institution generally must investigate and determine whether an error has occurred within ten business days of receiving a notice of error.[160] This period is extended to twenty business days if the EFT was not initiated within the United States or if it resulted from a POS debit card transaction.[161] If the institution cannot complete its investigation within the allotted time, it may extend the investigation period, provided, as a general matter, that the institution provisionally credits the customer's account within ten business days.[162]

[vi] *Unauthorized EFTs.*The EFTA and Regulation E provide consumers with certain protections in the event of unauthorized EFTs. An unauthorized EFT is an EFT from a consumer's account initiated by a person, other than the consumer, without actual authority to initiate the transfer and from which the consumer receives

---

[154] *Id.* § 205.9(a)(1)-(6).

[155] *Id.* § 205.9(b). Statements are issued on a monthly cycle unless no transfer has occurred, in which case quarterly statement issuance is acceptable.

[156] *Id.* § 205.9(b)(1)(i)-(v).

[157] *Id.* § 205.9(b)(3), (4).

[158] The term "error" includes: (i) an unauthorized EFT; (ii) an incorrect EFT to or from the consumer's account; (iii) the omission of an EFT from a consumer's periodic statement; (iv) a computational or bookkeeping error relating to an EFT on the part of the financial institution; (v) the consumer's receipt of an incorrect amount of money from an electronic terminal; (vi) an EFT not properly identified in a consumer's receipt received at an electronic terminal or in connection with a preauthorized EFT (*i.e.,* a "direct deposit"); and (vii) a consumer's request for documentation or for additional information or clarification concerning an EFT. *Id.* § 205.11(a)(1).

[159] *Id.* § 205.11(b)(1). A financial institution may require a consumer to give written confirmation of an error within 10 business days of an oral notice. *Id.* § 205.11(b)(2).

[160] *Id.* § 205.11(c)(1).

[161] *Id.* § 205.11(c)(3).

[162] *Id.* § 205.11(c)(2).

no benefit.[163] Unauthorized transactions include transfers where the customer is forced to initiate the transfer or has lost control of the access device as a result of fraud or robbery.[164] They also include erroneous or fraudulent transfers initiated by financial institution employees.[165] A transaction is not considered unauthorized if: (i) the consumer intentionally furnished another person with the access device, unless the consumer has notified the institution that transfers by that person are no longer authorized; or (ii) the transaction involves fraudulent intent by the consumer or any person in concert with the consumer.[166]

Regulation E generally limits a consumer's liability for unauthorized EFTs to the lesser of (i) $50 or (ii) the actual amount transferred prior to the time the customer notifies the financial institution if the consumer notifies the financial institution within two business days after learning of the loss or theft of the access device.[167] If a consumer fails to notify the financial institution within two business days after learning of the loss or theft of the access device, the consumer's liability for unauthorized transfers will not exceed $500.[168]

Regulation E also provides that a consumer must, in order to avoid liability for subsequent transfers, report an unauthorized EFT appearing on a periodic statement within sixty days of the financial institution's transmittal of that statement.[169] If the consumer fails to notify the institution during the sixty day time period, the consumer's liability shall not exceed the amount from the unauthorized transfers (i) that occur after the close of the sixty days and before notice to the institution, combined with the amount (ii) that the institution establishes would not have occurred had the consumer notified the institution within the sixty day period.[170]

[c] Preauthorized EFTs. Regulation E establishes certain rules for recurring preauthorized EFTs involving a consumer's account.[171] For example, consumers may establish preauthorized EFTs for receiving their pay or for making regular payments such as loan payments.[172] Preauthorized EFTs from a consumer's account may be authorized only by a writing signed or similarly authenticated by the consumer.[173] In amending Regulation E in 1996 to allow an authorization to be "similarly authenticated," the FRB noted that it intended

---

[163] 15 U.S.C. § 1693a(11); 12 C.F.R. § 205.2(m).

[164] 12 C.F.R. pt. 205, supp. I § 205.2(m)(3), (4).

[165] *Id.* pt. 205, supp. I § 205.2(m)(1).

[166] *Id.* § 205.2(m)(1), (2).

[167] *Id.* § 205.6(b)(1). Negligence by a consumer (such as writing the PIN on a debit card or on a piece of paper kept with the card) cannot be the basis for imposing greater liability than is permissible under Regulation E. *Id.* pt. 205, supp. I § 205.6(b)(2).

[168] *Id.* § 205.6(b)(2).

[169] *Id.* § 205.6(b)(3).

[170] If an access device is involved in the unauthorized transfer, the consumer may also be liable for the amounts provided in 12 C.F.R. § 205.6(b)(1), (2).

[171] A preauthorized EFT is an EFT authorized in advance to occur at substantially regular intervals. 12 C.F.R. § 205.2(k).

[172] The FRB takes the position that one-time transfers do not qualify as preauthorized transfers for purposes of Regulation E. Electronic Fund Transfers, 61 Fed. Reg. 19,678, 19,684 (1996). These one time transfers are usually initiated by telephone when a consumer provides an account number to a teller and authorizes a draft or an ACH debit to be submitted against the consumer's account.

[173] 12 C.F.R. § 205.10(b).

to address developments in home banking. The FRB noted that this change would, among other things, allow preauthorized transfers in an electronic payment system to be authenticated by a digital signature or a security code.[174] In order to satisfy these requirements there must be some means to identify the consumer and to make available a paper copy of the authorization, either automatically or on request.[175] The text of the electronic authorization would have to be displayed on a computer screen or other visual display that enables the consumer to read the communication.

Regulation E gives a consumer the right to stop a preauthorized EFT from the consumer's account by notifying the originating institution orally or in writing at least three days before the scheduled date of the transfer.[176] If a stop payment order is given orally, the institution may request written confirmation within fourteen days.[177] If the consumer fails to deliver written confirmation, the oral stop-payment order ceases to be binding upon the institution.

Financial institutions are required, under Regulation E, to provide the consumer with notice that a preauthorized transfer occurred resulting in a credit to the consumer's account, unless the payor bears the responsibility of providing such notice.[178] That notice may be given orally or in writing, and must be given within two business days of the scheduled transfer, whether the transfer occurred or not.[179] Alternatively, the financial institution may provide, and disclose the provision in its initial disclosures and periodic statements, a telephone line that consumers can contact to ascertain whether or not the transfer occurred.[180]

Regulation E also addresses preauthorized EFTs from a consumer's account that vary in amount. In the case of such a varying payment, the designated payee or financial institution is required to send the consumer written notice of the amount and date of the transfer at least ten days before the scheduled date of the transfer.[181] Although such notice is generally required, the designated payee or financial institution may give the consumer the option of receiving a notice only when a transfer falls outside of a specified range of amounts or only when a transfer differs from the most recent transfer by more than an agreed upon amount.[182]

[d] Confidentiality Policies. Regulation E requires a financial institution to disclose the circumstances under which, in the ordinary course of business, it may provide information concerning the consumer's account to third parties.[183] This provision covers any information regarding an account to or from which EFTs are

---

[174] Electronic Fund Transfers, 61 Fed. Reg. 19,662, 19,667 (1996).

[175] 12 C.F.R. pt. 205, supp. I § 205.10(b)(5).

[176] *Id.* § 205.10(c)(1).

[177] *Id.* § 205.10(c)(2).

[178] *Id.* § 205.10(a).

[179] *Id.* § 205.10(a)(i), (ii).

[180] *Id.* § 205.10(a)(iii).

[181] *Id.* § 205.10(d)(1).

[182] *Id.* § 205.10(d)(2).

[183] *Id.* § 205.7(a)(9). *See also* L. RICHARD FISCHER, THE LAW OF FINANCIAL PRIVACY: A COMPLIANCE GUIDE, ¶ 6.02 & form 6.1 (2d ed. 1991 & 1995 Supp.). Regulation AA, which sets forth consumer complaint procedures, is also relevant in this area. *See* 12. C.F.R. pt. 227.

permitted, not just those concerning EFTs.[184] The FRB takes the position that the term "third parties" includes a financial institution's affiliates, including other subsidiaries of the same holding company.[185] The model disclosure clauses include at least four categories of ordinary course release of information:

- when disclosure is necessary for completing an electronic fund transfer;

- in order to verify the existence and condition of a consumer's account for a third party, such as a credit bureau or merchant;

- in order to comply with governmental or court orders; or

- when the consumer gives consent.[186]

[e] Penalties for Failing to Comply with Regulation E and the EFTA. The FRB promulgated Regulation E, effective March 30, 1979, to implement the EFTA.[187] Failure to comply with Regulation E and the EFTA may result in civil or criminal liability. EFTA's civil liability provision states that, any person who fails to comply with Regulation E and the EFTA with respect to a consumer may be liable to such consumer for actual or statutorily prescribed damages, plus costs and attorneys fees.[188] In addition, a financial institution or other person may incur criminal liability under the EFTA for knowing or willful violations of the EFTA or for giving false or inaccurate information.[189]

[8] STATE EFT LAWS AND REGULATION E

There is a significant body of state law that may apply to EFTs.[190] State U.C.C. laws, particularly Articles 3 and 4,[191] largely govern the rights and liabilities of participants in paper-based payment systems, and to the extent applicable to EFTs, could, to some degree, provide a substantive body of law. Most courts, however, have generally held that Articles 3 and 4 do not apply to electronic payment messages that are not evidenced by a writ-

---

[184] 12 C.F.R. pt. 205, supp. I § 205.7(b)(9).

[185] *Id.*

[186] *Id.* pt. 205, app. A-2(f).

[187] For additional discussions of the provisions and operation of the EFTA and Regulation E, see FISCHER, *supra* note 183, ¶ 6.02; BAKER & BRANDEL, *supra* note 13, ¶ 12.04-12.06, chs. 14-17. In addition to Regulation E, the FRB has prepared (beginning in 1981, and updated in 1996), an Official Staff Commentary to Regulation E that provides guidance on specific technical points and examples of the application of Regulation E's requirements. Official Staff Interpretations, 12 C.F.R. pt. 205, supp. I. The Commentary substituted for prior individual staff interpretations and was designed to facilitate compliance with the EFTA and provide protection from civil liability under § 915(d)(1) of the EFTA for financial institutions that act in conformity with the Interpretations. *See* Electronic Fund Transfers, 61 Fed. Reg. 19,678 (1996) (adopting 12 C.F.R. Part 205, Supplement I - Official Staff Interpretations). In 1996, the FRB replaced the question and answer format of the Official Staff Interpretations to Regulation E with a narrative format in order to provide guidance of more general applicability. *Id.*

[188] 15 U.S.C. §1693m.

[189] *Id.* § 1693n. Penalties for violations include fines up to $10,000 and imprisonment, not to exceed 10 years, for knowing or willful violations. *Id.*

[190] For a comprehensive review of state EFT laws, see BAKER & BRANDEL, *supra* note 13, ¶ 12.06.

[191] Article 3 of the U.C.C. governs the rights and liabilities of various participants (holders, holders in due course and transferees) with regard to the use of commercial paper. Article 4 of the U.C.C. governs bank deposits and collections and the relationship between payor banks and their customers. *See generally* WHITE & SUMMERS, 2 UNIFORM COMMERCIAL CODE 69-70, 349-50 (4th ed. 1995).

ing.[192] Nonetheless, state U.C.C. principles may still have relevance to EFT transactions, because of the extensive decisional and policy authority that undergirds the development and operation of the U.C.C. State contract law principles will govern the relationship between financial institutions and the automated clearing house ("ACH") Network concerning EFTs.[193] For example, the NACHA Operating Rules provide that NACHA debit entries are "items" within the meaning of U.C.C. 4-104(g) and incorporate Article 4 of the U.C.C. by reference, except when such article is inconsistent with NACHA Rules.[194]

State EFTA laws that directly regulate EFT transactions generally follow the model of the federal EFTA. Typically, these laws generally apply to consumer asset accounts and do not apply to consumer credit accounts or business accounts.[195] State EFT laws also focus primarily on consumer rights, and provide consumer protections that match, or in some cases exceed, the protections contained in the federal EFTA. Colorado, Illinois, Iowa, Kansas, Massachusetts, Michigan, Minnesota, Montana, and New Mexico all have enacted EFT statutes of this type.[196] State consumer protections generally include limitations on consumer liability for unauthorized transactions, restrictions on unsolicited issuance of cards or other access devices, and initial and periodic disclosure requirements.[197]

[9] FEDERAL PREEMPTION OF STATE EFT LAW

The EFTA provides that it does not annul, alter, or affect similar state EFT laws, unless such state provisions are inconsistent with the EFTA. In any event, such state laws are preempted only to the extent of such inconsistency.[198] In addition, the EFTA grants the FRB the authority to exempt by regulation any class of EFTs within any state if the FRB determines that the state laws provide consumer protections that are

---

[192] *See Sinclair Oil Corp. v. Sylvan State Bank*, 869 P.2d 675 (Kan. 1994); *Bradford Trust Co. v. Texas Am. Bank*, 790 F.2d 407 (5th Cir. 1986); *Evra Corp. v. Swiss Bank Corp.*, 673 F.2d 951, 955 (7th Cir. 1982) ("Maybe the language of Article 4 could be stretched to include electronic fund transfers, . . . but they were not in the contemplation of the draftsmen."); *Delbrueck & Co. v. Manufacturers Hanover Trust Co.*, 609 F.2d 1047, 1051 (2d Cir. 1979).

[193] *See* BAKER & BRANDEL, *supra* note 13, ¶ 12.06, at 12-45.

[194] *See id.* ¶ 12.02[2][a], at 12-5 (citing NACHA RULES, *supra* note 22, § 14.11).

[195] *See id.* ¶ 12.06[3][a], at 12-46.

[196] COLO. REV. STAT. §§ 11-6.5-101 to 11-6.5-111 (commercial banks), 11-48-101 to 11-48-107 (savings associations, credit unions, and industrial banks); 205 ILL. COMP. STAT. 616/1 to 616/80; IOWA CODE § 527.1-.12 (savings associations); KAN. STAT. ANN. § 9-1111d (banks), § 17-5565 (savings and loan associations); MASS. ANN. LAWS ch. 167B, §§ 1-24; MICH. STAT. ANN. §§ 23.1137(1)-23.1138; MINN. STAT. §§ 47.61-47.74; MONT. CODE ANN. §§ 32-6-101 to 32-6-402; N.M. STAT. ANN. §§ 58-16-1 to 58-16-17.

[197] *See, e.g.*, MASS. GEN. LAWS. ch. 167B, § 1 (defining terms); § 6 (issuance of access devices); § 8(a) (initial disclosures of terms and conditions); § 8(b) (disclosure of change in terms); § 9 (periodic statements requirements); § 18 (liability of consumer for unauthorized transfer).

[198] 15 U.S.C. § 1693q provides:

This subchapter does not annul, alter, or affect the laws of any State relating to electronic fund transfers, except to the extent that those laws are inconsistent with the provisions of this subchapter, and then only to the extent of the inconsistency. A State law is not inconsistent with this subchapter if the protection such law affords any consumer is greater than the protection afforded by this subchapter. The Board shall . . . determine whether a State requirement is inconsistent or affords greater protection. If the Board determines that a State requirement is inconsistent, financial institutions shall incur no liability under the law of that State for a good faith failure to comply with that law, notwithstanding that such determination is subsequently amended, rescinded, or determined by judicial or other authority to be invalid for any reason. This subchapter does not extend the applicability of any such law to any class of persons or transactions to which it would not otherwise apply.

substantially similar to those provided under the EFTA and Regulation E.[199] According to the FRB's Official Staff Commentary, a state law which is inconsistent may be preempted even if the FRB has not yet issued a formal determination.[200]

The FRB, either on its own motion or at the request of an interested party, may determine whether or not a state law is consistent with the EFTA.[201] The FRB has indicated that an inconsistency may exist when a state law:

- requires or permits a practice or act prohibited by the EFTA or Regulation E;

- provides for consumer liability for an unauthorized EFT that exceeds the limits imposed by the federal law;

- provides for longer time periods than those under federal law for the investigation and correction of billing errors, or fails to provide for the recrediting of the consumer's account during the institution's investigation of errors under the extended time limits allowed by Regulation E; or

- provides for initial disclosure, periodic statements, or terminal receipts that are different in content, except to the extent that the disclosures relate to rights granted under the state law and not the EFTA or Regulation E.[202]

The FRB has made two determinations that state EFT law is preempted under the EFTA's preemption provision. In the first instance, the FRB determined that certain provisions of Michigan law concerning the definition of unauthorized use and consumer liability for such use were preempted under the EFTA.[203] In making the determination, the FRB indicated that it used the following analysis of preemption:

> If a state law is the same as federal law, no preemption occurs. If state law is different from federal law, but financial institutions can comply with both, state law is not preempted and institutions must comply with both laws. If a state law is different from federal law, and institutions may violate state law when complying with federal law, the state laws are inconsistent within the meaning of [Regulation E]. In this case, if state law is more protective of the consumer, state law is not preempted. Otherwise, federal law preempts state law and institutions need comply only with federal law.[204]

---

[199] 15 U.S.C. § 1693r.

[200] 12 C.F.R. pt. 205, supp. I § 205.12(b).

[201] BAKER & BRANDEL, *supra* note 13, ¶ 12.02[3][a], at 12-46.

[202] 12 C.F.R. § 205.12(b).

[203] Electronic Fund Transfers, 46 Fed. Reg. 19,216, 19,217 (1981) (codified at 12 C.F.R. pt. 205 supp. I § 205.12(b)(2)).

[204] *Id.* at 19,217.

In the second instance, the FRB found that the Massachusetts EFT law,[205] which had been amended in response to a preliminary FRB determination that certain provisions of the law were preempted, must be looked at as a whole and was thus not preempted by the federal EFTA because the Massachusetts law was, on balance, more protective than federal law.[206]

---

[205] MASS. GEN. LAWS. ch. 167B, §§ 1-24.

[206] Electronic Fund Transfers; Determination of Effect on Massachusetts Law, 48 Fed. Reg. 43,671 (1983). *See also* BAKER & BRANDEL, *supra* note 13, ¶ 12.02[3][a], at 12-47.

PART II

"Money makes the world go around. . ."

Money

—Joel Grey

Federal, state, and international legislative and regulatory bodies, as well as professional and trade associations, have begun to address the challenges and risks presented by computer-based commerce and banking. The complexity of the issues, and the multiplicity of authorities and jurisdictions, pose a substantial challenge to uniformity and consistency.

Lack of uniformity is endemic to the national/state and national/international arenas; furthermore, historical accident combined with public policy has created a complex multi-agency federal regulatory regime. This lack of uniformity may provide more opportunities for creative regulatory responses to emerging issues and simultaneously help regulated entities play one agency or government against another through regulatory arbitrage. Different philosophies about the role of government with respect to electronic banking and commerce amplify the consequences of these variations. At one end of the spectrum, some agencies have established broad parameters and allowed the private-sector markets to design solutions that satisfy general regulatory interests. At the other end of the spectrum, some agencies have specified in minute detail the rules and regulations applicable to selected activities. Many agency approaches fall in between. The first approach has been challenged as letting private markets operate without appropriate government supervision for protection of the public; the second as stifling innovation and misdirecting precious technological resources. Regulators face the daunting goal of navigating between these shoals in the uncharted waters of electronic commerce and banking. This Part charts their course.

Chapter 5 focuses on early collaborative efforts by the federal regulatory agencies in addressing electronic commerce. Chapter 5 also provides a timeline of electronic banking and commerce developments beginning in January 1996. The next four Chapters highlight the activities of the Office of Comptroller of the Currency (Chapter 6), the Board of Governors of the Federal Reserve System (Chapter 7), the Federal Deposit Insurance Corporation (Chapter 8), and the Office of Thrift Supervision (Chapter 9). Chapter 10 then rounds out Part II by summarizing the activities of other interested parties, including federal and state governments, international organizations, and professional entities, with regard to electronic banking and commerce.

CHAPTER 5

INTERAGENCY ACTIONS ADDRESSING ELECTRONIC FINANCIAL PRODUCTS AND SERVICES

§ 5.01   INTRODUCTION

Governments achieve their goals in ways that can either create new markets and underwrite new products, or effectively foreclose certain markets and products. If regulators intervene too soon or too aggressively, they risk skewing the development of the market and stifling the creativity of the banking industry's innovators. That would only fortify the view that banking is too tightly regulated and too conservatively operated to survive in a technologically diverse financial services market. In addition, the opportunity to explore ingenuity would be left to nonbanks, which, much like the money funds of the late 1970's and early 1980's, could take advantage of the economic and technological environment to grow from a *de minimus* business relative to the banking industry to a major competitor for consumer assets. This Chapter discusses the collaborative efforts of federal agencies with respect to electronic banking and commerce, and then includes a timeline of recent government actions impacting on the development of electronic banking and commerce.

§ 5.02   INTERAGENCY STATEMENT ON RETAIL SALES OF NONDEPOSIT INVESTMENT PRODUCTS

Providing consumers with disclosure of the existence or nonexistence of deposit insurance coverage is a matter of continuing concern to the Federal Deposit Insurance Corporation ("FDIC") and the other federal bank regulatory agencies, as well as to Congress.[1] Because FDIC-insured depository institutions offer products that are insured for up to $100,000 per depositor,[2] those institutions have a responsibility to ensure that their

---

[1] *See Retail Nondeposit Investment Sales*, OCC Banking Circular 274 (July 19, 1993); *Sales of Nondeposit Investments*, FDIC FIL-71-93 (Oct. 8, 1993); *Separation of Mutual Fund Sales Activities from Insured Deposit Taking Activities*, FRB SR 93-35 (FIS) (June 17, 1993). *See also Securities Regulatory Equality: Hearing Before the Subcomm. on Telecommunications and Finance of the House Comm. on Energy and Commerce*, 103d Cong. (1994); *Bank Sales of Mutual Funds: Hearing Before the Subcomm. on Financial Institutions Supervision, Regulation and Deposit Insurance of the House Comm. on Banking, Finance and Urban Affairs*, 103d Cong. (1994).

[2] *See* 12 U.S.C. § 1821(a).

customers are fully informed when the institution offers products that are not so insured. The potential for customer confusion regarding the insured status of investment products sold at a depository institution has been the subject of ongoing congressional, regulatory, and judicial review.[3] In order to address these concerns, on February 15, 1994, the Board of Governors of the Federal Reserve System ("FRB"), the Office of the Comptroller of the Currency ("OCC"), the FDIC, and the Office of Thrift Supervision ("OTS") (together, the "bank regulatory agencies") issued the Interagency Statement on Retail Sales of Nondeposit Investment Products ("NDIP Statement").[4] In response to questions raised by bank trade associations and financial institutions about the application of the NDIP Statement, the bank regulatory agencies issued an interpretation of the NDIP Statement in September 1995 ("NDIP Interpretation").[5] This Section will discuss these two releases.

[1] THE NONDEPOSIT INVESTMENT PRODUCTS STATEMENT

The NDIP Statement provides uniform guidance to depository institutions engaged in recommending or selling nondeposit investment products, such as mutual fund shares, other securities, or annuities, to retail customers, either directly or through various types of arrangements with third parties. The NDIP Statement requires that, at a minimum, retail customers be made aware of three disclosures concerning nondeposit investment products, namely that: (i) they are not insured by the FDIC; (ii) they are not deposits or other obligations of the institution and are not guaranteed by the institution; and (iii) they are subject to investment risks, including possible loss of the principal invested.[6] These disclosures must be made orally and in writing before investment accounts are opened, orally during sales presentations, and orally when investment advice is given concerning nondeposit investment products.[7] Generally, a statement signed by the customer should be obtained at, or prior to, the time that an investment account is opened, acknowledging that the customer has received and understands the disclosures.[8]

---

[3] *See In re American Continental Corp./Lincoln Sav. & Loan Sec. Litig.*, 794 F. Supp. 1424 (D. Az. 1992); *Shipp v. NationsBank Corp.*, No. 19,002 (D. Tex. Mar. 7, 1996); *Hanson v. NationsBanc Sec.*, No. 95-00120C1 (Fla. Cir. Ct. filed Feb. 28, 1995); *Asbury v. Germania*, No. 90-CV-03513 WLB (S.D. Ill. filed Aug. 20, 1990); *Moore v. Germania*, No. 90-CV-03859 WLB (S.D. Ill. filed Aug. 20, 1990). *See also Business Practices of FDIC-Insured Institutions Selling Nondeposit Investment Products: Hearing Before the Subcomm. on Capital Markets, Securities, and Government Sponsored Enterprises of the House Comm. on Banking and Financial Services*, 104th Cong. (1996).

[4] *Interagency Statement on Retail Sales of Nondeposit Investment Products* (Feb. 15, 1994) [hereinafter NDIP Statement]; *see also Sales of Nondeposit Investments*, FDIC FIL-9-94 (Feb. 17, 1994).

[5] *Retail Sales of Nondeposit Investment Products: Clarification of Interagency Guidelines*, OCC Bull. 95-52 (Sept. 25, 1995); *Interagency Nondeposit Investment Products Interpretation*, OCC News Release 95-94 (Sept. 13, 1995). *See also New Examination Procedures for Retail Nondeposit Investment Product Sales*, FDIC FIL-48-97 (May 7, 1997).

[6] NDIP Statement, *supra* note 4, at 7.

[7] *Id.* The NDIP Statement applies when recommendations or sales of nondeposit investment products are made by: (i) employees of the depository institution; (ii) employees of a third party, which may or may not be affiliated with the institution, occurring on the premises of the institution (including telephone sales or recommendations by employees from the institution's premises and sales or recommendations initiated by mail from its premises); and (iii) sales resulting from a referral of retail customers by the institution to a third party when the depository institution receives a benefit for the referral. *Id.* at 2-3.

[8] *Id.* at 7.

The bank regulatory agencies believe that "recommending or selling nondeposit investment products to retail customers should occur in a manner that assures that the products are clearly differentiated from insured deposits."[9] The NDIP Statement also emphasizes that "conspicuous and easy to comprehend disclosures concerning the nature of nondeposit investment products and the risk inherent in investing in these products are one of the most important ways of ensuring that the differences between nondeposit products and insured deposits are understood."[10] Similarly, advertisements and other promotional and sales material, written or otherwise, about nondeposit investment products should "conspicuously include at least the minimum disclosures discussed above and must not suggest or convey any inaccurate or misleading impression about the nature of the product or its lack of FDIC insurance."[11]

Stored value products may, in some circumstances, be likened to the sale of a nondeposit investment products.[12] The FDIC has opined that certain types of stored value systems would not constitute "deposits" under the Federal Deposit Insurance Act ("FDIA"), and thus would not be eligible for deposit insurance.[13] At the same time, stored value products can be designed in a manner such that they qualify for FDIC insurance.[14] Banks may decide, however, that the marketing benefits of offering insured stored value products will be negligible because of the small denominations likely to be involved at the level of an individual consumer. They may also decide that any such benefits would be outweighed by the prospect of paying deposit insurance on stored value that they issue and the undertaking of extra requirements and expenses associated with establishing and maintaining an insured deposit relationship.[15] Certain non-insured stored value products (or other information-related services that might be confused for stored value in the minds of customers) may be subject to limitations on permanent locations and nature of sales, as well as associated disclosure requirements.

Consistent with the spirit of the NDIP Statement, the FDIC has stated that it expects depository institutions to make clear to consumers whether or not stored value obligations are insured deposits under the FDIA.[16] Two additional points contained in the NDIP Statement are relevant to the likely course of regulation of stored value products and their status as insured or non-insured deposits under the FDIA. First, because of the possibility of customer confusion, nondeposit investment products must not have names that are identical to the name of the depository institution.[17] Thus, a bank's marketing strategy for a stored value product, which is

---

[9] *Id.* at 6.

[10] *Id.*

[11] *Id.* at 8.

[12] The term "stored value" is often used to refer to a payment method wherein a prepaid balance of funds, the value, is recorded on a device in the consumer's possession, and the balance on that device is decreased when it is used for payment. Stored value is the subject of Chapter 16.

[13] General Counsel's Opinion No. 8; Stored Value Cards, 61 Fed. Reg. 40,490 (1996) [hereinafter FDIC Opinion].

[14] Task Force on Stored-Value Cards, Am. Bar Ass'n, *A Commercial Lawyer's Take on the Electronic Purse: An Analysis of Commercial Law Issues Associated with Stored Value Cards and Electronic Money,* 52 BUS. LAW. 653, 675 (1997).

[15] A depository institution's total insured deposits must be reported for purposes of determining its assessment base. 12 U.S.C. § 1817(a).

[16] FDIC Opinion, 61 Fed. Reg. at 40,494 ("[T]he FDIC would expect that institutions clearly and conspicuously disclose to their customers the insured or non-insured status of their stored value products, as appropriate.").

[17] NDIP Statement, *supra* note 4, at 9. *See* Karen Talley, *Union Bank, Feeling Heat, Will Rename Mutual Funds,* AM. BANKER, Jan. 28, 1994, at 1.

not an insured product, may raise issues under the spirit of the NDIP Statement. Second, the bank regulatory agencies require that, in instances where other types of insurance is provided for nondeposit investment products (such as by the Securities Investor Protection Corporation, a state insurance fund, or a private insurance company), which at some point in the future might apply to some stored value products, such coverage must be clearly and accurately disclosed to customers, so as to avoid any possible confusion with FDIC insurance.[18]

[2] THE NONDEPOSIT INVESTMENT PRODUCTS INTERPRETATION

In September 1995, in response to questions regarding the application of the NDIP Statement, the bank regulatory agencies issued the NDIP Interpretation. The NDIP Interpretation, along with a letter to the American Bankers Association ("ABA(Bankers)"), which it incorporates by reference, provides guidance as to the scope of the NDIP Statement's application. Further, the NDIP Interpretation clarifies the joint agency position on when the disclosures outlined in the NDIP Statement need not be provided, or when abbreviated disclosures may be used instead.

The bank regulatory agencies assert that they issued the NDIP Statement out of concern for the potential confusion when nondeposit investment products, which are not FDIC insured, are recommended and sold to a depository institution's retail customers either on the depository institution's premises or in adjacent premises. They rejected an ABA(Bankers) suggestion that the NDIP Statement apply only to the sale of mutual funds and annuities because many depository institutions advertise and offer a broader range of nondeposit investment products. The NDIP Interpretation clarifies that the NDIP Statement will apply to: (1) sales made to individuals by either depository institution or third-party personnel in or adjacent to the depository institution's lobby; (2) sales by affiliated broker-dealers when those sales occur on the depository institution's premises; and (3) sales made by an affiliated broker-dealer that result from the referral of the retail customer by the depository institution to the broker-dealer. The NDIP Statement does not apply in situations where a broker sells government and municipal securities from a location other than the area in or around the depository institution's lobby, or to fiduciary accounts administered by the depository institution, except that disclosures must be provided for self-directed fiduciary accounts.

The bank regulatory agencies set forth four specific situations where disclosures are not required: (1) radio broadcasts of thirty seconds or less; (2) electronic signs, which the NDIP Interpretation defined as the billboard type signs that are electronic, time and temperature signs, and ticker tape signs; (3) signs, such as banners and posters, when used only as location indicators; and (4) when inclusion of the name of the financial institution, though for a valid business purpose, is made by a third party vendor relating to a nondeposit investment product confirmation or account statement, and the inclusion is incidental in nature.

Short form disclosures, which may be used in visual media, such as billboards and television broadcasts, must include the fact that the product is not FDIC insured, that there is no bank guarantee,

---

[18] NDIP Statement, *supra* note 4, at 9.

and further, that the product may lose value. The full written disclosures described in the NDIP Statement still must be given to the customer on the written acknowledgment forms that the customer signs.

§ 5.03   CONSUMER ELECTRONIC PAYMENTS TASK FORCE

The Consumer Electronic Payments Task Force ("Task Force") is an interagency task force established by Secretary of Treasury Robert E. Rubin in the fall of 1996. The Task Force is chaired by Comptroller of the Currency Eugene A. Ludwig, and consists of representatives of the OCC, FDIC, FRB, Federal Reserve Bank of Atlanta, Federal Trade Commission, Financial Management Service of the Department of Treasury, and OTS. The Task Force's stated mission is to identify issues affecting consumers raised by emerging electronic money technologies and to explore innovative responses that are consistent with the needs of a developing market.[19] The Task Force has also set forth specific objectives:

- Identify the issues raised by electronic money.

- Evaluate the extent to which such issues are addressed by state and federal laws and regulations and voluntary industry guidelines.

- Identify innovative, nonregulatory approaches that would best help the electronic money industry address identified consumer issues as well as the need for public education about electronic money.[20]

To meet those objectives and fulfill its mission, the Task Force will gather information from the technology and financial services industries, consumers, and public interest organizations. This process will include informal discussions, surveys, and public meetings. Once the information collection process is complete, the Task Force plans to "prepare a report that identifies areas of consumer interests, summarizes existing laws and regulations and industry guidelines relevant to those interests, and, if appropriate, recommends areas to be addressed by voluntary industry action and public education."[21] The Task Force has deferred making final decisions regarding the scope, nature, and date of its final report until after it completes the information gathering and analysis process.[22]

The Task Force has also requested comment on the appropriate balance between technological efficiency and consumer privacy protection. Specifically, the Task Force has asked the following questions:

1. What information is generated about users of electronic money products and their transactions?

2. Who collects and has access to that information, and what is done with it?

---

[19] *Consumer Electronic Payments Task Force – Mission Statement and Objectives* (visited June 26, 1997) <http://www.occ.treas.gov>.

[20] *Id.*

[21] *Id.*

[22] *Consumer Electronic Payments Task Force – Summary of Principals Meeting,* Feb. 6, 1997 (visited June 26, 1997) <http://www.occ.treas.gov>.

3. What are customers told about how this information is used?

4. What sorts of privacy concerns, if any, have customers raised about the collection and use of this information?

5. How can these privacy concerns be addressed?[23]

[1] THE PUBLIC HEARINGS

The Task Force held its first public hearing on June 9, 1997.[24] In its request for comment and statements for the hearing, the Task Force, in addition to soliciting comments on generally meeting its objectives, identified three general issues for comment: (i) consumer disclosures and protection; (ii) access by consumers to electronic money; and (iii) questions related to the stability of electronic money systems and the financial conditions of system participants.[25]

Comptroller Ludwig opened the hearing with remarks emphasizing that the acceptance and success of electronic money products depend on consumers understanding "both the risks and benefits of the new products,"[26] and that "their interests have been considered and addressed by industry in providing these products."[27] Comptroller Ludwig also stressed the importance of studying the impact that electronic products would have on access to financial services by low- and moderate-income individuals, as well as those without financial institution relationships.[28]

The June 9, 1997, public hearing consisted of four panels. Industry representatives participating in the first panel made presentations on Internet and stored value payment activities, and the pace of industry developments. The remaining three panels, which included academics, consumer advocates, and financial service providers, focused on (1) disclosures and consumer protections, (2) issuer financial condition and reliability, and (3) access.

The July 17, 1997, public hearing focused on privacy and security issues. Panel participants represented electronic value providers, consumer advocacy organizations, and representatives of financial institutions and the government. The primary thrust of the privacy panel presentations was that the government should supply electronic financial services participants with guidelines regarding appropriate consumer protection measures rather than issuing standards, because standards may not accommodate technological developments and may

---

[23] Consumer Electronic Payments Task Force; Public Meeting; Comment Request, 62 Fed. Reg. 29,392 (1997).

[24] Another hearing was held on July 17, 1997, focusing on privacy concerns in addition to the issues addressed at the June 9th hearing.

[25] Consumer Electronic Payments Task Force; Public Meeting; Comment Request, 62 Fed. Reg. 19,173, 19,174 (1997).

[26] *Consumer Electronic Payments Task Force Hearing: Opening Remarks by Comptroller Eugene A. Ludwig* (visited June 26, 1997) <http://www.occ.treas.gov>.

[27] *Id.*

[28] *Id.*

stifle electronic commerce altogether. The security panel presentations, which focused on the technical aspects of electronic commerce, reflected a similar concern regarding overregulation. One panelist, CyberCash's Russell Stevenson, in his presentation identified three points of vulnerability in electronic commerce to which the government should give primary consideration when creating its guidelines: (1) authentication of users; (2) security of communications; and (3) computer systems security.

§ 5.04   YEAR 2000 INITIATIVES

The financial services industry has come to rely heavily on computer systems. These systems perform a wide range of internal operations, in addition to communicating with other banks, third party service providers, and bank customers. Beyond the challenge of increasingly moving this continuously developing computer technology to the retail side of the payments and banking systems, there is the challenge of technology itself. In that regard, the Year 2000 poses a serious challenge to the industry.[29]

A substantial portion of the computer operating systems and programs in use today use six digit data fields (YYMMDD) incapable of reading or expressing a date past December 31, 1999. For example, 010228 would be read not as February 28, 2001, but as February 28, 1901, thereby threatening the operation of computer systems around the world. The problem is magnified by the fact that an institution cannot truly solve its Year 2000 problems unless every computer system with which it networks also solves its Year 2000 difficulties.

[1]   FEDERAL FINANCIAL INSTITUTIONS EXAMINATION COUNCIL

In an effort to assist the financial services in addressing the Year 2000 problem, the Federal Financial Institutions Examination Council ("FFIEC")[30] has issued three statements that provide Year 2000 management guidance.

[a]   June 1996, "The Effect of Year 2000 on Computer Systems." The FFIEC's first statement, entitled "The Effect of Year 2000 on Computer Systems," issued in June 1996, set forth the FFIEC's concerns regarding the industry's readiness for the Year 2000.[31] It recommended that financial institutions conduct a risk assessment of their processing systems and create an action plan for addressing vulnerable systems.

---

[29]   *See* Robert G. Gerber, *Computers and the Year 2000: Are You Ready?*, 30 JOHN MARSHALL L. REV. 837 (1997); Gary E. Clayton, John W. Lanius, & Greg Nosch, *The Year 2000 Headache "Two Thousand Zero-Zero. Party's Over. Oops, Out of Time,"* 28 TEX. TECH. L. REV. 753 (1997).

[30]   The Federal Financial Institutions Examination Council ("FFIEC") is a statutorily created interagency body empowered to prescribe uniform principles, standards, and report forms for the federal examination of financial institutions by the Federal Reserve Board, the Federal Deposit Insurance Corporation, the National Credit Union Administration, the Office of the Comptroller of the Currency, and the Office of Thrift Supervision, and to make recommendations to promote uniformity in the supervision of financial institutions. *See generally* <http://www.ffiec.gov>.

[31]   *See Year 2000 Programming Code Risks,* OCC Advisory Letter 96-4 (June 17, 1996).

[b] May 1997, "Year 2000 Project Management Awareness." On May 5, 1997, the FFIEC issued a statement entitled "Year 2000 Project Management Awareness" ("Interagency Year 2000 Statement") updating its previous statement and providing guidance for Year 2000 conversion efforts.[32] The Interagency Year 2000 Statement is divided into four parts:

- an outline of the Year 2000 project management process;

- identification of three external risk issues that Year 2000 conversion plans should consider;

- a discussion of other operational issues that may be relevant to an institution's Year 2000 planning; and

- a description of the federal financial institution regulatory agencies' supervisory strategy.[33]

[i] Project Management Processes. The Interagency Year 2000 Statement outlines five management phases necessary for complete Year 2000 computer conversion: awareness, assessment, renovation, validation, and implementation. During the awareness and assessment phases, which the FFIEC recommends concluding by the end of the third quarter of 1997, institutions should develop a Year 2000 team and strategy, in addition to completing an assessment of the size and complexity of the program. Financial institutions are also expected to consider the effects of the Year 2000 problem on strategic business planning.

The renovation phase includes code enhancements, hardware and software upgrading, and system replacements. The FFIEC strongly recommends that changes to mission-critical applications be largely completed, and testing well underway, by December 31, 1998. The deadline for completing the renovation phase is crucial to the success of the validation phase. Testing upgraded components, incremental changes, connections to other systems, and user acceptance is a difficult task that could easily take one year. When the validation phase is complete, the process enters the implementation phase wherein systems should be Year 2000 certified.

[ii] External Issues. Following the discussion of project management processes, the Interagency Year 2000 Statement identifies three external issues that should be considered during Year 2000 conversion process. It notes that financial institutions' reliance on vendors poses a risk to successful process implementation. The FFIEC recommends that financial institutions evaluate vendor agreements, monitor vendor activities, and consider alternate vendors, where necessary. Because much of the data transferred electronically by financial institutions is date sensitive, financial institutions should monitor the impact of Year 2000 processes on that information. Finally, financial institutions should monitor the Year 2000 efforts and progress of their corporate customers and consider including Year 2000 compliance representations in loan documents.

---

[32] *Year 2000 Project Management Awareness*, May 5, 1997 [hereinafter *Interagency Year 2000 Statement*]; *see Year 2000 Issues and Examination Approach*, OCC Advisory Letter 97-6 (May 16, 1997).

[33] *Interagency Year 2000 Statement, supra* note 32, at 1.

[*iii*] *Operating Issues.* The third part of the Interagency Statement addresses operating issues. Financial institutions will have to consider both cost and timing in deciding whether to replace or repair their computer systems. Attracting and retaining personnel qualified to confront the Year 2000 presents an additional factor for consideration. Year 2000 problems should also be taken into account in merger and acquisition decisions. Successful Year 2000 conversions will depend on awareness of Year 2000 issues by appropriate staff members throughout the entire financial institution organization. It is particularly important that remote or overseas operations receive thorough review during the process. Financial institutions should modify contracts to address Year 2000 compliance by vendors. Finally, all Year 2000 plans must take leap years into account.

[*iv*] *Supervisory Strategy.* The federal financial institution regulatory agencies will conduct a supervisory review of the Year 2000 progress of all financial institutions by mid-1998. The FFIEC has provided uniform examination procedures that the bank regulatory agencies will follow, and suggests that institutions use the procedures in conducting self-evaluations of their own computer systems.[34] Supervisory reviews will extend to third party service and software providers.

[c] December 1997, "Safety and Soundness Guidelines Concerning the Year 2000 Business Risk."
The FFIEC issued a third statement regarding the Year 2000 problem on December 17, 1997. The "Safety and Soundness Guidelines Concerning the Year 2000 Business Risk" ("Year 2000 Guidelines") were intended to supplement the Interagency Year 2000 Statement, and to be used as an aid to senior management and boards of directors of financial institutions in addressing Year 2000 issues.[35]

The Year 2000 Guidelines offer five suggestions for boards of directors of financial institutions to implement, in dealing with the Year 2000 problem:

- ensure that management is viewing Year 2000 as an enterprise-wide challenge, not merely as a technology issue;

- require quarterly status reports on Year 2000 efforts from senior management;

- ensure that there is communication with all vendors regarding Year 2000 systems and require due diligence inquiries of vendors and internal testing of vendor products and services;

- adopt an enterprise-wide project plan, including tasks, resource requirements, target dates, and strategies for responses to inquiries; and

- work towards industry-wide cooperation among financial institutions.

---

[34] FEDERAL FINANCIAL INSTITUTIONS EXAMINATION COUNCIL, INFORMATION SYSTEMS EXAMINATION HANDBOOK, at 1-1 (1996).

[35] *Safety and Soundness Guidelines Concerning the Year 2000 Business Risk*, Dec. 17, 1997 [hereinafter *Year 2000 Guidelines*]; *see Year 2000 Business Risk*, OCC Advisory Letter 97-10 (Dec. 17, 1997).

[*i*] *Enterprise Challenge.* The Year 2000 Guidelines stress the importance of sufficient attention to, and funding of, Year 2000 programs. Year 2000 programs must be enterprise-wide, not limited solely to information systems analysis, but encompassing accounting and risk control systems, as well as any interaction with outside vendors' systems, and customer account and credit risk systems. Financial institutions also must budget resources for testing all internal and external systems.[36]

[*ii*] *Reporting to the Board.* Boards of directors of financial institutions must monitor the progress of Year 2000 projects. The FFIEC suggests that the board require at least quarterly status reports on Year 2000 programs. These reports, which should be noted in the board minutes and available for review by bank regulatory agency examiners, should include:

- overall progress, including any new developments or efforts;

- comparisons of actual progress to the project plan;

- reports on the status of Year 2000 projects of key vendors, business partners, counter parties, and major loan customers;

- results of internal and external testing of information processing applications, databases, and systems;

- contingency plans;

- total number of applications inventoried, and details on the status of mission critical applications in each stage of the five step project management process;[37]

- reports on the progress of renovation, testing, and implementation of mission critical applications; and

- summaries of the results of all internal and external testing for Year 2000 systems.[38]

[*iii*] *Clarification of Certification Requirement (Vendors).* The Interagency Year 2000 Statement dealt with the relationship between financial institutions and their vendors.[39] The Year 2000 Guidelines reiterate the importance of monitoring and testing vendor Year 2000 solutions. The FFIEC indicates in the new guidelines, however, that formal certification of vendor systems is not required. Instead, financial institutions should communicate with vendors concerning target dates for implementation of Year 2000 systems; products that will not be converted in time; required coordination efforts between the vendor and the institution; and testing

---

[36] *Year 2000 Guidelines, supra* note 35.

[37] This process was outlined in the *Interagency Year 2000 Statement, supra* note 32.

[38] *Year 2000 Guidelines, supra* note 35.

[39] See Section 5.04[2][b] for additional information on FFIEC's suggestions regarding Year 2000 planning and vendors.

of renovated products and services. Financial institutions also should create contingency plans in case vendors' systems are not ready on time, and set trigger dates for implementation of those alternative plans.[40]

[*iv*] *Project Planning and Management.* The FFIEC suggests formal adoption of a Year 2000 project plan by all financial institutions. Under the Year 2000 Guidelines, any project plan should include:

- tasks to be accomplished throughout the term of the project;

- resource requirements and a list of the individuals responsible for implementation of the phases of the project;

- target dates for completion of key elements of the project;

- strategies for responding to inquiries from customers and business partners; and

- processes for monitoring the progress of Year 2000 programs of vendors, business partners, counter parties, and major loan customers.[41]

[*v*] *Industry Coordination.* Finally, the Year 2000 Guidelines urge the entire financial institutions industry to work together on solutions to the Year 2000 problem. The FFIEC points out the potential benefits of lower costs, increased competitiveness with other industries, and increased bargaining power with vendors, if financial institutions and industry associations work together to solve the problems posed by the Year 2000.

[2] YEAR 2000 ENFORCEMENT ACTIONS

In an action that further signals regulatory concern and resolve in this area, on November 17, 1997 the FDIC and the Georgia Department of Banking and Finance announced the joint issuance of cease and desist orders against three affiliated Georgia banks ("Banks").[42] Simultaneously, the FRB announced the issuance of a cease and desist order against their parent bank holding company.[43] The cease and desist orders were issued to ensure that: (1) adequate information systems are in place; (2) adequate internal controls are maintained; and (3) computer related operations will function effectively on and after January 1, 2000.

The FDIC orders charged that the Banks had engaged in unsafe or unsound banking practices and violations of laws and regulations by, among other things:

- Operating the Banks with an inadequate and unreliable electronic information systems and systems service provider.

---

[40] *Year 2000 Guidelines, supra* note 35.

[41] *Id.*

[42] *Orders to Cease and Desist Issued Against Georgia Banks*, FDIC Press Release PR-83-97 (Nov. 17, 1997).

[43] *Putnam-Greene Financial Corporation*, FRB Press Release (Nov. 17, 1997).

- Failing to take measures to ensure that the electronic information systems and other automated systems could correctly perform automated data processing operations involving dates later than December 31, 1999.

The FDIC orders, which were agreed to by the Banks, require the Banks to take a range of corrective measures, including:

- Adopting a Year 2000 plan to determine that all information systems can correctly perform automated data processing operations involving dates later than December 31, 1999. The Year 2000 plan must include:

  — An assessment of the actual and potential Year 2000 problems posed by the information systems that the Banks use.

  — An assessment of the potential credit risk that results from reliance of commercial loan customers on electronic information systems and other automated systems.

The Banks must meet the following timelines in attaining Year 2000 compliance:

- By August 1998, the Banks must complete all renovations of electronic information systems necessary to correct Year 2000 compliance deficiencies identified in the assessment.

- By December 31, 1998, the Banks must test all electronic information systems to ensure that all systems can correctly perform all operations involving dates later than December 31, 1999.

- By July 1, 1999, the Banks must use only information systems capable of performing all operations involving dates later than December 31, 1999, as demonstrated by a written determination that all such systems have been successfully tested.

The orders also provide that the Banks may only acquire or contract for the use of electronic information services, hardware, systems software, and/or applications software that has been successfully tested for Year 2000 compliance (including interactions or interdependencies with other systems used by the Banks, their customers, their affiliates, and their vendors) prior to use by the Banks.

Depository institutions and their information technology providers (which, in many instances, are subject to examination under the Bank Service Corporation Act)[44] should expect intensive scrutiny by federal and state bank regulatory agencies in regard to Year 2000 compliance.

---

[44] For a discussion of the Bank Service Corporation Act, see Chapter 6, Section 6.04[2].

[3]   LEGISLATIVE INITIATIVES

On November 10, 1997, Senator Robert Bennett introduced the Year 2000 Computer Remediation and Shareholder Protection Act of 1997 ("Act").[45] The Act includes findings that (1) most computer systems in the U.S. and around the world are not prepared to operate successfully after January 1, 2000; (2) that the failure of such systems threatens the financial results of U.S. corporations and the continued soundness of the global economy; and (3) that corporations have not provided adequate disclosure in regard to Year 2000 compliance issues. Under the Act, the Securities and Exchange Commission would be required, within 120 days of enactment, to adopt regulations that would require issuers registered under the Securities Exchange Act of 1934 to include in each quarterly report information on:

- Progress in completing the five phases of Year 2000 remediation by business unit.

- Costs incurred and anticipated additional costs in regard to remediation efforts.

- Anticipated litigation costs and liability outlays associated with the defense of legal actions against the issuer (or directors or officers of the issuer) as a result of Year 2000 problems, including breach of contract, tort, shareholder class action, and product liability actions.

- The existence of insurance policies of the issuer that cover specific Year 2000 problems.

- Contingency plans developed by the issuer itself or by a vendor, partner, or affiliate of the issuer.

[4]   ACTION PLAN FOR FINANCIAL INSTITUTIONS

Year 2000 compliance has rapidly emerged as a critical challenge for financial institutions and the economy as a whole.[46] For a further discussion of the steps that institutions should consider in this regard, see Appendix A.

§ 5.05   DEVELOPMENTS IN ELECTRONIC COMMERCE

The following timeline identifies selected developments involving electronic banking and commerce since January 1, 1996. These developments are discussed in greater detail elsewhere in this Chapter and in Chapters 6-10.

---

[45] S. 1518, 105th Cong. (1997).

[46] *See, e.g., Zap! How the Year 2000 Bug will Hurt the Economy*, BUS. WK., Mar. 2, 1998, at 93.

DATE	ACTOR	DEVELOPMENT
January 1996	OCC	Comptroller Eugene Ludwig challenges the banking industry to take a leadership position in the development and distribution of new electronic money and payment technologies.
February 1996	FRB	Approves bank holding company proposal to acquire an interest in a computer software company engaged partially in non-financial applications.
	OCC	Amends interpretive rulings to provide that national banks may perform, provide, or deliver electronically any authorized activity, function, product, or service and may market and sell to third parties excess electronic capacities acquired or developed in good faith for banking purposes.
	FDIC	Releases two opinions regarding regulatory treatment of a system for making purchases on the Internet.
March 1996	Congress	House Banking Subcommittee holds hearing on the Future of Money.
	OCC	Approves proposal by a group of national banks to dispense "alternative media" (including public transportation tickets; event and attraction tickets; gift certificates; prepaid phone cards; promotional and advertising materials; electronic benefits transfer script; and credit and debit cards) from ATMs.
April 1996	Congress	Enacts Debt Collection Improvement Act of 1996 requiring that all federal agencies convert from checks to electronic fund transfers for all federal payments, including salaries, retirement payments, and entitlements.
	OCC	Amends and reorganizes its interpretive rulings concerning permissible national bank activities incidental to the business of banking.
May 1996	FRB	Adopts a comprehensive revision to Regulation E and to the Official Staff Commentary thereunder. Proposes amendments to Regulation E to address stored value products.
	OCC	Confirms that a national bank may acquire and hold a minority interest in a company that is engaged in the design, development, marketing, and maintenance of a network for electronic data interchange and electronic fund transfers.
	FRB	Approves bank holding company's proposal to acquire a computer software company and thereby engage in data processing activities to provide banking and financial services over the Internet.

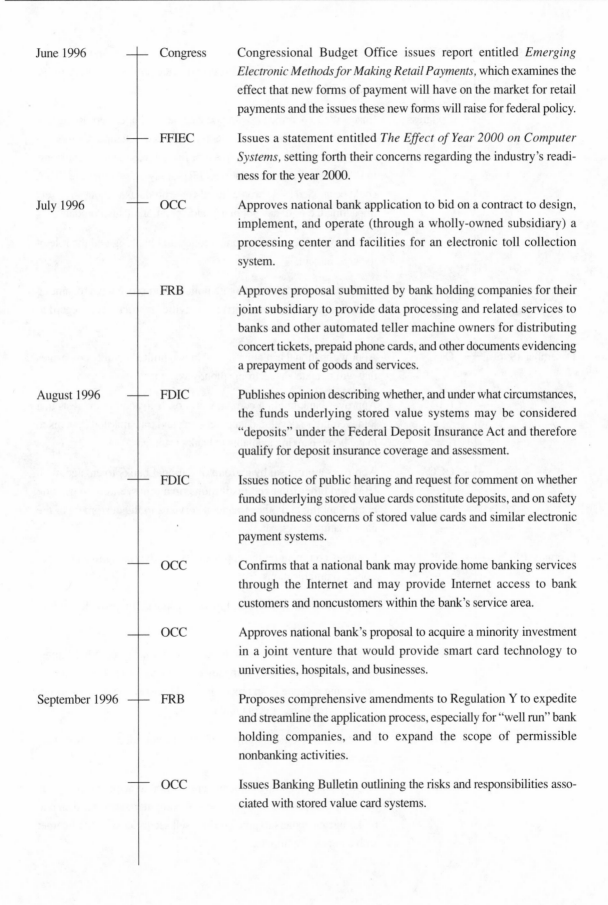

June 1996   Congress   Congressional Budget Office issues report entitled *Emerging Electronic Methods for Making Retail Payments,* which examines the effect that new forms of payment will have on the market for retail payments and the issues these new forms will raise for federal policy.

FFIEC   Issues a statement entitled *The Effect of Year 2000 on Computer Systems,* setting forth their concerns regarding the industry's readiness for the year 2000.

July 1996   OCC   Approves national bank application to bid on a contract to design, implement, and operate (through a wholly-owned subsidiary) a processing center and facilities for an electronic toll collection system.

FRB   Approves proposal submitted by bank holding companies for their joint subsidiary to provide data processing and related services to banks and other automated teller machine owners for distributing concert tickets, prepaid phone cards, and other documents evidencing a prepayment of goods and services.

August 1996   FDIC   Publishes opinion describing whether, and under what circumstances, the funds underlying stored value systems may be considered "deposits" under the Federal Deposit Insurance Act and therefore qualify for deposit insurance coverage and assessment.

FDIC   Issues notice of public hearing and request for comment on whether funds underlying stored value cards constitute deposits, and on safety and soundness concerns of stored value cards and similar electronic payment systems.

OCC   Confirms that a national bank may provide home banking services through the Internet and may provide Internet access to bank customers and noncustomers within the bank's service area.

OCC   Approves national bank's proposal to acquire a minority investment in a joint venture that would provide smart card technology to universities, hospitals, and businesses.

September 1996   FRB   Proposes comprehensive amendments to Regulation Y to expedite and streamline the application process, especially for "well run" bank holding companies, and to expand the scope of permissible nonbanking activities.

OCC   Issues Banking Bulletin outlining the risks and responsibilities associated with stored value card systems.

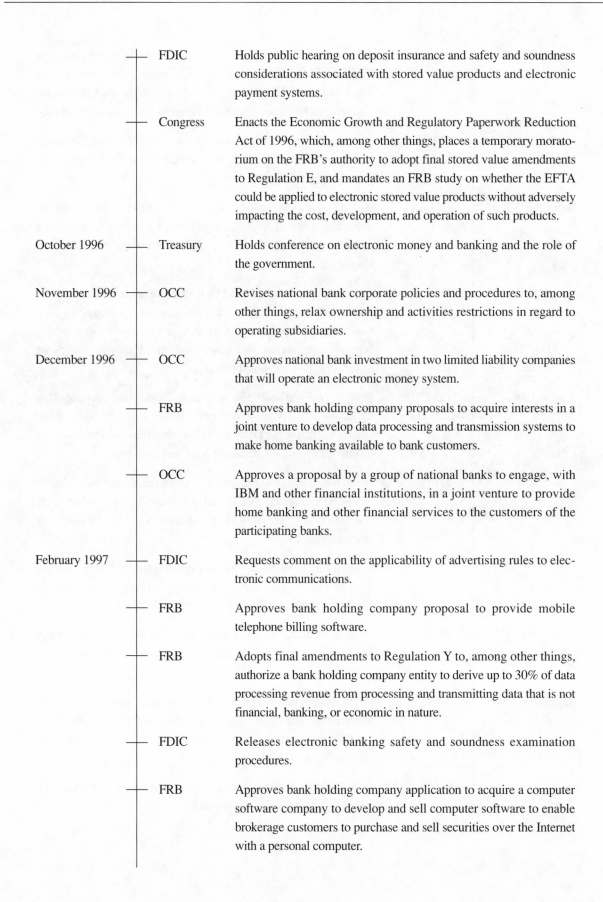

	FDIC	Holds public hearing on deposit insurance and safety and soundness considerations associated with stored value products and electronic payment systems.
	Congress	Enacts the Economic Growth and Regulatory Paperwork Reduction Act of 1996, which, among other things, places a temporary moratorium on the FRB's authority to adopt final stored value amendments to Regulation E, and mandates an FRB study on whether the EFTA could be applied to electronic stored value products without adversely impacting the cost, development, and operation of such products.
October 1996	Treasury	Holds conference on electronic money and banking and the role of the government.
November 1996	OCC	Revises national bank corporate policies and procedures to, among other things, relax ownership and activities restrictions in regard to operating subsidiaries.
December 1996	OCC	Approves national bank investment in two limited liability companies that will operate an electronic money system.
	FRB	Approves bank holding company proposals to acquire interests in a joint venture to develop data processing and transmission systems to make home banking available to bank customers.
	OCC	Approves a proposal by a group of national banks to engage, with IBM and other financial institutions, in a joint venture to provide home banking and other financial services to the customers of the participating banks.
February 1997	FDIC	Requests comment on the applicability of advertising rules to electronic communications.
	FRB	Approves bank holding company proposal to provide mobile telephone billing software.
	FRB	Adopts final amendments to Regulation Y to, among other things, authorize a bank holding company entity to derive up to 30% of data processing revenue from processing and transmitting data that is not financial, banking, or economic in nature.
	FDIC	Releases electronic banking safety and soundness examination procedures.
	FRB	Approves bank holding company application to acquire a computer software company to develop and sell computer software to enable brokerage customers to purchase and sell securities over the Internet with a personal computer.

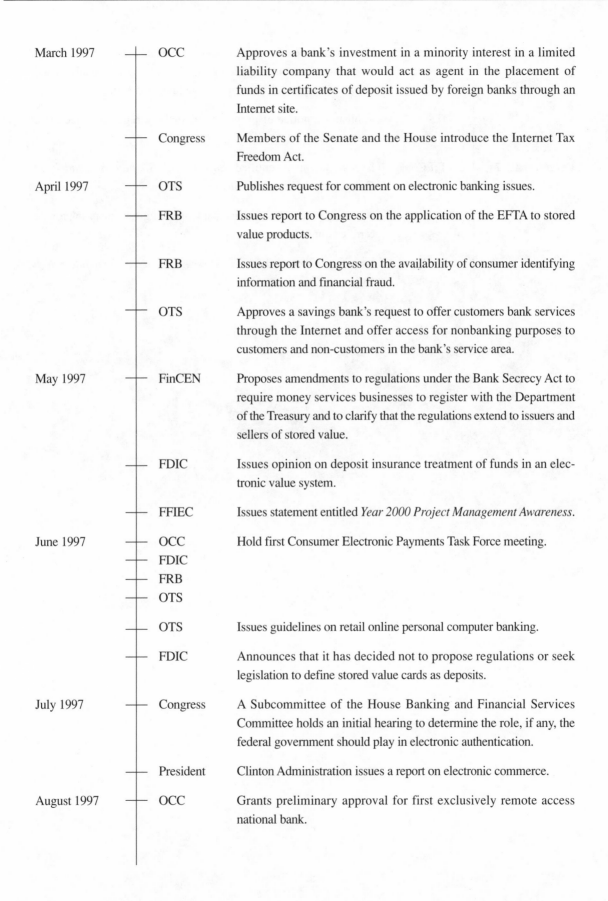

March 1997	OCC	Approves a bank's investment in a minority interest in a limited liability company that would act as agent in the placement of funds in certificates of deposit issued by foreign banks through an Internet site.
	Congress	Members of the Senate and the House introduce the Internet Tax Freedom Act.
April 1997	OTS	Publishes request for comment on electronic banking issues.
	FRB	Issues report to Congress on the application of the EFTA to stored value products.
	FRB	Issues report to Congress on the availability of consumer identifying information and financial fraud.
	OTS	Approves a savings bank's request to offer customers bank services through the Internet and offer access for nonbanking purposes to customers and non-customers in the bank's service area.
May 1997	FinCEN	Proposes amendments to regulations under the Bank Secrecy Act to require money services businesses to register with the Department of the Treasury and to clarify that the regulations extend to issuers and sellers of stored value.
	FDIC	Issues opinion on deposit insurance treatment of funds in an electronic value system.
	FFIEC	Issues statement entitled *Year 2000 Project Management Awareness*.
June 1997	OCC FDIC FRB OTS	Hold first Consumer Electronic Payments Task Force meeting.
	OTS	Issues guidelines on retail online personal computer banking.
	FDIC	Announces that it has decided not to propose regulations or seek legislation to define stored value cards as deposits.
July 1997	Congress	A Subcommittee of the House Banking and Financial Services Committee holds an initial hearing to determine the role, if any, the federal government should play in electronic authentication.
	President	Clinton Administration issues a report on electronic commerce.
August 1997	OCC	Grants preliminary approval for first exclusively remote access national bank.

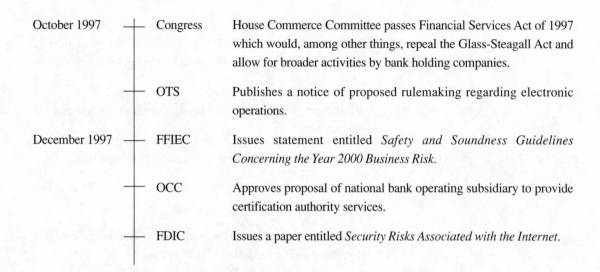

October 1997 — Congress — House Commerce Committee passes Financial Services Act of 1997 which would, among other things, repeal the Glass-Steagall Act and allow for broader activities by bank holding companies.

OTS — Publishes a notice of proposed rulemaking regarding electronic operations.

December 1997 — FFIEC — Issues statement entitled *Safety and Soundness Guidelines Concerning the Year 2000 Business Risk.*

OCC — Approves proposal of national bank operating subsidiary to provide certification authority services.

FDIC — Issues a paper entitled *Security Risks Associated with the Internet.*

CHAPTER 6

OFFICE OF THE COMPTROLLER OF THE CURRENCY'S PERSPECTIVE ON ELECTRONIC FINANCIAL PRODUCTS AND SERVICES

§ 6.01   INTRODUCTION

Chapter Two provided a brief history of the Office of the Comptroller of the Currency ("OCC") and the creation of the national banking system. It also reviewed the defining principles applicable to the breadth of national bank activities, from OCC interpretations of the National Bank Act[1] to the Supreme Court's decision in *NationsBank v. Variable Annuity Life Insurance Company* (*"VALIC"*).[2] This Chapter explores how the OCC has adapted to the evolution of the business of banking in general and its manifestation in electronic form in particular. Section 6.02 examines the process of analytical disaggregation and how the OCC uses this process in determining the permissibility of banking activities. Section 6.03 focuses on the OCC's approach to the data processing developments of the 1980s and 1990s to show that the OCC has given careful consideration to the issues presented by new forms of technology. Section 6.04 discusses the OCC's position on the various business arrangements that will play a pivotal role in the development and delivery of new products and services. Section 6.05 focuses on OCC supervision of electronic banking systems in their current form. Finally, Section 6.06 addresses the new phenomenon of virtual banks.

§ 6.02   ANALYTICAL DISAGGREGATION

While the other bank regulatory agencies often engage in what we will call "analytical disaggregation" to reach conclusions concerning whether activities are incidental, reasonably related, or closely related to the business of banking, the OCC makes the best and most consistent use of it. "Analytical disaggregation" is the process of dividing a complex question or activity into its many component issues and operations. Thus, launching the space shuttle may be viewed broadly as the business of shuttle launching or may be disaggregated

---

1   National Bank Act, June 20, 1864, c. 343, §1, 18 Stat. 123 (codified as amended at 12 U.S.C. §§ 21-216).

2   *NationsBank v. Variable Annuity Life Ins. Co.*, 513 U.S. 251 (1995) (*"VALIC"*).

to include the individual businesses of storing liquid fuel, igniting it, steering the shuttle, providing life support systems, and so on.

Similarly, a financial activity may be viewed as one integral business or the combination of a number of component financial activities. Thus, if each of the component activities may be viewed as a permissible banking activity, the totality of them must necessarily be viewed as a permissible banking activity. The recent OCC decision allowing national banks to engage in the development, creation, and maintenance of electronic toll collection systems for highways, discussed in Section 6.03[4][e], is a good example of this. The following discussion of OCC decisions demonstrates how the OCC disaggregates financial activities and evaluates them for permissibility. Generally, analytical disaggregation leads to a flexible view of what constitutes permissible banking activities.

Federal bank regulatory agencies must constantly evaluate whether technology is the means by which a financial product is distributed or, if at some point, it actually becomes the product itself. The former approach tends to provide more flexibility in determining what constitutes permissible banking activities. It is also the approach taken fairly consistently by the federal bank regulatory agencies. As the lines between financial services and technology continue to be blurred by the movement of business and commerce to the Internet, it may at times become difficult to adhere to the doctrine that technology is not the product, but the means by which a product is distributed. Indeed, the point at which analytical disaggregation and this technology versus product analysis becomes somewhat attenuated is when it is used to suggest that nonbanks, which are functionally providing financial services to consumers, are not in the banking business and should not be regulated as banks.

§ 6.03   NATIONAL BANK DATA PROCESSING AND ELECTRONIC SERVICES

The OCC's consistent and long-standing position regarding electronic banking has been to allow banks to employ new technologies in providing existing or emerging customer services that fall within the services historically associated with the business of banking, as broadly construed by the Comptroller.

The OCC amended and reorganized its interpretive rulings concerning permissible national bank activities as of April 1, 1996.[3] Electronic activities are addressed in 12 C.F.R. § 7.1019, entitled "Furnishing of Products and Services by Electronic Means and Facilities" ("Electronic Means and Facilities Rule"). Before evaluating this latest rule, it is useful, however, to review the predecessor rulings and the OCC's reasoning regarding the scope and nature of electronic products.

---

[3]   Interpretive Rulings, 61 Fed. Reg. 4849 (1996) (codified at 12 C.F.R. §§ 7.1000-7.1021). For an extensive discussion of the development of the OCC's actions regarding the business of banking see, Julie L. Williams & Mark P. Jacobson, *The Business of Banking: Looking to the Future*, 50 Bus. Law. 783 (1995) and Julie L. Williams & James F.E. Gillespie, Jr., *The Business of Banking: Looking to the Future - Part II*, 52 Bus. Law. 1279 (1997).

[1]   THE OCC'S 1984 INTERPRETIVE RULING ON DATA PROCESSING

In 1982, the OCC expressed concern that its original 1974 interpretive ruling regarding data processing activities failed to address technological advances and provide adequate guidance at a time of rapid advances in data processing and growth of the electronic payments system; it therefore proposed a new interpretive ruling on data processing.[4] The 1974 data processing interpretive ruling, in effect at the time of the OCC's 1982 proposal, stated that:

> A national bank may use data processing equipment and technology to perform for itself and other all services expressly or incidentally authorized under the statutes applicable to national banks. For example as part of its banking business and incidental thereto, a national bank may collect transcribe, process, analyze, and store, for itself and other, banking, financial, or related economic data. In addition, incidental to its banking business, a national bank may (1) market a by-product (*e.g.*, program, output, etc.) of an above-described data processing activity; and (2) market excess time on its data processing equipment so long as the only involvement by the bank is furnishing the facility and necessary operating personnel.[5]

Prior to issuing its proposal to revise this ruling, the OCC had issued an advanced notice of proposed rulemaking soliciting comments on five alternative approaches to be used in determining the appropriate interpretation:

- Revise the ruling to reflect changes in technology (Option 1).

- Revise the ruling to reflect current and future needs of financial institutions and other sectors of the economy for data processing capacity and services provided by banks (Option 2).

- Revise the ruling to eliminate differences with Regulation Y of the Board of Governors of the Federal Reserve System ("FRB") (Option 3).

- Retain the existing ruling but make it more understandable through question and answer bulletins or educational sessions (Option 4).

- Implement a formal regulation (Option 5).[6]

---

[4]   Data Processing by National Banks, 47 Fed. Reg. 46,526 (1982) (to be codified at 12 C.F.R. § 7.3500) (proposed Oct. 19, 1982) [hereinafter Data Processing Proposal].

[5]   12 C.F.R. § 7.3500(a). Paragraph (b) subjected the provision of data processing services to the prohibitions contained in 12 U.S.C. § 1972 against tying arrangements, reciprocal dealing and price discrimination. In the final interpretive ruling adopted in 1984, the OCC eliminated this paragraph. It determined that the paragraph had been adopted in 1974 at a time when the OCC believed that a formal interpretation regarding the applicability of 12 U.S.C. § 1972 was necessary because banks were relatively unsophisticated in matters related to data processing. The OCC determined that since 1974 banks had gained sufficient experience in providing data processing services, so that a codified opinion regarding the applicability of 12 U.S.C. § 1972 to data processing activities was no longer required. Data Processing Proposal, 47 Fed. Reg. at 48,527. *See also* Data Processing by National Banks, 49 Fed. Reg. 11,157 (1984) (codified at 12 C.F.R. § 7.3500) [hereinafter Data Processing Rule].

[6]   Data Processing Services, 45 Fed. Reg. 40,613 (1980).

Ultimately, the OCC declined to adopt any of the five proposed options.[7] It rejected Option 1 for two reasons. First, it determined that a technologically oriented ruling would quickly become outdated because state of the art data processing applications evolve at a rapid rate. Second, the OCC noted that a technologically oriented ruling would detract from the primary purpose of the interpretive ruling, to provide banks with the OCC's opinion regarding the legal permissibility of national banks' data processing activities.[8]

The OCC found that banks viewed themselves as the ultimate beneficiaries of any expansion of permissible bank data processing activities under Option 2, while nonbank processors felt they would be further disadvantaged by banks' increasing presence in that market. Because Option 2 could be misinterpreted as an OCC endorsement of bank data processing activities that are not incidental to the business of banking, or otherwise permissible under laws applicable to national banks, the OCC rejected Option 2.[9]

The OCC decided that legal considerations precluded conforming its interpretive ruling on data processing activities to the relevant provisions of FRB's Regulation Y, as proposed in Option 3. Regulation Y interprets and applies the provisions of the Bank Holding Company Act, a statute applicable to bank holding companies and their nonbank subsidiaries, entities not subject to the incidental powers provision of 12 U.S.C. Section 24(Seventh). Because the primary purpose of the proposed interpretive ruling was to interpret the applicability of Section 24(Seventh) to the data processing activities of national banks, the OCC reasoned that it could not achieve that purpose by revising its interpretive ruling to conform to the FRB's regulation.[10]

The OCC did not categorically reject Option 4, which proposed to retain the existing ruling and supplement it with additional aids, such as question and answer bulletins. It concluded, however, that ongoing litigation and the rapid pace of technological development made it unlikely that more specific guidelines would be possible or desirable in the near future. The OCC noted that the second and third sentences of the then existing interpretive ruling, which provided examples of permissible data processing activities, had led to confusion regarding permissible activities.[11] The OCC proposed to, and in its final interpretive ruling ultimately did, delete these two sentences for two reasons. First, it found the language of the bank data processing field generally imprecise, thereby making it difficult for the OCC to formulate examples of permissible activities that illustrate the full range of a national bank's authority to provide data processing activities without being subject to misinterpretation. Second, the OCC noted that any listing of permissible activities would quickly become obsolete because of rapid technological change.[12] It should be noted, however, that the OCC did not delete the

---

[7] Data Processing Proposal, 47 Fed. Reg. at 46,526.

[8] *Id.* at 46,528.

[9] *Id.*

[10] *Id.*

[11] *Id.*

[12] *Id.* at 46,529. *See also* Data Processing Rule, 49 Fed. Reg. at 11,157.

processing of banking, financial, and economic data as an activity incidental to the business of banking. Indeed, the OCC continues to recognize such activities as part of banking.[13]

The OCC decided not to promulgate a formal regulation as proposed in Option 5. It provided three reasons for that decision, based on comments by parties responding to the advance notice of proposed rulemaking. First, data processing is too dynamic to be bound by artificial restraints. Second, a regulation would hamper or retard the development of new banking technologies. Finally, a formal regulation would encourage an increasing regulatory presence. The OCC determined that no purpose would be served by a formal regulation that could not be achieved by an interpretive ruling.[14]

The final rule regarding data processing activities of national banks that the OCC adopted in 1984 ("Data Processing Rule") provided that:

> It is the opinion of the Comptroller that, in general, data processing is a technology rather than a service distinct or different from the underlying services or functions to which the technology is applied. A national bank may use data processing equipment and technology to perform for itself and others all services expressly or incidentally authorized under the statutes applicable to national banks.[15]

The language of the Data Processing Rule reflects an agency sensitive to the changing nature of technology and to the limitations of overly specific rules in a dynamic industry lacking precise terminology. The OCC's decision to delete specific examples is consistent with the position proposed, and subsequently adopted, that "[i]t is the opinion of the Comptroller that, in general, data processing is a technology rather than a service distinct or different from the underlying services or functions to which the technology is applied."[16] The OCC noted that such a statement was implicit in the 1974 rule, but should be made explicit in the Data Processing Rule because it is a fundamental element of the Office's position regarding the data processing activities of national banks.[17] Furthermore, deletion of the 1974 rule's last two sentences, which contained specific examples, did not change the OCC's view that the sale of by-products and excess processing capacity are activities legitimately incidental to the business of banking. The OCC stated its preference for analyzing permissible activities on a case-by-case basis on the facts and circumstances prevailing at the time of its evaluation.[18]

---

[13] *See* Conditional Approval Letter No. 221 (Dec. 4, 1996), 1996 OCC Ltr. LEXIS 139; OCC Interpretive Letter No. 653, [1994-1995 Transfer Binder] Fed. Banking L. Rep. (CCH) ¶ 83,601, at 71,801 (Dec. 22, 1994).

[14] Data Processing Proposal, 47 Fed. Reg. at 46,529.

[15] Data Processing Rule, 49 Fed. Reg. at 11,158-59.

[16] Data Processing Proposal, 47 Fed. Reg. at 46,530; Data Processing Rule, 49 Fed. Reg. at 11,158-59.

[17] Data Processing Proposal, 47 Red. Reg. at 46,529.

[18] Data Processing Rule, 49 Fed. Reg. at 11,158.

A final notable feature of the Data Processing Rule is the OCC's decision not to replace "data processing" with "information processing and communication," though it noted a change might be appropriate at a later date.[19] The OCC was concerned that a change in terminology at that time could lead to confusion. Moreover, it noted that the OCC has never adopted a restrictive or highly technical definition of data processing.[20]

[2] OCC DECISIONS REGARDING DATA PROCESSING AND ELECTRONIC ACTIVITIES

The OCC's opinions and decisions under both the original and revised data processing rules regarding the appropriateness of certain data processing activities and services as "incidental to banking" and therefore proper for national banks under 12 U.S.C. Section 24(Seventh), provide valuable guidance for banks as they explore new electronic products and services. A number of general principles emerge from the OCC's application of the Data Processing Rule:

1. Banks may use their excess data processing capacity to provide services incidental to permissible banking services.

2. Banks may sell their excess data processing capacity to non-financial institutions where that excess capacity was acquired in good faith to serve the bank's own needs.

3. Banks may provide data processing services to other financial institutions.

4. Banks may sell by-products of their data processing activities, such as software programs, where they are incidental to the data processing.

5. Banks may share technology platforms used in customer service operations with other service providers in order to serve their customers.

This Section provides a discussion of the OCC rulings that have established these principles.

[a] Services Incidental to Permissible Banking Services. A number of OCC decisions under the 1974 and 1984 data processing rules are described below.

[i] Mail Sorting Services. In May 1981, Interpretive Letter No. 196 addressed whether a national bank could be a member of an organization that provides credit card processing, related financial accounting and information services, and mail sorting services to its members if that organization also provides mail sorting services to nonmembers in connection with activities lacking any other connection to financial services or credit cards.[21] The organization in question was a not-for-profit, non-stock corporation organized to provide credit

---

19 *Id.* As discussed further herein, on April 1, 1996 the OCC did modify the Data Processing Rule to refer to "activities, functions, products, and services provided via electronic means and facilities rather than data processing" and changed the title of 12 C.F.R. § 7.1019 to "Furnishing of Products and Services by Electronic Means and Facilities." Interpretive Rulings, 61 Fed. Reg. 4849, 4853 (1996) (codified at 12 C.F.R. § 7.1019).

20 Data Processing Rule, 49 Fed. Reg. at 11,158.

21 OCC Interpretive Letter No. 196, [1981-1982 Transfer Binder] Fed. Banking L. Rep. (CCH) ¶ 85,277, at 77,415 (May 18, 1981).

card services to its members, which were national and state banks. The banks paid fees to the membership organization for the services that it rendered to the member banks. The OCC first addressed whether the membership organization should be subject to the Bank Service Corporation Act ("BSCA").[22] The BSCA provides for supervision and examination by federal bank regulatory agencies of bank service corporations ("BSCs") and entities that are not BSCs, that perform BSCA-authorized activities for banks. The OCC noted that the statutory definition of BSC referred to a corporation organized to perform services for two or more banks, each of which owns part of the capital stock of the BSC. It found that the membership fees paid to the organization by the member banks represented service payments and could not be characterized as the ownership of stock. As a result, the OCC concluded that the organization was not a BSC and, therefore, to that extent, the BSCA did not apply.

The membership organization was, however, still subject to the BSCA to the extent that it provided services to banks. This raised for the OCC a second question, namely, whether a national bank was permitted to be a member of the organization. The prevailing rationale for national bank membership in the organization was that it provided services for the member banks that they could themselves perform. The OCC found providing credit card services to be a permissible activity for national banks. The provision of mail sorting services in connection with the credit card services is incidental to a permissible bank activity and, therefore, itself permissible. The OCC determined, however, that providing mail sorting services on a stand-alone basis to companies that are not banks, where such services are not performed in a banking related context, is not an activity incidental to the business of banking. Such activities exceed the authority of national banks. As a result, the OCC required that a national bank with a membership in an organization providing such stand-alone mail sorting services must either withdraw from the membership organization or cause it to cease the impermissible activity.[23]

[ii] *Selling Excess Capacity Acquired in Good Faith.* In 1983, the same OCC official who had written Interpretive Letter No. 196 examined the provision of mail sorting services by a national bank from the perspective of excess capacity and found the services allowable.[24] The bank in question was a member of a not-for-profit, non-stock corporation organized to provide credit card and financial data processing services to its members, which were national and state chartered banks. The membership organization also sorted an oil company's bills by ZIP code to enable the oil company to obtain lower postage rates. The OCC, referencing its earlier analysis in Interpretive Letter No. 196, concluded that the mail sorting service, in and of itself, was not part of the business of banking. Noting, however, that its interpretive ruling at 12 C.F.R. § 7.3500(a) permitted a national bank to market excess time on its data processing equipment, the OCC concluded that the sale of the

---

[22]   12 U.S.C. §§ 1861-67.

[23]   OCC Interpretive Letter No. 196, *supra* note 21, at 77,417. The letter specifically reminded national banks of the prohibition against membership in organizations conducting activities other than those expressly authorized by statute or that are incidental to the business of banking.

[24]   Letter from Peter Liebesman, Assistant Director, Legal Advisory Services Division (Dec. 13, 1983) (unpublished).

mail sorting service to the oil company might be permissible.[25] The OCC permitted continued bank membership in the organization on the basis that selling appropriately acquired excess data processing capacity is an incidental activity permissible for a national bank and, therefore, is permissible for an organization of which a national bank is a member.

The OCC also relied on the excess capacity doctrine to allow a bank to sell excess capacity on its security service's automated console to other financial institutions. In No Objection Letter No. 86-15, the OCC stated that the excess capacity resulted from a good faith acquisition of a console designed to meet the bank's own security requirements and thus did not represent an attempt at a deliberate entry into a separate business.[26]

In adopting its Electronic Means and Facilities Rule in 1996, the OCC clarified the authority of a national bank to sell excess data processing capacity acquired or developed in good faith for the legitimate needs of the bank itself.[27]

[*iii*] *Financial Institutions Providing Data Processing Services to Other Financial Institutions.* In Interpretive Letter No. 513, the OCC approved a national bank's provision of clerical and support services, including the design of data processing forms, to other financial institutions through its BSC.[28] In this case, the OCC did not rely on the excess capacity rationale. Rather, the OCC found designing forms for use in data processing services provided to other financial institutions incidental to the business of banking. The OCC reasoned that such activity represented the provision of correspondent services, a traditional banking activity.[29]

The OCC followed similar reasoning and reached a broader result in another case where it found an impermissible stand-alone activity permissible when incidental to an allowed activity.[30] The bank in question owned a subsidiary that served as a general partner in a data processing business that provided processing for medical insurance claims and arranged for the transfer of funds in connection with such claims.[31] The OCC permitted the data processing activity because it found fund transfers to be the primary purpose of the service and the medical data processing only an incidental service.

[*iv*] *The OCC Permits Sale of Data Processing By-Products.* The OCC has found certain activities to be by-products of, and thereby incidental to, permissible activities. In one instance, in 1984, a bank proposed to form a subsidiary to acquire a software company and a software program owned by that company. The bank

---

[25] The OCC did not have enough information to determine, and did not determine, that the excess capacity of equipment providing the mail sorting service had in fact been acquired in good faith.

[26] OCC No Objection Letter No. 86-15, [1988-1989 Transfer Binder] Fed. Banking L. Rep. (CCH) ¶ 84,021, at 76,620 (June 6, 1986). The security system is required by the Bank Protection Act (12 U.S.C. §§ 1881-84). *See also* Letter from Stephen B. Brown, Attorney, Southwest District Office, (Dec. 20, 1989) (unpublished) (bank permitted to resell to unaffiliated third parties excess capacity on bank's private telecommunications network).

[27] Interpretive Rulings, 61 Fed. Reg. 4849, 4853 (1996) (codified at 12 C.F.R. § 7.1019).

[28] OCC Interpretive Letter No. 513, [1990-1991 Transfer Binder] Fed. Banking L. Rep. (CCH) ¶ 83,215, at 71,270 (June 18, 1990).

[29] *Id.* at 71,271. The OCC left open the question of whether the activity would be permissible if all customers were not financial institutions.

[30] OCC Interpretive Letter No. 419, [1988-1989 Transfer Binder] Fed. Banking L. Rep. (CCH) ¶ 85,643, at 78,013 (Feb. 16, 1988).

[31] The OCC found the bank's participation in the joint venture permissible because the bank enjoyed limited liability, veto power, and unanimous consent requirements for joint ventures. The partnership was also subject to examination.

planned to use the program to enhance the bank's own internal data processing. In addition, the bank would make the program available to parties purchasing access to the bank's banking, financial, and economic data-bases and sell the program on a stand-alone basis as a by-product. The OCC found the acquisition permissible to the extent it accomplished the first two purposes.[32] As to the by-product sales, the OCC issued no final determination because it lacked necessary information. It noted, however, that the sale of software was permissible to the extent that it was developed in-house, rather than purchased from a third party and then resold. This interpretation suggested that a bank's acquisition of a company to acquire that company's software and then sell it as a by-product would not be permissible, while a bank's acquisition of a software company that later developed software that could be sold as a by-product, would be permissible.

The OCC confirmed this result in 1988, when a bank asked the OCC whether the bank could sell or lease its self-developed software to financial institutions and corporations. The OCC responded that the sale of self-developed software constituted a permissible activity.[33]

[v] *Sale of Data Processing Hardware.* In 1985, the OCC faced the question of whether to permit a national bank subsidiary to sell data processing hardware in conjunction with the provision of permitted data processing services. The data processing subsidiary had been permitted to sell computer hardware to data processing customers pursuant to Regulation Y when the bank's parent holding company owned the subsidiary directly.[34] The subsidiary provided correspondent banking services that required bank customers to own the hardware in question. The OCC agreed with the rationale used by the Court of Appeals for the D.C. Circuit in upholding the FRB's authority to permit bank holding companies to engage in computer hardware sales pursuant to Regulation Y.[35] The OCC, however, distinguished between hardware that could be used exclusively in connection with the permitted correspondent services and hardware adaptable to other uses.[36] Where adaptable, the OCC required, that when taken as a whole package, the hardware must be subordinate to permitted services. The OCC opted for a case-by-case determination of the subordinate nature rather than the cost ratio used by the FRB.[37] The OCC maintained this rationale when reviewing a 1996 request regarding bank authority to provide Internet access.[38]

The OCC has historically taken a case-by-case approach to emerging electronic services rather than publishing generalized lists that may rapidly become obsolete. As new electronic and data processing services have emerged, the OCC's decisions illustrate its efforts to facilitate the delivery of financial services through new technologies so as to allow national banks to remain competitively relevant and viable.

---

[32]   OCC Interpretive Letter No. 284, [1983-1984 Transfer Binder] Fed. Banking L. Rep. (CCH) ¶ 85,448, at 77,610 (Mar. 26, 1984).

[33]   OCC Interpretive Letter No. 416, [1988-1989 Transfer Binder] Fed. Banking L. Rep. (CCH) ¶ 85,640, at 78,002 (Feb. 16, 1988).

[34]   OCC Interpretive Letter No. 345, [1985-1987 Transfer Binder] Fed. Banking L. Rep. (CCH) ¶ 85,515, at 77,799 (July 9, 1985).

[35]   *Id.* at 77,800. *See Association of Data Processing Serv. Org., Inc. v. Board of Governors of the Fed. Reserve Sys.*, 745 F.2d 677, 692-95 (D.C. Cir. 1984).

[36]   OCC Interpretive Letter No. 345, *supra* note 34, at 77,800.

[37]   *Id.* at 77,801.

[38]   *See* Section 6.03[4][d].

[3] THE 1996 ELECTRONIC MEANS AND FACILITIES RULE

On February 9, 1996, the OCC promulgated a final rule, effective April 1, 1996, that amended and recodified its interpretive rulings.[39] Subpart A of Part 7 sets forth the OCC's interpretive rulings regarding the powers of banks, including, under 12 C.F.R. § 7.1019, the authority of national banks to furnish products and services by electronic means and facilities. As originally proposed, the interpretive ruling read as follows:

> In general, data processing is a technology rather than a service distinct or different from the underlying services or functions to which the technology is applied. A national bank may use data processing equipment and technology to perform for itself and others all services expressly or incidentally authorized under the statutes applicable to national banks. Further, when a national bank uses data processing equipment or technology to perform authorized services, the bank may market and sell any legitimate excess capacity in that equipment or technology.[40]

In the Electronic Means and Facilities proposal, the OCC, noting that significant advances in data processing technology had occurred during the ten years since the interpretive ruling was last amended, [41] solicited comments with respect to two specific issues. First, it asked whether it should be more specific in describing the services a national bank may provide using data processing equipment and technology.[42] The majority of commentators stated that greater specificity in describing permissible services would not be useful.[43] The OCC also recognized that banks were engaging in an increasing range of activities through electronic means and facilities beyond simply "data processing."[44] It, therefore, modified the language of its proposed ruling to refer to "activities, functions, products, and services provided via electronic means and facilities" rather than to "data processing." Correspondingly, it modified the title of the interpretive ruling.

Second, the OCC asked for comments regarding the necessity of including the proposed language discussing the authority of national banks to sell excess capacity of data process equipment and technology.[45] In the final ruling, the OCC responded to commentators' concerns regarding the language, "legitimate excess capacity" and instead opted for a "good faith" standard.[46] Finally, the OCC noted that the express language of

---

[39] Interpretive Rulings, 61 Fed. Reg. 4849 (1996) (codified at 12 C.F.R. pts. 7, 31) [hereinafter Electronic Means and Facilities Rule].

[40] Interpretive Ruling, 60 Fed. Reg. 11,924, 11,936 (1995) (to be codified at 12 C.F.R. § 7.1019) (proposed Mar. 3, 1995) [hereinafter Electronic Means and Facilities Proposal].

[41] *Id.* at 11,927.

[42] *Id.*

[43] Electronic Means and Facilities Rule, 61 Fed. Reg. at 4853.

[44] *Id.*

[45] Electronic Means and Facilities Proposal, 60 Fed. Reg. at 11,927.

[46] Electronic Means and Facilities Rule, 61 Fed. Reg. at 4853-54.

the final ruling, that sales of excess capacity are appropriate for a bank to optimize the use of the bank's resources, parallels the standard applied by the OCC in cases involving sales to nonbank users.[47]

The OCC's ruling provides as follows:

> A national bank may perform, provide or deliver through electronic means and facilities
> any activity, function, product or service that it is otherwise authorized to perform,
> provide, or deliver. A national bank may also, in order to optimize the use of the bank's
> resources, market and sell to third parties electronic capacities acquired or developed by
> the bank in good faith for banking purposes.[48]

The 1996 Electronic Means and Facilities Rule preserves the fundamental premises of the Data Processing Rule. It thereby embraces the specific rulings and opinions that were examined earlier in this Section and sets the stage for future OCC rulings related to electronic banking and commerce based on the authority of 12 U.S.C. Section 24(Seventh), as interpreted by the OCC.

As illustrated by a number of recent OCC decisions, the regulatory approach for analyzing national banks' involvement in electronic banking and commerce is not limited to the Electronic Means and Facilities Rule. The following Section examines a variety of issues that have arisen during the last several years, among them the issue of banks providing access to, and offering services over, the Internet. It also examines the authority of national banks to engage in electronic banking and commerce on the basis of the bank's status as a finder or correspondent banker.

[4]   INTERNET-BASED AND OTHER EMERGING SERVICES

In a speech in January 1996, Eugene Ludwig, the Comptroller of the Currency, addressed some of the significant effects that technology will have on financial modernization.[49] He chided elected officials, policy-makers, and banking leaders for equating financial modernization with changes to, or elimination of, the Glass-Steagall Act, when, in his view, the changes to financial institutions caused by technology will be much more momentous and pervasive in at least three areas. First, the Comptroller noted that the Internet is only the tip of the iceberg in a world where totally electronic market trading, electronic money, a paperless payments system, and vastly more sophisticated pricing and risk control models are on the horizon. Second, technology increasingly blurs the distinctions between the products and producers of financial services and intensifies global competition among banks, nonbanks, and international financial institutions. Finally, Mr. Ludwig noted, technology is having a major impact on questions related to geography. The existing legal infrastructure,

---

[47] *Id.* at 4854 (citing Letter from Peter Liebesman, Assistant Director, Legal Advisory Services Division (July 24, 1987) (unpublished) and cases cited therein, *Wingert v. First Nat'l Bank of Hagerstown, Md.,* 175 F. 739 (4th Cir. 1909), *aff'd,* 223 U.S. 670 (1912); *Brown v. Schleier,* 118 F. 981 (8th Cir. 1902), *aff'd,* 194 U.S. 18 (1904)).

[48] 12 C.F.R. § 7.1019.

[49] Eugene A. Ludwig, Comptroller of the Currency, Financial Modernization, Remarks Before the Exchequer Club, Washington, D.C. (Jan. 24, 1996), *in* 15 O.C.C.Q.J. 33 (June 1996).

which ties the activities of banks to state laws, is under increasing strain as virtual products and even virtual banks emerge. The scope and extent of the impact of technology on banking is illustrated by the OCC decisions discussed below.

[a] Shared Platforms of "Smart Phones." In 1992, the OCC authorized a national bank to use the "platform" of "smart phones," which were already providing customers with banking and other financial services, to provide other data processing and communication services.[50] The bank sought to make its "platform" available to its correspondent financial institutions, which would, in turn, make banking services available to their customers. It also intended to enhance the package by allowing other service and information providers to access the "platform." Finally, the national bank would offer the "platform" to other financial institutions as a gateway for financial settlement services. The OCC found each of these ancillary uses incidental to banking, falling squarely within the area of traditional correspondent services.

In permitting the other service and information providers' use of the bank's smart phone platform, the OCC noted that such services constituted less than 20% of the banking and financial activity.[51] The OCC, however, based its approval for these other services on the authority of a national bank to act as a finder in bringing together a buyer and seller, and to market goods or services to the bank's customers on a promotional basis, rather than on the basis that this portion of the services constituted a *de minimis* portion of the total services and thus was incidental to a banking service.[52] The OCC determined that bringing together customers and suppliers is a traditional banking activity of a national bank, and recognized that banks invariably do, and must be permitted to, form alliances with non-financial institutions.[53]

[b] Providing Information and Payments Interface. In 1994, a bank proposed to offer, through a wholly owned operating subsidiary, an informational and payments interface between insurance underwriters, on the one hand, and general insurance agencies and their individual agents on the other.[54] The OCC determined that the operating subsidiary would not be an insurance agent or broker because the operating subsidiary would not sell or otherwise market insurance policies to potential policyholders nor would it represent underwriters in selling policies or dealing with policyholders. The proposal identified the following specific activities in which the subsidiary would engage:

- Providing information and consulting services to the general agency in negotiating contracts with underwriters;

- Collecting commissions from the underwriters and making appropriate disbursements;

---

[50] OCC Interpretive Letter No. 611, [1992-1993 Transfer Binder] Fed. Banking L. Rep. (CCH) ¶ 83,449, at 71,572 (Nov. 23, 1992).

[51] *Id.* at 71,573.

[52] *Id. See also* 12 C.F.R. § 7.1002 (ability of national bank to act as a finder); OCC Interpretive Letter No. 339, [1985-1987 Transfer Binder] Fed. Banking L. Rep. (CCH) ¶ 85,509, at 77,792 (May 16, 1985) (although a national bank cannot be a travel agent, it can market other entities' tour packages to its customers).

[53] OCC Interpretive Letter No. 611, *supra* note 50, at 71,573.

[54] OCC Interpretive Letter No. 653, [1994-1995 Transfer Binder] Fed. Banking L. Rep. (CCH) ¶ 83,601, at 71,801 (Dec. 22, 1994).

- Providing periodic reports to the general agency concerning insurance sales by its individual agents and maintaining records pertaining thereto; and

- Disbursing supplies (such as policy applications) and information authorized by nonaffiliated insurers concerning their policies to the individual agents on behalf of the general agency.

These proposed services involved finder services, data processing services, and payment services, all of which represent permissible activities for either a national bank or its operating subsidiary. Relying on its interpretive ruling with respect to finder services and the OCC's precedents in interpreting that ruling, the OCC found that providing information is one of the fundamental activities of a finder.[55] It also found consulting to be a permissible activity where it consists, as in the case at hand, of the provision of financial advice, including credit analysis, recommendations, and appraisals.[56]

One-half of the proposed operating subsidiary activities consisted of keeping financial and other records, activities that easily fit under the Data Processing Rule as permissible activities. The operating subsidiary proposed to maintain information regarding the license status of each agent.[57] The OCC concluded that such information is "banking, financial, or related economic data," important to the operating subsidiary in its role as a finder, because an agent's ability to sell a product depends on their license status.[58] Finally, the OCC found the collection and disbursement of commissions analogous to operating a lockbox, an activity traditionally performed by banks.[59]

[c] ATM Machines May Dispense Alternative Electronic Media. In early 1996, a group of banks requested OCC approval to dispense alternative media through their network ATMs. The media forms included (1) public transportation tickets, (2) event and attraction tickets, (3) gift certificates, (4) prepaid phone cards, and (5) similar products such as promotional materials and debit/credit cards. In its decision approving the activities, the OCC referenced its three-part test for determining whether activities may be considered within the business of banking. That test addresses whether the activity:

- is the functional equivalent to or a logical outgrowth of a recognized banking activity;

- benefits bank customers, or is convenient or useful to banks; or

- presents risks of a type similar to those already assumed by banks.[60]

---

[55] *Id.* at 71,802 (citing 12 C.F.R. § 7.7200 and OCC Interpretive Letter No. 472 [1989-1990 Transfer Binder] Fed. Banking L. Rep. (CCH) ¶ 83,008, at 71,111 (Mar. 2, 1989) (quoting Letter from James Kane, District Counsel, Central District Office (Oct. 24, 1985) (unpublished)).

[56] *Id.* (citing Letter from David Barris, Regional Counsel (Apr. 7, 1982) (unpublished)).

[57] Insurance agents must be licensed for each product and company in every state where they sell such products.

[58] OCC Interpertive Letter No. 653, *supra* note 54, at 71,802. The OCC also noted that even if the information regarding agents' license appointments is not viewed as strictly banking, financial or related economic information, this activity would still be permitted as an incidental part of the general provision of data processing services, just as the sale of hardware usable for services beyond those provided by a bank is permitted as an incidental subordinate part of the permissible services.

[59] *Id.* at 71,803 (citing Letter from Coreen Arnold, Senior Attorney, Central District Office, to Rolland Kelley at 2 (June 30, 1988) (unpublished), which cited *United States v. Philadelphia Nat'l Bank*, 374 U.S.321, 327 n.5 (1963)).

[60] OCC Interpretive Letter No. 718, [1995-1996 Transfer Binder] Fed. Banking L. Rep. (CCH) ¶ 81-033, at 90,299, 90,301 (Mar. 14, 1996).

The OCC noted, in keeping with its long-standing perspective on technology, that a bank may use any equipment or technology to perform an authorized activity. Thus, the issuance of credit and debit cards was clearly viewed as a traditional bank service.[61]

Concerning the remaining activities, the OCC concluded that the alternative media represented the "logical outgrowth of the recognized bill payment and funds transfer functions of national banks."[62] To reach this determination, the OCC relied on a two step analysis. First, it characterized the items in question as "prepayment media" representing two related but distinct traditional roles banks play in the payments system. In dispensing prepayment media, a bank fills the same role as when it acts as an "Issuing Bank" in the case of a credit card: it is providing the bank customer with a vehicle to make purchases from participating merchants.[63] The OCC reasoned that, in dispensing alternative media, the bank also provides a means of payment analogous to a credit card. The bank also plays the role of a "Clearing Bank," one that receives payment on behalf of and remits payment to a merchant. In the case of the alternate prepayment media, a bank is simply playing both roles simultaneously.[64] Thus, the first prong of the test was met.

The second step in the OCC's analysis recognized that the "sale" occurred not at the merchant's place of business, but at a consumer banking computer terminal ("CBCT"),[65] branch, or automated teller machine ("ATM"). Further, the transfer of the media is distinguishable from the transfer of the goods or services that are exchangeable for the media. The media merely provide evidence of a form of contractual value that the consumer and the seller agree to use in exchange for the goods and services. The sale of goods or services is consummated, the OCC held, only when the consumer obtains them from the merchant. Moreover, the OCC concluded that the availability of the alternative media at banks, in connection with the core banking activity of funds transfer, would be a benefit and convenience to consumers and merchants.[66] The second prong of the test was thereby met. Finally, the OCC noted that the proposal met the third prong of the test because it posed no risk not already present in traditional payment and funds transfer services provided by banks.[67]

[d] Providing Internet Access Services. In June 1996, Apollo Trust Company requested OCC confirmation that, as a service incidental to providing home banking via the Internet, a national bank operating subsidiary is permitted to provide Internet access (i) to the bank's customers, and (ii) to persons who are *not*

---

[61] *Id.* at 90,301.

[62] *Id.*

[63] Credit card transactions are discussed in greater detail in Chapter 4, Section 4.04.

[64] OCC Interpretive Letter No. 718, *supra* note 60, at 90,302. It is also possible for the bank to play both roles in the case of a credit card where both the consumer and merchant are customers of the same bank.

[65] *Id.* Interestingly, the OCC analyzed this situation from the perspective of the consumer using the terminal rather than from the perspective of the dispensing bank.

[66] *Id.*

[67] *Id.* at 90,303.

customers of the bank.[68] The OCC supplied that confirmation in an August 1996 Interpretive Letter, No. 742, in which it relied on its Electronic Means and Facilities Rule and on its historical interpretation of activities incidental to the business of banking under 12 U.S.C. Section 24(Seventh).[69]

[*i*] *Internet Access By Bank Customers.* The OCC deemed providing bank customers with full Internet access an appropriate activity on the basis that it was incidental to the provision of Internet home banking services. It gave three primary reasons for this determination. First, consistent with the OCC's reasoning in the smart phone and hardware rulings, the OCC noted that the full access service added virtually nothing to the cost of providing Internet home banking and did not dominate the bank's home banking package.[70] Second, providing full Internet access satisfied customer demand and provided the bank with an alternative means to successfully market its home banking services, which were nothing more than traditional banking services in electronic form. This position is consistent with the OCC's long held view that the provision of products and services by electronic means is not a separate service whose authority must be found in 12 U.S.C. § 24.[71] Third, the OCC found that providing full Internet access was a permissible use of the bank's excess capacity, which was acquired in good faith to support a traditional banking service. The OCC concluded that providing Internet access to customers presented no unique risks to the bank.[72]

[*ii*] *Internet Access for Non-Customers.* The OCC has also concluded that providing Internet access to non-customers in the bank's service area was incidental to the business of banking.[73] National banks generally may engage in activities to promote their reputation, goods, and services. Using excess capacity to offer Internet access to the public at large, the OCC reasoned, would establish goodwill and serve community needs.[74] In this respect, the OCC relied first on the authority of a national bank to promote its services and then, only derivatively, on its authority to do so electronically pursuant to 12 C.F.R. § 7.1019. Further, the OCC found that serving non-customers was a valid incidental distribution of excess capacity, although it did not offer extensive analysis on this point. Indeed, projecting the rationale underlying the Apollo decision, one can foresee a wide range of activities that national banks could undertake that would generally promote the bank and its permissible customer services and, at the same time, utilize excess capacities available to those banks.

---

[68] Apollo Trust is a state chartered bank. It sought the OCC's opinion in connection with its request for FDIC approval under 12 U.S.C. § 1831a(d) to establish a wholly owned subsidiary. Section 1831a(d)(1) provides that a subsidiary of an insured state chartered bank may not engage as principal in any type of activity that is not permissible for a subsidiary of a national bank unless the FDIC determines that the activity poses no risk to the insurance fund and the bank meets applicable capital standards.

[69] OCC Interpretive Letter No. 742, [1996-1997 Transfer Binder] Fed. Banking L. Rep. (CCH) ¶ 81-106, at 90,215 (Aug. 19, 1996).

[70] *Id.* at 90,218.

[71] *Id.* at 90,218-19.

[72] *Id.* at 90,219 (emphasis added). The OCC found that Internet servers provide no banking functions not provided by conventional banking means and thus there is no increased risk from unauthorized access as compared to these conventional means.

[73] *Id.* The applicant bank uses a local telephone number to provide access to the service in order to limit its non-customer base. The OCC did not address whether there might be a point at which the bank's marketing strategy and actual customer base might raise an issue as to the continued applicability of the incidental to banking doctrine as the rationale for the OCC's approval.

[74] The OCC cited *Franklin Nat'l Bank v. New York,* 347 U.S. 373 (1954), which recognized the authority of national banks to advertise.

[e] Operation of a Highway Toll Plaza. On July 1, 1996, the OCC issued an interpretive letter allowing a bank to establish a subsidiary to design, build, and operate a system of toll plazas pursuant to a contract with a consortium of public authorities.[75] Under its proposal, the bank would enter into a contract with a public authority to design, build, and operate an electronic toll collection facility.[76] In addition, the bank would operate a customer service center and collect funds from customers to open toll accounts. Alternatively, stored value cards could be used by customers to pay tolls. The "toll accounts" would not represent deposit accounts in the bank but prepaid toll fees that the bank would hold as an agent for the consortium of public authorities. The bank would not own or finance the facilities. The processing of toll payments by a bank clearly involved a financial function, and therefore raised little question regarding its relation to banking.[77] The bank would also, however, through a subcontractor, design and install the electronic receivers that communicate with the toll transponders and arrange for the design and construction of the customer service center. The construction activities could be conducted through a joint venture rather than a subcontract. The OCC approved the venture with its subcontract provision, even though this meant the bank would be the primary party carrying out the construction. The OCC found "the ability to arrange for, by means of subcontracting, the one-time design, construction, and installation of facilities and equipment necessary to conduct the activities" incidental to permissible banking activities.[78]

[f] Computer Networking Services as Correspondent Banking Services. The OCC has found the provision of computer networking services to other financial institutions to be a correspondent banking service permissible for a national bank.[79] In some instances, a national bank proposed to establish an operating subsidiary to provide a package of services. The operating subsidiary would assist its customers in the installation and maintenance of local computer area networks ("LANs") and wide area computer networks ("WANs") designed to facilitate the customer's financial services businesses by allowing computer systems to communicate with one another. The proposed comprehensive networking packages of services included:

- hardware and software;

- consulting services, including assessment of customers' needs, technical information and strategic planning, and installation and configuration of equipment; and

- support services, including employee training and ongoing system maintenance.

---

[75] OCC Interpretive Letter No. 731, [1995-1996 Transfer Binder] Fed. Banking L. Rep. (CCH) ¶ 81-048, at 90,339 (July 1, 1996).

[76] At the time of the proposal, the bank was entering a bid on the proposed contract. If the bid was successful, the bank intended to transfer the contract to an operating subsidiary or to subcontract with an operating subsidiary to perform the services under the contract. The OCC approved, noting that "the proposal as described would be legally permissible for a national bank and its operating subsidiary." *Id.* at 90,342. The OCC did not specifically address whether the bank could carry out the contract in its own name without any involvement of an operating subsidiary.

[77] Under the OCC's and FRB's analyses, if technology is only a tool that may be used to carry out any permitted activity, may a bank staff the toll booths with human collectors? In the financial services business, the technology required to deliver a product is, in some cases, becoming an inextricable part of the product itself. This will naturally broaden what regulators are prepared to categorize as the business of banking.

[78] OCC Interpretive Letter No. 731, *supra* note 75, at 90,342.

[79] OCC Interpretive Letter No. 754, [1996-1997 Transfer Binder] Fed. Banking L. Rep. (CCH) ¶ 81-118, at 90, 268 (Nov. 6, 1996).

The OCC found that the proposed services were designed to meet specific banking needs and that they satisfied the three general "business of banking" principles. First, the proposed activities are the functional equivalent to or a logical outgrowth of the smart phone and other data processing and communication services that the OCC had previously authorized for national banks. Second, the services respond to customer needs or otherwise benefit the bank or its customers. Third, the activities proposed involve risks similar to those risks the bank already assumes in running its own network.

With respect to the first "business of banking" principle, the OCC identified services that were substantively similar to the computer networking services proposed. Furthermore, the OCC found that LANs and WANs "are merely another technological vehicle by which electronic data is transferred, an activity the OCC has held to be a permissible correspondent activity."[80] It noted that the Supreme Court has recognized the long history of banks providing services to correspondents, and that the range of such services is extensive and constantly expanding.[81]

[g] Integrion Financial Network, LLC. In December 1996, the OCC approved a proposal by twelve national banks to engage, with IBM and with certain other financial institutions, in a joint venture to provide home banking and other financial services to the customers of the participating banks.[82] Each of the participating banks would make a minority investment in Integrion Financial Network, L.L.C. ("Integrion"), through an operating subsidiary. Integrion would establish an electronic gateway and design, develop, license, and market services that would enable participating financial institutions to offer their customers an electronic distribution channel with three types of services. First, the banks would make available traditional home banking and financial services such as bill paying and electronic statements. Second, Integrion's gateway would enable customers of participating institutions to access the home pages of other onlines services by providing links to third party vendors' websites. Finally, the gateway would provide the customers of the participating institutions a platform for access to the Internet.

With respect to the first activity, the OCC found that providing home banking services falls squarely within the business of banking because it involves banking, financial, and economic data. It noted that the removal of a reference to such data from its original data processing interpretive ruling merely reflected the OCC's reluctance to use examples and in no way reversed its long-standing position that collecting, transcribing, processing,

---

[80] *Id.* at 90,271.

[81] *See United States v. Citizens & Southern Nat'l Bank*, 422 U.S. 86, 114 (1975) (citing Austin & Solomon, *A New Antitrust Problem: Vertical Integration in Correspondent Banking*, 122 U. Pa. L. Rev. 366, 367-368 (1973)).

[82] Letter from Julie L. Williams, Chief Counsel, to Gerald P. Hurst, Assoc. Gen'l Counsel, NationsBank Corp., Conditional Approval No. 221 (Dec. 4, 1996) [hereinafter OCC Integrion Letter]. Integrion[SM] was formed in September 1996 as a limited liability company owned and operated by IBM, ABN AMRO North America, Bank One, Bank of America, Barnett Bank, Comerica, First Bank Systems, First Chicago NBD, Fleet Financial Group, Key Corp, Mellon Bank, Michigan National Bank, NationsBank, PNC Bank, Royal Banc of Canada, and Washington Mutual, Inc. *See 15 North American Banks and IBM Form Company to Offer Electronic Banking and Commerce Services*, Integrion[SM] News Release (Sept. 9, 1996) <http://www.integrion.net>. Thereafter, in 1997, First Union National Bank and Citibank joined Integrion. *Citibank Joins Integrion Financial Network*, Integrion[SM] News Release (Sept. 25, 1997); *First Union Joins Integrion Financial Network*, Integrion[SM] News Release (Sept. 25, 1997) <http://www.integrion.net>.

analyzing, and storing banking, financial, or economic data is a permissible activity for national banks.[83] In connection with the operation of the gateway, Integrion would provide participating institutions with software to distribute to their customers so that such customers could access and navigate the gateway. It would also provide software to third-party services providers to enable such third-party providers to access and navigate the gateway. The OCC found the sale of such software by participating national banks incidental to the business of banking because the software allows the banks' customers to access permissible services and, as such, is a necessary adjunct to the gateway service.[84] The OCC also found the fact that the browser and dialer software provided by Integrion could be used for other purposes such as access to the public Internet, to be only a minor and incidental part of the package of services Integrion would be providing. In this regard, the OCC noted that Integrion was providing the browser and dialer software to participating institutions at cost.[85]

Integrion's gateway would allow customers of participating institutions to access third-party vendors' websites, an activity that the OCC determined to be both part of the business of banking and incidental to the business of banking. The OCC reasoned that the link to third-party vendor websites represents the use of modern technology to provide the well-recognized finder function of banks.[86] The OCC also noted that providing links to third-party vendor websites was permissible as an incidental activity because it represents the sale of excess data process capacity acquired in good faith.[87] It analogized the links to these websites to the insertion of "statement stuffers" into a bank's regularly scheduled mailings.

The OCC found providing access to the Internet to be a valid incidental activity because an ancillary nonbanking service is permissible when it is necessary to successfully package and promote other permissible banking services.[88] The OCC based its conclusion, in part, on the results of a consumer survey that showed that consumers overwhelmingly demand public Internet access as part of a package of electronic financial management services. It found that blocking the provision by Integrion's participating institutions of public Internet access would create a hobbled home banking product, unlikely to meet consumer demand, especially in light of the fact that Integrion's competitors would be offering such a feature.

[h] Operating the Mondex™ Electronic Stored Value System. In December 1996, the OCC issued an important decision with respect to permissible activities by a limited liability company ("LLC") owned by banks and nonbanks, proposing to operate the stored value system originated by Mondex.[89] The OCC approved applications from four national banks (Wells Fargo Bank, N.A., Michigan National Bank, First National Bank

---

[83] OCC Integrion Letter, *supra* note 82, at 8.

[84] *Id.* at 9.

[85] *Id.* at 9 n.15.

[86] *Id.* at 9-11. The OCC noted that earlier OCC opinions had sometimes characterized acting as a finder as an incidental powers activity. It emphasized, however, that in light of the Supreme Court's analysis in *VALIC,* the finder function is a part of the business of banking. For a discussion of the *VALIC* decision, see Chapter 2, Section 2.04[2][a].

[87] OCC Integrion Letter, *supra* note 82, at 11-12.

[88] *Id.* at 12-14.

[89] OCC Corp. Decision, Conditional Approval No. 220 (Dec. 2, 1996) [hereinafter OCC Mondex Letter]. For a further discussion of the Mondex system, see <http://www.mondexusa.com>.

of Chicago, and Texas Commerce Bank), each proposing to establish an operating subsidiary that would participate as an owner of a minority interest in each of two LLCs. The nonbank LLC membership included AT&T Universal Bancorp Services, Inc., which at the time operated the third largest credit card program in the United States.[90]

Under the proposal, the originating LLC ("OLLC") would originate the electronic stored value ("ESV"), denominated in U.S. dollars, and sell it to (and redeem it from) participating financial institutions that are licensed as members ("Members"). The OLLC would then take the cash proceeds and invest them in U.S. government securities, cash, and certain cash equivalents in order to provide the resources to redeem the ESV.[91] The Members would then market electronic stored value to consumers and retailers, charging transaction fees for downloading or uploading the ESV. Mondex™ ESV can circulate indefinitely without clearing or settling.

The servicing LLC ("SLLC") would act as a licensing and servicing entity in order to implement the Mondex™ system in the United States. Thus, it would enter into licensing agreements with Members; coordinate the purchase of equipment from third-party manufacturers; and collect, assemble, and evaluate transaction data generated by the Mondex™ system.

In its analysis of how the origination and distribution of electronic stored value fit within the business of banking, the OCC determined that the proposed Mondex™ system was an advanced version of well-recognized clearing and settlement functions, similar to those performed in connection with, among others, credit and debit cards and electronic fund transfer systems.[92] The OCC noted that banks were integrating into adjacent businesses that supply technological expertise and resources to engage in a segment of the payments business in a new way.

The OCC premised its approval of the national bank investments in the Mondex™ system on the fact that the participating national banks would simply be participating in an additional facet of the payments system.[93] It also concluded that the investment by the national banks would meet the four OCC standards for non-controlling, minority interests.[94] In addition, the applicant banks committed to the development of asset and

---

[90] OCC Mondex Letter, *supra* note 89, at 2 n.4.

[91] The OCC noted that the applicant banks anticipated that the U.S. government securities and other assets purchased with the proceeds from the sale of the ESV would be pledged to the trust department of a commercial bank that would hold such assets for the benefit of the holders of the ESV. *Id.* at 3 n.7.

[92] *Id.* at 8.

[93] *Id.* at 7. The OCC had also approved, at the time the OCC Mondex letter was issued, the establishment and operation by a national bank of a closed stored value system on a university campus. *See* OCC Interpretive Letter No. 737, [1996-1997 Transfer Binder] Fed. Banking L. Rep. (CCH) ¶ 81-101, at 90,201 (Aug. 19, 1996). At an earlier point, a university stored value system was found to have been operating in violation of state banking laws. *See* Thomas P. Vartanian & Robert H. Ledig, *The Business of Banking in the Age of the Internet: Fortress or Prison*, BANKING POL'Y REP., Mar. 4-18, 1996, at 6.

[94] OCC Mondex Letter, *supra* note 89, at 6. See Section 6.04[3] for a discussion of the OCC's requirements for ownership of a minority interest in an entity.

liability management systems to ensure that the OLLC can redeem the ESV.[95] The OCC conditioned approval of the banks' investment through operating subsidiaries on, among other things:

- the performance of the services provided by the LLCs to national banks being subject to regulation, supervision and examination by the OCC;

- for purposes of 12 U.S.C. §§ 1813 and 1818, the LLCs stipulate that they are "institution-affiliated parties" with respect to all national banks that became investors in one of the LLCs;[96] and

- the LLCs will notify the OCC and obtain consent of the OCC before material changes are made to the LLC Agreements.

[i] Automated Loan Machines. In March 1997, the OCC ruled that banks can operate automated loan machines ("ALMs") without regard to state geographic restrictions under the National Bank Act.[97] Prior to the enactment of the Economic Growth and Regulatory Paperwork Reduction Act ("EGRPRA"), which took effect September 30, 1996, automated teller machines ("ATMs") operated by national banks were subject to the branching restrictions of 12 U.S.C. § 36. EGRPRA, however, amended Section 36(j) to exclude from the definition of branch ATMs. ALMs are designed to take loan applications, process the application in approximately ten minutes, and, where the application is approved, disburse the proceeds into the borrower's bank account or print out a check. The OCC noted that in order for an ATM to have been included in the prior definition of, and excluded from the revised definition of, a branch, it necessarily must have had the capacity to engage in one of the core banking functions of taking deposits, dispensing withdrawals or lending money. It found that an ALM is an unmanned facility engaging in the core function of lending money. Accordingly, the OCC concluded that an ALM is not a branch for purposes of the branching restrictions of 12 U.S.C. § 36.[98] It did not address whether state laws might restrict the authority of a national bank to operate ALMs, because the applicant bank had not cited any specific state laws potentially conflicting with the federal statute. The OCC, however, noted that the Supreme Court has repeatedly interpreted "grants of both enumerated and incidental powers to national banks as grants of authority not normally limited by, but rather ordinarily pre-empting, contrary state laws."[99]

[j] Internet Access to Certificate of Deposits Issued by Foreign Banks. In March 1997, the OCC approved a bank's[100] investment in a minority interest in a limited liability company ("LLC") that would act

---

[95] OCC Mondex Letter, *supra* note 89, at 3 n.7.

[96] 12 U.S.C. § 1813(u)(3) includes in the definition of institution-affiliated party "any shareholder (other than a bank holding company), consultant, joint venture partner, and any other person as determined by the appropriate federal bank regulatory agency (by regulation or case-by-case) who participates in the conduct of the affairs of an insured depository institution."

[97] OCC Interpretive Letter No. 772, [1996-1997 Transfer Binder] Fed. Banking L. Rep. (CCH) ¶ 81-136, at 90,323 (Mar. 6, 1997).

[98] *Id.* at 90,325.

[99] *Id.* at 90,324 (quoting *Barnett Bank v. Nelson*, 517 U.S. 25 (1996)).

[100] The bank in question was chartered under the laws of the District of Columbia and as such was subject to the jurisdiction of the OCC as its primary federal regulator.

as agent in the placement of funds in certificates of deposit issued by foreign banks through traditional means of service as well as through an Internet site linked to the bank's own Internet site.[101] The OCC found that the proposed activity and the structure of the LLC met the four-part test governing the ownership of minority interests by national banks.[102] First, the LLC's activity of placing deposits on behalf of customers is an activity that is part of, or incidental to, the business of banking. Second, the structure of the LLC and the bank's 49% ownership prevent the LLC from engaging in activities other than those permissible for national banks. Third, the investing bank's loss exposure was limited from both a legal and accounting standpoint. Finally, the activity was convenient and useful to the bank in carrying out its business because it allowed the bank to diversify its services. In this regard, the OCC found that some of the bank's existing depositors had become depositors through the Internet and that offering its customers the opportunity to invest in certificates of deposits issued by foreign banks was a natural extension of the bank's Internet business.[103]

[k] Internet-Based Auto Sales. As a result of the merger of a number of sister banks into a single bank, Barnett, and a reorganization of the activities of the parent company, Barnett Banks, Inc., Barnett became the 100% owner of Oxford Resources Corp. ("Oxford"), a specialized auto finance subsidiary. Oxford owned 80% of a technology company, Electronics Vehicle Remarketing, Inc. ("EVRI"). EVRI had developed an Internet-based system, known as Price Auto Outlet ("PAO"), that allows consumers to locate specific models of used cars offered for sale from Oxford's inventory, which consisted of vehicles that had come off lease or been repossessed. Barnett proposed to make the PAO system available to unaffiliated third party dealers to list their available vehicles for sale. When a potential buyer's search request could be matched, information about the buyer would be referred to the seller who would then contact the potential buyer directly. EVRI would earn a finder's fee for resulting sales. EVRI could also earn referral fees for referring buyers to certain services provided by the third parties, for example, vehicle warranty and service contracts. EVRI would disclose in all cases whether EVRI was acting as a principal for Barnett or Oxford, or as a finder for an unaffiliated third party.

In approving Barnett's application,[104] the OCC took note of Oxford's enhanced ability to sell its financing products as a result of EVRI's activities. It based its approval, however, not on this incidental benefit accruing from a clear banking activity (financing) but rather on the well-established authority of national banks to act as finders, as recognized by 12 C.F.R. § 7.1002.[105] This current version of the finder ruling distinguishes the activities of a finder from those of a broker on the basis that the former brings the parties together but does not

---

[101] OCC Interpretive Letter No. 778, [1997 Transfer Binder] Fed. Banking L. Rep. (CCH) ¶ 81-205, at 90,210 (Mar. 20, 1997).

[102] See Section 6.04[3] for a discussion of the elements of this test.

[103] The OCC also addressed the requirements that the bank comply with securities and consumer laws, deposit broker regulations, and the Interagency Statement on Retail Sales of Nondeposit Investment Products. OCC Interpretive Letter No. 778, *supra* note 101, at 90,215-17. Branching issues were not implicated because the LLC was located in the same building as the bank's main office and the bank was not receiving deposits within the meaning of 12 U.S.C. § 36(j), but was accepting funds for placement in a non-depository custodial account in order to have the bank wire the funds to an unaffiliated foreign bank. *Id.* at 90,216.

[104] OCC Corp. Decision No. 97-60 (July 1, 1997) the [hereinafter Barnett Banks Letter].

[105] *Id.* at 4-5.

negotiate or consummate the transaction.[106] In promulgating the final regulation, the OCC expressly noted that the authority to act as a finder does not include activities that would characterize the bank as a broker under applicable law.[107] In approving Barnett's request, the OCC cited its previous approval for a national bank to operate, as a finder, a telephone center for new and used vehicles through which potential purchasers could access databases containing information on the new and used vehicle inventories of dealers.[108] In this prior approval the OCC noted that the bank would receive a fee for its referrals, which, according to the OCC, would place this activity squarely within the finder authority of 12 C.F.R. § 7.1002. In the Barnett case, the OCC found the service to be identical except that it is delivered by a different technology, the Internet.

[l] Acting as a Certification Authority. On January 12, 1998, the OCC issued a letter approving the application of Zions First National Bank ("Zions") to establish an operating subsidiary to act as a certification authority ("CA") and repository for certificates used to verify digital signatures.[109] In the application, Zions proposed that its subsidiary, Digital Signature Trust Co. ("DST"), would act as a "trusted third party" and provide a "complete public key infrastructure" for electronic commerce.[110] DST, which had previously obtained a license to act as a certification authority under Utah law,[111] would (i) issue digital certificates that vouch for digital signatures offered by senders and recipients of electronic messages, (ii) provide a database (or repository) of digital certificates and information about such certificates (*i.e.*, user identities and public key information), and (iii) maintain a certificate revocation list available to registered users of the certificate repository.[112] DST also received OCC approval to engage in the incidental sale of hardware, such as smart cards and card readers, used with computers.[113]

In approving the plan for DST's operations, the OCC found that the activities of a certification authority, as well as those of a repository and key escrow agent, fall squarely within the scope of the "business of banking"

---

[106] 12 C.F.R. § 7.1002(b).

[107] Interpretive Rulings, 61 Fed. Reg. 4849, 4850 (1996) (codified at 12 C.F.R. § 7.1002(b)).

[108] Barnett Banks Letter, *supra* note 104, at 4-5 (citing OCC Interpretive Letter No. 741, [1996-1997 Transfer Binder] Fed. Banking L. Rep. (CCH) ¶ 81,105, at 90,213 (Aug. 19, 1996)).

[109] *See* Letter from Julie L. Williams, Chief Counsel, OCC, to Stanley F. Farrar, Esq., (Jan. 12, 1998) (copy available at the OCC's website, <http://www.occ.treas.gov/ftp/release/98-4.txt>) [hereinafter Zions OCC Letter]. Zions First National Bank ("Zions") and Digital Signature Trust Co. ("DST") must submit a description of their information and back office systems to the OCC for approval, as well as notify all third party software/hardware vendors of the OCC's regulatory authority. *See id.* at 20.

[110] *Id.* at 2-3.

[111] *See* Utah Digital Signature Act, UTAH CODE ANN. §§ 46-3-101 *et seq.* According to the OCC's letter, one of the first activities of DST will consist of the transmission and authentication of filings made in Utah's state courts. *See* Zions OCC Letter, *supra* note 109, at 4 n.9.

[112] To accomplish these functions, DST will maintain data processing, storage, and communications facilities, and provide and sell software that generates public/private key pairs to participants in electronic commerce. Zions OCC Letter, *supra* note 109, at 3. The OCC noted that the sale of software capable of being used generally for message encryption was permissible only as incidental to certification authority ("CA") activities. A separate application to the OCC would be required if DST wished to offer message encryption as a separate service. *Id.* at 4 n.8. The OCC's letter also notes that DST may, as a separate service unrelated to its CA activities, "hold in escrow keys that are used in encryption," such as keys used for internal data storage at a business which are held by certain employees. *Id.* at 5. The OCC found this service itself to be equivalent to safekeeping services rather than finding it to be incidental to CA activities.

[113] *Id.* at 4. The sales are incidental because they will be made only in connection with CA activities. *Id.* at 4 n.10. The OCC uses a case-by-case approach to determine that the sale of hardware is subordinated to permitted services, rather than the cost ratio test used by the FRB. *See* Chapter 7, Section 7.03[1], [6].

as determined by the three-part test applied by the OCC:[114] (1) whether the service or activity is functionally equivalent to or a legitimate outgrowth of a recognized banking activity; (2) whether it responds to customers' needs or otherwise benefits the bank or the bank's customers; and (3) whether it involves risks similar in nature to the risks already assumed by banks.[115]

The OCC concluded that DST's certification authority activities are permissible activities for national banks and their operating subsidiaries to engage in, because the activities are the "functional equivalent of notary and other authentication services already performed by banks."[116] The OCC also characterized CA activities as a "logical outgrowth" of the identification and verification skills that are "a core competency of banks."[117] The OCC noted that "the role of banks in identifying customers and parties to financial transactions has been central in conducting the business of banking," both in the United States and around the world, and relied upon other extensions "into the electronic realm" of banks' traditional "identification and authentication competencies."[118] The OCC distinguished CA activities from the broader "performance-type guarantees" that have previously been deemed by courts to constitute impermissible activities for national banks.[119] It emphasized that signature guarantee services by banks acting as stock transfer agents, a traditional banking activity, is similar to a notary's attestation to the authenticity of a *signature* on a document rather than the authenticity of the *document* itself. In contrast, in the case of performance-type guarantees, a bank promises to answer for the payment of some debt or the performance of some obligation of another party in the event that party defaults on its obligation.[120]

The OCC also approved DST's proposed key repository and escrow services, analogizing them to traditional safeguarding activities (such as renting a safe deposit box) of national banks.[121] Finally, the OCC concluded that DST's key escrow activities would not involve acting in one of the roles specified in 12 C.F.R. Part 9 as those requiring trust powers for a fiduciary activity that must be approved by OCC under the National Bank Act.[122]

---

[114] *See* Chapter 2, Section 2.04[2].

[115] Zions OCC Letter, *supra* note 109, at 9 (citing, for the judicial development of the doctrine, *Merchants' Bank v. State Bank*, 77 U.S. 604, 648 (1871) (certification of checks has grown out of the business needs of the country and involves no greater risks than a bank giving a certificate of deposit); *M&M Leasing Corp. v. Seattle First Nat'l Bank*, 563 F.2d 1377, 1382-83 (9th Cir. 1977), *cert. denied*, 436 U.S. 987 (1978) (personal property lease financing is "functionally interchangeable" with the express power to loan money on personal property); *American Ins. Ass'n v. Clarke*, 865 F.2d 278, 282 (D.C. Cir. 1988) (standby credits to insure municipal bonds is "functionally equivalent" to the issuance of a standby letter of credit)).

[116] *Id*. at 10. The OCC noted that such activities also resemble other authentication services traditionally performed by banks, such as letters of reference or of introduction. *Id*. at 11 (citing prior OCC decisions).

[117] *Id*. at 12-14.

[118] *Id*. at 14-16 (citing examples, among others, of check and credit check identification services and signature guarantees).

[119] *Id*. at 15 n.33 (citing *Bowen v. Needles Nat'l Bank*, 94 F. 925 (9th Cir. 1889) and *Border Nat'l Bank v. American Nat'l Bank*, 282 F. 273 (5th Cir.), *cert. denied*, 260 U.S. 701 (1922)).

[120] *Id*.

[121] *Id*. at 16.

[122] *Id*. at 18-19. The OCC noted, however, that DST's key escrow service would likely be held to give rise to a fiduciary relationship under most state laws. *Id*. at 19 n.44.

The OCC placed a great deal of emphasis on risk management controls proposed for adoption by DST and Zions.[123] In this regard, DST and Zions asserted that they would develop a "certificate practice statement" ("CPS") to address procedures for customer identification, the registration process, any planned uses of customer's personally identifiable information, and details regarding the number and types of certificates that may be issued.[124] The OCC noted that "[DST] recognizes that one of its most serious risks is that its private key might be compromised."[125] To protect against this possibility and safeguard certificates from unauthorized tampering or compromise, DST would utilize a variety of hardware, software, and procedural measures — to be certified as functional by an independent consulting firm in advance — designed to detect and prevent any unauthorized access.[126] In addition to these measures, Zions indicated that it would take advantage of the liability limitations of Utah's Digital Signature Act (*e.g.*, through "choice of law" provisions), disclaimers in its CPS, and insurance coverage to limit its liabilities in the event of fraud or unauthorized access/tampering.[127]

The Zions operating subsidiary letter, which has been heralded as a "watershed decision,"[128] is clear evidence of the OCC's interest in fostering national bank involvement in electronic commerce. In the OCC's press release accompanying the release of the Zions letter, Comptroller Eugene Ludwig noted that "[t]he ability to verify and authenticate electronic signatures is essential to the development of electronic commerce and electronic banking, [b]anks, which have long played a role as trusted intermediaries in financial transactions, are ideally situated to provide this type of service."[129]

§ 6.04   BUSINESS ARRANGEMENTS

The success of the banking industry's journey into the world of electronic financial products and services and electronic commerce will depend on banks being able to forge the business relationships necessary to deliver the new financial products and services that the marketplace demands. As businesses become more and more technologically driven, it becomes increasingly likely that, in order to survive in this new world, companies will have to do business with their competitors (both banks and nonbanks). It is an axiom that companies as

---

[123] *See id.* at 5-7.

[124] *Id.* at 6. These details will include, among other things, liability limits on certificates, relevant expiration dates and transaction limits (types, dollar amounts and frequency) on the use of certificates. *Id.*

[125] *Id.* at 6.

[126] *Id.*

[127] *Id.* at 6-7. Zions also assured the OCC that both it and DST will conform their operations to relevant security standards established by the National Institute of Standards and Technology and the National Security Agency. *Id.* at 6.

[128] *See* R. Christian Bruce, *Regulators Clear National Bank's Bid to Identify Parties in Electronic Commerce*, 70 Banking Rep. (BNA) 79 (Jan. 19, 1998).

[129] *See OCC Approves a National Bank to Certify Digital Signatures*, OCC Press Release 98-4, Jan. 14, 1998, *available at* (visited Jan. 19, 1998) <http://www.occ.treas.gov>.

powerful as Microsoft clearly understand and act upon.[130] Banks are likely to find that it will be necessary to form joint ventures, alliances, or partnerships in order to have access to the broad technical knowledge necessary to succeed in the electronic manifestations of traditional banking functions. They will also need the authority to engage in a wider range of activities, activities that may not look like the traditional business of banking, but that will be a critical component of the financial servicer's delivery systems of the future. Moreover, the recognition in *VALIC* of the broad nature of the National Bank Act's grant of authority to engage in the business of banking may play a decisive role in deciding whether banks will be allowed to evolve as real competitors of nonbanks.[131] Construing national bank powers narrowly could relegate banks to a more limited role as defined by the traditional business of banking, while competitors not so constrained would be free to evolve to meet customers' future needs as defined by the marketplace and technology.

The OCC has long recognized that, in order for banks to compete with nonbanks, it must, among other things, maintain "an analytical framework broad and flexible enough to be applicable to any question regarding the permissibility of particular data processing activities."[132] The following discussion shows how recent OCC actions are accommodating banks' needs to engage in business ventures through a variety of legal forms and structures.

[1]   OPERATING SUBSIDIARIES OF NATIONAL BANKS

On November 18, 1996, the Comptroller issued a final rule, effective December 31, 1996, substantially revising the OCC's entire Corporate Activities Rules codified in Part 5 of 12 C.F.R., including the operating subsidiary regulation.[133] The rules governing permissible activities for operating subsidiaries of national banks are codified at 12 C.F.R. § 5.34. Most notable from the perspective of the increasing trend toward computer- and Internet-based products and delivery systems, the revised operating subsidiary rule holds out the prospect for national bank operating subsidiaries to engage in activities not authorized for their parent banks, and for national banks to control less than 80% of their operating subsidiaries' voting securities.[134] In the regulation, the OCC also provided for operating subsidiaries to be established as limited liability companies.[135]

[a] Legal Form and Control of Operating Subsidiaries. Under the OCC's revised regulation, a bank need only hold a controlling interest in a subsidiary, compared to the 80% interest previously required, in order

---

[130] For example, in August 1997, Bill Gates and Steve Jobs announced a $150 million investment by Microsoft in its struggling rival, Apple Computer Inc. *See* Michael Krantz, *If You Can't Beat 'em . . . Will Bill Gates' Bailout Save Apple – or Just Strengthen Microsoft's Hand in the Web Wars*, TIME, Aug. 18, 1997, at 35 (noting the intellectual property gains and competitive advantage in the Web market arising out of Microsoft's investment); Allan Sloan, *Bill Does What's Good for Bill*, NEWSWEEK, Aug. 18, 1997, at 31 (opining that Microsoft's investment was based on antitrust concerns). *See also*, Bill Gates, *Bill Collector*, FORTUNE, Oct. 13, 1997, at 157.

[131] See Chapter 2, Section 2.04[2][c] for a discussion of the incidental powers of national banks.

[132] Data Processing Proposal, 47 Fed. Reg. at 46,529.

[133] Rules, Policies, and Procedures for Corporate Activities, 61 Fed. Reg. 60,342, 60,348 (1996) (codified at 12 C.F.R. pt. 5) [hereinafter Corporate Activities Rules].

[134] 12 C.F.R. § 5.34(d)(2), (f).

[135] 12 C.F.R. § 5.34(d)(2).

for the subsidiary to qualify as an operating subsidiary.[136] An ownership interest greater than 50% of the subsidiary's voting authority will thus suffice. Furthermore, a subsidiary will qualify if the parent bank does not own more than 50% of the voting interest in the subsidiary but otherwise controls the subsidiary and no other party owns a greater than 50% voting interest in the subsidiary. Where, however, the parent bank owns 50% or less of the voting interest of the subsidiary, the notice only or expedited approval provisions will not be available and the bank must file a standard application with the OCC.[137] The OCC imposed this requirement in recognition of the fact that effective control of an entity could come in a variety of forms. The standard application process affords the OCC the opportunity to conduct a case-by-case review to ensure that the national bank has effective control over the subsidiary and that the bank is not exposed to undue risks.[138]

The new regulation revised the former requirement that an operating subsidiary be a corporation, permitting other legal forms such as a limited liability company or a "similar entity."[139] The OCC identified a business trust as an example of a similar entity.[140] The operating subsidiary regulation exempts from operating subsidiary status subsidiaries in which the bank's investment is made pursuant to specific statutory or regulatory authorization, and those in which the bank's investment was acquired through a foreclosure on collateral in connection with a previously contracted debt.

[b] Notice and Application Requirements. The operating subsidiary regulation sets forth the basic information that a national bank must supply regarding its investment in, and the proposed activities of, its operating subsidiary.[141] It establishes three levels of notice to, or approval by, the OCC, depending on the status of the bank making the request and the type of activity involved. An "eligible bank," one that is adequately capitalized or well-capitalized and has not been notified that it is in troubled condition, may engage in certain specific activities through an operating subsidiary, if it provides written notice to the OCC within ten days after acquiring or establishing an operating subsidiary engaged in those activities or commencing such activities in an existing operating subsidiary.[142] The activities that are subject to the notification provision include:

- furnishing services for the internal operations of the bank or its affiliates, including accounting, auditing, appraising, advertising, public relations, data processing and data transmission services, databases, or facilities;[143]

---

[136] 12 C.F.R. § 5.34(d)(2).

[137] 12 C.F.R. § 5.34(e)(1)(i)(B).

[138] Corporate Activities Rule, 61 Fed. Reg. at 60,350. This applies whether the subsidiary is "a corporation, limited liability company, or similar entity."

[139] 12 C.F.R. § 5.34(d)(2).

[140] Corporate Activities Rule, 61 Fed. Reg. at 60,350.

[141] 12 C.F.R. § 5.34(e)(1).

[142] 12 C.F.R. § 5.34(e)(2)(i). *See* 12 C.F.R. pt. 6 (definitions of "adequately capitalized" and "well capitalized"); 12 C.F.R. § 5.51.

[143] 12 C.F.R. § 5.34(e)(2)(ii)(B).

- data processing and warehousing products, services, and related activities, including associated equipment and technology, for the operating subsidiary, its parent bank, and their affiliates;[144]

- acting as an investment or financial adviser or providing financial counseling;[145] and

- making, purchasing, selling, or servicing loans.[146]

The notice only provision may not be used, however, in any lending or leasing activities involving the direct or indirect acquisition by the bank from an affiliate of a low quality asset, as defined in Section 23A of the Federal Reserve Act.[147]

Eligible banks are eligible to engage in certain specified activities subject to an expedited thirty-day review of an application.[148] These specified activities include:

- data processing and warehousing products and services, and related activities, including associated equipment and technology permissible under 12 U.S.C. Section 24(Seventh) and 12 C.F.R. § 7.1019;[149]

- providing securities brokerage and related activities;[150] and

- permissible securities underwriting and dealing activities.[151]

Inclusion of data processing activities and services on both the notification only and expedited approval lists evidences the OCC's recognition that national banks are increasingly engaging in a broadening range of activities and processing consistent with the OCC's historical open-ended definition of data processing as related to the business of banking.[152]

[c] Operating Subsidiary Activities not Permissible for the Parent Bank. The operating subsidiary regulation permits an operating subsidiary of a national bank to engage in activities:

---

[144] *Id.* § 5.34(e)(2)(ii)(H).

[145] *Id.* § 5.34(e)(2)(ii)(I).

[146] *Id.* § 5.34(e)(2)(ii)(L).

[147] *Id.*

[148] *Id.* § 5.34(e)(3).

[149] *Id.* § 5.34(e)(3)(ii)(F).

[150] *Id.* § 5.34(e)(3)(ii)(A).

[151] *Id.* § 5.34(e)(3)(ii)(B).

[152] Corporate Activities Rule, 61 Fed. Reg. at 60,349 (codified at 12 C.F.R. § 5.34(d)(1)).

authorized under § 5.34(d) for the subsidiary *but different from that permissible for the parent national bank*, or may perform such activities in an existing operating subsidiary subject to the following additional requirements.[153]

Permissible activities for operating subsidiaries under 12 C.F.R. § 5.34(d)(1) are: (i) activities that are part of, or incidental to, the business of banking as determined by the OCC pursuant to 12 U.S.C. § 24(Seventh); and (ii) other activities permissible for national banks or their subsidiaries under other statutory authority. In adopting the regulation, the OCC noted that its determinations would be made on a case-by-case basis and must involve an "activity within the business of banking or incidental thereto."[154] Such a situation could occur where, for example, either a specific prohibition against conducting the activity applies to a parent bank or the legal authority for conducting the activity is otherwise restricted to the subsidiary.[155]

[i] *Notice, Comment and Corporate Requirements.* 12 C.F.R. § 5.34(f) provides notice, comment, and certain corporate requirements for activities that are authorized under 12 C.F.R. § 5.34(d) but that are different from those that are permissible for the parent national bank. If the activity in which an operating subsidiary proposes to engage is one that the OCC has not previously approved, then the OCC will publish a notice in the *Federal Register* and provide an opportunity for comment on the application. For subsequent applicants to conduct the same activity, the OCC may, but is not required to, publish notice of the application in the *Federal Register.*[156]

In the case of activities that are subject to Section 5.34(f), in order to avoid confusing customers, and to ensure that the obligations of the operating subsidiary are not erroneously perceived as obligations of the parent national bank, the regulation establishes the following requirements for the operating subsidiary and its parent bank:

- the subsidiary must have physically separate and distinct operations with subsidiary employees compensated by the subsidiary;[157]

- all written marketing materials must clearly state that the subsidiary is a separate entity whose obligations are not obligations of the bank;[158]

- the subsidiary must have a different name from the parent bank and, where the names are similar, the subsidiary must act to minimize the risk of confusion of the two entities, especially with respect to federal deposit insurance;[159]

---

[153] 12 C.F.R. § 5.34(f) (emphasis added).

[154] Corporate Activities Rule, 61 Fed. Reg. at 60,352.

[155] *Id.* at 60,351.

[156] 12 C.F.R. § 5.34(f)(1).

[157] *Id.* § 5.34(f)(2)(i).

[158] *Id.* § 5.34(f)(2)(ii).

[159] *Id.* § 5.34(f)(2)(iii).

- the subsidiary must be adequately capitalized by industry standards;[160]

- the subsidiary must maintain separate accounting and corporate records;[161]

- the subsidiary must conduct its business pursuant to independent policies and procedures;[162]

- contracts between the subsidiary and the bank must be based on market terms and conditions;[163]

- the subsidiary must observe appropriate separate corporate formalities;[164]

- at least one-third of the subsidiary's directors shall not be directors of the bank; and[165]

- the parent bank and subsidiary must maintain internal controls to manage the operational and financial risks of the subsidiary.[166]

[*ii*] *Legal Authority for 12 C.F.R. Section 5.34(f).* In conjunction with the adoption of the revised operating subsidiary rule, the OCC's Chief Counsel wrote a memorandum to the Comptroller setting forth the legal basis for allowing an operating subsidiary to engage, under certain circumstances, in activities prohibited for its national bank parent ("Operating Subsidiary Opinion").[167]

First, the Operating Subsidiary Opinion noted that it is the powers section of 12 U.S.C. § 24(Seventh) that allows national banks to own subsidiaries as an incident to their being in business.[168] The grant of authority contained therein, to exercise "all such incidental powers as shall be necessary" to carry on the business of banking involves two distinct categories of incidental activities. The first category involves activities incidental to the delivery of banking products or services, for example, lending on personal security. The second category of incidental activities involves those activities that, although not substantively banking activities, relate to the fact that the bank is in business and can do things that a business does. Examples falling into this category include hiring employees, renting equipment, raising capital, and borrowing money. The OCC found that a national bank's authority to own a subsidiary to deliver services to customers also falls within this second category, but there is a limitation on such authority because it derives from the powers sentence of 12 U.S.C. § 24(Seventh). The OCC concluded that because such statutory authorization limits a national bank to the conduct of the banking business and the exercise of powers incidental thereto, this same

---

[160] *Id.* § 5.34(f)(2)(iv).

[161] *Id.* § 5.34(f)(2)(v).

[162] *Id.* § 5.34(f)(2)(vi).

[163] *Id.* § 5.34(f)(2)(vii).

[164] *Id.* § 5.34(f)(2)(viii).

[165] *Id.* § 5.34(f)(2)(ix).

[166] *Id.* § 5.34(f)(2)(x).

[167] *Legal Authority for Revised Operating Subsidiary Regulation*, Memorandum from Julie L. Williams, Chief Counsel, to Eugene A. Ludwig, Comptroller of the Currency (Nov. 18, 1996) [hereinafter Operating Subsidiary Opinion].

[168] *Id.* at 2-4.

limitation is the logical boundary for determining the boundary for activities permissible for a national bank's operating subsidiaries.[169]

Second, the Operating Subsidiary Opinion reviewed additions to Section 24(Seventh) made by Congress in enacting the McFadden Act in 1927 and the Glass-Steagall Act in 1933. The OCC concluded that these statutory changes acknowledged, rather than limited, the authority of national banks to own operating subsidiaries.[170]

Third, the Operating Subsidiary Opinion noted that the McFadden Act and Glass-Steagall Act regulate the dealings between national banks and their operating subsidiaries and affiliates. In each case, where the legislation imposed controls or limitations on intercompany dealings, it assumed the lawfulness of the parent-subsidiary relationship. For example, Section 13 of Glass-Steagall added a new Section 23A to the Federal Reserve Act that imposed qualitative limitations and collateral requirements on national and state member banks' equity investments in, and loans to, affiliates. As enacted, Section 23A exempted from the qualitative limitations and collateral requirements those affiliates of the bank meeting certain criteria. The opinion noted that, in providing for restrictions on activities among affiliates, and exceptions to those restrictions, Congress assumed that national banks possess the authority to own and carry on activities through operating subsidiaries. Congress was merely controlling the exercise by national banks of such authority.[171]

Fourth, the Operating Subsidiary Opinion noted that Congress, the courts, and the OCC have, since 1933, consistently recognized that national banks are permitted to engage in the business of banking through the ownership of subsidiaries. Congress, for example, has expressly authorized the ownership of certain types of subsidiaries.[172] The OCC in 1966, in promulgating regulations governing operating subsidiaries, found that 12 U.S.C. Section 24(Seventh) allowed national banks to own corporations as an incident to and to facilitate the banks' conduct of their banking business.[173] Likewise the OCC found that courts have consistently recognized that national banks can conduct their business either directly or through operating subsidiaries.[174]

Finally, the Operating Subsidiary Opinion noted that the courts, the OCC, and other federal bank regulatory agencies have found that operating subsidiaries may engage in banking activities or activities incidental to banking that the parent national bank is prohibited by statute from conducting.[175] For example, the Supreme

---

[169] *Id.* at 4.

[170] *Id.* at 4-11.

[171] *Id.* at 11-14.

[172] *Id.* at 14-15 (citing statutory authorizations: 12 U.S.C. § 1861 *et seq.* (bank service corporations); 15 U.S.C. § 682(b) (small business investment companies); 12 U.S.C. § 24(Eleventh) (community development corporations)).

[173] *Id.* at 15-16 (citing 39 Fed. Reg. 11,459 (1966)).

[174] *Id.* at 18 (citing *VALIC* (an operating subsidiary of a national bank may lawfully sell annuities); *Clarke v. Securities Indus. Ass'n,* 479 U.S. 388 (1989) (operating subsidiaries of national banks can engage in securities brokerage business at various nonbank locations); *American Ins. Ass'n v. Clarke,* 865 F.2d 278 (D.C. Cir. 1987) (a national bank's operating subsidiary can be a municipal bond insurance company); *Independent Bankers Ass'n of Ga. v. Board of Governors of the Fed. Reserve Sys.,* 516 F.2d 1206 (D.C. Cir. 1975) (Citizens and Southern National Bank could lawfully own a holding company which in turn owned a majority interest in 8 banks and a minority interest in 27 other banks in Georgia)).

[175] *Id.* at 19-23.

Court upheld the FRB's determination that an investment advisor to a closed-end investment company, owned by the same bank holding company that owned a bank, could provide advisory services because the services were so closely related to banking as to be a proper incident thereto. Furthermore, the advisor could provide such services without regard to whether the affiliated bank itself could provide them.[176] Similarly, a federal court had upheld a Federal Deposit Insurance Corporation regulation authorizing an insured non-member bank to own a securities subsidiary even though Section 21 of Glass-Steagall prohibited the parent bank from engaging directly in the securities business.[177]

The OCC concluded that an operating subsidiary could engage in an activity prohibited for a national bank if the limitation imposed on the bank, and its rationale, do not apply to the operating subsidiary; and if the ability of the operating subsidiary to engage in the activity would not frustrate a congressional purpose of preventing the parent bank itself from engaging in the activity. The OCC set forth three factors for evaluating operating subsidiary applications involving an activity that a national bank may not conduct directly. First, it would consider and weigh the form and specificity of the restriction applicable to the parent bank. Second, it would examine why the restriction was applied to the parent national bank. Third, it would weigh whether it would frustrate the congressional purpose underlying the restriction to permit an operating subsidiary of a bank to engage in the particular activity.[178] In its evaluation of these three factors, the OCC would take into account regulatory safeguards applicable to the operating subsidiary and activity, conditions imposed in connection with the OCC's approval and undertakings by the bank or operating subsidiary that address the three factors noted above.

[iii] *Applications to Date.* Several applications have been submitted under the new authority provided by Section 5.34(f).

[A] *Limited Real Estate Development.* In April 1997 the OCC published a request for comment concerning an application by NationsBank, N.A. ("NationsBank") to engage through a wholly owned operating subsidiary in limited real estate development activities in connection with bank premises pursuant to 12 C.F.R. Section 5.34(f).[179] NationsBank's application proposed to build a forty-five unit residential condominium on land most of which the bank had owned for over twenty-five years and which was the site of a branch office of the bank. The bank was in the process of developing an office building on the site to be used as bank premises. The bank argued that the development of the condominiums would enable it to better contribute to its community and to make a safer, more pleasant work environment for employees. The value of the office building and land is estimated at $56 million and the cost of constructing the condominium is estimated at $13 million.

---

[176] *Board of Governors of the Fed. Reserve Sys. v. Investment Co. Inst.*, 450 U.S. 46, 58-64 (1981) ("bank affiliates may be authorized to engage in certain activities that are prohibited to banks themselves"). *See also Securities Indus. Ass'n v. Board of Governors of the Fed. Reserve Sys.*, 839 F.2d 47 (2d Cir. 1988), *cert. denied*, 486 U.S. 1059; *Securities Indus. Ass'n v. Board of Governors of the Fed. Reserve Sys.*, 847 F.2d 890 (D.C. Cir. 1988) (both holding that a member bank's affiliate may engage in some securities activities that would be prohibited to the member bank itself).

[177] *See* Operating Subsidiary Opinion, *supra* note 167, at 21 (citing *Investment Co. Inst. v. FDIC,* 606 F. Supp. 683 (D.D.C. 1985)).

[178] *Id.* at 24.

[179] Operating Subsidiary Notice, 62 Fed. Reg. 16,213 (1997).

In its Operating Subsidiary Opinion, the OCC set as a requirement for approving activities under 12 C.F.R. § 5.34(f) that it find the activity be part of, or incidental to, banking and that approval of the activity for an operating subsidiary not frustrate Congress' purpose in prohibiting a national bank from engaging in the activity directly.

NationsBank argued that its application met the first of these requirements because the proposed activities satisfy the three-prong test set forth by the OCC for determining activities are incidental to banking, namely the activities:

- are functionally equivalent to, or a logical outgrowth of, a recognized banking activity;

- respond to customer needs or otherwise benefit the bank or its customers; and

- involve risks similar in nature to those already assumed by banks.[180]

First, the bank noted that developing condominiums was integrated with, and ancillary to, the commercial development already under construction for use as bank premises. NationsBank argued that because the OCC has held that the development of banking activities is incidental to the conduct of the banking business,[181] and the condominium development will be ancillary to and integrated with the NationsBank premises, the authority to engage in the condominium development is likewise ancillary, and therefore incidental, to the authority to develop bank premises. Second, the bank noted that the proposed activities directly benefit its employees and customers by making the bank premises safer and more pleasant. Finally, the bank argued that because it would be selling the condominium units, the risk it was undertaking was the same as making a loan to a third party developer to construct the project, an activity permissible for national banks.

The bank contended that it met the second requirement for OCC approval because the proposed activities are not inconsistent with Section 29 of the National Bank Act, which prohibits national banks from holding real estate except for certain specified purposes. According to the Supreme Court, the purpose of this statutory prohibition is to:

- "keep the capital of banks flowing through the daily channels of commerce;"

- prevent banks from engaging in "hazardous real estate speculation;" and

- prevent banks from accumulating large amounts of real estate.[182]

The bank noted that the Bank Holding Company Act contains no similar prohibition, and while the FRB had not determined that the proposed activities are permissible for a bank holding company or its nonbank

---

[180] Letter from Richard K. Kim, Assistant General Counsel, NationsBank Corp., to Steven J. Weiss, Deputy Comptroller, Office of the Comptroller of the Currency 4-6 (Mar. 26, 1997).

[181] Operating Subsidiary Opinion, *supra* note 167, at 3.

[182] *Union Nat'l Bank v. Matthews*, 98 U.S. 621 (1875). *See also* OCC Interpretive Letter No. 758, [1996-1997 Transfer Binder] Fed. Banking L. Rep. (CCH) ¶ 81-122, at 90,285 (Apr. 6, 1996); OCC Interpretive Letter No. 556, [1991-1992 Transfer Binder] Fed. Banking L. Rep. (CCH) ¶ 83,306, at 71,407 (Aug. 6, 1991); OCC Unpublished Interpretive Letter (July 8, 1993); OCC Unpublished Interpretive Letter (June 8, 1987).

subsidiaries, there was no federal statute that prevented the FRB from making such a determination. The OCC, it argued, would therefore not frustrate congressional intent by approving the bank's application. Furthermore, the bank would not frustrate the intent of the statute as interpreted by the Supreme Court. The bank had stipulated in its application that its investment in, and advances to, the proposed operating subsidiary would be limited to two percent of the bank's Tier 1 capital and, therefore, the proposed activity would have no discernible impact on the liquidity or lending capacity of the bank. Likewise, the bank argued that developing condominiums would not frustrate the second purpose of preventing hazardous real estate speculation as the two percent cap represents a *de minimis* investment. Furthermore, the bank committed that if it ceased to be well capitalized for two consecutive quarters, it would submit an acceptable plan to become well capitalized or would divest or otherwise terminate the proposed activities of the operating subsidiary. Finally, the bank would be prevented from accumulating large amounts of real estate because the aggregate development would represent only a fraction of the real estate currently owned and occupied by the bank. Furthermore, the condominiums would be sold, not held, once completed.

[B] *Real Estate Lease Financing.* NationsBank has also submitted an application under Section 5.34(f) to form a wholly owned operating subsidiary to engage in real estate lease financing.[183] The structure of the proposed leases meets the requirements for real estate leasing by nonbank subsidiaries of bank holding companies under the FRB's recent revisions to Regulation Y.[184] It also meets the requirements for leases of personal property by national banks.[185] All transactions would be nonoperating leases with an initial term of at least ninety days. The leases would be structured as full payout leases designed to yield a return from rental payments, estimated tax benefits, and the estimated residual value of the property — that compensates the operating subsidiary for at least the full amount of its investment plus the estimated total cost of financing the property over the lease term. For the purpose of determining whether a given lease is a full payout lease, the estimated residual value of the property will not exceed 25% of the acquisition cost of the property to the operating subsidiary. As outlined in the application, NationsBank contemplates that the scope of operation of the proposed activities will be nationwide.

In addition, NationsBank's application commits that the operating subsidiary would acquire property only in connection with a proposed lease transaction. In other words, the operating subsidiary will not incur the risk of acquiring property with the expectation of being able to lease the property after its acquisition. The bank also commits that, upon the termination or expiration of any lease, if the lessee does not acquire the property, the operating subsidiary will enter into a new lease with the lessee or a third party or will reclassify the property as other real estate owned ("OREO") and dispose of the property in accordance with the OCC's OREO guidelines. In addition, NationsBank commits in its application that it would comply with the corporate safeguard requirements of Section 5.34(f)(2). NationsBank's application argues that when real estate lease

---

[183] Operating Subsidiary Notice, 62 Fed. Reg. 16,214 (1997).

[184] *See* Bank Holding Companies and Change in Bank Control (Regulation Y), 62 Fed. Reg. 9290, 9335 (1997) (to be codified at 12 C.F.R. § 225.28(b)(3)).

[185] Leasing, 61 Fed. Reg. 66,564 (1996) (codified at 12 C.F.R. pt. 23).

financing transactions are conducted as described in the application, they will be the functional equivalent of mortgage loans made by the operating subsidiary.

NationsBank based its arguments that its proposed real estate lease financing activities are a permissible activity for an operating subsidiary of a national bank on two basic premises. First, real estate financing is the functional equivalent of real estate lending and, as such, is part of the business of banking. Second, it argued that the reasons restricting ownership of real estate by national banks under 12 U.S.C. Section 29, as interpreted by the Supreme Court, apply only to national banks and not to their operating subsidiaries. Furthermore, the bank noted that as to legal and policy concerns, real estate lease financing as the functional equivalent of lending should not implicate these concerns.[186]

The bank noted that the operating subsidiary would be structured to minimize risks to the bank. The bank's investment will be limited and the subsidiary will maintain equity capital that is adequate by industry standards. In addition, the operating subsidiary will not acquire beneficial ownership of large amounts of real estate because property not released to the original lessee or a subsequent third party lessee at the expiration of a lease will be treated in accordance with the OCC's guidelines governing OREO. NationsBank further noted that there should be no supervisory concerns regarding its application because the OCC has allowed the leasing of real estate by national banks with respect to municipalities and the risks from the proposed activity are similar to those banks already assume.

[C] *State and Municipal Revenue Bonds.* On April 8, 1997, Zions First National Bank ("Zions") filed an application with the OCC seeking authority to engage in underwriting, dealing, and investing in securities of states and their political subdivisions through an existing operating subsidiary.[187] Specifically, the operating subsidiary would engage in such activities with respect to: (i) obligations defined by the OCC as general obligations of states and political subdivisions ("General Obligation Securities"); (ii) other obligations of states and political subdivisions that do not qualify as General Obligation Securities, known as "Revenue Bonds."

Zions already engaged in the aforementioned activities with respect to General Obligation Securities and marketed those products to institutional investors. Zions proposed that its operating subsidiary carry out the same activities with respect to Revenue Bonds. Zions, acting as agent, would provide brokerage and investment advice to institutional clients with respect to those Revenue Bonds. Zions pledged that, in all cases, its sales representatives would fully disclose that the securities are underwritten by the operating subsidiary and that Zions is acting as an agent of the subsidiary. The subsidiary would clear transactions through Zions, and Zions would fully disclose in public contacts, including confirmations, that it acts solely as clearing agent and that the operating subsidiary acts as the underwriter or dealer, as appropriate.

---

[186] Letter from Gerald Hurst, Asst. General Counsel, NationsBank, to Steven J. Weiss, Deputy Comptroller, OCC, at 7 (Mar. 26, 1997) (citing *M & M Leasing Corp. v. Seattle First Nat'l Bank*, 563 F.2d 337 (9th Cir. 1977)).

[187] Operating Subsidiary Notice, 62 Fed. Reg. 19,171 (1997).

In promulgating its final regulation regarding operating subsidiaries in 1996, the OCC noted that the Securities and Exchange Commission ("SEC") had expressed no opposition to the proposal regarding expanded operating subsidiaries activities subject to the understanding that: (i) the OCC intended that such expanded securities activities be subject to regulation under the federal securities laws; and (ii) the OCC did not intend to provide a steppingstone whereby activities not previously permissible for a bank to conduct itself could be shifted from an operating subsidiary to the bank. The OCC confirmed that these understandings would be correct if securities activities are approved for an operating subsidiary.[188]

In its application, Zions argued that underwriting and dealing in Revenue Bonds may properly be considered part of the business of banking as demonstrated by the legislative histories of the McFadden and Glass-Steagall Acts, which impose restrictions on bank activities. Furthermore, Zions noted that statutory restrictions were not intended to apply to the operations of national bank subsidiaries. Zions based its argument on four primary points: (i) that courts have recognized underwriting and dealing in revenues as functionally similar to traditional activities, a point that the McFadden and Glass-Steagall Acts' legislative histories make clear;[189] (ii) that in determining whether an activity is permissible, courts have looked at whether such activity is convenient and useful to the business of the bank;[190] (iii) that Zions' proposed activities are convenient and useful to the bank's customers because they allow Zions to respond to customers' needs on a competitive basis; and (iv) that the proposed activities do not threaten the safety and soundness of the bank, as any risk of piercing the operating subsidiary's corporate veil to the potential detriment of the bank is mitigated by the corporate requirements of Section 5.34(f)(2), with which Zions has agreed to comply.

As to statutory restrictions on the proposed activities, Zions argued that permitting an operating subsidiary to conduct the proposed activities would not frustrate congressional intent –and thus would be permissible under the test of the Operating Subsidiary Opinion — based on the plain language of Sections 20 and 32 of the Glass-Steagall Act as read in conjunction with Section 16 of that Act. In essence, Zions argued that the prohibitions under Section 16 of Glass-Steagall would make no sense as an absolute bar to underwriting and dealing to the extent that Section 20 of Glass-Steagall allows member bank subsidiaries to underwrite and deal in securities under certain circumstances. In fact, Zions argued, Congress clearly created different rules for banks engaged in underwriting and dealing in securities than for bank subsidiaries doing the same. Zions further argued that such a reading of the statute is consistent with any safety and soundness concerns embodied in the

---

[188] Corporate Activities Rule, 61 Fed. Reg. at 60,351 n.1 (1996).

[189] Memorandum from Zions to the Office of the Comptroller of the Currency 7-8 (Apr. 8, 1997) (filed in support of Zions' Application to Commence New Activities Through an Operating Subsidiary) (citing *First Nat'l Bank of North Bennington v. Bennington*, 9 F. Cas. 97 (C.C.D. Vt. 1879) (suit brought by national bank to enforce interest coupons issued by municipality); *Newport Nat'l Bank v. Newport Bd. of Educ.*, 70 S.W. 186 (Ky. 1902) (suit brought by national bank for breach of contract to purchase municipal bonds; found that power to negotiate evidence of debt includes power to deal in municipal bonds); Comptroller of the Currency Ann. Rep. 12 (1924) (recommending amendment of Section 24 of the Federal Reserve Act to permit national bank to buy and sell investment securities, which "would make very little change in existing practice, because a great number of national banks now buy and sell investment securities and the office of the comptroller has raised no objection because this has become a recognized service which a bank must render")).

[190] *Id.* at 9 (citing, among others, *Franklin Nat'l Bank v. New York*, 347 U.S. 373, 377 (1954) (power to advertise services was permissible as incidental power because "modern competition for business finds advertising one of the most usual and useful" practices); *M & M Leasing*, 563 F.2d at 1382 (leasing of personal property is permissible because it is "convenient and useful" to the banking business)).

legislation, for there is less risk to the bank (and a defined amount of risk) when an activity is restricted to an operating subsidiary. Finally, Zions noted that courts may not override congressional intent by imposing on bank subsidiaries the restrictions imposed by the statutory scheme on banks themselves.[191] In sum, Zions urged the OCC to find that the statutory restrictions placed on banks with respect to dealing in Revenue Bonds do not extend to bank subsidiaries, and that the prudential concerns motivating the statutory restrictions are limited to banks.

Zions made a further argument that public policy considerations support its application because the proposed activities would increase competition, resulting in attendant lower costs for state and political subdivision borrowers, and increase the ability of Zions to meet its responsibilities under the Community Reinvestment Act.

On December 11, 1997, the OCC issued its decision approving Zions' proposal, subject to certain conditions.[192] In summary, the OCC found that the proposed operating subsidiary activities are authorized by Section 24(Seventh) of the National Bank Act and, as proposed, are permitted for an affiliate of a national bank under Section 20 of the Glass-Steagall Act, provided that the affiliate is "not engaged principally in underwriting or dealing in the type of securities not permitted for the bank itself."[193] The OCC found that the different treatment afforded banks and their affiliates in the Glass-Steagall Act is explicit and unambiguous.

The OCC based its conclusion, in part, on three major findings supporting its determination that underwriting and dealing in Revenue Bonds is part of the business of banking under 12 U.S.C. § 24(Seventh). First, it found that underwriting and dealing have historically been a part of the business of banking.[194] It noted that such activities were already a customary part of the business of banking at the time the national bank system was created. Furthermore, both the McFadden Act's quantitative limits on investment banking activities with respect to debt securities of a single issuer, and the Glass-Steagall Act's limits on investment banking activities with respect to a broader range of securities, recognized that national banks were already engaged in these activities under their existing bank powers.

Second, the OCC found that underwriting and dealing in Revenue Bonds is part of the business of banking under Section 24(Seventh)'s enumerated powers to discount and negotiate promissory notes and other evidences of debt.[195] It noted that "evidences of debt" include Revenue Bonds. Furthermore, the OCC noted that the power to discount and negotiate includes the power to buy and sell as principal. Indeed, the OCC emphasized that prior to the enactment of the McFadden Act and the Glass-Steagall Act, this power to "discount and negotiate" provided the legal basis for many of the long-standing investment banking activities of national banks.

---

[191] *Id.* at 16 (citing *Investment Co. Inst. v. FDIC*, 606 F. Supp. 683, 686 (D.D.C. 1985), *cert. denied*, 486 U.S. 847 (1987)).

[192] Decision of the Comptroller of the Currency on the Application by Zions First National Bank, Salt Lake City, Utah to Commence New Activities in an Operating Subsidiary (Dec. 11, 1997) [hereinafter Zions Revenue Bond Decision].

[193] *Id.* at 5.

[194] *Id.* at 6-8.

[195] *Id.* at 8-9.

Third, the OCC found that underwriting and dealing in Revenue Bonds is also part of the general business of banking.[196] In this regard, the OCC noted that the activities in question are the functional equivalent of lending, a traditional banking activity. Additionally, such activities potentially benefit local governments (by increasing the competition for and availability of such activities) and banks (by increasing and diversifying banks' sources of income). Moreover, underwriting and dealing in Revenue Bonds entail the same traditional risks that banks already assume in underwriting and dealing in bank-eligible securities and in investing in Revenue Bonds.

Having concluded that the activities of underwriting and dealing, as proposed by Zions, fall within the business of banking, the OCC next examined the authority of national banks to own operating subsidiaries as an activity incident to the business of banking. It concluded that national banks have long had such authority.[197] It rested this determination on three findings. First, there is a long line of OCC rulings affirming such authority for national banks. Second, the OCC noted that the courts have consistently upheld such rulings by the OCC. Finally, it pointed to repeated recognition in legislative enactments of the authority of national banks to own operating subsidiaries. For example, in the case of both the McFadden Act and the Glass Steagall Act, the statutes placed limitations on the activities of bank subsidiaries, presupposing the authority of national banks to own such subsidiaries.

In reaching its decision on the Zions application, the OCC also relied, in part, on the existing distinction made in Sections 16 and 20 of the Glass-Steagall Act.[198] The former Section expressly prohibits national banks from underwriting and dealing in certain types of securities, including Revenue Bonds. Section 20, on the other hand, prohibits national banks from affiliating with other entities engaged in such underwriting and dealing activities only to the extent that such affiliated entities are "principally engaged in such activities." The statute defines "affiliate" to include any corporation, business trust, association, or similar organization of which a national bank directly or indirectly controls a majority interest.[199] The OCC also noted that the FRB had likewise applied the plain meaning of Section 20 of Glass-Steagall in determining that affiliates of national banks are permitted to underwrite and deal in securities in which a national bank is prohibited from underwriting and dealing.[200]

The OCC also found that its rulings and court decisions have recognized, in various contexts, that the limitations on activities applied to banks do not necessarily apply to banks' subsidiaries or affiliates.[201] Similarly,

---

[196] *Id.* at 9-14.

[197] *Id.* at 14-16.

[198] *Id.* at 17-19.

[199] *Id.* at 18 (citing 12 U.S.C. § 221a(b)(1)).

[200] *Id.* at 18 n.51.

[201] *Id.* at 21 (citing *Board of Governors of the Fed. Reserve Sys. v. Investment Co. Inst.*, 450 U.S. 46 (1981)).

a federal court had upheld a regulation of the FDIC permitting a subsidiary of a nonmember bank to engage in activities prohibited for the parent bank.[202]

In reviewing Zions' application the OCC also addressed safety and soundness issues and, based on four findings, concluded that the proposed activities of the operating subsidiary should be approved. First, it found that the proposed activities would not result in a significant or excessive risk to the bank or operating subsidiary because the application proposed limited expansion of current activities. Second, the OCC found that its regulations, and those of the FRB with respect to transactions with affiliates, ensure that the operating subsidiary will be adequately capitalized, transactions will be appropriately controlled, and the risk that customers may confuse activities and obligations of the operating subsidiary with those of the bank will be minimized. Third, the OCC found that the operating subsidiary would be subject to comprehensive supervision and regulation by both the OCC and the SEC. Finally, the OCC noted that its regulations governing operating subsidiaries approved under Section 5.34(f) impose a number of general requirements, and its Zions Revenue Bond decision imposes a number of specific requirements, designed to ensure the safe and sound operation of the subsidiary and to protect consumers. Several of the specific requirements imposed by the OCC are patterned after the FRB's regulations applicable to Section 20 subsidiaries of bank holding companies engaged in underwriting and dealing in securities.[203]

The OCC also addressed two regulatory and policy issues in approving the Zions application.[204] First, the OCC found that courts had specifically held that the Bank Holding Company Act ("BHCA")[205] does not govern the permissible activities of banks or their subsidiaries.[206] Consequently, the OCC determined that the Zions application is not subject to approval by the FRB under BHCA Section 4(c)(8). Second, the OCC found that consumer protections were adequate because the operating subsidiary had registered with the SEC as a broker-dealer, and thus would be subject to the federal securities laws, including the rules of the Municipal Securities Rulemaking Board.

[iv] *Objections by Congress and the FRB.* It is possible that Congress may take action to roll back national bank operating subsidiary authority under Section 5.34(f). A bill currently pending in the House of Representatives, the Financial Services Competitiveness Act of 1997 ("H.R. 10"), would make sweeping changes to current law by, among other things, removing the current Glass-Steagall prohibitions against affiliation by banks, securities firms, and insurance companies.[207] Under H.R. 10, bank holding companies meeting certain requirements would be able to engage in a much broader range of financial activities than is currently permissible for a bank holding company. In addition, within certain limitations, financial companies and

---

[202] *Id.* (citing *Investment Co. Inst. v. FDIC*, 606 F. Supp. 183 (D.D.C. 1985)).

[203] *Id.* at 27 & nn.75-76.

[204] *Id.* at 28-30.

[205] 12 U.S.C. §§ 1841 *et seq.*

[206] Zions Revenue Bond Decision, *supra* note 192, at 29.

[207] Financial Services Competitiveness Act of 1997, H.R. 10, 105th Cong. (1997).

commercial businesses would be able to affiliate. In the version of H.R. 10 passed by the House Commerce Committee on October 30, 1997, there are restrictions imposed on the activities of operating subsidiaries of national banks.[208] Section 121 of H.R. 10 would prohibit a subsidiary of a national bank from engaging in, or owning any share of, any company engaged in any activity that is not permissible for a national bank to engage in directly, or that is conducted under terms or conditions other than those that would govern the conduct of such activity by a national bank.

In response to the OCC's notice and solicitation of comments regarding NationsBank's applications to engage in real estate development and real estate leasing, the FRB submitted a letter strongly objecting to the OCC's approving real estate development activities of a national bank subsidiary.[209] The FRB noted that Congress has prohibited national banks from engaging in real estate development since 1864 and pointed to the recent experience with the thrift industry as one that should not be repeated with the national banking system.[210] According to the FRB, approval of the NationsBank proposal would turn national banks into real estate owners, competing with the developers to whom the banks lend. The FRB noted that the application contemplates much broader authority than sought for the specific project that was the subject of the NationsBank application. Further, approval would represent a precedent that would be impossible to contain or reverse.

In its legal analysis, the FRB raised several issues regarding the NationsBank application. It contended that the application was inconsistent with the National Bank Act and public policy. Further, it argued that approval of the application would appear inconsistent with Section 24 of the Federal Deposit Insurance Act, because it would remove the FDIC's authority to limit real estate development activities of state bank subsidiaries, as these activities would, if the application is approved, be permissible for subsidiaries of national banks. The FRB also found the proposal inconsistent with the Bank Service Corporation Act, which authorized subsidiaries to engage in banking or activities closely related to banking, a test real estate development fails.[211] In sum, the FRB argued that it would be inconsistent with all three cited statutes to permit national banks to engage, through a subsidiary, in an activity prohibited to the bank itself.

[v] *Implications.* Because the OCC has to date acted under Section 5.34(f) only on the application of Zions with respect to underwriting and dealing in Revenue Bonds, the full contours of the activities that might ultimately be approved remain to be seen. Yet, from the objections raised by the FRB to the real estate development application of NationsBank and to the potential risks to the banking system and federal safety net, it is clear, whether or not one agrees with the FRB, that the potential reach of the OCC's new rule could be great. The outcome will depend in the final analysis on two factors: (1) how broadly the OCC construes the business of banking and activities incidental thereto under 12 U.S.C. Section 24(Seventh) (recall, that any activity to be

---

[208] H.R. REP. NO. 105-164, pt. 3 (1997).

[209] Letter from William W. Wiles, Secretary, Board of Governors of the Federal Reserve System, to Eugene Ludwig, Comptroller of the Currency (May 5, 1997).

[210] *Id.* at 1.

[211] The FRB did note that NationsBank's proposal to engage in real estate lease financing appears to be permissible under the Bank Service Corporation Act because this activity has been found to be closely related to banking. *Id.* at 3-4.

approved under Section 5.34(f) must fall within such statutory authority); and (2) how the OCC construes congressional intent and purpose in examining statutory provisions that prohibit a bank from engaging in an activity that falls within the business of banking.

[2] BANK SERVICE CORPORATIONS

The Bank Service Corporation Act ("BSCA")[212] is a statute administered in part by the applicable federal bank regulatory agencies in their role as primary regulator,[213] and in part by the FRB in cases where the bank service corporation ("BSC") is engaging in activities permissible under Section 4(c)(8) of the BHCA.

[a] **Definition and Form.** A BSC is a corporation or limited liability company owned entirely by one or more insured banks and engaging in activities permitted by the BSCA.[214] Because there is not a limit on the number of banks that may own an interest in a BSC, individual banks may hold minority investments in BSCs. A bank's investment in a BSC is limited to the lesser of 10% of its capital and 5% of its assets. Investments include any extensions of credit.[215]

[b] **Activities and Restrictions.** There are three kinds of BSCs. They are defined by the activities in which they engage and the geographic scope of such activities. The first type performs services only for depository institutions and only the following designated services: check and deposit sorting and posting, computation and posting of interest and other credits and charges, preparation and mailing of checks, statements, notices, and similar items, or any other clerical, bookkeeping, accounting, or statistical and similar functions.[216] Banks may invest in this first type of BSC without prior notice to or approval from their primary regulator.[217]

The second type of BSC is much like a bank operating subsidiary. It may perform, for any person, any service (other than accepting deposits) its national or state bank owners could perform, though only at locations where the parent banks, all of which must be located in one state, could perform them.[218] Where the owners of the BSC include both national and state banks, its services are limited to those permissible for both.[219] Prior to investing in this second type of BSC, the insured bank must obtain the approval of the appropriate federal bank regulatory agency.[220] The third type of BSC may perform at any geographic location any service (other than accepting deposits) that the FRB has determined by regulation to be permissible for a bank holding

---

[212] 12 U.S.C. §§ 1861-67.

[213] The primary regulator of the BSC's principal investor, the bank with the largest dollar amount invested in the BSC's equity or, where investment amounts are equal, the bank chosen by the BSC as its principal investor, serves as the BSC's regulator. 12 U.S.C. § 1867(a).

[214] 12 U.S.C. § 1861(b)(2).

[215] *Id.* § 1862.

[216] *Id.* § 1863.

[217] *Id.*

[218] 12 U.S.C. § 1864(a), (b), (c), (d).

[219] *Id.* § 1864(e).

[220] *See id.* §§ 1864(c), (d), (e), 1865(a).

company under BHCA Section 4(c)(8).[221] The FRB must approve a bank's investment in this third type of BSC.[222]

BSCs, regardless of their type, are statutorily prohibited from unreasonably discriminating against depository institutions that do not own stock in the BSC but that compete with a stockholding depository institution, subject to the following exceptions: (1) providing services to the nonstockholder is beyond the BSCs practical capacity; and (2) comparable services are available from another source at a competitive cost. It is not considered unreasonable discrimination for a BSC to refuse to provide services at a price other than one that fully reflects the costs of offering those services.[223] A BSC is subject to examination and regulation by the appropriate federal bank regulatory agency of its principal investor.[224]

[c] Application to Third-Party Service Providers. The BSCA extends regulatory jurisdiction to third parties who are neither banks nor BSCs, but who have contracted to perform BSCA-authorized services for a bank.[225] Thus, even in cases where a bank opts to participate in shared activities or alliances through a contractual arrangement, rather than by retaining an ownership interest in the service provider, third parties providing the types of services that BSCs may provide will find themselves subject to oversight by banking regulators. Under the BSCA, when a third party performs BSCA-authorized services for a bank, that third party is subject to regulation or examination by the appropriate federal bank regulatory agency to the same extent as if the services were being performed by the bank itself. The bank must notify the agency of the existence of the service relationship within thirty days of either making the service contract or the performance of the service, whichever occurs first. The authority to examine and regulate these third parties extends only to the performance of designated services, as defined above in subsection [b], not to other third party affairs, and not to the full scope of businesses.[226]

[3]   MINORITY INTEREST INVESTMENTS

In 1985, the OCC issued an interpretive letter regarding the permissible activities of a partnership formed by a bank's wholly owned operating subsidiary and a nonfinancial institution.[227] The partnership was formed for the purposes of providing electronic information and transaction services, and serving as an electronic

---

[221] *Id.* § 1864(f).

[222] *Id.* § 1865(b).

[223] *Id.* § 1866(1).

[224] *Id.* § 1867(a). *See supra* note 212 (discussing the determination of "principal investor").

[225] 12 U.S.C. § 1867(c).

[226] *See* Letter from Robert B. Serino, Deputy Chief Counsel (Policy) (July 26, 1989) (unpublished); Letter from Billy L. Dowdle, Director for Trust Activities, 1987 OCC Ltr. LEXIS 104 (Nov. 10, 1987); OCC Interpretive Letter No. 196, [1981-1982 Transfer Binder] Fed Banking L. Rep. (CCH) ¶ 85,277, at 77,415 (May 18, 1981); Asset Management, OCC Banking Cir. 254 (June 14, 1991); Decision of the Office of the Comptroller of the Currency on the Application to Charter CompuBank, National Association, Houston, Texas, Aug. 20, 1997. Legislation has been introduced in the House that would extend the same types of notification, examination, and regulation provisions to parties providing certain services to savings associations, their service corporations, holding companies, and affiliates. Examination Parity and Year 2000 Readiness for Financial Institutions Act, H.R. 3116, 105th Cong. (1998). *See also* Contracting for Data Processing Services or Systems, OTS Thrift Bull. 46 (May 1, 1990).

[227] OCC Interpretive Letter No. 346, [1985-1987 Transfer Binder] Fed. Banking L. Rep. (CCH) ¶ 85,516, at 77,801 (July 31, 1985).

gateway for financial settlements in connection with commodities transactions. The OCC had no difficulty determining that these activities were properly incidental to the business of banking. Entering into partnership with an entity lacking federal deposit insurance, however, raised "legal, policy and prudential concerns."[228] In that regard, the OCC expressed a concern that, despite the absence of legal liability, the bank might feel compelled to honor obligations of the partnership so as to preserve the bank's reputation or protect future business opportunities.

The OCC approved the bank's indirect 50% ownership interest in the partnership subject to three conditions. First, the partnership must be subject to regulation, supervision, and examination by the OCC. Second, the investment by the bank and the bank's affiliates in the partnership must be limited to no greater than 5% of the bank's primary capital. Finally, the partnership must fully delineate its activities and give the bank's subsidiary veto power over whether the partnership may engage in certain types of activities and over certain major business decisions. The OCC also required that it be notified of any changes in the agreement, activities, or membership of the partnership. Under these conditions, the bank's indirect ownership of a general partnership interest satisfied the OCC's safety and soundness concerns.[229]

Over the last decade, the OCC has developed a set of requirements for national banks wishing to acquire minority ownership interests in business entities. These minority investments have evolved into an important method by which banks may align themselves with other banks and nonbanks to develop important electronic technologies used in providing competitive financial services. An early example of the analytical approach to minority investment came in the OCC's response to Bank of America's indication of an intention to establish a wholly owned subsidiary that would serve as general partner with a 33% interest in a partnership providing data processing and related services to ATM networks owned and operated by others.[230] The remaining 67% interest in the partnership would be held by three nonbank entities. The OCC approved the venture because its activities were related to basic banking services and its structure insulated the bank from unlimited liability. The partnership agreement contained a number of provisions designed to address the OCC's concerns regarding Bank of America's indirect involvement with the partnership. Specifically, the partnership agreement:

- specified the activities of the partnership and required unanimous consent to implement changes in its activities;

- provided the bank's operating subsidiary with veto power over basic business decisions;

- included a "regulatory impairment" provision allowing the bank's operating subsidiary to veto any existing or proposed activity that would cause the bank not to be in compliance with laws and regulations or, alternatively, would allow the bank's operating subsidiary to withdraw from the partnership without penalty;

---

[228] *Id.* at 77,803.

[229] *Id.*

[230] OCC Interpretive Letter No. 381, [1988-1989 Transfer Binder] Fed. Banking L. Rep. (CCH) ¶ 85,605, at 77,917 (May 5, 1987).

- acknowledged that the partnership and its members were subject to extensive state and federal regulation;[231] and

- limited the bank's investment to no more than 5% of its primary capital.[232]

In its ruling, the OCC distinguished its approval of a bank's activities when participating in a minority ownership role in a venture involving permissible bank activities from situations where a bank is selling excess capacity. In that regard, the OCC's approval states that "the [b]ank clearly is entering the Partnership as a means of developing and performing its lawful banking activities . . . and not merely as an investment."[233] By comparison, when selling excess capacity, the bank cannot have acquired the capacity in order to actively market the service to third parties, but must be a passive investor.[234] The OCC's rationale with respect to the sale of excess capacity is consistent with the position it took with respect to Bank of America's investment through an operating subsidiary in a partnership. In both the minority partnership and excess capacity cases, the bank's primary motivation and activity must focus on basic banking activities rather than on a new activity unrelated to banking. Ultimately, the OCC developed a general rule to apply to bank participation in both corporate and non-corporate entities involving a minority ownership interest by a bank operating subsidiary.

OCC Interpretive Letter No. 697 sets forth the following standards for banks wishing to have their operating subsidiaries participate in ventures as minority interest holders:[235]

- the business of the venture must be part of, or incidental to, the business of banking;[236]

- the bank must be able to prevent the venture from engaging in activities that do not meet the foregoing standard;[237]

- the bank's loss exposure must be limited, as a legal and accounting matter, and the bank must not have open-ended liability for the obligations of the enterprise;[238] and

---

[231] *Id.* at 77,918.

[232] *Id.* at 77,920.

[233] *Id.*

[234] *Id.*

[235] OCC Interpretive Letter No. 697, [1995-1996 Transfer Binder] Fed. Banking L. Rep. (CCH) ¶ 81-012, at 90,241 (Nov. 15, 1995).

[236] *Id.* at 90,244 (citing OCC Interpretive Letter No. 380, [1988-1989 Transfer Binder] Fed. Banking L. Rep. (CCH) ¶ 85,604, at 77,909, 77,913 n.8 (Dec. 29, 1986); Letter from Robert B. Serino, Deputy Chief Counsel (Nov. 9, 1992) (unpublished) [hereinafter Serino Letter]; Letter from John E. Shockey, Deputy Chief Counsel (June 7, 1976) (unpublished)).

[237] *Id.* (citing OCC Interpretive Letter No. 625, [1993-1994 Transfer Binder] Fed. Banking L. Rep. (CCH) 83,507, at 71,617 (July 1, 1993); Letter from Peter Liebesman, Assistant Director, Legal Advisory Services Division (Jan. 26, 1981 and Jan. 4, 1983) (unpublished)).

[238] *Id.* at 90,245 (citing *Merchants National Bank v. Wehrmann*, 202 U.S. 295 (1906); OCC Interpretive Letter No. 289, [1983-1984 Transfer Binder] Fed. Banking L. Rep. (CCH) ¶ 85,453, at 77,616 (May 15, 1984)).

- the investment must be convenient or useful to the bank in carrying out its business and not a mere passive investment unrelated to that bank's banking business.[239]

The OCC applied the same analysis when presented with a situation where the bank's interest at the outset was not a minority interest but could become one. OCC Interpretive Letter No. 677 addressed a request by two banks to form an equally owned joint venture in the form of a limited liability company ("LLC").[240] The LLC in question proposed to develop and distribute home banking and financial management software and to provide data processing services. The LLC anticipated increasing its membership to include additional banks, thus leading to potential minority ownership interests. The OCC found the proposed activities fit the "related to banking" provision of 12 U.S.C. Section 24(Seventh). Further, it determined that the proposed entity structure protected the banks from engaging in impermissible activities and from unlimited risks to the banks.[241]

§ 6.05   OCC GUIDANCE REGARDING SAFETY AND SOUNDNESS CONSIDERATIONS FOR STORED VALUE CARD SYSTEMS

On September 10, 1996, the OCC issued Banking Bulletin No. 96-48 to provide basic information concerning stored value card ("SVC") systems.[242] The Bulletin outlines the risks associated with these systems and emphasizes that banks and their managers have a responsibility to identify and manage the risks of SVC systems.[243]

The Bulletin identified the many different roles that national banks may play in emerging SVC systems, including: (i) an investing bank (holding an equity stake in a stored value system); (ii) an issuing bank (*i.e.*, the creator of or obligor for electronic cash); (iii) a distributing or redeeming bank (selling SVCs to consumers and contracting with merchants to convert their electronic cash receipts into currency or a deposit account balance); and (iv) a transaction authorizing or archiving bank (*i.e.*, either approving consumer transactions

---

[239] *Id.* at 90,245-46 (citing OCC Interpretive Letter No. 543, [1990-1991 Transfer Binder] Fed. Banking L. Rep. (CCH) ¶ 83,255, at 71,336 (Feb. 13, 1991); OCC Interpretive Letter No. 554, [1991-1992 Transfer Binder] Fed. Banking L. Rep. (CCH) ¶ 83,301, at 71,401 (May 7, 1990); OCC Interpretive Letter No. 427, [1988-1989 Transfer Binder] Fed. Banking L. Rep. (CCH) ¶ 85,651 (May 9, 1988); OCC Interpretive Letter No. 421, [1988-1989 Transfer Binder] Fed. Banking L. Rep. ¶ 85,645, at 78,018 (Mar. 14, 1988); Serino Letter, *supra* note 236; Letter from James M. Kane, Central District Counsel (June 8, 1988); Letter from John E. Shockey, Deputy Chief Counsel (Dec. 19, 1975)).

[240] OCC Interpretive Letter No. 677, [1994-1995 Transfer Binder] Fed. Banking L. Rep. (CCH) ¶ 83,625, at 71,851 (June 28, 1995). Congress recently enacted changes to the Bank Service Corporation Act, 12 U.S.C. §§ 1861-1867, to allow service companies to be organized as limited liability companies. This legislation does not change the requirement that all the equity holders in a bank service company must be insured banks. Nonetheless, it offers banks greater flexibility in entering into joint ventures. Economic Growth and Regulatory Paperwork Reduction Act, Pub. L. No. 104-208, § 2613, 1996 U.S.C.C.A.N. (110 Stat.) 3009, 3009-476.

[241] OCC Interpretive Letter No. 677, *supra* note 236, at 71,854.

[242] *Stored Value Card Systems*, OCC Banking Bull. No. 96-48 (Sept. 10, 1996).

[243] *Id.* at 3.

and/or maintaining transaction records); or (v) a clearing or settling bank (*i.e.*, transmitting funds and information through a payments system).[244]

§ 6.06   VIRTUAL BANKS

[1]   OCC GRANTS CHARTER TO A "VIRTUAL BANK"

On August 20, 1997, the OCC granted preliminary approval for a national bank charter to CompuBank, a Houston-based institution that intended to commence banking operations in February 1998.[245] CompuBank plans to offer a variety of traditional and electronic banking services, such as checking and savings deposit products, ATM services, and electronic bill payment, over the telephone or through a customer's personal computer. CompuBank will initially conduct its banking business from a single location, a "call center," that will provide for phone and computer dial-up connections with its customers. CompuBank does not intend, at least initially, to make loans.

CompuBank is the third "virtual" bank to receive approval to commence operations since 1995. The Office of Thrift Supervision has granted thrift charters to two "Internet" banks, Security First Network Bank and Atlanta Internet Bank.[246] CompuBank is, however, the first such "virtual" institution to win preliminary OCC approval (after a lengthy review period) for a national bank charter. Several aspects of the OCC's preliminary approval are significant for the continued development of "virtual" banks in the U.S.

In its preliminary approval, the OCC analyzed its traditional licensing factors for the operation of the proposed bank, such as (i) sound management, (ii) capital sufficiency, and (iii) its business plan, prospects for profitability, and likelihood of safe and sound operation. Acknowledging the continuing growth trends in electronic banking in U.S. retail banking markets, the OCC found that CompuBank's growth and revenue projections, notwithstanding its limited product scope, were reasonable and consistent with the granting of the bank charter.

Before it may commence operations, CompuBank must convince the OCC that its computer systems will be secure. This "functionality and security" review will include various tests of the bank's computer system, including a review by an independent security firm that will attempt to gain unauthorized access to the system. Prior to the grant of final approval, the OCC will conduct a "pre-opening" examination of CompuBank's "information systems environment." CompuBank also represented to the OCC that its computer systems will be fully Year 2000 compliant.

---

[244] *Id.* at 4-8. OCC Banking Bulletin 96-48 also referred to the general types of risks described in the OCC Supervision by Risk program which are present in stored value systems (*i.e.*, transaction, strategic, reputation, compliance, credit, liquidity, interest rate, and foreign exchange risks). It is discussed in greater detail in Chapter 16, Section 16.05[2].

[245] Decision of the Office of the Comptroller of the Currency on the Application to Charter CompuBank, National Association, Houston, Texas, Aug. 20, 1997.

[246] CompuBank initially will not offer Internet access.

During its first three years of operations (or until the bank reports two consecutive profitable quarters), CompuBank must also seek OCC approval to add any new banking products or services, such as Internet banking, loans, or stored value card products. Finally, under Community Reinvestment Act ("CRA") regulations, the OCC granted the bank's request to be treated as a "limited purpose" bank because of its intent not to offer loan products. To satisfy its CRA obligations, CompuBank intends to focus on providing personal computer availability and access to online banking services for low and moderate income individuals in the Houston area.

Banking industry observers will be watching new ventures like CompuBank to see if consumer acceptance of electronic banking has reached the point where the business strategy and economics of a virtual bank will succeed.

[2] UNAUTHORIZED INTERNET BANKS

One part of the OCC's Internet enforcement strategy includes issuing OCC Alerts to inform other federal and state banking agencies about unauthorized Internet banks. On April 26, 1995, the agency first addressed this phenomenon when it announced that the First Bank of Internet may be operating a banking business without authorization.[247] Since that time, the OCC has issued similar letters about the European Union Bank;[248] The Freedom Star National Bank of Arizona;[249] Netware International Bank;[250] Dunbar National Bank of Maryland;[251] and Focus International, Ltd.[252] In its Alerts, the agency warned that these entities lacked necessary charters and that any deposits made with these institutions would not be eligible for FDIC deposit insurance.

---

[247] Unauthorized Banking: The First Bank of Internet, OCC Alert 95-11 (Apr. 26, 1995).

[248] Unauthorized Banking: European Union Bank, OCC Alert 96-40 (Oct. 22, 1996).

[249] Suspicious Transactions: The Freedom Star National Bank of Arizona, OCC Alert 97-11 (May 15, 1997).

[250] Suspicious Transactions: Netware International Bank, OCC Alert 97-14 (June 24, 1997). The Federal Bureau of Investigation raided Netware International Bank's North Carolina offices following publication of the OCC Alert. *See* Dean Anason, *Charterless On-Line Banks Raise Regulatory Red Flags*, AM BANKER, July 18, 1997, at 3.

[251] Unauthorized Banking: Dunbar National Bank of Maryland, OCC Alert 97-23 (Aug. 29, 1997).

[252] Unauthorized Banking: Focus International, Ltd., OCC Alert 97-27 (Oct. 10, 1997).

CHAPTER 7

FEDERAL RESERVE BOARD'S PERSPECTIVE ON ELECTRONIC FINANCIAL PRODUCTS AND SERVICES

§ 7.01 INTRODUCTION

The Federal Reserve System is an independent central bank subject to legislative oversight. Its operations are directed by the Board of Governors of the Federal Reserve System ("FRB"). The FRB's duties fall into four general areas:

- Supervising and regulating bank holding companies and certain banking institutions to ensure the safety and soundness of the nation's banking and financial system and to protect the credit rights of consumers;

- Maintaining the stability of the financial system and containing systemic risk that may arise in financial markets;

- Conducting the nation's monetary policy by influencing the money and credit conditions in the economy in pursuit of full employment and stable prices; and

- Providing certain financial services to the U.S. government, to the public, to financial institutions, and to foreign official institutions.

Chapter 5 explored this last duty and it will be addressed further in Part IV. The focus of this Chapter is on the first two of these duties. The FRB achieves its goals in these areas through a system of regulation and supervision.

Section 7.02 provides an overview of the regulations governing bank holding companies. Section 7.03 focuses particularly on the FRB's actions regarding electronic banking and commerce activities of bank holding companies and state member banks. Section 7.04 discusses the FRB's rules regarding joint ventures and minority interest investments with respect to nonbanking activities. Section 7.05 discusses the FRB's supervisory role. Section 7.06 analyzes whether and how electronic financial products and services implicate the consumer protection requirements set forth in the Electronic Fund Transfer Act[1] ("EFTA") and the FRB's Regulation E.[2] Finally, Section 7.07 addresses the FRB's 1997 Stored Value Report.

§ 7.02   REGULATION OF BANK HOLDING COMPANIES AND THEIR ACTIVITIES

[1]   PERMISSIBLE ACTIVITIES AND OWNERSHIP INTERESTS

Subject to certain exceptions, a company that controls a bank is deemed to be a bank holding company ("BHC"),[3] pursuant to Section 2(c)(1) of the Bank Holding Company Act of 1956 ("BHCA").[4] Bank holding companies are subject to comprehensive regulation, supervision, and examination by the FRB under the BHCA. The FRB administers the provisions of the BHCA governing permissible BHC activities through Regulation Y, which is discussed in greater detail below.

The BHCA strictly limits the activities in which BHCs and their subsidiaries may engage. Apart from owning banks and managing and providing services to banks and other permissible subsidiaries, the principal authorization for BHC activities is set forth in Section 4(c)(8) of the BHCA. Section 4(c)(8) allows BHCs and their nonbank subsidiaries to engage in activities that the FRB has determined to be so "closely related to banking, or managing or controlling banks, as to be a proper incident thereto."[5] The FRB may make such determinations by order or by regulation.[6]

[2]   REGULATION Y

The FRB's Regulation Y provides the regulatory framework for its supervision of BHCs. Regulation Y includes a list of activities that the FRB has determined to be closely related to banking and, therefore, permissible activities for BHCs ("Reg Y List"). The FRB completed its most recent revision of Regulation Y in February 1997.[7] This Section discusses the activities listed in that revision.

[a] Permissible Activities. Over the years, the FRB interpretations of activities closely related to banking have substantially broadened the permissible activities for BHCs and their nonbank subsidiaries. Among the most significant aspects of the FRB's 1997 revision of the Reg Y List was its expansion of BHC authority to

---

[1]   Electronic Fund Transfer Act, Pub. L. No. 95-630, tit. XX, 1978 U.S.C.C.A.N. (92 Stat.) 3641, 3728 (codified at 15 U.S.C. §§ 1693-1693r) [hereinafter EFTA].

[2]   Electronic Fund Transfers (Regulation E), 12 C.F.R. pt. 205.

[3]   12 U.S.C. §§ 1841-49.

[4]   12 U.S.C. § 1842(a)(1). A company is considered to control a bank if, among other things, it has the power to vote 25% or more of any class of voting stock of the bank or controls in any manner the election of a majority of the directors of the bank. *Id.* § 1842(a)(2).

[5]   *Id.* §1843(c)(8).

[6]   *Id.*

[7]   Bank Holding Companies and Change in Bank Control (Regulation Y), 62 Fed. Reg. 9290 (1997) (to be codified at 12 C.F.R. pt. 225) [hereinafter Regulation Y].

engage in data processing activities. This will have a significant impact on the role BHCs play in the development of electronic banking and commerce. A discussion of the Reg Y List follows:[8]

[*i*] *Extending Credit and Servicing Loans.* BHCs may participate in the making, acquiring, brokering, and servicing of loans and other extensions of credit.[9]

[*ii*] *Activities Related to Extending Credit.* BHCs may conduct any activity incidental to making, acquiring, brokering, or servicing loans or extensions of credit.[10] Such activities include appraising real and personal property, arranging real estate equity financing, and providing real estate settlement services (other than providing title insurance as a principal, agent, or broker), as well as check-guaranty, collection agency, and credit bureau services. Asset management, servicing, and collection are also permissible activities, provided they do not include real property management or brokerage. Finally, a BHC may, subject to certain limitations, acquire debt in default at the time of acquisition.

[*iii*] *Leasing Personal or Real Property.* BHCs may participate in leases that are on a non-operating basis and for a minimum term of ninety days.[11] In the case of real property, there is an additional requirement that the lease be a full pay-out lease with the estimated residual value of the leased property representing no more than 25% of the property's original cost. BHCs may act as an agent, broker, or advisor in leasing property that is deemed permissible for leasing under the regulation.

[*iv*] *Operating Nonbank Depository Institutions.* A BHC may own, control, or operate an industrial bank, Morris Plan bank or industrial loan company, or a savings and loan association that engages only in activities permissible for BHCs under Regulation Y.[12]

[*v*] *Trust Company Functions.* A BHC or a subsidiary may perform fiduciary, agency, or custodial trust services permissible for a trust company under federal or state law, provided the company is not a bank under Section 2(c) of the BHCA.[13]

[*vi*] *Financial and Investment Advisory Activities.* BHCs may engage in a broad range of advisory services.[14] For example, a BHC may act as investment advisor to both open-ended and closed-ended investment companies.[15] In the case of the closed-ended investment companies, the BHC may sponsor, organize, and manage such investment companies. A BHC may also provide general economic information, statistical forecasting services, and industry studies. The regulation permits a BHC to provide advice with respect to mergers,

---

[8]   References to activities permissible for BHCs also extend to the performance of such activities by nonbank subsidiaries of a BHC.

[9]   Regulation Y, 62 Fed. Reg. at 9335 (to be codified at 12 C.F.R. § 225.28(b)(1)).

[10]   *Id.* (to be codified at 12 C.F.R. § 225.28(b)(2)).

[11]   *Id.* (to be codified at 12 C.F.R. § 225.28(b)(3)).

[12]   *Id.* (to be codified at 12 C.F.R. § 225.28(b)(4)).

[13]   *Id.* (to be codified at 12 C.F.R. § 225.28(b)(5)).

[14]   *Id.* (to be codified at 12 C.F.R. § 225.28(b)(6)).

[15]   As defined in § 2(a)(20) of the Investment Company Act of 1940, 15 U.S.C. § 80a-2(a)(20).

acquisitions, financing, and similar transactions as well as advice and informational services related to foreign exchange, swaps, commodities, futures, options, and similar derivative instruments. Finally, the regulation permits a BHC to provide individuals with instructional materials regarding financial management and to provide tax-planning and tax-preparation services to any person.

[*vii*] *Agency Transactional Services for Customer Investments.* A BHC may act for customers in an agency, or equivalent, capacity in five broad areas:[16] (1) a BHC may provide securities brokerage and clearing activities, either separately or in conjunction with investment advisory services; (2) it may buy or sell for its own account in a riskless principal transaction in order to fill a buy or sell order of a customer; (3) it may act as an agent for the private placement of securities;[17] (4) it may act as a futures commission merchant for unaffiliated entities to execute and clear futures contracts and options on futures contracts traded on an exchange; and (5) it may, acting as an agent, provide transactional services to customers in connection with a variety of option, futures, and forward contracts, swaps, and similar transactions permissible either under Section 4(b) of the BHCA or the regulations applicable to a state bank that is not a member bank.

[*viii*] *Investment Transactions As Principal.* A BHC may act as investment principal in three broad areas:[18] (1) a BHC may underwrite and deal in government obligations and money market investments; (2) it may deal as principal in forward contracts, options, futures, swaps, and similar derivatives; and (3) it may engage in buying and selling bullion and related activities.

[*ix*] *Management Consulting and Counseling Activities.* A BHC may provide management consulting advice on any matter to unaffiliated depository institutions and may provide management consulting advice regarding financial, economic, accounting, or audit matters to *any* company.[19] Regulation Y also permits a BHC to provide consulting services to, and in connection with, employee benefit plans. Further, a BHC may provide certain career counseling services to financial institutions, persons seeking employment at financial institutions, and employees of financial institutions seeking employment in the finance, accounting, or auditing department of any company. Finally, the regulation permits a BHC or a BHC's nonbank subsidiary to derive up to 30% of its management consulting revenue from "*services provided to any customer on any matter.*"[20] This grant of unrestricted authority is likely to be of significant strategic importance as BHCs increasingly seek to utilize their banking and commerce expertise.

---

[16] Regulation Y, 62 Fed. Reg. at 9336 (to be codified at 12 C.F.R. § 225.28(b)(7)).

[17] The private placement must be made in accordance with the requirements of the Securities Act of 1933 and the rules of the Securities and Exchange Commission. The BHC must not hold such securities for its own account.

[18] Regulation Y, 62 Fed. Reg. at 9336 (to be codified at 12 C.F.R. § 225.28(b)(8)).

[19] *Id.* (to be codified at 12 C.F.R. § 225.28(b)(9)). The regulation does prohibit the advising company from (a) owning more than 5% of the voting securities of the advised company or (b) providing its official to serve as an official of the advised company. *Id.* at 9337 (to be codified at 12 C.F.R. § 225.28(b)(9)(i)(B)(1) and (2)).

[20] *Id.* at 9312, 9337 (to be codified at 12 C.F.R. § 225.28(b)(9)(i)(C)) (emphasis added).

The revision of the management consultant and counseling activities provision incorporates two significant changes. The prior version restricted management consulting clients to depository institutions.[21] The revised regulation permits any company (and individuals in certain cases) to be the client where advice is rendered with respect to financial, economic, accounting, or auditing matters. The new regulation also carves out a 30% basket for any kind of management consulting service rendered to any type of client. With this change, major BHCs can be expected to reexamine their previous approach to consulting activities and to attempt to reach a much broader range of clients than they can now serve.

[*x*] *Support Services.* A BHC may provide courier services for checks and other instruments, as well as for banking, financial, and related documents.[22] In addition, printing and selling magnetic ink character recognition ("MICR") encoded items constitute permissible activities.

[*xi*] *Insurance Agency and Underwriting.* Unlike the other activities contained in the Reg Y List, insurance activities of BHCs[23] are subject to congressionally-established parameters.[24] The Regulation Y insurance provision permits a BHC to act as principal, agent, or broker of credit life, disability, or unemployment insurance offered in connection with an extension of credit by the BHC or its subsidiaries. A BHC may also act as agent or broker for any insurance in connection with an extension of credit by a finance company subsidiary of the BHC. The regulation permits BHCs to engage in any insurance agency activity from a town where the BHC or a subsidiary has a lending office, the town's population is not greater than 5,000, and the FRB determines, after notice and hearing, that the town has inadequate insurance agency facilities. In addition, the regulation grandfathers certain insurance activities and allows a BHC to supervise insurance agents dealing in certain policies that protect the property and employees of the BHC and its subsidiaries.

[*xii*] *Community Development Activities.* A BHC may make equity and debt investments in corporations and projects that promote community development in low-income areas.[25] It may also provide advisory and related services to such community development activities.

[*xiii*] *Money Orders, Savings Bonds, and Traveler's Checks.* A BHC may provide these traditional banking services which include "[t]he issuance and sale at retail of money orders *and similar instruments*."[26] Regulation Y thus also implies the authority to deal in a number of emerging consumer products, including stored value.

[*xiv*] *Data Processing.* The Reg Y List includes a significantly broadened version of the FRB's prior data processing rule by, among other things, incorporating select FRB orders issued since the promulgation of

---

[21] 12 C.F.R. § 225.25(b)(11) (1997).

[22] Regulation Y, 62 Fed. Reg. at 9312, 9337 (to be codified at 12 C.F.R. § 225.28(b)(10)).

[23] *Id.* (to be codified at 12 C.F.R. § 225.28(b)(11)).

[24] 12 U.S.C. § 1843(c)(8).

[25] Regulation Y, 62 Fed. Reg. at 9338 (to be codified at 12 C.F.R. § 225.28(b)(12)).

[26] *Id.* (to be codified at 12 C.F.R. § 225.28(b)(13)) (emphasis added).

the prior regulation.[27] The historical development and future implications of the FRB's data processing rule are discussed in Section 7.03[3]-[5].

[b] Procedural Requirements for Nonbanking Activities and Acquisitions. Regulation Y establishes procedural requirements for BHCs seeking to engage in nonbanking activities. As discussed below, these requirements vary depending on the condition of the BHC and the type of activity involved.

[i] Nonbanking Activities Conducted De Novo by BHCs Without Prior Notice. A BHC may establish a new entity to conduct any of the nonbanking activities on the Reg Y List (other than owning or operating an insured depository institution), and may also commence such activities through any existing entity without prior notice to the FRB, provided that the BHC (i) is well-capitalized and well-managed, (ii) conducts the activity in compliance with all FRB orders and regulations governing the activity, and (iii) provides written notice to its regional Federal Reserve Bank within ten business days of commencing the activity. That notice must describe the activity; identify the company engaged in the activity; and certify that the activity will be conducted in accordance with the FRB's orders and regulations, that the BHC meets the well-capitalized and well-managed tests, and that the BHC has not been the subject of a supervisory action during the previous twelve months.[28] The requirements of this "notice only" provision are discussed further below.

[A] Well-capitalized. Use of the notice only provision, and the expedited approval provision discussed below, requires that the well-capitalized test be met by the BHC and its insured depository institutions ("IDI"), both before and after the new activity or subsidiary is added.[29] A BHC is well-capitalized if, on a consolidated basis, it has a total risk-based capital ratio of 10% or greater, a Tier 1 risk-based capital ratio of 6%, and is not subject to any written order or directive to meet and maintain a specific capital level.[30] In order to meet the test, the BHC must show that (i) its lead IDI is well capitalized, (ii) that the IDIs that control at least 80% of the total risk-weighted assets of all of the BHC's IDIs are well-capitalized, and (iii) no BHC-controlled IDI is less than adequately capitalized.[31]

[B] Well-managed. Use of the notice only or expedited approval procedures requires that (i) the acquiring BHC, its lead IDI, and IDIs controlling at least 80% of risk-weighted assets of all IDIs must be well-managed, and (ii) no IDI controlled by the BHC has received one of the two lowest composite ratings in either its most recent examination or subsequent review by the appropriate federal bank regulatory agency, whichever came later.[32] Depository institutions acquired during the previous twelve months are excluded from the test if there is an acceptable plan to restore quality management and such IDIs constitute less than 10% of the risk-weighted

---

[27] *Id.* (to be codified at 12 C.F.R. § 225.28(b)(14)).

[28] *Id.* at 9330 (to be codified at 12 C.F.R. § 225.22(a)).

[29] *Id.* at 9331-9332 (to be codified at 12 C.F.R. § 225.23(a)(1) (notice only activities) and (c)(1) (activities subject to expedited approval)).

[30] *Id.* at 9321 (to be codified at 12 C.F.R. § 225.2(r)(1)). Special rules apply to BHCs with consolidated assets of less than $150 million. *Id.* at 9343 (to be codified at 12 C.F.R. pt. 225, app. C).

[31] *Id.* at 9332 (to be codified at 12 C.F.R. § 225.23(c)(1)(ii)).

[32] *Id.* (to be codified at 12 C.F.R. § 225.23(c)(2)(i) and (ii)).

assets of all IDIs controlled by the BHC.[33] A company, IDI, branch, or agency of a foreign banking organization is well-managed if it has received, in either its most recent inspection or examination by the appropriate federal bank regulatory agency, at least a "satisfactory" composite rating and, if applicable, a "satisfactory" rating for management and compliance or, where not yet examined, the FRB has determined after a review that the institution qualifies to be deemed to be well-managed.[34]

[ii] *Acquisitions Not Subject to Prior Notice.* In addition to the authorization for certain BHCs to engage *de novo* in Reg Y List activities without prior notice, a similar authorization applies to certain BHC acquisitions of the assets or business of a going concern. Prior approval is not required when a BHC acquires a company engaged solely in providing services to the BHC and its subsidiaries.[35] Further, no prior approval is necessary when a BHC acquires the following assets or securities: those arising from debts previously contracted; fiduciary assets; securities eligible for investment by national banks under Section 4(c)(5) of the BHCA; securities representing 5% or less of a company's voting securities; securities of investment companies owning no more than 5% of a company's voting securities; assets acquired in the normal course of business of a previously approved activity; and, subject to certain limitations, asset acquisitions by a lending company or industrial bank subsidiary.[36]

[iii] *Criteria for "Closely Related to Banking."* To approve a BHC application to engage in nonbanking activities, the FRB must find that the proposed activity (i) is so closely related to banking or controlling or managing banks as to be a proper incident thereto, and (ii) can reasonably be expected to produce benefits to the public, such as greater convenience and increased competition, or gains in efficiency that outweigh adverse effects, such as undue concentration of resources, decreased or unfair competition, conflicts of interests, or unsound banking practices.[37] The "closely related" finding may be made by regulation or order and, therefore, activities on the Reg Y List will meet this requirement. The FRB makes the public benefits determination on a case-by-case basis. FRB regulations require, in addition to consideration of the aforementioned factors, an evaluation of both the applicant's and target company's financial and managerial resources.[38] The FRB may also impose conditions on any approval to address issues raised by the consideration of the factors used in the evaluation.[39]

[iv] *Expedited Action for Certain Nonbanking Activities Conducted De Novo or by Acquisition.* Well-capitalized and well-managed BHCs may apply for expedited processing of nonbanking proposals for *de novo*

---

33   *Id.* (to be codified at 12 C.F.R. § 225.23(c)(2)(iii)).

34   *Id.* at 9321 (to be codified at 12 C.F.R. § 225.2(s)(1)). A foreign banking organization may qualify as well-managed if its combined operations in the United States have received at least a satisfactory composite rating at its most recent annual assessment. *Id.* at 9321 (to be codified at 12 C.F.R. § 224.2(s)(2)).

35   *Id.* at 9330 (to be codified at 12 C.F.R. § 225.22(b)).

36   *Id.* at 9330-9331 (to be codified at 12 C.F.R. § 225.22(d)).

37   12 U.S.C. § 1843(c)(8).

38   Regulation Y, 62 Fed. Reg. at 9339 (to be codified at 12 C.F.R. § 225.26(b)).

39   *Id.* (to be codified at 12 C.F.R. § 225.26(e)).

activities, or for acquisition of voting securities or company assets, provided the activity set forth in the proposal is permitted by order or regulation, meets certain criteria with respect to the competitive effects of the activity, and is within certain absolute and relative size parameters.[40] The BHC must submit to the appropriate Federal Reserve Bank: (i) a certification that it meets the well-capitalized, well-managed, and other requirements of Section 225.23(c); (ii) a description of the transaction and parties involved; (iii) market and competitive information; (iv) a statement of public benefits; and (v) certain pro forma financial information.[41] Within twelve business days, the Federal Reserve Bank will either approve the proposed activity or advise the applicant that action must be taken by the FRB pursuant to its regular procedures for processing proposals that do not qualify for expedited treatment.[42]

[v] *Standard Review of Proposals.* If a proposal for a nonbanking activity is not eligible for notice only or expedited processing, such proposal must be submitted to the Federal Reserve Bank for approval. The notice and information filed will vary depending on a variety of factors, including whether the notice seeks approval to (1) engage *de novo* in a Reg Y List activity, (2) acquire a company or engage in an activity on the Reg Y List, or (3) engage in an activity or acquire a company engaged in an activity not on the Reg Y List.[43] In addition to the information required when filing for the notice only or expedited reviews, the applicant seeking approval of an activity not on the Reg Y List must file evidence that the proposed activity is so closely related to banking, or managing or controlling banks, as to be a proper incident thereto. Where the FRB has previously approved the activity only by order, the applicant must commit to comply with all the conditions established by the FRB in that order.[44]

The Federal Reserve Bank will either approve an application within thirty days or, when the use of its delegated authority is not appropriate, refer it to the FRB.[45] The FRB will seek to act on every application within sixty days of the original notice date, but may extend such period for an additional thirty days, and for yet another ninety days in the case of activities not on the Reg Y List.[46] The FRB shall provide an advisory opinion regarding the scope of any permissible activity within forty-five days of receiving a written request.[47] Where the FRB is considering the permissibility of a new activity, it will publish notice thereof and invite interested parties to comment for at least thirty days.[48]

---

[40] *Id.* at 9331 (to be codified at 12 C.F.R. § 225.23(c)(3), (4), (5)).

[41] *Id.* (to be codified at 12 C.F.R. § 225.23(a)(1)).

[42] *Id.* (to be codified at 12 C.F.R. § 225.23(b)).

[43] *Id.* at 9332-33 (to be codified at 12 C.F.R. § 225.24(a)).

[44] *Id.* at 9333 (to be codified at 12 C.F.R. § 225.24(a)(3)(i)).

[45] *Id.* (to be codified at 12 C.F.R. § 225.24(d)(1)). The FRB, for example, noted in the preamble to its recent revisions to Regulation Y that all initial approvals to engage in underwriting debt and/or equity securities, whether *de novo* or by acquisition should be reviewed under the regular, rather than the expedited, procedures which will allow for a Federal Reserve System-wide review of applicants' risk-management systems. *Id.* at 9312.

[46] Regulation Y, 62 Fed. Reg. at 9333 (to be codified at 12 C.F.R. § 225.24(d)(2)(ii)(A) and (B), respectively).

[47] *Id.* at 9334 (to be codified at 12 C.F.R. § 225.27(a)(2)).

[48] *Id.* (to be codified at 12 C.F.R. § 225.27(b)(3)).

§ 7.03   THE FRB'S DATA PROCESSING RULE

As noted in Section 7.02, the FRB amended its rule regarding data processing activities that are permissible for BHCs in its 1997 revision of Regulation Y.[49] The final version of the regulation was greatly influenced by three notable sources of authority: (1) statutory authority, as interpreted by the FRB and the courts for those activities that are closely related to banking; (2) an FRB order (and its related revision of Regulation Y) made in connection with a request by Citibank to engage in the sale of time-sharing and certain related services; and (3) a series of rulings and interpretations entered prior to the finalization of the current Regulation Y. Understanding the development of these three sources is helpful to developing an understanding of how the regulation might be applied to future situations where novel facts give rise to questions about the limits to data processing activities permissible for BHCs, especially within the context of electronic banking and commerce.

[1] THE NATIONAL COURIER DECISION

As with any nonbanking activity, to be permissible under Section 4(c)(8) of the BHCA, data processing services must be "closely related" to banking. The Court of Appeals for the District of Columbia Circuit in *National Courier Association v. Board of Governors of the Federal Reserve System* has set forth the criteria to be used in making such a determination.[50] In *National Courier*, companies engaged in the courier services industry appealed an FRB order permitting BHCs to engage in four types of courier services. In affirming the FRB's order as to three of the four categories of service,[51] the court noted that there were at least three bases for the FRB to find that activities are closely related to banking:

- Banks have generally provided the proposed services.

- Banks have generally provided services that are operationally or functionally similar to the proposed services.

- Banks have generally provided services that are so integrally related to the proposed services as to require their provision in a specialized form.[52]

The court acknowledged that permissible activities include those that are not closely related to banking but which are incidental to carrying on an activity that itself is closely related to banking.

---

[49] *Id.* at 9338 (to be codified at 12 C.F.R. § 225.28(b)(14)).

[50] *National Courier Ass'n v. Board of Governors of the Fed. Reserve Sys.*, 516 F.2d 1229 (D.C. Cir. 1975). See Chapter 2, Section 2.04[3] for further discussion of the *National Courier* decision.

[51] The court upheld providing courier services (i) for the internal operations of the BHC and its subsidiaries, (ii) for transporting checks, commercial papers and documents and written instruments, and (iii) for transporting audit and accounting media of a banking or financial nature and other business records and documents. *National Courier Ass'n* at 1237-1239. The court reversed the FRB's order to the extent that it was based on the notion that nonfinancially related courier services were incidental to a permissible activity and, therefore, were themselves permissible for BHCs. *Id.* at 1241.

[52] *Id.* at 1237.

[2] BANKAMERICA

A related aspect to the development of permitted data processing activities was the FRB's conclusion that technology is a means and not itself an activity. BankAmerica Corporation applied to the FRB to expand geographically the data processing activities of its subsidiary, Decimus.[53] In 1975, the FRB had approved Decimus' processing of banking, financial, and related economic data, activities that the FRB determined to be closely related to banking. The approval confined Decimus' activities to an area within a 150 mile radius of Piscataway, New Jersey. The expansion of its services area to a 500 mile radius, the subject of BankAmerica's 1980 application to the FRB, was to be accomplished by means of remote satellite batch processing facilities. Parties protesting the application objected that there had not been proper publication of notice because the means of rendering the service (*i.e.*, by means of remote batch processing centers that could transmit data to a central site for processing) had not been adequately disclosed. The FRB found the means of providing a data processing service irrelevant because approval of an activity would not be limited to any particular method of providing the service or product. The FRB concluded that a BHC and its nonbank subsidiaries could use any technologically feasible method of providing a service that represented a permissible activity under the BHCA.[54]

[3] THE CITICORP APPLICATION

In 1980, Citicorp applied to the FRB for permission to establish a subsidiary, Citishare Corporation, to provide a broad range of data processing and transmission services to banks, institutions, and consumers. Citishare's application identified eight major functions that the subsidiary would perform:

1. data processing for affiliates;

2. data processing and transmission services through timesharing (covering financial, banking and economic related data, including financial modeling and record-keeping services);

3. packaged financial systems for installation;

4. systems for institutions to manage banking, financial and related data;

5. systems to electronically provide consumers with traditional products and enhanced information services;

6. hardware and software for authentication of interbank identifications for electronic fund transfers;

7. providing by-products from permissible data processing activities; and

8. selling excess data processing computer capacity.

---

[53] *BankAmerica Corp. (Decimus)*, 66 FED. RESERVE BULL. 511 (June 1980).

[54] *Id.* at 513.

At the time the FRB considered Citibank's application, two provisions of the FRB's regulations were particularly relevant. The first, found in Regulation Y, classified as a permissible BHC activity "storing and processing other banking, financial, or related economic data."[55] The second, also found in Regulation Y, was the FRB's interpretation that it regarded as incidental and, therefore, permissible the following data processing activities: "(1) making excess computer time available to anyone so long as the only involvement by the holding company is furnishing the facility and necessary operating personnel; [and] (2) selling a byproduct of the development of a program for a permissible data processing activity."[56] Although Citibank's request covered a broad range of activities, Citibank crafted it to fit, for the most part, within the definition of activities related to processing permissible data as then defined by the FRB.[57] Citicorp's proposal deviated from the then-existing definition of data allowed to be processed in that it proposed to process "economic related data" (*i.e.,* data-bases) rather than "related [to banking and financial] economic data." The application met with protests from the Association of Data Processing Service Organizations ("ADAPSO"), among others.

In order to address the protesters' concerns, the FRB held a hearing on the application before an administrative law judge. After analyzing the Citicorp application using the three tests for "closely related to banking" set forth in *National Courier,* the FRB issued an order approving Citishare's application in its entirety.[58] The key aspects of the FRB's order include the following points:

- Addressing the opposition to Citishare's request regarding timesharing technology, the FRB responded that technology is not a service in itself but a means of providing services.[59] It reiterated its conclusion from its *BankAmerica (Decimus)* order that a company may utilize any technologically feasible method of providing the designated services.[60]

- Rejecting the argument that economic related data should not be considered closely related to banking, the FRB concluded that banks had provided economic statistics, forecasts, and analyses by newsletter for many years and that providing such data by computer time-sharing was closely related to banking.

- Finding expanded home banking services to be functionally similar to corporate cash management services, a clear historical banking function, the FRB held that such services were closely related to banking and therefore permissible.

---

[55]   12 C.F.R. § 225.4(a)(8)(ii)(1980).

[56]   *Id.* § 225.123(e)(1980).

[57]   The Citicorp application proposed a slight variation on the language of the regulations since it asked for the right to process banking, financial, and economic related data. Protesters objected that the formulation "economic related data" was too broad and included data that was not closely related to banking, thereby implying an expansion of the type of data permitted to be processed and transmitted by BHC. The FRB approved the application as proposed on the basis that the administrative law judge's recommended decision did not address the issue but the record supported a finding that banks engage in the processing and transmitting of economic data. *Citicorp (Citishare)*, 68 FED. RESERVE BULL. 505, 507, n.8 (Aug. 1982) [hereinafter *Citishare Order*].

[58]   *Id.*

[59]   *Id.* at n.11. This approach corresponds with the OCC's view in regard to its analytical approach to the use of technology.

[60]   *BankAmerica Corp. (Decimus)*, 66 FED. RESERVE BULL. at 513.

- The FRB found that the sale of excess computer capacity and by-products to be incidental to closely related permitted activities.[61]

- The FRB found that customers often demanded integrated packages of software and hardware and thus allowed the sale of hardware, provided that its cost did not exceed 30% of the cost of the total package.

[4] FINAL RULES REFLECT CITISHARE ORDER

Contemporaneously with issuing its Citishare Order, the FRB published a final rule concerning permissible BHC activities ("Data Processing Rule") that, among other things, adopted the positions taken by the FRB in its Citishare Order.[62] The Data Processing Rule codified an expansion of the type of data that BHCs could process. Opponents of the regulation claimed that economic data, by definition, were not banking data and, therefore, by definition, not closely related to banking. The FRB acknowledged that its decision represented an expansion of the data processing authority for BHCs, with respect to the type of data that could be processed and transmitted, and that the administrative law judge's recommended decision (which the FRB followed) included no conclusion or finding supporting such expansion.[63] The FRB took the position that the record supported a finding that banks do process economic data and that the order, therefore, satisfied the standards of *National Courier*.[64] Furthermore, as the FRB had noted in its order, the only novel aspect of the data processing services being proposed in this particular case arise not from a broader reading of the business of banking but from a change in technology, namely, the fact that data could now be transmitted electronically from remote sites rather than processed in only a batch mode requiring physical delivery of the data to the computer site.[65]

In 1984, ADAPSO challenged the FRB's Citishare Order and the Data Processing Rule.[66] ADAPSO argued that no bank had historically provided computer services on the scale or sophistication that Citibank proposed and, therefore, the proposal could not meet the *National Courier* standard, which allows BHCs to perform any service that banks had generally performed. The Court of Appeals for the District of Columbia Circuit, relying upon *National Courier*'s tests for evaluating whether an activity is closely related to banking, ruled that the FRB's determination was not arbitrary and capricious.[67] The court noted that the BHCA's purpose was not to confine banks to the same level of simple previously existing services.[68]

---

[61] The excess capacity was found to result from the necessity in a time-sharing environment to cover peak needs thereby inevitably leaving unused capacity while the sale of by-products was a necessary incident to providing data processing services.

[62] Bank Holding Companies and Change in Bank Control, Data Processing, and Electronic Funds Transfer Activities, 47 Fed. Reg. 37,368 (1982) (codified at 12 C.F.R. §§ 225.4, 225.123) [hereinafter Data Processing Rule].

[63] Data Processing Rule, 47 Fed. Reg. at 37,369.

[64] *Id.* at 37,369 n.7.

[65] *Citishare Order*, 68 FED. RESERVE BULL. at 507.

[66] *Association of Data Processing Serv. Org., Inc. v. Board of Governors of the Fed. Reserve Sys.*, 745 F.2d 677 (D.C. Cir. 1984).

[67] *Id.* at 689.

[68] *Id.* at 691.

Both the FRB and the appeals court recognized a need to read the law broadly when dealing with technological change. Both emphasized that technology is a tool and not itself an activity to be calibrated against the "closely related to banking" standard in the BHCA.

[5]   ORDERS AFTER THE DATA PROCESSING RULE

[a] Computer Output to Microfilm. The FRB's 1987 approval of a BHC acquisition of a data processing company illustrates how the FRB's Data Processing Rule and the evolution of technology combined to expand the range of data processing services permissible for BHCs. In 1987, MCorp proposed acquiring Kalvar Corporation and offering computer output to microfilm ("COM") services.[69] Additionally, it proposed to sell certain equipment and supplies needed by customers to utilize the processed microfilm or microfiche resulting from the COM services.[70] In a 1975 regulation, the FRB had permitted COM services only as an output option for data otherwise permissibly processed and not as a separate line of business. In approving MCorp's application, the FRB noted that the COM services proposed differed materially from those proposed more than a decade earlier and, as a result of technological change, it intended to revoke its 1975 regulation.[71] In so doing, the FRB stated that ". . . technological improvements in the COM industry allow for the manipulation, sorting and arranging of data in a way that constitutes a substantive change to data, which is the touchstone of the [FRB's] definition of data processing."[72]

[b] Internet Banking Services. In 1996, the FRB approved the acquisition of Five Paces Software, Inc. ("Five Paces") by Cardinal Bancshares, Inc. Five Paces engaged nationwide in providing data processing and transmission activities involved in making banking and financial services available over the Internet.[73] Because Five Paces conducted all of its activities in connection with transactions for accounts maintained at depository institutions, the activities fell squarely within the financial, banking, or economic information contemplated by Regulation Y.[74] Anticipating a surge of new technological financial products about to offer consumers direct interactive access to their banks, the FRB expressed its concern regarding the new levels of bank security that will be required to protect both customers and banks. The FRB noted that the services provided by Five Paces would expose customers to the risks of electronic fraud and invasion of privacy. While it concluded that these risks are similar to those encountered in traditional banking operations, the FRB underscored that the burden of ensuring that the institution and holding company were adequately protected by prudent security measures fall squarely on the shoulders of management.[75] Specifically, the FRB stated that

---

[69] *MCorp*, 73 FED. RESERVE BULL. 933 (Dec. 1987).

[70] *Id.* at 934.

[71] *Id.* at 934 n.4.

[72] Data Processing Activities; Bank Holding Company Act, 52 Fed. Reg. 45,160 (1987).

[73] *Cardinal Bancshares, Inc.*, 82 FED. RESERVE BULL. 674 (July 1996).

[74] *Id.* at 675.

[75] *Id.* at 676.

"[t]he Board also expects financial institutions, as part of this evaluation, to implement any modifications to their information security procedures and controls that appear to be necessary or appropriate in light of the risks associated with Internet-based services."[76]

The FRB's admonition is one not to be taken lightly. As computer technology becomes an increasingly important retail delivery mechanism between depository institutions and customers, it will be elevated from a back office discipline, where the concern is communication and security, to a board room issue, where the focus will be on product development and marketing strategy. Whereas in the past, technology might have been analogized to plugging in the computer, the copier, and the fax machine, today and in the future, it will be the backbone of every banking product and delivery system. This shift creates a new business model with concomitant new responsibilities for management.

[c] PC-Based Personal Financial Software. Does the development and creation of financially-oriented software constitute (1) the manufacturing of a separate nonbanking product, (2) the production of a product that is closely related to the business of banking, or (3) a distribution vehicle that facilitates banking and, therefore, may be considered closely related to it? The FRB addressed this question in February 1996, when it approved an application by the Royal Bank of Canada ("RBOC") to acquire 20% of the voting shares of MECA Software, L.L.C. ("MECA"). MECA, a software development firm, is owned jointly by subsidiaries of NationsBank and Bank of America and is engaged in data processing activities related to its PC-based personal finance program, "Managing Your Money."[77] MECA's software products enable customers to pay bills, reconcile checking account registers, access their checking and savings account statements, transfer funds between accounts, receive stock quotations, and engage in tax and financial planning.[78] Because MECA was primarily involved in the processing of financial, economic, and banking data contemplated under the data processing provisions of Regulation Y, the FRB considered this portion of MECA's activities to be "closely related to banking" under Section 4(c)(8) of the BHCA.[79]

The FRB also considered whether to approve RBOC's application despite MECA's development, manufacture, and marketing of a medical reference library and non-financial software, such as video and arcade games, which on their face did not fall within the scope of the existing Regulation Y data processing rule. Although MECA's existing ownership by subsidiaries of national banks had been approved by the OCC, the FRB did not view this as binding upon its own determination. The FRB reasoned that the aforementioned activities were incidental to the primary activities of MECA, which were closely related to banking. In reaching this conclusion, the FRB relied on two findings. First, MECA did not devote any employees exclusively to the nonfinancial activities in question and had no plans to do so in the future. In other words, MECA was not developing these activities as a separate line of business. Second, the nonfinancial activities produced only 7% of MECA's revenues, an amount

---

[76] *Id.* at 676 n.15.

[77] *Royal Bank of Canada*, 82 FED. RESERVE BULL. 363, 364 (Apr. 1996).

[78] *Id.* at 364 n.3.

[79] 12 U.S.C. § 1843(c)(8).

that the FRB considered to be *de minimis*, making them only incidental to MECA's financial services related activities that were closely related to the business of banking.

Just over a year after the RBOC order, the FRB dramatically shifted its approach in this area. Rather than requiring a showing that non-financial data processing activity did not represent a significant aspect of the data processing entity's activities, on an application-by-application basis, the FRB shifted to a broad regulatory safe-harbor for non-financial data processing. Under the amended data processing regulation promulgated in 1997, the FRB now allows an entity's revenues from non-financial data processing services to comprise up to 30% of total data processing revenues.[80]

[d] Providing Billing Services. In February 1996, the FRB approved Compagnie Financiere de Paribas' ("Paribas") application to engage *de novo* (through a network of several foreign subsidiaries) in the provision of customer account billing services or software, or both, to digital mobile phone network operators ("operators") throughout the United States.[81] Paribas' U.S. subsidiary planned to provide an integrated software program for account billing features. The computer software and hardware provided would be separate and distinct from the hardware and software running the telephone operating and switching system.[82] The software's principal function would be to collect data necessary to prepare and transmit bills on behalf of operators to their customers.

The FRB considered the performance of these billing functions to be within the range of data processing activities permissible under Regulation Y.[83] Moreover, the FRB found that the software's nonfinancial data processing functions, which included (i) generation of fraud control reports and (ii) the transmission of customer identification and account information to the operators' verification files, played only a limited role in the overall operation of the software's billing functions and would not be provided apart from the billing functions. The FRB noted that, when data processing activities were first added to the Reg Y List in 1971, performing billing services was specifically included in the rule as an example of processing banking, financial, or related economic data. When Regulation Y was revised in 1982 and the FRB promulgated its Data Processing Rule, the removal of examples from the earlier rule was intended to expand the delineation of permissible data processing activities. The *Paribas* order also noted that Paribas had pledged that general purpose hardware included in any packaged offering would not exceed 30% of total revenues.[84]

---

[80] Regulation Y, 62 Fed. Reg. at 9338 (to be codified at 12 C.F.R. § 225.28(b)(14)(ii)). In promulgating the regulation the FRB noted in the preamble that "this 30 percent basket would not include revenue derived from the use of excess capacity or the sale of general purpose hardware that is currently permitted in accordance with the Board's [FRB's] regulation and policies governing those activities." *Id*. at 9304 n.5.

[81] *Compagnie Financiere de Paribas*, 82 FED. RESERVE BULL. 348 (Apr. 1996).

[82] *Id*. The Paribas subsidiary product prepared customer billing information based upon customer call information provided by the operators, including time and duration of the call, terms of the customer's service contract, and account balances. In addition, the software also performed general accounts receivable and payable functions.

[83] *Id*. at 349.

[84] *Id*. at 349 n.7.

[e] Dispensing Alternative Media. In 1996, a group of BHCs sought FRB approval for their jointly owned subsidiary to engage in certain data processing activities that would allow ATMs to dispense alternative media.[85] This proposal had already been approved by the OCC, which addressed the issue from the perspective of whether banks were authorized to dispense the alternative media. The FRB analyzed and approved the application as one to engage in data processing services. The FRB noted that it had already concluded that services that allowed customers to use an ATM card to access a deposit account or line of credit, and that supported customers' use of credit cards, are activities that fall within the scope of permissible data processing activities.[86] The FRB found that the proposed activities were the same type as it had previously approved for credit card and more traditional ATM transactions and, therefore, were permissible.

[f] Integrion Financial Network. In December 1996, the FRB approved the participation of BHCs in the Integrion Financial Network ("Integrion").[87] Integrion is currently owned and operated by its eighteen "owner" banks, in conjunction with their information technology partner, IBM.[88] It plans to offer interactive banking and financial and electronic commerce services to consumers and businesses, including data processing and transmission services as well as Internet access.[89] Integrion is designed to be a banking industry friendly alternative platform to existing online banking systems and products. Its chief goals are to permit banks to take a greater role in the development of the emerging "online" payments system and to share a common platform for electronic banking that will allow banks to protect their brand values and retain market share in the face of increased competition from nonbanks.[90]

IBM and Integrion's member banking organizations anticipate that the venture's integrated financial services platform will permit commercial banks to set the standards for new electronic banking services and coordinate such services with their existing lines of products and services. In granting its approval, the FRB found that the proposed data processing and transmission activities were closely related to banking.[91] Further, the FRB found that (i) the general provision of Internet access is incidental to such activities, and (ii) offering

---

[85] *Banc One Corp.*, 82 FED. RESERVE BULL. 848 (Sept. 1996). *See* OCC Interpretive Letter No. 718 [1995-1996 Transfer Binder] Fed. Banking L. Rep. (CCH) ¶ 81-033, at 90,299, 90,301, (Mar. 14, 1996). See Chapter 6, Section 6.03[4][c] for a further discussion.

[86] *Banc One Corp.*, 82 FED. RESERVE BULL. at 849 (citing *Bank of New York Company et al.*, 80 FED. RESERVE BULL. 1107, 1109 (Dec. 1994)).

[87] *Royal Bank of Canada*, 83 FED. RESERVE BULL. 135 (Feb. 1997) [hereinafter *Integrion Order*].

[88] *Id.* at 137. IBM will provide additional systems integration and networks services to member banks, including firewall, directory, and network services to link banks to the network. The Integrion Financial Network will be organized as a for-profit limited liability company owned and operated by IBM and its sixteen member banks: ABN AMRO, Banc One, Bank of America, Barnett Banks, Comerica, First Bank Systems, First Chicago NBD, Fleet Financial Group, KeyCorp., Mellon Bank, Michigan National Bank, NationsBank, Norwest, PNC Bank, Royal Bank of Canada, U.S. Bancorp, Visa U.S.A., Inc. and Washington Mutual, Inc. With over 60 million consumer accounts, these banking institutions claim to have a customer base of over half the total consumer accounts in North America. *See IBM Press Release*, Sept. 9, 1996.

[89] For a further discussion of the scope of services to be provided by the Integrion network and its implications for electronic banking, see Thomas P. Vartanian, Robert H. Ledig & Edward B. Whittemore, *Integrion Financial Network: A New Stage for Electronic Banking*, ELECTRONIC BANKING L. AND COM. REP., Oct. 1996, at 6.

[90] The disintermediation of banks from their customers and their assets is not a new phenomenon. *See* Thomas P. Vartanian, *Technology's Silver Lining and Banking's Dark Clouds*, AM. BANKER-FUTURE BANKING, Mar. 18, 1996, at 14A.

[91] *Integrion Order*, 83 FED. RESERVE BULL. at 137-138.

Internet access to member depository institutions is an acceptable business accommodation. The FRB did not find providing Internet access to be a separate activity subject to approval.[92]

[g] Internet Access Services. In a ruling where a banking service was to be provided over the Internet, the FRB based its decision that the activity was permissible on the nature of the activity and not the means of delivery. Shortly after the FRB revised its data processing rule under Regulation Y in 1997, the FRB authorized Toronto-Dominion Bank and its wholly-owned subsidiary, Waterhouse Investor Services, Inc., to purchase 50% of Marketware International, Inc. ("Marketware"), a company that proposed to develop, market, and sell computer software to financial institutions.[93] The software would enable purchasers to offer to *their* customers a means to purchase and sell securities over the Internet through the use of personal computers. The FRB, as authority for its approval of Toronto-Dominion's application, cited, among other things, its 1986 decision allowing Citicorp to offer online processing services involving transactions and quotation data for financial instruments.[94]

The sale of the software appeared to be one step removed from the provision of processing services. The FRB made no mention of this distinction, but in addressing the public benefits from the proposal, it noted that the entry of Marketware into the market would increase the level of competition among "existing providers of these software products."[95] The FRB's decision supports the proposition that a BHC may engage in traditional software development and sales to third parties, provided that the software is used by its purchasers to process banking, financial, or economic data.

[6] 1997 CHANGES TO PERMISSIBLE DATA PROCESSING ACTIVITIES

The data processing regulation promulgated by the FRB in 1997 reflects two major and one minor change from its predecessor.[96] The FRB increased the amount that the cost of the hardware may represent, when it is provided as part of a packaged offering of software and hardware, from 10% to 30%. The FRB gave no explanation for this increase, although it should be noted that the FRB permitted equipment to represent 30% of the cost of the total package in the case of its approval of Citibank's 1980 application to provide data processing through time-sharing. This change enhances the ability of BHCs to compete with nonbanking companies which sell packaged systems, including hardware, representing a turn-key solution to clients' needs.

The FRB also removed the requirement that data processing services and facilities must be designed,

---

[92] This continues a trend that has been embraced by various federal bank regulatory agencies, for example, the OCC views the Internet as a means of distributing a financial product rather than as a separate product in and of itself. *See* OCC Interpretive Letter No. 742, [1996-1997 Transfer Binder] Fed. Banking L. Rep. (CCH) ¶ 81,106, at 90,215 (Aug. 19, 1996).

[93] *Toronto-Dominion Bank*, 83 FED. RESERVE BULL. 335 (Apr. 1997).

[94] *Id.* at 335 n.8 (citing *Citicorp*, 72 FED. RESERVE BULL. 497 (July 1986)). The software to be developed and marketed by Marketware would reside on host computers operated by brokers, who would purchase the software from Marketware. *Toronto-Dominion Bank, Id.* at 335.

[95] *Id.* at 336.

[96] Prior to the 1997 amendments, the regulation was found at 12 C.F.R. § 225.25(b)(7) (1997).

marketed, and operated for processing and transmitting only financial, banking, or economic data. As noted above, the regulation now permits an individual BHC or BHC subsidiary to derive up to 30% of its data processing and transmission revenues from services without regard to the type of data involved.[97] The FRB had, in an earlier ruling, permitted a BHC to derive a *de minimis* amount of revenue from such activity.[98] The FRB offered two reasons for the change.[99] First, the restriction was inhibiting the ability of BHCs to compete with other providers, who often combine financial and nonfinancial products. Second, strict limitations have hindered the ability of BHCs to recruit qualified employees whose expertise and interests include both financial and nonfinancial matters.[100]

In addition, the FRB eliminated the requirement that data processing services must be rendered pursuant to a written contract.[101] The FRB offered no specific explanations for this change. The FRB imposed the requirement in 1982 when it promulgated the Data Processing Rule allowing processing of only banking, financial, and economic related data. The written contract requirement was designed to meet the objections of protesters to Citibank's application, who argued that equipment could easily be used to process impermissible data.[102] With the relaxation of the rule regarding permissible data, the rationale for the written contract rule is substantially diminished.

§ 7.04 INVESTMENTS AND ACTIVITIES THROUGH JOINT VENTURES AND MINORITY INTERESTS

The FRB pays special attention to transactions wherein a bank holding company or its subsidiary engages in nonbanking activities, through partial acquisition, or in a joint venture context. Such transactions may involve either activities that are not permissible for BHCs under the BHCA, or those that are permissible.

[1] INVESTMENTS PURSUANT TO SECTION 4(c)(6) OF THE BHCA

The prohibition in Section 4(a) of the BHCA against a BHC owning or controlling the shares of any company that is not a bank or in the business of managing banks is subject to certain exceptions. One such exception is Section 4(c)(6), which permits a BHC to own up to 5% of the outstanding voting shares of any company, regardless of the type of activities in which it engages. The operation of this provision was addressed by the FRB when a group of BHCs proposed that, pursuant to Section 4(c)(6), each BHC would acquire 100% of a separate class of voting securities with no BHC owning more than 5% of the total voting shares of an

---

[97] Regulation Y, 62 Fed. Reg. at 9312, 9338 (to be codified at 12 C.F.R. § 225.28(b)(14)(ii)).

[98] *See* Section 7.03[5][c].

[99] Regulation Y, 62 Fed. Reg. at 9304.

[100] For the same reasons, the FRB allowed up to 30% of management consulting revenues to be derived from providing advisory services other than in connection with financial, accounting, and similar matters. *Id.*

[101] State statutes based on the Statute of Frauds may still require written contracts in many cases.

[102] Data Processing Rule, 47 Fed. Reg. at 37,370 (codified at 12 C.F.R. § 225.4(a)(8)(ii)(A)). The FRB reasoned that a written contract setting forth the services to be provided would allow for a means to monitor whether the actual services rendered involved permissible data processing services.

insurance company to be formed to underwrite and reinsure credit life and credit accident insurance.[103] As a group, the BHCs would own 100% of the insurance company's voting shares. The FRB found the proposal inconsistent with Section 4(c)(6) of the BHCA.[104] In its analysis, the FRB applied the restriction from Section 2(a)(2)(A) of the BHCA that deems a company to control a bank, and therefore be a BHC, if it owns or controls 25% or more of any class of stock. The FRB reasoned that its application of Section 2(a)(2)(A) to Section 4(c)(6) was appropriate because Section 4(c)(6) must be viewed as permitting 5% ownership only when that ownership does not result in control. The FRB concluded that because each applicant BHC would in this case control a class of voting stock, the exception under Section 4(c)(6) was not available.[105]

The FRB took a similar position in a case where a BHC proposed to acquire 4.9% of the voting stock and 100% of the class B floating-market-rate, non-voting preferred stock of an insurance holding company whose subsidiaries would underwrite life insurance and annuities.[106] Attached to the preferred shares were warrants to purchase a significant number of shares of the insurance holding company's common stock. A group holding 95% of the insurance holding company's voting common stock had entered into an agreement granting the BHC the right to purchase up to 70% of the common voting shares or, under certain alternative conditions, to demand redemption of the preferred stock at a premium of 20%. The FRB evaluated the request on the basis of its compliance with the FRB's policy statement on minority equity investments by BHCs.[107] The FRB found that the terms of the preferred stock and the related agreements raised the potential of the BHC controlling the activities of the insurance holding company by effectively restricting the shareholders of 95% of the common stock from selling their shares. The stock acquisition agreement, the FRB found, "appears to give the bank holding company an entrepreneurial rather than a passive interest in the long-term success and operation of the company."[108]

The 5% exemption under Section 4(c)(6) does not prohibit a non-voting interest larger than 5% where the investment is passive, does not involve engaging in an activity permissible under the BHCA, and does not establish a control relationship. In a seminal decision applying these concepts, the FRB approved Sumitomo Bank, Ltd.'s investment in Goldman, Sachs & Co., a major investment bank, through a non-voting limited partnership interest and subordinated debt instruments.[109] The FRB's approval was subject to a number of

---

[103] Fed. Reserve Reg. Serv., Bd. Ruling 4-551, at 4-246 (Dec. 10, 1976).

[104] *Id. See also* 12 C.F.R. § 225.137.

[105] *Id.*

[106] Fed. Reserve Reg. Serv., Staff Op. 4-305.1, at 4-204 (Nov. 5, 1984).

[107] *See* Bank Holding Companies and Change in Bank Control; Statement of Policy on Nonvoting Equity Investments by Bank Holding Companies, 47 Fed. Reg. 30,965 (1982) (codified at 12 C.F.R. § 225.143).

[108] Staff Op. 4-305.1, *supra* note 106.

[109] *Sumitomo Bank, Ltd.*, 73 FED. RESERVE BULL. 24 (Jan. 1987). See also Staff Op. 4-305.1, *supra* note 106, in which the FRB emphasized the criterion of less than 25% ownership and the passive nature of the investment.

conditions that changed or deleted certain terms governing the investment included in the original application. These conditions included:

- The investment would represent less than 25% of the capital of the investee.

- Sumitomo would not acquire stock in, or have directors on the board of, any Goldman, Sachs affiliates.

- Sumitomo employees would not become trainees at Goldman, Sachs.

- Sumitomo's name would not be used as a part of the name of any Goldman, Sachs affiliate, and vice versa.

- Sumitomo would not solicit business for Goldman, Sachs, and vice versa, except under limited conditions.

- Normal business relationships would be maintained on an arm's length basis.

The FRB has likewise approved ownership by a BHC of a noncontrolling 24.9% equity interest in a leveraged corporate acquisition fund, an activity that generally would not be permissible for a BHC, where the BHC committed in its application that it would have no role in advising or financing the fund and agreed to limit its lending to companies that were investees of the fund.[110]

More recently, in another variant of the application of Section 4(c)(6), the FRB approved Meridian Bancorp's proposal to control a series of partnerships that would hold no more than 5% of any class of voting securities of any issuer and not own more than 25% of the total equity of any issuer, an activity that generally would be permissible for a BHC.[111]

[2]   MINORITY INTEREST INVESTMENT AS AN ACTIVITY PURSUANT TO SECTION 4(C)(8) OF THE BHCA

Where BHCs have made minority interest investments or participated in joint ventures in connection with activities that are permissible nonbank activities under Section 4(c)(8) of the BHCA, the FRB has often imposed conditions to ensure that the enterprise in which the BHC is investing does not involve itself in activities that are not permissible for BHCs. For example, Cardinal Bankshares, Inc. ("Cardinal") applied to the FRB in 1994 for permission for its subsidiary to invest in a joint venture with Compulife Investors Services, Inc. ("Compulife"), which would engage in securities brokerage and riskless principal activities.[112] To avoid the risk that the joint venture might mingle permissible and nonpermissible securities activities, the FRB imposed as a condition of its approval, among other things, requirements that: (i) the joint venture not engage in any additional

---

[110] Fed. Reserve Reg. Serv., Bd. Ruling 4-271.2, at 4-196 (Dec. 7, 1989).

[111] *Meridian Bancorp, Inc.*, 80 FED. RESERVE BULL. 736, 737 (Aug. 1994).

[112] *Cardinal Bancshares, Inc.*, 80 FED. RESERVE BULL. 447 (May 1994).

activities without Cardinal's knowledge and consent, and the prior authorization of the FRB; (ii) Cardinal not solicit business on behalf of Compulife; and (iii) Cardinal and its subsidiaries act on an arm's length basis in deciding whether to extend credit to Compulife or Compulife's competitors.[113]

The FRB imposed similar restrictions in the approval of an application by two foreign BHCs to retain control of Charterhouse North America, Inc. ("Charterhouse"), and to conduct certain private placement and investment advisory activities through Charterhouse pursuant to Section 4(c)(8) of the BHCA.[114] The applicants committed, among other things, to separate the operations of Charterhouse from those of a securities firm owned by one of the applicants that was permitted, on the basis of a grandfather exemption under the BHCA, to engage in activities not permissible for Charterhouse.

In another instance, a BHC applied for authorization for a subsidiary to acquire a limited partnership interest in a partnership formed to engage in investment advisory services, a permissible activity under Section 4(c)(8).[115] The limited partnership would include a second unaffiliated limited partner and a general partner, both of which engaged only in activities permissible for BHCs at the time of the application. Because affiliates of the general partner and the second limited partner engaged in activities not permissible for BHCs, the FRB imposed conditions on its approval. The applicant BHC represented that no employee, officer, or director of the general partner or the other limited partner would serve as an employee, officer, or director of the BHC or any of the BHC's affiliates, including the subsidiary of the bank investing in the partnership. In addition, the BHC agreed to notify the FRB if the partnership, the general partner, the other limited partner, or any affiliate of any of them was determined to engage in any securities underwriting or dealing activities not permissible for a BHC.

The FRB clarified its requirements for bank holding company joint ventures on December 26, 1996.[116] It delegated to the Reserve Banks the authority to approve joint ventures where: (1) the BHC would have a no greater than 5% voting interest in the joint venture; (2) the joint venture is *not* structured as a partnership; and (3) there are no issues regarding securities activities. The Reserve Bank is expected to pay particular attention to the effect on competition, the potential for engaging in impermissible activities, the allocation of profits and losses among co-ventures, and the treatment of regulatory capital. These items reflect the FRB's concern that joint ventures can break down the legally mandated separation of banking and commerce.[117] Of special concern in this respect are ventures between a BHC and a securities firm, which might lead the BHC to engage in impermissible securities activities.[118]

---

[113] *Id.* at 448 n.10.

[114] *Credit Commercial de France, S.A. & Berliner Handels-und Frankfurter Bank*, 81 FED. RESERVE BULL. 390 (Feb. 1995).

[115] *Creditanstalt-Bankverein*, 80 FED. RESERVE BULL. 828 (Sept. 1994).

[116] Joint Venture Proposals Pursuant to Regulation Y: Guidance Regarding Issues, and Criteria for Delegation, SR 96-39 (Dec. 26, 1996) [hereinafter Joint Venture Guidelines].

[117] *See, e.g., The Maybaco Co. and Equitable Bancorp.*, 69 FED. RESERVE BULL. 375 (May 1983).

[118] *See The Chuo Trust and Banking Co. Ltd.*, 78 FED. RESERVE BULL. 446 (June 1992); *Amsterdam-Rotterdam Bank, N.V.*, 70 FED. RESERVE BULL. 835 (Nov. 1984).

The FRB now requires that, in all joint venture applications, each BHC make two commitments.[119] The applicant, the joint venture company, and the co-venturer must commit that they do not conduct or anticipate conducting any activities or relationships that would cause the applicant, its affiliates, or the joint venture company to be engaged in any of the activities of the co-venturer or its affiliates (other than the joint venture company). The joint venture would also be treated as an affiliate for purposes of Sections 23A and 23B of the Federal Reserve Act and as a subsidiary of a BHC under the BHCA.

In summary, the nature and scope of the business of an enterprise in which a BHC makes a minority or joint venture investment will be determined in part by whether the investment is authorized under Section 4(c)(6) or 4(c)(8) of the BHCA. In the case of the former, the investment must be passive and limited to no more than 25% of the total capital, and 5% of the voting shares, of the enterprise. In such cases, the scope of permissible enterprise activities is very broad, including activities that have no connection with banking or finance. In the case of approval under Section 4(c)(8), the enterprise activities must be ones that are permissible for a BHC and closely related to banking. Furthermore, the FRB will impose specific conditions to ensure that the investee enterprise does not later engage in impermissible activities where the circumstances indicate a risk that the enterprise could involve the applicant BHC, or the BHC's affiliates, in activities not permissible under the BHCA.

[3] OWNERSHIP OF MINORITY INTERESTS BY STATE MEMBER BANKS

As discussed in Chapter 6, Section 6.04[3], the OCC has permitted national banks to own minority interests in entities found to be part of, or incidental to, the business of banking. Likewise, the FRB has permitted BHCs to own minority interests in an enterprise such as the Integrion Financial Network. The question arises, therefore, as to whether a state chartered bank that is a member of the Federal Reserve System, where permitted under state law to own a minority interest in an enterprise engaged in a permissible activity under the BHCA, would be permitted under federal law to own such a minority interest. State banks that are members of the Federal Reserve System ("state member banks") are subject, under the Federal Reserve Act, to the same restrictions on stock purchases under 12 U.S.C. Section 24(Seventh) that are applicable to national banks.[120]

Historically the FRB has taken the view that a state member bank may engage in activities permissible for such a bank through a subsidiary only if the subsidiary were wholly owned.[121] More recently, the FRB staff has indicated that a state member bank may acquire a minority interest in an entity engaged in activities that are permissible for the investing state member bank, provided three conditions are met.[122] First, where the investing state member bank will own a minority interest it must be in a position to prevent the entity from

---

[119] Joint Venture Guidelines, *supra* note 116.

[120] 12 U.S.C. § 335.

[121] 12 C.F.R. § 250.141.

[122] Memorandum from J. Virgil Mattingly, Jr., General Counsel, to Federal Reserve Bank General Counsels (Oct. 10, 1996). The memorandum addressed five investments made by three banks that requested no-action rulings in connection with such investments.

engaging in impermissible activities or be able to withdraw if the entity does engage in impermissible activities. This ability may be provided by means of charter, or by-law provisions, or otherwise. Second, the investing state member bank must not be exposed to unlimited liability. This requires that the bank's risk of loss be limited as both a legal and an accounting matter. A minority interest accounted for on the equity method of accounting under generally acceptable accounting principles would meet such a requirement, provided the investing bank did not otherwise obligate itself to be responsible for the liabilities of the entity in which it has invested. Finally, the FRB staff has indicated that the minority investment should be related to the bank's banking business and not merely a passive investment. In the case of the specific investments that gave rise to the staff ruling, the General Counsel of the FRB found the investments were not merely passive "[b]ecause each of these investments were convenient or useful to the bank in carrying out its banking business."[123]

§ 7.05   SUPERVISION

Traditional examinations by the federal bank regulatory agencies have focused considerable attention on verifying the credit quality of loan and investment security portfolios. Such credit risk evaluation remains an important part of the FRB examination procedure. The FRB has recognized that new electronic banking products, distribution systems, and services, "which allow institutions to adjust their yields, risks, and liquidity much quicker than ever before," present new or different types of risks "that are not best addressed by examination on a transaction by transaction basis or by simply verifying balance sheet values."[124] As a result, bankers and examiners may be forced to concentrate greater resources on the process of risk management.[125]

One FRB member has noted that Internet-based home banking services and new payment products expose institutions to significant liability if security measures are breached. Thus, he notes, an examination of a bank must necessarily extend to a review of its information systems, security controls, and contingency arrangements.[126] Examiners' evaluations of the processes banks use to manage risks are illustrated by the considerable attention paid to the area of assessing risk in the area of derivatives.[127]

---

[123] *Id.* at 3.

[124] *Risk Assessment: Hearing Before the House Comm. on Banking and Financial Services*, 104th Cong. (1996) (statement of Richard Spillenkothen, Director, Division of Banking Supervision and Regulation, Board of Governors of the Federal Reserve System), *reprinted in*, 82 Fed. Reserve Bull 397, 401 (May 1996) [hereinafter *Risk Assessment Hearing*].

[125] Susan M. Phillips, Governor, Board of Governors of the Federal Reserve System, Regulatory Policy Changes: Supervisory and Regulatory Responses to Financial Innovation and Industry Dynamics, Remarks Before the Bank Administration Institute, Washington, D.C. (Nov. 25, 1996).

[126] Edward W. Kelley, Jr., Governor, Board of Governors of the Federal Reserve System, Remarks Before the CyberPayments '96 Conference, Dallas, Texas (June 18, 1996).

[127] *See, e.g., Framework for Supervisory Information about the Derivative Activities of Banks and Securities Firms*, Joint Report by the Basel Committee on Banking Supervision and the Technical Committee of the International Organization of Securities Commissions (May 1995) (*available in* FRB Press Release, May 16, 1995). *See also Foreign Bank Supervision and The Daiwa Bank: Hearing Before the Subcomm. on Financial Institutions and Consumer Credit of the House Comm. on Banking and Financial Services*, 104th Cong. at 7 (1995) (statement of Alan Greenspan, Chairman, Board of Governors of the Federal Reserve System), *reprinted in* 82 FED. RESERVE BULL. 133 (Feb. 1996); Susan M. Phillips, Governor, Board of Governors of the Federal Reserve System, Risk Management for Banks and Banking Regulators in the 21st Century, Remarks Before the Atlanta Society of Financial Analysts (Feb. 14, 1997).

While technology has generated new product opportunities and risks for banks, it has also produced the means to more effective and efficient examination. For example, the examiner workstation allows off-site examiners to download data from banks' data processing systems and analyze such data, thereby reducing the amount of time spent on manual operations.[128] There is a consensus view that internal risk modeling by banks, and the examination by regulatory authorities of the effectiveness of the banks' systems and models, will become increasingly common and essential to effective examination as technology produces new products and risks.

[1] SOUND PRACTICES GUIDANCE FOR NETWORK INFORMATION SECURITY

The FRB took a step at addressing the risks associated with computer networks at financial institutions on December 4, 1997, when it issued a paper containing guidelines for sound banking practices pertaining to information security.[129] The key points of the FRB paper are:[130]

- *A strong information security program is essential.* A strong comprehensive information security program establishes the necessary structure and accountability to manage risks, and fosters awareness throughout the organization that information security is an important cultural value. A strong information security program includes active board and management oversight, policies and procedures, measurement and monitoring systems, and ongoing internal controls. Boards of directors and senior management are responsible for ensuring that spending on information security is appropriate to the magnitude and nature of the risks.

- *Internal network security issues need special attention.* The vulnerabilities of internal networks may be less obvious to banking organizations than networks connected to the Internet, yet these internal systems are vulnerable to a wide variety of intrusion tactics. Internal attacks are potentially the most damaging because an institution's personnel, which can include consultants as well as employees, may have authorized access to critical computing resources.

- *Confidential information needs to be encrypted.* The confidentiality of data transmitted over public networks is vulnerable to risks in addition to those identified for internal networks. "Dedicated" or "leased" lines may provide an inappropriate sense of security. These lines use the infrastructure of public networks and therefore are vulnerable to the same attacks as the public networks themselves.

- *Internet connections need to be carefully constructed.* An institution's Internet site is exposed to worldwide attack. As more products and services are offered via the Internet, the opportunities for attack increase. The greatest risk is associated with sites that have a path to the institution's internal

---

[128] *Risk Assessment Hearing, supra* note 124, 82 FED. RESERVE BULL. at 401.

[129] *Sound Practices Guidance for Information Security for Networks*, FRB SR 97-32 (SUP) (Dec. 4, 1997).

[130] Letter of Richard Spillenkothen, Director of the Division of Banking Supervision and Regulation, to the Officer in Charge of Supervision at each Federal Reserve Bank, Appropriate Supervisory Personnel, and All Domestic and Foreign Banking Organizations Regulated by the FRB at 2-3 (Dec. 4, 1997).

network, thereby providing unauthorized individuals with a link, however convoluted, to attack internal networks and gain access to an institution's information assets.

- *The backgrounds of employees in especially sensitive positions need to be checked.* Information technology personnel such as systems administrators, telecommunications support staff, systems programmers and others may have access to sensitive information, detailed knowledge about security methods and procedures, or both. Therefore, it is important to subject them to rigorous background checks.

- *Management must decide on benefits and costs.* Protecting networks to minimize financial, operational, reputational, and legal risks can require the dedication of significant resources. Senior management is responsible for evaluating the costs and benefits of alternative security measures and deciding the best allocation of the institution's resources.

The FRB has stated that guidance provided by the paper does not constitute a regulation and should not be interpreted as such.[131] In the absence of laws, regulations, or case law, however, agency guidelines are likely to be consulted in circumstances where questions arise regarding what constitutes sound banking practices in the area of computer system security. The FRB's paper, along with other agency pronouncements, are likely to play a role in establishing the standard of care against which the conduct of a financial institution and its officers will be measured.

§ 7.06   CONSUMER PROTECTION

[1]   APPLICATION OF REGULATION E TO STORED VALUE PRODUCTS

An important regulatory issue in the introduction of electronic banking and commerce in the United States has been the question of how the FRB's consumer protection regulation, Regulation E, which implements the EFTA, would be applied to stored value cards and similar products.[132] Industry representatives have consistently stated that the manner in which Regulation E applies to these products could dramatically influence the way in which they are developed and marketed.[133] This section traces the administrative and congressional efforts to adapt the EFTA and Regulation E to address electronic banking and commerce.

[a] Initial FRB Proposal. In March 1994, the FRB issued a proposal concerning Regulation E designed to simplify the language and format of the regulation and its staff commentary, to delete obsolete provisions, and

---

[131] FRB SR 97-32, *supra* note 129, at 1.

[132] Regulation E and the EFTA are discussed in greater detail in Chapter 4.

[133] *See Treasury Report Explores Approaches to Regulating Electronic Money,* BANKING POL'Y REP., Dec. 15, 1997, at 4; Jaret Seiberg, *Fed: Consumer Rules Shouldn't Be Imposed On Stored-Value Cards*, AM. BANKER, Apr. 3, 1997, at 3.

to reduce regulatory burdens on financial institutions.[134] The proposal discussed the FRB's position regarding the application of Regulation E to "smart cards," with the following statement:

> Questions have arisen about Regulation E coverage of smart cards. Generally, smart cards are plastic cards that have the capacity to either compute or communicate information. At one time, it was believed that smart card systems were not subject to Regulation E because no account existed within the definition of the act or regulation. With advances in smart card technology, that assumption is less clear. Increasingly more uses are available for smart cards. The FRB believes that smart cards are subject to Regulation E if the cards are used to access an account. A similar analysis might be applied to value-added or prepaid cards.[135]

The FRB adopted its proposed revisions to Regulation E as a final rule on May 2, 1996.[136] At the same time, the FRB issued a proposal specifically addressing Regulation E's application to stored value products. The proposal is discussed in Section 7.06[3].

[2] RELATED LEGISLATIVE ACTIVITY

On September 25, 1995, Senator Robert F. Bennett, (R-UT), introduced S. 1270 to provide an exemption for stored value cards ("SVCs") from coverage under the EFTA and Regulation E.[137] S. 1270 would, quite simply, have exempted all consumer transactions that occur after the issuance of a stored value card from the provisions of the EFTA and Regulation E. The bill provided that the EFTA's definition of "accepted card or other means of access" would not apply to "any card, device or computer that may be used by a person to pay for a transaction though the use of value stored on, or assigned to, that card device or computer." The bill would also have amended the EFTA's definition of "account" in a similar fashion. Use of a stored value card by a person to pay for a transaction would thus not trigger an electronic fund transfer within the meaning of EFTA. Neither the EFTA nor Regulation E's consumer protections would apply to the use of such an instrument to store and transmit value. The Senate considered an identical provision to the exemption contained in S. 1270 again in December 1995, as Section 601 of S. 650.[138] Neither bill was ultimately passed by the Senate.

In July 1995, Representative James A. Leach (R-IA) proposed H.R. 1858, which included a similar exemption under which stored value card transactions would be exempt from the EFTA and Regulation E. The bill included an exception for those instances, presumably at the initial purchase or issuance of such a

---

[134] Electronic Fund Transfers (Regulation E), 59 Fed. Reg. 10,684 (1994) (to be codified at 12 C.F.R. pt. 205) (proposed Mar. 7, 1994).

[135] *Id*. at 10,685.

[136] Electronic Fund Transfers (Regulation E), 61 Fed. Reg. 19,662 (1996) (codified at 12 C.F.R. § 205.1-.15) [hereinafter Reg. E Final Rule].

[137] Electronic Fund Transfer Act; Stored Value Cards, S. 1270, 104th Cong. (1995).

[138] Economic Growth and Regulatory Paperwork Reduction Act, S. 650, § 601, 104th Cong. (1995).

card to a consumer, where the SVC was "actually used to access an account" to effect transfers of value.[139] The proposed legislation would also have amended the EFTA's definition of "accepted card or other means of access" by providing that:

> such term does not include a card, device, or computer that a person may use to pay for transactions through the use of value stored on, or assigned to, the card device or computer itself, except for those transactions where such card, device or computer is actually used to access an account to effect such transaction.[140]

H.R. 1858 also included a similar amendment to the EFTA's definition of "account."[141] Like S. 1270, H.R. 1858 sought to provide a broad exemption for SVCs from the EFTA and Regulation E. The bill did not exclude from coverage those transactions that loaded or reloaded value onto card systems, because such transactions involve the "actual" access to a consumer's account for purposes of the EFTA. Accordingly, H.R. 1858 would have applied the consumer protections of the EFTA at the initial stage of purchase or issuance of SVCs, when the "value" is first embedded on such cards and would have also subjected later transactions that added additional or replacement value onto their SVCs to the EFTA's protections. As with the Senate version, House bill to exempt SVCs from the EFTA was not ultimately enacted.

[3]   FRB PROPOSAL CONCERNING REGULATION E'S APPLICATION TO STORED VALUE PRODUCTS

Consumers are exposed to a variety of risks when using electronic retail payment and transfer systems, including the risk of loss, unauthorized access or use by a third party, and payment processing errors. One purpose of the EFTA, as implemented by Regulation E, is to protect consumers from risks associated with electronic payments systems. The EFTA achieves this objective by imposing disclosure, recordkeeping, and error resolution requirements on providers of EFT services. Regulation E applies only to electronic fund transfers that authorize a financial institution to debit or credit a consumer's demand deposit, savings, or other asset account.[142] The EFTA provides the FRB with the authority to adjust Regulation E's coverage to accommodate new electronic products and services.

---

[139] *See* Financial Institutions Regulatory Relief Act of 1995, H.R. 1858 § 143, 104th Cong., H.R. REP. NO. 104-193 (1995). Representative Leach (R-IA), Chairman of the House Committee on Banking and Financial Services, has introduced a variety of regulatory and other reforms in the banking law field, as well as the regulation of the securities markets. The stored value card exemptive provision was first proposed by Congressman Leach on March 30, 1995, in Section 135 of H.R. 1362, Representative Leach's first version of the Financial Institutions Regulatory Relief Act of 1995. Indeed, this proposed amendment to EFTA was contained in numerous versions of Representative Leach's legislative efforts in the 104th Congress to enhance and streamline the regulation of the financial services industry. *See also* Financial Services Competitiveness and Regulatory Relief Act of 1995, H.R. 2158 § 107, 104th Cong. (1995); Financial Services Competitiveness and Regulatory Relief Act of 1995, H.R. 2520 § 443, 104th Cong. (1995); Federal Deposit Insurance Funds and Regulatory Relief Act of 1996, H.R. 3567 § 343, 104th Cong. (1996).

[140] H.R. REP. NO.104-193, *supra* note 139, § 143(a), at 63.

[141] *Id.*

[142] 12 C.F.R. § 205.3(a).

On May 2, 1996, the FRB took an important step in the development of a legal framework for the use of electronic financial products and services ("EFS") in the United States by issuing proposed amendments to Regulation E ("SVC Proposal").[143] The SVC Proposal, addressed a number of topics, including the treatment of stored value cards under Regulation E, the use of electronic means for providing disclosures and other documentation for home banking services, and error resolution procedures for electronic accounts.

[a] Stored Value and Electronic Fund Transfer Rules. In what the FRB staff described as a "lighthanded" approach, the FRB proposed to largely exempt off-line and low denomination stored value products from the requirements of Regulation E. According to remarks by a FRB member, the rationale for the SVC Proposal is that most electronic money and smart card products involve relatively small amounts of money and, thus, do not pose inordinate risks to consumers.[144] Noting the increased interest of the financial services industry in adopting stored value technologies, the FRB indicated in its SVC Proposal that the question of whether stored value systems were covered by the EFTA and Regulation E depends upon whether a stored value transaction involves an electronic fund transfer ("EFT") from a consumer's asset account.[145] The FRB cites the legislative history of the EFTA,[146] and Section 904(d) of EFTA itself,[147] to support its discretion to determine the scope of EFTA's coverage in regard to new products such as stored value systems.

Representing a first cut at a complex issue, the SVC Proposal places stored value products into three general categories, depending upon the particular architecture and function of the product: (1) "off-line unaccountable" systems; (2) "off-line accountable" systems; and (3) "online" systems. These three categories all involve transactions in which value "stored" on a card is drawn down to purchase goods and services or to transfer value.[148] Under the SVC Proposal, products in each category would be subject to different regulatory treatment under Regulation E. The SVC Proposal also distinguishes between the treatment given to cards that have a maximum value of $100 or less at any given time, and those that have a value exceeding $100.

---

[143] Electronic Fund Transfers (Regulation E), 61 Fed. Reg. 19,696 (1996) (to be codified at 12 C.F.R. pt. 205) (proposed May 2, 1996) [hereinafter SVC Proposal].

[144] Edward J. Kelley, Jr., Governor, Board of Governors of the Federal Reserve System, Remarks before the Digital Commerce Conference, Washington, D.C. (May 6, 1996).

[145] SVC Proposal, 61 Fed. Reg. at 19,698.

[146] The Senate Banking Committee report on the EFTA stated that "the definitions of 'financial institution' and 'account' are deliberately broad so as to assure that all persons who offer equivalent EFT services involving any type of asset account are subject to the same standards and consumers owning such accounts are assured of uniform protection." *See* S. REP. NO. 95-915, at 9, *reprinted in* 1978 U.S.C.C.A.N. 9403, 9411; *see also* SVC Proposal, 61 Fed. Reg. at 19,699.

[147] Section 904(d) of the EFTA provides that if EFT services "are made available to consumers by a person other than a financial institution holding a consumer's account, the Board shall by regulation assure that the disclosures, protections, responsibilities and remedies created by this title are made applicable to such persons and services." *See* 15 U.S.C. § 1693b; *see also* SVC Proposal, 61 Fed. Reg. at 19,699.

[148] These three categories do not match the categories established by the FDIC in General Counsel's Opinion No. 8. The divergence among the federal bank regulators may reflect the differences in the statutes they administer, or may be the product of the multiple conceptual ways to view stored value.

[*i*] *Off-line Unaccountable Systems.* "Off-line unaccountable" systems are systems where the record of value is maintained only on the card itself and not at the financial institution or a central database. Common examples of these systems are transit farecards and library copier cards. Transaction data involving a particular card is recorded on the card and captured at merchant terminals. However, the merchant terminals transmit only the aggregate amount of transactions for a specific time period (likely on a daily basis) to the financial institution or other entity.

According to the FRB, the lack of a centrally maintained, ongoing record of individual card balances in "off-line unaccountable" systems makes it difficult to conclude that an "account" exists with regard to such a product for purposes of Regulation E.[149] The FRB also noted that such "off-line unaccountable" systems currently involve small dollar amounts and single-use payments. Therefore, this type of product would not be covered by Regulation E, although the FRB solicited comment on whether coverage of these systems, for very limited requirements such as initial disclosures, would be advisable.[150] The FRB also noted that if there are concerns about consumer protections, it does have the ability to bring such "off-line unaccountable" systems within the coverage of the EFTA, to a limited extent, such as by requiring initial disclosures, without much compliance, difficulty, or cost.[151]

[*ii*] *Off-line Accountable Systems.* In an "off-line accountable" system, the balance of funds available on the stored value card is recorded not only on the card, but is also maintained at a financial institution or other location. Transactions are not authorized online, instead transaction data is periodically transmitted to and maintained by a data facility.[152] The distinction between "accountable" and "unaccountable" systems is not made by defining these terms in the proposed regulation. Rather, it is made by including in the definition of "off-line stored value account" a requirement that the balance of funds be maintained on a separate database, as well as the card.[153] As a result, if the balance is not maintained on a separate database, the card does not fall within the definition of an off-line stored value account.[154]

The FRB proposed to treat "off-line accountable" systems as involving an account for purposes of Regulation E. In characterizing the nature of this arrangement, the FRB offered the following observation that may be significant to the future legal treatment of stored value products:

> As in the case of the traditional consumer deposit account accessed by a debit card, in
> these stored value card systems, a consumer has the right to draw upon funds held by an

---

[149] SVC Proposal, 61 Fed. Reg. at 19,701-02.

[150] *Id.* at 19,702.

[151] *Id.* at 19,701.

[152] Put more simply, off-line unaccountable systems are those in which a party cannot be identified or there are no records of the transaction maintained at a central database. Off-line accountable systems are those in which the cardholder can be identified and records of all transactions will provide regulators, and law-enforcement, with an audit trail. *See* David B. Lipkin, *The Development of Smart Cards, An Electronic Substitute for Cash, Raises a Host of Regulatory Issues that the Federal Reserve Board is Just Beginning to Address,* NAT'L L.J., June 10, 1996, at B6.

[153] SVC Proposal, 61 Fed. Reg. at 19,704 (to be codified at 12 C.F.R. § 205.16(b)(1)) (proposed definition of "off-line stored value account").

[154] *See* Barbara E. Mathews, *Reg. E and Stored Value Cards: Fed Is On the Right Track,* BANKING POL'Y REP., July 15, 1996, at 4.

institution. The maintenance of a record of value and of transactions for a given card . . . so that transactions are traceable to the individual card . . . strongly parallels the functioning of a deposit account. The Board believes that the facts support a finding that such systems involve an account for purposes of the EFTA.[155]

Although "off-line accountable" systems would not be exempt from Regulation E under the SVC Proposal, such systems would not be subject to the provisions restricting unsolicited issuance of cards, requiring notification of changes in terms, requiring transaction receipts and periodic statements, limiting consumer liability for unauthorized transfers, or establishing error resolution procedures.[156] Issuers of these types of cards would be subject to a modified version of the general Regulation E initial disclosure requirement.[157] They would be required to provide only initial disclosures regarding only those terms and conditions that the FRB considered relevant for such cards, including disclosure of consumer liability for unauthorized transfer, the types of transfers available, transaction charges, if any, and available error resolution procedures.[158] At the same time, the SVC Proposal would exempt from all provisions of Regulation E, including the modified initial disclosure requirement, off-line accountable cards that are limited to a maximum value of $100 at a given time.[159]

[iii] *Online Systems.* The SVC Proposal defines an online system as one where the balance is maintained on a separate database maintained at the financial institution or data facility and is not recorded on the card itself. Further, the transactions are authorized by means of online communication similar to the function of a debit card. Under these systems, a transaction is authorized through online communication with a data facility, where the transaction data is stored. Unlike a debit card, the value associated with the card is an amount chosen by the cardholder rather than the balance in a deposit account, and the value associated with the card is accessible only by using the card, rather than through other means such as check or telephone transfer.

The SVC Proposal treats "online" systems as "accounts" subject to Regulation E. Under the SVC Proposal, these systems would be subject to a greater degree of coverage under Regulation E. Specifically, online systems would be subject to the restriction on unsolicited issuance, a modified version of the general requirement for initial disclosures, the limitations on consumer liability for unauthorized transactions, and to a modified obligation in regard to periodic statements.[160] They would be exempt from the requirement for notice of a change in terms for receipts or periodic statements and for error resolution procedures.[161] As with low value off-line accountable cards, online access cards would be exempt from all provisions of Regulation E, provided their maximum value was limited to $100 at any given time.[162]

---

[155] SVC Proposal, 61 Fed. Reg. at 19,699.

[156] *Id.* at 19,699-01.

[157] *See* 12 C.F.R. § 205.7.

[158] SVC Proposal, 61 Fed. Reg. at 19,700.

[159] *Id.* at 19,701.

[160] *Id.* at 19,702-03.

[161] *Id.* at 19,702.

[162] *Id.* at 19,703.

[b] Electronic Disclosure and Documentation. The SVC Proposal, in the context of home banking and other financial services, responded to financial institution inquiries regarding the circumstances under which written disclosures, such as initial disclosures under Section 205.7 and periodic statements under Section 205.9, may be provided to consumers by electronic means.[163] In this regard, the SVC Proposal defined an "electronic communication" as an "electronically transmitted text message between a financial institution and a consumer's home computer or other electronic device possessed by the consumer."[164] The SVC Proposal, however, would limit the term "electronic communication" to those communications in a form that can be displayed as visual text, such as on a computer monitor or screen phone.[165] Recognizing that electronic documents that are produced, stored, or communicated by computer are generally considered to be "in writing," the FRB proposed that Regulation E be amended to allow electronic communication to satisfy the written communication requirements of Regulation E, subject to a consumer's right to receive paper-based information upon request within one year.[166] The FRB requested comment on the extent to which electronic communication should be permitted to substitute for paper disclosures and other required paper messages for EFT services.[167] The issue of the utilization of electronic communications is a separable issue from the broader question of the treatment of various types of stored value products and one that the FRB should be able to act on in the near future even if it needs more time to study the other issues involved with stored value.

[c] Computer-Network Payment Products. Finally, as part of its SVC Proposal, the FRB also took note of the increasing interest in systems that would allow for payments to be made over computer networks, including the Internet. The FRB requested comment on how Internet and other computer-network based payment products should be treated for purposes of Regulation E.[168] Noting the differences in various proposed network payment systems, the FRB concluded that "the same principles should apply to network payment products as to stored value card products in analyzing coverage under Regulation E."[169] The FRB noted that some of these network payment products involve online access to consumer accounts at financial institutions and, accordingly, would be fully subject to Regulation E. On the other hand, the FRB commented that other products may involve various procedures for authorizing and carrying out transactions, and may or may not be subject to Regulation E.

---

[163] *Id.* at 19,704-05.

[164] *Id.* at 19,696.

[165] *Id.*

[166] *Id.* at 19,697.

[167] *Id.* at 19,696-97.

[168] *Id.* at 19,703.

[169] *Id.*

[d] **Reaction to the SVC Proposal.** The FRB's proposal on the application of Regulation E to stored value cards generated a substantial amount of commentary from legal commentators and industry members.[170] It has been criticized for distinguishing between "online" and "off-line" systems in a manner that would subject substantially similar activities to different regulatory treatment in a manner that is arguably not related to protecting consumer interests.[171] It has also been noted that developing technologies may make it possible for issuers to blend "off-line" and "online" characteristics in a single stored value product, making it difficult and confusing for consumers, regulators and courts to determine which category applies to the product. Some critics have argued that the FRB's SVC Proposal improperly creates an unlevel playing field between developing systems by imposing the heaviest regulation on online stored value systems, which arguably provide a higher level of benefits and protections to consumers than those offered by off-line systems. As a consequence, online systems may be disfavored by companies developing stored value products and merchants and other parties to whom they are trying to market such systems. Some believe that the FRB should consider whether stored value products should be regulated at all under Regulation E, in light of its historical interpretation not to apply Regulation E to pre-paid services, such as subway tokens, traveler's checks and gift certificates.

§ 7.07   THE FRB STORED-VALUE REPORT

Although Congress did not adopt the proposals to amend the EFTA to largely exempt stored value from its coverage, it did take action regarding the FRB's proposed rulemaking. Section 2601(c) of the Economic Growth and Regulatory Paperwork Reduction Act of 1996 ("EGRPA")[172] barred the FRB from taking final action on the SVC Proposal for a period of either three months from the date on which the FRB delivered a report on the options in regard to the regulation of stored value to Congress, or nine months from the date of enactment of the EGRPA, September 30, 1996.[173] EGRPA specifically directed the FRB to determine whether provisions of the EFTA could be applied to electronic stored value ("SV") products "without adversely affecting the cost, development, and operation of such products."[174] The EGRPA also directed the FRB to consider whether there

---

[170] Commentary on the FRB's SVC Proposal includes: Brian Nixon, *E-Cash*, AMERICA'S COMMUNITY BANKER, June 1996, at 34; David B. Lipkin, *The Development of Smart Cards, An Electronic Substitute for Cash, Raises a Host of Regulatory Issues that the Federal Reserve Board is Just Beginning to Address*, NAT'L L.J., June 10, 1996, at B6; *Stored Value Issuers Brace for a Reg. E. Ruling*, DEBIT CARD NEWS, July 16, 1996; Barbara E. Mathews, *Reg. E and Stored Value Cards: Fed Is On the Right Track*, BANKING POL'Y REP., July 15, 1996, at 4; Sharon B. Heaton, Comment: *The Perils of the Fed's Approach to Stored Value*, AM. BANKER, Apr. 29, 1996, at 18; Ira H. Parker, Comment: *Fed's Stored Value Proposal is a Blow to Card Industry*, AM. BANKER, Apr. 17, 1996, at 3; Niles S. Campbell, *Fed Proposes Stored-Value Card Rules; Regulation E to Cover New Technology*, 66 Banking Rep. 498 (BNA) (Mar. 25, 1996).

[171] The FDIC's General Counsel's Opinion No. 8 on stored value products utilizes four entirely different categories to identify the treatment of stored value products under the Federal Deposit Insurance Act ("FDIA"). These categories are (i) bank primary –customer account systems; (ii) bank primary –reserve systems; (iii) bank secondary –advance systems; and (iv) bank secondary – pre-acquisition systems. The FDIC notes that its use of different categories from those used by the FRB is not intended as a criticism or rejection of the FRB's classification system, but rather indicates the different issues involved in evaluating whether or not stored value obligations are "deposits" for purposes of the FDIA. *See* Stored Value Cards and Other Electronic Payment Systems, 61 Fed. Reg. 40,494, 40,495 (notice Aug. 2, 1996).

[172] Omnibus Consolidated Appropriations Act, 1997, Pub. L. No. 104-208, § 2601, 1996 U.S.C.C.A.N. (110 Stat.) 3009-469 [hereinafter EGRPA].

[173] EGRPA § 2601(c), (110 Stat.) 3009-469.

[174] *Id.*

are alternatives to regulation that are capable of achieving the consumer protection objectives of the EFTA and Regulation E.[175]

The FRB issued its *Report to Congress on the Application of the Electronic Funds Act to Electronic Stored-Value Products* ("Stored-Value Report") on April 2, 1997.[176] The Stored-Value Report begins with an intriguing discussion of the relationship between technological progress and social welfare. It then turns to an examination of the impact of technological developments on the financial services industry.

The Stored-Value Report then discusses the current status of SV products. In that regard, the Stored-Value report finds that both the costs of installing the necessary infrastructure to implement SV systems, and the likely product acceptance, are highly uncertain at this stage, particularly for general purpose SV cards. The Stored-Value Report next examines who should bear the risks of using SV products and the costs and benefits of various regulatory approaches to SV products. The FRB concludes, among other things, that full application of Regulation E to SV products would "likely impose substantial operating and opportunity costs of compliance." Having drawn that conclusion, the FRB analyzed the effects of four different approaches for the selective application of Regulation E to SV products:

(i)   requiring only initial disclosure of information concerning SV product characteristics;

(ii)   uniformly applying a subset of critical Regulation E provisions to all SV products;

(iii)   variably applying selected Regulation E provisions on the basis of product usage or characteristics; or

(iv)   variably applying selected Regulation E provisions on the basis of the underlying technology's ability to comply with regulatory requirements.

The Stored-Value Report presents a number of alternatives to such applications of Regulation E. These include: (i) relying on a combination of the existing legal framework and market incentives in place of regulation;[177] (ii) relying on government-issued policy statements and government-sponsored consumer education programs about SV products;[178] and (iii) passing new federal or state legislation to address SV products and consumer concerns.[179] The Stored-Value Report does not, however, endorse or recommend any specific

---

[175] EGRPA § 2601(a)(2), (110 Stat.) 3009-469.

[176] BOARD OF GOVERNORS OF THE FEDERAL RESERVE SYSTEM, REPORT TO THE CONGRESS ON THE APPLICATION OF THE ELECTRONIC FUND TRANSFER ACT TO ELECTRONIC STORED-VALUE PRODUCTS, Mar. 1997, at 1 [hereinafter Stored-Value Report]. For purposes of the Stored-Value Report, the FRB defined SV products as retail payment products intended primarily for consumer payments with some or all of the following characteristics: (i) it is a card or other device that electronically stores or provides access to a specific amount of funds available for payment to others; (ii) it is the only means of routine access to the funds; and (iii) the issuer does not record the funds stored on the device as an account in the name of, or credited to, the holder. *Id.* at 20.

[177] *Id.* at 65-69.

[178] *Id.* at 70-73.

[179] *Id.* at 74-75.

course of action. The Report appears to underscore that, at this stage of SV product development and consumer usage, there is no ideal solution for balancing the law, technology, and consumer expectations.

It seems likely that the FRB's view is influenced by the initial perception that SV alone will not be the engine that drives the smart card market. In this regard, it is natural for regulators to delay the public articulation of policies and procedures until the market has had a fair chance to mature and define its digital products and their optimal uses.

The Stored-Value Report's other major findings and conclusions include the following:

- The wide variety of existing and planned SV products makes it unlikely that a single set of consumer protections would be appropriate for all SV products.

- SV products, if successful, will create an additional payment option that will compete with payment alternatives already well-established among both consumers and merchants.

- SV products have the potential to increase the efficiency and security of the retail payment system, but are not likely to be widely accepted for some time.

- In general, SV products give rise to the same types (but potentially differing degrees) of risk that are present in other methods of retail payments including, risk of loss, unauthorized use, processing errors, dishonor, payment mechanism failure, and unauthorized use of consumer-specific payment information.

- Certain SV products fall within the scope of the EFTA and Regulation E; other types of SV products may not, however, because they do not involve EFTs from consumer asset accounts.

- While early government regulation of SV products may accelerate SV product development by removing regulatory uncertainties, it could also cause higher regulatory costs. Waiting too long to regulate SV products on the other hand could prove costly because issuers might be forced to adapt existing regulatory requirements to the emerging products.

- Given the limited experience with SV products to date, it is difficult to assess the extent to which the benefits to consumers from the application of any particular Regulation E provision might outweigh the corresponding costs of compliance.

- Even partial application of Regulation E's requirements to SV products could impede development of the new payment products, and thereby adversely influence the payment options available to market participants in the future.

- The existing legal framework provides considerable incentives for providers of SV products to avoid unconscionable or unfair terms and to make adequate disclosures about SV products.[180]

By providing a report that reads as a fair review of the full range of possibilities for arriving at the appropriate governmental role in regard to SV products, the FRB has clearly responded to Congress' directive. At the same time, the FRB used the report as a vehicle to make the case for its SVC Proposal.

---

[180] *Id.* at 75.

CHAPTER 8

FEDERAL DEPOSIT INSURANCE CORPORATION'S PERSPECTIVE ON ELECTRONIC FINANCIAL PRODUCTS AND SERVICES

§ 8.01   INTRODUCTION

The Federal Deposit Insurance Corporation ("FDIC") is best known for its role as the provider of deposit insurance for the nation's banks and savings associations. In that capacity, the FDIC ultimately deals with all types of depository institutions — national banks, state member banks, state nonmember banks, and federal and state savings associations.

The FDIC, as a result of its role as insurer, has greater experience in analyzing the causes of depository institution failures than any of the other federal bank regulatory agencies. Due to this presumed expertise, the FDIC has increasingly been given the responsibility for guarding the financial system against risks that are likely to expose institutions to failure. For example, during the past decade Congress has given the FDIC: (i) authority to determine whether a state savings association may engage in activities not permissible for federal savings associations;[1] (ii) authority to determine whether a state bank may engage in activities not permissible for national banks;[2] (iii) backup authority to take enforcement action against any type of insured institution;[3] and (iv) authority to issue regulations regarding golden parachutes and indemnification agreements that are applicable to all insured institutions.[4]

Electronic banking and commerce will reconfigure the spectrum of risks to which banks must be sensitive. If bank managements' efforts to respond to new risks are inadequate or unsuccessful, the FDIC, as insurer, will

---

[1]   Financial Institution Reform, Recovery & Enforcement Act of 1989, Pub. L. No. 101-73, § 222, 1989 U.S.C.C.A.N. (103 Stat.) 183, 269 (codified as amended at 12 U.S.C. § 1831e) [hereinafter FIRREA].

[2]   Federal Deposit Insurance Corporation Improvement Act of 1991, Pub. L. No. 102-242, § 303, 1991 U.S.C.C.A.N. (105 Stat.) 2236, 2349 (codified as amended at 12 U.S.C. § 1831a) [hereinafter FDICIA].

[3]   FIRREA § 912, 1989 U.S.C.C.A.N. (103 Stat.) at 482 (codified as amended at 12 U.S.C. § 1818(t)).

[4]   Crime Control Act of 1990, Pub. L. No. 101-647, § 2523, 1990 U.S.C.C.A.N. (104 Stat.) 4789, 4868 (codified as amended at 12 U.S.C. § 1828(k)).

bear the ultimate loss. The FDIC has been in the forefront of the federal bank regulatory agencies in addressing the issues raised by electronic financial products and services ("EFS"). Its efforts in this regard include not only applying the statutes and regulations under FDIC jurisdiction to new electronic products, but also identifying and responding to the broad safety and soundness considerations that relate to EFS.

This Chapter reviews the FDIC's efforts to adapt to the emergence of EFS. Section 8.02 discusses the safety and soundness considerations associated with electronic value. Section 8.03 discusses the FDIC's application of deposit insurance to stored value products. Section 8.04 considers the role that private insurance may play in electronic value systems. Section 8.05 looks at the FDIC's actions in connection with Internet value transfer systems. Section 8.06 addresses the FDIC's evolving position regarding disclosures of FDIC insurance in Internet-based forums. Section 8.07 details the new safety and soundness examination procedures that address EFS. Finally, Section 8.08 discusses FDIC warnings regarding uninsured Internet banks.

§ 8.02   ELECTRONIC VALUE AND DEPOSITORY INSTITUTION SAFETY AND SOUNDNESS

Emerging forms of electronic value raise the specter of potential depository institution failures as a result of the use of fraudulent, but apparently valid, stored value cards or computer-based electronic value products.[5] It is important to recognize that the risks associated with electronic value are qualitatively and quantitatively different from the types of risks that banks have previously faced; for example, banks routinely cope with the risks posed by stolen or forged checks. Such risks are inherently limited because, among other things, checks draw on the amounts held in a particular depositor's account and the bank has the opportunity to prevent unauthorized access to a depositor's funds. Similarly, risks associated with credit cards can be contained by a variety of techniques, including authorization limits and purchaser verification.

Electronic value that is issued by a bank presents an entirely different type of risk. Electronic value is the equivalent of a direct claim on the general assets of the bank rather than a claim on the individual account balance of a particular depositor. The ability to create illegitimate electronic value (presumably in unlimited amounts), that mimics legitimate electronic value is the ability to plunge a bank into insolvency. When a bank receives cash in exchange for issuing electronic value, the asset and liability sides of its balance sheet both increase in equal (or nearly equal) amounts. On the other hand, placing illegitimate electronic value in circulation would effectively increase the liability side of the bank's balance sheet, while the asset side of the balance sheet remains unchanged. In that direction lies insolvency.

Illegitimate electronic value arguably need not even be placed into circulation to produce harmful effects. The mere existence of a credible threat that such illegitimate value exists could be enough. Consider the choices

---

[5]   *See* CONGRESSIONAL BUDGET OFFICE, EMERGING ELECTRONIC METHODS FOR MAKING RETAIL PAYMENTS 40-41 (June 1996) [hereinafter CBO STUDY]. Similarly, to the extent that banks participate in the issuance and distribution of stored value, they may be subject to the operational and reputational risks that will arise if the issuer of a stored value system fails. *See also* Thomas P. Vartanian, *Doing Business on the Net Sure to Change Risk Profiles*, AM. BANKER – FUTURE BANKING, Feb. 18, 1997, at 18A.

that a bank that has issued electronic value would face if it believes that its electronic value system has been compromised. Ideally the bank would be able to take countermeasures that would prevent or contain the use of the illegitimate electronic value. Such countermeasures, however, may not be available or effective; and the bank may be faced with two quite unpalatable choices.

The bank could take steps to prevent further use of the electronic value issued by the bank. Such a move, though intended to protect the bank from fraudulent claims, would at the same time repudiate the legitimate electronic value in the hands of bona fide customers. Complicating such a scenario is the possibility that much of the electronic value will no longer be in the hands of the initial party to whom it was legitimately issued. There may be little or no way to show whether downstream parties had knowingly acquired illegitimate electronic value. As a consequence of preventing further transfers of outstanding electronic value, banks could expect to face a wide range of claims from parties whose expectations have been disappointed. Moreover, given that customer confidence and market credibility are probably the most important assets a bank has, an announcement that a bank is "disavowing" to some extent its own obligations is likely to create a serious crisis for the institution.

The bank could also make the decision that it will honor all the stored value that appears to have been issued by it, regardless of whether it is actually legitimate or illegitimate. Several disturbing scenarios could arise as a result of this decision. The bank's capital could be quickly wiped out by a flood of fraudulent but undetectable claims, forcing the bank into receivership. Alternatively, if the bank suspected that it was receiving illegitimate claims, the bank would treat this as criminal activity and file a suspicious activity report. At this point, the bank, its federal bank regulatory agency, and law enforcement officials would have a number of strategic choices in responding to the problem. They could decide to allow the bank to continue issuing and processing stored value, without any public announcement of the apparent breach or compromise of the integrity of the bank's stored value system, with the hope that they will be able to apprehend the responsible parties and contain the extent of the penetration. This approach, however, would put the bank and the government in a difficult position from a wide range of legal perspectives. New stored value purchasers would be exchanging their funds for stored value that the bank and the government know is not FDIC-insured and was issued by a bank threatened by imminent failure. Taking another approach, the bank could also announce that it will no longer issue stored value, though this would likely raise questions in the banking community and among the public as to the financial condition of the institution and perhaps cause a run on the institution. As these scenarios illustrate, banks that issue stored value face potentially catastrophic risks if the stored value system is compromised. The implications of a problem faced by a single institution for the broader banking system would depend, among other things, on the size and activities of the bank in question, and how its stored value products interact with other financial system participants.

The issuer of stored value may not be a bank; it may be a nonbank entity, perhaps one owned by a consortium of banks. Banks, including investors in the nonbank entity, are likely to be retail distributors of the stored value issued by the nonbank entity. Stored value issued in such a system will likely flow among the retailing banks, consumers, and merchants. Though a compromise of nonbank issued stored value would not directly implicate the assets of the banks, it would still likely have an adverse impact on banks. Banks investing in the nonbank issuer could suffer the loss of their investment. Perhaps more significantly, parties who bought stored value from a bank, particularly where the bank's name appears on the stored value card, may be surprised and disturbed to learn that the bank disavows any liability for the potentially valueless instrument. Alternatively, the bank may have undertaken an obligation to redeem stored value from its customers, thereby leaving it as the creditor of the nonbank issuer.

It is difficult to predict how the electronic value industry will develop. It is not hard, however, to predict that such electronic value systems will be an attractive target for a range of parties, such as hackers, organized crime, or a hostile foreign nation. Given the risks that may be presented by electronic value products, however hypothetical they may be, and the roles that insured depository institutions are likely to play, it is likely that the deposit insurance treatment of such instruments, and the risks that they present to depository institutions, are likely to remain under active consideration for some time.

Under extreme conditions, problems with electronic value systems may threaten one or more depository institutions, thereby placing additional risks on the deposit insurance fund.[6] In recognition of the new types of concerns presented by these systems, the FDIC has published new examination procedures to address the related safety and soundness concerns.[7]

§ 8.03   DEPOSIT INSURANCE FOR STORED VALUE PRODUCTS

Insured depository institutions are increasingly utilizing technology to offer customers new retail payment products, including a variety of stored value products. These emerging forms of electronic value raise a range of issues with regard to the interpretation and application of the Federal Deposit Insurance Act ("FDIA")[8] and the FDIC's regulations thereunder.[9] At a basic level, it is necessary to determine whether the value underlying stored value products fits within the statutory definition of "deposit."[10] This will depend upon a number of

---

[6]   *See* CBO Study, *supra* note 5, at 41. The undetected counterfeiting of stored value cards that results in ballooning issuer liabilities is known as "spawning." For additional discussion of actual and potential spawning scenarios, see FRIED, FRANK, HARRIS, SHRIVER & JACOBSON ET AL., THE MANAGEMENT OF RISKS CREATED BY INTERNET-INITIATED VALUE TRANSFERS 39-40 (1997) (a report prepared for the National Automated Clearing House Association). *See also National Security Agency Report Raises Systemic Security Issues Related to Anonymous Electronic Money,* 21ST CENTURY BANKING ALERT® No. 96-10-17, Oct. 17, 1996; *Security in Electronic Money Systems Under Scrutiny,* 21ST CENTURY BANKING ALERT® No. 96-10-8, Oct. 8, 1996, *available at* <http://www.ffhsj.com>.

[7]   Electronic Banking Safety and Soundness Examination Procedures (Feb. 1997). *See* Stored Value Cards and Other Electronic Payment Systems, 61 Fed. Reg. 40,494 (1996) [hereinafter SVC Notice]. In the SVC Notice, the FDIC stated that "[t]he emergence of stored value cards and other electronic payment systems raises certain safety and soundness concerns for depository institutions and regulators. For example, institutions must take steps to ensure that the stored value or similar system in which they are participating has adequate safeguards to prevent counterfeiting or other fraudulent activities which could harm the institution, its customers, or other participants in the system." SVC Notice, 61 Fed. Reg. at 40,497.

[8]   12 U.S.C. §§ 1811-35a.

[9]   12 C.F.R. pts. 303-67. *See also* General Counsel's Opinion No. 8; Stored Value Cards, 61 Fed. Reg. 40,490 (1996). For a description of stored value products and an analysis of how existing commercial laws might apply to their use, see Task Force on Stored-Value Cards, Am. Bar Assn., *A Commercial Lawyer's Take on the Electronic Purse: An Analysis of Commercial Law Issues Associated with Stored Value Cards and Electronic Money,* 52 BUS. LAW. 653 (1997).

[10]   12 U.S.C. § 1813(l).

factors including: (i) the type and design of the card, computer, or other architecture used; and (ii) the availability and adequacy of the card or other storage device to store sufficient information to identify an account, an account-holder, and the nature of any fiduciary or deposit relationship between the stored value holder and the issuer of the stored value obligation.[11] Whether deposit insurance covers the new forms of electronic payment is an important consideration in the design of such products. It can also ultimately have a significant impact on depositors and other purchasers and issuers of stored value products, and ultimately on the entire financial system.

[1]   STATUTORY CRITERIA OF DEPOSITS

Under the FDIA, the term "deposit" has a five-part definition. The most commonly referred to definition is provided in 12 U.S.C. § 1813(l)(1), which states, in part, that a deposit includes:

> [T]he unpaid balance of money or its equivalent received or held by a bank or savings association in the usual course of business and for which it has given or is obligated to give credit, either conditionally or unconditionally, to a commercial, checking, savings, time, or thrift account, or which is evidenced by its certificate of deposit, thrift certificate, investment certificate, certificate of indebtedness . . . or a check or draft drawn against a deposit account and certified by the bank or savings association, or a letter of credit or a traveler's check on which the bank or savings association is primarily liable.[12]

In interpreting Section 1813(l)(1), the Supreme Court, in *FDIC v. Philadelphia Gear Corp.,* imposed the requirement that a deposit of money or its equivalent be "hard earnings" that businesses and individuals have entrusted to banks.[13] In that regard, the Court found that a standby letter of credit backed by an unsecured promissory note does not fall within the meaning of Section 1813(l)(1) because the standby letter of credit was only a contingent obligation and did not represent "hard earnings."[14] Under this part of the definition, if money or its equivalent is collected by a depository institution in the "normal course" of its business of operating an electronic payments system, the insured depository institution may have a deposit liability, if the other provisions of applicable law are met.[15]

Several of the other prongs of the "deposit" definition may arguably be applicable to stored value card obligations. For example, Section 3(l) of the FDIA also defines the term "deposit" as:

---

[11]   *See* Sharon P. Sivertsen, *Legal and Regulatory Issues in Stored Value Card Technologies,* ELECTRONIC BANKING L. & COM. REP., May 1996, at 9-10.

[12]   12 U.S.C. § 1813(l)(1). An "insured deposit" is defined as "the net amount due to any depositor for deposits in an insured depository institution as determined under §§ 1817(i) and 1821(a) of this title." 12 U.S.C. § 1813(m)(1).

[13]   *FDIC v. Philadelphia Gear Corp.,* 476 U.S. 426, 435 (1986).

[14]   *Id.* at 440.

[15]   *See* Sivertsen, *supra* note 11, at 2-10.

- trust funds [as defined within the FDIA] received or held by such bank or savings association, whether held in the trust department or held or deposited in any other department;[16]

- money received or held by a bank or savings association, or the credit given for money or its equivalent received or held by a bank or savings association, in the usual course of business for a special or specific purpose regardless of the legal relationship thereby established, including without being limited to escrow funds, funds held as security for an obligation due to the bank or savings association or others (including funds held as dealers reserves) or for securities loaned by the bank or savings association, funds deposited by a debtor to meet maturing obligations, funds deposited as advance payment on subscription for United States Government securities, funds held for distribution or purchase of securities, funds held to meet its acceptances or letters of credit, and withheld taxes;[17]

- outstanding draft . . . cashier's check, money order, or other officer's check issued in the usual course of business for any purpose, including, but without being limited to those issued in payment for services, dividends, or purchases;[18] and

- such other obligations of a bank or savings association as the [FDIC] Board of Directors, after consultation with the Comptroller of the Currency, Director of the Office of Thrift Supervision, and the Board of Governors of the Federal Reserve System, shall find and prescribe by regulation to be deposit liabilities by general usage.[19]

Items that are deemed to be deposits for purposes of the FDIA are insured up to the applicable limits established by the FDIA.[20]

[2] JUDICIAL DECISIONS REGARDING DEPOSITS UNDER THE FDIA

It is important to recognize that the five paragraphs of 12 U.S.C. § 1813(*l*) define "deposit" in a far-reaching fashion and cover a number of relationships that may not be considered deposits by a lay person.[21] Under ordinary circumstances, statutory interpretation of the term "deposit" is left to the FDIC on a case-by-case basis.[22] Courts, however, have been called upon in a handful of decided cases to interpret the meaning of the

---

[16] 12 U.S.C. § 1813(*l*)(2).

[17] 12 U.S.C. § 1813(*l*)(3).

[18] 12 U.S.C. § 1813(*l*)(4). *See also FDIC v. McKnight*, 769 F.2d 658, 661-62 (10th Cir. 1985) (outstanding and unpaid cashier's check of failed institution converted by operation of law into "deposits" under Section 1813(*l*)(4) upon appointment of FDIC as receiver).

[19] 12 U.S.C. § 1813(*l*)(5).

[20] 12 U.S.C. § 1821(a)(1).

[21] *See FDIC v. Fedders Air Conditioning, USA, Inc.*, 35 F.3d 18, 22 (1st Cir. 1994) (dicta).

[22] *See FDIC v. European Am. Bank & Trust Co.*, 576 F. Supp. 950, 953 (S.D.N.Y. 1983).

"technical" provisions of 12 U.S.C. § 1813(*l*).[23] According to one district court, the statute confirms that Congress did not intend the definition "to comprise a set of rigid and unchanging categories."[24]

In *Philadelphia Gear*, the only Supreme Court decision specifically to address the meaning of the term "deposit" under 12 U.S.C. § 1813(*l*), the Court, agreeing with the FDIC's position, found that a standby letter of credit backed by a contingent promissory note did *not* qualify as a "deposit" under Section 1813(*l*)(1).[25] In that case, a bank customer had obtained a standby letter of credit for the benefit of the customer's supplier, Philadelphia Gear ("PG"), and executed an unsecured promissory note in the bank's favor.[26] After the bank's failure, PG presented for payment, on the letter of credit to the FDIC as receiver for the bank, $700,000 in unpaid customer drafts.[27] The FDIC returned the drafts unpaid. PG then sued the FDIC, alleging that the standby letter of credit was an insured deposit under 12 U.S.C. § 1813(*l*)(1) as "money or its equivalent."[28] The district court and the U.S. Court of Appeals for the Tenth Circuit agreed that the standby letter of credit qualified as a "deposit" under the FDIA, and that PG was entitled to $100,000 from the FDIC.[29]

Reversing these decisions, the Supreme Court held that the FDIC's interpretation, that standby letters of credit backed by unsecured promissory notes were not "hard assets" and thus did not qualify as a deposit under Section 1813(*l*)(1) as "money or its equivalent," was entitled to deference.[30] In reviewing the elements of the banking crisis that reached its climax in 1933 and the legislative history of the Banking Act of 1933, the *Philadelphia Gear* Court stated:

> Congress' purpose in creating the FDIC was clear. Faced with virtual panic, Congress attempted to safeguard the hard earnings of individuals against the possibility that bank failures would deprive them of their savings. Congress passed the 1933 provisions "[i]n order to provide against a repetition of the present painful experience in which a vast sum of assets and purchasing power is 'tied up.'" The focus of Congress was therefore

---

[23] *Fedders*, 35 F.3d at 21-22 (holding that a "phantom" escrow account in connection with a sale of real estate was not a deposit under the "escrow or held in trust" definition of "deposit," 12 U.S.C. § 1813(*l*)(3), but that the bank's promise to establish such an account created a "deposit" under the "obligated to give credit" language of 12 U.S.C. § 1813(*l*)(1)).

[24] *European Am. Bank & Trust Co.*, 576 F. Supp. at 953 (wherein the court stated that the "[c]ourt should respect the [FDIC's] efforts to adapt the statutory language to new developments," quoting *A.G. Becker Inc. v. Board of Governors of the Fed. Reserve Sys.*, 693 F.2d 136, 140 (D.C. Cir. 1982)). In this regard, the courts are likely to defer, in most cases, to the FDIC's interpretation of what a "deposit" is. For example, in *European American Bank*, the district court held that a CHIPS electronic fund transfer was a "deposit" within the meaning of 12 U.S.C. § 1813(*l*)(1) and (*l*)(3). In *Seattle-First Bank v. FDIC*, 619 F. Supp. 1351, 1359-60 (D. Okla. 1985), another district court concluded that monies wired by a loan participant to the lead bank, at the lead banks direction, for the purpose of funding a participated loan, may become "deposits" within the meaning of 12 U.S.C. § 1813(*l*)(3) if the wired funds are not drawn by the intended borrower.

[25] *Philadelphia Gear*, 476 U.S. at 438 (FDIC's conclusion entitled to deference). *See also FDIC v. Irving Trust Co.*, 137 F. Supp. 145, 162-63 (1955) (ordinary letters of credit are "deposits" under the Federal Deposit Insurance Act).

[26] Under the terms of the letter of credit, nothing was considered due on the note, and no interest was charged, unless PG presented drafts to the bank affirming nonpayment of bills by the customer. *Philadelphia Gear*, 476 U.S. at 428.

[27] *Id*. at 428-429.

[28] *Id*. at 429.

[29] *Id*. The Tenth Circuit reversed an award of prejudgment interest to Philadelphia Gear, but otherwise affirmed the judgment of the district court. *Id*.

[30] *Id*. at 438-439.

upon ensuring that a deposit of hard earnings entrusted by individuals to a bank would not lead to a tangible loss in the event of a bank failure.[31]

The Court further explained the purpose of the creation of the FDIC and the system of deposit insurance as follows:

> Congress' focus in providing for a system of deposit insurance — a system that has been continued to the present without modification to the basic definition of deposits that are "money or its equivalent" — was clearly a focus upon safeguarding the assets and "hard earnings" that businesses and individuals have entrusted to banks. Congress wanted to ensure that someone who put tangible assets into a bank could always get those assets back. The purpose behind the insurance of deposits in general, and especially in the section defining deposits as "money or its equivalent," therefore, is the protection of assets and hard earnings entrusted to a bank.[32]

Relying on these principles, the Supreme Court in *Philadelphia Gear* agreed with the FDIC that the goals of the FDIA would not be served by extending deposit insurance to cover the standby letter of credit backed by the contingent promissory note that involved no such surrender of assets or hard earnings to the custody of the bank.[33]

In addition to the enumerated definitions, the FDIC has the authority to prescribe by regulation that "such other obligations of a bank or savings association . . . by general usage" are "deposits" within the meaning of the FDIA.[34] The FDIC must consult with the other bank regulatory agencies, however, prior to expanding, in this manner, the definition of "deposit" under the FDIA.[35] Under current law, the FDIC will look to the books and records of the depository institution to determine whether or not funds qualify as an insured deposit. In determining the amount of insurance available to each depositor, the FDIC "shall presume that deposited funds are actually owned in the manner indicated on the deposit account records of the insured depository institution."[36] If these records are unambiguous, then they shall be considered binding on the depositor. If, however, the records as to how funds are owned are "ambiguous or unclear," the FDIC may, in its sole discretion, "consider evidence other than the deposit account records of the insured depository institution for the purpose of establishing the manner in which the funds are owned."[37]

---

[31] *Id.* at 432 (citing S. REP. NO. 77, 73d Cong., at 12 (1933)).

[32] *Id.* at 435.

[33] *Id.*

[34] 12 U.S.C. § 1813(*l*)(5). Congress provided the FDIC with the authority to promulgate regulations, by which the FDIC may recognize (in collaboration with the other banking agencies) that certain obligations of insured depository institutions may develop through general usage to be deposit liabilities of such institutions. *Id.*

[35] *Id. See also* 12 C.F.R. § 330.2 (describing the FDIC's authority and purpose to define terms under the FDIA).

[36] 12 C.F.R. § 330.4(a).

[37] *Id.*

[3]   DEPOSIT INSURANCE AND STORED VALUE PRODUCTS

[a] **General Counsel's Opinion No. 8.** The FDIC, in its General Counsel's Opinion No. 8 ("SVC Opinion"), addressed and clarified whether federal deposit insurance applies to the unpaid balances maintained on stored value cards ("SVCs") or other electronic payment systems prior to the use of the funds by consumers.[38] Issued on July 16, 1996, the SVC Opinion constituted the FDIC's first official formal regulatory action in regard to stored value products.[39] Specifically, the SVC Opinion described the FDIC's legal position on whether, and under what circumstances, the funds underlying stored value cards may be considered "deposits" under the FDIA[40] and therefore qualify for deposit insurance coverage and assessment.

The Opinion identifies four types of stored value systems: (1) "Bank Primary – Customer Account Systems"; (2) "Bank Primary – Reserve Systems"; (3) "Bank Secondary – Advance Systems"; and (4) "Bank Secondary – Pre-Acquisition Systems."[41] It divides SVCs into two basic types; "primary," in which the bank holds the funds underlying the electronic value directly, and "secondary," in which a third party (likely the issuer) holds the funds underlying the electronic value represented by the SVC.

In a Bank Primary – Customer Account System, the funds underlying the stored value card remain in a customer's deposit account until the value is transferred to a merchant or other third party, who collects the funds from the customer's bank. In a Bank Primary – Reserve System, funds are withdrawn from a customer's account (or paid directly) and data representing the withdrawn amount is placed onto a card. The funds themselves are allocated to a reserve or general liability account maintained by the institution to pay merchants and other payees as they make claims for payment.

In a Bank Secondary – Advance System, electronic value created by a third party and provided to an institution is made available to customers who exchange funds for such value, with the institution holding the funds briefly and then forwarding them to the third party. Finally, in a Bank Secondary – Pre-Acquisition

---

[38] This question has been addressed by a number of commentators. *See, e.g.,* Sivertsen, *supra* note 11; Thomas P. Vartanian, *Key Question for Emerging Systems: Where is the Money?,* AM. BANKER – FUTURE BANKING, June 17, 1996, at 6A. *See also* Thomas P. Vartanian, Statement before the Federal Deposit Insurance Corporation Concerning Stored Value Cards and Electronic Payment Systems (Sept. 12, 1996), *available at* <http://www.ffhsj.com>. There are advantages and disadvantages of having FDIC deposit insurance coverage for stored value or other retail payment products. For example, the bank issuer of an insured stored value card ("SVC") could use FDIC coverage as a marketing tool, allowing its products to be promoted as government-insured. However, covering stored value products with FDIC insurance would add to an institution's deposit base and thus could increase the insurance premium paid to the FDIC. *See FDIC Decides to Look Before it Leaps on Covering Stored Value Cards,* BANK NETWORK NEWS, July 26, 1996.

[39] General Counsel's Opinion No. 8; Stored Value Cards, 61 Fed. Reg. 40,490 (1996) (notice Aug. 2, 1996) [hereinafter SVC Opinion]. On the same day, the FDIC issued a notice of public hearings and request for comment on the issues contained in the SVC Opinion. *See* Stored Value Cards and Other Electronic Payment Systems, 61 Fed. Reg. 40,494 (1996). The FDIC had previously issued opinions on two related topics – deposit insurance for funds held by a company that provides payment services for Internet purchases and the status of such a company as a deposit broker under Section 29 of the FDIA. 12 U.S.C. § 1831f(f). *See* Interpretive Letter from Jeffrey M. Kopchik on Internet payments (Oct. 20, 1995); Interpretive Letter from Joseph A. DiNuzzo on sponsoring company as a deposit broker under the FDIA (Oct. 20, 1995). *See also FDIC Issues First Opinions on Internet Deposit Insurance Issues,* 21ST CENTURY BANKING ALERT® No. 96-2-12, Feb. 12, 1996, *available at* <http://www.ffhsj.com/bancmail/bancpage.htm>.

[40] *See* 12 U.S.C. § 1813(*l*)(1)-(5).

[41] SVC Opinion, 61 Fed. Reg. at 40,490.

System, an institution exchanges its own funds for electronic value from a third party and, in turn, exchanges the electronic value for funds with its customers.

[*i*] *Bank Primary – Customer Account Systems.* The SVC Opinion concluded that funds in the Bank Primary – Customer Account System "appear to be" deposits.[42] In making this determination, the FDIC reasoned that in Bank Primary – Customer Account Systems, the stored value remains credited to the customer's account until the payee makes a claim on the funds.

[*ii*] *Bank Primary – Reserve Systems.* On the other hand, the SVC Opinion found that, as a general matter, funds in the Bank Primary – Reserve System are not insured deposits. It noted that such products appear to be structured so that the institution does not credit any of the types of accounts identified in Section 1813(*l*)(1). Rather, the cardholder's funds are paid into a general liability account maintained by the institution. The SVC Opinion indicated that the FDIC does not consider such accounts, which institutions routinely create and maintain, to be within the statutory meaning of "deposit."[43] The FDIC's view in this regard was reinforced by the fact that its review of sample agreements did not indicate that the parties to SVC agreements (the insured depository institution and the purchaser of the SVC) intended the stored value funds to fit within the statutory definition of "deposit."[44] Furthermore, the SVC Opinion found that the funds underlying a Bank Primary – Reserve System are not held for a special or specific purpose such as those delineated in Section 1813(*l*)(3) (*i.e.*, escrow funds, funds held as security for a transaction or set of related transactions). In reaching this conclusion under the "special purpose" prong, the FDIC noted that funds in a Primary Reserve type of system appear to be held by an institution in order to meet its obligations to payees as they make claims on the funds in connection with miscellaneous and unrelated transactions undertaken within the system. The SVC Opinion compared the judicial interpretation of this prong, that funds must be held for a purpose associated with a particular transaction or two or more related transactions, with its view of the nature of Bank Primary – Reserve systems:

> [A] customer [in a Bank Primary – Reserve System] who transfers funds to an institution in exchange for electronic value may engage in any of a number of unrelated transactions. Indeed, when a customer has electronic value loaded onto a card he may have no idea as to what transactions he will use the card to engage in, nor whom the transferees will be. Thus, unlike the examples listed in the statute, funds held by an institution to redeem electronic value could be associated with general or miscellaneous unrelated transactions.[45]

---

[42] *Id.* at 40,494. Once the FDIC determines that funds fall within the definition of "deposit," it looks to the books and records of the depository institution to determine whether the funds are maintained in a manner that makes them eligible for FDIC insurance, limited to an aggregate $100,000 for funds held by a depositor in the same capacity and right in a single depository institution. 12 U.S.C. § 1813(m)(1).

[43] SVC Opinion, 61 Fed. Reg. at 40,492, 40,494.

[44] *Id.* at 40,492.

[45] *Id.* at 40,493.

As a result, the SVC Opinion concluded that funds in this type of system do not qualify as a deposit held for a specific or special purpose.

[*iii*] *Bank Secondary – Pre-Acquisition Systems.* The SVC Opinion concluded that funds underlying the stored value in a Bank Secondary – Pre-Acquisition Systems also do not qualify as deposits. The FDIC reasoned that the funds underlying the stored value in such systems are received or held by a third party issuer and are not "received or held by a depository institution" within the meaning of either Section 1813(*l*)(1) or (*l*)(3). In this regard, the FDIC stated that "[t]he institution in effect advances these funds on behalf of its customers and later collects funds from its customer in exchange for electronic value loaded onto stored value cards."[46] Therefore, the FDIC concluded that the requirement for an unpaid balance of money or its equivalent received or held by an institution would not be satisfied by such systems.[47]

[*iv*] *Bank Secondary – Advance Systems.* Finally, the SVC Opinion applied a two part analysis to the Bank Secondary – Advance System. It found that the funds held by an institution in such a system would not create a deposit liability owed to the customer because the liability is owed to a third party for whom the institution is temporarily holding the funds. The SVC Opinion noted that funds may initially be received by the institution but later transferred to a third party. This raises the issue of whether the holding of such funds, even for a short time, involves the creation of a deposit liability to the third party. The FDIC concluded that such funds would meet the tests set forth in Section 1813(*l*)(1) and (3), that they be "an unpaid balance of money or its equivalent received or held" by an institution. The FDIC found that the Bank Secondary – Advance System was indistinguishable from the situation where an institution sells travelers' checks issued by others. In that context, the FDIC's legal division has held that the proceeds from such sales are deposits while held by the selling institution. The SVC Opinion noted that any deposit liability to a third party issuer would be extinguished upon transfer of the funds to the third party. The SVC Opinion further noted that the parties may intend that the institution credit an account within the meaning of Section 1813(*l*). However, even if the institution is not obligated to credit such funds to an account and thus the funds do not qualify as a deposit under Section 1813(*l*)(1), the funds may be deemed to be held for the specific purpose of transferring the funds to the third party, and thus would be considered a deposit under Section 1813(*l*)(3).

[*v*] *Other Possible Bases for "Deposit" Treatment.* The SVC Opinion also addressed several other possible grounds for funds underlying stored value to be treated as deposits.[48] It commented that while trust funds are deposits under Section 1813(*l*)(2), the FDIC staff was not aware of stored value systems in which funds are held by an institution in a fiduciary capacity. It noted that while Bank Primary – Reserve Systems operate

---

[46] *Id.* at 40,491.

[47] The SVC Opinion noted that in some Bank Secondary Systems an insured institution may, by contract, undertake a contingent liability to redeem electronic value for consumers and merchants. It recognized that that this liability might be considered to represent an unpaid balance of money, or its equivalent, received or held by an institution. The SVC Opinion concluded that such a contingent liability would not constitute "hard earnings" as required by the *Philadelphia Gear* decision. In the view of the SVC Opinion, in Bank Secondary Systems the "hard earnings" are ultimately held by the third party issuer rather than the institution. *Id.* at 40,491-40,492.

[48] *Id.* at 40,493-40,494.

much like cashier's checks and money orders, both of which are expressly identified as deposits in Section 1813(*l*)(4), there are significant distinctions between these instruments and such forms of stored value. For example, a stored value card is not a negotiable instrument. Furthermore, a stored value card is not the equivalent of an institution drawing a check on itself, rather the cardholder transfers the right to a sum of money being held at the institution. The SVC Opinion concludes that Section 1813(*l*)(4) was not intended to include payment instruments other than the negotiable instruments enumerated in the statute. Finally, the SVC Opinion noted that while Section 1813(*l*)(5) gives the FDIC the authority, in consultation with the other federal bank regulatory agencies, to establish by regulation that particular obligations of insured depository institutions will be deemed to be deposits, no such regulation has been adopted.

The initial impact of the SVC Opinion was to give depository institutions and stored value card industry participants prompt and clear guidance that allowed them to design their products without uncertainty as to the deposit insurance treatment of particular approaches that they might take.

[b] Stored Value Card and Other Electronic Payment Systems Notice. On August 2, 1996, in addition to publishing the SVC Opinion, the FDIC issued a notice of public hearing and request for comment on whether, and under what circumstances, it should issue a regulation on whether funds underlying stored value card systems or other similar electronic payment systems are insured deposits ("SVC Notice").[49] The SVC Notice stated that the SVC Opinion set forth the FDIC's view concerning the application of Sections 1813(*l*)(1)-(4) to stored value products. At the same time, it noted the possibility that the FDIC may issue a regulation finding that some or all of a depository institution's stored value card obligations are deposit liabilities by general usage under Section 1813(*l*)(5). The FDIC indicated that, while it had no plans to issue such a regulation, it wished to solicit comments regarding the policy considerations surrounding whether it should consider doing so in the future.[50]

The SVC Notice indicated that while it was primarily directed at stored value cards, the FDIC staff believed that the analysis would, in general, apply to a variety of electronic payments, including Internet banking and the use of electronic cash. The SVC Notice identified a number of policy considerations that the FDIC believed should influence its evaluation of whether to issue a regulation regarding the deposit insurance treatment of stored value, including: (i) whether stored value is likely to constitute a significant portion of the payment system; (ii) whether consumers are likely to expect that stored value cards be covered by deposit insurance protection; (iii) what impact the presence or absence of deposit insurance could have on competitive equality between insured depository institutions and non-depository institutions; and (iv) the implications of the expectation that stored value card balances may be limited to $100 to $200.

---

[49] Stored Value Cards and Other Electronic Payment Systems, 61 Fed. Reg. 40,494 (1996) [hereinafter SVC Notice].

[50] *Id.* at 40,495. The SVC Notice stated that the request for comments is independent of, and will in no way effect or undermine, the analysis or conclusions in the SVC Opinion. *Id.*

The SVC Notice requested comment on a number of specific issues, including:

- Should funds underlying stored value cards be analogized to funds held to meet letters of credit, which are deposits under Section 1813(*l*)(3)?

- Should funds underlying stored value cards be analogized to money orders or cashier's checks drawn on an institution, which are deposits under Section 1813(*l*)(4)?

- What are the expectations of consumers in regard to whether stored value cards are insured products?

- Should a regulation distinguish between reloadable and disposable cards, or between single and multiple function cards?

- What types of disclosure should the FDIC require with respect to the insured or non-insured status of these products?

- What safety and soundness concerns are raised by the development of stored value cards and other electronic payments systems.[51]

As provided for in the SVC Notice, the FDIC held a public hearing on the matters addressed in the SVC Notice on September 12, 1996.[52] Witnesses generally supported the approach that the FDIC had taken in the SVC Opinion.[53]

On June 24, 1997, the FDIC announced that, for the time being, it had decided not to propose regulations or seek legislation to define stored value cards as deposits.[54] The FDIC instead would continue to rely on the principles contained in the SVC Opinion. The FDIC cautioned depository institutions that they were expected to clearly and conspicuously disclose to customers the insured or non-insured status of stored value cards they offer to the public. It noted that if the FDIC finds that customer confusion regarding the insurance status of stored value cards impedes the cards' acceptability or customers' ability to meaningfully distinguish differing card systems, it would reconsider the need for regulation.

---

[51]   SVC Notice, 61 Fed. Reg. at 40,497.

[52]   *FDIC Public Hearing Concerning Stored Value Cards and Other Electronic Payment Systems* (Sept. 12, 1996). Testifying at the hearing were: Valerie J. McNevin, Esq.; Diane M. Casey, Grant Thornton LLP; Edgar D. Brown, First Union Corporation; James Rudd, Wells Fargo Bank & Company; Frank O. Trotter, III, Mark Twain Bank; Michael T. Bradley, E-Money, Inc.; Thomas P. Vartanian, Fried, Frank, Harris, Shriver & Jacobson; Eric Hartz, Security First Network Bank; Rev. James H. Daniel, Jr., 21st Century Partnership; Rev. Charles R. Stith, Organization for a New Equality; Leland M. Stenehjem, Jr., Independent Bankers Association of America; Hal D. Lingerfelt, State of North Carolina; Janice C. Shields, Ph.D., U.S. Public Interest Research Group; and David H. Wells, America's Community Bankers. A summary and transcript can be found at <http://www.fdic.gov>.

[53]   *See* Celia Viggo Wexler, *Banks Seen Needing Help on Net - But Not FDIC Coverage on Cards*, AM. BANKER, Sept. 13, 1996, at 3; *Keep Regs Loose on Smart Cards, Bankers Urge the FDIC*, REGULATORY COMPLIANCE WATCH, Sept. 23, 1996, at 1; *FDIC Hearing on Stored-Value and Electronic Payment Systems*, ABA BANK COMPLIANCE, Oct. 1996.

[54]   *FDIC Will Continue To Rely On General Counsel Opinion Rather Than Issue Rules On Stored-Value Cards*, FDIC Press Release 44-97 (June 24, 1997), available at <http://www.fdic.gov>. *See* Dean Anason, *FDIC will Keep Hands Off Stored Value Cards For Now,* AM. BANKER, June 25, 1997, at 2.

The SVC Opinion represents a major step in the process of applying existing law and regulations to the new, and still evolving, technologies of stored value and computer network payment systems. It appears to provide broad flexibility to electronic commerce pioneers to structure products outside the regulated environment of insured deposit instruments. While this flexibility is welcome, product designers and participating depository institutions also need to take into account a variety of factors, including the potential collateral implications of the failure of another issuer, and the disclosure issues associated with the sale of non-insured products.

§ 8.04   PRIVATE INSURANCE

As illustrated by the preceding section, stored value and other electronic payment products may not fall within the clear parameters of insurability. Without the availability of federal deposit insurance for many versions of these products, it is possible that private insurance markets could develop for products like SVCs. Depository institutions, non-depository issuers, consumers, and merchants could all benefit if the marketplace were to develop private forms of insurance as a supplement to the existing system of deposit insurance.

Allowing depository institutions to offer privately-insured electronic value products, either in bank primary or bank secondary systems, would give such institutions the option to offer the benefits of an insured product to customers who might typically expect such a feature in a product offered by their banks. It would also help depository institutions avoid being potentially placed at a competitive disadvantage versus nonbank issuers, which may offer privately-insured products. Moreover, the experience with such a system could also be valuable to the FDIC in testing hypotheses regarding the likely performance of private deposit insurance on a more widespread basis.[55]

Perhaps most importantly, the use of private insurance might avoid potentially destablizing situations where the failure of a depository institution leaves large amounts of unredeemable stored value in the hands of consumers who, by virtue of holding uninsured obligations of an institution, will be left with subordinated claims against a receivership. Under the national depositor preference provision, holders of such claims would be

---

[55]   Various proposals for reform of the bank regulatory structure, including the deposit insurance system, have been made since the 1930s. These efforts have included consideration of the potential benefits of alternative deposit insurance systems, including a system of privately capitalized deposit insurance. Studies by Congress, the FDIC, or other entities have included, in chronological order: The Brookings Study in 1937; the Hoover Commision in 1949; the President's Commission on Financial Structure and Regulation in 1971 (known as the Hunt Commission) (advocating the establishment of a Federal Deposit Guarantee Administration to oversee the various deposit insurance funds); and the *Financial Institutions and the Nation's Economy (FINE) "Discussion Principles"* report in 1975 (recommending consolidation of bank regulatory agencies). In 1983, a report of the Federal Home Loan Bank Board, *Agenda for Reform, a Report on Deposit Insurance to the Congress from the Federal Home Loan Bank Board,* was published pursuant to Section 712 of the Garn-St Germain Depository Institutions Act of 1982. It advocated, among other things, a transfer of all or part of the deposit insurance system to the private sector as an alternative to the existing regulatory structure. In 1987, the FDIC published a study entitled *Mandate for Change, Restructuring the Banking Industry,* in which the FDIC took the position that deposit insurance in the existing scheme is underpriced, giving banks a competitive advantage. Finally, in 1991, the Treasury Department published its study *Modernizing the Financial System: Recommendations for Safer, More Competitive Banks,* pursuant to Section 1001 of the Financial Institutions Reform, Recovery and Enforcement Act of 1989. The Treasury report did not advocate privatization of the deposit insurance system, but did contain a discussion of the merits of a privately capitalized deposit insurance scheme. *See* Treasury Report, Ch. VII, Alternatives to Federal Deposit Insurance. *See also* PETER J. WALLISON, BACK FROM THE BRINK: A PRACTICAL PLAN FOR PRIVATIZING DEPOSIT INSURANCE AND STRENGTHENING OUR BANKS AND THRIFTS (1990) (advocating the creation of a supplemental deposit protection system, backed by the capital of banking institutions and administered through a series of Deposit Guarantee Associations).

unlikely to recover their funds.[56] The presence of private insurance in such circumstances might help avert a run by holders of uninsured store value on off-line stored value acceptance devices. Unless checked by another factor, such a reaction by consumers could result in lots of station wagons filled with cans of soda and numerous recipient merchants now holding claims of little or no value against the failed issuer because the off-line merchants may not be able to act promptly enough to protect themselves in the event of the failure of the stored value issuer.

Anticipating the adverse impact that such problems would have on consumer and merchant perception of stored value, groups of depository institution stored value issuers may find themselves in the position of acting as guarantors of stored value issued by other institutions. Under those circumstances, the institutions involved may have to advance substantial amounts of funds to head off the adverse impact that would be associated with consumers being unable to use their cards, and merchants not receiving value for purchases made with cards, with little or no prospect that the depository institutions will recover the funds that they contribute. If this were to occur during a period of stress on depository institutions, a series of failures of large depository institution issuers of stored value could exacerbate the pressure on the industry in general by causing other solvent institutions to incur losses in order to maintain confidence in an important product offered by depository institutions. For these reasons, the FDIC should consider whether it might be in the interest of the deposit insurance funds to encourage the development of private insurance for non-FDIC insured electronic value.

§ 8.05   FDIC OPINIONS REGARDING INTERNET VALUE TRANSFER SYSTEMS

[1]   THE CYBERCASH OPINIONS

On October 20, 1995, the FDIC took some of the first steps in clearing the way for the payments side of electronic banking and commerce. It issued opinions to a company (generally understood to be CyberCash) on two issues: (1) whether deposit insurance would pass through CyberCash, as agent, to its customers whose funds were in the CyberCash™ agency account at an insured institution; and (2) whether CyberCash would be considered a "deposit broker" under Section 29 of the FDIA.

In its letter regarding the pass-through of deposit insurance coverage, the FDIC described CyberCash's system of "agency accounts" for account-based cash transactions[57] as follows:

> Customers wishing to purchase goods and services over the Internet would enter into an agreement with the Company. The Company plans to establish agency accounts at insured depository institutions. These accounts would be entitled "[Company] as agent

---

[56] A depositor preference statute was enacted as part of the budget bill in 1993. *See* Omnibus Budget Reconciliation Act of 1993, Pub. L. No. 103-66, § 3001, 1993 U.S.C.C.A.N. (107 Stat.) 312, 336 (codified at 12 U.S.C. § 1821(d)(11)).

[57] CyberCash also had a credit card payment system that was already operational and not the subject of the pass-through insurance opinion request.

for its customers." Upon establishing a relationship with the Company, customers would transfer funds from their personal accounts to the Company's agency account. Once a customer has established a relationship with the Company, and funded their [Company] account or "wallet", the customer may purchase an item offered for sale over the Internet by selecting the [Company] payment option on the customer's computer screen. The Company will then debit the appropriate amount from the customer's account, which the Company maintains as agent for the customer, and credit that amount to the merchant's account, which the Company maintains as agent for the merchant. The Company would like its customers to receive the benefit of pass-through deposit insurance for the funds held in its agency accounts.[58]

The FDIC responded affirmatively to CyberCash's request. It noted the two conditions for "pass-through" insurance coverage: (1) deposit account records of an insured depository institution must expressly disclose, by way of specific reference, the existence of any fiduciary relationship;[59] and (2) assuming that such a fiduciary relationship is disclosed, the interests of the other parties must be ascertainable either from the deposit account records of the insured institution or records maintained in good faith and in the normal course of business by the depository or some other person or entity that has undertaken to maintain such records for the depositor.[60]

The FDIC found that CyberCash's proposal to title the accounts "[Company] as agent for its customers" satisfied the first condition of disclosing the existence of a fiduciary relationship. The FDIC then determined that CyberCash's proposal to maintain records indicating the legal name, ownership capacity, and address of parties on whose behalf funds have been deposited, satisfied the second requirement.[61]

The FDIC noted that if a CyberCash customer maintains any other accounts at the same institution that maintains the agency account, and those accounts are held in the same right and capacity as the agency account (*i.e.,* as an individual account), those accounts would be aggregated for deposit insurance purposes with the customer's interest in the CyberCash™ agency account. The FDIC cautioned that if the company chooses to include a reference to FDIC insurance in its communications with customers, the FDIC would expect that all statements and representations in that regard would be accurate and complete. Finally, the FDIC noted that its opinion is intended to address only the deposit insurance aspects of the company's proposal, and it is not intended to approve or sanction CyberCash's™ agency account system, which may raise issues that should be discussed with other federal agencies or departments.

---

[58] Interpretive Letter from Jeffrey M. Kopchik on Internet payments (Oct. 20, 1995), at 1 [hereinafter Internet Payment Op.].

[59] *Id.* at 2; 12 C.F.R. § 330.4(b)(1).

[60] Internet Payment Op., *supra* note 58, at 2; 12 C.F.R. § 330.4(b)(2).

[61] Internet Payment Op., *supra* note 58, at 3. The FDIC noted that in multi-tiered fiduciary accounts, every level of fiduciary relationship would have to be disclosed. *Id.*

In the second interpretive letter, the FDIC concluded that CyberCash would not be treated as a "deposit broker" by virtue of its role in the agency account system.[62] In reaching this conclusion, the FDIC considered the definition of deposit broker, and whether CyberCash's proposed activities fit within that definition or whether it qualifies for an exclusion from that definition.

A party deemed to be a deposit broker must give written notice to the FDIC that it is acting in such capacity.[63] It must maintain records regarding its placement of deposits with insured institutions and may be required to make periodic reports to the FDIC concerning such deposits.[64] Institutions that are not deemed to be well-capitalized are generally not authorized to accept brokered deposits.[65]

Section 29 of the FDIA defines "deposit broker," in the relevant part, as "any person engaged in the business of placing deposits or facilitating the placement of deposits of third parties with insured depository institutions."[66] The statutory definition of deposit broker contains an exclusion for "[a]n agent or nominee whose primary purpose is not the placement of funds with depository institutions."[67]

In interpreting the primary purpose test, the FDIC typically looks at three key characteristics to determine whether an entity is a deposit broker: (1) whether the depository institution pays a fee to the party for placing the funds with the institution; (2) whether the overall activity would not have been established but for the purpose of placing funds with the institution; and (3) whether there exists a "substantial purpose" for the activity, other than the placement of funds with the insured institution.[68]

The FDIC concluded that CyberCash qualified for the "primary purpose" exclusion.[69] It found that CyberCash's primary purpose was not to provide a deposit placement service to customers but rather to facilitate its business of providing them with an Internet payment mechanism. Furthermore, the FDIC noted that the participating depository institutions would not pay interest on the agency accounts, thus indicating that the arrangements did not involve a situation where funds were being channelled to an institution paying high rates of interest to attract deposits. In sum, the FDIC concluded that CyberCash establishes the agency account as a tool to accomplish its goal of enabling customers to buy and sell goods and services over the Internet, rather than as the focal point of its business.

---

[62]   Interpretive Letter from Joseph A. DiNuzzo on sponsoring company not constituting a deposit broker under the FDIA (Oct. 20, 1995).

[63]   12 C.F.R. § 337.6(h)(1).

[64]   *Id.* § 337.6(h)(2)-(3).

[65]   *Id.* § 337.6(b)-(e).

[66]   12 U.S.C. § 1831f(f)(1).

[67]   *Id.* § 1831f(f)(2)(I). *See also* 12 C.F.R. § 337.6(a)(5)(ii)(I).

[68]   FDIC Advisory Opinion 92-51 (Aug. 3, 1992).

[69]   The FDIC noted that it had determined that "primary purpose" does not mean "primary activity," but instead means the "primary intent" of the party engaging in the activity.

[2] ECASH™ OPINION

The FDIC applied the principles set forth in the SVC Opinion, described in Section 8.02[3][a] in its May 12, 1997 opinion regarding whether accounts offered by a bank under the ecash™ program fell within the meaning of deposit (the "ecash Opinion").[70] As described in the FDIC opinion, the ecash™ program operates in the manner described below.

The bank requesting the FDIC opinion had entered into an agreement with a company to offer consumers and merchants the opportunity to participate in the program, which provides a method of payment from one personal computer to another. Consumers and merchants would pay fees to participate in the system. A customer first opens a money market account known as a World Currency Account ("WCA"). The bank, in turn, establishes an ecash™ Mint account for every customer who transfers funds into the ecash™ Mint. A customer may transfer funds from the WCA account to her ecash™ Mint account by phone, fax, mail, or e-mail. The bank maintains account records of each customer's ecash™ Mint account. Once the funds are in the individual ecash™ Mint account, participants can make payments using those funds by contacting the ecash™ Mint via the Internet and downloading the desired amount onto their hard drive. Once this occurs, the underlying funds are placed in a pooled ecash™ Mint account. The bank maintains only aggregate records for the pooled account. Once ecash™ is transferred to a customer's hard drive, the customer can transfer ecash™ to merchants or other individuals over the Internet. When a payor wishes to transfer ecash™, the payor will typically address the ecash™ to the payee's ecash™ account identification. The payee's software sends the ecash™ to the mint. The mint then verifies that the ecash™ is valid and asks whether the payee wishes to accept the payment. If the payment is accepted, the ecash™ is deposited into the payee's individual ecash™ Mint. It is at this stage that the anonyomous feature of ecash™ comes into play. In Internet transactions, the bank can only identify the validity of the ecash™ and the payee's ecash™ individual account. The bank, however, is never able to determine the identity of the payor. In addition, even where a customer returns unspent coins to the ecash™ Mint, the bank does not have the ability to link the ecash™ with a particular customer.[71]

A customer at any time may use their computer to return ecash™ on her hard drive to her ecash™ Mint individual account. Once ecash™ is in the ecash™ Mint individual account, the customer may request by phone, fax, or e-mail that funds be transferred from the ecash™ Mint individual account into the customer's WCA account. The bank pays interest on the WCA accounts. It does not pay interest on funds in the customer's ecash™ account, whether in the ecash™ Mint individual account or on the customer's hard drive when it is in

---

[70] Letter from Marc J. Goldstrom, May 12, 1997. Ecash™ is a product of DigiCash. Although the opinion does not identify the bank participating in the program, Mark Twain Bank appears to be the sole U.S. participant in the program. *See DigiCash Taps New Strategy for U.S. Market,* FINANCIAL SERV. ONLINE (Faulkner & Gray N.Y.), July/Aug. 1997; *Mark Twain's Internet Adventure,* ELECTRONIC PAYMENTS INT'L, June 1997, at 11. Ecash™ is also in use in Finland and Germany. *See Finnish Bank Moves Boldly onto Internet,* BANK TECH. NEWS (Faulkner & Gray N.Y.), Apr. 1997; Jennifer Kingson Bloom, *Deutsche Bank Helps Digital Coin Make its Mark,* AM. BANKER, May 7, 1996, at 1.

[71] The opinion also noted that the ecash™ system, in limited circumstances, offers the payor the option, known as the Wild Card Option, to send ecash™ by e-mail without linking the ecash™ to the intended payee's ecash™ individual account. This option is never available when purchasing merchandise through a merchant's website. If a third party were to intercept the e-mail and deposit the ecash™ in his ecash™ Mint individual account, the payor would have no recourse. Accordingly, the bank recommends that the Wild Card Option only be used to send small amounts of ecash™.

the pooled ecash™ Mint account. The bank invests funds in the ecash™ Mint and all income earned through such investment is the property of the bank.

The ecash Opinion reviewed the features of the agreement that ecash™ participants enter into. It states, among other things, that:

- the ecash™ Mint is not a deposit with the bank, but represents a general obligation of the bank;

- any "account" set up in the ecash™ system is not a deposit with the bank but represents cash held by the customer in his/her personal computer under the ecash™ system;

- the money held in the ecash™ Mint is not insured by the FDIC;

- the customer is an unsecured creditor of the bank as to all money held in the ecash™ Mint; and

- the customer will treat ecash™ as though it was cash that was under "risk of attack."

The agreement also provides that the software for the ecash™ system is being provided gratutiously by a third party for testing purposes only, and that the customer shall bear all risks including nonperformance, loss, or corruption of data.

The ecash Opinion noted that, notwithstanding the disclaimers in the agreement, the bank is internally treating all funds in the ecash™ system as deposits and that they appear as such on the bank's general ledger. It also noted that the bank's letter states that the Board of Governors of the Federal Reserve System is treating such funds as deposits and is requiring that reserves be held on funds in the ecash™ system.

The bank that requested the ecash Opinion asked whether and to what extent the funds or obligation underlying ecash™ constitute deposits within the meaning of Section 1813(l), and are, therefore, assessable for purposes of insurance premiums and also qualify for deposit insurance.[72]

The FDIC first analyzed the treatment of ecash™ Mint individual accounts in the context of Sections 1813(l)(1) and (3). Section 1813(l)(1) treats as deposits funds that the institution is obligated to credit to a commercial, checking, savings, time, or thrift account. The ecash Opinion noted that arguments may be advanced both in support of and against the proposition that funds in the ecash™ Mint individual accounts qualify under this section. It was not necessary to reach a conclusion on this question, however, because ecash™ Mint individual accounts qualify as funds held for a special or specific purpose and therefore come within the meaning of Section 1813(l)(3).

In order to qualify as a deposit under Section 1813(l)(3), the funds credited to an ecash™ Mint individual account must represent: (1) money or its equivalent, received or held by an institution in the usual

---

[72]   In responding to the bank's request, the FDIC noted that there are other possible issues associated with ecash™, that are not addressed by the opinion, which include consumer disclosure matters, systemic risk, security, electronic fund transfer matters, reserve requirements, counterfeiting, monetary policy, and money laundering.

course of business; (2) for a special or specific purpose. The ecash Opinion found that the first requirement was satisfied and that the second prong of the requirement was at issue. It discussed the principles set forth in the SVC Opinion, noting, among other things, that in the case of Bank Secondary – Advance systems, funds received in order to pay the third party may be considered to be held for a special or specific purpose and thus insured under Section 1813(*l*)(3), and found that ecash™ Mint individual accounts were in an analogous posture. Funds held in such accounts are being held either (1) to be transferred to the ecash™ Mint pooled account (when the customer downloads funds to his hard drive), or (2) to be transferred to the customer's WCA account. In either case, the ecash Opinion stated that the funds represent an obligation owed to a predetermined specific party — the bank's customer. Furthermore, the funds were associated with only two possible transactions. On that basis, the FDIC ruled that the funds underlying an ecash™ Mint individual account appear to be for a specific purpose, like the examples given in the statute, and therefore such funds would be held for a special or specific purpose within the meaning of Section 1813(*l*)(3). Accordingly, such funds qualify for deposit insurance and are subject to assessment.

The ecash Opinion then turned to funds held in the ecash™ Mint pooled account. It noted that when a customer downloads ecash™ onto her hard drive, the underlying funds are paid into a reserve or general liability account to pay merchants and other payees as they make claims for payments. In the FDIC's view, the Bank Primary - Reserve system is exactly like the ecash™ system once the funds have been transferred to the ecash™ Mint pooled account and thus funds in the pooled account would be treated the same way as funds that had been transferred onto a stored value card in a Bank Primary - Reserve system. Such funds do not qualify as deposits because they are not credited to one of the types of accounts identified in Section 1813(*l*)(1) and because they do not qualify as funds held for a special or specific purpose as required in Section 1813(*l*)(3).

The ecash Opinion stated that the FDIC expected the bank to clearly and conspicuously disclose to its customers that funds are insured up to applicable limits until the ecash™ is downloaded to their computer, at which point such funds are no longer insured.

§ 8.06 INSURED INSTITUTION STATUS DISCLOSURES ON THE INTERNET

In February 1997, the FDIC published a proposed rule and request for comments to amend its regulations on the requirements applicable to the advertisment of FDIC membership by insured depository institutions ("Advertising Proposal").[73] In the Advertising Proposal, the FDIC sought comment on the applicability of FDIC advertising rules to electronic communications systems, such as the Internet. Both the current rule and the proposed rule mandate that insured depository institutions include the official advertising statement, "Member FDIC" or an acceptable variant, in their advertisements, subject to certain exceptions.

The FDIC noted that many financial institutions have established World Wide Web sites through which

---

[73] Advertisement of Membership, 62 Fed. Reg. 6142 (1997) (to be codified at 12 C.F.R. pt. 328) (proposed Feb. 11, 1997).

customers may obtain information about the institution, and, in some cases, transact business with the institution. It stated that the proliferation of bank websites raises the questions of whether, and under what circumstances, the advertisement regulation should apply to the Internet or other computer networks.[74]

The FDIC acknowledged that neither the existing nor proposed rule define the term "advertisement" in connection with these new media. It then set forth several points that reflect guidelines that the FDIC's staff have developed in this area.

- An "advertisment" can include transmission via computer networks such as the Internet.

- Every institution's home page is, to some extent, an advertisement.

- Home pages should contain the official advertising statement to the extent required by the rule.

- Each subsidiary web page that contains an advertisement regarding insured deposit products should include the official statement, unless one of the exceptions apply.

The FDIC sought comments on whether, and in what circumstances, it should require insured depository institutions to display the official FDIC advertising statement on their website, and whether the determination should vary based on whether business can be transacted through the site.

§ 8.07   FDIC ELECTRONIC BANKING SAFETY AND SOUNDNESS EXAMINATION PROCEDURES

The FDIC, reacting to the increasing importance of electronic financial products and services ("EFS") and the associated risks posed to the safety and soundness of insured depository institutions offering such products, issued electronic banking examination procedures ("Examination Procedures") in February 1997 for its staff.[75] The Examination Procedures include five parts: (1) an introduction; (2) a discussion of electronic capabilities; (3) an identification of risks; (4) a discussion of risk management techniques; and (5) an explanation of the examination program. The highlights of each of the five parts are discussed below.

---

[74] *Id.* at 6145.

[75] Electronic Banking Safety and Soundness Examination Procedures (Feb. 1997) [hereinafter Examination Procedures]. The Examination Procedures are the first element of what the FDIC sees as a four-part approach to evaluating the wide-ranging risks associated with EFS. The other three remaining parts involve:

    (1) The creation of a training program to educate FDIC examiners on how to use the new procedures;

    (2) The institution of a program to develop internal technical expertise; and

    (3) The development of procedures addressing the technical aspects of electronic banking for information system specialists.

[1]   INTRODUCTION

The FDIC cited three reasons that underscore its concern regarding the use of electronic systems to deliver financial services:

- the increasing competition from nonbank financial service companies, the telecommunications industry, and systems or software developers;

- the demand for more efficient and convenient capabilities; and

- the widening cost and delivery differentials between electronic capabilities and traditional delivery channels.[76]

The FDIC emphasized that new opportunities created by EFS also mean new risks to depository institutions.

[2]   ELECTRONIC CAPABILITIES

For purposes of examination, the FDIC divided electronic capabilities provided by depository institutions into three categories based on the degree of functionality:

- "information-only" systems;

- "electronic transfer" systems; and

- "electronic payment" systems.

In information-only systems, the publisher, usually the bank, makes available general purpose, marketing, or other publicly available information.[77] Websites represent the most common information-only system. The FDIC recognizes websites not only as effective publishing devices, but as a means of collecting information about site visitors and thus enhancing marketing efforts.[78]

The second category, electronic information transfer systems, allow users to interact with the system by transmitting messages, documents, and files.[79] E-mail is one example of an electronic information transfer system. Another example is a bank website that enables site visitors to submit loan or deposit account applications online. The FDIC noted that secure communications will play a vital role in the success of products in this category.[80]

---

[76] Examination Procedures, *supra* note 75, at 1.

[77] This is the same information traditionally communicated through print and other media. Electronic systems can offer greater flexibility in terms of audience, content, and geography, in addition to greater cost efficiency.

[78] Examination Procedures, *supra* note 75, at 3.

[79] *Id.*

[80] *Id.*

The final category, electronic payment systems, includes the electronic components of traditional payment systems; payment entry, settlement, and distribution. The only difference is that their execution may be affected through the Internet.[81]

The FDIC highlighted six criteria that consumers will use to evaluate electronic payment system products:[82]

- Trust;

- Confidence;

- User privacy;

- Transactions legitimacy, security, and non-repudiation;

- System dependability; and

- Merchant acceptance and conveyance.

Noting that risks will vary depending on system implementation, administration, and controls,[83] the FDIC provided a categorization system for the three characteristics of electronic payment systems that must be evaluated when conducting a basic risk evaluation:

---

[81]   *Id.*

[82]   *Id.* at 3-4.

[83]   *Id.* at 5.

CHARACTERISTICS OF ELECTRONIC PAYMENT SYSTEMS	
System Components:	Chip versus magnetic strip technology Card versus computer-based systems System hardware (i.e., PC, card reader, ATM, etc.)
Process Methodology:	Batch versus real-time processing Online versus offline access
System Structure:	Legal currency versus branded (proprietary) value Single versus multiple currency Debit- versus credit-based systems Open versus closed systems* Reloadable versus single use systems Controlled versus secured access Single versus multiple purpose Integrated versus stand alone systems User anonymity Payment mechanics (buyer and seller interaction) Payment system settlement (processing) Transaction size (micro or large-dollar payments) Geographic reach

*With respect to payment systems, open systems are characterized by broad geographic presence and acceptance by a large number of merchants or programs. Closed systems generally involve a smaller geographic presence and/or a single or limited purpose use.

Note: The table is intended to show the primary decision areas in developing a payment system. Software is not specifically included because it is what converts the decisions regarding components, methodology, and structure into an operative system. Indirectly, software decisions are imbedded throughout the table.

Note: The subcategorizations do not necessarily present "either . . . or . . ." decisions. In many ways, the decisions run along a continuum, such as the degree of security or system integration. Technology also allows for systems to be accessed via multiple access media, such as electronic kiosks, PC dial-up programs and Internet services.

Source: FDIC Safety and Soundness Electronic Banking Examination Procedures

The electronic payment system discussion concludes with a reminder to depository institutions that they may perform any one, or a combination of roles, in the electronic payments system.[84] Further, many of these roles may be unfamiliar and thus may present unfamiliar risks.

[3]   RISKS

The third part of the Examination Procedures highlights the risks associated with EFS. In that regard, there are risks inherent in all electronic interfaces (*e.g.,* e-mail distribution errors, system failures due to power outages, alterations by unauthorized parties). But there are also unique risks related to the increased operating speed and broad access base of the Internet. The chart below details the electronic delivery risks associated with the six review areas of the Examination Program:

SUMMARY OF SPECIFIC RISKS Electronic Delivery and Payment Systems	
Area of Concern*	**Specific Risks and Concerns**
Planning and Deployment	• Inadequate decision processes while considering, planning, and implementing electronic capabilities • Impact of technology cost and pricing decisions on financial position • Strategic implications of interstate and global activities • System design and capabilities may not meet customer demands • Implications of increasing competition from/involvement with non-financial entities • Uncertain applicability of blanket bond/other insurance coverages to electronic activities
Operating Policies and Procedures	• Managerial or technical incompetence relative to electronic activities • Existing controls may not adequately protect confidential electronic information • Existing policies and procedures may not address the transaction speed and broad reach of electronic channels
Audit	• Audit trails may be lacking in electronic systems

---

[84] *Id.* Roles include owner/investor, system developer, issuer, distributor/redeemer, transaction authorizers and processors, recordkeepers, transaction archiver, and trusted third party.

Area of Concern* *(cont'd)*	Specific Risks and Concerns *(cont'd)*
Legal and Regulatory	• Uncertain enforceability of digital contracts, agreements, and signatures • User privacy issues • Contingent liabilities may result from user or participant claims • Uncertain legal jurisdiction with respect to taxation, criminal, and civil laws • Implications for interstate and international commerce • Uncertain regulatory environment (local, national, and international; financial services and other areas) • Uncertain applicability of reserve requirements to electronic money • Uncertain applicability of financial recordkeeping, disclosure, and other requirements • Uncertain acceptability of electronic documentation/disclosures under various regulations
Administration and System Operations	• Hardware and/or software failures or disruptions • System and/or data base compromise • Inadequate system capacity • System obsolescence • Administration of multiple standards and protocols • Inadequate protection of electronic communications • Inadequate system security and controls
Vendors and Outsourcing	• Reliance on vendor competence to perform critical functions • Internal controls may not extend to third party vendors • Weak system support among vendor group • Maintenance and administration of multiple inter-related systems, activities • Failure to monitor inter-relationships among multiple financial institutions, vendors or originators, and participants within a payment system
*These Areas of Concern are generally consistent with the six Review Areas of the Safety and Soundness Electronic Banking Examination Procedures.	

Source: FDIC Safety and Soundness Electronic Banking Examination Procedures

The Examination Procedures emphasize that threats of compromise and failure are greater in an environment of connected computers.[85] Depository institutions will need to pay special attention to these threats. The open architecture of the Internet presents operational failure and fraud exposures that differ from those that depository institutions are accustomed to in the relatively closed environment of the current payments system.

[4] RISK MANAGEMENT

According to the Examination Procedures, "risk management is the ongoing process of identifying, measuring, monitoring, and managing potential risk exposure."[86] Depository institutions will have to modify their risk management programs to accommodate the specific risks presented by electronic systems. The FDIC specifically recommends that institutions' risk management processes address economic, legal, regulatory, and technological risk areas associated with electronic delivery and payment systems.[87] The following areas should be considered in a risk management program:

- General supervision, as evidenced by: planning and analysis, policies and procedures, accountability and authority, regulatory compliance and legal framework, human resources, and audits;[88]

- Transaction processing, as seen in: user legitimacy, information integrity, nonrepudiation of transactions, and data confidentiality;[89] and

- Systems administration, as evidenced by: resource requirements, system security, system reliability and contingency planning, system capacity, outsourcing policies, and systems update control.[90]

The FDIC suggests integrating the results of the risk management process into:

- Strategic planning and feasibility analysis;

- Management supervision and internal controls;

- Incident response and preparedness plan;

- Operating policies and procedures;

- System administration, audit and testing;

- Physical, transaction, and system security;

---

[85] *Id.* at 7.

[86] *Id.* at 8.

[87] *Id.*

[88] *Id.* at 9.

[89] *Id.*

[90] *Id.*

- Vendor due diligence, and vendor internal support terms;

- Disaster recovery, business resumption; and contingency plans; and

- Ongoing review of technological developments and capability enhancements.[91]

On December 18, 1997, the FDIC issued a paper entitled "Security Risks Associated with the Internet," designed to "complement" the FDIC's safety and soundness examination procedures for electronic banking activities.[92] Providing an overview of the types of risks associated with the use of the Internet as a delivery channel for information, products and services, the paper illustrates five categories of risks present by the use of the Internet — data privacy and confidentiality, data integrity, authentication, non-repudiation, and access control/system design.[93] The paper also notes that "security breaches due to [the five factors] may currently be rare, but as banks expand their role in electronic commerce they could potentially become prominent targets of malicious activities."[94]

[5] EXAMINATION PROGRAM

The Examination Procedures are designed for use in conjunction with traditional examination procedures. Examiners will conduct the safety and soundness examination for each electronic product and service offered by the financial institution. The three levels of examination, geared to the varying levels of system complexity and related risk that a depository institution's electronic products and services may create, are cumulative. For simple systems, such as information only websites, the examiner will only conduct a Level 1 review.

Systems capable of accessing and transferring data, files, or messages receive both Level 1 and 2 reviews. Systems that enable users to direct or process financial transactions receive Level 1, 2 and 3 reviews.

In addition to examining the specific electronic products and services, examiners will review general electronic banking capabilities.[95] The Examination Program sets forth seven review areas:

1. Planning and Deployment;

2. Operating Policies and Procedures;

3. Audit;

4. Legal and Regulatory Matters;

5. Administration;

---

[91] *Id.*

[92] Division of Supervision, Federal Deposit Insurance Corporation, *Security Risks Associated with the Internet* (Dec. 18, 1997).

[93] *See id.* at 1.

[94] *Id.*

[95] Examination Procedures, *supra* note 75, at 14.

6. Vendors; and

7. Outsourcing.[96]

Examination findings will be incorporated into the Risk Management section of the safety and soundness report. Findings will be factored into the management component rating for safety and soundness examination,[97] with the impact depending upon a number of factors, including:

- The specific issues in relation to the volume and trends in transactions, dollars, and customers;

- The apparent risk to the bank's financial and informational assets, including customer data, regardless of the volume and trends in activity;

- Anticipated growth in volume, whether dollars, transactions, or customers; and

- Anticipated expansion of products, services, or platforms.

Copies of bank documents supporting the findings will be included in the report for future reference. The FDIC Examination Procedures will consider a lack of supporting documentation and information to be a weakness in the bank's electronic capabilities.[98]

§ 8.08   FDIC ALERTS – UNINSURED INTERNET BANKS

One part of the FDIC's Internet enforcement strategy includes issuing financial institution letters ("FILs") to inform other federal and state banking agencies about uninsured Internet banks. Because Internet websites offer wide geographic reach for a low startup cost, some promoters have established unauthorized Internet "banks" purporting to provide high rates of return on deposits.

On April 10, 1997, the agency first addressed this issue when it announced in FIL-29-97 that the European Union Bank was soliciting on the Internet and that the bank's deposits were not insured by the FDIC.[99] Since that time, the FDIC has issued similar letters about The Freedom Star National Bank of Arizona;[100] Netware International Bank;[101] Dunbar National Bank of Maryland;[102] Focus International, Ltd.[103] and The Excelsior Bank.[104] In its FILs, the agency warned that these entities lacked necessary charters and that any deposits made with these institutions would not be eligible for FDIC deposit insurance.

---

[96] Examiners are expected to seek assistance from specialists for clarification.

[97] Examination Procedures, *supra* note 75, at 15.

[98] *Id*. at 16.

[99] European Union Bank, FDIC FIL-29-97, 1997 FDIC Interp. Ltr. LEXIS 26 (April 10, 1997).

[100] Entities that may be Conducting Banking Operations in the United States Without Authorization, FDIC FIL-66-97, 1997 FDIC Interp. Ltr. LEXIS 62 (July 11,1997).

[101] Entities that may be Conducting Banking Operations in the United States Without Authorization, FDIC FIL-71-97, 1997 FDIC Interp. Ltr. LEXIS 66 (July 18, 1997).

[102] Entities that may be Conducting Banking Operations in the United States Without Authorization, FDIC FIL-99-97, 1997 FDIC Interp. Ltr. LEXIS 84 (Sept. 26, 1997).

[103] Focus International, Ltd., FDIC FIL-114-97, 1997 FDIC Interp. Ltr. LEXIS 105 (Oct. 27, 1997).

[104] The Excelsior Bank / The Excelsior Bank International Corp., FDIC FIL-134-97, 1997 FDIC Interp. Ltr. LEXIS 118 (Dec. 31, 1997).

CHAPTER 9

THE OFFICE OF THRIFT SUPERVISION'S PERSPECTIVE ON ELECTRONIC FINANCIAL PRODUCTS AND SERVICES

§ 9.01   INTRODUCTION

The Office of Thrift Supervision ("OTS") regulates federal and state chartered savings institutions. Established as an office of the Department of Treasury on August 9, 1989,[1] OTS stated mission is to "effectively and efficiently supervise thrift institutions to maintain the safety and soundness of institutions and to ensure the viability of the industry."[2] OTS aims to create a regulatory framework flexible enough to accommodate change without sacrificing safety and soundness.[3] OTS has taken a number of actions, both in the form of regulations and supervisory guidance in connection with specific applications, that address electronic banking issues. This Chapter highlights those actions.

§ 9.02   OTS ACTIONS

[1]   OTS APPROVES INTERNET BANKS

On May 8, 1995, OTS issued an order providing conditional approval of the establishment of Security First Network Bank, FSB ("SFNB"), the first Internet bank.[4] SFNB offered potential customers nationwide the opportunity to visit SFNB's World Wide Web site, to open deposit accounts, and then to view account information and engage in transactions. In order to satisfy OTS safety and soundness concerns, prior to opening

---

[1]   The Office of Thrift Supervision was created as one of the successors to the Federal Home Loan Bank Board by the Financial Institutions Reform, Recovery, and Enforcement Act of 1989, Pub. L. No. 101-73, tit. III, 1989 U.S.C.C.A.N. (103 Stat.) 183, 277 (codified as amended in scattered sections of 12 U.S.C.).

[2]   Office of Thrift Supervision – OTS Mission and Functions (visited June 17, 1997) <http://www.ots.treas.gov>.

[3]   *Id.*

[4]   *See Kentucky Thrift Given Authority to Offer Services Over Internet*, OTS News Release 95-33 (May 10, 1995); Approval of Purchase of Assets and Assumption of Liabilities, OTS Order No. 95-88 (May 8, 1995) [hereinafter SFNB Order]. For more information on SFNB, including the possible sale of the bank, see Chapter 1, Section 1.03[3][b], note 17.

for business, SFNB had to obtain independent tests of the functionality and security of its operations. The pioneering role played by SFNB and OTS received wide attention.[5]

OTS approved a second Internet bank, Atlanta Internet Bank ("AIB"), on July 11, 1997.[6] In approving the establishment of AIB, OTS set conditions similar to those for approving SFNB. OTS required an independent security review and an AIB attestation that the computer system "does not allow unauthorized or undetected access to customer accounts, with reasonable certainty," by August 31, 1997.[7] Further, OTS required that AIB comply with the OTS "Statement on Retail On-Line Personal Computer Banking."[8]

[2] OTS PROPOSALS FOR UPDATING REGULATIONS ADDRESSING ELECTRONIC OPERATIONS

In order to meet its goal of creating a flexible regulatory framework, in 1995, OTS undertook a comprehensive review of its regulations. As part of that review, in the spring of 1997, OTS started to specifically address the impact of its regulations on electronic banking activities. On April 2, 1997, OTS published an advance notice of proposed rulemaking regarding the adequacy of OTS regulations concerning electronic banking ("Electronic Banking Notice").[9] In that notice OTS recognized that while entirely new regulations may be more appropriate than simple updates, it intended to focus primarily on the potential for updating the three regulations currently impacting directly on electronic operations: (1) remote service units ("RSUs");[10] (2) home banking services;[11] and (3) data processing.[12] Then, on October 3, 1997, having reviewed the comments on the Electronic Banking Notice, the OTS published a notice of proposed rulemaking ("Electronic Operations Proposal")[13] to eliminate the existing regulations and replace them with a single new subpart that would focus on electronic operations.

[a] **Electronic Banking Notice.** In the Electronic Banking Notice, the OTS identifies three existing regulations that affect a federal savings association's ability to engage in electronic activities. The first two regulations govern the type of facility that such an institution can use to deliver services: 12 C.F.R. § 545.141, Remote Service Units; and 12 C.F.R. § 545.142, Home Banking Services (together, "Facilities Regulations"). The third

---

[5] *See Banks Service on the Internet Cleared by U.S. Regulators*, WALL ST. J., May 11, 1995, at B4; *Kentucky Thrift Gets Green Light to Offer Banking Services on the Internet*, AM. BANKER, May 12, 1995, at 3; *Internet Bank Plan Wins Federal OK*, LEXINGTON HERALD-LEADER, May 10, 1995, at A13.

[6] *OTS Approves Internet Bank to Provide Range of Services*, News Release 97-44 (July 14, 1997); Approval of Holding Company Acquisition and Purchase of Assets and Assumption of Liabilities, Order No. 97-66 (July 11, 1997) [hereinafter *AIB Order*].

[7] *AIB Order, supra* note 6, at 3.

[8] *Id.*

[9] Deposits and Electronic Banking, 62 Fed. Reg. 15,626 (1997) (to be codified at 12 C.F.R. pts. 545, 556, 557, 561, 563 and 563g) (proposed Apr. 2, 1997).

[10] 12 C.F.R. § 545.141.

[11] 12 C.F.R. § 545.142.

[12] 12 C.F.R. § 545.138.

[13] Electronic Operations, 62 Fed. Reg. 51,817 (1997) (to be codified at 12 C.F.R. § 545.92, §§ 545.140-545.144) (proposed Oct. 3, 1997).

regulation establishes parameters for permissible federal savings association data processing activities; 12 C.F.R. § 545.138, Data Processing.[14] The Electronic Banking Notice divides the discussion into sections concerning facilities, permissible activities, and other issues, a format reflecting the current regulatory framework.

[*i*] *Facilities.* Facilities through which a federal savings association may deliver services to customers include: home offices, branches, agency offices, data processing or administrative offices, RSUs,[15] and home banking.[16] In the Electronic Banking Notice, OTS questioned whether automated loan machines ("ALMs"), which permit customers to apply for a consumer loan up to a specific limit by entering certain information by keypad into a machine resembling an ATM, should be considered branches or RSUs. The issue is significant because different rules govern the establishment of branches and RSUs, with the establishment of branches being subject to application requirements, and the establishment of RSUs not being subject to such requirements. In 1981, the Federal Home Loan Bank Board replaced the enumerated activities permissible for RSUs with a statement that RSUs could not be used to establish a loan account.[17] OTS queried whether it should broaden the definition of RSU to include ALMs and then adjust other facility definitions accordingly.[18] OTS is also considering whether a full range of banking services may be offered under the home banking services regulation.[19] At the time the regulation was drafted, home banking was defined to include only the "transfer of funds or financial information" and "the performance of other transactions initiated by the customer."[20] Accordingly, the OTS raised the question of whether this definition is broad enough to cover the opening of new accounts or the processing of credit applications using electronic banking systems.

[*ii*] *Data Processing.* OTS issued its data processing regulation,[21] at a time when the OTS interpreted data processing to mean the performance of nondiscretionary functions, such as maintenance of bookkeeping or accounting records.[22] Data processing technology now is capable of making risk-based decisions, for example, ALMs process loan applications. OTS indicated that it intends its regulations to reflect and accommodate such changes. In addition, OTS is reconsidering the necessity of restricting thrifts in the sales or marketing of services, software, and excess data processing capacity. In this regard, the OTS noted that the Office of the Comptroller of the Currency ("OCC") has afforded national banks broader authority to sell electronic services,

---

[14]   12 C.F.R. § 545.138.

[15]   12 C.F.R. § 545.141. A remote service unit ("RSU") is an information processing device not on the premises of a federal savings association.

[16]   12 C.F.R. § 545.142.

[17]   Deposits and Electronic Banking, 62 Fed. Reg. at 15,631. *See* Debit Cards; Remote Service Unit Amendments, 46 Fed. Reg. 8438, 8440 (1981); 12 C.F.R. § 545.141(b).

[18]   Deposits and Electronic Banking, 62 Fed. Reg. at 15,631.

[19]   *Id.* at 15,632.

[20]   Data Processing Activities of Federal Associations; Home Banking Services, 48 Fed. Reg. 7428, 7431 (1983).

[21]   *See* 12 C.F.R. § 545.138.

[22]   Deposits and Electronic Banking, 62 Fed. Reg. at 15,632.

products, and excess capacity than OTS has afforded federal savings associations.[23] OTS is seeking comment on whether it should provide similarly broad authority.

[*iii*] *Other Issues*. OTS requested comment on a variety of additional issues including the applicability of OTS regulations to stored value cards and how the "borderless nature of electronic banking will affect thrift responsibilities under the Community Reinvestment Act ("CRA").[24]

Current OTS regulations do not address stored value technology. OTS requested comment on all aspects of stored value technology. In addition, OTS requested specific comment on the following questions:

- How extensively will the industry use stored value cards?

- Do certain kinds of stored value programs present greater safety and soundness concerns than others?

- Do stored value cards present special issues that OTS should consider in examining the liabilities of a savings association?

- What kind of OTS guidance, if any, is appropriate for the industry?[25]

OTS requested comment on what factors should be considered, and how much weight each should be afforded, in determining what constitutes a community for CRA purposes when banking takes place electronically. OTS questioned whether (1) the location where the thrift is chartered, (2) where its brick and mortar branches stand, or (3) where its customers reside, should define the community. Further, OTS requested comment on how an institution can demonstrate that it is meeting the credit needs of widely dispersed customers.

[b] Electronic Operations Proposal. In reviewing the comments it received following the Electronic Banking Notice, the OTS discerned two broad guiding principles for the drafting of regulations to govern emerging electronic services provided by federal savings associations:

- The public and insured depository institutions will best be served if statutory and regulatory restrictions are kept to a minimum. Commenters feared that the premature imposition of restrictive operational standards would impede the development of improved financial services.

- Savings associations should be permitted to compete effectively with other regulated financial institutions and unregulated firms offering financial and related services.[26]

---

[23] *Id. See* Chapter 5, Section 5.03. *See, e.g.*, OCC Interpretive Letter No. 611, [1992-1993 Transfer Binder] Fed. Banking L. Rep. (CCH) ¶ 83,449, at 71,572 (Nov. 23, 1992) and OCC Interpretive Letter No. 742, [1996-1997 Transfer Binder] Fed. Banking L. Rep. (CCH) ¶ 81-106, at 90,215 (Aug. 19, 1996). *See also* OCC Interpretive Letter No. 196, [1981-1982 Transfer Binder] Fed. Banking L. Rep. ¶ 85,277, at 77,415 (May 18, 1981); Interpretive Letter No. 284, [1983-1984 Transfer Binder] Fed. Banking L. Rep. (CCH) ¶ 85,448, at 77,610 (Mar. 26, 1984); OCC Interpretive Letter No. 419, [1988-1989 Transfer Binder] Fed. Banking L. Rep. (CCH) ¶ 85,643, at 78,013 (Feb. 16, 1988).

[24] 12 C.F.R. pt. 563e. Under the Community Reinvestment Act, institutions are encouraged to help meet the credit needs of the local community.

[25] Deposits and Electronic Banking, 62 Fed. Reg. at 15,633.

[26] Electronic Operations, 62 Fed. Reg. at 51,817.

Consistent with these guiding principles, the Electronic Operations Proposal sets forth the text of a new subpart B to part 545 that would consolidate current regulations addressing electronic operations and describe how a federal thrift may provide products and services through electronic means and facilities. The substantive portion of the new subpart is broken down into four components:

- 545.141 How may I use electronic means and facilities?

- 545.142 When may I sell electronic capacities and by-products that I have acquired or developed?

- 545.143 How may I participate with others in the use of electronic means and facilities?

- 545.144 What security precautions must I take?

The Electronic Operations Proposal presents a summary of the goals and comments supporting the development of the each of these components.

[i] *How may I use electronic means and facilities*? In its discussion of the formulation of this section, the OTS emphasized the restrictive nature of the authority given to federal savings associations by the facilities regulations. As an example, the OTS noted that an RSU may not be used to open a savings or demand deposit account or to establish a loan account.[27] Further, the OTS stated that it remained unclear whether the home banking services regulation would permit the opening of new accounts or the processing of credit applications.[28] Commenters had requested that the OTS clarify and expand the range of permitted activities in a manner that would enable thrifts to compete more effectively with other financial service providers. The OTS responded by proposing to permit federal savings associations to "use electronic means or facilities to perform any authorized function or provide any authorized product or service."[29] Specifically, the OTS stated that electronic facilities include, but are not limited to, telephones, ATMs, ALMs, PCs, the Internet, and the World Wide Web. The OTS went on to note that electronic facilities are not considered branch offices and that the branch office regulations will be revised accordingly.[30]

[ii] *When may I sell the electronic capacities and by-products that I have acquired or developed*? In analyzing the existing regulations governing the sale of electronic capacities and by-products, the OTS emphasized the significant constraints imposed by those regulations, such as prohibiting data processing that encompasses risk-based decision making.[31] Commenters addressing those regulations suggested a more flexible approach that would make them more competitive with other financial institutions, an approach more in line with that taken by the OCC. The proposal permits federal savings associations to market and sell electronic

---

[27] *Id.* at 51,818.

[28] *Id.*

[29] *Id.*

[30] *Id.*

[31] *Id.*

capacities and by-products to third parties, so long as they are acquired or developed in good faith as part of the provision of financial services, a condition consistent with that imposed on national banks by the OCC.[32]

[*iii*] *How may I participate with others in the use of electronic means and facilities?* The OTS states that an entity that is not subject to regulation by a federal bank regulatory agency may participate with a federal savings association in the provision of electronic operations only if that entity agrees, in writing, to permit OTS to examine its electronic means and facilities. Further, the entity must agree to pay all fees relating to the examination and make all relevant records available to the OTS. The OTS noted that these requirements are not new. The existing electronic operations regulations contain similar provisions.

[*iv*] *What security precautions must I take?* The OTS, after considering some comments promoting the use of specific security measures and other comments suggesting that security should be part of a safety and soundness evaluation, chose not to codify static security requirements. Instead, the OTS, in the Electronic Operations Proposal, proposed to require that federal savings associations should adopt standards and policies designed to ensure secure operations.[33] Further, the provision would establish a requirement that security measures employed by federal savings associations must prevent unauthorized access to their records and their customer's records, and also must take steps "to prevent financial fraud through the use of electronic means or facilities."[34]

[3] INTERNET ACCESS SERVICES TO BE PROVIDED BY A FEDERAL SAVINGS BANK

In April 1997, OTS granted a savings bank permission to provide Internet access to customers and non-customers through a subsidiary.[35] OTS found the authority for providing these services in the OTS home banking services regulations[36] and the OTS data processing regulation.[37]

The OTS home banking services regulations allow federal savings associations to provide customers with home banking services through any electronic means.[38] The OTS found that providing customers with Internet access to their accounts in order to transfer funds, make account inquiries, and conduct other banking activities fell squarely within the scope of regulation.

---

[32] *Id.* at 51,819.

[33] *Id.*

[34] *Id.*

[35] Letter from Dwight C. Smith, III, Deputy Chief Counsel (Apr. 14, 1997) [hereinafter Home Banking Op.] The OTS did condition the approval on the non-customer accounts being part of a safe and sound implementation strategy approved by the appropriate regional OTS office. *See also* OCC Interpretive Letter No. 742, [1996-1997 Transfer Binder] Fed. Banking L. Rep. (CCH) ¶ 81-106, at 90,215 (Aug. 19, 1996).

[36] *See* 12 C.F.R. § 545.142.

[37] *See id.* § 545.138.

[38] *See id.* § 545.142.

The OTS data processing regulation allows federal savings associations to use data processing technology and equipment to perform any permissible activity.[39] Permissible data includes financial, economic, thrift-related, home financing, and data from other activities conducted by depository institutions. The processing must be for the savings bank itself, a subsidiary, another depository institution, or a person with whom the bank has an established loan or deposit relationship. The OTS found that providing customers with Internet access as a means of performing banking operations meets the requirements that the data be financial and that the processing be for a person with whom the savings association has an established relationship.

The OTS also found that the data processing regulation supplies the authority for extending the provision of Internet access to non-savings bank customers. The regulation permits the marketing of excess data processing capacity.[40] That permission is limited, however, by the requirements that the excess capacity not be artificially created and that the involvement not extend beyond the provision of access to facilities and operating personnel.[41] In applying these requirements to the facts presented by the savings bank, OTS determined that the savings bank subsidiary's plans regarding the amount and type of equipment to acquire appropriately met the savings bank's foreseeable needs.[42] OTS approved of the savings bank's efforts to limit access to its market area by offering only a local access number.[43]

[4] OTS GUIDANCE TO SAVINGS ASSOCIATIONS ON RETAIL ON-LINE PC BANKING

On June 23, 1997, OTS issued a statement of guidance to savings associations entitled Statement on Retail On-Line PC Banking ("PC Banking Guidelines") concerning retail online personal computer banking ("PC banking").[44] In a cover memorandum issued with the statement, John Downey, Executive Director of Supervision of the OTS, emphasized the importance of risk analysis and the implementation of appropriate risk controls.[45] Further, Downey urged institutions to consult with their OTS Regional Office regarding the implementation of PC banking programs.[46]

The PC Banking Guidelines begin with a background section defining PC banking and conclude with a section emphasizing the importance of planning, testing, and monitoring PC banking activities "as part of the system development methodology and the risk management process."[47] The main body of the PC Banking

---

[39] 12 C.F.R. § 545.138. An operating subsidiary of the federal savings bank may be the actual provider of the Internet access. Operating subsidiaries of federal savings associations can perform any activity that is permissible for the federal savings association to perform. 12 C.F.R. § 559.3(e)(1).

[40] 12 C.F.R. § 545.138(c).

[41] 12 C.F.R. § 545.138(c)(2).

[42] Home Banking Op., *supra* note 35, at 6.

[43] *Id.*

[44] *OTS Issues Guidance to Thrifts on Retail On-Line PC Banking, Statement on Retail On-Line PC Banking*, OTS News Release 97-39 (June 23, 1997) [hereinafter *PC Banking Guidelines*].

[45] Memorandum from John Downey to Chief Executive Officers on OTS Statement on Retail On-Line PC Banking (CEO Letter No. 70) (June 23, 1997).

[46] *Id.*

[47] *PC Banking Guidelines, supra* note 44, at 8.

Guidelines, entitled "Risks and Controls," focuses on the (i) strategic, (ii) legal/regulatory, and (iii) operational risks inherent in offering PC banking to customers. In its discussion of these risk areas, OTS explores traditional risks, as well as those unique to PC banking.

In assessing the strategic risks of implementing PC banking, the OTS recommends that financial institutions address four specific concerns:

- developing a business plan which justifies the program;

- making sufficient resources available to support the program;

- deciding whether to outsource certain functions or perform them in-house; and

- staying abreast of technological developments.[48]

OTS notes that these four areas should be addressed for any new product or service.

The legal/regulatory section emphasizes the risks resulting from uncertain impact of the electronic environment on the existing legal framework, jurisdiction, and regulatory compliance. OTS encourages management to consider the use of detailed contracts, digital signatures, and comprehensive disclosures as a means of mitigating the risks associated with these new products. With regard to jurisdiction, OTS advises institutions to consult with legal counsel and to develop policies governing whether and how they will conduct business with customers in different states and countries. Finally, OTS reminds institutions that though the existing regulations remain in force, new interpretations may require updating policies, procedures, and programs.

OTS defines operational risk as that arising "from the potential that inadequate information systems, operational problems, breaches in internal controls, fraud, and unforeseen events will result in unexpected losses."[49] The Statement's Operational Risk Section is divided into discussions of security and operations. OTS presents security as the paramount issue. The security section emphasizes the controls that management could implement to ensure customer data is protected from unauthorized access or alteration during the transmission process as well as in the internal systems. OTS specifically suggests the implementation of the following controls: authorization, access controls, authentication, secure data storage, encryption, and firewalls.[50] OTS, in its discussion of operations, reminds institution management that they have "little or no control over the performance of the Internet,"[51] and urges institutions to take action to ensure the reliability of their PC banking programs. OTS recommends the establishment of a PC banking program including program specific policies and procedures, client accounting, contingency plans, back up training, and audit procedures.

---

[48] *Id.* at 2.

[49] *Id.* at 5.

[50] *Id.* at 6.

[51] *Id.* at 7.

§ 9.03   OTS UPDATE OF EXAMINATION GUIDELINES FOR THE USE OF INFORMATION TECHNOLOGY

On October 15, 1997, the OTS issued a Regulatory Bulletin attaching a revised Thrift Activities Regulatory Handbook Section 341.[52] The OTS titled the new Section "Information Technology," replacing the prior title "Electronic Data Processing Controls," to "more accurately reflect the scope of these safety and soundness examination procedures."[53] The Information Technology Section incorporates guidance for savings associations on the employment of emerging information technologies. The OTS plans, in conjunction with the release of these new guidelines, to conduct a national training effort to educate examiners on information technology and its impact on safety and soundness.

The Information Technology Section is broken into three primary components: (1) Introduction; (2) Examination Objectives; and (3) Examination Procedures.[54] In addition, the Information Technology Section includes references to relevant federal regulations, OTS supervisory bulletins and memoranda, and other federal bank regulatory agency resources, as well as appendices that provide specific guidance in the areas of outsourcing contracts and the corporate business resumption and contingency planning process.

[1]   INTRODUCTION

The Introduction to the Information Technology Section, following a preliminary discussion of the need for a risk-based approach to examinations of institutions, breaks the discussion down further into four parts: (1) Information Technology and Electronic Banking in Financial Institutions; (2) Management Controls for Evaluating and Controlling Risks; (3) Examination Comments and Rating; and (4) Distinction Between Information Systems and Safety and Soundness Examinations.

[a] **Information Technology and Electronic Banking in Financial Institutions.** The OTS in this section focused on how the widespread use of personal computers changed information processing from a traditional, centralized operation to a decentralized or distributed network operation. While recognizing the benefits inherent in decentralization, such as increased productivity and enhanced information access, the OTS emphasized that decentralization changes the nature of the risks involved in information processing.[55] Because PC users may engage in program development, data manipulation, and data origination directly from their desktop computer, and each of these activities can and will affect decisions regarding corporate strategies and customer relationships, the OTS stressed the importance of operational controls at the PC user level. Recognizing that institutions may require more sophisticated information technology systems than they are capable of supporting efficiently internally, the OTS also addressed the risks inherent in outsourcing arrangements. The OTS warned institutions that the use of facilities management arrangements and service bureaus

---

[52] *Information Technology*, Regulatory Bulletin (RB) 32-6 (Oct. 15, 1997).

[53] *Id.*

[54] THRIFT ACTIVITIES REGULATORY HANDBOOK § 341 (Oct. 1997).

[55] *Id.* § 341.2.

may expose the institution to "excessive operating costs, poor outsourcing contracts that do not protect the institution in case of termination of service, loss of customer data, lack of data communications security, and lack of contingency planning."[56] It goes on to provide institutions with guidance for the contracting process.

[b] **Management Controls for Evaluating and Controlling Risks.** The OTS indicated that current institution operations may not adequately address many of the "unique aspects of the electronic environment,"[57] including transaction speed, geographic reach, and user anonymity. Specifically, the OTS recommended that management consider the adequacy of audit procedures, the effectiveness of outsourcing contracts in protecting the institution's interests, and the impact of new computer hardware and software on internal security. The OTS highlighted the importance of control practices governing input and use of information. Further, recognizing the interactive nature of technology and the potential for a compromise of security in one area to impact on other areas, the OTS recommended developing a risk management control program that could minimize the negative effects of a problem situation. The OTS emphasized the need for strategic planning in incorporating, and care in the deployment and operation of, new technology. It called for the establishment of input and output controls, information security systems, contingency plans, and an audit procedure specifically designed to evaluate the use of information technology.

[c] **Examination Comments and Rating.** The OTS in this section provided specific guidance for examiners in conducting their information technology examinations. Specifically, it called on examiners to consider:

- specific issues in relation to the volume and trends in transactions, dollars, and customers;

- apparent risk to the institution's financial and informational assets, including customer data, regardless of the volume and trends in activity;

- anticipated growth in volume, whether dollars, transactions, or customers; and

- anticipated expansion of products, services, or platforms.[58]

[d] **Distinction Between Information Systems and Safety and Soundness Examinations.** The information technology component of the safety and soundness examination is supplemented by information systems ("IS") examinations conducted by specially trained IS examiners in accordance with the policies and procedures of the Federal Financial Institutions Examination Council ("FFIEC").[59] IS examiners working under those policies and procedures are responsible for the "identification and reduction of unwarranted risks that could threaten a healthy system of financial institutions,"[60] such as IS conversion failures, inadequate management

---

[56] *Id.* § 341.3.

[57] *Id.* § 341.5.

[58] *Id.* § 341.10.

[59] FFIEC Information Systems Examination Handbook (1996). The Federal Financial Institutions Examination Council ("FFIEC") is discussed in Chapter 5.

[60] *Id.* at 2-1.

of information reporting systems, and catastrophic disasters.[61] IS examiners have traditionally been responsible for examining in-house data centers, service bureau, and other high risk situations. IS examiners will continue to examine national, regional, multiregional, and local service bureaus. Safety and soundness examiners will examine "the information systems and technology controls of institutions that have information systems services provided primarily by a service bureau, but are increasingly using internal information systems and technology to perform daily operations and provide products and services."[62] The OTS emphasized the importance of consultation between information system examiners and safety and soundness examiners.

[2]   EXAMINATION OBJECTIVES

In revised Section 341 the OTS provided a list of objectives to be taken into account by the safety and soundness examiners. It directed examiners to determine: (1) if management analyzed the investment, opportunities, and risk involved with deploying electronic capabilities; (2) if management policies, procedures, and internal controls are adequate to monitor and control information technology risk; and (3) whether the institution is in compliance with information technology related regulations. It also requires the examiner to assess: (1) the adequacy of security controls over computer and microcomputer terminals used for information technology services; (2) management's guidelines for selecting, evaluating, and monitoring service bureau performance; and (3) the adequacy of internal audit review of related information technology. Finally, the OTS instructs the examiner to recommend corrective action when internal control policies, procedures, and practices are deficient.[63]

[3]   EXAMINATION PROCEDURES

The OTS set forth a two level approach for the examination of information technology. In the first level, the examiner is expected to obtain and review information relating to technology controls, Internet activities, and outsourcing arrangements. An extensive review of the procedures for auditing information technology systems also occurs at this level. In the second level of review, the examiner is to select one or two departments that employ information systems and technology and evaluate the adequacy of the operational controls in place. As part of that evaluation the examiner is expected to examine the strategic planning mechanisms, outsourcing arrangements, insurance, operating controls, information security, contingency planning, and training programs in place in those departments. In the final phase of the examination, the examiner is expected to discuss the adequacy of the institution's information systems with other examiners and identify any significant problems.

---

[61]   *Id.* at 1-2.

[62]   *Id.*

[63]   THRIFT ACTIVITIES REGULATORY HANDBOOK, *supra* note 54, at § 341.12

CHAPTER 10

OTHER GOVERNMENTAL AND NONGOVERNMENTAL ENTITIES INFLUENCING ELECTRONIC FINANCIAL PRODUCTS AND SERVICES

§ 10.01 INTRODUCTION

The five preceding Chapters review how the federal bank regulatory agencies are shaping the environment for depository institutions that are planning to offer electronic financial products and services ("EFS"). As participants in EFS readily acknowledge, one thing that makes EFS so interesting and challenging is their interdisciplinary nature. As a practical matter this means that it is essential to recognize that the parties with an interest or a role in the structuring of the EFS industry, and its regulation, in many instances will extend far beyond the federal bank regulatory agencies. Moreover, just as EFS requires bank regulators to consider how new technologies interact with laws and policies enacted well before such technologies were contemplated, EFS likewise requires other governmental and non-governmental entities to accommodate new technologies. Other federal entities, state governments, private domestic organizations, and international organizations are all actively engaged in developing laws, regulations, and policies that will govern the EFS and other aspects of electronic commerce.

Section 10.02 reviews the balance between the government's interest in preventing money laundering and the public's interest in the protection of financial privacy and how these issues are addressed by the Financial Crimes Enforcement Network, the Department of the Treasury's regulatory arm, that has asserted jurisdiction over stored value and electronic payment products under the Bank Secrecy Act. Section 10.03 discusses the restrictions on banking organizations engaging in financial transactions, including those associated with EFS, with certain nations and individuals. Section 10.04 focuses on the role of the states in facilitating the development of EFS and electronic commerce and in regulating interactive activities, including electronic signature legislation, securities regulation, state consumer protection laws, and state commercial laws. Section 10.05 addresses the principles that will likely apply to taxation involving EFS and electronic commerce, and certain initial developments regarding new principles to govern taxation of such activities. Section 10.06 discusses the United Nations initiatives to provide an international framework for EFS and electronic commerce. Finally,

Section 10.07 reviews the efforts of the American Bar Association relating to financial electronic data interchange, digital signatures, and stored value.

§ 10.02   Financial Crimes Enforcement Network

The very features that make EFT so exciting — the ability to move "money" from computer to computer, or from computer to card, or from a card in one wireless phone to a card in another wireless phone — are the transformations that make EFS a concern to law enforcement. Such mechanisms could allow electronic value to be transferred freely from individuals to businesses, from business to business, and, most intriguingly, between individuals. If EFS develop in a way that allows them to operate (either within or outside of the banking system) in a manner that does not generate records showing the identities of the parties and the amounts involved in their transactions; and if the products allow for the cross border flow of money, then such developments may jeopardize law enforcement tools for surveillance, investigation, and prosecution of financial and other crimes.

On the other hand, a means of conducting transactions that do not create a permanent record may be something that is highly desirable. Today, in many transactions, individuals have the option to pay cash in exchange for goods. In most instances, no record is made of the identity of the individual engaging the purchase of goods or services. No implication of illegality or illegitimacy is imputed to the use of cash. There are a whole range of transactions of which, while perfectly legal, an individual may not wish to create an easily traceable record. Examples include purchases of certain books or publications, purchases of certain substances (*e.g.,* cigarettes or alcohol), purchases of certain types of apparel, payment for particular types of medical services, or just transactions, no matter that how innocuous, that place a person in a particular place at a particular time. The power of such information or its potential availability was demonstrated during the Supreme Court confirmation hearings for Robert Bork when a claim that he had rented adult videotapes set off an intensive effort to determine if there was any record of such a rental. In reaction, Congress concluded that the protection of personal privacy outweighed whatever benefit might come from allowing unlimited access to such information, and passed a law restricting access to videotape rental store records.[1]

[1]   A Cashless World

Imagine the world in 2020. You walk into a convenience store to buy a soda and a newspaper. You reach into your pocket and pull out your New York Yankees brand smart card with a stored value feature. You put the card in the reader on the counter and $5.50 is deducted from it (you think to yourself, I can remember when this would have only cost $1.15). You could also have paid with a debit card or credit card. But what you could not do was to pay with paper cash or coins.

How did this come to pass? As debit cards gained greater consumer acceptance, more merchants installed

---

[1]   Video Privacy Protection Act of 1988, Pub. L. No. 100-618, 1988 U.S.C.C.A.N. (102 Stat.) 3195 (codified at 18 U.S.C. § 2710).

equipment that allowed them to accept them for purchases. Smart cards with stored value features that provided loyalty benefits rapidly attracted consumers who appreciated the opportunity to get something extra with each purchase. Merchants began to consider whether the benefits of accepting cash — not losing a sale because a potential purchaser did not have an alternative form of payment available — still outweighed the burdens associated with cash. As the benefits began to shrink, the burdens loomed ever larger in the equation. In response, the government altered the legal tender laws, discontinuing the required acceptance of cash and coins as payment for any debt.

Merchants who dealt in cash, such as the convenience store, faced a range of problems associated with that medium. The use of cash put businesses at risk of employee theft. Furthermore, each cash transaction created the possibility for an innocent error in the change making process (one that was less likely to be corrected if it was in the customer's favor). Once the cash was collected it had to be counted and reconciled against the register receipts. Management effort was allocated to this process to deal with situations where the register receipts exceeded the cash actually turned in. Then the cash either was left on the premises overnight or taken by an employee to a bank night deposit window, either of which carried a security risk. In addition, the risk of robbery cast a shadow over many cash businesses. Television viewers are all too familiar with black and white video-camera views of clerks being shot even after they have turned over the small amount of money they had in the register. In addition to the tragedy to the employees involved and their families, the spillover effect was substantial. Employees were harder to attract and retain, thereby increasing costs, and customers did not want to expose themselves to being in the wrong place at the wrong time, thereby decreasing revenues. Merchants faced the need to incur additional expenses by increasing security both in terms of technology and on-site security personnel. Moreover, they faced the prospect of lawsuits by injured employees or customers.

[2]   A CURRENT PERSPECTIVE

As EFS develop, merchants may decide that a no-cash policy may be beneficial from a variety of perspectives. The government may foster the adoption of such policies by facilitating the use of stored value cards by government benefit recipients, and thereby reduce concerns that merchants will lose some part of their market by shifting away from cash.

The government may also have a number of direct incentives to reduce, isolate, stigmatize, or eliminate the use of cash. Businesses and individuals who operate on a cash basis may now participate in a vast underground network that exists outside of the reach of federal, state, and local tax authorities. Pursuing these enterprises now is a largely futile task. At some point in the future, however, businesses that accept cash may find that they are the exception rather than the rule and find themselves the targets of intensive, and unwelcome, scrutiny. Similarly individuals who hold cash, especially large amounts of cash, may find themselves the object of additional scrutiny in their contacts with law enforcement or tax authorities. Ultimately the government may eventually stop minting coins or printing cash and begin the process of retiring the supply in circulation.

At that point, the structure of electronic value will have a great deal of significance. Debit card and credit card transactions provide a direct documented link between a particular individual and a particular transaction. Will electronic value evolve in the same way, leaving your financial affairs accessible to whoever can review the records associated with your payment methods?

Although the issue of the privacy of transactions conducted through the use of electronic value has received relatively little attention among the general public, its has been at the forefront of concerns among the designers of electronic value systems either on philosophic grounds or as a marketing and security consideration. Dr. David Chaum, the inventor of ecash™ and other pioneering products in the world of electronic value, was drawn to design a system that enabled a bank customer to make an Internet purchase from a merchant, allowing the merchant to obtain value from the bank without letting the bank know which of its customers made the purchase. Dr. Chaum was motivated by concerns of how governments could misuse information regarding their citizens and how a system without cash might leave citizens no protection from an all-inquiring, all-knowing, government.[2]

Although the cash versus electronic value debate may not be held in earnest for some time, the stakes are high. What balance will be struck between moving cash, with its current relatively anonymous characteristics, into a digital form with the same anonymous characteristics or having it become the equivalent of an electronic tracking device?

In addition to electronic value product designers, the traceability of electronic value transactions has begun to emerge as a major concern for law enforcement in the U.S. and around the world. In the United States, the Financial Crimes Enforcement Network ("FinCEN"), an office of the Department of the Treasury, has taken the leading role in formulating government policy regarding the money laundering concerns relating to electronic value. This Section describes the type of threats that FinCEN can envision in this regard.

[3] A Fictitious Money Laundering Scenario

Mr. Smith stares at his piles of greenbacks, accumulated from his vast illicit drug enterprise spanning the Northeast. He frowns as he tries to figure out a way of getting all his cash out of the United States to his compatriots in Shangri-La, so that the cash can eventually "legitimately" return and fund his campaign to take over the world. All of his current options — banks, wire transfer services, currency exchangers, and the like — result in the production of records and reports that are accessible to the nosy United States government. It looks as if Mr. Smith will have to bring out the false-bottomed suitcases and hope that the Customs Service's currency-sniffing dogs develop the flu.[3]

---

[2] Alan Deutschman, *Money Wants to be Anonymous*, WORTH, Oct. 1995, at 95.

[3] In an effort to make money laundering and money smuggling more difficult, the government has stopped printing large denomination bills. As a result, the movement of large amounts in cash form has become quite conspicuous. This was recently illustrated by the story of an armored car driver who stole $20 million from his truck and then had the practical problem of how to move cash that filled three duffel bags. It was clear that this would present a true logistical quandary: would he trust it to checked baggage or try to put it in the overhead bin? *See* Thomas W. Lippman, *Suspect in $21 Million Armored Car Haul Arrested in Texas*, WASH. POST, Aug. 31, 1997, at A7; Karl Vick, *Have You Seen This Man? He's 33, Single, Lonely, Grouchy, Rumpled and Very Possibly the Richest Thief Who Ever Lived*, WASH. POST, July 27, 1997, at F1.

Mr. Smith's despair fades when he spies an advertisement in his favorite tech magazine for "A-Cash," issued by XYZ Corp. "Fully anonymous," "within seconds," and "around the world" are but a few of the phrases that reel in the usually skeptical Mr. Smith. He decides to visit with his local XYZ Corp. agent, and subsequently signs up for the A-Cash Electronic-Money Smart-Card and Internet program. Mr. Smith proceeds to transfer his ill-gotten profits into his new XYZ Corp. account and, in return, receives a small card that can be loaded with electronic value. Because the electronic money business is so new, XYZ Corp. is not yet subject to United States anti-money laundering information-collecting regulations. Soon, Mr. Smith's A-Cash account contains more than $10 million. He has several options for getting this money out of the United States.

1. He may put A-Cash on his smart card, take the card over to the A-Cash smart card reader installed in his personal computer, press a few keys, and instantaneously transfer the value of the card to one of his many offshore bank accounts. No financial intermediary is needed, and there is no paper trail.

2. He may put A-Cash on his smart card, and then transfer that value to his portable A-cash electronic wallet. He may then give the wallet to one of his couriers, who can discreetly take the wallet out of the country.

3. Or, if he feels nostalgic for the "good old days," he may just take one or many smart cards loaded with electronic value out of the country in a baseball card box. With no need to carry bulky cash, Mr. Smith finally has room in his suitcase for his tennis racket.

If Mr. Smith does not wish to utilize the smart card feature of XYZ Corp.'s A-Cash system, he may simply authorize an electronic money transfer from his account directly through his personal computer. In one short period, Mr. Smith may "load up" with electronic money and send the money anywhere an electronic mail message can go.[4]

Finally, Mr. Smith might convince his "customers" to join the A-Cash program. The customers may pay him in A-Cash by simply transferring "purchasing power" from their electronic wallets right into Mr. Smith's electronic wallet.[5] From there, transferring the money out of the U.S. is easy. Again, Mr. Smith does not require a financial intermediary, and now he does not have to deal in paper currency at all.

Such a "launderer-friendly" electronic value system is not likely to ever be available to the public. However, Mr. Smith's situation provides a cursory view of the kind of technology that has been developed for electronic money systems. In theory, electronic money can provide both the anonymity of currency and the speed of wire transfer. Such characteristics could provide a new way to transform "dirty" money into

---

[4]   *See* Steven Levy, *E Money (That's What I Want)*, WIRED, Dec. 1994, *available at* (visited Jan. 28, 1998) <http://www.wired.com/wired/2.12/features/emoney.html>.

[5]   *See* Glenn Wahlert, *Money Laundering, the Perils of Cyberpayments*, TECH. CRIME BULL., Sept. 1996, *available at* (visited June 18, 1997) <http://www.rcmp>.

"clean" money.

[4]   MONEY LAUNDERING

Money laundering involves disguising the sources and amounts of cash derived from illegal activities. The money launderer transforms illegally obtained proceeds into funds with an apparently legal source.[6] Thus, the actions performed in the course of money laundering tend to be "not only legal but commonplace."[7] Money laundering can be as simple as transporting and depositing money in an offshore bank account. FinCEN warns that money laundering has "devastating social consequences . . . . [M]oney laundering provides the fuel for drug dealers, terrorists, arms dealers, and other criminals to operate and expand their operations . . . . Left unchecked, money laundering can erode the integrity of our nation's and the world's financial institutions."[8]

The process of money laundering can be broken down into three parts:

1. Placement – Physically placing cash proceeds into "legitimate repositories . . . with as little trace of the source and beneficial ownership as possible."[9]

2. Layering – Further separating the proceeds of criminal activity from their origins through layers of complex transactions.

3. Integration – Providing an apparently legitimate explanation for the illicit proceeds.[10]

In order to have a successful money laundering operation, a criminal must avoid a paper trail that can link the three steps together. This paper trail, which usually consists of records and reports filled out each time large amounts of cash pass through different points in the financial system, is the government's primary weapon in the fight against money laundering.[11] Much of this transactional recordkeeping is mandated by anti-money laundering legislation enacted in the United States and around the world.

The most familiar way money launderers avoid a paper trail is by physically smuggling illegal cash proceeds out of the country of their illegal origin and into jurisdictions with staunch financial secrecy or weak anti-money laundering legislation.[12] The risk and bulk of this type of activity, however, has forced potential launderers to seek other means of transport. Rather than attempt to sneak large amounts of currency past the eyes, ears, and noses of the United States Customs Service, launderers have resorted to other tactics. Their primary focus has been the manipulation of the financial institution system. Because banks and other financial

---

[6]   *See* FINCEN, *What is Money Laundering?*, *available at* (visited May 30, 1997) <http://www.treas.gov>.

[7]   Stephen R. Kroll, *Some Thoughts on Law Enforcement and Stored Value Products*, 12 BUTTERWORTHS J. INT'L. BANKING & FIN. L. 1 (1997).

[8]   FINCEN, *The Global Fight Against Money Laundering*, *available at* (visited May 30, 1997) <http://www.treas.gov>.

[9]   Sarah Jane Hughes, *"Cyberlaundering" Poses Threat to Controls*, MONEY LAUNDERING ALERT, Apr. 1995, at 1.

[10]   *See* OCC, *Money Laundering - Background*, *available at* (visited June 16, 1997) <http://www.occ.treas.gov>.

[11]   The points at which financial institutions record large cash transfers are commonly referred to as "chokepoints." *See Money in Cyberspace*, *available at* (visited May 30, 1997) <http://www.treas.gov>.

[12]   Countries such as these are often referred to as money-laundering "havens."

intermediaries are "the linchpin of any effective anti-money laundering strategy,"[13] any disabling of an institution's watchdog system leaves the door wide open for successful money laundering.

The most blatant misuse of the banking system involves the possible complicity of bank employees.[14] In some instances, there have been findings that individual depository institutions failed to meet the obligation to police possible money laundering occurring at their institution.[15] If a launderer convinces an employee who is required to report large cash transfers to look the other way, that launderer avoids a traceable paper trail. In other instances, launderers may hire "smurfs," whose function is to break down large amounts of illicit funds into smaller increments, such that subsequent transfers of the cash do not trigger the various cash reporting limits set by governmental agencies.[16] Other traditional money laundering methods include the purchase and transport of foreign currency with proceeds of illegal activity, the wire transfer of criminal funds, the purchase and transport of assets using criminal cash (followed by a subsequent sale of the assets overseas), the purchase and shipping of money orders, criminal investment in "legitimate" companies, and more complicated schemes such as "reverse flips"[17] and "loanbacks."[18] No matter what form the activity takes, however, the overall thrust is always to thwart the government's ability to "follow the money."[19]

[a] Laundering Electronic Money in a World Without Regulation. Traditional forms of electronic fund transfer have not been alluring to money launderers, because of the records generated by each transaction. Electronic money, however, may be attractive to money launderers and legitimate consumers alike because of its potential for facilitating untraceable transactions.[20] Electronic money systems with "peer-to-peer" capability — which allows customers to transfer electronic money amongst themselves without the intervention of a financial intermediary — are potentially the most vulnerable to money laundering. In theory, a money launderer using electronic money could transfer criminal proceeds out of the country without having to pass

---

[13] Ann Davis, *Nations Worry About a Rise in On-Line Money Laundering*, WALL ST. J., Mar. 17, 1997, at B1 (quoting Stanley Morris, Director of the Department of the Treasury's Financial Crimes Enforcement Network ("FinCEN")).

[14] *See* Michelle Celarier, *Citi and the Mexican Millions*, EUROMONEY, May 1997, at 12.

[15] *See* Fox Butterfield, *Bank in Boston Fined on Shifts in Cash Abroad*, N.Y. TIMES, Feb. 8, 1985, at A1; James Vicini, *High Court Lets Stand Bank of New England Conviction, Fine,* REUTER BUS. REP., Nov. 9, 1987, *available in* LEXIS, Nexis Library, News File.

[16] *See Money Laundering, A Preventive Guide for Small Business & Currency Exchanges in Canada, available at* (visited July 11, 1997) <http://www.rcmp-grc.gc.ca/html/launder.htm> (published by the Royal Canadian Mounted Police, Proceeds of Crime Unit).

[17] A "reverse flip" occurs when a money launderer negotiates a below market value purchase price with a seller, who then accepts the difference under the table. It enables the money launderer to purchase a $2 million item for $1 million. The money launderer then sells the property for its stated value. *See* Holger Jensen, *The Laundering Game*, MACLEAN'S, Oct. 23, 1989, at 54. *See also Money Laundering and the Drug Trade: Hearing Before the Subcomm. on Crime of the House Comm. on the Judiciary,* 105th Cong. (1997).

[18] A "loan-back" results when a launderer establishes an off-shore corporation. The launderer then purchases a business in his or her own country with money borrowed from the offshore corporation. The launderer makes scheduled payments on the loan, and pays interest to the off-shore corporation. Jensen, *supra* note 17.

[19] United States Department of Treasury Conference, *An Introduction to Electronic Money Issues*: *Toward Electronic Money and Banking: The Role of Government,* Sept. 19-20, 1996, at app. 2 [hereinafter Electronic Money Issues].

[20] *See, e.g.,* Jon W. Matonis, *Digital Cash and Monetary Freedom, available at* (visited July 8, 1997) <http://www.info.isoc.org> (describing anonymity as one of the "key elements" of a marketable digital cash system).

through any financial system chokepoints.[21] Once launderers convert cash into electronic value, the technology exists to design off-line systems that do not trace the path taken by the electronic money.

If an electronic money system utilizes an "electronic key" mechanism, for instance, then the issuer does not see the numbers that make up each batch of electronic cash issued (outgoing electronic money).[22] Thus, the issuer can only trace incoming electronic money to the redeemer at the tail end of that electronic money's journey. If a launderer were to take out a batch of electronic money, and then send it through a variety of channels, it is unlikely that the electronic money issuer could ever trace the electronic money back to the launderer. The very cornerstone of money laundering countermeasures — information — would be largely bypassed.

The potential proliferation of off-shore "cyberbanks" poses yet another challenge for anti-money laundering authorities: the diminished effectiveness of "know your customer" directives to financial institutions. For example, prior to its failure in August 1997 amidst allegations that it had come under the control of Russian mob figures, The European Union Bank of Antigua, a widely publicized Internet-based bank, allowed potential customers to open accounts merely by filling out an electronic form, mailing or faxing a copy of some form of identification to the bank, and sending in a deposit of as low as $2,500.[23] This lack of face-to-face contact could make it difficult for cyberbanks or other electronic money providers to distinguish between "the largest international conglomerate and the smallest garage business . . . and . . . next to nothing may be revealed about the organization's actual activities."[24] Again, the government is deprived of its money laundering informational countermeasure.[25]

Though the technology exists for such untraceable transactions, it is still unclear whether these type of transactions will become generally available. The ongoing debate centers around the balance between the collection of transactional information for law enforcement purposes and consumer privacy and security.[26] Both governments and members of the electronic money industry are contemplating measures which would either restrict the amount of anonymity in electronic money systems or limit the value of electronic money transactions to the point that the use of electronic money would become economically unfeasible for launderers. Governments are also attempting to determine whether current anti-money laundering regulations can be successfully applied to electronic money, or if more industry-specific regulation will have to be developed once the electronic

---

[21] *See, e.g., FATF Highlights Money Laundering Trends: E-Cash Could Hamper Law Enforcement*, Banking Daily (BNA), Feb. 10, 1997, at D2 (discussing the conclusions of the February 1997 money laundering report released by the multilateral Financial Action Task Force).

[22] *See* Levy, *supra* note 4. In an "electronic key" system, the customer's request for electronic money is concealed within a digital "envelope." The issuer signs its authorization on the outside of the digital "envelope." Thus, the authorization is transferred directly onto the electronic key within the "envelope," and the issuer never sees the set of numbers which makes up that particular electronic money. *Id.*

[23] *See Antigua Cyberbank Tests Laundering Curbs*, MONEY LAUNDERING ALERT, June 1, 1996, at 1 ("The methods the bank uses to verify identity are unclear."); Larry Rohter, *New Bank Fraud Wrinkle in Antigua: Russians on the Internet*, N.Y. TIMES, Aug. 20, 1997, at A4; Jeanne Whalen, *Russians Linked to Collapsed Caribbean Bank*, MOSCOW TIMES, Aug. 23, 1997.

[24] *Cyberlaunderers: A First Look*, MONEY LAUNDERING L. REP., Mar. 1997, at 5.

[25] United States taxpayers are required to report any foreign bank account holdings on Schedule B, line 11a of Form 1040.

[26] *See, e.g., NSA: On the Costs of Anonymity*, AM. BANKER, Dec. 23, 1996, at 6A (describing the difference between "privacy" and total "anonymity").

money industry is more widespread and better understood.

[5]   UNITED STATES MONEY LAUNDERING REGULATION AND ITS POTENTIAL APPLICABILITY TO ELECTRONIC MONEY

Anti-money laundering legislation in the United States centers around the Bank Secrecy Act ("BSA"), enacted in 1970.[27] The original purpose of the BSA was to prevent the use of bank accounts to conceal tax fraud, gambling operations, and other activities typical of organized crime.[28] The BSA did not actually criminalize money laundering,[29] but rather created an information trail for the government's pursuit of criminal actors. The BSA required financial institutions to fill out Currency Transaction Reports for cash transactions in amounts over $10,000, and required the reporting of any cross-border transport of more than $5,000 in cash using Reports of International Transportation of Currency or Monetary Instruments.

Gradually, Congress amended and expanded the scope of the BSA, increasing the number of activities and types of financial institutions covered. Money laundering actually became a criminal activity with the passage of the Money Laundering Control Act of 1986 ("MLCA"),[30] which criminalized all transactions conducted with the proceeds of illegal activity if the actor knew of the illegal underlying derivation of the funds used.[31] The MLCA also strengthened the BSA by criminalizing the structuring of transactions to avoid BSA reporting and recording thresholds. At least one circuit court has found that a person may be found guilty of money laundering even if that person has no knowledge of the specific illegal activity underlying the funds.[32] Rather, knowledge that the laundered money was *somehow* illegally obtained is sufficient for conviction.[33]

In 1988, the Kerry Amendment attempted to expand the BSA record keeping requirements to the international level.[34] The amendment required the United States to pursue bilateral information-sharing agreements with other nations concerning anti-money laundering transaction reporting and recording.[35] This provision was the first notable recognition of the fact that money laundering is a problem that stretches across national borders.[36]

---

[27] Bank Records and Foreign Transactions, Pub. L. No. 91-508, 1970 U.S.C.C.A.N. (84 Stat. 1114) 1301 (codified as amended at 12 U.S.C. §§ 1829b, 1951-59, 31 U.S.C. §§ 5311-30). For a further discussion of the Bank Secrecy Act and implementing regulations thereunder, see JOHN K. VILLA, BANKING CRIMES, ch. 6 (1997) and CLIFF E. COOK, BANK SECRECY (1991).

[28] *See In re Grand Jury No. 76-3*, 555 F.2d 1306, 1309 (5th Cir. 1977).

[29] The Bank Secrecy Act did, however, mandate civil and criminal penalties for violations of its provisions and implementing regulations.

[30] Money Laundering Control Act of 1986, Pub. L. No. 99-570, tit. 1, 1986 U.S.C.C.A.N. (100 Stat.) 3207 (codified as amended in scattered sections of 12, 18, and 31 U.S.C.).

[31] *See* 18 U.S.C. §§ 1956-57.

[32] *See United States. v. Maher*, 108 F.3d 1513, 1526 (2d Cir. 1997).

[33] *Id.*

[34] International Narcotics Control Act of 1988, Pub. L. No. 100-690, tit. IV, 1988 U.S.C.C.A.N. (102 Stat.) 4261 (codified in scattered sections of 18, 22, 31 U.S.C.).

[35] *Id.* § 4407, 1988 U.S.C.C.A.N. at 4277 (codified at 22 U.S.C. § 2291).

[36] The provision was repealed in 1992, when the Department of State was given responsibility for international anti-money laundering cooperation.

In 1992, the Annunzio-Wylie Anti-Money Laundering Act authorized the Secretary of the Treasury to require financial institutions to report any suspicious transactions by customers.[37] It also absolved financial institution employees of any liability for reporting suspicious transactions to the government and forbade them from notifying the customers who were engaging in the suspicious transactions that a report had been filed regarding their activities.[38] This combination of reporting and non-disclosure, at a minimum, puts financial institutions in an awkward position. If the bank tries to end or scale back its relationship with the customer in question, it may have a very difficult time doing so without giving some indication of the nature of its concerns regarding the customer. Where the bank's actions do not appear to be justified by objective financial criteria, it may find itself facing customer claims based on lender liability or prohibited discrimination theories.

In the same legislation, Congress also sought to focus the attention of depository institutions on their responsibilities for combating money laundering. It provided that a national bank or federal savings association that is convicted of a money laundering or cash transaction reporting offense could be subject to the forfeiture of its charter.[39] A state chartered depository institution that is convicted of a money laundering or cash transaction reporting offense could be subject to the termination of its FDIC insurance.[40] In the event of such a conviction, the Attorney General is directed to notify the Office of the Comptroller of the Currency, in the case of national banks; the Office of Thrift Supervision, in the case of federal savings associations; and the Federal Deposit Insurance Corporation, in the case of state chartered depository institutions.

Upon receipt of such notice, federal bank regulatory agencies are required to take a number of factors into account in deciding whether the institution's charter should be forfeited or insurance terminated. These factors include:

- The extent to which director or senior officers of the institution knew of, or were involved in, the commission of the offense.

- The extent to which the offense occurred despite the existence of policies and procedures designed to prevent the occurrence of such offense.

- The extent to which the institution fully cooperated with law enforcement authorities with respect to the offense.

- The extent to which the institution has implemented additional internal controls since the commission of the offense of which it was convicted.

---

[37] Annunzio-Wylie Anti-Money Laundering Act, Pub. L. No. 102-550, § 1517, 1992 U.S.C.C.A.N. (106 Stat.) 4044, 4059 (codified at 31 U.S.C. § 5314(g)).

[38] 31 U.S.C. § 5318(g)(2), (3).

[39] Annunzio-Wylie Anti-Money Laundering Act § 1502(a), (b), 1992 U.S.C.C.A.N. at 4045 (codified at 12 U.S.C. §§ 93(c), 1464(w)).

[40] Id. § 1503, 1992 U.S.C.C.A.N. at 4048 (codified at 12 U.S.C. § 1818(w)).

- The extent to which the interest of the local community in having adequate deposit and credit services available would be threatened by the forfeiture or termination of insurance.[41]

This "death penalty" for depository institution money laundering has made compliance with the BSA and its implementing regulations a critical priority for every institution.[42]

In 1994, Congress enacted the Money Laundering Suppression Act as an amendment to the BSA.[43] The Act included provisions authorizing the Treasury to designate a single agency to receive suspicious activity reports and requiring all money transmitting businesses to register with the Treasury.[44] The latter provision came as a recognition of the increasing use of wire transfer services by money launderers.

FinCEN has the responsibility for adopting regulations to implement the BSA. The regulations provide the current monetary thresholds for transaction recording and reporting by financial institutions. Generally, $10,000 is the reporting threshold for cash transactions.[45] For anti-money laundering purposes, financial institutions that conduct cash transactions greater than $10,000 must fill out Currency Transaction Reports.[46] In addition, the regulations mandate a $5,000 threshold for suspicious transaction reporting by banks, as well as a $3,000 reporting floor for sellers of financial instruments such as traveler's checks and money orders.[47] Because money launderers appear to increasingly utilize nonbank financial institutions, such as wire transferors, for their laundering activities, FinCEN has increased its focus on such institutions. This focus is clearly represented in three recently proposed amendments to the BSA regulations. These amendments, among other things, address the potential relationship between electronic money and money laundering for the first time.

[a] The New BSA Amendments and Electronic Money. On May 19, 1997, FinCEN proposed three new rules as amendments to its regulations implementing the BSA. Through increased informational requirements for nonbank financial institutions, the amendments expand the audit trail currently used to track and control money laundering. The amendments also bring a new class of financial institutions, deemed "money services businesses," within the scope of the BSA's application. These proposed rules are the result of four factors: (1) a 1994 BSA amendment mandating registration of money services businesses; (2) a 1992 BSA amendment mandating the reporting of suspicious transactions, such as structured "smurf" transactions;

---

[41] 12 U.S.C. §§ 93(c)(2), 1464(w)(2), 1818(w)(2).

[42] As of this date, the death penalty provision with respect to depository institutions has not been triggered. *See Money Laundering Hearing, supra* note 17 (testimony of Michael Zeldon, Partner, Price Waterhouse).

[43] Money Laundering Suppression Act of 1994, Pub. L. No. 103-325, tit. IV, 1994 U.S.C.C.A.N. (108 Stat.) 2243 (codified in scattered sections of 31 U.S.C.).

[44] *Id.* § 403, 1994 U.S.C.C.A.N. at 2245 (codified at 31 U.S.C. § 5318(g)(4)). The government later named FinCEN as this agency.

[45] 31 C.F.R. §§ 103.22, 103.23.

[46] Currency Transaction Report, Form 4789 (Rev. Oct. 1995).

[47] 31 C.F.R. §§ 103.21(a)(2), 103.29. These thresholds do not apply in cases of insider abuse. *See, e.g.,* 12 C.F.R. § 563.180(d)(3)(i).

(3) the successful implementation of a FinCEN Geographic Targeting Order ("GTO") in New York City during 1996;[48] and (4) the emergence of stored value and electronic money products.[49]

The first proposed amendment to the BSA regulations requires "money services businesses"[50] to register with the Department of the Treasury and to maintain a current list of their agents for periodic governmental examination. The purpose of the amendment is to assist law enforcement and to prevent money services businesses from engaging in illegal activities.[51] The proposed amendment would, for the first time, address the treatment of stored value under the BSA. Under the proposal, FinCEN would consider stored value to be similar to money orders and traveler's checks, and thus to fall within the scope of the BSA. Issuers and sellers of stored value would generally be treated as being engaged in the money services business and would be subject to proposed registration requirements applicable to such entities. They would also be subject to other provisions of the BSA and its implementing regulations.

Issuers and sellers of stored value must register with the government only if they surpass a transactional threshold of $500 per person/per day.[52] The purpose of this threshold, according to FinCEN Director Stanley Morris, is to single out only those businesses that are plausible conduits for efficient money laundering.[53] Under the proposal, stored value would be defined as "funds or monetary value represented in digital electronic format and stored, or capable of being stored, on electronic media in such a way as to be retrievable and transferable electronically."[54]

---

[48] A GTO is a tool used to combat money laundering in specific areas with noted laundering problems. Title II of the BSA gives the Secretary the authority, through GTOs, "to obtain additional information on specified transactions within a geographical area 'if the Secretary [of the Treasury] finds . . . that reasonable grounds exist for concluding that additional record-keeping and reporting requirements are necessary to carry out the purposes of [the BSA]." Steven Tabackman, *Tips on What to Do About Those Geographical Targeting Orders*, MONEY LAUNDERING L. REP., Sept. 1996, at 1, 6 (citing 31 U.S.C. § 5326(a)). The Secretary, subsequently, "has delegated his statutory authority to the [U]ndersecretary for enforcement; actual administrative activity within Treasury rests with [FinCEN]." *Id. See also* 31 U.S.C. § 5318(a)(1) (discussing the Secretary's power to delegate his/her duties under the BSA to "an appropriate supervising agency").

The Secretary's "reasonable grounds" for the New York GTO, which began in August, 1996, were largely statistical. A community of about 25,000 households in New York City was wiring approximately $1.2 billion to South America, mostly to Colombia. Ronald Powers, *Crackdown Takes Aim at Drug-Money Smugglers*, WASH. DATELINE, March 12, 1997. This broke down to roughly $50,000 per year per household in a community where the median household income was $27,000. This anomaly led FinCEN to impose strict reporting requirements in the New York City metropolitan area. The GTO mandated that wire money transmitters record and report all transfers greater than $750. *See* David E. Sanger, *U.S. Plans Tighter Rules to Curb Money Transfers by Drug Cartels*, N.Y. TIMES, May 19, 1997, at A1. The previous reporting threshold for money transactions and transfers was $10,000. Having to break up large drug money transfers into increments of $749 or less imposed a significant burden on drug traffickers.

[49] *See Stored Value Systems Brought Under BSA by New Rules*, MONEY LAUNDERING ALERT, June 1997, at 1.

[50] Definition and Registration of Money Services Businesses, 62 Fed. Reg. 27,890 (1997) (to be codified at 31 C.F.R. pt. 103) (proposed May 21, 1997) [hereinafter MSB Proposal]. The term "money services businesses" includes "currency dealers or exchangers; check cashers; issuers of traveler's checks, money orders or stored value; sellers or redeemers of traveler's checks, money orders, or stored value; and money transmitters." *Id.* at 27,891 (to be codified at 31 C.F.R. § 103.11(uu)).

[51] *See id.*

[52] *Id.* at 27,897-98 (to be codified at 31 C.F.R. § 103.11(uu)(3), .41(a)).

[53] *See* Financial Crimes Enforcement Network, Public Meeting, Money Services Businesses: Proposed Anti-Money Laundering Rules, Aug. 15, 1997 (copy on file with the authors).

[54] MSB Proposal, 62 Fed. Reg. at 27,898 (to be codified at 31 C.F.R. § 103.11(vv)).

In proposing to make stored value expressly subject to the BSA, FinCEN stated that it intends to elimi-nate any lingering doubt that offerors and operators of advanced electronic payment systems are subject to the BSA.[55] At the same time, it stated that its treatment of stored value for purposes of the BSA should not be taken as expressing a view by the Treasury regarding whether stored value should fall within the scope of state laws applicable to money transmitters and similar entities.

FinCEN recognized that, as mechanisms for the issuance and transmission of stored value develop, the appropriateness of any particular characterization for BSA purposes may change. It also recognized that the characteristics of such advanced electronic payment systems may present special issues as specific BSA recordkeeping and reporting requirements for such systems are formulated. In this regard, FinCEN asked for comments on a number of issues regarding stored value including:

- The manner in which BSA rules should be applied to advanced electronic payment systems.

- The potential impact of BSA compliance on the design and operation of such systems.

- Whether products such as telephone cards or other closed system products, or products that are limited to facilitating micropayments, should be treated differently than other stored value products for purposes of the registration requirements of the rule.[56]

The second proposed amendment requires "money transmitters and issuers, sellers, and redeemers of money orders and traveler's checks to report suspicious transactions involving at least $500 in funds or other assets."[57] In effect, this amendment applies to all money services businesses except for those dealing in stored value. Banks, broker-dealers, and casinos are not subject to this $500 threshold. The businesses under the scope of this amendment tend to transact in much lower increments. The $500 threshold reflects the codification of a previously informal governmental presumption of drug-related activity. This amendment also reflects the evolving international posture regarding money laundering, as articulated in the central recommendations of the Financial Action Task Force ("FATF").[58] FATF Recommendation Fifteen states that "[i]f financial institutions suspect that funds stem from a criminal activity, they should be required to report promptly their suspicions to the competent authorities."[59]

---

[55] *Id.* at 27,893.

[56] *Id.* at 27,893-94.

[57] Requirement of Money Transmitters and Money Order and Traveler's Check Issuers, Sellers, and Redeemers to Report Suspicious Transactions, 62 Fed. Reg. 27,900 (1997) (to be codified at 31 C.F.R. § 103.20) (proposed May 21, 1997) [hereinafter Suspicious Transactions Proposal].

[58] The Financial Action Task Force ("FATF") is a multilateral organization established by the Group of Seven Nations ("G-7"), whose purpose is to develop and promote of policies to combat money laundering. Its members currently consist of: Australia, Austria, Belgium, Canada, Denmark, Finland, France, Germany, Greece, Hong Kong, Iceland, Ireland, Italy, Japan, Luxembourg, the Netherlands, New Zealand, Norway, Portugal, Singapore, Spain, Sweden, Switzerland, the United Kingdom, the United States, the European Commission and the Gulf Cooperation Council. *See* FinCEN, *Money in Cyberspace* (last modified Feb. 3, 1997), *available at* <http://www.treas.gov>.

[59] *See* Suspicious Transactions Proposal, 62 Fed. Reg. at 27,901. *See also* FATF-VII: THE FORTY RECOMMENDATIONS OF THE FINANCIAL TASK FORCE ON MONEY LAUNDERING, Annex I, at ¶ 22 (discussing FATF recommendations requiring anti-money laundering compliance programs) [hereinafter FATF REPORT].

FinCEN exempted stored value issuers and sellers from the second proposed amendment because "it is not appropriate given the infancy of the use of stored value . . . to propose a rule specifically dealing with suspicious transaction reporting by nonbanks with respect to stored value *at this time*."[60] As noted, stored value *is* specifically included in the overall scope of the BSA, under the definition of "money services businesses."[61] This leaves the door open for FinCEN to require stored value dealers to report suspicious transactions — and comply with other BSA provisions — once stored value technology is better developed and understood.[62] However, one commentator has stated that BSA informational requirements would "generate little compliance" due to the potential for untraceable peer-to-peer transactions.[63]

The third proposed amendment to the BSA requires "money transmitters" to report and maintain records of all international transfers between $750 and $10,000, and to verify the identities of the senders.[64] As used here, "money transmitters" is intended to refer only to wire transmitters, such as those covered by the New York GTO.[65] This proposed amendment effectively extends the $750 GTO reporting threshold to all money transmitting businesses nationwide.

Shortly after it proposed the new regulations, FinCEN announced that it would hold a series of four public hearings across the country in July and August 1997.[66] The hearing and comment process brought forth criticism of the proposal from stored value industry participants.[67]

Ultimately the key question will be how FinCEN seeks to apply its BSA regulations to the documentation and reporting of transactions involving stored value and other electronic payment systems. At least one FinCEN representative has suggested that a bank could be acting inconsistently with, and possibly in violation of, the BSA, if it participates in an electronic value system that is designed in a manner such that it does not allow the bank to scrutinize transactions occurring within the system, and therefore does not allow the bank to file

---

[60] Suspicious Transactions Proposal, 62 Fed. Reg. at 27,904.

[61] *See* MSB Proposal, 62 Fed. Reg. at 27,893 (defining stored value for the purposes of the BSA).

[62] Indeed, in the Suspicious Transaction Proposal, FinCEN invites specific comments regarding the manner in which the suspicious transactions rule can be applied to stored value transactions. The comment period initially was to end on August 19, 1997, but was later extended to September 30, 1997. Bank Secrecy Act Regulations; Money Services Businesses – Definition and Registration; Suspicious Transaction Reporting; Currency Transaction Reporting, 62 Fed. Reg. 40,779 (1997).

[63] J. Orlin Grabbe, *Part II, End of Ordinary Money, available at* (visited June 17, 1997) <http://www.en.com/users/bthomas/cs/grabbe/money2.htm>.

[64] Special Currency Transaction Reporting Requirement for Money Transmitters, 62 Fed. Reg. 27,909 (1997) (to be codified at 31 C.F.R. pt. 103) (proposed May 21, 1997).

[65] In a recent public meeting held by FinCEN regarding the proposed registration amendment, several parties raised concerns that FinCEN's definition of "money transmitters" is too broad, and could include entities such as common carriers. However, FinCEN Director Morris assured meeting participants that the definition is not meant to be that broad.

[66] Bank Secrecy Act Regulations; Money Services Businesses; Open Working Meetings, 62 Fed. Reg. 36,475 (1997); Bank Secrecy Act Regulations; Money Services Businesses – Stored Value Products and Issuers, Sellers, and Redeemers of Money Orders or Traveler's Checks; Open Working Meetings, 62 Fed. Reg. 40,778 (1997).

[67] *Public Meetings to Discuss Proposed Anti-Money Laundering Rules*, FinCEN Press Release, July 2, 1997, *available at* <http://www.treas.gov>. Russell Stevenson, General Counsel of CyberCash, took the position that "the burden is on the government to show that any imposition it makes on the private sector, however small, has some legitimate purpose behind it and I don't think, in our case, that registration would serve any useful purpose because I don't think our system is subject to money laundering abuses." Harvey Berkman, *Dirty Money Regs Spark Biz Uproar*, NAT'L L.J., Sept. 15, 1997, at B1.

reports required under the BSA. The FinCEN representative also noted the dilemma that FinCEN is faced with in regard to evolving stored value systems. On one hand, if FinCEN establishes detailed guidelines for permissible systems it may be accused of prematurely locking stored value technology into place. On the other hand, if FinCEN does not provide such guidelines, the stored value industry runs the risk of investing heavily in a technology that FinCEN ultimately may determine to be inconsistent with the requirements of the BSA.[68]

[6]   INTERNATIONAL ANTI-MONEY LAUNDERING REGULATION AND ELECTRONIC MONEY

Nations around the world have vastly different levels of anti-money laundering regulation, the specifics of which are beyond the scope of this Chapter. However, a discussion of the actions of the Financial Action Task Force ("FATF") in this area is important, because it has served as the leading multinational source of information regarding money laundering around the world. FATF provides this information primarily through its annual public reports on money laundering typologies.[69] A recent report summarizing the FATF meeting held in November 1996 ("FATF Report" or "Report") deals with issues such as the estimates of the size of the money laundering problem worldwide, the principal illegal sources of laundered proceeds, traditional and "trendy" money laundering methods and counter-measures, and the emerging problem of cyberlaundering.[70]

The FATF Report focuses most of its discussion around its "40 Recommendations" for the international fight against money laundering.[71] Annex I of the FATF Report focuses upon the application of traditional money laundering countermeasures to new technologies such as electronic money.[72] New technologies are referenced

---

[68]   *See* Kroll, *supra* note 7.

[69]   *See FATF Report Highlights Money Laundering Trends*, Feb. 6, 1997, *available at* (visited June 17, 1997) <http://www.treas.gov>.

[70]   *See id.*

[71]   The 40 Recommendations were initially issued in 1990, and were updated in 1996. *See FATF Updates Anti-Money Laundering Standards*, FinCEN News Release, June 28, 1996, *available at* (visited May 30, 1997) <http://www.treas.gov>.

[72]   The FAFT provides a useful internationally-oriented review of the current status of stored value and electronic value products. The FAFT Report notes that there is currently no formally adopted international terminology with respect to electronic money, and that terms in use include stored value cards, smart cards, electronic money, digital cash, cybermoney, cybercurrency, and cyberpayments. For purposes of its report the FAFT divided these systems into three general categories.

   • Stored Value Cards. Cards which use either magnetic, optical or chip technology. The state of the art is microchip technology which are much more difficult to counterfeit or tamper with than optical or magnetic strips. With these types of stored value cards the transfer of value takes place at the time and place of the transaction.

   • Network-Based Systems. These systems use the Internet as a means of transfer. Some systems require that there be an account held at a financial institution through which the value clears. Other systems contemplate the use of digital value or tokens, where the value is purchased from an issuer and then stored on the computer rather than held in an account. Even when a transaction leaves an electronic trail as it makes it way through the Internet, it may not necessarily be traceable back to a particular person or entity.

   • Hybrid Systems. Systems are now being developed that would allow stored value cards to be used interchangeably, regardless of issuer. Other developing systems would permit cards to be used in connection with network-based systems.

The FAFT Report also described four types of issuer and open/closed environments.

   • Merchant-Issuer Model - Card issuer and seller of goods are the same, such as the Hong Kong Transit system.

   • Bank-Issuer Model for Closed and Open Systems - Merchant and card issuer are different parties. Transactions are cleared through traditional banking mechanisms. Examples are Banksys' Proton card in Belgium and the Danmont card in Denmark.

Continued on next page

in only one recommendation. Recommendation 13 states that "[c]ountries should pay special attention to money laundering threats inherent in new or developing technologies that might favour anonymity, and take measures, if needed, to prevent their use in money laundering schemes."[73]

The Report notes that the FATF has been looking to foster increased cooperation with the nonbank financial services sector, echoing FinCEN's concern that money launderers are turning increasingly to nonbank institutions, including electronic money providers, for their laundering needs. However, referring specifically to the electronic money industry, the Report states that "to date, there have been no reported instances of money laundering through these systems. Therefore, it is premature to consider prescriptive solutions to theoretical problems. However, it would be a disservice . . . for law enforcement and regulators not to continue to frame the issues that should be considered as markets and technologies mature."[74] Thus, the FATF has taken a general position on electronic money regulation very similar to that of the United States.[75]

While FinCEN is leaving the door open for the application of the information-based BSA to electronic money providers, however, the FATF appears to be somewhat pessimistic about the potential effectiveness of informational requirements as countermeasures to money laundering. For example, the Report notes that FATF Recommendations 10-12 and 14-19, which promote registration requirements and mandatory suspicious transaction reporting (much like the recent FinCEN proposed regulations), would be difficult to apply to electronic money systems.[76] This language cites the potential danger of untraceable peer-to-peer transactions, as well as the financial impossibility of monitoring such transactions. Finally, the FATF Report puts the potential problem of cyberlaundering monitoring in perspective. It notes that SWIFT, the primary wholesale wire transfer clearing house system used by commercial banks, carries 580 million messages per year, while the Internet carries approximately over 1 billion email messages every *month*.[77] As such, monitoring the ranks of potential electronic money transfers over the Internet appears to be a daunting task.

Footnote continued

- nonbank Issuer Model - In these systems users would buy electronic cash from issuers using traditional money and spend the electronic cash at participating merchants. The issuer will subsequently redeem the electronic cash from the merchant. Examples include CyberCash's electronic coin product.
- Peer-to-Peer Model - Bank or nonbank issued electronic cash would be transferable between users. The only point of contact between the traditional payments system and electronic cash would be the initial purchase of electronic cash from the issuer and redemption of electronic cash from individuals or merchants. Examples include the Mondex™ system.

FATF REPORT, Annex I, *supra* note 59, at ¶ 10-15.

[73] Financial Action Task Force, *The Forty Recommendations of the Financial Action Task Force on Money Laundering*, June 28, 1996, at 5.

[74] FATF REPORT, Annex I, *supra* note 59, ¶ 6, at 20. *Compare* Richard Waddington, *Drug Gangs Laundering Cash on Web*, THE SCOTSMAN, June 11, 1997, at 3 (reporting that "[b]ig crime syndicates are using the Internet to launder dirty money and there isn't much the authorities can do about it.").

[75] It should be noted that the 1996-97 Director of the FATF is Stanley E. Morris, the Director of FinCEN.

[76] *See* FATF REPORT, *supra* note 59, ¶ 22, at 24.

[77] *Id.* ¶ 36-37, at 26.

The Nations of the Group of Ten ("G-10") also recently released a report ("G-10 Report") discussing electronic money.[78] The G-10 Report devotes part of its discussion to law enforcement issues such as money laundering, taking a stance very similar to that of the FATF regarding cyberlaundering, and asserting that the electronic money products currently in use are too low-value and consumer-oriented to present a serious money laundering concern as of yet.[79] It also points out that cyberlaundering will only be difficult to detect if electronic money becomes very popular among consumers, because if the overall volume of electronic money transactions is low, "irregularities in payment activity due to criminal usage are likely to be more easily detected."[80]

The G-10 Report also contains a vague compromise that the organization feels can satisfy the balance between law enforcement needs and consumer privacy/protection. This compromise provision claims that advances in technology can improve the terms of the trade-off between record-keeping and privacy. The G-10 Report hypothesizes an intermediate level of privacy "where codes or serial numbers are used in transactions, and consumers' identities could be found only by cross-reference, and potentially only in certain law enforcement situations."[81] A compromise so heavily dependent upon technology necessitates the cooperation of the electronic money industry itself.

Though reluctant to regulate the development of actual electronic money systems, European authorities are contemplating measures that would allow only banks to deal in electronic money. For example, as of October 1996, the German Finance Ministry has adopted this "bank-only" proposal as policy.[82] This position contrasts with the emerging situation in the United States, as illustrated by FinCEN's proposed amendment to its BSA regulations. By including issuers and sellers of stored value as a separate category within "money services businesses," FinCEN appears to recognize that some electronic money providers will be nonbank institutions. In this regard, one member of the Board of Governors of the Federal Reserve System has stated that "[t]he Federal Reserve has not subscribed to the European view that only banks should issue prepaid cards, or by extension other stored-value payments products."[83]

[7]   SELF-IMPOSED ELECTRONIC MONEY CONTROLS

Regulators to date have taken a somewhat restrained approach to the regulation of the electronic money industry, giving market innovations precedence over regulation. This attitude can be simultaneously

---

[78] GROUP OF TEN, ELECTRONIC MONEY: CONSUMER PROTECTION, LAW ENFORCEMENT, SUPERVISORY AND CROSS BORDER ISSUES (1997) [hereinafter G-10 REPORT].

[79] *Id.* at 17. *See also id.* at 12 ("G-10 countries have not seen evidence of this type of activity in connection with electronic money systems.").

[80] *Id.* at 15.

[81] *Id.* at 17 n.16.

[82] *See* Simon Reeve, *The Euro: Yet to Launch But Already Outdated,* THE EUROPEAN, Oct. 28, 1997, at 28; Michelle Celarier, *What a Tangled Web,* EUROMONEY, Oct. 1996, at 85, 86 (quoting Edward Kelley, member of the Federal Reserve Board).

[83] Celarier, *supra* note 82, at 88.

characterized as cautious, because regulators are being careful not to stifle technological advancement,[84] and risky, because the approach could have significant consequences if criminals take advantage of government restraint in this area and are able to accomplish a major security breach in the interim.[85] Such a scandal in the United States could have a twofold negative effect: (i) regulators would have to answer to Congress as to why they did not identify the specific vulnerability that was in fact exploited, or if they had identified the vulnerability, why they did not take steps to prevent depository institutions from being exposed to the risk in question or to take effective steps to control the risk; and (ii) consumers may lose confidence in an industry that has not yet gained a true market foothold.

Security-based concerns such as these have been addressed by the electronic money providers themselves through self-imposed controls. Companies such as DigiCash and Mondex International, Ltd. have devoted part of their marketing material to informing the public about their security measures.[86] The most simple control is the placing of value limits on electronic money vehicles. Currently, in the trials under way in New York City, the Citibank VISA Cash Money Card has a limit of $500 on the card at any one time,[87] and the Chase Smart Card using Mondex™ is limited to $200 on the card at any one time.[88] Mondex states that its value limits work as an effective barrier to money laundering.[89] Such limits would not necessarily prevent a launderer from conducting a series of numerous smaller transactions.[90] The G-10 has commented that value limits do not actually prevent money laundering, but rather merely add cost and time to the launderer's activities.[91]

The other main security feature touted by electronic money providers is monitoring or auditability. However, the more capability an electronic money provider has to monitor customer transactions, the less "cash-like" their products become. Because any increase in monitoring shifts the balance away from privacy, electronic money providers have been a bit vague as to the exact amount of auditability inherent in their systems. For example, different Mondex officials have made various statements regarding the auditability of their electronic money system, although this may be attributable to changes in the system over time or in different countries.[92] Janet Crane, President and CEO of Mondex International, has stated that "[t]he Mondex™ card system

---

[84] *See* Dean Anason, *Regulating E-Commerce: Damned if You Do...*, AM. BANKER, June 20, 1997, at 3 (describing Comptroller of the Currency Eugene A. Ludwig's desire to not "kill[] the golden goose before it lays any eggs").

[85] *See id.*

[86] *See, e.g., Keeping Cash Clean*, MONDEX™ MAG., Dec. 1996, at 29 (asserting that the structure of Mondex™ is incompatible with money laundering); *Digicash E-Cash: About E-Cash and Crime, available at* (visited July 8, 1997) <http://www.digicash.com> (stating that Digicash is "not at all well suited" for criminals).

[87] Citibank VISA Cash Money Card Agreement, Aug. 1997.

[88] Chase Standalone Smart Card Agreement, Oct. 1997.

[89] *See Keeping Cash Clean, supra* note 86, at 30.

[90] "[I]f [a] micro-transaction could be repeated 186,000 times per second — sooner or later that's 'real money'." Kroll, *supra* note 7, at 3.

[91] *See* G-10 REPORT, *supra* note 78, at 14.

[92] Additionally, Mondex changed its advertising to remove the word "anonymous" after it was sued by Privacy International for false advertising. *See Privacy International Complaint is Upheld - Electronic Cash is Anything but Anonymous*, June 21, 1996, *available at* <http://www.privacy.org>. *See also* Niall McKay, *Mondex's Double Life: E-Cash Both "Private" and "Fully Auditable,"* INFOWORLD CANADA, May 7, 1997, at 2, *available at* <http://insight.mcmaster.ca>.

is fully auditable. There is an electronic record of the time, date, amount, and participants of each transaction."[93] The vice-president of product management and marketing for Mondex USA has stated that though Mondex™ is auditable, "[Mondex does] not keep a record of every transaction."[94] The manager of the Mondex division of the Royal Bank of Canada has noted that "[t]here is no way that [Mondex™] can keep a full audit trail . . . Everything happens off-line. It's not fully auditable."[95] Users of the Chase Standalone Smart Card, which is a Mondex™ system card, are told:

> Like when you use cash, Chase will have no record of your Smart Card Purchase so
> you will not receive information about the transaction on a monthly statement nor will
> Chase have any responsibility for errors, claims or mistakes which may occur related to
> such merchant or such Smart Card Purchase.[96]

Digicash takes the position that, while it allows anonymous transfers of electronic value, its system is launder-proof because "all the amounts each person receives are known to their bank."[97] Digicash's monitoring mechanism does identify the entities that redeem ecash™.

Users of the Citibank Visa Cash Money Card are told that they can get information about the dollar amount of their last ten purchases and the last three load/unload transactions at terminals at participating branches and specified merchant locations where value may be loaded onto the card. Merchant point of sale terminals will also display a card's balance, purchase amount, and remaining balance. The card's pocket balance checker will display purchase, load/unload, and balance information. It appears that a cardholder's deposit account statement will show the amount of value loaded onto the card from their deposit account and the amount of value deposited into the cardholder's deposit account, but will not show any information regarding individual transactions.[98]

[8]   CONCLUSION

Currently, money laundering via stored value and electronic value is still a problem waiting to happen. Illicit use of electronic money instruments is not likely to proliferate until the electronic money industry acquires a stronger foothold with legitimate consumers. It appears that regulators such as FinCEN will continue to be very concerned about the possibility that money launderers will be able to use some aspect of the stored value and electronic value industry in order to serve their objectives.

---

[93] David Jones, *Mondex: A House of Smart-Cards?*, THE CONVERGENCE, July 12, 1997, at 3, *available at* (visited July 12, 1997) <http://insight.mcmaster.ca>.

[94] McKay, *supra* note 92.

[95] *Id. See also Mondex Makes Waves,* BANK TECH. NEWS, Jan. 1997.

[96] Chase Standalone Smart Card Agreement, Oct. 1997.

[97] *First Bank to Launch Electronic Cash* (released Oct. 23, 1995), *available at* <http://www.digicash.com>.

[98] Citibank VISA Cash Money Card Agreement, Aug. 1997.

From there, we are likely to see attempts to apply current money laundering informational counter-measures to electronic cash. Two questions then arise. First, will electronic money providers *be able* to collect enough transactional information to satisfy the government? Second, will launderers be able to circumvent all reporting thresholds due to the speed with which smaller transactions may be conducted? As is the pervasive theme in this Chapter, we must wait and see.

§ 10.03 OFFICE OF FOREIGN ASSET CONTROL

The Office of Foreign Asset Control ("OFAC") of the Department of the Treasury is another player that should command the attention of banking institutions and other industry participants as they develop and deploy electronic financial products and services ("EFS"). OFAC is primarily responsible for the administration and enforcement of United States economic sanctions and embargo programs.[99] These sanction and embargo programs, which vary depending on the nature of the United States' foreign policy and national security goals, impose controls regarding with whom parties under OFAC jurisdiction may conduct business. OFAC has jurisdiction over all United States citizens and permanent residents, companies located in the United States, overseas branches of United States companies, and certain subsidiaries of United States companies.[100] OFAC routinely publishes, by both conventional and electronic media, a list of countries, entities, and individuals covered by the sanctions and embargo programs.[101]

OFAC is not a bank regulatory agency, but banking institutions must comply with OFAC regulations.[102] OFAC regulations define "banking institution" as any "person engaged primarily in the business of banking, of granting or transferring credits, or purchasing or selling foreign exchange, or procuring purchasers and sellers thereof, as principal or agent, or any person holding credits for others as a direct or incidental part of [their]

---

[99] Embargo and sanction programs are established pursuant to Executive Orders of the President acting under wartime or national emergency powers or pursuant to specific statutory authority, including, Trading with the Enemies Act, ("TWEA") Act of Oct. 6, 1917, c. 106, 40 Stat. 411 (codified as amended at 50 U.S.C. App. §§ 1-44); International Emergency Economic Powers Act ("IEEPA"), Pub. L. No. 95-223, tit. II, 91 Stat. 1626 (1977) (codified as amended at 50 U.S.C. §§ 1701-06); Iraqi Sanctions Act ("ISA"), Pub. L. No. 101-513, 1990 U.S.C.C.A.N. (104 Stat.) 2047-55; United Nations Participation Act ("UNPA"), Act of Dec. 20, 1945, c. 583, § 5, 59 Stat. 620 (codified as amended at 22 U.S.C. § 287c); International Security and Development Cooperation Act ("ISDCA"), Pub. L. No. 99-83, tit. V, § 504, 99 Stat. 221 (1985) (codified as amended at 22 U.S.C. § 2349aa-8); Cuban Democracy Act ("CDA"), Pub. L. No. 102-484, tit. XVII, 1992 U.S.C.C.A.N. (106 Stat.) 2575 (codified as amended at 22 U.S.C. §§ 6001-10; Cuban Liberty and Democratic Solidarity Act of 1996 ("LIBERTAD"), Pub. L. No. 104-114, 1996 U.S.C.C.A.N. (110 Stat.) 785 (codified as amended at 22 U.S.C. §§ 6021-6091); Antiterrorism and Effective Death Penalty Act of 1996 ("AAEDPA"), Pub. L. No. 104-132, § 321, 1996 U.S.C.C.A.N. (110 Stat.) 1214-1319 (codified as amended at 18 U.S.C. § 2332d); and the U.S. Criminal Code codified at 18 U.S.C. § 1001.

[100] 31 C.F.R. § 500.329. Department of the Treasury, *Foreign Assets Control Regulations for the Financial Community*, at 4 (Aug. 25, 1997) [hereinafter *OFAC Financial Community Regulations*].

[101] Changes to List of Specially Designated Nationals and Blocked Persons since January 1, 1997, Doc. No. 1004 (July 30, 1997); Changes to List of Specially Designated Nationals and Blocked Persons during 1996, Doc. No. 1005 (Dec. 4, 1996); List of Specially Designated Nationals and Blocked Persons - Partial List (A-R), Doc. No. 1013 (July 30, 1997); List of Specially Designated Nationals and Blocked Persons - Partial List (S-Z) (July 30, 1997). The primary List of Specially Designated Nationals and Blocked Persons contains approximately 5,000 names and variations. It includes a disclaimer, however, that it is not complete and warns banking institutions to exercise caution when dealing with anyone from a restricted country. The list is available from OFAC in paper form or electronically from the Department of the Treasury at (visited Sept. 9, 1997) <http://www.treas.gov>.

[102] Office of Foreign Assets Control, 31 C.F.R. pts. 500-595; *see also* Office of Foreign Assets Control, 62 Fed. Reg. 45,098 (1997) (to be codified at 31 C.F.R. pts. 500-596).

business, or any broker; and, each principal, agent, home office, branch or correspondent of any person so engaged."[103] Banking institutions are expected to monitor their operations in order to block or reject covered transactions. Almost any normal banking activity, including letters of credit, checking accounts, bank cards, and wire transfers constitute an OFAC-covered transaction.[104]

[1] BLOCKING AND REJECTING

Whether a banking institution is required to block or reject an account or transaction will depend on the mandate of the specific governing sanctions. Blocking means that no covered transaction of any kind may be conducted with regard to the assets in question, which are in fact frozen and held by the banking institution in special interest bearing accounts that cannot be accessed without OFAC authorization.[105] Title to the blocked assets remains with the designated entity; the powers and privileges normally associated with ownership, such as transferability and alienability, however, are prohibited.[106] Banking institutions must block accounts in which any designated country or any national thereof has any interest.[107] Further, they must block transactions where called for by the governing sanctions.

Governing sanctions may call for banking institutions to reject transactions rather than blocking them. A rejected transaction does not require the establishment of a separate interest bearing account. Rather, the banking institution needs merely to refuse to process the transaction and to notify the originator that the transfer cannot be processed. A banking institution rejects a transaction by simply refusing to process it and notifying the originator and OFAC of that decision. Examples of transactions currently requiring rejection include: (1) transfers in the form of gifts or charitable contributions from the government of Syria;[108] and (2) transfers of interests in blocked accounts.[109] Banking institutions need to consult with the specific sanction programs to determine whether blocking or rejecting is appropriate.

[2] EXCEPTIONS

There are transactions with designated countries, entities, individuals or citizens of designated countries ("designated entities") that require neither blocking or rejecting. Transactions with these designated entities may

---

[103] 31 C.F.R. § 500.314.

[104] *See* Steve Cocheo, *Tips from ABA's Compliance Conference*, ABA BANKING J., Sept. 1996, at 36.

[105] *See OFAC Financial Community Regulations, supra* note 100, at 4. *See also* 31 C.F.R. § 500.205. A covered transaction is any payment or transfer to any designated foreign country or citizen of that country, any export or withdrawal from the United States to the designated country, and any transfer of credit, or payment of an obligation made in the currency of that designated foreign country. 31 C.F.R. §§ 500.201, 500.205.

[106] *See OFAC Financial Community Regulations, supra* note 100, at 4.

[107] 31 C.F.R. § 500.319.

[108] 31 U.S.C. § 2332d; 31 C.F.R. pt. 595.

[109] 31 C.F.R. § 505.508(a).

be permitted under either a general or specific licensing authority depending on the particular sanction or embargo program.[110]

[a] **General Licenses.** General licenses typically permit transactions consistent with normal banking practices,[111] such as debiting a blocked account for normal account service charges or to cover customs duties, taxes, and other fees owed to the United States.[112] General licenses may address activities with a specific country, entity, or individual or they may address a particular type of payment of transfer. Examples of general licenses include: (1) authorizing payments to North Korea for services provided by the Government of North Korea in connection with flights over, or emergency landings in, North Korea by airplanes registered in the United States or owned or controlled by persons subject to the jurisdiction of the United States;[113] (2) permitting overflight payments to Iran;[114] and (3) permitting telecommunications service between the United States and Cuba.[115] A party interested in conducting a transaction covered by a general license need not file an application with OFAC.

[b] **Specific Licenses.** Specific licenses are issued by OFAC on a case-by-case basis to permit the party requesting the license to perform an activity that would otherwise be prohibited by an embargo or sanctions program. A request for a specific license must be submitted to OFAC and must disclose the names of all parties concerned with or interested in the proposed transaction.[116] If a request for a specific license is approved, the licensee may be required to file reports with OFAC with regard to the transaction covered by the license.[117] Telecommunications companies that are permitted to provide telecommunications services between the United States and Cuba under the general license discussed above must obtain specific licenses in order to receive payment for services rendered.[118] Entities under OFAC jurisdiction must also obtain specific licenses from OFAC to receive overflight payments involving Cuba.[119]

---

[110] Reporting and Procedures Regulations: Consolidation of Information Collections; Annual Reports on Blocked Assets and Retained Transfers; Reports on Rejected Transfers; Reports on Litigation; Procedure for Releasing Funds Believed to Have Been Blocked Due to Mistaken Identity; Procedure for Removal from the Lists of Blocked Persons and Vessels, 62 Fed. Reg. 45,098, 45,104 (1997) (to be codified at 31 C.F.R. § 501.801) [hereinafter Reporting and Procedures Regulations]. See also 31 C.F.R. §§ 500.502-.584 for general licensing provisions.

[111] *OFAC Financial Community Regulations, supra* note 100, at 4.

[112] 31 C.F.R. §§ 505.509, 500.510.

[113] Overflight Payments to North Korea, 62 Fed. Reg. 17,548 (1997) (to be codified at 31 C.F.R. § 500.585).

[114] *OFAC Financial Community Regulations, supra* note 100, at 13.

[115] 22 U.S.C. § 6004(e)(1).

[116] Reporting and Procedures Regulations, 62 Fed. Reg. at 45,104 (to be codified at 31 C.F.R. §§ 501.801(b)(2), (3)).

[117] *Id.* (to be codified at 31 C.F.R. § 501.801(b)(5)).

[118] 22 U.S.C. § 6004(e)(3). The United States has issued eight licenses authorizing payments related to telecommunications between Cuba and the United States. Report to the Congress of the United States, 33 WKLY. COMP. PRES. DOC. 1314 (Sept. 10, 1997).

[119] *OFAC Financial Community Regulations, supra* note 100, at 6.

[3]   FAILURE TO BLOCK OR REJECT

If banking institutions fail to block or reject a transaction as required, they may be subject to criminal fines, imprisonment, or civil monetary penalties.[120] Penalties, which depend upon the specific sanctions or embargo program violated, are steep.[121] Compliance responsibility cannot be delegated.[122] Furthermore, each banking institution or agent preceding the one in the chain that does not block the transaction will incur liability for not blocking it itself.[123] The amount of money involved in the transaction bears no relevance in the determination of whether a violation has occurred.[124]

[4]   ADMINISTRATIVE REQUIREMENTS FOR BLOCKED AND REJECTED TRANSACTIONS

OFAC regulations impose reporting and recordkeeping requirements that require banking institutions to report on blocked and rejected transactions.[125] Reports on blocked or rejected payments or transfers must be filed within ten days and must include the date on which the block occurred, the identity of the property owner, and a description of the property that gives its location and actual or estimated value.[126] In addition to the recordkeeping and initial reporting requirements, a comprehensive report on all blocked transactions must be filed annually.[127] Banking institutions must prepare full and accurate records of each blocked transaction and must retain those records for at least five years.[128]

---

[120] Banking institutions will not be penalized for processing transactions based on guidance received from OFAC on a specific transaction. *See* "*Specially Designated Who?" A Primer on OFAC Compliance*, ABA BANK COMPLIANCE, Mar./Apr. 1996, at 29, 36. Institutions acting in good faith and in conformity with OFAC regulations may also not be penalized for inadvertent errors. *See* Cocheo, *supra* note 104, at 40.

[121] TWEA provides for ten years imprisonment, a $1 million fine for corporations, and a $100,00 fine for individuals as well as forfeiture of funds or other property involved; IEEPA provides for 10 years imprisonment, a $50,000 fine for corporations and individuals; ISA provides for 12 years imprisonment and a $1 million corporate or personal fine; UNPA provides for a ten year prison term and a $10,000 corporate and person fine; CDA imposes the same fines as TWEA; LIBERTAD imposes the same fines as TWEA; AAEDPA provides for criminal penalties of $500,000 for corporations, ten years imprisonment and/or a $250,000 per count for willful violations by individuals; ISDCA provides for no criminal penalties but other penalty provisions may apply in particular circumstances. Depending on the violations, criminal penalties may be imposed up to $1 million while civil penalties could be imposed up to $275,00,000. *See OFAC Financial Community Regulations*, *supra* note 100, at 2.

[122] *See* ABA BANK COMPLIANCE, *supra* note 120, at 30.

[123] *See* Cocheo, *supra* note 104, at 40. For more information on OFAC compliance, see 31 C.F.R. parts 500 and 515 and see the OFAC website.

[124] *See* Cocheo, *supra* note 104, at 40.

[125] OFAC amended its regulations in August 1997 to consolidate and standardize reporting and recordkeeping requirements. Reporting and Procedures Regulations, 62 Fed. Reg. 45,098 (1997) (to be codified at 31 C.F.R. pt. 501). Previously, reporting and recordkeeping requirements were codified in the individual chapters of part 500 that dealt with specific sanction programs.

[126] *Id.* at 45,102 (to be codified at 31 C.F.R. §§ 501.603, 501.604).

[127] *Id.* at 45,103 (to be codified at 31 C.F.R. § 501.603(b)(2)). Banking institutions may be required to file reports on specific transactions under oath, from time to time, as requested. *Id.* at 45,102 (to be codified at 31 C.F.R. § 501.602).

[128] *Id.* at 45,103 (to be codified at 31 C.F.R. § 501.601).

[5] ENSURING COMPLIANCE

The bank regulatory agencies cooperate with OFAC to ensure banking institution compliance by periodically issuing OFAC regulations and notices to banking institutions within their jurisdictions.[129] They also encourage banking institutions to establish compliance programs and internal audit procedures to avoid violations of OFAC regulations.[130] The adequacy of a banking institution's compliance and audit programs are evaluated during bank examinations to determine whether policies and procedures are in place. The evaluation includes a determination of: (i) whether the bank maintains a current list of OFAC countries, entities, and individuals; (ii) whether it provides its foreign offices with updated OFAC information; (iii) whether new accounts are compared to OFAC listings; and (iv) whether international accounts are compared to OFAC lists.[131]

Commercially available software products can assist banks in complying with OFAC regulations.[132] These products screen transactions for names of blocked parties and references to blocked countries. The software products also provide audit trails, thus leaving evidence of an institution's efforts to comply.[133]

OFAC compliance applies to traditional activities conducted by banking institutions as well as to EFS. The anonymity associated with many of these EFS will make OFAC compliance an even greater challenge for banking institutions. For example, the Internet can carry live financial instruments, electronically executed legal contracts, electronic value, and airline tickets, all of which are traditionally blocked by OFAC.

[6] OFAC POLICY INTERPRETATION FOR THE ACH NETWORK

In March 1997, OFAC, in response to a request from the National Automated Clearing House Association ("NACHA"), stated its position on the "purely domestic account-to-account Automated Clearing House ("ACH") system that involves originating depository financial institutions ("ODFIs") and receiving depository financial institutions ("RDFIs"), but does not involve any intermediary financial institutions."[134] OFAC will hold liable any ODFI that initiates ACH credits by permitting debits to blocks on restricted accounts. Further, OFAC expects ODFIs that themselves batch or rebatch items for transmission to take care, to the extent possible given available information, not to process transactions in violation of OFAC's regulations. OFAC places the remainder of the compliance burden on RDFIs. OFAC anticipates that NACHA will, as previously discussed between OFAC and NACHA, revise its rules to require originators and ODFIs to acknowledge that the ACH

---

[129] Blocking Accounts Associated with Narcotics Traffickers, FDIC FIL-41-97 (Apr. 30, 1997) and FDIC FIL-84-97 (Aug. 19, 1997); Office of Foreign Assets Control: Availability of OFAC Issuances on OCC Information Line, OCC Bull. 95-54 (Oct. 6, 1995); Foreign Assets Control Regulations, FRB Supervisory Release No. 88-30 (Oct. 20, 1988).

[130] *Id.*

[131] *See* Cocheo, *supra* note 104, at 36.

[132] *See* Matt Schulz, *Software Helps Banks Steer Clear of Bad Guys*, AM. BANKER, Aug. 24, 1995, at 8.

[133] *See id.*

[134] Letter from R. Richard Newcomb, Director, OFAC, to Elliott C. McEntee, President and Chief Executive Officer, NACHA (Mar. 20, 1997), *available at* <http://www.nacha.org>. The ACH system is described in greater detail in Chapter 4.

system "may not be used for transactions in violation of U.S. law, including sanctions administered by OFAC," and that NACHA's sample authorization agreements will reflect that requirement.

§ 10.04   STATE ACTIVITIES

On the one hand, individual states can function as "laboratories" for conducting limited experiments in the emerging field of electronic commerce and banking.[135] On the other hand, actions by individual states can rapidly complicate the legal landscape by adopting conflicting or overlapping approaches, in particular in the battle over the permissible level of state control over Internet-based activities, including electronic financial products and services.[136] States have used litigation, legislation, and regulation to address electronic commerce issues.

In this regard, at least one federal court has suggested that because of the unique multi-directional nature of the Internet, states should have little or no leeway in imposing their legislative preferences on parties operating in the Internet. This ruling came in the case of *American Library Association v. Pataki*, which involved a challenge to a New York State criminal statute that made unlawful the transmission to minors of computer data that included certain sexual-related information ("New York Act").[137] In this case, Judge Loretta Preska issued a preliminary injunction preventing enforcement of the New York Act, finding that the plaintiffs had made a sufficient showing that the New York Act represented an unconstitutional intrusion into interstate commerce.

Given the nature of the Internet, the court determined that the New York Act could not effectively be limited to purely intrastate communications over the Internet because there is no way for a user to reliably restrict the flow of communications.[138] The court noted that this feature of the Internet leaves a party potentially subject to haphazard, uncoordinated, and inconsistent regulation by states the party never intended to reach. The court determined that the transmission of information and ideas over the Internet falls within the scope of the Commerce Clause of the Constitution.[139]

The court gave three grounds for its decision:

- The New York Act represents an unconstitutional projection of New York law into conduct that occurs wholly outside of New York.[140]

---

[135] *See New State Ice Co. v. Liebman*, 285 U.S. 262, 311 (1932).

[136] This same concern applies at the national/international level. See Chapter 19 for a discussion of this topic.

[137] *American Library Ass'n v. Pataki*, 969 F. Supp. 160 (S.D.N.Y. 1997).

[138] *Id.* at 177.

[139] *Id.*

[140] *Id.*

- Even if the New York Act is not a *per se* violation of the Commerce Clause, because it imposes burdens on interstate commerce that are excessive in relation to the benefits it confers, it is invalid indirect regulation of interstate commerce.[141]

- Finally, and most significantly, the Internet is one of those areas of commerce that must be marked off as a national preserve to protect users from inconsistent legislation that, taken to its most extreme, could paralyze development of the Internet altogether.[142]

States have also addressed the use of digital signatures and Internet securities offerings. Some have also dealt with consumer protection issues. Moreover, committees on model state laws have proposed amendments to the Model Business Corporation Act ("MBCA") and to the Uniform Commercial Code ("U.C.C.")[143] to accommodate these technological changes, as well as new model laws for other electronic topics.[144] In addition to these legislative and regulatory efforts, some state Attorneys General have brought actions against parties who, in their view, have used the Internet for illegal purposes such as gambling or pornography.

[1] DIGITAL SIGNATURE/ELECTRONIC SIGNATURE LEGISLATION

[a] State Law. In an effort to spur the development of electronic commerce, state legislators across the country are enacting or considering legislation governing the use of "electronic signatures" and "digital signatures." The term "electronic signature" generally refers to any letters, characters, or symbols manifested by electronic means and intended to authenticate a writing. The more narrow term "digital signature" refers to a specific type of electronic signature generated by public key cryptography.[145] To date, at least thirty-nine states have taken up the issue of electronic signatures, and more states are likely to follow suit.

In 1995, Utah became the first state to enact any type of electronic signature law. The Utah Digital Signature Act[146] accords digital signatures generally the same legal effects as handwritten signatures. The Act establishes a "public key infrastructure" in which the Utah Department of Commerce licenses and regulates certification authorities.[147] The Act specifies the duties of certification authorities and digital signature creators, and it enables certification authorities to limit their liability. In addition to Utah, Minnesota and Washington have enacted digital signature legislation that establishes a public key infrastructure.[148]

---

[141] *Id.*

[142] *Id.* at 183.

[143] *U.C.C. Article on Licenses Makes Debut as ACI Members Focus on Articles 2 and 9*, Banking Rep. (BNA) 1096 (June 9, 1997).

[144] *Uniform State Law Commissioners Eyeing Electronic Commerce Projects*, Banking Rep. (BNA) 906 (May 12, 1997); *New Draft Electronic Transactions Act Aims to Clarify Status of Electronic Records*, Banking Rep. (BNA) 427 (Sept. 15, 1997); *Electronic Contracting Group Begins Translating Paper-Based Cyberspace Law*, Banking Rep. (BNA) 584 (Oct. 13, 1997); *NCCUSL Group to Develop Uniform Law for Non-Bank Financial Service Providers*, Banking Rep. (BNA) 680 (Nov. 3, 1997).

[145] See Chapter 13 for a discussion of encryption systems and digital signatures.

[146] UTAH CODE ANN. §§ 46-3-101–504.

[147] Certification authorities are entities that certify particular digital signatures.

[148] *See* 1997 Minn. Laws 173; WASH. REV. CODE ch. 19.34.

Several states have taken alternative approaches to electronic signature legislation. Some have enacted or are considering legislation that gives legal effect to electronic signatures generally, but does not focus on digital signatures in particular. Florida is one example of a state that has enacted such a law.[149] Other states, including California,[150] have enacted or proposed legislation whose scope is limited to communications with state agencies.

Somewhat paradoxically, as states increasingly enact laws to authorize and regulate the use of electronic signatures, they may inadvertently hinder the development of efficient electronic commerce. The possibility that fifty states may enact fifty different electronic signature laws raises a specter of uncertainty, particularly in multi-party, multi-jurisdictional transactions. In response to this problem, states are pursuing plans for uniform laws. Representatives from forty-seven states have tentatively agreed that a basic uniform law should track the Model Law on Electronic Commerce adopted by the United Nations Commission on International Trade Law.[151] The states also plan to work with The National Conference of Commissioners on Uniform State Laws to draft a uniform law on complex electronic commerce issues.[152]

[b] Federal Legislation and Regulations. The prospect of various state laws governing electronic signatures has prompted some proponents of electronic commerce to urge Congress to establish federal standards for electronic authentication.[153] A subcommittee of the House Banking and Financial Services Committee held a hearing in July 1997 to determine the role, if any, the federal government should play in electronic authentication.[154] In November 1997, Representatives Richard H. Baker (R-LA) and David Dreier (R-CA) introduced a bill in the House that would govern digital signatures and other forms of electronic authentication. In February 1998, Senator Robert F. Bennett (R-UT) introduced a similar bill in the Senate. In addition, one federal agency — the Food and Drug Administration ("FDA") — has adopted regulations concerning electronic signatures.

[i] The House Bill. H.R. 2937, the Electronic Financial Services Efficiency Act of 1997 (the "Act"),[155] would provide for the recognition of digital and other forms of electronic authentication as an alternative to existing paper-based methods and define and harmonize the practices applicable to the conduct of electronic authentication.

The Act would grant legal validity to qualifying forms of electronic authentication in three respects:

- First, the Act authorizes a digital signature, accompanied by a certificate issued by a trusted third party, as defined by the Act, to be used in lieu of a paper-based, written signature in any

---

[149] *See* FLA. STAT. §§ 282.70-74.

[150] *See* CAL. GOV. CODE § 16.5.

[151] *See Baker Bill's CA Licensing Regime Faulted as Overly-Restrictive, Premature*, Banking Rep. (BNA), at 20 (Jan. 5, 1998).

[152] *See id.*

[153] *See* Bill McConnell, *In Focus: On-Line Bankers Ask Congress for a Hand, But With Light Touch*, AM. BANKER, Mar. 31, 1997, at 3.

[154] *Federal Role in Electronic Authentication: Hearing Before the Subcomm. on Domestic and International Monetary Policy of the House Comm. on Banking and Financial Services,* 105th Cong. (1997). Testimony of the witnesses is available at <http://www.house.gov>.

[155] H.R. 2937, 105th Cong. (1997).

communication that requires a signature with any federal agency, U.S. court, or other instrumentality of the United States government ("Federal Communication").[156]

• Second, the Act provides that all forms of qualified electronic authentication (a category intended to extend beyond digital signatures) shall have the same standing as a paper-based, written signature in any Federal Communication.[157] Therefore, any rule of law that requires a Federal Communication to be in writing or signed would be satisfied by a qualified electronic authentication under the Act.[158]

• Third, the Act provides that unless expressly prohibited by state law, all forms of qualified electronic authentication shall have the same standing as traditional paper-based, written signatures, so that any rule of law which requires a record to be in writing or signed would be similarly satisfied.[159]

Under the Act, any form of electronic authentication would be valid and entitled to legal recognition if it "reliably establishes" both the identity of the maker, sender, or originator of a document or communication in electronic commerce and the fact that the document or communication has not been altered.[160] In addition, in order for technological authentication applications to be valid under the Act, any application must be (i) unique to the person making, sending, or originating a document or communication, (ii) capable of verification, (iii) under the sole control of the person using it, and (iv) linked to data or communication transmitted in such a manner that if such data or communication has been altered, the authentication becomes invalid.[161]

The Act would establish a National Association of Certification Authorities ("NACA"),[162] with which any person or group wishing to provide electronic authentication services in the United States must register.[163] The Act would require NACA to form an Electronic Authentication Standards Review Committee (the "Standards Review Committee"), which would establish and enforce criteria governing the electronic authentication industry.[164] Any party aggrieved by an order of the Standards Review Committee could obtain a review of such order in a United States Court of Appeals by filing a petition within thirty days after the entry of an order.[165]

---

[156] *Id.* § 4.

[157] *Id.* § 5(a).

[158] *Id.*

[159] *Id.* § 5(b).

[160] *Id.* § 6(a).

[161] *Id.* § 6(b).

[162] *Id.* § 7(a).

[163] *Id.* § 7(b).

[164] *Id.* § 7(e).

[165] *Id.* § (7)(e)(6).

The Secretary of the Treasury would oversee and review the Standards Review Committee's activities and would be required to approve all guidelines, standards, and codes of conduct before they are adopted.[166] The Act would not impair the rights afforded a consumer under the provisions of any law applicable to an underlying transaction or communication that is authenticated by a digital signature or other form of qualified electronic authentication.[167]

H.R. 2937 exposes many issues by what it says and does not say. The issues include the types of technology authorized under the Act, the reliability of authentication applications, the liability of parties that provide certification services, the need for a government agency or self-regulatory organization to monitor the performance of parties engaged in the chain of electronic commerce, and the control of authentication methods.

[A] *Technology Neutrality*. While unquestionably validating public key cryptography and signature dynamics technology, the Act also affirmatively recognizes the need to provide a mechanism to validate other technology applications for authentication. Such flexibility is necessary given the pace at which technological changes are occurring and the need for the government to avoid the explicit or implicit endorsement of one authentication product over another.

[B] *Uniformity and Federal Preemption*. As described above, a significant number of states have enacted or are considering enacting digital signature or other electronic authentication laws. Because these statutes lack uniformity in both scope and application, they invite consideration of uniforms laws or federal preemption. Section 5(b) of the Act provides for an opt-out form of federal preemption and, thus, would not necessarily ensure a uniform national standard for electronic authentication and its legal effect. Moreover, given recent court decisions on the scope of the Commerce Clause, the assertion of federal preemption in regard to transactions that will have a purely local character may be subject to challenge.

[C] *Reliability of Electronic Authentication Applications*. The Act requires that electronic authentication technologies be able to "reliably establish" the identity of parties and the integrity of the transmitted communication.[168] The Act does not, however, establish a standard regarding what would constitute such reliability (arguably, implementing regulations would establish such a standard). The problems associated with identification verification in this country are well documented. Efforts to establish more secure, universal methods of identification have repeatedly failed. Testimony on identification verification that accompanied the enactment of legislation on this issue in 1996 demonstrated that neither birth certificates, social security cards, passports, nor drivers' licenses are a reliable form of identification.[169] If these forms of identification are the best we

---

[166] *Id.* §§ 7(e)(2), 8.

[167] *Id.* § 9(a).

[168] *Id.* § 6(a).

[169] *See* Thomas P. Vartanian, *The Case for National ID Verification Standards*, AM. BANKER, Sept. 24, 1997, at 14. For example, in Texas, more than 900 state offices reportedly issued certified birth certificates without a consistent format being required. In some states, by law, the state is required to issue a certified birth certificate to whomever requests it, as long as the appropriate fee is paid. Moreover, there are 265 million social security cards outstanding today, issued in 16 different formats.

have to rely and build upon for electronic authentication, there may be no greater reliability of identity in Cyberspace than there is in the physical world today.

[D] *Liability for Certification.* The "assurance" provided by a certification authority ("CA") that a particular digital signature is tied to an individual is unclear. In an environment where it is difficult to verify the identity of a person with absolute certainty, what responsibility does the CA that issues a certificate to an individual bear? At best, a CA can assure only that the person to whom it provides a certificate has produced certain evidence of identification. It cannot actually assure that X is X, and the law needs to recognize that fact. Without certainty as to the liability or non-liability of the CA under each set of laws (*i.e.*, federal, state, international) that may apply, it becomes difficult to implement and price certification products.

[E] *The Need for a Government Agency or Self-Regulatory Organization.* The Act creates the NACA but does not explain what it is, how it is staffed, or what its nexus to the federal government is, if any. Similar issues exist with regard to the Standards Review Committee and the meaning of Treasury's "oversight" responsibilities with respect to that Committee. The Act raises critical questions that must be explored. Should CAs be licensed? Who, if anyone, would license and supervise them? If some entity must do so, to what extent, if any, is a cradle-to-grave bureaucracy required?

[F] *Control of the Authentication Method.* Section 6(b)(3) of the Act requires that, among other things, to qualify as an approved form of electronic authentication, identification technology must be "under the sole control of the person using it." This requirement raises interesting questions regarding the use of PCs by more than one person and the extent to which a business entity may qualify as a "person" so that various individuals in the organization can use the same certificate to transact business over the Internet.

[ii] *The Senate Bill.* Another bill, S. 1594, the "Digital Signature and Electronic Authentication Law of 1998" ("SEAL of 1998"), was recently introduced in the Senate by Senator Robert F. Bennett (R-UT).[170] SEAL of 1998 would amend the Bank Protection Act of 1968,[171] in order to facilitate the use of digital signature technology and other electronic authentication techniques by financial institutions.[172] According to Senator Bennett, his bill would make electronic signatures "as valid as [signatures] created with pen and paper."[173] Unlike H.R. 2937, S. 1594 would only apply to financial institutions.[174]

[iii] *FDA Regulations.* One federal agency — the Food and Drug Administration ("FDA") — has adopted regulations setting forth the criteria under which it will accept electronic records and electronic signatures.[175]

---

[170] S. 1594, 105th Cong. (1998).

[171] 12 U.S.C. § 1881.

[172] S. 1594 § 3. See 144 CONG. REC. S271-03 (daily ed. Feb. 2, 1998) (statement of Sen. Bennett).

[173] *See* Scott Barancik, *Banks Plug for Law to Establish Standard for Digitatl Signatures*, AM. BANKER, Mar. 12, 1998, at 3.

[174] Because of this limitation, some alternative service providers are criticizing Senator Bennett's bill. *See id.* (according to Harris N. Miller, president of the Information Technology Association of America, "[b]anks are not the only providers of financial services . . . [a]ll companies and their customers should be able to benefit from the same secure electronic authentication scheme afforded to banks and their affiliates").

[175] *See* Electronic Records; Electronic Signatures, 62 Fed. Reg. 13,430 (1997) (to be codified at 21 C.F.R. pt. 11), *available at* <http://www.fda.gov>.

The regulations apply to records in electronic form that are created, modified, maintained, archived, retrieved, or transmitted under any records requirements set forth in FDA regulations. The regulations also apply to electronic records submitted to the agency under the Federal Food, Drug, and Cosmetic Act[176] and the Public Health Service Act.[177] The FDA will consider electronic signatures to be equivalent to handwritten signatures if they meet certain requirements designed to ensure their trustworthiness and reliability. For example, electronic signatures not based upon biometrics must employ at least two distinct identification components, such as an identification code and password. In addition, persons using electronic signatures based upon identification codes and passwords must employ specific controls to ensure their security and integrity. The FDA regulations took effect August 20, 1997.

[c] International Developments. While uniform state laws or federal standards may be a solution for purely domestic transactions, such laws and standards will not resolve issues raised by international electronic contracts. Governments understand that they must think globally about electronic commerce, and they have begun efforts to coordinate national policies and develop regional and international guidelines. For example, the Commission of the European Communities solicited proposals in 1996 to prepare a study on the legal aspects of digital signatures.[178] The Organization for Economic Cooperation and Development ("OECD") adopted Cryptography Policy Guidelines in March 1997 to assist governments in formulating cryptography policies and legislation.[179] In July 1997, the Clinton Administration issued a report on global electronic commerce that, among other things, supports the development and adoption of international model laws.[180] Finally, UNCITRAL adopted a Model Law on Electronic Commerce in December 1996,[181] and released the latest version of its Draft Uniform Rules on Electronic Signatures in December 1997.[182]

A number of governments have also undertaken studies, issued guidelines, or proposed or enacted legislation that addresses electronic signatures. These include Canada, Denmark, France, Germany, Italy, Japan, Malaysia, and the United Kingdom. Companies planning to conduct global electronic commerce will have to consider the impact of foreign laws and monitor international developments.

---

[176] 21 U.S.C. §§ 301-92.

[177] 42 U.S.C. §§ 201 *et seq.*

[178] Tender Specifications: Invitation to Tender No. XV/96/51/E; Study on the Legal Aspects of Digital Signatures, *available at* (visited Nov. 21, 1997) <http://www2.echo>.

[179] Council of the European Union, Organization for Economic Cooperation and Development, *Crytography Policy Guidelines* (Mar. 26, 1997), *available at* <http://www.oecd.org>. The OECD's Guidelines are intended, among other things, to promote the use of cryptography and raise awareness of the need for internationally compatible cryptography policies and laws.

[180] PRESIDENT WILLIAM J. CLINTON & VICE PRESIDENT ALBERT GORE, JR., A FRAMEWORK FOR GLOBAL ELECTRONIC COMMERCE (1997), *available at* <http://www.iitf.nist.gov/electronic_commerce.htm>. *See White House Releases Report on Electronic Commerce*, 21st CENTURY BANKING ALERT® No. 97-7-2, July 2, 1997, *available at* <http://www.ffhsj.com/bancmail/bancpage.htm>.

[181] *UNICTRAL Model Law on Electronic Commerce*, G.A. Res. 162, U.N. GAOR 6th Comm., 51st Sess., 85th plen. mtg. (1996), *available at* (visited Jan. 28, 1998) <http://www.un.or.at/uncitral/>.

[182] UNITED NATIONS COMMISSION ON INTERNATIONAL TRADE LAW, WORKING GROUP ON ELECTRONIC COMMERCE, DRAFT UNIFORM RULES ON ELECTRONIC SIGNATURES (Dec. 12, 1997), *available at* (visited Jan. 28, 1998) <http://www.un.or.at/uncitral/>.

[2] INTERNET SECURITIES OFFERINGS

On January 7, 1996, the North American Securities Administrators Association ("NASAA"), the association of state securities regulators, adopted a resolution regarding securities offered on the Internet ("Resolution").[183] The Resolution recognized in its preamble that state securities administrators should adopt a uniform policy concerning offers of securities on the Internet that is consistent with the goals of investor protection and access to capital markets. To date, thirty-two states have adopted some form of the Resolution; it is pending in fifteen other states.[184]

The Resolution contained three core principles, that NASAA would: (1) develop a pilot program to monitor Internet offers and subsequent sales; (2) encourage states to exempt Internet offers from the registration provisions of their state securities laws if (a) the offer indicates, directly or indirectly, that the securities are being offered only to the residents of a particular state, and (b) the offer is not otherwise specifically directed to any person in a state by, or on behalf of, the issuer of securities; and (3) encourage states to take appropriate steps to allow sales of securities if either (a) no sales were made in any state until the offering has been registered and declared effective and the final prospectus has been delivered to the investor prior to such sale, or (b) the sales are exempt from registration.

Internet based securities fraud has accelerated rapidly.[185] In response, several states have brought enforcement actions alleging that securities-related Internet activity violated state anti-fraud provisions.[186]

[3] CONSUMER PROTECTION

The new and unfamiliar nature of the Internet has caused several states to amend and refine their consumer protection statutes or test the applicability of existing laws. Such laws, assuming that they pass constitutional requirements, may require either that entities operating on the Internet, particularly on the World Wide Web, comply with the requirements imposed by numerous jurisdictions or that these entities take steps to ensure that they do not engage in business with residents of other jurisdictions, which may impose requirements with which they are not in compliance.

For example, effective January 1, 1997, California amended its catalog/telemarketing consumer law to protect California residents who conduct transactions over the Internet.[187] The law extends the delivery, refund, or substitution requirements of California's existing law to any vendor conducting business over the Internet or over other means of electronic communication when the transaction involves buyers located in California.[188]

---

[183] *Resolution Regarding Securities Offered on Internet*, NASAA Rep. (CCH) ¶ 7040, at 7046-47 (Jan. 7, 1996).

[184] *See NASAA Internet Resolution, available at* (visited Jan. 29, 1998) <http://www.nasaa.org/bluesky/guidelines/resolu.html>.

[185] *See* Leslie Eaton, *Investing It; Fraud Case Focuses on the Internet*, N.Y. TIMES, Sept. 14, 1997, § 3, at 5; Jerry Knight, *Penny Stock Promoter Is Indicted; Nev. Man Cited for Role in Collapse*, WASH. POST, Sept. 19, 1997, at G2.

[186] *See, e.g.*, Alexander C. Gavis, *The Offering and Distribution of Securities in Cyberspace: A Review of Regulatory and Industry Initiatives*, 52 BUS. LAW. 317 (1996).

[187] CAL. BUS. & PROF. CODE § 17538.

[188] *Id.* § 17358(a).

It also establishes consumer disclosure obligations for online vendors, including specific locations on a vendor's page where disclosures must be included.[189]

Minnesota's Attorney General has been in the forefront in defending state prerogatives in regard to the application of state gambling restrictions to online gambling activities involving residents of a particular state.[190] In December 1996, a Minnesota court denied a motion for dismissal for lack of jurisdiction in *State of Minnesota v. Granite Gate Resorts,*[191] wherein the State of Minnesota alleged that a Nevada company, Granite Gate Resorts, and its president engaged in deceptive trade practices, false advertising, and consumer fraud by advertising in Minnesota, through its Belize-based WagerNet site, that Internet gambling is legal in Minnesota.

Although the WagerNet website advises readers to "consult your local, county and state authorities regarding restrictions on off-shore sports betting via telephone before registering," the court gave this disclaimer little weight. Instead, the court found that once the defendant put an ad on the Internet, he knew that it had to reach national markets, including Minnesota. The court also found that the state's jurisdictional claim was buttressed by WagerNet's statement that it had the right to apply for an injunction or other relief with regard to the customer's state. The court also took note of the fact that Minnesota residents were regular visitors to the site. The Minnesota Court of Appeals, after applying a five part minimum contacts test, affirmed the lower court's finding of personal jurisdiction.[192]

In another case involving state enforcement of gambling laws, *Missouri v. Interactive Gaming & Communications Corp.*, investigators with the Missouri Attorney General's Office telephoned a Pennsylvania-based company offering gambling through an off-shore affiliate and were advised by the company that the gambling services offered were legal.[193] The court found that the actions of the company violated Missouri gambling law. The court also found that the company had failed to provide notice in any of its communications, including its website, that the gambling service and a customer's participation in them were illegal in Missouri. The fact that the company had represented that those activities were legal in Missouri also violated a Missouri deceptive trade practices statute.

The court entered a permanent injunction against the company prohibiting it from doing business in Missouri or providing Missouri residents the ability to participate in any form of casino gambling. The court

---

[189] *Id.* § 17358(d).

[190] See Chapter 19 for a discussion of jurisdiction. Online gambling is also receiving attention at the federal level. *See* Internet Gambling Prohibition Act of 1997, H.R. 2380, S. 474, 105th Cong. (1997); *Hearing Before the Subcommittee on Technology, Terrorism, and Government Information of the Senate Comm. on the Judiciary,* 105th Cong. (1997); United States Attorney's Office for the Southern District of New York, Press Release, Mar. 4, 1998 (announcing the indictment of owners and managers of six off-shore sports betting companies).

[191] *Minnesota v. Granite Gate Resorts*, No. C6-95-7227 (D. Minn. filed Dec. 6, 1996), *aff'd*, No. C6-97-89, 1997 WL 557670 (Minn. App. Sept. 5, 1997).

[192] *Minnesota v. Granite Gate Resorts, Inc.*, No. C6-97-89, 1997 WL 557670 (Minn. App. Sept. 5, 1997).

[193] *Missouri v. Interactive Gaming & Communications Corp.*, No. 97-7808 (Mo. App. May 22, 1997). *See also Growth of Internet-Based Gambling Raises Questions for Bank Systems,* Banking Rep. (BNA) 406 (Mar. 3, 1997); Dean Starkman, *U.S. Indicts 14 Over Gambling on the Internet,* WALL ST. J., Mar. 5, 1998, at A8.

required the company (i) to reject all applications from Missouri, by whatever means necessary, including programming its software to perform a check for the state of residence of each applicant, (ii) to reject and return any funds sent to the company to participate in casino gambling by a Missouri resident, (iii) to post a prominent notice on its homepage and all application pages stating that the company is prohibited from accepting applications or funds from Missouri residents, and (iv) to allow an independent entity selected by the Attorney General's Office to conduct unannounced audits of the company's compliance with the injunction.[194]

[4] MODEL BUSINESS CORPORATION ACT

The Committee on Corporate Laws of the Section of Business Law of the American Bar Association ("ABA") recently proposed changes to the Model Business Corporation Act ("MBCA"), which are intended to accommodate the use of electronic means for transmitting and filing corporate documents with Secretaries of State.[195]

The proposed amendments would permit corporations to file documents electronically and exempt electronic filings from requirements for submitting multiple originals to the state.[196] The amendments would also allow the state to deliver copies of approved documents and rejection notices to an applicant electronically.[197] A state would be similarly permitted to issue a good standing certificate electronically.[198] The penalty for false signatures would be expanded to include false electronic signatures.[199] Finally, companies would be permitted to provide electronic notice to a shareholder if the shareholder specifically authorized the use of electronic means.[200]

[5] UNIFORM COMMERCIAL CODE REVISIONS

The process of adapting the paper-based Uniform Commercial Code ("U.C.C.") to electronic commerce by amending existing Articles and adding new Articles is already underway.[201]

---

[194] *Id.* The court also imposed monetary penalty of approximately $66,500 on the company. *See Judge Rules Internet Business Can't Offer On-line Gambling to Missourians, Must Pay $66,000 in Penalties and Costs*, Mo. Attorney Gen'l' Office, Press Release, May 23, 1997, *available at* <http: www.state.mo.us>.

[195] Am. Bar Ass'n, Comm. on Corp. Laws, *Changes in the Model Business Corporation Act - Amendments Pertaining to Electronic Filings,* 52 BUS. LAW. 991 (1997).

[196] *Id.* § 1.20, at 992.

[197] *Id.* § 1.25, at 996.

[198] *Id.* § 1.27, at 997.

[199] *Id.* § 1.29, at 998.

[200] *Id.* § 1.41, at 999.

[201] *See generally* Amelia H. Boss & Jane Kaufman Winn, *The Emerging Law of Electronic Commerce*, 52 BUS. LAW. 1469 (1997) (providing an overview of the U.C.C. revisions and related legislation which is being prepared to "respond to the demands of an electronic age").

With respect to the payments system,[202] Article 4A governs certain electronic movements of funds via wire transfer.[203] With respect to investment securities products,[204] Article 8 was revised in 1994 ("Revised Article 8")[205] to closely reflect industry practices such as book-entry securities[206] and physical, immobilized share certificates.[207] This same immobilization approach has been implemented by the developers of the privately held Mortgage Electronic Registration Systems ("MERS") for single-family residential mortgages to help mortgage industry participants simplify the transfer and servicing of these obligations.[208]

With respect to electronic communications, efforts have been made to address whether these communications qualify as "signatures" and "writings" under the U.C.C. For example, Article 2 currently defines a "signature" as "any symbol executed or adopted by a party with present intention to authenticate a writing,"[209] and a "writing" as any "printing, typewriting, or any other intentional reduction to tangible form."[210] The scope of these definitions are critical in determining whether a contract is within the Statute of Frauds, which provides that "a contract for the sale of goods for the price of $500 or more is not enforceable . . . unless some *writing* sufficient to indicate that a contract for sale has been made between the parties and *signed* by the party against whom enforcement is sought or by his authorized agent or broker."[211] The case law and the

---

[202] See Chapter 4 for a comprehensive discussion of this topic.

[203] Article 4A governs a closed system involving the transfer of funds among participants with established, structured, and ongoing relationships. Verification, authentication, and compliance procedures are easier to promote and maintain here than in open systems, such as the Internet.

[204] For a comprehensive discussion of current wire transfer systems, see DONALD I. BAKER & ROLAND E. BRANDEL, THE LAW OF ELECTRONIC FUND TRANSFER SYSTEMS, ch. 11 (3d ed. 1996).

[205] As of June 5, 1997, Revised Article 8/9 has been adopted by 33 states and the District of Columbia. *See* Alan M. Christenfeld & Shepard W. Melzer, *Corporate Update: Secured Transactions* (June 5, 1997).

[206] A "book entry security" is issued electronically through entries in the accounts of the relevant financial institutions. After issuance, the financial institution records transactions by debiting and crediting appropriate accounts. No physical certificate exists for these securities. Effective in early 1997, federal agencies, such as the Department of Treasury, and government sponsored entities, such as the Federal National Mortgage Association ("Fannie Mae") and the Federal Home Loan Mortgage Corporation ("Freddie Mac"), adopted regulations that preempt state laws which do not conform with Revised Article 8 with respect to the hypothecation and perfection of security interests in their book entry securities. See the Secretary of HUD's Regulation of the Federal National Mortgage Association (Fannie Mae) and the Federal Home Loan Mortgage Corporation (Freddie Mac): Book Entry Procedures, 62 Fed. Reg. 28,975 (1997) (to be codified at 24 C.F.R. pt. 81).

[207] A "physical, immobilized certificate" is a share of a publicly traded stock or debenture held of record by the Depository Trust Company through its own nominee partnership, Cede & Co., or GNMA pass-through certificates held of record by the Participation Trust Company. When customers trade these securities, no certificate changes hands — the trust company makes a book entry to reflect the purchase and sale.

[208] The Mortgage Electronic Registration Systems ("MERS") is operated by a Delaware nonstock corporation, Mortgage Electronic Registration Systems, Inc., which is owned by its members, who are usually its users. Members pay an annual fee to execute electronic transactions on the MERS System. When a mortgage loan is registered on the MERS System, it receives a unique mortgage identification number (MIN). Typically, the borrower executes a traditional paper mortgage naming the lender as mortgagee and the lender assigns the mortgage to MERS. From that point on, no additional mortgage assignments will be recorded because MERS will remain the mortgagee of record throughout the life of the loan; transfers of the servicing rights are permissible, however, and will take place through MERS. For more on this topic, see R.K Arnold, *Yes, There is Life on MERS*, PROB. & PROP., July/Aug. 1997, at 33.

[209] U.C.C. § 1-201(39).

[210] *Id.* § 1-201(46).

[211] *Id.* § 2-201 (emphasis added).

views of commentators on this issue is divided,[212] and several proposals have been made to expressly broaden the scope of these terms.[213]

With respect to licensing of information and software contracts, a new Article 2B has been proposed, that would significantly expand the scope of the Code and bring within its coverage types of transactions typically encountered in the conduct of electronic commerce.[214] This proposed Article introduces new concepts into the U.C.C., such as the use of the term "record" rather than "writing" to permit the use of electronic documents[215] and the term "authentication" rather than "signature" to limit repudiation of electronic agreements.[216] It addresses several issues of interest to the software community, including mass market transactions,[217] and electronic employing agents.[218] The current draft of Article 2B is scheduled for consideration by the National Conference of Commissioners on Uniform State Laws and the American Law Institute in 1998.

§ 10.05 TAXATION

Through their choice of tax policy, states have the potential to exert significant influence over the growth and development of electronic commerce. There are, by one estimate, more than 6,500 taxing authorities and 30,000 taxing jurisdictions in the United States at the state and local level.[219] Because of the radically decentralized nature of the Internet, even a very simple transaction between two parties can be routed through a Byzantine series of channels, with the parties generally having no knowledge of, or control over, the particular routing.[220] The sequence of digital electronic instructions (or "packets," in Internet parlance) comprising a single transaction may pass through a number of different servers or other hardware components, each located in a different city and state. This has raised concerns in some quarters that multiple, overlapping state-level taxation of electronic transactions could seriously impede the growth of the Internet as a new avenue for conducting commerce. State- and local-level taxing authorities are drawing complaints of opportunism, if not

---

[212] *See* Thomas P. Vartanian, *Comment: Digital Certification: New Wrinkles in Managing Risk*, AM. BANKER, July 1, 1997; Glenn T. Oxton, *Digital Signatures: Potentials and Pitfalls*, N.Y.L.J., July 21, 1997, at 56.

[213] *See* NATIONAL CONFERENCE OF COMMISSIONERS ON UNIFORM STATE LAWS, UNIFORM ELECTRONIC TRANSACTIONS ACT (draft Aug. 15, 1997); INFORMATION SECURITY COMM., AM. BAR ASS'N, DIGITAL SIGNATURE GUIDELINES: LEGAL INFRASTRUCTURE FOR CERTIFICATION AUTHORITIES AND SECURE ELECTRONIC COMMERCE (1996).

[214] *See* NATIONAL CONFERENCE OF COMMISSIONERS ON UNIFORM STATE LAWS, UNIFORM COMMERCIAL CODE ARTICLE 2B, LICENSES (Nov. 1997 Draft) [hereinafter ARTICLE 2B PROPOSAL]. *See also* Boss & Winn, *supra* note 201, at 1483.

[215] *See* ARTICLE 2B PROPOSAL § 2B-102(35), at 44.

[216] *See id.* § 2B-102(3), at 36.

[217] *See id.* § 2B-102(29), at 42.

[218] *See id.* § 2B-102(16), at 39.

[219] *See* 143 CONG. REC. S442 (daily ed. Mar. 13, 1997) (remarks of Sen. Wyden).

[220] *See* Howard E. Abrams, *How Electronic Commerce Works*, 13 STATE TAX NOTES 123 (1997).

buccaneerism.[221]   However, many states and municipalities have a different story to tell: a real concern about the impending loss of an important tax base. Whether state taxation of electronic commerce is opportunistic is debatable. What is clear, however, is that it lacks uniformity. Different states tax different aspects of electronic commerce in different ways and at different rates. Some states have declared the Internet a tax-free zone, while others impose taxes on multiple aspects of electronic commerce.

The power of states to assess and collect taxes is not unlimited. In order to subject a transaction — electronic or otherwise — to taxation, the state must be able to assert territorial jurisdiction over a particular transaction and over the parties thereto ("taxing jurisdiction"). The scope of this taxing jurisdiction is defined and limited by two sources. At the state level, there is the definitional requirement found in many state statutes of an in-state "taxable event." At the federal level, the relevant limitations are those that the Supreme Court has imposed based on two constitutional provisions: the Due Process Clause of the Fourteenth Amendment and Interstate Commerce Clause. The scope of these restrictions has already been litigated (and, in at least once instance, ruled upon by the Court) in the context of a commercial activity that pre-dates, and is in certain ways analogous to, electronic commerce — mail order sales.

Some commentators feel that this two-fold limitation is too prohibitive with regard to electronic commerce, and that a new framework is needed. Certain public-sector organizations have begun to consider extensive restructuring of the current system of state taxation of electronic commerce to increase state taxing jurisdiction, through such measures as a uniform taxation statute. To the extent that such reform efforts run afoul of constitutional principles, they are unlikely to be successful, unless, as some urge, Congress chooses to aid states in their efforts by placing its imprimatur on such uniform legislation. Currently, however, the only pending congressional action is to exactly the opposite effect: a broad moratorium on all state taxation of the Internet.

[1]   CURRENT STATE SALES AND USE TAX LAWS

Since their inception during the Great Depression, sales and use taxes[222] have provided an important source of revenue for many states and municipalities.[223]   In fact, sales taxes have become the principal revenue source for many states.[224]   Sales and use taxes are separate, reciprocal excise taxes imposed on the privilege of

---

[221] *See* John Simons, *Battle Over Internet Taxes Heats Up as Congress Considers a Plan for Moratorium on New Levies,* WALL ST. J., Oct. 23, 1997, at A20 (noting that, "[t]he [Internet] industry has formed a lasting impression of government as a ham-fisted ogre, eager to over-regulate and strangle the growth of electronic commerce. It doesn't trust the nation's 30,000 taxing jurisdictions to arrive at a uniform solution for taxing billions of dollars of Internet transactions.").

[222] States also derive revenue from income taxation and other sources. The following discussion is limited to sales and use tax issues.

[223] *See* Steven J. Forte, *Use Tax Collection on Internet Purchases: Should the Mail Order Industry Serve as a Model?*, 15 J. MARSHALL J. COMPUTER & INFO. L. 203 (1997).

[224] *See* Edward A. Morse, *State Taxation of Internet Commerce: Something New Under The Sun?*, 30 CREIGHTON L. REV. 1113, 1129 ("In 1992, states collected more than $107 billion in sales taxes, representing 32.8% of the total state tax revenues.").

buying (sales tax)[225] and using, storing, or consuming (use tax)[226] property within a state. Sales taxes are targeted at in-state purchases of goods. They are imposed on the consumer, the merchant, or some combination of the two.[227] Use taxes cover purchased goods that are subsequently brought in-state for use or consumption. Unlike sales taxes, use taxes are imposed on the possessor or "user" of the property, not the seller.[228] They are designed to prevent in-state consumers from tax "forum shopping" (seeking out merchants located in jurisdictions without sales taxes).[229] Most of the states that have sales taxes have also adopted corresponding use taxes to cover those transactions that sales taxes do not cover.[230]

[a] Electronic Commerce as Analogous to Mail Order. At one level, electronic commerce represents merely an extension of an already well-established form of interstate commerce — mail order sales. As such, it poses (and threatens to exacerbate) the same impediment to state use tax collection efforts posed by mail order transactions. As discussed above, use taxes are generally assessed in situations involving an in-state consumer and an out-of-state merchant. States would, of course, much prefer to tax the out-of-state merchant but are often prohibited to doing so by a lack of taxing jurisdiction. Although the tax can be assessed against and collected directly from in-state consumers, the administrative difficulties involved in doing so has led many states to forgo this alternative.[231] In fact, it is estimated that as much as $3.3 billion in tax revenues are lost each year, due primarily to consumer substitution of mail order vendors for local vendors.[232] Currently, mail order sales are estimated to represent about 3% (or $60 billion) of the more than $1 trillion total retail market.[233] As the volume of electronic commerce increases, so will the number of opportunities for in-state consumers to choose out-of-state vendors. This could result in serious erosion of sales tax bases.

[b] Novel Issues Raised by Electronic Commerce. Electronic commerce is not merely a 21st Century version of mail order.[234] It is also an entirely new form of commerce, raising novel definitional issues under existing state tax statutes. State efforts to interpret and to rewrite these statutes to reflect these

---

[225] 68 AM. JUR. 2D *Sales and Use Tax* § 5 (1993).

[226] *Id.* §§ 190-192.

[227] Different states allocate the sales tax burden differently as between these two parties. *Id.* § 6.

[228] *Id.* § 236.

[229] *Henneford v. Silas Mason Co.*, 300 U.S. 577 (1937) (Justice Cardozo stated that one purpose of a challenged use tax was to allow in-state merchants "to compete upon terms of equality with retail dealers in other states who are exempt from a sales tax or any corresponding burden." He also noted a revenue preservation motive on the part of the state: "[a]nother effect, or at least another tendency, must be to avoid the likelihood of a drain upon the revenues of the state, buyers being no longer tempted to place their orders in other states in the effort to escape payment of the tax on local sales.").

[230] *See* Gregory A. Ichel, *Internet Sounds Death Knell for Use Taxes: States Continue to Scream Over Lost Revenues*, SETON HALL L. REV. 643, 645 (1997).

[231] *See* Kaye K. Caldwell, *Solving State and Local use Tax Collection Problems: A Necessary First Step Before Dealing With Use Tax Problems of Electronic Commerce*, available at (visited July 28, 1997) <http://www.softwareindustry.org/issues/docs-htm/usetaxwp.html>.

[232] *See* Daniel J. Langin, *The Economics of the Internet: Insurance and Risk Management, Advertising and Other Business Models, Valuation and Tax Issues*, 482 PRAC. L. INST. 447, 462 (1997).

[233] *See* Karl A. Frieden & Michael E. Porter, *The Taxation of Cyberspace*, 11 STATE TAX NOTES 1363, 1375 (1996).

[234] *See* David Cowling & Andrew M. Ferris, *Internet Taxation Reviewed*, 13 STATE TAX NOTES 41 (1997).

unprecedented changes have lacked uniformity. Widespread uncertainty predominates and may be impeding the evolution of electronic commerce.[235]

Electronic commerce should not be viewed as a unitary process. Rather, it is a series of discrete, but related, components, each of which may be subject to separate and differing taxation. At the most foundational level, there is the basic access to the channels of electronic commerce, such as telephone lines and Internet connections. In that regard, some states adhere to a narrow definition of "telecommunications," while others attempt to distinguish between basic telecommunications services and "value added" services.[236] Another component is the transfer of electronic "content," such as software or information, through those channels. Finally, there is electronic marketing and solicitation of sales by online vendors. State approaches to the taxation of each of these components vary.[237]

Electronic commerce did not create the thorny definitional distinction between goods and services.[238] It does, however, heighten the problem because of the difficulty, in many instances, in distinguishing between online service and digitized content. For instance, the downloading of information from an online information retrieval service might be characterized as either the provision of a service or the delivery of electronic content, with vastly different tax results.[239] Similarly, "canned" (as opposed to custom-designed) computer software has been described as both an intangible (*e.g.*, an embodiment of knowledge or intellectual services) and therefore not subject to tax, and as a series of magnetic impulses stored in a tangible medium and therefore taxable.[240] Moreover, even though many states exempt from tax the commissioning of certain custom-designed software, such as World Wide Web pages, these programming services might nevertheless become subject to tax if the programmer's work product is ultimately embodied in a tangible item delivered to the consumer, such as a printout or a diskette.[241]

[c] Differing Approaches: New York and Texas. For illustrative purposes, it is interesting to note that although New York and Texas have structurally similar sales and use tax statutes,[242] the two states take vastly different approaches to the taxation of the Internet and of electronic commerce. Both statutes impose sales[243]

---

[235] A July 1996 survey of top executives at companies engaged in electronic commerce cited uncertainty regarding state-level tax exposure as a major factor inhibiting further growth in the volume of on-line transactions. *American Companies Forecast Huge Growth in Electronic Commerce, But Study Uncovers Concern About the Impact of Ambiguous State Tax Laws*, available at (visited Apr. 17, 1997) <http://www.ice.kpmg.com/news/news6-96b.html>.

[236] *See* Frieden & Porter, *supra* note 233, at 1369.

[237] *See Internet Taxes: Hearing Before the Subcomm. on Telecommunications, Trade and Consumer Protection of the House Comm. on Commerce*, 105th Cong. (1997).

[238] *See* Morse, *supra* note 224, at 1130 ("[T]he difference between a good (presumptively taxed) and a service (presumptively not taxed unless enumerated in the taxing statute) presents a long-standing controversy which is not uniformly resolved among the states.").

[239] *See* Frieden & Porter, *supra* note 233, at 1371-04.

[240] *See* Linda A. Sharp, *Computer Software or Printout Transactions as Subject to State Sales or Use Tax,* 36 ALR 5th 133.

[241] *See* Frieden & Porter, *supra* note 233, at 1374.

[242] N.Y. TAX LAW § 1101 *et seq.*; TEX. TAX CODE ANN. Ch. 151.

[243] N.Y. TAX LAW § 1105; TEX. TAX CODE ANN. § 151.0051.

and use[244] taxes on "tangible personal property"[245] and certain enumerated services.[246] With regard to electronic commerce, this is where the similarities end. New York has declared the Internet a largely tax-free zone.[247] Texas employs a more aggressive approach.[248]

Under the New York statute, "tangible personal property" is defined to include "pre-written computer software,"[249] which includes all software that is not custom-designed for the purchaser.[250] Enumerated services subject to taxation include: (1) creation or fabrication of "tangible personal property;"[251] (2) installation, service and repair of "tangible personal property;"[252] and (3) furnishing of information, except for personal information and advertising services.[253] The New York Department of Taxation and Finance has, in a number of recent Advisory Opinions, taken the position that these definitions do *not* include: (1) web page development services;[254] (2) Internet access subscriptions, including such "incidental" features as e-mail;[255] (3) advertising on "Virtual Storefronts;"[256] or (4) customized reports listing web page hits.[257]

Under the Texas statute, "tangible personal property" is defined to include "a computer program,"[258] which is, in turn, defined as a set of computer-readable instructions.[259] "Taxable services" include: (1) telecommunications services;[260] (2) information services;[261] (3) data processing services;[262] and (4) services involved in the creation, installation, maintenance and repair of computer programs, except where not rendered by the

---

[244] N.Y. Tax Law § 1110; Tex. Tax Code Ann. § 151.0101.

[245] N.Y. Tax Law §§ 1105, 1110; Tex. Tax Code Ann. § 151.0010.

[246] N.Y. Tax Law §§ 1105; Tex. Tax Code Ann. § 151.00101.

[247] *See* Deborah R. Bierbaum, *The New Media Industry and Electronic Commerce: Developing a Tax Policy for New York,* 12 State Tax Notes 1533, 1534 (1997).

[248] *See* L.J. Kutlen, *Software - and Net - Taxation in the Lone Star State,* 13 State Tax Notes 559, 560 (1997) ("Texas is very aggressive regarding taxation of any and all Internet transactions. Your working assumption should be that if it involves the Internet, it is taxable.").

[249] N.Y. Tax Law § 1101(b)(6).

[250] *Id.* § 1101(b)(14). There are additional provisions concerning custom-designed enhancements or modifications to pre-written software.

[251] *Id.* § 1105(c)(2).

[252] *Id.* § 1105(c)(3).

[253] *Id.* § 1105(c)(1).

[254] TSB-A-97(41)S (July 23, 1997), *available in* 1997 WL 538527 (N.Y. Dept. Tax. Fin.), TSB-A-97(35)S (June 25, 1997), *available in* 1997 WL 417156 (N.Y. Dept. Tax. Fin.).

[255] TSB-A97(49)S, TSB-A-97(17)(C) (July 23, 1997), *available in* 1997 WL 538529 (N.Y. Dept. Tax. Fin.), TSB-A-97(30)S (May 28, 1997), *available in* 1997 WL 358997 (N.Y. Dept. Tax. Fin.).

[256] TSB-A-95(33)S (Aug. 14, 1995), *available in* 1995 WL 559665 (N.Y. Dept. Tax. Fin.).

[257] TSB-A-97(56)S (Sept. 3, 1997), *available in* 1997 WL 611816 (N.Y. Dept. Tax. Fin.).

[258] Tex. Tax Code Ann. § 151.009.

[259] *Id.* § 151.0031.

[260] *Id.* § 151.0101(a)(6).

[261] *Id.* § 151.0101(a)(10).

[262] *Id.* § 151.0101(a)(12).

vendor thereof.[263]   Together these definitions arguably cover every major aspect of electronic commerce, including: (1) Internet access; (2) web page design; and (3) electronic delivery of software.[264]

[2]   TAXING JURISDICTION

[a]   State Law: "Taxable Event."   Under many current state sales and use tax statutes, a necessary prerequisite for taxation is the occurrence of an in-state "taxable event."[265]   Many state sales tax statutes include the explicit phrase "in this state."[266]   The "taxable event" when assessing sales taxes has been described as the transfer of title of ownership for consideration.[267]   The "taxable event" when assessing use taxes is the in-state use, storage, or consumption of the goods or services.[268]   Application of the "taxable event" standard to online transactions involving purely electronic content such as online software or digitized information presents difficult sourcing problems.   In the inherently borderless world of cyberspace, it is often difficult to pinpoint the location or source of the (1) purchase, (2) delivery, (3) storage, or (4) consumption.   This creates the potential for two equally unpalatable results.

On the one hand, an online consumer might take possession of electronic content in more than one geographical location simultaneously, creating the potential for multiple taxation.   On the other hand, the ease with which electronic content can be moved or relocated might create incentives for taxpayers to accept delivery, store, or use the electronic content on a network server located in a "tax haven."[269]   New sourcing tests may be necessary.   The New York State Department of Taxation and Finance's Internet Working Group considered precisely this issue, but did not reach consensus as to the appropriate alternative sourcing test.[270]

[b]   Federal Constitutional Law.   Currently, the most significant federal constraints on state-level taxation are those that the Supreme Court has established based on two clauses of the Constitution: the Due Process

---

[263] *Id.* § 151.0101(a)(5)(D).

[264] *See supra* note 248.

[265] *See, e.g., Savemart, Inc. v. State Tax Com'n of State of N.Y.*, 482 N.Y.S.2d 150 (N.Y. S.Ct. 1984); *South Dakota v. Dorhout*, 513 N.W.2d 390 (S.D.N.Y. 1994); *Kellogg Co. v. Department of Treasury*, 516 N.W.2d 108 (Mich.App. 1994) ("taxable moment").

[266] 68 AM. JUR. 2d *Sales and Use Tax* § 20 (1993).

[267] *See, e.g., Sullivan v. United States*, 395 U.S. 169, 175 (1969) (construing Connecticut tax statute).

[268] 68 AM. JUR. 2D *Sales and Use Tax* §§ 190-192.

[269] Under current rules, the parties have some ability to control by contract how certain sales are sourced.   Courts will often look to the terms of the sales contract executed by the parties in determining the locations of delivery and the transfer of title. 68 AM. JUR. 2D *Sales and Use Tax* § 21. Under the Uniform Commercial Code, parties have substantial latitude to specify by contract how and when title to purchased "goods" passes from the buyer to the seller in a general commercial context. *See* U.C.C. § 2-401(1).   In the context of sales tax assessments, the scope of this latitude may be narrower. *See* U.C.C. § 2-401, Official Comment 1 ("This section, however, in no way intends to indicate which line of interpretation should be followed in cases where the applicability of 'public' regulation depends upon a 'sale' or upon location of 'title' without further definition.").

[270] *See* Bierbaum, *supra* note 247, at 1535-36.   The group put forward three alternative tests, which would, respectively, source the sale or use: (1) to the location of the drafting, negotiation, and signing of the sales contract; (2) to the location of the computer server; or (3) based on a ratio of in-state customers to out-of-state customers.

Clause of the Fourteenth Amendment and the Interstate Commerce Clause. Although sometimes overlapping, these are independent limitations on state taxing jurisdiction, each reflecting different constitutional concerns.[271]

[*i*] *The Due Process Clause: "Minimum Contacts."* The Due Process Clause demarcates the general limits of a state's authority to subject persons (including legal persons, such as corporations) to that state's jurisdiction. This includes not only the power to tax, but also the power to exert *in personam* jurisdiction over an individual in a state's courts (*e.g.* civil lawsuit). In the landmark case of *International Shoe Co. v. Washington,*[272] the Court stated that the relevant question was whether the individual had "minimum contacts" with the state such that the maintenance of the suit in that state's court does not offend "traditional notions of fair play and substantial justice."[273] Subsequently, in *Hanson v. Denckla,*[274] the Court rephrased this test to ask whether a party "purposefully avails itself of the privileges of conducting activities within the forum State, thus invoking the benefits and protections of its laws."[275]

With regard to specific issue of use taxes, the Court in *Quill Corp. v. North Dakota*[276] held that: "[t]he Due Process Clause requires some definite link, some minimum connection, between a state and the person, property or transaction it seeks to tax, and that the income attributed to the State for tax purposes must be rationally related to values connected with the taxing state."[277] The *Quill* case involved an out-of-state mail order vendor that had neither in-state offices nor employees. The Court held that a law requiring this vendor to collect and remit use taxes violated the Commerce Clause. However, the Court found the law consistent with the Due Process Clause. In reaching this latter conclusion, the *Quill* Court saw as determinative the "continuous and widespread solicitation of business within a State" and concluded that "[i]n this case, there is no question that Quill has purposefully directed its activities at North Dakota residents . . . ."[278]

Electronic commerce presents novel wrinkles for the purposefully directed formulation, the most notable of which is the question of whether an out-of-state merchant who maintains a website that can be accessed by in-state users is "purposefully direct[ing] its activities" at in-state users. The handful of lower courts that have considered this issue (in varying contexts) have split.[279] In any individual case, the result may depend on the relative passivity or interactivity of the site. The Sixth Circuit has found "purposeful availment" where a defendant shareware vendor entered into an online contract to upload its product to a computer information

---

[271] *See Quill Corp. v. North Dakota,* 504 U.S. 298, at 305-06 (1992). For a further discussion of jurisdictional issues, see Chapter 19.

[272] 326 U.S. 310 (1945).

[273] *Id.* at 316.

[274] 357 U.S. 235 (1958).

[275] *Id.* at 253.

[276] 504 U.S. 298 (1992).

[277] *Id.* at 306 (citations and internal quotation marks omitted).

[278] *Id.* at 308.

[279] *See* Michael Davidson, *Internet Vendors - Nexus or Not?,* 12 STATE TAX NOTES 1613, 1614 (1997); *see also* Thomas H. Steele, *State and Local Taxation of Electronic Commerce: The Current Landscape,* ELECTRONIC BANKING L. & COM. REP., Sept. 1997, at 7; Howard G. Zaharoff & Thomas W. Evans, *Cyberspace and the Internet: Law's Newest Frontier,* BOSTON BAR J., May/June, 1997, at 24; David Cowling & Andrew M. Ferris, *Internet Taxation Reviewed,* 13 STATE TAX NOTES 41, 44 (1997).

service and then repeatedly transferred and advertised its product online.[280] The Ninth Circuit reached a contrary result in a situation where the defendants maintained an "essentially passive home page," and "entered into no contracts in Arizona, made no sales in Arizona, received no telephone calls from Arizona, earned no income from Arizona, and sent no messages over the Internet to Arizona."[281] In a non-electronic commerce context, a plurality of the Supreme Court stated that "a defendant's awareness that the stream of commerce may or will sweep the [defendant's] product into the forum State does not convert the mere act of placing the product into the stream into an act purposefully directed toward the forum State."[282]

[ii] *The Commerce Clause: "Substantial Nexus."* While the Due Process Clause is concerned with preventing states from unfairly imposing their jurisdiction on individuals, the Interstate Commerce Clause is aimed at preventing the states from unfairly burdening interstate commerce and commercial activities as a whole.[283] In *Quill,* the Supreme Court reiterated its previously-formulated four prong test for assessing whether a particular state tax unduly burdens Interstate Commerce.[284] A state tax will be upheld if it "[1] is fairly applied to an activity with a substantial nexus with the taxing State, [2] is fairly apportioned, [3] does not discriminate against interstate commerce, and [4] is fairly related to the services provided by the State."[285] With regard to the first prong, the *Quill* Court expressly reiterated its position that physical presence in-state, however slight or fleeting, is a necessary prerequisite for taxation.[286]

[A] *Physical Presence.* "Physical presence" does not require that the taxpayer (either individual or corporate) actually set foot within the borders of the state. Instead, the Court has, in a series of cases, left open the possibility that certain factors might serve as proxies for the taxpayer's physical presence in-state. First and foremost is a line of cases in which the Court held that the in-state presence of the taxpayer's agents or representatives (sometimes referred to as "drummers"[287]) might satisfy the nexus requirement.[288] Other such proxies that both the Supreme Court and lower courts have considered include in-state: (1) offices or other places of business; (2) property ownership; (3) telephone listings; (4) advertising; and (5) bank accounts.[289] In *Goldberg v. Sweet,*[290] the Court indicated that sufficient nexus to tax telecommunications would be found where a

---

[280] *CompuServe, Inc. v. Patterson,* 89 F.3d 1257 (6th Cir. 1996).

[281] *Cybersell, Inc. v. Cybersell, Inc.,* 130 F.3d 414, 419 (9th Cir. 1997).

[282] *Asahi Metal Indus. Co. v. Superior Court,* 480 U.S. 102, 112 (1987).

[283] *Quill,* 504 U.S. at 312 ("We have, therefore, often identified 'notice' and 'fair warning' as the analytical touchstone of due process nexus analysis. In contrast, the Commerce Clause and its nexus requirement are informed not so much by concerns about fairness for the individual defendant as by structural concerns about the effects of state regulation on the national economy.").

[284] *Id.* at 311.

[285] *Complete Auto Transit, Inc. v. Brady,* 430 U.S. 274, 279 (1977).

[286] *Quill,* 504 U.S. at 317-18 (affirming the presence requirement first formulated in *National Bellas Hess, Inc. v. Department of Revenue of Ill.,* 386 U.S. 753 (1967)).

[287] *See Quill,* 504 U.S. at 308 ("phalanx of drummers").

[288] *See* Saba Ashraf, *Virtual Taxation: State Taxation of Internet and On-line Sales,* 24 FLA. ST. U. L. REV. 605, 620 (1997).

[289] *See* Richard G. Cohen & Paul Terry, *Online Taxation Issues Undergo Federal Scrutiny,* NAT'L L.J., May 5, 1997, at B16; KPMG, *Perspectives in State and Local Taxation – An Update on Current Issues and Trends,* BUS. MONITOR (N.Y.), Jan. 7, 1997.

[290] 488 U.S. 252 (1989).

long-distance telephone call or other communication signal originates or terminates in the taxing state and is either directed at an in-state resident or billed to an in-state billing address.[291]

Application of this framework to electronic commerce has engendered several different, and novel, theories. Some commentators have taken the position that Internet services providers ("ISPs") act as in-state "agents" of their customers when they furnish these customers with Internet access.[292] A related theory is that signing up with an ISP for Internet access is the effective equivalent of "leasing" the ISP's in-state hardware.[293] This theory can be — and has been — expanded beyond tangible property such as computer hardware to include clearly intangible property.[294] In the context of licensing intellectual property, one court has found sufficient nexus where the only contact with the taxing state was the in-state presence and use of the taxpayer-licenser's tradename.[295] Another theory posits that the entire notion of "presence" should be redefined to take account of the possibility of "virtual presence," an online interactive experience of such realism that it is essentially equivalent to physical presence.[296]

[B] *Fair Apportionment.* The Supreme Court has stated that "the central purpose behind the apportionment requirement is to ensure that each State taxes only its fair share of an interstate transaction."[297] The analysis involves two distinct issues: internal consistency and external consistency.[298] Internal consistency essentially requires that the challenged state tax law must not, as written, pose the threat of multiple taxation.[299] External consistency, by contrast, requires that there be no substantial threat of actual multiple taxation.[300]

---

[291] *Id.* at 263. This statement is technically dictum because the *Goldberg* parties stipulated that sufficient nexus existed. *Id.* at 260. In a subsequent decision, the Court stated "[w]e recently held that a State in which an interstate telephone call originates or terminates has the requisite Commerce Clause nexus to tax a customer's purchase of that call as long as the call is billed or charged to a service address, or paid by an addressee, within the taxing state." *Oklahoma's Tax Comm'n v. Jefferson Lines, Inc.*, 514 U.S. 175, 185 (1995).

[292] *See* Zaharoff & Evans, *supra* note 279, at 26 (noting that under this theory, "every company that does business over the Internet has agents in every state and therefore must collect and remit sales or use taxes").

[293] *See* Thomas H. Steele, *State and Local Taxation of Electronic Commerce: The Current Landscape*, ELECTRONIC BANKING L. & COM. REP., Sept. 1997, at 10-11.

[294] *See id.* at 4-6.

[295] *See Geoffrey, Inc. v. South Carolina Tax Comm'n.*, 437 S.E.2d 13 (D.S.C. 1993) *cert. den.* 510 U.S. 992 (noting that the taxpayer-licensor had purposefully directed its commercial activities at South Carolina where it was "aware of, consented to, and benefited from" the licensee's in-state use of the tradename).

[296] *See* Ashraf, *supra* note 288, at 627 (concluding that as online Virtual Reality software improves, "[c]onsumers will be able to virtually walk through a showroom or mall, drive a car, use a computer, or talk to technical support personnel using the Web").

[297] *Goldberg*, 488 U.S. at 260-1.

[298] *Id.*

[299] *Jefferson Lines*, 514 U.S. at 185 (stating that the internal consistency "test asks nothing about the degree of economic reality reflected by the tax, but simply looks to the structure of the tax at issue to see whether its identical application by every State in the Union would place interstate commerce at a disadvantage as compared with commerce intrastate").

[300] *Id.* ("External consistency, on the other hand, looks not to the logical consequences of cloning, but to the economic justification for the State's claim upon the value taxed, to discover whether a State's tax reaches beyond that portion of value that is fairly attributable to economic activity within the taxing state. . . . Here, the threat of real multiple taxation (though not by literally identical statutes) may indicate a State's impermissible overreaching.").

The requirement of external consistency can in some instances be satisfied if a state sales or use tax statute provides a credit for any sales or use tax paid in other jurisdictions.[301]

The Court has upheld as both internally and externally consistent a state tax on gross receipts for the sale of tickets for interstate bus trips.[302] The Court considered and dismissed the argument that the interstate nature of the bus trip might subject the passengers[303] to multiple taxation in each state along the bus route.[304] This conclusion was based, at least in part, on the Court's observation that "[t]he taxable event comprises agreement, payment, and delivery of some of the services in the taxing State; no other State can claim to be the site of the same combination."[305] The Court further noted that "[t]he analysis should not lose touch with the common understanding of a sale; . . . the combined events of payment for a ticket and its delivery for present commencement of a trip are commonly understood to suffice for a sale."[306] However, as discussed above, electronic commerce threatens to blur this "common understanding of a sale" by making it difficult to pinpoint the locations of (1) purchase, (2) delivery, (3) storage, or (4) consumption.[307]

In *Goldberg* the Court upheld as internally and externally consistent a state excise tax on interstate telephone calls. Regarding the former, the Court concluded that "[t]he Tax Act is internally consistent, for if every State taxed only those interstate phone calls which are charged to an in-state service address, only one State would tax each interstate telephone call."[308] Regarding external consistency, the only possibility that the Court saw for actual multiple taxation was a situation where "the service address and billing location of a taxpayer are in different States."[309] The Court concluded that this "limited possibility of multiple taxation" was not enough to render it externally inconsistent.[310] The *Goldberg* Court also distinguished certain precedents involving "the movement of large physical objects over identifiable routes" in which the Court had "endorsed apportionment formulas based upon the miles a bus, train, or truck traveled within the taxing state," noting that "[a]n apportionment formula based on mileage or some other geographic division of individual telephone calls

---

[301] 68 AM. JUR. 2D *Sales and Use Tax* § 206.

[302] *Jefferson Lines,* 514 U.S. at 175.

[303] Although taxpayer/respondent Jefferson Lines was a carrier engaged in the sale of bus tickets, the Court focused on the incidence of the challenged tax upon individual passengers, using this distinction to distinguish a prior contrary result in *Central Greyhound Lines, Inc. v. Mealey,* 334 U.S. 653 (1948). *Jefferson Lines,* 514 U.S. at 190.

[304] *Jefferson Lines,* 514 U.S. at 192 ("The taxpayer has failed to raise any specter of successive taxes that might require us to reconsider whether an internally consistent tax on sales of services could fail the external consistency test for lack of further apportionment (a result that no sales tax has ever suffered under our cases).").

[305] *Id.* at 190.

[306] *Id.* (internal citation to *Goldberg* omitted).

[307] *See supra* note 269.

[308] *Goldberg,* 488 U.S. at 261.

[309] *Id.* at 263.

[310] *Id.* at 264.

would produce insurmountable administrative and technological barriers."[311] One lower court has struck down as both internally and externally inconsistent a tax on interstate pager services.[312]

[C] *No Discrimination Against Interstate Commerce.* As with the fair apportionment prong, the discrimination prong of the test also has two components. A state tax statute must not discriminate against interstate commerce either on its face, or as applied, absent certain extraordinary justification.[313] The Court has, for example, found facial discrimination in a case involving a state excise tax statute that provided a tax credit only for ethanol produced in-state (and in a limited number of other enumerated states),[314] and discriminatory application of an otherwise neutral state tax statutes where state-wide use tax that was purportedly a "compensatory" equivalent to the corresponding sales tax in some instances actually resulted in higher tax rates as assessed by particular municipalities.[315] In finding a challenged telecommunications tax non-discriminatory, the *Goldberg* Court distinguished a prior precedent to the effect that a flat tax imposed on the operation of all trucks on Pennsylvania's highways "imposed a disproportionate burden on interstate trucks, as compared with intrastate trucks, because the interstate trucks traveled fewer miles per year on Pennsylvania highways."[316] In making this distinction, the *Goldberg* Court looked to the practical difficulties of measuring exactly the interstate versus intrastate portion of a long-distance phone call, as well as the remedies afforded by state-level political processes to aggrieved taxpayers.[317]

[D] *Fair Relation to Services Provided by State.* The fair relation prong looks to the services or other benefits that the taxpayer derives from the taxing state. For instance, the Court has upheld the assessment of an airport service charge upon passengers traveling through the airport where the revenues therefrom were used to fund improvements of the airport facilities.[318] However, the connection between the tax imposed and the benefits received need not be so direct. In *Goldberg*, the Court noted that, "[t]he benefits that Illinois provides cannot be limited to those exact services provided to the equipment used during each interstate telephone call."[319] Some of the other "benefits" that these consumers of these telecommunications services received included "police and fire protection" and "other general services."[320]

---

[311] *Id.*

[312] *Radio Common Carriers v. New York*, 601 N.Y.S.2d 513 (N.Y. S.Ct. 1993).

[313] *See Limbach*, 486 U.S. at 274 (clear discrimination against interstate commerce forbidden unless "demonstrably justified by a valid factor unrelated to economic protectionism.") One form of permissible discrimination is a "compensatory" use tax. *Associated Industries of Missouri v. Lohman*, 511 U.S. 641, 677-8 (1994). *See also West Lynn Creamery, Inc. v. Healy*, 512 U.S. 186 (1994) (proceeds of a uniform milk tax were used to subsidize only in-state producers).

[314] *New Energy Company of Indiana v. Limbach*, 486 U.S. 269 (1988) (finding "patent" discrimination against interstate commerce).

[315] *Lohman*, 511 U.S. 641.

[316] *Goldberg*, 488 U.S. at 266.

[317] *Id.*

[318] *Evansville-Vanderburg Airport Authority District v. Delta Airlines*, 405 U.S. 707 (1972).

[319] *Goldberg*, 488 U.S. at 267.

[320] *Id.*

[3]   FUTURE DIRECTIONS

[a] Congress. On March 13, 1997, parallel bills known as the Internet Tax Freedom Act ("ITFA") were introduced in the House of Representatives and the Senate.[321] The most significant operative provision of the ITFA is a moratorium on state and local taxation of "(1) the Internet or interactive computer services; or (2) the use of the Internet or interactive computer services."[322] In the words of one sponsor, "[t]he purpose of th[is] bill . . . is to allow everyone to step back and take a deep breath. It says let's suspend this crazy tax quilting bee so that everyone can come together in a rational way to figure out what policy makes the most sense."[323]

The moratorium that would go into effect under the ITFA does not, however, purport to suspend all state and local taxes on electronic commerce. Rather, it contains an important series of exceptions that preserve the rights of state and local governments to tax certain aspects of electronic commerce.[324] At hearings before the House Subcommittee on Telecommunications, Trade, and Consumer Protection of the Committee on Commerce, some witnesses complained that the ITFA could have unintended consequences and might cripple state and local taxing authority.[325]

In the House, a markup of the ITFA was held in the Subcommittee on Telecommunications, Trade, and Consumer Protection of the Committee on Commerce on October 9, 1997. At that markup, Representative Cox (R-CA) introduced a substitute amendment that received Subcommittee approval. In the Senate, the Committee on Commerce, Science, and Transport approved a substitute amendment offered by Senators McCain (R-AZ), Wyden (D-OR), Burns (R-MT), and Kerry (D-MA) on November 4, 1997. Both of the substitutes vary from the ITFA in that they expand the scope of the moratorium to include Internet "transactions" as well as Internet use and access, and they expand the list of state and local taxes that are exempt from the moratorium.

[b] The Administration. To date, the Clinton Administration has made three important policy statements about electronic commerce and the related tax issues — one drafted by a working group headed by Ira Magaziner, one drafted by the Treasury Department, and most recently, a statement issued by President Clinton supporting a moratorium on state and local Internet taxes.

[i] The Working Group's Statement. Entitled "A Framework For Global Electronic Commerce" (the "Framework"), the statement prepared by the working group discusses a number of legal, political, and financial aspects of electronic commerce. The discussion begins with the assertion of the following five principles:

1. The private sector should lead.

---

[321] Internet Tax Freedom Act, S. 442 and H.R. 1054, 105th Cong. (1997) [hereinafter ITFA].

[322] ITFA § 3.

[323] 143 CONG. REC. S442 (daily ed. Mar. 13, 1997) (remarks of Sen. Wyden).

[324] ITFA § 3(b).

[325] *Internet Tax Freedom Act: Hearing on H.R. 1054 Before the Subcomm. on Commercial and Administrative Law of the House Comm. on the Judiciary,* 105th Cong. (1997) (testimony of Brian O'Neil, First Vice President, National League of Cities; Stanley Arnold, Commissioner, New Hampshire Department of Revenue Administration; Walter Hellerstein, Professor, University of Georgia School of Law).

2. Governments should avoid undue restrictions on electronic commerce.

3. Where governmental involvement is needed, its aim should be to support and enforce a predictable, minimalist, consistent and simple legal environment for commerce.

4. Government should recognize the unique qualities of the Internet.

5. Electronic Commerce over the Internet should be facilitated on a global basis.[326]

The body of the Framework is devoted to an application of these principles to various issues raised by electronic commerce.

With regard to tax policy, the bulk of the discussion in the Framework is devoted to international tax issues. The Framework concludes that the World Trade Organization ("WTO") should declare the Internet a "tariff-free environment" and that any international sales taxes imposed on electronic commerce should be "simple and transparent" and not "discriminate among types of commerce, nor . . . create incentives that will change the nature or location of transactions."[327] With regard to state and local taxation of electronic commerce, the Framework states that: "[t]he Administration believes that the same broad principles applicable to international taxation, such as not hindering the growth of electronic commerce and neutrality between conventional and electronic commerce, should be applied to subfederal taxation."[328]

[ii] *The Treasury Department's Statement.* The Treasury Department's contribution comes in the form of a discussion paper, circulated by the Office of Tax Policy in November 1996, entitled "Selected Tax Policy Implications of Global Electronic Commerce" ("Treasury Discussion Paper").[329] Although it contains a disclaimer stating that subfederal taxation is outside the scope of its analysis[330], the Treasury Discussion Paper makes a number of assertions that seem equally applicable to both federal and subfederal taxation. Among the most significant of these are proposals for: (1) replacement of source-based taxation (such as sales taxes) with residence-based taxation (such as that imposed by the federal income tax); and (2) adoption of copyright principles for classification of income derived from sale of digitized information.

The Treasury Discussion Paper favors residence-based taxation because it avoids the risk of multiple taxation.[331] It notes that many current tax treaties (including certain of the forty-eight such treaties to which the United State is a signatory) preclude taxation unless an individual maintains a "permanent residence" in the

---

[326] PRESIDENT WILLIAM J. CLINTON & VICE PRESIDENT ALBERT GORE JR., A FRAMEWORK FOR GLOBAL ELECTRONIC COMMERCE, *available at* (visited Oct. 1, 1997) <http://www.iitf.nist.gov/eleccomm/ecomm.htm>.

[327] *Id.* at § I.1.

[328] *Id.*

[329] OFFICE OF TAX POLICY, DEP'T OF THE TREASURY, SELECTED TAX POLICY IMPLICATIONS OF GLOBAL ELECTRONIC COMMERCE, *available at* (visited Dec. 9, 1996) <ftp://ftp.fedworld.gov/pub/tel/internet.txt>.

[330] *Id.* at n.1.

[331] *Id.* at § 7.15 ("In the world of cyberspace, it is often difficult, if not impossible, to apply traditional source concepts to link an item of income with a specific geographical location. Therefore, source based taxation could lose its rationale and be rendered obsolete by electronic commerce. By contrast, almost all taxpayers are resident somewhere.").

taxing country.[332] In the United States, for instance, certain foreign business entities are only subject to taxation if they maintain "permanent residence" in the United States, even if their activities are extensive enough to constitute a "U.S. trade or business."[333]

For business entities, "permanent residence" generally requires a "fixed place of business" in the United States. However, two exceptions exist that are closely analogous to two of the exceptions to the aforementioned physical presence requirement of the Commerce Clause. First, the Treasury Discussion paper notes that ownership or utilization of a computer server in the United States may or may not constitute a "permanent establishment," depending on such factors as whether the use of the server is limited to "storage, display, or delivery of goods."[334] Second, "[a] U.S. trade or business or permanent establishment can also arise by imputation from the activities of an agent."[335] Regarding the possibility that an Internet service provider ("ISP") could be deemed to be the agent of a foreign individual, the Treasury Discussion Paper says, "[e]ven if an agency relationship were deemed to exist, the service provider would likely be considered an independent agent, with the result that a U.S. trade or business or permanent establishment would not arise."[336] In both cases, it recommends further clarification.

With regard to the second issue, the Treasury Discussion Paper notes that the current approach is inadequate "in light of the ease of perfectly reproducing and disseminating digitized information," proposing instead a rights-based analysis founded on principles of copyright law.[337] Under current rules, income realized in respect of the transfer of digitized information and software may be classified as derived either from the sale of goods or from payment of royalties, depending upon relatively mutable factors such as whether the vendor makes multiple copies for the consumer or merely licenses the consumer to makes his or her own copies. The Treasury Discussion Paper favors "a more complex analysis that disregards the form of the transaction without regard to whether tangible property is involved in favor [of] an analysis of the rights transferred."[338] It notes that such a rights-based approach is expressly adopted in proposed Internal Revenue Code regulations regarding computer program transactions.[339]

[*iii*] *The President's Statement.* On February 26, 1998, in remarks at the Technology '98 Conference in San Francisco, President Clinton explicitly endorsed the ITFA, "because it takes into account the

---

[332] *Id.* at § 7.2.

[333] *Id.*

[334] *Id.*

[335] *Id.* at § 7.2.4.

[336] *Id.* at § 7.2.5.

[337] *Id.* at § 7.3.1.

[338] *Id.*

[339] Classification of Certain Transactions Involving Computer Programs, 61 Fed. Reg. 58,152 (1996) (to be codified at 26 C.F.R. § 1.861-18); 62 Fed. Reg. 2633 (1997). The proposed rule draws a distinction between income derived from the sale of the right to copy and distribute a computer program (a "copyright right") and the sale of the computer program itself (a "copyrighted article"). 61 Fed. Reg. at 58,155 (to be codified at 26 C.F.R. §§ 1.861-18(c)(2), (c)(3)).

rights of consumers, the needs of businesses and the overall effect of taxation on the development of Internet commerce."[340]

[c] Other Groups. The federal government is not alone in seeking to develop a new framework for addressing electronic commerce taxation issues. A number of state-level organizations have begun to address the issue. The range of approaches varies greatly. At one extreme, the Multistate Taxing Commission ("MTC") has adopted an expansive interpretation of in-state presence.[341] Under the MTC approach, any presence other than "the slightest presence" provides sufficient taxing nexus.[342] Also, the Executive Director of the MTC publicly opposed the Treasury Discussion Paper shortly after its publication, noting that many states consider residence-based taxation to be a "dead end."[343]

A more moderate alternative is the so-called "knee deep nexus" theory that has reportedly been under discussion in closed-door negotiations between the Direct Marketing Association (consisting of a number of large mail order firms) and representatives from fifteen states. Under this theory, mail order retailers would agree to cooperate in state tax collection in exchange for the ability to engage in certain in-state activities while still qualifying for simplified tax administration.[344]

In a similar vein, a number of states are considering embodying such new approaches to taxation in uniform state-level legislation. Three major approaches have emerged:[345] (1) enforce existing use taxes against in-state consumers on the basis of customer information furnished by online vendors;[346] (2) "reverse-engineer" current nexus rules to establish nexus on the basis of the consumer's billing address;[347] and (3) give the federal government and the states concurrent taxing jurisdiction over any merchant having a substantial presence in the United States.[348]

All three proposals present potential constitutional problems. To the extent that they run counter to the Supreme Court's Due Process and Commerce Clause precedents, they are likely to fail. Several commentators have therefore called upon Congress to ratify such uniform statutes by exercising its plenary legislative powers

---

[340] President William J. Clinton, Remarks Before the Technology '98 Conference, San Francisco (Feb. 26, 1998), *available at* <http://library.whitehouse.gov>. *See also* Jackie Calmes, *Clinton, as Expected, Says He'll Support Moratorium on Taxing Internet Sales*, WALL ST. J., Feb. 27, 1998, at B6; Nicholas Denton, *Clinton Backs Bill to Halt Internet Taxes*, FIN. TIMES, Feb. 17, 1998, at 1.

[341] *See* Kim Marshall & Marc Lewis, *What We Know Today About Substantial Nexus,* 13 STATE TAX NOTES 967 (1997).

[342] *See id.*

[343] *See* Amy Hamilton, *MTC Debates Treasury on Electronic Commerce*, 96 TNT 231-4.

[344] *See* David Cay Johnson, *Mail-Order Group Agrees to Collect State Sales Taxes*, N.Y.TIMES, Nov. 6, 1997 at A1. *See also* Amy Hamilton, *Electronic Commerce-Knee Deep in Nexus*, 12 STATE TAX NOTES 1597, 1600 (1997).

[345] *See* Kendall L. Houghton, *Imposing and Collecting Sales and Use Taxes on Electronic Commerce: How?*, TAX NOTES, Oct. 13, 1997, at 237.

[346] *Id.* at 233.

[347] *Id.*

[348] *Id.* at 237.

under the Commerce Clause. [349] Whether Congress will do so remains to be seen. Furthermore, even if Congress were so inclined, the extent to which it could obviate Due Process Clause concerns is uncertain.[350]

§ 10.06 UNITED NATIONS

[1] UNITED NATIONS MODEL LAWS: MODEL LAW ON INTERNATIONAL CREDIT TRANSFERS AND MODEL LAW ON ELECTRONIC COMMERCE

The United Nations Commission on International Trade Law ("UNCITRAL") is engaged in an ongoing effort to establish, before disparate national laws are developed and implemented, mutually agreed upon international rules in the area of electronic commerce.[351] With this in mind, over the past five years UNCITRAL has composed, and the United Nations General Assembly has adopted, two important legal texts designed to help promote uniformity in international electronic banking and commercial law. The United Nations General Assembly adopted the first of the two model laws, the United Nations Model Law on International Credit Transfers ("MLICT"), on November 25, 1992.[352] It deals primarily with the movement of funds electronically.[353] UNCITRAL developed the second model law, the United Nations Model Law on Electronic Commerce ("MLEC"). It was adopted on December 16, 1996, and concerns the use of electronic messages in international trade.[354]

The MLICT is broken down into four chapters. Chapter I concerns general provisions of applicability and interpretation. Chapter II concerns the obligations of the parties involved in an international credit transfer, specifically defining when and how parties are bound by a payment order, as well as when and how a payment order is accepted or rejected. It also addresses certain rules regarding the receipt of payment, timing requirements, and revocation of payment orders. Chapter III defines the rules of failed, delayed or erroneous credit transfers, focusing on assistance, refund, correction, restitution, and liability. Finally, Chapter IV provides suggested text for a rule regarding the completion of a credit transfer.

The MLEC delineates the basic rules of electronic messages in commerce. Pursuant to Chapter I, Article 1, the term "commercial" is to be given a broad interpretation so as to make the MLEC applicable to all manners of commercial relationships, whether contractual or not. It is comprised of two parts, "Electronic Commerce in General" and "Electronic Commerce in Specific Areas." Part One deals with rules on the validity, attribution,

---

[349] *See* Forte, *supra* note 223; Ichel, *supra* note 230.

[350] *See* Walter Hellerstein, *State Taxation of Electronic Commerce: Preliminary Thoughts on Model Uniform Legislation*, 12 STATE TAX NOTES 1315, 1323 (1997).

[351] *See* Harold S. Burman, *United Nations: UNCITRAL Model Law on Electronic Commerce, Introductory Note*, 36 I.L.M. 197, at 199 (1997) [hereinafter *Electronic Commerce Note*].

[352] *See Model Law on International Credit Transfers, Report of the United Nations Commission on International Trade Law,* 25th Sess., UN Document No. Supplement No. 17 (A/47/17), at 48 (1992), 32 I.L.M. 587 (1993).

[353] *See Electronic Commerce Note, supra* note 351.

[354] *See Model Law on Electronic Commerce, Report of the United Nations Commission on International Trade Law,* 29th Sess., UN Document No. Supplement No. 17 (A/51/17), Annex I (1996), 36 I.L.M. 197 (1997).

and effect of electronic messages generally, while the Part Two sets forth the first of many rules for particular areas of commerce that UNCITRAL expects to develop.[355]

Part One is divided into three chapters. Chapter I contains general rules of interpretation as well as certain definitions. Chapter II is designed to prevent electronic messages from being denied legal effect because they are not paper communications. It spells out the rules of interpretation of other law in the context of electronic messages, and states the requirements for the validity, applicability, and evidentiary status of electronic messages. For instance, it defines the methods one must utilize to meet such legal requirements as a writing, a signature, the presentation of originals, and the retention of data messages.[356] Chapter III contains rules that address the fundamental issues associated with communications between parties as they apply to electronic messages, including contract formation, attribution, acknowledgment, and time and place of dispatch.[357] Part Two of the MLEC is currently comprised of one chapter that deals with the use of electronic messages in the area of carriage of goods. Further rules will be added as they are developed.[358]

The MLICT and the MLEC were designed to promote uniformity in national legislation and to aid in the removal of obstacles to the flow of international trade. Accordingly, in their resolutions of adoption, the United Nations General Assembly recommended that all states either give favorable consideration to the model laws when enacting new legislation, or consider enacting legislation based on the model laws themselves.[359]

§ 10.07   AMERICAN BAR ASSOCIATION

[1]   MODEL FINANCIAL ELECTRONIC DATA INTERCHANGE AGREEMENT

Electronic data interchange ("EDI") is the computer-to-computer exchange of data from one company to another. The type of data exchanged is that which otherwise would appear on a purchase order, invoice, or other paper document. Companies have been using EDI for over twenty years. Over time, companies have combined EDI with ACH payments, resulting in payment and remittance information traveling together electronically, a process referred to as financial EDI ("FEDI"). Realizing that FEDI was becoming an increasingly significant factor in everyday commercial transactions, and that no legislation or model agreement addressed the rights and responsibilities of FEDI participants, the American Bar Association ("ABA(Bar)") in 1990 set out to create an applicable model agreement for "trading partners" using FEDI. This Section focuses on that agreement.

---

[355] *See Electronic Commerce Note, supra* note 351, at 198.

[356] *Id.*

[357] *Id.*

[358] *Id.*

[359] *See Assembly Would Urge States to Become Parties to Conventions Emerging from UNICITRAL's Work by Legal Committee Draft*, Press Release GA/L3030, Nov. 26, 1996.

The EDI and Information Technology Division ("Division") of the Section of Science and Technology of the ABA(Bar) worked with industry, banks, and fund transfer professionals to develop the Model Electronic Payments Agreement and Commentary (For Domestic Credit Transfers) ("Model Agreement"). The Model Agreement uses as its foundation U.C.C. Article 4A, which pertains to the relations between banks and the fund transfers system but does not govern trading partner relations.[360] The Model Agreement focuses solely on the relations between trading partners.[361] The Division included an Introduction with the Model Agreement that explains the processes involved and the roles of the parties in FEDI. The Introduction then explores the proper use of the Model Agreement.

The Model Agreement presumes the existence of separate purchase and sale agreements that include relevant due dates, discounts, and other commercial terms. Agreements based on the model should therefore provide trading partners with the flexibility to change terms without creating a whole new FEDI agreement. The Model Agreement addresses the following:

- the disclosure of the recipient's bank account information;

- the terms regarding notification of payment and the discharge of payment obligations;

- payment, timing and float, thus providing parties the opportunity to consider the impact of delayed payment and any related remedies;

- the mechanisms of funds transfer and who bears the cost of their use;

- the data format and content of the remittance information;

- security procedures to be employed by the trading partners;

- electronic return of payment to show nonacceptance and avoid waiver.

The ABA(Bar), in addition to providing a sample agreement structure, intended the Model Agreement and associated comments to serve as an educational planning tool and strategic planning guide for parties considering implementing electronic payments systems.

[2]   STORED VALUE TASK FORCE REPORT

In February 1997, the ABA(Bar)'s Business Law Section published a report entitled *A Commercial Lawyer's Take on the Electronic Purse: An Analysis of Commercial Law Issues Associated with Stored-Value Cards and Electronic Money* ("ABA(Bar) SV Report").[362] The ABA(Bar) SV Report was the product of a year-

---

[360] Article 4A thus provides the relevant definitions for the Model Agreement. *See* AM. BAR ASS'N, *Model Electronic Payments Agreement and Commentary* 32 (1992).

[361] Parties must look to other sources for models regarding agreements with banks and third-party service providers.

[362] Task Force on Stored Value Cards, Am. Bar Ass'n, *A Commercial Lawyer's Take on the Electronic Purse: An Analysis of Commercial Law Issues Associated with Stored-Value Cards and Electronic Money,* 52 BUS. LAW. 653 (1997) [hereinafter *ABA(Bar) SV Report*].

long study and drafting effort conducted during 1996 by the Stored Value Task Force, a group comprised of ABA(Bar) members including representatives of the legal, banking, and financial services communities ("ABA(Bar) Task Force").[363] The ABA(Bar) Task Force's primary objective was to consider and analyze the commercial law principles that will likely govern new electronic and stored value retail payments media.

The ABA(Bar) SV Report recognized several principles which underlie the evaluation of stored value ("SV") products from the point of view of existing commercial laws. First, the ABA(Bar) Task Force recognized that participants in emerging retail payment systems will seek to determine clear sets of rules to govern their commercial activities using new payment products and that, as a consequence, the legal and regulatory system for such products should try to achieve a balance. This balance will weigh the need for, structure of, and clarity of the laws, system contracts, and other rules that will likely govern emerging payment products, to the degree applicable, and the need for flexibility to permit such products to develop in accordance with the dictates of the marketplace and consumer preferences. In this regard, the ABA(Bar) SV Report contemplated that existing commercial law principles likely will be used to resolve disputes that arise with emerging payment media, but that private contract and systems rules will also govern the use of such products, at least in their initial stages.[364]

By way of background, the ABA(Bar) SV Report defines certain terms relevant to the emerging payments media, provides an overview of the history of money in the United States, and compares and contrasts "open" versus "closed" systems of "stored obligations."[365] The ABA(Bar) SV Report also provides a useful historical perspective on the meaning of the term "money," addressing the related issues of what constitutes "legal tender" or a "bank deposit."[366]

---

[363] The members of the Task Force were drawn largely from the ABA(Bar)'s Uniform Commercial Code Committee, the Subcommittee on Payments and EFT Transactions, the Banking Law Committee and the Committee of Law and Commerce in Cyberspace. The Task Force reporters were Thomas C. Baxter, Jr. and Stephanie Heller of the Federal Reserve Bank of New York, and Henry Wysocki of the New York Clearing House. Robert H. Ledig and Edward B. Whittemore of Fried, Frank, Harris, Shriver & Jacobson participated as members of the Task Force in drafting the Task Force Report. Other members of the Task Force included Lee S. Adams, Morrison & Foerster; Patricia Allouise, Federal Reserve Bank of Boston; Lynne Barr, Goodwin, Procter & Hoar; Robert Egan, Chemical Bank; Thomas Fox, Schwartz & Ballen; Prof. Henry Gabriel, Loyola Law School; Thomas Greco, American Bankers Association; Michael Kadish, Rudnick, Partus & Kadish; Loren Karnick, Citicorp Services, Inc.; Mary Karr, Federal Reserve Bank of St. Louis; Michael Kenny, Citibank/Citicorp; Ann Marie Kohlligian, Board of Governors of the Federal Reserve System; John Jin Lee, Wells Fargo Bank; Keith Ligon, Federal Deposit Insurance Corporation; David Lipkin, Drinker, Biddle & Reath; Jordan Luke, Davis, Polk & Wardwell; Ed Mahon, Federal Reserve Bank of Philadelphia; Margaret Marquette, U.S. Treasury Department, Bureau of Public Debt; Stephanie Martin, Board of Governors of the Federal Reserve System; Colleen McCall, Bank of America; Norman Nelson, New York Clearing House; Prof. Spencer Neth, Case Western Reserve University; Ira Parker, Alston & Bird; Henry Polmer, Bell, Boyd & Lloyd; Judith Rinearson, American Express Travel Related Services Company, Inc.; Dolores Smith, Board of Governors of the Federal Reserve System; H. Grant Stephenson, Porter, Wright, Morris & Arthur; Marcia Sullivan, Consumer Bankers Association; Anne Wallace, U.S. Treasury Department, Financial Management Services; and David Whitaker, Bank of Oklahoma.

[364] *ABA(Bar) SV Report*, *supra* note 362, at 655.

[365] *Id*. at 656-667. The ABA(Bar) SV Report defines a "stored obligation" as the "intangible claim that is transferred when a party uses one of the new payment products. The claim is represented by data stored either on a computer chip embedded within a card, a computer hard drive, or within another storage device." *Id*. at 657.

[366] *Id*. at 664-74. In so doing, the ABA(Bar) SV Report introduces the various barriers that exist, including assorted state "business of banking" and "money transmitter" statutes, and Section 21(a) of the Glass-Steagall Act, to nonbank firms engaging in the issuance of "stored obligations." *Id*. at 676-77.

The bulk of the ABA(Bar) SV Report addresses commercial law issues in three principle parts, which make up the "Life Cycle of a Stored Value Electronic Obligation."[367] This approach covers, from a legal perspective, the issues raised by the creation or "birth" of a SV obligation, how it is transferred from one party to another (its "growth"), and ultimately how it is settled and discharged (its "death").[368] In regard to the creation phase, the ABA(Bar) SV Report identifies several significant issues for issuers and users of stored obligations, including (i) when and how the obligation is created, (ii) the disclosures required at the time of issuance or sale, and (iii) most importantly, the ability of the consumer to identify the issuer/obligor of the stored obligation (*i.e.,* that party on whose books the liability of the stored obligation is carried).[369]

With regard to the transfer phase of a stored obligation's life cycle, the ABA(Bar) SV Report discusses issues including the accomplishment and the effectiveness of the transfer, authentication, the resolution of disputes, liability, or loss resulting from systems or card errors, payment finality, and the levy, attachment, and pledge of stored obligations.[370] It also addresses a variety of commercial law issues raised by discharge and settlement, such as "redemption" of a stored obligation to money or a bank deposit, the problem of counterfeiting (or "spawning") of stored obligations, and the threat of, and systemic risk implications raised by the failure of an issuer of stored obligations.[371]

Finally, the ABA(Bar) SV Report provides an overview of other relevant commercial law issues that may need to be addressed by legislatures and/or systems participants with regard to emerging payment products; including, the risk of loss associated with theft, damage to the instrument or disputed transactions, the use of choice of law provisions, and the possibility that stored obligations may "expire" without being spent by the holder, and whether, under such circumstances such value would "escheat" to the state.[372]

[3]   DIGITAL SIGNATURE GUIDELINES

In August 1996, the Information Security Committee ("ISC") of the Science and Technology Section of the ABA(Bar) published Digital Signature Guidelines ("DS Guidelines").[373] The ISC's goal in drafting the DS Guidelines was to foster the development of digital signatures as a tool for conducting secure electronic commerce.[374] The DS Guidelines are not intended to serve as a model statute, but rather to assist in the

---

[367] For a further discussion of stored value and electronic money, see Chapter 16.

[368] Specifically, the ABA(Bar) SV Report's "Life Cycle" approach consists of the following parts: (1) the creation of the obligation; (2) its transfer; (3) and the discharge and settlement of the stored obligation. *ABA(Bar) SV Report, supra* note 362, at 674-715.

[369] *Id.* at 680-83.

[370] *See id.* at 689-709.

[371] *Id.* at 709-15.

[372] *Id.* at 715-27.

[373] INFORMATION SECURITY COMM., AM. BAR ASS'N, DIGITAL SIGNATURE GUIDELINES: LEGAL INFRASTRUCTURE FOR CERTIFICATION AUTHORITIES AND SECURE ELECTRONIC COMMERCE (Aug. 1, 1996) [hereinafter DS GUIDELINES]. The DS Guidelines have not been approved or endorsed by the House of Delegates or Board of Governors of the American Bar Association, the Council of the Section of Science and Technology, or its Electronic Commerce and Information Technology Division. The DS Guidelines represent only the position of the Information Security Committee.

[374] DS GUIDELINES, *supra* note 373, at 20.

drafting and interpretation of digital signature legislation.[375] They contain a wealth of information concerning digital signatures and numerous citations to other relevant publications. With an increasing number of states enacting or considering digital signature legislation or other types of electronic signature laws, the DS Guidelines provide a useful introduction to the subject of digital signatures.

[a] The DS Guidelines. The DS Guidelines contain two types of information: the DS Guidelines proper, which are general statements of principle intended to provide a common basis for more precise rules; and Comments on the DS Guidelines, which may explain the intent of the DS Guidelines, offer cautionary notes, or provide practical illustrations or other useful information.[376] The DS Guidelines are organized into five parts: (1) definitions; (2) general principles; (3) certification authorities ; (4) subscribers; and (5) relying on certificates and digital signatures.

Part 1 defines the terms used in the DS Guidelines. Part 2 addresses general matters including interpretation of the DS Guidelines and parties' right to define, by agreement, their duties more precisely. Part 3 provides the basic rules governing certification authorities.[377] Notably, it provides for no liability on the part of a certification authority for the breach of any duty not specified in the DS Guidelines.[378] Part 4 sets forth the duties and obligations of subscribers, including the duty to safeguard private keys.[379] Finally, Part 5 addresses the legal effect of digital signatures and addresses the reasonableness of reliance on them.[380]

[b] Focus on Digital Signatures. As the name suggests, the DS Guidelines focus exclusively on "digital signatures," which are a particular type of electronic signature based on a branch of cryptography known as "public key cryptography." Public key cryptography employs algorithms to generate pairs of mathematically related keys that can be used to create and verify digital signatures. Each "key pair" includes a "private key" and a "public key." The private key is known only to the message originator, who uses the key to create a digital signature. The public key is available to the public generally. The message recipient uses the public key to verify the digital signature. The public key enables the message recipient to verify that the message came from the message originator (authenticity) and was not altered (integrity).[381]

The DS Guidelines seek to establish digital signatures as secure, computer-based equivalents of traditional pen and ink signatures.[382] The ISC predicts that digital signatures will:

- minimize the incidence of electronic forgeries;

---

[375] *Id.*

[376] *Id.* at 19.

[377] *Id.* at 63.

[378] *Id.* at 77.

[379] *Id.* at 78.

[380] *Id.* at 82.

[381] See Chapter 13 for a further description of digital signatures.

[382] *See* DS GUIDELINES, *supra* note 373, at 18.

- enable and foster the reliable authentication of documents in computer form;

- facilitate commerce by means of computerized communications; and

- give legal effect to the general import of the technical standards for authentication of computerized messages.[383]

In furtherance of these goals, the DS Guidelines envision and describe a legal infrastructure for certification authorities, entities that play a critical role in digital signature systems.[384] Certification authorities issue certificates which associate or "bind" a given key pair with the identity of a particular person. Reference to a certificate is intended to enable the recipient of a digitally signed message to verify the identity of the message originator, thereby making reliance on the message commercially feasible.

[c] Relationships Among Subscribers, Certification Authorities and Message Recipients. The DS Guidelines are devoted in large part to establishing the legal duties of the three types of parties playing primary roles in a system of authentication based on digital signatures: (1) persons who sign electronic communications with digital signatures ("subscribers"); (2) certification authorities; and (3) persons who rely on certificates and digital signatures. Under the DS Guidelines, the relationships of these parties are governed primarily by traditional legal doctrines of contract and tort.[385] For example, the relationship between a certification authority and a subscriber is primarily contractual, while the relationship between a certification authority and a person relying on a certificate is defined in part by proscriptions against tortious conduct, such as negligent misrepresentation.[386] Finally, the duties of a subscriber to a person who relies on the subscriber's digital signature arise under both contract and tort law.[387]

---

[383] *Id.*

[384] See Chapter 13 for a further discussion of certification authorities.

[385] DS GUIDELINES, *supra* note 373, at 19.

[386] *Id.* at 19.

[387] *Id.*

PART III

"Why rob banks? Because that's where the money is."

—Willie Sutton

Regulatory approval does not ensure the success of new products and services; it is but one piece of the puzzle. Another vital piece is consumer acceptance. Individuals have an emotional relationship with their money; thus acceptance is not a simple matter. A new product or service must be cost effective to use. It must also be convenient. And the consumer must be confident that the product or service does what it promises. Consumers and businesses will not simply take leaps of faith with their money. They require assurances.

People store wealth in assets that hold value. And people place those assets in places that they think are safe. As assets accumulate in a single location, that place becomes an increasingly attractive and vulnerable target. Characters like Willie Sutton attacked vaults containing physical assets, such as paper and gold. The digitized financial assets existing in cyberspace soon will be pursued with equal zeal. Electronic commerce, however, poses even greater risks because it supports the exchange of not only digital value but also digitized personal and corporate information, which has its own commercial value.

Electronic financial products and services, because of their potential vulnerability, will further require assurances as to the privacy and security of transactions in order to achieve consumer acceptance.

Chapter 11 explores the three C's of consumer acceptance: Cost, Convenience, and Confidence. A discussion of privacy principles and legislation follows in Chapter 12. Finally, Chapter 13 provides an introduction to the security and risk management techniques available to electronic financial service participants.

CHAPTER 11
COST, CONVENIENCE & CONFIDENCE

§ 11.01 INTRODUCTION

Successful introduction and adoption of new technology is rarely just a function of supply. Frequently, demand dictates which technological innovations succeed and which fail. Demand for electronic financial products and services ("EFS") will be a function of, among other things, consumer acceptance. While consumers may discover important uses for stored value cards and other EFS, they might be unprepared to pay for these alternative, unfamiliar forms of money. Consumers comfortable with their current use of checks, credit cards, debit cards, and cash may not initially realize or appreciate the convenience associated with EFS. Further, consumers will require assurance that EFS, which have the potential to collect vast amounts of personal information about consumers, will address their concerns regarding privacy and confidentiality. This Chapter focuses on how cost, convenience, and confidence will govern the acceptance of EFS. Section 11.02 provides a comparative analysis of the costs associated with traditional banking practices and the anticipated reduced costs associated with electronic financial products and services. Section 11.03 explores how EFS will make financial transactions more convenient for consumers. Finally, Section 11.04 discusses the role consumer confidence plays in the consumer acceptance equation.

§ 11.02 COST

Cost will be one of the key elements in the acceptance of EFS. In banking, technology's greatest promise probably lies in its potential to decrease costs and provide customers with better products and lower account and transaction fees. To the extent that customers move away from a dependence on physical branches, cash, and checks and move toward online banking and other electronic payment products, banks should be able to reduce costs and pass some of the resulting savings on to the customers. In order for suppliers of EFS to succeed, and banks to enjoy the benefits offered by these new products and services, they "will have to deliver [products] that consumers want to use at a price they are willing to pay, and that merchants see as a desirable additional way to conduct business."[1]

---

[1] Edward W. Kelley Jr., *The Future of Electronic Money: A Regulator's Perspective*, IEEE SPECTRUM, Feb. 1997, at 22 (Mr. Kelley is a Governor of the Federal Reserve Board).

Traditional methods of providing banking services incur substantial transaction costs. For example, while consumers perceive cash as an attractive payment instrument, costs associated with the use of cash, including transportation and protection costs, make it a costly payment mechanism for banks.[2] An examination of the range of costs associated with alternative bank service delivery mechanisms illustrates the magnitude of cost-saving opportunities associated with EFS. The average cost of a teller assisted branch transaction is $1.07.[3] Telephone transactions typically cost $0.54 and ATM transactions $0.27.[4] By comparison, the estimated costs of a similar transaction executed through personal computer ("PC") banking is $0.02 and through a smart card is $0.01.[5] The costs associated with EFS may include any or all of the following: the cost of cards; the cost of terminals; the cost of creating and maintaining software; the cost of obtaining funds and settlement.[6] These costs are likely to decrease continuously as technology advances.[7]

Beyond cost reductions, EFS may provide banks with significant revenue enhancement opportunities. Banks can use the World Wide Web to reach broader audiences. They can also conduct highly targeted marketing efforts based on the information collected during electronic transactions. Banks may need to compensate, however, for the loss of sales traditionally triggered through in-person branch contacts. Depending on their strategy, they may also need to consider means of promoting name recognition, confidence, and legitimacy in markets where they decide to establish or retain few, if any, brick-and-mortar branches.

§ 11.03 CONVENIENCE

Consumers are likely to respond favorably to new payment products and services that are convenient with respect to time, location, and method of use. They have repeatedly shown their appreciation of convenience in the ways they use traditional payment methods. For example, point of sale ("POS") terminals at gas pumps have become a popular method of payment because they eliminate the need to wait for a cashier to accept payment and make change or request a signature. Debit cards make it possible to leave the checkbook at home and cash in the bank. Purchases of everything from monthly Internet access fees to newspaper subscriptions are automatically billed to credit cards. Telephone and PC banking programs have enabled customers to do their banking anytime, anywhere.

Banks and industry now face the challenge of creating EFS that provide the convenience that consumers have come to expect. The widespread accessibility of interactive personal computer technology now makes it practical for banks to meet consumer demands for round-the-clock financial services. Banks are now able to

---

[2] *See* David Chaum & Stefan Brands, *"Minting" Electronic Cash*, IEEE SPECTRUM, Feb. 1997, at 30.

[3] *See* BOOZ-ALLEN & HAMILTON INC., FINANCIAL SERVICES GROUP, INTERNET BANKING: A SURVEY OF CURRENT AND FUTURE DEVELOPMENT, at III-3F (1996).

[4] *See* BILL BURNHAM, PIPER JAFFREY RESEARCH, ELECTRONIC COMMERCE REPORT 163 (1997).

[5] *See id.*

[6] *See* Kelley, *supra* note 1, at 22.

[7] *See id.*

provide online, near real time access to a range of banking information whenever and wherever the customer desires that access. Technology enables customers to effectuate a wide range of transactions with the bank without requiring any direct attention from bank personnel. This round-the-clock flexibility is enhanced where it is coupled with prompt access to knowledgeable bank customer service staff who are available to answer questions and resolve issues. Twenty-four hour financial services present banks with a new market opportunity. The key to success will be the quality and efficiency of the customer service provided.

Electronic value products must meet consumer and merchant convenience expectations. They will need to be simple in operation and error-free. Issuers of these products must enjoy a high degree of financial stability, for a product is not convenient if it becomes worthless. Stored value cards must be inexpensive and easy to obtain and replenish. Consumers must be given a wide range of opportunities to use them. Merchants will require that staff training in the use of the card be a simple process. Further, settlement must occur efficiently and quickly.[8]

§ 11.04   CONFIDENCE

Consumers must achieve a certain level of confidence in the new electronic financial products and services in order for them to succeed. Confidence will come from the assurance that the relevant product or service is recognizable and stable.[9] Finally, confidence will depend on whether consumers perceive that these products and services provide adequate protection in terms of confidentiality, privacy, and security. These concepts are discussed below in general terms and the legal and technical aspects are explored further in Chapters 12 and 13.

[1]   CONFIDENCE BASED ON PERCEPTIONS OF CONFIDENTIALITY, PRIVACY, AND SECURITY

One commentator recently described the implications of electronic money in the following manner: "The widespread use of electronic currency generates the risk of the creation of a mutual and constant surveillance society where all actions are taken in view of employers, marketers and government."[10]

Financial institutions probably will seek to provide consumers with a sufficient level of assurance that the security protections in place will adequately protect the consumer interest in maintaining the confidentiality of certain pieces of information. In choosing a security system, financial institutions will balance the system's cost against the cost of the loss of security.[11] It is unlikely that "perfect" security will be employed because of the associated costs.[12] Consumers will have to evaluate whether the level of protection that they

---

[8]   *See id.*

[9]   *See id.* at 21.

[10]   L. Jean Camp, *Opportunities, Options, Obstacles for Payment in Internet Commerce*, EDI FORUM, Vol. 10, No. 2, at 19 (1997).

[11]   *See id.*

[12]   *See id.*

are afforded in the event of unauthorized transactions — whether as a matter of law, regulation, organizational rule, contract, or practice — is within their risk tolerance.

There are many examples in commerce and banking where perfect security is not achieved, but business is able to continue without significant disruption. Large numbers of fraudulent or otherwise invalid checks pass through the banking system every day, yet signature authenticity or authorization is verified in only a small fraction of checks.[13] On a risk/cost analysis basis, it is just not cost effective or feasible to put into place a system that would entirely prevent check fraud. Similarly, cellular phone authorization information is notoriously subject to unauthorized interception that is estimated to cost between $300 and $350 million in lost revenue each year.[14] Yet the cellular phone business shows no indication that it is unable to cope with the widespread existence of cellular phone fraud.[15]

Recent experience with debit cards demonstrates that consumer concern regarding the potential exposures created by a new product can quickly threaten its viability by undermining consumer confidence in the product. During the first half of 1997, increasing media attention was directed at the risks associated with debit cards, risks greater and different from those associated with ATM cards.[16] For example, unlike ATM cards, debit cards typically allow a customer to access funds based solely on a signature receipt rather than a personal identification number ("PIN") and are not subject to transaction limits (other than the limits imposed by funds availability); and, therefore, the prospect that funds in a consumer's deposit account could be rapidly depleted increases with the use of debit cards. Faced with mounting concern regarding the risks associated with debit cards, the industry moved to reassure consumers and head off possible legislative action by largely eliminating consumer liability for unauthorized debit card transactions and taking steps to speed up the process of recrediting accounts of affected consumers.[17]

In another context, if a bank has issued large amounts of stored value or electronic money, and someone is able to counterfeit additional amounts, depending on the system the bank has used, it may be faced with the

---

[13] *See* Barkley Clark Shook, *Can Clearinghouse Rules Reallocate Check Fraud Losses?*, CLARK'S BANK DEPOSITS & MONTHLY PAYMENTS (Com. L. Inst. Kansas City, Mo.), Apr. 1996.

[14] *See* Dep't of Consumer Affairs (New York City), *Avoiding Cellular Phone Fraud, available at* (visited Jan. 21, 1997) <http://www.ci.nyc.ny.us/html/dca/html/dcacellu.html>. Forrester Research, a Massachusetts research firm, has estimated that losses in the cellular phone business average $20 for every $1,000 of revenue generated. In contrast, Forrester predicts that Internet commerce will result in roughly $1 of fraud losses for every $1,000 of revenue. *See* Steve Lohr, *Business Gets Nervous Over Computer Security: Internet Opens Up a World of Danger*, VANCOUVER SUN, Mar. 19, 1997, at D15.

[15] According to Ameritech, the costs of fraud are not being passed along to customers in the form of higher prices. Average monthly air-time bills actually dropped between 1988, going from $95-$100 to $51. *See* <http://www.ameritech.com:1080/news/releases/may_1996/cellularfraud.html>. The use of PIN numbers has also assisted in a decrease in cell phone fraud.

[16] *See* David J. Morrow, *Handy? Surely, but Debit Card has Risks, too*, N.Y. TIMES, July 13, 1997, at A1.

[17] *See* Lisa Fickenscher, *MasterCard to Cap Consumer Debit Card Liability*, AM. BANKER, July 31, 1997, at 1; Charles Keenan, *Visa One-Ups Rival on Consumer Card Liability*, AM. BANKER, Aug. 14, 1997, at 1. *See also* H.R. 2319, 2234, 105th Cong. (1997) (two bills that were introduced in the House prior to the voluntary actions of Visa and MasterCard).

choice of unilaterally dishonoring outstanding validly issued stored value or electronic money, or treating both valid and counterfeit forms of stored value and electronic money as equally valid.[18]

The coming onset of the age of electronic banking and commerce has also coincided with an increasing interest in, and concern regarding, the protection of individual privacy. This evolving world is filled with possibilities for massive illegal or unauthorized acquisition, manipulation, and use of personal data, including financial information. Much of this concern is a result of the understanding of the both the advantages and disadvantages of interactive communications. While it is convenient to be able to transmit personal financial information over the Internet to the website of a business partner, this approach correspondingly exponentially increases the number of parties who may have the opportunity to have access to the same information as it passes across the Internet, or even once it reaches the destination web server.

There may be somewhat of an emotional quality to how people react to these issues. When an individual gives her credit card to a waiter at a restaurant, it is possible that during the time the waiter is gone the individual's credit card number will be recorded and subsequently passed on to be used in unauthorized transactions. At the same time, if an individual enters a credit card number on an order form on a World Wide Web site and transmits it through the Internet, it is possible that the credit card information will be intercepted and then used in unauthorized transactions. In either instance the individual's liability for unauthorized transactions will generally be limited to $50.[19] While from a liability perspective the outcome is the same regardless of the how the diversion of credit card information occurs, it appears that many consumers view the two situations differently. While few individuals would hesitate when the waiter offers to take their credit card to pay the bill, a significant percentage of consumers to date have been unwilling to type their credit card number into a prospective seller's website. This reluctance has emerged as an important, if transitory, barrier to the widespread acceptance of electronic commerce.

Another aspect of electronic confidentiality is the financial and personal fingerprints that electronic consumers will leave behind. This is attractive information to those who are interested in learning more about a particular individual, whether for purposes of marketing to that individual, or for any other number of legitimate or improper purposes. Consumers have little knowledge of when and how such information is collected and the circumstances under which it may be used or transferred to other parties. There is little law at the federal or state level addressing the information privacy rights of an individual. The handling of this information will be an important consideration in the design of a variety of electronic banking and commerce products. Moreover, privacy considerations are likely to play a significant role in the public policy discussions that will occur regarding the development of legislation to accommodate developments in electronic banking and commerce. In one such discussion, the American Bankers Association recently adopted a set of privacy

---

[18]   *See* Steve Glain, *Pinball Scam Costs Japanese Firms $588 Million*, WALL ST. J., May 22, 1996, at A18; *Pachinko Counterfeit Scam Illustrates the Threat of Spawning*, 21ST CENTURY BANKING ALERT® No. 96-7-1, July 1, 1996, *available at* <http://www.ffhsj.com/bancmail/bancpage.htm>. *See also* Chapter 8, Section 8.02.

[19]   *See* 12 C.F.R. § 226.12(b).

principles to encourage financial institutions to consider, create, supplement, or improve their policies regarding privacy.[20] These are discussed in detail in Chapter 12.

Today's EFS pioneers should bear in mind the importance of cost, convenience, and confidentiality as they strive to develop the electronic commerce world of the next century.

---

[20] *See ABA Board Approves Privacy Principles*, ABA(Bankers) Press Release, July 21, 1997; *American Bankers Association Approves Privacy Principles*, 21ST CENTURY BANKING ALERT® No. 97-7-25, July 25, 1997, *available at* <http://www.ffhsj.com/bancmail/bancpage.htm>.

CHAPTER 12

PRIVACY

§ 12.01 INTRODUCTION

In 1890, Samuel Warren and Louis Brandeis first identified the right to privacy.[1] After exploring the nature and scope of the right to privacy, they concluded that "[i]t is the unwarranted invasion of individual privacy which is reprehended, and to be, so far as possible, prevented."[2] Common law privacy law gradually evolved to mean the right to enjoy life — "the right to be left alone."[3] In 1960, a distinguished legal commentator contributed to the development of privacy law when he asserted that while no right to privacy existed under United States constitutional law, various tortious invasions of privacy are recognized under state common law.[4] Today, the tort of "invasion of privacy" consists of four separate and distinct rights, as outlined in the Restatement (Second) of Torts, Section 652A: (i) the unreasonable intrusion upon the seclusion of another; (ii) the appropriation of another's name or likeness; (iii) the unreasonable publicity given to another's private life; and (iv) publicity that unreasonably places another in a false light before the public.[5] These torts exist in some form or another, under common or statutory law, in the overwhelming majority of the states.[6] This patchwork approach means that an individual's privacy rights may vary widely based on the state in which they live and the type of infringement involved.

For purposes of this Chapter, the term "privacy" will be used chiefly in two contexts, "informational privacy" and "financial privacy." The term "informational privacy" has been defined as the "claim of individuals, groups or institutions to determine for themselves when, how, and to what extent information about them

---

[1] Samuel Warren & Louis Brandeis, *The Right to Privacy*, 4 HARV. L. REV. 193, 213 (1890). *See also* Richard C. Turkington, *Legacy of the Warren and Brandeis Article: The Emerging Unencumbered Constitutional Right to Informational Privacy*, 10 N. ILL. U. L. REV. 479, 482 n.5 (1990) (indicating that a 1881 Michigan case and other sources discussed the right to privacy prior to the publication of the Warren and Brandeis article).

[2] Warren & Brandeis, *supra* note 1, at 215.

[3] *Id.* at 193. Professor Lawrence Tribe describes the essence of an individual's right to privacy, the "right to be left alone," as "nothing less than society's limiting principle . . . It is a right which has meaning only within the social environment from which it would provide some degree of escape. *See generally* LAWRENCE TRIBE, AMERICAN CONSTITUTIONAL LAW 1302 (2d ed. 1988).

[4] William L. Prosser, *Privacy*, 48 CAL. L. REV. 383 (1960).

[5] *See* RESTATEMENT (SECOND) OF TORTS § 652A (1979).

[6] *See* William L. Prosser, *Privacy*, 48 CAL. L. REV. 383, 386 (1960) (describing privacy torts recognized in 47 states); W. PAGE KEETON ET AL., PROSSER AND KEETON ON THE LAW OF TORTS 849-69 (5th ed. 1984).

is communicated to others."[7] The concept of informational privacy is closely related to the concept of "financial privacy," the rights of individuals to control the collection, storing, use, and dissemination of information concerning their personal financial affairs by their financial institutions and third parties. Section 12.02 explores informational privacy generally and its application to electronic financial products and services. Section 12.03 focuses on financial institutions' duty of confidentiality regarding customer financial records. Section 12.04 discusses the degree of privacy consumers may reasonably expect in cyberspace. Section 12.05 explores government and industry efforts to meet those expectations. Section 12.06 provides an overview of the federal and state laws currently defining the boundaries of privacy in cyberspace. Finally, Section 12.07 details recent legislative efforts in the United States Congress and the European Union that focus on electronic commerce and the Internet.

§ 12.02 THE CONCEPT OF INFORMATIONAL PRIVACY

Informational privacy in the age of computers and electronic fund transfers is not an unlimited or absolute right.[8] As noted above, the components of informational privacy are: (i) what personal information is collected; (ii) the circumstances in which someone may access such information; and (iii) how the personal information is protected.[9] A financial institution's use of a customer's personal financial information may be completely acceptable in one context, such as the submission of a loan application, and an unacceptable invasion of privacy in another, such as the disclosure of account or transaction history to a third party. Concerns about privacy, as well as confidentiality, include concerns about unauthorized access to one's personal or financial information and concerns about the nature of the information maintained by financial institutions and the consequences that flow from the loss of control of personal information.[10]

Individuals who choose to participate in commercial transactions, and society in general, must be prepared to give up some control of their personal information in order to have access to banking, credit, and other financial services.[11] Indeed, at some level, for the purposes of increased security, many individuals would be willing to forego some aspect of privacy. For example, if you sat in an audience with 100 other people and were asked how much privacy each of you should have, the responses likely would be nearly universal in

---

[7] ALAN WESTIN, PRIVACY AND FREEDOM 7 (1967). *See also* ALAN WESTIN, THE EQUIFAX REPORT ON CONSUMERS IN THE INFORMATION AGE, at XVIII (1990).

[8] *See* DONALD L. BAKER & ROLAND E. BRANDEL, THE LAW OF ELECTRONIC FUNDS TRANSFER SYSTEMS, LEGAL AND STRATEGIC PLANNING ¶ 19.01, at 19-2 (3d ed. 1996).

[9] *See* Jonathan P. Graham, *Privacy, Computers, and the Commercial Dissemination of Personal Information*, 65 TEX. L. REV. 1395, 1397 n.7 (1987).

[10] *See* Oscar H. Gandy, Jr., *Legitimate Business Interest: No End in Sight? An Inquiry into the Status of Privacy in Cyberspace*, 1996 U. CHI. LEGAL F. 77, 78.

[11] Although individuals may refuse to disclose certain facts about themselves, such disclosure is often either required by law (*e.g.*, tax returns) or required if the individual wishes to participate in society in a meaningful way (*e.g.*, disclosing financial information to obtain a mortgage or releasing medical information to obtain insurance benefits). As a practical matter, individuals cannot participate fully in society without revealing vast amounts of personal data. *See generally* INFORMATION POLICY COMM., NATIONAL INFORMATION INFRASTRUCTURE TASK FORCE, OPTIONS FOR PROMOTING PRIVACY ON THE NATIONAL INFORMATION INFRASTRUCTURE (1997) (Draft for Public Comment), *available at* <http://www.iitf.nist.gov/ipc/privacy.htm> [hereinafter NIITF 1997 DRAFT REPORT].

favor of nearly absolute privacy, unless waived by the individual. But if you were told that two of the 100 people in the room with you were terrorists, it is likely that many people would change their minds about the shroud of privacy that each of those 100 people should be able to maintain.

In a world where privacy interests must be balanced against other legitimate interests, individuals should, however, have some control over how and for what purposes their personal information will be made available. They should also have an opportunity to assure that whatever information does circulate will be at all times accurate, complete, and timely.[12] Harmonizing individual concerns about privacy with institutional needs for information is at the heart of the debate over the right to informational and financial privacy.[13] This struggle between the desire of individuals to protect their privacy and society's need for information is most readily apparent in the financial realm, where an individual's desire to maintain data privacy may conflict with law enforcement's need to prevent criminal activities, such as money laundering and counterfeiting.

Information about a consumer, including everything from a person's age and address to favorite products and services, has value.[14] Normally, how valuable that information is depends, at least in part, on how descriptive it is and how the information can be used.[15] Government, of course, has long been a major collector and possessor of extensive amounts of personal information about U.S. citizens. In recent years, the private sector has increased dramatically its acquisition and use of personal information.[16]

The rapid development of computer systems and software has made the collection, storage, retrieval, processing, and dissemination of personal information cheaper and easier than ever before.[17] Computers can now bring together in centralized databases information gathered by a variety of sources (credit, driving and voting histories, for example), thus facilitating the generation of personal profiles.[18] Computers also make possible the processing of large amounts of personal data and drastically reduce the costs and time required to transmit personal data to third parties.[19]

---

[12] See BAKER & BRANDEL, supra note 8, ¶ 19.01, at 19-2.

[13] Alan Greenspan, Chairman of the Board of Governors of the Federal Reserve System ("FRB"), recently acknowledged the delicate balance between privacy concerns, the needs of commerce, and the needs of government to administer the laws and provide for public safety. See Alan Greenspan, Chairman of the FRB, Remarks at the Conference on Privacy in the Information Age, Salt Lake City, Utah (Mar. 7, 1997) available at (visited Jan. 6, 1998) <http://www.bog.frb.fed.us/boarddocs/speeches>.

[14] See BOARD OF GOVERNORS OF THE FEDERAL RESERVE SYSTEM, REPORT TO CONGRESS CONCERNING THE AVAILABILITY OF CONSUMER IDENTIFYING INFORMATION AND FINANCIAL FRAUD 4 (Mar. 1997) [hereinafter FRB CONSUMER REPORT]. The FRB's Report was commissioned by Congress in Section 2422 of the Economic Growth and Regulatory Paperwork Reduction Act of 1996, subtitle D of Pub. L. No. 104-208, 110 Stat. 3009 (1996). Congress instructed the FRB to conduct a study to determine whether organizations which are not subject to the provisions of the Fair Credit Reporting Act "are engaged in the business of making sensitive consumer identification information, including Social Security numbers, mother's maiden names, prior address, and dates of birth, available to the general public," and whether such "activities create a potential for fraud." FRB CONSUMER REPORT, supra, at 14.

[15] See id. at 4.

[16] The National Information Infrastructure Task Force ("NIITF") was created in 1993 by President Clinton and Vice-President Gore to address concerns regarding a variety of consumer and business issues regarding the National Information Infrastructure. See NIITF 1997 DRAFT REPORT, supra note 11.

[17] See Graham, supra note 9, at 1395-99.

[18] See id. at 1399.

[19] See id. at 1399-1401 (citing the "loss of [personal] privacy [as] the most serious casualty of the information age").

Fundamentally, there are three sets of distinct participants in the information industry — government entities (federal, state, and local), direct marketers, and reference services.[20] Typically these participants both gather and distribute personal identifying information. Government entities retain information such as property ownership and legal judgments in public records. Direct marketers and reference services have developed a business of creating and selling dossiers on individuals.[21] These services gather in one place a variety of facts about individuals.[22] In many instances, the information may be gathered for one purpose, then sold and used for another.[23] According to some estimates, the average American is on at least twenty-five (and often as many as one hundred) of these computer lists or databases at any one time.[24] Although the vast amount of stored information about business and consumers has both positive and negative implications, the sheer magnitude of information collection, storage, and dissemination increases the probability that information will be used in a manner not reasonably contemplated or desired by the consumer, or "data subject."[25]

Not surprisingly, the past decade has witnessed a growing concern among our society regarding the use of personal information in commerce, government, and the private sector.[26] A recent episode involving the establishment of a website by the Social Security Administration ("SSA") illustrates this point. In March 1997, the SSA began offering personal information to present and potential Social Security recipients at its website. The system made available information about personal earnings and/or benefits received for Social Security participants, going back, in some cases, decades. By providing a Social Security number, mother's

---

[20] *See* FRB CONSUMER REPORT, *supra* note 14, at 5.

[21] *See, e.g.*, Saul Hansell, *Getting to Know You,* INSTITUTIONAL INVESTOR, June 1991, at 71 (describing efforts by credit card and other financial services companies to improve their marketing and selling efforts by data mining and storing techniques).

[22] According to the FRB CONSUMER REPORT, one Internet reference service sells what it calls a "comprehensive dossier report." The service provides the name, age, date of birth, Social Security number (including the state and date of issuance), any alias, current and previous address, and telephone listing, as well as the names, telephone numbers, and addresses of relatives and neighbors. *See* FRB CONSUMER REPORT, *supra* note 14, at 8.

[23] *See* FRB CONSUMER REPORT, *supra* note 14, at 5. Litigation concerning the misuse of information gathered in a permissible manner, but misused by the compiler of the data, is on the rise. In one recent example, a federal jury in Nebraska awarded $23.7 million in damages against Trans Union Corp., finding that the credit bureau had breached its contract with the First National Bank of Nebraska by selling names of the bank's customers to third parties for direct marketing and solicitation purposes harmful to the bank's credit card operations. *See First Nat'l Bank of Omaha v. Trans Union Corp.*, Case No. 8:95CV57, Aug. 29, 1997 (order entering judgment); Complaint, *First Nat'l Bank of Omaha v. Trans Union Corp.*, Case No. 8:95CV57, filed on Feb. 3, 1995 (copies on file with the authors). Trans Union has said it will appeal the verdict. *See Jury Orders Trans Union to Pay $23.7 Million to Nebraska Bank,* PRIVACY TIMES, Sept. 8, 1997, at 2.

[24] *See* NIITF 1997 DRAFT REPORT, *supra* note 11, at 6.

[25] *Id.* at 7. The NIITF notes that increased data mining can lead to targeted marketing efforts, lower prices for goods and services, and increased competition, all of which may benefit consumers. The NIITF also notes, however, that many potential misuses of such consumer and business information exist, such as improper denial of benefits or financial services based upon a consumer's medical history, demographic information, or data "profile." *Id.*

[26] According to the NIITF's 1997 Draft Report (citing LOUIS HARRIS AND ASSOCIATES, INC., THE 1996 EQUIFAX/HARRIS CONSUMER PRIVACY SURVEY (1996)), 65% of those surveyed consider consumer privacy protection "very important," up from 61% in 1995. Threats to personal privacy concerned 64% of the respondents in 1978, 79% in 1990 and 1993, 82% in 1995, and 87% in 1996. *Id.* Recently, Time magazine ran a cover story feature on the demise of privacy in the lives of U.S. consumers. *See* Joshua Quittner, *The Death of Privacy,* TIME, Aug. 25, 1997, at 29-35. *See also Secrets for Sale*, FUTUREBANKER, Aug. 4, 1997, at 38 ("Privacy is an illusion cloaked by bureaucracy and ambivalence . . . . Individual [data] summaries will be packaged and sold [online] like Cheerios in the supermarket."); Nina Bernstein, *OnLine, High-Tech Sleuths Find Private Facts,* N.Y. TIMES, Sept. 15, 1997, at A1 (websites such as Dig Dirt and SpyForU will find unlisted phone numbers for $69, bank account numbers for $55, beeper numbers for $59, an individual's salary for $75, and a summary of an individual's stock portfolio for $200).

maiden name, and date and place of birth, a visitor to the website could access the corresponding financial information online.[27]

When the news media publicized this new means of obtaining information from the SSA, an outcry ensued. Critics claimed that the site made available a host of information about an individual's financial background to anyone who typed in the required information, which privacy advocates claim, is readily available from information vendors.[28] Critics noted that the possibility of unauthorized third-party access could lead to widespread "identity theft" or fraud.[29] Several U.S. senators sent a letter to the SSA urging it to suspend the operation of the website unless and until the privacy concerns of consumers could be properly addressed through the use of encryption or passwords.[30] Within days, SSA suspended the operation of the website in order to study in detail the privacy concerns relating to the operation of the site.[31] This episode demonstrated that the public is becoming aware of, and concerned about, perceived threats to individual financial and informational privacy.[32] Likewise, consumers increasingly are asserting that the unauthorized dissemination of personal information violates state law.[33]

---

[27] *See* John Schwartz & Barbara J. Saffir, *Social Security Website Takes Hit Over Access*, WASH. POST, Apr. 8, 1997, at A1.

[28] *See* Simson L. Garfinkel, *Social Insecurity: Few Key Bits of Info Open Social Security Records*, USA TODAY, Apr. 7, 1997, at A1.

[29] "Identity theft" typically refers to the illegal use of personal identifying information – including name, address, Social Security Number, financial account numbers, and birth date – to commit financial fraud. One particular type of identity theft occurs when the criminal "takes over" a consumer's account, for example, by changing the consumer's address for an existing account or submitting a fraudulent credit application to open an account in the consumer's name, but giving a different address as the place to send the card. *See* FRB CONSUMER REPORT, *supra* note 14, at 18 n.14.

[30] *See* M.J. Zuckerman & Peter Eisler, *Senators Say Shut Web Site*, USA TODAY, Apr. 9, 1997, at A1.

[31] On September 4, 1997, the SSA announced that its online Personal Earning and Benefit Estimate Statement (PEBES) service would be relaunched in January 1998. Unlike its predecessor, the revamped service will not make taxpayer information or workers' earning histories available online. Under the revised system, members of the public will request their personal earnings and benefit estimate information online, and subsequently receive a password via e-mail from the SSA to be used to retrieve the information from the website. *See* Rebecca Vesely, *Social Security Unveils New Online Data Plan*, WIRED NEWS, Sept 4, 1997, *available at* (visited Jan. 8, 1998) <http:// www.wired.com/news/news/politics/story/6617.html>.

[32] In another recent development, Experian, one of the country's largest credit reporting bureaus, began offering customers the opportunity to view their credit reports over the Internet. *See* Robert O'Harrow, Jr. & Rajiv Chandrasekaran, *Credit Reports Made Available Online*, WASH. POST, Aug. 15, 1997, at D1. By visiting Experian's website, interested consumers could view their credit report information, including loans, payment patterns, Social Security Numbers, overdue credit card bills, former addresses, and other financial details. *Id.* Experian officials noted that they had delayed the rollout of the service for several months to address confidentiality concerns. However, operation of the website was abruptly canceled by Experian, after only 48 hours, when at least four consumers, including a Washington Post reporter, received credit reports pertaining to other individuals in error. *See* Robert O'Harrow, Jr., *Privacy Lapses Force Shutdown of Online Credit Reporting Service*, WASH. POST, Aug. 16, 1997, at A1.

[33] At least one consumer has made a recent, and highly publicized, attempt to prevent the unauthorized dissemination of his personal information. In August 1995, Ram Avrahami filed suit in Virginia state court against U.S. News & World Report, challenging the right of the magazine to sell or rent his name to another publication without his express written consent. Ram Avrahami claims that the magazine has benefited commercially from his name (by selling his name on a list to a direct marketing firm), thus violating a Virginia law which protects every person from having his/her name being used for commercial purpose without consent. *See* Plaintiff's Motion for Judgment, *Avrahami v. U.S. News & World Report, Inc.* (G.D.C. Arlington (VA), 1995) (Civ. Action No. 95-7479), *available at* (visited Jan. 6, 1998) <http://www.eff.org/ftp/pub/privacy/credit_junkmail_commercial/Avrahami-v-USNWR/>; *see also* G. Bruce Knecht, *Privacy: Junk-Mail Hater Seeks Profits From Sale of His Name*, WALL ST. J., Oct. 18, 1995, at B1. On June 13, 1996, the Arlington County Circuit Court ruled that Mr. Avrahami did not have a property right in various spellings of his name, that individual names have no value, and that the inclusion of names in a mailing list did not constitute a "use for the purpose of trade" for purposes of the Virginia statute. See the website of the Electronic Privacy Information Center for more information on the Avrahami case, <http://washofc.epic.org/privacy/junk_mail>. In late 1996, Mr. Avrahami filed a petition of appeal in the Virginia Supreme Court, which was denied. *See* Va. Sup. Ct. No. 961837 (1996).

[1] INFORMATIONAL PRIVACY; ELECTRONIC BANKING AND EMERGING PAYMENT PRODUCTS

In the context of electronic banking and commerce, informational privacy means control over the collection, storage, retrieval, and dissemination of financial information, account numbers, activities, transactional and credit histories, and purchasing and spending patterns. A number of the Internet's special characteristics — the potential anonymity of buyer and seller, the capacity for multiple small transactions, and the difficulty of associating online activities with physically defined locations — appear, at first glance, to represent a boon for the protection of informational privacy. Yet, the Internet facilitates the collection, re-use, and instantaneous transmission of information, which can, if not managed carefully, diminish personal privacy.[34] A closer look at the use and characteristics of the Internet, combined with the existing information and database marketplace, suggests that it may constitute a growing threat to the informational privacy of citizens and businesses.

A potential risk to consumers in electronic banking and commerce is that information regarding the form, amount, and location of electronic payments they make will be collected and used by merchants, financial institutions, or other third parties for purposes unknown to or unauthorized by them.[35] For example, information regarding a particular consumer's spending and payment habits could be captured by an electronic payment system, such as a stored value card system (*e.g.*, a merchant's card reader terminal at the point-of-sale) and stored in a computer database for later resale to a marketing firm or reference service. Generally, electronic payments are more susceptible to this kind of compilation because of the relative ease with which electronic payment data may be captured, stored, compiled, and accessed in a database.[36]

Consumer concern about the use of personal information is likely to increase as more information is compiled.[37] In our current payments system, only nonbank consumer transactions conducted with cash are typically somewhat anonymous.[38] The use of paper checks, electronic fund transfers, credit, and debit purchases all leave some record of the transaction. "Online" stored value card products[39] will operate through existing automated teller machine ("ATM") or point-of-sale ("POS") networks, and may be subject to the same (or similar) audit trail that currently exists for credit and debit card systems.

---

[34] *See* PRESIDENT WILLIAM J. CLINTON & VICE PRESIDENT ALBERT GORE, JR., A FRAMEWORK FOR GLOBAL ELECTRONIC COMMERCE (July 1997), *available at* <http://www.whitehouse.gov/WH/New/Commerce/>.

[35] *See* BOARD OF GOVERNORS OF THE FEDERAL RESERVE SYSTEM, REPORT TO THE CONGRESS ON THE APPLICATION OF THE ELECTRONIC FUND TRANSFER ACT TO ELECTRONIC STORED-VALUE PRODUCTS (Mar. 1997), at 36-37 [hereinafter STORED-VALUE REPORT].

[36] *See id.* at 36.

[37] *See* Udo Flohr, *Electric Money: Cash, Checks, and Coupons Are All Going Digital*, BYTE, June 1996, at 74, 80 ("What's the danger [of access to personal information]? If unchecked, all our transactions, as well as our spending habits could eventually reside on the corporate databases of individual companies, like those that now track our credit histories.").

[38] Certain electronic payment products may be designed to simulate the anonymity of individual currency transactions.

[39] By "online" card system, we mean a system in which the information containing the balance of funds on a stored value card (and possibly, the account information) is maintained, not on the card itself, but rather on a separate database. Transactions made by use of a stored value card will be authorized by means of online communication with such database or storage facility. For a discussion of stored value cards, see Chapter 16. *See also* Electronic Fund Transfers, 61 Fed. Reg. 19,696, 19,698-99 (1996) (to be codified at 12 C.F.R. pt. 205) (proposed May 2, 1996) [hereinafter FRB Stored Value Proposal].

"Off-line" stored value products,[40] as well as Internet or other computer network-based payment products, may generate substantial amounts of consumer spending information at the merchant and/or retail level. As noted in Chapter 7, whether the full panoply of consumer protections of the Electronic Fund Transfer Act[41] and the Board of Governors of the Federal Reserve System's Regulation E,[42] or similar consumer protections and disclosures, whether government-mandated or self-imposed by the industry, will apply to emerging electronic and stored value payment products is still under consideration by Congress, the federal bank regulatory agencies, the credit/debit card associations, and the banking industry.[43]

Users of stored value or other electronic payment products face a range of threats to the security of their personal or account information, the integrity of their financial transactions, and their own personal expectations of privacy.[44] To understand the likely application of existing federal laws concerning the security and privacy of consumer information to the advent of stored value and other electronic payment products, a review of the "haphazard" coverage under these statutes, as more fully detailed in Section 12.06 below, is essential.

§ 12.03   A FINANCIAL INSTITUTION'S DUTY OF CONFIDENTIALITY AT COMMON LAW TO PREVENT DISCLOSURE OF CUSTOMER FINANCIAL RECORDS

[1]   STANDARDS

In many jurisdictions, a bank is considered to owe a duty of confidentiality to a customer to protect the customer's financial records from unauthorized disclosure of information regarding a customer's finances, transactions, and financial condition, without the customer's actual or implied consent.[45] This rule, which was espoused in a 1920's English case, has now been adopted, in some form, by most states.[46] Courts have generally

---

[40]   An "off-line" system is one where the balance of funds is recorded on the card itself and there is no online authorization of transactions by communication to a database maintained at a financial institution or other issuer. *See* FRB Stored Value Proposal, *supra* note 39, at 19,701.

[41]   Electronic Fund Transfer Act, Pub. L. No. 95-630, tit. XX, § 2001, 1978 U.S.C.C.A.N. (92 Stat.) 3728 (codified as amended at 15 U.S.C. §§ 1693-1693r).

[42]   Electronic Fund Transfers, Regulation E, 12 C.F.R. pt. 205.

[43]   See Chapters 4 and 7 for discussions of Regulation E.

[44]   At least one commentator has called the privacy battle the "first Holy War of the Information Age." *See* Marcia Stepanek, *Administration Sparks New Battle Over Internet Privacy*, TIMES UNION, May 25, 1997, at A10 (quoting Stanford University computer expert Eric Roberts).

[45]   *See* Donald A. Doheny, Sr. & Graydon John Forrer, *Electronic Access to Account Information and Financial Privacy*, 109 BANKING L.J. 436 (1992); Roy Elbert Huhs, Jr., *To Disclose or Not to Disclose Customer Records*, 108 BANKING L.J. 30 (1991); Thomas C. Russler & Steven H. Epstein, *Disclosure of Customer Information to Third Parties: When Is the Bank Liable?*, 111 BANKING L.J. 258 (1994). Increasingly, banks have felt an increased ethical, as well as legal, obligation to safeguard their customers financial records. *See* Cheryl B. Preston, *Honor Among Bankers: Ethics in the Exchange of Commercial Credit Information and the Protection of Customer Interests*, 40 KAN. L. REV. 943, 970-71 (1992).

[46]   *See Peterson v. Idaho Nat'l Bank*, 367 P.2d 284 (Idaho 1964) (holding that an implied contractual duty of confidentiality exists between a bank and its depositor); *Milohnich v. First Nat'l Bank of Miami Springs*, 224 So. 759 (Fla. Dist. Ct. App. 1969) (same) (citing to *Peterson* and to *Tournier v. National Provincial & Union Bank of England*, 1 K.B. 461 (1924), an English privacy case); Russler & Epstein, *supra* note 45, at 259-64.

found that banks implicitly warrant to maintain customer account information in the strictest confidence.[47] Under the depositor's "right of secrecy," a bank may be liable, under appropriate circumstances, for disclosing customer account information to third parties negligently, willfully, maliciously, or intentionally. Case law has provided a range of exceptions to the general rule of implied confidentiality.[48] Courts also may differ as to the range of customers to whom the implied duty of confidentiality runs from the bank; with some courts holding that the duty protects only a bank's depositors, and others holding that the duty protects all of a bank's customers (such as borrowers or loan applicants).[49] Certain states, such as New York and Nebraska, provide few confidentiality protections.[50]

The increasing use of technology in the delivery of banking services, such as the use of World Wide Web sites and remote banking (via telephone, modem, and personal computer),[51] has raised a host of questions concerning the adaptation of common law principles of the bank/customer relationship. These questions include: How, when, and under what circumstances would a bank be liable when a criminal uses covert (electronic) means to break into the bank's computer records and access a customer's account without the bank or the customer's knowledge? What standard of care would be used to determine if a bank would be liable to a customer for a breach of its duty of confidentiality when an unauthorized user gains access, steals, or modifies, for example, a customer's account, or recent loan application with the bank?

[2] IDENTITY THEFT: UNDER WHAT CIRCUMSTANCES COULD A BANK BE LIABLE?

The standards that have generally been developed in this area have been aimed at intentional communication of customer information by bank employees to third parties rather than circumstances where access to such information is gained without the direct involvement of any bank employees. Standards aimed at individual behavior do little to explain how, when, and under what circumstances, deliberate and unauthorized third-party attempts to break into a bank's computer systems could be found to violate this duty. Banks can be expected to argue that the unauthorized tampering of third parties with customer account balances or information do not constitute disclosures "made" by the bank.

---

[47] On the other hand, the Supreme Court found that depositors do not have a legitimate expectation of privacy with respect to the bank records maintained by the bank pursuant to the Bank Secrecy Act and pertaining to their depository accounts and related transactions. *See United States v. Miller*, 425 U.S. 435 (1976). This decision spurred Congress to offer a degree of protection to depositors from Federal Government access to their deposit records by enacting the Right to Financial Privacy Act.

[48] *See Peterson*, 367 P.2d at 290 (customer authorization of disclosure and disclosures required by law*); Barnett Bank of West Fla. v. Hooper*, 498 So.2d 923, 925 (Fla. 1986) (exceptions to the general rule include disclosures under compulsion of law, pursuant to the public interest, pursuant to a bank's interest, and where expressly or impliedly authorized by customer).

[49] *See Russler & Epstein, supra* note 45, at 261-62 (discussing the *Peterson, Milohnich,* and *Barnett Bank* cases). The cases often turn on the court's characterization of whether the relationship between the bank and its customer is that of a fiduciary or agent (*i.e.,* for a depositor) or merely that of a debtor/creditor. *See e.g., United States v. First Nat'l Bank of Mobile*, 67 F. Supp. 616, 624 (S.D. Ala. 1946) (finding a fiduciary duty to prevent disclosures); *Graney Dev. Corp. v. Tasken*, 400 N.Y.S.2d 717 (Sup. Ct. 1978), *aff'd* 411 N.Y.S.2d 756 (App. Div. 1978) (confidentiality duty did not extend to information received by bank from a party to a loan agreement).

[50] *See Russler & Epstein, supra* note 45, at 267.

[51] *See generally* Chapter 14.

A September 1995 civil award in federal court in Texas illustrates possible risks to banks and financial institutions of being involved in the unauthorized access and use of a customer's financial records. In a "theft-of-identity" case, a federal judge awarded $1.45 million in damages and attorney's fees against a former loan officer at a Houston bank to a retired couple whose financial and credit records had been fraudulently used by the loan officer.[52] According to news reports, the loan officer (who had the same last name as the couple) obtained their personal and financial information by using the bank's credit terminal to access their credit report.[53]

Armed with this information, the alleged defrauder opened bank, finance, gas, and other credit accounts under the couple's identity. The alleged defrauder also paid bills on the accounts for brief periods to build up the credit lines on the accounts. Although the court awarded damages against the (presumably judgment-proof) alleged defrauder, the couple also sued (in a separate action) thirteen credit bureaus, banks, department stores, collection agencies and other creditors on grounds of violations of privacy, defamation, violations of the Fair Credit Reporting Act, and other federal and state debt collection laws.

The threat of identity theft in the banking business has been greatly increased by the growth of online services, dissemination of personal information, and the increasing use of technology in the delivery of banking services.[54] Other types of criminal fraud are made easier by the advent of online banking. As depositors and other bank customers gain increased access to their accounts and related information through use of computers and other electronic means, banks must bear in mind the increasing likelihood that third parties may seek to access such information as well. The increased likelihood that criminals will seek to capture and use deposit or account information of a bank's customers poses a growing threat to both banks and their customers.

§ 12.04 PRIVACY IN CYBERSPACE

[1] OVERVIEW

The treatment of e-mail, voice mail, and computer files in the context of the private workplace provides a useful template for the analysis of privacy rights in the information age. A growing reliance of businesses on

---

[52] See McBride v. McBride, No. H-95-1037 (S.D. Tex. Oct. 2, 1995) (unpublished). See also Albert B. Crenshaw, Identity Crisis: The Theft That's Tough to Thwart, WASH. POST, Aug. 25, 1996, at H1; Kelly McMurry, Judge Favors Plaintiffs in Theft-of -Identity Case, TRIAL, Jan. 1, 1996; Biggest Yet! Texas Couple Wins $1.45 Million for 'ID Theft,' PRIVACY TIMES, Oct. 5, 1995, at 1.

[53] See Biggest Yet!, supra note 52, at 2.

[54] See U.S. PUBLIC INTEREST RESEARCH GROUP, THEFT OF IDENTITY: THE CONSUMER X-FILES (1996) (describing case studies of identity theft and the consequences to consumers); Ann Cavoukian, Information and Privacy Commissioner (Ontario), Identity Theft: Who's Using Your Name?, June 1997, available at (visited Jan. 6, 1998) <http://www.ipc.on.ca/web_site.eng/matters/sum_pap/papers> (citing statistic that U.S. banks lost up to $90 million during 1995 in cases involving bank customer identity theft).

e-mail[55] and voice mail communications systems has created many new opportunities for private sector employers to monitor the performance, behavior, and online activities of employees either without their knowledge or without disclosing when such monitoring is occurring. According to a survey conducted by *MacWorld* magazine of 301 private sector employers, at least 22% of the companies searched employees' computer files, voice mail and e-mail, or other networking communications systems.[56] Of the 22% respondents admitting to the monitoring of electronic communications, slightly more than 66% of them confirmed that they conducted employee monitoring without employee knowledge or consent.[57] The American Civil Liberties Union has estimated that twenty million employees have their e-mail, computer files, and voice mail searched by their employers.[58] This Section will briefly address the legal theories that may be applicable to such electronic monitoring as a model for the users and providers of electronic banking and other financial services, and as an outline of the legal protections afforded to consumers engaged in electronic commerce and to private sector employees.

A recent spate of scholarly literature has addressed the propriety of e-mail and voice mail monitoring in the workplace and evaluated the legal protections available to protect the online communications of private sector workers.[59] To date, there is not a great deal of law on e-mail privacy other than several state court decisions and one particularly relevant federal statute, the Electronic Communications Privacy Act of 1986.[60]

---

[55] E-mail allows an individual to send an electronic message to another individual or group of individuals. The message is stored electronically until the recipient accesses his or her mailbox. *See Reno v. American Civil Liberties Union*, 521 U.S. __, 117 S. Ct. 2329, 138 L. Ed. 874, 884-85 (1997). In 1994, 776 billion e-mail messages passed through U.S.-based computer networks. Projections are for 2.6 trillion e-mail messages to pass through U.S. networks in 1997, and for 6.6 trillion e-mail messages to pass through U.S. networks in 2000. *See* Susan E. Gindin, *Lost and Found in Cyberspace: Informational Privacy in the Age of the Internet*, 34 SAN DIEGO L. REV. (forthcoming in 1998), Draft *available at* (visited Jan. 6, 1998) <http://www.info-law.com/lost.html> (citing a Time magazine estimate).

[56] *See* Charles Piller, *Bosses with X-Ray Eyes*, MACWORLD, July 1993, at 118, 120.

[57] *See id.* at 118, 123. *See also* Thomas R. Greenberg, *E-Mail and Voice Mail: Employee Privacy and the Federal Wiretap Statute*, 44 AM. U. L. REV. 219, 222 (1994).

[58] *See* Anne L. Lehman, *E-mail in the Workplace: Questions of Privacy Property or Principle*, 5 COMMLAW CONSPECTUS 99 (1997) (citing a Wall Street Journal article).

[59] *See generally* Bruce Gaylord, *E-mail Issues in the Workplace: How to Develop Effective Policies*, COMPUTER L. STRATEGIST, Vol. XI, No. 2, at 1; Albert Gidari, *Privilege and Confidentiality in Cyberspace*, 13 COMPUTER L. 1 (1996); Thomas R. Greenberg, *E-Mail and Voice Mail: Employee Privacy and the Federal Wiretap Statute*, 44 AM. U. L. REV. 219 (1994); Anne L. Lehman, *E-mail in the Workplace: Questions of Privacy Property or Principle*, 5 COMMLAW CONSPECTUS 99 (1997); Donald H. Seifman & Craig W. Trepanier, *Evolution of the Paperless Office: Legal Issues Arising out of Technology in the Workplace, Part I. E-mail and Voicemail Systems*, 21 EMP. REL. L.J. 5 (1995); Parry Aftab, *Monitoring Communications on the Internet; Big Brother or Responsible Business?*, N.Y.L.J., Sept. 30, 1996, at S2.

[60] 18 U.S.C. § 2510-22. *See also* Section 12.06[5].

[2] PRIVACY E-MAIL CASES

E-mail is the transfer of messages, usually text or other files, sent from one person to another via the Internet or other networked computers.[61] Because, in a practical sense, e-mail users "voluntarily" communicate their messages to system administrators in addition to the intended recipient as part of their e-mail use agreement, the legal treatment of e-mail presents a difficult case for courts and lawmakers because it falls somewhere between a telephone call and written correspondence. Discussed below are a number of recent cases involving the privacy rights of users of e-mail and similar computer-based communications.

Current law tends to favor employers when it comes to monitoring e-mail in the workplace. In *Smyth v. Pillsbury Company*,[62] an at-will employee sued his employer under Pennsylvania law for the tort of "intrusion upon seclusion" after the employer intercepted and read the employee's e-mail messages made on the company's e-mail communications system. Notwithstanding the company's guidelines regarding the use of corporate e-mail,[63] Pillsbury dismissed Smyth for "inappropriate and unprofessional" comments made to a supervisor via e-mail messages. In attempting to overcome Pennsylvania's strict "at-will" employment rule, Smyth argued that his termination was in violation of the public policy of protecting against tortious invasions of privacy by employers.[64]

The *Smyth* court dismissed Smyth's complaint with prejudice, on the grounds that there was no reasonable expectation of privacy in e-mail communications voluntarily made by an employee to his supervisor over the company e-mail system, notwithstanding the company's assurances to the contrary.[65] The *Smyth* court noted that "[o]nce [Smyth] communicated the alleged unprofessional comments to a second person (his supervisor) over an e-mail system which was apparently utilized by the entire company, any reasonable expectation of privacy was lost."[66] The *Smyth* court, emphasizing the voluntary nature of Smyth's e-mail comments, noted that voluntary e-mail messages bore no similarity to either urinalysis or personal property searches of employees. It also noted that, even if Smyth had a reasonable expectation of privacy in his e-mail communications, Pillsbury's monitoring of these messages could not have been a substantial and highly offensive invasion of his

---

[61] *See* MORGAN STANLEY & CO., THE INTERNET REPORT, at 13-2 (1996) (defining commonly used Internet terms). "E-mail enables an individual to send an electronic message — generally akin to a note or letter — to another individual or to a group of addressees. The message is generally stored electronically, sometimes waiting for the recipient to check her "mailbox" and sometimes making its receipt known through some type of prompt. A mail exploder is a sort of e-mail group. Subscribers can send messages to a common e-mail address, which then forwards the message to the group's other subscribers. Newsgroups also serve groups of regular participants, but these postings may be read by others as well." *See Reno*, 521 U.S. __, 117 S. Ct. 2329, 138 L. Ed. 874, 884-85 (1997).

[62] *Smyth v. Pillsbury Co.*, 914 F. Supp. 97 (E.D. Pa. 1996).

[63] The Pillsbury Company had issued guidelines concerning the use of the company's e-mail system, repeatedly assuring employees that all e-mail communications would remain confidential and privileged and that e-mail communications could not be intercepted and used by the company as grounds for termination or reprimand of its employees. *Id.* at 98.

[64] *Id.* at 100. The court noted that the tort of "intrusion upon seclusion" required a showing of an intrusion which is "highly offensive" to a reasonable person. *Id.*

[65] *Id.* at 101. *See also Bourke v. Nissan Motor Corp.*, No. B068705 (Cal. Ct. App., July 26, 1993) (unreported decision) (summary judgment for defendant corporation, which monitored sexually explicit e-mail of an employee who was subsequently terminated by the corporation); *Shoars v. Epson America, Inc.*, No. B073243 (Cal. Ct. App.) (unreported decision), *review denied*, No. S040065, 1994 Cal. LEXIS 3670 (June 29, 1994) (finding no violations of the California wiretapping statute from eavesdropping on electronic communications).

[66] *Smyth*, 914 F. Supp. at 101.

privacy.[67] The Smyth court explained that Pillsbury's interest in "preventing inappropriate and unprofessional comments or even illegal activity over its e-mail system outweigh[ed] any privacy interest the employee may have in those comments."[68]

In *Bohach v. City of Reno*,[69] plaintiffs claimed violations of the Fourth Amendment and the federal Electronic Communications Privacy Act ("ECPA")[70] based upon monitoring by the Reno, Nevada police department of messages transmitted by the plaintiffs (police employees) over the department's "Alphapage" electronic messaging system.[71] The police department had stored and retrieved on its computer system the plaintiffs' objectionable messages.[72] The *Bohach* court found that the employees who sent electronic communications over the department's computer network, had no reasonable expectation of privacy in their communications, and were, therefore, not protected by the Fourth Amendment.[73] The court also rejected the employees' claims that by reading their electronic communications, the employer violated the ECPA because it found that reading the employee communications did not constitute "interception" within the meaning of the Act.[74]

There has been at least one case recognizing users' objective expectations of privacy in cyberspace in the criminal context of whether searches and seizures of computer data or e-mail by state or federal law enforcement or other government officials comply with the Fourth Amendment. In *United States v. Maxwell*,[75] an Air Force Court of Criminal Appeals addressed the validity under the Fourth Amendment of a warrantless search of anonymous e-mail messages and other information stored in computers of a bulletin board service provider, which resulted in federal pornography charges.[76] The search in question resulted in a colonel's dismissal from service.

Colonel Maxwell allegedly used his personal computer to receive and transport graphic depictions of child pornography and other obscene materials by means of anonymous "screen names" by sending electronic mail to other users of America Online's computer bulletin boards.[77] Another user informed the FBI and America Online ("AOL") of these activities, providing them with a list of screen names whose users were thought to be engaged in the transmission of child pornography. Following an FBI investigation, a search warrant was

---

[67] *Id.*

[68] *Id.*

[69] 932 F. Supp. 1232 (D. Nev. 1996).

[70] Electronic Communications Privacy Act of 1986, Pub. L. No. 99-508, 1986 U.S.C.C.A.N. (100 Stat.) 1848 (codified as amended at 18 U.S.C. §§ 2510-21 (Title I), 2701-11 (Title II)).

[71] *Id.* at 1233.

[72] *Id.* at 1234.

[73] *Id. at* 1234-35.

[74] *Id.* at 1236-37 (reviewing the Electronic Communications Privacy Act definition of an "interception").

[75] *United States v. Maxwell*, 42 M.J. 568 (A.F.C.C.A. 1995), *rev'd on other grounds*, 45 M.J. 406, 1996 CAAF LEXIS 116 (C.A.A.F. Nov. 21, 1996).

[76] *Id.* at 572-3.

[77] *Id.* at 573.

issued to find and seize the electronic mail of the users on the list of screen names, which included one of Colonel Maxwell's screen names.[78]

Anticipating execution of the warrant, employees of AOL designed software and searched its databases to extract the electronic mail information prior to the execution and presentment of the warrant.[79] After seizure of his home computers and files by military officials, Colonel Maxwell was tried, convicted, and court-martialed on the federal pornography charges.[80] On appeal, he argued that the seizure of electronic information from America Online's computers and from his personal computer was unlawful under the Fourth Amendment and should have been suppressed. A military judge examined the ECPA and concluded that, while Colonel Maxwell had a subjective expectation of privacy in his e-mail communications, he had no objective expectation of privacy because of the manner in which the transmissions were made and disseminated.[81]

Although the appeals court concluded that the search was valid because the warrants had been issued with probable cause, it disagreed with the military judge and ruled that Colonel Maxwell would have a reasonable objective expectation of privacy in e-mail transmissions, under certain circumstances.[82] The appeals court agreed that Colonel Maxwell may well have forfeited his right to privacy to any e-mail transmissions that were downloaded from the computer by another subscriber or removed by a private individual from America Online. It held however, that Colonel Maxwell maintained an objective expectation of privacy in any e-mail transmission he made so long as they were stored in America Online's computers.[83] The appeals court found compelling the fact that private e-mail transmissions to other users by means of individually assigned passwords

---

[78] *Id.*

[79] When the warrant was presented, an America Online official turned over approximately 13,000 pages of printed e-mail messages and 39 high density computer disks containing visual transmissions. *Id.* at 574. Although a transcription error was made in presenting the list of screen names for the warrant, America Online had used a proper list, which contained two of Colonel Maxwell's screen names. *Id.*

[80] *Id.* at 573.

[81] The judge based his conclusion on the following factors: (1) the e-mail could not be erased or recalled once it was dispatched and the user was powerless to prevent it being forwarded; (2) the e-mail messages were transferred to screen names rather than known third parties; and (3) the forwarding of messages to multiple individuals made the situation analogous to bulk mail. *Id.* at 576.

[82] *Id.* at 576 (so long as e-mail messages were stored in America Online's computers, Colonel Maxwell had a reasonable expectation of privacy in the messages). Colonel Maxwell appealed his convictions to the U.S. Court of Appeals for the Armed Forces, *see United States v. Maxwell*, 45 M.J. 406, 1996 CAAF LEXIS 116. The Court of Appeals affirmed the convictions of Colonel Maxwell on the federal obscenity and child pornography trafficking charges, but reversed Colonel Maxwell's convictions on the counts involving the communication of indecent language. *Id.* at *40-42. The Court of Appeals concluded that the results of the FBI's search and seizure of files under the screen name "Zirloc" were outside the scope of the warrant, and thus inadmissible under the Fourth Amendment. *Id.* at *42.

[83] *Id.* This finding was upheld by the Court of Appeals, which held that "under the circumstances, [as an AOL® subscriber, Colonel Maxwell] possessed a reasonable expectation of privacy, albeit a limited one, in the e-mail messages that he sent and/or received on AOL." *Maxwell*, 45 M.J. 406, 1996 CAAF LEXIS 116, *22. The Court cautioned that the reasonableness of this expectation of e-mail privacy diminishes as public access becomes more certain in cyberspace. The Court of Appeals noted:

  Drawing from [letter and telephone call] parallels, we can say that the transmitter of an e-mail message enjoys a reasonable expectation that police officials will not intercept the transmission without probable cause and a search warrant. However, once the transmissions are received by another persons, the transmitter no longer controls its destiny. In a sense, e-mail is like a letter. It is sent and lies sealed in the computer until the recipient opens his or her computer and retrieves the transmission. The sender enjoys a reasonable expectation that the initial transmission will not be intercepted by the police. The fact that an unauthorized "hacker" might intercept an e-mail does not diminish the legitimate expectation of privacy in any way.

  Id. at *26-27.

entailed "virtually no risk that the computer transmissions would be received by anyone other than the intended recipients," distinguishing e-mail messages from cordless telephone messages.[84]

In *Steve Jackson Games, Inc. v. United States Secret Service* ("*Games*"),[85] an action brought under the civil recovery provisions of the ECPA by the operators and users of a computer bulletin board service ("BBS"), a district court addressed the question of whether the seizure of stored electronic mail constituted an unlawful "interception" within the meaning of the ECPA. In *Games*, federal law enforcement officers discovered that a sensitive document belonging to a telecommunications company was available on a computer bulletin board service run by the plaintiff's corporation.[86] The Secret Service sought and received a warrant to search the premises of the plaintiff, based on its belief that an employee of the defendant had been involved in the theft and uploading of the document and related codebreaking activity.[87] The Secret Service seized the computer that operated the BBS, 162 items of unread e-mail of a user contained on the hard drives of the computer, as well as other stored data (including a draft book intended for publication, and magazine articles).[88]

Following a bench trial, the district court found that the Secret Service had read all of the seized e-mails, including private e-mails not mentioned in the warrant or affidavits, and had also deleted some of the seized files.[89] The court found that the seizure and later review of the e-mail did not constitute the unlawful "interception" of the private e-mails under Title I of the ECPA.[90] The court, however, did find that the Secret Service's conduct violated Title II of the ECPA, because its agents had unlawfully disclosed the contents of stored electronic communications in violation of 18 U.S.C. § 2703 and they could not rely upon the good faith exception contained in Title II of the ECPA.[91] The plaintiffs appealed the holding regarding Title I liability.

The Fifth Circuit affirmed,[92] holding that the seizure of a computer used to operate a computer bulletin board system containing private e-mail sent to and stored by the bulletin board service, but not read or retrieved by the intended recipients, did not constitute an unlawful "intercept" under Title I of the ECPA.[93] The Fifth Circuit found that the plain language of the statute and its legislative history supported the conclusion that

---

[84] *Id.* at *27.

[85] *Steve Jackson Games, Inc. v. United States Secret Serv.*, 816 F. Supp. 432 (W.D. Tex. 1993), *aff'd*, 36 F.3d 457 (5th Cir. 1994) [hereinafter *Games I*]. *See generally* Gregory L. Brown, *Steve Jackson Games, Inc. v. United States Secret Service: Seizure of Stored Electronic Mail is Not an "Interception" Under the Federal Wiretap Act*, 69 TUL. L. REV. 1381 (1995).

[86] *Games I*, 816 F. Supp. at 435.

[87] *Id.* at 436.

[88] *Id.* at 439-40.

[89] *Id.* at 438.

[90] *Id.* at 441-42.

[91] *Id.* at 443. The court awarded $1,000 in statutory damages, $195,000 in attorneys fees, and $57,000 in costs to the plaintiffs.

[92] *Steve Jackson Games, Inc. v. United States Secret Serv.*, 36 F.3d 457 (5th Cir. 1994) [hereinafter *Games II*].

[93] *Id.* at 460-61. *See also Seizure of Stored Electronic Communications Upheld*, COMPUTER L. STRATEGIST, Vol. XI. No. 7, at 7 (discussing the *Games II* holding).

Congress did not intend Title I to apply to "interceptions" of electronic communications when those communications are in "electronic storage," within the meaning of the applicable provisions of the ECPA.[94]

§ 12.05 PUBLIC AND PRIVATE EFFORTS TO MEET PRIVACY EXPECTATIONS

[1] GOVERNMENT ONLINE PRIVACY INITIATIVES

[a] National Information Infrastructure Task Force Privacy Principles. In 1993, President Clinton and Vice President Gore established the National Information Infrastructure Task Force ("NIITF") to "articulate and implement" the Clinton Administration's vision for the National Information Infrastructure ("NII").[95] High-level representatives of the federal agencies playing a major role in the development and application of information and telecommunications technologies serve on the NIITF.[96]

The NIITF's security report identified five primary expectations held by NII users.[97] NII users expect to have: (i) the ability to control who sees (or cannot see) their information and under what terms, (ii) the ability to know with whom they are communicating, (iii) the ability to know that information stored or transmitted is unaltered, (iv) the ability to know when information and communication services will (and will not) be available, and (v) the ability to block unwanted information or intrusions. These expectations have proved elusive in practice.[98] For example, there has been an explosion of Internet e-mail and marketing firms that direct unsolicited e-mail towards subscribers of Internet service providers ("ISPs").[99] In addition, the widespread use of "cookies," a type of text file sent by a website to the web browser that resides on an individual's hard drive

---

[94] *Games II,* 36 F.3d at 461.

[95] The President's 1993 AGENDA FOR ACTION defined the NII as a "seamless web of communications networks, computers, databases, and consumer electronics that will put vast amounts of information at users' fingertips." *See* NATIONAL INFORMATION INFRASTRUCTURE: AGENDA FOR ACTION, *available at* (visited June 9, 1997) <http://sunsite.nuc.edu/nii/NII-Executive-Summary.html>.

[96] See generally the web page of NIITF (visited June 9, 1997) <http://www.iitf.nist.gov/about.html>. William M. Daley, the Secretary of Commerce, chairs the NIITF. In addition to the NIITF, the Clinton Administration has established the U.S. Advisory Council on the NII, which consists of representatives from industry, labor, state and local governments, and public interest groups. Through Executive Order No. 12864, the President established an Advisory Council on the National Information Infrastructure. *See* Exec. Order No. 12864, 3 C.F.R. pt. 634 (1994). The Advisory Council advises the Secretary of Commerce on issues relating to the NII, including security and privacy issues. *See generally* NII SECURITY: THE FEDERAL ROLE (1995) *available at* <http://www.IITF.nist.gov/sif/sif-pub.html>.

[97] *See* Draft Security Tenets for the National Information Infrastructure, 60 Fed. Reg. 8100 (1995) [hereinafter Draft Security Tenets].

[98] *Id.* The Draft Security Tenets noted that none of the five principles could or should be absolute. Rather, they recognized that there exist valid societal reasons to condition each of the tenets under appropriate circumstances and that each tenet requires NII participants to take responsibility for constructing the rules under which they will exchange information on the NII.

[99] Litigation involving such firms and Internet service providers ("ISPs") has been growing. *See* David Hilzenrath, *Judge Rules AOL Can Block Direct-Marketing Firm's Ads,* WASH. POST, Nov. 5, 1996, at C1 (describing how America Online, a major ISP, obtained an injunction against the efforts of a "junk mail" firm to send thousands of e-mail messages daily to AOL® subscribers). *See also Cyber Promotions, Inc. v. America Online, Inc.,* 948 F. Supp. 436 (E.D. Pa. 1996); *Cyber Promotions, Inc. v. America Online, Inc.,* 948 F. Supp. 456 (E.D. Pa. 1996) (subsequent proceedings); *Compuserve Inc. v. Cyber Promotions, Inc.,* 962 F. Supp 1015 (S.D. Ohio 1997) (preliminary injunction granted to Compuserve, another large ISP). For more information on the litigation between America Online and Cyber Promotions, see *infra* notes 528-36 and the accompanying text.

and tracks data on the individual, indicates that many types of information disclosures related to the Internet and use of the World Wide Web are involuntary.[100]

The NIITF's Privacy Working Group works to develop proposals to protect individual privacy in the face of the rapid increase in the collection, storage, and dissemination of personal data in electronic form. In June 1995, the Privacy Working Group developed a set of privacy principles, entitled the "Principles for Providing and Using Personal Information" ("Privacy Principles"), to guide the promotion and adoption of privacy policies and standards for both government and the private sector.[101]

The Privacy Principles "reflect a recognition that the nature of the electronic medium itself must shape development of a workable privacy policy."[102] They were premised upon several widely understood truths about the "information marketplace" in the United States. First, the private sector now rivals the government in acquiring and using personal data. Second, individuals actively participating in the Internet will create volumes of data containing the content of communications as well as transactional data. Third, the transport vehicles of personal information — the networks — are vulnerable to abuse, thus the security of the networks are critical to the Internet's future success. Finally, the rapidly evolving information environment makes it difficult to apply existing ethics rules, even ones that are well understood and accepted, when dealing with tangible records and documents.

The Privacy Principles identified three fundamental principles — information privacy, information integrity, and information quality — that should guide all uses of personal information on the NII.[103] In addition, the Privacy Principles include ten core concepts:

- Personal information should be acquired, disclosed, and used only in ways that respect an individual's privacy.

- Personal information should not be improperly altered or destroyed.

- Personal information should be accurate, timely, complete, and relevant for the purpose for which it is provided and used.

- Information users should assess the impact on privacy in deciding whether to acquire, disclose, or use personal information and acquire and keep only information reasonably expected to support current or planned activities.

---

[100] The term "cookies" generally refers to data files that allow a website operator or advertiser to record the trail of sites that a person visits as well as online purchases, or other transaction information. *See, e.g., Big Brother Meets the Cookie Monster*, MACUSER, July 1997, at 96, 99; Julia Angwin, *Online 'Cookies' May Not Be So Sweet*, DENVER POST, Apr. 14, 1997, at E9.

[101] *See* NIITF PRIVACY WORKING GROUP, PRIVACY AND THE NATIONAL INFORMATION INFRASTRUCTURE TASK FORCE: PRINCIPLES FOR PROVIDING AND USING PERSONAL INFORMATION (1995) [hereinafter NIITF PRIVACY PRINCIPLES], *available at* (visited June 9, 1997) <http://www.IITF.nist.gov/ipc/ipc-pub.html>.

[102] NIITF 1997 DRAFT REPORT, *supra* note 11, at 3.

[103] NIITF PRIVACY PRINCIPLES, *supra* note 101, at 4.

- Information users who collect personal information directly from the individual should provide adequate, relevant information about: why they are collecting the information; what the information is expected to be used for; what steps will be taken to protect its confidentiality, integrity, and quality; the consequences of providing or withholding information; and any rights of redress.

- Information users should use appropriate technical and managerial controls to protect the confidentiality and integrity of personal information.

- Information users should not use personal information in ways that are incompatible with the individual's understanding of how it will be used, unless there is a compelling public interest for such use.

- Information users should educate themselves and the public about how information privacy can be maintained.

- Individuals should be able to safeguard their own privacy by having: a means to obtain their personal information and to correct their personal information that lacks sufficient quality to ensure fairness in its use; the opportunity to use appropriate technical controls, such as encryption, to protect the confidentiality and integrity of communications and transactions; and the opportunity to remain anonymous, when appropriate.

- Individuals should, as appropriate, have a means of redress if harmed by an improper disclosure or use of personal information.[104]

The NIITF noted that its Privacy Principles, although lacking the force of law and not creating any substantive legal rights, should be used by both providers and users of information on the NII to strike a meaningful balance between "abstract concepts and a detailed code."[105] In trying to achieve the balance between the privacy rights of individuals and the legitimate commercial and governmental uses of personal information, the NIITF recommended consideration of several factors, including the extent to which the provision of information is voluntary, the sensitivity of the information, the potential harm of its disclosure, and the cost and effort required to protect against harmful disclosures of individuals' personal information.[106]

[b] NIITF April 1997 Report. In April 1997, the NIITF Privacy Working Group published a draft paper entitled "Options for Promoting Privacy on the National Information Infrastructure" ("NIITF 1997 Draft Report").[107] The NIITF 1997 Draft Report is centered around a crucial, but complex, question: what is the best mechanism and mix of government and private sector initiatives to balance the informational needs of government, commerce, and individuals on the Internet, keeping in mind the value placed upon both the free

---

[104] *Id.* at 5-10.

[105] *Id.* at 2.

[106] *Id.*

[107] The NIITF 1997 DRAFT REPORT, *supra* note 11, is available at the NIITF's website, <http://www.IITF.nist.gov/ipc/privacy.htm>.

flow of information and the protection of consumer information privacy? The NIITF 1997 Draft Report provides a useful overview of United States privacy laws and the structure and makeup of the information marketplace. It also considers a variety of industry efforts at self-regulation to carry out the NIITF's Privacy Principles. Most importantly, the NIITF 1997 Draft Report identifies and evaluates four separate options for government and private sector action to attain the optimal balance of information privacy and freedom of information in the electronic marketplace. The NIITF 1997 Draft Report evaluated each of these four options in detail, identifying the potential advantages and drawbacks of each approach.

The first option is to continue to support and improve upon the current "sectoral" approach to regulating and protecting privacy in the United States. By sectoral approach, the NIITF 1997 Draft Report refers to the co-extensive efforts of federal and state governments, as well as private industry, to identify privacy concerns of American consumers and to develop privacy laws, standards, and policies designed to address these concerns.[108] Under this approach, the NIITF would work with government agencies, industry, and others, to foster the growth of privacy awareness and the development of new privacy standards.[109] The remaining three options discussed in the NIITF 1997 Draft Report involve the creation of a federal privacy agency, with varying powers, composition, and mandates.

Under the second option, the NIITF discusses whether it would be advisable to create a federal privacy agency to: (i) drive development of privacy policies; and (ii) "direct traffic" for the various privacy initiatives now underway in the private sector.[110] This agency could be created as an executive branch agency, like the Environmental Protection Agency, or an independent regulatory body, like the FRB or the Securities and Exchange Commission, with authority to exercise a broad range of powers to initiate, monitor, and coordinate the regulation of one or more sectors of the economy, and to implement, promulgate, and enforce privacy regulations in the U.S. economy. Under a third option, a federal privacy agency could be established without regulatory authority, perhaps by an Executive Order of the President.[111] Finally, the Draft Report considers the option of creating a non-governmental or advisory privacy body, like the National Security Telecommunications Advisory Committee, which would be able to function in either (or both) the private or public sectors.[112] An advisory privacy agency would offer advice to government agencies and the private sector, perhaps assisting both sectors in compliance with the NIITF's privacy principles.[113]

[c] Federal Trade Commission Privacy Initiatives. During the past several years, the Federal Trade Commission ("FTC") has begun to take a leading role among federal agencies in scrutinizing the privacy and

---

[108] As the NIITF 1997 DRAFT REPORT notes, however, the "sectoral" approach is not without its critics. *See* NIITF 1997 DRAFT REPORT, *supra* note 11, at 25-26 (listing criticisms, and discussing the European approach to privacy regulation).

[109] *Id.* at 26-29. The NIITF 1997 DRAFT REPORT also identifies several concrete steps, including congressional action to adopt the Privacy Principles as the policy of the federal government, to take the lead in the enhanced sectoral approach. *Id.* at 28.

[110] *Id.* at 29-31.

[111] *Id.* at 31-34.

[112] *Id.* at 34-35.

[113] *Id.* at 35.

confidentiality concerns associated with electronic commerce and use of the Internet. The FTC's Bureau of Consumer Protection undertook a Consumer Privacy Initiative in June 1995 to educate consumers and businesses about the use of personal and financial information on the Internet. The FTC held a two-day set of hearings in June 1996 to address consumer information and privacy issues related to the Internet, interactive computer services, and participants in the data marketplace.[114]

The FTC's June 1996 hearings resulted in the publication in December 1996 of an FTC staff report entitled the "Public Workshop on Consumer Privacy on the Global Information Infrastructure" ("FTC Staff Report").[115] The FTC Staff Report concluded that notice, access, choice, and security are recognized as necessary for the development of fair information practices online, and are the crucial issues for participants in the online marketplace to address in the near future. After surveying and describing the current state of the information marketplace, the FTC Staff Report highlighted the potential for technological solutions, combined with industry self-regulation, to address online privacy concerns.[116] Finally, the FTC Staff Report considered the special concerns raised by the online gathering of data from and about children.

In June 1997, the FTC held another set of hearings in Washington, D.C., on a broad range of privacy issues.[117] Over the course of a two-day period, the FTC conducted panel discussions with a variety of industry participants, privacy advocates, and other experts. Topics addressed during the June 1997 hearings included: (i) the operation and sources of information regarding consumers of proprietary computer databases, such as LEXIS/NEXIS, the National Credit Information Network, and Metromail Corp.; (ii) consumers' views on online privacy; (iii) industry self-regulation; (iv) industry and consumer initiatives for protecting children's privacy online; and (v) the FTC's role in supervising privacy developments and enforcement efforts.

In July 1997, the FTC issued a letter ruling on the permissible use of online data collection by merchants on the World Wide Web who gather such information from children.[118] In its letter, the FTC concluded that many Internet websites collect personal information from children without proper disclosure of the practice to their parents.[119] The FTC staff concluded that it would likely constitute an unfair practice in violation of Section 5 of the Federal Trade Commission Act to collect personally identifiable information (such as name, e-mail address, home address, or phone number) from children and sell or otherwise disclose such identifiable

---

[114] Federal Trade Commission, *Public Workshop on Consumer Privacy on the Global Information Infrastructure,* June 4-5, 1996. Copies of testimony are available at the FTC's website, (visited Sept. 16, 1997) <http://www.ftc.gov/WWW/bcp/privacy 2/index.html>.

[115] *See* FEDERAL TRADE COMMISSION, PUBLIC WORKSHOP ON CONSUMER PRIVACY ON THE GLOBAL INFORMATION INFRASTRUCTURE [hereinafter FTC STAFF REPORT], *available at* (visited June 27, 1997) <http://www.ftc.gov/ WWW/reports/privacy/privacy1.htm>.

[116] *Id.* at 6. The FTC noted that recent Harris polls have indicated that 85% of Americans polled are concerned about privacy and emerging threats to their personal privacy from online activities.

[117] *See* Federal Trade Commission, *Public Workshop on Consumer Information Privacy*, June 10-11, 1997, *available at* (visited Sept. 16, 1997) <http://www.ftc.gov/WWW/bcp/privacy 2/index.html>.

[118] *See* Letter from Jodie Bernstein, Director of the FTC Bureau of Consumer Protection, to the Center for Media Education (July 15, 1997) [hereinafter FTC Letter]; Rajiv Chandrasekaran, *FTC Rules on Online Data Collection*, WASH. POST, July 17, 1997, at C3.

[119] The FTC gave the example of KidsCom™, a website operated by the KidsCom Company, which was soliciting the following information online from children: name, sex, birthday, e-mail address, home address, number of family members and grade. FTC Letter, *supra* note 118, at 2. KidsCom also was making such information available to third parties on an aggregate basis. *Id.* at 3.

information to third parties without providing parents with adequate notice, as described above, and an opportunity to control the collection and use of the information. The FTC warned site operators to provide clear notices on their websites of their information gathering practices and also stated that such sites must obtain parental consent before releasing personal information to third parties.[120] Such notice, in the FTC's view, should contain: (i) who is collecting the personally identifiable information; (ii) what information is being collected; (iii) its intended use(s); (iv) to whom and in what form it will be disclosed to third parties; and (v) the means by which parents may prevent the retention, use, or disclosure of such information.[121]

In December 1997, fourteen credit information companies and individual reference services (collectively, the "IRSG") agreed to voluntarily place limits upon the availability of personally identifiable information online.[122] In the wake of the announcement of the IRSG, the FTC published its staff report, entitled "Individual Reference Services: A Report to Congress," recommending that Congress not enact new legislation at this time regarding consumer privacy and the online gathering, storage, or dissemination of personally identifiable information.[123] In the report, the FTC also noted that a number of important issues concerning consumers' access to public information obtained or compiled by IRSG members remain to be addressed by both the private sector and government.[124]

[d] Privacy and Confidentiality Guidelines of Federal Bank Regulatory Agencies. As discussed above, privacy and confidentiality concerns are a "front burner" issue for Americans today.[125] Recent commentary on the related issues of online privacy and electronic commerce has indicated that the banking and financial service industries must increasingly address consumer privacy issues from a compliance perspective.[126] Until recently, privacy issues have not been a particular focus of bank examiners and regulators.[127] The federal bank regulatory agencies, however, have increasingly begun to develop and articulate policies regarding the obligations of regulated entities with regard to consumer privacy.

---

[120] *See* Chandrasekaran, *supra* note 118, at C3. The FTC declined to take enforcement action against KidsCom, because of several modifications KidsCom made to its site, and because KidsCom does not release personally identifiable information to third parties without prior parental approval. FTC Letter, *supra* note 118, at 7.

[121] FTC Letter, *supra* note 118, at 4.

[122] *See Information Industry Voluntarily Agrees to Stronger Protections for Consumers*, FTC Press Release, Dec. 17, 1997; John Simons, *Credit Companies Agree to Set Limits for OnLine Data*, WALL ST. J., Dec. 18, 1997, at B10.

[123] *See* Federal Trade Commission, *Individual Reference Services: A Report to Congress*, December 1997, at i-ii, *available at* <http://www.ftc.gov>.

[124] *Id.* at 31-32. Such issues include the frequency of database errors, the ability of consumers to identify and correct such errors, and the availability of audit trails of the precise records accessed by each user.

[125] *See, e.g.*, Nina Bernstein, *The Erosion of Privacy — a Special Report — Personal Files Via Computer Offer Money and Pose Threat*, N.Y. TIMES, June 12, 1997, at A1 (describing the use of Texas prison inmates to process consumer surveys for Metromail Corp., a leading seller of direct marketing information, which resulted in a lawsuit by a woman against Metromail Corp. for violations of her privacy after an inmate who was a convicted rapist sent her sexually explicit letters containing the woman's personal information). The class action suit against Metromail Corp., which reportedly maintains a database containing up to 40 items of personal data on over 85 million Americans, is ongoing. *See* Saul Hansell, *Getting to Know You*, INSTITUTIONAL INVESTOR, June 1991, at 71; Nancy Millman, *Questionable Data Sale to Hinder Metromail IPO? R.R. Donnelly Says Unit No Longer Fits In*, CHI. TRIB., June 4, 1996, at 1.

[126] *See* JoAnn S. Barefoot, *The Next Compliance Controversy: Privacy*, ABA BANKING J., Jan. 1997, at 22; Lisa Fickenscher, *Passive Banks Seen Inviting Rules on Data Privacy*, AM. BANKER, Mar. 27, 1996, at 16; *Q&A: Privacy Advocate Sees Value in Anonymity*, AM. BANKER - FUTURE BANKING, Oct. 21, 1996, at 14A (interview with Marc Rotenberg, Director of the Electronic Privacy Information Center).

[127] These concerns, however, have been the subject matter of litigation by consumers. *See* Section 12.03, and cases cited therein.

[e] Board of Governors of the Federal Reserve System. In assessing the likelihood that the provision of banking and financial services over the Internet would pose a threat to the safety and soundness of banks, the Board of Governors of the Federal Reserve System ("FRB"), in one instance, indicated that it expects banking organizations to consider carefully the risks associated with Internet banking and urged banking organizations to "evaluate carefully whether those risks are consistent with their policies relating to the security of customer information and other data."[128] The FRB also made clear that it expects financial institutions, as part of this evaluation, to "implement any modifications to their information security procedures and controls that appear necessary or appropriate in light of the risks associated with Internet-based services."[129]

Regulation E, promulgated by the FRB under the Electronic Fund Transfer Act of 1978 ("EFTA"),[130] mandates that financial institutions disclose to consumers their policies regarding the confidentiality of the consumer's personal information.[131] The regulation requires the financial institution to disclose, in general terms, the situations in which, and the persons or entities to whom, it ordinarily will disclose to third parties consumer information relating to an account from which electronic fund transfers ("EFTs") are permitted, not just information concerning the EFTs themselves.[132] The Appendix to Regulation E indicates that at least four types of disclosures are within the ordinary course of business:

- When disclosure is necessary for completing an electronic fund transfer;

- In order to verify the existence and condition of a consumer's account for a third party, such as a credit bureau or merchant;

- In order to comply with governmental or court orders; or

- When the consumer gives consent.[133]

The Official Staff Commentary to Regulation E also indicates that the term "third parties" for purposes of Section 205.9 includes affiliates of the financial institution, such as subsidiaries of the same holding company.[134] Once a financial institution has disclosed its policies concerning the use of consumer information, amendments to such policies must take into account applicable requirements for notifying customers.[135]

---

[128] *Cardinal Bancshares, Inc.*, 82 FED. RESERVE BULL. 674, 676 (July 1996).

[129] *Id.* at 676 n.15.

[130] Pub. L. No. 95-630, tit. XX, 1978 U.S.C.C.A.N. (92 Stat.) 3728 (codified at 15 U.S.C. §§ 1693-1693r).

[131] 12 C.F.R. § 205.7(b)(9). Other federal laws contain similar notification requirements. *See, e.g.*, The Privacy Act of 1974, 5 U.S.C. § 552a(e)(3) (requiring that Federal agencies advise the subjects of federal records of the intended use of such records), Cable Communications Policy Act of 1984, 47 U.S.C. § 551(a) (entitling cable subscribers to an annual notice of the cable company's information practices).

[132] Electronic Fund Transfers, 61 Fed. Reg. 19,678, 19,690 (1996) (to be codified at 12 C.F.R. pt. 205). *See also* L. RICHARD FISCHER, THE LAW OF FINANCIAL PRIVACY: A COMPLIANCE GUIDE, ¶ 6.02[1], at 6-4 (2d ed. 1991 & Supp. 1995).

[133] 12 C.F.R. § 205, app. A, § A(7). Neither the EFTA nor Regulation E prevent financial institutions from adopting their own definitions of the "ordinary course of business." *See* FISCHER, *supra* note 132, ¶ 6.02[1], at 6-4.

[134] *See* Electronic Funds Transfers, 61 Fed. Reg. 19,678, 19,690 (1996) (codified at 12 C.F.R. pt. 205, supp. I).

[135] *See* FISCHER, *supra* note 132, ¶ 6.02[1], at 6-5.

Outside its bank supervisory role, the FRB recently issued a study on financial privacy issues required by the Consumer Credit Reporting Reform Act of 1996.[136] In this legislation, Congress instructed the FRB to conduct a study to address a number of issues: (i) whether customer identifying information is widely available in the United States; (ii) whether that information can be used to commit financial fraud; and (iii) whether there is an undue risk of loss to insured depository institutions resulting from such financial fraud.[137]

In reviewing the current information marketplace, the FRB report noted that participants in both the primary and secondary information markets are regularly engaged in the gathering and dissemination of consumer-identifying personal information; but that there are differences as to what types of information are "sensitive."[138] The report also stressed that an increase in the availability of consumer information has resulted in an increase in instances of "identity theft."[139]

Among the conclusions that the FRB reached are that: (i) information about consumers is widely available from both government and private sources; (ii) few legal constraints exist regarding the collection, use, and dissemination of information about individuals; (iii) such information can be used to facilitate identity theft and financial fraud, but that (iv) at present, the risk of loss from such fraud does not pose a significant risk to insured depository institutions.[140]

[f] Office of the Comptroller of the Currency. Other federal bank regulatory agencies have also been emphasizing the importance of maintaining the confidentiality of consumers' personal financial information. For example, in 1994 the Office of the Comptroller of the Currency ("OCC") addressed the issue of a national bank's use of sensitive customer financial information in the context of the sale of annuities and other investment products. In Bulletin No. 94-13, the OCC stated that:

> Examiners should determine that bank customer information policies address the permissible uses of such information for any purpose associated with bank-related retail investment sales activity. In particular, if the bank intends to use customer lists to telephone depositors whose certificates of deposit are due to mature to inform them about alternative investment products, the policies should outline steps the bank will take to avoid confusing customers as to the risks associated with nondeposit investment products, including their uninsured nature.
>
> Banks may also supply customer information lists to a third party vendor. Supplying such information should only occur, however, after bank management has evaluated

---

[136] FRB CONSUMER REPORT, *supra* note 14, at 2.

[137] *Id.* at 1.

[138] *Id.* at 14.

[139] *Id.*

[140] *Id.* at 20-21.

steps the third party is taking to avoid confusing customers and after determining such steps are consistent with bank policy. Bank management also may wish to consider obtaining a legal opinion concerning the bank's authority to share customer information with third parties.[141]

Most recently, the OCC has taken the following approach to bank customer privacy, in the context of national bank annuities sales activities. In its Advisory Letter 96-8, the OCC noted that:

> [i]n the course of providing banking and other services, banks will acquire various types of financial and personal information about their customers. Bank management should be sensitive to privacy expectations of the bank's customers regarding this information. Management should take appropriate internal measures to safeguard the security of customer information as well as developing internal policies on the use of customer information. These considerations apply generally to all aspects of a bank's operations. Insurance and annuity sales activities are but one context in which questions regarding the use and sharing of customer information arise. Nor are banks unique in facing issues relating to customer privacy.

> Banks' policies on use of customer information should also recognize that different types of information can present different degrees of sensitivity from a customer perspective. Information of an especially personal nature, such as information regarding the health or physical well-being of a customer, may be viewed as particularly sensitive and thus warrant safeguards or restrictions under the bank's policies.[142]

[g] Federal Home Loan Bank Board and the Office of Thrift Supervision. In addition to the statements of the OCC and the FRB, the Federal Home Loan Bank Board ("FHLBB"), a former regulator of the savings and loan industry (now regulated by the Office of Thrift Supervision ("OTS")) adopted a rule in 1989 governing the release of customer financial information by federally-chartered savings associations which had a lengthy regulatory history.

In 1987, as part of its efforts to address a range of corporate governance issues for federally chartered thrifts, the FHLBB proposed a rule pursuant to which third parties would be prohibited from obtaining, inspecting, or copying any books or records of a federal savings association containing: (1) a list of depositors or borrowers from the thrift; (2) their addresses; (3) individual deposit or loan balances; or (4) any data from which such information could be reasonably constructed.[143]

---

[141] *Retail Nondeposit Investment Sales Examination Procedures*, OCC Bull. No. 94-13, at 3-4 (Feb. 24, 1994) (Insert for the Handbook for National Bank Examiners).

[142] *Guidance to National Banks on Insurance and Annuity Sales Activities*, OCC AL 96-8, at 11-12 (Oct. 8, 1996).

[143] *See* Federal Home Loan Bank Board, Corporate Governance, Parts III and IV, 52 Fed. Reg. 25,876, 25,883 (1987) (to be codified at 12 C.F.R. pt. 545).

In February 1989, the FHLBB withdrew the Corporate Governance proposal and substituted a proposed rule permitting broader disclosure of customer financial identifying information by federally-chartered thrifts.[144] This proposal distinguished customer identification information (*i.e.*, names and addresses) from customer financial information (information regarding balances or transactional information related to customer deposit or other accounts).[145] Under the proposed rule, thrifts could, unless prohibited by a customer in writing, release customer identification information to third parties, provided that such disclosure consisted of a complete list of such customers.[146] Thrifts were prohibited, however, with certain exceptions, from disclosing customer records to third parties in the absence of the customer's written authorization permitting such disclosure.[147]

The FHLBB's proposed rule met with stiff opposition from the thrift industry.[148] After receiving numerous comments, the FHLBB modified the proposed rule on customer financial records, to strike a "more reasonable balance between the privacy concerns of the customers and the business needs of federal associations."[149] Under the revised rule, federal savings associations were permitted to disclose certain "customer identification" information to any subsidiary or service corporation of the federal association, as long as the customers of the association had been previously notified by the association of their right to object to the release of their information and were given a reasonable time within which to notify the association of their objection to such release.[150]

The amended rule also permitted federal associations to disclose to third parties "customer information" (*i.e.*, a customer's name and address, plus deposit, account, and transaction information), if such information was contained in public records maintained by governmental entities. Finally, the rule permitted federal associations to disclose to third parties this broader type of "customer information" if the customer was provided with a detailed "informed consent form" which notified the customer of their "opt-out" right and contained a description of the types of organizations to which the information would be disclosed, and the applicable time periods of such disclosure.[151]

---

[144] *See* Federal Home Loan Bank Board, Release of Customer Financial Records by Federal Associations, 54 Fed. Reg. 5629, 5632 (1989) (proposing new 12 C.F.R. § 545.132 "disclosure of customer records").

[145] *Id.* at 5632.

[146] *Id.* at 5635 (to be codified at 12 C.F.R. § 545.132(c)).

[147] *Id.* (to be codified at 12 C.F.R. § 545.132(e)(1)). The FHLBB indicated that the consent had to be procured in advance from the customer in a "timely manner." *Id.*

[148] *See* Federal Home Loan Bank Board, Release of Customer Financial Records by Federal Associations, 54 Fed. Reg. 33,859, 33,861-62 (1989) (discussing the negative comments from the thrift industry).

[149] *Id.* at 33,862. The final FHLBB rule took effect on December 15, 1989.

[150] *Id.* at 33,868 (including a new proposal for 12 C.F.R. § 545.132, "disclosure of customer records"). The amended rule also provided enumerated exceptions to the restrictions on disclosure in instances of, for example, a valid court order or after the customer's affirmative written consent. *Id.* at 33,869.

[151] *Id.* at 33,869 (including 12 C.F.R. § 545.132(f)). The rule required the association to wait fifteen days after the mailing of the customer consent form to the customer, provided the disclosures were made with respect to only those customers who did not object to the disclosures. *Id.* at 33,868.

In August 1990, the OTS removed the regulation and announced its intention to promulgate its own rule relating to the release of customer financial information.[152] In September 1992, the OTS announced that it did not intend to propose a replacement for the prior regulation, in light of the fact that such a regulation "would not significantly further OTS policies and would duplicate state law."[153]

The OTS noted the importance of computer and customer data security in a 1995 order approving a federal savings institution's Internet operations.[154] In October 1997, the OTS proposed amendments designed to streamline and update its regulations relating to electronic operations of federal savings associations.[155] Under proposed 12 C.F.R. § 545.144, a federal savings association "should adopt standards and policies that are designed to ensure secure operations" and "implement security measures adequate to prevent unauthorized access to its records and its customers' records."[156]

[h] Other Agencies; Self-Regulatory Organizations. On September 11, 1997, Department of Health and Human Services ("HHS") Secretary Donna Shalala released a report to Congress, pursuant to Section 264 of the Health Insurance Portability and Accountability Act of 1996, recommending the enactment of federal medical privacy legislation. The recommendations of HHS are included in its report, "Confidentiality of Individually-Identifiable Health Information," submitted to a number of House and Senate committees.[157] The report is intended to assist the various congressional committees in drafting a comprehensive measure to protect the privacy of health care information and medical records, to guarantee to consumers the right to inspect their records, and to punish unauthorized disclosures of personal health data by hospitals, insurers, health plans, drug companies, or other third parties.[158] The HHS recommendations center upon five principles: boundaries, security, consumer control, accountability, and public responsibility. The recommendations, however, have been met with criticism by consumer groups.[159]

One securities self-regulator organization has recently addressed the issue of the use of customer financial information by its member organizations. In March 1997, NASD Regulation, Inc. requested comment on new National Association of Securities Dealers ("NASD") Rule 3121 that would govern NASD members' use

---

[152] *See* Release of Customer Financial Records by Federal Associations, 55 Fed. Reg. 34,698 (1990) (rescinding the newly adopted rule).

[153] *See* Regulatory Review, 57 Fed. Reg. 40,350, 40,354 (1992).

[154] *See Security First Network Bank, FSB*, OTS Order No. 95-88 (May 8, 1995) (requiring applicant to provide assurances of adequate security over the Internet, including adequate encryption and independent testing of computer network vulnerabilities).

[155] *See* Electronic Operations, 62 Fed. Reg. 51,817, 51,819 (1997) (to be codified at 12 C.F.R. § 545.144) (noting the need for adequate security measures, but proposing not to "codify static security requirements"); *see also* Dean Anason, *OTS Rule Would Give a Free Hand in Electronic Banking*, AM. BANKER, Oct. 2, 1997, at 2.

[156] Electronic Operations, 62 Fed. Reg. at 51,819 (1997).

[157] *See* HEALTH AND HUMAN SERVICES, CONFIDENTIALITY OF INDIVIDUALLY-IDENTIFIABLE HEALTH INFORMATION (Sept. 1997), *available at* (visited Jan. 7, 1998) <http://aspe.os.dhhs.gov/admnsimp/pvcrec0.htm> [hereinafter HHS REPORT].

[158] *Health Care Portability and Accountability: Hearing Before the Senate Comm. On Labor and Human Services*, 105th Cong. (1997) (testimony of Donna Shalala, Secretary of HHS), *available at* the HHS website, (visited Jan. 6, 1998) <http://www.hhs.gov>.

[159] *See* American Civil Liberties Union, *Clinton Privacy Recommendations Open Medical Records to Desktop Snooping*, Press Release, Sept. 11, 1997 (arguing that the recommendations do not go far enough to prevent the widespread storage of medical data in databases, and objecting to the use of "unique health identifiers," a type of national medical I.D. which includes information obtained from individuals' medical records).

and release of customer confidential financial information.[160] The Rule would apply to all members that use customer "confidential financial information"[161] obtained from a "business affiliate,"[162] including financial institutions, insurance companies, finance companies; and to members who release customer confidential financial information to any third party, whether affiliated or unaffiliated. Under proposed Rule 3121, a member would be generally prohibited from releasing such information without a customer's prior informed written consent.[163] The Rule may, however, permit members to disclose confidential financial information to government agencies, regulatory bodies, or courts.[164]

[2] BANKING INDUSTRY PRIVACY AND CONFIDENTIALITY GUIDELINES

Increasingly, participants in the banking and financial services industries (such as banks and credit card issuers), as well as technology firms and trade associations, are publicizing their commitment to protect the privacy rights of consumers, including those engaging in online financial transactions. Efforts by the banking and financial services industries have focused on voluntary privacy codes and industry self-regulation, an approach that is designed to promote consumer confidence and discourage government regulation of electronic commerce and the Internet. The Clinton Administration strongly encouraged this approach in its recent report on electronic commerce.[165]

Many of the industry efforts at self-regulation attempt to address a number of core principles that are typically considered to make up model "fair information" practices. These include: (i) collection principles, which operate to limit the collection of personal information to that which is genuinely necessary;

---

[160] Nat'l Ass'n of Securities Dealers, *Use and Release of Confidential Financial Information*, 1997 Notice to Members 12, 1997 NASD LEXIS 15 (March 1997) [hereinafter NASD Proposal].

[161] The term "confidential financial information" would be defined as any financial information concerning a customer, but not including (i) a customer's name, address, and telephone number(s), unless the customers specifies otherwise, or (ii) information that can be obtained from unaffiliated credit bureaus or similar companies in the ordinary course of business. *Id*. at *13 (proposed NASD Rule 3121(d)(1)).

[162] The term "business affiliate" is defined as a person with whom the member maintains a control relationship or has a contractual arrangement for the purpose of servicing customers. This definition thus includes entities that maintain "networking" arrangements with member firms but no other type of corporate affiliation. *Id*. at *5, *13-14.

[163] Proposed NASD Rule 3121(a) would provide that:

> A member shall not release confidential financial information regarding any customer to any person other than a business affiliate unless: (A) the member clearly and conspicuously discloses to the customer that: (i) the information may be released to a person other than a business affiliate; and (ii) the customer has the right to object to the release of the information; and (B) following such disclosure, the customer has consented in writing to the release of such information to such other person.

Subsection (b) of proposed NASD Rule 3121 would provide:

> A member shall not release confidential financial information regarding any customer to a business affiliate unless the member: (1) clearly and conspicuously discloses to the customer that: (A) the information may be released to a business affiliate; and (B) the customer has the right to object to the release of the information; (2) provides the customer with an opportunity, a reasonable period of time before the time that the information is released, to object to the release of the information; and (3) has not received an objection from the customer to the release of the information.

Id. at *12-13.

[164] In addition, Proposed Rule 3121(e) provides exceptions for the sharing of customer information "pursuant to clearing, custodial, or transfer arrangements with member firms necessary to service customer accounts" or "pertaining to customers other than natural persons." *Id*. at *14.

[165] A FRAMEWORK FOR GLOBAL ELECTRONIC COMMERCE, *supra* note 34.

(ii) transparency principles, which assure that individuals are informed about the manner in which information is to be collected, stored, and used by businesses and other organizations; (iii) access and correction principles, which assure that individuals have access to, and the ability to correct when inaccurate, the information that businesses and other organizations have compiled; (iv) use principles, which govern how and under what circumstances businesses and other organizations make use of personal information in ways other than those for which the information was initially collected; and (v) disclosure principles, which may require that some type of consent is granted by individuals to businesses and other organizations prior to the disclosure of such information to third parties.[166]

[a] Banks and Other Card Issuers. Until recently, many banks and financial services firms did not maintain formal privacy policies governing their range of services.[167] The privacy policies of Citibank's Europe/North America Cards Privacy Policy and VISA's Issuer Privacy Principles are frequently cited as examples of leading policies maintained today by the banking and financial services industries.[168] Many other financial service providers are developing similar privacy policies, as are trade and industry associations, in the hopes of averting regulatory or other legal problems concerning customer privacy.[169]

The Citicorp and Visa privacy policies contain the following core concepts:

* Strictly maintain the privacy and confidentiality of customer financial records.

* Use customer information only to the extent needed in the conduct of their business.

* Maintain accurate information according to strict security standards.

* Limit employee access to those with a need to know or see the information.

* Honor customer/cardholder requests to be removed from telemarketing and mailing lists.

* Maintain cardholder privacy in relationships with third parties.

* Require third parties accessing identification information (*i.e.*, name, address, phone number) to maintain equivalent privacy protections with regard to the information disclosed.[170]

[b] Banking Trade Associations. The Bankers Roundtable, an industry group made up of the nation's 125 largest banking institutions, issued a "Statement of Industry Principles" in November 1996 ("Bankers Roundtable Statement"), which addresses, among other topics, the issue of the privacy and confidentiality of

---

[166] *See* Oscar H. Gandy, Jr., *Legitimate Business Interest: No End in Sight? An Inquiry into the Status of Privacy in Cyberspace*, 1996 U. Chi. Legal F. 77, 136 (1996).

[167] *See* Lisa Fickenscher, *Passive Banks Seen Inviting Rules on Data Privacy*, Am. Banker, Mar. 27, 1996, at 16 (noting the estimate of the newsletter, Privacy and American Business, that only a dozen or so of the 6,000 U.S. banks that issue credit cards have card member privacy policies).

[168] *See* Citibank, Europe/North America Cards Privacy Policy (1996); Visa Issuer Privacy Principles (1996).

[169] *See e.g.*, John M. Moran, *The Battle Over Online Privacy; Can the Internet Police Itself?*, Hartford Courant, June 23, 1997, at A1 (noting the debate between advocates of new privacy laws and regulations to protect online privacy and advocates of industry self-regulation).

[170] Both Visa's and Citicorp's privacy policies indicate that consumers may "opt-out" of any disclosure regime in place at a member organization.

consumer information.[171] The Bankers Roundtable Statement treats privacy and security of consumer information as important public policy goals. Specifically, the statement recommends that Roundtable members should:

- Abide by all applicable federal and state laws regulating privacy issues.

- Train employees on bank requirements concerning consumer privacy, security, confidentiality, and data encryption, and address rule violations by employees promptly.

- Inform users of electronic financial services of consumer obligations and rights and methods for protecting their privacy.

- Act to maintain confidentiality of current and former customer information and protect customer confidentiality in all account and account transfer information outside of and within their institutions, except in cases where the member is compelled to meet legal requirements which compel otherwise or where disclosure is made at the request or with the consent of the customer.

- Develop and employ technologies that will enhance confidentiality in the transmission of consumer information.

- Disclose to their customers account and other information in conformance with all applicable banking laws.[172]

The Consumer Bankers Association ("CBA") released its own set of principles ("Best Practices - Use of Customer Information") regarding the use of customer information in 1996. The CBA's principles include having members pledge to:

- Limit the use and collection of information about customers to what is necessary to administer our business, provide superior service, and offer opportunities to customers.

- Restrict employee access to customer information to those employees with a business need to know the information.

- Limit the instances in which the member will permit other companies to offer their products and services to the member's customers (*i.e.*, when the member will provide customer information to third parties).

---

[171] The guidelines of the Bankers Roundtable are designed to address a broad range of issues, providing guidance for banking organizations to follow in their use of technology and the provision of financial and information services. *See* BANKERS ROUNDTABLE, BANKING AND TECHNOLOGY: STATEMENT OF INDUSTRY PRINCIPLES 1 (1996). The Bankers Roundtable notes that the principles serve as a "guide" for banking institutions, consumers of retail and wholesale financial products, government officials and the public. *Id.*

[172] *Id.* at 13-15.

- Tell customers how to remove their names from telemarketing and mailing lists when they open accounts and maintain such information and provide it to customers upon request.

- Hire only those firms (*e.g.*, to provide operational support to the member) which agree in writing to safeguard customer information according to the CBA's guidelines.[173]

The American Bankers Association ("ABA(Bankers)") is engaged in an ongoing study of the effects of technological advances upon all aspects of the banking and financial services industry. For example, in 1996 the Payments System Task Force of the ABA(Bankers) studied payments system issues relating to the increasing use of technology in the banking business and issued a report calling for banks to play a leading role in the payments system of the future.[174] In July 1997, the ABA(Bankers) released its voluntary guidelines for member banks to follow to protect the personal information of consumers in Internet banking and other online financial transactions.[175]

In September 1997, major bank trade groups developed a unified set of privacy guidelines. On September 18, 1997, the House Subcommittee on Financial Institutions held hearings on electronic commerce and consumer financial privacy.[176] Representatives from the CBA, ABA(Bankers), the Bankers Roundtable, and the Banking Industry Technology Secretariat ("BITS") testified at the hearings, urging caution before Congress drafts additional regulation of the banking industry and unveiling the set of industry privacy guidelines to be followed by five bank industry trade groups (ABA(Bankers), CBA, BITS, the Independent Bankers Association of America, and the Bankers Roundtable).[177] These guidelines are as follows:

- **Recognition of a Customer's Expectation of Privacy.** Financial institutions should recognize and respect the privacy expectations of their customers and explain principles of financial privacy to their customers in an appropriate fashion. This could be accomplished, for example, by making available privacy guidelines and/or providing a series of questions and answers about financial privacy to those customers.

- **Use, Collection, and Retention of Customer Information.** Financial institutions should collect, retain, and use information about individual customers only where the institution reasonably

---

[173] CONSUMER BANKERS ASSOCIATION, BEST PRACTICES, USE OF CUSTOMER INFORMATION (1996).

[174] *See* PAYMENTS SYSTEM TASK FORCE, AM. BANKERS ASS'N, THE ROLE OF BANKS IN THE PAYMENTS SYSTEM OF THE FUTURE (1996).

[175] The American Bankers Association's ("ABA(Bankers)") Privacy Principles recognized eight core principles: (i) recognition of a customer's expectation of privacy, (ii) the use, collection, and retention of customer information only if the institution believes that the customer will benefit, (iii) maintenance of accurate customer information, (iv) limiting employee access to such information, (v) protecting information via established security procedures, (vi) restricting the disclosure of account information, (vii) maintaining customer privacy in business relationships with third parties, and (viii) making an institution's privacy policies known to the consumer. *See American Bankers Association Approves Privacy Principles,* 21ST CENTURY BANKING ALERT® No. 97-7-25, July 25, 1997, *available at* <http://www.ffhsj.com>; *ABA To Issue Consumer Privacy Guidelines*, FIN. NETNEWS, May 26, 1997, at 6.

[176] *See Consumer Financial Privacy: Hearing Before the Subcomm. on Financial Institutions of the House Comm. on Banking*, 105th Cong. (Sept. 1997) [hereinafter *Privacy Hearing*].

[177] *See Privacy Hearing, supra* note 176 (statement of Marcia Z. Sullivan, Vice President, Consumer Bankers Association) (urging that Congress refrain from considering additional legislation and stating that the current legal and regulatory framework "adequately protects consumer privacy through an effective interplay of consumer demands, federal and state laws and regulations, and the electronic commerce marketplace itself.").

believes it would be useful (and allowed by law) to administer that organization's business and to provide products, services, and other opportunities to its customers.

- **Maintenance of Accurate Information.** Financial institutions should establish procedures so that a customer's financial information is accurate, current, and complete in accordance with reasonable commercial standards. Financial institutions should also respond to requests to correct inaccurate information in a timely manner.

- **Limiting Employee Access to Information.** Financial institutions should limit employee access to personally identifiable information to those with a business reason for knowing such information. Financial institutions should educate their employees so that they will understand the importance of confidentiality and customer privacy. Financial institutions should also take appropriate disciplinary measures to enforce employee privacy responsibilities.

- **Protection of Information via Established Security Procedures.** Financial institutions should maintain appropriate security standards and procedures regarding unauthorized access to customer information.

- **Restrictions on the Disclosure of Account Information.** Financial institutions should not reveal specific information about customer accounts or other personally identifiable data to unaffiliated third parties for their independent use, except for the exchange of information with reputable information reporting agencies to maximize the accuracy and security of such information, or in the performance of bona fide corporate due diligence, unless (1) the information is provided to help complete a customer-initiated transaction; (2) the customer requests it; (3) the disclosure is required or allowed by law (*e.g.*, subpoena, investigation of fraudulent activity, etc.); or 4) the customer has been informed about the possibility of disclosure for marketing or similar purposes through a prior communication and is given the opportunity to decline (*i.e.*, "opt out").

- **Maintaining Customer Privacy in Business Relationships with Third Parties.** If personally identifiable customer information is provided to a third party, the financial institutions should insist that the third party adhere to similar privacy principles that provide for keeping such information confidential.

- **Disclosure of Privacy Principles to Customers.** Financial institutions should devise methods of providing a customer with an understanding of their privacy policies. Customers that are concerned about financial privacy will want to know about an institution's treatment of this important issue. Each financial institution should create a method for making available its privacy policies.[178]

---

[178] *See id.*

[c] Smart Card Forum Guidelines. The Smart Card Forum ("SCF"), a trade organization of more than 200 businesses and organizations committed to the development and promotion of smart card applications, issued a set of cross-industry privacy guidelines for industry and government issuers of smart cards in May 1997, that set forth "responsible information practices," governing the use of consumer data obtained through the smart card applications.[179] The SCF stated that "smart card technology, if properly designed and implemented, can enhance both the fact and the perception of the consumer's ability to exercise a much greater degree of control over personal information than is the case with any comparable delivery system."[180] The SCF also characterized the smart card as not only an efficient and secure delivery system, but also an "empowerment tool," by which individuals can control the access to and dissemination of information about their lives, spending, or other commercial activities.[181]

The SCF urged its members to: (i) adopt consumer privacy principles and make them known to their customers; (ii) incorporate into smart card applications the consumer privacy protections available from today's technologies; and (iii) adopt a code of responsible information practices or similar policies covering the use of consumer data.[182] The SCF's guidelines encompass the following key points:

- Identify, recognize, and respect the privacy expectations of consumers and make applicable privacy guidelines available to them.

- Establish procedures to ensure that consumer data — information directly related to the consumer's use of the card — is as accurate, up to date, and complete as possible. Promptly honor requests from consumers for information the company has about them as a result of the consumer's use of their cards and provide a procedure for them to correct inaccurate personally identifiable information.

- Limit the use, collection, and retention of information about consumers to what is necessary in order to administer their accounts, provide superior service, and offer consumers new opportunities.

- If personally identifiable consumer information is to be provided to unaffiliated third parties for marketing or similar purposes, inform the consumer of that purpose and provide the consumer with the opportunity to decline (*i.e.* "opt-out"). If personally identifiable consumer information is provided to a third party, require the third party to adhere to equivalent privacy standards with respect to that information. This would not apply to situations where information is disclosed in

---

[179] *Consumer Privacy and Smart Cards - A Challenge and an Opportunity, available at* (visited June 3, 1997) <http://www.smartcrd.com>.

[180] *Id.* at 1.

[181] For example, with a smart card, a consumer could control what information is placed on the smart card, who may have access to it and when, and "compartmentalize" information about his or her personal or spending habits maintained on a card, so that one merchant or service provider does not gain access to all the information stored on the card as a result of one transaction. *Id.* at 2.

[182] *Id.* at 3.

order to complete a transaction or pursuant to legal process, including the investigation of fraud or criminal activity.

- Inform consumers of data disclosure policies and provide an opportunity to "opt-out," whereby consumers may remove their names from the company's telemarketing, online, mailing, and other solicitation lists.

- Maintain appropriate security standards and procedures regarding access to personally identifiable consumer information.

- Implement policies and procedures to limit employee access to personally identifiable consumer information to a need-to-know basis; educate employees about privacy standards and employees' responsibilities to protect consumer privacy, monitor employee compliance, and take appropriate disciplinary measures with employees who fail to adhere to such standards.[183]

[d] Open Profiling Standard. In May 1997, a group of about sixty companies and organizations led by Netscape Communications Corp., proposed a standard known as the "Open Profiling Standard" ("OPS"), to govern the dissemination and use of personal information supplied by consumers using the World Wide Web on the Internet.[184] Under the OPS, Internet site developers will have available a uniform architecture for protecting consumers' disclosure of personal information when using the Web and Web browsers. Consumers will establish personal "preferences" on their personal computers and be able to tailor these preferences to manage what personal information is disclosed or withheld when the consumer visits a particular website. Consumers would be notified by OPS what information is being requested of them upon visiting a website and could choose to disclose all, some, or none of the information requested by the website.[185]

[e] The "Opt-out" vs. "Opt-in" Debate. In each of the instances of self-regulatory efforts described in this Section 12.05, an important issue is whether consumers will be able to control the use of personal data disseminated to banks, merchants, and other third parties by an "opt-out" mechanism — whereby consumers' personal information is available for use by the collectors of the data, unless the consumer affirmatively opts (usually in writing) not to have such data shared with affiliates or third parties — or by an "opt-in" mechanism, whereby the collectors of personal data about consumers are prohibited from providing such data to third parties, unless the consumer opts (in writing after advance notice) to permit such disclosure.[186] Under

---

[183] *Id.* at 3-4.

[184] *See* Don Clark & John R. Wilke, *Firms to Unveil Plans to Protect OnLine Privacy,* WALL ST. J., June 9, 1997, at B9; G. Christian Hill, *Group of Firms Propose Standard for Privacy on the Net,* WALL ST. J., May 27, 1997, at B11A. Microsoft also agreed to support the plan in early June 1997. *See* Don Clark, *Rivals Microsoft and Netscape Team Up to Protect Consumer Privacy on the Web,* WALL ST. J., June 12, 1997, at B14.

[185] *See Netscape, Firefly and VeriSign Propose Open Profiling Standard (OPS) to Enable Broad Personalization of Internet Services,* Press Release (May 27, 1997), *available at* (visited Jan. 9, 1998) <http://www.netscape.com/newsref/pr/newsrelease411.html>.

[186] The Center for Democracy and Technology ("CDT") maintains a chart outlining the information practices of each of the major online service providers, America Online, CompuServe Information Service, the Microsoft Network, and Prodigy. According to the research of the CDT, three of the four online service providers maintain policies whereby: (i) consumers may "opt-out" of disclosures of their personally identifiable transaction data to third parties, and (ii) consumers may limit (by an "opt-out") the disclosure of subscription data to third parties. *See Privacy Policy Chart - Online Service Providers, available at* (visited Oct. 2, 1997) <http://www.cdt.org/privacy/online_services/chart.html>.

the self-imposed guidelines recommended by the bank trade groups and the SCF, consumers would have to rely on the "opt-out" approach. Only the OPS scheme for consumer online appears to adopt a form of the "opt-in" approach by providing consumers the opportunity to dictate what information (or none) a website may retrieve from their personal computer.

§ 12.06 FEDERAL LAWS DEFINING THE BOUNDARIES OF PRIVACY AND CONFIDENTIALITY IN CYBERSPACE

[1] OVERVIEW

As described previously, privacy protections under U.S. law are relatively limited and may vary significantly from state to state.[187] Current federal privacy protections form an incomplete framework and may not adequately address the privacy concerns of users of computer network systems and products.[188] In an April 1997 Privacy Discussion Paper, the NIITF described the United States informational privacy policy as follows:

> [I]nformation privacy policy in the United States consists of various laws, regulations and practices, woven together to produce privacy protection that varies from sector to sector. Sometimes the results make sense, and sometimes they do not. The degree of protection accorded to personal information may depend on the data delivery mechanism rather than on the type of information at issue. Moreover, information privacy protection efforts in the United States are generally reactive rather than proactive: both the public and the private sector adopt policies in response to celebrated incidents of nonconsensual disclosure involving readily discernible harm. Sometimes this approach leaves holes in the fabric of privacy protection.[189]

Many critics of the current United States privacy regime believe a regulatory or legal overhaul of existing federal privacy law, or the adoption of a comprehensive new federal privacy statute,[190] may be necessary to address new informational privacy concerns accompanying the development of electronic financial products and

---

[187] *See generally* Section 12.01.

[188] A number of commentators have noted these concerns and remarked on the effect of computer networks and open systems on informational privacy and security. *See, e.g.*, Gindin, *supra* note 55; Graham, *supra* note 9 (surveying applicable federal statutory privacy law); Richard D. Marks, *Legal Issues in the Information Revolution: Security, Privacy and Free Expression in the New World of Broadband Networks*, 32 HOUS. L. REV. 501 (1995) (reviewing federal statutory framework and exploring issues concerning fraud); Randolph S. Sargent, *A Fourth Amendment Model for Computer Networks and Data Privacy*, 81 VA. L. REV. 1181 (1995) (describing a model of how the Fourth Amendment could be applied to computers, search and seizures, and data privacy); Catherine M. Downey, Comment, *The High Price of a Cashless Society: Exchanging Privacy Rights for Digital Cash?*, 14 J. MARSHALL J. OF COMPUTER & INFO. L. 303 (1996) (reviewing primary federal privacy statutes and applying those laws to the advent of digital cash).

[189] NIITF 1997 DRAFT REPORT, *supra* note 11, at 1.

[190] For one author's call for a new federal privacy statute, *see* Downey, *supra* note 188 (arguing for the adoption of new federal privacy standards). *See also* Gindin, *supra* note 55 (discussing the need for new legislation).

services.[191] There are a number of "targeted" federal privacy statutes which illustrate the United States' sectoral approach to the protection of privacy rights and the fact that privacy rights under federal law often are the result of specific problems perceived by the public and Congress.[192]

For example, in 1994 Congress passed the Driver's Privacy Protection Act ("DPPA") to address its increasing concerns over state governments selling their public information records to direct marketing firms and other third parties.[193] One major exception is that a motor vehicle department may provide bulk distribution of information for surveys, marketing, or solicitations if individuals have a clear right to opt-out; in which case such surveys, marketing, or solicitations will not be directed to those who opt-out.[194] Motor vehicle departments may also release such information upon informed individual consent, for public safety purposes, or by request on an individual consumer basis.[195] Similarly, in 1988 Congress passed the Video Privacy Act ("VPA"), which protects video tape rental records form disclosure.[196] Under the VPA, video tape service providers who knowingly disclose any personally identifiable information concerning a consumer to a third party may be subject to civil damages in an action by the consumer.[197]

This Section describes some of the current federal statutes that may affect the privacy policies of companies that create and issue electronic financial products and services. This Section also discusses some of the relevant state law provisions in this area.

---

[191] *See* Joshua B. Sessler, Note & Comment, *Computer Cookie Control: Transaction Generated Information and Privacy Regulation on the Internet*, 5 J.L. & POL'Y 627, 645-50 (1997) (discussing new legal regimes, industry self-regulation, and technological "fixes" as possible solutions to the growing problem of "transaction generated" information on the Internet).

[192] *See, e.g.,* Family Educational Rights and Privacy Act of 1974, 20 U.S.C. § 1232g (protecting student records); Telephone Consumer Protection Act of 1991, 47 U.S.C. § 227(b)(1)(A)(iii) (regulating telemarketing practices); Cable Communications Policy Act of 1984, 47 U.S.C. § 521 (protecting cable television subscriber information); Telecommunications Act of 1996, 47 U.S.C. § 153 et seq. (safeguarding customer information held by telecommunications carriers). *See generally* Gindin, *supra* note 55.

[193] Driver's Privacy Protection Act of 1994, Pub. L. No. 103-322, 1994 U.S.C.C.A.N. (108 Stat.) 2099 (codified as amended at 18 U.S.C. § 2721). The Driver's Privacy Protection Act ("DPPA") restricts the release of motor vehicle records, and provides that, with certain enumerated exceptions, a state department of motor vehicles may not knowingly disclose or otherwise make available to any third party information about an individual obtained by the department in connection with the individual's motor vehicle records. *Id.* § 2721(a). According to a recent report, Illinois makes $10 million per year selling its public records. *See* Nina Berstein, *A Profitable Invasion: More and More are Making a Living Collecting, Selling the Data of Our Lives*, SAN DIEGO UNION & TRIB., Sept. 30, 1997, at 4. The state of Colorado makes about $4.4 million annually by selling its motor vehicle information. *See Privacy Bills Up Next: Should Sale of Driver's License Info Continue?*, DENVER POST, May 5, 1997, at A1.

[194] 18 U.S.C. § 2721(b)(12).

[195] *Id.* § 2721(b)(11). The DPPA was scheduled to take effect on September 13, 1997. Two states, however, Oklahoma and South Carolina, recently initiated legal challenges to the DPPA, arguing that the law constituted an unconstitutional infringement of state sovereignty under the Tenth Amendment. *See* John Gibeaut, *Keeping Federalism Alive*, ABA J., Jan. 1998, at 38. On Sept. 11, 1997, the U.S. District Court for the District of South Carolina permanently enjoined the enforcement of the DPPA. The court held that Congress had chosen not to assume responsibility for the conduct of motor vehicle records, and that it could not permissibly command "the states to implement federal policy by requiring them to regulate the dissemination and use of [such] records," consistent with the Tenth Amendment. *Condon v. Reno*, 972 F. Supp. 977, 984-85 (D.S.C. 1997), *appeal filed. See also Oklahoma ex rel. Oklahoma Dep't of Public Safety v. United States*, 1997 U.S. Dist LEXIS 14455, at *20-2 (Sept. 17, 1997) (enjoining enforcement of the DPPA on Tenth Amendment grounds), *appeal filed.*

[196] 18 U.S.C. § 2710.

[197] *Id.* § 2710(b)(1). Video tape rental providers may provide personally identifiable information concerning a consumer if the provider has provided the consumer with clear details of such planned disclosure, and the opportunity for the consumer to opt out, but only if the disclosure does not identify the title or subject matter of any video tapes rented to the consumer. *Id.* § 2710((b)(2)(D).

[2]   THE FAIR CREDIT REPORTING ACT

[a] Statute – Exceptions. Congress passed the Fair Credit Reporting Act ("FCRA"), the first major piece of federal privacy legislation, in 1970.[198] The FCRA is one of several federal statutes governing credit transactions that have privacy overtones or components.[199] It was enacted in response to consumer complaints of abuses of privacy in the consumer credit industry, and the lack of responsiveness on the part of many credit reporting bureaus and other collection agencies that collect and disseminate credit and other personal information.[200] FCRA requires credit bureaus and other similar entities to adopt reasonable procedures for meeting the commercial need for information about individuals in a manner that is fair and equitable to the consumer.[201] As detailed below, FCRA restricts the dissemination of consumer reports to "permissible purposes," but does not generally grant consumers the right to prevent the disclosure of personal information. It does, however, prohibit the maintenance or disclosure of obsolete or inaccurate information about consumers.[202]

FCRA generally governs the collection, evaluation, maintenance, and dissemination of reports on consumers collected for the purpose of evaluating their qualifications for credit, insurance, employment, and certain other transactions.[203] It only applies, however, to "consumer credit reports"[204] issued by "consumer

---

[198] Fair Credit Reporting Act, Pub. L. No. 91-508, § 601, 1970 U.S.C.C.A.N. (84 Stat.) 1301, 1316-27 (codified at 15 U.S.C. §§ 1681-1681u, a subtitle of the Consumer Credit Protection Act, 15 U.S.C. §§ 1601-1691r) [hereinafter FCRA]. For a discussion of the provisions and operation of the FCRA, see FISCHER, *supra* note 132, ¶ 1.01 *et seq.*; GEORGE B. TRUBOW, PRIVACY LAW AND PRACTICE ¶ 3.02[2] (1991); Ronald C. Clairborne, *Credit Reports and the Fair Credit Reporting Act*, 28 J. MARSHALL L. REV. 365 (1995); Elwin Griffith, *The Quest for Fair Credit Reporting and Equal Credit Opportunity in Consumer Transactions*, 25 MEM. ST. U.L. REV. 37 (1994).

[199] *See, e.g.*, the Fair Credit Billing Act, Section 162(b) of the Truth in Lending Act, 15 U.S.C. §§ 1666-1666j, enacted in 1976 to regulate credit billing practices, and the Equal Credit Opportunity Act, 15 U.S.C. § 1691-91f, enacted in 1974 to prohibit discriminatory credit granting on the basis of gender, marital status, race, color, religion, and age. The Fair Credit Billing Act supports consumer's financial privacy interests because it provides a procedure for resolving billing disputes designed to foster the accuracy of stored information. The Equal Credit Opportunity Act also supports consumers' financial privacy rights because it requires credit grantors to give reasons for denials of credit, thus giving the individual consumer a chance to discover what adverse information is being stored and circulated about him. *See* BAKER & BRANDEL, *supra* note 8, ¶ 19.02[1][c], at 19-20 to 19-21.

[200] *See* FISCHER, *supra* note 132, ¶ 1.01, at 1-4.

[201] *See id.*

[202] *See* 15 U.S.C. §§ 1681c, 1681k, 1681*l*. *See also* FISCHER, *supra* note 132, ¶ 1.01, at 1-4.

[203] 15 U.S.C. § 1681b(3). Credit reporting agencies maintain records on a vast number of consumers. This information shows the accounts that a consumer has, how a consumer has made payments on the accounts, the total amounts owed by the consumer, whether the accounts are up to date or overdue, whether action has been taken against a consumer, and whether a consumer has been "marked" for collection purposes. *See* Clairborne, *supra* note 198 (describing the overall operation of the credit bureau and reporting agency marketplace).

[204] Under the FCRA, the term "consumer report" means:

[A]ny written, oral, or other communication of any information by a consumer reporting agency bearing on a consumer's credit worthiness, credit standing, credit capacity, character, general reputation, personal characteristics, or mode of living which is used or expected to be used or collected in whole or in part for the purpose of serving as a factor in establishing the consumer's eligibility for (1) credit or insurance to be used primarily for personal, family, or household purposes, or (2) employment purposes, or (3) other purposes authorized under section 1681b of this title. The term does not include (A) any report containing information solely as to transactions or experiences between the consumer and the person making the report; (B) any authorization or approval of a specific extension of credit directly or indirectly by the issuer of a credit card or similar device; or (C) any report in which a person who has been requested by a third party to make a specific extension of credit.

15 U.S.C. § 1681a(d).

credit agencies."[205] Generally, a person or entity that regularly prepares reports to enable third parties to evaluate consumers, based on information not derived from that person's or entity's experiences with the consumer is a "consumer reporting agency" under FCRA, and is subject to all of FCRA's substantive provisions.[206] These provisions include:

- Standards for maintaining the currency and accuracy of information and restrictions on the purposes for which that information may be released.[207]

- Consumers' rights of access to information in their files and procedures for exercising those rights.[208]

- Consumers' rights to have consumer reporting agencies reinvestigate information in their files believed by the consumer to be inaccurate, and to have such information corrected if it is in fact inaccurate.[209]

- The rights to include statements of dispute in their files when they disagree with consumer reporting agencies about the accuracy of information in their files.[210]

- Requirements that consumer reporting agencies disseminate corrected information and consumer statements of dispute to certain prior users of their consumer reports.[211]

- Civil[212] and criminal[213] penalties for violation of the FCRA's procedural and substantive requirements, as well as limitations on consumers' legal rights in connection with consumer reports.[214]

---

[205] Under the FCRA, the term "consumer reporting agency" means:

[A]ny person which, for monetary fees, dues, or on a cooperative non-profit basis, regularly engages in whole or in part in the practice of assembling or evaluating consumer credit information or other information on consumers for the purpose of furnishing consumer reports to third parties, and which uses any means or facility of interstate commerce for the purpose of preparing or furnishing consumer reports.

Id. § 1681a(f).

[206] *Id.* § 1681a(f).

[207] *See Id.* §§ 1681b, 1681c, 1681e, 1681k, 1681l.

[208] *Id.* §§ 1681g, 1681h.

[209] *Id.* § 1681i(a).

[210] *Id.* § 1681i(b).

[211] *Id.* §1681i(d).

[212] *Id.* §§ 1681n, 1681o.

[213] *Id.* §§1681q, 1681r.

[214] *Id.* § 1681h(e).

Other than prohibiting the reporting of obsolete[215] or inaccurate information,[216] FCRA does not impose substantive limits on the types of information that may be put in a consumer report.[217] Under the FCRA, however, a credit reporting agency may only furnish a consumer report for one of five enumerated purposes: (i) in connection with a credit transaction involving the consumer; (ii) for employment purposes involving the consumer; (iii) in connection with the underwriting of insurance involving the consumer; (iv) for determination of the consumer's eligibility for government benefits; and (v) for "other legitimate business needs involving a business transaction."[218]

FCRA contains other privacy protections, including a requirement that consumer reporting agencies disclose to consumers the "nature and substance" of all information (except medical information) in its files on the date of the consumer's request, the source of the information, and the names of each recipient of a consumer report during the preceding two-year period.[219] Consumer reporting agencies need not generally permit a consumer to see his or her file, but must investigate any information contained in the file that a consumer disputes.[220] The consumer reporting agency must either rectify errors or augment the consumer's file with a description of the fact that the dispute is unresolved.[221] All future credit reports must indicate the deletion or existence of a continuing dispute. Moreover, the consumer reporting agency must, on the consumer's request, send notice of the deletion or resolution of any dispute to recipients designated by the consumer, who received the report during the last two years for employment purposes, and those who received the report during the last six months for any other purpose.[222]

FCRA obligates users of consumer reports to notify a consumer of any adverse action taken on the basis of nonexperience information.[223] Users of consumer reports must also notify a consumer if adverse action is taken on the basis of the information contained in the consumer's credit report, the name and address of the credit reporting agency that prepared the reports, and the fact that the consumer has the right to obtain, without

---

[215] Under 15 U.S.C. § 1681c, obsolete information generally includes adverse information that antedates the consumer report by more than seven years, with two exceptions: (i) bankruptcy cases may be reported up to ten years after filed; and (ii) suits and judgments for which the statute of limitations is longer than seven years. *See* 15 U.S.C. § 1681c(a)(1)-(6). *See also* TRUBOW, *supra* note 198, ¶ 3.02[2], at 3-37.

[216] *See* 15 U.S.C. §§ 1681c, 1681e(b).

[217] *See* BAKER & BRANDEL, *supra* note 8, ¶ 19.02[1][c], at 19-17.

[218] 15 U.S.C. § 1681b(3). An example of "other legitimate business needs" is the furnishing of microfiche lists of consumer check use information provided to merchants for the purpose of determining when to accept a check from a consumer as payment for goods and services. *See Greenway v. Information Dynamics, Ltd.*, 399 F. Supp. 1092 (D. Ariz. 1974), *aff'd*, 524 F.2d 1145 (9th Cir. 1975), *cert. dismissed*, 424 U.S. 936 (1976).

[219] 15 U.S.C. § 1681g.

[220] *Id.* § 1681i(a).

[221] *Id.* § 1681i(b).

[222] *Id.* § 1681i(d). *See also* BAKER & BRANDEL, *supra* note 8, ¶ 19.02[1][c], at 19-17.

[223] *See* 15 U.S.C. § 1681a(d)(A) (exclusion of experience information from the definition of "consumer report"); *Id.* § 1681m (requiring notification after adverse action).

charge, a copy of the consumer report from the applicable consumer reporting agency.[224] The creditor is not required, however, to disclose its credit criteria or standards.[225]

In general, FCRA establishes a three-pronged enforcement scheme that includes: (i) civil liability through private rights of action against consumer reporting agencies and users of consumer reports;[226] (ii) criminal liability for certain knowing or willful violations of FCRA;[227] and (iii) administrative enforcement by the FTC.[228] Under the FCRA's civil liability provisions, a consumer reporting agency or user may be found liable for negligent[229] or willful[230] noncompliance with the provisions of FCRA. A consumer may generally recover any actual damages sustained and costs of the action. The court may also award punitive damages in cases of willful noncompliance.[231] Actions must be brought within two years of the date of the inaccurate report, or, in cases of willful noncompliance, two years after discovery in willful cases.[232]

FCRA contains two types of criminal penalties. First, it prohibits any person from knowing and willfully obtaining information on a consumer from a consumer reporting agency under false pretenses.[233] Second, the FCRA proscribes the knowing and willful release of information concerning an individual to an unauthorized person by an officer or employee of a consumer reporting agency.[234] Finally, violations of the FCRA are considered unfair or deceptive trade practices within the meaning of Section 5 of the Federal Trade Commission Act,[235] and such violations are subject to FTC administrative remedies.[236] The FTC has its normal procedural, administrative, and subpoena powers to enforce FCRA, but does not have the authority to issue binding regulations and interpretations of the Act's provisions.[237]

[b] 1996 FCRA Amendments. In September 1996, Congress passed, as part of Title II of the fiscal year 1997 Omnibus Consolidated Appropriations Act, the "Consumer Credit Reporting Reform Act of 1996"

---

[224] *Id.* § 1681m(a)(1)-(2). Under § 1681m(b), the user of such information from a source other than a consumer reporting agency must also notify the consumer of the nature of the information upon which the adverse action was based.

[225] Federal Trade Commission, Statement of General Policy or Interpretation; Commentary on the Fair Credit Reporting Act, 55 Fed. Reg. 18,804, 18,826 (1990) (codified at 16 C.F.R. pt. 600) [hereinafter FTC FCRA Commentary].

[226] 15 U.S.C. §§ 1681n, 1681o.

[227] *Id.* §§ 1681q, 1681r.

[228] *Id.* §§ 1681s(a) (authorizing the FTC to enforce compliance with FCRA, unless specifically delegated to another federal agency).

[229] 15 U.S.C. § 1681o. In negligence actions under the FCRA, a consumer plaintiff must establish that the defendant was negligent in failing to follow reasonable procedures designed to assure the maximum possible accuracy of the report about the plaintiff, that the information reported was inaccurate, that the plaintiff was injured, and that the defendant's negligence was the proximate cause of the injury. *See Morris v. Credit Bureau of Cincinnati*, 563 F. Supp. 962, 968 (S.D. Ohio 1983).

[230] 15 U.S.C. § 1681n.

[231] *Id.* § 1681n(2).

[232] *Id.* § 1681p.

[233] *Id.* § 1681q.

[234] *Id.* § 1681r. Penalties under § 1681q and § 1681r include a fine of not more than $5,000, imprisonment for one year, or both. *Id.*

[235] 15 U.S.C. §§ 41-77.

[236] *Id.* § 1681s(a).

[237] *See* FISCHER, *supra* note 133, ¶ 1.07, at 1-117. The FTC also issues advisory opinion letters in response to inquiries concerning the FCRA. *See id.*

("Reform Act").[238] The Reform Act contains amendments to the FCRA, effective as of September 30, 1997, that have several implications for banks and electronic banking.[239] The Reform Act places significant new restrictions on parties who use credit reports and who furnish information to credit reporting agencies, gives new enforcement authority to the FTC, and increases the amount of required disclosures to consumers regarding credit information practices.[240]

By restricting access to consumer credit information and by providing new privacy protections and disclosure requirements, as discussed below, the Reform Act provides additional protections to consumers. It also clarifies that affiliated companies (those within the same corporate family or structure) may share, without limitation under the FCRA, "experience information" concerning consumers, *i.e.*, that information which relates solely to transactions or experiences between the consumer and the person making the report.[241] A bank may thus share a consumer's transaction records with its affiliates without triggering the rules governing consumer reports. In addition to the relaxation of restrictions on "experience information," the Reform Act permits affiliates to share *any information* (such as application information, demographic information, and credit reports from credit bureaus) concerning a consumer, if it is "clearly and conspicuously" disclosed to the consumer that the affiliates intend to share such information, and the consumer is given the right, prior to the sharing of any information, to "opt-out" of the scheme.[242] Further, when actions adverse to a consumer are based upon information shared among affiliates, the Reform Act requires that the consumer be notified of the adverse action (in writing or electronically) and given sixty days to request from the affiliate the nature of the information upon which the adverse action was based.[243]

With the passage of the Reform Act, consumers gain new privacy and disclosure rights with regard to "firm offers" of credit or insurance products sent by banks. For example, under Section 2404(e) of the Reform Act, consumers may elect to have their names excluded from the lists that are used to generate firm offers of credit or insurance products.[244] A consumer credit agency that provides consumer information for firm offers of credit or insurance must set up an elaborate system of notification including a toll-free telephone number, publication of notices in the area served by the agency, and a duty to respond to consumer requests for removal within five business days.[245] Consumers also enjoy increased disclosure rights regarding the users of credit

---

[238] Economic Growth and Regulatory Paperwork Reduction Act of 1996, Pub. L. No. 104-208, tit. II, subtit. D, §§ 2401-22, 1996 U.S.C.C.A.N. (110 Stat.) 3009, 3009-426 [hereinafter FCRA Amendments].

[239] *See generally* Peter Swire, *The Consumer Credit Reporting Reform Act and the Future of Electronic Commerce Law*, ELECTRONIC BANKING L. & COMMERCE REP., Nov. 1996, at 4.

[240] *See id.*

[241] *See* FCRA Amendments, § 2402(e), 1996 U.S.C.C.A.N. (110 Stat.) at 3009-428 (adding new exclusions to the definition of "consumer credit report" under 15 U.S.C. § 1681a(d)). The Reform Act completely preempts any state law or regulation governing information sharing among affiliated companies. *Id.* § 2419, 1996 U.S.C.C.A.N. (110 Stat.) at 3009-452.

[242] FCRA Amendments, § 2404(e), 1996 U.S.C.C.A.N. (110 Stat.) at 3009-432.

[243] *See id.* § 2411(e), 1996 U.S.C.C.A.N. (110 Stat.) at 3009-445; Swire, *supra* note 239, at 5.

[244] FCRA Amendments, § 2404(e), 1996 U.S.C.C.A.N. (110 Stat.) at 3009-432.

[245] *Id.* § 2404(e)(5), 1996 U.S.C.C.A.N. (110 Stat.) at 3009-433. *See also* Swire, *supra* note 239, at 5.

reports, including banks. These rights include the right to see all information contained in a credit report about the consumer and the right to request a free copy of the credit report from the user of the report after an adverse action has been taken.[246] In addition, the user of the credit report must notify the consumer after any adverse action that the consumer credit agency did not make the adverse decision and is unable to provide information regarding the decision to the consumer.[247]

Under the Reform Act, furnishers of credit information are under a heightened duty to ensure that consumer credit report information is accurate, as well as a duty to update and correct such information when a consumer makes a request.[248] The new standard of liability under the Reform Act is whether the furnisher of information knew or consciously avoided knowing that the information furnished was inaccurate.[249] The furnisher of consumer credit information must therefore, upon learning that such information is inaccurate, contact the consumer credit reporting agency and make any necessary corrections to the information. Further, the furnisher of credit information may not thereafter furnish to the agency any of the information that remains incomplete or inaccurate.[250] Upon notice of a dispute as to information provided to a reporting agency, the furnisher of the information must investigate the dispute within thirty days and must thereafter furnish corrected information to any national credit reporting agency to which it previously furnished inaccurate data.[251]

Under the Reform Act, consumer credit reports that contain medical information may be provided to a requesting party only if a consumer consents to the furnishing of the report.[252] The Reform Act has also increases the FTC's enforcement powers, permitting that agency to seek civil money penalties in federal court from persons subject to an injunction resulting either from a knowing or willful FCRA violation, or from a "pattern or practice" of such violations.[253] State officials may also sue for violations of the FCRA in federal court. On balance, the Reform Act provides an indication of the likely balance between consumer rights, especially privacy and notifications of disclosures, and the business requirements of banks and merchants in the area of electronic commerce and banking.[254] The Reform Act also demonstrates an inclination on the part of Congress to address consumer protection issues with regard to the privacy and confidentiality of consumer information.

---

[246] FCRA Amendments, § 2411(a)-(b), 1996 U.S.C.C.A.N. (110 Stat.) at 3009-443 to -445.

[247] Id § 2411(a), 1996 U.S.C.C.A.N. (110 Stat.) at 3009-443.

[248] See id. § 2413, 1996 U.S.C.C.A.N. (110 Stat.) at 3009-447.

[249] Id. at § 2413(a)(1), 1996 U.S.C.C.A.N. (110 Stat.) at 3009-447. The FCRA Amendments have increased the civil liability provisions of the FCRA, now permitting the recovery of punitive damages, and the greater of $1,000 or actual damages, in cases of willful or knowing violations of the FCRA. See id. § 2412, 1996 U.S.C.C.A.N. (110 Stat.) at 3009-446.

[250] Id. § 2413(a)(2). 1996 U.S.C.C.A.N. (110 Stat.) at 3009-447.

[251] Id. § 2413(b), 1996 U.S.C.C.A.N. (110 Stat.) at 3009-448.

[252] Id. § 2405, 1996 U.S.C.C.A.N. (110 Stat.) at 3009-434.

[253] Id. § 2416, 1996 U.S.C.C.A.N. (110 Stat.) at 3009-450.

[254] See Swire, supra note 239, at 7.

[c] FCRA's Application to Electronic Banking and Commerce. The FCRA should not have direct application to the marketing and use of stored value and other electronic payment products for three reasons.[255] First, as noted above, the term "consumer reporting agency" primarily determines FCRA's coverage. An institution is not a "consumer reporting agency" unless it "regularly engages" in the practice of reporting consumer *credit* information.[256] This definition can still create problems for financial institutions. For example, a depository or other financial institution may fall under the definition of "consumer reporting agency" inadvertently if the institution regularly furnishes nonexperience credit information about consumers to third parties.[257]

Because most providers of stored value or electronic payment products (and participating merchants) are not likely to be engaged in the business of gathering credit information about consumers, such providers and merchants should not ordinarily run the risk of being deemed a "consumer reporting agency" under FCRA.[258] The degree to which bank or nonbank issuers of stored value or other types of electronic retail payment systems intend to collect and disseminate consumer credit information is presently unclear, although currently conceived and/or operational stored value and electronic money products are not regarded as involving the provision of credit to consumers.[259] Clearly, merchant payment and transaction information plays a role in online verification of consumer transactions, enables consumers to track their own expenditures, and will be invaluable to marketing and advertising firms interested in deciphering consumer spending and payment patterns.[260]

Second, the information (related to the provision of credit or otherwise) generated by merchants (and stored by merchants or issuers) regarding consumers' use of stored value or other electronic money products, either at the point-of-sale or over the Internet, should likely fall within the "transaction or experience" that the issuer or merchant has with the consumer, and thus should likely come within the "transaction or experience" exception from the definition of "consumer report" provided in Section 1681a(d) of the FCRA. Under this exception, the term "consumer report" does not include any report containing information relating "solely as

---

[255] The FCRA will continue to be applicable, however, to all those activities conducted by banks and other financial institutions which involve the provision of credit to consumer which are done in cyberspace, as opposed to more traditional outlets. For a discussion of bank lending operations and credit products available on the Internet and Web, see Chapter 14.

[256] 15 U.S.C. § 1681a(f).

[257] *See* FISCHER, *supra* note 132, ¶ 1.03, at 1-24. Alternatively, a financial institution will be deemed a "consumer reporting agency" under FCRA if it regularly provides to other creditors information obtained from local retail merchants regarding a customer's retail credit accounts. One court has also suggested that a financial institution might become a consumer reporting agency under the FCRA by producing nonexperience consumer records to the IRS pursuant to a summons prior to an enforcement order. *United States v. Puntorieri*, 379 F. Supp. 332 (E.D.N.Y. 1974).

[258] Put another way, if an issuer of electronic money or stored value obtained possession of credit information (either as an intermediary in the payment system, or during verification of the electronic value for the merchant), the issuer might be liable under FCRA if it subsequently disseminated such payment and transaction information to third parties without compliance with FCRA requirements.

[259] *See Visa Cash Usage Soars During 1996 Summer Olympic Games*, PR NEWSWIRE, July 25, 1996 (press release describing monthly transaction information, including volume, dollar amounts, and location(s)); Task Force on Stored-Value, Am. Bar Ass'n, *A Commercial Lawyer's Take on the Electronic Purse: An Analysis of Commercial Law Issues Associated with Stored Value Cards and Electronic Money,* 52 BUS. LAW. 653, 658-60 (1997) (describing data retention role of the "originator" (issuer) of Mondex value in pilot program, but noting that holders of Mondex value may circulate Mondex value outside of the settlement system for indefinite periods).

[260] *See* James Gleick, *Dead as a Dollar*, N.Y. TIMES, June 16, 1996, (Magazine) at 26, 50 ("[T]his could also be a world where vast computer databases keep track of every magazine you buy, every bus you ride, every hot dog you eat, every beer you drink, every video you rent, every sawbuck you borrow. . . . In the money business, knowledge is power: your spending habits, your likes and dislikes, are valuable to marketers.").

to transactions or experiences between the consumer and the person making the report."[261] According to the FTC's Commentary, this exception applies directly to, among other entities, banks and credit unions.[262] By contrast, the exception does not apply "to report[s] by these entities of information beyond their own transactions or experiences with the consumer."[263]

Assuming that consumer credit information is involved in some manner, it is unclear whether issuers of stored value or other retail electronic payment products will be protected from application of FCRA under the "own transactions and experiences" exemption under 15 U.S.C. § 1681a(d)(A). The crucial question, therefore, for coverage under FCRA is not whether the consumer information passed on by a financial institution comes from its own files, but who is the original source of that information.[264] If the source of information was not a transaction or experience between the depository institution and its customer, then the institution may be found to be a consumer reporting agency under FCRA if it regularly passes on consumer information to third parties.[265]

Finally, as noted in Section 12.06[2][a] above, FCRA is premised on the notion that financial information will be pooled into large databases, such as those operated by the major credit bureaus in the United States. However, developments in cyberbanking and computer networking suggest that the past efficiencies of large databases may not be nearly as great in the future. In the event that large numbers of individual merchants choose to report information on their transactions with consumers directly to other merchants, it will be possible to create detailed financial profiles on consumers that may escape any protection under the FCRA.[266]

[3] THE PRIVACY ACT OF 1974

The Privacy Act of 1974 ("Privacy Act") regulates the practices of federal agencies regarding personal information.[267] It governs how such information is collected and how it is applied to decision-making. The Privacy Act, together with its companion statute, the Freedom of Information Act,[268] represent the most comprehensive attempt by the federal government to regulate information access, processing, and dissemina-

---

[261] 15 U.S.C. § 1681a(d)(A). Case law supports the principle that when a bank furnishes information based solely on its own experiences with the consumer, the information is not a consumer report and the bank is not under those circumstances a consumer reporting agency within the meaning of FCRA. *See, e.g., Nikou v. INB Nat'l Bank*, 638 N.E.2d 448, 453 (Ind. Ct. App. 1994) (holding that information provided about a consumer's payment history, including late payment information, as co-maker on a note to the bank, did not come within the definition of a "consumer report" under the FCRA); *Freeman v. Southern Nat'l Bank*, 531 F. Supp. 94, 95 (S.D. Tex. 1982) (acknowledging that a bank could be, under certain circumstances, a consumer reporting agency, but finding that a bank's provision of collection information regarding a car loan to one of its customers was excluded from the definition of a "consumer report" under the FCRA).

[262] FTC FCRA Commentary, *supra* note 225, at 18,811 (commentary on the definition of "consumer report").

[263] *Id.* An example would be a creditor's or an insurance company's report of the reasons it canceled credit or insurance, based on information from an outside source.

[264] *See* FISCHER, *supra* note 132, ¶ 1.03[3][a], at 1-25.

[265] *See id.*

[266] *See Privacy Hearing, supra* note 176 (statement of David Medine, Associate Director for Credit Practices, FTC).

[267] Privacy Act of 1974, Pub. L. No. 93-579, 88 Stat. 1896 (1974) (codified as amended at 5 U.S.C. § 552a).

[268] Freedom of Information Act, Pub. L. No. 89-487, 80 Stat. 250 (1978) (codified as amended at 5 U.S.C. § 552(f)). The Freedom of Information Act governs third-party access to federal records, including personal information in the control of federal agencies.

tion.[269] The Privacy Act was passed in response to the Nixon administration's use of political opponents' tax records.[270] It was also the first federal legislation to recognize the need to balance an individual's concern for informational privacy with the institutional practice of storing information in a computerized record-keeping system.[271] The Privacy Act has three goals: (i) to protect individuals' interest in government records concerning those individuals; (ii) to regulate practices of federal agencies regarding personal information; and (iii) to balance an individual's need for privacy with the government's need for information about the individual in order to perform its legitimate functions.[272]

[a] Disclosures – Exceptions. The Privacy Act prohibits, with certain exceptions, a federal agency from disclosing any record[273] contained in its system to any other person or agency without the written request or consent of the subject individual.[274] It obliges federal agencies (i) to store only such personal information as is relevant and necessary;[275] (ii) to collect information to the greatest extent practicable from the subject individual;[276] (iii) to maintain records with accuracy and completeness;[277] and (iv) to establish appropriate administrative and technical safeguards to assure the security of records.[278] The Privacy Act also authorizes an individual to have access to, and an opportunity to amend, government records of which he is the subject.[279] Additionally, an individual may request that the agency correct information which is not timely, accurate, or complete.[280] If the agency disagrees with the individual, and refuses to amend its records, the individual has the right to request a review of such refusal.[281] That review must be completed by the agency within thirty days from the date of the request.[282] Finally, the Privacy Act provides for civil remedies against federal

---

[269] *See* SCHWARTZ AND REIDENBERG, DATA PRIVACY LAW § 5-1, at 92 (1996).

[270] *See* Graham, *supra* note 9, at 1419 n.141.

[271] *See* Downey, *supra* note 188, at 309.

[272] *See* Financial Institutions Regulatory and Interest Rate Control Act of 1978, H.R. REP. No. 1383, 33, 34 (1978), *reprinted* in 1978 U.S.C.C.A.N. 9273, 9305.

[273] "[T]he term record means any item, collection, or grouping of information about an individual that is maintained by an agency, including, but not limited to, his education, financial transactions, medical history, and criminal or employment history and that contains his name, or the identifying number, symbol, or other identifying particular assigned to the individual, such as a finger or voice print or a photograph." 5 U.S.C. § 552a(a)(4).

[274] Section 552a(b) provides that "[n]o agency shall disclose any record which is contained in a system of records by any means of communication to any person, or to another agency, except pursuant to a written request by, or with the prior written consent of, the individual to whom the record pertains, unless disclosure would be [permitted under the twelve enumerated exceptions]." 5 U.S.C. § 552a(b).

[275] 5 U.S.C. § 552a(e)(1). *See MacArthur Foundation v. FBI*, 1996 U.S. App. LEXIS (D.C. Cir. Dec. 24, 1996) (rejecting argument that the FBI violated the Privacy Act when it held records related to an individual's First Amendment activities longer than necessary for current law enforcement purposes).

[276] 5 U.S.C. § 552a(e)(2).

[277] *Id.* § 552a(e)(5).

[278] *Id.*

[279] *Id.* § 552a(d)(1)-(2). *See also* SCHWARTZ & REIDENBERG, *supra* note 269, § 5-2(a), at 94.

[280] 5 U.S.C. § 552a(d)(2)-(d)(4).

[281] *Id.* § 552a(d)(3).

[282] *Id.*

agencies.[283] Available remedies include: (i) an order instructing an agency to amend a record; (ii) reasonable costs and attorneys fees; (iii) an injunction from withholding records from an individual; and (iv) actual damages sustained by an individual in cases of willful or intentional agency action.[284]

The Privacy Act contains an extensive list of exemptions to the general prohibition on disclosure of agency records regarding individuals without their request or consent.[285] The most controversial and frequently used of these exemptions is the "routine use" exemption contained in 5 U.S.C. § 552a(b)(3).[286] Federal agencies have cited this exemption to justify a wide range of disclosures of personal information without the individuals' permission.[287] A government sponsored privacy study criticized agency use of the routine use exemption as a "catchall" exemption early in the life of the Privacy Act.[288]

---

[283] *Id.* § 552a(g)(1) (defining agency actions for which civil remedies are available).

[284] *Id.* § 552a(g)(2)(A)-(4)(A). The Privacy Act also contains criminal penalties for agency employees or officers who make willful disclosures in violation of the Act. *Id.* § 552a(i). In late 1992, officials in the Bush administration were accused of making improper inquiries of the passport files of then-Presidential candidate Bill Clinton. An independent counsel, Joseph E. DiGenova, was appointed to investigate the charges, but no prosecutions were ever brought. *See* Walter Pincus, *Prosecutions Unlikely in Passport Case*, WASH. POST, Dec. 14, 1993, at A16. After President Clinton took office, the State Department was asked to investigate whether officials of the Clinton White House examined and disseminated FBI personnel files of former Bush administration officials. *See* Walter Pincus, *State Dept. to Probe Access to Personnel Files: Possible Privacy Act Violations Cited in Check of Bush Appointees*, WASH. POST, Sept. 3, 1993, at A1. Separately, a lawsuit filed on behalf of several former Reagan and Bush White House aides, alleging violations of the Privacy Act in connection with the examination and dissemination of the FBI files, was allowed to proceed to discovery in June 1997. *See Alexander et al. v. Clinton*, Civ. Action No. 96-2123 (D.D.C.); Tom Squitieri, *Hillary Clinton May Have to Testify about FBI Files*, USA TODAY, June 1, 1997, at 8A.

[285] These exceptions include disclosures made:

    (1) to those officers and employees of the agency which maintains the record who have a need for the record in the performance of their duties; . . .

    (3) for a routine use as defined in subsection (a)(7) of this section and described under subsection (e)(4)(D) of this section; . . .

    (5) to a recipient who has provided the agency with advance adequate written assurance that the record will be used solely as a statistical research or reporting record, and the record is to be transferred in a form that is not individually identifiable; . . .

    (7) to another agency or to an instrumentality of any governmental jurisdiction within or under the control of the United States for a civil or criminal law enforcement activity if the activity is authorized by law, and if the head of the agency or instrumentality has made a written request to the agency which maintains the record specifying the particular portion desired and the law enforcement activity for which the record is sought; . . .

    (9) to either House of Congress, or, to the extent of matter within its jurisdiction, any committee or subcommittee thereof, any joint committee of Congress or subcommittee of any such joint committee;

    (10) to the Comptroller General, or any of his authorized representatives, in the course of the performance of the duties of the General Accounting Office;

    (11) pursuant to the order of a court of competent jurisdiction; or

    (12) to a consumer reporting agency in accordance with section 3711(e) of title 31.

5 U.S.C. § 552a(b)(1)-(12).

[286] This provision permits disclosures which fall under the definition of "routine use." Under 5 U.S.C. § 552a(a)(7), a "routine use" means, with respect to the disclosure of a record, "the use of such record for a purpose which is compatible with the purpose for which it was collected." 5 U.S.C. § 552a(e)(4)(D) requires each federal agency to publish in the *Federal Register* a description of each "routine use of the records contained in [its] system, including the categories of users and the purpose of such use."

[287] *See* SCHWARTZ & REIDENBERG, *supra* note 269, § 5-2(a), at 95; Todd Robert Coles, *Does the Privacy Act of 1974 Protect Your Right of Privacy? An Examination of the Routine Use Exemption*, 40 AM. U. L. REV. 957, 990 (1991) (evaluating the success of the Privacy Act in safeguarding individual privacy).

[288] PRIVACY PROTECTION STUDY COMMISSION, THE PRIVACY ACT OF 1974: AN ASSESSMENT 91-93 (1977).

[b] Application of Privacy Act to Electronic Banking and Commerce. The Privacy Act applies only to agencies of the federal government. It creates no right for consumers against other private parties. Thus a depository institution or a nonbank that issues stored value other electronic retail payment products will not face regulation or potential civil liability under the Privacy Act. The Privacy Act may apply if a federal department or agency becomes an issuer of electronic value and retains records concerning the holders of that value. To date, no such government-issued electronic payment products are clearly foreseen at this time.[289]

[4] RIGHT TO FINANCIAL PRIVACY ACT

The Right to Financial Privacy Act ("RFPA")[290] was enacted in response to the Supreme Court's ruling in *United States v. Miller.*[291] The RPFA limits federal government access to the financial records of individuals and gives individuals standing to challenge the release of personal financial information by financial institutions to government agencies and officials.[292] According to the House Report on the RFPA, the purpose of RFPA is "to protect the customers of financial institutions from unwarranted intrusion into their [financial] records while at the same time permitting legitimate law enforcement activity."[293] RFPA therefore, "strikes a balance between customers' right of privacy and the need of law enforcement agencies to obtain financial records pursuant to legitimate investigations."[294]

Under the RFPA, the government generally may have access to, or obtain copies of, information contained in a customer's financial records from a financial institution only if the customer authorizes the disclosure, the government obtains an administrative or judicial subpoena or summons, or the records are sought pursuant to a search warrant or formal written request.[295] The RFPA includes procedural requirements that must be satisfied

---

[289] *See, e.g.,* Edward W. Kelley, Jr., Federal Reserve Board Governor, Remarks at the CyberPayments '96 Conference, Dallas, Texas (June 18, 1996) ("As I have mentioned on previous occasions, however, I do not anticipate that the Federal Reserve will seek to provide a new retail electronic payment product in this emerging industry."); *The Future of Money II: Hearing Before the Subcomm. on Domestic and International Monetary Policy of the House Comm. on Banking and Financial Services,* 104th Cong. (1995) (statement of Philip N. Diehl, Director, U.S. Mint) ("[T]he idea of a Treasury-issued, 'universal' stored-value card presents the potential for recouping the lost seignorage revenue from a lower demand for coinage, especially considering the high value that could be stored on such a card. . . . [this idea] is worth exploring."). *See also* CONGRESSIONAL BUDGET OFFICE, EMERGING ELECTRONIC METHODS FOR MAKING RETAIL PAYMENTS 45 (June 1996).

[290] Right to Financial Privacy Act of 1978, Pub. L. No. 95-630, tit. XI, 1978 U.S.C.C.A.N. (92 Stat.) 3641, 3697-3710 (1978) (codified as amended at 12 U.S.C. §§ 3401-3422) [hereinafter RFPA]. The RFPA was passed as Title XI of the Financial Institutions Regulatory and Interest Rate Control Act of 1978. For a comprehensive overview of the provisions and disclosure procedures of, and the exceptions to, the RFPA, see FISCHER, *supra* note 132, ¶¶ 2.01 *et seq.*

[291] *United States v. Miller,* 425 U.S. 435 (1976) (holding that a bank depositor had no reasonable expectation of privacy in the contents of checks and deposit slips held by his financial institution, largely because the institution, not the customer, had physical possession of the records). *See also* Donald A. Doheny, Sr. & Graydon John Forrer, *Electronic Access to Account Information and Financial Privacy,* 109 BANKING L.J. 436, 443-47 (describing the *Miller* holding and rationale).

[292] *See* FISCHER, *supra* note 132, ¶ 2.01, at 2-6.

[293] H.R. REP. No. 95-1383, at 33-34 (1978), *reprinted in* 1978 U.S.C.C.A.N. 9273, 9305.

[294] *Id.*

[295] *See Anderson v. La Junta State Bank,* 115 F.3d 756 (10th Cir. 1997) (holding that a bank officer's oral response to a government investigator's request, without compliance with the RFPA's procedures, related to the customer's records and thus violated the RPFA).

by the federal government prior to seeking financial institution customer records, as well as procedural require-ments the institution must follow prior to disclosure.[296] Subject to certain exceptions, the government must provide the financial institution with a certificate of the government's compliance with RFPA prior to disclosure of the requested information.[297] The government's request for information triggers a waiting period,[298] during which the customer is notified of the request and given the opportunity to challenge the disclosure by either filing a motion to quash a subpoena or seeking an appropriate injunction against the government's written request.[299]

The RFPA covers only disclosure requested by "any agency or department of the United States, or any officer, employee or agent thereof,"[300] not disclosure made by financial institutions to state or local governments or to private parties. The Act also is limited in its coverage in that it covers only specified "financial institu-tions"[301] and specified customers, namely individuals and partnerships with five or fewer individual partners.[302] Thus the availability of the RFPA's protections depends upon the type of person whose records are sought.[303]

[a] Permitted Disclosures Under the RFPA. There are a number of exceptions to RFPA's disclosure prohibitions and required procedures. Disclosures under the RFPA may be made, pursuant to (i) written customer authorizations,[304] (ii) administrative subpoenas and summonses,[305] (iii) search warrants,[306] (iv) judicial subpoenas,[307] and (v) formal written requests by the government.[308] RFPA establishes a series of

---

[296] Under the RFPA, a "customer" means a person, an individual, or a partnership with five or fewer partners, or an authorized representative of that person who uses a financial institution's services in relation to an account maintained in the individual's name. 12 U.S.C. § 3401(4)-(5). Under the RFPA, "'financial record' means "an original of, a copy of, or information known to have been derived from, any record held by a financial institu-tion pertaining to a customer's relationship with the financial institution." 12 U.S.C. § 3401(2). Under the RFPA, a "financial institution" includes any office of a depository institution or a card issuer as defined under the Consumer Protection Act (15 U.S.C. § 1602(n)). 12 U.S.C. § 3401(1).

[297] Under the RFPA, a financial institution "shall not release the financial records of a customer until the Government authority seeking such records certi-fies in writing to the financial institution that it has complied with the applicable provisions of this chapter." 12 U.S.C. § 3403(b). The government may also seek to demonstrate exigent circumstances necessitating disclosure and submit a formal written request to a financial institution or seek an ex parte order of an appropriate court delaying notification to the customer for specified periods. 12 U.S.C. §§ 3408, 3409(b).

[298] 12 U.S.C. § 3410(a) (generally, within ten days of service or fourteen days of mailing).

[299] *Id.* § 3410 (customer challenges).

[300] *Id.* § 3401(3).

[301] Under the RPFA, a "financial institution" means any "office of a bank, savings bank, card issuer as defined in section 1602(n) of Title 15, industrial loan company, trust company, savings association, building and loan, or homestead association (including cooperative banks), credit union, or consumer finance institution, located in any State or territory of the United States, the District of Columbia, Puerto Rico, Guam, American Samoa, or the Virgin Islands." 12 U.S.C. § 3401(a).

[302] *See* FISCHER, *supra* note 132, ¶ 2.01, at 2-4.

[303] *See id.* ¶ 2.03[3], at 2-17 (explaining that corporations, unincorporated associations, and large partnerships are not protected by the RFPA).

[304] 12 U.S.C. § 3404.

[305] *Id.* § 3405.

[306] *Id.* § 3406.

[307] *Id.* § 3407.

[308] *Id.* §§ 3402, 3408.

criteria for written customer authorizations, including limited duration and customer right of revocation.[309] Blanket written customer authorizations cannot be required as a condition of doing business with a financial institution,[310] and appear to be generally prohibited.[311] The scope of a written authorization will normally be evaluated in light of a customer's reasonable expectations as to the purpose of the authorization and the scope of the records covered by the authorization.[312] In instances where the authorization is deficient on its face, a financial institution's disclosure of customer records to the government may cast doubt on the institution's good faith, and thus it may be unable to rely on the good faith defense in the RFPA.[313] Moreover, a customer has the right to obtain a copy of a record that indicates all instances when that customer's records were disclosed to the government under the RFPA.[314]

The government may only obtain disclosure of a customer's financial records pursuant to an administrative subpoena or summons if: (i) the subpoena or summons is authorized by law; (ii) there is "reason to believe that the records sought are relevant to a legitimate law enforcement inquiry;" and (iii) the government follows the specified procedures for obtaining the records, namely, that the ten or fourteen day period for customer challenge of the subpoena or summons has passed.[315] Provided that the government has subpoena power, the federal agency must also serve a subpoena on the customer before, or concurrently with, service on the financial institution.[316] The requirements for disclosure pursuant to a judicial subpoena are substantially similar to those for an administrative subpoena or summons.[317] The government may only obtain disclosure pursuant to a search warrant if: (i) the warrant has been issued upon a showing of probable cause and signed by a federal judge or magistrate; (ii) the warrant is executed within ten days of its issuance; (iii) the agency provides a

---

[309] The RFPA provides, in relevant part:

A customer may authorize disclosure under [the RFPA] if he furnishes to the financial institution and to the Government authority seeking to obtain such disclosure a signed and dated statement which:

(1) authorizes such disclosure for a period not in excess of three months;

(2) states that the customer may revoke such authorization at any time before the financial records are disclosed;

(3) identifies the financial records which are authorized to be disclosed;

(4) specifies the purposes for which, and the Government authority to which, such records may be disclosed; and

(5) states the customer's rights under this chapter.

12 U.S.C. § 3404(a).

[310] *Id.* § 3404(b).

[311] *See* FISCHER, *supra* note 132, ¶ 2.04[1], at 2-30.

[312] *See id.*

[313] The RPFA provides, in relevant part, that "[a]ny financial institution or agent or employee thereof making a disclosure of financial records pursuant to this chapter in good-faith reliance upon a certificate by any Government authority or pursuant to the provisions of section 3413(l) of this title shall not be liable to the customer for such disclosure under this chapter, the constitution of any State, or any law or regulation of any State or any political subdivision of any State." 12 U.S.C. § 3417(c).

[314] *Id.* § 3404(c).

[315] *Id.* § 3405(1)-(3).

[316] *Id.* § 3405(2).

[317] *Compare* 12 U.S.C. § 3407, *with* 12 U.S.C. § 3405.

certificate of compliance to the financial institution; and (iv) the agency notifies the customer within ninety days after the search, unless it has obtained a delaying order for such notification.[318]

The final method whereby disclosure is authorized under the RFPA is the formal written request by the government.[319] Under this method, disclosure is permissible only if (i) no administrative summons or subpoena "reasonably appears" available; (ii) the request is authorized under appropriate agency regulations; and (iii) there is reason to believe that the records sought are relevant to a legitimate law enforcement inquiry.[320] Financial institutions, increasingly aware of their privacy obligations and potential liabilities for improper disclosures as a result of RFPA, will likely be reluctant to permit these voluntary disclosures.[321]

[i] *Exceptions to the Disclosure Requirements.* RFPA provides numerous exceptions to its disclosure prohibitions based on the type of transaction and purpose of the disclosure.[322] For example, RFPA contains exceptions relating to the perfection of security interests[323] and for government loan programs.[324] There are also exceptions for disclosures required by federal laws, such as the Bank Secrecy Act and Federal Deposit Insurance Act, as well as exceptions for disclosures in national security situations.[325]

The RFPA also contains an exception for supervisory investigations and proceedings of federal agencies, such as the Federal Deposit Insurance Corporation, the Office of Thrift Supervision, and the Securities and Exchange Commission.[326] Under this exception, the RFPA excepts disclosures to supervisory agencies in the exercise of their supervisory, regulatory, or monetary functions, including conservatorship and receivership, with respect to financial institutions, their holding companies, or subsidiaries.[327] In *Adams v. Board of Governors of Federal Reserve System,*[328] the plaintiff consumer claimed the FRB violated the RFPA by obtaining certain loan information about the consumer from the bank and from the Office of the Comptroller of the Currency without complying with the notification and procedural requirements of the RPFA.[329] Granting the FRB's motion for summary judgment, the district court concluded that the FRB was a supervisory agency conducting

[318] 12 U.S.C. § 3406(a)-(c).

[319] *Id.* § 3408 (which replaced the past practice of informal requests by government). *See* FISCHER, *supra* note 132, ¶ 2.05[4], at 2-45 to 2-46.

[320] 12 U.S.C. § 3408(1)-(3) .

[321] *See* FISCHER, *supra* note 132, ¶ 2.05[4], at 2-46.

[322] For a further discussion of the operation of each of the RFPA's exceptions, see FISCHER, *supra* note 132, ¶ 2.05, at 2-66 to 2-85.

[323] 12 U.S.C. § 3403(d)(1).

[324] 12 U.S.C. §§ 3403(d)(2), 3413(o) (disclosure to Federal Housing Finance Board or Federal Home Loan Banks).

[325] *Id.* § 3414(b) (disclosures permitted in emergency situations); *Id.* § 3414(a) (disclosures to the Secret Service and intelligence agencies).

[326] *Id.* § 3413(b).

[327] *Id.; see id.* § 3401(7) (definition of "supervisory agency").

[328] *Adams v. Board of Governors of Fed. Reserve Sys.,* 659 F. Supp. 948 (D. Minn. 1987), *aff'd*, 855 F.2d 1336 (8th Cir. 1988).

[329] *Adams,* 659 F. Supp. at 949. The FRB's investigation of the plaintiff began with the plaintiff's efforts to acquire a Montana bank and the FRB's review of the plaintiff's proposal under the provisions of the Change in Bank Control Act, 12 U.S.C. § 1817(j)(1). *Id.*

its supervisory and regulatory functions and thus was within the supervisory exception to the requirements of the RFPA.[330]

Finally, there is a general exception for the disclosure of "any financial records or information which is not identified with or identifiable as being derived from the financial records of a particular customer."[331] This exception is consistent with the general RFPA policy that if an individual's privacy is not at stake in a particular disclosure, then the RFPA does not restrict that disclosure.[332] The Eighth Circuit, applying this exception in *Donovan v. National Bank of Alaska*,[333] explained that financial records not identified with, or identifiable as being derived from, a particular customer may be disclosed without compliance with the RFPA.[334] In *Donovan*, the Department of Labor had requested documents concerning the employee benefit plan of a national bank. The court found that the plan was not a person within the coverage of RFPA.[335] It noted, however, that if the Labor Department sought particular records of bank customers covered by the plan, then the RFPA would be implicated.

[*ii*] *Preemption of State Law – Penalties.* Except for disclosures permitted in connection with suspected criminal activity, the RFPA does not expressly preempt state laws.[336] Absent specific preemptive provisions or a clear intent in a federal law, federal preemption of state law rests upon one of two theories: (i) an express or implied congressional intent to "occupy the field" governed by the federal legislation; and (ii) a conflict between state and federal law, or between state law and federal operations duly authorized by federal law.[337] Therefore, where states have statutory restrictions on disclosure of customer financial information that exceed the RFPA or other federal law, a bank's disclosure of account or other customer financial information to third parties may still make the bank subject to damages under state law even when such disclosure would be permitted under federal law.[338]

Under the RFPA, financial institutions or governmental agencies "obtaining or disclosing financial records or information contained therein" in violation of the RFPA's provisions may incur civil liability to the customer to whom the records relate.[339] Penalties include: (i) $100 for the first violation without regard to the volume of records involved; (ii) actual damages sustained by the customer; (iii) punitive damages in cases of willful or

---

[330] *Id.* at 955-57; *see also Adams v. Board of Governors of the Fed. Reserve Sys.*, 855 F.2d at 1341-42.

[331] 12 U.S.C. § 3413(a).

[332] *See* FISCHER, *supra* note 132, ¶ 2.05[1], at 2-67.

[333] *Donovan v. National Bank of Alaska*, 696 F.2d 678 (9th Cir. 1983).

[334] *Id.* at 683.

[335] *Id.*

[336] 12 U.S.C. § 3403(c). See Section 12.06[8] for a discussion of state financial privacy laws.

[337] *See generally* TRIBE, *supra* note 3, §§ 6-25, 6-26, 6-27.

[338] *See* Donald A. Doheny, Sr. & Graydon John Forrer, *Electronic Access to Account Information and Financial Privacy*, 109 BANKING L.J. 436, 447 (1992).

[339] 2 U.S.C. § 3417(a).

intentional violations; and (iv) costs and attorneys fees.[340] As noted above, the government's certificate of compliance generally acts as a shield to liability for financial institutions.[341]

[b] Application of RFPA to Electronic Banking and Commerce. RFPA applies to agencies of the federal government as well as to "financial institutions." The term encompasses a broad range of financial services providers including banks, credit unions, savings and loans, and other depository institutions, as well as credit card issuers.[342] The RFPA will, therefore, apply to claims made by consumers of electronic retail payment products against issuers of those products for violations of their privacy rights. There are two limitations in RFPA's applications. First, RFPA does not apply to all voluntary disclosures made by financial institutions, but only to those disclosures made to agencies of the federal government. The RFPA does not prohibit voluntary disclosures by financial institutions to local or state governments, including law enforcement officials, or to private third parties such as employers or credit bureaus. Thus, a stored value issuer might contract to provide spending and payment transactional information about its customers' spending habits. If derogatory (or neutral) information about a customer's spending and payment habits were disclosed in this manner, for example, for marketing or other purposes to third parties, the consumer would have no cause of action under the RPFA against either the issuer of the stored value product or the user of the information. In addition, to the extent that a stored value issuer is not a "financial institution" for purposes of RFPA, the notification and procedural safeguards of RFPA will not apply, either to disclosures to the federal government or to third parties.

Finally, like the Privacy Act, the RFPA does not create rights for consumers against private third parties who tamper with, steal, modify, or misappropriate consumers' funds or account information. Individuals who are victims of privacy violations or computer fraud or theft must instead look to other federal statutes, such as the Electronic Communications Privacy Act[343] and the Computer Fraud and Abuse Act of 1986.[344]

[5] ELECTRONIC COMMUNICATIONS PRIVACY ACT OF 1986

Congress addressed the broader issue of individuals' electronic privacy rights in the Electronic Communications Privacy Act ("ECPA").[345] Passed in 1986 to amend Title III of the Omnibus Crime Control and Safe Streets Act,[346] the ECPA clarified the scope of federal privacy protections in light of changes in computer and telecommunications technologies. The ECPA is a comprehensive privacy statute that addresses,

---

[340] 12 U.S.C. § 3417(a)(1)-(4).

[341] *See* FISCHER, *supra* note 132, ¶ 2.08, at 2-136.

[342] 12 U.S.C. § 3401(1) (definition of "financial institution"). *See also* 15 U.S.C. § 1602(n) (definition of "card issuer" under the Fair Credit Reporting Act).

[343] *See* Section 12.06[5].

[344] *See* Section 12.06[7].

[345] Electronic Communications Privacy Act of 1986, Pub. L. No. 99-508, 1986 U.S.C.C.A.N. (100 Stat.) 1848 (codified as amended at 18 U.S.C. §§ 2510-21 (Title I), 2701-11 (Title II)) [hereinafter ECPA]. For a further discussion of the provisions of the ECPA, see FISCHER, *supra* note 132, ¶ 6.06[1], at 6-21 to 6-31; *see also* BAKER & BRANDEL, *supra* note 8, ¶ 19.02[1][d], at 19-21 to 19-26.

[346] Pub. L. No. 90-351, 1968 U.S.C.C.A.N. (82 Stat. 213) 253 (codified at 18 U.S.C. §§ 2510-20 (1968)).

in two separate titles, electronic surveillance and interception, and record-keeping concerns related to (i) real-time oral, wire or electronic communications, and (ii) stored electronic transmissions.[347] The statute has a broad scope, regulating the information practices of a wide range of communications companies serving the public.[348] The law also reaches the conduct of both public and private sector firms. Unlike the Privacy Act and the RFPA, the ECPA is not limited to the access rights of federal agencies for disclosure of consumer information stored or transmitted by financial institutions.

According to the Senate Report on the ECPA ("Senate ECPA Report"), Congress intended ECPA to protect against the "unauthorized interception of electronic communications."[349] The Senate ECPA Report noted that "tremendous advances" in telecommunications and computer technologies have "carried with them comparable technological advances in surveillance devices and techniques," making possible spying techniques that would permit the interception of personal and proprietary communications.[350] It also recognized generally the effect of computer data processing and storage on individual Americans' privacy rights, stating:

> The Committee also recognizes that computers are used extensively today for the storage and processing of information. With the advent of computerized recordkeeping systems, Americans have lost the ability to lock away a great deal of personal and business information.[351]

[a] Title I — Surveillance and Interception Concerns. The ECPA amended federal wiretap provisions[352] to bring private individuals' access and privacy rights into line with modern technological developments. Title I addresses generally the interception of wire, oral, and electronic communications.[353] It thus directly applies to most of the data and communications made between parties using the Internet and other open computer networks.[354] Under the statute, subject to enumerated exceptions, it is illegal to intercept the contents of wire, oral, or electronic communications or to disclose the contents of a communication that one

---

[347] Title III of the ECPA governs the use, application, and issuance of orders for pen registers and trap and trace devices. *See* 18 U.S.C. §§ 3121-27; FISCHER, *supra* note 132, ¶ 6.06[1]1, at 6-21 to 6-22.

[348] *See* BAKER & BRANDEL, *supra* note 8, ¶ 19.02[1][d], at 19-21.

[349] S. REP. No. 99-541 (1986), *reprinted in* 1986 U.S.C.C.A.N. 3555.

[350] *Id.* at 3557.

[351] *Id.* The Senate Report also spoke in broad terms of the defense of Fourth Amendment privacy rights, stating:
Most importantly, the law must advance with the technology to ensure the continued vitality of the [F]ourth [A]mendment. Privacy cannot be left solely to depend on physical protection, or it will gradually erode as technology advances. Congress must act to protect the privacy of our citizens. If we do not, we will promote the erosion of this precious right.
Id. at 3559.

[352] 18 U.S.C. § § 2501 *et seq.* ("Wire Interception and Interception of Oral Communications").

[353] *See* FISCHER, *supra* note 132, ¶ 6.06[1], at 6-21.

[354] *See* Downey, *supra* note 188, at 312-13.

knows to have been illegally intercepted.[355] The term "intercept" means "the aural or other acquisition of the contents of any wire, electronic, or oral communication through the use of any electronic, mechanical, or other device."[356]

An "electronic communication" includes certain defined data transfers that "[affect] interstate or foreign commerce."[357] As a general rule, a communication is an "electronic communication" if it is not carried by sound waves and cannot fairly be characterized as containing the human voice.[358] The term "electronic communication" includes transmissions which are transmitted by electronic mail, bulletin boards, computer-to-computer communications, remote computer services, cellular telephones, portions of cordless telephone communications, pen registers, trap and trace devices, and certain kinds of pager and satellite transmissions.[359] The

---

[355] The ECPA provides, in relevant part:

(1) Except as otherwise specifically provided in this chapter any person who —

(a) intentionally intercepts, endeavors to intercept, or procures any other person to intercept or endeavor to intercept, any wire, oral, or electronic communication;

(b) intentionally uses, endeavors to use, or procures any other person to use or endeavor to use any electronic, mechanical, or other device to intercept any oral communication when (i) such device is affixed to, or otherwise transmits a signal through, a wire, cable, or other like connection used in wire communication; or (ii) such device transmits communications by radio, or interferes with the transmission of such communication; or (iii) such person knows, or has reason to know, that such device or any component thereof has been sent through the mail or transported in interstate or foreign commerce; or (iv) such use or endeavor to use (A) takes place on the premises of any business or other commercial establishment the operations of which affect interstate or foreign commerce; or (B) obtains or is for the purpose of obtaining information relating to the operations of any business or other commercial establishment the operations of which affect interstate or foreign commerce; or (v) such person acts in the District of Columbia, the Commonwealth of Puerto Rico, or any territory or possession of the United States;

(c) intentionally discloses, or endeavors to disclose, to any other person the contents of any wire, oral, or electronic communication, knowing or having reason to know that the information was obtained through the interception of a wire, oral, or electronic communication in violation of this subsection;

(d) intentionally uses, or endeavors to use, the contents of any wire, oral, or electronic communication, knowing or having reason to know that the information was obtained through the interception of a wire, oral, or electronic communication in violation of this subsection; or

(e)(i) intentionally discloses, or endeavors to disclose to any other person the contents of any wire, oral, or electronic communication, intercepted by means authorized by [the ECPA] (ii) knowing or having reason to know that the information was obtained through the interception of such a communication in connection with a criminal investigation, (iii) having obtained or received the information in connection with a criminal investigation, and (iv) with intent to improperly obstruct, impede, or interfere with a duly authorized criminal investigation, shall be punished as provided in [the ECPA].

18 U.S.C. § 2511.

[356] 18 U.S.C. § 2510(4). The term "oral communication" means "any oral communication uttered by a person exhibiting an expectation that such communication is not subject to interception under circumstances justifying such expectation, but such term does not include any electronic communication." *Id.* § 2510(2). The term "wire communication" means:

any aural transfer made in whole or in part through the use of facilities for the transmission of communications by the aid of wire, cable, or other like connection between the point of origin and the point of reception (including the use of such connection in a switching station) furnished or operated by any person engaged in providing or operating such facilities for the transmission of interstate or foreign communications or communications affecting interstate or foreign commerce and such term includes any electronic storage of such communication.

Id. § 2501(1).

[357] *See* 18 U.S.C. § 2510(12). Under the statute, the term "electronic communication" means any "transfer of signs, signals, writing, images, sounds, data, or intelligence of any nature transmitted in whole or in part by a wire, radio, electromagnetic, photoelectronic or photooptical system that affects interstate or foreign commerce, but does not include (a) any wire or oral communication; (b) any communication made through a tone-only paging device; [or] (c) any communication from a tracking device (as defined in section 3117 of this title)." *Id.*

[358] *See* FISCHER, *supra* note 132, ¶ 6.06[1], at 6-22.

[359] S. REP. No. 99-541 (1986), *reprinted in* 1986 U.S.C.C.A.N. 3562-65.

protection for electronic communications could include at least some components of an electronic payment system, depending upon how it is structured. For example, computer to computer communications over the Internet would be covered by the ECPA.[360]

The Title I prohibition regarding interception of oral, wire, or electronic communications is subject to a number of exceptions. First, the statute does not prohibit a communications service provider from disclosing communications or information with the "lawful" consent of either the originator or the intended recipient of the communication.[361] It also permits broadly the interception of oral, wire, or electronic communications by a party to the communication if one of the parties to such communication consents to the interception, unless the interception is done for purposes of committing a criminal or tortious act.[362]

Title I of the ECPA permits a communications service provider to disclose information to other communications service providers that are involved in the transmission of the communication.[363] In a related exception, the statute does not prohibit the interception, disclosure, or use of a protected communication by an officer, employee, or agent of a provider of communications services whose facilities are used in the transmission of the communication, if such interception, disclosure, or use occurs "in the normal course of his employment while engaged in any activity which is a necessary incident to the rendition of [the communications] service" or to the protection of the property rights of the service provider.[364] Under this "normal course" of business exception, the service provider is not permitted to engage in random monitoring of its system other than to check for mechanical problems or service quality.[365]

Under the ECPA, it is permissible to intercept electronic communications made through an "electronic communications system"[366] configured so that the communication is "readily accessible to the general public."[367] The statute also permits a communications service provider to intercept communications that "appear to pertain to the commission of a crime," and subsequently disclose such communications to a law enforcement agency if the communications service provider "inadvertently obtained" the transmission.[368] In addition, the ECPA contains a number of specific exemptions where persons (or government agencies)

---

[360] Under the consent exception, 18 U.S.C. § 2511(2)(d), however, the ECPA likely would not prohibit a merchant who is a party to an Internet electronic payment transaction from retaining and disclosing information regarding the communication. BD. OF GOVERNORS OF THE FED. RESERVE SYSTEM, REPORT TO THE CONGRESS ON THE APPLICATION OF THE ELECTRONIC FUND TRANSFER ACT TO ELECTRONIC STORED-VALUE PRODUCTS 37 (March 1997).

[361] 18 U.S.C. § 2511(3)(b)(ii).

[362] Id. § 2511(2)(d).

[363] Id. § 2511(3)(b)(iii).

[364] Id. § 2511(2)(a)(i).

[365] Id. § 2511(2)(a)(i).

[366] The term "electronic communications system" means "any wire, radio, electromagnetic, photooptical or photoelectronic facilities for the transmission of electronic communications, and any computer facilities or related electronic equipment for the electronic storage of such communications." 18 U.S.C. § 2510(14).

[367] Id. § 2511(2)(g).

[368] 18 U.S.C. § 2511(3)(b)(iv).

are authorized by law to intercept a wire, oral, or electronic communication if the person is a party to the communication.[369]

The ECPA generally prohibits the disclosure of electronic communications by electronic communications service providers after any interception thereof.[370] For example, subject to certain enumerated exceptions provided by the statute, a person providing an electronic communications service to the public shall not "intentionally divulge" the contents of any communication to any person or entity other than the addressee or intended recipient, or an agent thereof.[371]

Title I of the ECPA provides civil and criminal penalties for unauthorized interception of protected communications by parties in the private sector. As a general rule, a statutory violation of the ECPA is punishable by a five-year term of imprisonment and a fine of up to $250,000 for individuals or $500,000 for organizations.[372] The ECPA distinguishes as to, and provides lesser criminal penalties for, first time offenders.[373] Under the statute, injunctive relief is also available to the federal government in cases of certain violations.[374]

The ECPA authorizes any person whose wire, oral, or electronic communication is intercepted, disclosed, or intentionally used in violation of the statute to file a civil action for compensatory damages and statutory damages in amounts ranging from $50 to $10,000 depending upon the particular circumstances.[375] Courts may also award punitive damages in appropriate cases, and award attorneys' fees and litigation costs reasonably incurred.[376] Civil actions brought under Title I of the ECPA are subject to a two-year statute of limitations.[377] Finally, the statute provides for injunctive relief against persons who are about to engage in interceptions or uses of oral, wire, or electronic communications in violation of the statute.[378]

[b] Title II — Stored Communications. ECPA Title II — "Stored Wire and Electronic Communications and Transactional Records" — governs the storage of wire or electronic communications. Title II makes it a criminal offense to "intentionally access without authorization a facility through which an electronic communications service is provided,"[379] or to "intentionally exceed an authorization to access that facility; and thereby obtain, alter, or prevent authorized access to wire or electronic communication while it is in electronic

---

[369] *See e.g.,* 18 U.S.C. § 2511(2)(a)(ii) (pursuant to the Foreign Intelligence Surveillance Act of 1978), § 2511(2)(b) (Federal Communications Commission).

[370] 18 U.S.C. § 2511(3)(a).

[371] *Id.* The exceptions set forth in 18 U.S.C. § 2511(3)(b), include the "necessary incident" exception of § 2511(2)(a).

[372] *See* FISCHER, *supra* note 132, ¶ 6.06[1], at 6-23.

[373] 18 U.S.C. § 2511(4)(b).

[374] *Id.* § 2511(5)(a)(ii).

[375] *Id.* § 2520(a)-(c). *See* FISCHER, *supra* note 132, ¶ 6.06[1], at 6-24.

[376] 18 U.S.C. § 2520(b).

[377] *Id.* § 2520(e).

[378] *Id.* § 2521.

[379] *Id.* § 2701(a)(1).

storage in such system."[380] In order to constitute a crime under Title II, a person must obtain, alter, or prevent authorized access to a wire or electronic communication while it is in "electronic storage."[381] The term "'electronic storage" means: "(a) any temporary, intermediate storage of a wire or electronic communication incidental to the electronic transmission thereof; and (b) any storage of such communication by an electronic communication service for purposes of backup protection of such communication."[382] According to the ECPA Senate Report, The definition of "electronic storage" is not intended to prohibit public access to electronic storage facilities such an "electronic bulletin board,"[383] nor to preclude a subscriber to a computer mail facility from accessing information in that subscriber's portion of the computer facility.[384]

Title II also contains a prohibition against disclosure of the content of an electronic communication while in electronic storage similar to that contained in Title I.[385] Title II prohibits the "knowing" disclosure of such communications.[386] The statute's prohibition against disclosure of a stored communication is subject to certain exceptions. These exceptions include where the disclosure is made (i) with the lawful consent of the originator of the communication, (ii) to the employees or authorized agents "whose facilities are used" to forward the communication to its destination, (iii) in a response to a court order, (iv) as a "necessary incident" to the rendition of the electronic storage services, or (v) to law enforcement agencies, if the communication was inadvertently obtained by the communications service provider and "appears to pertain to the commission of a crime."[387]

Title II provides that any entity, either an individual communications service provider or "other person aggrieved by any violation" of Title II, may institute a civil action to recover damages for violations of the statute.[388] Title II distinguishes between those acts committed for purposes of commercial advantage, malicious destruction, or private personal gain.[389] In such cases, Title II provides for a fine of not more than $250,000 or imprisonment of one year, or both, or lesser penalties if the violation was not committed for such purposes.[390] In all other cases, the statute provides lesser penalties.[391]

---

[380] *Id.* § 2701(a)(ii).

[381] FISCHER, *supra* note 132, ¶ 6.06[1], at 6-25.

[382] 18 U.S.C. § 2510(17).

[383] *See* S. REP. No. 99-541, *supra* note 359, *reprinted in* 1986 U.S.C.C.A.N. at 3590.

[384] *Id.* Whether Title II's definition of "electronic storage" would include a web server is unclear.

[385] 18 U.S.C. § 2702(a)(1). Title I extends such protection to electronic communications while they are in transmission. *See* S. REP. No. 99-541, *supra* note 359, *reprinted in* 1986 U.S.C.C.A.N. at 3591 (citing 18 U.S.C. § 2511(3)).

[386] 18 U.S.C. § 2702(a)(1)-(2). *See also Andersen Consulting, LLP v. UOP and Bickel & Brewer*, 1998 U.S. Dist. LEXIS 1016 (N.D. Ill. Jan. 23, 1998) (holding that defendants' intentional disclosure of plaintiff's e-mails to the Wall Street Journal did not violate § 2702).

[387] 18 U.S.C. § 2702(b)(1)-(6).

[388] *Id.* § 2707(a).

[389] *Id.* § 2701(b)(1).

[390] *Id.* § 2701(b)(1).

[391] *Id.* § 2701(b)(2).

[c] ECPA Case Law. Case law regarding ECPA provisions have involved wireless (*i.e.*, cordless) and cellular phone communications, financial institutions facilitating customer electronic fund transfers ("EFTs"), and the search and/or seizure of e-mail, CD-ROMs, and other computer files. Civil actions brought for ECPA violations sometimes fail on the grounds that the makers of the communications via a wireless or cellular telephone have no reasonable expectation of privacy in their communications conducted over radio waves.[392]

For example, in *Edwards v. State Farm Insurance Company*, the plaintiff initiated a telephone call from his automobile with his attorney over a mobile phone.[393] A listener using a radio scanner overhead the transmission and provided a recording to the local United States Attorney's Office, which used it in a pending criminal trial in Louisiana.[394] The plaintiff brought an action under Title I of the ECPA for unlawful interception of the telephone call, and under Louisiana state law for violations of his right to privacy.[395] In *Edwards*, the Fifth Circuit found that the eavesdropping and disclosure to the government did not violate the ECPA or state privacy law because the call was, in essence, an "oral communication which lacked a reasonable expectation of privacy."[396]

Similarly, in *United States v. Carr*, a defendant, whose cordless phone conversations regarding cocaine trafficking were intercepted by police authorities, argued that the interception of the cordless telephone conversations was a violation of Title I of the ECPA and of the Fourth Amendment.[397] The *Carr* court rejected this argument, reasoning that the cordless telephone call was not protected under the ECPA as a "wire" or "electronic" communication.[398] It also concluded that the defendant did not have a reasonable expectation of privacy in his cordless telephone communications under the Fourth Amendment.[399]

In 1994, Congress amended Title I of the ECPA to bring cordless phone calls within the ECPA's protections.[400] Since 1994, Title I of the ECPA protects both the "radio and wire portion of cordless [telephone] communications" from unlawful interception or disclosure.[401] By contrast, cellular telephone communications,

---

[392] *See e.g., Tyler v. Berodt*, 877 F.2d 705 (8th Cir. 1989), *cert. denied,* 493 U.S. 1022 (1990); *Edwards v. State Farm Ins. Co.*, 833 F.2d 535 (5th Cir. 1987).

[393] *Edwards*, 833 F.2d at 536.

[394] *Id.* at 536.

[395] *Id.* at 537.

[396] *Id.* at 539-40.

[397] *United States v. Carr*, 805 F. Supp. 1266, 1267 (E.D.N.C. 1992).

[398] *Id.* at 1271-72.

[399] *Id.* at 1276.

[400] The provision in 18 U.S.C. § 2510(1) expressly excluding the radio portion of a cordless telephone communication from the protection of the Act was deleted by amendment in 1994. Communications Assistance for Law Enforcement Act, Pub. L. No. 103-414, § 202(a)(1), 1994 U.S.C.C.A.N. (108 Stat.) 4279, 4290. *See Askin v. McNulty*, 47 F.3d 100, 103 (4th Cir.), *cert. denied*, 116 S. Ct. 382 (1995) (before Congressional amendments in 1994, cordless telephone communications were "neither a wire nor electronic communication" under Title I of the ECPA) (citations omitted).

[401] *See Askin*, 47 F.3d at 104. In December 1996, a Florida couple using a police scanner taped a portion of a telephone conference call involving Speaker Newt Gingrich and other ranking House Republican officials discussing strategy related to congressional ethical investigations of Speaker Gingrich. *See* George Archibald, *GOP Seeks Probe of Piracy of Phone Call*, WASH. TIMES, Jan. 11, 1997, at A1 (discussing the episode and possible ECPA violations).

which operate in a different manner than cordless telephone calls, have always fallen squarely within the protection of Title I of the ECPA as "wire communications."[402]

A series of related cases has interpreted the meaning of the ECPA's provisions involving the transfer and/or seizure of funds involving EFTs.[403] Typically, these cases involved investigations by the government of criminal activities (such as money laundering) related to bank accounts, the forfeiture of assets in connection with such investigations, and the use of the EFTs in criminal activities under investigation. For example, in *Manufacturas International, Ltda. v. Bank of New York* (*"Manufacturas"*), a group of Columbian business concerns brought suit against the U.S. government and a number of banks for their role in the government's investigation of drug trafficking and seizure of funds transmitted in a large number of wire transfers from Europe to South America, passing through New York banks.[404] The defendant banks had seized the funds transmitted by the EFTs and paid the funds over into a court-supervised bank account.[405]

The plaintiffs in *Manufacturas*, intended beneficiaries of the EFTs, brought suit claiming violations of, among other statutes, the ECPA. Granting summary judgment to the banks, the court ruled that the seizure of the funds, which were transmitted by means of the EFTs, by the banks (following government and court orders to do so) did not fall within the range of conduct prohibited by the ECPA.[406] Noting that "[f]orfeiture proceedings are not surveillance,"[407] the court stated that "since the funds and the transfers were being claimed in good faith as belonging to the government, obtaining information on their destination and taking them into government possession was not a violation of the [ECPA]."[408]

The court also found that, even if the ECPA applied to the seizure of the wire transfers, the banks were not liable because of the application of the "color of law" exception for Title I liability under the ECPA.[409] The court found, therefore, that the government's intent was to seize its own funds, and that the banks "had no

---

[402] *See United States v. Carr*, 805 F. Supp. at 1270 (citing S. REP. No. 541, at 11, *reprinted in* 1986 U.S.C.C.A.N. at 3565).

[403] *See Organizacion JD Ltda. v. United States Dep't of Justice*, 18 F.3d 91 (2d Cir.), *cert. denied*, 512 U.S. 1207 (1994), *on remand*, 1996 U.S. Dist. LEXIS 4347 (E.D.N.Y. Apr. 2, 1996) (plaintiffs had no standing under Title II of the ECPA to sue government for alleged ECPA violations), *aff'd*, 1997 U.S. App. LEXIS 22614 (2d Cir. Aug. 26, 1997).

[404] *Manufacturas Int'l Ltda. v. Manufacturers Hanover Trust Co.*, 792 F. Supp. 180, 184 (E.D.N.Y. 1992) [hereinafter *Manufacturas*]; *see also United States v. All Funds on Deposit in Any Accounts Maintained at Merrill, Lynch, Pierce, Fenner & Smith*, 801 F.Supp. 984 (E.D.N.Y. 1992) [hereinafter the *All Funds* case], *aff'd, United States v. Daccarett*, 6 F.3d 37 (2d Cir. 1993).

[405] *Manufacturas*, 792 F. Supp. at 186.

[406] *Id*. at 191.

[407] *Id*.

[408] *Id*. Put another way, the court declined to read the seizure of the funds to be transmitted to the plaintiffs as ECPA violations because the statutes governing forfeiture of assets in criminal activities deem the forfeiture proceeds to belong to the government at the moment of their illegal use. *See id.*; 18 U.S.C. § 981(b).

[409] *Manufacturas*, 792 F. Supp. at 192 (citing 18 U.S.C. § 2511(2)(c)).

independent intention other than to follow the directions of the United States Attorney," but were merely following their perceived legal obligations to cooperate with federal investigators.[410]

In *Organizacion JD Ltda. v. United States Department of Justice*,[411] several plaintiffs from the *Manufacturas* case appealed the dismissal of their complaint against the government and the banks in a separate (but related) action brought against two agencies and two private banks.[412] The Second Circuit in *Organizacion JD* rejected the plaintiffs claims for violations of Title I of the ECPA based upon the seizures of the wire transfers, because the court found that no "interception" within the meaning of Title I had occurred and no "device" was used to seize the funds, as required by the statute.[413] The Second Circuit also held that the defendant banks could not be found liable for damages under Title II of the ECPA because of their good faith reliance on orders concerning the EFT seizures.[414] The Second Circuit found, however, that the government agencies could be held liable for violations under Title II of the ECPA as an "entity," but remanded the case for factual development.[415]

On remand, the district court found that the plaintiffs did not have standing as "customers" within the meaning of Title II of the ECPA to sue the government for its seizures of the funds transferred by the EFTs, because the plaintiffs were merely customers of foreign banks, which were, in turn customers of the United States banks involved in the case.[416] Comparing the definition of "customer" in Title II of the ECPA to a similar definition in the RFPA, the court concluded that the plaintiffs were not "customers," subscribers, or providers under the ECPA.[417] On this basis, the court found that they did not fall within the range of parties able to recover for ECPA violations.[418]

As discussed previously, case law is gradually defining the evolving notions of an individual's "reasonable expectations of privacy" with regard to e-mail communications and in cyberspace generally.[419] Several recent cases have addressed the application of the ECPA's provisions to computer records and communications.

---

[410] *See Manufacturas*, 792 F. Supp. at 192; 18 U.S.C. § 2511(2)(c). These holdings were largely upheld on appeal in the *All Funds* case. *See United States v. Daccarett*, 6 F.3d 37 (2d Cir. 1993) (no "interception" within the meaning of the ECPA occurred when the government seized wire transfers because the government did not conduct an "interception" involving a "device" under the ECPA) (appeal of related action involving complaint filed by government for forfeiture).

[411] *Organizacion JD Ltda. v. United States Dep't of Justice*, 18 F.3d 91 (2d Cir. 1994).

[412] *Id.* at 93.

[413] *Id.* at 94; 18 U.S.C. § 2510(4).

[414] *Organizacion JD*, 18 F.3d at 94.

[415] *Id.* at 95; 18 U.S.C. § 2707(a).

[416] *Organizacion JD Ltda. v. United States Dep't of Justice*, 1996 U.S. Dist. LEXIS 4347 (E.D.N.Y. Apr. 2, 1996), at *7.

[417] *Id.* at *11.

[418] *Id.* at *11-12 ("In the world of electronic fund transfers, with virtually instantaneous movement of large amounts of cash, delay or frustration of government investigations is equivalent to failure. It is reasonable to assume that Congress intended to incorporate one of the RFPA's most salient features into the ECPA — a highly restricted notion of "customer" tailored to insure effective government investigation.").

[419] *See* Section 12.04, and the cases discussed therein.

For example, in *Oklahoma ex rel. Macy v. One Pioneer CD-ROM Changer* ("*Macy*"), the state of Oklahoma brought suit against defendant Davis seeking forfeiture of certain computer equipment allegedly used by Davis to sell pornography.[420] Davis argued, among other things, that the state violated Title I of the ECPA based upon the state's seizure of certain computer equipment, which the state contended was being used to photograph, print, exhibit, sell, publish, and distribute pornography in violation of state law.[421] The equipment seized included computer workstations, monitors, CD-ROM drives, and modems.[422] Davis argued that the state should have, but failed to, comply with the specific warrant requirements for government seizures contained in the ECPA.[423] Davis also argued that the seized materials contained over 150,000 e-mail messages, many of which were private messages of subscribers of the bulletin board system operated by Davis, and that the state had therefore "intercepted" the electronic mail in violation of the statute.[424]

Relying upon *Steve Jackson Games, Inc. v. United States Secret Service*,[425] the *Macy* court found that, even if the seizure of the e-mail in connection with the seizure of the computer equipment could have been an "interception" within the meaning of the ECPA, that such a conclusion was not a bar to the state's enforcement of its forfeiture statute.[426]

Following the civil forfeiture and his criminal conviction under state law, Davis, his corporation, and several users of e-mail services at the BBS run by his business argued in *Davis v. Gracey*,[427] that the individual Oklahoma City police officers violated Title II of the ECPA and the Fourth Amendment in seizing the computer equipment and e-mails, and thereby "preventing authorized access" to the e-mails.[428] The Tenth Circuit, in resolving what it termed a "question of first impression in this or any circuit," found that the seizure of the e-mails related to the seizure of the computer equipment was an "incidental seizure of electronic communications" and did not violate Title II of the ECPA.[429] The Court assumed that the conduct described constituted

---

[420] *Oklahoma ex rel. Macy v. One Pioneer CD-ROM Changer*, 891 P.2d 600, 603 (Okla. Ct. App. 1994) [hereinafter *Macy*].

[421] *Id.* at 603.

[422] The defendant operated his online adult information service via a bulletin board system whereby individuals could send and receive e-mail and access text and graphic files. *Id.* at 604.

[423] 18 U.S.C. § 2518.

[424] *Macy*, 891 P.2d at 605-06; 18 U.S.C. §§ 2518, 2510(4).

[425] *Steve Jackson Games, Inc. v. United States Secret Serv.*, 816 F. Supp. 432 (W.D. Tex. 1993), *aff'd*, 36 F.3d 457 (5th Cir. 1994).

[426] *Macy*, 891 P.2d at 606. *See also Bohach v. City of Reno*, 932 F. Supp. 1232, 1236 (D. Nev. 1996) (storage, and later retrieval, of messages contained in police department "alphanumeric" paging communications system during internal affairs investigation did not constitute an unlawful "interception" under the ECPA).

[427] *Davis v. Gracey*, 111 F.3d 1472 (10th Cir. 1997).

[428] *Id.* at 1484.

[429] *Id.* at 1482-84. In dismissing Davis' argument, the Tenth Circuit noted that "[t]he argument appears to draw its force from plaintiffs' efforts to distinguish between the computer hardware — the 'container' — and its contents. They repeatedly urge that the seizure was unlawful because no probable cause was asserted to seize the contents independent of the probable cause asserted to seize the computer equipment. The question then is whether the incidental temporary seizure of stored electronic materials invalidated the seizure of the computer within which they were stored. We hold that it did not." *Id.* at 1480.

"intentional access" within the meaning of the statute,[430] but found that the good faith exception to liability under ECPA Title II applied under the facts of the case.[431]

[d] Application of ECPA to Electronic Banking and Commerce. The application of the ECPA's prohibitions to electronic banking and commerce may depend most directly upon the application of its definitions to the emergence of the new computer technologies involved, and the continued growth of e-mail and voice mail.

E-mail and voice mail are ubiquitous in corporate America today.[432] Consumer and business use of e-mail as a communications medium is booming, rising from approximately five million users and ten million daily e-mail messages in 1992, to an anticipated seventy-five million users and 225 million daily e-mail messages in 1998.[433] E-mail and other electronic communications will play a primary role in the development of online banking and payment systems. As one commentator notes, the application of the ECPA's provisions to e-mail and voice mail will depend upon which point in the "lifecycle" of the electronic communications the challenged interception or access occurs.

> While the distinction between the terms "intercept" and "access" has little significance for forms of communication that only exist as transmissions, and are never stored, the distinction is critical when a transmitted communication is later electronically stored, because it is at the time of storage that a communication becomes subject to different provisions of the ECPA. This is the case with both e-mail and voice mail messages, both of which have a transmission phase and a storage phase. During the transmission phase, any protection against unlawful interception under Title III is governed by § 2511. On arrival in storage, the same messages are subject to § 2701. Thus, the same message is subject to differing standards of protection merely because it exists in a different statutorily defined medium.[434]

The application of Title I of the ECPA's prohibition against the unlawful interception of electronic communications and Title II's prohibition against unlawful actions with regard to stored electronic communications remains largely untested. With the advent and wider adoption of stored value cards, Internet-based banking firms, and other financial service providers, resulting in an increase in the number and frequency of online financial transactions at the retail level a range of issues relating to the ECPA will undoubtedly be addressed in future cases involving e-mail and other computer-to-computer communications.

---

[430] 18 U.S.C. § 2701(a).

[431] *Davis,* 111 F.3d at 1484; 18 U.S.C. § 2707(e) (exception to Title II ECPA liability for party relying, in good faith, upon a warrant).

[432] In addition, many feel that the line between voice mail and e-mail are already beginning to blur. *See* Thomas E. Weber, *Line Between E-Mail and Voice Mail Fades,* WALL ST. J., Feb. 13, 1997, at B6 (describing the advent of "unified" messaging and communications systems).

[433] *See* Jon G. Auerbach, *Reaching Out: Getting the Message,* WALL ST. J., June 16, 1997, at R22 (citing estimates of Forrester Research, Inc.).

[434] *See* Thomas R. Greenberg, *E-mail and Voice Mail: Employee Privacy and the Federal Wiretap Statute,* 44 AM. U. L. REV. 219, 248 (1994).

[6]   BANK SECRECY ACT

[a] Overview. The Bank Secrecy Act ("BSA")[435] is a federal law which affects consumer financial privacy indirectly.[436] Enacted in 1970 as the Bank Records and Foreign Transactions Act,[437] the original purpose of the BSA was to "avoid secrecy," by preventing the use of bank accounts to conceal tax fraud, gambling operations, and other activities associated with organized crime through a variety of record keeping and disclosure requirements for banks.[438] The BSA authorizes the Secretary of the Treasury to require "financial institutions"[439] to keep records and file reports that are determined to have usefulness in criminal, tax, and regulatory matters, and to implement counter-money laundering procedures.[440] Specifically, the BSA requires financial institutions to fill out Currency Transaction Reports ("CTRs") for cash transactions over $10,000, and requires the reporting of any cross-border transport of more than $5,000 cash using Reports of International Transportation of Currency or Monetary Instruments ("CMIRs").[441] Gradually, Congress has amended and expanded the scope of the BSA, increasing the number of activities and types of financial institutions covered.[442]

[b] Application of the BSA to Electronic Banking and Commerce. Although strictly speaking not a financial privacy law, the BSA and its regulations have implications for electronic banking and commerce. In the view of the Financial Crimes Enforcement Network ("FinCEN"), the branch of the U.S. Treasury charged with responsibility for the BSA and regulations thereunder, the BSA's provisions are generally applicable to stored value and other emerging electronic money products.[443] As discussed in Chapter 10, on May 19, 1997,

---

[435] Bank Secrecy Act ("BSA"), Pub. L. No. 91-508, 1970 U.S.C.C.A.N. (84 Stat. 1114) 1301 (codified as amended at 12 U.S.C. §§ 1829b, 1951-59; 31 U.S.C. §§ 5311-26).

[436] For a further discussion of the BSA, see Chapter 10. For a comprehensive overview of the BSA, see FISCHER, *supra* note 132, ¶¶ 4.01 *et seq.*

[437] Bank Records and Foreign Transactions Act, Pub. L. No. 91-508, 1970 U.S.C.C.A.N. (84 Stat. 1114) 1301 (codified as amended at 12 U.S.C. §§ 1829b, 1951-59, 31 U.S.C. §§ 5311-30) (this Act over time came to be known as the Bank Secrecy Act). In *California Bankers Ass'n v. Schultz*, 416 U.S. 21 (1974), the Supreme Court upheld the constitutionality of the BSA's record-keeping requirements under the First and Fourth Amendments.

[438] *See In re Grand Jury No. 76-3*, 555 F.2d 1306, 1309 (5th Cir. 1977).

[439] Under the BSA regulations, a "financial institution" is defined to include "agent, agency, branch, or office within the United States of any person doing business, whether or not on a regular basis or as an organized business concern, in one or more of the capacities listed below: (1) A bank (except bank credit card systems); (2) A broker or dealer in securities; (3) A currency dealer or exchanger, including a person engaged in the business of a check casher; (4) An issuer, seller, or redeemer of traveler's checks or money orders, except as a selling agent exclusively who does not sell more than $150,000 of such instruments within any given 30-day period; (5) A licensed transmitter of funds, or other person engaged in the business of transmitting funds; and (6) a telegraph company." *See* 31 C.F.R. § 103.11(n).

[440] *See generally* 31 C.F.R. pt. 103.

[441] For a discussion of the BSA's other record keeping and reporting requirements, *see* ROBERT E. POWIS, BANK SECRECY ACT COMPLIANCE 29-126 (4th ed. 1994).

[442] *See* Money Laundering Control Act of 1986, Pub. L. No. 99-570, tit. I, subtit. H, 1986 U.S.C.C.A.N. (100 Stat.) 3207-18 (codified as amended in scattered sections of 12, 18, and 31 U.S.C.) (criminalizing money laundering and the structuring of such transactions to avoid the BSA's requirements); Annunzio-Wylie Anti-Money Laundering Act of 1992, Pub. L. No. 102-550, tit. XV, § 1517, 1992 U.S.C.C.A.N. (106 Stat.) 4059 (codified at 31 U.S.C. § 5314(g)) (authorizing financial institutions to report any suspicious activities believed to involve money laundering); Money Laundering Suppression Act of 1994, Pub. L. No. 103-325, tit. IV, 1994 U.S.C.C.A.N. (108 Stat.) 2243 (codified in scattered sections of 31 U.S.C.) (requiring, *inter alia*, all money transmitting businesses to register with the Treasury).

[443] Proposed Amendment to the Bank Secrecy Act Regulations - Definition and Registration of Money Services Businesses, 62 Fed. Reg. 27,890 (1997) (to be codified at 31 C.F.R. pt. 103) [hereinafter MSB Proposal].

FinCEN proposed three new rules as amendments to its regulations implementing the BSA.[444] These are: (i) the definition and registration of a new type of entity, "money service businesses";[445] (ii) the requirement for money transmitters, sellers, and redeemers to report suspicious transactions involving at least $500;[446] and (iii) the requirement for money transmitters and their agents to report and retain records of currency transactions of at least $750.[447]

In its "money services businesses" proposal, FinCEN took the position (for the first time) that, as a general matter, the BSA is applicable to the issuance and use of "stored value."[448] In stating that it was bringing stored value within the scope of the money services businesses rule, FinCEN stated that such products are "generally comprehended within the [BSA] statutory reference to be instruments 'similar' to money order and traveler's checks."[449] As such, issuers and sellers of stored value, subject to certain exceptions, would be required to register with FinCEN.

Because the regulation regarding the application of the BSA to stored value remains in the proposal stage, its effect on the emerging electronic commerce and banking systems remains an outstanding issue. FinCEN's proposal has proven controversial. Those who are interested in the extent to which stored value and electronic money will be permitted to circulate as an anonymous electronic substitute for cash should be aware that this may depend largely on actions taken by FinCEN.

[7] COMPUTER FRAUD AND ABUSE ACT

The most important federal law designed to prevent breaches of computer security and resulting damage or loss is the Computer Fraud and Abuse Act of 1986 ("CFAA").[450] The CFAA was enacted as amendments

---

[444] *See id.;* Proposed Amendment to the Bank Secrecy Act Regulations - Requirement of Money Transmitters and Money Order and Traveler's Check Issuers, Sellers, and Redeemers to Report Suspicious Transactions, 62 Fed. Reg. 27,900 (1997) (to be codified at 31 C.F.R. § 103.20) [hereinafter Suspicious Transactions Proposal]; Proposed Amendment to the Bank Secrecy Act Regulations - Special Currency Transaction Reporting Requirement for Money Transmitters, 62 Fed. Reg. 27,909 (1997) (to be codified at 31 C.F.R. pt. 103) [hereinafter Special Currency Transaction Proposal].

[445] The term "money services businesses" includes "currency dealers or exchangers; check cashers; issuers of traveler's checks, money orders or stored value; sellers or redeemers of traveler's checks, money orders, or stored value; and money transmitters." MSB Proposal, 62 Fed. Reg. at 27,891 (to be codified at 31 C.F.R. § 103.11(uu)).

[446] *See* Suspicious Transactions Proposal, 62 Fed. Reg. at 27,900.

[447] *See* Special Currency Transaction Proposal, 62 Fed. Reg. at 27,909.

[448] The MSB Proposal defines the term "stored value" as "[f]unds or monetary value represented in digital electronics format (whether or not specially encrypted) and stored or capable of storage on electronic media in such a way as to be retrievable and transferable electronically." MSB Proposal, 62 Fed. Reg. at 27,898.

[449] FinCEN noted that neither of its other May 1997 proposed rules would apply to stored value and that, as stored value and other electronic money develop, FinCEN would be open to reevaluating its regulatory position to take account of the unique characteristics of such products. *Id.* at 27,893.

[450] Computer Fraud and Abuse Act of 1986, Pub. L. No. 99-474, 1986 U.S.C.C.A.N. (100 Stat.) 1213 (codified as amended at 18 U.S.C. § 1030).

to the Counterfeit Access Device and Computer Fraud Abuse Act of 1984 ("1984 Computer Act").[451] The CFAA is the first comprehensive legislation to address growing government and private sector concerns regarding proliferation of computer fraud and crime.[452] The CFAA had initially been limited to those instances of computer crimes and fraud in which Congress found that there was a compelling federal interest, *i.e.*, where computers of the federal government or certain financial institutions were involved, or where the crime itself was interstate in nature.[453]

In 1996, Congress passed the National Information Infrastructure Protection Act ("NIIPA"), which amended the CFAA and, broadened its scope to apply to many other forms of conduct that are committed by or through the use of the Internet, World Wide Web, or other computer networks.[454] The CFAA provides for misdemeanor and felony penalties, as well as civil remedies, including damages and injunctive relief for parties who suffer damages due to conduct prohibited by the CFAA.[455] In light of the recent evidence showing the explosion of computer fraud and crimes perpetrated through the use of the Internet and other networks,[456] the CFAA has potential application for all participants in electronic commerce, including consumers, merchants, and financial institutions, as discussed below.

[a] CFAA Prohibitions and Penalties. In passing the CFAA in 1986, Congress intended to proscribe additional illegitimate computer-related conduct and to impose significant penalties for the growing problem of computer-related crimes.[457] It chose, however, to limit the reach of CFAA to those instances where there is a clear "compelling [f]ederal interest," or where the crime itself is "interstate in nature."[458] CFAA

---

[451] Counterfeit Access Device and Computer Fraud Abuse Act of 1984, Pub. L. No. 98-473, 1984 U.S.C.C.A.N. (98 Stat.) 2190 (codified as amended at 18 U.S.C. § 1030) [hereinafter 1984 Computer Act]. For a discussion of the legislative history, goals and passage of the 1984 Computer Act, and the 1986 amendment thereto, see Dodd S. Griffith, *The Computer Fraud and Abuse Act of 1986: A Measured Response to a Growing Problem*, 43 VAND. L. REV. 453, 456-473 (1990).

[452] S. REP. No. 99-432, at 2 (1986), *reprinted in* 1986 U.S.C.C.A.N. 2479, 2480.

[453] *Id.* at 4, *reprinted in* 1986 U.S.C.C.A.N. at 2483.

[454] National Information Infrastructure Protection Act, Pub. L. No. 104-294, tit. II, 1996 U.S.C.C.A.N. (110 Stat.) 3491 (codified at 18 U.S.C. § 1030).

[455] *See* 18 U.S.C. § 1030(c) (providing a range of misdemeanor and felony penalties of 1-10 years of imprisonment and fines up to $250,000); § 1030(g) (providing that any person who suffers damage or loss by reason of a violation of the CFAA, except for reckless violations of subsection (a)(5), may obtain compensatory damages, injunctive and other equitable relief against a violator).

[456] *See* Jo-Ann M. Adams, Comment, *Controlling Cyberspace: Applying the Computer Fraud and Abuse Act to the Internet*, 12 SANTA CLARA COMPUTER & HIGH TECH. L.J. 403, 409-10 (1996) (describing how the number of computer crimes, such as hacking, worms and viruses, electronic break-ins, and frauds, has doubled each year since 1989). *See* Sharon Walsh and Robert O'Harrow Jr., *Trying to Keep a Lock on Company Secrets — Law Enforcement Officials Fear Rise in Computer Crimes, Made Easier by Technological Advances*, WASH. POST, Feb. 17, 1998, at D1, D4. During 1996, several notorious instances of the "hacking" of major government computer networks were detailed in the media. *See, e.g.*, Associated Press, *Hackers Penetrate Justice Department Home Page*, WASH. POST., August 18, 1996, at A22 (describing how hackers tampered with Web page of the Department of Justice, placing pornography, swastikas and criticism of the Communications Decency Act of 1996 on the site); Sewell Chan, *Electronic Vandals Tamper with Web Pages*, WALL ST. J., June 26, 1996, at B1. Pierre Thomas and Elizabeth Corcoran, *Argentine, 22, Charged With Hacking Computer Networks*, WASH. POST, Mar. 30, 1996, at A4 (describing the investigation and arrest of Argentine citizen who used the Internet to hack into computer networks at Department of Defense installations, NASA and the Los Alamos National Laboratory).

[457] "This technological explosion has made the computer a mainstay of our communications system, and it has brought a great many benefits to the government, to American businesses, and to all of our lives. But it has also created a new type of criminal — one who uses computers to steal, to defraud, and to abuse the property of others. The proliferation of computers and computer data has spread before the nation's criminals a vast array of property that, in many cases, is wholly unprotected against crime." *See* S. REP. No. 99-432, at 2, *reprinted in* 1986 U.S.C.C.A.N. at 2480.

[458] *Id.* at 4, *reprinted in* 1986 U.S.C.C.A.N. at 2482.

subsection (a)(1) protects classified federal government information by prohibiting the knowing access to a computer without authorization, or exceeding authorization, in order to obtain information relating to national defense or foreign relations, with an intent that the information obtained be used to injure the United States.[459] A violation of subsection (a)(1) is a felony offense and requires only that the defendant "obtain information." This requirement may be satisfied by a person merely reading the information; physically copying or removing the information is not required.[460] Violations of CFAA subsection (a)(1) are punishable by up to twenty years imprisonment, depending upon the defendant's prior record.[461]

Prior to the 1996 amendments to the CFAA, the prohibition contained in subsection (a)(2) focused solely on the protection, for privacy reasons, of computerized credit records and information relating to a customer's relationship with his financial institution. As amended, CFAA subsection (a)(2) is now directed at those who "intentionally" access a computer, or "exceed authorized access,"[462] and thereby obtain information contained in a "financial record"[463] of a customer at a "financial institution,"[464] or information in a file of a "consumer reporting agency" as defined under the FCRA.[465] The statute's legislative history also makes clear that the term "obtains information" under subsection (a)(2) does not require physical removal of the information, in the sense of physically taking away and removing the computer data from the financial institution records. Rather, the statutory prohibition is triggered when an unauthorized party merely observes the computer data or records.[466]

As amended, CFAA's subsection (a)(2) also prohibits the intentional accessing of a computer without authorization and thereby obtaining information from any U.S. agency or department. It is directed at persons who intentionally access a "protected computer"[467] without, or in excess of, authorized access, and thereby

---

[459] *See* 18 U.S.C. § 1030(a)(1). The statute describes such "classified" information to include information determined by the government or by an Executive Order to require protection against unauthorized disclosure for reasons of national defense or foreign relations. *See Id.*.

[460] *See* Scott Charney & Kent Alexander, *Computer Crime*, 45 EMORY L.J. 931, 950-51 (1996).

[461] 18 U.S.C. § 1030(c)(1).

[462] Under the CFAA, the term "exceed authorized access" means to "access a computer with authorization and to use such access to obtain or alter information in the computer that the accessor is not entitled so to obtain or alter." *Id.* § 1030(e)(6).

[463] Under the CFAA, the term "financial record" means "information derived from any record held by a financial institution pertaining to a customer's relationship with the financial institution." *Id.* § 1030(e)(5).

[464] Under the CFAA, the term "financial institution" includes: an institution with deposits insured by the Federal Deposit Insurance Corporation; the Federal Reserve or any members of the Federal Reserve including any Federal Reserve Bank; a credit union with accounts insured by the National Credit Union Administration; a member of the Federal Home Loan Bank System and any Home Loan Bank; any institution of the Farm Credit System under the Farm Credit Act of 1971; broker-dealers registered under the Securities Exchange Act of 1934; the Securities Investor Protection Corporation; or a branch or agency of a foreign bank and an organization operating under section 25 or section 25(a) of the Federal Reserve Act. *Id.* § 1030(e)(4).

[465] Subsection (a)(2) applies to the financial records of all customers of financial institutions, not merely customers who are natural persons. *See* S. REP. NO. 99-432, at 6, *reprinted in* 1986 U.S.C.C.A.N. at 2484. *See also* 12 U.S.C. § 3401(4) (defining a "person" under the RFPA).

[466] S. REP. NO. 99-432, at 6, *reprinted in* 1986 U.S.C.C.A.N. at 2484.

[467] Under the CFAA, the term "protected computer" means a computer "(A) exclusively for the use of a financial institution or the United States Government, or, in the case of a computer not exclusively for such use, used by or for a financial institution or the United States Government and the conduct constituting the offense affects that use by or for the financial institution or the Government; or (B) which is used in interstate or foreign commerce or communication." 18 U.S.C. § 1030(e)(2).

obtain information from such computer if the conduct involved an "interstate or foreign communication."[468] As described below, this provision when read in conjunction with the recently amended penal provisions of the CFAA,[469] may extend the reach of CFAA's criminal penalties to a wide range of electronic communications using the Internet. Violations of CFAA subsection (a)(2) are punishable as felonies, depending upon the value of the information obtained, or the use to which the information is put.[470] For example, the recent amendment of subsection (c)(2) makes any violation of subsection (a)(2) a felony punishable by five years imprisonment or a fine if a person intentionally accessed a computer without authorization and obtained information under certain circumstances.[471] The NIIPA amendments are consistent with the view of Justice Department officials, who had, prior to the amendments, expressed the view that the CFAA, as well as other federal criminal statutes, should be amended to respond to the vast increases in computer crime and fraud in the intangible environment of "cyberspace."[472]

CFAA subsection (a)(3) prohibits the intentional access (without authorization) of a nonpublic computer of a department or agency of the United States.[473] It is designed to apply primarily against "outsiders" who attack government computers, but also brings within its scope those government employees who exceed their permitted computer access.[474] Congress amended the intent requirement of subsection (a)(3) in 1986, by substituting the term "intentionally" for "knowingly."[475] As amended, the subsection no longer requires that the person's use "adversely" affect the government's use of the computer.[476] Violations of CFAA subsection (a)(3) are felonies punishable by up to ten years imprisonment.[477]

---

[468] *Id.* § 1030(a)(2)(B); *See also* Economic Espionage Act of 1996, Pub. L. No. 104-294, § 201, 1996 U.S.C.C.A.N. (110 Stat.) 3491, 3492.

[469] *See* 18 U.S.C. § 1030(c)(2).

[470] *Id.* § 1030(c)(2). As amended, the CFAA appears to criminalize certain torts and noncomputer crimes under other federal or state law by enlarging the scope of CFAA subsection (c)(2) to punish subsection (a)(2) offenses which are (i) "committed for purposes of commercial advantage or private financial gain;" (ii) "committed in furtherance of any criminal or tortuous act in violation of the Constitution or laws of the United States or of any State," or (iii) committed in instances where the information obtained exceeded $5,000 in value. *Id.* § 1030(c)(2)(B).

[471] *Id.* §§ 1030(a)(2) (intentionally access without authorization or exceed authorized access); 1030(c)(2)(B) (providing for fines and/or five year imprisonment under three circumstances). The effect of this amendment is that the CFAA may broadly prohibit use of the Internet to commit a crime or tort under other federal or state law, making the use of a "protected computer" a separate federal computer offense. *See* Adams, *supra* note 456, at 433.

[472] *See* Scott Charney, *Computer Crime*, at 21 (Jan. 24, 1996) (paper presented at the American Bar Association 1996 Annual Meeting, by the Chief of the Computer Crime Unit of the Criminal Division, U.S. Department of Justice) (calling for (i) the amendment of the CFAA, (ii) a new forfeiture provision addresses specifically to computer crimes, and (iii) an amendment to the Interstate Transportation of Stolen Property statute, 18 U.S.C. § 2314, to apply that statute to the theft and movement of computer source code or information over the Internet). *See also United States v. Brown*, 925 F.2d 1301 (10th Cir. 1991) (holding that 18 U.S.C. § 2314 does not apply to the interstate transportation of computer source code because the statute only applies to "goods, wares and merchandise" and does not cover intangible property).

[473] 18 U.S.C. § 1030(a)(3).

[474] S. REP. NO. 99-432, at 8, *reprinted in* 1986 U.S.C.C.A.N. at 2486.

[475] Congress made this change because it wanted to proscribe only intentional acts of unauthorized access and not mistaken, inadvertent or careless acts and because they felt that a "knowing" standard was too strict a standard in light of the particular circumstances in cases involving computer technology. *See id.* at 5-6, *reprinted in* 1986 U.S.C.C.A.N. at 2484.

[476] *Id.* at 8-9, *reprinted in* 1986 U.S.C.C.A.N. at 2486; *see also* Charney & Alexander, *supra* note 460, at 951.

[477] 18 U.S.C. §§ 1030(c)(2)(A), 1030(c)(2)(C).

CFAA subsection (a)(4) prohibits an individual from knowingly, and with intent to defraud, accessing a "protected computer" without or in excess of authorization, and by means of such conduct furthering the intended fraud and obtaining anything of value.[478] The term "protected computer" is significant, because it "allows a computer owned by a private company to be a 'protected computer' and thus be protected by the [statute's general fraud prohibition]."[479] Subsection (a)(4) thus reaches all "thefts of property via computer that occur as part of a scheme to defraud."[480] Unlike the mail and wire fraud statues,[481] in creating a federal computer fraud offense, Congress provided that subsection (a)(4) requires a showing that the use of the computer or computers in question was "integral to the intended fraud and was not merely incidental" to the fraud.[482] The computer use must further the intended fraud.[483]

CFAA subsection (a)(5) creates three separate offenses, two felonies and a misdemeanor, depending on the intent and authority of the actor.[484] It prohibits any person (*e.g.*, an insider or an outsider) from "caus[ing] the transmission of a program, information, code or command" if such transmission causes "damage"[485] to a protected computer without authorization.[486] Subsection (a)(5) "is designed to penalize those who intentionally alter, damage, or destroy certain computerized data belonging to another" person.[487] Any knowing access which results in damage to a protected computer is a felony under the statute. By contrast, intentional access by an outsider resulting in only reckless damage to a protected computer is a lesser felony; while intentional access by an outsider merely causing damage is a misdemeanor under the statute.[488]

---

[478] *See* Charney & Alexander, *supra* note 460, at 951 (discussing § 18 U.S.C. § 1030(a)(4)).

[479] *Id.* at 951.

[480] *See* S. REP. No. 99-432, at 9, *reprinted in* 1986 U.S.C.C.A.N. at 2486-87. 18 U.S.C. § 1030(a)(4) creates a violation where any person:

knowingly and with intent to defraud, accesses a protected computer without authorization, or exceeds authorized access, and by means of such conduct furthers the intended fraud and obtains anything of value, unless the object of the fraud and the thing obtained consists only of the use of the computer and the value of such use is not more than $5,000 in any 1-year period.

[481] 18 U.S.C. § 1341 (mail fraud); 18 U.S.C. § 2511(1)(a) (wire fraud).

[482] S. REP. No. 99-432, at 9, *reprinted in* 1986 U.S.C.C.A.N. at 2487.

[483] *Id.*

[484] *See* Charney & Alexander, *supra* note 460, at 952.

[485] Under the CFAA, the term "damage" means "any impairment to the integrity or availability of data, a program, a system, or information, that — (A) causes loss aggregating at least $5,000 in value during any 1-year period to one or more individuals; (B) modifies or impairs, or potentially modifies or impairs, the medical examination, diagnosis, treatment, or care of one or more individuals; (C) causes physical injury to any person; or (D) threatens public health or safety." 18 U.S.C. § 1030(e)(8).

[486] *Id.* § 1030(a)(1)(C). Subsection (a)(5) provides that any person who:

(A) knowingly causes the transmission of a program, information, code, or command, and as a result of such conduct, intentionally causes damage without authorization, to a protected computer; (B) intentionally accesses a protected computer without authorization, and as a result of such conduct, recklessly causes damage; or (C) intentionally accesses a protected computer without authorization, and as a result of such conduct, causes damage; . . . shall be punished as provided in subsection (c) of the CFAA.

[487] S. REP. No. 99-432, at 10, *reprinted in* 1986 U.S.C.C.A.N. at 2488.

[488] 18 U.S.C. §§ 1030(a)(5)(B) and (C); 1030(c)(1), (2).

CFAA subsection (a)(6) prohibits the knowing trafficking in computer passwords or similar information.[489] The trafficking must involve passwords that relate to computers used by or for the United States Government or affect interstate commerce.[490] Finally, CFAA subsection (a)(7), added in the 1996 amendments, prohibits an individual from, with the intent to extort from person any money or other thing of value, transmitting a threat intended to cause damage to a protected computer.[491] This provision is intended to deal with an emerging threat of "hackers" who threaten to "crash" computer systems if they are not given system privileges, money, or other items of value.[492] Violations of subsections (a)(6) and (a)(7) are punishable as felonies.[493]

In addition to the penalties, private parties who have suffered damage or loss by reason of a violation of the CFAA may maintain a civil action against the violator to obtain compensatory damages and injunctive or other equitable relief.[494] Damages, as defined under the statute, are limited to economic damages. Such an action must be brought within two years of the act complained of or the date of discovery of the damage caused by the violation.[495]

[b] CFAA Prosecutions – _United States v. Morris_. Prior to 1986, the Justice Department did not prosecute a single case under the predecessor of the CFAA, the 1984 Computer Act.[496] Although relatively rare, reported prosecutions under the CFAA have resulted in a number of cases construing the meaning of the statute's criminal prohibitions.[497] These cases demonstrate that courts are broadly construing the scope of prohibited conduct under the CFAA in an era of increasing use of computer technologies.

In _United States v. Morris_, the Court of Appeals for the Second Circuit, in applying and construing the CFAA, upheld the conviction of a Cornell University graduate student who had created and released a computer

---

[489] Subsection (a)(6) prohibits "knowingly and with intent to defraud traffi[cking] (as defined in section 1029) in any password or similar information through which a computer may be accessed without authorization, if – (A) such trafficking affects interstate or foreign commerce; or (B) such computer is used by or for the Government of the United States." _Id._ § 1030(a)(6).

[490] _Id._

[491] Subsection (a)(7) prohibits any person, "with intent to extort from any person, firm, association, educational institution, financial institution, government entity, or other legal entity, any money or other thing of value, [from transmitting] in interstate or foreign commerce any communication containing any threat to cause damage to a protected computer." _Id._ § 1030(a)(7).

[492] _See_ Charney & Alexander, _supra_ note 460, at 953.

[493] 18 U.S.C. §§ 1030(c)(2)(A), 1030(c)(2)(C).

[494] _Id._ § 1030(g).

[495] _Id._

[496] _See_ Adams, _supra_ note 456, at 426.

[497] _See United States v. Coleman_, 1991 U.S. App. LEXIS 14833, at *2 (9th Cir. July 3, 1991) (aiding and abetting computer fraud under the CFAA, 18 U.S.C. § 1030(a)(4) and (a)(2) in connection with scheme to defraud the government of $9,469,348 by cashing fraudulent government check); _United States v. Carron_, 1991 U.S. App. LEXIS 4838 (9th Cir. May 20, 1991) (unauthorized computer access in connection with fraudulent credit card scheme); _United States v. Lewis_, 872 F.2d 1030 (6th Cir. 1989) (defendant embezzled approximately $47,000 from a federally insured bank); _United States v. Fernandez_, 1993 U.S. Dist. LEXIS 3590, at *3 (S.D.N.Y. Mar. 25, 1993) (involving various computer-related crimes, including accessing a federal-interest computer without authorization and altering or damaging information contained in the computer); _United States v. Rice_, 1992 U.S. App. LEXIS 9562 (4th Cir. May 2, 1992) (violation of CFAA subsection (a)(3) in connection with the unauthorized access of the computer system of the IRS).

virus (or "worm") over the Internet that infected a number of university and military computer systems.[498] The Court held that the statute did not require proof that the defendant intentionally caused damage to the range of "infected" computers.[499]

Morris was convicted of deliberately releasing the "worm" from Cornell into computers at M.I.T. and other academic and government institutions, by means of the Internet. Morris had intended to test the security systems of other host computers connected to the Internet, but miscalculated the rate at which the worm would replicate itself and the other computer systems.[500] The virus quickly spread to many computers around the United States causing the systems to crash or rendering those computers "catatonic."[501] The virus prevented other host computers connected to the Internet from functioning properly; despite Morris' efforts to provide other systems administrators with instructions on how to kill the virus program.[502] Morris caused damage ranging from $200 to $53,000 at the various computer facilities and was convicted of violating 18 U.S.C. Section 1030(a)(5).[503]

In affirming the conviction, the Second Circuit rejected Morris' argument that the government had to prove Morris intended not only to access the computer (or exceed his access, in this case), but that he also "intentionally" intended to prevent authorized users from using the computers, thus causing a loss.[504] The Second Circuit reviewed the legislative history of CFAA, holding that the structure, purpose, and language of subsection (a)(5) indicated that the intent requirement of subsection (a)(5) applied only to the "access" language, not to both the conduct of accessing and damaging.[505] Because he was authorized to access computers (via the SENDMAIL and "finger demon" programs) at Cornell, Harvard, and the University of California (Berkeley), Morris also argued that his conviction was improper because (a)(5) required "unauthorized access" and he had, at most, merely "exceeded authorized access."[506] The Second Circuit also rejected this claim.[507]

---

[498] *United States v. Morris*, 928 F.2d 504, 505 (2d Cir.), *cert. denied,* 502 U.S. 817 (1991). The graduate student in the *Morris* case had developed a computer virus to demonstrate the inadequacies of the security features of networked computers. Released through the Internet, the worm attacked and infected computer systems at many leading universities, educational institutions, and military sites, causing the systems to "crash" and cease functioning. *Morris*, 928 F.2d at 505. The Government prosecuted Morris under subsection (5)(A) of the statute (18 U.S.C. § 1030(a)(5)(A)), contending that Morris intentionally caused damage and loss to the computer systems.

[499] *Morris*, 928 F.2d at 509.

[500] *Id*. at 505-6. Morris had originally programmed the worm to make it difficult for others to detect and read so other programmers would not be able to "kill" the worm easily. *Id*.

[501] *Morris*, 928 F.2d at 505-6; *see also* Catherine T. Clarke, *From CrimiNet to Cyber-Perp: Towards an Inclusive Approach to Policing the Evolving Criminal Mens Rea on the Internet*, 75 OR. L. REV. 191, 214-15 (1996) (describing the facts of the *Morris* case).

[502] *Id*. at 506.

[503] *Id*.

[504] *Id*. at 504.

[505] *Id*. at 509.

[506] *Id*. at 509-10.

[507] *Id*. at 510 ("Morris did not use either of those features in any way related to their intended function. He did not send or read mail nor discover information about other users; instead he found holes in both programs that permitted him a special and unauthorized access route into other computers.").

By contrast to *Morris*, the prohibitions in the CFAA have been held inapplicable to the unauthorized "browsing" of computer files. For example, in *United States v. Czubinski*, the Court of Appeals for the First Circuit reversed the conviction of a IRS representative on four counts of computer fraud in violation of subsection (a)(4) of the CFAA.[508] Czubinski, an alleged white supremacist, accessed and borrowed IRS taxpayer files with a valid password, certain search codes, and taxpayer social security numbers.[509] By means of this access, Czubinski was able to retrieve income tax return information regarding "virtually any taxpayer," including that of former and current political adversaries, relatives and acquaintances.[510] Indicted on four counts of unauthorized access computer fraud under CFAA subsection (a)(4), Czubinski was convicted after a jury trial.

In reversing the lower court's denial of Czubinski post-trial acquittal motion, the First Circuit found that Czubinski's browsing of files "unquestionably" constituted "exceed[ing] authorized access to a [protected] computer," but that, by such browsing, Czubinski did not obtain "anything of value" in violation of CFAA subsection (a)(4).[511] The First Circuit specifically noted that, in order to sustain a conviction under CFAA subsection (a)(4), the defendant must have been shown to have obtained something more than merely the "unauthorized use" of the computer itself.[512] The court noted that Czubinski did not print out, compile or otherwise retrieve the information contained in the accessed taxpayer records. On these grounds, the First Circuit held that Czubinski could not have been found to have participated in a fraudulent scheme in violation of CFAA subsection (a)(4).[513]

A number of CFAA prosecutions have involved some form of financial fraud.[514] In one case, *United States v. Sykes*, the Fourth Circuit affirmed the sentence of a defendant convicted of computer access fraud under CFAA subsection (a)(4) for the unauthorized use of an automated teller machine and personal identification number.[515] The statute, however, has been applied to unauthorized conduct involving computer systems at a bank. In *United States v. Sablan*,[516] the Ninth Circuit, in a case involving access to a bank's computer files by a former bank employee which construed the meaning of CFAA subsection (a)(5) (prior to its 1996 amendment),

---

[508] *United States v. Czubinski*, 106 F.3d 1069, 1073 (1st Cir. 1997) (reversing computer and wire fraud convictions).

[509] *Id.* at 1071.

[510] *Id.* at 1071-72.

[511] *Id.* at 1078. The First Circuit also concluded that Czubinski's browsing of the IRS computer files was not part of a criminal scheme to defraud under the wire fraud statute, under either of two theories, that Czubinski defrauded the IRS of its property or that he defrauded taxpayers of their nonproperty right to honest government services. *Id.* at 1075-77.

[512] The First Circuit noted that "[t]he plain language of section 1030(a)(4) emphasizes that more than mere unauthorized use is required: the 'thing obtained' may not merely be the unauthorized use. It is the showing of some additional end — to which the unauthorized access is a means — that is lacking here." *Id.* at 1078.

[513] *Id.* at 1079 (reversing conviction on all counts).

[514] *United States v. Sykes*, 4 F.3d 697, 698 (8th Cir. 1993) (unauthorized use of an automated teller machine and personal identification number); *United States v. DeMonte*, 1992 U.S. App. LEXIS 11392 (6th Cir. 1992) (per curiam), *aff'd in part, rev'd in part, and remanded*, 25 F.3d 343 (6th Cir. 1994) (a Veterans Administration ("VA") accountant made more than 50 fictitious computer entries defrauding the VA of more than $46,000, and during the investigation admitted that he had earlier defrauded the VA of $30,000).

[515] *Sykes*, 4 F.3d at 698, 700.

[516] *United States v. Sablan*, 92 F.3d 865 (9th Cir. 1996).

adopted the *Morris* reasoning and concluded that the intent (*"mens rea"*) requirement of subsection (a)(5) applied only to the access language, not to the defendant's infliction of "damage."[517]

In *Sablan*, a former employee of the Bank of Hawaii gained access to her former employer's computer systems with a stolen key and old passwords.[518] Sablan changed several computer files and deleted others, "severely damag[ing]" the bank's computers.[519] After a conditional guilty plea, Sablan challenged her conviction under CFAA subsection (a)(5), on the grounds that the statute required proof of her intent to damage the bank's files.[520] The Ninth Circuit, following *Morris*, concluded that subsection (a)(5) did not require proof that the defendant intentionally damaged the computer data, only proof of intent to access the computer without authorization.[521]

A number of civil actions have attempted to address the right to recover damages under CFAA. For example, in *North Texas Preventive Imaging, L.L.C. v. Eisenberg* (*"Imaging"*), a district court in Texas construed the meaning of the term "knowingly cause the transmission," added by the 1994 CFAA amendments.[522] In *Imaging*, a medical diagnostics firm licensed computer software from a vendor and, after seeking a refund for the software, disputed the terms and conditions of the license.[523] After the medical firm canceled its contract with the software provider, and demanded the return of payments made, the software developer transmitted an update disk which contained "disabling codes" which would have disabled the medical firm's computers.[524]

The district court reviewed what it described as a question of first impression under CFAA subsection (a)(5) — whether the software firm, in providing the disks containing the disabling codes, which acted as a "time bomb," to an authorized computer user, who then unwittingly loaded the codes onto a computer system and thereby suffered damages stated a claim for relief under the CFAA.[525] The court found that the use of a "time bomb" on the diskette was likely within the CFAA's prohibition against the knowing transmission of a "program, information, code or command," if the transmission was accompanied by the intent to do harm.[526] The court therefore denied the software firm's motion to dismiss, finding that the medical firm had sufficiently pleaded each element of a violation of CFAA subsection (a)(5).[527]

---

[517] *Sablan*, 92 F.3d at 868.

[518] *Id.* at 866.

[519] *Id.* at 867.

[520] *Id.*

[521] *Id.* at 868.

[522] 18 U.S.C. §§ (a)(5)(A), (B). *See North Texas Preventive Imaging, L.L.C. v. Eisenberg*, 1996 U.S. Dist. LEXIS 19990, at *15 (S.D. Cal. Aug. 19, 1996) (finding that an allegation that defendant transmitted a disk containing software disabling codes, which acted as a "time bomb," to an authorized computer user, who then unwittingly loaded the codes onto a computer system and thereby suffered damages, stated a claim for damages under subsection (a)(5) of the CFAA).

[523] *Id.* at *6-7.

[524] *Id.* at *6.

[525] *Id.* at *10-11.

[526] *Id.* at *16.

[527] *Id.* at *20-21.

In a recent widely-publicized case,[528] a major Internet service provider, America Online ("AOL") and Cyber Promotions, Inc. ("Cyber"), an e-mail marketing and solicitation firm, asserted similar claims against one another under subsection (a)(5) of the CFAA.[529] After receiving complaints from its membership about Cyber's dissemination of unsolicited e-mail, America Online sent a number of "e-mail bombs" to Cyber's Internet service providers ("ISP").[530] Cyber filed suit against AOL in response to AOL's "e-mail bombing" of Cyber's ISPs, alleging that two of Cyber's ISPs terminated their relationship with Cyber and a third ISP refused to enter into a contract with Cyber, and that AOL committed violations of the CFAA.[531]

In its own complaint, AOL alleged that Cyber:

> transmi[tted] . . . one or more programs, . . . codes or commands related to the unsolicited e-mail transmission to AOL's computer facilities, . . . [and thereby] caused damage to the . . . computer systems . . . and furthermore caused the withholding and denial of use of the computers, computer services, systems, networks information, data and programs of AOL's computer facilities, thereby causing injury to AOL.[532]

AOL also alleged that Cyber transmitted the e-mails to AOL's subscribers without authorization, and with "reckless disregard of a substantial and unjustified risk, that its transmission would damage, or cause damage to, a computer, computer system, network, information, data or program of AOL's computer facilities."[533]

After consolidation of the cases, the district court granted summary judgment to AOL, ruling that, because AOL was not a "state actor" for purposes of the First Amendment, AOL had the right to prevent Cyber's unsolicited e-mail which was sent to AOL subscribers through its own computer facilities.[534] In a subsequent opinion, the court denied Cyber's motion for a temporary restraining order based on Cyber's antitrust claims

---

[528] *See Cyber Promotions, Inc. v. America Online, Inc.*, 948 F. Supp. 436 (E.D. Pa. 1996) (involving cross claims by both parties under the CFAA between an e-mail advertising firm and an Internet service provider over the advertiser's practice of sending unsolicited e-mail to the ISP's subscribers and the ISP's use of an e-mail "bomb" in response to the messages); *America Online Has Not Violated First Amendment by Blocking E-mail*, COMPUTER LAW., Nov. 1996, at 23; David S. Hilzenrath, *Judge Rules AOL Can Block Direct-Marketing Firm's Ads*, WASH. POST, Nov. 5, 1996, at C1.

[529] *America Online, Inc. v. Cyber Promotions, Inc.*, No. 96-462 (E.D. Va.) ("AOL Complaint") (subsequently consolidated with Cyber Promotions' action filed in the Eastern District of Pennsylvania); *Cyber Promotions, Inc. v. America Online, Inc.*, C.A. No. 96-2486, 1996 WL 565818 (E.D. Pa. Sept. 5, 1996) (Cyber granted temporary restraining order), *rev'd* (3d Cir. 1996) (unpublished opinion); *Cyber Promotions, Inc. v. America Online, Inc.*, 948 F. Supp. 436 (E.D. Pa. 1996) (AOL granted partial summary judgment on First Amendment issues), *recons. denied*, 948 F. Supp. 436, 447 (1996); *Cyber Promotions, Inc. v. America Online, Inc.*, 948 F. Supp. 456 (E.D. Pa. 1996) (denial of temporary restraining order on Cyber's antitrust claim).

[530] *Cyber Promotions, Inc*, 948 F. Supp. at 437.

[531] *Id.*

[532] *See* AOL Complaint, *supra* note 529, at ¶ 102.

[533] *Id.*

[534] *Cyber Promotions, Inc.*, 948 F. Supp. at 445.

against AOL.[535] The case was recently settled out of court.[536] Under the settlement, AOL members will be able to effectively block unsolicited e-mail from Cyber.[537]

[c] Application of CFAA to Electronic Banking and Commerce. As a result of the 1996 amendments to the CFAA, subsections (a)(4) and (a)(5) of the statute — which respectively prohibit computer fraud regarding "protected computers" and the knowing or intentional transmission of access information pertaining to a protected computer, such that it results in damage or destruction of computer information or data — most likely will be applicable to instances of criminal fraud affecting electronic commerce conducted on the Internet.[538] An Internet user's attempt at theft or fraud may fall within the reach of CFAA because a thief must generally use a computer to access the Internet and such "use" of the computer in interstate commerce would arguably make the computer a "protected computer" under the statute.[539] As one commentator has observed, any attempt at theft or fraud affecting the Internet should fall within the CFAA's definition of a protected computer because most, if not all, messages sent via the Internet are properly viewed as interstate communications.[540]

Indeed, with over ninety million personal computers in homes in the United States today, and an estimated thirty-four million households online worldwide, this interpretation of protected computer appears sound.[541] It may, however, run counter to the original intent CFAA, *i.e,* to limit federal jurisdiction of computer crime to those cases in which there is a "compelling federal interest."[542]

[8] STATE FINANCIAL PRIVACY LAWS

To the extent federal law does not "occupy the field" of financial privacy, state laws will apply. The Right to Financial Privacy Act ("RFPA") governs requests or orders from the federal government but does not cover requests from private entities or financial institutions.[543] The Fair Credit Reporting Act ("FCRA") regulates the sharing of financial information about customers by private entities that fall within the definition of consumer reporting agency and places limited obligations on other entities.[544] Financial institutions,

---

[535] *Cyber Promotions, Inc.*, 948 F. Supp. at 456.

[536] *See Cyber Promotions, Inc. v. America Online, Inc.*, No. 96-2486 (E.D. Pa. Feb. 1997) (unpublished) (order approving settlement).

[537] *See* Courtney Macavinta, *Spam King, AOL Agree to Disagree*, THE NET, Feb. 4, 1997, *available at* (visited Oct. 17, 1997) <http://www.news.com/News/Item/0,4,7648,00.html>.

[538] *See* Adams, *supra* note 456, at 429-31.

[539] 18 U.S.C. § 1030(e)(2)(B).

[540] *See* Adams, *supra* note 456, at 430.

[541] *See Internet Privacy and H.R. 2265, The "No Electronic Theft Act": Hearing Before the Subcomm. On Courts and Intellectual Property of the House Comm. on the Judiciary*, 105th Cong. (Sept. 1997) (testimony of Cary H. Sherman, Senior Executive Vice President and General Cousnel, Recording Industry Associaton of America) (discussing the number of PCs in U.S. homes, and estimating that by the year 2000 there will be over 154 million home PCs in the United States, and worldwide there will be over a half billion PCs); Peter McGrath, *The Web: Infotopia or Marketplace*, NEWSWEEK, Jan. 27, 1997, at 82.

[542] S. REP. NO. 99-432, at 4, *reprinted in* 1986 U.S.C.C.A.N. at 2482.

[543] 12 U.S.C. §§ 3401-22. *See* Section 12.06[4].

[544] 15 U.S.C. §§ 1681-81u. *See* Section 12.06[2].

therefore, need to consider the privacy laws of each state in which they conduct operations. Further, they need to consider the impact of state privacy laws as they develop new products and services. While a full review of state privacy laws is beyond the scope of this work, this section provides a discussion of the three primary types of state laws that govern financial privacy: (1) state constitutions; (2) state common law; and (3) state statutes and regulations.

[a] State Constitutions. Most state constitutions include prohibitions against improper search and seizure similar to that of the Fourth Amendment. At the state level, those provisions protect against actions by state and local governments. They do not apply to actions by private entities. Some states have incorporated more specific privacy provisions into their constitutions. For example, the New York State Constitution prohibits the "unreasonable interception of telephone and telegraph communications";[545] the California Constitution provides that "the right of the people to be secure in their persons, houses, papers, and effects against unreasonable seizures and searches may not be violated";[546] and the Florida Constitution recognizes an individual's "right to be let alone and free from governmental intrusion into his private life."[547]

[b] Common Law. Common law is the body of law that develops over time as a result of the case-by-case resolution of controversies.[548] There are three basic common law theories that support the right to privacy: (1) invasion of privacy; (2) defamation; and (3) implied contract.

[i] Invasion of Privacy. The four separate and distinct rights that make up the tort of "invasion of privacy," as outlined in the Restatement (Second) of Torts, § 652A, are: (i) the unreasonable intrusion upon the seclusion of another; (ii) the appropriation of another's name or likeness; (iii) the unreasonable publicity given to another's private life; and (iv) publicity that unreasonably places another in a false light before the public.[549] These offer limited protection to financial institution customers, however, because disclosures need to rise to the level of unreasonable, false, or embarrassing. The one area where these rights are of some assistance is in providing protection in the information collection process.

[ii] Defamation. The common law of defamation protects individuals against the dissemination of false information. It is, therefore, likely to be limited in its application to financial institution disclosures.

[iii] Implied Contract. The custom of confidentiality in the banking industry and generally accepted principles of common law, which are discussed in section 12.03[1], may give rise to a right of privacy based on implied contract.

[c] Statutes. In addition to constitutional provisions and common-law doctrines, many states have

---

[545] N.Y. CONST. art. I, § 12.

[546] CAL. CONST. art. I, § 13.

[547] FLA. CONST. art. I, § 23.

[548] *See* BLACK'S LAW DICTIONARY 276 (6th ed. 1990) (definition of "common law").

[549] *See* RESTATEMENT (SECOND) OF TORTS § 652A (1977).

specific statutes governing financial privacy. These statutes vary widely in coverage, but generally speaking, they are more specific in application than the broad general principles enunciated in state constitutions and the common law. A leading authority on the law of financial privacy suggests that state financial privacy laws, though varying in the range of their coverage, can be effectively analyzed by taking into consideration six basic issues: (1) the type of financial institutions governed by the statute; (2) the type of entity requesting the disclosure of financial information; (3) the type of customer that receives protection; (4) the methods by which confidential financial information may be accessed; (5) the sanctions imposed for improper disclosure; and (6) the recovery of costs associated with disclosures.[550] A number of state financial privacy laws are discussed below.

[i] *California.* Chapter 20 of California's Government Code,[551] the California Right to Financial Privacy Act ("CRFPA"), regulates requests for, and receipt of, customer "financial records"[552] by state and local governments upon a broad range of financial institutions.[553] Under Section 7470, employees, officers, directors, and agents of state or local agencies may not, in connection with criminal or civil investigations, "request or receive copies of, or the information contained in, the financial records of any customer from a financial institution unless the financial records": (i) are described with particularity; (ii) are consistent with the scope of the investigation; and (iii) meet the statute's procedural requirements (*i.e.,* the records are sought pursuant to a valid administrative or judicial subpoena or search warrant), or are otherwise authorized by the customer.[554]

Under California Government Code § 7471, financial institutions (and their employees, directors and agents) are prohibited from disclosing customer financial records (or the information contained therein) to state or local agencies if the financial institution or individual "knows or has reasonable cause to believe" that such records are sought in connection with a civil or criminal investigation of the customer.[555] This section does not prohibit the disclosure by the financial institution of the financial records of a customer (or the information contained therein) "incidental to a transaction in the normal course of business of such financial institution."[556]

Under California Government Code § 7485, the *mens rea* standard for violations of the CRFPA is knowing and purposeful violations.[557] The penalties apply to (i) any person who, "with the intent to violate, knowingly participates in a violation" [of the CRFPA] (*i.e.,* unlawfully making prohibited disclosures); and (ii), any

---

[550] FISCHER, *supra* note 132, ¶ 5.05, at 5-40.

[551] CAL. GOV'T CODE §§ 7460-93.

[552] *Id.* "Financial records" include "any original or any copy of any record or document held by a financial institution pertaining to a customer of the financial institution." *See id.* § 7465(b).

[553] Under California's Act, a "financial institution" includes state and national banks, state and federal savings and loan associations, state and federal credit unions, and trust companies. *See id.* § 7465(a).

[554] *Id.* § 7470(a).

[555] *Id.* § 7471(a).

[556] *Id.* § 7471(b).

[557] *Id.* § 7485.

person who "knowingly induces or attempts to induce a violation."[558] The statute also provides injunctive relief for customers of financial institutions "aggrieved by" a violation of the statute.[559]

California Government Code Section 7480 provides that certain types of disclosures will not violate the CRPFA. These disclosures include: (1) dissemination of financial information which is not identified with, or identifiable to, the financial records of a particular customer; (2) disclosures to police departments or prosecutors related to investigations of "alleged fraudulent use" of checks, drafts, or orders drawn upon a financial institution; (3) investigations by federal or state banking regulatory agencies; and (4) investigations of other state regulatory agencies.[560]

[ii] *Utah.* Chapter 14 of the Financial Institutions Act, entitled Credit Information Exchange, permits financial institutions and credit reporting agencies to exchange with any other such entity certain specific types of information.[561] They may disclose that an account relevant to a transaction has been closed, the reasons for the closure, and the identity of the depositor or account holder. They may also disclose, upon the request of another financial institution, their credit experience with regard to a specified customer and any information relating to a customer's efforts to defraud the institution. Depository institutions, which are defined for the purposes of this statute as those entities authorized by state or federal law to accept and hold accounts used to effect third party payment transactions, are granted immunity for communications containing errors or omissions when made to an authorized recipient. Utah also has statutory provisions specifically dealing with financial information privacy that address the type of "person" who may request the information,[562] the procedural requirements associated with making the disclosure (including the notice that must be given prior to the disclosure),[563] the admissibility of such disclosures, and the reimbursement of costs associated with making such disclosures.[564]

[iii] *Maryland.* Maryland has a comprehensive statute covering a range of financial institutions.[565] It refers to the disclosure of "financial records," which are defined to include documents granting signature authority, account records, checks, drafts, or money orders drawn on or issued by and payable by or through such fiduciary institution, and any other debit or credit items relating to a customer's account.[566] The Maryland Confidential Records Act modified and expanded this definition to include information relating to loan accounts and transactions at electronic terminals. Maryland financial institution laws only expressly permit disclosures

---

[558] *Id.*

[559] *Id.* § 7487.

[560] *Id.* § 7480.

[561] Utah Code Ann. § 7-14-3.

[562] *Id.* § 78-27-45.

[563] *Id.* § 78-27-46.

[564] *Id.* §§ 78-27-48, -49.

[565] Md. Code Ann., Fin. Inst. tit. 1, subtit. 3; *see id.* § 1-301(b) (definition of "fiduciary institution"). Connecticut and Maine have similar statutes. *See* Conn. Gen. Stat. Ann. § 36a-41 to § 45; Me. Rev. Stat. Ann. tit 9-B, §§ 161-64.

[566] Md. Code Ann., Fin. Inst. § 1-301(c).

where either the customer has provided authorization, which can be waived, or the Department of Human Resources requires the information to verify public assistance eligibility.[567] The term customer is not defined in the statute, but the breadth of the statute suggests a broad reading of the term. Though the statute does not explicitly provide for damages or injunctive relief, under Section 1-305, any officer, employee, agent, or director of a financial institution who "knowingly and willfully" discloses or induces the disclosure of financial records in violation of the statute is guilty of a misdemeanor and is subject to a fine of $1,000 upon conviction. The statute also penalizes those (outsiders) who "knowingly and willfully" induce or attempt to induce any officer, employee, agent, or director of a financial institution to disclose customer financial information.[568]

[iv] *Florida.* Under Florida Banking Law § 655.059(2)(b), financial institution customer records must be kept confidential, subject to enumerated exceptions.[569] There are three exceptions. First, information relating to any loan may be released by the financial institution, without the customer's authorization, "for the purpose of meeting the needs of commerce and for fair and accurate credit information."[570] Second, information about customer accounts may also be released without the customer's authorization to verify or corroborate the existence or amount of a customer's account when such information is reasonably provided to meet the needs of commerce and to ensure accurate credit information.[571] Third, a financial institution and its subsidiaries may furnish information to one another that relates to customers, subject to the requirement that each receiving institution treats information received from an affiliate as confidential and does not disclose such information to any unaffiliated person or entity.[572] The *mens rea* standard for violations of § 655.059(2)(b) is a "willful" violation.[573] Florida also has a statute dealing with access to credit cards, lists of subscribers, and account information that contains similar standards.[574]

[v] *Michigan.* Michigan law addresses privacy concerns in connection with electronic fund transfers.[575] The statute calls for electronic fund transfer facilities to be operated in a manner that ensures the privacy of personal financial information.[576] Further, it prohibits disclosure, by either the relevant financial institution or the facility, of information about a customer's deposit account or transactions conducted through the electronic

---

[567] *Id.* § 1-302.

[568] *Id.* § 1-305.

[569] FLA. STAT. ANN. § 655.059(2)(b). Generally "[t]he books and records pertaining to the deposit accounts and loans of depositors, borrowers, members, and stockholders of any financial institution shall be kept confidential by the financial institution and its directors, officers, and employees and shall not be released except upon the express authorization of the account holder as to his own accounts, loans, or voting rights."

[570] *Id.*

[571] *Id.*

[572] *Id.*

[573] Section 655.059(2)(c) provides that "[a] person who willfully violates the provisions of this section that relate to unlawful disclosure of confidential information is guilty of a felony of the third degree [and shall be punished according to state criminal penalty statutes]."

[574] *Id.* § 817.646.

[575] MICH. COMP. LAWS ANN. ch. 488.

[576] *Id.* § 488.8.

funds facility to outside parties unless that disclosure is made with the consent of the customer or is provided for by law.[577]

§ 12.07   LEGISLATIVE EFFORTS REGARDING FINANCIAL AND INFORMATION PRIVACY

[1]   105TH CONGRESS

In January 1997, Representative Bruce F. Vento (D-MN) introduced the Consumer Internet Privacy Protection Act of 1997 ("CIPPA").[578] The bill proposed to prohibit interactive computer services from disclosing to third parties any "personally identifiable information" provided by the subscriber without the subscriber's prior informed written consent, which could be revoked at any time.[579] The term "personally identifiable information" includes any information about a subscriber that is not aggregate data, which does not identify specific persons.[580] CIPPA would also require interactive computer services to, at a subscriber's request, provide the subscriber's personally identifiable information to the subscriber in order to permit the subscriber to verify and correct the information. Finally, CIPPA grants the FTC jurisdiction to "examine and investigate" prohibited practices under the Act.[581]

In a separate piece of legislation, Representative Bob Franks (D-NJ) proposed to regulate interactive computer services' use of Social Security numbers and related personally identifiable information.[582] The Social Security Online Privacy Protection Act of 1997 would require interactive computer services to obtain a customer's written informed consent prior to disclosing a customer's Social Security number or other personally identifiable information which is identifiable by means of a Social Security number.[583]

A third piece of legislation which was introduced in both the Senate and House, the Personal Information Privacy Act of 1997 ("PIPA"), would provide a range of protections for consumers' personally identifying information.[584] PIPA would amend the Fair Credit Reporting Act to prohibit credit bureaus from giving out Social Security numbers, unlisted phone numbers, dates of birth, past addresses, and mother's maiden names without the individual in question's written consent.[585] It would further prohibit dissemination of names, addresses, and

---

[577] *Id.* § 488.12.

[578] H.R. 98, 105th Cong. (1997).

[579] H.R. 98, § 2(a).

[580] *See id.* § 4(3); 47 U.S.C. § 551(a)(2).

[581] H.R. 98, § 3(a).

[582] H.R. 1287, 105th Cong. (1997).

[583] H.R. 1287, § 2(a). This bill would also authorize the Federal Trade Commission to exercise regulatory jurisdiction over interactive computer services and issue cease and desist orders, and fines or penalties for knowing violations of the Act. *See id.* § 3(b).

[584] *See* S. 600, 105th Cong. (1997) (introduced by Senator Feinstein (D-CA)); H.R. 1813, 105th Cong. (1997) (introduced by Rep. Kleczka (D-WI) and Rep. Franks (D-NJ)).

[585] *See* S. 600, § 3; H.R. 1813, § 3.

phone numbers if such information is not listed in local phone directories.[586] PIPA would also amend the Social Security Act to prohibit the commercial acquisition or distribution of an individual's Social Security number, and the use of a personal identification number without the individual's written consent.[587] PIPA would also prohibit state motor vehicle departments from disseminating Social Security numbers for bulk distribution in surveys, marketing, or solicitations.[588] Under PIPA, victims may bring a cause of action to recoup the greater of actual damages or liquidated damages,[589] as well as attorneys' fees and costs.[590]

[2] EUROPEAN PRIVACY INITIATIVES - EU DIRECTIVE 95/46/EC

The nations of the European Union historically have taken a different approach to personal and informational privacy than that of the United States.[591] Most European nations have laws that are designed to regulate both private and public sector use of personal information.[592] Such laws generally establish a comprehensive set of rights and responsibilities regarding the collection, use, storage, and disclosure of personal information.[593]

In mid-1995 the European Commission[594] adopted a Council Directive ("EU Directive") "on the protection of individuals with regard to the processing of personal data and on the free movement of such data."[595] This EU Directive embraces four core principles of data use and protection: (i) the establishment of obligations and responsibilities for personal information; (ii) the maintenance of transparent processing of personal information; (iii) the creation of special protections for sensitive types of personal data; and (iv) the

---

[586] *See* S. 600, § 2; H.R. 1813, § 2.

[587] *See* S. 600, § 3; H.R. 1813, § 3. Under PIPA, an individual's "consent" is not deemed to have been obtained unless (i) the service provider informs the consumer of all the purposes for which the Social Security number will be utilized and the persons to whom the number will be made known, and (ii) the service obtains the consumer's affirmatively expressed consent in writing. S. 600, § 3(c), H.R. 1813, § 3(c).

[588] S. 600, § 4; H.R. 1813, § 4.

[589] Liquidated damages are available up to $25,000, or if the violation is willful and resulted in profit or monetary gain, $50,000. S. 600, § 3; H.R. 1813, § 3.

[590] S. 600, § 3; H.R. 1813, § 3.

[591] For a comprehensive discussion of the differences between the European Union and the U.S. in the privacy arena, see PETER P. SWIRE & ROBERT E. LITAN, NONE OF YOUR BUSINESS: WORLD DATA FLOWS, ELECTRONIC COMMERCE, AND THE EUROPEAN PRIVACY DIRECTIVE (forthcoming Spring 1998), Interim Report *available at* <http://www.acs.ohio-state.edu/units/law/swire.htm>. The 15 member states of the European Union are Austria, Belgium, Denmark, Finland, France, Germany, Greece, Ireland, Italy, Luxemberg, Netherlands, Portugal, Spain, Sweden, and the United Kingdom.

[592] *See* SCHWARTZ & REIDENBERG, *supra* note 269, §§ 2-2 to 2-2(d), at 12-17 (providing an overview of the European approach to regulation of personal information practices, as compared to the U.S. approach).

[593] Among the European nations, Austria, Belgium, Denmark, France, Germany Ireland, Luxembourg, the Netherlands, Spain, Sweden and the United Kingdom have such laws. *See id.* § 2-2, at 12 n.11.

[594] The European Commission is one of the ten institutions of the European Union. Its functions are to initiate proposals for legislation, serve as the guardian of Treaties, and act as the manager and executor of Union policies and of international trade relationships.

[595] Council Directive 95/46/EC (on the Protection of Individuals with Regard to the Processing of Personal Data and on the Free Movement of Such Data), 1995 O.J. (L 281) 31 [hereinafter EU Directive].

establishment and enforcement of rights and effective oversight of the treatment of personal information.[596] The EU Directive is scheduled to go into effect in October 1998.[597]

The EU Directive provides a general framework for information practices regarding the "processing"[598] at least in part by automatic means of "personal data," which is defined as "any information relating to an identified or identifiable natural person."[599] It provides that such processing shall be "transparent," meaning that the subject of the data processing is given notice of the use of their personal information and an opportunity to make decisions in that regard.[600] Subject to certain exceptions, the EU Directive requires generally that personal data may be processed only "if the data subject has unambiguously given his consent."[601] It further requires that, when personal data is collected from an individual, he or she must be informed of (i) the identity of the "controller" of the data,[602] (ii) the purposes for which processing of the data is intended, and (iii) any other information that guarantees "fair processing" of the data.[603]

Article 6 of the EU Directive requires that personal data must meet certain quality standards. For example, Article 6 provides that personal data must be (i) processed fairly and lawfully, (ii) collected for "specified, explicit and legitimate purposes," (iii) "adequate, relevant and not excessive" to the purposes for which it was collected, (iv) accurate and, where necessary, up to date, and (v) kept in a form which permits identification of data subjects only for such time periods as are "necessary" for the purposes for which the data was collected.[604]

The EU Directive gives individuals a right of access to personal data that is subject to processing by the controller of that data, as well as the ability to correct inaccuracies or to erase or block personal data that is processed in a manner inconsistent with the EU Directive's standards.[605] Under Article 14 of the EU Directive, the data subject has the right (i) to object on "compelling legitimate grounds" to the processing of personal data, (ii) to be informed of personal data to third parties prior to the disclosure, and (iii) to be expressly offered

---

[596] *See* SCHWARTZ & REIDENBERG, *supra* note 269, § 2-2, at 13.

[597] *See* FEDERAL TRADE COMM'N, STAFF REPORT - PUBLIC WORKSHOP ON THE GLOBAL INFORMATION INFRASTRUCTURE, app. B (1996) (discussing the European Directive on the Protection of Personal Data) [hereinafter FTC STAFF REPORT, app. B], *available at* (visited Sept. 16, 1997) <http//www.ftc.gov/reports/privacy/APPENDIXb.htm>.

[598] "Processing" is defined as "any operation or set of operations which is performed upon personal data, whether or not by automatic means, such as collection, recording, organization, storage, adaptation or alteration, retrieval, consultation, use, disclosure by transmission, dissemination or otherwise making available, alignment or combination, blocking, erasure or destruction." EU Directive, art. 2(b), *supra* note 595.

[599] *Id.* art. 2(a).

[600] *Id.* art. 7. *See also* FTC STAFF REPORT, app. B, *supra* note 597.

[601] EU Directive, art. 7(a), *supra* note 595. Under Article 7 of the EU Directive, member states may also permit personal data to be processed if (i) necessary for (i) the controller to comply with a legal obligation (ii) the performance of a task in the public interest, or (iii) if the processing is necessary for the purposes or the legitimate interests pursued by the controller and third parties to whom the data are disclosed. *Id.* art. 7.

[602] "Controller" is defined as the "the natural or legal person, public authority, agency or any other body which alone or jointly with others determines the purposes and means of the processing of personal data." *Id.* art. 2(d).

[603] *Id.* art. 10. *See* FTC STAFF REPORT, app. B, *supra* note 597 ("Similar protections apply where personal information about a data subject is not obtained directly from him or her.").

[604] EU Directive, *supra* note 595, art. 6(1).

[605] *Id.* art. 12.

the right, free of charge, to object to such disclosure.[606] The EU Directive requires member states to provide individuals with judicial remedies and a right to compensation for damages suffered by reason of a controller's violation of an individual privacy rights under the EU Directive.[607]

Article 25 of the EU Directive governs the transfer of personal data to countries outside the European Union. It thus may have important implications for the United States and other nations doing business with residents of EU member states. Article 25 allows member states to permit the "transfer to a third country of personal data which are undergoing processing or are intended for processing after transfer . . . only if . . . the third country in question ensures an adequate level of protection."[608] This requirement is subject to exceptions enumerated in Article 26, including an exception where the controller of the data must be able to demonstrate that "adequate safeguards," such as appropriate contractual provisions, for protecting the privacy and fundamental rights of individuals.[609] Under the EU Directive, the "adequacy" standard is to be assessed in light of the particular facts and circumstances of the proposed data transfer, and with regard to "the rules of law, both general and sectoral, in force in the third country in question, as well as the professional rules and security measures that are complied with in that country."[610] Where, with respect to a particular proposed data transfer, a country is found not to have an "adequate" level of data protection, the EU Directive requires member states to prevent any transfer of the same type of data to the country in question.[611]

Currently there is an increasing focus on whether United States data privacy protections conform with the EU Directive's "adequacy" standard.[612]

In June 1996, the European Council agreed to extend the principles contained in the EU Directive to the context of digital telecommunications networks, particularly the development of integrated services digital networks ("ISDN") and mobile digital networks.[613] This proposed Directive would establish rules related to the security and services of such ISDN networks, the confidentiality of communications, the uses of data collected during data traffic, and restrictions on calling and connected line identification.[614]

---

[606] *Id.* art. 14.

[607] *Id.* art. 22-24.

[608] *Id.* art. 25.

[609] *Id.* art. 26(2). Under Article 26, member states may also permit the transfer of personal data to countries whose level of data protection is not deemed "adequate" where: the data subject has "unambiguously" consented to the proposed transfer; the transfer is necessary for the performance of a contract between the controller of the data and the data subject or is necessary to protect the data subject's vital interests; the transfer is required to support a legal claim. *See id.* at art. 26(1). *See also* FTC STAFF REPORT, app. B, *supra* note 597.

[610] EU Directive, art. 25(2), *supra* note 595.

[611] FTC STAFF REPORT, app. B, *supra* note 597.

[612] *Id. See also* Lisa Fickenscher, *Information Industry Keeping Its Cool About Talk of a Federal 'Privacy Czar,'* AM. BANKER, Oct. 15, 1996, at 1; William L. Fishman, *The Privacy Problem; European Concerns About U.S. Protections Threaten Commerce,* FULTON COUNTY DAILY REP., Sept. 26, 1997; Doug Sweet, *Differences Evident at Convention: U.S., Europe Disagree on Privacy Directive,* THE GAZETTE (Montreal), Sept. 27, 1997, at A7.

[613] *See* Council Common Position 57/96 (concerning the Processing of Personal Data and the Protection of Privacy in the Telecommunications Sector), 1996 O.J. (L 315) 3.

[614] *Id.*

Chapter 13

Security

§13.01 Introduction

Financial institutions are under continual competitive pressure to offer new products and services. These new products and services now frequently take the form of new and emerging forms of electronic banking and commerce and include the use of the Internet to provide information and interactive transactional services. Some of the underlying technologies may be new and unproven. The vendors may also be new and thinly capitalized. Accordingly, financial institutions may, in implementing these new technologies, be exposing themselves to considerable risk, often with limited ability to assess and manage this risk.

It is possible to make information, such as market summaries, analyses, investment opportunities, and other marketing information available over the Internet at low risk to an institution, particularly if offered through a third party online service provider. Actively providing financial services over the Internet, however, creates much greater risk. Internet-based services may require an institution to allow external access to a server within the institution. This opens the server to the potential for external attack in the form of fraudulent activity or malicious damage. To the extent that the server is linked to other computers within the enterprise, those computers also may be vulnerable. The potential for monetary loss and/or loss of the capability to maintain continuity in the conduct of business can be great. The specific risks related to particular forms of electronic commerce — automated teller machines ("ATM"), point-of-sale ("POS") systems, stored value cards, smart cards, financial electronic data interchange ("FEDI"), and others — may be different but still have the potential for significant business impact from fraud and other attacks, as well as from system errors and failures.

The previous two Chapters discussed the benefits as well as the potential "privacy" cost pertaining to electronic financial products and services ("EFS"). Just as the financial services industry invested time and provided education to encourage consumers to embrace ATM technology, at a minimum, a similar investment will be needed to facilitate the use of a new generation of EFS. The American Bankers Association, through its Payments System Task Force, recognizes the importance of consumer concerns, and the need for financial institutions and vendors to take steps to recognize and address these concerns. The Task Force's report notes that:

> Customers' acceptance of new technologies will be driven largely by traditional concerns about liability, unauthorized access, exposure to fraud, fees, privacy and finality of payment. The Task Force believes that the banking industry must take the lead in prescribing standards of practice for dealing with these customer concerns in a way that promotes acceptance of new products and successful banking relationships.[1]

Security concerns are not limited to consumers. During the past two years, issues and concerns regarding the security of systems that offer EFS have drawn significant attention from state, federal, and international bank regulators. The Federal Deposit Insurance Corporation, the Office of Thrift Supervision, and the National Credit Union Administration have already issued regulatory compliance or examination guidelines relating to these new business paradigms.

This Chapter will explain the security associated with EFS through the use of a proprietary information security model. It will demonstrate the need for security not only at the technology level but at the organizational and business levels as well.

§ 13.02 INFORMATION SECURITY FRAMEWORK

Information technology, and its integration into service delivery and relationship management, has forced financial institutions to rethink their approach to information security. The desire to have open access to information is countered by ever increasing threats from inside and outside the organization. This conflict cannot be adequately resolved using traditional information security concepts and practices. It requires a structured, comprehensive perspective that addresses the business risks with the right combinations of security techniques in place throughout an organization. The Information Security Framework[SM] ("ISF")[2] is a model designed to provide this perspective, and to provide decision makers with a cost-effective approach to address information security related business risks.

[1] THE ISF BALANCE

ISF is based on the simple concept of balance: information security risk management techniques should create a balance between benefits and opportunities derived from undertaking risks and the cost of risk mitigation strategies. This optimum balance is illustrated by the following diagram:

---

[1] PAYMENTS SYSTEM TASK FORCE, AM. BANKERS ASS'N, THE ROLE OF BANKS IN THE PAYMENTS SYSTEM OF THE FUTURE, at iii (1996).

[2] Additional information regarding the Arthur Andersen ("AA") Information Security Framework ("ISF") can be obtained from the AA website <http://www.arthurandersen.com>. Financial institutions can employ various models that use existing technology differently for maintaining security. This Chapter discusses only the ISF model.

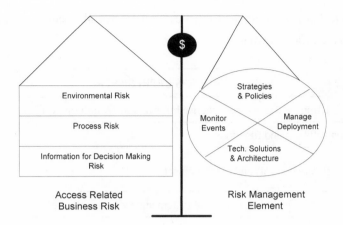

The left side of the scale reflects the business risks faced by the organization.[3] Risk Management Elements ("RME"), the right side of the scale, represent actions taken to mitigate the business risks.

[2]   CATEGORIZING RISK MANAGEMENT ELEMENTS

RME's fall into four categories. The name of the category and a brief description are provided in the following matrix:

RME	BRIEF DESCRIPTION
Strategies and Policies	Management strategies for information security and relevant policies, standards, guidelines, or directives used to communicate these strategies to the organization.
Manage Deployment	Proactive processes that turn policies into action — professional education and awareness programs, change management and control, security administration, and other necessary activities.
Monitor Events	Reactive processes that enable management to measure how well policies are implemented and followed, and to identify when policies need change.
Technology Solutions and Architecture	The technologies needed to provide the appropriate protection and support critical processes. These security risk management elements are then evaluated for each security access layer.

[3]   IDENTIFYING THE SECURITY ACCESS LAYER

It is insufficient to consider only the RME when addressing enterprise-wide electronic money and banking security concerns. Each of the RMEs must be considered in conjunction with a Security Access Layer ("SAL").

---

[3]   A thorough discussion of business risks and the use of a business risk model may be obtained from "Managing Business Risks – An Integrated Approach," The Economist Intelligence Unit, 1995.

The SAL reflects various technological processes that can impact overall security. SALs and the process they represent are described in the following matrix:

SAL	PROCESS REPRESENTED
Process	Business functions and processes that use Information Technology ("IT")
Application	Application software and functions
Data Management	Database software controls and related objects
Platform	Hardware platform including operating system and system software
Network	Local Area Network ("LAN"), Wide Area Network ("WAN"), Internet, Intranet and support systems
Physical	Components that house, support and process IT

[4] INTERRELATIONSHIP BETWEEN RISK MANAGEMENT ELEMENTS AND SECURITY ACCESS LAYERS

It is important to note that each SAL and each RME must be addressed to mitigate security risks. The following diagram illustrates the relationship between each RME and each SAL.

Information Security Framework^{SM}

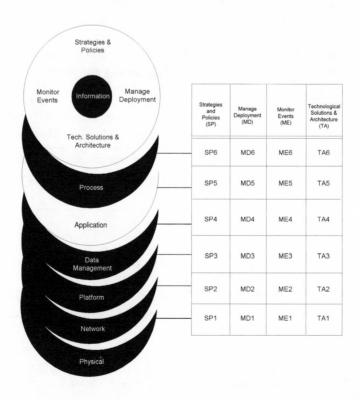

In evaluating these risks it is helpful to use a matrix that compares each RME and each SAL. The following matrix provides a simple illustration:

	Strategies and Policies (SP)	Manage Deployment (MD)	Monitor Events (ME)	Technology Solutions and Architecture (TA)
Process (6)	SP6	MD6	ME6	TA6
Application (5)	SP5	MD5	ME5	TA5
Data Management (4)	SP4	MD4	ME4	TA4
Platform (3)	SP3	MD3	ME3	TA3
Network (2)	SP2	MD2	ME2	TA2
Physical (1)	SP1	MD1	ME1	TA1

The following matrix summarizes the issues to be considered for each matrix component:

	Strategies and Policies (SP)	Manage Deployment (MD)	Monitor Events (ME)	Technology Solutions and Architecture (TA)
Process (6)	Management supported comprehensive enterprise-side information asset protection program with cornerstone of individual user identification and authentication along with access based on need-to-know for job function.	Effective and efficient procedures to establish and maintain logical access control over computerized information assets, including user administration that transcends individual platforms and applications.	Procedures and automated tools to identify and address systems security and business process risks stemming from information technology used to deliver products and services.	Automated tools to support and facilitate establishment and ongoing security administration for information systems supporting key business processes.

Continued on next page

Continued from previous page

	Strategies and Policies (SP)	Manage Deployment (MD)	Monitor Events (ME)	Technology Solutions and Architecture (TA)
	Application (5)	Formal management directive to assess information security and business process risks and exposures as part of application development process obtaining application owner sign-off on security design.	Control over application maintenance through change control and source code management, as well as control over users through logical access control software.	Systems development life cycle and source code management software. Application specific or host-based logical access control system which also logs and reports access activities.
Unauthorized attempted application access and transaction activities are identified and	addressed, along with periodic selective review of successful access activities. Audit trail of all	significant business transactions are retained to facilitate detective controls.	**Data Management (4)**	Accountability and responsibility for database access control and data administration.
Management authorization for database reorgani-zation or use of data altering utilities.	DBMS specific logical access control system and monitoring utilities.	Manual or automated audit trails of direct database access and the use of data altering utilities.	**Platform (3)**	Platform specific standards and procedures to secure access to information assets consistent with overall policy.
Access administration for operating system and security software to maintain access based on need.	Platform specific logical access control software, including monitoring of unauthorized access and selected successful access.	Identify unauthorized attempts or actual access to platform and take appropriate technical and disciplinary action.	**Network (2)**	Policies for the establishment of inter and intra company network connections with standards for minimum acceptable security standards.

Continued on next page

Continued from previous page

	Strategies and Policies (SP)	Manage Deployment (MD)	Monitor Events (ME)	Technology Solutions and Architecture (TA)
Risk assessment process and methodology to access the security and control impact of all new network connections and to recommend control enhancements prior	to implementation.	Access control over remote access and network monitoring software.	Network intrusion detection software and utilities.	**Physical (1)**

The following examples demonstrate the use of the ISF.

<u>Example 1</u>

Institution X's concern about security is limited to network connections only. In this particular situation, Institution X would only address matrix boxes SP2, MD2, TA2, and ME2. That is, it would need only to consider all four RMEs as they relate to the network level. If one of the RMEs proves ineffective, there would be a security exposure that would need to be remedied.

	Strategies and Policies (SP)	Manage Deployment (MD)	Monitor Events (ME)	Technology Solutions and Architecture (TA)
Process (6)	SP6	MD6	ME6	TA6
Application (5)	SP5	MD5	ME5	TA5
Data Management (4)	SP4	MD4	ME4	TA4
Platform (3)	SP3	MD3	ME3	TA3
Network (2)	SP2	MD2	ME	TA2
Physical (1)	SP1	MD1	ME1	TA1

Example 2

Institution X's concern is limited to whether it has the appropriate strategies and policies in place to effectively manage technology and to comply with the strategy and policy components of the Federal Financial Institutions Examination Council.[4] Institution X therefore should consider how the RME, "Strategies and Policies" affected each SAL (SP1, SP2, SP3, SP4, SP5, and SP6). As in the last example, if one of the SALs was omitted or ineffective, Institution X would have incomplete strategies and policies.

	Strategies and Policies (SP)	Manage Deployment (MD)	Monitor Events (ME)	Technology Solutions and Architecture (TA)
Process (6)	SP6	MD6	ME6	TA6
Application (5)	SP5	MD5	ME5	TA5
Data Management (4)	SP4	MD4	ME4	TA4
Platform (3)	SP3	MD3	ME3	TA3
Network (2)	SP2	MD2	ME2	TA2
Physical (1)	SP1	MD1	ME1	TA1

Example 3

Institution X is concerned with the impact of electronic financial products and services on the overall security environment of the financial institution. This concern would necessitate that Institution X consider all RMEs and all SALs.

	Strategies and Policies (SP)	Manage Deployment (MD)	Monitor Events (ME)	Technology Solutions and Architecture (TA)
Process (6)	SP6	MD6	ME6	TA6
Application (5)	SP5	MD5	ME5	TA5
Data Management (4)	SP4	MD4	ME4	TA4
Platform (3)	SP3	MD3	ME3	TA3
Network (2)	SP2	MD2	ME2	TA2
Physical (1)	SP1	MD1	ME1	TA1

---

[4] For additional information concerning FFIEC requirements, see generally FEDERAL FINANCIAL INSTITUTIONS EXAMINATION COUNCIL, INFORMATION SYSTEMS EXAMINATION HANDBOOK (1996) [hereinafter IS EXAMINATION HANDBOOK].

Experience shows that where financial institutions fail to effectively implement a strong enterprise security program, it is because they do not consider the proper mix of RMEs and SALs in their strategy development.

§ 13.03 THE BUSINESS PROCESS

The previous Section introduced the ISF and the concepts of SALs and RMEs. This Section shows how these concepts impact a typical financial institution business process. The following diagram provides a process review of the typical loan cycle.

[1]   THE LOAN CYCLE AND SALS

Process Loans, Mortgages, Credit Cards

The diagram, along with the ISF, show how the various sub-processes of the loan cycle interact with the ISF. As illustrated in the previous Section, each SAL and its risks must be mitigated to achieve effective enterprise security.

SAL	EXAMPLES OF SUB-PROCESSES OF THE LOAN CYCLE HAVING A SECURITY IMPACT
Process	• Security administration throughout the loan process is provided by authentication tools, encryption, and logging facilities • Customers must successfully identify themselves in order for the system to recognize them and allow them access to the information • Underwriting process authenticates customers and their ability to repay loans
Application	• Loan management system would receive the account setup information, approvals, third party information, queries, loan activity, and reports • Loan management system submits the journal entries to the general ledger and loan performance analysis to a report writing tool
Data Management	• Database would hold data such as customer information and customer balances • Customers can access only their information by access controls implemented at the database level
Platform	• Operating system running the loan management system processes loan transactions and coordinates the other system facilities processing the loan information
Network	• Firewalls, proxy servers, routers, web servers, and Internet services that facilitate the connection between the customer and the bank • Customers submit their loan application electronically to the bank • Bank sends a return/response and a contract electronically to the customer • Customers sign the contract through a trusted certification service, which may include digital signatures • Customer Service disburses funds via a payment system • Customers have their banks send payments and interest to the bank's account management through a payment system • Customers can access the bank's Web page or system in order to review statements and balances online • Third party information such as foreign exchange rates send data over the Internet directly to the bank's system
Physical	• Physical access to the servers and systems running the loan management system, general ledger system, and other related systems

Section 13.04 through 13.09 will analyze each SAL in detail. The authors assume a general familiarity with security, especially where electronic financial products and services would have a minimal impact on the SALs security effectiveness. A management control checklist for each of these areas is included at Appendices B and C.

§ 13.04   THE PROCESS SAL

The Process SAL reflects most of the functions commonly known as end-user computing. The introduction of electronic commerce does not significantly change RME use or application. As a result, this discussion is limited to the chart below, which identifies RME strategies to mitigate the security risks associated with the Process SAL:[5]

RME	EXAMPLES OF RME TO MITIGATE PROCESS SAL CONCERNS
Strategies and Polices (SP6)	• Clear definition of management's security expectations documented in policies • Organizational infrastructure and security administration to carry out policies • Assignment of responsibilities and accountability for information assets through identified "owners"
Manage Deployment (MD6)	• Clear definition of management's security expectations documented in policies • Organizational infrastructure and security administration to carry out policies • Assignment of responsibilities and accountability for information assets through identified "owners" • Accountability and responsibility for systems activities through individual user identification and authentication • Classification scheme to protect information assets based on sensitivity and value • Access to information assets based on need-to-know to perform job function
Monitor Events (ME6)	• Audit trails of information security activities • Criteria for determining which activities constitute a violation • Proactive identification and follow-up of violations • Service level agreements and monitoring of security administration tasks to assure delivery of quality information security service • Regular management review of users' access capabilities
Technology Solutions and Architecture (TA6)	• User registration system to track basic systems access capabilities of each user with ultimate goal of single point for user authentication • Interface between user registration system and Human Resources to identify terminated users • Regular reporting allowing managers to review their staff's basic access authorities with deletion of inappropriate access • Asset inventory linking each information asset to an asset owner • Regular reporting allowing asset owners to review access to their assigned assets

---

[5]   For information on end-user computing risks, see IS EXAMINATION HANDBOOK, *supra* note 4, at chapter 16.

§ 13.05   APPLICATION SAL

The Application SAL is concerned with ensuring the integrity of the application and the accuracy and completeness of application systems data.

This SAL addresses whether:

- only complete, accurate, and valid data is entered and updated in a computer system;

- processing accomplishes the correct task;

- processing results meet expectations; and

- data integrity is maintained.

The controls may consist of edit tests, validations checks, total reconciliations, and identification and reporting of incorrect, missing, or exception data. In the electronic financial products and services ("EFS") environment, automated controls are the primary means to ensure proper identification and investigation of exceptions. Many EFS applications rely on client-server systems. In such systems, both application code and data files may be distributed among a number of different types of processors. These processes work together to provide the user with the information and systems processes needed, regardless of the user's location and type of computer, and the location and type of computers holding the requested data and application processing code. Traditional approaches to managing application security are unlikely to provide the assurances needed by management responsible for the client-server systems.

As a result, more sophisticated application controls will need to be developed in the Application SAL to accommodate the expected increase in activity and potential direct customer access. The following chart identifies RME strategies to mitigate the security risks associated with the Application SAL:

RME	EXAMPLES OF RME TO MITIGATE APPLICATION SAL CONCERNS
Strategies and Policies (SP5)	• Owner identified for all applications • User identification and authentication required for application access • Users' access capabilities assigned based on need in order to perform job functions • Security requirements for application defined and approved by owner and corporate information security group • Formal risk acceptance process for applications that do not meet security requirements
Manage Deployment (MD5)	• Program management software to secure and manage program source code • Security review and approval of program changes to ensure enhancement does not introduce risk or exposure into business process • Formal change control procedures with authorization requirements for migrating new or enhanced programs into production • Security review of business process to map and assess controls effectiveness
Monitor Events (ME5)	• Manual or automated audit trails of significant business transactions • Review and follow-up of application access and transaction failures • Periodic management review of users' application access authorities with deletion of inappropriate access
Technology Solutions and Architecture (TA5)	• Program library management and change control software and/or procedures • Risk assessment methodology • Risk acceptance procedures and approval process • Systems development life cycle incorporating security as a critical path milestone • Application specific security including user id identification, user authentication and access authorization checking • Utilities to report user access authorities

§ 13.06   DATA MANAGEMENT SAL

Data is created and stored in large volumes, representing millions of records and transactions. In electronic banking, internal users and external customers access the data directly through internal or external networks, telephone lines, the Internet, and satellites. The data is therefore vulnerable to possible unauthorized access and mishandling. Controls must be implemented to minimize the vulnerability of all information.

Data management challenges associated with EFS are greater than those associated with most traditional banking products and services because in EFS outside parties are permitted to directly access the data. This requires heightened practices to effectively validate users and to determine if they are appropriately authorized to initiate certain transactions. Although subsequent Sections will discuss RMEs related to external networks, effective data management strategies need to be implemented to enhance protection over critical information.

Management Information System ("MIS") policies and procedures should cover accountability and responsibility for database access control and data administration. The database administrator ("DBA") is responsible for the activities that affect the development, use, and maintenance of the database. The DBA's functions include maintenance of data definition, database design, data operations, and security.

Database security policies should cover the following:

- investigating all known security violations as well as suspicious activity;

- establishing the levels of authority appropriate for various users;

- maintaining security codes, passwords, etc.;

- monitoring adherence to security procedures; and

- performing periodic audits on security.

There should also be formal procedures for database recovery in the event of hardware and software failure. In addition, adequate disaster recovery considerations should be documented and tested.

Changes to the data dictionary should be authorized through the DBA, approved by users where applicable, adjusted in user documentation, adequately tested, and reviewed for audit trails and controls. There should be procedures ensuring that the data dictionary is current and accurate. The DBA should determine which software exits are allowed, as well as approve programs that access the database.

It is essential that the DBMS maintains an automated audit trail of direct database access and the use of data altering utilities. These logs should have enough detail to allow for recovery from failures and damaged files as well as supervisory review. Administrative and operator messages should also be included. The log should give transaction history to allow for an investigation of an error. Activity reports and exception reports should be reviewed daily.

The following are essential elements of database security:

- There should be an audit trail for prompt detection of loss.

- User actions should be reviewed for any suspicious or unauthorized behavior.

- Access should be available only to identified, authorized individuals.

- Data should be protected from physical hazards, such as fire and theft.

- Data should be recoverable in case of intentional or accidental loss.

- The system should not allow programmers to bypass controls.

- The system must have the ability to verify whether user actions are authorized.

Database management systems can be controlled by authorization and processing controls. Authorization controls involve granting general system access as well as access to specific files, programs, and records. Processing controls include edit checks and reasonable tests. Data confidentiality can be protected through encrypting data and archives, having strict controls on authorizations, and maintaining logical access.

The following chart summarizes the RME strategies for the Data Management SAL:

RME	EXAMPLES OF RME TO MITIGATE DATA MANAGEMENT SAL CONCERNS
Strategies and Policies	• Assigned accountability and responsibility for each database through DBA • End-user database access controlled through application • Formal documentation of database utilities assigned to DBAs • User identification and authentication for accessing any DBMS
Manage Deployment	• Formal process and management authorization procedures for database reorganization • Regular review to verify assigned DBA is appropriate
Monitor Events	• Manual or automated audit trails of usage of data altering utilities • Review and follow-up of direct access to databases
Technology Solutions and Architecture	• DBMS specific logical access control system over ORACLE, SYBASE and INFORMIX

§ 13.07 THE PLATFORM SAL

The rapid evolution of information technology has carried financial institutions (as well as business in general) from the traditional, centralized, large, and monolithic data centers to business environments that include centralized large computers linked to midsize and minicomputers, as well as to stand-alone and inter-connected end-user computing systems. New application technologies, including digital image processing and the use of electronic data interchange for both internal operations and customer service, are increasingly important to financial intermediary productivity and, ultimately, even to the protection of an institution's market share and its competitive survival. The variety of technological environments and their ubiquitous distribution throughout virtually all business functions and locations makes the assessment of technology-related controls a difficult task.

Whereas the traditional data center, because of its isolated nature, allowed for a single point of management control over, for example, physical access, application systems development and maintenance, and disaster recovery, today's distributed environments rely heavily on departmental and branch management to achieve these same objectives. The security concerns in these environment must not only address centrally managed systems but must also address the numerous and varied end-user systems not directly managed by the information systems, to the extent that these systems impact relevant and significant business events and financial transactions. In such situations, a major portion of this assessment responsibility necessarily rests with line management in all areas of the financial institution. At the Platform SAL, a variety of risks need to be considered, risks that largely focus on the integrity of programs and data. For example:

1. Environmental Integrity – Ensuring that applications and databases that support critical processes cannot be easily modified or altered outside of the application system itself. Sound information and network security practices are critical to managing this risk.

2. Application Change Control – Ensuring that system changes have been appropriately tested is critical to ensuring the consistency of information. Similarly, the timely distribution of client-side software to the various local and distributed client machines is important.

3. System Management & Monitoring – Making sure that platforms, databases and networks run smoothly, efficiently, and when needed requires effective IT business processes.

A financial institution can process on a variety of platforms. Typical operating system platforms include OS/900, OS/400, DEC/VAX, Windows NT, and UNIX. To illustrate the concerns relating to operating system security, the authors analyze UNIX. There are many variants of UNIX (depending on the vendor). UNIX is used by many financial service institutions in their client/server environments. The checklist included in Appendix C is typical of various platform checklists used to help identify security exposures.

As indicated in the checklist included in Appendix C, the following major concerns must be addressed to enhance security over the Platform SAL:

- default password and administration values must be changed;

- critical security features of the operating system must be implemented;

- access for privileged users and temporary guests must be controlled and monitored; and

- programs, routines, or applications that can circumvent normal processing should be identified and reconciled to approved plans.

The following chart summarizes other RME Strategies for the Platform SAL:

RME	EXAMPLES OF RME TO MITIGATE PLATFORM SAL
Strategies and Policies	• Assigned accountability and responsibility for each major platform • Individual user identification and authentication for access to the platform • Formal documentation of authorization assigning special privileges to users
Manage Deployment	• Formal process and management authorization procedures for operating system changes • Planning to facilitate consistency between operating/security system and business systems needed • Process to identify and apply operating and security system maintenance in a timely manner
Monitor Events	• Manual or automated audit trails of usage of data altering utilities • Review and follow-up of failed systems access or failed access against critical operating system files
Technology Solutions and Architecture	• Operating system level logical access control software • Report writer to extract and format audit information for system logs

§ 13.08 SECURING THE NETWORK LAYER IN THE INFORMATION TECHNOLOGY RISK FRAMEWORK

Security is critical to the reliable functioning of EFS systems. At the same time, it is continually subject to being compromised either internally or externally. As recognized in a recent government report, "there is no single magic" technology or technique that can ensure that the Global Information Infrastructure will be secure and reliable. Accomplishing that goal requires a range of technologies (encryption, authentication, password controls, firewalls, etc.) and effective consistent use of those technologies, all supported globally by trustworthy key and security management infrastructures.[6]

Before implementing an EFS system that involves a network, one priority must be to develop a strategy for the management, development, implementation and maintenance of the network. It is important to implement policies and procedures for the type of internal (ATM, Ethernet, Token Ring, etc.)[7] and external (Internet, electronic fund transfer (EFT) networks, FEDWIRE, CHIPS) network that will be used, the type of transactions allowed on the networks, and the financial institution's objective in implementing the new system.

---

[6] PRESIDENT WILLIAM J. CLINTON & VICE PRESIDENT ALBERT GORE, JR., A FRAMEWORK FOR GLOBAL ELECTRONIC COMMERCE (July 1997), *available at* <http://www.iitf.nist.gov/eleccomm/ecomm.htm>.

[7] ATM (Asynchronous Transfer Mode), Ethernet, and Token ring are types of network architectures. These architectures specify the types of computer hardware, wires, and software a network participant needs to use.

Security measures such as firewalls,[8] encryption, proxy servers[9], and de-militarized zones[10], should also be incorporated into strategy to optimize the development of the network's topology. A well designed strategy will help reduce the risk of obsolescence of the network and ensure that it is stable and secure enough to satisfy business needs.

[1] THE NEED FOR POLICIES AND MONITORING

Totally preventing unauthorized activity (including fraud or other illegal activity) in a network is likely to prove to be impractical and very expensive. Yet security can be paramount for a total customer relationship. An effective way to administer networks is to develop appropriate strategies and communicate them to key network personnel. Policies that would implement the identified strategies should include:

- security settings to be used for each type of network;

- use of intruder detecting measures;

- determining the how, when, why, where, and by whom each network will be used;

- determining the types of information that can be distributed on the network and how; and

- hardware and software security practices to reduce the risk of fraud and illegal activities.

Establishing standardized policies and procedures for network administration allows for enhanced monitoring of the system and provides users with a reference as to the security of the system. Ideally, such policies and procedures allow administrators to focus on proper implementation of management's security directives and enable management and security administrators to significantly reduce the risk of fraud or illegal activity.

Contingency planning for network failure is also extremely important. Even with the high reliability of current networks, network unavailability can be expected from time to time potentially causing significant damage to business operations or reputation. In businesses where time is money, quick recovery is a paramount consideration.

Monitoring may be one of the most difficult and important jobs in adequately controlling the network environment. It is important also to recognize that with the different types of networks different monitoring techniques must be used.

---

[8] A firewall is a combination of computer hardware and software that is used to protect an internal network from any external networks to which it may be connected. The basic function of a firewall is to filter data coming into a network.

[9] A proxy server is used to screen and limit access from the Intranet to the Internet.

[10] A De-Militarized Zone ("DMZ") is a part of the firewall. It is a region designated as an intermediary between the Intranet and the Internet. Hardware included in the DMZ are proxy servers, application servers, mail servers and domain name servers. Other types of computers may also be part of the DMZ, but its main function is to screen information going out from the Intranet to the Internet and prevent access from the Intranet to the Internet.

Monitoring all Internet activity involving a financial institution is likely to prove impractical. Firewalls, proxy servers, demilitarized zones and encryption can however be used to manage a financial institution's risk in using the Internet for customer service transactions and other business. These techniques will be discussed later in the Chapter. Firewalls and proxy servers can be used to monitor information coming in and out of an organization and to provide relevant information as to the status of a bank's domain. It is important to recognize that periodic review of this information is necessary to provide value to an organization. Security policies dictated by management directives should address what information should be monitored and how.

Most network operating systems have options available for monitoring the traffic on a financial service firm's internal network and reporting certain unusual activities in system reports. These system reports should also be reviewed on a periodic basis and a management strategy should be prepared and approved by appropriate management specifying types of activities to be flagged and the review methodology to be employed.

Network monitoring is composed of many factors, including network availability. Many network operating systems have an intruder detection option. This option limits the number of times a potential user can make unsuccessful attempts to log onto a network. Some operating systems have the capability of tracking these repeated failed attempts and bringing them to the system administrator's attention. Monitoring the current EFS environment and the current security exposures is also important. Being aware of the new techniques used by hackers can aid a system administrator in reducing an organization's exposure to such attacks.

EFS is a dynamic function within the financial industry. It is important to realize that in order to keep up with the changes in standards, demands, and usage of EFS, the networks that are used to provide these services must also change rapidly. Implementing a clearly defined and documented change management process should facilitate the rapid changes necessary to offer EFS in a controlled and secure environment. A change management process will also elevate the level of accuracy and completeness in change implementation reducing the amount of down time for the networks and decrease the costs involved with changes.

[2]   TYPES OF NETWORK ACCESS

As previously discussed, multiple types of external networks are used for EFS. The primary external networks in use today are public telephone lines, private dedicated lines, and the Internet. Each network uses a different type of protocol to connect the external network with the internal network of a business. A typical business will use a combination of these networks to provide services cost-effectively in the electronic community.

[a] Private Dedicated Lines. The most secure, but also the most expensive way, of conducting electronic business is through private dedicated lines. These private networks are used to connect one or more organizations' computers in geographically dispersed locations and are often used for large transfers of data. The Clearing House Interbank Payment System (CHIPS) is a good example of a dedicated line network that handles over one trillion dollars a day in transactions.[11] A dedicated line is usually purchased from a communications company such as a regional or long distance telephone provider. These lines are either completely dedicated to a particular organization or group of organizations or they can be portions of a line called bandwidth dedicated by the provider to the company. Security over such networks is tightly controlled by the service provider and usually stipulated contractually when a private dedicated line is purchased. It is important to recognize, however, that organizations using such dedicated lines remain susceptible to fraudulent activity and must still properly restrict highly sensitive information. For example, even where dedicated lines are used, encryption of highly sensitive information is recommended to provide optimal security.

[b] Public Telephone Lines. Another method of providing access to corporate networks for EFS is through remote access using public telephone lines. When a corporation uses this method, it has to protect access to its data and authenticate the user. Registering users of remote access is imperative to providing a degree of authentication and assurance that sensitive data is secure. Remote access to internal networks should be strictly limited on a business need only basis and monitored closely. Additionally, all modem[12] connections to internal networks should be centralized and a modem server should be set up to require a user to authenticate to the modem server in addition to authenticating to the network server. Public dial in access, such as online banking, should have similar controls to business need only access as well as some additional safeguards to enhance data security. Publicly distributed telephone numbers should be changed on a regular basis to reduce the exposure to remote break-ins. Call-back systems can also be implemented to authenticate users by calling back at preset numbers. An optimal situation is to allow dial in access to a stand-alone computer completely isolated from the internal network containing only the information the dial in users need. However, it is important to recognize that a trade-off in connectivity must be made for security, and an adequately designed strategy will need to address these issues and provide guidance as to an acceptable level of risk.

[c] Foundations of Internet Security. The Internet is the fastest growing method of conducting electronic business in today's market. The open and anonymous nature of the Internet accentuates the importance of focusing on the issues of authentication and protection of internal networks and data in systems that are connected to the Internet. Most of the current discussions about security in regard to electronic commerce on the Internet are concerned with authentication and data protection. However, it is important to recognize that it is also extremely important to protect internal networks from unauthorized access, as these are the systems that are used to account for, and initiate, electronic commerce. The growing importance of the links between the Internet and internal system was recently described in the following manner:

> The Internet is a vital resource that is changing the way many organizations and individuals communicate and do business. However the Internet suffers from significant and widespread security problems. Many agencies and organizations have been attacked or probed by intruders, with resultant losses to productivity and reputation. In some cases,

---

[11] *See* THE BANKERS ROUNDTABLE, 2 BANKING'S ROLE IN TOMORROW'S PAYMENTS SYSTEM 61 (1994).

[12] A modem is a device with which computers can communicate over regular telephone lines.

organizations have had to disconnect from the Internet temporarily, and have invested significant resources in correcting problems with system and network configurations.[13]

[3] FIREWALLS

Protecting an internal network from unauthorized intrusion via the Internet is usually the function of a firewall. Firewalls are a combination of computer hardware and software that act as an electronic gatekeeper allowing desired information in and out and rejecting undesired information. In addition to a firewall, a simplified diagram of the technologies used to protect internal networks is set forth below. The firewall protects the internal network from the Internet using both hardware and software to segregate the network from the Internet. The firewall hardware consists mainly of a computer with three separate network cards for the following regions:

- Internet;

- De-Militarized Zone ("DMZ"); and

- Internal network.

The firewall software dictates how data is transferred between network cards and what data is accepted from the Internet. The purpose of using these three network cards in conjunction with software is to centralize the control over traffic between these areas. Incoming traffic, *i.e.*, e-mail and application requests, are directed by the firewall, to the mail and application servers in the DMZ. The firewall can also be configured to authorize users coming in from the Internet before directing them to the DMZ by using either user name and passwords, one time passwords, or digital certificates.[14] Outgoing traffic to the Internet is controlled using the proxy server and Domain Name Server[15] ("DNS") to restrict access to acceptable locations and monitor what data is being exchanged between the internal network and the Internet.[16] This type of firewall is known as an Application Gateway and is considered one of the most secure methods for a company to connect itself to the Internet.[17]

Use of a firewall, and other associated hardware and software, can provide a level of protection for an internal network if properly configured, monitored, and maintained. New technology for attacking firewalls is consistently being developed and the preventative technology must continually be upgraded to respond to new types of attacks. Accordingly, as a detective measure, firewalls provide a monitoring function that has the

---

[13] Information Technology Laboratory, Computer Security Division, National Institute of Standards and Technology, *Internet Security Policy: A Technical Guide*, at 8 (1997)

[14] *Id.* at 67-68

[15] A Domain Name Server ("DNS") is a device that is used to convert Internet names like www.site.com to an Internet protocol number 129.100.10.2. This conversion is necessary in order for the machines to locate and talk to one another.

[16] *Internet Security Policy: A Technical Guide*, *supra* note 13, at 68.

[17] *Id.* at 68.

capability of reporting all activity occurring between the Internet, the DMZ, and the internal network. As discussed above, it is essential that responsibility be assigned for monitoring these reports and taking the corrective actions necessary to contain damage and losses.

Network Security Control Points

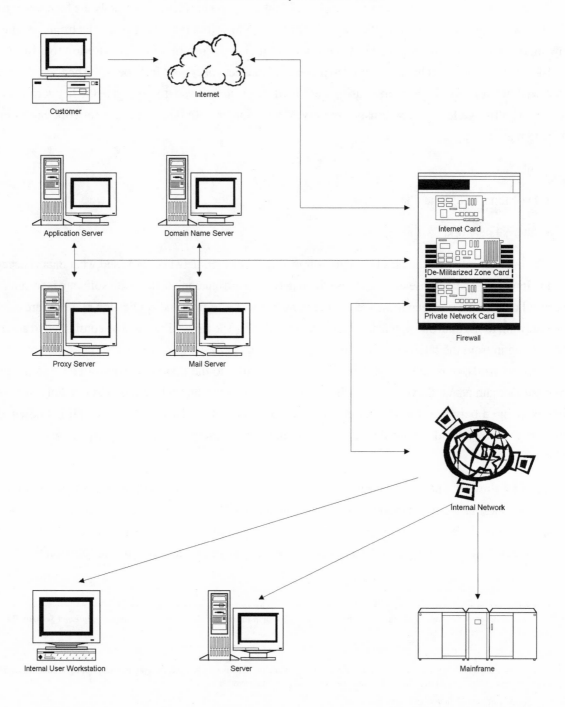

[4]   ENCRYPTION

Information privacy and authentication are topics in the forefront of discussions on electronic commerce security, because they are integral to one of the key foundations of business which is trust. As a general matter, in order to provide trust on the Internet, all parties must be able to identify themselves and believe that their information is private.

Encryption is a process by which a message is encoded using a mathematical formula to render a message transmitted on the Internet or any other network unreadable to anyone but individuals with the keys to unlock the message. An extremely common standard for encryption utilized on the Internet is RSA public key encryption. Public key encryption allows a party that wishes to receive confidential data to widely disseminate a "public" key with which senders of such information may encrypt it. The receiving party maintains a "private" key, which allows only the owner of the key to decode the information. The Data Encryption Standard (DES®) is another type of encryption, which uses the same key to encrypt and decrypt messages. The length of the key used for encryption determines the amount of security provided by these techniques. The longer the key, the harder it is to "crack" the encryption code.[18] "Cracking" the encryption code can be done using a brute force guessing approach, which with the aid of modern computers can take from seconds to years depending on the key length and the speed of the computer. As computers get faster, it is important to create keys with longer lengths to protect against this brute force guessing.

An interesting application of encryption to achieve data privacy is the Virtual Private Network™ ("VPN") concept. It is meant to replicate the security and privacy features of dedicated networks while incorporating the cost efficiency of the Internet. A VPN is software used by parties on both ends of a data transmission that both encrypts the data being transmitted and creates a direct channel or tunnel between the sender and the receiver. The combination of the tunnel and the encryption creates a network with security similar to that of a private network but does not exactly match it. An interesting feature built into the VPN concept is digital signature validation and digital certificate acceptance. VPNs are a new technology that should receive extensive analysis before implementation in major banking operations. Additional information on encryption systems is included in Appendix D.

[5]   DIGITAL SIGNATURES

Digital signatures are the electronic world's equivalent of the pen and ink signature in that they should be unique to an individual. However, it is commonly known that pen and ink signatures can be easily forged but forging a digital signature should be far more difficult. Digital signatures use encryption as an authentication measure. A private key is used to encrypt the signature and anyone with the corresponding public key can decrypt it and thereby verify the signature since only the signer should have access to their private key. A description of digital signature technology is included in Appendix E.

---

[18] *See* WARWICK FORD & MICHAEL S. BAUM, SECURE ELECTRONIC COMMERCE 103-05 (1997). *See also* Dave Kosiur, *Unlocking the Internet Security Puzzle,* ZD INTERNET MAG., Feb. 10, 1997, *available at* <http://www.zdint.com/zdimag>.

[6] KEY MANAGEMENT

Verification of real life signatures can be done using a driver's license or passport. These items are issued by a well known certifying authority, a state department of motor vehicles, and the United States Government. Much like a driver's license, a digital certificate is issued by a certificate authority to verify the identity of the holder of the certificate. Use of digital certificates has become widespread throughout the various electronic commerce networks. MasterCard and Visa have both made agreements with Spyrus and CERTCO to provide the Root Certificate Authority system for their Secure Electronic Transaction™ (SET) network.[19] In this new network, MasterCard and Visa will serve as the certifying authorities, assuring all parties that individuals and entities are who they say they are. Digital Certificates also use encryption to safeguard against tampering and the creation of false certificates. Basically what MasterCard and Visa are doing is acting as a public key verifying service. The mechanism is somewhat more complicated and varies with different systems but the concept is the same. Appendix C contains a generic management control checklist that can be used to help evaluate security issues pertaining to firewall and Web server administration:

The following summarize RME strategies for the Network APL:

RME	EXAMPLES OF RME TO MITIGATE NETWORK APL CONCERNS
Strategies and Policies	• Overall policy for securing internal and external network connection • Standards for minimum acceptable security for internal and external network connections, including remote access and inter-connections with value added network
Manage Deployment	• Formal process and management authorization procedures for network configuration changes • Effective network management allowing network to remain responsive to business needs and processes
Monitor Events	• Network intrusion monitoring • Monitoring access/use via remote access dial-in portals • Monitoring PBX systems • Network infrastructure configurations (e.g. router configuration)
Technology Solutions and Architecture	• Internet firewall products • Challenge/response smart cards for remote users • Router/bridges/gateway configuration

---

[19] *Visa and Mastercard Select CertCo/Spyrus to Create Root Certificate Authority for SET Electronic Commerce*, Mastercard® Press Release, May 13, 1997, *available at* <http://www.mastercard.com/press>.

§13.09   PHYSICAL LAYER SAL

The Physical SAL refers to the actual computers, wires, cables, batteries, tapes and other hardware. Controlling the physical layer consists of:

- restricting access to the hardware;

- providing adequate environmental control;

- backing up data, programs and operating system on a regular basis;

- properly maintaining backups and safeguarding the information on them; and

- having adequate and fully tested disaster recovery plans.

It is important to recognize that these controls are no different from the controls currently recommended for financial services computing systems.[20] It is extremely important, however, to recognize that the areas of data backup and proper storage, and security over those backups along with disaster recovery plans, are especially important in EFS.

Moving toward EFS increases a financial institution's exposure to risk if the computer-based systems fail. As more and more reliance is placed on data storage devices, it is important for management to recognize that these devices are not infallible. Data loss is a risk inherent in implementing a computer-based information system. Most banks have implemented backup procedures to mitigate these risks. However, it is important to note that EFS in many instances completely eliminate almost all manual procedures in the banking transaction process, thereby increasing an institution's reliance on the integrity of the data stored in computer systems. EFS will increase the rate at which transactions can be made, thus increasing the volume of transactions. As millions of transactions a day turn into trillions, daily backups will no longer be sufficient.

Most financial institutions recognize the importance of disaster recovery planning and the need to include computer operation resumption in these plans. The increased reliance on these computer systems increases the importance of properly implementing and testing these plans. Considerations for implementing a hot site become more important as financial institutions provide customers with continuous instantaneous access to their accounts.[21]

---

[20] For a detailed discussion of the physical and environmental controls recommended for financial institution computing systems, see IS EXAMINATION HANDBOOK, *supra* note 4.

[21] A "hot site" is a second redundant computer facility that provides an organization with the ability to resume computer operations in a minimum amount of time. These sites are extremely expensive to own and operate and many companies are using third party vendors or are collaborating with other organizations to create these sites.

RME	KEY RME FACTORS TO CONSIDER IN THE PHYSICAL SAL CONCERNS
Strategies and Policies	• Policy on physical protection of information assets and the hardware used to process and store these assets • Minimum acceptable standards for perimeter controls, localized physical access and environmental controls • Formal documentation of risk acceptance for deviation from standards • Standard regarding the level of access to computing facilities based on individual job functions
Manage Deployment	• Formal process to review physical security and control mechanism for new or enhanced locations to ensure • Standards for the removal of physical assets • Standards for the secure destruction or "decommissioning" of physical assets
Monitor Events	• Automated surveillance of physical premises • Automated or manual audit trail of access to restricted areas • Inventory of physical information processing assets with formal authorization to remove assets • Procedures to render all obsolete media unreadable prior to destruction or re-sale • Periodic review of access privileges by "owner" • Identifying "owner" of physical areas
Technology Solutions and Architecture	• Surveillance equipment • Physical locks, including card key access system • Effective erasure utilities for all media • "Electronic" property tags • Bar coding physical assets

§ 13.10 U.S. CRYPTOGRAPHY POLICY

The application of encryption technology to electronic transactions provides users with the ability to conduct secure and private transactions. That same technology, however, provides the means for criminal enterprises, terrorist groups, and hostile nations to plan and conduct criminal operations, terrorist attacks, and espionage.[22] In response to this dilemma, the Clinton Administration has supported "key recovery" or "key escrow" arrangements that would provide law enforcement agencies with the ability to access encrypted messages.

Under key recovery arrangements, cryptography users would be required to store, or escrow, their decryption keys with "trusted third parties" ("TTPs"). In some instances, "self-escrow" arrangements might be used, in which the TTP would be a party within a user's own organization. TTPs would be required to disclose decryption keys to law enforcement officials acting on warrants or other proper authority. Thus, law enforcement agencies would be empowered to combat the use of cryptography for illicit purposes.

Key recovery is closely tied to U.S. policy on the export of encryption products.[23] Historically, the U.S. has classified most encryption products as "munitions," subject to strict export controls under the Arms Export Control Act ("AECA").[24] Strong encryption products, including DES®, were largely barred from export.[25] In November 1996, President Clinton, in an effort to ease export controls, ordered the removal of most encryption products from the U.S. Munitions List.[26] Subsequently, the Department of Commerce issued an interim rule permitting the export of encryption products of unlimited strength, provided the products contain key recovery features.[27] The interim rule also relaxes export controls on 56-bit key length non-recovery and key escrow encryption items. The rule is designed to encourage the development and use of recoverable encryption systems and a key management infrastructure (intended to protect intelligence gathering, anti-terrorism and law enforcement interests of the Government), while also encouraging the growth of electronic commerce and promoting the U.S. software industry's competitive standing.

---

[22] *See* THE INTERNET AND CRIME: A REPORT TO THE INTERNET WORKING GROUP OF THE NATIONAL ASSOCIATION OF ATTORNEYS GENERAL (June 1997). According to the National Information Fraud Center, Internet fraud totals approximately $100 million per year. *See* Taylor & Jerome, *Cyberscam,* PC COMPUTING, Aug. 1997, at 87, *available at* <http://www.zdnet.com/pccomplopinion/>. In testimony before a Senate subcommittee, the Secret Service reported that a survey conducted by the Computer Security Institute of San Francisco found that 75% of the 563 United States companies, government agencies, financial institutions, and universities surveyed suffered computer fraud losses. *Internet Crimes Affecting Consumers: Hearing Before the Subcomm. on Terrorism, Technology, and Government Information of the Senate Judiciary Comm.,* 105th Cong. (1997) (statement of Michael C. Stenger, Special Agent in Charge – Financial Crimes Div., Dep't of the Treasury, United States Secret Service).

[23] The federal government played a preeminent role in the development of key recovery technology. In 1993, the Clinton Administration unveiled a new encryption algorithm incorporating key recovery. A hardware version of the algorithm was dubbed the "Clipper" chip.

[24] 22 U.S.C. §§ 2751 *et seq.*

[25] *See* Sean M. Flynn, Note, *A Puzzle Even the Codebreakers Have Trouble Solving: A Clash of Interests Over the Electronic Encryption Standard,* 27 LAW & POL'Y INT'L BUS. 217, 225 (1995).

[26] Exec. Order No. 13,026, 3 C.F.R. 228 (1997). Most encryption products were transferred to the Commerce Control List ("CCL"), which is administered by the Department of Commerce.

[27] Encryption Items Transferred from the U.S. Munitions List to the Commerce Control List, 61 Fed. Reg. 68,572, 68,573 (1996) (Dep't of Commerce Interim Rule).

[1]   FINANCIAL TRANSACTION EXCEPTION TO KEY RECOVERY REQUIREMENTS

While maintaining its general commitment to key recovery, in May 1997 the Commerce Department announced that it would permit the export of non-key recovery products — of any strength — specifically designed to support financial transactions.[28] This exception to key recovery requirements is based in part on the historical cooperation of financial institutions with law enforcement agencies. As stated by the Commerce Department, "[b]ecause banks and other financial institutions are subject to explicit legal requirements and have shown a consistent ability to provide appropriate access to transaction information in response to authorized law enforcement requests, key recovery will not be required for the financial-specific products covered by today's export announcement."[29] The Commerce Department identified home banking software as among the products covered by the new rule, but did not identify other products.[30] In June 1997, the Department granted Microsoft Corporation and Netscape Communications Corporation licenses to export 128-bit encryption products to certified banks worldwide and to enable export versions of browsers to communicate at 128 bits with certified banks.[31] Thus, while encryption controls remain a matter of much debate, banks and other financial institutions enjoy relatively greater freedom than most other entities to employ the strongest encryption products available.

[2]   PROPOSED LEGISLATION

Several encryption-related bills have been introduced in the 105th Congress that reflect the varying concerns of privacy advocates, the software industry, and law enforcement agencies. These include:

- the Promotion of Commerce OnLine in the Digital Era (Pro-CODE) Act of 1997;[32]

- the Encrypted Communications Privacy Act of 1997;[33]

- the Security and Freedom through Encryption (SAFE) Act;[34] and

- the Secure Public Networks Act.[35]

With the exception of the Secure Public Networks Act, these bills generally would liberalize export controls on encryption products and prohibit mandatory key recovery requirements. By contrast, the Secure Public Networks Act, which is supported by President Clinton and law enforcement authorities, promotes the

---

[28]   Revisions and Clarifications to the Export Administration Regulations, 62 Fed. Reg. 25,451 (1997) (to be codified at 15 C.F.R. pts. 730 *et seq.*).

[29]   Encryption Exports Approved for Electronic Commerce, BXA-97-12 (May 8, 1997), *available at* (visited Dec. 31, 1997) <http://www.bxa.doc.gov/banks2.htm>.

[30]   *Id.*

[31]   *Netscape Granted Federal Approval to Export Netscape Communicator with Strong 128-BIT Encryption to Customers Worldwide*, Netscape Press Release, June 24, 1997, *available at* (<http://www.netscape.com>; *Microsoft Obtains Government License for Export of 128-BIT Encryption*, Microsoft Press Release, June 24, 1997, *available at* <http://www.microsoft.com>.

[32]   S. 377, 105th Cong. (1997).

[33]   S. 376, 105th Cong. (1997).

[34]   H.R. 695, 105th Cong. (1997).

[35]   S. 909, 105th Cong. (1997).

use of key recovery systems. Given the strong differences in views among members of Congress, a legislative resolution of this issue does not appear imminent at this point.

[3]   CASE LAW

Two federal courts have considered challenges to export controls on encryption products. Although the courts were presented with similar facts and issues, they reached different results as to the constitutionality of the export controls.

[a] Karn v. United States Department of State. In March 1996, the U.S. District Court for the District of Columbia ruled in *Karn v. United States Department of State* that State Department export limitations as applied to a computer disk containing source codes for cryptographic algorithms did not violate the Constitution.[36] *Karn* arose out of the State Department's designation of the computer disk as a "defense article,"[37] pursuant to the AECA[38] and the International Traffic in Arms Regulations ("ITAR").[39] The State Department made the designation even though it decided that a book containing the same source codes was not subject to export controls. The plaintiff, who owned the computer disk, claimed that the designation was arbitrary and capricious and an abuse of discretion in violation of the Administrative Procedure Act ("APA").[40] The plaintiff also raised two constitutional arguments. He claimed that the designation violated his First Amendment right to freedom of speech and arbitrarily treated the disk differently from the book in violation of his Fifth Amendment right to due process.[41]

The court rejected all of the plaintiff's claims. First, the court dismissed the APA claim, finding that the AECA precluded judicial review of the State Department's designation of the computer disk as a defense article.[42] Second, while noting that the AECA did not bar constitutional challenges, the court rejected the plaintiff's First Amendment claim, holding that regulation of the disk was justified as a narrowly tailored measure designed to effect the significant governmental interest of limiting the proliferation of cryptographic products.[43] Finally, the court rejected the plaintiff's Fifth Amendment claim, ruling that the State Department's stringent treatment of the disk as compared to the book was rational, given the relative ease with which the disk could be used to encrypt data.[44] In deciding the case, the court noted its reluctance to "substitute its policy judgments for that of the President, especially in the area of national security."[45]

---

[36] *Karn v. United States Dep't of State*, 925 F. Supp. 1, 9 (D.D.C. 1996).

[37] A defense article is any item or technical data designated on the Munitions List. 22 C.F.R. § 120.6 (1997).

[38] 22 U.S.C. §§ 2751-96d.

[39] 22 C.F.R. pts. 120-30.

[40] 5 U.S.C. § 706(2)(A).

[41] *Karn*, 925 F. Supp. at 3.

[42] *Id*. at 5-8.

[43] *Id*. at 12.

[44] *Id*. at 14.

[45] *Id*. at 13 (omitting citations).

The plaintiff in *Karn* appealed to the U.S. Court of Appeals for the District of Columbia Circuit. In light of President Clinton's November 1996 Executive Order transferring regulatory authority of dual-use encryption products to the Commerce Department's Bureau of Export Administration ("BXA"), and the BXA's promulgation of its interim rule effecting the transfer, the appeals court in January 1997 remanded the case to the district court. The appeals court ordered the district court to consider the reviewability and, if appropriate, the merits of the plaintiff's claims under the APA in the context of the BXA's export control regime and without the statutory ban on judicial review found in the AECA.[46]

[b] Bernstein v. United States Department of State. In a similar case involving export controls on encryption products, the U.S. District Court for the Northern District of California reached a decision opposite that in *Karn*. In December 1996, the court in *Bernstein v. United States Department of State*[47] struck down the ITAR provisions applicable to licensing the export of cryptographic software. The court reasoned that the ITAR provisions constituted a prior restraint on speech in violation of the First Amendment.[48] However, the impact of that decision was largely blunted by the transfer of export control authority over dual-use encryption products from the State Department to the Commerce Department's BXA. The plaintiff in *Bernstein* therefore amended his complaint to address the BXA regulations. On August 25, 1997, the court found that the BXA regulations, like the ITAR provisions, constituted an impermissible prior restraint on the plaintiff's freedom of speech.[49] While this decision may be challenged on appeal, the ruling and the reasoning that supports it could have an important impact on the regulation of exports of technical data generally.

The plaintiff in *Bernstein*, while a Ph.D. candidate in mathematics at the University of California at Berkeley,[50] developed an encryption algorithm, created two related software programs (one for encryption, the other for decryption), and authored an academic paper on the algorithm. In 1992 and 1993, he asked the State Department's Office of Defense Trade Controls ("ODTC") to determine whether the computer programs and the academic paper were defense articles covered by Category XIII(b) of the Munitions List.[51] Dissatisfied with the ODTC initial determinations that the programs were defense articles, Dr. Bernstein, in early 1995, filed an action in U.S. district court claiming, among other things, that the export regime violated the First Amendment guarantee of freedom of speech.

---

[46] *Karn v. United States Dep't of State*, No. 96-5121, 1997 U.S. App. LEXIS 3123 (D.C. Cir. Jan. 21, 1997) (per curiam). The court declined to review plaintiff's constitutional challenges absent resolution of his APA claims.

[47] *Bernstein v. United States Dep't of State*, 945 F. Supp. 1279 (N.D. Cal. 1996) (*Bernstein II*).

[48] *Id.* at 1290. Previously, in *Bernstein I*, 922 F. Supp. 1426 (N.D. Cal. 1996), the court found that the plaintiff's encryption and decryption software constituted speech protected by the First Amendment. *Bernstein I*, 922 F. Supp. at 1436.

[49] *Bernstein v. United States Dep't of State*, 974 F. Supp. 1288 (N.D. Cal. 1997) (*Bernstein III*).

[50] Dr. Bernstein is now at the University of Illinois at Chicago as a Research Assistant Professor in the Department of Mathematics, Statistics and Computer Science. *Bernstein III*, 974 F. Supp. at 1292.

[51] This category then encompassed "cryptographic (including key management) systems, equipment, assemblies, modules, integrated circuits, components or software with the capability of maintaining secrecy or confidentiality of information or information systems...." 22 C.F.R. §121.1(c), category XIII(b) (1996).

In its August 1997 decision, the Bernstein court emphasized the "heavy presumption" against upholding any prior restraint on expression.[52] First, the court noted that "encryption software [had been] singled out and treated differently than other software regulated" by BXA.[53] The court found that BXA's license exception for the source code in printed form, but not in electronic form, was both unreliable (because BXA reserved its right to control scannable source code) and "irrational," especially in light of evidence that scholarly journals are now increasingly being published electronically as well as printed. The court also rejected as an inadequate justification for prior restraint the government's claim that regulation of encryption is required in the interest of national security.

In analyzing the BXA's licensing regime, the court found that it failed the three tests established by the Supreme Court for assessing the permissibility of a prior restraint on speech, even if content-neutral. Characterizing the BXA's regulations as "woefully inadequate," the court found that they contained (i) no requirement for issuing a licensing decision within a reasonable time,[54] and (ii) no standards for reviewing a licensing application. Moreover, there is no time limit on administrative appeals of a license denial, and, the court concluded, no opportunity for judicial review if a license is denied. For these reasons, the court found BXA's encryption software licensing regime ran afoul of the First Amendment as an impermissible prior restraint. The court granted only a narrow injunction pending appeal, prohibiting the Commerce Department from enforcing BXA's regulations against Bernstein or others seeking to "use, discuss or publish" *his* encryption program.

[*i*] *Impact of the Bernstein Decision.* The government can be expected to appeal the court's decision, perhaps on an expedited basis. While the injunction runs only to Dr. Bernstein's software, the declaratory relief is much broader.[55] The infirmities found by the court go to the heart of BXA's encryption licensing regime. Moreover, because these infirmities are, in the district court's view, constitutional in nature, Congress may not be able to remedy them in the current legislative tug-of-war over encryption controls merely by enacting a statute explicitly overturning the court's decision. Rather, unless the court's ruling is overturned on appeal, future export licensing of encryption software and technology will have to be attended by significant new procedural safeguards which render the prior restraint permissible, including expeditious licensing decisions, judicial review, and the government's bearing the burden to justify license denial. In sum, while encryption software may, by being ineligible for certain licensing exceptions, remain substantively disadvantaged in the export licensing process vis-a-vis other software (although the court's decision certainly invites the Government to revisit that approach), such software must henceforth be granted a greater degree of procedural review than other items subject to BXA export licensing controls.

---

[52] *Bernstein III*, 974 F. Supp. at 1303 (citing *Organization for a Better Austin v. Keefe*, 402 U.S. 415, 419 (1971)).

[53] *Id.* at 1306. Of particular moment are the inapplicability to encryption software and technology of the license exceptions for foreign availability, public availability, and "de minimis" contributions to value.

[54] *Id.* at 1308. Instead, the BXA regulations provide only that a license application must go to the President for disposition if no licensing decision is made within 90 days of its receipt.

[55] Among the court's conclusions are that all of BXA's "rules, policies and practices promulgated or pursued [under BXA's regulations] insofar as they apply to or require licensing for encryption and decryption software and related devices and technology are in violation of the First Amendment . . . and are, therefore, unconstitutional." *Id.* at 1310.

In addition, if it is upheld, the court's decision may, in the context of export control legislation now before the Congress, lead to broader reconsideration of license review procedures afforded all software and technology that is subject to First Amendment protection as expression. The court's decision may also have an impact on the pending *Karn* case.

Accordingly, export controls over encryption remain in a state of flux, so much so that policy makers concerned about the use of encryption by terrorists and criminals may decide that export controls are no longer their preferred means to deter the technology's spread, and may seek instead statutory authority to impose more expansive controls on domestic development, manufacture, use, and sale of such software. Again, however, to the extent the court's First Amendment analysis is adopted by the federal courts, such domestic regulation would appear to be subject to similar strict constitutional scrutiny.

§ 13.11 FINANCIAL MARKET IMPLICATIONS

Up to this point, this Chapter has addressed the security risks faced by financial institutions involved with electronic commerce. Some institutions will find these risks and their associated risk mitigation strategies costly or technically burdensome compared to current service delivery strategies. Other institutions will leverage the risk mitigation strategies discussed to enhance their service delivery efforts. Pioneering institutions will generate additional fees from the risk mitigation strategies by offering new products and services to existing and new customers.

This Section will identify some of the key security-related market opportunities available to financial institutions that choose to implement EFS to expand services and revenues. The opportunities leverage off the trust, reliability, reputation, and daily experiences developed by financial institutions during the past two centuries. These opportunities are directly correlated with technology investments, and, in many cases, require further consolidation and joint ventures than are currently seen.

- *Certificate Authority* – A financial intermediary could "vouch" for a business or individual. This could encompass vouching for both identity and creditworthiness, thus mitigating a party's risk in entering into a transaction with that individual or business. In many respects this is very similar to the use of credit cards and letters of credit.

- *Payment Solutions* – Although some consider this key banking "franchise" to be under attack, institutions should be able to respond to this perceived threat. A recent Piper Jaffrey analysis concluded that "[l]arge, highly scaled firms with an aggressive focus on expanding their business into all aspects of electronic payments, an international growth strategy, and an intense but diplomatic drive appear best positioned to survive in this challenging environment."[56]

---

[56] BILL BURNHAM, PIPER JAFFRAY RESEARCH , THE ELECTRONIC COMMERCE REPORT 142 (1997).

- ***Electronic Bill Presentment and Payment*** – Recent efforts, such as those of Integrion Financial Network, demonstrate how banks can leverage their trusted role and reengineer their service delivery processes, and through joint development begin to regain traditional services. According to one commentator, Integrion "is melding network services, message standards and home banking applications in a generic package that can be customized by each user bank. The idea is to capture economies of scale while preserving individual bank brand identities and overall banking industry control of the new realm of electronic payments."[57]

- ***Trust and Custodial Services*** – Banks may be able to expand on their traditional trust and custodial roles. For example, they can provide repository or escrow services for encryption key or critical software component vendors. Banks could also provide custodial services for new payment mechanisms, such as stored value. This would help minimize the risks that stored value products would loose their value due to the bankruptcy or mismanagement of a stored value vendor. Given their reputation, banks could also issue and/or market stored value products.

- ***Relationship Management*** – EFS and related security fears will provide additional opportunities for financial institutions to expand existing relationships. Banks are entering this market by developing customized customer interfaces that promote cross-selling opportunities. EFS provides banks with the opportunity to provide customized products using mass-market economic models. As described in a recent Yankee Group Internet Market Strategies Division survey, "with more than 85% of top commercial banks launching significant Internet-based services by 1999, offering localized content and personalizing the online experience are the brick and mortar for building the successful cyber branch."[58]

In addition to the above, there are many other opportunities. Financial institutions that focus on their core strengths and cost-effectively leverage their investments in new technology will find ample opportunities to increase profits.

§ 13.12   CONCLUSION

Some financial institutions will look at the security issues and shy away from the opportunities. Most institutions are hopeful that the risks associated with EFS can be profitably managed. EFT networks, PC banking, and automated clearing house transactions are just a few examples of how intermediaries have successfully integrated earlier versions of electronic commerce into their service delivery strategies. We anticipate that through this experience, institutions will adopt the risk management strategies needed to capitalize on the new forms of commerce.

---

[57] Steve Klinkerman, *Throwing the Switch,* BANKING STRATEGIES, Nov./Dec. 1997, at 113. For a further discussion of Electronic Bill Presentment and Payment, see Chapter 14.

[58] *Web Banks Must Personalize or Perish, Yankee Group* States, Yankee Group Press Release, Mar. 11, 1997, *available at* <http://www.yankeegroup.com>.

PART IV

"In a bank, in a box, money talks
In the black, on the rocks, money talks. . ."

Money Talks
—Alan Parsons

What will banks offer customers in the 21st Century? In creating products and services, banks have historically balanced complying with regulatory requirements and meeting consumer demands. Some banks sought joint venture partners with complementary expertise to accomplish these objectives.

Technology, however, is causing banks to rethink many fundamental business assumptions. Part II explored the new regulatory aspects of electronic commerce and banking and Part III analyzed consumer appetite for these goods. This Part focuses on emerging electronic financial products and services. Physical location no longer constrains market area because banks can now operate without boundaries in cyberspace. A combination of technological advances and competitive forces is leading to the development and use of new products, such as various forms of remote financial services (Chapter 14), Internet payment systems (Chapter 15), stored value and electronic money systems (Chapter 16), and electronic benefits transfers (Chapter 17).

CHAPTER 14

REMOTE BANKING AND FINANCIAL SERVICES

§ 14.01   INTRODUCTION

Audio, video, and text are rapidly converging into a single digital stream that permits banks and financial service providers to offer customers the flexibility to conduct traditional financial services activities "remotely," that is, without visiting a physical branch. Until recently, remote banking consisted primarily of automated teller machines and telephone banking. From these origins, remote banking is evolving quickly and dramatically — offering the potential for a host of sophisticated services, via new technologies, such as smart phones, personal computers, and the Internet.

This Chapter focuses on the personal banking activities of the retail customer in the United States. It also places a heavy emphasis on the channels through which a retail customer can reach the bank (the "customer access channels"), rather than bank central processing (or "glass house") operations. Finally, this Chapter utilizes familiar technological constructs, such as "television" and "telephone," to organize customer access products into useful categories, even though rapid technological changes are blurring the distinction between these traditionally distinguishable devices (*e.g.*, the close functional similarities between the Internet and WebTV™ that reduce the differences between television and the personal computer).

From this perspective, this Chapter explores four basic remote financial services delivery themes. Section 14.02 reviews the economic factors underlying the recent flurry of remote banking activity. Section 14.03 surveys available remote banking services. Section 14.04 analyzes the remote banking delivery systems that support these services. Finally, Section 14.05 considers the regulatory challenges, security issues, and privacy concerns that affect remote financial services delivery.

§ 14.02   REMOTE BANKING ECONOMICS

Remote banking demand and remote banking supply interact to establish the market for remote banking services. This Section summarizes and analyzes the trends in these areas.

[1] REMOTE BANKING DEMAND

Somewhere between 88% and 94% of the U.S. adult population holds at least one bank account.[1] Estimates of the number of households banking or paying bills via personal computer in 1997, however, range from 2.6 million[2] to 4.5 million.[3] This relatively small remote banking customer base has been projected for rapid growth. According to some estimates, remote banking will reach sixteen million households by 2000.[4]

Probably the most important, and most obvious, factor increasing the demand for remote banking products is the power of remote banking to make the concept of "bank office hours" irrelevant. Using remote services such as the telephone or the Internet, a customer can access "the bank" at any time — during regular business hours or after midnight. This convenience makes remote banking an attractive alternative to traditional physical branches.

Remote banking products also reduce the importance of geography. Traditionally, a bank's potential customer base has been limited to the population living or working within driving distance of the bank. Remote banking enables a bank to interact electronically with a new customer who might live thousands of miles away. Moreover, the bank can interact with a customer who is at home, on vacation, anywhere. This change, however, is a double-edged sword — on the one hand, remote banking affords banks a potentially huge new customer market; on the other hand, it challenges banks to protect their existing, and increasingly fickle, customer base from competitors attempting to grab market share using the same technology.

Another critical factor increasing remote banking demand is the downward trend in remote access fees. Basic online banking fees and bill payment fees have fallen as banks recaptured their infrastructure costs and recognized the negative marketing effect of fees on the growth of these new customer access products. Just two years ago, customers paid as much as $20 per month for remote online banking and bill payment.[5] Informal surveys show that, although some banks now charge up to $7-$10 per month for online banking and for online bill payment,[6] many banks offer these remote access channels free, especially to preferred customers.[7] Broader

---

[1]   *See* Caroline Wilson, *Tapping the Unbanked*, AMERICA'S COMMUNITY BANKER, Aug. 1997, at 22.

[2]   *See* Sidney Hill, *Banking's Bridge to OnLine Brokerage*, FIN. SERV. ONLINE, Dec. 1997 (citing to FAULKNER & GRAY'S 1998 DIRECTORY OF HOME BANKING & ONLINE FINANCIAL SERVICES). For a comprehensive discussion of PC banking see STEVEN C. DAVIDSON, THE COMMUNITY BANKER'S GUIDE TO THE INTERNET AND HOME BANKING (1997).

[3]   *See* Jodi Rave, *Online Banking Is Catching On; More Than 4.5 Million Americans Expected To Use It This Year*, SALT LAKE TRIB., Oct. 18, 1997, at B7 (citing a recent study by Jupiter Communications℠ Co.); Lisa Reilly Cullen, *Finally, You Could Profit By Banking Online*, MONEY, Sept. 1997, at 31.

[4]   *Retail Delivery '97 Promotes Back-End Integration*, RETAIL DELIVERY SYS. NEWS, Dec. 5, 1997 (citing a recent payments study by Bank Administration Institute (BAI)); Mark Grossman, *The Web: Now You Can Bank On It*, LEGAL TIMES, Dec. 1, 1997, at 27 (citing a recent study by Booz-Allen & Hamilton).

[5]   *See* Cullen, *supra* note 3.

[6]   *See id. See also* Craig Stoltz, *Put Your Money Where Your Mouse Is*, WASH. POST WEEKEND, Mar. 28, 1997, at 37.

[7]   *See Bank of America Enhances Its Popular HomeBanking Service With Free Online Account Access and Reduced Price For Online Bill Payment*, BUS. WIRE, Nov. 20, 1997.

use of the World Wide Web has also driven down the costs consumers pay for other remote banking and financial services. For example, online securities trading can be found for as low as $12 a trade.[8]

The final factor, addressed more comprehensively in Section 14.04, is the increasing growth of the personal computer market and the rise of personal financial management software, both of which have combined to increase customer demand for remote access to financial data, such as bank balances and account transaction histories.

[2] REMOTE BANKING SUPPLY

Banks supply many kinds of remote banking services. For example, nearly every bank offers automated teller machines ("ATMs"). Similarly, many offer telephone, PC, and Internet banking. Banks that offer these products and services typically do so after analyzing the cost increases and savings in several related areas of bank operations, including (1) labor, (2) storage, (3) computer systems, (4) marketing, and (5) customer service centers.[9] Recently, banks have added two other factors to this analysis: (i) the rapidly occurring mergers in the banking industry, along with the resulting need to standardize and integrate different data management systems and hardware; and (ii) the Year 2000 compliance of existing and proposed computer systems. The opportunities for cost savings are potentially substantial. At least one study concluded that remote banking greatly reduces the cost per transaction to the bank from $1.07 by teller, to $0.54 by telephone, to $0.27 by ATM, to $0.02 by proprietary computer system, and finally, to $0.01 by World Wide Web.[10]

In theory, a well-crafted and implemented remote banking long-term strategy should generate greater returns for bank shareholders, higher interest rates for depositors, and lower rates for borrowers. To date, however, industry analysts have yet to settle on the likely effect of online banking on the bottom line of those banks that have invested heavily in this technology.[11]

[a] **Joint Ventures and Strategic Alliances.** As discussed in Section 14.04, any remote banking strategy should focus on which customer access devices, if any, a bank is willing to support. Once this initial decision is made, the bank should determine the appropriate internal staffing, joint venture partners, and strategic alliances to efficiently and profitably deliver those chosen devices to its customers.

With respect to internal staffing, banks have adopted several different structures. At one end of the spectrum, several banks have addressed remote banking issues on an ad hoc basis, forming separate business groups to handle the development of each product. At the other end of the spectrum, Huntington Bancshares

---

[8] See Industry Pros: Schwab Must Compete on Price, NET NEWS, Dec. 22, 1997. Among the current discount brokerage firms offering World Wide Web trading services are Waterhouse Securities, Suretrade, Ameritrade, E*trade, Wit Capital, and Tradingdirect. Wit Capital is scheduled to begin offering its customers a Digital Stock Market in 1998 through which investors can trade NASDAQ shares directly with other investors reducing the spreads charged by traditional market makers.

[9] See Drew Clark, People Need Costly Hand-Holding To Use Home Banking, Experts Say, AM. BANKER, Aug. 1, 1997, at 14.

[10] Grossman, supra note 4.

[11] See CyberBanking – Part One: An Evolving Landscape for PC Banking, GOLDMAN SACHS U.S. RESEARCH, Dec. 9, 1996, at 13.

of Columbus, Ohio recently consolidated all of its electronic commerce products, including its Internet banking, call center, smart card, and related "virtual activities" under a single, separate business unit called Direct Access® Financial Services.[12]

In addition, recognizing the high level technological expertise that exists outside of the banking industry, and potentially high startup costs, several banks have sought marketing alliances and outsourced technology needs.[13] This approach, however, raises its own concerns, such as how to structure the relationship to best allocate the risks and returns of the project; how to structure copyright, licensing, and other intellectual property agreements; and, most significantly to many institutions, how to maintain control over the "customer interface," the medium through which the bank relates to its customers.[14] Furthermore, some outsourcers have been wary of the short term profitability of some remote banking venues, such as the Internet, and have opted to wait until these markets mature.[15]

§ 14.03 REMOTE BANKING SERVICES

Remote banking services have been a part of the banking landscape since ATMs were launched in the 1970s.[16] These early terminals allowed customers to perform basic account functions, such as viewing bank balances, depositing funds, and withdrawing funds during off-hours, from remote locations, all without waiting in line. Subsequent regulatory changes and technological advances allowed banks to introduce more sophisticated services, such as electronic bill payment, credit card applications, loan applications, securities trading, and insurance. During the next few years, new services, such as electronic bill presentment, electronic cash, and others yet to emerge, will become commonplace. Each of these remote banking services raise a range of compliance and disclosure issues, which, although familiar in the physical world, relate uneasily to cyberspace. As the variety of services continues to expand, and as regulatory barriers to entry continue to fall, banks will have to compete aggressively to maintain and grow market share, relative both to other banks and to nonbank competitors. The following subsections discuss existing and emerging remote banking services.

[1] DEPOSIT ACCOUNTS

All basic deposit account functions can, to some degree, be performed remotely. The four main deposit account functions are: (a) opening an account; (b) inquiring about balances and historical banking activity; (c) transferring funds between accounts and to third parties; and (d) depositing and withdrawing funds. Other

---

[12] *See* Jeffrey Kutler, *Huntington Forms Stand-Alone Electronic Banking Unit*, AM. BANKER, Aug. 14, 1997, at 19.

[13] *See* JOHN L. DOUGLAS, BANKING ORGANIZATIONS: RELATIONSHIPS WITH AND INVESTMENT IN TECHNOLOGY COMPANIES, STRUCTURAL AND OTHER CONSIDERATIONS (1996).

[14] *See* Robert E. Zahler & Jennifer P. Clasby, *Structuring Relationships Between Banks and Technology Providers Entering the Electronic Banking Market*, ELECTRONIC BANKING L. & COM. REP., Oct. 1996, at 2.

[15] *See* Steven Marjanovic, *Internet Profits Elude Outsourcers*, AM. BANKER, Oct. 27, 1997, at 12.

[16] For a discussion of the development of ATMs, see Chapter 4.

important account functions include overdraft protection, check order requests, and stop payment requests. The four main functions are discussed below.

[a] Opening an Account. Offering customers the ability to open accounts remotely exacerbates certain consumer protection, disclosure, and money laundering concerns already addressed by federal laws such as the Truth In Savings Act ("TISA")[17] and the Board of Governors of the Federal Reserve System's ("FRB's") Regulation DD thereunder,[18] the Electronic Fund Transfer Act ("EFTA"),[19] Regulation E,[20] the Bank Secrecy Act,[21] and the related "Know Your Customer" policies.[22] The critical, yet unresolved, question of whether an electronic communication constitutes a "writing" runs through a variety of consumer banking disclosure statutes including the TISA and the EFTA. This uncertainty can lead banks, at least for the short term, to adopt a hybrid electronic-paper strategy, which can lengthen the time before a new customer gains online access. While the need to verify identity via off-line communications may eventually be supplanted by digital certificates or biometric identification, the current technology reinforces the need for this hybrid strategy.

[b] Balance and Historical Banking Activity. The most frequently used and simplest remote deposit account features are balance and historical banking inquiries. Because no funds are transferred, the EFTA and Regulation E do not apply. These services are being integrated rapidly into personal financial management software to provide real-time account reconciliation and seamless interoperability between actual financial data and future projections.

[c] Transfers. Electronic fund transfers by retail customers, both within accounts at a single bank (*e.g.,* a transfer between a checking and a savings account held by the same person) and to third parties, have a long history rooted in ATM transfers, written direct deposit authorizations for paychecks, and preauthorized electronic fund transfers to mortgage lenders, utility companies, and other recurring billers. Banks have recently been spurred to offer additional non-recurring electronic fund transfer services to retail customers. For example, electronic bill payment, described in Section 14.02, is an example of a non-recurring electronic transfer that, because of improved technology, is increasingly attractive to banks. Although the FRB has tried to keep pace with the recent evolution of remote banking systems,[23] such as the growth of the Internet, many important regulatory issues, including whether electronic communications constitute "writings" under Regulation E, remain unresolved.[24]

---

[17] 12 U.S.C. §§ 4301 *et seq.*

[18] 12 C.F.R. pt. 230.

[19] 15 U.S.C. §§ 1691 *et seq.*

[20] 12 C.F.R. pt. 205.

[21] 12 U.S.C. §§ 1951-59; 31 U.S.C. §§ 5311-22.

[22] Board of Governors of the Fed. Reserve Sys., *Know Your Customer Policies, reprinted in* CLIFF E. COOK, BANK SECRECY 241 (1991).

[23] *See, e.g.,* Electronic Fund Transfers (Regulation E), 61 Fed. Reg. 19,696 (1996).

[24] See Chapter 4, Section 4.07[7] for more information on Regulation E's requirements.

[d] Deposits and Withdrawals. Deposits and withdrawals can be performed through ATMs.[25] These transactions, however, cannot be conducted using other customer access devices, such as the phone or the personal computer. This state of affairs will change rapidly when PC card readers and similar devices, which can transfer value to or from stored value cards, are introduced later this decade.[26]

[2] BILLS

Businesses in the United States generate over fifteen billion consumer bills each year.[27] The vast majority of these consumer bills are currently delivered by the Postal Service. The billing process occurs in two stages. The first stage — bill presentment — involves the transmission, usually by mail, of a bill from a business to a consumer. The second stage — bill payment — involves the transmission of a payment from a consumer to a business, also usually by mail, frequently accompanied by remittance data identifying the bill received and the consumer's account information.

While both bill presentment and bill payment can be conducted electronically, until recently, the focus has been on electronic bill payment. Many banks and nonbanks, however, have announced plans to enter the bill presentment market.

[a] Bill Payment. Electronic bill payment was initially available over the telephone, but the cumbersome telephone interface limited its acceptance until it became available via the personal computer. Structurally, electronic bill payment involves six elements: a customer access device (for example, a telephone or personal computer); the customer's bank; a bill payment processor that processes bill payments on behalf of the customer's financial institution; a "lockbox" or "concentrator" that collects and processes payments on behalf of a merchant;[28] the merchant's bank; and the merchant.

Electronic bill payment usage has increased dramatically from 800,000 users in 1995, to 1.8 million users in 1996, to a predicted 3.5 million in 1997.[29] Although several companies are active in the bill payment segment of remote banking, CheckFree currently processes nearly 70% of the electronic bill payment transactions.[30]

---

[25] For a discussion of ATMs, see Chapter 4.

[26] For a discussion of stored value and related legal issues, see Chapter 16.

[27] *See ATM Cardpay Introduces New Bill Payment Idea*, RETAIL DELIVERY SYS. NEWS, Jan. 16, 1998. The Postmaster General is concerned about the effect that new billing and payment technology will have on the Postal Service. *See* John Greenwald, *Zapping the Post Office*, TIME, Jan. 19, 1998, at 46; *Business Center: US Postal Service Leads in Moving Mail and Packages* (CNBC television broadcast, Nov. 3, 1997), *available in* LEXIS, Nexis Library, News File (statement of Marvin Runyon, Postmaster General) ("We stand in jeopardy of losing about 25% of our business. We can see that [sic] coming, and we have to figure out: How do we deal with that?"). *See also* Steven Marjanovic, *Postal Service Effort Could Rival Banks in Bill Processing*, AM. BANKER, June 13, 1997, at 1 (discussing Remitco, the Postal Service's newly formed bill payment unit).

[28] See Chapter 15, Section 15.03[2] for a definition of "lockbox."

[29] *See* BILL BURNHAM, PIPER JAFFRAY RESEARCH, THE ELECTRONIC COMMERCE REPORT 116 (1997).

[30] *See id.* at 118; Steve Weber, *Online Bill Presentment Set to Explode, Study Predicts*, ONLINE BANKING NEWSL., Aug. 11, 1997, at 1. Companies active in the bill payment and bill presentment industry include Blue Gill Technologies, CheckFree®, Electronic Funds & Data Corp., MSFDC (a joint venture between Microsoft and First Data Corp.), Online Resources & Communications Corp., Princeton Telecom, Travelers Express, and Visa Interactive (recently acquired by Integrion℠).

The largest marketing barrier facing banks is the "mental shift" that the customer must make from paying bills directly to the vendor through the mail, to paying bills through the new bank-branded customer access device. Bill payment systems currently face three main hurdles: (1) they are not integrated — properly delivering remittance information frequently requires expensive custom connections to merchant databases; (2) they lack synchronization — payments are not posted in real time to customers' accounts, thus creating the possibility of overdraft; and (3) they are not standardized — the participating industries have not yet adopted a standard message format, which could alleviate some of the compatibility problems within a single bill payment transaction and across bill payment networks.[31]

Aside from these broad issues, three other areas of concern are: the five-day lag time required by most banks between payment order and posting for paper checks;[32] the immediate debit to the customer's account that reduces the ability of customers to manage the "float" on their checking accounts; and the need to convert electronic bill payment requests to paper form. For example, surveys have indicated that between 65% and 85% of all electronic bill payments are actually converted to paper checks before they are sent to the biller.[33]

Despite these concerns, bill payment is emerging as one of the fastest growing remote banking services. The next step that will probably accelerate this trend is the rise of electronic bill presentment, as described below.

[b] Bill Presentment. Despite the fact that electronic bill presentment is essentially an untried service, many banks and nonbanks have announced plans to offer this service beginning in 1998.[34] Surveys have estimated that up to 534 million bills, or 3.5% of the total number of bills, will be presented electronically in 2001.[35] Electronic bill presentment offers several benefits, including (1) reduced mailing costs, (2) reduced customer service costs, (3) increased electronic payments, (4) increased customization of the bill to create the desired "look and feel" (which could be further modified to appeal to different customer groups), and (5) cross-sales and advertising revenues through the electronic equivalent of paper "statement stuffers." Although cost savings estimates vary, one survey estimated that an electronic bill would cost the biller $0.45 cents per transaction, well below the $1.10 cost for a paper transaction.[36] Also, a larger customer base would allow a bank to achieve significant economies of scale and to amortize the fixed costs of the project (which account for 70% to 80% of the customer interface costs)[37] over a larger group.

---

[31] See BURNHAM, *supra* note 29, at 116.

[32] See Drew Clark, *OnLine Banking: Electronic Bill Payment: One User's Perspective*, AM. BANKER, Aug. 21, 1997, at 10.

[33] See BURNHAM, *supra* note 29, at 115.

[34] See, e.g., *Internet Banking on the Cards for Chase*, DIRECT DELIVERY INT'L, Nov. 1997, at 5; *Chase to Become First U.S. Bank to Offer Electronic Bill Presentment; Chase and CheckFree Join To Deliver and Pay Bills Over the Internet*, PR NEWSWIRE, Oct. 9, 1997; *Mbanx to Offer Bill Presentment*, FIN. NETNEWS, Sept. 8, 1997.

[35] See *ATM Cardpay Introduces New Bill Payment Idea, supra* note 27.

[36] See Jeffrey Kutler, *Strategic Value of Electronic Wallets Debated*, AM. BANKER, Sept. 23, 1997, at 8.

[37] See *id.*

Currently, at least four different electronic bill presentment models are being developed: (1) presenting the bill at the biller's Internet site; (2) presenting the bill at the customer's financial institution's Internet site; (3) presenting the bill directly to the customer through personal finance management software; and (4) presenting the bill directly to the customer through a formatted e-mail message. Each method has its benefits and drawbacks. For example, a model using a financial institution's site will require billers to establish relationships with multiple banks. Alternatively, a model relying on delivery to the biller's Internet site will require customers to visit several billing sites. Layered on top of these design issues is the primary battle over control of the customer interface.

Several third-party vendors are offering turn-key bank-branded electronic bill presentment services based on the aforementioned models, and banks are forming strategic alliances with the vendors.[38] In the short term, however, some banks are still analyzing whether to create in-house expertise or to outsource, and many are adopting a "wait-and-see" attitude.[39]

Although bill presentment may spur the growth of the bill payment market, the use of "electronic return addresses" on individual bills may squeeze out bill processing intermediaries and their elaborate translation databases.

[3] CREDIT CARDS

Credit cards are likely to form a backbone of electronic commerce. They represent a convenient method of making payments via the Internet. Recognizing lingering consumer security concerns, the major credit card associations collaborated in the development of an Internet value transfer protocol, Secure Electronic Transaction ("SET").[40] Increasingly, banks and nonbanks are using the World Wide Web to attract potential new customers and to accept online applications.

[4] LOANS

Consumers now routinely make loan payments remotely through the electronic fund transfers, as described in Section 14.03[2][a]. Of greater interest and press attention, however, has been the recent spate of remote loan origination services offered through the Internet.[41] Many banks include on their websites preformatted loan application templates, payment calculators, rate sheets, and other data covering a wide variety of loans, including

---

[38] *See, e.g., Chase to Become First U.S. Bank to Offer Electronic Bill Presentment, supra* note 33; *Microsoft-First Data: Good For Bill Presentment, But Is It Good For Banks?*, FUTUREBANKER, Aug. 1997; Lisa Greim, *Online Billing Venture to Be Based in Denver: Microsoft, First Data Test Program Allowing Consumers to Receive, Pay Bills on Internet*, ROCKY MOUNTAIN NEWS, June 27, 1997, at 1B.

[39] *See Mbanx to Offer Bill Presentment, supra* note 34.

[40] For a comprehensive discussion of these topics, see Chapter 15.

[41] *See, e.g.,* Jane Bowar Zastrow, *Home Loans, Contractors, Realty Agents Available on the Internet*, S.F. EXAMINER, Oct. 19, 1997, at E1; Scott Kersnar, *Planning Leads to More Active Websites*, NAT'L MORTGAGE NEWS, Oct. 6, 1997, at 110; Robert Sharoff, *Borrowers Adjust to Mortgage Market Changes; On the Web, A Net Gain for Finding Loan Data,* WASH. POST, Oct. 18, 1997, at E1; *E-Loan Awarded Top Real Estate Website; Leading OnLine Provider Chosen for IRED Top Ten Real Estate Websites*, BUS. WIRE, Oct. 6, 1997.

mortgages, home equity, personal credit lines, boat loans, and automobile loans. Although the number of Internet-initiated loans is currently low — observers have indicated that the Internet accounts for less than 1% of the $789 billion mortgage business — approximately 1,500 mortgage companies are doing business on the Internet.[42]

As the remote loan origination services have proliferated, customers have been receptive to tools that aggregate and compare different Internet loan alternatives. In response, software vendors have developed search engines and intelligent agents to analyze the vast pool of available services and to provide comparative real-time mortgage information, personalized mortgage rate quotations, and other ancillary services based on individual customer profiles.[43]

Remote loan origination raises a variety of legal issues, including those arising under federal statutes and regulations, such as the Equal Credit Opportunity Act,[44] the FRB's Regulation B,[45] the FRB's Regulation C,[46] the Truth in Lending Act ("TILA"),[47] the FRB's Regulation Z,[48] and the false loan application criminal statutes.[49]

[5]   BROKERAGE/SECURITIES TRADING

In the past five years, the increased use of the World Wide Web by various participants in the securities market has prompted operational and regulatory advances that today provide banks and their regulators with a body of experience from which to draw.[50] Moreover, as the financial services industries converge and more banking organizations acquire securities brokerage firms,[51] banking organizations are increasingly becoming familiar with the regulatory regime directly. Mutual funds, broker-dealers, investment advisors, and companies that issue publicly traded securities ("corporate issuers") have established presences on the World Wide Web;

---

[42] *See* Sharoff, *supra* note 41.

[43] *See, e.g., Chase Manhattan Mortgage Corporation Teams With Intuit as a Charter Lender For QuickenMortgage*, PR NEWSWIRE, Oct. 14, 1997; *OnLine Battle Extends to Mortgages*, MORTGAGE MARKETPLACE, Oct. 13, 1997, at 1.

[44] 15 U.S.C. §§ 1691 *et seq. See also* Chapter 4, Section 4.07[4].

[45] 12 C.F.R. pt. 202.

[46] 12 C.F.R. pt. 203.

[47] 15 U.S.C. §§ 1601 *et seq. See also* Chapter 4, Section 4.07[3].

[48] 12 C.F.R. pt. 226.

[49] 18 U.S.C. §§ 1005, 1006, 1014.

[50] Members of the securities regulation community, as well as the press, have begun to analyze and document the impact of the World Wide Web on the field. *See, e.g.,* John C. Coffee, Jr., *Brave New World?: The Impact(s) of the Internet on Modern Securities Regulation*, 52 BUS. LAW. 1195 (1997); Joseph J. Cella, III & John Reed Stark, *SEC Enforcement and the Internet: Meeting the Challenge of the Next Millennium*, 52 BUS. LAW. 815 (1997); Alexander C. Gavis, *The Offering and Distribution of Securities laws in Cyberspace: A Review of Regulatory and Industry Initiatives*, 52 BUS. LAW. 317 (1996); Gloria Santona, *More Corporations Using Net to Reach Investors*, NAT'L L.J., July 14, 1997, at B16; Joseph McLaughlin, *'Booting' the Federal Securities Laws into the 21st Century*, INSIGHTS, July 1997, at 21; Gary Weiss, *Web of Hype and Glory*, BUS. WK., June 16, 1997, at 108; Leslie Eaton, *Slow Transition For Investing: Stock Market Meets Internet*, N.Y. TIMES, Nov. 11, 1996, at A2.

[51] For example, NationsBank recently acquired Montgomery Securities, a San Francisco partnership, for approximately $1.2 billion; Bank of America acquired Robertson Stephens for $540 million; and Bankers Trust acquired Alex Brown for $1.7 billion. *See* Larry Light, *Wall Street Deals That Aren't So Pricey*, BUS. WK., July 28, 1997, at 4; *see also* Jill Barshay, *U.S. Bancorp Agrees to Buy Piper Jaffray: Piper Workers See Windfall, Chance to Build Tougher Bank*, STAR TRIB., Dec. 16, 1997, at 1A.

and have taken advantage of tools such as e-mail and proprietary software to communicate with customers and offer new services, including online trading.[52] The Securities and Exchange Commission ("SEC") has enthusiastically embraced the World Wide Web and has begun to address both its potential to increase the efficiency of the securities markets and the accessibility of such markets to a broader sector of investors. At the same time, it has moved to combat novel forms of market manipulation and securities-related fraud.[53] The low cost, instant access to a wide range of information available over the World Wide Web complements a regulatory regime like the federal securities laws, whose bedrock principle is disclosure.

Securities market participants have developed a host of new financial tools in response to the World Wide Web's potential to reach a greater number of participants in a faster, cheaper, and sometimes more interactive manner. These tools include online brokerage accounts, investor chat rooms, electronic trading and bulletin boards,[54] public offerings over the World Wide Web,[55] and electronic delivery of documents.[56] This Section will first examine how the SEC and the self-regulatory organizations ("SROs")[57] that govern the stock exchanges and over the counter trading services have responded to the World Wide Web. They have done so primarily by adjusting and enhancing certain elements of the existing regulatory regime to accommodate the new technology rather than altering the fundamental precepts of the regime itself. This form of response reveals the regulators' determination that World Wide Web technology has not yet realigned the relationships among market participants to the point that the very character of the securities markets requires a different set of regulatory incentives in order to protect investors and preserve the supply and liquidity of capital available to enterprises. After looking at the regulatory responses, this Section will examine some of the more recent operational advances and products available to securities market participants through the World Wide Web.

[a] **Regulatory Developments.** The regulatory approach developed by the SEC and the SROs combines the intent to nurture beneficial innovations on the World Wide Web with a concern that new web-based fraudulent activities be deterred.[58] The SEC and the SROs have simultaneously adapted existing disclosure and recordkeeping regulations to address changes brought about by the new electronic medium while developing new strategies within the current legal structure to protect online investors from new methods of fraudulent

---

[52] One commentator has noted that over seventy mutual funds have established pages on the World Wide Web which provide investors with information on their portfolios and portfolio managers, and some which permit investors to download prospectuses and applications. *See* Gavis, *supra* note 50, at 321 (citing Sana Siwolop, *Now, The Superhighway Leads to Mutual Funds*, N.Y. TIMES, Aug. 13, 1995, at F5).

[53] *See* Gavis *supra* note 50; Ruth Simon, *An SEC Commissioner Sizes Up the Net's Pros and Cons for Investors*, MONEY, Oct. 1, 1996, at 29; Steven M.H. Wallman, *Regulation for a New World*, BUS. L. TODAY, Nov./Dec. 1996, at 8.

[54] *See* Section 14.03[5][c].

[55] *See* Section 14.03[5][a][ii].

[56] *See id.*

[57] For purposes of this discussion, the self-regulatory organizations ("SROs") include the New York Stock Exchange, Inc. ("NYSE"); American Stock Exchange, Inc., ("AMEX"); and the National Association of Securities Dealers, Inc. ("NASD"). NASD Regulation, Inc. ("NASD-R"), a subsidiary of the NASD, which monitors the trading activity in NASDAQ markets.

[58] *See generally* Harvey L. Pitt, Mark J. Dorsey, & Peter H. Schwartz, *Protecting the OnLine Investor and the Markets: SEC and SRO Activities*, *in* SECURITIES IN THE ELECTRONIC AGE (John F. Olson & Harvey L. Pitt eds., 1998).

manipulation using the World Wide Web.[59] Some foreign authorities have adopted this same adaptive approach to the use of the World Wide Web by securities market professionals to deliver information to investors. For example, Canadian regulators proposed changes to their own regime that follow principles established by the SEC and SROs, including standards of sufficient notice of, and access to, evidence of the electronic delivery of any information required to be delivered to investors.[60]

[*i*] *The EDGAR® System.* The establishment of the Electronic Data Gathering and Analysis ("EDGAR®") system, and its availability via the World Wide Web, has made perhaps the broadest impact on the securities markets of any web-related initiative undertaken by the SEC. Every corporate issuer and mutual fund registered under the federal securities laws must now submit their filings in electronic format to the SEC via EDGAR®, with few exceptions.[61] These filings, previously available from private data retrieval services or SEC reading rooms located in metropolitan centers, can now be accessed by the public over the World Wide Web within twenty-four hours of the actual filing.[62] EDGAR® filings include Registration Statements under the Securities Act of 1933, as amended (the "Securities Act"), and Quarterly and Annual Reports filed pursuant to the Securities Exchange Act of 1934, as amended (the "Exchange Act"). Providing the EDGAR® database to investors over the World Wide Web effectively creates a new channel for distributing such information to the public, and does so at a far lower cost. Information previously available only in paper form can be accessed from a computer terminal anywhere in the world, at any hour, at no direct cost to the user. EDGAR's link to the World Wide Web, and the subsequent availability of documents, also enhances the SEC's integrated disclosure system, which provides for uniform disclosure under the Securities Act and the Exchange Act. The EDGAR® service is so useful to investors, analysts, and market observers that corporate issuers and mutual funds themselves have undertaken to create hyperlinks from their own websites to the SEC website in order to provide customers and prospective investors with instant access to the issuer's or the fund's filings.

Despite the positive impact of EDGAR®, the system's full potential is limited by its current technology. Materials such as pictures, graphs, symbols, and charts that companies are accustomed to using in other

---

[59] This adaptive approach is similar to the SEC's treatment of past technological changes which impacted the securities markets. As one author noted, "the SEC has not instituted, nor sought from Congress, fundamental changes to the federal securities laws in response to changing uses of technology by market participants. Instead, it has updated and revised its rules and regulations incrementally to address new forms of communication and technologies." Gavis, *supra* note 50, at 323.

[60] *See Canadian Securities Regulators Eye Internet*, INTERACTIVE FIN. SERV., July 15, 1997, at 3. The proposals were adopted by the Canadian Securities Administrators, which includes the relevant regulatory body of each Canadian province. Regulation of securities in Canada is governed by provincial and not federal law.

[61] *See* Rule to Provide that the Commission will not Accept Paper Filings that are Required to be Filed Electronically, SEC Release No. 33-7472, 62 Fed. Reg. 58,647 (1997). Under this rule, any filers after January 1, 1998 must qualify for temporary or continuing hardship exemptions (as defined in Rules 201 and 202 of Reg. S-T) in order to file in paper form.

[62] Two private companies currently hold the exclusive contractual rights to disseminate SEC filings on a real-time basis, one in EDGAR® format and the other on microfiche, CD-ROM, and an online feed. Filings are only available without fee on the SEC's own Internet site after a twenty-four hour delay. *See* DAN FRISA, WHAT'S UP WITH EDGAR? THE PROSPECTS FOR PRIVATIZING THE SEC'S ELECTRONIC DATE GATHERING, ANALYSIS AND RETRIEVAL SYSTEM ("EDGAR"), at 28 (Feb. 1996) (report prepared for Rep. Jack Fields, Chairman, Subcommittee on Telecommunications and Finance).

documents delivered over the World Wide Web cannot be delivered in the ASCII format demanded by EDGAR®, and therefore are summarized instead. Firms wishing to produce more sophisticated documents for delivery over the World Wide Web must produce two sets of materials. Converting from textual formats, such as the standard word processing systems, into ASCII is also a costly burden to firms. As a result, the SEC is currently grappling with calls from industry participants for technological improvements to EDGAR® that would permit the filing of more sophisticated documents, eliminate the costly need for production of the same document in two formats, and more easily accommodate a broader range of textual formats.

[*ii*] *Interpretive Guidance.* The SEC has published, received comments on, and implemented a number of regulatory releases that address other uses of World Wide Web technology in the securities markets. These initiatives go beyond the implementation of the EDGAR® system to address compliance with other disclosure and recordkeeping requirements imposed by the federal securities laws. Specifically, the SEC has issued releases to address how electronic media can be used in compliance with the federal securities laws: (i) by corporate issuers, mutual funds, and other market participants to deliver information such as prospectuses and shareholder reports to investors; (ii) by broker-dealers, investment advisors, and transfer agents to provide investment services and information to clients and customers; and (iii) by broker-dealers and corporate issuers to operate trading systems for securities. The releases provide comprehensive guidance on topics first examined by the SEC in No-Action Letters to participants who sought advice from the SEC staff on certain specific issues.[63]

For instance, the staff of the SEC's Division of Corporation Finance first articulated its position that the term "prospectus," as defined and used in the Securities Act, includes an electronic prospectus in a February 1995 No-Action Letter ("Brown & Wood Letter"). That ruling allowed broker-dealers to deliver a final prospectus to customers by electronic means, thus overcoming the logistical difficulties of delivering the document prior to or at the same time as delivery of a confirmation of a trade or sale in connection with under-written transactions as required by law.[64] The SEC staff also agreed with the requesting parties that the delivery of an electronic prospectus would satisfy the Securities Act requirement that a prospectus be "sent or given," and that delivery of an electronic document need not be accompanied by proof that the customer actually received the prospectus, just as broker-dealers need not prove that a customer actually received a paper prospectus by mail or that the customer read such material.[65] At the same time, the SEC did require that any party who wished to deliver a prospectus by electronic means include the same information as contained in a paper prospectus, establish procedures to provide investors with the option to receive a prospectus by electronic means, notify those who make such an election when the prospectus is available, and provide investors with continuous access

---

[63] "No-Action Letters" are written assurances from the SEC that the agency will not take enforcement action against a market participant should the participant undertake a certain transaction or method of operation.

[64] Brown & Wood, SEC No-Action Letter, [1994-1995 Transfer Binder] Fed. Sec. L. Rep. (CCH) ¶ 77,000, at 78,841, 78,845 (Feb. 17, 1995).

[65] *Id.* at 78,845.

to the prospectus.[66] The issuance of the Brown & Wood Letter signaled that the SEC would take an incremental approach to electronic media and the World Wide Web, deriving regulation of these emerging technologies from existing definitions and their interpretations. Hence, the new technology of electronically formatted documents is subsumed into the existing regulatory term "written prospectus."[67]

The SEC followed the Brown & Wood pronouncement by issuing an interpretive release, which constitutes an official regulatory guidance, in October 1995 ("October Release").[68] The October Release expressly superseded the Brown & Wood Letter and permitted the electronic delivery of documents such as prospectuses, annual and semiannual reports, and proxy solicitation materials under the Securities Act, the Exchange Act, and the Investment Company Act of 1940, as amended ("Investment Company Act"). The SEC further acknowledged that the federal securities laws do not prohibit the delivery by electronic means of prospectuses and other information, and that such electronic means represent an equal alternative to paper-based media and should not be disfavored.[69] The SEC argued that electronic delivery may be more useful to investors than paper-based media, because it enhances individual investors' ability to access, research, and analyze information and generally facilitates the provision of information to the marketplace.[70]

In the October Release, the SEC identified three factors that should be considered by market participants when delivering documents by electronic means: (i) whether the issuer's electronic communications provide adequate and timely notice to the investor that the information is available; (ii) whether the investor's access to the electronic document is comparable to that provided in paper format; and (iii) whether there is some evidence to provide "reasonable assurance" that the investor actually received the information.[71] The agency stressed, however, that these factors are not exclusive and that others may be relevant to actual compliance with the federal securities laws, which continue to apply equally to both electronic and paper-based media.[72] The release then provided fifty-two hypothetical fact patterns to illustrate how the SEC sought to apply these concepts to actual situations.[73] The agency suggested, for example, that a corporate issuer or fund may need to provide an investor with separate notice that a document is available on its website in order to meet notice requirements, and that the

---

[66]   *Id.* at 78,845-46.

[67]   The requesting parties backed up their arguments with the fact that the definition of "written" contained in Section 2(9) of the Securities Act includes "graphic communications," a term which the SEC has defined in Rule 405 as "magnetic impulses or other forms of computer data compilation." *Id.* at 78,843.

[68]   Use of Electronic Media for Delivery Purposes; SEC Release No. 32-7233, 60 Fed. Reg. 53,458 (Oct. 13, 1995) [hereinafter October Release]. This release was accompanied by SEC Release No. 32-7234, 60 Fed. Reg. 53,468 (Oct. 13, 1995), which proposed technical amendments to existing regulations that do not contemplate distribution of electronic prospectuses.

[69]   "[N]one of the federal securities statutes exclusively require paper delivery of information. Accordingly, issuer or third party information that can be delivered in paper under the federal securities laws may be delivered in electronic format." October Release, 60 Fed. Reg. at 53,458.

[70]   *Id.*

[71]   *Id.* at 53,460.

[72]   *Id.*

[73]   *Id.* at 53,461-67.

corporate issuer or fund must ensure that accessing a document electronically is not more burdensome to the investor than requesting a paper document.[74] Furthermore, a corporate issuer or fund should consider whether the chosen electronic means allows investors to "retain the information or have ongoing access equivalent to personal retention."[75] Finally, the agency provided several suggestions for how an issuer or fund could ensure delivery had actually been made to an investor; for example, by getting an informed consent from the investor or an electronic mail return-receipt or other form of confirmation or by providing hyperlinks from another document.[76]

In response to industry comments on the October Release, the SEC published a follow-up interpretative release in May 1996 (the "May 1996 Release"),[77] providing seven additional examples that clarified some of the agency's earlier interpretations. For example, the SEC acknowledged that strict compliance with each requirement applicable to printed material may not be possible in all electronic media, and expressly allowed for some variation in electronic formats.[78]

The May 1996 Release also provided guidance to broker-dealers, transfer agents, and investment advisors on how to fulfill certain statutory obligations regarding information delivery.[79] Some of these issues had been raised in No-Action Letters issued previously by the SEC. In 1983, the SEC provided assurances that the Depository Trust Company could comply with its regulatory obligation under Exchange Act Rule 10b-10, to issue securities trading confirmation slips to its institutional clients if it replaced paper slips with copies transmitted by electronic means.[80] Later that year the SEC issued similar No-Action relief (the "OASYS Letter") regarding Rule 10b-10 to a broker-dealer requesting to operate an electronic post-trade confirmation network called OASYS® Global for its institutional clients, which included domestic and foreign broker-dealers as well as institutional investors.[81] The relief was conditioned on the broker-dealer taking several measures, including ensuring that: (i) a subscriber could download and print an electronic confirmation; (ii) a customer could

---

[74] *Id.* at 53,460.

[75] *Id.*

[76] The agency's embrace of World Wide Web technology is evident in its willingness to recognize that a document hyperlinked to another text is delivered along with that original text in the same manner as if it were an attachment or exhibit to a paper document. *Id.* at 53,460-61.

[77] Use of Electronic Media by Broker-Dealers, Transfer Agents, and Investment Advisers for Delivery of Information; SEC Release No. 33-7288, 61 Fed. Reg. 24,644 (May 15, 1996) [hereinafter May 1996 Release]. This release was accompanied by Securities Act Release No. 7289, 61 Fed. Reg. 24,652 (May 15, 1996) whereby the SEC adopted certain technical amendments to existing regulations that had not contemplated distribution of electronic prospectuses and which the agency had previously proposed in Securities Act Release 7234, 60 Fed.Reg. 53,468 (Oct. 13, 1995).

[78] May 1996 Release, 61 Fed. Reg. at 24,644.

[79] *Id.*

[80] Depository Trust Co., SEC No-Action Letter, 1983 SEC No-Act. LEXIS 1909 (Feb. 28, 1983). The requesting party is a clearing agency registered with the SEC under Section 17A of the Exchange Act that effects the transfer and pledge of securities by book-entry for participants and performs settlement of securities transactions.

[81] Thompson Financial Services, Inc., SEC No-Action Letter, 1993 SEC No-Act. LEXIS 1241 (Oct. 8, 1993). OASYS® Global provided for the broker-dealer operating the systems and its subscribers to communicate electronically from the moment a securities trade was executed to the time it was settled.

affirm or reject a trade through the system once receiving confirmation; (iii) the system did not permit automatic deletion of a trade confirmation; and (iv) both parties to a transaction had a capacity to receive an electronic confirmation.[82]

In the OASYS Letter, the Divisions of Market Regulation and Investment Management differed over the use of electronic storage to comply with recordkeeping requirements. The Division of Market Regulation was unable to grant its assurance that OASYS® Global's participants, all of which are publicly traded companies, could electronically store confirmation messages in order to comply with Exchange Act recordkeeping requirements. The Division of Investment Management expressly permitted investment advisor and investment company participants registered under the Investment Company Act and the Investment Advisers Act of 1940, as amended ("Advisers Act"), to use electronic storage of confirmations to meet their separate recordkeeping requirements.[83]

The May 1996 Release built on the earlier No-Action Letters by stating which rules or requirements under the Exchange Act, the Investment Company Act, and the Advisers Act could be complied with using electronic means of delivery. Beyond Rule 10b-10, addressed in the earlier No-Action Letters, regulated market participants, with assurances from their regulators, could thereafter use electronic media to comply with some twenty-three other specific rules governing certain types of communications with clients, customers, and securities holders.[84] The May 1996 Release expressly did not cover unregulated communications with clients and customers transmitted by broker-dealers, investment advisers, and transfer agents using electronic means and thus left advertisements disseminated by electronic means outside its purview.[85] Investment advisers who use a publicly available electronic medium to advertise their services, however, run the risk that they may not qualify for the exemption from registration under the federal securities laws granted to advisers with fewer than fifteen clients. Any advertisement disseminated electronically also remains subject to the same anti-fraud provisions of the federal securities laws applicable to other forms of advertisement.[86] In other words, the SEC has laid down a general principle that communications transmitted by electronic means would be regulated in the same manner as other forms of communication, *i.e.,* by their content. The agency also called upon the SROs to provide more specific guidance regarding electronic communications among market participants.[87]

---

[82]   *Id.* at *7-8.

[83]   *Id.* at *8. The relief granted to investment companies registered under the Investment Company Act went beyond the scope of the original request.

[84]   The delivery requirements covered by the release are Exchange Act Rules 8c-1, 9b-1, 10b-5, 10b-10, 10b-16, 10b-17, 11Ac1-3, 15a-6, 15c1-5, 15c1-6, 15c2-1, 15c2-5, 15c2-8, 15c2-11, 15c2-12, 15c3-2, 15c3-3, 15g-2 through 15g-9, 17a-3, 17a-4, 17a-5, 17Ad-5 and Advisers Act Rules 204 and 206. May 1996 Release, 61 Fed. Reg. at 24,648-49.

[85]   *Id.* at 24,647.

[86]   *Id.* at 24,648.

[87]   *Id.* at 24,645.

The SEC has also issued a series of No-Action Letters permitting the operation of electronic bulletin board systems that facilitate the purchase and sale of securities.[88] The staff of the SEC has not been inclined to regulate such operations as "exchanges." Instead, they have examined whether registration as a broker-dealer might be required.[89] Traditionally, the SEC requires proprietary trading systems to register as broker-dealers because they match, cross, or otherwise facilitate agreement between participants to the basic terms of a sale of securities through the system itself. Bulletin boards must limit themselves to dispensing information to avoid registering as broker-dealers. Thus far, the SEC's Division of Market Regulation has insisted that operators adhere to certain limitations and conditions before permitting a bulletin board trading system to go forward. These include refraining from: (i) participation in negotiations between potential sellers and buyers or making buy/sell recommendations; (ii) taking possession of subscribers' funds or securities; (iii) effecting transactions within the system; or (iv) charging fees per transaction.

Similarly, the SEC permits companies to use the World Wide Web to provide information and other online enrollment in unregistered direct stock plans, commonly known as bank plans, as well as issuer sponsored direct stock plans.[90] The SEC also permits the development of so-called "online road shows" whereby a private network may distribute video transmissions concerning public offerings to subscribers, principally registered broker-dealers, and investment advisers.[91]

[b] The World Wide Web and Securities Enforcement. The SEC has sought to harness the World Wide Web as a tool for protecting investors as well as one for facilitating standard disclosure under the securities regime. The SEC now includes Internet and electronic communications as one of the areas for review during its regular inspections and examinations of brokers and dealers.[92] Beyond accommodating the medium to review practices, the agency has also been proactive in its approaches to the Internet. Investors can now communicate directly with the SEC via the agency's website, to ask questions of the regulatory staff or to file formal

---

[88] *See, e.g.,* Real Goods Trading Corporation, SEC No-Action Letter, [1996-1997 Transfer Binder] Fed. Sec. L. Rep. (CCH) ¶ 77,226, at 77,131 (June 24, 1996); Spring Street Brewing Co., SEC No-Action Letter, 1996 SEC No-Act. 435 (Mar. 22, 1996) (listing of investment opportunities; distributed electronically via a PC and modem connection, by mail and by fax); Farmland Industries, Inc., SEC No-Action Letter, [1991 Transfer Binder] Fed. Sec. L. Rep. (CCH) ¶ 79,803, at 78,609 (Aug. 26, 1991) (listing of Farmland securities; distributed through an electronic mail system and by mail); Investex Investment Exchange, Inc., SEC No-Action Letter, [1990-1991 Transfer Binder] Fed. Sec. L. Rep. (CCH) ¶ 79,649, at 77,952 (Apr. 9, 1990) (listing of limited partnership interests; distributed over dedicated telephone lines via a PC or by newsletter); Troy Capital Services, Inc., SEC No-Action Letter, [1989 Transfer Binder] Fed. Sec. L. Rep. (CCH) ¶ 78,975, at 78,858 (Apr. 28, 1989) (listing of limited partnership interests in equipment leasing programs; method of distribution not disclosed); Real Estate Financing Partnership, SEC No-Action Letter, [1989 Transfer Binder] Fed. Sec. L. Rep. ¶ 78,994, at 78,903 (Apr. 4, 1989) (listing of commercial real estate financing opportunities, including real estate limited partnerships; distributed over dedicated telephone lines via a PC).

[89] Banks are statutorily exempted from broker-dealer registration. 15 U.S.C. §§ 78c(a)(4) & (5). *See also* Securities Exchange Act of 1934 Release No. 13,195, 11 SEC Docket (CCH) 1552 (Jan. 21, 1977).

[90] Securities Transfer Association, SEC No-Action Letter, 1997 SEC No-Act. LEXIS 967 (Oct. 24, 1997). Other shareholder services offered by issuers and banks include certificated share deposits, book-entry registration of a shareholder's ownership interest, certification of book-entry shares on request of the shareholder and confirmation-based share purchases and sales of the issuer's securities. *See, e.g.,* Bank-Sponsored Investor Services Programs, SEC No-Action Letter, 1995 SEC No-Act. LEXIS 707 (Sept. 14, 1995).

[91] Private Financial Network, SEC No-Action Letter, 1997 SEC No-Act. LEXIS 406 (Mar. 12, 1997). The SEC staff said they would not consider such transactions to be deemed a "prospectus" under Section 2(a)(10) of the Securities Act, thereby avoiding regulation as a prospectus and the attendant liabilities. *See also,* Stephen M. Cutler, *Paving the Way for a Successful Road Show Online,* WALLSTREETLAWYER.COM, July, 1997, at 1.

[92] *SEC to Include the Net in Routine Exams,* FIN. NETNEWS, Apr. 28, 1997, at 1, 10.

complaints online.[93] The SEC also publishes daily and weekly World Wide Web access statistics on its site.[94] Several employees in the Division of Enforcement have been assigned to continuously monitor the World Wide Web in search of misleading sales literature, investment scams, and activities that require registration with the SEC.[95]

Similarly, Mary Schapiro, the President of the regulatory arm of the National Association of Securities Dealers ("NASD-R"), has stated that members of her unit now regularly monitor electronic investment forums for stock tips, and cross checks them against what is happening in the NASDAQ market.[96] NASD-R has developed a search engine designed to monitor and detect stock manipulation on the Internet.[97] The NYSE and the AMEX also operate sites on the World Wide Web that offer access to information about the exchanges, their regulation, online publications, and historical data.[98]

To date, the SEC and SROs approaches to the regulation of World Wide Web usage among market participants has not addressed the potential for the World Wide Web to disaggregate and realign market functions. The World Wide Web allows individual entities to specialize in increasingly narrower aspects of what has been collectively identified as "the securities market," and may enable less centralized associations of those specialized entities to effectively replicate a securities exchange on the World Wide Web using online technology.[99] The SEC and the SRO initiatives leave open a further set of issues including the scope of regulatory jurisdiction,[100] the emerging role of electronic money,[101] and the need for investor confidence in a broader online securities marketplace.[102]

The SEC's and the SRO's adaptive approaches welcome the introduction of World Wide Web technology, a factor whose consequences are unknown, into the known, stable securities regulatory regime that is already familiar and reasonably predictable in most of its outcomes to those governed by it. To date, these regulators view the use of World Wide Web technology as an extension or evolution of the way market actors have interacted and conducted commercial relations in the past. These evolutionary approaches allow market participants to explore new technological tools without destabilizing the market's operations or shaking investor

---

[93] The SEC's website address is <http://www.sec.gov>.

[94] *See* <http://www.sec.gov/stats/>.

[95] *See* Ruth Simon, *An SEC Commissioner Sizes Up the Net's Pros and Cons For Investors*, MONEY, Oct. 1996, at 29; Mary Ann Gadziala, *Regulatory Talk,* COMPLIANCE REP., Aug. 19, 1996, at 9.

[96] *See* Jerry Knight, *Tracking Stock Cyberscams: NASD Regulators Go On-Line to Warn Investors of Dangers*, WASH. POST, Aug. 23, 1996, at F1.

[97] *See* Adam Rombel, *NASDR Gears up Search Engine to Sweep Web for Stock Manipulation*, COMPLIANCE REP., Feb. 3, 1997, at 1.

[98] *See* <http://www.nyse.com>; <http://www.amex.com>.

[99] *See* Pitt, Dorsey & Schwartz, *supra* note 58, at 11-34.

[100] See Chapter 19 for a discussion of jurisdiction. *See also* William S. Byassee, *Jurisdiction of Cyberspace: Applying Real World Precedent to the Virtual Community*, 30 WAKE FOREST L. REV. 197. For a discussion of the extraterritorial application of the securities registration provisions of Section 5 of the Securities Act of 1933, and of the broker-dealer registration provisions of Section 15(a) of the Securities Exchange Act of 1934, see Harvey L. Pitt, Mark Dorsey, Lawrence Bard & Ted Whittemore, *Beyond the Blue Horizon*, L.A. LAW., Sept. 1996, at 33.

[101] *See* Chapter 15.

[102] *See* Pitt, Dorsey & Schwartz, *supra* note 58, at 11-35.

confidence. However, these evolutionary approaches will become insufficient if the market itself changes because the technology alters the very relationships and incentives among participants. Such changes will demand more profound revisions to the current regulatory structure.

[c] Current Securities Activity on the Internet. The Internet provides another channel for banks, brokerage houses, and insurance companies[103] to offer retail trading and investment in securities and mutual funds. With the erosion of regulatory barriers between these three competitors, financial institutions increasingly may offer a variety of products worldwide from a single location, the World Wide Web. A tremendous surge in online securities activity in 1997 brought forth securities and related product offerings, including initial public offerings,[104] stock and options trading, mutual funds, annuities, U.S. Treasuries, and government bonds.[105] In addition, the financial services industry started to provide a broad range of services, such as real time stock quotes,[106] financial calculators, investment advice, research reports, asset allocation toolkits, online applications,[107] tombstone ads,[108] and prospectuses. Some noteworthy issues related to online securities trading include: (i) whether traders who use bulletin boards to trade securities are dealers subject to regulation under the Exchange Act;[109] (ii) whether the bulletin board itself is a securities exchange subject to registration requirements;[110] (iii) how offerors of securities may comply with disclosure and document delivery obligations of the Securities Act, the Exchange Act, and the Investment Company Act using the World Wide Web;[111] and (iv) the jurisdictional ramifications of online securities trading and the concomitant obligations under state blue sky and foreign law governing securities.

[i] Bank Brokerages. A competitive advantage for banks in the financial services industry is their ability to aggregate a customer's financial information and present it to the customer in a single format. Banks may

---

[103] NYLIFE Securities, a full-service brokerage subsidiary of New York Life Insurance Co., intends to launch Internet securities trading, the first insurance-owned brokerage to offer online trading. *Insurance Brokerage Opens Up for Web Trading*, FIN. NETNEWS, Sept. 15, 1997, at 2.

[104] The first Internet-based initial public offering ("IPO") was made by Spring Street Brewing Co., a New York City microbrewery. The attention given to the Spring Street Brewing IPO spurred many other small companies to launch Internet-based IPOs, with varying degrees of success. *See* Michelle V. Rafter, *The Cutting Edge: Online IPOs Falling Short of Expectations*, L.A. TIMES, May 26, 1997, at D1. *See also* Spring Street Brewing Co., SEC No-Action Letter, 1996 SEC No-Act. LEXIS 435 (Mar. 22, 1997). In 1996, the SEC issued a No-Action Letter to IPONET, a Web-based trading facility run by a registered dealer, Leo J. Feldman and W.J. Gallagher & Company, Inc. The SEC allowed the dealer to offer Regulation D exempt securities to investors, if online information is furnished and the investor is certified as an accredited investor. 1996 SEC No-Act. LEXIS 642 (July 26, 1996). Wit Capital, an online investment bank, permits retail investors to participate in IPOs. Its first offering, in September 1997, allowed investors to purchase shares of Radcom Ltd., a Tel Aviv, Israeli-based data communications and network producer. *See Bookmarks*, FIN. NETNEWS, Sept. 29, 1997, at 5.

[105] First Chicago NDB Investment Services and Fleet Investment Services are planning to offer Treasuries and First Union Brokerage is considering selling Treasuries as well as other government bonds via the Internet. *See Bank Brokerages Offer Treasury Products Online*, FIN. NETNEWS, July 28, 1997, at 1.

[106] Charles Schwab & Co. uses automated telephones with speech recognition capabilities to return stock quotes. *See Speech Recognition: Think Positive But Proceed With Caution*, INTERACTIVE FIN. SERV., June 1, 1997, at 1.

[107] NASD Regulation granted interpretive relief to MEK Securities, a start-up Internet brokerage, to begin accepting electronic account applications. *See NASDR Gives Okay to Electronic Accounts*, FIN. NETNEWS, Aug. 4, 1997, at 1.

[108] *See, e.g.,* NetSource's® website at <http://www.netsource.com/wsm/lrg00326.html>.

[109] 15 U.S.C. § 78c(a)(5).

[110] See 15 U.S.C. § 78c(a)(1) for a definition of exchange.

[111] *See* Use of Electronic Media For Delivery Purposes, 60 Fed. Reg. 53,458 (Oct. 13, 1995).

present a customer's checking, savings, and investment portfolio along with stock quotes, market activity, and research reports in a way that is cost effective and easy to use.[112] The Internet allows investors to instantly compare product offerings of a variety of entities. This commoditization of the financial services industry increases the pressure on institutions to provide competitive products to its customer base.

First Chicago NBD Investment Services ("NBD") was the first bank brokerage to offer trading as part of its bank website.[113] Banks have been relatively cautious in moving to online securities activities. As of April 1997, only six of the top 120 U.S. bank and thrift sites on the World Wide Web offered transactional services.[114] However, the Integrion member banks, including Citibank, NationsBank, Comerica, PNC Bank, and First Chicago have established a partnership to discuss how bank-owned brokerages can take better advantage of the Internet.[115] Citibank offers online brokerage services, while Wells Fargo provides its customers with a trading interface within the Prodigy network.[116] Wachovia Corporation, Security First Network Bank (the first bank to offer its services exclusively over the Internet) and a group of Texas banks are all developing online trading services for their customers on their websites using a system called MoneyXpress.[117] Wachovia plans to wed its investment services with its traditional banking services and popular personal financial software produced by Intuit and Microsoft.[118] Wachovia also acquired a financial information company that will provide research ratings on some 9,000 stocks and 4,000 mutual funds to Wachovia's investment customers.[119]

[ii] *Brokerage Firms.* Securities brokerages firms have enthusiastically taken advantage of the Internet and embraced online trading. One of the industry leaders in this area is Charles Schwab & Co. ("Schwab"). More than one million Schwab clients have completed at least one online or Internet based trade since October 1996. Nearly 40% of trades executed by Schwab are received online, compared to 26% in 1996.[120] Merrill Lynch is expected to begin offering securities trading online early in 1998.[121] E*Trade Securities, a pioneering newcomer to the brokerage industry, has an online customer base of 225,000.[122] E*Trade has received approval from SEC to offer after hours trading on the Internet, which would make it the first online brokerage firm to

---

[112] *See Chat Room*, FIN. NETNEWS, Sept. 8, 1997, at 9 (statement of Terry Ransford, Vice President, First Chicago NBD Investment Services).

[113] *See First Chicago First with Web Securities Trading*, INTERACTIVE FIN. SERV., June 1, 1997, at 1.

[114] *See CSFB Sees Only Six Top Banks with Transactional Sites*, FIN. NETNEWS, Apr. 28, 1997, at 3.

[115] *See Integrion Banks Pursue On-Line Brokerage Biz*, FIN. NETNEWS, Oct. 27, 1997, at 5.

[116] *See* Daniel McQuillen, *Banks Prepare to Offer Trading on Internet*, AM. BANKER, May 21, 1997, at 6.

[117] *See id.* For a discussion of Security First Network Bank, see Chapter 1, Section 1.03[3][b].

[118] Wachovia's software was designed by Netvest of Rockville, Maryland. *Id.*

[119] *See Banks Prepare to Open Internet Brokerages*, INTERACTIVE FIN. SERV., July 1997, at 3. Interestingly, Wachovia's management reportedly considered it necessary to provide such services in order to serve existing brokerage customers and not as a means for attracting new customers.

[120] *See Schwab, DLJ Hold the Line on Commissions*, FIN. NETNEWS, Oct. 20, 1997, at 1, 2.

[121] *See Electronic Stock Trades Cut Commission Costs For Investors: Execution Isn't Swifter, But Commissions Are Smaller With Computers*, STRATEGIES, Jan. 19, 1998, at F3. Merrill Lynch® OnLine is "clearly looking at giving [the] ability [to trade online] to customers with cash management accounts, priority clients with a minimum $250,000 in accounts and asset power and wrap account holders." *Chat Room*, FIN. NETNEWS, Sept. 22, 1997, at 9 (statement of Frank Zammataro, Director, Merrill Lynch).

[122] *See E*Trade Looks to Improve Customer Service*, FIN. NETNEWS, Sept. 29, 1997, at 2.

provide this feature, and the first firm ever to provide after hours trading to retail customers.[123] However, E*Trade does not intend to begin after hours trading until October 1998.[124] Typically, online account holders are required to maintain a minimum balance ranging from $1,000 to $5,000.[125] A new stock execution service called Trade Fast allows customers to execute orders directly on the floors of the stock exchanges and can be tailored for any institutional investor.[126] Current software permits investors to access real-time stock and mutual fund updates from services that provide a constant feed of new information.[127]

Online brokerage firms experienced their first test of high volume on October 27-28, 1997 when the Dow Jones Industrial Average fell 554 points, its largest one day point loss ever, and then rebounded the following day with its highest volume of trades ever.[128] As a result of the heavy trading volumes experienced by the exchanges on October 27-29, 1997, the SEC launched an inquiry into the capacity of brokerages to meet their client's demand for online trading.[129]

[iii] *Mutual Funds.* The mutual fund industry is also moving towards fully functional websites. According to a survey of mutual funds by the Investment Company Institute, 35% of mutual funds that are online established an Internet presence as an additional sales channel.[130] About 29% provide educational materials to their clients, 11% were exclusively designed for broker dealers who sell load funds, while only 3% of the sites are intended to provide clients with transactional capabilities. The most prevalent features on mutual fund sites are sales literature, e-mail capabilities, fund prospectuses and net asset values.[131] Charles Schwab & Co., Fidelity Investments, and T. Rowe Price have developed mutual fund supermarkets providing investors with the option to purchase shares in hundreds of funds from various fund families.[132] TIAA-CREF, the largest provider of retirement services to education professionals, permits fund holders to access real-time information about their portfolio over the Internet, in addition to prospectuses and annual reports.

[iv] *Investor Tools and Resources.* The cost savings features of the Internet permit discount brokerages to provide increased services to their clients. For example, Charles Schwab & Co. has teamed up with Microsoft

---

[123] *See E*Trade Receives Approval for After Hours Trading*, FIN. NETNEWS, Sept. 15, 1997, at 1.

[124] *See id.*

[125] *See Online Investing Finds Favor*, FIN. POST, Jan. 13, 1998, at 32.

[126] Customers can also access real-time information about their portfolio, gains and losses during the day, a listing of trading orders, daily statistics on account balances and value of holdings, as well as e-mail and telephone customer service. *See The Next Wave: Internet Brokerage*, FUTUREBANKER, Aug. 1997, at 28.

[127] For instance, Wall Street Access originally sold its StockTracker portfolio software to approximately 30,000 investors for $59.95, but now offers it free to users in an effort to increase its marketing database. In the words of Managing Director Eric Alexander, the free offer of software is "a generous but self-serving offer. The Names go into our database. You'll get e-mail from us." *Software Giveaway at Web Brokerage*, INTERACTIVE FIN. SERV., June 1, 1997, at 3.

[128] *See* Greg Ip, *Bloody Monday: Stocks Plummet 7% As Pros Seek Cover to Protect 1997 Gains*, WALL ST. J., Oct. 28, 1997, at A1. Suzanne McGee, *Stocks Burst Back by 337.17 Points on Record Volume as Bonds Drop*, WALL ST. J., Oct. 29, 1997, at C1.

[129] *See SEC Checks Into On-Line Broker Capacity*, FIN. NETNEWS, Nov. 17, 1997, at 2.

[130] See the Investment Company Institute's website at <http://www.ici.org>.

[131] *See ICI Finds Most Fund Sites are Still Basic*, FIN. NETNEWS, Oct. 13, 1997, at 4.

[132] *See T. Rowe to Introduce Fund Supermarket on Web Site*, FIN. NETNEWS, July 21, 1997, at 1.

to allow Schwab's customer account information to be downloaded into the Microsoft Investor website.[133] Microsoft's Investor site provides users with financial planning tools and reference charts to measure portfolio performance while doing research on the website.[134]

Merrill Lynch® OnLine deploys software applications that allow it to customize the Web content sent to its clients based on their profiles and preferences. The software allows Merrill Lynch to track a client's online activities to determine the products and services that would interest that particular client.[135] Merrill Lynch provides password protected areas to its clients to access research, track securities, and send e-mail communications to Merrill Lynch's financial consultants. Interactive technologies also permit Merrill Lynch's financial consultants to communicate with clients over the Internet.[136]

[v] *Regulatory Costs and Technological Benefits.* Discount brokerage houses and Internet trading have dramatically lowered the cost of executing retail trades. The reduction in work hours spent fielding telephone calls due to trading automation has corresponded with steep reductions in the commissions charged by online trading firms. Consumers, however, must weigh the added benefit derived from lower commissions against the loss of value added services, not provided by many discount brokerages.[137]

Though the Internet is reducing the costs associated with trading, regulatory costs make traditional telephone services more attractive than electronic messaging in certain instances. The SEC and the NASD-R have issued guidelines requiring brokerages to retain all e-mail messages sent and received.[138] The New York Stock Exchange, Inc. ("NYSE") has also issued proposed rules to govern its brokers' communications with customers by e-mail.[139] The NYSE rules will guide and impact the supervisory policies of most Wall Street firms. The SEC responded to the NYSE proposal with a letter requesting more specific guidelines for firms in deciding what constitutes reasonable procedures for supervision of incoming and outgoing messages.[140] The regulators consider e-mail to be the equivalent of correspondence that must be retained for a three-year period. Regulatory requirements associated with e-mail have reportedly led Dreyfus Service Corporation to encourage its representatives to respond by telephone rather than e-mail.[141] Responses by telephone merely require a

---

[133] *See* <http://www.investor.msn.com/>.

[134] *See Schwab Strikes Deal With Microsoft*, FIN. NETNEWS, Sept. 22, 1997, at 2.

[135] *See Merrill Plans Customized Web Content*, FIN. NETNEWS, Sept. 22, 1997, at 1.

[136] *See Chat Room*, FIN. NETNEWS, Sept. 22, 1997, at 9 (statement of Frank Zammataro, Director, Merrill Lynch). See Section 14.03[5][a][ii] for a discussion of SEC regulation of those communications.

[137] *See Schwab, DLJ Hold the Line on Commissions*, FIN. NETNEWS, Oct. 13, 1997, at 1.

[138] *See* May 1996 Release, 61 Fed. Reg. at 26,645 (noting that the supervision requirements for electronic communications should be based on the content and audience, not the medium); NASD Notice To Members 95-80, at 503 (Sept. 26, 1995) ("Members are reminded that they have the same obligations under the [NASD Conduct Rules] relative to communications with the public sent electronically via computer as they do with regard to any other type of communication covered by these rules."); *NASD Offers Members Acid Test on E-mail Adverting*, COMPLIANCE REP., Oct. 30, 1995, at 7.

[139] *See* Self-Regulatory Organizations, SEC Release No. 34-39511, 63 Fed. Reg. 1135 (1998) (SEC order approving NYSE's proposed rule changes).

[140] *See* Dominic Bencivenga, *SEC Weighs Tighter Control of Alternative Systems*, N.Y.L.J., June 5, 1997, at 5; *NYSE Told to Toughen Email Rules*, FIN. NETNEWS, Apr. 28, 1997, at 1.

[141] *See Dreyfus Offers Alternative to E-Mail*, FIN. NETNEWS, Sept. 15, 1997, at 7.

firm to maintain its recorded lines, whereas a registered principal must approve outgoing e-mail.[142] Other firms are looking toward e-mail surveillance software to monitor broker e-mail for compliance with firm and regulatory policies.[143]

[6] INSURANCE

The business of insurance on the Internet has entered a phase of explosive growth. Studies estimate that by the year 2000, between $1.4 and $2.4 billion of automobile, homeowners, and life insurance will be sold over the Internet.[144] This volume is expected to double, and perhaps triple, by the year 2005.[145] One reason for this rapid commercial expansion is a shifting of insurance consumer behavior from more traditional, intermediary-based, purchasing methods to direct-to-insurer purchasing techniques.

Insurance transactions are well-suited to the electronic medium. Like banking and other financial services, the business of insurance is information-intensive. The insurance "product" itself — a promise to pay upon the happening of a contingent future event — is embodied in the terms of the policy contract, terms that can be easily converted into electronic data. At each stage of the insurance transaction — solicitation and application, underwriting and policy issuance, and claims adjusting and payment — the necessary information exchange can take place almost entirely online.

Mass-marketed personal lines, such as automobile, homeowners, life, and health insurance, make particularly good candidates for online transactions. These less complex types of insurance are standard commodities, written in high volumes to take advantage of the "law of large numbers," and generally do not require the same level of underwriting or servicing expertise as commercial lines. Accordingly, personal lines insurance transactions are a natural fit with Internet commerce, and the online insurance market is quickly evolving in this direction.

Private passenger automobile insurance is particularly well-suited to Internet sales because: (1) it is relatively simple to understand compared to other products, such as retirement planning and life insurance products; (2) the application process for automobile insurance requires less personal and confidential information than that for most other types of insurance products; and (3) automobile insurance must be purchased by virtually all households because it is required by law in most of the fifty states.[146] At least one personal lines insurer is

---

[142] *See* Exchange Act Release No. 37182, 61 Fed. Reg. 24,644, 24,645 (1996).

[143] *See GKN Securities Mulls Automated E-Mail Surveillance*, FIN. NETNEWS, June 23, 1997, at 6; *OPCO, Friedman Billings to Automate E-Mail Oversight*, FIN. NETNEWS, June 30, 1997, at 1.

[144] *See* CONNING & CO., ELECTRONIC COMMERCE AND THE INTERNET (1997) [hereinafter CONNING/INTERNET]; DATAMONITOR, INSURANCE ON THE INTERNET 1996-2000 (1996).

[145] *See* CONNING/INTERNET, *supra* note 144.

[146] *See* DATAMONITOR, *supra* note 144.

currently binding automobile insurance coverage online based entirely on information submitted by the applicant to the insurer by means of the company's website.[147]

A recent study concluded that the types of insurance products with the greatest Internet sales potential are as follows: [148]

Type of Insurance	% of Computer-Owning Households Who Have This Type of Insurance	# of Computer-Owning Households Who Have This Type of Insurance
1. Automobile	92%	32.1 million
2. Health	88%	30.7 million
3. Life	84%	29.3 million
4. Home/Renters	80%	27.9 million

[a] Insurance Transactions on the Internet. This Section provides a brief description of how Internet technology is currently being applied in each stage of the typical personal lines insurance transaction, followed by a discussion of several emerging business issues raised by electronic insurance commerce. It concludes with a review of current legal and regulatory issues, including the efforts of the National Association of Insurance Commissioners (the "NAIC") to evaluate the present and future challenges facing state authorities responsible for regulating insurance transactions over the Internet.

[i] Solicitation and Application. The first step in the typical insurance transaction is solicitation — attracting the prospective insured's interest in purchasing insurance. When solicitation is successful, the prospective insured submits an application to the insurer's underwriting department. Both solicitation and application are currently taking place on the Internet in several well-developed formats.

Insurers have traditionally employed both "passive" solicitation methods, such as television and print advertising, and "active" methods, such as personal sales. Both of these insurance industry marketing techniques have translated well to the Web.

Passive solicitation elements that are now commonplace on the Web include extensive information about available product benefits and prices, insurers' financial ratings, advertising graphics, video and audio support, answers to frequently asked questions ("FAQs"), and hypertext links to related websites.[149] The Internet

---

[147] See Progressive Casualty Insurance Co.'s website at <http://www.auto-insurance.com>.

[148] *See* JUPITER COMMUNICATIONS[SM] & FIND/SVP, EMERGING TECHNOLOGIES RESEARCH GROUP, THE AMERICAN HOME FINANCIAL SERVICES SURVEY: MANAGEMENT REPORT (1996) [hereinafter FIND/SVP QUANT].

[149] One example of a website containing both passive and active solicitation elements, in addition to many other features, the Insweb site, located at <http://www.insweb.com>. InsWeb is a Web-based independent intermediary that provides a broad spectrum of information regarding insurers, insurance products, and other items of current interest to both consumers and the industry.

provides far more than traditional passive insurance advertising, however, it provides the consumer with a low-cost opportunity to take a self-guided tour through the information she finds most relevant and interesting. The Internet thus probably has a better chance than television or print media of catching and holding the consumer's interest. Targeting marketing efforts to the areas in which the consumer is most interested saves time and money for both the consumer and the insurer.

Active solicitation elements on the Web allow insurers and potential insureds to interact electronically in real time. Interactive insurance sites may feature request for quotation pages ("RFQs") that allow users to enter detailed information and obtain "instant quotes" from a multitude of insurers. The RFQ improves the insurer's efficiency and flexibility in soliciting new customers. Insurance intermediary sites, operated by brokers and agents with multiple insurer relationships (as contrasted with insurer sites dedicated solely to a single insurer), allow access to competitive quotes from a large number of insurers through a single RFQ, saving the consumer and the insurer time and money.[150]

Many interactive insurance sites also allow the user to send e-mail requesting information on a broad range of topics, including local area agency referrals. After the policy is in force, e-mail can continue to be used during the policy period to respond to policyholder questions, claims inquiries, and renewal requests. With these interactive tools, the Internet has now evolved into an extensive electronic "insurance marketplace."

"Agency system insurers" have traditionally solicited business through intermediaries, such as company agency forces, independent agents, managing general agents, and brokers.[151] Intermediaries typically earn commissions that are charged to the insurer at policy inception as "acquisition costs." These costs typically constitute a significant portion of an agency system insurer's policy expenses. "Direct writers," in contrast to agency system insurers, mass-market and issue policies directly to insureds (through mass media such as television, telephone, and the mail) without the use of intermediaries. Some direct writers have successfully reduced acquisition and other transaction costs by, in effect, "cutting out the middleman."

Internet insurance providers are expected to reduce acquisition costs even further. One study concludes that Internet insurers have a 23% overall cost advantage over agency insurers and a 5.1% cost advantage over direct writers.[152] This is especially important in the personal lines market, because consumers buy basic "commodity-type" insurance products such as private automobile and homeowners based on price considerations in many cases.[153] Although acquisition costs can be reduced by insurance companies that are able to exploit the Internet cost structure, many insurers may be reluctant to fully adopt Internet

---

[150] *See id.*

[151] Company agency forces, or so-called "captive" agents, represent a single insurer. Independent agents often represent multiple insurers. Managing general agents ("MGAs") have contractual relationships with insurers through which the MGA may perform limited underwriting functions and bind the insurer under certain circumstances (this is sometimes referred to as "holding the pen" of the insurer). Brokers are insurance intermediaries that specialize in representing insureds.

[152] DATAMONITOR, *supra* note 144.

[153] *See id.*

solicitation and servicing techniques because they are worried about the impact on their existing valuable agency networks.[154]

Innovative Internet content providers specializing in insurance have begun to create large-scale online insurance "marketplaces" by entering into partnerships with large personal lines carriers. For example, InsWeb, a leading Internet insurance technology provider, and State Farm Insurance, the nation's largest automobile insurer (with 17,000 agents), recently announced a nationwide agreement that enables consumers to obtain an automobile insurance premium quote from a State Farm agent in most states in the nation.[155] Intuit, Inc., has recently agreed to provide consumers with real-time rate quotes for term life policies as well as agent referral services through its Quicken® InsureMarket™ service, part of Intuit's Quicken website, which is designed to provide individuals with objective information and interactive tools to make sound financial decisions.[156]

[*ii*] *Underwriting and Policy Issuance.* After the prospective insured submits an application to the insurer, the insurer must decide whether to underwrite (*i.e.*, select and price) the risk. In the personal lines market, agents are typically authorized by insurers to issue "binders," or evidence of temporary coverage, to applicants who appear to meet the insurer's underwriting guidelines. The insurer reserves the right to decline the risk within a certain time period if the underwriting department denies the application. If the insurer decides to accept the risk, a policy is then issued that sets forth the requested coverage.

For many personal lines insurance transactions, underwriting and policy issuance can occur almost instantaneously online. The application can be transmitted by e-mail, in a format similar to (and somewhat more elaborate than) an RFQ. The application information can then be automatically measured against the insurer's guidelines by means of underwriting software. If the information contained in the application is acceptable under the insurer's guidelines, the agent can automatically issue a binder or policy.

At least one automobile insurer, Progressive Casualty Insurance Company, currently underwrites automobile insurance risks and issues binders in minutes over the Internet. Through a series of data entry screens, the Progressive website compiles the necessary application information This service is currently limited to the State of Minnesota.

Of course, not all personal lines underwriting can be accomplished by software — insurers recognize that an intermediary's expertise and judgment can be critical in selecting risks that will ultimately experience acceptably low losses. Accordingly, insurers may use the Internet as a powerful tool to enhance agency-insurer communication.

---

[154] *See* CONNING/INTERNET, *supra* note 144. Some existing agency networks add significant value to insurer operations because of the extensive consumer relationships and referral contacts the agencies have developed.

[155] *See State Farm and InsWeb Form Partnership*, PR NEWSWIRE, Sept. 16, 1997.

[156] *See Intuit's Quicken InsureMarket Now Offers Prudential Insurance Term Life Rate Quotes*, BUS. WIRE, Sept. 16, 1997. *See also* <http://www.quicken.com>.

Prior to the widespread availability of the Internet, some insurers had developed their own proprietary interfaces to enhance and safeguard the use of information by their exclusive agencies. Other insurers made use of the Insurance Value Added Network Service ("IVANS"), which enabled them to receive, bundle, and store a high volume of agency/company information. Still other services, developed to improve insurance company administration in the paper era, have adapted to their customers' Internet related needs. For example, the Agency Company Organization for Research and Development ("ACORD"), a nonprofit organization with agency, insurer, and service provider members, has developed standards for displays and formats for insurance information to reduce the number of necessary procedures and forms, and to thereby decrease the likelihood of errors in the application and underwriting process.[157]

Many of the advances made in agency/company interface have been driven by the industry's goal of achieving "single-entry multi-company interface," or "SEMCI," to reduce the errors and inefficiencies associated with data entry (that is often duplicative) from multiple sources within the independent agency system.[158] These systems have also arisen out of the insurance industry's need to process enormous quantities of information. Now that the Internet has increasingly sound data security and sufficient capacity to adequately serve many of these agency-insurer communication needs, the Internet will play an increasingly important role in replicating or enhancing these agency/company network systems and standards.

Regarding policy issuance, insurers continue to issue policies by mail, facsimile, and other remote means. Although no insurer appears to actually be issuing electronic policies at this time, with the adoption of electronic signature laws and improvements in data security, the capability to issue insurance policies quickly and safely by electronic means should become a reality in the near future.

[*iii*] *Claims Adjustment and Payment.* Claims adjusting and payment do not necessarily require the physical presence of the insurer. It is not uncommon for out-of-state insurers to adjust claims entirely from their home offices by fax and telephone, with the assistance of local inspectors and automobile repair or residential construction facilities. Thus, many parts of the claims adjustment process can occur online, including communication between the insurer, the insured, and local third parties, verification of claim information, and electronic transmittal of claims payments. As digital cameras become more available, insureds or adjusters will be able to transmit digitized photographs of losses over the Internet.

At least one insurer offers complete automobile claims adjusting services on the Internet.[159] The insured provides standard information regarding the vehicle, date, time and location of loss, on an electronic claim form. The claim form also provides spaces for narrative descriptions of damage and injuries, and can be submitted to the insurer by a simple "point-and-click."

---

[157] See Agency Company Organization for Research and Development's website at <http://www.acord.com>.

[158] *See* GATZA, TURNER & STONE, AMERICA INSTITUTE FOR CERTIFIED PROPERTY/CASUALTY UNDERWRITERS, MANAGING INFORMATION RESOURCES 86 (1995).

[159] *See* Centurion Corporation, *Insurance Underwriters & Counselors, available at* <http://www.centcorp.com/c.auto.claim.html>.

In summary, virtually every phase of the basic personal lines insurance transaction can be accomplished more quickly and efficiently by means of the Internet. Website and e-mail technology provide the necessary support for insurance solicitation, applications, underwriting, policy issuance, claims adjusting, and payment. A recent study concluded that consumers perceive the Internet as a useful tool to accomplish many of these tasks:

ELECTRONIC INSURANCE FEATURES — RATINGS BY CONSUMERS[160] *Ratings based on a 1-10 scale where 10 equals "most useful"*			
	Rated 9 or 10	**Rated 6-8**	**Rated <6**
Compare company policies	32%	26%	42%
Inquire about claim status	30%	27%	43%
Submit claims	29%	24%	47%
Get In-Depth Policy Information	21%	27%	52%
E-Mail local agents/customer service	19%	24%	57%
Make changes to policies	19%	22%	59%
Securely purchase/pay for policies	18%	22%	60%

[b] Business Issues. Many observers believe that Internet insurance commerce is on the verge of a period of unprecedented growth, certain business and regulatory hurdles will need to be addressed in order to provide an appropriate economic and legal climate for such expansion.

[i] Changing Relationships with Policyholders. From an informational perspective, the Internet brings insurers and insureds closer together. However, it also has the potential to separate the insurer from its policy-holders. A recent study concluded that today's increasingly fragmented and mobile society, combined with the proliferation of consumer "access points" for interacting with companies, has weakened the links between companies and their customers.[161]

Another study found that 45% of computer-owning households reported they rarely or never visited an agent or broker in person, and 40% said they had never even phoned an agent or company representative. This lack of client contact presents a potential problem for insurance companies that struggle to maintain a branded relationship with their customers. In response, insurers have embraced online distribution as a way to keep a continuing stream of product and service information flowing to the desirable segment of consumers that comprise the current and prospective interactive marketplace.[162]

---

[160] *See* FIND/SVP QUANT, *supra* note 148.

[161] *See* CONNING/INTERNET, *supra* note144.

[162] *See* FIND/SVP QUANT, *supra* note 148.

[*ii*] *Agent/Company Relations.* The insurance industry now recognizes that electronic commerce has the potential to provide tremendous cost savings in distribution and elsewhere.[163] Most insurers are careful, however, not to take a public position that the Internet is a useful tool to "cut out" valuable but expensive intermediary networks. Some carriers have made the decision to place only select agents on the company's website. Agency groups have argued that because some insurers' cyberspace efforts are being directed only to the top producers, the resulting discrimination leads to division and unhappiness within their sales forces.[164] Accordingly, insurers must bear these factors in mind to gain the increased efficiencies of the Internet while at the same time preserving the substantial value of existing intermediary networks.

[*iii*] *Privacy and Security of Personal Information.* Privacy of information on the Internet is a significant concern for consumers. Of the 9,000 consumers who responded to a recent online survey, more than 70% are more concerned about privacy on the Internet than they are about information transmitted by telephone or mail.[165] Study findings also indicate that consumers are more willing to reveal personal and financial information to companies that provide disclosure of information gathering and dissemination policies.[166] Insurers and intermediaries can respond to these concerns by developing and disclosing adequate safeguards for private, confidential, or otherwise sensitive insurance information.

[*iv*] *Bank Sales of Insurance.* Reflecting their significant concerns about security, consumers generally appear to show a preference for traditional vendors, such as large financial institutions, over Internet-only vendors.[167] Accordingly, the Internet may provide established banks and other financial institutions with increased opportunities to gain the trust of Internet insurance consumers. Banks have already established significant electronic transaction facilities — one study indicates that at year-end 1997, 80% of the top twenty banks will offer electronic transaction processing for their customers, and 45% will offer Internet transaction processing.[168]

Booz-Allen & Hamilton's recent survey of 170 insurers found that "consumers' expectations are raised by other industries' online product offerings, and they are already requesting services far in excess of what the vast majority of insurance companies are offering."[169] The Booz-Allen survey found that insurers' plans to offer Internet services compared to what their customers want as follows:

---

[163] *See* R. Lent, *Insurers close to Net-ting customers*, J. OF COM., Sept. 30, 1997.

[164] *See* Daniel Hayes, *Dividing the Information Highway*, BEST'S REVIEW (LIFE/HEALTH ED.), Sept. 1997, at 95.

[165] *See* BOSTON CONSULTING GROUP, E-TRUST INTERNET PRIVACY STUDY (1997).

[166] *Id.*

[167] *See* GEORGIA TECH RESEARCH CORP., GRAPHICS, VISUALIZATION & USABILITY CENTER'S 6TH ANNUAL WWW USER SURVEY (1996).

[168] BOOZ-ALLEN & HAMILTON, INC., INTERNET INSURANCE: A STUDY OF CURRENT USE AND FUTURE TRENDS (1997).

[169] *Id.*

Type of Service	% of Insurers Whose Customers Want Service	% of Insurers Planning to Offer Service by 1998
Online Price Quotes	68%	26%
Personal Information Changes	63%	37%
More Agent Information	32%	70%
Policy Purchase	32%	9%
Provider Directory	22%	22%

Source: BOOZ-ALLEN & HAMILTON, INC., INTERNET INSURANCE: A STUDY OF CURRENT USE AND FUTURE TRENDS, at V-3F (1997).

Banks have been eager to compete for insurance sales for many years and have recently made substantial inroads into the insurance brokerage market. By developing powerful Internet and Electronic Data Interchange tools, banks appear to have gained a substantial competitive advantage in the market for electronic financial services. Consumers are now demanding the more sophisticated transaction capabilities of the Internet, but in many instances continue to feel comfortable purchasing financial products and services only from major financial institutions. Accordingly, if insurance companies fail to respond quickly to customer electronic transaction needs, banks may become even more formidable competitors for insurance sales than they already are by fulfilling this need.

While insurers continue to face certain Internet business issues, these issues are not insurmountable, and the industry may once again find creative ways to convert perceived potential problems into significant opportunities.

[c] Legal and Regulatory Issues. While insurers have made considerable progress in resolving technological and business issues, they have not been as successful resolving legal and regulatory issues. The legal and regulatory environment of the Internet is developing rapidly. Insurers, therefore, may redouble their efforts to promote the development of an acceptable regulatory environment before regulators and possibly private plaintiffs step in to fill the void.

[i] Fifty-State Regulation and Licensing Requirements. Insurance regulation focuses primarily on insurer solvency and market conduct. Under the McCarran-Ferguson Act,[170] persons transacting the "business of insurance" are regulated primarily at the state level by fifty different departments of insurance, resulting in a highly complicated regulatory environment. To enforce solvency and market conduct laws and regulations, state regulators have relied on an extensive licensing system under which insurers must be separately licensed in their "domiciliary" state — where they are legally organized — as well as every other state in which they transact insurance. Individual states impose insurance policy content and rate requirements that may vary substantially

---

[170] 15 U.S.C. §§ 1011-15.

from those of other states. Other participants in the insurance industry, including intermediaries, adjusters, and administrators, must also be licensed by individual states.

Although the National Association of Insurance Commissioners ("NAIC") has made significant strides in achieving greater uniformity of state insurance laws, the existing "crazy quilt" of state insurance laws and regulations does not lend itself well to the "borderless" transactional environment of global electronic commerce.

At the most fundamental level, each state requires licensure for any activity that constitutes "doing an insurance business" or "transacting" insurance. Such activities are defined by state laws typically in very broad terms to include any conduct relating to the issuance of a policy; solicitation, preliminary negotiations, execution, post-execution activities, and claims handling.[171]

Persons transacting insurance on the Internet must comply with the same byzantine legal requirements that have historically been faced by insurers and intermediaries transacting insurance in person, by mail, or over the telephone. As a result, many websites that offer RFQs display state law disclaimers.[172] The only automobile insurer currently binding coverage over the Internet limits its sales to the state of Minnesota.[173]

Consumers, insurers, and regulators must recognize that Internet insurance sales do not occur in a legal vacuum. If the industry does not take action to self-regulate in a consistent way, individual state regulators will develop their own rules based on problems unique to their jurisdictions. The industry will then be faced with another system of fifty different sets of laws and regulations, raising costs for consumers, insurers, state agencies, and ultimately taxpayers. At this time, no uniform model state law exists on the subject of Internet insurance (see NAIC discussion, *infra*, subsection [*iv*]), and federal lawmakers have not yet entered the fray. Meanwhile, the industry continues to expand its Internet activities at a rapid pace. Thus, the currently existing opportunity to create workable standards of consumer protection may only be a temporary one.

[*ii*] *The "Situs" Issue.* The fifty-state insurance regulatory environment in the United States hinges upon distinct geographical concepts: the "domiciliary state" of an insurer, the residence of a policyholder, the "situs" of a risk, *etc.* The Internet, however, does not have a distinct "location." In the past, state insurance commissioners have asserted broad regulatory powers to attempt to exercise extra-territorial jurisdiction over unlicensed, out-of-state and off-shore insurers deemed to be "transacting" insurance in their jurisdictions (the so-called "non-admitted" market). More recently, insurance commissioners have endeavored to protect domestic policyholders by regulating the intermediaries that sell insurance written by non-admitted insurers

---

[171] *See, e.g.,* CAL. INS. CODE § 35 ("'Transact' as applied to insurance includes any of the following: (a) Solicitation. (b) Negotiations preliminary to execution. (c) Execution of a contract of insurance. (d) Transaction of matters subsequent to execution of the contract and arising out of it."); N.Y. INS. LAW § 1101(b)(1)(A) ("making, or proposing to make, as insurer, any insurance contract, including either issuance or delivery of a policy or contract of insurance . . . or solicitation of applications for any such policies").

[172] *See, e.g.,* <http://www.insweb.com/cgi-bin/newauto.exe> ("InsWeb cannot currently offer quotes to residents of Connecticut, Massachusetts and Rhode Island. We are adding new quoting companies and states regularly - please check back soon.").

[173] *See* <http://www.auto-insurance.com>.

(called "surplus line" brokers).

On May 30, 1996, the California Department of Insurance released Bulletin 96-4, which sets forth, among other things, the parameters by which licensed California surplus line brokers can transact electronic insurance business with non-admitted insurers:

- Unless and until the Legislature authorizes otherwise, any surplus line transaction conducted via electronic media must be performed through a licensed California surplus line broker, rather than directly between an insured and a nonadmitted insurer. . . .

- [S]urplus line brokers must comport with the statutory requirement that policy issuance by the nonadmitted insurer or its representative occur outside of California. One example of an acceptable electronic transaction would involve all of the following steps:

Step 1 — A California surplus line broker, on his or her terminal in California, contacts a nonadmitted insurer's computer. The nonadmitted insurer's computer must be located outside of California.

Step 2 — On his or her computer terminal, the surplus line broker calls up an input screen from the nonadmitted insurer's computer or server located outside this state (or from the nonadmitted insurer's website located on the server of an independent Service provider) which contains a program or template of the insurer's underwriting and rating guidelines. Those guidelines must have been established by the insurer outside California.

Step 3 — The surplus line broker inputs the data about the applicant required for the insurer's computer to perform underwriting and rating of the applicant.

Step 4 — Assuming the nonadmitted insurer's program approves binding on specified terms and at a specified rate, the computer may automatically transmit a policy, bearing electronic facsimile signatures. The policy may be printed in the surplus line broker's California office and the surplus line broker may deliver the policy to the insured or the insured's representative.

- All of the foregoing may be performed automatically by the nonadmitted insurer's computer, so long as that computer or server is located outside California (or from the nonadmitted insurer's website located on the server of an independent Service provider).[174]

California's Bulletin 96-4 is limited to "surplus line" transactions, in which the insurance sought is an "exportable" coverage not readily available in the admitted market. More difficult questions are likely to arise as the marketplace begins to interpret Bulletin 96-4 in practice, stretching the limits of permissible licensed broker involvement (or non-involvement) in nonadmitted insurance transactions.

---

[174] Affiliation with Nonadmitted Insurers; Permissible Transactions by Surplus Line Brokers and Nonadmitted Insurers, Bulletin No. 96-4 (Cal. Dept. of Ins. 1996).

[*iii*] *Insurance Fraud.* Internet transactions lack a discrete or easily identifiable location, and because websites are relatively easy to construct and dismantle, insurance regulators and prosecutors may have difficulty in preventing insurance fraud over the Internet. A perpetrator's lack of physical presence in a jurisdiction, and the lack of a reliable evidentiary trail to identify fraudulent operations, will make discovery and prosecution challenging.

To the extent that data transmitted over the Internet is not secure, Internet insurance transactions may facilitate unauthorized modification of policy terms, forgery by alteration of electronic signatures, and defalcations of electronic premium or claims payment funds. Accordingly, ancillary rules and regulations regarding data security, electronic signatures, and wire fraud will play critical roles in the success of insurance on the Internet.

[d] NAIC Activities. The NAIC is a national group of state insurance regulators that meets at least quarterly to discuss emerging insurance industry issues and to draft and promote model laws and regulations aimed at increasing uniformity of regulation and efficiency of administration. The NAIC first formed an Internet subgroup to begin examining Internet issues in 1995. Since then, the NAIC has produced a draft "white paper" entitled "The Marketing of Insurance over the Internet" (the "NAIC White Paper").[175]

The NAIC White Paper contains an appendix with a forty-eight state survey of insurance regulators, addressing Internet insurance sales issues. The regulators indicated that the three most important areas of concern regarding Internet insurance sales are: (i) unlicensed/unauthorized companies and producers; (ii) fraud; and (iii) misleading or deceptive advertising and marketing. The NAIC White Paper also addresses the issues of data security, information privacy, and advantages and disadvantages of Internet insurance sales for consumers, insurers, and regulators.

The current draft of the NAIC White Paper provides a general framework for discussion of Internet marketing issues and catalogs some recent legal and regulatory developments. The draft, however, stops short of proposing any definitive solutions. When the NAIC White Paper is completed, it is likely to lead to the development of a model law by the NAIC. In some cases, NAIC model laws have taken several years to draft and complete, after which time they are presented to interested state legislatures to consider. If state legislators are favorably disposed to an NAIC model law, the model, with modifications by the state, must still be enacted through the state legislative process before it actually becomes law. In view of the rapid development of online insurance markets, state legislators may find it necessary to take steps to regulate Internet insurance commerce before the NAIC has completed its work.

§ 14.04 REMOTE BANKING DELIVERY SYSTEMS

Remote banking delivery systems consist of three basic parts: (a) a "front-end" customer access device (also known as an "access channel"), such as a phone or personal computer; (b) a "back-end" proprietary device,

---

[175] The latest version of the National Association of Insurance Commissioners' ("NAIC") White Paper can be accessed through the NAIC's website at <http://www.naic.org>.

such as a bank server or a third party processor system; and (c) middleware, which links the front-end device to the back-end device. Banks can use either proprietary formats or industry standards to transmit financial data among these system components. This Section explores the different types of customer access channels, middleware products, back-end devices, and industry standards that banks and nonbanks use to support remote banking.

[1]   CUSTOMER ACCESS CHANNELS

Until recently, the traditional "customer access channel" for most bank customers has been the teller window. Today, banks can reach customers many other ways, including through ATM and point-of-sale ("POS") systems, telephones, televisions, and personal computers. One recent study predicted the percentage of transactions delivered by each channel would change, as customers increasingly move away from branch-based transactions:[176]

	1995	1998
Branches	56%	41%
ATMs	28%	31%
Telephones	10%	15%
Home Banking	1%	6%
Other	5%	7%

The authors of the study also argue that the technology decisions to support or minimize certain access channels have "moved from the back room to the board room."[177] Not every bank will employ the same remote banking strategy. Some will offer an entire suite of channels, while others concentrate on particular channels. Each bank, however, must answer a basic question — how does the bank want to utilize the electronic options that are available to it? This subsection explores how banks and customers have incorporated today's remote customer access channels into routine financial activities, and what trends may emerge in the future.

[a] ATM/POS. The ATM networks and the POS networks were among the first devices to allow customers to make withdrawals, third party transfers, deposits, and balance inquiries in publicly accessible locations without visiting an actual branch.[178] Some banks have emphasized this strategy by establishing

---

[176] Philip Lawrence & John Karr, *Technology Spending – and Alliances: New Highs in Financial Services Firms*, J. OF RETAIL BANKING, Sept. 1996, at 47.

[177] *Id.*

[178] For a further discussion of the evolution of this customer access channel, see Chapter 4.

interactive video kiosks in grocery stores, shopping malls, and other high traffic volume areas that offer additional services, such as access to bank officers.[179]

[b] Telephone. The omnipresent, and transportable, telephone is another attractive access channel. The home touch-tone phone, the public touch-tone phone, and the cellular phone each offer more flexibility than geographically fixed ATM/POS devices. By pressing a series of keys, a customer can check balances, transfer accounts, even pay bills using any touch–tone phone. Many banks offer 24-hour customer service, allowing customers to conduct telephone remote banking at any time. Traditional touch-tone phone remote banking, however, has two drawbacks: (1) as banks offer more services, the response menu that guides the customer will become increasingly cumbersome and complex; and, (2) the phone cannot immediately provide consumers with currency, or its digital equivalent.

New breeds of screen phones and smart card reader-phones may soon overcome these obstacles. Several companies are designing screen phones that, in addition to video images, will offer e-mail; and a smaller number of these screen phones will also provide home banking and limited Web access.[180] Full function screen phones will soon retail for about $200 to $300.[181] Jupiter Communications has predicted that the installed base of screen phones will rise from approximately one million in 1996 to over ten million households by 2002, and that a quarter of these phones will have Web-browsing capabilities.[182] Similarly, the Mondex™ smart card trials have used telephone/card readers that allow customers to transfer value onto smart cards by phone.[183] As these new technologies enter the marketplace, they will further increase the power of the telephone as an important remote banking customer access channel.

Many banks incorporate telephone banking as part of an overall remote banking strategy. One bank, interestingly, has decided to rely almost exclusively on the telephone as the means for interacting with its consumers. TeleBank, based in Arlington, Virginia, has no physical branches.[184] Its customers contact the bank exclusively by phone and by mail. Whether such a banking model will be adopted to any significant extent remains to be seen — clearly, at least one bank, and its investors, believe that the remote telephone banking channel has the ability to operate profitably as a stand-alone bank.

---

[179] *See, e.g.,* James E. Causey, *News Focus: Stop, Shop and Refinance,* MILWAUKIE J. SENTINEL, Jan. 5, 1998, at 6; *Huntington is Banking on Marketing Strategy,* PLAIN DEALER, Dec. 30, 1997, at 2C; Tami Luhby, *Full-Motion Video Puts Face on Remote Delivery,* AM. BANKER, Dec. 23, 1997, at 15; John J. Jedlicka, *Marine Midland Kiosks to Offer Market Data via Web,* AM. BANKER, July 30, 1997, at 11; Liz Moyer, *Video-Equipped Off-Site Banking Comes to Mellon,* AM. BANKER, July 30, 1997, at 4.

[180] *See, e.g., Screen Phones Seek Their Niche,* INTERACTIVE HOME, June 1, 1997.

[181] *See id.*

[182] *Id.*

[183] *See* Lynn Waldsmith, *Card Moves U.S. Closer to Cashless: Mondex System Will be Used Mostly for Purchases Under $20,* DET. NEWS, Jan. 14, 1998, at B1.

[184] *See* Laurance P. Greenberg & Arthur M. Domingo, *A Bank No One Visits – TeleBank,* J. OF RETAIL BANKING, Sept. 1996, at 15.

[c] Television. Interactive television has long been an alluring access channel for the banks. Televisions, like telephones, are in virtually every home in the United States — and the cable wires and direct satellite equipment that support most of them can transmit data at a rate many times faster than telephone wires.

Many banks and nonbanks have begun to explore the applicability of television to remote banking. For example, Barnett Bank began exploring cable home banking in 1996.[185] More recently, Wells Fargo and First Commerce Bank announced that they will be offering simplified television versions of their online home banking websites.[186] Under these proposals, customers would be able to connect to banks using cable box top sets which would retail for about $250. The bank software would detect whether the customer is connecting via the TV or the Internet and automatically provide the correct customer interface. Industry analysts estimate that the cost of designing and maintaining a companion television version of an online home banking website will range between 25% and 40% of the amount spent to build the original website.[187] If these television-based remote banking channels prove successful, many other banks may follow suit.

Many technology companies are competing aggressively in this market. For example, Microsoft bought WebTV Networks™ Inc., manufacturer of WebTV™ boxes, in the spring of 1997 for about $425 million.[188] Similarly, Oracle, through its Network Computer, Inc. affiliate ("NCI"), has designed an alternative WebTV™ box, NetChannel®.[189] These products, and perhaps many others, will challenge each other for a share of this untapped market.

Television probably is the most underdeveloped remote banking channel. Its familiarity and widespread availability, however, provide it with perhaps the greatest potential for future growth and customer acceptance.

[d] Personal Computer. The remote banking channel that has received the most press coverage is the personal computer. Approximately 40.4 million households in the United States have computers (approximately 40%).[190] Several studies have concluded that personal computer ownership and use correlate strongly with demographically attractive segments of the banking market. Approximately twenty-one million households in the United States have access to the Internet.[191] This number will probably grow dramatically in the next few years.

---

[185] *See* Julie Monahan, *Is Barnetts' Interactive TV Banking too Late?*, COMPUTERWORLD, Oct. 1, 1996, at F6.

[186] *See Internet-TV: Banking's Next Channel*, FUTUREBANKER, Aug. 1997, at 26 [hereinafter *Internet-TV*]; Drew Clark, *Wells, Ga. Bank Offering Service Through WebTV*, AM. BANKER, June 26, 1997, at 16.

[187] *See Internet-TV, supra* note 186.

[188] *See It Sounds Great But Will Web TV Ever Take Off?*, CAMPAIGN, Nov. 7, 1997, at S14.

[189] *See* Don Clark, *Intel and Microsoft Split Over Internet-TV Gear*, WALL ST. J., Oct. 3, 1997, at A3.

[190] *See* Michelle Matassa Flores, *The Set-Top Revolution*, SEATTLE TIMES BUS. REP., Dec. 21, 1997, at E1. For a comprehensive discussion of PC banking, see STEVEN C. DAVIDSON, THE COMMUNITY BANKER'S GUIDE TO THE INTERNET AND HOME BANKING (1997).

[191] *E-Commerce Just Scratching Surface of Market Potential*, MEDIA DAILY, Dec. 9, 1997.

Customers use personal computers to access three remote banking services: direct dialup PC banking, commercial online provider PC banking, and Internet banking.[192]

[*i*] *Direct Dialup Software ("PC Banking")*. Direct dialup software typically offers account information, intrabank transfers, bill payment, and formatted e-mail communications with the bank. Banks that have evaluated the marketing and economic effects of different direct dialup software models have reached different conclusions. For example, some banks offer software that is exclusively bank-branded, while others offer a co-branded product in conjunction with a personal financial management software package such as Quicken® or Managing Your Money. One significant benefit of direct dialup access, however, is that, in exchange for these higher production and mailing costs, the bank can maintain exclusive control of the customer interface without the involvement of an Internet service provider or other intermediary.

In this rapidly shifting direct dialup software market, some players have recently been acquired, scaled back their presence, or repositioned their offerings. For example, Checkfree has been trying to sell or license Bank Street®, a PC Banking product it acquired when it purchased Servantis in 1996.[193] Also, some banks, in crafting their remote banking strategies, have opted not to offer a PC Banking product, but to reach their potential and existing customers exclusively through the Internet.

[*ii*] *Commercial Online Provider PC Banking*. Major Internet service providers ("ISPs") also provide access to home banking. For example, America Online ("AOL"), has created a co-branded banking "channel" for participating financial institutions, called the AOL Banking Center[SM].[194] This product, started in September 1996, relies on the Intuit system known as BankNow™. BankNow™, available for nineteen institutions, offers an all-in-one-screen format that allows customers to use their personal computer to check bank account balances, transfer funds between accounts, and make payments without switching screens.[195] Intuit has also recently offered BankNow™ for co-branding on bank websites.[196]

Depending on the contract with the participating financial institution, the AOL Banking Center[SM] also permits customers to conduct more complex financial transactions either through bank websites or separate software, which must be separately acquired from the bank.

Whether online service providers can continue to perform such intermediary services remains to be seen.

[*iii*] *Internet*. In addition to direct dialup software and online service provider alternatives, customers can access bank-operated websites via the Internet. These sites, and the applications contained within them, may

---

[192] Responding to increasing use of this channel, Travelers Bond, a unit of Travelers Property Casualty Corp., offers financial institutions an insurance policy against cyberfraud on PC-banking customers. *See* Carol Power, *Travelers Unit Introduces PC Banking Insurance*, AM. BANKER, Sept. 24, 1997, at 15.

[193] *See CheckFree Settles In, After Bulking Up*, BANK TECH. NEWS, Apr. 1997.

[194] *See* Doug Anderson, *PC Banking: A Brief Overview*, CREDIT WORLD, Mar./Apr. 1997, at 32-34; *AOL Reports FY 97 2nd Quarter Revenues Up 64% With Record Membership & System Usage*, M2 PRESSWIRE, Feb. 7, 1997.

[195] *See* Russell Redman, *Intuit Product Caters to Transactions-Only Users*, BANK SYS. + TECH., June 1997 [hereinafter *Redman*].

[196] *See Intuit on the Net*, STAR TRIB., June 8, 1997, at D1.

be bank-branded or co-branded. Many technology providers sell turn key, bank-branded systems.[197] Other providers offer applets, which are branded, customizable plug-ins for bank sites.[198] If a bank decides to use an applet, the bank will control where the applet appears on its Web page and the vendor will build and maintain the applet software.[199] For example, Intuit offers an applet version of its BankNow product, which several banks currently offer and others plan to add in the near future.[200] Finally, some banks design their own, proprietary websites.

One survey classified Internet remote banking sites based on the types of services provided to remote banking clients.[201] The simplest, "entry level" sites offer only static information about a bank and its products; "basic" sites offer some basic interactive tools, such as loan payment calculators, and often allow customers to download loan applications; "intermediate" sites offer more advanced features, such as online credit card applications and the ability to display deposit account balances; and "advanced" sites offer online account transfers, bill payment, and account opening services. According to that survey, the sample of 285 banks fell into the following categories: "entry level" (70%); "basic" (14%); "intermediate" (15%); and "advanced" (1%).[202] Since that time, these ratios have probably changed as more banks have incorporated more sophisticated services into their Internet offerings.

Like TeleBank® in the area of telephone banking, two banks were formed as solely Internet banks. These banks, Security First Network Bank ("SFNB") and the Atlanta Internet Bank, obtained approval orders from the Office of Thrift Supervision to operate without any physical branches.[203] Customers communicate with the banks solely by mail and by the Internet. Avoiding the operating costs associated with maintaining physical branches allows these banks to offer higher interest rates to attract customers. Some commentators, however, have questioned the long-term viability of these single channel financial institutions. SFNB, which opened its electronic doors in October 1995, reportedly had only 7,000 customers after a two years of widespread, free publicity.[204] Whether or not these specialized banks survive, traditional banks will continue to incorporate Internet access into their suite of remote banking services. This trend will probably accelerate when PC/smart card readers, which will allow electronic deposits and withdrawals, become common personal computer accessories.[205]

---

[197] *See* BANK ADMINISTRATION INST., ONLINE BANKING AND BILL PAYMENT BUYERS GUIDE (1997).

[198] *See Intuit on the Net, supra* note 187.

[199] *See Redman, supra* note 186.

[200] *See BankNow Makes its Debut on the Internet*, REP. ON HOME BANKING & FIN. SERVICES, May 30, 1997.

[201] Michael K. O'Neal, *Cyberbanking*, CONSUMER FIN. L.Q. REP., Summer 1996, at 221.

[202] *Id.*; *See, e.g.*, Bill Burnham, *The Internet and Retail Banking: Hold On For The Ride*, ELECTRONIC BANKING L. & COM. REP., June 1996, at 16.

[203] For a further discussion of the history and agency approval orders for these banks, see Chapters 6 and 9.

[204] *See, e.g.*, Steve Weber, *Houston Banker Plans National Online Bank*, ONLINE BANKING NEWSLETTER, Sept. 8, 1997, at 1.

[205] *See PC/SC Workgroup Releases First Specifications for Integration of Smart Cards With Personal Computers*, BUS. WIRE, Dec. 10, 1997.

[2] MIDDLEWARE

Middleware connects multiple customer access channels to the bank servers, third-party processors, and other legacy systems, primarily by translating from one message format to another. Because these products are highly system-specific, analysis of particular systems would not yield any general observations; properly functioning routing systems, however, are a critical, yet extremely non-standardized, piece of the remote banking puzzle.

[3] BANK SERVERS AND THIRD-PARTY PROCESSORS

The final piece of a remote banking delivery system is the collection of bank servers and third-party processors. Each bank must decide what tasks it will perform on its own systems and what tasks will be performed by a third party.

Bank servers typically execute customer transactions, generate periodic statements, and maintain customer data. Each bank owns a unique set of legacy systems, which have been amassed through internal expansion and by merger with other banks. These servers raise many of the Year 2000 issues discussed earlier in this book.[206] In addition to this problem, these systems frequently require translators and inefficient data reentry to move information across the bank network.

Third-party processors typically perform a host of services that banks find more economical to outsource to third parties, such as warehousing (storing future payment instructions until the appropriate payment date); scheduling (sequencing payments to ensure the correct arrival date); payment execution (initiating consumer payments and ensuring payments are made at the lowest cost and risk to the bill payment processor); and remittance delivery (delivering remittance information to biller so that it knows which customers paid what bill).

[4] STANDARDS AND PROTOCOLS

Currently, most remote banking systems use a patchwork of customer access channels, custom middleware products, proprietary back-end systems, and multiple interfaces to stitch together a workable remote banking product. Individual banks and the banking industry, however, are exploring several options for standardizing many elements of remote banking, especially in the areas of messaging standards, platforms, security, and programming languages.

Perhaps the largest, and most ambitious effort in this area is the Integrion Financial Network ("Integrion"). On September 9, 1996, International Business Machines ("IBM") and fifteen major North American commercial banks announced that they intended to form a joint venture, Integrion[SM], through which they would collectively construct a "bank-friendly" alternative to then existing online banking systems and products. This effort, which was a significant step because the participating banks represented nearly 60% of the assets held

---

[206] For a discussion of Year 2000 issues, see Chapter 5 and Appendix A.

by the industry, grew out of two trends: the attempt to aggressively engage emerging technology and to block nonbank entities from accruing market share, and the accelerating disintermediation by inserting themselves between the banks and their customer base.

The members of Integrion anticipated that the joint venture would permit banks to set the standards for new electronic banking services and coordinate such new services with existing product lines and services. As described below, Integrion has been especially active in the fields of message standards and platforms. While many other collaborative efforts, such as the alliance supporting Open Financial Exchange, are pursuing the same general standardization objectives, multiple groups can, at least, in the short term, generate incompatible results. Despite these potential problems, almost all of the participants in this standardization effort have demonstrated a commitment to provide "open" architectures, translators, and other devices which smooth over most of the differences between the different approaches. One thing is clear, however, Integrion has provided the large banks with a powerful voice in this somewhat esoteric, but fundamentally important, debate.[207]

[a] Messaging Standards. Messaging standards allow banks and other participants to exchange data instructions using a single, universal format, thus reducing the need for conversion programs and for maintaining legacy systems.[208] Currently, two messaging standards are competing for dominance; Open Financial Exchange ("OFX™") and Integrion Gold[SM].[209]

The OFX™ specification, which was jointly developed by Microsoft, Intuit, and Checkfree, applies only to data generated and transmitted by personal computer.[210] Several companies in different sectors of the remote banking industry, such as personal financial management, home banking technology providers, and financial service providers, have announced a commitment to developing OFX-compliant products.[211]

Integrion Gold[SM], developed by Integrion, supports multiple customer access devices, such as touch-tone phones and PCs.[212] Banks and designers of personal financial management software have announced a commitment to Integrion Gold[SM], although not in the same numbers as OFX™.[213]

---

[207] For more information about the Integrion[SM] Financial Network, see Thomas P. Vartanian, Robert H. Ledig & Edward B. Whittemore, *Integrion Financial Network: A New Stage for Electronic Banking*, ELECTRONIC BANKING L. & COM. REP., Oct. 1996, at 1.

[208] *See Adding Fuel to the Specification Fire*, REP. ON HOME BANKING & FIN. SERVICES, May 30, 1997.

[209] Previously, three protocols were competing in this market: OFX™, Integrion[SM], and Visa Interactive's Access Device Messaging Standard. In August 1997, however, Integrion acquired Visa Interactive from Visa International. *See* Drew Clark, *Integrion Cuts Deal for Visa's Shaky Remote Banking Unit*, AM. BANKER, June 23, 1997, at 1; Robert Tie, *And Then There Were Two: Integrion Buys Out Visa Interactive*, INVESTMENT DEALERS' DIG., Sept. 1, 1997.

[210] *See Intuit, Microsoft and CheckFree Create Open Financial Exchange*, BUS. WIRE, Jan. 16, 1997; *Spec Should Spur Internet Commerce*, WINDOWS MAG., Apr. 1, 1997, at 310.

[211] *See* Frank Cerne, *Which Road Map To Read?*, FIN. SERVICE ONLINE, July/Aug. 1997; Jeffrey Kutler, *CoreStates, Wells Among Backers of Microsoft's Internet System*, AM. BANKER, Sept. 9, 1997, at 1.

[212] *See IBM Weighs In With New Online Banking Standard*, MEDIA DAILY, Mar. 24, 1997; *Integrion Rolls Out Plan For New Banking System*, ELECTRONIC PAYMENTS INT'L, Apr. 1997.

[213] *See* Cerne, *supra* note 211.

The proponents of OFX and Integrion Gold^{SM} have asserted that the differences between the two standards will be ironed out shortly. In the meantime, these two competing messaging systems add complexity to the process, and may have slowed down the standardization of the remote banking infrastructure. Some banks and some vendors have chosen sides; others have tried to straddle the two standards by developing multiple versions of a product or by using translators; and some have opted to wait on the sidelines until a single standard emerges.

[b] Platforms. Microsoft's Internet Finance Server Toolkit (code name "Marble") and IBM's Goldrush compete in the remote banking platform business. Marble, released in 1997, offers a pre-packaged set of turn-key services to banks and other financial institutions. Wells Fargo, CoreStates, and PaineWebber have agreed to use Marble for their computer needs.[214] Goldrush, on the other hand, operates in a Lotus Notes® environment with a Lotus® Domino™ server.[215]

[c] Security Protocols. The existence of several different security protocols, such as https, SSL, and SET also complicate the delivery of remote banking services.[216]

[d] Programming Languages. Finally, technology providers are competing to determine which programming language will dominate the future remote banking computer marketplace. For example, in the smart card industry, Visa uses Java® while Mondex uses the Multos™ smart-card programming language. Java®, which has received substantial press coverage, allows programmers to design "applets," plug-in executable files that, when certified as "100% Pure Java," will run on any Java®-enabled platform.[217] At least one study has predicted a bright future for Java®, stating that about 10% of the financial institutions in the survey supported online commerce with Java® applets today, and that number is expected to reach over 30% in three years.[218] At present, no single language has become dominant, and it is conceivable that none will.

---

[214] *See* Kutler, *supra* note 211.

[215] *See* Russell Redman, *IBM Crafts Lotus-Based Web Banking Package*, BANK SYS. + TECH., Aug. 1997.

[216] For a more comprehensive discussion of these and other security issues, see Chapter 13.

[217] *See* Steven Marlin, *First Tennessee to Build 'Pure Java' Cyberbank*, BANK SYS. + TECH., Aug. 1997.

[218] *See Vendors Prepare for Java Revolution*, RETAIL DELIVERY SYS. NEWS, June 6, 1997.

CHAPTER 15

INTERNET VALUE TRANSFER SYSTEMS

§ 15.01 INTRODUCTION

At the dawn of the next millennium, it is estimated that nearly 55 million homes[1] and 1.1 million businesses in the United States will have access to the Internet.[2] Industry analysts have offered a wide range of predictions as to how quickly the market for consumer-to-business and business-to-business Internet commerce will grow. According to one estimate, by the year 2000, the value of consumer transactions on the Internet will rise to $7.3 billion.[3] By 2001, another projection suggests that the consumer market may grow to $26 billion.[4] This growth in Internet commerce is dependent upon the development of convenient and secure methods of electronic payment. This Chapter explores several Internet value transfer systems ("IVT Systems") that are likely to serve as the foundation for the expected growth in payments made over the Internet. Financial intermediaries, merchants, and customers will each want to weigh the costs and benefits that a particular system provides for various transactions,[5] because IVT Systems vary by method of payment, level of security, and economic terms.

This Chapter reviews three types of payment methods currently in use, or intended for use, over the Internet. Section 15.02 examines credit card payments over the Internet and the economic advantages and security features related to their use. Section 15.03 focuses on IVT Systems in which third-party processors

---

[1] Scott Smith, *Internet Payments Report,* JUPITER COMM., Jan. 1997, Fig. 1.3, at 7.

[2] Anita Karve, *Internet Commerce Makes the Sale, Part 1*, NETWORK, May 1997, at 79.

[3] Smith, *supra* note 1, at 17-18.

[4] *Questions Surround SET Pilots: Industry Analysts Aren't Convinced Internet Payment System Will Fly*, ELECTRONIC COMMERCE NEWS, Aug. 18, 1997 (citing the ELECTRONIC COMMERCE REPORT, published by the Minneapolis based Piper Jaffray Research, which projects that $228 billion in goods and services will be purchased and paid for on the Internet by 2001. Of that amount, $202 billion will consist of business-to-business online trade and the remainder will consist of consumer-to-business purchases.). *See also First Virtual Holdings and Firefly Announce Agreement to Offer Convenient E-Commerce Solution*, BUS. WIRE, Aug. 11, 1997 (citing a study by TRUSTe and the Boston Consulting Group which concluded that consumer Internet commerce could increase by $6 billion by 2000 if widespread consumer privacy could be assured).

[5] For further discussion of the risk considerations associated with Internet value transfer systems ("IVT"), see THE MANAGEMENT OF RISKS CREATED BY INTERNET-INITIATED VALUE TRANSFERS, a report prepared for the Internet Council of the National Automated Clearing House Association®, co-authored by Thomas P. Vartanian, Robert H. Ledig, Edward B. Whittemore, and Peter H. Schwartz of Fried Frank, Harris, Shriver & Jacobson; Marilyn Bruneau, Lee Ann Summers, and Joel Lanz of Arthur Andersen; and Peter Wayner. FRIED, FRANK, HARRIS, SHRIVER & JACOBSON ET AL., THE MANAGEMENT OF RISKS CREATED BY INTERNET-INITIATED VALUE TRANSFERS (1997) [hereinafter FRIED FRANK, THE MANAGEMENT OF IVT RISKS].

enable users to access their deposit or asset accounts held by financial institutions. Section 15.03 also explores the banking industry's efforts to develop an IVT System that enables direct Internet access to deposit or asset accounts through the existing wholesale and retail payments system, either using electronic checks or electronic fund transfers. Section 15.04 examines merchant billing and payment processing systems. Section 15.05 analyzes IVT Systems created by third-party processors acting as agent for consumers and merchants.

§ 15.02 CREDIT CARD IVT SYSTEMS

The credit card is one natural form of payment for purchases on the Internet. As discussed in greater detail in Chapter 4, a credit card transaction occurs in three steps. A consumer presents the credit card to the merchant to initiate a purchase. The merchant communicates with a payment processor to obtain authorization. Finally, the payment processor credits the merchant's account and debits the cardholder's account. Today, merchants and consumers can buy and sell goods and services by communicating credit card information via the Internet. Upon receipt of the credit card information, the merchant relays the payment information and the charge amount to the existing credit card processing network. After receiving online authorization from the credit card processor, the merchant sends a confirmation of the transaction to the consumer either by e-mail or through an online reply to the consumer's web browser.

Conducting financial transactions over the Internet raises numerous concerns regarding personal privacy and financial security. Transmission of credit card and personal data from a consumer's PC to a merchant's server over the Internet's open network subjects the data to the risk of interception, alteration, and subsequent unauthorized use. IVT Systems, including credit card systems, must incorporate measures to prevent, detect, and contain such security breaches. A discussion of security measures available to IVT Systems, such as cryptography, digital signatures, and certificates, is contained in Chapter 13. Privacy issues, and relevant statutory and case law, implicated by the growth of electronic commerce transactions are addressed in Chapter 12. The following Sections present a survey of the security, legal, and economic characteristics of credit card IVT Systems.

[1] SECURE ELECTRONIC TRANSACTIONS™ PROTOCOL

Participants in electronic commerce recognize that widespread consumer acceptance of credit card use for Internet purchases is likely to be a key element in spurring the development of electronic commerce. Although consumers generally are comfortable with credit card use, in many instances they have a strong resistance to using credit cards to undertake Internet-transactions. Moreover, the anonymous nature of the Internet, and the potential volume of Internet-based transactions, creates the risk that merchants and card issuers could become victims of widespread fraud.

It is widely believed that consumers are concerned about the possibility that their credit card data, traveling over the Internet's open network, could be intercepted and then used for unauthorized transactions. As a practical matter, the risk of intercepting individual transmissions of unencrypted credit card data is relatively low.

The nature of the Internet, and its millions of transmissions each day, affords the general public some protection — there is safety in numbers.[6] A hacker's attempt to intercept and read transmissions to find valuable information is similar to an attempt to meet a person in Manhattan without knowing her name, what she looks like, where to meet her, and what time to meet her. A hacker can, however, pinpoint likely sources of credit card and other payment data by "trolling" electronic commerce sites in an attempt to purloin unencrypted messages.[7] Even if a consumer's credit card information was obtained, the credit card customer would still have the general liability limitation protections offered by the Truth in Lending Act[8] and Regulation Z.[9] Nevertheless, given the broad public concern about the security of Internet credit card transactions, the industry has moved to address these concerns.[10]

Visa International and MasterCard International, after some initial hesitation, agreed to work together to establish an open standard for secure credit card transactions.[11] These two leaders of the U.S. credit card industry cooperated in formulating the design of the Secured Electronic Transaction™ ("SET®") protocol.[12] SET® is designed specifically for consumers who want to use their credit cards to buy merchandise or services on the Internet.[13] SET® technology may be integrated into standard web browser software for consumers, requiring businesses to install the SET® protocol by upgrading their Internet servers to interact with a consumer's web browser. The current SET® design provides the merchant bank with the option to allow its merchants to have access to the cardholder's credit card number or other personal data.[14] This feature is intended to reduce security risks associated with new merchants, and their employees, who set up shop on the Internet.[15]

---

6   Richard Behar, *Who's Reading Your E-mail*, FORTUNE, Feb. 3, 1997, at 58 (stating that over 200 million e-mail messages traverse the Internet each day).

7   *See* Steve Ginsberg, *Security for Internet Sales Still Case of 'Buyer Beware,'* S.F. BUS. TIMES, Feb. 14, 1997, at A10; Mark Grossman, *Trolling for Bottom-Dwellers on the Net*, RECORDER, Oct. 9, 1997, at 4.

8   Truth in Lending Act, Pub. L. No. 90-321, 82 Stat. 146 (1968) (codified at 15 U.S.C. §§ 1601 *et seq.*).

9   12 C.F.R. pt. 226.

10   *See Questions Surround SET Pilots, supra* note 4 (quoting Frank Taylor, President and Chief Executive Officer of TriNet Services, who questioned the need for SET® in light of the liability policies and other protections afforded consumers by federal regulations).

11   *Credit-Card Companies OK Internet Security Deal*, S.F. EXAMINER, Feb. 1, 1996, at A1 (noting the initial competition between Visa International, which formed an alliance with Microsoft Corp., and MasterCard International, which paired up with Netscape Communications Corp.); Jeff Pelline & Michelle Quinn, *Mastercard, Visa Accord on Internet: Credit Card Giants Agree on Security Standard*, S.F. CHRON., Feb. 1, 1996, at A1. *See SET Secure Electronic Transaction — Setting the Stage for Safe Internet Shopping, available at* <http://www.mastercard.com/set/>; *Electronic Commerce, available at* <http://www.visa.com/cgi-bin/vee/nt/ecomm/main.html?2+0>. *See also NationsBank Enters Electronic Commerce Marketplace with Successful Completion of First [Interoperable] SET 1.0 Transaction in the United States*, MasterCard Press Release, Jan. 13, 1998, *available at* <http://www.mastercard.com/press/980113a.html>.

12   *See* FRIED FRANK, THE MANAGEMENT OF IVT RISKS, *supra* note 5, at 15-20 (describing Internet credit card transactions and the SET® protocol).

13   SET® technology may eventually be integrated with the IPsec protocol to accommodate corporate credit card transactions. This will allow purchasing departments to acquire goods and services from their suppliers.

14   A merchant's bank reserves the right to supply the payment information to the merchant upon request when there is a problem with an order or if the merchant is large enough to handle settlement internally via a direct connection to VisaNet. Some consumer and privacy advocates have objected to this feature, while merchants contend that it allows for more efficient transactions. Merchants argue that the inability to receive the personal data hampers customer service. Rivka Tadjer, *Give Your Site Some Credit; Preparing Your Website to Handle Credit-Card Transactions*, COMPUTER SHOPPER, Sept. 1997. Other Internet communications security protocols do protect the transmission of information during its transfer, however, they do not prevent a merchant from reviewing the information upon receipt.

15   *See* FRIED FRANK, THE MANAGEMENT OF IVT RISKS, *supra* note 5, at 20 n.50.

A graphic representation and description of a SET® transaction appears below.

The SET
Transaction

STEPS IN A SET® TRANSACTION:

① **OBTAIN DIGITAL CERTIFICATES AND SET® SOFTWARE** – The cardholder, the merchant, and the Payment Gateway obtain digital certificates and copies of the necessary SET® software.[16]

---

[16] This Model depicts a single certification authority ("CA"). A number of digital signature and certificate schemes envision the use of a certification chain, whereby a series of CAs verify one another's digital signatures until sufficient assurance of authenticity (which may depend upon the value of the underlying commercial transaction) is provided to the parties to a transaction. *See, e.g.,* Philip S. Corwin, *The Virtual Dotted Line: Understanding Digital Signatures,* BANKING POL'Y REP., Feb. 17, 1997, at 1; Thomas J. Smedinghoff, *Digital Signatures: The Key to Electronic Commerce, reprinted in* Glasser LegalWorks (eds.), *Second Annual Conference on Emerging Law of Cyberbanking and Electronic Commerce* 217 (1997). The American Bar Association's Digital Signature Guidelines reserves the term "certification authority" for the entity that issues digital certificates to "end users," not to certificate-issuing authorities above this entity. *See* INFORMATION SECURITY COMM., AM. BAR ASS'N, DIGITAL SIGNATURE GUIDELINES: LEGAL INFRASTRUCTURE FOR CERTIFICATION AUTHORITIES AND SECURE ELECTRONIC COMMERCE § 3.6 (Aug. 1, 1996) (availability of certification authority's certificate) [hereinafter DS Guidelines]. *See generally* BILL BURNHAM, PIPER JAFFRAY RESEARCH, THE ELECTRONIC COMMERCE REPORT 21-39 (1997) (providing a description of the interaction of digital certificates, digital signatures, public and private key cryptography, and CAs). *See* FRIED FRANK, THE MANAGEMENT OF IVT RISKS, *supra* note 5, at 16.

Once this step is completed, the parties can use SET®. A typical SET® transaction consists of a Purchase, an Authorization and a Payment (in SET® parlance, a "Capture").

(2) **SET® PURCHASE** has four subparts:

- *Initiate Request* - The cardholder searches the Internet, finds an item to purchase, completes an online order form provided by the merchant, selects a credit card for payment, and forwards the request to the merchant.

- *Initiate Response* - The merchant receives the request and responds with the certificates of the merchant and the Payment Gateway and includes a unique transaction identifier for this purchase. This identifier will accompany every subsequent step in this transaction.

- *Purchase Request* - After verifying the authenticity of the certificates, the cardholder sends to the merchant a Purchase Request which includes an encrypted order instruction ("Order Instruction") that only the merchant can read, and an encrypted credit card payment instruction ("Payment Instruction") that only the Payment Gateway can read.

- *Purchase Response* - The merchant verifies the authenticity of the cardholder and the integrity of the Order Instruction and sends a digitally-signed, encrypted Purchase Response to the cardholder. The cardholder verifies the identity of the merchant and the integrity of the Purchase Response, maintains the Purchase Response for reconciliation with the statement from the Issuing Bank, and awaits delivery.

(3) **SET® AUTHORIZATION** has two subparts:

- *Authorization Request* - The merchant digitally signs an encrypted Authorization Request and forwards the request, along with the Payment Instruction, to the Payment Gateway. The Payment Gateway verifies the identity of the cardholder, the identity of the merchant and the integrity of the Payment Instruction. The Payment Gateway "hands off" the information in the Payment Instruction for clearing and settlement when it seeks authorization from the Issuing Bank.

- *Authorization Response* - The Payment Gateway forwards to the merchant a digitally signed, encrypted Authorization Response. If the Authorization Response approves the Authorization Request, the Payment Gateway will include an encrypted capture token ("Capture Token") that the merchant will use to seek payment. The merchant verifies the identity of the Payment Gateway, the integrity of the Authorization Response, and the integrity of the Capture Token.[17]

---

[17] If the Authorization Response approves the Authorization Request, the merchant will commence delivery of the requested goods to the cardholder at this time. However, the timing of the merchant's delivery can vary without affecting the sequence of other events in the model. *See* FRIED, FRANK, THE MANAGEMENT OF IVT RISKS, *supra* note 5, at 16.

④ **SET® Capture** has two subparts:

- *Capture Request* - The merchant seeks payment by forwarding a digitally signed, encrypted capture request ("Capture Request"), along with the Capture Token, to the Payment Gateway. The Payment Gateway verifies the identity of the merchant and the integrity of the Capture Request and the Capture Token. The Payment Gateway "hands off" to the traditional credit card clearing and settlement system when it seeks payment from the Issuing Bank.

- *Capture Response* - The Payment Gateway digitally signs and encrypts a Capture Response which it forwards to the merchant. Finally, the merchant verifies the identity of the Payment Gateway and the integrity of the Capture Response, and keeps the Capture Response for reconciliation with the merchant's account at the Merchant Bank.

The advantage that SET® provides over current security protocols is the authentication feature that validates the credit card and permits the use of a digital signature. However, the entire SET® process takes up to thirty seconds due to the number of encryption and decryption calculations involved.[18] Business-to-business transactions will likely continue to employ other security protocols until SET® is modified to provide for business-to-business transactions.[19]

For consumers, SET® technology is only as secure as their personal computers. For example, the identity of a person using a PC to initiate a SET® transaction cannot be ascertained. SET® only authenticates the digital signature attached by a PC to the payment and order information, without verifying that the person who is initiating or authorizing the communication is, in fact, the party to whom the digital signature belongs. Thus, unauthorized access to another's PC, and subsequent use of that person's web browser, will now be the primary instances where fraud occurs.

[2] Legal Issues Related to Credit Card Transactions on the Internet

Credit card payment systems operate through the legal interplay of consumer protection statutes and the interlocking contractual relationships among merchants, card issuers, participating financial institutions, cardholders, and credit card associations. In this equation, credit card associations play a pivotal role in establishing the rules that govern the rights and responsibilities of all parties involved in credit card transactions. Significantly, the contractual and economic rights and liabilities of the parties to a credit card transaction are

---

[18] *See* Saul Hansell, *New Security System for Internet Purchases has its Doubters*, N.Y. Times, Nov. 24, 1997, at D1 (noting several burdens that SET® places on electronic commerce, including delay, increased costs, and cumbersome processes). According to one commentator, SET® is "so slow it will lead to the electronic equivalent of arterial sclerosis." *Id.* (quoting Gary S. Roboff, senior vice president of the Chase Manhattan Bank). *See also* Burnham, *supra* note 16, at 68-69 (labeling the time delays involved in the encryption and decryption process as "latency," while noting that most people using the Internet are used to delays and will probably attribute the delayed processing to inherent problems in the structure of the Internet).

[19] The initial developers of SET® viewed the consumer-to-business credit card payments as the primary market niche and focused the development of SET® on that market rather than addressing business-to-business corporate credit card purchases. SET® is currently being upgraded to include business-to-business transactions as well as integrating its encryption processes for ACH debit transactions. *See* Kelly Jackson Higgins, *Getting SET*, Internet Wk., Oct. 20, 1997, at 83.

frequently based upon whether there is a writing and a properly verified signature of the cardholder giving rise to the cardholder's contractual obligation to pay.[20]

The issue of whether the electronic transmission of credit card information constitutes a writing and whether a digital signature contractually binds a cardholder will play an important role in allocating liability in the case of purportedly unauthorized transactions.[21] Under most circumstances, consumer liability for the unauthorized use of a credit card may not exceed fifty dollars.[22] The card issuer bears the burden of proving that the cardholder authorized the credit card transaction, and typically proves this by requiring the merchant to supply a copy of its paper charge slip with the cardholder's signature.[23] Unlike a consumer's repudiation of credit card transactions that occur over the phone where the merchant is unable to provide a written signature, merchants participating in SET® transactions will have the benefit of an authenticated digital signature as proof of the transaction.

§ 15.03 IVT SYSTEMS UTILIZING DEPOSIT AND ASSET ACCOUNTS VIA ELECTRONIC CHECKS AND ACH TRANSFERS

American businesses and consumers currently write approximately sixty-four billion checks per year in payment for goods and services.[24] As described in Chapter 4, a drawer writes a check ordering its depository institution to pay a particular sum of money to a payee.[25] The payee accepts and then deposits the check into the payee's depository financial institution ("PDFI") and receives provisional credit from the PDFI pending payment by the drawer's depository financial institution ("DDFI"). The settlement process requires the PDFI to present the check to the DDFI. The manual labor associated with the transportation and processing of billions of paper checks each year places a burden on the banking industry that it would like to reduce or eliminate. The banking industry is now looking eagerly to advances in electronic technology as a means to reduce costs and improve the efficiency and accuracy of the check payments system.[26] Though Interbank Check Imaging, described in Chapter 4, is expected to yield significant cost savings through the digitization of paper checks,

---

[20] *See* Henry H. Perritt, Jr., *Legal and Technological Infrastructures for Electronic Payment Systems*, 22 RUTGERS COMPUTER & TECH. L. J. 1, 20-28 (1996) (discussing credit card processing and the legal implications of Internet transactions).

[21] *See, e.g.,* FLA. STAT. ANN. §§ 282.70 *et seq.* (giving electronic signatures legal force and effect); UTAH CODE ANN. §§ 46-3-201 *et seq.* (describing the role of certification authorities under Utah law); VA. CODE ANN. §§ 59.1-467 *et seq.* (providing bases for authentication of digital signatures). *See generally* 12 C.F.R. § 226.12; DS Guidelines, *supra* note 16.

[22] 15 U.S.C. § 1643(a)(1)(B).

[23] *Id.* § 1643(b).

[24] *See* COMM. ON THE FED. RESERVE IN THE PAYMENTS MECHANISM, FEDERAL RESERVE SYSTEM, THE FEDERAL RESERVE IN THE PAYMENTS MECHANISM 12 (Jan. 1998) (describing the Federal Reserve System's role in the check presentment and clearing system and its view of electronic check presentment and imaging) [hereinafter THE FEDERAL RESERVE IN THE PAYMENTS MECHANISM].

[25] *See generally* U.C.C. § 3-104.

[26] Booz, Allen & Hamilton performed a study that estimated that an Internet transaction will cost approximately $.01 to process, versus $1.07 for a bank teller transaction, $.85 for a staffed call center transaction, $.44 for an automated call center transaction and $.27 for an ATM transaction. BOOZ-ALLEN & HAMILTON, INTERNET BANKING: A SURVEY OF CURRENT AND FUTURE DEVELOPMENTS, at III-3F (1996). *See also* CS First Boston, *Banking in the Information Age, An Investor's Guide to the Impact of Technology on Financial Services and the Payments System*, Nov. 14, 1996, at 30.

electronic checks may offer a means to complete the dematerialization of paper checks into electronic form.[27]

[1] ELECTRONIC CHECKS

"Electronic checks" are a recent initiative by one segment of the banking industry in an effort to dematerialize paper checks in favor of electronic payments. The electronic check is still in the early development and pilot testing phases, and thus, the following discussion is necessarily preliminary and generic in nature.[28] An electronic check is a specially formatted e-mail message sent over the Internet. The message contains the same information carried on a paper check, such as the identity of the drawer, recipient, amount, account number, bank transfer number, and date. Instead of a handwritten signature, it includes a digital signature with the message. Electronic checks contain additional data fields that allow drawers to attach lengthy memoranda. In addition, the time of payment and other information may be included depending on the versatility of the bank's electronic check system.[29] The drawer's use of an electronic check to pay debts varies depending on the design of the bank's electronic check payment system. Electronic check payment systems may incorporate a variety of payment procedures for drawers. Some basic electronic check models include: (1) a traditional check payment flow; (2) cash and transfer; (3) lockbox arrangements; and (4) electronic bill presentment.

In the check payment flow transaction, upon either electronic receipt of a bill or invoice from a creditor, the review of the bill on the creditor's website, or otherwise, the drawer creates an electronic check with PC based payments software. This software encrypts the electronic check, digitally signs it, attaches a digital certificate provided by the drawer's institution or other certificate authority ("CA"), and transmits it over the Internet to the intended recipient. The digital certificate represents a CA's certification of the validity of the drawer's digital signature.[30] Upon receipt of the electronic check, the payee's software verifies the digital signature of the drawer and the authenticity of the accompanying digital certificate prior to depositing the

---

[27] *See* FRIED FRANK, THE MANAGEMENT OF IVT RISKS, *supra* note 5, at 21-24 (describing the transactions involving deposit/asset accounts).

[28] The term "electronic check" has been used in a variety of contexts ranging from the transmission of the digital image of a paper check, the transmission of debit payment information from a point of sale terminal, and, as used in this Section, the transmission of a specially formatted e-mail message created by a PC software application designed to be the functional equivalent of the paper check. *See generally Electronic Check Project Details,* Financial Services Technology Consortium, *available at* <http://fstc.org/projects/echeck/echeck2.html> (generally describing the proposed electronic check system, its benefits, business model, architecture, and technological components). *See also* Letter from Julie Williams, Chief Counsel, Office of the Comptroller of the Currency, to Stanley F. Farrar, Esq. at 17 (Jan. 12, 1998), *available at* <http://www.occ.treas.gov/ftp/release/98-4.txt>; Task Force on Stored-Value Cards, Am. Bar Ass'n, *A Commercial Lawyer's Take on the Electronic Purse: An Analysis of Commercial Law Issues Associated with Stored-Value Cards and Electronic Money,* 52 BUS. LAW. 653, 663 (1997); John Doggett, *Electronic Checks - a Detailed Preview,* J. OF RETAIL BANKING, June 22, 1996, at 1 (describing the technical process, characteristics, and the benefits and disadvantages of electronic checks).

[29] *See generally* PETER WAYNER, DIGITAL CASH: COMMERCE ON THE NET (1996).

[30] *See generally* Philip S. Corwin, *Administration Entangles Digital Signatures with Encryption Policy,* BANKING POL'Y REP., Apr. 21, 1997, at 1; Keywitness Canada, *Role of the Certificate Authority, available at* <http://www.keywitness.ca/english/role.htm>.

electronic check into the payee's PDFI. The PDFI initiates an automated clearing house ("ACH") debit for clearing and settlement of the electronic check.[31] This check flow scenario mirrors the typical paper check transaction flow. Electronic check software applications, however, have the versatility to provide alternative methods of fund transfer.

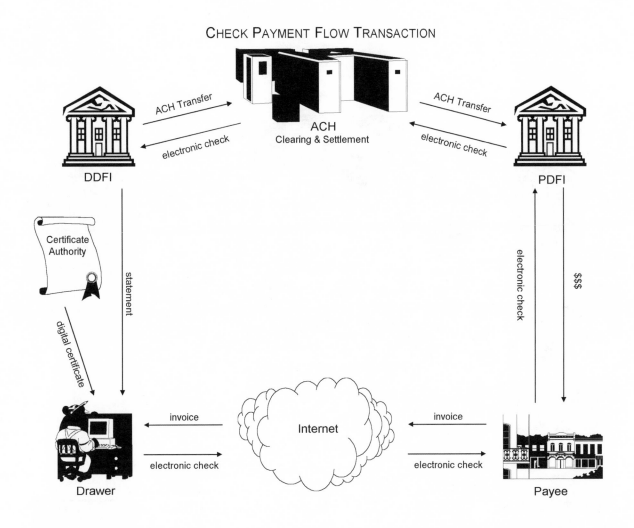

CHECK PAYMENT FLOW TRANSACTION

---

[31]   *See* BURNHAM, *supra* note 16, at 106-07 (describing the electronic check process).

The cash and transfer method departs from the transaction flow associated with a typical check present-ment and clearing process. In a cash and transfer transaction, the drawer receives a bill or invoice from its creditor and sends an electronic check by transmitting it to the creditor. The creditor then presents the electronic check via the Internet directly to the DDFI. The DDFI may transfer funds from the drawer's account to the creditor's account at the PDFI via an electronic fund transfer through the ACH Network.

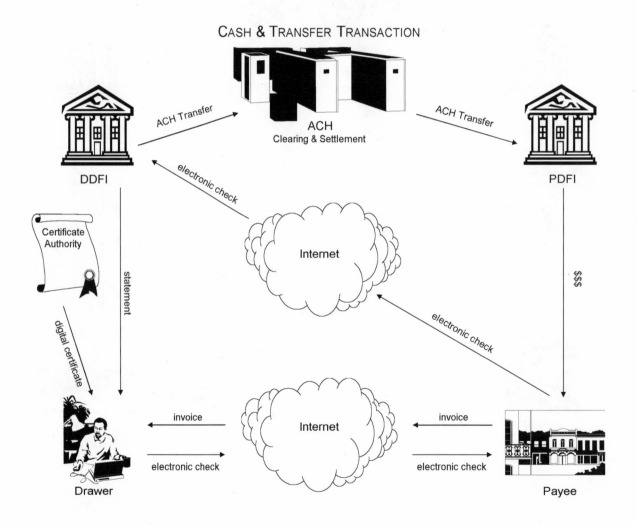

CASH & TRANSFER TRANSACTION

A lockbox arrangement permits the drawer to transmit the electronic check to a creditor's PDFI via a "lockbox" located on the PDFI's server. As used currently, a lockbox is a cash management system whereby a creditor's customers mail payments to a specified post office near the creditor's PDFI. The PDFI collects the paper checks from the lockbox, deposits them into the creditor's account, generally for a fee, and transmits the accounts receivable information to the creditor. As discussed below in Section 15.03[2][b], faster deposit of incoming checks minimizes the drawer's float and puts the cash to work more quickly for the payee. In the electronic check environment, the post office is eliminated and the electronic check is sent directly to the PDFI. The PDFI sends the electronic check to the DDFI for clearance and settlement without the creditor's endorsement, and then electronically transmits the relevant accounts receivable information to the creditor.

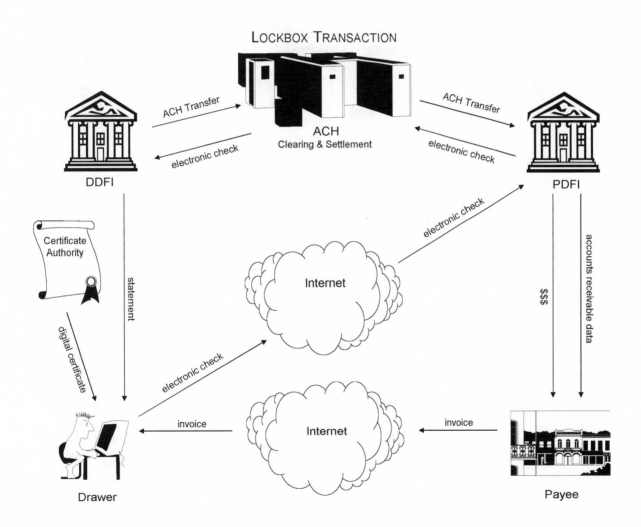

A DDFI may set up an electronic bill presentment feature. In this arrangement, a creditor electronically forwards its invoices to a DDFI, which, in turn, transmits the invoices individually to its customers or posts them on a password-accessible website. The customer transmits an electronic check to the DDFI. That DDFI then transfers funds to the creditor's account at its PDFI.

DRAWER BANK BILL PRESENTMENT AND PAYMENT PROCESSING

Alternatively, a PDFI may provide an electronic bill presentment system. In this scenario, a creditor electronically forwards its billing information to the PDFI, which, in turn, transmits the invoices individually to the creditor's customers or posts them on a password-accessible website. The customer transmits an electronic check to the PDFI. The PDFI then presents the electronic check to the DDFI for payment. Electronic bill presentment and payment processing is examined further in Section 15.04. In addition to the variety of electronic check transfer methods available, other advantages of electronic checks relative to their paper-based counterparts include greater security, speed, and ease of processing.

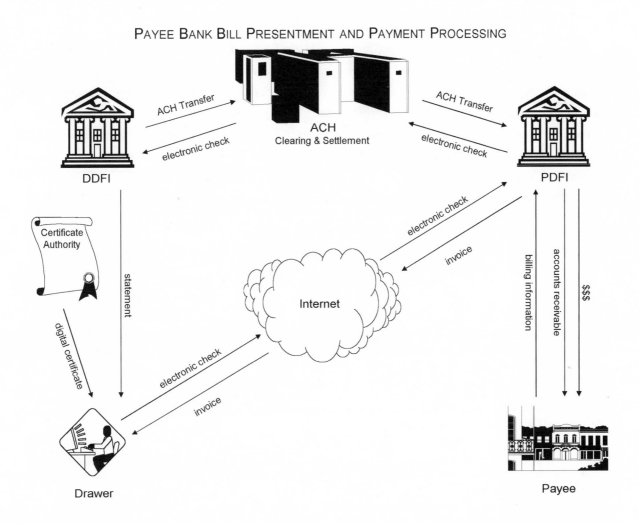

PAYEE BANK BILL PRESENTMENT AND PAYMENT PROCESSING

[a] Electronic Check Fraud Issues. The law governing the use of paper checks as a payment vehicle is well-established. State laws define the rights and liabilities between the parties to a check transaction, and the rights and liabilities between a bank and its customers.[32] These rights and liabilities generally depend on the existence of a statutory writing and a valid drawer signature giving rise to the statutory remedies for the payee of a paper check.[33] As in many other legal questions in electronic commerce, the issue of how an electronic transmission will be treated under current law, which typically is designed to accommodate physical transactions, is critical to whether a new non-physical system can function under such laws. It is well settled that paper checks are susceptible to fraud in a variety of ways, including the risks associated with the unauthorized use of the drawer's signature and the unauthorized alteration of information on a check. Electronic checks have their own unique set of fraud risks.[34] One risk inherent in many electronic payment systems is the unauthorized use of the consumer's PC to effectuate transactions.

[i] Unauthorized Use of a Digital Signature on an Electronic Check. Electronic checks present significant, and as yet unresolved, liability issues. Customers, whether individuals or corporate treasurers, must treat the computer systems that generate electronic checks and digital signatures in a secure manner. Unauthorized access to a customer's PC may place the customer at risk for losses resulting from the unauthorized use of the customer's electronic checks. Unlike a forged paper check that can be identified by handwriting experts, an unauthorized electronic check will be digitally identical to one validly issued by the customer. Under U.C.C. Article 3, a bank generally bears the risk of loss for paying on a forged paper check, although a bank has the right to seek recourse against the forger, if the forger is identified.[35]

---

[32] *See generally* U.C.C. Article 3 (governing the check transaction); U.C.C. Article 4 (governing the relationship between a bank and its customer).

[33] The U.C.C. definition of "writing" requires reduction to a tangible form. U.C.C. § 1-201(46). *See also* U.C.C. §§ 1-201(43), 3-404, 4-406 (provisions regarding "signatures").

[34] *See* U.C.C. § 3-407(2)(a) (discharging the drawer from the full amount of a debt owed, when the payor fraudulently alters the payment terms of a paper check). It remains to be seen whether such a sweeping statutory protection for drawers will apply to electronic checks. Without an adequate legal framework governing electronic checks, the parties sending, receiving, and clearing electronic checks will largely rely on contracts to define the rights and liabilities of the parties in the interim.

[35] U.C.C. Article 3 provides, in relevant part:

> Any unauthorized signature is wholly inoperative as that of the person whose name is signed unless he ratifies it or is precluded from denying it; but it operates as the signature of the unauthorized signer in favor of any person who in good faith pays the instrument or takes it for value.

U.C.C. § 3-404. In other words, as a general matter, the forger is liable to the bank for forging the signature and the bank is liable to the drawer for paying funds from the customer's account on an instrument that the customer did not sign. However, the U.C.C. provides an exception where the customer is negligent, that may be applied when the customer's negligence results in unauthorized access to the PC and digital signature of the customer:

> Any person who by his negligence substantially contributes to a material alteration of the instrument or to the making of an unauthorized signature is precluded from asserting the alteration or lack of authority against a holder in due course or against a drawee or other payor who pays the instrument in good faith and in accordance with the reasonable commercial standards of the drawee's or payor's business.

U.C.C. § 3-406.

It is unclear, however, how the allocation of liability would be assessed in the case of an unauthorized use of a digital signature.[36]

[b] Electronic Check Processing Speed and the Reduction in Float. The speed of electronic check transfers may reduce the float associated with the processing of paper checks. This Section examines the treatment of float in the Federal Reserve System, then discusses the manner in which float benefits debtors. Float is money that appears simultaneously in the accounts of two depository institutions or in the accounts of both a debtor and a creditor.

[i] Float and Check Clearing in the Federal Reserve System. Funds that are in the process of collection may appear simultaneously in customer accounts at both the institution that receives the checks for deposit and the institution upon which the checks are drawn. This occurs when check clearing is delayed, and causes the amount of money in the banking system to be temporarily inflated. When a bank receives a check for deposit, it credits the account of the check depositor on a provisional basis, and then collects the funds from the drawer's financial institution.[37] PDFIs transfer many checks to their district Federal Reserve Bank for collection, rather than independently sorting every deposited check and presenting individual checks to the particular institution for settlement.

When a Federal Reserve Bank receives checks from a bank, it credits the bank's reserve account for the funds deposited according to a pre-arranged funds availability schedule, which is based, in part, on the location of the Federal Reserve Bank relative to the depositing bank. Banks receive credit for checks depending on the time it normally takes to process and present the check to the bank upon which it was drawn. A Federal Reserve Bank gives credit for most checks the next business day. For all other checks, credit is generally given within two days. The Federal Reserve does not debit the DDFI's reserve account until it presents the check to the DDFI.[38]

[ii] Float in the Realm of Debtors and Creditors. Customers enjoy float when they pay by paper check. When the merchant receives a customer's payment, that customer's debt is extinguished.[39] The merchant removes the customer's account receivable from its books and enters the increase in cash in its ledger. The merchant does not, however, begin to earn interest on the funds associated with the check until it deposits the check into its checking account. Even then, the merchant must wait one to seven days before the merchant has

---

[36]   *See generally* C. Bradford Biddle, *Misplaced Priorities: The Utah Digital Signature Act and Liability Allocation in a Public Key Infrastructure*, 33 SAN DIEGO L. REV. 1143, 1167-86 (1996) (discussing the allocation of liability for the unauthorized use of a digital signature under the Utah digital signature statute and the potential preemption of the Utah statute by application of the Electronic Fund Transfer Act ("EFTA")); Richard L. Field, *The Electronic Future of Cash: Survey: 1996: Survey of the Year's Developments in Electronic Cash Law and the Laws Affecting Electronic Banking in the United States,* 46 AM. U.L. REV. 967 (1997); U.C.C. § 4-406 (1991) (describing bank customers' obligation to report unauthorized signatures). *See also* U.C.C. Article 4A (governing electronic fund transfers, but specifically excluding consumer transactions governed by the EFTA. U.C.C. § 4A-108). The EFTA may provide the liability rules for electronic checks. *See* 15 U.S.C. §§ 1693-1693r.

[37]   U.C.C. §§ 4-201, 4-215.

[38]   *See* BOARD OF GOVERNORS OF THE FEDERAL RESERVE SYSTEM, THE FEDERAL RESERVE SYSTEM: PURPOSES AND FUNCTIONS 38, 99-102, 117-18 (8th ed. 1994) [hereinafter THE FEDERAL RESERVE SYSTEM].

[39]   *See* U.C.C. § 2-511 cmts. 4-5.

access to those funds.[40] The customer on the other hand still has the funds in its account until the Federal Reserve Bank presents the check to the customer's DDFI. The float associated with the delayed deposit and the subsequent settlement and clearing of paper checks may be eliminated, or substantially reduced, by the speed of electronic check transfer and electronic settlement.

Customers using electronic checks may no longer state that "the check is in the mail" and thereafter enjoy a three-day respite from a creditor demanding payment. By integrating an electronic payment system with its depository institution, a creditor can assure itself that the customer's funds have been deposited into the creditor's institution promptly upon receipt of the payment made over the Internet. Electronic check and fund transmission may be instantaneous (particularly if electronic money or stored value is used), same day, or next day depending on the services offered by the creditor's financial institution and expected technological enhancements to the ACH Network. Customers may, however, insist on receiving the benefit of float as a pre-condition to their use of electronic checks. As illustrated in Section 15.04, creditors may completely automate their billing services by using the Internet to gain immediate access to incoming receivables.

The use of electronic checks could eliminate the manual handling associated with the processing of paper checks. A computer processes, sorts, and stores electronic checks and simultaneously transmits the essential payment data into the clearing and settlement system. This reduces not only the transportation and handling costs but also largely eliminates human error from the process. If the payment system is adapted to permit instantaneous transfer of funds once an electronic check clears, the settlement and clearing of electronic checks could occur quite rapidly following deposit. The process by which electronic checks will be integrated into the existing bank payments infrastructure is the focus of the FSTC's Bank Internet Payments System project, which is discussed in the next Section.[41] Direct presentment of electronic checks, bypassing the check clearing system is possible, however, payment must still be made through the Federal Reserve or ACH Network.

[2] BANK INTERNET PAYMENTS SYSTEM

In 1997, a consortium of U.S. banks, technology firms, government agencies, and industry organizations established the Bank Internet Payments System ("BIPS") project.[42] This project culminated in the creation of specifications for the design of a secure server that would act as a conduit connecting the Internet to bank information systems and to the wholesale and retail payment networks. Until BIPS is deployed, Financial Electronic Data Interchange ("FEDI") will continue to provide corporations with electronic access to financial institutions. FEDI is a complex electronic translator that enables corporations to electronically transfer payment instructions and financial information in corporate documents to financial institutions. In the initial versions, BIPS secure servers will ease access for corporations to the wholesale and retail payment networks. Future

---

[40] 12 U.S.C. § 4002.

[41] *See* Charles Davis, *Payments: the Final Countdown*, ELECTRONIC PAYMENTS INT'L, Apr. 1997, at 12 (discussing future changes in the ACH network).

[42] *The Bank Internet Payment System (BIPS): Leading the Way to Electronic Commerce, available at* (visited Nov. 17, 1997) <http://www.fstc.org/projects/bips/index.html>.

versions will enable consumers to access banking networks for electronic check transactions and stored value transfers via the Internet.

BIPS is a set of access specifications for connecting to the bank payment systems infrastructure from the Internet. BIPS servers must comply with uniform messaging standards, such as OFX Wizard™ and Integrion™ Gold, which are described in Chapter 14. These standards create an accessible and open transfer and messaging system. The open nature of BIPS specifications permits any vendor to design the front-end computer servers that will access the bank payments system using any messaging standard.[43] Banks may lease or purchase these servers to provide their customers with transaction services via the Internet.

When integrating BIPS secure servers with the bank, vendors must safeguard the integrity of the bank's internal systems. Surrounding the BIPS server with a secure design will help protect the bank's internal systems from hackers. A server with proper security permits payment instructions initiated over public networks to travel safely to the BIPS server. The BIPS standard interface relays these instructions to the existing bank payment systems. The standard interface guarantees that bank information systems may exchange data with any vendor's system. This interoperability allows for the transmission of information to the bank's closed network from the Internet's open network. Until BIPS is fully deployed, corporations will have to continue using FEDI and EDI to communicate with each other and with financial institutions.

[a] Electronic Data Interchange. Electronic Data Interchange ("EDI") is the electronic transfer of business documents between corporate trading partners based on an agreed upon process.[44] This agreement details the use of messaging standards, the exchange of information, the use of a Value Added Network ("VAN"), and the schedule for the transfer of information. EDI relies on computer translators that reformat documents, such as invoices, remittance advices, purchase orders, and shipping notices, into the agreed upon EDI standard.[45] The translator places the EDI document into an envelope and places the receiving corporate trading partner's ID on the envelope. This envelope remains in an electronic mailbox pending retrieval by the receiving trading partner. The receiving trading partner's computer establishes a modem connection to the VAN that connects to the receiving trading partner's electronic mailbox in the sending trading partner's computer. The EDI translator opens the EDI document into a format read by the receiving trading partner's computer application. The computer application reads the EDI information and executes a series of preprogrammed operations. For example, if the EDI document is an invoice, the receiving trading partner's computer will automatically open the receiving trading partner's financial books and increase accounts payable to reflect the debt. Thereafter,

---

[43]   *See* Steven Marjanovic, *Group Will Test Linking Companies, Payment System Through the Internet*, AM. BANKER, July 1, 1997, at 17.

[44]   An agreement governing the enforceability of electronic transactions provides the legal certainty required to perform business transactions in the sale of goods. The sale of goods is governed by Article 2 of the Uniform Commercial Code, which provides that contracts for the sale of goods in excess of $500 are unenforceable unless evidenced by a writing sufficient to indicate that a contract exists between the parties. U.C.C. § 2-201(1). EDI agreements typically have a provision by which the parties specifically waive any defense based upon a claim that the electronic messages did not comply with the Statute of Frauds' writing and/or signature requirement. Electronic Messaging Services Task Force, *The Commercial Use of Electronic Data Interchange-A Report and Model Trading Partner Agreement*, 45 BUS. LAW. 1645, 1680 (1990).

[45]   Marc E. Szafran, Note, *A Neo-Institutional Paradigm For Contracts Formed in Cyberspace: Judgment Day For the Statute of Frauds*, 14 CARDOZO ARTS & ENT. L.J. 491 (1996).

the receiving trading partner's computer will decrease cash and accounts payable, and then, generate a paper check for payment of the invoice.[46]

Corporations in ongoing business relationships that transfer documents on a recurring basis can reduce costs with the efficient use of EDI. Efficiencies result from one-time data entry that initiates automated procedures for invoicing, accounting, shipping, and managing numerous aspects of a business. Once the data is entered, the system transfers the data to a corporate trading partner without intervention. EDI allows corporate trading partners to transfer data between different computer systems and applications. Thus, a corporation that uploads documents into its partner's mailbox by a wordprocessor may transfer the documents to its partner's spreadsheet software.

[b] Financial Electronic Data Interchange. Currently, corporate access to the wholesale and retail payment systems is through proprietary treasury management products supplied by banks. These products use FEDI, which enables automated transfer of payment and handling instructions for letters of credit, accounts receivable, accounts payable, and other payment functions. Each corporation must prearrange with its DDFI for the transfer of payment information via a specialized EDI translator that permits the transfer of payment information between corporate trading partners and financial institutions.[47]

A debtor corporation that receives an invoice via EDI may use a FEDI translator to process the payment information. The FEDI translator then communicates the payment information to the debtor's DDFI. The DDFI's server processes this information and initiates an ACH credit entry in favor of the debtor's trading partner. Though there are enormous savings and efficiencies to be gained by the use of EDI and FEDI, the savings and efficiencies are not necessarily available to smaller scale entities with non-recurring payments. For example, small to midsize government contractors may submit paper invoices to the government for payment processing. The Treasury Department inputs the invoice data for purposes of an electronic fund transfer and electronically transmits the remittance information to the contractor's PDFI. The PDFI, in turn, uses its FEDI translator to reconstruct the remittance information and payment data onto a paper printout to be sent to the government contractor. Banks are looking to the Internet to provide these same cost savings and efficiencies to all payment transactions by the use of BIPS.

[c] BIPS Transactions. BIPS will expand corporate access to the bank payment systems through software for the Internet, including third-party bill payment and bill presentment software. BIPS specifications will permit technology vendors to create software that provides corporations with the freedom to choose among the different payment vehicles. Each payment vehicle will provide settlement at different speeds and costs.[48]

---

[46] *See What is EDI?, available at* (visited Nov. 5, 1997) <http://www.phxcon.com/whatis.htm>.

[47] *See generally* ABA ("Bar"), *Model Electronic Payments Agreement and Commentary* 32 (1992); Bankers EDI Council, *Corporate Financial EDI User Guide* (1995). For further discussion of FEDI, see Chapter 10, Section 10.07[1].

[48] *See* Steven Marlin, *Internet: Bank Group Plans Web-based Solution,* BANK SYS. + TECH, Sept. 1997, at 9, *available at* (visited Jan. 23, 1998) <http://www.financetech.com/banktech/homepage.htm>.

BIPS secure servers will allow contracting parties with access to multiple bank payments systems to agree on payment terms and payment vehicles. BIPS technology provides the capacity to permit customers and banks to choose the most cost-effective payments system for the drawer based on its requirements for speed of settlement.[49]

In the first BIPS pilot tests, financial institutions will set up debit authorization accounts for corporate participants. BIPS secure servers will provide corporate participants with access to invoices posted on the Web or sent via e-mail. To pay an invoice, a corporation will initiate a payment authorization via the Internet to its bank's secure server. The BIPS secure server will provide online authentication of the drawer and payee. Then, the BIPS secure server will convert this payment request into an ACH debit to transfer funds from the corporation's DDFI account to the payee's PDFI account. Immediately, the BIPS secure server will instruct the bank's information systems to execute an electronic fund transfer to the payee's PDFI. Eventually, all consumers and businesses may be able to use BIPS to send payment instructions via the Internet, including retail ATM transactions by consumers.

[d] BIPS Pilots. The initial BIPS pilot test occurred in late 1997 demonstrating the "push model" in which Glenview (Ill.) State Bank designed a BIPS secure server that interfaced with the Internet. Cummins-Allison Corp., a manufacturer of bank and business hardware products and the parent corporation of Glenview Bank, sent an electronic request to Glenview to distribute dividends to Cummins-Allison's shareholders. The request contained information about all the necessary payments to be made and Glenview's BIPS server converted that information into multiple ACH funds transfers to the shareholders.[50] Another test of the BIPS system will occur between Mellon Bank and Pennsylvania Power and Light demonstrating the "pull model." The server will route the payment instructions to the Mellon's back-end information systems which will translate the instructions into an ACH debit transaction.

BIPS will allow corporations to issue ACH debit instructions to the BIPS secure server to retrieve payments from customers. The BIPS secure server processes the debit instructions and verifies the parties to the transactions using public keys and digital certificates. This process is known as the "pull model," because the party initiating the transaction issues an ACH debit that "pulls funds away from" the other party. In the "push" model, the initiating corporation will issue ACH credits via an Internet interface to the bank's BIPS server that push funds toward its creditors or shareholders. The BIPS server instructs the bank's internal systems to execute a fund transfer from this corporation's account to its various payees. The pull model has yet to be demonstrated and must be properly implemented before BIPS can be fully deployed.[51]

BIPS software is easier to use than EDI because its online interface capability allows bank customers to initiate electronic payments from the Internet without knowing anything about EDI, the ACH Network, or the

---

[49] *Financial Services Technology Consortium Announces Formation of Bank Internet Payment System Project*, FSTC Press Release, June 18, 1997, *available at* <http://fstc.org/press/june18.html>.

[50] Steven Marjanovic, *FSTC Demonstrates Protocol for Internet Transfers*, AM. BANKER, Dec. 4, 1997, at 22.

[51] *Financial Services Technology Consortium Announces Formation of Bank Internet Payment System Project*, *supra* note 49.

payments system generally.[52] The BIPS server will prompt the user for its payment instructions and provide the necessary formatting of those instructions to initiate the payment.[53] In this manner, corporate billing departments may access the ACH Network directly without the complex instructions required for FEDI transfers. This automation of a corporate billing department will produce substantial cost savings to corporations, such as insurance companies, that have a substantial number of recurring receivables.

[3] LEGAL ISSUES REGARDING ELECTRONIC CHECKS

Until legislatures enact applicable statutes and regulatory bodies promulgate applicable regulations, the rights and responsibilities of the parties to an electronic check transaction may be defined largely by contract and association rules. In addition, judicial application and adaptation of principles that govern paper checks may be applied to disputes regarding electronic checks. Article 3 of the Uniform Commercial Code, which governs the transfer of negotiable instruments, including paper checks, may not apply to electronic check transactions because, by definition, Article 3 only applies to written instruments.[54] The Electronic Fund Transfer Act ("EFTA"),[55] Regulation E,[56] and Regulation CC[57] may apply to electronic checks, particularly in those instances where the drawer sends the check to a financial institution directly for payment to a creditor. Legal scholars, the banking industry, and legislatures are evaluating necessary modifications to the law governing negotiable instruments and the scope of the EFTA to address the technological advances affecting the payments system.[58]

§ 15.04 MERCHANT BILLING AND PAYMENT PROCESSING SYSTEMS

[1] INTRODUCTION

Electronic bill presentment and payment processing systems present a tremendous opportunity for merchants to obtain cost savings in both time and money spent on collecting and depositing payments into financial institutions. As described in Section 15.04[2], the market for electronic bill presentment and payment processing is still under development. However, the market has tremendous potential as our society changes from paper checks to electronic payment systems and as participants in the payments system increasingly acquire electronic transactional capabilities. Section 15.04[3] describes the capabilities and functions of bill

---

[52] Szafran, *supra* note 45.

[53] *Fed, Treasury Hound for EDI Lure, Government Mandate Prompts Industry Action,* EDI NEWS, Aug. 18, 1997.

[54] Under Article 3, a "negotiable instrument" is "an unconditional promise or order to pay a fixed amount of money." U.C.C. § 3-104(a). "Promise" and "order" require a "writing," which must be in tangible form. U.C.C. §§ 1-201(46), 3-103(a)(6), 3-103(a)(9).

[55] 15 U.S.C. §§ 1693-1693r.

[56] 12 C.F.R. pt. 205.

[57] 12 C.F.R. pt. 229.

[58] *See* Gregory E. Maggs, *New Payment Devices and General Principles of Payment Law,* 72 NOTRE DAME L. REV. 753 (1997); Catherine Lee Wilson, *Banking Law Symposium: Banking on the Net: Extending Bank Regulation to Electronic Money and Beyond,* 30 CREIGHTON L. REV. 671 (1997); NATIONAL CONFERENCE OF COMMISSIONERS ON UNIFORM STATE LAWS, DRAFT UNIFORM ELECTRONIC TRANSACTIONS ACT (Aug. 1997), *available at* (visited Jan. 22, 1998) <http://www.law.upenn.edu/library/ulc/uecicta/ect897.htm>.

presentment and payment processing software that enables merchants to increase marketing to their existing customer base while simultaneously obtaining feedback on customer preferences and complaints. Section 15.04[4] describes how the use of third party payment processors may loosen the relationship between merchants and their banks.

[2]   THE MARKET FOR ELECTRONIC BILL PRESENTMENT AND PAYMENT PROCESSING

The sixty-five billion checks written during 1997 accounted for 77% of all noncash payments, far outstripping the number of credit card, debit card, and ACH transactions combined.[59] The banking industry, technology firms, and government agencies are developing various technological solutions to decrease the use of this vast amount of paper. The essential ingredient to these solutions is a secure technological bridge between the Internet and the existing retail and wholesale payments network, one that will electronically link a merchant's back-end payment processing with its depository institution. As electronic bill presentment and electronic check transfer features are integrated into merchants' payment processing, the number of electronic payments by consumers and businesses will continue to rise. In 1996, the number of consumers paying bills electronically rose to 1.8 million from 800,000 in 1995, and that number was expected to rise to 3.5 million in 1997.[60] The growth of this market has spurred the development of nonbank payment processors.[61]

[a] **Third-Party and Bank Payment Processing.** In this burgeoning market for electronic processing of check payments, Checkfree Corporation has become a market leader, claiming to process 50% or more of electronic bill payments.[62] Currently, most payments initiated electronically are not processed electronically. More than two thirds of such payment orders are converted into paper checks because the payees and their PDFIs are not yet prepared to accept automated transactions. This situation should change due to a rule adopted by the National Automated Clearing House Association ("NACHA"), requiring that its member financial institutions with business accounts become EDI compliant by September 18, 1998.[63] EDI enables financial institutions to process transactions and payment information electronically through the retail and wholesale payments systems on behalf of their corporate customers. Because EDI provides for the transfer of any electronic data, including transactional information associated with the payment being processed, control over this information will dictate which participants will dominate the payments system.

---

[59] Drew Clark, *Wired Billing: The (Electronic) Check is Still in the Mail*, AM. BANKER, Aug. 13, 1997, at 22; Steven Marjanovic, *Nacha Targets $3B of Savings with Rule Changes*, AM. BANKER, Sept. 12, 1997, at 12. *See also* <http://www.nacha.org/resources/elec-payments/us-payments-96.gif> (showing that check transactions accounted for ten-thirteenths of all non-cash transactions in 1996).

[60] Clark, *supra* note 59, at 22 (citing to BURNHAM, *supra* note 16).

[61] *See* Davis, *supra* note 41 (quoting John McGann, the banking program manager of INPUT, a New York electronic commerce research firm, stating that "[t]oday, about 55 percent of global corporate banking business is still handled by paper. In 2001, over 95 percent of all banking transactions and message traffic will be electronic.").

[62] *See Online Resources: Integrating Financial Services*, EFT REP., Aug, 30, 1995. *See also* Checkfree's website at <http://www.checkfree.com>.

[63] Steve Marjanovic, *Nacha Rule to Make Banks Process EDI Payments in '98*, AM. BANKER, Oct. 24, 1997, at 3 (noting that NACHA® officials were prompted to adopt the rule in light of the 1996 electronic benefits transfer law mandating all federal payments be delivered electronically by 1999). See Chapter 17 for a detailed discussion of electronic benefits transfer.

MasterCard's Remittance Processing Service ("RPS"), which is utilized by 90% of consumer bill payment services, serves as an example of back-end payment processing.[64] RPS is a network of interbank payment connections that serve as a pipeline for the transmission of payment instructions and related information. Third party payment processors, such as Checkfree, rely on RPS and the Federal Reserve to relay electronic remittances to merchants and merchants' banks.[65]

[3] ELECTRONIC BILLING AND PAYMENT PROCESSING SYSTEMS

The automation of a merchant's billing and payment processing should not only save time and money, but also may enable merchants to increase marketing to their existing customer base while simultaneously obtaining feedback on customer preferences and complaints. Financial institutions and technology vendors can integrate a merchant's billing and payment processing system with its marketing, promotions, online order capabilities, and customer feedback forms into one full service website. A merchant's website can be configured to post invoices and monthly billing statements for customer access, review, and payment. A website can enable customers to e-mail questions or concerns to the merchant. Interactive bill presentment and payment features provide customers with better service and potentially customized billing services to enhance customer relationships.

Financial institutions and technology vendors are encouraging Internet merchants and billers to accept electronic payments directly on their websites. Electronic bill presentment permits merchants to reinforce their customer relationships through interactive billing websites. Online billing and payment processing can deepen the customer relationship with cross-selling opportunities via advertisements on the merchant's web page. Electronic bill presentment and payment also allows merchants to offer services to their customers while simultaneously permitting merchants to reduce back-end processing costs associated with the receipt of invoices and paper checks. A more sophisticated website could analyze a particular customer's transaction history to determine whether to offer one or more products at a reduced price to induce the customer to purchase products while paying bills online. Merchants can create what appear to be personalized communications with individual customers through electronic advertisements presenting products and services for sale or high-lighting upcoming product offerings based on a customer's buying history. Financial institutions can assist their corporate customers in evaluating, selecting, and implementing a system that reduces back-end processing costs while maximizing the corporation's relationship with its customers.[66]

Technology vendors provide several "storebuilder" applications that facilitate a merchant's design of its website. Storebuilder software integrates bill presentment and payment processing with product presentation, order and purchase processing, product fulfillment and distribution, and secure financial transactions, all on a

---

[64] Clark, *supra* note 59, at 22.

[65] *See* <http://www.checkfree.com/products/abt/faq.html>.

[66] Price Waterhouse, *Price Waterhouse and CyberCash Form Agreement to Provide Internet Currency Solutions*, M2 PRESSWIRE, July 25, 1997 (stating that "Price Waterhouse will provide financial institutions and their billers with advisory services for evaluating their electronic currency options and identify a solution that positions the financial institution for the commercial marketplace of the future").

real-time basis. The software supports a customer's choice of payment method and allows Internet merchants to receive instant and secure online payments. Such software will enhance a merchant's flexibility to deliver goods depending on the payment options provided to the merchant's customer base. A merchant's website, with its integrated financial software, assumes the role of a completely automated point-of-sale system for Internet transactions. The software supports secure links over the Internet to the existing electronic payment infrastructure of banks and payment processors. Furthermore, the software should provide back office functions to manage transactions, accounts, inventory and all other aspects of the merchant's cash cycle. The merchant should consider whether the software offers its customers an Internet commerce experience that is functionally comprehensive. The software should be able to be upgraded to implement leading technological developments. Finally, the electronic commerce system should have the scalability to meet increasing demand.[67] The continued globalization of many corporations with large customer bases requires the use of computers with large data storage capacity and fast processing capability to service the corporation's worldwide customers. This technology holds the prospect of enabling merchants to increase revenues, decrease costs, and enhance their customer service by providing high quality products and services to their worldwide distributors, resellers, suppliers, and customers year round.[68]

[4]   WHO PROCESSES THE TRANSACTION: BANKS OR NONBANKS?

As one observer has noted, "electronic bankers view money transfers, clearing and settlement as a key source of fee income and the last line of defense in the battle against nonbank competitors."[69] Some financial institutions offer financial software to merchants to maintain their books and communicate payment data directly to financial institutions. However, of the 5000 banks receiving EDI messages, only 1200 banks are able to use the EDI message content.[70] Beyond posting the transaction, most banks are unable to use any of the remaining remittance information.[71] If merchants find that third party technology vendors are better equipped than banks to meet the need for bill presentment and payment processing, the banking industry may suffer another attenuation of its relationship with its traditional commercial customer base.[72]

Nonbank technology vendors are quickly becoming intermediaries for electronic payment processing services on behalf of merchants and other billers. In the face of this competition, banks should consider whether and how to position themselves to compete for this business. Otherwise, the lost opportunity to process the information contained in thousands of transactions may leave banks in the role of a back-end processor of

---

[67]   Scalability is the ability of a computer system to incrementally increase in its capacity in proportion to increases in demands upon that capacity.

[68]   *InterWorld Adds Secure, Real-Time Payment Transaction Technology to its Leading Internet Commerce System*, PR NEWSWIRE, Aug. 25, 1997.

[69]   Davis, *supra* note 41, at 12. "The last great area of banking control is the payments system, particularly the wholesale clearing and settlement system." *Id.* (quoting Thomas P. Vartanian).

[70]   *Id.* (quoting Bob Allen, Vice-President of the Federal Reserve Bank of Kansas City and Chairman of the Federal Reserve's EDI task force).

[71]   *Id.* (citing Bob Allen).

[72]   *See* Thomas P. Vartanian, *Technology's Silver Lining and Banking's Dark Clouds*, AM. BANKER - FUTURE BANKING, Mar. 18, 1996, at 1.

Internet payment instructions.[73] Banks appreciate this threat because they have already lost such opportunities and control in other areas, such as the processing of point of sale and ATM transactions. Banks can place themselves in the middle of the electronic commerce equation by leveraging their existing reputation for trust and confidence and their relationships with depositors and borrowers.

§ 15.05 THIRD-PARTY IVT SYSTEMS

Nonbanks have become active in developing payment systems for Internet commerce by establishing agency accounts and notational currency for Internet transactions. Rather than creating stored value, these nonbanks have developed payment systems that allow customers to transfer funds to the nonbank that holds the funds pending payment instructions to pay a merchant. Two entities, First Virtual Holding Company and CyberCash™ Inc. have created this type of payments system.[74]

[1] FIRST VIRTUAL AND VIRTUALPINS®

One of the earliest Internet payment systems established for the purchase of digital information such as newsletters, software, or other documents was designed by First Virtual Holding Company ("First Virtual").[75] The First Virtual system, as described in its website, uses an e-mail system to transfer payment instructions without requiring checking or credit card account information to accompany the e-mail. To use First Virtual's system, both parties to the transaction must have accounts at First Virtual.[76] A First Virtual consumer pre-establishes an information profile with First Virtual by providing name, both e-mail and residential addresses, telephone number, and choice of a Personal Identification Number ("PIN"). The consumer supplies this information via e-mail and thereafter receives an e-mail message from First Virtual containing an application number and instructions to call First Virtual's toll free number. To protect the consumer, credit card information is supplied over the telephone to First Virtual rather than through the Internet. After processing this information and charging an account fee, First Virtual issues a VirtualPIN® via e-mail to its consumers.

A VirtualPIN® is an alias for the consumer that permits First Virtual to access the consumer's account information. The alias contains a prefix of letters or numbers and a hyphen prior to the consumer's chosen PIN to ensure the uniqueness of the VirtualPIN®, used for consumer purchases from First Virtual merchants. A merchant sets up a First Virtual seller's account by paying a fee by paper check to First Virtual. First Virtual

---

[73] *Smoke Signals Surround Microsoft, WebTV Deal*, 2 RETAIL DELIVERY SYS. NEWS, Apr. 11, 1997 (describing Microsoft's planned purchase of WebTV and the implication that Microsoft will process payments to web merchants by incorporating smart card readers into consumer televisions, which will come bundled with Microsoft software such as Internet Explorer, Microsoft Money, and other products).

[74] *See* FRIED FRANK, THE MANAGEMENT OF IVT RISKS, *supra* note 5, at 29-32 (describing the transactions involving sub-deposit/asset accounts).

[75] The First Virtual Holdings Inc. website is located at <http://www.fv.com>.

[76] As of March 1997, FV had 3,300 participating merchants and 215,000 VirtualPINS® assigned to consumers. FV's partners, First Data Corp. and First USA Paymentech, have purchased 350,000 VirtualPINS® for distribution to consumers and 200 accounts for merchants respectively. Jennifer Kingson Bloom, *First Virtual's President Resigns; AT&T Exec. Takes Marketing Post*, AM. BANKER, June 16, 1997, at 1.

deposits the check and records the merchant's bank account number. First Virtual uses the bank account number for subsequent transfers of funds from the consumer's credit card account to the merchant's bank account.

Upon ordering an item, the consumer supplies a VirtualPIN® to the merchant. The merchant confirms the VirtualPIN® with First Virtual via e-mail. Consumers can remain anonymous because the merchant never receives any information regarding the consumer's identity. Of course, the merchant may require the consumer to supply identifying information on its order form. First Virtual sends an e-mail message to the consumer to confirm the purchase by supplying the seller's name, the consumer's name, the price and a description of the product. The consumer may respond "YES" to authorize the transaction, "NO" to cancel the purchase, or "FRAUD" to cancel the VirtualPIN®.

First Virtual merchants only sell digital goods and services. Unlike the purchase of a book in a bookstore, customers generally may not peruse information products on the Internet before making a purchase. The First Virtual system, however, permits consumers to receive the product, whether it is a piece of software, a newspaper article or report, before agreeing to pay. Following the receipt of digital products from a merchant, the customer may negate the transaction by responding "NO" to the confirmation sent by First Virtual. The First Virtual business model, thus, seeks to encourage purchases by providing a risk free opportunity to review a product. First Virtual protects participating merchants from abusive consumers who frequently disaffirm their orders by withdrawing the validity of an abusive consumer's VirtualPIN®.[77]

[2]   CYBERCASH, INC.

According to CyberCash's website, CyberCash provides three payment options for electronic commerce. Consumers may use their bank issued credit card with CyberCash merchants for higher value transactions. The CyberCoin® Service is available for micropayments. Finally, CyberCash's™ PayNow™ electronic checks provide for electronic fund transfers from the customer's checking account to the merchant's bank account. For the transfer of information, CyberCash relies on secure conduits created by Secure Sockets Layer ("SSL") or Secure HyperText Transfer Protocol ("S-HTTP").

To use the CyberCash payment system for online purchases, merchants may download the CyberCash CashRegister. This software is integrated with the merchant's Internet storefront. The CashRegister can accept payment via a variety of methods including SSL forms, customized payment methods, or existing Wallet software, such as the CyberCash Wallet, the Checkfree Wallet, and the Microsoft Wallet. Currently, the vast majority of transactions with CyberCash merchants occur through the transmission of consumer credit card data over an SSL link to a merchant, which, in turn, uses the CyberCash Register to transmit the credit card and payment information with the more secure CyberCash Cash Register. Essentially, the CyberCash CashRegister serves the same function as a POS terminal and connection used by merchants in the physical world.

---

[77]   For further description of FV's system, see WAYNER, *supra* note 29, ch. 6, at 85.

Consumers may also download the CyberCash™ Wallet software ("Wallet") from CyberCash or from participating CyberCash merchants. The Wallet interacts with the consumer's web browser. Upon activating the Wallet, the consumer is taken through a series of dialogs that obtain information from the consumer for future transactions. The Wallet secures this information in an encrypted file on the consumer's PC. The encryption process provides the consumer's PC with a private key to encrypt future payment instructions. CyberCash retains the public key for future decryption of consumer payment instructions.

[a] Credit Card Transactions with CyberCash. A consumer initiates a credit card transaction by transmitting an electronic order form to the merchant's website.[78] The transmission is customarily made through a web browser that supports SSL or S-HTTP security protocols. The merchant returns a summary of the order to the consumer including the selected item, price, shipping address, and order number for the consumer's verification. Upon approval, the consumer clicks on the Pay icon, activating the consumer's CyberCash™ Wallet. The Wallet encrypts the order and shipping data into one compartment and the payment data into another compartment. The Wallet attaches the sender's digital signature and then transmits the encrypted file to the merchant. Separate encryption of the payment data ensures that the merchant is unable to view the card-holder's credit card number. The CyberCash system permits the merchant to view only the shipping data when a customer uses Wallet software. The merchant uses its CyberCash CashRegister software to decrypt the ordering and shipping data and to transmit the encrypted payment data to CyberCash for decryption. CyberCash designed the system to place itself between the merchant and the credit card processing association to protect a consumer's payment data.

CyberCash decrypts and processes the payment data on its computers behind its Internet firewall. CyberCash then submits the payment data to the merchant's bank for credit card processing over the existing credit card processing network. The merchant bank transmits an authorization request to the card issuer for approval or denial. The card issuer transmits the approval or denial to the merchant bank, which transmits it to CyberCash, who then relays it to the merchant. The merchant issues a confirmation to the consumer and ships the goods or provides the online service as requested.

CyberCash intends to make its credit card payment option compliant with SET® technology.[79] The upgrade to SET® technology will permit CyberCash to authenticate the validity of the credit card and other consumer account information, a capability the current system does not offer.

[b] CyberCoin® Service. CyberCash has developed a "notational" IVT System permitting micropayments in the range between 25¢ and $10.00 to be made over the Internet.[80] To use the CyberCoins® Service, a consumer must link a checking account or credit card account to the consumer's CyberCash™ Wallet. The

---

[78] *See Six Steps of a Secure Internet Credit Card Payment, available at* (visited Oct. 17, 1997) <http://www.cybercash.com/cybercash/shoppers/shopsteps.html>.

[79] *See CyberCash SET Complete Payment Solution, available at* (visited Dec. 19, 1997) <http://www.cybercash.com>. *See also* Section 15.02[3].

[80] *See CyberCoin FAQ, available at* (visited Nov. 12, 1997) <http://a.dn.cybercash.com/cybercash/shoppers/coinfaq.html> (answers to frequently asked questions about CyberCoin® Service). See also Chapter 8, Section 8.05[1] describing Federal Deposit Insurance Corporation opinions regarding the treatment of the CyberCoin® Service for purposes of deposit insurance and deposit broker regulations.

consumer can use the Wallet to send an order to CyberCash to withdraw funds from the checking account or to charge the credit card currently limited to $20 increments. If the funds are charged to the consumer's credit card, they are immediately available for purchases. If the funds are to be withdrawn from the consumer's checking account, the consumer must wait three to seven days for processing of the electronic funds transfer.

The Wallet creates a record of the money transferred for use as "CyberCoins." "CyberCoins" are not stored value in the sense that the consumer does not download computer-coded value for the payment of goods and services that other token based systems rely on such as Mondex and Digicash. The Wallet merely makes a notational entry into the customer's transaction log that reflects the amount held by CyberCash for the customer in an agency account it maintains at an FDIC insured institution. When a consumer decides to buy goods from a merchant who accepts CyberCash payments and maintains an account with CyberCash, the customer clicks the "Pay" icon on the merchant's web page. This initiates the consumer's CyberCash™ Wallet software that issues payment instructions to CyberCash to transfer funds to the merchant's account with CyberCash. The Wallet records the reduction in the balance of the consumer's sub-account and keeps a log of all transactions.

[c] PayNow™ Secure Electronic Check Service. CyberCash has also developed its PayNow™ secure electronic check service to provide consumers and merchants with the ability to pay for goods and services over the Internet by electronic fund transfer.[81] A customer or merchant must register to use the PayNow™ service with a third party bill payment service.[82] After registering for the PayNow™ service, a consumer's checking account information is stored in an encrypted format in the CyberCash™ Wallet on the consumer's PC. The consumer accesses the merchant's website to pay a bill or to purchase goods with the PayNow™ Service. The consumer transmits a pre-assigned user ID and password to access the merchant billing account. The consumer clicks on the Pay button to pay a portion or entire amount of the balance. After entering the amount of the payment, the CyberCash™ Wallet prompts the consumer for another password. The consumer chooses the PayNow™ check option in the Wallet and confirms the payment instructions with the password. The Wallet transmits the payment instructions to CyberCash. CyberCash, working with the payment service, executes the transaction through the existing ACH Network by transferring funds electronically from the consumer's checking account to the billing party. PayNow™ checks may only be used to pay merchants who are currently registered with the CyberCash pilot. CyberCash intends to modify this service to permit person-to-person fund transfers via the PayNow™ check service.

Unlike the electronic check systems described in Section 15.03[2], PayNow™ is not a check. A customer's utilization of the PayNow™ check service is merely a consumer authorization to transfer funds electronically from the consumer's checking account to the merchant's checking account via the ACH Network. Unlike stored value systems, the consumer's funds remain in the consumer's FDIC-insured account

---

[81] *PayNow™ Secure Electronic Check Service Pilot Program Frequently Asked Questions, available at* (visited Nov. 1, 1997) <http://a.dn.cyber-cash.com/cybercash/paynow.html/paynowfaq.html> (noting that the PayNow™ pilot began in February 1997 and is presently available for use with a limited number of merchants and bill provider services).

[82] *See* Section 15.04.

CHAPTER 16

A NEW PAYMENT SYSTEM:
STORED VALUE/ELECTRONIC MONEY

§ 16.01   INTRODUCTION

Stored value ("SV") and electronic money systems raise a variety of unresolved legal and business issues.[1] As discussed below, attempts to fit SV into the current statutory and regulatory structure are, in many instances, like trying to place square pegs into round holes. Regulatory uncertainty has not, however, prevented banks and nonbanks from developing and marketing SV systems. Currently, a variety of SV systems in the United States either are being tested in initial pilot programs or are already underway in small scale operations. Although they share some common characteristics, many of these systems differ quite markedly in regard to their operational features and the business models involved.

The terms stored value and electronic money are frequently used to describe the same products or types of products. "Electronic money" may be considered a subset of SV products that allow multiple transfers among individuals without requiring the direct involvement of a third party, in a manner similar to the person-to-person exchange of dollar bills. On the horizon, SV entrepreneurs foresee worldwide interoperability of their systems. Interoperability and the potential for person-to-person SV transfers raise a number of domestic and international public policy concerns regarding the potential impact on international efforts to curtail money laundering and other financial crimes — topics that are discussed in greater detail in Chapter 10.

This Chapter discusses the legal issues and developments that affect these innovative payment systems. Section 16.02 provides a framework for that discussion, defining stored value and explaining various stored value systems. Section 16.03 explores policy issues regarding which entities should be permitted to create SV systems. Section 16.04 examines possible legal restrictions on who may issue SV. Section 16.05 analyzes the impact of various federal and state statutes governing the banking and money transmitter industries on SV issuers.

---

[1]   For an extensive analysis of the commercial law issues that arise with the use of stored value ("SV") in commercial transactions, see Task Force on Stored-Value Cards, Am. Bar Ass'n, *Report: A Commercial Lawyer's Take on the Electronic Purse: An Analysis of Commercial Law Issues Associated with Stored-Value Cards and Electronic Money*, 52 BUS. LAW. 653, 654 (1997) (stating that "[t]he existing legal framework and regulatory apparatus for retail payments seems ill-equipped to deal with an electronic future, if it unfolds as anticipated") [hereinafter ABA(Bar) SV Report].

§ 16.02 WHAT IS STORED VALUE?

Stored value is a recent innovation to the electronic payments system. The most common existing SV systems are prepaid telephone cards, mass transit cards, and university multiapplication cards. These systems are referred to as "closed systems" because they allow the SV product to be used only in a limited community. In contrast, an "open system" allows the use of SV to make payments to a wide range of parties, including merchants and other individuals. The open SV systems that are being developed are still in the testing stages.[2] Often characterized as "money," SV is an intangible electronic obligation that can be stored on a computer, SV card, or other hand held storage device.[3] SV transactions typically involve the following parties:

- **Issuer/Originator** - creates, sells, and redeems SV denominated in a single currency or multiple currencies;

- **Users** - customers and merchants; and

- **SV Service Providers (SVSPs)** - intermediaries between the Issuer and Users.

Open and closed SV systems differ in the type of technology that they utilize. Open SV systems use computer chip technology, installed in a smart card, for the transfer of SV. Magnetic stripe cards, similar to those used by credit and debit cards, are primarily used in closed payment systems such as transit and university systems.[4]

SV systems also vary in the funds transfer model they employ. SV system providers must determine whether the services of an intermediary will be required. Some smart cards enable two users, even two customers, to transfer electronic value between their storage devices. Some SV system models transfer funds between electronic storage devices without the need for an intermediary, though not necessarily excluding intermediaries. Other models include contact with an intermediary as part of the SV system. The remainder of this Section will describe various SV systems and their method of SV transfer.

---

[2] The Congressional Budget Office foresees a market of $20 billion in SV issuance. CONGRESSIONAL BUDGET OFFICE, EMERGING ELECTRONIC METHODS FOR MAKING RETAIL PAYMENTS 45-46 (June 1996) [hereinafter CBO STUDY].

[3] ABA(Bar) SV Report, *supra* note 1, at 657 (defining a SV obligation as an intangible claim represented by data stored on a microprocessor chip, computer harddrive, or within another storage device, that may be transferred in payment of a monetary obligation); PAYMENTS SYSTEM TASK FORCE, AM. BANKERS ASS'N, THE ROLE OF BANKS IN THE PAYMENTS SYSTEM OF THE FUTURE, at G-7 (Sept. 1996) (defining stored value as "[e]lectronically stored information and monetary value to pay for goods and services" that includes prepaid cards and electronic purses) [hereinafter PAYMENTS SYSTEM TASK FORCE]; BOARD OF GOVERNORS OF THE FEDERAL RESERVE SYSTEM, REPORT TO CONGRESS ON THE APPLICATION OF THE ELECTRONIC FUND TRANSFER ACT TO ELECTRONIC STORED-VALUE PRODUCTS 19 (Mar. 1997) (stating that "[t]here is no generally accepted definition of an electronic stored-value product. The term 'stored-value' is often used to refer to payment methods in which a prepaid balance of funds, or 'value,' is recorded on a device held by the consumer; this balance is decreased, or debited, when the device is presented for payment") [hereinafter FRB SV REPORT]; Amendment to the Bank Secrecy Act Regulations-Definition and Registration of Money Services Businesses, 62 Fed. Reg. 27,893 (1997) (to be codified at 31 C.F.R. pt. 103) (defining stored value as "funds or monetary value represented in digital electronic format (whether or not specially encrypted) and stored or capable of storage on electronic media in such a way as to be retrievable and transferable electronically"). *See also Stored Value Cards Systems*, OCC Banking Bull. No. 96-48 (Sept. 10, 1996).

[4] ABA(Bar) SV Report, *supra* note 1, at 658.

[1]   STORED VALUE SYSTEMS

Transfers of stored value in open systems typically operate via smart cards. A smart card is a wallet-sized plastic card with an embedded microprocessor. The microprocessor contains software that runs on an internal operating system. The software performs calculations, stores and processes data, and may interface with other access devices.

[a] Smart Cards. Though smart cards are most often associated with the electronic payments industry, they are not necessarily pure payment vehicles. The ability of smart cards to provide multifunctional capability may greatly enhance their value to users in everyday situations beyond retail payment transactions.[5] Smart cards offer several benefits over magnetic stripe cards, including larger memories, stronger security features, and the ability to store additional data, such as an individuals' medical history and identification data (*e.g.*, drivers license data and digital signatures). Smart cards are capable of holding SV or electronic money, records of transactions, and retail information, such as frequent flier miles and loyalty program information.[6] They may perform ATM, credit card, or debit card transactions, in addition to enabling two users to transfer SV between themselves without the assistance of a third party intermediary. By contrast, traditional ATM, credit card, and debit card transactions involve third-party intermediaries, such as banks, credit card processors, or the automated clearing house ("ACH") Network.

Smart cards must be properly authenticated before customer purchases will be accepted. The smart card computer chip stores a digital certificate that authenticates the user data in the smart card. The authentication of smart card data requires a smart card reader (*e.g.,* a retrofitted POS terminal) to perform the public key encryption calculations, which are discussed in Chapter 13.[7] As one commentator has noted, however, smart cards are facing the classic "chicken or the egg" quandary. Customers are not purchasing smart cards in large numbers because smart card readers are not widely available at locations convenient for smart card use; manufacturers of smart card readers are hesitant to manufacture adequate numbers of readers until they are sufficiently certain that there will be a market for them; and merchants are reluctant to invest in smart card technology until they are convinced that customer demand will be sufficient to justify the investment.[8]

SV system designers must decide whether to create "online" or "off-line" systems. In an off-line system, the balance of funds is recorded on the card itself and no further authorization takes places. An online system maintains the balance in a separate database and does not record that information on the card itself. Transaction authorization occurs through online communications with the database facility. Off-line systems allow

---

[5]   *See* BILL BURNHAM, PIPER JAFFRAY RESEARCH, THE ELECTRONIC COMMERCE REPORT 51-53, 111 (1997) (providing a description of smart cards and PC smart cards).

[6]   *See generally* SMART CARD FORUM, SMART CARDS: SEIZING STRATEGIC AND BUSINESS OPPORTUNITIES (Catherine Allen & William J. Barr eds., 1997); Walter A. Effross, *Putting the Cards Before the Purse?: Distinctions, Differences, and Dilemmas in the Regulation of Stored Value Card Systems*, 65 UMKC L. REV. 319 (1997).

[7]   *See* BURNHAM, *supra* note 5, at 51.

[8]   *Id*. at 52 (noting Hewlett-Packard's acquisition of Verifone, the leading manufacturer of credit card POS terminals and a producer of several smart card readers). *See HP Completes $1.29 Billion Merger with Verifone, VeriFone Becomes HP Subsidiary* (June 25, 1997), *available at* (visited Feb 6, 1998) <http://hpcc923.external.hp.com/retail/v1/pr129mil.html>.

transactions to be completed without incurring the communications and other costs associated with online authorization, and therefore, off-line systems may offer cost advantages. Online systems, however, may offer improved security because such systems offer greater opportunity to implement a centralized response to potentially fraudulent transactions. The distinction between online and off-line payment functions and accountable and unaccountable systems is discussed further in Chapter 7.

[*i*] *Security Considerations in SV Systems.* There are significant fraud risks associated with any computerized system that has the potential for creating stored value.[9] Emerging SV systems raise two significant security issues: (1) the ability to tamper with SV cards, hard drives, or other access and origination devices; and (2) the ability to counterfeit stored value, which can create fraudulent obligations. These concerns have been noted by security experts.[10] For example, scientists at the Bell Communications Research (Bellcore) lab have reportedly discovered a design flaw that could affect certain smart cards.[11]

[*ii*] *SV System Components.* SV systems utilize a variety of hardware and software components. Current SV systems are either card-based or computer-based. Advances in computer technology will soon permit the use of smart cards in PCs. Some SV cards permit users to transmit value immediately without authentication or intervention by a financial intermediary or online communications network. Users can also transfer SV online or off-line with SV card readers similar to traditional POS card readers. These SV readers can be installed in automated retail and governmental locations, such as soda machines, pay phones, parking meters, and toll booths.

At least one SV system incorporates personal hand-held transfer devices that are comprised of a microprocessor, a multifunctional keypad, and a SV card interface. Users of this system may transfer SV between the hand-held device and the SV card. The device displays the current balances that remain on the SV card and in the device. The device retains a limited record of completed transactions. Generally, both the SV card and the device can be "locked" with a personal identification number (PIN). Another type of system that is being tested involves Internet-initiated SV card transactions.[12]

---

[9] *See* FRIED, FRANK, HARRIS, SHRIVER & JACOBSON ET AL., THE MANAGEMENT OF RISKS CREATED BY INTERNET-INITIATED VALUE TRANSFERS, at 39-40 (1997) (a report prepared for the Internet Council of the National Automated Clearing House Association®, co-authored by Thomas P. Vartanian, Robert H. Ledig, Edward B. Whittemore, and Peter H. Schwartz of Fried Frank, Harris, Shriver & Jacobson; Marilyn Bruneau, Lee Ann Summers, and Joel Lanz of Arthur Andersen; and Peter Wayner) [hereinafter FRIED FRANK, THE MANAGEMENT OF IVT RISKS].

[10] *See generally* Laurie Law, Susan Sabett & Jerry Solinas, *How to make a Mint: The Cryptography of Anonymous Electronic Cash*, National Security Agency, Office of Information Security Research and Technology; Cryptography Division, June 18, 1996, at 23-28. For further discussion of the risk of counterfeit SV and the threat this poses to insured depository institutions, see Chapter 8, Section 8.02.

[11] See Chan Pak Woo, *Bellcore Discovers Security Hole in Smart Card: Mondex, Visa, MasterCard, and Other Banks Involved in a Stored Value Card Pilot in Manhattan are Quick to Repudiate* (Aug. 20, 1997), *available at* (visited Feb. 7, 1998) <http://www.cosmo21.com/netcash/nc1997/n0897_03.htm>. Richard Lipton, a Bellcore researcher, discovered the flaw by forcing a smart card to perform a faulty computation that disclosed information on how that calculation was made. This method of "reverse engineering" revealed the structure of the algorithm or secret key that protected the integrity of the smart card. *Id. See also Security in Electronic Money Systems Under Scrutiny*, 21ST CENTURY BANKING ALERT® NO. 96-10-8, Oct. 8, 1996, *available at* <http://www.ffhsj.com/bancmail/bancpage.htm>.

[12] For a discussion of other types of Internet value transfer systems, see Chapter 15.

[b] A Model Card-Based Stored Value System. The foundation of a stored value system rests upon the integrity and stability of the SV issuer. This SV issuer establishes a new SV payments system for the transfer of its SV. The SV payments system may be a network of stored value service providers ("SVSPs"), or a single SVSP. The SVSP purchases a license from a SV issuer for the distribution of the issuers SV. Although any party could be a SV issuer, as discussed in Section 16.03[7], European and United States regulators are currently debating whether governments should limit the types of entities that can play this role, possibly restricting it to depository institutions or entities affiliated with depository institutions.[13] A diagram and description of a model SV system follows:

CARD-BASED STORED VALUE TRANSFER SYSTEM

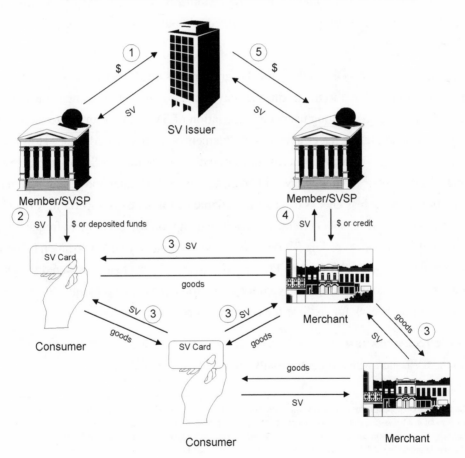

---

[13] *See* CBO STUDY, *supra* note 2 (discussing the issue of non-depository institutions issuing SV); PAYMENTS SYSTEM TASK FORCE, *supra* note 3, at 17 (arguing that the issuance of SV should be limited to regulated depository institutions) and at 20 (citing the view espoused by the *Report to the Council of The European Monetary Institute on Prepaid Cards, infra* note 107, which proposed that only depository institutions should be permitted to issue third-party stored value devices with exceptions for non-depository institutions willing to subject themselves to equivalent regulation). See also Section 16.03[7] for the European viewpoint.

SV TRANSFERS FROM:

① SV ISSUER TO SVSP - Each SVSP pays the SV issuer a contractual amount for the right to sell SV. The SVSP then purchases SV from the SV issuer. The SV issuer invests these funds in some form of liquid instruments.[14]

② SVSP TO USER - The SVSP sells SV to users.

③ USER TO USER - Users with the necessary hardware can exchange SV for goods and services. For example, a customer can select items for purchase and present a SV card to the merchant, either in person, over a "smart" phone, or on the Internet. The merchant's card reader will verify the authenticity of the customer's SV and, if authentic, the reader will transfer funds to the merchant's SV receiving device. Alternatively, customers can engage in "peer-to-peer" transactions by transferring SV directly from one customer SV card to another using an electronic wallet. Both types of transactions can be performed without the aid of a bank or other financial intermediary.

④ USER BACK TO SVSP - One of the critical characteristics of SV transactions is the indeterminate transfer point of SV into the traditional payments system for clearance and settlement. Frequent transfers of SV among users or aggregation of SV before transfer to an SVSP, can delay, or even indefinitely defer, clearance and settlement of the transferred value. However, cash management or other financial concerns may compel users to transfer SV back to an SVSP in exchange for deposits.[15] Whether SV will be cleared by SVSPs later and less often than other financial products, such as checks or other negotiable instruments, is uncertain. Conceivably, SV may become a high velocity currency, in that its redemption will occur more frequently due to the speed and ease of downloading SV onto cards and computers from any location in the world. A customer could download SV onto a PC, "log on" to the Internet to access a creditor's website and transfer the SV to pay a bill. The creditor's electronic payments program can immediately transfer the SV to its bank for credit to the creditor's deposit account.[16]

⑤ SV BACK TO SV ISSUER - A SVSP can either retain the SV for future resale or transfer the SV back to the SV issuer, which is contractually obligated to redeem the SV.

---

[14] For example, the Mondex USA Originator has assured the Office of the Comptroller of the Currency ("OCC"), in its letter seeking approval for national bank investment in a SV issuer, that the funds received in exchange for Mondex SV would be invested in "U.S. government securities and, to the extent necessary to satisfy short-term liquidity needs, cash and certain cash equivalents," pending redemption by SVSPs. *See* OCC Corp. Decision, Conditional Approval No. 220 (Dec. 2, 1996) [hereinafter "OCC Mondex Letter"].

[15] The point at which SV enters the existing clearing and settlement process will depend on the cash management policies of the user. Until an SV product is developed that can compensate its holder at a market rate of interest for the time value of its holding period, from an economic perspective, the transfer point of SV into the existing clearing and settlement process will occur when the benefits of investment exceed the costs of maintaining an inventory of SV. Incorporating the ability to provide a "rate return" mechanism into SV systems would require enhancements that have not been discussed by any system designer. *See* Thomas P. Vartanian, *Doing Business on the Net Sure to Change Risk Profiles*, AM. BANKER - FUTURE BANKING, Feb. 18, 1997, at 18A [hereinafter *Risk Profiles*].

[16] Section 16.05 discusses regulatory issues that may arise depending upon the location of the value in the payment cycle, and upon whether a transaction is online or off-line.

[c] Card-Based Products. In the United States, two card-based products, Mondex™ and Visa Cash®, are currently the most prevalent forms of SV payments systems. There are also other SV systems in use, undergoing initial testing, or being developed throughout the world.

[i] Mondex. Mondex International Ltd.'s ("Mondex") SV system was first conceived in March 1990 by two bankers at National Westminster Bank ("NatWest") in England, who were working on smart card applications. The Mondex SV system was developed through the joint efforts of NatWest and Midland Banks.[17] Mondex is a U.K. limited liability company ("LLC") that has established a franchise system whereby it licenses institutions or consortiums granting them the right to develop and operate the Mondex system in their respective countries.[18] The first Mondex pilot has been ongoing in Swindon, England since July 1995.[19] Additional pilot programs are planned or currently underway in New York City, San Francisco, Hong Kong, Australia, New Zealand, and Guelph, Canada. A broader Mondex rollout in the United States is also planned for 1998.[20]

The U.S. licensees of Mondex have established two LLCs to implement the Mondex system.[21] The originating LLC creates, sells, and redeems Mondex electronic stored value ("ESV") in exchange for dollars. Another LLC acts as the licensing and servicing agent for the Mondex USA system. The servicing LLC licenses the bank and nonbank entities that intend to distribute ESV to customers. The licensees must purchase the ESV that will be distributed on Mondex ESV cards from the originating LLC. The originating LLC is required to purchase the ESV at par when a licensee tenders it for redemption.[22] Licensees contract with customers and merchants for the use and acceptance of ESV in daily transactions. Mondex smart cards are capable of combining credit, debit, and SV functions on a single card that stores up to five different currencies and is reloadable from specially designed ATMs or telephones, or via the Internet onto computer disks.[23]

A unique attribute of this system is that Mondex SV can be transferred from a SV card to a SV wallet in off-line transactions. The system allows both customers and merchants (in the form of a POS reader) to have wallets. Individuals are able to transfer Mondex ESV without any interaction with a third party, thus making the transaction nearly equivalent to a customer handing a $10 bill to a merchant.

---

[17] See *The Mondex Story* at Mondex International's website <http://www.mondex.com>. MasterCard International acquired a 51% stake in Mondex in February 1997, and is presently involved in several pilots. *See* Jeffrey Kutler, *MasterCard to Control Mondex's Asian Ventures*, AM. BANKER, Mar. 4, 1997, at 14.

[18] OCC Mondex Letter, *supra* note 14, at 2 & n.3.

[19] As of February 1997, over 700 retail outlets and 13,000 cardholders use the system in Swindon, England. See *The Mondex Story,* at Mondex International's website <http://www.mondex.com>.

[20] *See* Dudley M. Nigg, *How Wells Fargo and Partners are Developing Mondex in the U.S; Wells Fargo and Co.; Electronic Cash Payments System Using 'Smart' Cards*, J. OF RETAIL BANKING SERV., June 22, 1997.

[21] *See id.* at 2-3. The U.S. licensees are currently comprised of AT&T Universal Card Services, Inc. (recently acquired by Citibank, subject to regulatory approval), Texas Commerce Bank (a subsidiary of Chase Manhatten Corp.), Morgan Stanley Dean Witter, MasterCard International, Wells Fargo Bank, N.A., Michigan National Bank, and First National Bank of Chicago NDB. *See Smarty Smart Card Reader Receives Mondex International "Seal of Approval,"* BUS. WIRE, Dec. 2, 1997 [hereinafter *Smarty Smart Card*].

[22] OCC Mondex Letter, *supra* note 14, at 4.

[23] *See Smarty Smart Card, supra* note 21; *Oki Value-Checker Personal Smart Card Readers Approved for Mondex Electronic Purse Systems*, BUS. WIRE, Jan. 5, 1998.

[*ii*] *Visa Cash®*. Visa International offers "Visa Cash®" SV cards that are either disposable, stand-alone reloadable, or adaptable to existing bank cards.[24] Disposable Visa Cash® cards are sold in specific monetary denominations. These cards may be given as gifts, serve as spending money for business travelers and tourists, or act as admission tickets to special events. Stand-alone reloadable Visa Cash® cards have no pre-set face value. The cardholder loads or reloads money onto the card from an ATM or a special value-loading terminal. Soon, special telephone and cash-to-card terminals will permit customers to load their cards with value. Finally, the Visa Cash® feature may be added to an existing bank card, enabling customers to have the advantage of stored value on a credit, debit, or ATM card. Customers who already have a bank relationship and carry cards will have the convenience of SV functionality without adding another card to their wallet.

The Visa Cash® transaction flow differs quite markedly from a debit card transaction. Visa member financial institutions issue Visa Cash® cards to customers. A customer's purchase of value to load onto the Visa Cash® card may be paid for by cash, by a withdrawal from a deposit account, or by credit card. Customers use the cards in retail transactions. Merchants collect and transmit the transactional information to Visa, which performs settlement among the participants. This collection and settlement process is similar to the process used in Visa credit card transactions, where the merchant's computer aggregates numerous transactions into batches on a daily basis and then sends the batch to Visa at the end of the day. Visa credits merchants the total value of their Visa Cash® transactions. The principal difference between a bank issued Visa Check Card™, a debit card that initiates an electronic fund transfer from the customer's account, and the Visa Cash Card® is that the Visa Cash® card stores "funds" in the card's microprocessor. Unlike the Visa Check Card™, no online authorization using a telecommunication service is required for a Visa Cash® transaction to take place. Functioning both as a security device and automatic calculator, the SV cash card authenticates the value to be transferred before the transaction. A significant difference between Visa Cash® and Mondex, is that at this time, Visa Cash® does not envision peer-to-peer transactions (*i.e.* between two individuals), while such transactions are a part of the Mondex pilot in Swindon, England and remain a possibility in U.S. Mondex applications.

[A] *Visa Cash® Pilots*. The first Visa Cash® pilot began in April 1995, when Bank of America issued disposable cards for use by more than 2,000 Visa employees and guests at the cafeterias and vending machines at Visa headquarters.[25] Visa introduced its reloadable cards in early 1996 and the first phase of Visa's largest launch of SV cards occurred during the 1996 Olympic Games in Atlanta, Georgia. The three largest banks in the southeastern United States, First Union National Bank, NationsBank, and Wachovia Bank, joined Visa to introduce Visa Cash® to the world. Each bank chose which of the three types of Visa Cash® SV to offer: a disposable card; a reloadable card; or a reloadable SV feature on an existing Visa bank card.

In Atlanta, Visa Cash® disposable cards were available in $10, $20, $50, and $100 denominations from the participating banks. Cardholders loaded funds onto the cards at participating banks and at various terminals

---

[24]   *See* Visa International's website <http://www.visa.com>; *see also* (visited Nov. 9, 1997) <http://www.cardshow.com/applications/VisaCash/pilots.html>. Visa Cash® is intended to function as "cash." *See* (visited Nov. 26, 1997) <http://www.visa.com/cgi-bin/vee/nt/cash/>.

[25]   *See* <http://www.cardshow.com/applications/VisaCash/pilots.html>.

located throughout Atlanta. Customers could purchase the cards from participating merchants or from card-dispensing machines in banks and shopping centers. Visa Cash® was accepted for the purchase of food and beverages at the main stadium venues and in the Olympic Village.[26] Over 1,500 locations in Atlanta, including fast food outlets, gasoline stations, convenience stores, cinemas, and railway stations still accept Visa Cash®. The Atlanta Visa Cash® program has received mixed reviews. Some believe that the increased awareness of SV technology and its widespread adoption by merchants throughout Atlanta were positive outcomes of the trial.[27] Others cast the Atlanta test in less glowing terms because it lacked critical mass in terms of the number of participating locations, and because customer usage at installed terminals was lower than expected.[28]

In 1993, Visa formed a working group of international market leaders in the customer payments industry to develop global specifications for the SV card. Composed of twenty representatives from thirteen nations, this group addresses the issues of interoperability, security, and interchange capability of SV programs. Worldwide, Visa continues to rollout its products with pilots in Argentina, Canada, Columbia, Australia, and Spain.[29] In addition, Visa is working with MasterCard and Europay to develop common global technical specifications for the integration of microchips in payment cards. The purpose of this cooperative effort is to facilitate the worldwide implementation of chip-based payment cards.[30] As discussed below, the first step towards interoperability is underway.

[iii] *MasterCard/Visa Interoperable Pilot.* MasterCard[31] and Visa launched a pilot program in October 1997, involving nearly 80,000 customers and more than 600 merchants in the Upper West Side of Manhattan.[32] Chase Manhattan Bank ("Chase"), on behalf of MasterCard, distributes the Chase Smart Card, a Mondex SV product, and Citibank distributes the Citibank Visa Cash® Money Card™. The pilot focuses primarily on joint interoperability by providing merchants with a single terminal to process both Mondex™ and Visa Cash® transactions. The pilot will be watched closely to see the extent to which this new payment mechanism is

---

[26] *See* Rod Newing, *Milestone in the History of Money*, FIN. TIMES (London), June 5, 1996, at 6.

[27] *See Olympic Cash Card Pilot Results are in: Merchants the Key to Program's Success*, BANK SYS. + TECH., Sept. 1996 (quoting Una Somerville, Senior Vice President of Visa International, who stated that the system "worked flawlessly"); Melanie Rigney, *The Smart Card Train Picks Up Steam*, CREDIT CARD MGMT., Jan. 1997.

[28] *See* Rigney, *The Smart Card Train Picks Up Steam*, *supra* note 27.

[29] *See Olympic Cash Card Pilot Results are in: Merchants the Key to Program's Success*, *supra* note 27. The Spanish smart card system complies with an international standard agreed to between Visa, MasterCard, and Europay. *Id.* Europay International is one of the main providers of traveler's checks, ATM services, and debit and credit card products throughout Europe. Europay has formed an alliance with MasterCard, under which Europay is the sole licensor of MasterCard products in Europe. In addition to the more traditional forms of financial services, Europay has developed a smart card, the Eurocard, which is part of the European Payments System Services electronic network. *See* <http://www.europay.com>.

[30] *See* Newing, *Milestone in the History of Money*, *supra* note 26, at 6.

[31] MasterCard bought a controlling interest in Mondex in February 1997. *See* Jeffrey Kutler, *MasterCard to Control Mondex's Asian Ventures*, AM. BANKER, Mar. 4, 1997, at 14.

[32] *No Clear Verdict Emerges So Far From A New York Smart Card Trial*, DEBIT CARD NEWS, (Dec. 16, 1997). Citibank has issued 39,000 Visa Cash® cards, 25,000 of which may be reloaded at various ATMs, whereas the remainder may be reloaded at kiosks at four Citibank branches and 20 merchant locations. *Id.* By late January 1998, Chase Manhattan issued 65,100 reloadable Mondex SV cards for its customers and 21,850 cards for non-customers who work in the area. CARDFAX, Jan. 27, 1998.

accepted by customers and merchants.[33] The participants in the pilot anticipate expanding the test to include other parts of New York City.[34]

[A] *The Chase and Citibank SV Card Agreements.* Under the pilot program, a stored value card purchaser receives an agreement from Chase or Citibank setting forth the rights and obligations of all program participants. Relevant provisions of the Chase and Citibank agreements are detailed below.

Several important provisions of the Chase Standalone Smart Card Agreement relate to card security, card ownership, maximum SV limits, payment finality, risk of loss, and warranty disclaimers. The Smart Card Agreement requires the cardholder to maintain the security of the Smart Card at all times and to take responsibility for any card use, including use not authorized by the cardholder. Under the agreement, Chase reserves the right to cancel Smart Card privileges, and the card remains the property of Chase, requiring the cardholder, upon the bank's request, to cut up the Smart Card and return it to Chase. The maximum value of the Chase Smart Card is $200. The agreement informs cardholders that purchases made with the Chase Smart Card are similar to cash in that Chase will not have a record of the transaction, and thus, a customer's monthly statement will not itemize Smart Card purchases. It also states that once the SV is transferred, the merchant receives title to the value transferred.

Under the agreement, customer liability for loss or theft of the Smart Card is the same as if the customer lost cash; in the event of loss or theft, the Smart Card will not be replaced. The agreement specifically states: "USE OF THE SMART CARD IS AT YOUR OWN RISK." Smart Cards may be "locked" with a code at the option of the holder. To operate the card, however, it must be unlocked until a transaction is completed. Chase disclaims all warranties, express and implied, and states that it shall have no liability associated with the use of its Smart Card, including any malfunction by the card, ATM, or Smart Card reader or other equipment. The agreement provides that Chase will replace any malfunctioning Smart Card so long as the cardholder did not cause the malfunction. In addition, Chase will assist in retrieving any SV remaining on a malfunctioning card. It disclaims, however, any liability in the event of its failure to retrieve the SV.

The Citibank Visa® Cash Money Card™ Agreement also requires the cardholder to maintain the security of the Money Card™ at all times and to take responsibility for all card use. Citibank states that it may cancel card privileges at anytime to maintain or restore the security of the Visa Cash® and Citibank operating systems. The maximum value of Citibank's Money Card™ is $500. The card retains information on the dollar amount

---

[33] *See* Chris Isadore, *Smart Card Fails 1st Test – Few Shoppers, Retailers Use Alternate to Cash,* CRAIN'S NEW YORK BUSINESS (Feb. 16-22, 1998). *See also The Real World,* CARDFAX, Jan. 14, 1998 (reporting comments of consumers who believe that sit-down restaurants are underrepresented in the pilot and that they are uncomfortable carrying around SV for which they will not be reimbursed if they lose the card, and reporting various training problems with merchant employees); *Snail's Pace,* CARDFAX, Jan. 8, 1998 (quoting two merchants regarding malfunctioning terminals, slow transaction times, and consumer ignorance about SV cards). Burger King has withdrawn from the Upper Westside trial, citing the time it takes to process a transaction. Burger King, however, has aligned itself with Mondex in a smart card test to be conducted on Long Island in the second quarter of 1998. *See* Antoinette Coulton & Jeffrey Kutler, *Smart Cards: Fast-Food Trials May Point to Killer Card App.; Mondex's Burger King Program Looks to Bring New Technology to Masses,* AM. BANKER, Feb. 11, 1998, at 15. Additionally, merchants are indicating they will not pay fees to offer the service to customers unless smart card traffic increases. *See 1998: The Year to Start Selling on the Web,* RETAIL DELIVERY SYS. NEWS, Jan. 16, 1998.

[34] *Id.* (quoting Ronald Braco, Chase Manhattan Senior Vice President, who stated that the program will be expanded in the second half of 1998).

of the previous ten purchases and the previous three loading or uploading transactions. This information may be displayed at load value terminals at specified merchants. Customer liability for loss or theft of the Money Card™ is the same as if the customer lost cash, and the card will not be replaced. Citibank's agreement does not indicate whether the Money Card™ can be locked. It does state, however, that card holders may receive a refund or credit for any SV remaining on the Money Card™ in the event of a malfunction.

[c] Computer-Based Products. Computer-based SV products use PC hard drives to store SV. Current users of these products must rely on a single bank to send and receive payments. That bank clears and settles all transactions by executing "on us" balance adjustments. Computer-based SV systems may evolve to include multiple banks and allow users to make payments without relying on a third-party clearance and settlement mechanism.

[i] *Ecash™*. An example of a computer-based SV is ecash™, developed by DigiCash, an Amsterdam-based SV developer. Ecash™ has been available to customers of Mark Twain Bank of St. Louis, Missouri, since October 1995.[35] Mark Twain, now known as a division of Mercantile Bank, maintains World Currency Accounts ("WCA") to facilitate ecash™ payments. These accounts for ecash™ users and merchants are FDIC-insured. Using a WCA, a customer instructs the bank to move funds to the "ecash™ Mint," which is a pooled ecash™ "location" on the bank's computer server. Each customer has an "account" in the ecash™ Mint, in the bank's secure server, that is accessible via the Internet. Once transferred to the ecash™ Mint, a customer may use ecash™ software to instruct the Mint to issue a set of "coins"[36] and transfer these "coins" to the customer's hard drive. At this point, the customer's funds are treated as being held in an individual ecash™ "location" on the bank's computer server. The bank's website states that ecash™ transferred to a customer's hard drive is no longer FDIC-insured and should be treated like cash in all respects.[37] Once coins are stored on the hard drive, a customer may make payments to other ecash™ participants over the Internet. The customer may spend the coins, store them for future use, or transfer the coins back from the hard drive to the pooled ecash™ Mint and can then request that the bank transfer the funds from the pooled ecash™ Mint to the customer's WCA account.[38]

Ecash™ is a payments system that is intended to facilitate tamper-proof, anonymous transfers of electronic money. Ecash™ software converts money into a digital form; money becomes a string of numbers, capable of transmission by any telecommunications medium. Transactions paid for with ecash™ do not reveal the name or address of the purchaser to the seller unless the purchaser has provided such information. Each ecash™

---

[35] *See* <http://www.digicash.com>. The merger of Mark Twain Bancshares Inc., the parent bank holding company of Mark Twain Bank, into Mercantile Bancorporation, Inc. was completed on April 25, 1997. *See* <http://www.mercantile.com/about/html/199704256696.html>. Mark Twain Bank has been renamed Mercantile Bank.

[36] Ecash™ coins are strings of characters sent in electronic messages from a bank to its account-holders' PCs over a network connection (*i.e.*, the Internet), in such a way that the bank cannot identify which coins were sent to the consumer. Each string corresponds to a different digital coin. *See* DigiCash's website <http://www.digicash.com> and Mark Twain Bank's website <http://www.marktwain.com>.

[37] *See* Letter from Marc J. Goldstrom, Counsel, FDIC, 17-18 (May 12, 1997) (stating that funds in the ecash™ Mint individual accounts are "deposits" for FDIC insurance purposes). *See also* Chapter 8, Section 8.05 (discussing the FDIC opinion letter on ecash™).

[38] See <http://www.digicash.com> for a more detailed description of an ecash™ transaction.

coin is secured by strong encryption intended to prevent any unauthorized party from depositing the ecash™ and obtaining cash value. Ecash™ software includes customer protection against losses resulting from PC crashes.[39] The ecash™ recovery procedure attempts to ensure that, even if the coins and other files on the customer's hard disk are corrupted or destroyed, the user will still be able to retrieve the full value of any lost ecash™ coins.

An explanation of an ecash™ withdrawal and its transfer illustrates the security features of ecash™. Each digital coin has a single "denomination." The ecash™ software manages a "purse" of digital coins contained on the customer's PC. When a customer purchases an item, the purse determines which denominations to use to pay for the item. The ecash™ purse maintains a number of smaller denomination digital "coins," and prompts the customer to contact the bank in the event that more coins are needed, allowing the customer to reconfigure coin denominations in the purse before the next transaction. When a merchant receives digital coins from a customer, the merchant's software automatically transmits the ecash™ to the bank for verification. The bank authenticates the coins and sends the merchant an electronic "acceptance" of the ecash™. The merchant then sends the merchandise to the customer along with an electronic receipt.

Systems exist to maintain the anonymity of customers within the ecash™ system. The bank's computer imprints a randomly generated serial number on each coin at the time it was originally minted and given to the customer. Due to the encryption method used in the ecash™ system, the bank does not know the serial number or the name of the recipient of a particular coin. As a result, the bank is unable to determine the identity of the customer who spent a particular coin with a particular merchant. To ensure that each coin it receives is used only once, the bank records the serial number of each coin it receives in its "spent coin" database.[40] If the bank receives a coin for verification, and the coin serial number is already recorded in the "spent coin" database, the bank can inform the merchant that it is a copy of a coin that has previously been spent. If, no such "spent coin" serial number has been recorded, the bank records the serial number and informs the merchant that the coin is valid. Under this system, the bank assumes that the first coin received is authentic, and the second coin received, with an identical serial number, is the counterfeit. If a thief copies and spends a customer's ecash™, the valid ecash™ will be rejected by the system when the customer later attempts to spend it.

"Peer-to-peer transactions" are not possible under the current ecash™ system. Whenever a customer receives ecash™ from another customer, the ecash™ software automatically deposits value received into the bank. If a customer prefers to have ecash™ available to spend immediately after receipt, the software must be preprogrammed to make an automatic withdrawal to the customer's hard drive of any money received.

An interesting encryption method protects payer privacy in the ecash™ system. It uses "blind signatures," rather than digital stamp validation. The blind signature concept, which is the foundation of the DigiCash's

---

[39] *See* (visited Nov. 9, 1997) <http://www.digicash.com/index_n.html>.

[40] *See* <http://www.digicash.com>.

privacy feature, prevents the bank from tracing the customer's money.[41] The customer's software creates multiple coins of the same value (*e.g.,* $1) with random serial numbers. Each coin is placed in a digital "envelope." The software transmits the envelopes to the bank and the bank opens all but one of the envelopes to assure itself that the purchaser of the ecash™ coin is submitting the same value for each envelope. The bank discards the nine opened envelopes, and takes the risk that the remaining envelope is for the same value. The bank withdraws one dollar from the customer's account and makes its digital validation like an embossed stamp on the remaining unopened envelope before returning it to the customer's computer.[42]

Similar to an emboss, the blind signature mechanism allows for the application of the validating signature through the unopened envelope. When the customer's computer removes the envelope, it obtains a coin of its own random choice, validated by the bank's stamp. When the customer spends the coin, the bank will honor it and accept it as a valid payment because the coin bears the bank's validation stamp. The bank, however, cannot identify the coin or the customer who made the payment because it was hidden in the envelope when it was stamped. The bank that signed the coin can verify that it made the signature, but it cannot link it back to a particular owner.[43]

[*ii*] *Digital Equipment Corporation's MilliCent*™. In March 1996, Digital Equipment Corporation ("DEC") introduced MilliCent™, an electronic microcommerce payment system designed to allow Internet merchants to charge customers for individual pieces of digital information, including news, articles, games, and music, for sums as low as $.001 (1/10 of a cent).[44] DEC designed the MilliCent™ system to make it feasible to handle transactions valued from less than a penny, up to five dollars. MilliCent™ opens up the potential for new information industries while allowing old industries, such as the music and newspaper publishing industry, to tap into a new payment stream for individual media services.

The MilliCent™ system design removes the need for Internet vendors to provide their customers with individual accounts. Brokers, who purchase a server from DEC, will create vendor specific "scrip" in amounts that the vendor licenses the broker to create. The broker purchases this vendor license at a discount. For example, for every $100 of vendor specific scrip that the broker purchases under the license, the broker may pay the vendor only $95. A customer purchases MilliCent™ broker scrip from the broker. The broker earns its profit when it exchanges its vendor specific scrip with customers who exchange at par their previously purchased broker scrip. The customer's MilliCent™ software will automatically transmit the required amount of broker scrip required to exchange for vendor specific scrip to make a purchase from the vendor. For example, if the customer desires to purchase a vendor's product for $1.25, the software will send $1.25 in broker scrip to the

---

[41] This anonymity is discussed in Chapter 10, Section 10.02, in the context of the Bank Secrecy Act and Financial Crimes Enforcement Network ("FinCEN").

[42] <http://www.digicash.com>. *See also* Financial Crimes Enforcement Network, U.S. Department of the Treasury, *Exploring the World of Cyberpayments, An Introductory Survey,* at 12 (Sept. 27, 1995) (containing a reprinted description of David Chaum's blind signature from *Worth* magazine).

[43] *See* <http://www.digicash.com>.

[44] *See DEC's Millicent Java Micro-Web Payment System Goes Into Beta,* COMPUTERGRAM INT'L., Dec. 10, 1997; *see also* <http://www.millicent.digital.com>.

broker's server. The broker's server will transmit $1.25 in vendor specific scrip to the customer's PC which, in turn, forwards the $1.25 in vendor specific scrip to the vendor. The MilliCent™ system does permit vendors to directly issue their scrip to customers in the form of rebates and loyalty rewards, however, the use of brokers permits customers to deal with one entity when purchasing material from multiple vendors.[45]

The components of the MilliCent™ system include the MilliCent™ Wallet, a MilliCent™ Broker Server, and a MilliCent™ Vendor Server. The wallet is client software that is logically integrated into a customer's web browser. When a customer chooses to make a purchase at a particular vendor, the wallet handles the conversion of broker scrip into vendor specific scrip, as needed, and spends it in exchange for the content purchased by the customer. The broker server is a software application that resides on the broker's host computer and converts customer's cash, check, or credit card payment into broker scrip. In addition, the broker server converts its broker scrip into vendor scrip whenever a customer is purchasing content from a vendor. The vendor server is a software application that resides on the vendor's host computer that administers the pricing for the content it sells and validates scrip used for payment by its customers.

The security of the MilliCent™ system relies on small transaction values that demand trust and a good reputation between brokers and vendors. Although DEC states that the MilliCent™ system does not use "industrial-strength encryption," DEC takes the position that its simpler encryption function is sufficient to validate scrip and prevent theft or counterfeiting.[46]

[iii] *Citibank EMS.* The Electronic Money System ("EMS"), currently under development by Citibank, is another example of a computer-based SV.[47] The EMS prototype creates and exchanges electronic notes that behave like paper cash in a wallet-based system called "Money Modules" (essentially a smart card embedded with EMS software that is interoperable with a party's computer). In the EMS, issuing banks generate electronic notes for distributing banks or their own customers and guarantee the notes' value. Correspondent banks (which license the EMS technology from Citibank) will accept EMS notes from the issuing banks and distribute the notes to users. Citibank's EMS notes may be created in any currency by a cash withdrawal from a demand deposit account or as a draw-down from an approved line of credit. The system has off-line capabilities, permitting peer-to-peer transactions, and offers a complete audit trail for traceability. For security purposes, the EMS system periodically "sweeps" electronic notes into the bank for validation and control and then returns new notes to users' Money Modules.[48]

---

[45] For a full description of the Millicent™ system, see *How the MilliCent System Works, available at* <http://www.millicent.digital.com/sell/white_papers/executive/index.html>.

[46] *See id.*

[47] *See* <http://citibank.com>.

[48] *See Citibank Awarded Key Technology Patents for Electronic Money*, CITIBANK TECH. BULL., (Citibank Technologists Worldwide), Vol. 12, No. 4, 1995-1996, at 15-18. *See also Know Technology, Process to Avoid Legal Troubles*, RETAIL DELIVERY SYS. NEWS, Feb. 14, 1997 (describing some of the features associated with Citibank's EMS that were discussed at the Second Annual Conference on Emerging Law of CyberBanking and Electronic Commerce in February 1997, in Washington D.C.).

§ 16.03   PUBLIC POLICY CONSIDERATIONS: WHO SHOULD ISSUE STORED VALUE?

As various forms of stored value and electronic money are created, tested, developed, and deployed throughout the world, the current regulatory structure for the payments system may be headed for a comprehensive overhaul. The current regulatory structure provides adequate legal certainty in regard to existing payment applications. For example, federal or state law specifies when an individual's or corporation's indebtedness is discharged by cash, check, or wire transfer, but generally current law does not address when a SV payment is complete.[49] Emerging electronic financial products and services are different from current payment mechanisms, and the unique features of these systems often were not contemplated by the drafters of the present regulatory structure.[50]

SV presents a range of legal, business, and public policy issues. Many of these issues stem from the difficulties in trying to fit SV products into existing legal definitions.[51] This Section presents a sample of current public policy perspectives on who should issue SV.

[1]   AMERICAN BANKERS ASSOCIATION PAYMENTS SYSTEM TASK FORCE

In 1995, the American Bankers Association ("ABA(Bankers)") formed a Payments System Task Force ("Task Force") to study SV and other payments systems. The Task Force released its report in September 1996 ("Task Force Report").[52] The Task Force Report has two main recommendations. It recommends that depository institutions should be the only financial service providers with direct access to the payments system currently maintained by the Federal Reserve System.[53] It also recommends that only regulated depository institutions should be allowed to issue SV products that "function as currency,"[54] such as those that operate in open SV systems. The Task Force Report notes, however, that exceptions could be made to this general principle

---

[49]   In any U.S. dollar-denominated indebtedness, U.S. currency and coins will discharge a debt upon tender. 31 U.S.C. § 5103; *see* 31 C.F.R. § 100.3. Under negotiable instruments law, when a negotiable instrument, such a personal check, is tendered in payment of a debt, that debt is temporarily suspended until the check clears at which point the debt is discharged. U.C.C. § 3-310. For a discussion of finality of payment rules for legal tender, bank credits, negotiable instruments, wholesale fund transfers, and the applicability of those concepts to the creation, transfer, and payment finality of SV, see ABA(Bar) SV Report, *supra* note 1, at 669-700, 709-13. *See also* Walter A. Effross, *The Electronic Future of Cash: Article: Piracy, Privacy, and Privatization: Fictional and Legal Approaches to the Electronic Future of Cash*, 46 AM. U.L. REV. 961 (Apr., 1997); *Legal and Regulatory Implications of Advanced Card Programs, available at* <http://www.smartcrd.com/info/more/lega/.htm>.

[50]   For a discussion of some of the issues facing SV issuers, see Thomas P. Vartanian, *Key Questions for Emerging Systems: Where is the Money?*, AM. BANKER - FUTURE BANKING, June 17, 1996, at 6A.

[51]   General Counsel's Opinion No. 8; Stored Value Cards, 61 Fed. Reg. 40,490 (1996) (indicating that some SV products will be eligible for deposit insurance while others will not).

[52]   PAYMENTS SYSTEM TASK FORCE, *supra* note 3.

[53]   *Id.* at 17. *See also* Orla O'Sullivan, *Payment System Should Stay as is*, TECHNOLOGY TOPICS, *available at* <http://www.banking.com/aba/tech_1296.htm> [hereinafter O'Sullivan].

[54]   PAYMENTS SYSTEM TASK FORCE, *supra* note 3, at 18.

on a case-by-case basis. The Task Force primarily based its recommendations on the threat to the overall payments system posed by the potential for failure of an unregulated SV issuer.[55]

At present, only the U.S. Treasury, state governments, certain government sponsored enterprises and depository institutions have direct access to the FedWire® component of the payments system.[56] The FedWire® system leaves the Federal Reserve temporarily exposed to nonpayment by its participants. The Federal Reserve wires funds to the receiving institution before it receives payment from the sending institution. To ensure the integrity of the payments system, the banking regulatory structure provides for federal examination of the depository institutions that participate in the system to determine the safety and soundness of each institution. This regulatory structure, governing depository institution participants in the FedWire® system, tempers the risk exposure to nonpayment by the sending institution.

The Task Force questioned how a nonbank could fit into the present bank regulatory scheme. It noted that the bank regulatory model would be difficult to apply to most nonbanks due to strict risk-based capital requirements and an extensive system of examination and supervision.[57] Further, the disclosure-based model used for the securities industry would not be appropriate for certain SV products.[58]

The Task Force focused on the roles that public trust and confidence play in the success of the payments system and the financial industry.[59] Such trust and confidence could erode if entities fail to meet their obligations either as a result of their inability or unwillingness to do so.[60] The Task Force suggested that fraud perpetrated by unregulated SV issuers would be a likely cause of the aforementioned loss of public trust and confidence. It also noted that nonbanks are not subject to the same regulatory burdens that are imposed on the banking industry. Banks, the Task Force noted, pay "billions of dollars every year . . . simply to do business as a bank."[61] The Task Force stated that to permit unregulated nonbanks to issue SV could place banks at a

---

[55] *Id.* The four principles of the report were to (1) maintain the integrity of the payments system; (2) protect the interests of consumers; (3) promote a competitive environment; and (4) strike the proper regulatory balance. *Id.* at i-ii. See also Chapter 8, Section 8.02 for a discussion of "spawning," the counterfeiting of electronic money.

[56] *See* The Depository Institutions Deregulatory and Monetary Control Act of 1980, Pub. L. No. 96-221, 94 Stat. 149 (March 31, 1980) (codified in scattered sections of 12 and 15 U.S.C.); Regulation J, 12 C.F.R. pt. 210. PAYMENTS SYSTEM TASK FORCE, *supra* note 3, at 17. The FedWire® is a high-speed communications network that connects all 12 Federal Reserve Banks, their branches, the FRB, the U.S. Treasury and the Commodity Credit Corporation. The FedWire® enables banks to transfer reserve balances from one another for immediate available credit and to transfer balances for business customers.

[57] *See generally* Walter I. Conroy, *Note: Risk-Based Capital Adequacy Guidelines: A Sound Regulatory Policy or a Symptom of Regulatory Inadequacy?*, 63 FORDHAM L. REV. 2395 (1995).

[58] PAYMENTS SYSTEM TASK FORCE, *supra* note 3, at 20. While a consumer may be motivated to understand the risks in an investment portfolio; the same is probably not true of a $25 smart card.

[59] *Id.* at 18. *See also* Chapter 11.

[60] PAYMENTS SYSTEM TASK FORCE, *supra* note 3, at 19 (citing Gautam Naik, *Sorry, Your Prepaid Phone Card Has Been Deactivated*, WALL ST. J., July 16, 1996, at B1). The increasing incidence of phone cards that prove to be worthless in the hands of purchasers illustrate how consumer confidence in new electronic value products can affect whether products, such as SV, ultimately achieve widespread acceptance. *See Prepaid Phone-card Scams Demonstrate the Risk of Fraud or Misuse of Stored Value*, 21ST CENTURY BANKING ALERT® NO. 96-7-25, July 25, 1996, *available at* <http://www.ffhsj.com/bancmail/bancpage.htm>; *see also Pachinko Counterfeit Scam Illustrates Threat of Spawning*, 21ST CENTURY BANKING ALERT® NO. 96-7-1, July 1, 1996, *available at* <http://www.ffhsj.com/bancmail/bancpage.htm>.

[61] PAYMENTS SYSTEM TASK FORCE, *supra* note 3, at 33.

competitive disadvantage, and may ultimately eliminate banks from the payments system or relegate them to back-office payment processors.[62] In the Task Force's view, the prospect of banks losing their "central role" in handling retail and wholesale payments to new contenders from the telephone, television, telecommunications, and computer industries presents serious systemic safety and soundness concerns.

Support for the Task Force's position has come from the Congressional Budget Office, whose report on payment systems reached conclusions similar to those reached by the ABA(Bankers).[63] A 1996 Congressional Budget Office study states that "the supervision and regulations covering depository institutions safeguard the safety and soundness of those institutions. Lacking those safeguards, an electronic payment method issued by an unregulated institution may be more likely to fail. Such a failure could undermine customers' confidence in other issuers."[64] One banking regulator has stated, "[a]ll firms offering liabilities used by the public for making payments should be required to obtain bank charters."[65]

Another essential component of understanding the public policy debate is understanding the business case for why banks and nonbanks might want to issue stored value. The following Section discusses the history and economics of issuing currency.

[2]   THE MONEY IN MAKING MONEY

At the time of the establishment of the U.S. Mint in 1792, the federal government did not charge a fee for the minting of coins.[66] Following English tradition, the Mint's policy of free coinage permitted the holder of any silver or gold bullion to have it coined into U.S. currency by the Mint without charge.[67] During the early 1800s, when banks frequently issued paper currency, state banks earned seigniorage on that issuance.

One financial incentive for banks and nonbanks to issue electronic currency arises out of the concepts of brassage and seigniorage. When depositors entrusted their precious metal to banks, the banks returned bank notes in an amount worth less than their deposits. The difference represented two charges to the depositor: (i) brassage, the fee a bank charged above the value of the notes issued to cover its operational costs, such as storing the gold;[68] and (ii) seigniorage, an additional fee levied to create a profit on the issuance of notes in

---

[62]   *Id.*

[63]   *See* O'Sullivan, *supra* note 53.

[64]   CBO STUDY, *supra* note 2, at 46.

[65]   R. Alton Gilbert, *Cyber-Payments: What Should the Government Do?; Federal Involvement is Inevitable*, BANKING STRATEGIES, Sept./Oct. 1996, at 16. Mr. Gilbert is a Vice President at the Federal Reserve Bank of St. Louis. *Id.*

[66]   *See* ARTHUR NUSSBAUM, A HISTORY OF THE DOLLAR 54 (1957). *See* Mint Act, Ch. 16, § 9, 1 Stat. 246, 248 (1792).

[67]   *See* NUSSBAUM, *supra* note 66, at 54 (citing STEWART, HISTORY OF THE FIRST UNITED STATES MINT 50 (1924)). The U.S. government chose not to charge seigniorage in order to buttress the U.S. legal rate for the dollar and its newly established gold silver ratio. If the holder of the metal wanted it coined immediately, .5% was deducted. *See id.* at 54.

[68]   *See id.* at 54. In the context of minting coins, brassage is the "[g]overnment charge for coining metals; covering only the actual cost." BLACK'S LAW DICTIONARY 188 (6th ed. 1990).

exchange for gold.[69] This type of seigniorage largely disappeared with the passage of National Bank Act,[70] when the federal government imposed a federal tax on state bank note issuance. Ultimately, the federal government became the sole issuer of paper currency. Currently, the federal government does not "charge" brassage or seigniorage fees for its issuance of federal reserve notes, but rather issues these notes at par. However, a more subtle form of seigniorage is stilled "earned" by the federal government on its issuance of paper money.

[a] Modern Seigniorage. An explanation of the seigniorage currently earned by the federal government requires an analysis of the economics of the issuance of currency in the United States. The total value of paper and metal currency issued by the U.S. government is estimated roughly at $425 billion.[71] Theoretically, the holders of this currency could invest this money in U.S. bonds or other interest bearing government securities rather than keeping it in their wallets and bank accounts. Because a holder of currency does not earn interest on the cash in the individual's wallet or purse, the holder is, in effect, lending to the government at zero interest, which is the economic equivalent of the government earning interest on the cash it issues.

[b] Seigniorage Accruing to SV Issuers. The potential revenue for SV issuers, apart from transaction fees, comes from essentially receiving interest free loans from SV users when they exchange U.S. currency or other funds for SV. SV issuers will earn "seigniorage" when they invest the proceeds of these "interest free loans." As a result, the government could lose an estimated twenty-five billion dollars or more each year in seigniorage if the entire outstanding amount of $425 billion of federal reserve notes were to be replaced by SV.[72] This estimate assumes that non-governmental SV issuers of the currency invest the proceeds from that sale of SV into government securities that yield a 6% return. Former Federal Reserve Board ("FRB") Governor Alan S. Blinder suggests that this seigniorage could accrue to the purchasers of stored value, because "[i]t may be technically feasible to pay interest on stored-value products."[73]

[c] Federal SV Issuance. The federal government could expand its current role as the sole issuer of coins and paper currency to include SV issuance. The U.S. Mint, a bureau of the U.S. Department of Treasury, has put forth a proposal to issue SV cards to retain the seigniorage the government would otherwise lose by the partial

---

[69] *See* NUSSBAUM, *supra* note 66, at 54. Seigniorage, a more commonly known fee, is defined as a "royalty or prerogative of the sovereign, whereby an allowance of gold and silver, brought in the mass to be exchanged for coin, is claimed." BLACK'S LAW DICTIONARY 1358 (6th ed. 1990).

[70] National Bank Act, Ch. 343, §1, 18 Stat. 123 (1864) (codified as amended at 12 U.S.C. §§ 21-216).

[71] *See* Thomas C. Meltzer, *Electronic Money, Inflation and the Role of the Fed in the Payments System,* Remarks at the Banking and the Internet Seminar, at Murray State University (April 25, 1997) [hereinafter Meltzer, *Electronic Money*].

[72] *See* Michael N. Castle, *Electronic Money and Banking: What Should Government's Role Be?,* USA TODAY (MAGAZINE), May 1997, at 26 (stating that "[t]heoretically, [the U.S. Treasury and the FRB] stand to lose $20,000,000,000 or so in annual earnings and a substantial measure of independence if electronic money were to supplant physical notes and coins completely"). Representative Castle (R. Del.) is the chairman of the House Banking Committee's Committee on Domestic and International Policy. *But see* Edward W. Kelley, Jr., Governor of the Federal Reserve Board, Remarks at CyberPayments '96 Conference, in Dallas, Texas (June 18, 1996), *available at* <http://www.bog.frb.fed.us/boarddocs/speeches/19960618.htm> (stating that over two thirds of U.S. issued currency circulates beyond U.S. borders) [hereinafter Kelley, CyberPayments '96 Remarks].

[73] *See* Alan S. Blinder, Vice Chairman, Board of Governors of the Federal Reserve System, Statement before the Subcommittee on Domestic and International Monetary Policy of the Committee on Banking and Financial Services, U.S. House of Representatives (Oct. 11, 1995).

replacement of cash and coins with SV.[74] Some believe that if the SV industry develops into a significant form of "currency" in the U.S., the government may be the most appropriate entity to issue SV, because government issuance would enhance customer confidence in SV as a payment vehicle, and alleviate concerns regarding the nonbank issuance of SV.[75] To date, the federal government has shown no inclination to expressly preclude certain parties from engaging in SV issuance. Nor does it appear to have immediate plans itself to become an SV issuer.[76] Federal Reserve Chairman Alan Greenspan, in addressing this topic, has noted that it may be difficult to determine whether SV products are actually efficient alternatives to official paper currency or simply a diversion of seigniorage from the government to the private sector. He suggested that the diversion of seigniorage may be an inevitable byproduct of developing a more efficient retail payment system,[77] and, as our monetary history has shown, there is a correlation between economic prosperity and payments efficiency.[78]

[3]   THE IMPACT OF SV ON FEDERAL RESERVE BANK MONETARY POLICY

The Federal Reserve System is operated by the Board of Governors, a central governmental agency, and twelve regional Federal Reserve Banks. Together these components supervise and regulate certain financial institution activities, provide services to depository institutions and the federal government, and ensure that adequate customer protection mechanisms are in place throughout the banking industry.[79] This Section focuses on the implementation of monetary policy, as determined by the Federal Open Market Committee ("FOMC").[80] The FRB implements monetary policy through three principal devices: (1) open market operations; (2) reserve requirements; and (3) discount rate policy. The primary issues faced by the FRB in light of the development of SV systems are: the potential impact that SV may have on the FRB's ability to monitor the money supply, and whether the issuance of SV by nonbanks could restrict the FRB's ability to effect monetary policy.

[a] Open Market Operations. The FRB primarily implements monetary policy through open market operations, which includes the buying and selling of U.S. government securities through the Federal Reserve

---

[74] *See* National Performance Review – Phase II, Department of the Treasury – Final Proposals, *Commission Study of Currency Smart Card* submitted by Philp N. Diehl, Director of the United States Mint, to the House Subcommittee on Domestic and International Monetary Policy "The Future of Money" Oct. 11, 1995 (proposing a study to determine the feasibility of the possible issuance of a federal SV card as part of Vice President Gore's National Performance Review on Reinventing Government).

[75] *See id.*

[76] *See* COMMITTEE ON THE FEDERAL RESERVE IN THE PAYMENTS MECHANISM, FEDERAL RESERVE SYSTEM, THE FEDERAL RESERVE IN THE PAYMENTS MECHANISM 38 (Jan. 1998) (indicating that the FRB's role should be to foster cooperation and information sharing among all retail payments system participants, including nonbank providers in an effort to structure a legal and regulatory framework that fosters the development of new and emerging retail payment systems, rather than promoting any particular payment method) [hereinafter THE FEDERAL RESERVE IN THE PAYMENTS MECHANISM].

[77] Alan Greenspan, Chairman, Board of Governors of the Federal Reserve System, Remarks at the U.S. Treasury Conference on Electronic Money & Banking: The Role of Government, in Washington, D.C. (September 19, 1996), *available at* <http://www.emoneyworld.com/html/greenspan.html> [hereinafter Greenspan, U.S. Treasury Conference Remarks].

[78] *See* ABA(Bar) SV Report, *supra* note 1, at 654.

[79] These activities are discussed in Chapters 4 and 7.

[80] The Federal Open Market Committee is comprised of the seven members of the Board of Governors and five of the twelve presidents of the regional Federal Reserve Banks, who serve on a rotating basis.

Bank of New York ("N.Y. Fed"). The FRB alters the volume of reserves in the depository system by buying or selling U.S. securities from FRB designated dealers. The N.Y. Fed purchases securities with a check issued on itself, and adds reserves to the depository system.[81] The N.Y. Fed honors the presentation of the check by increasing the reserves in the seller's reserve account at the N.Y. Fed without any decrease in reserves elsewhere. To reduce reserves in the system, the N.Y. Fed reduces the total reserves in the buyer's bank account by selling securities.

SV issuance could reduce the FRB's control over the monetary and credit aggregates in the financial system, thus making it more difficult to implement monetary policy, because non-depository institutions are not subject to the jurisdiction of the FRB.[82] Non-depository entities are not required, under current law, to report the amount of currency issued. The participation of such entities as SV issuers may reduce the FRB's ability to measure and influence the money supply unless these issuers voluntarily file reports with the FRB.[83] The expected size of the SV market, however, is sufficiently small that the FRB's conduct of monetary policy may not be affected.[84] Thus, the present state and anticipated development of SV systems may not present an obstacle to the FRB's open market operations.[85] Restricting the SV issuance to regulated depository institutions would assist in assuring that the FRB's monetary policy process is based on a reliable quantification of the money supply, that, although not the focus of monetary policy, is an important ingredient in proper decision making.[86]

[b] Reserve Requirements and SV. Reserve requirements imposed on depository institutions impact the economy in two ways: (1) through the practice of bank lending based on fractional reserves; and (2) through reserve requirements' interplay with the demand for money, the supply of money, and interest rates. When a bank lends money, it creates additional money in the overall economy beyond the amount it lent.[87] Fractional reserve lending is the process by which banks lend out a fraction of its deposits to borrowers. Assume that the FRB sets reserve requirements to 10% of all deposits on hand, and that all banks may lend up to their maximum

---

[81] *See* BOARD OF GOVERNORS OF THE FEDERAL RESERVE SYSTEM, THE FEDERAL RESERVE SYSTEM: PURPOSES AND FUNCTIONS 35 (8th ed. 1994) [hereinafter THE FEDERAL RESERVE SYSTEM].

[82] *See* CBO STUDY, *supra* note 2, at 46.

[83] *Id*. at 46; *see also* Kelley, CyberPayments '96 Remarks, *supra* note 72 (stating "[i]f new payment instruments were issued by non-banks, [the FRB] would expect to obtain voluntary reports from issuers, as [the FRB] traditionally [has] done with travelers checks").

[84] *See* CBO STUDY, supra note 2, at 46; *see also* Kelley, CyberPayments '96 Remarks, *supra* note 72, stating:

> [W]e would not expect that the expansion of electronic delivery of existing banking services will have appreciable effects on the money supply or the money markets. In contrast, "electronic cash" or other new electronic payment products, if successful, could gradually lead to shifts among different forms of money held by consumers and thus potentially affect the behavior of the monetary aggregates. Yet concerns about loss of "control" of the money supply are misdirected. In the last twenty years, major shifts caused by other financial innovations have led to some changes over time in the ways in which monetary policy is formulated, with the monetary aggregates now playing a lesser role. Moreover, financial innovation has not seriously undermined central banks' ability to implement policy, although adaptations have sometimes been called for.

[85] *See* PAYMENTS SYSTEM TASK FORCE, *supra* note 3, at 22.

[86] *See id. See also* Kelley, CyberPayments '96 Remarks, *supra* note 72 (stating that "growth rates of the money supply are no longer the central focus of monetary policy making," however, "the Federal Reserve still needs to monitor the monetary aggregates carefully in the policy process, and it will remain important that the aggregates accurately measure the various instruments that are being used as money").

[87] *See* JONATHAN R. MACEY AND GEOFFREY P. MILLER, BANKING LAW AND REGULATION 50 (1992).

reserves. Whenever a bank receives a deposit, it lends 90% of that deposit. The borrower deposits that money into its bank, which lends out 90% of that deposit *ad infinitum*. Thus, for every $1000 initially deposited into the system, an additional $8999.99 in money and credit is created. Unregulated nonbank SV issuers may "lend" their "deposits" when they invest the proceeds of the sale of SV in non-government securities. The possibility that a SV issuer with a significant segment of the market for SV could increase the money supply through fractional reserve lending is one issue with which the FRB may eventually have to contend.

[c] FRB's Discount Rate Policy and SV. The FRB determines the discount rate as part of the implementation of its monetary policy. The discount rate is the interest charged by Federal Reserve Banks on reserves lent to banks that have reserve shortfalls.[88] This rate fluctuates to complement the FRB's open market operations. The discount rate is lowered when expanding the credit supply, while the rate is increased when the FRB seeks a tightening of credit.[89] A change in the discount rate, if unanticipated, will cause a change in market rates to reflect the shift in monetary policy. When a bank is unable to meet its reserve requirements, it may borrow reserves directly from the Federal Reserve through the discount window.[90]

Throughout the 1920s, the FRB used the discount window as the primary tool for implementation of monetary policy. As U.S. financial markets evolved, however, open market operations became the most efficient tool for providing or restricting the supply of credit and money in the U.S. economy. Today, the discount window serves primarily to facilitate balance sheet adjustments of individual banks when the demand for reserves is unexpectedly high or its supply is unexpectedly low.[91] Nonbank SV issuers that might find themselves short on liquidity, which could occur as the result of unanticipated requests for redemption or a devaluation of the securities in which the SV issuer invested the proceeds from the SV sale, would not have the benefit of access to the FRB's discount window as the lender of last resort.

[4]   THE FEDERAL RESERVE BOARD'S VIEW

The FRB recognizes that competition in the field of electronic payment systems is healthy and will result in products that maximize efficiencies in the payments system.[92] The FRB views nonbanking organizations as contributing to the competitive environment and serving as an impetus to innovation,[93] and seems inclined to

---

[88] *See id.* at 46. Borrowing at the discount window can either be through the "discount of eligible paper (notes, drafts, and bills of exchange) or as an advance secured by collateral." The borrowing bank endorses eligible paper and transfers it to the Federal Reserve Bank, which credits "an amount equal to the discounted value of the eligible paper at the current discount rate." When the paper matures, the Federal Reserve Bank debits the borrower's account and returns the paper to the borrower. Alternatively, the Federal Reserve Bank can provide an advance of reserves to the borrower who provides a note secured by adequate collateral to the Federal Reserve Bank. Today, the Federal Reserve Bank provides credit in the form of advances due to their operational convenience. *Id.*

[89] *See id.* at 43-44.

[90] *See* THE FEDERAL RESERVE SYSTEM, *supra* note 81, at 43-44.

[91] *See id.* at 43.

[92] *See* Kelley, CyberPayments '96 Remarks, *supra* note 72.

[93] *See* THE FEDERAL RESERVE IN THE PAYMENTS MECHANISM, *supra* note 76, at 35.

take a light-handed approach to the possible regulation of SV products.[94] Because significant social or economic risks have not yet materialized, aggressive regulation would handicap innovation for no compelling reason. If, however, significant problems do arise affecting the economic interests and well-being of the public, the payments system, or the economy in general, it is likely that there would be a corresponding legislative and regulatory response.

In the emerging electronic payments arena, the FRB appears to be focused on ensuring that effective risk management systems are in place in the private sector. The increasing complexity of electronic financial products and services and their integration into the payments infrastructure requires that the government foster financial innovation, rather than inhibit it.[95] FRB Chairman Alan Greenspan is cognizant of the fact that the private sector will need the flexibility to experiment in developing new forms of payment without broad interference by the government.[96]

[5] THE OFFICE OF THE COMPTROLLER OF THE CURRENCY'S VIEW

The Comptroller of the Currency, Eugene Ludwig, views the private sector and the U.S. markets as the driving force behind the development of electronic financial products and services ("EFS"). However, in achieving leadership in the global development of electronic currency, the Comptroller sees the role of government as aiding the private sector and U.S. markets in the evolution of electronic currency.[97] Most importantly, the Comptroller believes that whether electronic currency will evolve to become an efficient substitute for the U.S. paper payments system will depend upon a continual dialogue between the government and industry. In his view, solutions to significant public policy issues can be created through such a discourse.

According to the Comptroller, three principles should guide the government in its regulation of EFS. First, the government should work with the private and public sectors wherever possible. The rapid development of EFS exceeds the pace by which the government can develop and retain the expertise required to accomplish its public policy objectives. Therefore, the electronic commerce industry must support the government in its efforts to ensure a sound payment system. Second, the government should avoid premature regulation. Government entry into an industry in its infancy could stunt its growth or promote inefficiencies. Regulations that may become outmoded could be detrimental to the evolution of EFS. Third, the government should be prepared to

---

[94] *See* FRB SV REPORT, *supra* note 3, at 59 (stating that "full application of Regulation E to electronic [SV] products would probably give rise to prohibitive costs"). The FRB has proposed a limited application of Regulation E to certain SV products. *See* Electronic Fund Transfers, 61 Fed. Reg. 19,696 (proposed May 2, 1996); *see also* Kelley, CyberPayments '96 Remarks, *supra* note 72.

[95] *See* THE FEDERAL RESERVE IN THE PAYMENTS MECHANISM, *supra* note 76, at 3-4, 35-39.

[96] Greenspan, U.S. Treasury Conference Remarks, *supra* note 77 (stating that "[g]overnment action can retard progress, but almost certainly cannot ensure it").

[97] Eugene A. Ludwig, Comptroller of the Currency, Remarks at the U.S. Treasury Conference on Electronic Money & Banking: The Role of Government, in Washington, D.C. (Sept. 19, 1996), *available at* <http://www.emoneyworld.com/html/ludwig.html> [hereinafter Ludwig, U.S. Treasury Conference Remarks].

act, and not hesitate to act when action is required. Though premature regulation may stifle product innovation, hesitating to address problems will also impede the proper development of this new market.[98]

[6]   THE FREE BANKING ERA AND ITS IMPLICATIONS FOR ELECTRONIC MONEY

Evolving electronic currency products suggest analogies to paper currency and coins.[99] Comparisons to an earlier period in U.S. history, when private currencies circulated widely, may be appropriate. Although there are limits to the policy conclusions that can be drawn from such comparisons, an understanding of our banking history will inform or broaden the analysis of SV products that, in some respects, function like currency.[100]

In the early 1800s, notes issued by state chartered banks became an increasingly important part of the nation's money supply.[101] Prior to the Civil War, lax state requirements for entry into the banking industry spurred a proliferation of state bank charters.[102] Requirements for the maintenance of specie, gold and silver, or other reserves to back the notes issued by state banks were minimal.[103] Confidence in the monetary system deteriorated to a point where state banks were suspending redemption of their notes, which then circulated at steep discounts. State legislatures supported their banks' reluctance to redeem notes by enacting protective statutes including one statute requiring the holder of any notes, before redemption would be authorized, to swear in court, in front of the bank's five directors and cashier, that he owned each note.[104]

Recent research suggests, however, that the problems of the free banking period were exaggerated. Analysis has shown, for example, that losses to bank note holders and bank failures were not out of line with comparable periods in U.S. banking history.[105] Because state bank notes were not legal tender, market forces helped to protect holders of bank notes. According to the Chairman of the FRB, "there was no obligation to accept the currency of a suspect bank, or to accept it at par value; accordingly, notes often were accepted and

---

[98] *Id.*

[99] *See generally* Robert E. Litan & Jonathan Rauch, *American Finance for the 21st Century*, United States Department of the Treasury (Nov. 17, 1977) (presenting numerous conceptual questions regarding electronic money, such as whether it is cash, who should issue electronic money, and whether it should be covered by deposit insurance). This Treasury Department report analyzes many of these issues in the context of the free banking era of the early 19th Century. *See also* Mondex International, *How Will The Scheme Operate?, available at* <http://www.mondex.com/mondex/cgibin/show.pl?english+global&../english/documents/global/ faq39493413.txt> ("Mondex is designed to be an electronic equivalent of cash").

[100] *See* Greenspan, U.S. Treasury Conference Remarks, *supra* note 77.

[101] The power to issue notes was a continuation of English common law permitting banks to issue notes without being considered an infringement upon the royal prerogative to coin money. *See* NUSSBAUM, *supra* note 66, at 14-15. In the pre-Civil War period, gold and silver coins minted by the federal government were the primary circulating medium of exchange.

[102] This period is known as the Free Banking Era. It is also discussed in Chapter 2.

[103] *See* NUSSBAUM, *supra* note 66, at 64.

[104] *See id.* at 66.

[105] *See* Greenspan, U.S. Treasury Conference Remarks, *supra* note 77. *See also* Lewis D. Solomon, *Local Currency: A Legal and Policy Analysis*, 5 KAN. J.L. & PUB. POL'Y 59 (1996). Professor Solomon notes that commentators recently found that most of the state bank failures were due to declining government bond prices. Many states enacted free banking statutes that granted charters to those entities willing to purchase state bonds to hold as reserves. When state government bond prices declined, some banks became insolvent. *Id.* at 62.

cleared at less than par."[106] Consequently, bank note reporters were published to provide the current market rates for notes of different banks based on their creditworthiness, reputation, and location, as well as to identify counterfeit notes. Banks competed for reputation, and advertised high capital ratios, often exceeding 33%, to attract depositors. Market forces spurred the private regulation that helped stem the inflation associated with the overissuance of notes.

Similar to state bank notes, electronic money may serve as a form of quasi-currency, usable as a form of payment, but not recognized as legal tender by the federal government. A loss or drop in confidence in a particular form of SV would raise the prospect that merchants or other parties may be unwilling to accept that particular type of SV or to accept it at par. The implications of this could go beyond an individual bank or nonbank SV issuer, and become systemic in nature. Assume that a particular form of SV gained widespread acceptance and then a news report appeared stating that either the issuer is in danger of failure or that there was a significant breach of the SV system's security. In either instance, this could trigger a run on the form of SV, here acting as a from of quasi-currency rather than a run on a particular depository institution. At this point, the federal government might feel compelled to step in to avoid an adverse systemic impact on the economy, because FDIC deposit insurance would likely have no effect in this circumstance. This might even turn into a contagion which would affect issuers and redeemers of other types of stored value. To the extent that this scenario does not necessarily include SV "issued" by a bank, it is not a perfect analogy, but it is similar in that it involves "currency" being issued by a party other than the federal government.

[7]   INTERNATIONAL SV INITIATIVES: THE EUROPEAN PERSPECTIVE

In February 1993, the Committee of Governors of the European Community ("EC") central banks requested the Working Group on EU Payment Systems to study the issues involved in the creation of multi-purpose prepaid SV cards.[107] On January 1, 1994, the European Monetary Institute ("EMI") was formed pursuant to the Maastricht Treaty. The EMI is comprised of the central banks of the twelve member countries of the European Union.[108] In May 1994, EMI published the Working Group's report ("EMI Report") discussing prepaid cards in the context of a European Single Market and the anticipated obligations of the future European System of Central Banks with regard to the functioning of the payment system.[109]

The EMI highlighted a number of issues in regard to SV. It stressed the importance that new payment instruments not adversely affect public confidence in the existing payment media or the payments system. Public confidence, it noted, could be shaken if non-regulated institutions issue SV, or if the SV system design

---

[106] Greenspan, U.S. Treasury Conference Remarks, *supra* note 77.

[107] Working Group on EU Payment Systems, *Report to the Council of The European Monetary Institute on Prepaid Cards*, ¶2 (May 1994) <http://www.systemics.com/docs/papers/EU_prepaid_cards.html> [hereinafter EMI Report].

[108] *See* PAYMENTS SYSTEM TASK FORCE, *supra* note 3, at app. B-15.

[109] EMI Report, *supra* note 107, ¶ 2. The Working Group's report refers to multipurpose prepaid cards and "electronic purses" to represent what is generally referred to herein as SV cards.

makes counterfeiting either easy to achieve or difficult to detect.[110] The EMI Report's conclusion states that SV would probably not hamper the central bank's ability to control the money supply. The EMI cautioned that new measures may be needed to implement monetary policy; policy that relies on the availability of accurate information concerning the outstanding currency.[111] Finally, the EMI noted that extensive use of SV might infringe on the revenues that central banks derive from the issuance of coins and paper currency (*e.g.,* brassage and seigniorage).[112]

The EMI also found that the issuance of value on a multipurpose prepaid card represents the economic equivalent of deposit taking by the issuer. The EMI Report states that a SV holder views the cash paid for the purchase of SV to be a deposit held by the issuer for later redemption. The EMI, therefore, proposed that the right to issue SV be restricted to depository institutions. It based the proposal on four policy rationales: (1) protecting the integrity of the retail payment system; (2) protecting customers against the consequences of a bankrupt issuer; (3) facilitating the conduct of monetary policy; and (4) ensuring fair competition between issuing institutions.[113]

The EMI Report notes that no EU central bank anticipated issuing prepaid cards in the near future. At the time of its publication, the degree of EU central bank involvement in the development of SV varied. Some central banks considered SV to be exclusively a matter for private operators. Others thought it preferable to be involved in interbank settlements, when appropriate. Some EU central banks hoped to encourage market participants to develop a common technical infrastructure with a view to promoting the interoperability of competing card schemes.[114]

The EMI Report's policy conclusions are listed below:

- Only credit institutions should be allowed to issue SV.[115]

- EU central banks should continue to monitor developments in the field of prepaid cards, possibly in cooperation with other central banks outside the EU.

---

[110] *Id.* ¶6.

[111] *Id.* ¶7.

[112] *Id.* ¶8.

[113] *Id.* ¶9.

[114] The EMI Report notes that:

> Protection against counterfeiting will be a very important element on which the future of electronic purses depend. Forgery will probably be more difficult to detect with this instrument, particularly if the card can be used anonymously, and is not personalized in any way. By virtue of their higher degree of built-in security, chip cards have a far greater potential than traditional cashless payment technologies and, although it is not the only option available, recent experience suggests that the chip card seems to be the most probable choice in this context; for security reasons, an electronic purse system implemented on the basis of cards containing magnetic stripes does not seem very realistic. There is no certainty however, that chip cards will provide an absolute protection against forgeries.

> *Id.* ¶ 20.

[115] Credit institutions are defined as European institutions subject to banking regulation, excluding mortgage institutions, multilateral development banks, and central banks. *See* International Financial Encyclopaedia, (visited on Jan. 24, 1998) <http://www.euro.net/innovation/Finance_Base/ Encyclopaedia/C.html#RTFToC907>.

- EU central banks should be kept informed, if possible at an early stage, of any major prepaid card scheme involving more than one good or service provider, to decide whether the scheme should be considered as "limited-purpose" or as "multi-purpose."

- Central banks may wish to examine carefully the security features of proposed prepaid card schemes. They may wish to discourage some initiatives in order to protect the integrity of the retail payment system.

In certain circumstances (*e.g.*, in the case of systems already in operation before the policy conclusions of the report were released), the local central bank may agree that SV issuers are not required to be credit institutions. Such exceptions would be granted if the issuer: (1) provides only domestic payment services; (2) is subject to appropriate regulations, in particular, with respect to liquidity requirements; and (3) is supervised by the regulatory body which supervises credit institutions.[116] According to the EMI report, EU central banks are of the view that the market should decide which payments systems can best serve customer needs. Therefore, they do not wish to interfere unnecessarily in the development of prepaid card systems.[117]

More recently, the EC Banking Advisory Committee has drafted a proposal for a directive on "Electronic Money Institutions." This proposal is intended to: (1) provide rules for non-credit institutions issuing electronic money; (2) provide a level playing field; (3) establish a supervisory regime covering electronic money risks; and (4) encourage the use and provision of electronic money.[118]

[a] The Netherlands Approach. Since the publication of the EMI Report in 1994, several developments in the field of electronic commerce occurred that have affected the European perspective.[119] With the rise of the Internet as a global communications system, SV providers emerged to furnish the means by which customers could execute transactions online.

In the Netherlands, nonbanks serve as major providers of computer-based SV.[120] Multi-purpose SV cards and computer-based SV have been found to be the legal equivalent of deposit taking.[121] This means that SV issuers should obtain a banking license and be subject to supervision. In 1997, Henny van der Wielen,

---

[116] EMI Report, *supra* note 107, ¶ 32.

[117] *Id.* ¶ 28.

[118] *See* P. Michael Nugent, General Counsel for Technology & IP, Citibank, *Electronic Money Products*, Remarks at the Third Annual Cyberbanking and Electronic Commerce Conference, in Washington, D.C., at 4 (Feb. 3, 1998); *see also Financial Services - Commission Agrees: Recommendation on Electronic Payment Instruments*, *available at* <http://europa.eu.int/comm/dg15/en/finances/banks/626.htm> (Oct. 23, 1997) (noting that the EC will assess member state compliance with the Recommendation, and if the member states do not adequately implement the minimum standards recommended with respect to electronic payment instruments, the EC will propose a Directive).

[119] The EMI Report is not binding on European central bankers, but merely an early perspective on the regulatory structure that regulators thought would be designed for the regulation of SV issuers and SV payment systems.

[120] *See, e.g.,* <http://www.digicash.com>. *See also Focus: Reductions in Working Hours Must be Negotiated*, SOCIETE GENERALE FRANCE: MONTHLY ECON. REP., Sept. 1997 (describing actions taken by banks in the Netherlands, in order to be competitive with nonbanks entering the market); Henny van der Wielan, Deputy Director of the central bank of the Netherlands, *Electronic Money: A European Perspective,* Remarks at the Seminar on Electronic Money, in London (Feb. 4, 1997), *available at* <http://jya.com/EU_perspective.html> (discussing the effects of increased nonbank competition in the prepaid card market) [hereinafter van der Wielan, *A European Perspective*].

[121] van der Wielan, *A European Perspective, supra* note 120, ¶ 13.

Deputy Director of the central bank of the Netherlands, commented that banking regulators should engage SV issuers in a dialogue to acquire relevant information on the SV system designed by the issuer. According to van der Wielen, in fulfilling their regulatory responsibilities, banking regulators should learn the general characteristics of the system, the institutional and organizational structure, the legal relationships among the system's participants, the issuing, accounting and administrative processes, float management, security, technical, and other internal features.[122]

Deputy Director van der Wielen proposed that banking regulators, as guardians of the payments system, should ensure that the management of SV issuers and operators possess the requisite competence and integrity.[123] He maintained that reporting and capital reserve requirements should be applicable to all SV issuers and the responsibilities and obligations of all SV system participants should be well-defined and communicated between the participants and the supervising agency. If the SV issuer is not a bank, banking regulators should be provided with the authority to extend their supervision to system operators and to subcontractors. In addition, Deputy Director van der Wielen stated that relevant international professional standards, such as accounting standards, best practices, and security standards should be applied to all SV issuers.[124]

Commenting on the approach taken by the EMI Report, Deputy Director van der Wielen raised the concern that limiting the issuance of SV to depository institutions may stifle competition. He noted, however, that the limits in the EMI Report do not necessarily restrict nonbank SV issuers from affiliating with depository institutions in the execution of their SV systems.[125] These depository institutions are not necessarily subject to the same requirements in terms of liquidity, solvency, and reporting as general-purpose banks in the Netherlands. The main requirement for the operation of a SV system by a nonbank is that its affiliated bank bears full responsibility for the money flows involved.[126] If a nonbank SV issuer intends to do no more than receive proceeds from the sale of SV and hold the float in a liquid form (*e.g.*, bank deposits or government securities), then only a small part of existing regulations would be applicable to this issuer.[127]

[b] Smart Card Products and SV Systems in Europe. Europe is widely viewed as being far more advanced in the use of smart cards and SV systems than the United States.[128] In particular, France and Germany

---

[122] *Id.* ¶ 14.

[123] *Id.* ¶ 15.

[124] *Id.* ¶ 14.

[125] *Id.* ¶ 26.

[126] *Id.*

[127] *Id.* ¶ 26.

[128] *See generally* The Tower Group, *Smart Cards in Banking, The Future of Money?*, Dec. 1996 (discussing the prospects of various SV ventures throughout Europe and the United States such as Mondex in the U.K. and elsewhere, Proton in Belgium, Danmont in Denmark, and SEMP in Spain). The Tower Group Report notes that over 95% of worldwide smart cards will be held in Europe through 1998. *Id.* at 3 (stating that the U.S. is 10 to 12 years behind Europe in its adoption of smart cards). In addition, the European Community's ESPRIT research program has begun field trials of Conditional Access for Europe ("CAFE"), a secure electronic payment system based on smart cards and electronic wallets with infrared transceivers. *See Europe Bucks Conventions,* BYTE, June 1996, at 80; *DigiCash BV, Bank Austria and Den norske Bank to Issue Ecash the Electronic Cash for the Internet*, M2 PRESSWIRE, Apr. 15, 1997; *Banks Issue DigiCash Wallets; Has Introduced Infrared Wallets Which Support Portable Transmission of Cash*, BANK SYS. + TECH., May 1996, at 10.

lead the world in the number of smart cards in circulation and number of transactions.[129] The success of the European approach appears to be attributable to the production and use of multifunctional smart cards, which permits the Europeans to combine credit, debit, and stored value features onto a single card.[130] Furthermore, the cooperation of the majority of banks, the national payment network and telecommunications companies to ensure interoperability provided the foundation for the success of smart cards in Europe.[131] The dramatic rise of smart card and SV systems in Europe, and their recent adoption in North America and Asia, have led to studies on a coordinated regulatory approach by the G-10 countries.

[c] International Regulation of SV Systems. The G-7 Heads of State and Governments, in an effort to promote international development of a coordinated approach to the regulation of SV systems, recently requested a cooperative study of retail electronic payments.[132] In the fall of 1996, the G-10 Deputies responded to the G-7 request by forming a Working Party to study three broad policy areas concerning SV: (1) customer issues; (2) law enforcement issues; and (3) supervisory issues.[133] The G-10 Report, published in April 1997, identifies broad policy objectives in these three areas and discusses approaches taken by various G-10 countries to date.[134]

[i] *Market Risks.* Before addressing private and government measures to regulate SV systems, the G-10 Report discusses several risks faced by SV issuers that constitute threats to the integrity of not only individual SV issuers, but of the payments system generally.[135] SV issuance creates liabilities on the issuer's balance sheet that are redeemable at face value by SV users. Such liabilities create operational and liquidity risks for the SV issuer.[136] In addition, credit and market risks can threaten the value of an SV issuer's assets purchasedwith the proceeds of the sale of SV. Some SV systems may attempt to protect the holders of SV against

---

[129] *See* The Tower Group, *supra* note 128, at 2 (noting that as of December 1996, over 25 million smart cards were in circulation in France, out of the 50 million circulating in Europe at that time, and that there were plans to place microprocessors on all 55 million eurocheque cards circulating in Germany).

[130] The Tower Group Report states that SV comprising the only function on a smart card has not been an overwhelming success in Europe as of December 1996, primarily because consumers derive very little benefit from the system. *Id.* at 4-5. However, the Report comments on what it considers the enormous advantages that accrue to banks such as the interest on the float of prepaid amounts, transfer of the risk of fraud to the consumer, potential retention of unused money on lost or stolen cards, and some benefits to merchants such as slightly faster transaction times, and elimination of black-lists associated with checks accepted on insufficient funds.

[131] *Id.* at 7 (noting that incompatible systems raise the prospect of project failure due to the lack of incentives for consumers and merchants to invest in a project that restricts the interoperability of a smart card or smart card readers).

[132] *See* GROUP OF TEN, ELECTRONIC MONEY: CONSUMER PROTECTION, LAW ENFORCEMENT, SUPERVISORY, AND CROSS BORDER ISSUES, at 1 (Apr. 1997), *available at* <http://www.bis.org> [hereinafter GROUP OF TEN, ELECTRONIC MONEY] (noting the G-7's request for the study at the Lyon Summit Economic Communiqué, June 28, 1996). The G-10, whose membership has grown to 11 countries, includes central bankers from Belgium, Britain, Canada, France, Germany, Italy, Japan, the Netherlands, Sweden, Switzerland, and the United States.

[133] *Id.* at 1.

[134] *Id.* The report did not focus on the monetary and seigniorage implications of SV because they have been the subject of extensive analysis under the auspices of the G-10 central bank Governors. *Id.* at 2.

[135] *Id.* at 18-19.

[136] *Id.* at 19.

these risks by accepting the risk of insolvency of another SV issuer by means of a loss sharing or guarantee agreement.[137]

The G-10 Report notes that market forces can reduce many of the risks associated with issuing SV. SV issuers have strong incentives to protect against financial and operational risks. The need for a reputation of stability and integrity, in order to attract new capital and to encourage the participation of financial institutions, merchants, and customers, should motivate SV issuers to institute effective risk management practices, such as the investment of proceeds in high-quality, short-term, liquid securities pending SV redemption. SV issuers may suffer, however, from a conflict of interest in their desire to gain higher returns by investing in assets with greater risk.[138]

[*ii*] *Regulatory Considerations.* The G-10 Report urges regulatory authorities to consider the degree to which market incentives will achieve public policy objectives.[139] Government supervision may enhance public confidence in SV payment systems, but may lead to public expectations of government support in case of market failure. Governments should determine, according to the G-10 Report, the extent to which licensing requirements will level the playing field and promote fair competition among SV issuers, while simultaneously examining the extent to which such requirements act as a barrier to entry, thus reducing competition.[140] These licensing requirements may be triggered by a regulatory agency's assessment that the issuance of SV is the economic equivalent of deposit-taking and thus subject to the established supervisory framework.[141]

The G-10 Report recommends that regulators take into consideration the risks confronted by SV issuers and the differences those risks pose from the set of risks applicable to standard banking organizations. Solvency requirements, liquidity standards, and other types of prudential guidelines developed for traditional banks may not be relevant or appropriate for SV issuers. The G-10 Report recommends that SV issuers should be limited in their investments to high-quality, short-term assets that can be liquidated at short notice to meet redemption obligations.[142] This will translate into a rather simple balance sheet and cash flow operation for the SV issuer, requiring less complex and less intensive supervisory examinations. Thus, a SV issuer, under the scheme laid out in the G-10 Report, may be exempted from several aspects of depository regulation if it does not engage in other banking functions.[143]

The G-10 Report asserts that systemic risks to the financial system whether in a single country, or globally, are negligible in the short term due to the limited size and scope of SV systems. If, however, SV develops to

---

[137] *See id.* at 19 (stating that a special purpose organization set up to issue SV may be owned by a group of banks).

[138] *Id.*

[139] *Id.* at 20.

[140] *Id.*

[141] *Id.*

[142] *Id.* at 22-23.

[143] *Id.* at 23. In Germany, regulators are considering modifications of supervisory rules and exemptions from others for specialized SV issuers that do not engage in other banking activities. *Id.* at n.22.

such a degree as to substantially replace a nation's currency, a loss of confidence in the SV system could conceivably have broader consequences for that country's and the world's financial system. Although the G-10 Report considers this to be only a remote possibility, it finds that the magnitude of the potential damage warrants continued monitoring and assessment of SV developments.[144]

§ 16.04 WHO MAY ISSUE STORED VALUE OR ELECTRONIC MONEY UNDER CURRENT LAW?

Stored value and electronic money systems vary and will continue to develop unique approaches that may result in differing legal treatment. These systems raise novel issues such as: Whether they are a new form of "currency" or just another type of payment instrument similar to traveler's checks or money orders? Are SV and electronic money issuers engaged in deposit taking and if so, are they engaged in the business of banking, subjecting them to a number of state and federal banking laws? Are these issuers and new payments systems subject to another regulatory regime such as money transmitter and sale of check statutes? This Section explores and discusses these and other issues.

[1] ISSUING CURRENCY AS A FUNCTION OF SOVEREIGNTY

In 1789, the U.S. Constitution provided Congress with the authority "[t]o coin Money, regulate the Value thereof, and of foreign Coin, and fix the Standard of Weights and Measures."[145] Congress established the dollar to be the money unit of the United States,[146] and similarly established a fixed rate of redemption of all U.S. currency, in both gold and silver.[147] The Constitution prohibits the states from coining money, emitting bills of credit, or making "any Thing but gold and silver Coin a Tender in Payment of Debts."[148]

[2] ISSUING NOTES AS A FUNCTION OF THE BUSINESS OF BANKING

[a] **National Banks.** In 1864, the National Bank Act[149] amended and expanded the provisions of the 1863 Currency Act. Among other provisions, the National Bank Act sets forth in specific detail the corporate

---

[144] *Id.* at 20-21.

[145] U.S. CONST. art. I, § 8, cl. 5.

[146] Act of Apr. 20, 1792, c. 16. The creation of paper currency was expressed by similar designations, sanctioned by law, and made legal tender in payment of debts. It was necessary to allow judgments to be entered for payment of coined dollars when that kind of money was specifically designated in contracts upon which suits were brought. *Trebilcock v Wilson,* 79 U.S. 687 (1872). The current codification may be found at 31 U.S.C. § 5101 ("[d]ecimal system: United States money is expressed in dollars, dimes or tenths, cents or hundreths, and mills or thousandths. A dime is a tenth of a dollar, a cent is a hundredth of a dollar, and a mill is a thousandth of a dollar").

[147] *See* NUSSBAUM, *supra* note 66, at 47. Recognizing the scarcity of U.S. coins, Congress on February 9, 1793 declared Spanish and Mexican dollars to be legal tender. Contrary to popular belief, the $ is of Spanish origin represented by two parallel vertical lines, the abbreviation of "P" for peso, with an "S" imprinted upon the lines indicating the plural. *See id.* at 56.

[148] U.S. CONST. art. I, § 10, cl. 1. *See also Briscoe v. Bank of the Commonwealth of Kentucky*, 11 Peters 326 (1837), wherein the Supreme Court held that a note issued by a state and backed by its full faith and credit was an impermissible bill of credit but a note issued by a state chartered bank was not.

[149] National Bank Act, ch. 106, 13 Stat. 100 (1864) (codified as amended at 12 U.S.C. § 21 *et seq.*). See Chapter 2 for a further discussion of the National Bank Act.

powers of national banks and various activities in which they may engage. One important power of a national bank is that it has "all such incidental powers as shall be necessary to carry on the business of banking."[150]

Congress, in establishing the national banking system, gave national banks the power to "obtain, issue and circulate notes."[151] In pursuit of a more stable currency than that of the free banking era, national banks issued notes backed by federal government bonds.[152] The necessity for national bank issuance of notes became obsolete when Federal Reserve notes replaced bank notes as United States currency in 1913.[153] Since then, "more modern substitutes for currency, such as traveler's checks, cashier's checks, and other bearer instruments issued or sold by banks, have developed as components of the payments system and as part of the business of banking."[154] The OCC, in the context of the proposed investment in Mondex through the operating subsidiary of national banks, concluded that "the issuance and redemption of stored value represents a new way of conducting one aspect of the payments business of banks: issuing and circulating notes."[155]

[b] State Banks. In 1865, Congress passed a tax on state bank notes in order to prompt state banks to convert to national banks; a tax that was upheld by the Supreme Court in 1869.[156] State banks responded with the development of the checking account as an effective substitute for circulating state bank notes. Presumably, state banks retain the power to issue notes as a function of the business of banking and, therefore, under state laws an analysis similar to that used by the OCC would apply to state bank notes.[157]

[3]   THE ISSUANCE OF ELECTRONIC MONEY AND RESTRICTIONS ON DEPOSIT TAKING AND THE BUSINESS OF BANKING

Due to the range of activities conducted by modern banks, the word "bank" has a variety of meanings in different legal contexts. Generally, receiving deposits is one indicia (in fact, probably the principal indicia)

---

[150] 12 U.S.C. § 24(Seventh). For a further discussion of the permissible scope of national banking activities, see Chapter 6.

[151] OCC Mondex Letter, *supra* note 14, at 8.

[152] *Id.*

[153] *Id.* "In 1994, Congress repealed the provisions in the National Bank Act dealing with the issuance of post notes by national banks (previously codified at 12 U.S.C. §§ 101 et seq.) because they believed that those provisions were obsolete. H.R. REP. No. 103-652, 103rd Cong., *reprinted in* 1994 U.S.C.C.A.N. 2035. Thus, the repeal did not indicate a congressional intent to restrict national bank powers." OCC Mondex Letter *supra* note 14, at n.11.

[154] OCC Mondex Letter, *supra* note 14, at n.11.

[155] *Id.* at 8.

[156] *Veazie Bank v. Fenno*, 75 U.S. (8 Wall.) 533, 548 (1869) (holding that the federal government could discriminate against an otherwise lawful industry for regulatory purposes).

[157] The tax remained in effect until it was repealed by the Tax Reform Act cf 1976. Pub. L. No. 94-455, 1976 U.S.C.C.A.N. (90 Stat.) 1520. For a further discussion of the history and legal treatment of national and state bank note issuance, see LEWIS D. SOLOMON, RETHINKING OUR CENTRALIZED MONETARY SYSTEM: THE CASE FOR LOCAL CURRENCIES 103 (1996).

that an entity is engaging in the business of banking.[158] A definition of "deposit" generally incorporates the concept of "account" or the bank's liability as a "debtor" to make payments to the depositor or third party.[159]

[a] Federal Law. As discussed below, federal banking statutes provide a number of definitions of the terms "bank" and "deposits" that might be relevant to the treatment of an SV issuer.

[i] Bank Holding Company Act. The Bank Holding Company Act ("BHCA") defines "bank" as an FDIC-insured institution or as an institution that accepts demand deposits and makes commercial loans.[160] The U.S. Supreme Court, in the context of the BHCA, has defined "demand deposit" as a deposit that may be withdrawn by depositor without prior notice or limitation.[161] If the FRB deems a SV issuer to be accepting demand deposits by virtue of its SV activities and the SV issuer is engaged in making commercial loans, it could be treated as a bank for purposes of the BHCA, thereby incurring significant restrictions on its activities and subjecting any parent company and its affiliates to the activities restrictions, and examination and supervision provisions of the BHCA.

[ii] Federal Deposit Insurance Act. The Federal Deposit Insurance Act ("FDIA") defines "bank" as a national bank and as any other banking institution "engaged in the business of receiving deposits."[162] The term "deposit" is given broad meaning under the FDIA.[163] The FDIC has taken the position that in certain instances, funds associated with a bank's role in a SV system qualify as deposits for purposes of the FDIA.[164]

---

[158] The EMI Report addresses this point and notes its relation to SV, stating that, in economic terms, it is clear that the money received by the issuer of an electronic purse is a bank deposit.

> It is indeed a claim which the card-holder (or account holder) has on a third party and which can be used to make cashless payments to a wide range of providers of goods and services. . . . Therefore, in economic terms, the reasons which led public authorities to reserve deposit-taking to a specific category of institutions should also apply to the issuers of electronic purses. These reasons relate both to the protection of the consumer and to the protection of the money transmission system. If corporations other than credit institutions were to issue electronic purses, banking regulations, which, in the end, seek to protect customers deposits, would not apply. Moreover, deposit guarantee schemes would not apply either. As far as the money transmission system is concerned, its stability could be threatened by the failure of one or several issuers; public confidence in other retail payment instruments (*e.g.*, debit cards) may also be affected. Therefore, it is very important that the liquidity regime which applies to credit institutions serves to ensure that the issuers of prepaid cards are able to meet their liabilities to retailers in the settlement of transactions made with the cards. Moreover, there would be an additional concern for central banks and banking supervisors if banks which were subject to prudential regulations (and in some countries to reserve requirements) were not able to compete on equal terms with other issuers of electronic purses.

EMI Report, *supra* note 107, ¶ 31.

[159] 5A MICHIE ON BANKS AND BANKING, ch. 9, § 1, at 22 (1994).

[160] Bank Holding Company Act of 1956, ch. 240, 70 Stat. 133 (1956) (codified as amended at 12 U.S.C. § 1841 *et seq.*). *See* 12 U.S.C. § 1841(c)(1) (defining a bank and excluding certain types of entities, such as savings associations, certain credit card banks, and trust companies from the definition of bank).

[161] *Board of Governors of the Fed. Reserve Sys. v. Dimension Financial Corp.*, 474 U.S. 361, 368 (1986).

[162] Federal Deposit Insurance Act of 1950, ch. 967, 64 Stat. 873 (codified as amended at 12 U.S.C. § 1811 *et seq.*). *See* 12 U.S.C. § 1813(a)(2)(A).

[163] 12 U.S.C. § 1813(*l*) (referring to, among other things, any money received or held by bank in the usual course of business and for which bank is obligated to give credit to a commercial, checking, savings, time, or thrift account; and includes letters of credit or traveler's checks on which the bank is primarily liable, escrow and trust funds, bank cashier's checks and money orders).

[164] General Counsel's Opinion No. 8; Stored Value Cards, 61 Fed. Reg. 40,490 (1996).

[*iii*] *National Bank Act.* The National Bank Act empowers national banks to conduct various activities, including receiving deposits.[165] A "branch" of a national bank is a place where "deposits are received, or checks paid, or money lent."[166] The Supreme Court, in the context of one state bank's attempt to redeem another state bank's notes, defined the term "deposit" as the depositor's parting with the title to money, by lending it to a banker. In this context, the banker, in consideration of the loan of the money and the right to use it for profit, agrees to refund the same amount or any part thereof, on demand.[167]

[*iv*] *Glass-Steagall Act.* In 1933, Congress, in an effort to address what were perceived to be risks associated with speculative securities practices by commercial banks, separated commercial banking from the investment banking industry by means of the Glass-Steagall Act.[168] The Glass-Steagall Act was intended to sharply limit the extent to which a national bank or a state member bank could engage as a principal in securities underwriting and dealing, or to affiliate with a securities firm. At the same time the act sought to preclude securities firms from engaging in the core banking activity of accepting deposits. Over the past two decades, a series of court decisions, regulatory actions, and product innovations have largely broken down the wall between commercial banking organizations and investment banking firms.[169]

[A] *Section 21 of the Glass-Steagall Act: A Prohibition on Deposit-Taking by Nonbanks.* Section 21 of Glass-Steagall contains two separate prohibitions on the acceptance of deposits by non-depository institutions.[170] If a particular SV or electronic money product were considered to be a "deposit," issues regarding the applicability of Section 21 to the SV issuer might arise. According to a recent report of the Treasury Department regarding electronic money,[171] "[t]he government has not definitively opined on [Section 21] issues. Because the statutes involved are criminal, the regulatory agencies must defer to the Department of Justice . . . As criminal statutes, the laws would be narrowly construed. Uncertainty over the application of Glass-Steagall Act has not, so far, appeared to have chilled the development of electronic [money]."[172]

---

[165] 12 U.S.C. § 24(Seventh).

[166] 12 U.S.C. § 36(f).

[167] *Marine Bank v. Fulton Bank,* 69 U.S. (2 Wall.) 252, 256 (1864) (addressing one state bank's attempt to redeem notes of another state bank whose market value had declined 50% from their face value).

[168] Glass-Steagall Act (1933), 48 Stat. 162 (codified in scattered sections of 12 U.S.C.).

[169] *See Regulatory Reform in Transition: The Dismantling of the Glass-Steagall Act,* 47 ADMIN. L. REV. 545, 552-559 (1995) (listing various actions and decisions which have limited the application of Glass-Steagall, including the decision of the FRB to increase the percentage of gross revenues that banks may receive from "ineligible activities," including underwriting).

[170] Section 21(a)(1) prohibits any person or entity that engages in a securities business from engaging "at the same time to any extent whatsoever" in the business of receiving deposits subject to check or repayment upon presentation of a passbook, certificate of deposit, or other evidence of debt, or upon request of the depositor. 12 U.S.C. § 378(a)(1). Section 21(a)(2) prohibits any person or entity from engaging, to any extent whatsoever, in the business of receiving deposits subject to check or repayment upon presentation of a passbook, certificate of deposit, or other evidence of debt, or upon request of the depositor, unless such person or entity (i) is incorporated under and authorized by federal or state law to engage in such business and subjected by such law to examination and regulation, or (ii) is permitted by the federal government or a state to engage in such business and subject, under federal or state law, to examination and regulations, or (iii) submits to periodic examination by the banking authority of the state where such business is conducted and publishes periodic reports of its condition. 12 U.S.C. § 378(a)(2).

[171] U.S. Department of Treasury, *An Introduction to Electronic Money Issues: Toward Electronic Money and Banking — The Role of Government,* Prepared for the U.S. Department of the Treasury Conference, Washington, D.C., Sept. 19-20, 1996 [hereinafter Treasury Report].

[172] *Id.* at 52.

The courts have not often had the occasion to interpret or to apply Section 21 with respect to nonbanks. A decision by the Court of Appeals for the Second Circuit is the only reported court decision that considered the application of Section 21's prohibitions to non-depository institutions. In *United States v. Jenkins*,[173] the Second Circuit upheld the conviction of an individual charged with violating Section 21(a)(2) after receiving $150,000 as part of a money-laundering scheme. The defendant argued that Section 21 did not apply because no actual bank existed and, in his version of events, the funds should be characterized as an investment in the creation of a bank (rather than a deposit in an existing one). The court rejected this argument, finding that by its very nature Section 21 clearly applies to persons and entities other than existing registered banks and their agents.[174]

[B] *What Constitutes a "Deposit" for Purposes of Glass-Steagall?* The term "deposit" is not expressly defined by the Glass-Steagall Act. Definitions of deposit in other areas typically contain a common principle: the physical receipt and possession of money or its equivalent, payable upon the demand of the depositor.[175] At common law, a deposit is money placed in the custody and safekeeping of a bank, subject to withdrawal at the will of the depositor (or pursuant to agreement).[176] In this regard, the Supreme Court has stated that "[h]aving a place of business where deposits are received and paid out on checks, and where money is loaned upon security, is the substance and business of a banker."[177]

Lying outside the traditional definition of deposit are a series of instruments that offer features similar to those associated with bank deposits. These instruments have been referred to as "non-deposit deposits."[178] These instruments include money orders and traveler's checks. Another prominent example of an instrument that has become widely viewed by the public as a deposit substitute are money market mutual fund ("MMF") shares. The Department of Justice, in a December 18, 1979 letter written to the Securities and Exchange

---

[173] 943 F.2d 167 (2d Cir. 1991).

[174] The Second Circuit implied in dictum, however, that the act of holding oneself out as a bank or as a banker was a significant element in any criminal violation of Section 21 by a nonbank. *Id.* at 173 (noting that "we are convinced that section 378(a)(2) prohibits any entity that claims to be a bank, or any person who purports to represent a bank, from engaging in the business of receiving deposits without proper authorization – regardless of whether an actual bank exists"). *See also* Banque Worms, S.A., Docket Nos. 93-060-WA/RB-FB; No. 93-060-WARB-FBS (FRB 1996) (prohibiting Banque Worms, S.A., and its New York subsidiary from engaging in violations of Section 21(a)(2) of the Glass-Steagall Act (12 U.S.C. § 378(a)(2)) and prohibiting the taking of deposits in the United States).

[175] Black's Law Dictionary defines a "deposit" as "[t]he act of placing money in the custody of a bank or banker, for safety or convenience, to be withdrawn at the will of the depositor or under rules and regulations agreed on." BLACK'S LAW DICTIONARY 438 (6th ed. 1990). *See also* BALLANTINE'S LAW DICTIONARY 121 (3d ed. 1969) (defining a "deposit" as a "contractual relationship ensuing from the delivery, by one known as the depositor, of money, funds, or even things into the possession of the bank, which receives the same upon the agreement to pay, repay, or return, upon the order or demand of the depositor, the money, funds, or equivalent amount.").

[176] *See* 5A MICHIE ON BANKS AND BANKING § 3 (perm. ed. 1973); 9 CJS BANKS AND BANKING § 268.

[177] *Warren v. Shook*, 91 U.S. 704 (1875) (examining the Congressional Acts of June 30, 1864 (13 Stat. 252), and March 3, 1865 (13 Stat. 472)).

[178] *See* Jonathan R. Macey and Geoffrey P. Miller, *Nondeposit Deposits and the Future of Bank Regulation*, 91 MICH. L. REV. 237 (1992).

Commission, opined that MMF shares, though subject to redemption by check, remain equity investments and, thus, do not constitute deposits for purposes of Section 21 of the Glass-Steagall Act.[179]

[b] State Law and the Business of Banking. States generally define what activities constitute the "business of banking." As a general matter, the "business of banking" is most clearly associated with organizations that both accept deposits and make loans. Of the two activities, however, it is deposit-taking that is most likely to raise the "business of banking" issue.[180] Most state "barrier statutes," which restrict the entities that may engage in banking activities, focus on the receipt of deposits.[181] Examples of these types of statutes and their potential application to stored value and electronic money follow.

[i] New York Law. Under New York law, a "deposit" is the transfer of money to a bank to be withdrawn on the depositor's demand or under rules and regulations agreed upon.[182] The relationship between a depositor and a bank is that of a creditor and a debtor.[183] New York's Banking Law prohibits, among other things, a person or corporation, except one expressly authorized under New York or federal banking law, from engaging in the business of receiving deposits.[184] Specifically, N.Y. Banking Law § 131 provides that:

> [n]o corporation, foreign or domestic, other than a national bank or a federal reserve bank, unless expressly authorized by the laws of this state, *shall employ any part of its property, or be in any way interested in any fund which shall be employed for the purpose*

---

[179] Letter from Philip B. Heymann, Assistant Attorney General, Criminal Division, DOJ, and Lawrence Lippe, Chief, General Litigation and Legal Advice Section, DOJ, to Martin Lybacker, Associate Director, Division of Marketing Management, SEC (Dec. 18, 1979) [hereinafter 1979 DOJ Letter]. The 1979 DOJ Letter opined that money market mutual funds offered by brokerage firms were not "deposits" for purposes of Section 21 of Glass-Steagall, recognizing the critical distinction between a "deposit" in which the holder was a creditor and an investment in "mutual fund shares" in which the purchaser was an owner.

[180] Thomas P. Vartanian & Robert H. Ledig, *The Business of Banking In the Age of the Internet: Fortress or Prison?*, 15 BANKING POL'Y REP., Mar. 4-18, 1996, at 6.

[181] Most states' "business of banking" statutes define the business of banking to include the acceptance of deposits. *See, e.g.,* CAL. FIN. CODE § 102 ("The soliciting, receiving or accepting of money or its equivalent on deposit as a regular business shall be deemed to be doing a commercial banking business whether such deposit is made subject to check or is evidenced by a certificate of deposit, a passbook, a note, a receipt, or other writing"); N.C. GEN. STAT. § 53-1 (defining a "bank" as any corporation, other than chartered depository institutions, "receiving, soliciting or accepting money or its equivalent on deposit as a business"); OR. REV. STAT. § 706.005 (defining the "business of banking" to include "soliciting, receiving or accepting money or its equivalent on deposit as a regular business"). *See also* FLA. STAT. ANN. § 658.12 (defining a "general commercial banking business" to include the "business of receiving demand and time deposits"); GA. CODE ANN. § 7-1-241 (prohibiting any person, except chartered banks, credit unions or other licensed firms, from engaging in the "business of banking" or receiving money for deposit or transmission); LA. REV. STAT. ANN. § 6:2 ("business of banking" defined as "lending money, and either receiving deposits, or paying checks anywhere within this state"); MASS. GEN. LAWS ch. 167, § 37 (prohibiting any corporation, individual, partnership or association from transacting business as a bank or "receiving money on deposit").

[182] *See Gimbel Bros. v. White*, 10 N.Y.S.2d 666, 667-68 (App. Div., 3d Dept., 1939) ("An ordinary bank deposit is made for the benefit of the depositor who loans his money to the bank 'and the latter, in consideration of the loan of the money and the right to use it for his own profit, agrees to refund the same amount, or any part thereof, on demand'") (quoting *Marine Bank v. Fulton County Bank*, 17 L. Ed. 785 (1864)). *See also* 9 N.Y. JUR. 2D *Banks and Banking* § 224 (1980).

[183] See *Reichling v. Continental Bank*, 813 F. Supp. 197, 198 (E.D.N.Y. 1993).

[184] *See, e.g.,* N.Y. BANKING LAW §§ 131(3), 180(1). Section 180(1) provides that "[e]xcept as authorized by this chapter [regarding private bankers], no individual, either for himself or as trustee, and no partnership or unincorporated associations shall [e]ngage in the business of receiving deposits." *Id.* § 180.

of receiving deposits, making discounts, receiving for transmission or transmitting money in any manner whatsoever.[185]

The powers of New York chartered banks are generally established by N.Y. Banking Law § 96. It provides that the business of banking, among other powers, shall include the power to "receive deposits of moneys, securities or other personal property upon such terms as the bank . . . shall prescribe; and exercise all such incidental powers as shall be necessary to carry on the business of banking."[186] A New York bank may also "designate one or more agents . . . to issue or sell its travelers checks or money orders at locations other than its principal office . . . ."[187]

[*ii*] *California Law.* Under California law, a "depositor" is one who transfers money to a bank in the usual course of business to the credit of the depositor and subject to the depositor's check.[188] The relationship created by a general deposit is that of a debtor-creditor.[189] The deposit is a debt of the bank, payable on demand to the depositor or the depositor's creditor.[190] Section 102 of the California Finance Code prohibits the unlawful conduct of a banking business, providing that:

> [t]he soliciting, receiving or accepting of money or its equivalent on deposit as a regular business shall be deemed to be doing a commercial banking business whether such deposit is made subject to check or is evidenced by a certificate of deposit, a passbook, a note, a receipt, or other writing; provided, that nothing herein shall apply to or include money or its equivalent left in escrow, or left with an agent pending investment in real estate or securities for or on account of his principal. It shall be unlawful for any corporation, partnership, firm or individual to engage in or transact a banking business within this state except by means of a corporation duly authorized for such purpose.[191]

[185] N.Y. BANKING LAW, § 131(1) (emphasis added). Section 131(1) permits the receipt of deposits if such activity is "expressly authorized by the laws of this state." Under its Blue Sky Laws, New York provides a comprehensive scheme (the "Martin Act") of registration for all individuals and entities who offer and sell securities, investment advisors, and all issuers of securities. *See* N.Y. GEN. BUS. LAW §§ 359-e to 359-eee. Under the Blue Sky regime, broker-dealers may receive moneys from customers for use in connection with securities transactions. *See* N.Y. GEN. BUS. LAW § 359-e(1)(a)-(b) (definitions of "dealer: and "broker"). *Brokers, Dealers and Salespersons*, 2A Blue Sky L. Rep. (CCH), ¶ 42,501 *et seq.* (1990).

[186] N.Y. BANKING LAW § 96(1).

[187] *Id.* § 96(11).

[188] *See Merchants Nat'l Bank v. Continental Nat'l Bank*, 277 P. 354, 357 (Cal. Dist. Ct. App. 1929).

[189] *See Union Tool Co. v. Farmers & Merchants Nat'l Bank*, 218 P. 424, 429 (Cal. 1923); *Bank of America Nat'l Trust & Savings Ass'n v. California Savings & Commercial Bank*, 22 P.2d 704, 709 (Cal. 1933).

[190] *See Union Tool*, 218 P. at 429.

[191] CAL. FIN. CODE § 102.

Under California law, a person who solicits or receives deposits is carrying on "the business of banking."[192] Thus, corporations formed for other purposes may inadvertently perform the essential functions of a banking business and become subject to the power of the state to regulate their activities.[193] Persons who conduct a banking business without proper authorization from the state are subject to fines that accrue daily and violators may be enjoined from transacting such business, in a proceeding brought by the superintendent of banks.[194]

[*iii*] *Applications of State "Business of Banking" Statutes to University Debit Card Systems.* In a few instances, state officials have issued opinions regarding the applicability of individual state's business of banking statutes to college-based debit card programs.[195]

[*A*] *Florida.* In 1990, the Comptroller of Florida issued an opinion holding that Florida State University's ("FSU") debit card program violated Florida banking statutes.[196] The FSU program enabled students to deposit funds with the university and receive a magnetic stripe debit card to be used for accessing those funds when making purchases at various campus locations. Students were also able to use the card at some bank ATMs to withdraw funds or deposit additional funds into their accounts. The Florida Comptroller found that FSU had solicited and received funds for deposit and engaged in the payment of "checks" on behalf of student cardholders, who used their cards to purchase goods and services and to withdraw cash from ATMs. For these reasons, the Comptroller concluded that FSU was conducting the business of banking without the requisite FDIC insurance and without state authorization in violation of the applicable Florida statutes.

[*B*] *Texas.* In 1995, the Attorney General of Texas reviewed numerous debit card programs in effect at public and private universities in Texas in response to an inquiry from the Texas Department of Banking. The Attorney General issued an opinion, in which he stated that it was unlikely that a court would conclude that a debit card program would constitute the sale of checks and thus, these programs did not violate the Texas Sale of Checks Act.[197] The Texas Attorney General found the Florida Comptroller's reliance on *Illinois ex rel.*

---

[192] See CAL. FIN. CODE § 3390, which provides that:

[N]o person which has not received a certificate from the superintendent authorizing it to engage in the banking business shall solicit or receive deposits, issue certificates of deposit with or without provision for interest, make payments on check, or transact business in the way or manner of a commercial bank or trust company.

Cf. Rosenblum v. Anglim, 135 F.2d 512 (9th Cir. 1943) (generally, receiving deposits constitutes carrying on "banking business").

[193] 9 CAL. JUR. 2d *Banks* §§ 47-48 (1993) (citing *In re Estate of Wellings*, 221 P. 628, 633 (Cal. 1923)).

[194] See CAL. FIN. CODE § 3395, which provides:

Any person or any bank violating any provision of the foregoing sections of this article shall be liable to the people of the state in the amount of one hundred dollars ($100) a day or part thereof during which such violation continues. Any court of competent jurisdiction in a proceeding brought by the commissioner may enjoin any person from using words in violation of the provisions of this article or from transacting business in violation of this division or in such a way or manner as to lead the public to believe that its business is that of a bank, commercial bank or trust company.

[195] *See* Thomas P. Vartanian, & Robert H. Ledig, *The Business of Banking in the Age of the Internet: Fortress or Prison?*, BANKING POL'Y REP., Mar. 4-18, 1996, at 6.

[196] Inter-Office Communication from J. Ashley Peacock, Assistant General Counsel to Terry Straub, Director, Division of Banking, November 16, 1990.

[197] Office of the Attorney General of Texas, Opinion No. DM-329, March 9, 1995 Tex. AG LEXIS (construing the Texas Sale of Checks Act codified at V.T.C.S. art 489d, §3).

Lignoul v. Continental Illinois Nat'l Bank & Trust Co.,[198] a case in which the court construed whether the withdrawal of funds from an ATM constituted branch banking for purposes of the National Bank Act, to be misplaced. The Texas Attorney General stated that although "an ATM withdrawal may constitute payment of a check for purposes of the National Bank Act, it does not necessarily constitute a check for purposes of the Commercial Code or the common commercial understanding of the term."[199] Furthermore, the Attorney General found that university debit card systems that did not permit students to withdraw funds from an ATM did not constitute the unauthorized business of banking.

[C] *North Carolina.* In 1993, East Carolina University sought an advisory opinion from the Office of the Attorney General concerning the application of North Carolina and federal business of banking statutes to closed debit card systems. The Attorney General found that these systems restricted purchases to the university campus, and therefore, did not implicate the business of banking statutes.[200] The opinion found that the students' "deposits" were no more than prepayment for goods and services provided by the university and thus, did not constitute the receipt of deposits under the banking statutes nor did it create the traditional debtor and creditor relationship. Instead, the Attorney General construed the relationship as that of a bailee and bailor whereby title to the funds does not pass to the university and, absent negligence on the part of the university, the student retains the risk of loss. The Attorney General concluded that this activity did not constitute the business of banking. The Attorney General stated, however, that if the university sought to expand access to the debit card system by permitting student to purchase goods and services from local merchants, the university would, at that point, be engaged in the business of banking, by placing itself in the role of an intermediary.

[D] *Idaho.* Recently, the Idaho legislature explicitly granted universities the authority to offer programs that permit payment cards to be used at campus locations to purchase goods or services, as long as those cards are not used for cash redemption, without being considered to be a bank or doing banking business under Idaho law.[201]

[iv] *Past Applications of State "Business of Banking" Statutes.* SV issuers should be cognizant of the possibility that financial products that resemble deposits in some respects may come under the scrutiny of state banking officials or attorneys general. For example, the scope of state business of banking statutes was tested in the late 1970s and early 1980s in regard to an innovative product offered by a leading securities brokerage firm. During the introduction of its Cash Management Account ("CMA") in late 1977, Merrill Lynch initially met resistance from a number of state banking regulators regarding the offering of CMAs.[202] Several states

---

[198] 536 F.2d 176 (7th Cir.), *cert. denied*, 429 U.S. 871 (1976).

[199] Office of the Attorney General of Texas, *supra* note 197, at 11.

[200] Office of the Attorney General of the State of North Carolina, 1993 N.C. AG LEXIS 75 (Oct. 4, 1993).

[201] University Debit Card Act, IDAHO CODE §§ 26-3001 to -3004.

[202] *See* Fredric H. Karr, *Is the Cash Management Account Innovative Brokerage or Unlawful Competition For Smaller Banks?*, 96 BANKING L.J. 301, 307-311 (1979).

had characterized these securities assets accounts as deposit accounts and took the position that Merrill Lynch was engaged in the unauthorized business of banking, although these rulings were eventually withdrawn.[203]

[c] Money Transmitter and Sale of Checks Laws. The drafters of current laws regulating banking and payment instrument activities, generally did not contemplate the development of SV and electronic money. In some instances, the issuance of SV or electronic money may appear to be similar to the acceptance of deposits. To the extent that this activity is deemed to be depository in nature, nonbank SV issuers may be faced with issues regarding compliance with business of banking laws. In many instances, nonbank issuers of SV or electronic money are likely to find themselves subject to state assertions that state money transmitter or sale of check statutes are applicable. To the extent that nonbank SV issuers are placed in a separate state regulatory basket, they may find that this separation adequately accommodates their operations while insulating them from the full range of bank regulatory provisions.

At least forty-five states have money transmitter laws, and in certain instances these laws[204] may be applicable to SV. These statutes, generally administered by state banking authorities, require a firm to obtain a license before engaging in the business of money transmission, and subject firms that fail to secure that license to various penalties.[205] In addition, the federal government has criminalized the failure of a money transmitting business to obtain a state license, where required to do so, or to comply with the money transmitter registration requirements of the Bank Secrecy Act.[206] State money transmitter statutes, generally perceived as "safety and soundness" measures, could also assist law enforcement efforts to curtail money laundering and other forms of organized crime.[207]

The possible classification of SV issuers as covered entities for purposes of state money transmitter laws must be examined based on the specific operational features of the SV system and the provisions of the state law

---

[203] *See, e.g.,* Opinion of William S. Gibbs, Special Assistant Attorney General of Utah to M.D. Brothick, Commissioner, Department of Financial Institutions, 1980 Utah AG LEXIS 40, Oct. 6, 1980 (finding the Cash Management Account to be a deposit account). *But see* John A. Adams, *Money Market Funds: Has Glass-Steagall Been Cracked?*, 99 BANKING L.J. 17 (1982) (noting the Utah Attorney General's withdrawal of the opinion).

[204] *See, e.g.,* ARIZ. REV. STAT. § 6-1202 (engage in the "business of receiving money for transmission or transmitting money"); OHIO REV. CODE ANN. § 1315.02 (same); COLO. REV. STAT. § 12-52-104 ("selling or issuing exchange or in the business of money transmission"); DEL. CODE ANN., tit. 5, § 2303 (business of selling or issuing checks or the business of receiving money for transmission); N.Y. BANKING LAW § 641 (same); TENN. CODE ANN. § 45-7-202 (same); VA. CODE ANN. § 6.1-371; GA. ANN. CODE § 7-1-681 (business of selling or issuing checks). *See generally State Legislation — Sale of Checks and Money Transmitter Statutes: Part One — Alabama to Kentucky,* ELEC. BANKING L. & COM. REP., Nov./Dec. 1996, at 13-17; *State Legislation — Sale of Checks and Money Transmitter Statutes: Part Two — Missouri to Wyoming,* ELEC. BANKING L. AND COM. REP., Jan. 1997, at 12-15 (providing a comprehensive list of relevant state statutes).

[205] *See, e.g.,* VA. CODE ANN. § 6.1-375 (sale of money orders without a license is a misdemeanor).

[206] 18 U.S.C. § 1960 (treating the operation of an "illegal money transmitting business" as a felony); *Anti-Money Laundering Act of 1993: Hearing Before the Subcomm. On Financial Institutions Supervision, Regulation and Deposit Insurance of the House Comm. on Banking, Finance and Urban Affairs,* 103d Cong. (1993). See also Chapter 10, Section 10.02 for a discussion of FinCEN and the application of the Bank Secrecy Act ("BSA") to SV issuers.

[207] *See* Ezra C. Levine, '*Safety and Soundness' Issues in High-Tech Funds Transfer,* MONEY LAUNDERING L. REP., Oct. 1996, at 1-2. *See also* Definition and Registration of Money Services Businesses, 62 Fed. Reg. 27,890, 27,893 (1997) (to be codified at 31 C.F.R. pt. 103) (proposing to make stored value expressly subject to the BSA, to eliminate any lingering doubt that offerors and operators of advanced electronic payment systems are subject to the BSA; stating that its treatment of stored value for purposes of the BSA should not be taken as expressing a view by the Treasury regarding whether stored value should fall within the scope of state laws applicable to money transmitters and similar entities).

in question.[208] Numerous states have informally indicated that they generally consider nonbank SV issuers to be subject to their money transmitter statutes.[209] Money transmitter statutes are principally intended to protect customers against the issuer's inability to make payment as promised. The statutory requirements typically include: (i) permissible investments standards (*i.e.*, the maintenance of a certain level of reserves in specifically authorized investments); (ii) annual reporting and audit requirements; (iii) restrictions on who may own and operate the business; and (iv) bonding requirements.

Money transmitter statutes generally exempt banks, credit unions, trust companies, government agencies, telegraph companies, and insurance companies from regulation.[210] Virginia also exempts "any person who receives money for transmission as an incident to the conduct of another business."[211]

[d] Stamp Payments Act. As noted above, lawmakers and regulators did not know about SV and electronic money when many of the laws and regulations that might apply to those products were written or last revised. Accordingly, how existing laws will be interpreted in light of these product developments is unclear. One interesting example of this juxtaposition of a paper past and an electronic future arises in the context of the Stamp Payments Act of 1862 ("Stamp Payments Act" or the "Act").[212]

The Stamp Payments Act, in its current form, states:

> Whoever makes, issues, circulates, or pays out any note, check, memorandum, token, or other obligation for a less sum than $1, intended to circulate as money or to be received or used in lieu of lawful money of the United States, shall be fined under this title or imprisoned not more than six months, or both.[213]

---

[208] *See, e.g.*, TENN. CODE ANN. § 45-7-203 (defining "money transmission" as the "sale or issuance of payment instruments or engaging in the business of receiving money for transmission or transmitting money within the United States or locations abroad, by any and all means, including, but not limited to, payment instrument, wire facsimile or electronic transfer"); VA. CODE ANN. § 6.1-370 (defining "money transmission" as receiving money from a person for transmission by wire, facsimile, electronic or other means"). *See also* Draft Nondepository Providers of Financial Services Act (proposing state regulation of the issuance, redemption, and sale of stored value, and the capital structure, and permissible investments by nondepository issuers of stored value), *available at* <http://www.law.upenn.edu/library/ulc/ndpfsa/ndp298.htm>; *See also* Uniform Money Transmitters Act § 3 (defining "money transmission" as the sale or issuance of payment instruments or the business of receiving money for transmission within the United States or abroad by any or all means, including, but not limited to the payment instrument, wire, facsimile, or electronic transfer).

[209] For recent efforts by individual states to regulate stored value, see generally A.B. 9218, 221st Leg., (N.Y. 1998) (proposing the criminalization of the fraudulent or unauthorized use of a stored value card; the form, content, and distribution of SV disclosure information; and limiting the liability for customer losses to $50 for the unauthorized use of a reasonably secure SV card); S.B. 2540 80th Leg. Sess. (Minn. 1997-98) (limiting customer losses to $50 for the loss or theft of a stored value card prior to the receipt of notification by the financial institution); H.B. 4095, 73rd Leg., 2d Reg. Sess (W.Va. 1998) (amending the current check seller statute to require, among other items, the licensing of entities engaged in "currency transmission" that would include SV Issuers, except for those that issue SV cards for the purchase of goods and services from that Issuer).

[210] *See, e.g.*, TENN. CODE ANN. § 45-7-204; VA. CODE ANN. § 6.1-371; DEL. CODE ANN. tit. 5, § 2304.

[211] VA. CODE ANN. § 6.1-371(vi).

[212] *See* Thomas P. Vartarian, Robert H. Ledig, & Yolanda Demianczuk, *Echoes of the Past with Implications for the Future: The Stamp Payments Act of 1862 and Electronic Commerce*, 67 Banking Rep. (BNA) 465-70 (Sept. 23, 1996) [hereinafter Vartarian *et al.*, *Echoes of the Past*].

[213] 18 U.S.C. § 336.

Given the plain language of the Act, an issue may arise as to whether the Act might be applicable to any SV or electronic money systems,[214] particularly systems used in connection with micropayments.[215] Although the Stamp Payments Act seems anachronistic today, Congress has not repealed the statute. Any effort to interpret the scope of the statute today raises a host of issues, for example, what does the word "money" mean in the context of this statute.[216] The Treasury Department recognized the possible significance of the Stamp Payments Act for SV systems, when, in a background paper prepared for the September 1996 Treasury Department Conference on electronic money, it stated: "[f]ederal criminal law also restricts the issuance of obligations intended to circulate as money or to be used in lieu of lawful money; this restriction applies equally to banks and nonbanks."[217] The Treasury Department paper also states that only the Department of Justice ("DOJ") can provide definitive interpretations of criminal statutes, including the Stamp Payments Act, and determine its application to SV and electronic money issuers.[218] An interpretation by the DOJ of the Act will likely take into account, at least in part, an examination of the concept of money, as it was perceived in 1862, along with the legislative history and judicial application of the Act.

[i] *A Short History on U.S. Coins.* The Stamp Payments Act applies to, among other things, the issuance of obligations intended to be used as money or in lieu of U.S. lawful money in sums less than $1. A number of economic, political, and social events occurring across several decades in U.S. history converged to cause the federal government to prohibit the private issuance of money in sums less than $1. A summary of relevant highlights follows.

In the pre-civil war period, a federal law established gold and silver coins ("specie") as legal tender for all debts and their value was dictated by statute rather than by market forces.[219] Variations between the market value and the statutory value inherently led to arbitrage, by which importers and exporters bought and sold the precious metals and coins to profit by the discrepancies between the different statutory and market values of the coins.[220]

President Jackson's veto of the extension of the Second Bank of the United States, together with crop failures and an English financial panic reducing foreign investments and credit in the U.S., led to a severe

---

[214] Some commentators on the subject argue that the Stamp Payments Act poses no bar to issuers of electronic currency relying in part on the fact that the private issuance of traveler's checks (American Express Traveler's Cheques)® has occurred without interruption since 1891. *See* Brian W. Smith and Ramsey J. Wilson, *The Electronic Future of Cash: Article: How Best to Guide The Evolution of Electronic Currency Law,* 46 AM. U. L. REV. 1105, 1110-11 (1997). In this regard, it should be noted that traveler's checks have historically been issued in amounts greater than $1, the threshold that determines the applicability of the Stamp Payments Act.

[215] The capacity to easily and economically complete small value transactions via the Internet may create new market opportunities for cyber entrepreneurs. Also, existing information industries may wish to utilize the Internet for the sale of news articles or other small bits of information like recipes for amounts less than $1.

[216] See Chapter 3 for a discussion of the evolving and ever changing concept of money.

[217] Treasury Report, *supra* note 171, at 50.

[218] *Id.*

[219] *See, e.g.,* Act of June 28, 1834, ch. 96, 4 Stat. 699. *See generally Legal Tender Cases,* 79 U.S. (12 Wall.) 457 (1870).

[220] Congress altered the statutory valuation of gold relative to silver above the market price in an effort to bring gold bullion and coins into the country. This, however, had the opposite effect of the export of silver coins. NUSSBAUM, *supra* note 66, at 73-78.

economic contraction and the bank panic of 1837. Private issuers responded to the scarcity of specie during this period by producing "hard time tokens."[221] Although there was an enormous increase in the amount of gold in the country in the 1840s, silver coins were less plentiful. In 1853, Congress attempted to remedy this situation by altering the statutory value of silver fractional coins, those less than $1, by a reduction in their silver content relative to market values; and, for a short time, this value alteration acted as a barrier against the export of fractional coins.[222] In 1857, however, Canada recognized U.S. currency as legal tender without differentiating between the full face value of fractional coins and their substandard silver content.[223] This led to the export of silver fractional coins to Canada in exchange for more valuable gold coins. The gold would return to the U.S. and be used to purchase silver bullion to be minted into silver fractional coins at the U.S. Mint free of charge, and the silver coins were subsequently exported to Canada, to complete arbitrage.[224] This arbitrage led to a proliferation of tokens, private notes, and other substitute currencies for use in everyday transactions.[225]

[ii] *The Legislative History of the Stamp Payments Act.* Politicians sought to enact legislation to impede the private issuance of currency valued at less than $1, believing it to be the cause of the flight of fractional silver coins from circulation, rather than a symptom of the government's inflationary policies. At the time of congressional consideration of the Stamp Payments Act, Secretary of the Treasury Salmon P. Chase drafted a letter read during the congressional debate, stating that "[t]he depreciation of the currency, result[ed], in great measure, from the unrestricted issues of non-specie paying banks and unauthorized associations and persons, [that] cause[d] the rapid disappearance from circulation of small coins." Secretary Chase's letter suggested two options for Congress to address this problem: (1) further reduce the weight of fractional coins, or (2) accept postage stamps as payment for government debts valued at less than five dollars.[226] Secretary Chase recommended a second provision that would enforce this "solution" by criminalizing the issuance of tokens and notes representing fractional parts of a dollar that were intended to circulate as money.[227]

Despite some opposition,[228] Congress adopted Chase's second solution to currency problem and enacted a criminal prohibition in the Stamp Payments Act of 1862. Section 1 of the Act provided for the use of postage stamps as currency for government debts valued at less than five dollars.[229] Section 1 created a postage stamp

---

[221] *See* NUSSBAUM, *supra* note 66, at 85-86 (providing a description of various forms of tokens and shinplasters used due to the scarcity of coins in the system).

[222] *See id.* at 83. Act of February 21, 1853, 1 Stat. 160. *See also Bollinger's Campagne,* 70 U.S. (3 Wall.) 560 (1865).

[223] *See* NUSSBAUM, *supra* note 66, at 96-97, 112; Statutes of Canada, 1857, ch. 18.

[224] *See* NUSSBAUM, *supra* note 66, at 112.

[225] *See id.* at 73. *See also* VIVIANNA A. ZELIZER, THE SOCIAL MEANING OF MONEY: PIN MONEY, PAYCHECKS, POOR RELIEF, AND OTHER CURRENCIES 13-15 (1994).

[226] Cong. Globe, 37th Cong., 2d Sess. 3405 (1862). *See also* Vartanian *et al., Echoes of the Past, supra* note 212, at 466.

[227] Vartanian *et al., Echoes of the Past, supra* note 212, at 466.

[228] Congressman Phelps sought to strike Section 2 arguing that it was unconstitutional, although he proclaimed that he was as firmly opposed as his colleagues to the circulation of "shinplasters." Phelps feared that congressional power to prohibit the circulation of currency in denominations less than one dollar, would allow the government to prevent any corporation from issuing paper money of any amount, which he opined was beyond the scope of the government's constitutional powers. 37 Cong. Globe, 37th Cong., 2d Sess. 3405 (1862).

[229] This provision was soon repealed by the Currency Act of 1863.

crisis, however, because postage stamps were not of sufficient material strength to handle numerous transactions. Thus, stamps were mutilated, destroyed, or lost in a short period, to the dismay of the Postmaster General, who sought the provision's repeal.[230] Section 2 of the Stamp Payments Act criminalized the issuance of notes and tokens in units under one dollar intended to pass as currency of the United States and remains in effect to this day. Congress created the Stamp Payments Act to prevent the private issuance of fractional currency substitutes,[231] but as one author noted, "the public did not care and the authorities proved unable to enforce these laws during critical years."[232]

[iii] *Summary of the Judicial Application of the Stamp Payments Act in the 19th Century and Legislative Revisions During the 20th Century.* In the 135 years since the passage of the Act, only a handful of reported criminal prosecutions were commenced under the Act, none of which resulted in convictions. Shortly after the passage of the Act, the Monongahela Bridge Company was prosecuted under the Stamp Payments Act based on its issuance of paper tickets for use on one of its toll bridges. In 1863, the United States District Court for the Western District of Pennsylvania held that the issuance of paper tickets for use on the toll bridge did not violate the criminal prohibition of the Stamp Payments Act.[233] In holding for the defendants, the court emphasized the ticket's lack of physical resemblance in size, design, or material to U.S. coins or postage currency protected by the Act. Because the tickets did not contain a promise to pay money nor did they represent money, the court found that the toll company could not have intended the tickets to circulate as money. The court concluded that the tickets were merely a permit to pass on the defendants' bridges, issued for the convenience of the bridge-crossing public, which in no way interfered with the passenger's duty to pay the toll.[234]

The United States Supreme Court addressed the scope of the Stamp Payments Act in 1877.[235] Although the Court was asked to address the constitutionality of the Act, the Court did not reach the issue because its ruling regarding whether notes redeemable in goods were prohibited by the Act resolved the case. The notes, issued by Bangor Furnace Company, bore the following inscription: "The Bangor Furnace Company will pay the bearer, on demand, fifty cents, in goods, at their store, in Bangor, Mich." The Court stated that Congress intended to protect the use of stamps as fractional currency substitutes by prohibiting competition from private issuers. The Court then distinguished small notes payable in specific goods from notes payable in U.S. currency, because the former could only reasonably circulate in a limited area and, thus, did not pose significant competition to the use of stamps as general currency.[236] The Supreme Court stated that the dollar is the standard of measure expressed in the statute. Therefore, it found that the law is inapplicable to the issuance of notes

---

[230] *See* NUSSBAUM, *supra* note 66, at 114.

[231] *See* Vartanian *et al.*, *Echoes of the Past, supra* note 212, at 465.

[232] NUSSBAUM, *supra* note 66, at 113.

[233] *United States v. Monongahela Bridge Co.*, 26 F. Cas. 1292 (W.D. Pa. 1863) (No. 15796).

[234] *Id.* at 1293.

[235] *United States v. Van Auken*, 96 U.S. 366 (1877).

[236] See generally Section 16.04[3][f] on the use of Ithaca Hours, local currency developed for use in the town of Ithaca, New York.

measured by a non-pecuniary standard.[237] Furthermore, because redemption of the notes was limited to the company's store, distribution of the note did not constitute a circulation of "money." The fifty-cent limit of the notes' value gave customers redemption options that were limited by the contents of the store. Because it found that the defendant's conduct did not violate the statute, the Court did not address the constitutionality of the statute.[238]

At the end of the last century, the Clark & Boice Lumber Co. was indicted for violating the Stamp Payments Act when it issued coins bearing an inscription of the company's name on one side and the inscription "Good for 50¢ in Merchandise" on the other side. The United States District Court for Minnesota distinguished the circular metal tokens from U.S. coins, because they differed in size and weight.[239] Relying on *Van Auken*, the Court held for the defendant because the obligation was redeemable in a sum of merchandise only and the likelihood that the tokens would be mistaken for U.S. coins was minimal.[240]

This limited case law provides a number of principles that may be used in the analysis of emerging electronic currencies. Fractional currencies that have limited areas of circulation do not threaten U.S. currency and, therefore, are not prohibited by the Act. Fractional currencies whose redemption is limited to merchandise, even if the value is for less than a dollar, do not constitute the circulation of money. Fractional currencies that lack physical resemblance to U.S. coins or other currency may be beyond the scope of the Act. However, physical resemblance may not be a necessary attribute for a violation of the Act, because the Act prohibits the use of any unauthorized form of currency. Finally, the Stamp Payments Act was intended to protect the use of stamps as fractional currency substitutes by its prohibition of competition from private issuers, a consideration that is no longer applicable.

In 1909, Congress revised and recodified the Stamp Payments Act as part of the first Criminal Code.[241] In 1948, Congress comprehensively revised, codified, and reenacted all criminal statutes into title 18, "Crimes and Criminal Procedure," of the United States Code.[242] The congressional motivation for this revision was to consolidate a growing body of uncodified criminal legislation within the original Criminal Code and to eliminate

---

[237] *Van Aucken*, 96 U.S. at 368.

[238] *Id.* The Supreme Court subsequently applied its holding in *Van Auken* to *Hollister v. Zion's Co-Operative Mercantile Institution*, 111 U.S. 62 (1884). The Collector of Internal Revenue was attempting to enforce tax assessments that the defendants alleged were imposed illegally under the National Bank Act. At issue before the Supreme Court was whether a note, redeemable for $5 in merchandise, had circulated as money so as to subject the note to taxation under the National Bank Act. Although this case was brought under a different statute, the court cited *Van Auken*, reasoning that the drafters of both the National Bank Act and the Stamp Payments Act were motivated by similar concerns. Applying the *Van Auken* rationale, the Court concluded that the potential danger to the national currency by notes redeemable in specific goods was minimal, because it was unlikely that obligations in anything other than money "would pass beyond a limited neighborhood." Thus, these obligations were not notes within the meaning of the National Bank Act and not subject to taxation under the law. *Id.* at 64. The U.S. Attorney General cited *Hollister* in an opinion in which he ruled that tickets issued by ice companies redeemable in goods were not "notes" within the meaning of the National Bank Act and, thus, were not subject to the 10% tax. *Tax on Notes Used for Circulation*, 19 Op. Atty. Gen. 98 (1888). *See* Vartanian *et al., Echoes of the Past, supra* note 248, at 467 n. 17.

[239] *United States v. Roussopulous*, 95 F. 977 (D. Minn. 1899).

[240] *Id.* at 978.

[241] Ch. 321, § 178, 35 Stat. 1122 (1909).

[242] H.R. Rep. No. 80-304, 80th Cong. (1948).

out-dated language used in the older statutes.[243] The legislative history of the 1948 revision indicates that minor alterations were made to simplify the text of the Stamp Payments Act.[244] A few members of Congress proposed the omission of the Stamp Payments Act from the Criminal Code as obsolete or, at least, a revision of the Act to exclude commercial obligations. Lawmakers rejected the proposals, finding that the revision posed no threat to commercial transactions and interpreting case law as plainly excluding checks in amounts under one dollar from the scope of the Act.[245] The legislative history cites *United States. v. Monongahela Bridge Co.* and *United States v. Stettinius*,[246] an 1839 case brought under a federal statute prohibiting the circulation of small notes in the District of Columbia, as support for this proposition. Although neither of these cases explicitly exclude checks from the scope of the Act, the legislators expressed their intent to do so.

Recently, Congress modified the Stamp Payments Act by passing amendments to the penalties of all crimes included in the Violent Crime Control and Law Enforcement Act of 1994.[247] Nothing in the legislative history of this Act indicates that this amendment reflected any substantive consideration of the present day application of the Act.[248]

[iv] *Application of the Stamp Payments Act to Stored Value and Electronic Money.* As described in Section 16.02, SV systems can be either card-based SV or computer-based SV, or a combination of both. Some SV issuers may intend to circulate SV in amounts less than $1 throughout the U.S. in everyday transactions both in person and on the Internet. Because different SV and electronic money systems have different architectures, and many remain under development, making precise statements regarding potential application of the Act to SV and electronic money difficult.

Some general observations can be made regarding the language of the Act. First, it arguably fits within the requirement that the issuer "make, issue, circulate, or pay" the note, check, memorandum, token or obligation, because SV is designed and created to be held by third parties. Second, whether SV or electronic money is a "note, check, memorandum, token, or other obligation" depends upon the configuration of the SV system. Legislative intent may be of little use. Congress in 1862 could not have contemplated an application of the Act to SV or electronic money. More recent congressional action provides arguments for and against the Act's

---

[243] *Id.*

[244] 18 U.S.C. § 336 (1948).

[245] H.R. REP. No. 80-304, 80th Cong. (1948).

[246] 22 F. Cas. 1322 (C.C.D.C. 1839) (No. 13387). The Act of July 7, 1838, ch. 212, 5 Stat. 297, provided: "it shall be unlawful for any individual, company, or corporation to issue *de novo*, or knowingly to pass, or procure to be issued, passed, or circulated within the District [of Columbia], any note, check, bank bill, or any other paper medium, of the denomination [less than five dollars] . . . evidently intended for common circulation, as for or in lieu of small change in gold or silver, or for any other pretense whatever . . . ." In this case, the court ruled that the bank bills the defendant was charged with passing were not "paper medium . . . evidently intended for common circulation," but provided little reasoning to support this conclusion. *Stettinius*, 22 F. Cas. at 1334.

[247] The original version of the Act provided for a fine of $500. *See* Act of July 17, 1862, ch. 196, § 2, 12 Stat. 592. The code provision as amended allows for a maximum fine of $5,000 per infraction for individuals, and $10,000 per infraction for organizations. Moreover, if the defendant derives a pecuniary gain or causes a pecuniary loss, the fine assessed can be as high as twice the amount of the gain or loss. 18 U.S.C. § 3571.

[248] Anecdotes circulating in the electronic commerce community suggest that the Secret Service visited Las Vegas casinos during the 1970s to discourage a local practice of allowing casino chips to circulate as cash in the area, which could have implicated the Stamp Payments Act.

application to SV. On the one hand, the 1994 amendment of the Act may indicate Congress' intent to apply the law to present day "obligations." On the other hand, because Congress failed to amend the Act to include "electronic cash or coins," "strings of binary digits," or "encrypted data," its recent inaction could be interpreted as support for the argument that the Act does not extend to electronic commerce.

Assuming that a unit of SV or electronic money could be considered a "token" or "other obligation," the issue becomes whether that unit represents "a less sum than one dollar." In *Van Auken*, the Supreme Court found that the "sum" of the note at issue was for "goods" valued for less than one dollar, not for money, because the token was not payable in cash. The Supreme Court in *Van Auken* and *Hollister* indicated that it is unlikely that obligations payable in anything other than money would pass beyond a limited neighborhood, and, therefore, would not threaten the national currency. Modern day equivalents of a merchant issuing an instrument that can only be used to obtain a specific product or service are transit farecards, and library copy cards.

On the other hand, it appears that many SV or electronic money systems do not anticipate that the SV or electronic money will be restricted to being exchanged with a particular merchant for a limited set of goods. Rather, the Internet and stored value cards ensure that SV will circulate beyond a limited neighborhood. Courts may view a particular form of SV as coming within the Act's concept of "money," as it gains widespread acceptance. Moreover, most systems will probably allow units of SV or electronic money to be converted into traditional forms of money, including forms that could allow a holder of electronic money to receive cash in exchange.

The final requirement of the statute is that the item issued be "intended to circulate as money or to be received or used in lieu of lawful money of the United States."[249] This branch of the test, in turn, relies upon the definition of "money." *United States v. Gellman*, a case involving an indictment alleging that defendants violated several criminal counterfeiting statutes,[250] adopted the following definition of "money":

> Any material that by agreement serves as a common medium of exchange and measure of value in trade . . . . [T]he essential, natural functions of money may be stated as including these three: 1. It is a commodity — having a value of its own. 2. It is a

---

[249] Under federal law, U.S. coins and currency (including Federal Reserve notes and circulating notes of Federal Reserve Banks and national banks) are legal tender for all debts, public charges, taxes, and dues. 31 U.S.C. § 5103. However, the possibility of valid transactions without the use of legal tender clouds our understanding of the concept "lawful money." See *Nemser v. New York City Transit Auth.*, 530 N.Y.S.2d 493 (N.Y. Sup. Ct. 1988), *aff'd mem.*, 542 N.Y.S.2d 1003 (N.Y. App. Div. 1989), in which a bus operator that required the use of tokens rather than dollar bills as payment for fares paid on its buses was found not to be in violation of the legal tender statute. The court applied a "reasonableness" test to conclude that the statute does not preclude a vendor from limiting the locations where cash payments can be made if the action is reasonable under the circumstances. *Nemser*, 530 N.Y.S.2d at 494.

[250] These statutes included former Section 281 of Title 18 of the United States Code. In its present form, this statute provides: "Whoever, except as authorized by law, makes or utters or passes, or attempts to utter or pass, any coins of gold or silver or other metal, or alloy of metals, intended for use as current money, whether in the resemblance of coins of the United States or foreign countries, or of original design, shall be fined under this title or imprisoned not more than five years, or both." 18 U.S.C. § 486.

common measure of value. 3. It has general exchangeability, and is, hence, a general medium of exchange.[251]

In *Gellman*, the defendants had manufactured circular tokens or slugs for amusement, bearing inscriptions "for amusement purposes only" and this token has "no cash value," but which also could be used in place of U.S. coins to operate vending machines, pay telephones, and parking meters. The court, applying the rationale of *Van Auken* and *Roussopulous*, determined that the metal tokens were not a medium of common exchange. Further, the court suggested that proper relief should be sought from Congress for the issues raised by the indictment were for violations of a statute enacted more than one hundred years ago, when coin-operated machines did not exist.[252]

Whether SV or electronic money is intended to circulate as money, may be the most difficult issue to determine. Is SV or electronic money: (1) a commodity having a value of its own; (2) a common representative measure of value; or (3) a general medium of exchange? If today's financial pioneers understand the characteristics and questions that are relevant, they should be able to design an electronic product around the proscriptions of the Act. One consideration to bear in mind in this regard is that private SV or electronic money is not likely to be accepted as money until customers and merchants feel that they can trust the issuer to stand behind the SV issued.

The foregoing analysis is necessarily clouded by our historical perceptions of money. Will intangible electronic "coins" or other units of value ever be accepted as money? Although an individual is capable of performing most financial transactions electronically today via credit and debit cards, ATMs, and other means, the prospect of a cashless society is nevertheless difficult for many people to conceptualize and accept.

Ultimately the question may come down to "where is the money?"[253] If SV or electronic money is viewed by a pragmatic court as simply a convenient way to transfer units of value in cyberspace, then it should not be viewed as the creation of a parallel currency that comes within the scope of the prohibition contained in the Act. As in *Gellman*, a court may be reluctant to find an archaic statute enacted before SV and electronic money had ever been contemplated to be applicable to their use.

Conversely, the more issuers describe and treat SV and electronic money as "cash" and enable it to have the finality of cash transactions, the more weight is provided to an argument that it, in fact, represents an independent instrument that was neither printed by the Federal Reserve nor minted by the U.S. Mint; and that, while it exists in an era far removed from that of the Second Battle of Manassas, it falls within the scope of the Act.

---

[251] *United States v. Gellman*, 44 F. Supp. 360, 365 (D. Minn. 1942) (citing FUNK & WAGNALL'S DICTIONARY and J.M. GREGORY, POLITICAL ECONOMY). However, the definition of money as it was understood in 1862, rather than 1942, or 1998 may be more appropriate under an originalist's interpretation of the plain meaning of the statute.

[252] *Gellman*, 44 F. Supp. at 365-66.

[253] Vartanian, *Key Questions for Emerging Systems, supra* note 50.

[e] Ithaca Hours. The prospective emergence of SV and electronic money is causing a reexamination of many of the key assumptions about money that our current society takes for granted. Foremost among these is the assumption that the government, rather than private sector entities, issues "money." From some perspectives, SV and electronic money, particularly where it can be transferred from customer-to-customer may function in the same manner as dollar bills or coins. Assume that the transfer of SV or electronic money can be accomplished without the immediate involvement of any other party and that it is treated for payment purposes as if one party had handed another party a dollar bill; thinking outside of our current paradigm in this manner is an interesting exercise. Analysis can be aided by looking at another type of system that functions as a private form of money. One emerging system involves local paper-based currencies, a leading example of which is the Ithaca Hour.

An Ithaca Hour is a unit of value that that has been in circulation in Ithaca, New York since 1991.[254] One Ithaca Hour is equivalent to $10 in U.S. currency. Merchants, who join the Ithaca Hours program and agree to accept Ithaca Hours, receive one or two Ithaca Hours simply for joining. A merchant's continued participation in the program earns another Hour every eight months which gradually increases the local money supply. Presently, over 2000 individuals and 360 local merchants, including a local credit union, use Ithaca Hours. Employees of these merchants may agree to receive part of their pay in Ithaca Hours, to promote their use in the local economy.[255] The total issuance for Ithaca Hours exceeds $62,000, with five denominations: 2 HRS ($20), 1 HR ($10), 1/2 HR ($5), 1/4 HR ($2.50), and an 1/8 HR ($1.25). Ithaca Hours have circulated in transactions totaling more than $2,000,000.[256]

Ithaca Hours are local tender rather than legal tender. The value inherent in an Ithaca Hour arises when an employee earns the Hour or when a merchant's product is sold in exchange for the Hour. According to the sponsor of Ithaca Hours, it is a legal form of currency.[257] In that regard, the issuer of Ithaca Hours has indicated that the Internal Revenue Service and "Fed" officials "have been contacted by media, and repeatedly have said there is no prohibition of local currency, as long as it does not look like [U.S.] dollars, as long as denominations are at least $1.00 value, and if it is regarded as taxable income."[258]

The idea of local currency based on the Ithaca standard has spread into small towns throughout the nation. The Ithaca Hour website offers a Hometown Money Starter Kit for communities interested in implementing a local currency. The kit provides a systematic procedure to establish and maintain an Hours

---

[254] *See* ITHACA HOUR FACT SHEET, *available at* <http://pciweb.baka.com/web/ithacahour>.

[255] *Id.*

[256] *Id.*

[257] *Id. See also* LEWIS SOLOMON, RETHINKING OUR CENTRALIZED MONETARY SYSTEM: THE CASE FOR LOCAL CURRENCY (1996) (providing an extensive study of the legal aspects of local currency).

[258] *See* ITHACA HOUR FACT SHEET, *supra* note 254. *See also* Ellen Graham, *Regions: Community Groups Print Local (and Legal) Currencies*, WALL ST. J., June 27, 1996, at B1 ("Local currency is legal, but the government stipulates that the notes must be smaller in size than dollar bills, issued in denominations valued at a minimum of $1 and reported as taxable income to the [I.R.S.]"). The reference that the denominations must exceed $1 implies that federal officials are mindful of the Stamp Payments Act.

system based on the Ithaca system. Over 1,000 communities in forty-seven states have received the kit and at least thirty-nine Hour systems have been established in North America.[259]

The significance of the Ithaca Hours program is that it demonstrates that a medium can function as "money" without being issued by a government and without the issuer promising to give anything in exchange for presentation of the instrument. As discussed in Chapter 3, the key point in determining whether an instrument has reached the point of functioning as money is whether a significant number parties are willing to accept the instrument as money. In light of the current developments relating to electronic commerce, we may see the same type of innovation that the Ithaca Hour represents in a physical world begin to appear in the virtual world.

§ 16.05   REGULATORY ISSUES CONCERNING SV ONCE ISSUED

At present, the application of federal or state laws or regulations to SV and electronic money is, in many respects unclear.[260] Increasingly, however, government agencies have been either proposing or adopting rules to apply to emerging SV or electronic money systems. For example, the FRB has proposed amendments to Regulation E to specifically address the application of the regulation to various types of SV systems.[261] The FDIC has also issued a General Counsel's Opinion regarding the application of deposit insurance to various types of SV systems.[262] Other legal and regulatory topics that have been addressed by commentators include: the relationship between SV and escheat (the power of a state to claim unused SV as "abandoned property"); the relationship between SV and privacy law; and whether SV issuers should be treated as engaged in the business of banking under applicable federal or state law.[263] Federal bank regulatory agencies appear to have taken, at least for the short term, a cautious approach to regulation and appear to have decided to let the market grow

---

[259] *See* Paul Glover, *Creating Community Economics with Local Currency*, updated from original article in 14850 MAG., *available at* <http://pciweb.baka.com/web/ithacahour>. *See also* Bill Minutaglio, *Barter Bucks: Local Currency System is Designed to Keep Money At Home*, DALLAS MORNING NEWS, June 3, 1996, at 1C ("Part bartering system, part economic [strategy] to skirt the tentacles of big business, the new currencies — in use in 30 cities from coast to coast, plus Canada and Mexico — are patterned after an Ithaca, New York-based organization that five years ago began issuing 'Ithaca Hours.'").

[260] *See, e.g.,* CBO STUDY, *supra* note 2, at xii (noting legal and regulatory uncertainties, such as deposit insurance and reserve requirements, for emerging payment products); Treasury Report, *supra* note 171, at Appendix I (describing application of current laws).

[261] *See* Electronic Fund Transfers, 61 Fed. Reg. 19,696 (1996) (codified at 12 C.F.R. pt. 205). Congress had imposed a moratorium on the FRB adoption of amendments to Regulation E with regard to SV payments systems prior to June 30, 1997. *See also* Omnibus Consolidated Appropriations Act of 1996, § 2601, Pub. L. No. 104-208, 1996 U.S.C.C.A.N. (110 Stat.) 3009, 3009-469. For a discussion of stored value products and Regulation E, see Chapter 7, Section 7.06, and for an overview of the Electronic Fund Transfer Act and Regulation E, see Chapter 4, Section 4.07[7].

[262] General Counsel's Opinion No. 8, Stored Value Cards, 61 Fed. Reg. 40,490.

[263] Thomas P. Vartanian & Robert H. Ledig, *The Business of Banking in the Age of the Internet: Fortress or Prison?*, BANKING POL'Y REP., Mar. 4-18, 1996; Ellen d'Alelio, *Smart Cards and Escheat: Can the States Reach "Abandoned" Funds Held to Pay Smart Card Liabilities?*," ELEC. BANKING L. & COM. REP., May 1996, at 15; In addition, the ABA(Bar) SV Report, *supra* note 1, addresses a host of legal and commercial issues regarding SV; including, the identity of the SV obligor, transferability of devices and claims, payment finality, allocation of the risk of loss, levy and attachment, escheat, choice of law, and the measure of damages.

and evolve first.[264] Federal bank regulators have, however, stressed the need for regulated institutions to identify and implement risk management strategies for participation in emerging payments systems, consistent with safety and soundness.[265]

The development of SV systems will also depend to a large extent on the contractual arrangements between the participants. These contracts include the agreements: (1) between the SV developer and the originators in each country; (2) between the Originator and the SV service providers ("SVSP") within a each country; (3) between the customer and its SVSP; and (4) between the merchant and its SVSP. Courts confronted with the issue of what rules to apply to electronic commerce may well look to private industry and government initiatives to provide guidance for the resolution of disputes, such as loss allocation, among participants in SV payments systems.[266]

Several issues regarding the development of the SV systems are likely to be important in determining the success of such systems. For example, disclosure of the characteristics of, and risks posed by, SV products in a manner that does not lead to customer confusion will be essential to the acceptance of SV. The legal framework governing SV systems should protect customers against fraud while promoting broad access to new products and technologies. Finally, the adoption of risk of loss rules that strike a reasonable balance among the parties involved will be essential. Regulators, when promulgating regulations and guidelines governing SV systems, should be mindful that the most important ingredient in the success of these emerging products is trust. All participants, but most especially customers, must have confidence in the SV system's dependability and integrity. The integrity of a SV system depends on the development of adequate risk management systems. Regulators are also concerned about the possibility that the interoperability of SV systems at an international level will present a significant risk that SV systems will be subject to misuse by organized crime. Some SV systems may facilitate financial crimes due to, among other things, the potential for some systems to provide transactional anonymity. Various regulatory officials have addressed these topics and agencies have proposed solutions to some of these problems.[267] A discussion of some of these initiatives now follows.

---

[264] For example, in its recent approval of the application of four national banks to establish subsidiaries to acquire 70% of two Delaware limited liability companies that will operate the U.S. Mondex franchise, the OCC did not discuss the implications of a variety of federal laws and regulations, noting only that "we do not address the important consumer protection and supervisory considerations that will arise when the Companies actually commence operations." *See* OCC Mondex Letter, *supra* note 14, at 2.

[265] *See Stored Value Card Systems*, OCC Bulletin 96-48 (Sept. 10, 1996) (describing various risks banks may face in SV systems); *Cardinal Bancshares, Inc.*, 82 FED. RESERVE BULL. 674 (May 21, 1996) (order approving Cardinal Bancshares acquisition of Five Paces Software, Inc. but noting the importance of risk management for Internet-based services); *Interagency Statement on Risk Management of Client/Network Computer Systems*, Federal Financial Institutions Examination Council, Oct. 24, 1996. *See also*, Thomas P. Vartanian, *Wanted: Standards and Codes for Allocating Liability; Regulatory Uncertainties Are Only Part of the Problem*, AM. BANKER - FUTURE BANKING, Jan. 21, 1997, at 8A.

[266] Numerous private and public bodies are developing and considering the publication of standards regarding various aspects of electronic systems, or have already published such standards. *See* ABA(Bar) SV Report, *supra* note 1. *See also* Thomas P. Vartanian, *Technology Advances Require New Kind of Code of Conduct*, AM. BANKER - FUTURE BANKING, Dec. 9, 1996, at 11A. (discussing four areas that institutions should address when adapting corporate codes of conduct to the age of cyberspace).

[267] *See* Ludwig, U.S. Treasury Conference Remarks, *supra* note 97 (concerning the need for a Consumer Electronic Money Task Force, comprised of federal governmental policy makers from the Treasury Department, the FRB, the FDIC, and the Federal Trade Commission, to address in detail many of the consumer issues raised at the Treasury Conference).

[1]   FEDERAL RESERVE BOARD PERSPECTIVE

The FRB is responsible for examining, and assessing the safety and soundness of, bank holding companies and state chartered banks that are members of a Federal Reserve Bank. New electronic financial products and services, including SV and electronic money systems, may expose these institutions to significant liability, as well as financial and reputational risks, if the organizations adopt inadequate security measures or other risk management procedures. The FRB has made it clear that it expects banking organizations to carefully analyze the risks associated with all types of electronic financial products and services.[268]

While the applicability of Regulation E to SV products remains an open issue, the FRB's Regulation E Proposal and its report to Congress on SV provide some indication to SV issuers of the potential level of regulation that may be applied to SV systems.[269] Another important area of banking regulation that the FRB oversees concerns the financial integrity and stability of its member institutions and depository institutions generally. This is an area of concern to customers and to regulators, who want to ensure that a SV issuer has the financial integrity to stand behind its issuance. In addition to deposit insurance, a level of protection is provided to depositors through the maintenance of reserves on hand to meet depositors' demands for funds, in accordance with Regulation D.

[a]   Reserve Requirements under Regulation D.

The FRB determines the reserve requirements of all depository institutions and implements these requirements through Regulation D. Bank reserves consist of cash on hand to pay depositor's withdrawals and cash or balances held at Federal Reserve Banks to meet reserve requirements.[270] Under the Depository Institutions Deregulation and Monetary Control Act of 1980,[271] all depository institutions, regardless of membership in the Federal Reserve System are subject to reserve requirements.[272] A depository institution that fails to meet these reserve requirements is subject to a penalty of an additional 2% added to the discount rate charged to the bank when it borrows from the Federal Reserve Discount Window to eliminate reserve deficiencies.[273] If a depository institution fails to rectify its reserve deficiency, the institution may be subject to enforcement actions, including cease and desist orders and/or assessment of civil money penalties.[274]

---

[268] *See, e.g., Cardinal Bancshares, Inc.*, 82 FED. RESERVE BULL. 674 (May 21, 1996) (order approving Cardinal Bancshares acquisition of Five Paces Software, Inc. but noting importance of risk management for Internet-based services); and *Royal Bank of Canada*, 83 FED. RESERVE BULL. 135 (Feb. 1997) (approving the investment by several banking organizations in Integrion Financial Network, L.L.C., a joint venture for the design, development, and operation of a data processing and transmission system through which depository institutions and their affiliates would make available home banking and other financial services to their respective customers.). In approving the investments, the FRB considered the security measures that Integrion and its owners committed to take to protect the account data and other financial information transmitted through the Integrion network from the risk of electronic interception, interference, or fraud. These measures included log-in passwords and encryption procedures to attempt to maintain the privacy and integrity of the data transmitted. *Id.* at n. 19.

[269] *See* Chapter 4, Section 4.07[7]; Chapter 7, Section 7.07 (discussing the EFTA and Regulation E and their application to SV).

[270] 12 U.S.C. § 461(c) and 12 C.F.R. § 204.3(b); *see also* THE FEDERAL RESERVE SYSTEM, *supra* note 81, at 18-20, 53-55.

[271] Pub. L. No. 96-221, 1980 U.S.C.C.A.N. (94 Stat.) 132 (codified in scattered sections of 12 and 15 U.S.C.).

[272] 12 U.S.C. § 461(b)(1)(A); 12 C.F.R. § 204.2(m)(1).

[273] 12 C.F.R. § 204.7(a).

[274] *Id.* § 204.7(b).

[*i*] *What Constitutes a "Deposit" for Reserve Requirements Purposes?* The term "deposit" is used throughout federal banking law and regulations. Of the various definitions of "deposit" applied by federal banking regulators, one of the broadest is that used in conjunction with the FRB's reserve requirements. This breadth is necessary because of the importance of bank reserves to both the safety and soundness of the banking industry and the FRB's own monetary policies.[275] Thus, the FRB has stated that "Regulation D currently defines a number of sources of funds [as deposits] that frequently are not classified as deposits for other purposes."[276]

Under Regulation D, a "deposit" is generally defined as the unpaid balance of money or its equivalent received or held by a *depository institution* in the usual course of business.[277] The depository institution must be obligated to give credit to an account or an instrument must evidence the deposit on which the depository institution is primarily liable.[278] A "deposit" for purposes of reserve requirements, includes:

- Money received or held by a depository institution, or the credit given for money or its equivalent received or held by the depository institution in the usual course of business for a special or specific purpose;

- Credit balances;

- An outstanding teller's check, or an outstanding draft, certified check, cashier's check, money order, or officer's check drawn on the depository institution, issued in the usual course of business for any purpose, including payment for services, dividends or purchases;

- Any due bill or, in some circumstances, a liability or undertaking on the part of a depository institution to sell or deliver securities to a customer (or to purchase securities for the account of a customer) involving the receipt of funds or a debit to an account of the customer before the securities are delivered;

- Any liability of a depository institution's affiliate that is not a depository institution, on any promissory note, acknowledgment of advance, due bill, or similar obligation (written or oral), with

---

[275] *See* OCC Interpretive Letter No. 378, [1988-1989 Transfer Binder] Fed. Banking L. Rep. (CCH) ¶ 85,602 (Mar. 24, 1987). In the March 1987 letter, the OCC stated that:

> [y]ou should consult with the Federal Reserve Board to determine whether the CMO transaction you describe would be considered by them to be a 'deposit' for purposes of the member bank reserve requirements in Regulation D . . . Even if the Federal Reserve concluded that the transaction is subject to reserve requirements, that does not mean that there is a deposit under the Comptroller's Interpretive Ruling. . . . The definition of deposit in Regulation D is an expansive one designed in large part to facilitate the Federal Reserve Board's monetary control policies.

Id. at 77,907 n.2.

[276] Reserve Requirements of Depository Institutions, 45 Fed. Reg. 56,009, 56,014 (1980) (codified at 12 C.F.R. pt. 204) (adopting revised Regulation D to implement the provisions of the Monetary Control Act of 1980).

[277] For Regulation D purposes, a "depository institution" means any FDIC-insured bank, any savings bank or mutual savings bank, any insured credit union, and any "insured institution" under the Federal Home Loan Bank Act, 12 U.S.C. § 1422(4). *See* 12 C.F.R. § 204.2(m)(1).

[278] 12 C.F.R. § 204.2(a)(1)(i).

a maturity of less than one and one-half years, to the extent that the proceeds are used to supply or to maintain the availability of funds (other than capital) to the depository institution;

- Any liability of a depository institution on any promissory note, acknowledgment of advance, banker's acceptance or similar obligation.[279]

The applicability of Regulation D to various SV systems will ultimately be determined on a case-by-case basis, depending on the nature of the system. The FRB has stated that the funds in the ecash™ system, in use by Mercantile Bank, are being treated as deposits for reserve requirement purposes.[280]

[2]   OFFICE OF THE COMPTROLLER OF THE CURRENCY PERSPECTIVE

The OCC is responsible for monitoring the safety and soundness of national banks.[281] In September 1996, the OCC published Banking Bulletin No. 96-48 which provides guidance to national banks and banking examiners, by describing SV systems and outlining the risks associated with those systems. The banking bulletin is discussed below.

[a]   **The Various Functions and Roles of Banks in SV Systems.** The OCC recognizes that national banks may participate in SV systems in a variety of capacities.[282] The bank may be a partial investor in an entity that issues SV, a non-investor participant, or the entity that issues the SV.[283] National banks may distribute and redeem SV, sell SV cards to customers, and contract with merchants to convert their SV into cash or to deposit the SV into the merchants' depository accounts. Banks may perform the functions of a transaction authorizer for those SV systems that require authorization before consummation of the transaction. If banks agree to accept SV issued by different entities, then a clearing house mechanism must be established to settle such transactions. Finally, SV systems are likely to include a bank or other entity to maintain a transaction archive for error resolution, and fraud, or counterfeit detection.[284]

The OCC notes that transactional rules governing the rights and liabilities of all parties involved in a SV transaction are not fully developed under current law. Until these rules are created, participants in a SV system will rely on contractual arrangements to distribute the risk of loss under various SV transaction scenarios.[285] Contracts that address these liability concerns in a clear and concise manner will alleviate the potential burden that failures in a SV system may place on banks. To draft these contracts, banks must understand the risks

---

[279] *Id.* § 204.2(a)(ii)-(vii).

[280] Letter from Marc J. Goldstrom, Counsel, FDIC, at 9-10 (May 12, 1997) (stating that the ecash™ system is subject to reserve requirements imposed by the FRB). See Section 16.02[1][b][i] for a discussion of the ecash™ system.

[281] See Chapter 6 for a discussion of the OCC.

[282] OCC Banking Bull. No. 96-48, *supra* note 3. For example, in December 1996, the OCC approved the investment of several national banks in two limited liability companies that would operate the Mondex SV system. OCC Mondex Letter, *supra* note 14.

[283] OCC Banking Bull. No. 96-48, *supra* note 3, at 3.

[284] *Id.* at 3-4.

[285] *Id.* at 4 (contracts should govern numerous potential system problems such as malfunctioning cards, lost cards, operational errors, and counterfeit SV or SV cards).

underlying SV systems and the threats they pose to various functions and roles that the banks play in the SV system. The OCC identifies seven roles that banks may play in a SV system.[286]

[*i*] *Investing Banks.* These banks have an equity stake in the SV system. They face strategic risks dependent upon the success or failure of the SV system. Additional liability may be derived from these banks' contractual obligations and the corporate structure of the SV entity in which these banks invest. This liability can be reduced, however, if banks use an ownership structure that limits their liability.

[*ii*] *Issuing Banks.* These banks create the SV that is sold to customers either directly or through another entity. They face strategic, transaction, compliance, and reputation risks associated with their operation of an SV system. The issuance of SV and the investment of the proceeds from the sale of SV pending redemption, pose credit, liquidity, interest rate, and foreign exchange risks for issuing banks. These risks should be addressed by the issuing bank's investment policy.[287]

[*iii*] *Distributing Banks.* These banks, which can include issuing banks, distribute or sell SV. They are exposed to transaction, compliance, reputation, credit, and liquidity risk. Distributing banks can limit their credit and liquidity risks if they only sell SV as agents for an issuing bank, because distributing banks do not have ownership rights in the SV they sell.

[*iv*] *Transaction Authorizing Banks.* These banks authorize the validity of the SV that customers wish to use in payment for goods and services. Similar to credit card transactions, merchants will obtain authorization from these banks before accepting the SV as a valid obligation of these bank. This function exposes banks to transaction risk.[288]

[*v*] *Redeeming Banks.* A redeeming bank may either act as collection agent or as principal. A collection agent is not required to purchase or redeem SV for depositors, but acts as the depositor's agent by presenting the SV to the issuer for redemption. The agent bank then credits the depositor's account with the funds received from the issuer. These banks face the transaction risk to effect proper presentment of the SV for redemption. If the bank provides provisional credit to the depositor pending redemption, the bank is exposed to the credit risk of the issuing bank's default before redemption.[289]

Redeeming banks that act as principal are obligated to redeem SV by crediting depositor's accounts or transferring funds to the presenter of SV. These banks are exposed to all the risks associated with ownership of SV that may be held for resale or presented to the issuer for redemption.[290]

---

[286] *Id.* at 4-9.

[287] These risks are described in Section 16.05[2][b].

[288] OCC Banking Bull. No. 96-48, *supra* note 3, at 6.

[289] *Id.* at 7.

[290] *Id.*

[*vi*] *Clearing and Settling Banks.* These banks transmit information and funds through a payments system's network to clear and settle transactions. These banks may be the redeeming banks or other banks that act as intermediaries between banks and issuers. They are exposed to transaction, credit, liquidity, and foreign exchange risk.[291] The banks are exposed to transaction and credit risks when acting as principal; whereas agent banks are limited to transaction risks for failure to properly process the redemption.

[*vii*] *Transaction Archiving Banks.* Two types of transaction archiving banks exist in SV systems. First, a fully auditable central system archives the records of every SV transaction of each SV card when it is executed. Second, a batch system archives the records of a bundle of merchant transactions in periodic sessions. The batch system is auditable, but at a greater expense than the central system. These systems provide the basis for settling disputes between customers, merchants, and participating banks, and for government investigation of criminal activity. Archiving banks are exposed to transaction, reputation, and compliance risks.

[b] Description of Risks in SV Systems. Participants in a SV system should be concerned with numerous risks inherent in the issuance of SV products. A discussion of eight of these risks follows.[292]

[*i*] *Transaction Risk.* Transaction risk is a function of adequate internal controls, data integrity, transaction rules, employee performance, and operating procedures in a SV system.[293] Issuing banks must prevent errors in the distribution of their SV. Distributing agent banks bear the responsibility of safeguarding the computer systems used to distribute an issuer's SV.[294] Inadequate commercial laws governing SV require effective contractual arrangements describing the rights and obligations of the parties.[295] Transaction authorizing banks must establish adequate controls to ensure the accuracy of the bank's information for proper authorization. Liability for improperly authorized transactions will fall onto the bank that has inadequate controls over data integrity and inadequate system capacity to authorize transactions on a timely basis.[296] A lack of internal controls and qualified staff can result in fraud and disruptions in SV operations. Archiving banks are exposed to the risk of data corruption that prevents error resolution, identification of fraud, or recognition of counterfeit SV.[297] Banks should implement contingency plans and back-up facilities to ensure timely restoration of computer functions and continuation of business operations.[298]

[*ii*] *Strategic Risk.* Strategic risk is the product of a bank's goals, strategies, and resources and the compatibility of these elements in implementation of a SV system. Proper design and pricing of SV products in

---

[291] *Id.* at 7-8 (including a description of various clearing arrangements for SV systems involving single or multiple issuers of SV). See OCC Banking Circular 271 (May 1993) for a detailed discussion of risks associated with clearing houses.

[292] OCC Banking Bull. No. 96-48, *supra* note 3, at app. 1-3.

[293] *Id.* at app. 1.

[294] *Id.* at 5-6.

[295] *Id.* at 5.

[296] *Id.* at 6.

[297] *Id.* at 8-9.

[298] *Id.* at app. 1.

accordance with market demand are essential to successful SV systems. A profitable SV venture requires cost effective SV readers and software systems.[299] Banks lacking in the expertise to design SV systems must rely on outsourcing. Outsourcing exposes banks to risks associated with poorly conceived service contracts, partnership agreements or other venture contracts.

Improper integration of the SV system into bank operations could not only cause the failure of the SV system, but may impair the bank's current operations. Interoperability of the computer systems running the SV system with the bank's systems demands standardization of SV processing, data communication, and transaction security. A lack of standardization will hamper the bank's efforts to achieve a critical mass necessary for the viability of the SV system.

[*iii*] *Reputation Risk.* The reputation of a distributing or issuing bank can be threatened by customer dissatisfaction or adverse public reaction to any aspect of a SV system. The reputation of a bank will be disparaged by litigation arising from customers' financial losses associated with the bank's SV system.[300] Archiving banks are exposed to public criticism for their improper or incompetent resolution of customer complaints.[301] Malfunctions and security breaches may damage a bank's reputation for integrity. Any of these problems may result in adverse media coverage of a bank's brand name.[302]

[*iv*] *Compliance Risk.* Compliance risk arises from the violation of laws, rules, regulations, business practices, or ethical standards. Banks must have SV systems designed with the ability to adapt to a dynamic regulatory environment. Several areas of uncertainty remain regarding the applicability of various laws and regulations.[303] SV distributors may be the primary point of contact with customers. Therefore, they bear the obligation to distribute any required disclosures.[304] Distributing agent banks may be liable to customers for the failure to properly disclose the true and limited function of the bank in relation to the SV product.[305] Archiving banks must maintain records in accordance with federal and state record keeping regulations.

[*v*] *Credit Risk.* The OCC defines credit risk as the risk that an obligor will fail to meet the terms of its contract with a bank. Credit risk occurs whenever the success of the contract depends on counter-party, borrower, or issuer performance. For example, the sale of SV exposes banks to credit risk when the payment for the SV is in a form other than cash or a deposit in that bank.[306] Banks also face credit risk in connection with its activities such as establishing a proper investment portfolio to fund the float of SV, foreign exchange

---

[299] *Id.* at app. 1.

[300] *Id.* at 5.

[301] *Id.* at 9.

[302] *Id.* at app. 2.

[303] *Id.* In this regard, the OCC notes the uncertain application of Regulation E, the Bank Secrecy Act, and state escheat and money transmitter laws.

[304] *Id.* at 5.

[305] *Id.* at 6.

[306] *Id.* at 5.

counter-party exposure, and sovereign exposure. A distributing bank carries the credit risk that a SV issuer may default on its obligations to redeem SV.[307]

[vi] *Liquidity Risk.* Liquidity risk is the inability to meet obligations as they come due, while incurring "acceptable" losses.[308] Banks are exposed to liquidity risk when payments for SV are delayed in their conversion to cash or deposit account balances.[309] SV issuers are obligated to maintain liquid investments sufficient to meet the ongoing and occasional unexpected demands for redemption.

[vii] *Interest Rate Risk.* The movement of interest rates affects the economic value of an issuer's investments held for redemption of the outstanding float of SV. The assessment of interest rate risk should consider both the effects on a bank's accrual earnings and on the market value of the bank's portfolio. SV issuers may face interest rate risk on the portfolio of investments held for redemption of their SV if the rate inflation exceeds their yield on those investments.

[viii] *Foreign Exchange Risk.* Banks that accept foreign currency in payments for SV or that construct SV systems to use multiple currencies are exposed to fluctuations of foreign exchange rates. Banks involved with these SV systems must possess the necessary expertise to conduct evaluations of foreign currency fluctuations before engaging these SV systems.

[ix] *Additional Observations on SV System Risk.* The authors note that the risks associated with SV are likely to change over time. During the early implementation of this technology, and until there is widespread adoption and acceptance of the SV obligations as a transferable form of money, there may be greater risks associated with the financial stability of a stored value issuer and indeed with the possible abandonment of particular forms of SV technology.[310] Should the technology gain widespread acceptance, the risks of a SV issuer's failure may decrease somewhat, particularly once regulations or payments system rules attempt to prevent a participant's possible insolvency or to mitigate effects of such an insolvency. To some extent the systemic risks associated with SV may be minimized, if SV largely remains a mechanism for settling low-dollar transactions or for purchasing specific services (*i.e.*, paying transit fares, bridge and highway tolls, and telephone charges).[311] The complexity and scope of systemic risks would increase if, over time, the SV gains

---

[307] *Id.* at app. 3.

[308] *Id.* at app. 3.

[309] *Id.* at 5.

[310] The operational failure or insolvency of a key issuer in an SV system could create a widespread loss of consumer and merchant confidence in other forms of SV, leading to additional issuer insolvency and/or a flight to legal tender. *See* Treasury Report, *supra* note 171, at 32; ABA(Bar) SV Report, *supra* note 1, at 710-12.

[311] While the potential market for SV payments systems is large, SV payment products may not enter widespread use in the immediate future. The CBO recently estimated the size of the potential SV marketplace. The CBO determined that the value of U.S. currency with a face value of $10 or less outstanding is roughly $50 billion, and that the total value of transactions is a multiple of this stock of coins and bills. By analyzing three likely markets for the introduction of SV cards in the near future (fast food restaurants, vending machines, and convenience stores), the CBO estimated the potential SV card marketplace at $20 billion annually, roughly comparable to the annual market for traveler's checks. *See* CBO STUDY, *supra* note 2, at 16-18.

widespread acceptance and begins to circulate as electronic money.[312]

[c] OCC Recommended Customer Disclosures for SV Systems. An essential feature that must accompany SV cards, or other SV systems, is appropriate customer disclosure. Functional and physical resemblance to existing debit and credit cards may create a certain degree of confusion until customers become fully educated in the use of SV cards and the distinct risks attendant with the use of SV products. Issuers, both banks and nonbanks, must take the appropriate steps to inform customers and merchants of their rights and responsibilities when consummating transactions with SV cards.[313]

The OCC suggested that national banks consider the basic disclosures needed for SV cards and provided the following topics that national banks should address when deciding how to adequately inform customers:

- How to use the card.

- Where and how the customer can increase the value on the card.

- Whether the electronic cash earns interest, dividends, or any other return.

- Where, how, and when the electronic cash can be redeemed.

- All fees charged in connection with obtaining or using the card or the electronic cash stored on it.

- The name of the entity that issues the electronic cash and its obligation to redeem it.

- Whether the customer is protected in case of a lost or stolen card.

- Whether the amount of the electronic cash transferred to the card is insured by the FDIC.

- Where does liability lie if a transaction is not properly consummated.

- What happens to electronic cash that is abandoned or expires under the terms of the agreement.

- How customers can resolve disputes involving electronic cash transactions.

- The circumstances under which information on a customer's electronic cash transactions may be disclosed to third parties.[314]

---

[312] When compared to existing methods of retail payments, SV issuers must develop and successfully market products with the right combination of features and protections and educate consumers and merchants about the benefits of adopting new payment technologies. At present, it is unclear whether and how existing retail payments methods will be affected by the adoption and increased use of SV payments systems, and the potential growth of peer-to-peer SV transactions. For a description of the retail payments system, see generally PAYMENTS SYSTEM TASK FORCE, *supra* note 3; CBO STUDY, *supra* note 2; NACHA, ACH RISK MANAGEMENT HANDBOOK (1994).

[313] *See generally* FRB SV REPORT, *supra* note 3, at 12-13; General Counsel's Opinion No. 8, Stored Value Cards, 61 Fed. Reg. 40,490 (1996).

[314] OCC Banking Bull. No. 96-48, *supra* note 3 (noting that banks should consider similar disclosures for the sale of SV via the Internet).

In considering customer disclosures, SV designers should also consider the range of options available to them in structuring their programs. In this regard the following scenario illustrates some of the issues that may arise.

A bank customer enters a downtown New York City bank branch. She hands a twenty dollar bill to a teller in return for a SV card on which twenty dollars of value has been loaded. The customer walks out of the branch holding the SV card in her hand. At that moment, a speeding bicycle messenger comes racing down the street. The bank customer leaps out of his way at the last second, but in the process drops her SV card down the sewer, consigning it forever to the proverbial legion of alligators that populate the New York City sewer system. This amazing incident is witnessed by the bank branch manager and the teller. Shaken, but unharmed, the customer returns to the teller and asks for the twenty dollars back. What is the teller's response? Will he say "I'm sorry, as your stored value card disclosure states, your stored value card is just like cash and the bank has no obligation to replace the card or the value that is on it if it is lost"; or will he say "if no claim is made for the value on the stored value card within five years, the money will be treated as unclaimed property and turned over to the state to be held for the rightful owner?" In either case the customer may say "but you have my money, what are you gong to do with it?"

Although the foregoing scenario is unlikely to occur, it illustrates a critical point in the SV equation — where is the money?[315] Can the money be on the card and at the same time be in the teller's drawer? Where customers have become accustomed to little or no loss in the event of unauthorized transactions involving their ATM cards or credit cards, will the SV industry find it feasible to shift the risk allocation balance almost completely to customers? These are questions that no doubt will be addressed by market forces, and by legislators and regulators.

[3]   OFFICE OF THRIFT SUPERVISION PERSPECTIVE

Presently, the Office of Thrift Supervision ("OTS") does not have any specific regulations covering SV. OTS has requested comment on all aspects of electronic banking activities and SV technology[316] and has published a notice of proposed rulemaking to replace existing regulations with a single subpart that would focus on electronic operations.[317]

[4]   FEDERAL DEPOSIT INSURANCE CORPORATION PERSPECTIVE

The Federal Deposit Insurance Corporation ("FDIC") insures the deposits of all depository institutions.[318] Beyond the FDIC's regulation of depository institutions and the protection of deposits held by those institutions,

---

[315] *See* Thomas A. Vartanian, *Key Questions for Emerging Systems, supra* note 50.

[316] Deposits and Electronic Banking, 62 Fed. Reg. 15,626, 15,627 (1997) (to be codified at 12 C.F.R. pts. 545, 556, 557, 561, 563 & 563g). For further discussion of the OTS see Chapter 9.

[317] Electronic Operations, 62 Fed. Reg. 51,817 (1997) (to be codified at 12 C.F.R. §§ 545.92, 545.140-545.144).

[318] For a discussion of the FDIC's position on the application of deposit insurance to SV systems, see Chapter 8, Section 8.03.

the FDIC also regulates the acceptance of deposits through deposit brokers. Under federal law, a "deposit broker" is very broadly defined.[319] Institutions seeking to issue computer- or card-based SV may look to deposit brokers to increase the circulation of their particular product, however, current law may limit that institution's ability to do so.

The Federal Deposit Insurance Act ("FDIA"), generally prohibits insured depository institutions that are not "well capitalized" from accepting brokered deposits.[320] The FDIC has the authority to grant an exemption to this brokered deposit restriction on a case-by-case basis, for an institution that is at least "adequately capitalized,"[321] upon a showing that the acceptance of such deposits would not constitute an unsafe or unsound banking practice.[322] The FDIC, however, does not have the authority to grant an exemption for undercapitalized or significantly undercapitalized institutions.[323] Thus, depository institutions that become SV issuers must be mindful of their capital levels if they seek to use deposit brokers to gain increased circulation of their SV.

Chapter 8, Section 8.05[1] provides a discussion of the FDIC's opinion regarding the application of the deposit broker regulation to the CyberCash program, in which CyberCash places customer funds in a depository institution for the purposes of facilitating Internet purchases.

[5] FEDERAL FINANCIAL INSTITUTIONS EXAMINATION COUNCIL PERSPECTIVE

In 1996, the Federal Financial Institutions Examination Council updated its Information Systems Examination Handbook to include, among other revisions, the need to establish examination procedures relating to what it characterizes as smart cards.[324] Some of these examination procedures include:

- Description of the smart card product;

- Review of procedures relating to the integrity of personal identification numbers;

---

[319] See 12 U.S.C. § 1831f(g); 12 C.F.R. § 337.6(a)(5). A deposit broker is any person "engaged in the business of placing deposits or facilitating the placement of deposits of third parties with insured depository institutions or the business of placing deposits with insured depository institutions for the purpose of selling interests in those deposits to third parties." For example, the FDIC has stated that the definition of "deposit broker" covers scenarios where the deposit broker "facilitates" the payment of deposits as well as a scenario where the broker places deposits in its name as nominee or agent for others. See FDIC Advisory Opinion 92-52, Aug. 3, 1992. If an entity is deemed to be a "deposit broker" it is required to register as a deposit broker with the FDIC and the FDIC may request written quarterly reports regarding its deposit brokerage activities. See 12 C.F.R. § 337.6(h) (deposit broker notification and recordkeeping requirements). See also FDIC Advisory Opinion 93-31, June 17, 1993.

[320] 12 U.S.C. § 1831f(a) provides that "[a]n insured depository institution that is not well capitalized may not accept funds obtained, directly or indirectly, by or through any deposit broker for deposit into 1 or more deposit accounts." For deposit brokerage purposes, the FDIC defines a "well capitalized" institution as one that: (i) has a total risk-based capital ratio of ten percent or greater, (ii) has a "Tier 1" risk-based capital ratio of six percent or better; and (iii) has a leverage ratio of five percent or greater. See 12 C.F.R. § 325.103(b)(1).

[321] A depository institution is "adequately capitalized" if it has a total risk-based capital ratio of 8.0 percent or greater, has a "Tier 1" risk-based capital ratio of 4 percent or greater and has a leverage ratio of 4 percent, or 3 percent under certain circumstances. See 12 C.F.R. § 325.103(a)(2).

[322] 12 U.S.C. § 1831f(c).

[323] The FDIC may grant a limited exception in the case of certain conservatorships. Id. at § 1831f(d).

[324] See FEDERAL FINANCIAL INSTITUTIONS EXAMINATION COUNCIL, INFORMATION SYSTEMS EXAMINATION HANDBOOK 20-4 (1996) (stating that "[r]egardless of the system employed, financial institutions should ensure that adequate internal controls are in place to minimize errors, discourage fraud, and provide an adequate audit trail").

- Review of customer agreements to ensure adequate disclosure of responsibilities and liabilities, especially as required by the Electronic Fund Transfer Act;

- Review of agreements between network operators to ensure adequate disclosure of responsibilities and liabilities of the parties;

- Review of internal audit trail procedures for compliance with examination requirements; and

- Review of the audit functions to determine whether periodic updates occur to inventory all smart card transfer points.[325]

[6]   FEDERAL TRADE COMMISSION PERSPECTIVE

[a] Authority Over Non-FDIC Insured Depository Institutions. The Federal Trade Commission ("FTC") may play a role in regard to SV and electronic money in the fields of consumer protection and antitrust.

The Federal Deposit Insurance Corporation Improvement Act ("FDICIA") added a provision to the FDIA, which granted the FTC the authority to regulate the deposit-taking operations of certain depository institutions that were not insured by the FDIC. The provision also gave the FTC the authority to determine what constitutes the business of "receiving or facilitating the receipt of deposits."[326]

Under the statute, any "depository institution (other than a bank or an unincorporated bank) lacking federal deposit insurance" that is determined by the FTC to be engaged in the business of "receiving or facilitating the receipt of deposits" and which is susceptible to being reasonably mistaken for a bank or depository institution by its current or prospective customers is prohibited from using interstate commerce to receive or facilitate deposits, unless the appropriate supervisor of the State in which the institution is chartered determines that the institution meets all of the eligibility requirements for FDIC insurance.[327]

At the time of its enactment, certain trade groups criticized the statute.[328] A news report at the time stated that the FTC staff indicated, at a meeting with members of a financial institutions trade group, that it would take a "very broad initial interpretation of the scope of the section," to reach wholesale banking operations of the U.S. offices of foreign banks, as well as money market mutual funds, and certain securities firms offering "deposit like products."[329] However, because of a continuing legislative ban on using appropriated

---

[325] *Id.* at 20-7 to 20-15.

[326] 12 U.S.C. § 1831t.

[327] *See* 12 U.S.C. § 1831t(e)(1); Treasury Report, *supra* note 171, at 53-54. This Federal Deposit Insurance Corporation Improvement Act ("FDICIA") provision, entitled "Depository Institutions Lacking Federal Deposit Insurance" was contained in Subtitle F of FDICIA, entitled "Federal Deposit Insurance for State-Chartered Depository Institutions" and was designed to force state chartered and state insured institutions into the FDIC insurance system, as part of the overall range of FDICIA reforms in 1991. *See* H.R. REP. NO. 102-33 (1991) *reprinted in* 1991 U.S.C.C.A.N. 1901, 1918.

[328] *See, e.g., International Banks Ask For Exemption From Law Against Non-Insured Lenders,* THOMSON'S INT'L BANKING REGULATOR, Apr. 27, 1992, at 5 (detailing the effort of the Institute of International Bankers to request assurances from the FTC that the agency would not apply the statute to the U.S. offices of international banks).

[329] *Id.*

funds to implement this statute,[330] the FTC has not promulgated any regulations under 12 U.S.C. § 1831t or otherwise issued any guidance under the provision.

[b] Approach to Electronic Banking and Commerce. In the evolving area of electronic commerce, FTC Chairman Robert Pitofsky has set forth his views concerning several issues regarding the dynamic technological changes in the conduct of commerce.[331] The new forms of electronic commerce can be exceptionally beneficial to customers and to competitive processes in the marketplace. Electronic commerce will provide customers with more options, greater convenience, and detailed information concerning products, including a greater breadth of price data. Mobility between markets should be facilitated by the technological developments, assuming that participants do not erect barriers to entry through private anti-competitive arrangements. Technological developments in electronic payment systems will provide the stimulus for this marketing revolution.

SV issuers must meet customer's demands to provide both convenience and security. The FTC recognizes that government's role in the development and deployment of new electronic payments systems is delicate balancing act between ineffective regulation and aggressive regulation. Regulation must provide sufficient public confidence in the security, effectiveness, and fairness of SV systems while not inhibiting voluntary private arrangements in support of electronic commerce by intervening prematurely, which prevents the market from developing optimal solutions.[332] In addressing governmental regulation, current customer protection and antitrust regulation is sufficiently flexible to address problems as they arise, however, the FTC is monitoring the development of electronic commerce to respond to problems that are not addressed by the current legal framework.

[c] Consumer Protection. Consumer protection is the primary concern of the FTC in the development of SV systems. The success of a SV system will depend on whether it is widely accepted, convenient, and secure.[333] Two principal consumer protection issues that Chairman Pitofsky has addressed are (1) liability rules for unauthorized use and dispute resolution procedures, and (2) access to SV systems by under-served populations.[334]

---

[330] *See* Semi-Annual Regulatory Agenda, 62 Fed. Reg. 22,692, 22,700 (1997) (noting no action under 12 U.S.C. § 1831t); Semi-Annual Regulatory Agenda, 60 Fed. Reg. 24,344 (1995).

[331] Unless otherwise indicated, the remaining portions of this subsection is drawn from Robert Pitofsky, Chairman U.S. Federal Trade Commission, *Competition and Consumer Protection Concerns in the Brave New World of Electronic Money*, Remarks at the U.S. Treasury Conference on Electronic Money & Banking: The Role of Government, in Washington, D.C. (Sept. 19, 1996) *available at* <http://www.ftc.gov/www/speeches/pitofsky/banking.htm> [hereinafter Pitofsky, *Competition and Consumer Protection*].

[332] Chairman Pitofsky has stated that his preference is for self-regulation because of the dynamic nature of the stored value industry. Robert Pitofsky, Chairman U.S. Federal Trade Commission, Remarks at the Third Annual Cyberbanking and Electronic Commerce Conference, in Washington, D.C. at 4 (Feb. 2, 1998) [hereinafter Pitofsky, Cyberbanking Conference, Feb. 2, 1998].

[333] *Id.* at 5-6.

[334] Pitofsky, *Competition and Consumer Protection, supra* note 331 (also commenting on privacy issues, particularly as they relate to the interaction between children and merchants on the Internet). Chairman Pitofsky has spoken further on the issue of privacy and related issues with respect to children. *See generally* Pitofsky, Cyberbanking Conference, *supra* note 332.

[*i*] *Liability Rules.* SV systems have a number of different payment models from which to create rules that allocate liability to participants in the system. Credit cards, debit cards, and ATM cards each provide unique rules that allocate losses differently among users. The credit card industry did not obtain broad market support for its payments system until federal legislation provided for billing dispute and unauthorized protections in the Truth in Lending Act ("TILA").[335] Following TILA, credit cards became a viable method of payment for small and large transactions alike due to the general $50 limitation on customer liability for unauthorized use.[336] The ability to dispute charges on customer bills provided customers with the freedom to deal with unknown merchants because the customer had recourse against their credit card issuer. Though these protections come at a cost to issuers, merchants, and ultimately customers, the benefits to all participants in the credit card payment system are far greater. The EFTA differs from TILA in that it protects the transfer process of the debit card payment system rather than the underlying transaction. Similar to credit cards, the EFTA provides for customer dispute resolution and limited customer liability for unauthorized use.[337]

Some industry analysts have expressed concerns that enhanced regulatory protections may inhibit the development of new SV systems. However, history has shown the reverse may be true when there are inadequate protections. Without customer confidence, no system will reach a critical mass of acceptance. Acceptance will only occur when the industry and government succeed in the challenge of educating customers about the various SV systems and the benefits and disadvantages of each system. Customers must learn that the functions of multifunction chip cards and features provided by different cards may vary although the cards may have a similar appearance, and perhaps the same corporate logos. Disclosure must also include discussions of the potential liability, fees, charges, float, frequent flyer points, and the many competing features of different SV systems. Proper disclosure will educate customers as to the new types of SV systems and enable customers to make informed decisions as to which payments system to use, whether SV, cash, credit cards, or ATM and debit cards.

Before designing a regulatory framework for SV issuers to operate under, private markets should be given an opportunity to design liability rules and disclosure standards. The new SV technology has the potential to address the policy objectives of the FTC. Encryption may solve some consumer protection problems such as loss due to theft. Receipts that are required under the EFTA[338] may be unnecessary because proof of payment may be recorded by the SV system on both the merchant's computer and the customer's SV card. Fraud associated with forgery and insufficient funds should be reduced substantially with the use of digital signatures, online verification, and other authentication devices. Thus, private industry may design SV systems that operate more efficiently and with greater protections to customers than cash.

---

[335] Truth in Lending Act, Pub. L. No. 90-321, 82 Stat. 146 (1968) (codified at 15 U.S.C. §§ 1601 *et seq.*).

[336] 15 U.S.C. § 1643(a)(1).

[337] 15 U.S.C. § 1693f & 1693g (generally limiting consumer liability to $50).

[338] 15 U.S.C. § 1693d.

[*ii*] *Competition Issues.* The antitrust laws express the nation's commitment to an economic policy that favors competition as the best means to allocate goods and services and to promote innovation and efficiency. Antitrust is based on a view that the free market, unimpeded by anti-competitive obstacles, will lead to the optimal allocation of goods and services.

The role of antitrust enforcement will evolve as the markets for electronic commerce continue to form. In the nascent state of electronic commerce, the government should exercise caution before intervening to enforce antitrust laws. Premature intervention may inhibit the efficient evolution of the market. However, antitrust enforcement will play a role to create a competitive marketplace for electronic commerce. Certain firms may possess control of critical "gateways" to the emerging market for electronic commerce. Other firms may control the standards that govern how participants compete in this new market. Control of both gateways and standards can be used to distort the competitive dynamics of the market in violation of the antitrust laws.

Electronic commerce poses many novel and cutting edge issues for antitrust enforcers, many of which were addressed in the FTC's recent hearings on competition and competition policy in the 21st Century.[339] The Commission held these hearings to assess whether the century-old antitrust laws need to be adjusted in response to the competitive challenges of the next century. The general conclusion of the staff report was that the antitrust laws are sufficiently durable and flexible to meet those challenges, although some adjustments are in order.[340]

[7] STORED VALUE AND MONEY LAUNDERING

SV may provide a new vehicle for organized crime to attempt to move their illegal proceeds beyond the nation's borders without detection. The prospect of anonymous transactions and the capacity to move small amounts of SV repetitively through the Internet raises new concerns for governments worldwide.[341]

[8] ESCHEAT

Escheat is the sovereign power of a state to take custody or assume title to abandoned personal property.[342] The issuance of SV raises concerns over a state's right to assume title to the funds underlying the SV in the event that a purchaser fails to redeem the SV. The failure to redeem SV may be due to the loss, abandonment, damage, or theft of an SV card or retention of the card as a collectible.[343] SV issuers should expect that states will be anxious to assert jurisdiction over these funds.[344]

---

[339] *See* Hearings on FTC Policy in Relation to the Changing Nature of Competition, 60 Fed. Reg. 66,802 (1995).

[340] Staff Report, *available at* <http://www.ftc.gov/opp/global.htm>.

[341] See Chapter 10, Section 10.02 for further discussion of money laundering and recent federal government and international regulation of money transfers.

[342] *Delaware v. New York*, 507 U.S. 490, 497 (1993) (stating that the sovereign right to abandoned personal property at common law was through *bona vacantia*, now more commonly known as escheat).

[343] *See* John L. Burke, Jr., *State Survey, Unclaimed Property Act Variations*, ELECTRONIC BANKING L. & COM. REP., Mar. 1997, at 20 (providing a compilation of the escheat statutes of the fifty states and the District of Columbia).

[344] *Id.*

Before a state may exercise its right to escheat abandoned funds, those funds must lie dormant for a statutorily defined period, generally three to five years.[345] The holder of the abandoned funds must file reports with the state following the dormancy period.[346] At the time the report is filed, or up to six months thereafter depending upon the state, the holder is required to deliver the property to the state, as "custodian" for the owner, at which time the holder is freed from further liability. The Uniform Unclaimed Property Act ("Uniform Act") and other state statutes, however, require the holder to maintain available records for such property for up to ten years after it has been reported.[347] Following the reporting period, the state claims the property from the holder as custodian in perpetuity until the rightful owner claims the property.[348] This property may be in the form of deposit or trust accounts and intangible property held or owing in the ordinary course of business by a financial institution.[349]

[a] Multiple Claims to Abandoned Intangible Property by Two States. Unlike tangible property located within a state, intangible property may give to competing claims by multiple states.[350] Generally, intangible property is subject to escheat by the state of the last known address of the rightful owner as indicated on the books and records of the holder.[351] If the rightful owner cannot be located or identified, the state in which the financial institution holding the funds is incorporated may exercise its right to escheat the funds belonging to the unidentifiable or unlocatable rightful owner.[352] However, a different rule is applied if the funds are held for payment of money orders and traveler's checks.[353] In that instance, the state in which the instrument was purchased, may claim the abandoned funds. If the books and records do not indicate the state of purchase, the state where the financial institution has its principal place of business may claim the funds.[354]

Most unclaimed property statutes provide penalties for the failure to report unclaimed property as abandoned or to comply with the statute's provisions. Under the Uniform Act, a holder must pay an interest penalty on the unclaimed property from the time it should have been reported.[355]

---

[345] *Id.; But see* N.Y. ABAN. PROP. LAW § 1310 (stating that under certain circumstances the property need only lie dormant for two years).

[346] *See generally* Ellen d'Alelio & John T. Collins, *Small Change and the Big Float: Smart Cards and Escheat, in* THE EMERGING LAW OF CYBERBANKING 182, 183-184 (Glasser Legal Works ed. 1996).

[347] UNIF. UNCLAIMED PROP. ACT 1981 § 31(a), 8B U.L.A. 567, 670 (1993).

[348] UNIF. UNCLAIMED PROP. ACT 1981 § 20, 8B U.L.A. 567, 643 (1993).

[349] d'Alelio & Collins, *Small Change, supra* note 346, at 186.

[350] *Id.* at 185.

[351] *Texas v. New Jersey*, 379 U.S. 674, 680-681 (1965); *see also Pennsylvania vs. New York*, 407 U.S. 206, 214 (1972).

[352] *Delaware v. New York*, 507 U.S. 490, 499-500 (1993).

[353] Disposition of Abandoned Money Orders and Traveler's Checks Act, 12 U.S.C. §§ 2501-03.

[354] *Id.* at § 2503(2).

[355] UNIF. UNCLAIMED PROP. ACT 1981 § 34, 8B U.L.A. 567, 676 (1993).

CHAPTER 17
ELECTRONIC BENEFITS TRANSFER

§ 17.01 INTRODUCTION

Chapter 4 detailed the development and structure of the payments system industry. The major feature of this industry has been the development of electronic fund transfer ("EFT") as a means of wholesale and retail payment. Federal and state benefit payments present another application of EFT. Benefit delivery through EFT occurs through one of two mechanisms:

(1) *Direct Deposit:* The agency disbursing benefits originates an Automated Clearing House ("ACH") credit to the recipient's preexisting account at the recipient's financial institution.

(2) *Electronic Benefits Transfer ("EBT"):* A mechanism whereby government benefits are distributed through a given EFT channel and are accessible only through electronic means. This mechanism is used to reach benefit recipients without accounts at financial institutions.[1]

Providing benefits electronically curtails fraud, enhances security, and dramatically reduces distribution costs.[2] The federal government, as part of its mandate to deliver all federal payments electronically by January 1, 1999, is developing a system for electronic benefits distribution.[3] State governments have also begun implementing electronic payments. The impact of these combined efforts include a significant increase in the volume of payments processed by the Automated Clearing Houses, greater use of the automated teller machine ("ATM") and point-of-sale ("POS") commercial infrastructure, a change in the relationship between financial institutions and their existing customers, and an opportunity to draw the unbanked into the financial services arena. Financial institutions must understand and prepare for these changes.

This Chapter provides a discussion of these areas. Section 17.02 provides a background discussion of the current benefits distribution systems. Section 17.03 explores the development of electronic benefits

---

[1] Electronic Benefits Transfer; Selection and Designation of Financial Institutions as Financial Agents, 62 Fed. Reg. 25,572 (1997) (to be codified at 31 C.F.R. pt. 207) (proposed May 9, 1997).

[2] *See* Cynthia A. Glassman & James R. Wells, Jr., *Government Electronic Payments: A Wakeup Call for Banks*, J. RETAIL BANKING SERV., Dec. 1996, at 53.

[3] Section 31001(x) of the Debt Collection Improvement Act, *infra* note 24, discussed in Section 17.02[2], amends 31 U.S.C. § 3332 to require federal agencies to convert from paper-based to electronic payment methods. Electronic benefits transfer is one part of that conversion.

distribution and its governing regulations. Section 17.04 explains the role intermediaries play in the system. Section 17.05 presents the impact and challenges that full implementation of electronic benefits distribution will have on system participants. Finally, Section 17.06 highlights the public policy concerns inherent in the transition to EBT and presents an action plan for implementing the new systems.

§ 17.02　CURRENT BENEFIT DISTRIBUTION SYSTEM

An understanding of the evolution of the benefit distribution system is essential to an appreciation of the impact of the transition to universal electronic benefit distribution. Both the federal and state governments distribute benefits. For purposes of clarity, the nature and delivery of federal and state benefits are explained separately. Then a summary presents the combined distribution statistics.

[1]　FEDERAL BENEFIT PAYMENTS

The United States Department of Treasury's ("Treasury's") Financial Management Service ("FMS") is responsible for the government's delivery systems for payments and collections, the central accounting and reporting systems, the government cash management programs credit, debt collection activities, and other financial services.[4] As the financial agent for the federal government, FMS distributes the following federally funded benefits: Social Security Old Age, Survivors, and Disability Insurance ("SSA"); Supplemental Security Income ("SSI"); Black Lung ("BL");[5] Railroad Retirement Board Retirement and Annuity ("RRB"); Department of Veteran's Affairs Compensation ("VA"); and Pension, Civil Services Retirement and Disability. The payment methods employed in the distribution process currently include paper checks and direct deposits. As of the mid-1970s, however, FMS paid all federally distributed benefits by check, either delivered directly at the workplace or sent through the postal service.[6] Necessity compelled the transition to electronic payments as the volume of paper checks and the forgery workload related to social security disbursements threatened Treasury's disbursement ability.[7] The transition from check to electronic payments enjoyed gradual growth as technology developed, recipient acceptance increased, and participants realized that electronic delivery presented a cheaper, safer, and easier payment mechanism than checks. As of May, 1997, roughly 57% of federal benefit disbursements were made through EFT, mostly through direct deposit.[8]

---

[4] There are other federal agencies that make their own disbursements. These agencies have delegated or statutory disbursing authority, and are referred to as Non-Treasury Disbursing Offices ("NTDO's"). The requirement that federal agencies disburse all funds electronically by January 2, 1999 applies to both Treasury and NTDO disbursed funds. For purposes of simplicity, only Financial Management Services ("FMS")/Treasury distributed benefits will be discussed herein.

[5] Black Lung benefits currently cost over $1.3 billion each year, with payments going to 75,000 former miners. *See Labor Secretary Names Committee to End Black Lung and Silicosis Among Coal Miners*, MSHA News Release No. 96-001 (Jan. 26, 1996); *see also Abolishing Black Lung*, 112 PUB. HEALTH REP. 20 (Mar./Apr. 1997).

[6] *See* Glassman & Wells, *supra* note 2.

[7] *Electronic Benefits Transfer: Hearing Before the Senate Comm. on Banking, Housing and Urban Affairs*, 104th Cong. (1997) (statement of John D. Hawke, Jr., Undersecretary for Domestic Finance, Dept. of Treasury) [hereinafter *EFT/EBT Hearing*]. This is particularly relevant because Social Security Old Age, Survivors, and Disability Insurance ("SSA") recipients represent 88% of all federal benefit payees. Over 64% of the 50 million SSA recipients now get their benefits through direct deposit, SSA expects to distribute benefits to 80 million recipients by 2020. *See Social Security Gears Up for Direct Deposit*, CORP. EFT REP., Oct. 16, 1996, *available in* LEXIS, Nexis Library, News File.

[8] *EFT/EBT Hearing, supra* note 7 (Hawke statement, at 1-2).

The electronic delivery of benefits provides the opportunity for tremendous savings by eliminating costs associated with fraud, theft, loss or damage, and processing associated with paper delivery. For example, 75,000 government checks on average each year are forged and fraudulently negotiated, costing the financial services industry $70 million.[9] Automating disbursements makes it possible to reduce such fraud and to identify and eliminate double claims and claims relating to deceased individuals.[10] Each year, Treasury handles over one million complaints associated with check payments.[11] It replaces over 800,000 checks that are lost, stolen, delayed, or damaged during delivery.[12] Electronic delivery should eliminate the majority of these complaints. Payments cannot be stolen or damaged when made electronically. A misrouted payment can typically be corrected within twenty-four hours at negligible cost.[13] In addition, taxpayers will realize savings of $500 million annually in postage and check production as a result of the conversion to electronic payments.[14] With the potential for such significant savings, the federal government has opted to make electronic payment a requirement rather than a mere goal.

[2]   STATE BENEFIT PAYMENTS

State distributed benefits fall in two general categories: (1) benefits that are fully funded and administered by the state, such as unemployment and general assistance; and (2) benefits that enjoy part or full federal funding yet are state administered, including Aid to Families with Dependent Children ("AFDC") (commonly known as welfare), Supplemental Nutrition Program for Women, Infants, and Children ("WIC"), and Food Stamps. States traditionally make these benefit payments by paper check, coupon, or stamp. State welfare agencies issue 120 million checks totaling approximately $30 billion each year.[15] In 1997, approximately $20.8 billion in food stamp benefits were delivered to 23.9 million people.[16] The costs associated with these traditional payment methods have led states to explore electronic payment methods. Forty states are currently at some stage in the implementation process, with eighteen states making electronic food stamp distribution. Many started with food stamps because of their high processing costs.[17]

---

[9]   *Id.* at 2.

[10]   *See* Ian Griffiths, *Lottery Firm May Help in Fraud Battle; Gtech is Offering its Technology to Aid the Government War on Benefit Cheats*, THE INDEPENDENT, Nov. 24, 1996, at 1.

[11]   *EFT/EBT Hearing, supra* note 7 (Hawke statement, at 2).

[12]   *Id.*

[13]   *Id.*

[14]   *See* Glassman & Wells, *supra* note 2 (citing "Good-bye Government Checks; Hello Electronic Payments" Fedtalk: Financial Services Updates, Federal Reserve Bank of Boston, Summer 1996, at 6).

[15]   *See* David Brindley & Fred Vogelstein, *The Check is Not in the Mail*, U.S. NEWS & WORLD REP., Apr. 14, 1997, at 66.

[16]   *Review of the Status of Electronic Benefit Transfer (EBT) for the Food Stamp Program Implementation: Hearing Before the Subcomm. on Dept. Operation, Nutrition, and Foreign Agriculture of the House Comm. on Agriculture*, 105th Cong. (1997) (statement of Roger C. Viadero, Inspector General, U.S. Dept. of Agriculture) [hereinafter *EBT Food Stamp Hearing*].

[17]   Food stamps are used only once. Costs associated with their use include printing, postage, and counting (food stamps must be counted at the points of distribution, retailer receipt, bank acceptance, and during the clearing process).

[3] THE COMBINED VOLUME OF FEDERAL AND STATE ELECTRONIC BENEFITS DISTRIBUTION

It took over twenty years to reach 57% electronic distribution of federal benefits.[18] The remaining 43% must be achieved by January 1, 1999.[19] In addition, state distributed food stamps must be electronically delivered by 2002. Combined, these benefits represent 850 million payments, and approximately one trillion dollars, each year.[20] These payments, along with individual state efforts to distribute state funded benefits electronically, will have an impact on financial institutions, recipients, and third party service providers/networks.

§ 17.03 THE DEVELOPMENT OF EBT AND REGULATORY COORDINATION

As electronic fund transfer developed gradually as a payment mechanism, proving a more efficient payment method than postal delivery of checks, the federal government realized its potential to streamline its payment system and produce real savings. It is not cost-effective, however, for the government to continue a dual system based on recipient choice. Thus in March 1993, President Clinton announced a comprehensive review of all federal agencies and systems to improve performance and efficiency in specific areas.[21] After a six-month study, conducted under the leadership of Vice President Gore, the Administration released its report.

The National Performance Review ("NPR") Report recommended increased use of electronic fund transfer for all government payments and reimbursements. The NPR Report also recommended the development of a nationwide electronic benefit transfer plan for government programs, such as Food Stamps, and other direct payments to individuals without bank accounts.[22] While the banking industry and public assistance agencies have been contemplating the idea of electronic benefits transfer for at least a decade, the NPR recommendation provided the push to get it off the ground. The Federal EBT Task Force, formed in November 1993, developed a plan for nationwide implementation of EBT. The Task Force plan, setting a 1999 goal for 100% federal electronic benefits payment, received the Vice President's approval in May 1994. On April 26, 1996, when President Clinton signed into law the Debt Collection Improvement Act of 1996 ("DCIA"), the 1999 goal became a mandate.[23] The 1996 welfare reform legislation, enacted on August 22, 1996, required states to deliver benefits electronically not later than October 1, 2002.[24]

---

[18] *EFT/EBT Hearing, supra* note 7 (Hawke statement, at 2).

[19] *See* discussion *supra* note 3 & Section 17.03. Personal Responsibility and Work Opportunity Reconciliation Act of 1996, Pub. L. No. 104-193, § 825, 1996 U.S.C.C.A.N. (110 Stat.) 2105, 2324 (codified at 7 U.S.C. § 2016(i)(1)) [hereinafter Welfare Reform Act].

[20] *See* Edward Blount, *Using Quality to Position EBT Services*, ABA BANKING J., Feb. 1997, at 54.

[21] Report of the National Performance Review, From Red Tape to Results; Creating a Government that Works Better and Costs Less (Sept. 7, 1993) [hereinafter NPR Report].

[22] *Id.* at 112-16.

[23] Debt Collection Improvement Act of 1996, Pub. L. No. 104-134, ch. 10, § 31001, 1996 U.S.C.C.A.N. (110 Stat.) 1321-358 (codified at 31 U.S.C. §§ 3701- 3711-12, 3716-19, 3720A-3720E, 7701) [hereinafter DCIA].

[24] Welfare Reform Act, *supra* note 19.

The April 1996 federal mandate brought EBT to the attention of many EBT stakeholders for the first time. Treasury and several states, however, have been developing and testing EBT programs since the mid-1980s.[25] Disparate development strategies led to variety in program specifications and governing regulations. As EBT programs developed, many participants realized a need for consistency and interoperability. For the federally distributed programs, consistency is a matter of having a clear set of federal standards. For state distributed programs, regulatory consistency presents a greater problem.

This Section details the federal regulatory initiative and its emerging standards. Then it focuses on the efforts of the U.S. Department of Agriculture ("USDA") and the EBT Council of the National Automated Clearing House Association ("NACHA") in promulgating operating rules for state distributed benefit payments. Financial institutions, as stakeholders in the EBT process, must be aware of both sets of rules as well as the potential for federal preemption of the EBT Council's QUEST® Operating Rules,[26] which are discussed in detail in Section 17.03[2][a].

[1] FEDERAL ELECTRONIC PAYMENTS

As noted above, on April 26, 1996, President Clinton signed DCIA into law, thus mandating electronic delivery of federal payments by January 1, 1999. This Act and the regulations promulgated under its authority regarding benefits distribution are the focus of this Section.

[a] **The Debt Collection Improvement Act.** The DCIA, applicable not only to benefit payments but to all federal electronic payments, provides a two phase approach for making the transition to electronic delivery. Phase One requires federal payment recipients becoming eligible on or after July 26, 1996, to receive payments electronically unless the recipient certifies that the recipient has no financial institution or authorized payment agent and the agency grants a waiver.[27] Phase Two calls for the conversion from checks to EFT for all federal payments, except those under the Internal Revenue Code,[28] or granted a waiver,[29] by

---

[25] In 1989, Treasury conducted a one-year pilot with approximately 300 SSI recipients in Baltimore, Maryland. Since 1992 Treasury has used direct payment cards to reach the unbanked federal benefit recipients throughout the state of Texas. *See EFT/EBT Hearing, supra* note 7 (statement of John Dyer, Principal Deputy Commissioner, Social Security Administration, at 3).

[26] The EBT Council worked with the USDA to incorporate its concerns into the QUEST® Operating Rules. However, USDA concerns regarding fraud and card safeguarding might lead to stricter card formatting requirements than currently called for in QUEST®.

[27] DCIA § 31001(x)(1), 1996 U.S.C.C.A.N. at 1321-376 (codified at 31 U.S.C. § 3332(e)). Management of Federal Agency Disbursements, 61 Fed. Reg. 39,254 (1996) (codified at 31 C.F.R. pt. 208) [hereinafter EBT Interim Rule]. Prior to the enactment of the DCIA, federal law required federal wage, salary, and retirement payments to individuals who began to receive such payments after January 1, 1995 to receive payment by electronic fund transfer, unless a recipient submitted a written request to receive another form of payment. *See* 31 U.S.C. 3332(a)-(d). Treasury was also authorized to grant waivers for a group of recipients on agency request. DCIA § 31001(x)(1)(A) (codified at 31 U.S.C. § 3332(e)(2)). These provisions remained effective until July 26, 1996, when they were superseded by DCIA. EBT Interim Rule, 61 Fed. Reg. at 39,256.

[28] *See* DCIA § 31001(x)(1)(B), 1996 U.S.C.C.A.N. at 1321-377 (codified at 31 U.S.C. § 3332(j)(3)). See EBT Interim Rule, 61 Fed. Reg. at 39,254, for agencies with financial responsibility.

[29] DCIA § 31001(x)(1)(A), 1996 U.S.C.C.A.N. at 1321-376 (codified at 31 U.S.C. § 3332(f)(2)).

January 1, 1999 ("EFT[99] mandate").[30] DCIA also authorizes Treasury to issue regulations to implement EFT requirements.[31]

Compliance with DCIA requires direct deposit of benefits to payment recipients with bank accounts and the provision of an alternate means of electronic delivery to unbanked recipients. In addition to the requirements imposed on government agencies, the DCIA places some responsibility on federal payment recipients. Recipients must designate one or more financial institutions or other authorized agents to receive payments on their behalf and must provide information to the federal agency that makes or authorizes payments so that the agency may implement electronic fund transfer payments to the recipients.

[b] EFT[99]. The two phase process of converting the majority of federal payments to electronic fund transfers began on July 26, 1996.[32] On that day, Treasury's FMS published the interim rule governing Phase One, in 31 C.F.R. Part 208. The rule was effective on its date of publication.[33]

[i] Interim Rule. The interim rule applies to payments made by all federal agencies and makes no distinction between agencies whose disbursements are made by Treasury and agencies with statutory or delegated disbursing authority, known as Non-Treasury Disbursing Offices ("NTDO's"). After providing the essential definitions (including benefit payment, federal payment, and financial institution), the interim rule sets forth the agency and recipient responsibilities for making and receiving federal payments electronically.

[A] Agency Responsibilities. The interim rule calls for federal agencies to disburse payments electronically under the following conditions:

- Benefit payments applied for on or after July 26, 1996;

- Federal wage or salary payments for which the recipient first becomes eligible or applies on or after July 26, 1996;

- Vendor payments made on a contract or purchase order resulting from a solicitation made on or after July 26, 1996.[34]

Agency heads may waive the electronic payment requirement for recipients who certify in writing that they have no financial institution account or authorized payment agent. Agencies that determine that they are incapable of making any or all required electronic payments are required to notify FMS in writing and submit a plan for solving the problem.

---

[30] *Id.* (codified at 31 U.S.C. § 3332(f)(1)).

[31] DCIA § 31001(x)(1)(B), 1996 U.S.C.C.A.N. at 1321-377 (codified at 31 U.S.C. § 3332(i)).

[32] Prior to enactment of DCIA, federal law already required recipients of federal wage, salary, and retirement payments, who began receiving those payments after January 7, 1995, to receive those payments by electronic fund transfer. *See supra* note 28.

[33] FMS promulgated the interim rule without providing opportunity for prior public comment pursuant to the Administrative Procedure Act, 5 U.S.C. § 553. FMS had determined that a comment period would be impracticable and contrary to public interest. EBT Interim Rule, 61 Fed. Reg. at 39,257.

[34] 31 C.F.R. § 208.3.

[*B*] *Recipient Responsibilities.* Section 208.4 of the interim rule places the responsibility for designating a financial institution or authorized payment agency to whom their payment may be made on the payment recipients. Further, recipients must provide written notice to the disbursing agency if no such institution or agent is available.

Prior to proposing the final rules for Phase Two of the EFT[99] mandate, the Department of Treasury conducted further research into the EFT process and policies. It met with consumer interest organizations and the financial services industry, held public meetings, and reviewed comments submitted in response to the interim rule. In addition, Treasury hired consulting and research groups to conduct two research studies related to the electronic payment mandate.[35] The result of these efforts is a proposal for a revised and expanded Part 208 that will apply to Phase Two.

[*ii*] *Proposed Final Rule.* As proposed, the rule for federal agency disbursements after January 2, 1999 offers an expanded definitions section, a thorough explanation of waiver requirements and procedures, and a discussion of account requirements and access.[36] It also includes provisions for monitoring agency compliance and more detailed descriptions of agency and recipient responsibilities. The major provisions of the proposed rule, and the ones most relevant to the discussion of electronic benefit distribution include:

- All federal payment recipients *with* an account at a financial institution (bank, credit union, or savings and loan) must designate that account to receive their payments electronically.

- Federal payment recipients *without* an account at a financial institution will be provided with an Electronic Transfer Account ("ETA[sm]") in their name at a federally-insured financial institution. These recipients may continue to receive paper checks until either these accounts are available or January 2, 2000, whichever is earlier. With an ETA[sm], recipients will be able to access their funds through automated teller machines (ATMs) or point-of-sale (POS) terminals with an access card. These ETAs will be provided at a reasonable cost and have the same consumer protections as other accounts at the financial institution. Similar to an ATM card, the card will give recipients a safe and convenient way to withdraw funds electronically. ETAs[sm] will only be provided to individual payment recipients, and not to vendors who contract with the government. Treasury encourages recipients to open an account at a financial institution on their own, and to designate that financial institution to receive their funds electronically.

- Recipients who were receiving Federal payments *before* July 26, 1996 and who certify that electronic payment would present a hardship because of a physical disability or geographic barrier will be eligible for a waiver. For example, recipients (or their legal representatives) may request a waiver if they would be physically unable to access their funds if they were delivered electronically, or if there is limited access to financial institutions, ATMs, or POS terminals in their area.

---

[35] These research studies are available at <http:www.fms.treas.gov/eft>.

[36] Management of Federal Agency Disbursements, 62 Fed. Reg. 48,714 (1997) (to be codified at 31 C.F.R. pt. 208) (proposed Sept. 16, 1997).

- Recipients who certify that they *do not* have an account at a financial institution *and* that payment by EFT would impose a hardship due to a physical disability, a geographic barrier, or a financial hardship, will be eligible for a waiver. These waivers are available to any recipient without an account at a financial institution, regardless of when they started receiving payments.

- In some cases, federal agencies will not be required to make payments via EFT for reasons such as military deployment, threats to national security, or certain other situations where EFT is impractical. In certain circumstances, agencies may choose to make payments to vendors by check, such as for certain one-time payments, where making the payment by EFT would be more expensive than making a check payment.[37]

[c] Treasury's Regulations for EBT. On July 26, 1996, FMS issued interim regulations to implement Phase One payments.[38] On May 9, 1997, FMS published its proposal for the rules governing federal EBT.[39] The highlights of the proposal include:

- FMS defines the term "Direct Federal electronic benefits transfer (EBT)" as a program for providing Direct Federal benefit payments to the unbanked through disbursements by financial institutions acting as financial agents of the United States.[40]

- FMS defines "Direct Federal payment" to include payments under any federally funded entitlement, pension, annuity, wage or salary program not administered by a state government.[41]

- Only financial institutions can qualify as financial agents of the government to perform the disbursement of public funds that is central to Direct Federal EBT.[42]

- The financial agent's disbursement function includes establishing an account in the name of the unbanked recipient; maintaining the account; crediting the Direct Federal payments to the account; and providing access to the account under the terms set forth by FMS.

- The financial agent may apply the operational or accounting convention of its choice, provided its records are clear as to the unbanked recipient's ownership rights.

---

[37] Fact Sheet: *31 C.F.R. 208: Management of Federal Agency Disbursements; Notice of Proposed Rulemaking, available at* <http/fms.worlweb.net.>.

[38] Management of Federal Agency Disbursements, 61 Fed. Reg. 39,254 (1996) (codified at 31 C.F.R. pt. 208).

[39] Electronic Benefits Transfer; Selection and Designation of Financial Institutions as Financial Agents, 62 Fed. Reg. 25,572 (1997) (to be codified at 31 C.F.R. pt. 207) (proposed May 9, 1997) [hereinafter EBT Proposal].

[40] The requirement that financial institutions act as the financial agent does not preclude a financial agent from working with non-financial institutions in providing the EBT services. EBT Proposal, 62 Fed. Reg. at 25,574 (to be codified at 31 C.F.R. § 207.2).

[41] *Id.*

[42] *See* Omnibus Consolidated Appropriations Act, 1997, Pub. L. No. 104-208, § 665, 1996 U.S.C.C.A.N. (110 Stat.) 3009 (amending 12 U.S.C. § 90) (pertaining to the Treasury Secretary's authorization to select national banking associations as financial agents for EBT).

- Financial agents issue each unbanked recipient a debit card bearing the FMS registered service mark, Benefit Security Card®.[43]

- FMS determines the services financial agents provide the cardholders.

- The Direct Federal EBT Rules provide for coordination with state and local EBT programs. The financial agent is permitted to credit state and local EBT payments, excluding non-cash payments such as Food Stamps, to the account established as part of the Direct Federal EBT program.[44] No other deposits, whether over-the-counter or by EFT, may be made to the account.[45]

- Financial agents must comply with Regulation E.

- The account may be closed only at the direction of FMS.

[d] Distinctions Between Direct Deposit and Direct Federal EBT. The two primary distinctions between Direct Deposit and Direct Federal EBT provide insight into the challenges system participants face in establishing EBT.[46] The first distinction relates to the manner in which the account is established. Direct Deposit recipients establish accounts at the financial institution of their choice, participate in determining the attributes of the account, and are free to change accounts at will. In contrast, Treasury designates a financial institution as its Financial Agent for an EBT and establishes an account in the name of an unbanked recipient. The second distinction relates to discretion. Direct Deposit recipients contract with their financial institution for desired means of accessing the account. EBT recipients would only access their benefit payments using a plastic card, the Benefit Security Card©,[47] at ATM and POS terminals. That access would be governed by the proposed rules in 31 C.F.R. Part 207 and in the agreement between Treasury and the financial agent. In summary, EBT creates a set of bank customers lacking the elements of control and choice enjoyed by traditional bank customers, as well as the access to many traditional financial services.

Treasury is encouraging banks to offer another alternative, Direct Deposit Too, for EBT recipients who desire direct control over their account. Section 17.05, discussing the impact of electronic benefits distribution on intermediaries, provides a more detailed review of Direct Deposit Too. Before discussing the intermediaries in the EBT process, however, it is important to look at the state benefits system. The payment volume and regulations governing state electronic benefits payment must be considered alongside the federal EBT program as intermediaries prepare for universal electronic delivery.

---

[43] The Patent and Trademark Office issued Registration number 1,946,344 to FMS on January 9, 1996, identifying FMS as the registered owner of Benefit Security Card. *See* EBT Proposal, 62 Fed. Reg. at 25,575-76 (to be codified at 31 C.F.R. § 207.3(a)(4)).

[44] EBT Proposal, 62 Fed. Reg. at 25,575 (to be codified at 31 C.F.R. § 207.3(a)(3)).

[45] *Id.*

[46] *Id.* at 25,573-74. *See* 31 C.F.R. pt. 207 for an explanation of the distinctions.

[47] *Id.* at 25,574 (to be codified at 31 C.F.R. § 207.2). Treasury registered this service mark for EBT on January 9, 1996.

[2] STATE ELECTRONIC BENEFIT PAYMENTS

Rampant fraud and high processing and transaction costs associated with food stamps, a state distributed federally funded benefit, led states to explore the development of electronic food stamp distribution alternatives. Perceiving a need for standardization, the USDA, in 1992, published the *Food Stamp Program: Standards for Approval and Operation of Food Stamp Electronic Benefit Transfer* ("USDA Standards"). At that time, however, no state had an electronic food stamp system to which to apply the USDA Standards. As electronic distribution programs developed, many states found the USDA Standards burdensome because they did not allow for the use of the existing commercial infrastructure. As a result states developed their own standards. Recipients, multistate merchants, and service providers soon called for the development of operating standards providing for interoperability and consistency between programs that worked within the parameters of existing commercial infrastructure. A voluntary association developed such standards, and that development is described below.

[a] **QUEST® – Uniform Operating Rules for EBT.** In 1995, perceiving a need for consistency in and EBT interoperability among states, NACHA spearheaded the creation of the EBT Council. The EBT Council is a not-for-profit voluntary association comprised of EBT stockholders such as financial institutions, EFT networks, merchants, associations, and government agencies. By April 1996 the Council had created and approved a set of operating rules for commercially compatible EBT programs nationwide.[48] These QUEST® Operating Rules focus on eleven key aspects of EBT:[49]

(1) Issuer Requirements;

(2) Card Specifications;

(3) Acquirer and Terminal Operator Requirements;

(4) Merchant Agreement Requirements;

(5) Adjustments, Chargebacks and Representments;

(6) Settlement;

(7) Third Party Service Provider Requirements;

(8) Arbitration and Grievance Procedures, Assessments;

(9) Security;

(10) Liabilities and Indemnification; and

(11) Licensing of the QUEST® Mark.

---

[48] The Council monitors EBT implementation and technological advancement to determine whether the Quest® Operating Rules adequately address the issues or whether amendment is required.

[49] *See* QUEST® OPERATING RULES (Version 1.1 Sept. 27, 1996).

QUEST® rules apply to state-funded assistance programs as well as state-administered federal programs such as food stamps[50] and AFDC. Adoption and use of the QUEST® rules is at the election of each state or coalition of states that choose magnetic stripe cards as their delivery mechanism. The rules become binding when states/coalitions include mandatory compliance with QUEST® in their EBT contracts with either prime contractors or government designated issuers. The QUEST® logo appears on cards issued in programs governed by the QUEST® Operating Rules and on POS and ATM machines where cardholders can make transactions.[51] The consistency they provide enables the federal program administrators to avoid the cost and inconvenience of maintaining different electronic programs and links for each state's program. The QUEST® rules only apply to magnetic stripe card systems.[52]

QUEST® will affect financial institutions in their roles as issuers, acquirers, processors, and network participants. Financial institutions should therefore gain familiarity with the QUEST® Operating Rules. Further, because QUEST® provides for consistency and interoperability and is modeled on existing commercial systems, it will benefit financial institutions to encourage QUEST's® adoption in states/regions in which they operate. Financial institutions should be aware, however, that FMS is in the process of developing federal standards that may pre-empt QUEST®.

Financial institutions, increasingly operating in several states, will appreciate the consistency of state regulation as they prepare for their roles in the EBT process. The impact on financial institutions in their various roles is discussed in Section 17.05.

[b] Implementation by October 1, 2002. Section 825 of the Personal Responsibility and Work Opportunity Reconciliation Act of 1996 ("Welfare Reform Act") amended Section 8(i) of the Food Stamp Act of 1977 to include a mandate for state implementation of electronic benefit transfer systems by October 1, 2002.[53] Waivers are available to state agencies that face unusual barriers to implementation.[54] State agencies are given the flexibility to procure and implement the EBT system under whatever terms, conditions, and design the state agency deems appropriate.[55] Section 825 does, however, instruct states that they should consider the needs for interstate operation, effective monitoring by law enforcement, and use of the existing commercial electronic funds transfer technology.[56]

---

[50]   The EBT Council worked with the USDA to incorporate food stamp requirements into the QUEST® Rules.

[51]   *See* QUEST® OPERATING RULES, *supra* note 49. Food Stamp benefits can only be redeemed at POS terminals of authorized food stamp merchants, consistent with USDA regulations.

[52]   Chapter 16 discussed the distinctions between magnetic stripe and smart card technology. The important distinctions for the purpose of EBT are (1) magnetic stripe cards are cheaper to produce than smart cards; (2) magnetic stripe transactions are online whereas smart card transactions are off-line; and (3) magnetic stripe cards cannot store the depth of information nor provide the multiple function capability of smart cards. The federal government and the majority of the state EBT programs in place employ the online magnetic stripe card system. Only Ohio and Wyoming have developed smart card systems, preferring the one-batch delivery system because it relieved merchants of the burden of excessive gateway and transaction fees as well as eliminating the need for additional phone lines.

[53]   7 U.S.C. § 2016(i).

[54]   Welfare Reform Act, 1996 U.S.C.C.A.N. at 2324 (codified at 7 U.S.C. § 2016(i)).

[55]   *Id.* (codified at 7 U.S.C. § 2016(i)(1)(C)).

[56]   *Id.* (codified at 7 U.S.C. § 2016(i)(1)(D)).

§ 17.04 THE ROLE OF INTERMEDIARIES IN THE BENEFITS DISTRIBUTION PROCESS

The type and role of intermediaries involved in the benefits distribution process will change as electronic benefits distribution reaches the January 1, 1999 deadline for universal electronic delivery. This Section explores the role check cashing intermediaries (financial institutions, the informal sector, and check cashing outlets) and the ACH Networks currently play in the benefits distribution process. Further, it considers the role these actors may play after the January 1, 1999 deadline. Then it introduces the additional parties necessary to the delivery of electronic benefits to the unbanked: issuing financial institutions ("IFIs"); acquiring financial institutions ("AFIs"); EBT service providers; merchants; and networks. The impact that universal electronic delivery will have on these entities is then discussed further in Section 17.05.

[1] CHECK CASHING INTERMEDIARIES

[a] Banks. Financial institutions currently accept direct deposit of benefit payments for those customers who have elected that method. The Social Security Administration and the Department of Veteran's Affairs estimate that over 64% and 50% of their recipients respectively already receive their benefits through direct deposit.[57] As part of the marketing effort to increase election of direct deposit, Treasury mailed inserts with the April 1997 check payment encouraging recipients to voluntarily switch to direct deposit prior to the January 1, 1999 deadline.[58] For many check recipients, however, direct deposit is not an attractive alternative. It is these recipients who present Treasury's great challenge.

Check recipients, those with and without bank accounts, use a variety of methods to process their checks. Recipients with bank accounts, the target of initial direct deposit promotion, may prefer receiving the check and then processing it in person or through the ATM at their own bank. They may also prefer one of the alternative methods that service the unbanked.[59] These fall primarily into two categories: the informal sector and check cashing outlets.

[b] The Informal Sector. Grocery stores, other retail outlets, friends, and relatives represent components of the so-called informal sector with whom a check recipient will process his benefit check. Benefit recipients currently taking advantage of these methods will be affected by the switch to electronic delivery. There is limited data, however, regarding the habits or size of this group. Financial institutions should, however, recognize that these individuals represent either potential bank customers or EBT recipients and that an estimate for informal sector users should be included in their planning for the overall transition process.

---

[57] *See Social Security Gears Up for Direct Deposit, supra* note 7. Management of Federal Agency Disbursements, 61 Fed. Reg. 39,254 (1996) (codified at 31 C.F.R. pt. 207), *EFT/EBT Hearing, supra* note 7 (statement of Stephen L. Lemons, Acting Under Secretary for Benefits, Veterans Benefits Administration, Department of Veteran Affairs; statement of Marcelyn Creque, Regional Volunteer Director Midwest Region, AARP; and statement of John D. Hawke, Jr., Undersecretary for Domestic Finance, Dept. of Treasury).

[58] *EFT/EBT Hearing, supra* note 7 (Hawke statement, at 30).

[59] Individuals with bank accounts may utilize alternative service providers for a variety of reasons, including avoiding creditors and nonsupporting parent laws. *See* JOHN P. CASKEY, FRINGE BANKING: CHECK-CASHING OUTLETS, PAWNSHOPS, AND THE POOR 73 (1994).

[c] Check Cashing Outlets. Check cashing outlets ("CCOs") play a significant role in the benefits process and may continue to do so to some extent after EBT utilization reaches 100%. Over 5,500 CCOs across the country cash approximately 200 million checks per year, amounting to $60 billion and earning approximately $1 billion in fees.[60] They depend on cashing paychecks, both private sector and government, and government benefit checks as the core of their business.[61] CCOs may partner with financial institutions to distribute benefits, receive authorization to serve as payment agents, or be eliminated from the process entirely. Given the strategic locations of CCOs and their significant customer base, CCOs are likely to continue to operate within a niche market. A closer look at CCOs follows.

[i] Growth of CCOs. CCOs entered the financial services arena in the 1930s. Until the mid-1970s, CCOs remained principally confined to Chicago, New York, and a small number of urban areas.[62] Though still largely concentrated in urban areas, the industry has expanded its geographic reach.[63] The rapid growth of CCOs since the mid-70s is related to changes in traditional bank services.

National Check Cashers Association reports the following growth in the industry between 1995 and 1997:[64]

Year	Number of CCOs
1985	2685
1990	4250
1995	5500
1997	5720

A 1989 survey of low-income households found that in many instances increased charges and balance requirements, as well as other factors, made maintaining a bank account either not worthwhile or beyond their means.[65] The following chart illustrates the changes in attitudes toward maintaining a bank relationship.

[60] *See* Lynn Waldsmith, *Check Cashers: Saints or Sinners?: Critics Say They Gouge Patrons With Big Fees; Others Say It's Service*, DETROIT NEWS, Apr. 6, 1997, at C1.

[61] In addition to cashing checks, check cashers also sell lottery tickets, money orders, car registration stickers, and mass transit tokens. *See Check Cashers: The Latest Players to Enter the Electronic Bill Payment Game*, REP. ON HOME BANKING & FIN. SERV., Apr. 20, 1997.

[62] *See* CASKEY, *supra* note 59, at 36.

[63] *See* CASKEY, *supra* note 59, at 63-65.

[64] Brindley & Vogelstein, *supra* note 15, at 66.

[65] BOARD OF GOVERNORS OF THE FEDERAL RESERVE, SURVEY OF CONSUMER FINANCES (1989).

SURVEY OF FAMILIES WITHOUT CHECKING ACCOUNTS

Reasons reported by families without a checking account for not having one, 1989, 1992, and 1995.

Response category	1989	1992	1995
Do not write enough checks to make it worthwhile	34.3	30.4	27.1
Minimum balance is too high	7.6	8.6	8.6
Do not like dealing with banks	15.0	15.3	22
Service charges are too high	8.4	11.2	7.9
No bank has convenient hours or location	1.2	.9	1.2
Do not have enough money	21.8	20.9	20.5
Cannot manage or balance a checking account	4.6	64	8.6
Other	7.1	10.1	3.4
Total	100	100	100

Source: Arthur B. Kennickell, Martha Starr-McCluer, and Annika E. Sunden, *Family Finances in the U.S.: Recent Evidence from the Survey of Consumer Finances*, 83 FED. RESERVE BULL. 7 (Jan. 1997).

NOTE: Total percentages may not add to 100 percent due to rounding.

Some have contended that the consolidation process in the banking industry has resulted in branch closings that have had a significant impact on predominantly minority and low-income areas of cities.[66] These closings, coupled with limited transportation alternatives, have led some individuals to seek alternative service providers.[67] The following chart reflects the decline in the percentage of households with deposit accounts of any type.[68]

[66] CASKEY, *supra* note 59, at 91-93.

[67] *Brindley & Vogelstein, supra* note 15, at 66.

[68] Later studies showed a slight increase in the percentage of account holders by 1992. *See* Arthur B. Kennickell & Martha Starr-McCluer, *Changes in Family Finances from 1989 to 1992; Evidence from the Survey of Consumer Finances*, 80 FED. RESERVE BULL. 886 (Oct. 1994).

PERCENTAGES OF HOUSEHOLDS WITH DEPOSIT ACCOUNTS OF ANY TYPE		
	1977	**1989**
All Households	90.5	86.5
Income (in 1991 $)		
Up to $11,969	70.3	59.2
$11,970-$21,545	86.2	85.8
$21,546-$29,925	93.7	92.5
$29,926-$47,875	95.9	97.2
$47,876-$83,780	99.6	98.3
Age		
Less than 25 years	88.6	70.7
25-64 years	91.4	85.6
65 years and older	87.8	91.8
Education		
0-8 grades	76.9	69.8
9-11 grades	83.9	77.2
High school	94.1	85.8
Some college	97.1	94.3
College degree	99.0	98.4
Race		
Minority	71.6	65.8
White	93.6	93.0

Source: JOHN P. CASKEY, FRINGE BANKING: CHECK-CASHING OUTLETS, PAWNSHOPS, AND THE POOR, ©1994 Russell Sage Foundation. Reprinted with permission of Russell Sage Foundation.

Though individuals may not desire a financial institution relationship and a deposit account, they must have a means of accessing their funds and making payments. CCOs provide these services.

[*ii*] *CCO Use.* The CCO customer base includes individuals with and without bank accounts. In fact, it is estimated that 50% of CCO users have bank accounts, and simply prefer CCOs.[69] There are several reasons why an individual might prefer a CCO to a traditional financial institution. Many find the hours and locations

---

[69] *See* Waldsmith, *supra* note 60.

of CCOs appealing.[70] For others it is the immediacy of payment.[71] Individuals moving to a new area may enjoy the services of CCOs, including making utility payments and getting money orders, until they are able to set up a bank account.[72] Still others may harbor a general mistrust of banks, perceive banks as being more expensive, or avoid banks because they wish to avoid drawing attention to their financial transactions for legal reasons.[73]

CCO customers, regardless of their reason for using CCOs, typically pay four to six times what a bank would charge for the same services.[74] The fees provide the CCO owner with a source of revenue for covering expenses including personnel costs, insurance, bank service fees, and other overhead.[75]

[d] Banks and CCOs Working Together. Direct deposit and affordable bank accounts can pose a competitive threat to the survival of CCOs. CCOs are, however, taking steps to ward off that threat. CCOs are forming alliances with banks to become part of the ATM networks, and in some instances, are engaging in lending activities.[76] Several factors indicate that EBT will provide a partnership opportunity for banks and CCOs that will change the nature of financial services, including: (1) CCOs are strategically located in low-income neighborhoods where a large number of benefit recipients reside; (2) banks already have business relationships with CCOs, providing check clearing and credit; and (3) there are expenses associated with building and maintaining new brick-and-mortar bank branches.

[2] COMMERCIAL POS AND ATM NETWORKS: NEW PLAYERS IN THE BENEFITS GAME

Unbanked electronic benefit payment recipients, whether through federal, state, or local programs, will access their benefits with plastic cards at ATM and POS machines. In order to understand the impact this will have, it is necessary to look at the existing commercial ATM and POS structure (referred to herein as the commercial EFT environment). This Section provides a basic description of the roles and relationships of the various participants. Then it looks at the transaction fee structure currently applied in ATM and POS transaction processing.

---

[70] *See* Kennickell & Starr-McCluer, *supra* note 68, at 19.

[71] *See id.*

[72] *See id.* at 76.

[73] *See* Kennickell & Starr-McCluer, *supra* note 68, at 19.

[74] *See* CASKEY, *supra* note 59, at 7. CCOs generally charge 1.5 to 2.5 percent of face value of paychecks, so a worker with an annual take home pay of $15,000 can spend $375 annually to convert his paychecks into cash. CCOs charge the fees by discounting the full face value of the check. *Id.* at 2.

[75] *See id.* at 55. *See also* Kennickell & Starr-McCluer, *supra* note 68, at 55-58, for a general discussion of the reasons behind the high costs of doing business with CCOs.

[76] *See* Brindley & Vogelstein, *supra* note 15, at 66.

[a] The Participants. The commercial EFT environment consists of six primary categories of participant:

- issuers;

- acquirers;

- third-party processors;

- networks;

- merchants; and

- gateway service providers.

A single participant may perform multiple roles depending on the range of services it provides.

[i] Issuers. Financial institutions serve as issuers. They issue debit and/or ATM cards. To process transactions using the commercial EFT network, the issuer must abide by the operating rules of the networks in which it chooses to participate as a member.

[ii] Acquirers. Acquirers are financial institutions responsible for warranting the capture of ATM and POS transactions and the transmission of requests to networks in which they participate. In addition to operating their own terminals, acquirers sponsor the deployment and/or operation of ATM and POS terminals by non-financial institutions.

[iii] Third-Party Processors. For issuers, third-party processors provide transaction authorization services. For acquirers, they provide front-end transaction processing services necessary to support terminal operations.[77] A third-party processor may own the ATM and/or POS terminal it operates. Third-party processors must enter a processor agreement with the commercial network, abide by its technical and operational requirements, and ensure that its merchants are sponsored by acquirers and that financial institutions are members.

[iv] Networks. Networks provide switching facilities for transaction routing between acquirers and issuers.[78] They transmit transaction requests and approval/denial messages between parties. In addition, networks settle transactions between issuer and acquirer by clearing accounts, settling fees, and ensuring standardization of operations and processing among members. Networks eliminate the need for direct physical connections between issuer and acquirer. Reciprocal relationships between networks provide members with extended geographic reach.

[v] Merchants. Acquirers sponsor merchants into the commercial EFT networks. Merchants with their

---

[77] They may also provide gateway services, as described in Chapter 4.

[78] *See* EBT Council, *Commercial POS and ATM Transaction Fees: A Compilation of Publicly Available Information,* Jan. 1997, at 4.

own processing capabilities make a direct connection to the network. Otherwise they take advantage of third party processing systems to access the network. When a merchant is a member of several networks, it can use a single third party processor to gateway to those networks.

[vi] *Gateway Service Providers.* Third-party processors and networks may also serve as gateways to accessing multiple networks. Acquirers, issuers, third-party processors, and networks may all contract directly with a gateway service provider.

[b] The Fees. Network fees are assessed and collected by each network. Since EBT users will be accessing their benefits through the ATM and POS machines that the networks service, and fee structures may be impacted by the new participants and the increased transaction volume they generate, it is worth taking a look at the fee structure.

Fees may be paid by the issuer or the acquirer, or both, depending on the nature of the transaction and the governing rules. Generally networks charge each participant four kinds of fees: (1) an initiation fee; (2) an annual membership fee; (3) monthly service fees; and (4) transaction fees. Initiation fees may cover the cost to connect, test, and certify the new participant's system. The amount may vary by type of participant, number of cards issued, number of terminals deployed, or service options selected. Because transaction fees are the greatest area of concern for EBT stakeholders, the remainder of this Section will focus on transaction fees.

Networks charge switch fees for processing services. These fees are retained to cover network services. Networks collect interchange fees on behalf of issuers and acquirers. Interchange fees for POS transactions are paid by the acquirer/terminal operator to the issuer, and those for ATM transactions are paid by the issuer to the acquirer/terminal operator.

Gateway fees are a subset of transaction fees. The network whose cardholder initiates an ATM transaction pays the gateway provider. The gateway provider retains its fee and then passes on the remainder to the acquirer/terminal operator. When a gateway is used in a POS transaction, the acquirer pays both the regional and national networks.

Issuers cover their fees with income generated through transaction fees and consumer account service fees. Acquirers in some instances impose surcharges on "foreign" cardholders.[79]

The roles of network participants and the fee structure system supporting the networks provide important insight into the commercial infrastructure on which EBT transactions will travel. Many of the issues surrounding EBT delivery remain unresolved. The potential impact on the participants and other EBT stakeholders is described below in Section 17.05.

---

[79] Surcharges are a topic of hot debate. *See* Olaf de Senerpont Domis, *ABA Organizes Meeting to Mobilize Support for Keeping ATM Access Fees,* AM. BANKER, Jan. 12, 1998; *D'Amato Proud of Banking Committee's 1997 Efforts, Vows to Continue Focus on Consumer Taxpayer Protections in 1998,* Cong. Press Release, Jan. 15, 1998, *available in* LEXIS, Nexis Library, News File.

§ 17.05   ELECTRONIC BENEFIT DISTRIBUTION: THE POTENTIAL IMPACT ON PARTICIPANTS

[1]   INCREASING DIRECT DEPOSITS

The anticipated increase in direct deposit payments will likely cause a concomitant increase in the volume of ACH network transactions. It is expected that ACH operators will be prepared to handle the increased volume.[80] Banks should prepare for a gradual increase in direct deposits in anticipation of the January 1, 1999 implementation target date. During this transitional period banks will likely incur additional expenses related to operational changes, marketing, and consumer education. Once the transition is completed, however, banks can be expected to realize savings in areas associated with paper payment processing. While the impact of increased direct deposit is likely to be significant, it is the new EBT system that poses a greater challenge to the parties and, is thus, the focus of the remainder of the Section.

[2]   NEW OPPORTUNITIES

Financial institutions will realize the greatest impact of EBT in their role as acquirers, processors, and network participants. When electronic delivery is complete, the unbanked will account for a significant increase in the number of ATM and POS transactions executed each month. As acquirers, financial institutions should recognize the opportunity to sponsor more merchants into the networks. As processors, the impact will be in terms of increased volume. As network participants, financial institutions must look at the current transaction fee structure and decide how EBT programs fit within that system.

The competition between banks and technology providers in developing and providing electronic banking services has been a factor in the evolution of EBT programs at both the state and federal levels. A series of legal challenges illustrates the competitive nature of the EBT market.

[a]   Transactive Challenges Treasury's Selection of Citicorp. In May 1994 an eight state coalition, known collectively as "the Southern Alliance of States" or "SAS," joined the Department of Treasury and a federal EBT task force in an effort to design and implement a joint EBT program.[81] Treasury's primary role in the program was to contract with a private party to maintain EBT account information, provide access to the ACH, ATM, and POS networks, and provide basic account services to EBT recipients. Treasury published an Invitation of Expression of Interest ("IEI") in order to solicit bids from interested parties.[82] The IEI was conducted under Treasury's authority to name certain financial institutions as "depositories of public money" and "financial agents" of the federal government.[83] It is an alternative to the more typical bidding process

---

[80]   *See Social Security Gears Up For Direct Deposit*, EFT REP., Oct. 16, 1996.

[81]   *See* William Claiborne, *Federal State Benefit Systems Move Toward Cashless Automation*, WASH. POST, June 1, 1994, at A8; Vice President Al Gore, Press Briefing, *Electronic Delivery of Government Funded Benefits* (May 31, 1994), *available in* LEXIS, Nexis Library, News File.

[82]   Invitation for Expressions of Interest to Acquire EBT Services for the Southern Alliance of States, AR-1-969 (JA 585-701) (Mar. 9, 1995).

[83]   12 U.S.C. § 90. *See* EBT Proposal, 62 Fed. Reg. 25,575; 31 C.F.R. pt. 202.

governed by the Competition in Contracting Act ("CICA").[84] Transactive Corporation, a technology services provider that services the Texas EBT program, but is not associated with any financial institution, objected to Treasury's use of the IEI because it excluded entities that are not financial institutions from competing for EBT. Transactive sued to enjoin the use of the IEI on March 29, 1995.[85]

The district court granted summary judgment in favor of Treasury on September 8, 1995.[86] Transactive appealed. While the appeal was pending, Treasury awarded the EBT contract, worth an estimated $200 to $400 million,[87] and representing perhaps more than 20% of the national market for EBT services,[88] to Citicorp. The United States Court of Appeals for the District of Columbia reversed the lower court's decision in August 1996.[89] The court found that Treasury had acted in an arbitrary manner in using the IEI proceeding to procure the EBT contractor. Further, the court found Treasury's position, that the EBT contractor must be eligible to serve as a financial agent for the government, to be inconsistent with its established policies regarding EFT, direct deposits, and disbursements; and that Treasury had failed to provide an adequate justification for that departure.

At the urging of the Treasury Department and the federal EBT task force, Congress effectively over-turned the court's rulings in September 1996, by adding the following language to the budget bill: "[T]he selection and designation of financial agents, the design of the pilot program, and any other matter associated with or related to" the SAS EBT pilot "shall not be subject to judicial review."[90] As a result, vendors such as Transactive are precluded from participating in EBT unless they do so as partners with, or subcontractors to, a financial institution. Transactive went before a congressional subcommittee and asked the subcommittee to initiate action to repeal the relevant legislation, eliminate the use of IEI as a method of future procurements, and review the use of federal funds in connection with EBT consulting activities.[91]

[b] Competition for EBT Contracts Nationwide. Transactive's challenge to the SAS EBT contract is one of a number of such challenges that have occurred throughout the United States.[92] Another famous challenge occurred in New York, where Transactive, along with the New York Check Cashers Association and six

---

[84] *See* Matt Barthel, *Treasury Using New Bid Process for EBT*, AM. BANKER, Oct. 11, 1994, at 22.

[85] *Transactive Corp. v. United States*, 91 F.3d 232 (D.C. Cir. 1996).

[86] *Id.* at 235.

[87] *See SAS Gains Treasury Approval; State Pilots Set for Testing*, CORP. EFT REP., Nov. 13, 1996, *available in* LEXIS, Nexis Library, News File; *see also* Valerie Block, *Banks Cleared to Provide Electronic Benefits Transfer*, AM. BANKER, Oct. 3, 1996, at 10.

[88] *Electronic Benefits for Food Stamp Recipients: Hearing Before the Subcomm. on Department Operations, Nutrition and Foreign Agriculture of the House Comm. on Agriculture*, 105th Cong. (Mar. 1997) (statement of Gregory L. Coler, President, Transactive Corp.) [hereinafter *EBT Food Stamp Hearing*].

[89] *Transactive*, 91 F.2d 232.

[90] Omnibus Consolidated Appropriations Act, 1997, Pub. L. No. 104-208, § 664, 1997 U.S.C.C.A.N. (110 Stat.) 3009, 3385 (codified at 31 U.S.C. § 3336(c)).

[91] *EBT Food Stamp Hearing, supra* note 89.

[92] Transactive also challenged awards of EBT contracts by the Western States EBT Alliance, the State of Colorado, and San Bernardino County, California.

check-cashing companies, challenged the state of New York's award of its EBT contract to Citicorp.[93] In April 1997, a New York State Supreme Court judge ruled that the state had acted illegally in procuring and evaluating the EBT contract proposals and in selecting Citicorp as the recipient of the contract.[94] In November 1997, however, a New York appellate court reversed the judgment based on its analysis of New York's competitive bidding statutes.

§ 17.06   PUBLIC POLICY CONCERNS

Financial institutions, retailers, and special interest groups have voiced a variety of concerns over the EFT[99] mandate and state electronic payment programs. A summary of some of these concerns follows:

- Financial institutions are getting a windfall in the benefit from the float.[95]

- Second class banking citizens are created when banks and Treasury decide on the account attributes.[96]

- Consumer education and customer service will play a vital role in the transition.[97]

- The DCIA term "authorized payment agents" needs to be liberally construed because of the absence of banks in low-income and rural areas, but not so liberally construed as to allow those with a financial interest in the recipients benefits to control and abuse them.[98]

- ATMs need to accommodate disabled, illiterate, and non-English speaking recipients.[99]

- ATMs should include crime prevention measures such as lighting and cameras.[100]

- Some areas provide limited access to reliable transportation to carry recipients to financial institutions.[101]

- Liability controls must be in place.[102]

---

[93] *See EBT Projects Slowed By Lawsuits*, CORP. EBT REP., Feb. 14, 1996, *available in* LEXIS, Nexis Library, News File. Citicorp purchased Transactive's EBT contracts and related assets in February 1998. *See* Charles Keenan, *Citi Seen Likely to Buy Transactive, EBT Nemesis*, AM. BANKER, Feb. 9, 1998, at 1; *Transactive's Wild Ride Ends: Confident Citicorp Moves Ahead Amid Questions About Lack of Competition in the Market*, 21 EFT Report No. 5.

[94] *Transactive Corp. v. New York State Dept. of Soc. Servs.*, CIV. NO. 03194-96 (NY. Sup. Ct. Apr. 22, 1997).

[95] *EFT/EBT Hearing, supra* note 7 (Creque statement, at 6).

[96] *See* Michelle Singletary, *Electronic World, Unchecked Problem? U.S. Move to Paperless Payments Raises Worries About Those Who Don't Use Banks*, WASH. POST, Mar. 4, 1997, at C1.

[97] *See id.*

[98] *EFT/EBT Hearing, supra* note 7 (Creque statement, at 4).

[99] *Id.*

[100] *Id.*

[101] *See* CASKEY, *supra* note 59, at 72; *see also* Blount, *supra* note 20.

[102] *See* BLOUNT, *supra* note 20, at 52.

- Canceling and replacing a card upon loss, theft, or damage should be easy.[103]

- Hardship waivers must remain available.[104]

- Some benefit recipients need a physical check in order to obtain and retain transitional housing.[105]

- Fraud is still a possibility. A clerk can swipe a card and distribute cash, keeping a cut as payment.

- ATM/POS fees will impose a burden on EBT recipients.[106]

- Benefit payments do not come in neat increments that an ATM can dispense in one withdrawal.[107]

---

[103] *See id.*

[104] *EFT/EBT Hearing, supra* note 7 (Creque statement, at 1).

[105] *Id.* (statement of Richard A. Wannemacher, Jr., Associate Legislative Director, Disabled American Veterans) at 1.

[106] *Id.* (statement of Margot Saunders, Managing Director, National Consumer Law Center) at 3-4 .

[107] *Id.* at 3.

PART V

"Money, money changes everything
We think we know what we're doin
We don't know anything. . ."

Money Changes Everything
—Cyndi Lauper

Any really challenging jigsaw puzzle has a few extra pieces in the box. The first four Parts of this book have fit together the critical pieces of electronic banking and commerce. This final Part addresses issues that are well understood in the physical world but that are far from settled in the virtual world. Chapter 18 explores how copyright, trademark, and patent laws operate in the national and international electronic environment. Chapter 19 addresses the jurisdictional issues that arise in the confluence between borderless cyberspace and our physically delineated world of nations and states.

Some of the pieces identified in this book will expand in importance while others will be diminished. Others, yet unforeseen, will emerge. How this fascinating, flexible electronic commerce and banking puzzle will transform itself by accommodating to these changes is an issue we hope to explore with you far into the 21st Century.

CHAPTER 18

INTELLECTUAL PROPERTY
CONSIDERATIONS

§ 18.01 INTRODUCTION

The advent of electronic banking and associated technology has enhanced the importance of intellectual property as an element of financial institution operations. For example, intellectual property laws serve to protect a whole array of a financial institution's property used in connection with its online services, smart cards, and stored value cards, including software, website text, graphics, corporate product/service names, logos, and encryption technology. With proper precautions, an online presence can enhance the value of a financial institution's intellectual property rights. Conversely, the Internet can present traps for those who do not take appropriate precautions, including the potential loss of certain rights and commission of online infringement.

There are currently no intellectual property laws that deal specifically with the Internet, though recently federal legislation has been proposed.[1] Thus, a bank wishing to protect its intellectual property rights for its online operations must look (for the moment) to conventional intellectual property laws for protection. This chapter identifies the relevant intellectual property laws that affect the provision of electronic financial products and services ("EFS"), including copyright, trademark, patent, trade secret, and unfair competition laws.

---

[1] Several federal bills have been introduced regarding copyright infringement and the Internet. *See* Digital Copyright Clarification and Technology Education Act of 1997, S. 1146, 105th Cong. (1997); Digital Era Copyright Enhancement Act, H.R. 3048, 105th Cong. (1997); On-Line Copyright Liability Limitation Act, H.R. 2180, 105th Cong. (1997). It is unlikely that any new Internet copyright law will be adopted until some consensus is reached on the complex issues surrounding copyright protection on the Internet. *See generally Issue: Cybercopyright*, 55 CONG. Q. WKLY. REP. 3008-09 (1997).

At least one state has attempted to impose broad restrictions on Internet transmissions. *See* GA. STAT. CODE ANN. § 16-9-93.1. However, a federal court enjoined enforcement of the statute stating that the statute's challengers were likely to prevail in establishing that it violated the First Amendment. *See American Civil Liberties Union of Georgia v. Miller*, Civ. A. 1:96CV2475MHS, 1997 WL 552487, at *5 (N.D. Ga. June 23, 1997). Specifically, the court determined that the statute would, among other things, unconstitutionally restrict the right to communicate anonymously and pseudony-mously over the Internet and would prohibit the use of web page links. *Id.* at *1-5.

§ 18.02 COPYRIGHTS

Banks that offer EFS must concern themselves with copyright issues. In particular, financial institutions should know how to protect their own copyrights in content made available over the Internet. Additionally, banks must be cognizant of the rights of others and avoid potential infringement of third-party copyrights.

[1] THE SCOPE OF COPYRIGHT PROTECTION

In order to assess how a bank can safeguard its copyright interest in connection with online activity, it is first necessary to understand the general scope of copyright protection. Traditional copyright laws protect original expression. While no copyright protection can be claimed in any "idea, procedure, process, system, method of operation, concept, principle or discovery," protection does extend to various types of expressive "works" including literary, musical, dramatic, pictorial, graphic, and sculptural works.[2] Within these categories, website text and software receive copyright protection as expressive literary works. Databases may be similarly protected, provided that there is some creativity in the selection and arrangement of information compiled.[3]

In general, the two requirements of copyrightability are (i) an original work of authorship and (ii) fixation in a tangible form.[4] With respect to the first requirement, there is a relatively low threshold for originality.[5] A Web designer's creation of a simple dot or box on a computer screen would probably not be copyrightable. But a design only slightly more complicated may be entitled to copyright protection.

The second requirement — fixation — mandates that the work be preserved in some type of media.[6] Information that is stored on a computer disk, or available on a server satisfies the fixation requirement. On the other hand, original information that is orally conveyed or publicly performed is not considered "fixed."[7]

Various aspects of a bank's website thus may include copyrightable subject matter. However, the question of what specifically constitutes protectable material, especially in the context of graphics and screen lay-outs, is often a complicated one. Copyright law draws a distinction between an idea itself and expression of the idea, giving protection only to the latter.[8] Moreover, when a feature is "as a practical matter indispensable,

---

[2] 17 U.S.C. § 102.

[3] *See Feist Publications, Inc. v. Rural Telephone Service Co.*, 499 U.S. 340 (1991).

[4] 17 U.S.C. § 102.

[5] *See Bleistein v. Donaldson Lithographing Co.*, 188 U.S. 239 (1903); *Alfred Bell & Co. v. Catalda Fine Arts, Inc.*, 191 F.2d 99 (2d Cir. 1951).

[6] Under the Copyright Act, a work is not fixed unless its embodiment in tangible form "is sufficiently permanent or stable to permit it to be perceived, reproduced, or otherwise communicated for a period of more than transitory duration." 17 U.S.C. § 101. "Copies" are defined as "material objects, other than phonorecords, in which a work is fixed by any method now known or later developed, and from which the work can be perceived, reproduced, or otherwise communicated." *Id.*

[7] However, the copyright laws may afford protection to "a work consisting of sounds, images or both," such as a broadcast, if the work is fixed simultaneously with transmission and other statutory conditions are met. *See* 17 U.S.C. § 411(b).

[8] *See Baker v. Selden*, 101 U.S. 99 (1879).

or at least standard, in the treatment of a given [idea]" it is treated as an idea and is not protected by copyright.[9] While the idea/expression dichotomy appears to be a relatively straightforward test, it is often difficult to apply in practice, as evidenced by the increasing copyright litigation over graphics, icons, screen display, menus, etc. Depending upon the website at issue, the copyright laws may only afford protection to the site's most artistic and individualized features. Thus, a financial institution desiring protection of the copyright laws for its website should strive to make its site as individualized and unique as possible.

[2]   OBTAINING COPYRIGHT

One important fact to keep in mind is that no action is required on the part of an "author" of a work to obtain copyright protection. A copyright is created at the moment that an original work of authorship is "fixed in a tangible form." For example, the moment that a would-be author jots down a poem on a piece of paper, the author enjoys copyright protection in that poem. Likewise, the moment that text is typed onto a website, the text, assuming it is original, is protected. Surprising to many, registration is *not* a requisite to copyright protection.[10]

While registration is not statutorily required to create a copyright interest, it is desirable for several reasons. Registration is required before an infringement action can be instituted.[11] It provides proof that a valid copyright exists.[12] Registration also may provide the copyright owner with some benefits in litigation — in the form of statutory damages and attorney's fees — if registration is accomplished *before* infringement occurs.[13]

Registration of a copyright is a relatively simple process. Indeed, it is easier than applying for a trademark or patent protection. An applicant may download forms from the Internet or obtain forms by contacting the U.S. Copyright Office,[14] or a corresponding office in a foreign country. The Copyright Office may require samples of the work, as well as a nominal fee, in connection with the application. Depending on the type of

---

[9]   *Frybarger v. IBM Corp.*, 812 F.2d 525, 530 (9th Cir. 1987) (affirming district court's determination that similar features in video games were unprotectable basic ideas of such games) (quoting *Atari, Inc. v. North Am. Philips Consumer Elecs. Corp.*, 672 F.2d 607, 616 (7th Cir. 1982)); *see also Apple Computer, Inc. v. Microsoft Corp.*, 35 F.3d 1435, 1444 (9th Cir. 1994) (explaining, among other things, that overlapping windows are a "clear preference" in graphic interfaces and the idea of such windows is not protectable); 37 C.F.R. § 202.1(d). Similarly, in *Lotus Development Corp. v. Borland International Corp.*, 49 F.3d 807 (1st Cir. 1995), *aff'd by an equally divided court*, 516 U.S. 223 (1996), an appeals court took up whether prominent features of the Lotus 1-2-3 spread sheet program were protectable subject matter. There, the defendant admitted copying the menus and submenus of the command hierarchy of the spread sheet program but denied copying any of the underlying code. The appeals court held that the command hierarchy was uncopyrightable because it was a method of operation. The U.S. Supreme Court affirmed the court's decision without opinion when it split 4-4 (Justice Stevens recused himself).

[10]   *See* 17 U.S.C. § 408(a).

[11]   17 U.S.C. § 412.

[12]   17 U.S.C. § 410(c).

[13]   17 U.S.C. § 412.

[14]   Forms may be downloaded from < http://www.lcweb.loc.gov/copyright > or by calling the U.S. Copyright Office at (202) 707-9100.

work, a registration is valid for seventy-five years from the date of first publication or the life of the author plus fifty years.[15]

Regardless of whether registration has been (or will ever be) obtained, a copyright notice can be used on a work in which a financial institution desires to claim copyright, such as its website.[16] Proper notice is accomplished by using the word "copyright" or the "©" symbol, the year the work was created, and the name of the copyright owner. For example, the copyright notice for the National Bank would read "© 1997 National Bank."

Providing notice of a copyrighted work is generally advisable. In addition to its deterrent value, if a copyright notice is used, an infringer cannot legitimately claim that it had no knowledge of the copyright. This may aid in the collection of damages in an infringement action.[17]

[3] PROTECTING A BANK'S COPYRIGHT RIGHTS

In order to further safeguard copyright interests, banks should be aware of potential ownership issues with respect to websites. Such issues may arise when a financial institution takes steps to design or modify a website. A financial institution should attempt to obtain any copyright interest in its website from any relevant third parties in order to prevent other entities, especially competitors, from setting up identical or strikingly similar sites.

For example, a bank that hires a design company to create its website will probably not own any copyright interest in the finished product unless the bank obtains such rights contractually. Under copyright law, the "author" of a copyrighted work is generally the person who creates the work, although an employer is entitled to any copyrights of works created by employees within the scope of their employment.[18] As for works created by independent contractors — such as a Web design company — the party using the independent contractor's services would only receive the copyright if agreed to in a written document.[19] Thus, financial institutions, where possible, should obtain assignment of any copyright interest in the website from the design company. This may require difficult negotiation, because Web design companies often use certain stock design elements in numerous websites, and they may be reluctant to give up such rights.

Once a website is created, a bank may want to, in certain situations, prevent dissemination of the copyrightable features or information on its site. This may be necessary if a financial institution makes

---

[15] 17 U.S.C. § 302. Before March 12, 1989, copyright protection could be forfeited if proper notice was not used on a work. The notice requirement was eliminated under United States copyright law when the United States became a signatory to, and implemented, the Berne Convention Treaty.

[16] 17 U.S.C. § 401.

[17] 17 U.S.C. § 402.

[18] *See* 17 U.S.C. § 201(b).

[19] *Id.*

available any third-party works on its website and is required by the third party to undertake certain protective measures. Banks can discourage dissemination of copyrighted materials by using restrictive legends, such as: "This material is licensed for your online viewing only. No further reproduction or distribution of this material is permitted." [20]

[4] AVOIDING COPYRIGHT INFRINGEMENT

As banks design and implement websites and otherwise use the Internet, they must be careful to avoid infringing existing copyrights. A copyright owner has exclusive rights under the copyright laws. These rights include, among other things, the right to reproduce the copyrighted work, prepare a derivative work, distribute copies of the work, and display the work publicly.[21] Accordingly, a copyright owner can prevent another from enjoying these rights by filing a lawsuit for infringement. To prevail in establishing copyright infringement a plaintiff must show "(1) ownership of a valid copyright, and (2) copying of constituent elements of the work that are original."[22] A plaintiff that has obtained a copyright registration will find it easier to satisfy the ownership requirement. As for copying, because it is usually difficult to obtain direct evidence, it may be proven by establishing that the accused infringer had access to the copyrighted work and created a work that was substantially similar.[23]

The infringement analysis becomes more complex when the alleged copying involves computer systems. In order to determine whether one computer program is "substantially similar" to another, most courts follow the "abstraction-filtration-comparison" test set forth in *Computer Associates International, Inc. v. Altai, Inc.*[24] The abstraction and filtration parts of the test generally require the isolation of copyrightable elements of a program. The comparison portion of the test requires a comparison of the copyrightable elements of the program with the accused infringing work.

---

[20] Steven R. Englund & David F. Noteware, *Banking on the Internet: Intellectual Property Pitfalls, Opportunities,* BANKING POL'Y REP., Sept. 16, 1996, at 1.

[21] 17 U.S.C. § 106.

[22] *Feist Publications,* 499 U.S. at 361. Another question that courts have grappled with in the world of computers and cyberspace is what constitutes "copying." The trend appears to be to interpret the term broadly for copyright purposes. For example, in *MAI Systems Corp. v. Peak Computer, Inc.,* 991 F.2d 511, 518 (9th Cir. 1993), the court held infringement may occur even where a copy of a work was only temporarily placed into random access memory.

[23] *See Feist Publications,* 499 U.S. at 361. While the "substantial similarity" test is traditionally applied to determine copyright infringement, courts have held that "when the range of protectable and unauthorized expression is narrow, the appropriate standard for illicit copying is virtual identity." *See, e.g., Apple Computer, Inc. v. Microsoft Corp.,* 35 F.3d 1435, 1439 (9th Cir. 1994).

[24] *Computer Associates Int'l, Inc. v. Altai, Inc.,* 982 F.2d 683 (2d Cir. 1992).

In order to avoid potential claims of infringement, financial institutions should carefully consider any applicable copyright issues before they display any works of third parties on their websites.[25] For example, banks may display select pieces from their art collections online. However, unless the institution owns the copyright, has permission from the copyright owner, or the work is in the public domain (*i.e.*, the copyright term has expired or the author has lost copyright protection for other reasons), the display of the work online may violate copyright laws.[26]

The best way for financial institutions to avoid copyright infringement is to separately evaluate the copyrightability of each feature, such as graphics, information, displayed art, and software, used on its website; and to determine whether any third party owns any copyright interest in each feature. If the answer is yes, the bank should seek permission, obtain a license, or secure an assignment of copyright, from the third party.

§ 18.03 TRADEMARKS

Banks developing online services, in addition to concerning themselves with copyright issues, must also pay special attention to trademark issues arising from Internet activity. Although recent case law regarding Internet trademark disputes does not specifically address the banking industry, banks need to consider its implications for their operations. Accordingly, the following Sections address trademark regulation in cyberspace and recent trademark case law relating to the Internet, and apply the foregoing to the banking industry.

[1] TRADEMARK REGULATION IN CYBERSPACE

In considering trademark issues, it is first instructive to distinguish between the primary types of property that are generally associated with or included within the rubric of trademark law. A trademark is any word, name, symbol, or combination of these things used in connection with a product that indicates the origin of the product and serves to distinguish it from the products of others.[27] A service mark includes the same components but is used in connection with a service rather than a product.[28] Similar to both a trademark and a service

---

[25] Financial institutions should also consider applicable defenses to copyright infringement. One frequently-raised defense is the doctrine of fair use. The doctrine provides that "the fair use of a copyrighted work . . . for purposes such as criticism, comment, news reporting, teaching (including multiple copies for classroom use), scholarship, or research, is not an infringement of copyright. In determining whether the use of a work is "fair" courts consider (i) the purpose and character of the use; (ii) the nature of the copyrighted work; (iii) the amount and substantiality of the portion of the copyrighted work used in relation to the work as a whole; and (iv) the effect of the use upon the potential market for or value of the copyrighted work. 17 U.S.C. § 107. Exact transmissions of copyrighted work will rarely be considered "fair use" especially where the work has commercial value. *See Sega Enterprises Ltd. v. MAPHIA*, 857 F. Supp. 679 (N.D. Cal. 1994); *Playboy Enterprises, Inc. v. Frena*, 839 F. Supp. 1552 (M.D. Fla. 1993). Thus, this defense may only be applicable on the Internet where a portion of another's copyrighted work is utilized.

[26] *See Sega Enterprises Ltd. v. MAPHIA*, 948 F. Supp. 923 (N.D. Cal. 1996); *Religious Technology Center v. Netcom OnLine Communications Serv., Inc.*, 923 F. Supp. 1231 (N.D. Cal. 1995). These cases lead to the conclusion that uploading a work onto the Internet constitutes a reproduction or distribution in violation of a copyright holder's rights.

[27] 15 U.S.C. § 1127.

[28] *Id.*

mark, a trade name is a name used to identify a business.[29] Finally, "trade dress is the totality of elements in which a product or service is packaged or presented."[30]

Each of these types of property can symbolize the consumer goodwill that a company has developed for a particular product, service, name, or packaging. For example, "Wells Fargo," "Wells Fargo Bank®," the stage-coach logo, and all page headers and button icons located at the Wells Fargo website are registered marks of Wells Fargo & Company.

[a] Domestic Federal Trademark Law. Unlike copyright and patent law, which are wholly federal, trademark rights are protected in the United States under both state and federal law. Federal trademark rights stem from use of a mark in commerce.[31] Even if no application has been filed, an entity that is using a name as a trademark will acquire common law rights in the name. This is different from most foreign countries where trademark rights are awarded to the first to file an application and not the first to use a mark. Thus, financial institutions which have or intend to develop international operations should file early in relevant countries abroad to ensure priority.[32]

While not compulsory, registration of the mark is advisable in most cases, as it can strengthen and bolster the trademark rights significantly. Under federal trademark law, there is also a mechanism to file an application to essentially reserve a trademark, if available, for a limited period of time until the applicant begins using the trademark.[33]

Once a mark is registered, federal trademark law proscribes the use in commerce of any reproduction, counterfeit, copy, or colorable imitation of the mark (broadly defined to include trademarks, service marks, trade names, trade dress, or any other device that serves as a source-identifying function) in connection with the sale, offering for sale, distribution, or advertising of any goods or services that is likely to cause confusion or to cause mistake or to deceive.[34] In addition, federal trademark laws prohibits (1) the use in commerce of any mark that is likely to cause confusion as to the source, sponsorship, or affiliation of goods or services, regardless of whether the goods or services are offered in connection with a federally registered mark, and (2) any false or misleading statement in commercial advertising and promotion that misrepresents the nature, characteristics, qualities, or geographic origin of the advertised or competitive goods or services.[35]

---

[29] 17 U.S.C. § 1127.

[30] J. THOMAS MCCARTHY, MCCARTHY ON TRADEMARKS § 8.1, at 8-2 (1996).

[31] *See* 15 U.S.C. § 1051(a)(1).

[32] Banks that seek to reach an international audience on the Internet should also consider foreign trademark laws. At the same time, banks should evaluate the impact of their actions on their jurisdictional status in applicable countries. For example, they should consider whether such registration would strengthen a claim that the bank is offering products or services in that country and thus subject the bank to its jurisdiction.

[33] 15 U.S.C. § 1051(b).

[34] 15 U.S.C. § 1114(1)(a).

[35] 15 U.S.C. § 1125(a)(1).

A trademark owner has the right to obtain damages for unauthorized use of the trademark and prevent third parties from using a word, name, symbol, or device that is likely to cause confusion with the trademark owner's mark.[36] Actual confusion, however, is not required, although evidence of actual confusion bolsters an infringement claim.[37] Courts generally look at a variety of factors to determine whether a likelihood of confusion exists, such as the strength of a trademark owner's mark, the degree of similarity between the marks in question, the proximity of the products, the likelihood that the trademark owner will begin selling products similar to those of the accused infringer, actual confusion, the accused infringer's good faith in adopting its own mark, the quality of accused infringer's product, and the sophistication of the buyers.[38] For example, ZZ Bank, a bank with a well-known trademarked logo, can prevent any other entity from using a confusingly similar logo to advertise financial services, because it is likely that consumers might confuse the other bank's service with ZZ Bank's services.

[b] Federal Trademark Dilution Act. On January 16, 1996, Congress enacted the Federal Trademark Dilution Act of 1995.[39] Unlike the traditional claim for trademark infringement, which turns on whether there is confusion between the plaintiff's use of a mark on similar goods or services, confusion is not an element of a dilution claim. Instead, the dilution doctrine is designed to remedy the injury that occurs when the distinctive value of a famous mark is whittled away or tarnished by use, typically on dissimilar or noncompeting goods or services.[40]

In order to prevail in a dilution claim, a trademark owner must establish that: (i) its mark is famous; (ii) the mark was famous before the defendant began using its mark; and (iii) the defendant's use will dilute the mark of the trademark owner.[41] Courts look at a variety of factors in determining whether a mark is "famous" including the degree of distinctiveness of the mark; the duration and extent of the trademark owner's use of its mark; the geographic extent to which the mark is used; the channels of trade within which the goods or services exist; the degree of recognition within the mark's channel of trade; the extent of use of same or similar marks by third parties; the extent of advertising and publicity of the trademark owner's mark; and whether the plaintiff's mark is federally registered.[42] If the defendant's mark is registered, a dilution claim cannot be made.[43] Returning to the ZZ Bank example, if ZZ Bank can prove that its trademarked logo was "famous" it may be able to prevent entities from using it even in connection with very dissimilar goods or services.

---

[36] 15 U.S.C. §§ 1114, 1116.

[37] *Eclipse Ass'n v. Data General Corp.*, 894 F.2d 1114 (9th Cir. 1990); *E. Remy Martin & Co., S.A. v. Shaw-Ross Int'l Imports, Inc.*, 756 F.2d 1525 (11th Cir. 1985).

[38] *Polaroid Corp. v. Polarad Electronics Corp.*, 287 F.2d 492 (2d Cir. 1961). Depending on the jurisdiction, other courts may use a slightly different list of factors. *See, e.g., AMF, Inc. v. Sleekcraft Boats*, 599 F.2d 341 (9th Cir. 1979); *see also* RESTATEMENT (THIRD) OF UNFAIR COMPETITION §§ 20-23 (1995).

[39] Federal Trademark Dilution Act of 1995, Pub. L. No. 104-98, § 3(a), 1995 U.S.C.C.A.N. (109 Stat.) 985 (codified at 15 U.S.C. § 1125(c)(1)).

[40] *See* J. THOMAS MCCARTHY, MCCARTHY ON TRADEMARKS § 28:67 *et seq.* (1996).

[41] 15 U.S.C. § 1125(c)(1). *See Toys "R" Us, Inc. v. Akkaoui*, 1996 WL 772709 (N.D. Cal. 1996) (granting preliminary injunction against pornographic materials sold under the mark "ADULTS 'R' Us").

[42] 17 U.S.C. § 1125 (c)(1).

[43] 17 U.S.C. § 1125(c)(3).

[c] State Trademark Law. Every state has enacted laws that provide for the registration and protection of trademarks. Although state trademark statutes seldom afford the registrant any greater substantive protection than those available under the federal trademark laws or common law, state registration can generally be procured faster than a federal registration and may therefore afford the owner of a mark some measure of protection while an application for federal registration is pending.[44]

[2]   DOMAIN NAMES

The trademark law principles of infringement and dilution described above are relevant to banking on the Internet in many respects, including the use of "domain names."[45] A domain name, or identifying address on the Internet, creates an expectation about who and what is located at that address. Communication over the Internet requires each computer and user to be distinguished in some manner. The vast majority of domain names are assigned by Network Solutions, Inc. ("NSI"), a private company that provides Internet addresses and registers domain names. The expanded usage of the Internet for commercial purposes has placed greater importance and significance on name recognition on the Internet. Because a domain name suggests identity, quality, and content, it may be closely related to, or function as, a trademark.[46]

Any bank that seeks to host a website and commence online banking services must register a domain name. Not surprisingly, the best choice of a domain name for a financial institution is one that is "guessable" by its customers. For this reason, most institutions register names that are identical or as close as possible to the institution's name. For example, the domain names for Wells Fargo Bank and Bank of America are www.wellsfargo.com and www.bankamerica.com, respectively.

Domain names are generally assigned on a first come, first served basis. This is done without determining whether the domain name infringes or dilutes any trademarks. This practice can create potential problems for trademark owners, some of whom have faced the unintentional or even intentional "pirating" of their trademarks by third parties.[47] In the face of such problems, the use of domain names on the Internet has rapidly created a new line of trademark case law. Such cases are not always consistently decided.

---

[44]   *See* KENT D. STUCKEY, INTERNET AND ONLINE LAW 7-32 (Law Journal Seminars Press 1996).

[45]   *See* Lloyd. L. Rich, *Trademark Protection in Cyberspace* (last modified July 8, 1996), *available at* <http://www.publaw.com/trade.htm>.

[46]   *Id.*

[47]   In May 1994, the list of "pirated" names included: McDonald's, Coke, Hertz, Nasdaq, Viacom, and MTV. In *The Princeton Review Management Corp. v. Stanley H. Kaplan Educational Center, Ltd.,* 94 Civ. 1604 (MGC) (S.D.N.Y. filed March 9, 1994) Kaplan Educational Center sued its competitor, The Princeton Review, for trademark infringement because The Princeton Review had obtained and used the domain name "kaplan.com" to publish comments which criticized the Kaplan Educational Center's program and praised that of The Princeton Review. The arbiter in that case agreed, and ordered the Princeton Review to relinquish the domain name. A similar result occurred in *Planned Parenthood Federation of America, Inc. v. Richard Bucci, d/b/a Catholic Radio,* 1997 U.S. Dist. LEXIS 3338; 42 USPQ 2d 1430 (S.D.N.Y. 1997). In that case, an anti-abortion advocate set up a website at www.plannedparenthood.com to promote a book opposing abortion. The court determined that there was a likelihood that persons seeking the Planned Parenthood website and information, actually located at www.plannedparenthood.org, would be confused and consequently granted Planned Parenthood's request for an injunction. *Id.*

For example, in *Actmedia, Inc. v. Active Media International, Inc.*,[48] a court held that the reservation alone of someone else's trademark as a domain name constitutes trademark infringement and dilution. In contrast, in *Lockheed Martin Corp. v. Network Solutions, Inc.*,[49] the court suggested in dicta that reserving a domain name was not sufficient to support an action under the Lanham Act. In that case, Lockheed Martin Corp. sued NSI alleging that NSI infringed and diluted its registered trademark, SKUNK WORKS®, by awarding registrations of the domain names skunkworks.com., skunkworks.net, skunkwrks.com, and skunkwerks.com to parties other than Lockheed. The court stated that it seemed unlikely that NSI's registration of SKUNK WORKS® type domain names, by itself, violated the Lanham Act. Consequently, the issue of whether registration alone constitutes trademark infringement remains open to dispute, although recent cases indicate that a choice of domain name that appears to be motivated purely by the desire for competitive advantage over a registered trademark owner will result in liability if it can be clearly established.

One lesson to take away from these disputes is that banks planning online activity should promptly register domain names of their choice. This will help to ensure availability of a bank's preferred domain name or names. Moreover, because domain names are given out on a first come, first served basis, preempting a third party's adoption of a domain name similar to a bank's trademark may make it less likely that a bank will have to engage in trademark infringement litigation.

[3] MAINTAINING AND STRENGTHENING RIGHTS THROUGH ONLINE TRADEMARK USE

Before adopting any word, name, symbol, or device in connection with an online product or service, or even a domain name in connection with a website, a bank should obtain a clearance opinion. This is typically done by a trademark attorney, who commissions a search and reviews the results to determine whether identical or similar trademarks or service marks are already in use. A bank should at least obtain a clearance opinion in every country where it has online customers (both at the present and in the foreseeable future). Depending on the outcome of the clearance search, the bank should apply for a federal trademark registration with the U.S. Patent and Trademark Office ("USPTO") and any other countries that may be applicable.

As with copyright law, there are a number of benefits afforded from obtaining a federal registration of a trademark. A registration is evidence of the validity of a mark and of the trademark owner's rights in such mark.[50] Moreover, the registration will deter others from seeking rights in an identical mark. Once a bank has secured its federal trademark, it should be careful maintain the validity of the mark with the timely filing of appropriate documents. For example, after a mark has been registered for five years, a trademark owner may obtain "incontestable" status in the mark upon filing an affidavit with the USPTO.[51] This prevents third

---

[48] *Actmedia, Inc. v. Active Media Int'l, Inc.*, No. 96C-3448, 1996 U.S. Dist. LEXIS 20814; 1996 WL 399707 (N.D. Ill. July 12, 1996).

[49] *Lockheed Martin Corp. v. Network Solutions, Inc.*, Case No. CV 96-7438 DDP (C.D. Cal. Oct. 22, 1996).

[50] 15 U.S.C. § 1057(b).

[51] 15 U.S.C. § 1065. This status may be sought within one year after a five consecutive year period subsequent to the date of registration where the mark is in continuous use. *Id.*

parties from challenging the validity of the mark on certain grounds. In addition, a trademark registration must be renewed every ten years in order to maintain it in force.[52]

In addition to registering any trademarks or service marks, a financial institution, as a mark owner, should provide notice to third parties in connection with any word, name, symbol, or device that it is using in a trademark or service mark capacity. The "™" or "SM" symbols may be used, depending upon whether the mark is a trademark or a service mark, where common law rights are being asserted (even if no application for registration has or will be filed). The "™" or "SM" may also be used when an application for registration is pending. The "®" designation can legally only be used when the USPTO has issued a federal registration of the mark, either for a trademark or service mark.[53] As with copyright law, providing notice of rights prevents an infringer from legitimately claiming that it had no knowledge of the asserted rights, which aids in the collection of damages in an infringement action.[54]

Once a financial institution has selected or is using a trademark, it should be alert to potential infringers. Banks should not allow third parties to infringe their trademarks. This can severely weaken trademark rights. One option is to hire a professional trademark watch service to monitor the market for similar trademark usage. In addition to checking for potential infringement, the watch service can monitor applications that have been filed in the USPTO, and corresponding offices in foreign countries, for potentially similar marks. It is also good practice to keep the trademark register clear of similar marks to the extent possible. If a bank discovers infringement by third parties or that an application for a similar mark has been filed, it should consult with a trademark attorney.

[4]   AVOIDING LANHAM ACT LIABILITY

In addition to protecting its own rights, a financial institution should take care to avoid infringing or diluting the trademark rights of others. Prudence and common sense are often the key. As discussed in Section 18.03[3], it is important to obtain clearance opinion for any product or service names, logos, slogans etc. used on the website. While clearance opinions are not infallible, they will substantially reduce the likelihood that an entity will be found to infringe or dilute the rights of a trademark owner.

In addition to infringement and dilution, banks must avoid other federally proscribed conduct. This other proscribed conduct includes passing off, false designation of origin, and false description.[55] These types of claims may arise if goods or services are improperly presented as endorsed or sponsored by some disassociated entity, or if false representations are made about particular goods or services. For example, it probably would not be surprising that a bank which used a famous financier's image on its home page without

---

[52]   15 U.S.C. § 1059. Renewal may be sought at any point within the window of six months preceding and three months following expiration of the ten year registration period. *Id.*

[53]   15 U.S.C. § 1111.

[54]   *See id.*

[55]   15 U.S.C. § 1125(a).

permission might get sued.[56] A financial institution could also face potential liability for less obvious conduct, such as listing its famous customers, which might be viewed as an implicit endorsement. Another situation that should be approached with caution is the use of third party marks on the website. While it is not improper to provide truthful comparisons to customers, it must be clear that there is no relationship between the two entities.

To avoid potential claims, a financial institution should ensure that it has permission before knowingly using a third party's intellectual property, including trademark, trade name, logo, image, or likeness.

§ 18.04   PATENTS

In the United States, patent rights constitute a unique species of protected intellectual property. The rights afforded by a U.S. patent can, in certain cases, prove exceptionally valuable to its holder.[57] In exchange for granting and providing enforcement mechanisms for these rights, however, the federal government — which has exclusive jurisdiction over patents — exacts strict compliance with detailed statutory and technical requirements for patent issuance and use. In view of the stakes — whether to an inventor or his employer attempting to avoid waiver of potential patent rights, or to a financial institution seeking to avert possibly-significant liability for infringement of another party's patent — careful attention to patent considerations is of particular importance to any institution utilizing rapidly-developing technologies, such as those at the heart of electronic banking.

[1]   PATENTABLE SUBJECT MATTER

[a] Generally. The U.S. Patent Code provides that "[w]hoever invents or discovers any new and useful process, machine, manufacture, or composition of matter, or any new and useful improvement thereof, may obtain a patent therefor, subject to the terms and conditions of" the Patent Code.[58]

The United States Patent and Trademark Office ("USPTO") examines all patent applications and issues those patents deemed allowable. A patent contains a written "specification" describing the invention in detail; figures illustrating the invention if it is capable of being drawn; and one or more claims, short sentences defining the boundaries of the subject matter for which the inventor has obtained exclusive protection. Only registered patent attorneys and patent agents may represent patent applicants before the USPTO.

---

[56]   In addition to violating federal trademark laws, such conduct may violate the right of publicity protected under state law.

[57]   *See, e.g.*, Robert Schaffer & Clarke Wixon, *Software Companies Implement Patent Strategies*, NATL. L. J., Oct. 20, 1997 (noting 1994 patent infringement verdict against Microsoft, in Civ. Case No. 93-0413 (C.D. Cal.), awarding patentee Stac Inc. $120 million for Microsoft's infringement of data compression patent); *see also* Lee Patterson, *Get Smart: Tools to raise your company's IQ*, FORBES ASAP, Apr. 7, 1997, at *2 ("Revenues from *patent licensing* and litigation are expected to reach $100 billion by the end of 1997. Companies stand to lose out on millions of dollars by failing to recognize the value of their patent portfolios.").

[58]   35 U.S.C. § 101.

From the statutory provision setting forth the right to a patent flow the three prerequisites for the patenting of any product or process. Patent practitioners use the terms (i) *novelty*, (ii) *utility*, and (iii) *non-obviousness* to refer to the three fundamental characteristics of a patentable invention.

[*i*] *Novelty*. The statute requires that an invention be "new" as compared to technology that has come before (referred to in the patent argot as the "prior art"). This novelty requirement means that the following events will preclude patentability of a claimed invention: (1) knowledge or use of the invention by others in the United States, or description of the invention in a printed publication anywhere, before the date the applicant made the invention;[59] or (2) a showing that the patent applicant did not invent the claimed subject matter at all,[60] or that he invented it only after some other inventor in the U.S.[61]

[*ii*] *Utility*. Stemming from the statutory requirement that a patentable invention be "useful," the utility mandate is typically not difficult to meet, as the USPTO in practice devotes little effort toward gauging the value of an invention, leaving it to the market to make such a determination once a patent issues.

[*iii*] *Non-obviousness*. Because a patented device or process must not merely be "new," but also represent an "invention," a patent applicant must show that his claimed subject matter would not have been obvious at the time of the invention, as viewed by one of ordinary skill in the art to which the patent application pertains.[62] A particular device could pass the novelty test (*i.e.*, because it contained an element not found in any previously-existing devices of its kind), but might still be deemed obvious if addition of that element would have readily suggested itself to workers in the particular technological field of the invention. Determinations of obviousness are inherently inexact, but because an inventor typically keeps abreast of the state of the art in his technological field, he may be able to provide accurate assessments of, or arguments for, the non-obviousness of his invention over previous devices or processes of its kind.

[b] Special Problems.

[*i*] *Statutory Subject Matter and Computer Inventions*. As noted above, the patent right extends only to processes, machines, manufactures, compositions of matter, or combinations of such classes. The abstract nature of many computer-related inventions, particularly software, led courts and the USPTO in the past to limit or deny patentability to many inventions involving electronic technology or computer processing functions.[63] Most of these decisions essentially held that a computer program, for example, represented nothing more than

---

[59] 35 U.S.C. § 102(a).

[60] 35 U.S.C. § 102(f).

[61] 35 U.S.C. § 102(g). For the purposes of U.S. patent law, "inventors" are those persons contributing significantly to the creation of the claimed subject matter. Determining who is and is not an inventor is important because the U.S., unlike most other nations, requires all patent applications to be made in the name of the original and first *individual* inventors, even if the property rights in the invention belong to the individual inventor's corporate employer or another assignee.

[62] 35 U.S.C. § 103; *Graham v. John Deere Co.*, 383 U.S. 1 (1966).

[63] *Gottschalk v. Benson*, 409 U.S. 63 (1972); *Diamond v. Diehr*, 450 U.S. 175, 186 (1981).

a series of mathematical expressions or algorithms, and that such mathematical expressions fell outside the ambit of the subject matter Congress had made protectable by patent.

Even when it was willing to concede that computerized devices could be the subject of a proper patent application, the Supreme Court expressed skepticism as to their patentability. In *Dann v. Johnston*,[64] the Court considered an inventor's application for a patent on a machine system for automatic record keeping of bank checks and deposits using large scale electronic computer processing while retaining the ability to use individual ledger format and bookkeeping methods. The Court held the system unpatentable, because it was obvious in view of existing banking recordkeeping systems.[65]

Such reflexive hostility toward computer-related patents has greatly waned in the past decade, however, and it is now clear that a computer program, while not patentable by itself, can qualify for patent protection in conjunction with the hardware used to execute it,[66] or with other expressed utility (such as a software-based process for identifying certain illnesses). While earlier decisions holding that algorithms, mathematical expressions, or mere ideas were not patentable remain in force as a legal matter, today an inventor can generally escape these prohibitions by embodying his algorithm or processing procedure in a computer system having processing and storage hardware, so the USPTO may without demur accept the physical aggregate of computer plus software as a single, patentable machine.

Accordingly, a mathematical formula for calculating creditworthiness, or a computer program for managing cash transfers, would be unpatentable as such, but, if made tangible by embodiment in a physical structure, which the inventor could describe as, for example, "a computer system for calculating, storing, and displaying credit or cashflow information in accordance with a specified algorithm," the system could qualify for patent protection as a machine.[67]

[2] VALUE OF PATENTS IN ELECTRONIC BANKING

[a] A Patent is a Valuable Property. Because patents represent valuable property rights, not only as against infringing parties in litigation, but as an additional, and sometimes significant asset for licensing to

---

[64] *Dann v. Johnston*, 425 U.S. 219 (1976).

[65] *Id.* at 229.

[66] The outlines of a clear doctrine for establishing patentability of software had coalesced by the mid-1990s. *In re Alappat*, 33 F.3d 1526 (Fed. Cir. 1994); *see also* Jack Brown, Address at the Thirteenth Annual Judicial Conference of the United States Court of Appeals for the Federal Circuit (May 25, 1995), *in* 166 F.R.D. 515, 584 (1995) ("The Allapat [sic] case . . . has in effect already moved to an acceptance of software, even if defined essentially as a series of mathematical algorithms, as patentable subject matter. The cases may still require at least a mention of some kind of hardware, usually a generic computer."); *see also In re Warmedam*, 33 F.3d 1354 (Fed. Cir. 1994); *Arrhythmia Research Tech., Inc. v. Corazonix Corp.*, 958 F.2d 1053 (Fed. Cir. 1992); *Atari Games Corp. v. Nintendo of Am., Inc.*, 975 F.2d 832, 839 (Fed. Cir. 1992) ("In conformance with the standards of patent law, [U.S.C.] title 35 provides protection for the process or method performed by a computer in accordance with a program."). The Patent Office has recently set forth detailed, and liberalized, rules for its patent Examiners to follow in determining the patentability of computer related inventions. *See* Examination Guidelines for Computer-Related Inventions, 61 Fed. Reg. 7478 (1996); *see also* MANUAL OF PATENT EXAMINING PROCEDURE § 2106.

[67] Or, alternatively, as a process; one might write a claim reading, for example, "a process for calculating creditworthiness consisting of the steps of entering selected credit data into a memory, computer processing such data in accordance with a particular algorithm, and displaying the results of such processing on a monitor."

third parties or as a price-enhancing element in any sale of a business, institutions should be aware of how far existent and potential patent rights extend.

Financial institutions should give serious consideration to patent protection for their proprietary software and other computer systems, when feasible, because patents often impart significantly stronger rights than do other categories of intellectual property rights that one might alternatively seek for the same subject matter.[68]

The patent law permits issuance of a separate patent for each distinct invention, and it is common for a single device or process to embody multiple patents. For example, a bank whose engineers developed a completely innovative ATM system would need to examine the possibility of separate patent protection for inventive advances contained in the main computer processing unit, the display devices, the storage system, the data input mechanism, the computer-processed data structure used in carrying out transactions, the cash transport mechanism, the security features, and the data communication means.

Patents may also serve a valuable defensive function. A company may wish to establish a patent position in an important technology simply to avoid the prospect that competitors could otherwise occupy the same ground and harass the company with patent litigation. Further, an institution can often avert potential disputes with other parties holding patents on related technology by entering into cross-licensing agreements permitting each party to use the other's complementary patents.

Although banks provide the channel through which electronic financial services are likely to be delivered, banking institutions may find that when it comes to the actual methods of delivery, banks will be left in the role of licensees of technology created by non-bankers.[69] However, banks are increasingly recognizing that control over the future shape of electronic financial services delivery, and the allocation of the revenue streams associated therewith, may turn on who has invented and licensed out the relevant technologies. Some banking organizations, in particular Citibank, have long recognized that they are better able to control their own destiny if they are in the position of creating and owning the technology that can be used most effectively to conduct their business.[70] More recently, other banks have begun to see the value of joining forces with each other and with technology providers in order to develop new financial technologies with their particular needs and revenue interests in mind. Notable examples of this phenomenon include: (i) Integrion[SM], which was established by leading banking institutions and IBM; and (ii) Mondex[TM], which was initially a collaboration between NatWestBank and British Telecom.

[b] Trends in Patenting of Electronic Banking Technology. In the past, financial institutions generally underutilized the protections of the patent system, but in recent years it has become more and more common

---

[68] *See* Section 18.02 (noting that copyright of material protects only a particular form of expression, and not the idea underlying the expression). *See also* Robert Schaffer & Clarke Wixon, *Software Companies Implement Patent Strategies*, NAT'L L. J., Oct. 20, 1997, at *1 ("[C]opyright law will prevent verbatim copying of a software program or copies made with minimal changes. Competitors, however, are free to exploit the facts, ideas, processes or methods of operation set forth in a copyrighted work. Patents provide a broader level of protection.").

[69] Licensing is discussed below in Section 18.07[3].

[70] *See generally* PHILLIP L. ZWEIG, WRISTON (1995).

for banks and brokerages (or individual inventors) to seek and obtain patents for their electronic finance innovations.[71] Institutions that do not affirmatively pursue patent protection as a tangible payoff for their investment in development of electronic banking technology may find themselves at a significant competitive disadvantage to more patent-savvy domestic and international competitors.[72]

In recent years, for example, Citibank has undertaken efforts at obtaining comprehensive patent protection for its central financial systems, including credit card processing and international fund transfers.[73] Several patents already issued to Citibank are expected to form the basis for its Electronic Monetary System ("EMS"), described by Citibank as the first fully secure retail and wholesale electronic payment system.[74]

In an indication of the international battle for primacy in electronic banking technology, a group of Japanese banks filed a protest with the Japanese patent office, seeking to block Citibank's Japanese patent applications for the EMS system. The Japanese banks — which appear to have lagged behind Western rivals in developing their own electronic banking technology — alleged that Citibank's patent applications improperly sought to claim both old and new technology. The dispute remains pending in the Japanese patent office.[75]

Numerous other inventors have succeeded in securing U.S. patents on financial transaction processing, including patents for:

- an apparatus for cashless purchases not requiring entry of PIN codes or interconnection to an external credit verification network;[76]

---

[71] See A Dose of Patent Medicine, ECONOMIST, Feb. 10, 1996, at 71 ("Some argue that financial institutions have until now simply undervalued their inventions, and so failed to exploit them.").

[72] See, e.g., Symposium: Information Issues: Intellectual Property, Privacy, Integrity, Interoperability, and the Economics of Information (Fred H. Cate, ed.), 48 FED. COMM. L. J. 5, 25 (1995) (quoting P. Michael Nugent , Vice-President and General Counsel for Technology and Intellectual Property, Citicorp):

All of these players are coming in and saying, "We own the system – the method – by which the Information Age is conducting itself, by which transactions will occur, and by which payments will be effectuated." And you have them wheeling and dealing between the parties and litigation. You have settlements. You have contracts being negotiated back and forth.

You are going to see this happen just like it did in the automobile industry, the chemical industry, and the engineering industry, where patent positions were maintained. Then there are dramatic cross-licensing agreements. A lot of small companies were kicked out. There are a lot of small companies that did not protect themselves. That is going to happen here.

See also Japanese Banks' Defeat In Electronic Money War Imminent: In Spite Of Contesting Citibank's Patent Application, NIHON KEIZAI SHIMBUN, Mar. 18, 1996 ("Because Japanese banks were too much involved in making real estate loans, they are now behind in research or investment in an interbank settlement system in the era of Cyber network communication. . . . The lack of foresight on the parts of both regulators and city banks is likely to cause a delay by which they cannot catch up with Western firms' technological advance in the 21st Century, said a leading manufacturer's spokesman.").

[73] See A Dose of Patent Medicine, ECONOMIST, Feb. 10, 1996, at 71.

[74] See U.S. Patents No. 5,453,601 ("Electronic-Monetary System") (1995), 5,557,518 ("Trusted Agents For Open Electronic Commerce") (1996), 5,455,407 ("Electronic-Monetary System") (1995), and 5,621,797 ("Electronic Ticket Presentation And Transfer Method") (1997); see also Citibank Awarded Key Technology Patents for Electronic Money, CITIBANK TECHNOLOGY BULLETIN, Vol. 12, No. 4 (1995-96), at 1.

[75] See Brian Bremner, Hold It Right There, Citibank, BUSINESS WEEK, Mar. 25, 1996, at 176; Tsutomu Wada, Citibank Patent Bid Catches Banks Napping, NIKKEI WEEKLY, Mar. 25, 1996, at 1.

[76] U.S. Patent No. 5,591,949 ("Automatic Portable Account Controller For Remotely Arranging For Payment Of A Debt To A Vendor") (1997) (individually owned).

- a system for small cashless purchases, permitting automatic refreshing of cash card balance at point of sale;[77]

- an early system utilizing cryptographic techniques in an electronic fund transfer ("EFT") system to prevent unauthorized obtaining or use of sensitive information;[78]

- a computerized consumer home banking system for checkless payments to merchants;[79]

- a cash card system claiming to provide highly effective security without continuous "online" connection to a central verification computer;[80]

- a computerized lending portfolio management technique;[81]

- a computerized debt restructuring system;[82]

- an anonymous trading system, matching bid/ask prices and credit information between buyers and sellers of financial instruments;[83] and

- an encrypted EFT system permitting secured check clearing by use of facsimile machine.[84]

Areas of particular continued interest in electronic banking, judging by recently issued U.S. patents, include refinements to electronic cash systems and improvements in security measures.[85]

While electronic banking technology poses certain peculiar challenges to acquiring patents, it is incumbent on managers of modern financial institutions to be attentive to the possibility of obtaining patent protection for (or defending against other concerns' patents on) banking functions that the institution has begun performing by means of electronic equipment.

---

[77] U.S. Patent No. 5,557,516 ("System And Method For Conducting Cashless Transactions") (1996) (owned by MasterCard International).

[78] U.S. Patent No. 4,302,810 ("Method And Apparatus For Secure Message Transmission For Use In Electronic Funds Transfer Systems") (1981) (owned by IBM Corp.).

[79] U.S. Patent No. 5,383,113 ("System And Method For Electronically Providing Customer Services Including Payment Of Bills, Financial Analysis And Loans") (1995) (owned by Checkfree Corp.).

[80] U.S. Patent No. 4,650,978 ("Off-Line Cash Card System And Method") (1987) (owned by RMH Systems, Inc.).

[81] U.S. Patent No. 4,742,457 ("System And Method Of Investment Management Including Means To Adjust Deposit And Loan Accounts for Inflation") (1988) (owned by Trans Texas Holdings Corp.).

[82] U.S. Patent No. 4,739,478 ("Methods And Apparatus For Restructuring Debt Obligations") (1988) (owned by Lazard Freres & Co.).

[83] U.S. Patent No. 5,375,055 ("Credit Management For Electronic Brokerage System") (1994) (owned by Foreign Exchange Transaction Services, Inc.).

[84] U.S. Patent No. 5,590,196 ("Secure Payment Method Using Facsimile") (1996) (owned by Connotech Experts Conseils, Inc.).

[85] *See, e.g.,* U.S. Patent No. 5,677,955 ("Electronic Fund Transfer Instruments") (1997) (owned by Financial Services Technological Consortium) (setting forth method of attaching unique "signatures" to electronic transactions for improved verification); U.S. Patent No. 5,671,279 ("Electronic Commerce Using A Secure Courier System") (1997) (owned by Netscape Communications Corp.) (claiming method of more secure online credit card payments); U.S. Patent No. 5,623,547 ("Value Transfer System") (1997) (owned by Jonhig Ltd.) (describing method of transferring electronic cash between virtual "purses").

[3] ACQUIRING AND PRESERVING PATENT RIGHTS

[a] Patent Applications and Corporate Invention Disclosure Programs. Diligence is the watchword in obtaining and protecting patent rights. A patent gives the owner the right to exclude others from making, using, selling, or offering to sell the patented invention for twenty years from the date of patent application.[86] In exchange for this "monopoly," the federal government requires that patent applicants apply for or "prosecute" their patents promptly and with full disclosure of the details for practicing the invention, so that once the patent expires, the public may have the full benefit of using, and further developing, the teachings of the patent.

[b] Role of the Patent Attorney. As noted earlier, only registered patent practitioners who have satisfied the USPTO's technical education requirements and passed its examination are permitted to represent inventors in the prosecution of patent applications.[87] Careful selection of a patent attorney and supervision of the application process is of great importance, because actions taken during claim drafting and prosecution may later limit or eliminate altogether a patentee's right to recover for infringement of his patent.[88]

In many actions for patent infringement, defendants will seek to escape liability by arguing that the patent is invalid or unenforceable, alleging, for instance, that the claims as drafted do not describe a novel and non-obvious invention vis-à-vis the prior art. Even though the USPTO, in issuing a patent, has presumably found that the invention *did* meet such requirements,[89] trial courts will give serious consideration to such allegations, and not infrequently will grant infringement defendants' motions to declare an issued patent invalid. Careful planning during prosecution can minimize the chances of later patent invalidation.

The patent attorney will typically take primary responsibility for:

- interviewing the inventor, so as to understand the advance he believes he has made in his field;

- conducting a search of prior art in the relevant field to aid in evaluating the likelihood of establishing novelty and non-obviousness;[90]

---

[86] 35 U.S.C. § 154(a)(1). The twenty year term from date of application applies to all patents issued on applications filed after June 8, 1995; earlier-filed patents may be subject to a term of seventeen years from the date of issuance. MANUAL OF PATENT EXAMINING PROCEDURE § 1309.01.

[87] As is true of most legal proceedings, an individual party may represent himself before the Patent Office; for corporate applicants, though, retention of registered patent counsel is a practical necessity.

[88] *See, e.g., Warner-Jenkinson Co. v. Hilton Davis Chem. Co.*, ____ U.S. ____, 117 S. Ct. 1040, 1051 (1997) (discussing doctrine of prosecution history estoppel, which may bar infringement recovery based on positions taken by patentee's attorney during prosecution of patent); *Hebert v. Lisle Corp.*, 99 F.3d 1109, 1115-16 (Fed. Cir. 1996) (setting forth grounds which may make patent unenforceable due to inequitable conduct during its prosecution). Additionally, the statutory bars of 35 U.S.C. § 102, discussed above, and the deadlines for filing various documents in the Patent Office during prosecution in order to avoid abandonment (see 35 U.S.C. § 133, setting a six month statutory time limit for response to Patent Office communications), place an additional premium on knowledge of, and diligent attention to, the sometimes arcane rules of Patent Office practice.

[89] 35 U.S.C. § 282 establishes a rebuttable presumption that a patent, once issued, is valid.

[90] Although a patent applicant and his attorney are obligated to disclose to the Patent Office prior inventions, of which they are aware, having significant relevance to the patentability of the inventor's claimed invention (37 C.F.R. § 1.56), an inventor is *not* under an obligation to make a patent search. In fact, as part of the patent application process, the Patent Office Examiner will conduct his own search of related prior art. Nonetheless, applicants and attorneys often choose to conduct pre-filing searches of the prior art to gauge the likelihood of obtaining a patent and weigh it against the costs involved in going forward with the application.

- drafting the specification and claims of a patent application and filing the application;

- taking care that the specification and claims meet all statutory and technical requirements;[91]

- planning for international patent filings, if desired by the applicant, no later than one year after the filing of a U.S. patent application;[92] and

- responding to communications from the USPTO regarding the application.

[i] *Role of the Inventor and the Financial Institution.* Other considerations necessary to maintaining patentability of inventions impose important responsibilities upon the inventor himself and his corporate employer, in consultation with patent counsel. These notable considerations include:

- Early and systematic recognition and disclosure of potentially-patentable innovations. Technical and in-house legal personnel should be instructed as to the importance of reporting significant developments in new technology or improvement of existing technology. Any employee with substantial technical responsibility is a potential inventor and should be among those inculcated with 'patent consciousness.' Many large companies give technical personnel standing instructions to fill out standard invention disclosure forms whenever an individual or technical team develops a notable new device or process. Supervisors, or a corporate patent committee, then

---

[91] For instance, 35 U.S.C. § 112 requires that the description of the invention in the patent be sufficiently detailed to permit one of ordinary skill in the invention's field to practice the invention, and that it set forth the best mode the inventor knows of practicing the invention.

[92] 35 U.S.C. § 119 permits inventors to file a United States patent application within one year of a foreign application on the same invention and claim the benefit of the earlier foreign filing date for certain purposes. The significance of this provision arises when, for example, a competitor files for a United States patent on the same device during the period between the applicant's foreign and United States filing dates. By using the "dating back" provisions of Section 119, the applicant can still establish patentability in the United States based on his earlier foreign filing date, even though the competitor technically filed in the United States before the applicant did. It is important to note that Section 119 does *not* operate to defeat the statutory bars of Section 102. For instance, if the applicant has placed the invention on sale in the United States, he *must* file a United States patent application within one year. Filing a foreign patent application within one year of sale, and later filing a U.S. application based on the foreign application, will *not* avoid the statutory bar. Filing an initial patent application anywhere outside the United States after a commercial use or offer for sale of the invention defeats patent protection in every country except the United States — absolute novelty has been destroyed by such activity.

Provisions similar to those of Section 119 obtain in many countries by treaty, so it is also possible to file a U.S. patent application first and follow it up within one year with foreign counterpart filings. Harmonization provisions for a world treaty include a proposal to make such foreign filing dates a basis for determining patent validity.

The Patent Cooperation Treaty (codified at 35 U.S.C. §§ 351 *et seq.*) permits applicants to use a single patent application as a launching point for multiple foreign patent filings. An applicant may either file a PCT application in the first instance, or file a regular U.S. (or other national) application and follow it up with a PCT application within one year. The PCT operates in two stages: an international stage, during which a search for related patents is conducted, and preliminary substantive examination may take place; and a national stage, at which point the applicant chooses in which of the individual states previously designated he wishes to pursue a national patent application. The advantages to the two-stage system are that it permits a more efficient single literature search, and that by the end of the international stage the applicant may have developed a better estimate of the value of the technology and likelihood of patentability so as to decide the advisability of the substantial additional outlay required for national stage prosecution in a host of countries.

Perhaps the most important factor to bear in mind when considering transnational patent applications is that the U.S. sets forth distinctive disclosure requirements not imposed by other countries, *e.g.*, the requirement that inventors disclose in the specification the best mode of practicing their invention. 35 U.S.C. § 112. Accordingly, any inventor contemplating basing a later U.S. application on an earlier foreign application must ensure that the foreign application meets the distinctive U.S. disclosure requirements, because in claiming priority from earlier patent applications inventors are *not* permitted to supplement or amend the earlier-filed specification.

evaluate — often in consultation with in-house or outside patent counsel — the financial and strategic benefits and costs of pursuing patent protection for such inventions.[93]

- Thorough documentation of inventors' research and development activities. Because establishing the timing and substance of an inventor's discoveries may prove crucial at a time far removed from the original invention,[94] detailed, contemporaneous inventor's notebooks charting the history of invention development can be decisive in future disputes. It is sound practice for inventors to ask a witness to sign their dated bench notes at the time they are written, in order to bolster even further their future evidentiary value.

- Securing the company's ownership rights in inventions. Workers in technological industries typically sign agreements to assign to their employer the right to ownership of any inventions made during the course of their employment. Assuring that such provisions are in place as to all personnel who may potentially make patentable inventions — and considering what covenants of confidentiality and non-competition the company ought to secure from technical employees — will be an increasingly important task for financial institutions as their business becomes more heavily reliant on development and implementation of electronic technology.

[c] The Statutory Bars. Companies must pay particular care to avoid the so-called "statutory bars" to patentability. In keeping with the Patent Code's mandate of diligence and early disclosure by inventors, an invention, even if otherwise novel and non-obvious, will be deemed unpatentable if:

- the invention has been put on sale or publicly used in the U.S. for more than one year before the date of filing a patent application;[95]

- the invention was patented or described in a printed publication here or abroad more than one year before the date of application;[96]

- the inventor obtained a foreign patent on the same invention by a foreign patent application, which was filed more than one year before the date of filing a U.S. application on the invention;[97] or

- the inventor has abandoned the invention.[98]

---

[93] While inventors are typically the primary source of information about the state of the art in their field, and can provide useful assessments of the magnitude of their own technological advances, evaluations of patentability should almost always include input from business and legal personnel to supplement technical evaluations of the invention. For instance, a new device may prove innovative but, for commercial reasons, may not justify the costs of patent prosecution. Similarly, a technical advance which a highly experienced engineer might evaluate as trifling in light of his own extraordinary command of the art may nevertheless prove sufficiently non-obvious, as viewed from the statutory perspective of *ordinary* technical skill, to win a patent.

[94] *See, e.g.*, 35 U.S.C. § 102(g) (providing that as between two unrelated inventors of the same subject matter, a patent will issue to the party shown to be first in time to reduce the invention to practice).

[95] 35 U.S.C. § 102(b).

[96] *Id.*

[97] *Id.* § 102(d).

[98] *Id.* § 102(e).

While evaluating whether particular forms of the statutory bar apply in a given case will usually require analysis by patent counsel,[99] technical and legal staff of the institution should be aware of two general precepts to avert statutory bars: (a) time is of the essence in disclosing, and applying for patents on, new technology; and (b) until a patent application is on file with the USPTO, any act of publicizing or commercializing an invention can start a clock running, which could end in forfeiture of potential patent rights if a patent application is not duly filed within a year of the first such act.

[d] Cost and Timing. It is difficult to generalize as to the cost and time required for prosecution of a patent, because the differing complexity of applications and various procedural actions the USPTO may take can cause substantial variance among applications. The USPTO halves most of its fees for small entities (*i.e.,* those having fewer than 500 employees).[100]

Few patent applications receive USPTO approval upon first submission. Almost universally, a patent applicant will instead receive an "Office Action" several months after the filing of his application, setting forth the Patent Examiner's rejections of, or technical objections to, the claims of the application.

Often initial and subsequent rejections occur because the inventor, or the inventor's counsel, in defining the scope of the protected invention, has set forth very broad claims in the as-filed application in the hopes of securing a sweeping patent. Particularly in a "crowded art," a technology in which many similar patents abut one another so as to leave space only for incremental improvement inventions, the Examiner will frequently reject such initial broad claims by the inventor as improperly overlapping with previous inventions in the field. The Examiner will, for instance, assert that the claims as written are not patentable because they define a device identical to,[101] or obvious in light of,[102] one or more pieces of prior art.

Such rejections or objections should not occasion despair, for it is typical that applicants go through several rounds of rejections and argument with the USPTO before securing allowance of claims. It is important to bear in mind that an invention may do nothing more than incrementally improve a device or process known in the prior art and still be fully patentable, so long as the invention, viewed as a whole, otherwise meets the

---

[99] For instance, the question under Section 102(b) of whether demonstrating a device at a trade show more than one year before filing a patent application for it amounts to a forbidden act of placing the device "on sale," or whether use, while perfecting an experimental technology can raise a "public use" statutory bar, may prove factually and legally complex.

[100] 35 U.S.C. § 41(h)(1).

[101] A rejection on the basis that a *single* prior art invention is identical to the claimed invention is founded on the novelty requirements of 35 U.S.C. § 102 and is referred to as an *anticipation* rejection.

[102] 35 U.S.C. § 103 is the basis for obviousness rejections of claims; such rejections, unlike Section 102 anticipation rejections, may be based on a combination of items in the prior art, which the Examiner asserts have combined to make the claimed invention obvious from the perspective of the man of ordinary skill in the art.

statutory requirements for patent protection.[103] Receiving an Office Action rejecting claims also does not diminish the inventor's rights in the invention. Patent applications are maintained in secrecy and, until the USPTO issues a final rejection and the applicant exhausts available administrative and judicial remedies for the Office's rejection, the application should be regarded as viable. Even in the event of abandonment or final failure to gain USPTO allowance of an application, the inventor or owner can, in some cases, preserve much of the value of his invention by practicing it under such conditions of secrecy as to qualify for trade secret protection.[104]

Sometimes the process of discussions with the USPTO will involve narrowing of claims to overcome the Examiner's belief that broad original claims were not distinct from the prior art. If prosecution does ultimately succeed, the patent issues upon payment of a further fee. All told, a time span of anywhere from two to four years from the date of filing the application to the date of patent issue is typical.

[e] Maintaining Patent Rights. Once a company secures a patent or patent portfolio, it must maintain and enforce its rights. Doing so requires, *inter alia*, "marking." By statute, to preserve his rights a patentee must put the public on notice of his patent on an article by affixing to the patented article the word "Patent" or abbreviation "Pat.," followed by the U.S. patent number.[105] Prominently displaying such a message on the screen of a patented electronic device would in most cases meet the marking requirement. Failure to mark a patented article can severely limit the damages available against even a clearly-infringing party.[106]

A patentee, or corporate assignee of the patent, must also pay periodic (and escalating) maintenance fees to keep the patent in force; this despite the nominal twenty year term of the patent. Failure to pay these fees, due four years, eight years, and twelve years after the date of issuance, results in expiration of the patent.[107] Accordingly, a company must periodically review its patent portfolio to evaluate which patents merit continuing payment of extension fees, and which may be deemed to have such limited remaining value that permitting them to expire would be the more economically sensible course.

---

[103] *See Pacific Technica Corp. v. United States*, 3 U.S.P.Q.2d 1168, 1180 (Cl. Ct. 1986) ("The test under section 103 is not whether an improvement or a use set forth in a patent would have been obvious or nonobvious. The test is whether *the claimed invention, considered as a whole*, would have been obvious or nonobvious."), *aff'd in part, vacated in part*, 835 F.2d 871 (Fed. Cir. 1987); *Grain Processing Corp. v. American Maize-Prods. Co.*, 840 F.2d 902, 907 (Fed. Cir. 1988) ("[Defendants'] effort to establish obviousness by showing that each element of the patented products may be found somewhere in the prior art is also unavailing. In determining [patentability], 'the inquiry is not whether each element existed in the prior art, but whether the prior art made obvious *the invention as a whole* for which patentability is claimed.'") (citations omitted).

Indeed, the Patent Office and courts recognize that few inventors create startlingly new devices *ex nihilo*; rather, most simply build upon the efforts of the prior art. The Patent Office even recognizes (but does not mandate) a special format for writing improvement claims so as to separate plainly the element of the claim which is simply the prior art, and the addition to that prior art element which is asserted to be the basis of patentable invention. *See Manual of Patent Examining Procedure* § 2129.

[104] *See* Section 18.05.

[105] 35 U.S.C. § 287(a).

[106] *Id.* In practice, a patentee who has failed to properly mark his product may only be able to recover those damages arising after the date of filing an infringement lawsuit, which could be only a fraction of the actual total infringement damages.

[107] 35 U.S.C. § 41(b).

[f] Enforcement. Enforcement of a valid patent takes place by a suit for patent infringement in federal district court.[108] Remedies potentially available to the owner of an infringed patent include: injunctions against infringement;[109] reasonable royalty damages or lost profits;[110] enhanced damages up to three times actual damages in the event of willful or deliberate infringement;[111] and, in exceptional cases, attorneys fees.[112] To date, little if any reported infringement litigation regarding electronic banking patents has taken place. The investments made by procurers of such patents, and the increasing interest of companies everywhere in suing to enforce their U.S. patents, suggests that such patents, once they have been in the marketplace long enough to spawn imitation or allegations of copying, will generate their share of lawsuits.

[4] AVOIDING PATENT INFRINGEMENT LIABILITY

Diligence is as important to preventing costly litigation or liability for infringement of another party's patent as it is to obtaining a patent portfolio of one's own. Liability for patent infringement arises when a party makes, uses, sells, or offers to sell an article exactly meeting the description of another party's patent claims, or differing from those claims in an only-insubstantial degree.[113]

In order to minimize the risk of patent infringement liability, a party should take the following into consideration.

[a] Awareness. Patents become publicly available immediately upon issuance. Technical and legal personnel should make an effort to keep abreast with patents currently in force within their technological field. While this may prove a daunting task as to the rapidly-developing electronic arts, there are commercial services and patent searching databases that can provide regular focused reports of newly-issued patents in particular technological categories.

[b] Designing Around. Assume a third-party patent has come to a financial institution's attention. It appears that the patent might cover electronic banking activities in which the institution is, or wishes to become, engaged. It may still prove possible to practice a device or process very similar to that of the claimed invention while avoiding infringement liability by "designing around" the patent. Designing around involves omitting or substantially modifying one or more key elements of the patent claims so as to assemble a device or

---

[108] 35 U.S.C. §§ 271, 284; 28 U.S.C. § 1338(a).

[109] 35 U.S.C. § 283; *Richardson v. Suzuki Motor Co.*, 868 F.2d 1226, 1247 (Fed. Cir.), *cert. denied*, 493 U.S. 853 (1989). As harm from ongoing infringement of a valid patent is presumptive, and likely to be severe and difficult to quantify, courts generally will grant permanent injunctions following a finding of infringement.

[110] 35 U.S.C. § 284; *Panduit Corp. v. Stahlin Bros. Fibre Works, Inc.*, 575 F.2d 1152, 1157-58 (6th Cir. 1978).

[111] *In re Hayes Microcomputer Prods., Inc. Patent Litig.*, 982 F.2d 1527, 1543 (Fed. Cir. 1992) (enumerating factors that would support a finding of willfulness infringement and imposition of multiple damages).

[112] 35 U.S.C. § 285; *see also Rohm & Haas Co. v. Crystal Chem. Co.*, 736 F.2d 688, 690 (Fed. Cir. 1984); *Kori Corp. v. Wilco Marsh Buggies & Draglines*, 761 F.2d 649, 656 (Fed. Cir.), *cert. denied*, 474 U.S. 902 (1985). Courts typically grant attorneys fees only in fairly egregious cases of willful infringement or abusive litigation.

[113] *Hilton Davis Chem. Co. v. Warner-Jenkinson Co.*, 62 F.3d 1512, 1518 (Fed. Cir. 1995), *aff'd in part, vacated in part*, 117 S. Ct. 1040 (1997), *remanded*, 114 F.3d 1161 (Fed. Cir. 1997).

process which, despite the modified or omitted element, still permits attainment of most or all of the desired advantages of the patented invention. Appropriately carried out, such "designing around" is a perfectly proper way to avoid infringement by not trespassing within the bounds marked off by the patentee's claims.

[c] Opinions of Counsel. One of the most fearsome spectres for companies operating in fields in which charges of patent infringement may arise, is the patent law's provision of the possibility of triple damages for willful patent infringement.[114] Fortunately, precedent establishes a relatively reliable safe harbor for institutions contemplating the vagaries of a jury considering charges of willful infringement. A defendant company that has obtained (preferably *before* commencement of the potentially-infringing activity or of litigation) a competent opinion of outside patent counsel stating that a particular patent issued to another party does not create infringement liability on the defendant company's part, will generally avoid imposition of enhanced damages, even if the opinion in hindsight turns out to have been ill-considered or inaccurate and defendant *is* found to have infringed.[115]

A soundly-reasoned analysis of a competitor's patent or patents by counsel schooled in patent prosecution and litigation can provide a legal defense to charges of willfulness in connection with later-commenced activity alleged to be willful. Such a legal opinion may also serve as a tool for avoiding *any* infringement liability. The opinion will often focus attention on the crucial patented elements of the invention, so as to permit effective designing around. In other cases, the opinion will establish that a company *cannot* hope to duplicate the desired features of the patented invention without infringing and so should simply refrain from any such effort. In this event, while the company is perhaps precluded from a entering a promising line of business, it is able to determine this fact at a far more modest price than that incurred in defending and losing an infringement trial.

§ 18.05   TRADE SECRETS

While trade secret law is probably not as important for financial institutions as copyright, trademark, and patent law, a basic understanding is helpful to further safeguard a financial institution's rights. Trade secret law protects information, such as technical or nontechnical data, formulae, patterns, compilations, programs, devices, methods, techniques, or processes, that provide some economic advantage to the owner and have not been made available to the public. A company may use trade secret laws to prevent another entity from stealing or utilizing company secrets. For the most part, trade secrets laws are creatures of state law.[116] Most states have adopted the Uniform Trade Secrets Act ("UTSA"), or a modified version thereof. The UTSA provides a range of remedies for trade secret misappropriation, including injunctive and monetary relief.[117]

---

[114] 35 U.S.C. § 284.

[115] *See Underwater Devices, Inc. v. Morrison-Knudsen Co.*, 717 F.2d 1380, 1389-90 (Fed. Cir. 1983).

[116] A federal criminal statute was enacted in 1995. *See* 18 U.S.C. § 1832.

[117] UNIF. TRADE SECRETS ACT §§ 2, 3 (1985 & 1990 Supp.).

The key concern under trade secret law for a financial institution with online banking activities is to ensure that it does not divulge to the public on its website, or by any other means, information that it may later wish to claim as proprietary. This is essential because under trade secret law an entity is required to make reasonable efforts under the circumstances to maintain the secrecy of the information that it claims as a trade secret.

§ 18.06 UNFAIR COMPETITION

In addition to trade secret laws, many states also proscribe, either by statute or common law, unfair competition.[118] Courts have construed this doctrine to include a wide range of conduct including: trademark/service mark infringement and dilution; use of confusingly similar trade names; use of confusing similar literary titles; appropriation of distinctive literary and entertainer characteristics; infringement of the right of publicity; "bait and switch" selling tactics; false advertising; "palming off" goods; theft of trade secrets; filing a frivolous lawsuit as a competitive weapon; an unreasonable rejection of goods shipped under contract; and obstructing the entrance to a competitor's place of business.[119]

Unfair competition is an additional, potential intellectual property related claim of which banks should be aware in maintaining online and other activity.

§ 18.07 DUE DILIGENCE

As recognition of the value of intellectual property rights grows, such rights play a greater and greater role in any corporate transaction entered into by a company. When technology-intensive (or copyright- and trademark-intensive) companies undertake stock or asset transactions, intellectual property rights of various sorts may be the driving force behind the transaction.[120] While intellectual property rights may not constitute as great a part of the value of financial institutions as of, say, semiconductor manufacturers, ensuring that due diligence includes attention to such rights remains important, particularly given the prevalence in recent years of mergers and consolidations in the banking industry.

The intellectual property due diligence inquiry has several dimensions. First, both purchaser and seller of a company or unit will desire accurate valuation of the intellectual property rights changing hands in order to set pricing for the deal. Such valuation is often the province of specialized accounting or audit practitioners.

---

[118] *See, e.g.,* CAL. BUS. & PROF. CODE §§ 17200 *et seq.* (defining "unfair competition" to include "any unlawful, unfair or fraudulent business act or practice and unfair, deceptive, untrue or misleading advertising").

[119] *See* MCCARTHY, *supra* note 30, § 1.10, at 1-22.

[120] *See* Christopher P. Bussert, *Acquisition and Sale of Intellectual Property, in Protecting Your Intellectual Property*, at 393, 397 (PLI Patents, Copyrights, Trademarks, and Literary Property Course Handbook Series No. G-468, 1997) ("In pursuing such a transaction, a primary goal of the parties' counsel and management is to ascertain what property rights the purchaser desires to acquire and what rights the seller is capable of delivering.").

More broadly, a desire to maximize long-term return on potential intellectual property acquisitions, and avoid assuming unforeseen liabilities, will animate any buyer's decision to investigate the legal state of the target's patent, trademark, copyright, and trade secret rights.

[1] EXTANT REGISTERED RIGHTS

A buyer should request a listing of all registered U.S. and foreign patents, trademarks, and copyrights used in connection with the seller's business. Counsel for the buyer should obtain and examine copies of the official registration documents (and, when pertinent, the records of the application process). The examination will look to such questions as: whether the seller still has good title to the patent, trademark, or copyright; whether any maintenance fees are currently paid up; and whether the registration has been canceled by the issuing authority or a court.

[2] PENDING AND UNREGISTERED RIGHTS

The buyer should also request a similar catalog of intellectual property rights and applications as to which prosecution is underway, or is not required (*e.g.,* common law trademarks or trade secrets). Again, counsel will scrutinize such records to assure the seller possesses a conveyable property right and has not forfeited or compromised the purported asset (*e.g.,* by running afoul of statutory bars, so as to doom a pending patent application; or by failing to maintain a putative trade secret in appropriate confidentiality).

[3] LICENSES

Owners and end-users of intellectual property rights often find it advantageous to enter into licensing agreements allowing the licensee to use the licensor's protected subject matter under specified conditions, often in exchange for a royalty indexed to the volume of the licensee's use of the subject matter. In complex technical fields, licensing and cross licensing often become necessary when no one player controls enough technology rights to market a product without making at least some use of another party's proprietary technology.[121]

Particularly in such a setting of extensive licensing, the buyer conducting due diligence for a corporate transaction must assure himself that the seller has not given third parties freedom under license agreements to use intellectual property rights the buyer believes he is obtaining on an exclusive basis. Conversely, the buyer must investigate any intellectual property licenses from third parties under which the seller purports to be operating to ensure the licenses are sound and will protect the buyer from any infringement charges on the part of the owner of third party rights.

---

[121] Sometimes, owing to the uncertainty of the scope or enforceability of various parties' technology rights, and a risk-averse desire to avoid litigation, parties enter into reciprocal technology cross licenses bearing essentially no royalties. While such arrangements might appear less than optimal if one is viewing a patent portfolio as a source of significant cash flow, many companies find the certainty provided by such arrangements, and the avoidance of disruptive and expensive litigation, to be significant, albeit difficult to quantify, benefits justifying a no-fee cross license.

[4] INFRINGEMENT CLAIMS

The buyer should obtain any correspondence the seller has received alleging that the seller is infringing a third party's intellectual property rights, or threatening suit for such infringement. The buyer may be able to ascertain likelihood of such suits by review of non-infringement opinions already in the seller's files, but in some cases the buyer may have to conduct its own search for latent liabilities of the seller, or commission its own expert counsel opinions on infringement and other topics relating to the seller's activities.

[5] WARRANTIES AND REPRESENTATIONS – INDEMNIFICATION

Buyers quite frequently require that sellers provide warranties and representations in connection with intellectual property conveyed. These warranties generally contain extensive recitation of the seller's rights in the asset, the absence of any known legal impediments to enforcement of the intellectual property rights, and kindred matters. Other contractual means of providing buyers with peace of mind include indemnification by the seller. The seller may contractually undertake to make the buyer whole for any litigation damages suffered on account of stepping into the seller's shoes and inheriting infringement liability, or other infirmities, in connection with the intellectual property and overall business conveyed by the seller.

§ 18.08 OTHER INTELLECTUAL PROPERTY CONSIDERATIONS

There are other intellectual property issues that are implicated by online banking activities that are not limited to the various disciplines of intellectual property law.

[1] LINKING

One unique feature of the Internet that banks must consider when analyzing intellectual property concerns is the ability of users to "link." Linking is generally understood as the ability to "click" on an icon and leap from that page in the site to another, either within the same site or in an unrelated site. It is common practice on the Internet for website hosts to provide links from their sites to the home pages of third parties. However, a practice that has recently been challenged and may ultimately be judged by courts to be impermissible is for a website host to provide a link to a page beyond the home page of a third party site. Among other concerns, this allows a user to jump past the advertisements and legal notice on the third party's home page.[122]

---

[122] The issue of unauthorized linking was raised by Ticketmaster in a case filed against Microsoft on April 28, 1997, which is presently pending. *See Ticketmaster Corp. v. Microsoft Corp.*, CV 97-3055 RAP (C.D. Ca., filed Apr. 28, 1997) (the Amended Complaint is available at <http://www.ljx.com/LJXfiles/ticketmaster>). In addition, at least one state statutorily attempted to prohibited unauthorized linking. *See* GA. STAT. CODE ANN. § 16-9-93.1. Enforcement of the statute was enjoined, however, when it was challenged on First Amendment grounds. *See American Civil Liberties Union of Georgia v. Miller*, Civ. A. 1:96CV2475MHS, 1997 WL 552487, at *5 (N.D. Ga. June 23, 1997). The court implied in a footnote that the statute would, among other things, unconstitutionally prohibit the use of web page links. *Id.* at *3 n.5.

By obtaining permission from the party hosting the linked site, a site that offers links to other sites can protect itself from unauthorized-linking claims. Additionally, linked sites should be visited regularly to determine whether continued linking is desirable.

It has also become common practice for site operators who offer links to disclaim any endorsement or responsibility for the content of linked sites. Banks that provide links to other sites should consider including such a disclaimer, along with any other legal notices, on their sites.

[2]   FRAMING

"Framing" is another feature of the Internet. Framing permits a second website to be viewed through a frame on a first website. Like linking, framing can be an issue for banks concerned about trademark and copyright infringement because the Uniform Resource Locator or website address does not change while a site is being framed. This creates the impression that the first website is an authorized provider of the framed content, when in fact it may not be.

In *Washington Post Co. v. Total News,* Total News' website featured a list of news services, identified by their trademarks, such as CNN® Interactive, The Washington Post, Time, The Los Angeles Times, Dow Jones and Co., and Reuters.[123] The Total News' site allowed the browser to click in the news service and its content appeared within the content window on the Total News site. When the framed site's content loaded, however, its advertisements were replaced by the Total News advertising banner. Several of the news services sued for trademark infringement arguing that a viewer could easily confuse the advertisements seen on Total News as those endorsed by the news services and vice versa. The case settled when Total News agreed to cease framing the news services websites in exchange for permission to link to the respective news sites using a method that did not obscure advertisements.[124]

There are preventive measures that a bank can undertake in order to prevent undesired framing. These included programming that prevents a site from being "framed" into a third party's site.

[3]   META-TAGS

Another arena for potential disputes on the Internet is over the unauthorized use of trademarks in "meta-tags." The text and graphics on a website contain hidden tags and markers that are written in hypertext markup language or HTML and cannot be perceived by website visitors. Certain tags known as "meta-tags" may be used to designate words identifiable to search engines. A website operator can bury a well-known competitor's name in its meta-tags so that, upon performing a search, Internet users will find its site, along with the well-known competitor's site.

---

[123] *Washington Post Co. v. Total News,* No. 97-1190 (S.D.N.Y. 1997).

[124] *See* Martin H. Samson, *Hyperlink at Your Own Risk,* N.Y.L.J., June 24, 1997, at 1; *Total News Inc. Deal Reached in Copyright over Web Sites,* CHI. TRIB., June 6, 1997, at 2.

Because this tactic is relatively new, very few courts have addressed its propriety. However, at least one court found it to be improper. In *Playboy Enterprises Inc. v. Calvin Designer Label*, the court preliminarily enjoined the defendants from, among other things, "using in any manner the PLAYMATE® or PLAYBOY® trademarks . . . in buried code or meta-tags on their home page or Web pages . . . ."[125] In granting the injunction, the court determined that plaintiff was likely to succeed in establishing trademark infringement and unfair competition.[126] Financial institutions should be aware that this tactic might be used by competitors and be vigilant.[127]

[4]   CONTRIBUTORY INFRINGEMENT

Another concern that arises with hosting a website is contributory infringement. In two recent cases, a computer bulletin board operator and a service provider were held contributorily liable for the infringing activities of their users. First, in *Sega Enterprises Ltd. v. MAPHIA*, an operator of a computer bulletin board was found liable for contributory copyright and trademark infringement when it allowed its users to upload and download Sega games through its bulletin board service.[128] Similarly, in *Religious Technology Center v. Netcom OnLine Communication Services, Inc.*, the court held that a service provider could be liable for a subscriber's infringement if the service provider knew of the infringing activity.[129] Prudence and common sense, along with the above cases, indicate that institutions should take care to avoid being placed in a position where they might appear to be condoning infringing activity by any entity in association with their websites.

[5]   WEBWRAPS

Among other considerations, banking institutions that operate websites should carefully consider the type of legal notice given in connection with their site. Obviously, a balance is required between protection of the institution's rights and discouraging end-users from visiting the site or undertaking online banking activities.

Banks that offer sophisticated online services should consider including a "webwrap" on their home page. A "webwrap" agreement in this context is a license agreement between a bank and the end-users of its website that sets forth the terms and conditions associated with use of the website. Although there is little case law at present addressing the enforceability of "webwrap" agreements, courts are likely to look to the precedent of shrink-wrap license agreements that are commonly used in connection with software. In *ProCD v. Zeidenberg*,[130] the Court of Appeals for the Seventh Circuit endorsed the use of a shrink-wrap license agreements under certain conditions. Applying the reasoning to online agreements, website hosts should ensure that

---

[125] *Playboy Enterprises Inc. v. Calvin Designer Label*, 1997 U.S. Dist. LEXIS 14345 (D. Cal. Sept. 8, 1997).

[126] *Id.*

[127] *See generally* Martin J. Elgison et al., *Trademark Cases Arise From Meta-Tags, Frames*, NAT'L L.J., Oct. 20, 1997, at C6.

[128] *Sega Enterprises Ltd. v. MAPHIA*, 948 F. Supp. 923 (N.D. Cal. 1996).

[129] *Religious Technology Center v. Netcom OnLine Communication Services, Inc.*, 907 F. Supp. 1361 (N.D. Cal. 1995).

[130] *ProCD v. Zeidenberg*, 86 F.3d 1447 (7th Cir. 1996).

site visitors are: (i) put on notice of the license agreement; (ii) provided with an opportunity to review the terms of the agreement prior to acceptance; and (iii) required to do some affirmative act (such as click on an "I accept" link), or be denied further access to the site. Institutions that intend to have visitors to their websites register and select a log-in name and password can set up their systems so that customers are only required to indicate their assent to the terms during the first log-in. After that point, the terms should be available behind a "Terms" icon on the home page, or elsewhere.

CHAPTER 19

THE CONFLUENCE OF INTERNATIONAL, FEDERAL, AND STATE JURISDICTION OVER INTERNET COMMERCE

§ 19.01   INTRODUCTION

The Internet is becoming the most ubiquitous telecommunications system the world has ever known. Its use of the existing and expanding telecommunications network for data transmissions has permitted the Internet to transcend state and national borders, increasing the globalization of information-intensive industries such as capital markets, news media, and computer applications. As financial institutions and other commercial entities venture forth into this marketplace, they must consider that their activities may unintentionally subject them to jurisdiction in states or nations far removed from the ones in which they typically consider themselves to be operating.

This Chapter surveys a range of issues relating to a sovereign's regulation of conduct within its territory, and limitations on the extraterritorial reach of a sovereign's statutes and its courts. Section 19.02 provides a summary of the nature of Internet communications and their effect on jurisdictional issues. Section 19.03 discusses issues pertaining to the international regulation of the Internet and the activities of various entities vis-à-vis a foreign forum.[1] Section 19.04 discusses the authority of the United States to regulate the Internet under the Commerce Clause and, by negative implication, the limitation the Commerce Clause places on individual states' ability to regulate interstate commerce. Finally, Section 19.05 discusses the authority of state courts to subject a foreign party to jurisdiction under state "long arm" statutes and the Due Process Clause of the U.S. Constitution.

---

[1]   Unless otherwise noted, "state" refers to one of the fifty states that comprise the United States of America. When referring to countries other than the United States, we refer to "nations" or "foreign states." "Forum" refers to a state or nation whose courts seek to assert their jurisdiction over a "foreign party." "Foreign party" refers to any person or entity that is not a citizen or resident of the forum, *e.g.,* a resident of the state of Montana is a foreign party when subject to the jurisdiction of an Idaho court.

§ 19.02   THE NATURE OF THE INTERNET

The Internet is a global network where local computer networks are connected to regional networks that combine to form national and international high capacity systems.[2] Communications between computers on the Internet are in the machine languages known as Internet Protocols ("IP").[3] Communications in IP eliminate geographic barriers by way of a packet switching network and "smart communications."

Transmissions over the Internet utilize a packet switching network that breaks up a communication into distinct packets of data that can be transmitted individually as capacity on the network connections permit. Each packet is labeled with the "address" of the final destination. A single transmission may follow a number of different routes from computer to computer until arriving at its final destination, where the packets are reassembled by the recipient computer server.[4] A stream of packets on one channel between two computers may carry parts of an e-mail message to an intended recipient within the same state, interspersed with parts of a software program downloaded from a server in another state, to a user in Tokyo along with a myriad of other packets that are parts of communications in the stream of data traversing the Internet worldwide.

The Internet architecture employs "smart communications." Every link in the network of computers is capable of using computer intelligence to monitor packet traffic on the network and route packets along the least congested route to the next computer. This process is generally repeated.[5] Each computer determines whether to send packets along a channel, to hold packets pending reduction of network traffic, or to reroute packets of data via different channels to their ultimate destination to maximize use of the available carrying capacity of the Internet. In sum, a single communication has the potential to be broken up into separate packets and sent through several different jurisdictions before reaching its final destination. With the exception of the jurisdiction in which the communication originates, and the jurisdiction in which the communication is received, only segments of the communication may pass "through" computer servers located in other territories, but not the entire communication.

Generally, there is no centralized control of data transmissions over the Internet. Each computer acts autonomously, coordinating data flow with its nearest connected computers, guided by the "invisible hand"

---

2   *See* Dan L. Burk, *Federalism in Cyberspace*, 28 CONN. L. REV. 1095, 1097 (1996).

3   *See id.* (citing *A Close-up of Transmission Control of Transmission Control Protocol/Internet Protocol (TCP/IP)*, DATAMATION (Aug. 1, 1988); ED KROL & PAULA FERGUSON, THE WHOLE INTERNET FOR WINDOWS 95 (1995)).

4   The address is not a geographical location such as a street address, but rather a logical address that designates a particular computer server that may be relocated in any part of the country or the world while retaining its same logical address. *See id.*

5   *See Is the Internet Ready for Prime Time? Skeptics Have Field Day With Shutdown*, ELECTRONIC MESSAGING NEWS, Aug. 6, 1997 (describing the one day shutdown caused by human error, in which modifications to one server's messaging system, in essence, communicated to the rest of the Internet that it had no traffic flow causing other computers to redirect their packets through that server, which caused an overload and enormous traffic at that server).

that arises from the interconnection of millions of independent actions on the Internet.[6] Though one author states that "there is no central authority to govern Internet usage, no one to ask for permission to join the network, and no one to complain to when things go wrong,"[7] the government of the People's Republic of China is making efforts to control the Internet within its borders.[8] However, the ability of a totalitarian regime to control of the free flow of information must also contend with the "telepresence" of the Internet.

Telepresence is the IP method of extending scattered resources to users worldwide without regard to geographic location. The Internet community frequently expands available resources by establishing "mirror sites," which are computer databases with precise replicas of the information stored on the original site. Depending on local data traffic, access to a distant mirror site may be faster than waiting in the congestion for the original site that may be closer geographically.[9] The Chinese government's effort to block out certain computer sites deemed "harmful" to its regime must also contend with mirror sites equally accessible from the Internet containing the same "harmful" information.[10]

§ 19.03 INTERNATIONAL SOVEREIGNTY AND COMITY

The sovereign authority of individual nations to assert jurisdiction over Internet activities within their own geographic borders is beyond question. Their practical ability to do so is a different matter altogether, given the borderless nature of the Internet. Complications arise when a nation's regulation of the Internet concerns foreign parties whose activities on the Internet may or may not be directed towards that nation. The prospect of inadvertently subjecting oneself to the regulation of a foreign nation should be of concern to financial institutions and Internet merchants alike. This Section addresses some of the legal issues implicated by such conflicting regulation.

[1] CRIMINAL JURISDICTION UNDER INTERNATIONAL LAW

There are a number of grounds for jurisdiction over extraterritorial crimes that are commonly recognized under International law. These include: (1) territorial jurisdiction, premised on the place where the offense was committed; (2) national jurisdiction, premised on the offender's nationality; (3) protective jurisdiction,

---

6   See Chapter 3, Section 3.02[2] for a description of the "invisible hand" at work in decentralized economic systems in which the economy attains coherence without centralized control.

7   Burk, *supra* note 2, at 1098.

8   *See* Section 19.03[4][a]. *See also* Greg Caressi, *China Begins*, ASIA COMPUTER WKLY., Sept. 1, 1997; Paul Gilster, *Internet Regulation Won't Come from Top*, NEWS & OBSERVER, Nov. 11, 1997, at D2.

9   *See* Burk, *supra* note 2, at 1098. "Caching" is the method by which servers on the Internet store partial or complete duplicates of frequently-accessed resources from a variety of sites on the Internet. This reduces the frequency of contact the original site has with the multitudes of Internet users worldwide. There is generally no method for distinguishing between cached materials and the original. *See American Library Ass'n v. Pataki*, 969 F. Supp. 160, 171 (S.D.N.Y. 1997).

10   *See China Holds Centralized Control of Internet: Interview*, NIKKEI ENG. NEWS, Mar. 12, 1997. *See also The Cutting Edge; Testing the Boundaries; Countries Face Cyber Control in their Own Ways*, L.A. TIMES, June 30, 1997, at D1 (discussing requirements placed on users of the Internet in China, including signing a written pledge not to "harm" Chinese national interests).

based on whether the national interest is injured; (4) universal jurisdiction, conferred in any forum that obtains physical custody of the perpetrator of certain offenses considered particularly heinous and harmful to humanity; and (5) passive personal jurisdiction, premised on the victim's nationality.[11] These principles must be considered in regard to a court's assertion of jurisdiction relating to Internet activities.

[2] APPLICATION OF PRINCIPLES OF INTERNATIONAL JURISDICTION TO THE INTERNET

The borderless nature of the Internet seemingly could confer territorial jurisdiction over every website and web page by every sovereign entity throughout the world because websites are capable of being accessed in every location in the world. For example, a website maintained in Antigua by an Antiguan Internet bank for the purpose of soliciting and accepting deposits worldwide could, arguably, subject the bank to assertions of jurisdiction by countries throughout the world. In fact, political subdivisions of sovereign nations could assert jurisdiction premised on the notion that the solicitation occurred within the territory of that political subdivision, simply because the Internet permeated that subdivision's borders. This was precisely the case in regard to the European Union Bank ("EUB") of Antigua.

[a] **European Union Bank and the Solicitation of Deposits in Idaho.** In 1997, the State of Idaho issued a cease and desist order, based on violations of Idaho banking law, in which it prohibited EUB from soliciting deposits from Idaho residents via the World Wide Web.[12] The Idaho banking authorities noted that the EUB was not FDIC-insured and found that it had violated two Idaho statutes[13] that prohibit the solicitation of deposits by any entity that is not chartered as a bank under the laws of Idaho or the United States. It appears

---

[11] *United States v. Yunis*, 681 F. Supp. 896, 899-900 (D.D.C. 1988) (finding United States jurisdiction over a foreign hijacker of a foreign registered airplane that never flew over U.S. soil based on the presence of three U.S. nationals aboard and universal recognition that hijacking airplanes is a heinous crime harmful to humanity). The five general principles listed were developed in 1935 by a Harvard Research Project in an effort to codify principles of jurisdiction under international law. *See* Harvard Research in International Law, *Jurisdiction with Respect to Crime*, 29 AM. J. INT'L L. 435, 445 (Supp. 1935).

[12] *See* Maria Seminerio, *These Banks May Be Virtual, But the Crime Is Real*, Aug. 22, 1997, *available at* (visited Jan. 9, 1998) <http://www.zdnet.com.au/zdnn/content/zdnn/0821/zdnn0003.html> (although not noted in the cease and desist order, Gavin Gee, Director of the Idaho Department of Finance, received notice from several Idaho residents regarding e-mail solicitations for deposits from European Union Bank).

[13] Section 26-202 of the Idaho Code states, in relevant part:

> It shall be unlawful for any person to engage in or transact any banking business in this state except by means of a corporation duly organized for that purpose and chartered under the bank act .... Except as specifically authorized by other laws of the state of Idaho, no person except a national bank shall engage in or transact any banking business except as is incidental or necessarily preliminary to its organization without the written approval of the director and without his written charter stating that it has complied with the provisions the bank act and all of the requirements of law and that it is authorized to transact banking business within the state.

> IDAHO CODE § 26-202. Idaho law contains a second prohibition on unauthorized banking which states that:

> It shall be unlawful for any person to engage in soliciting, receiving or accepting money or its equivalent on deposit as a regular business whether such deposit, however evidenced, is made subject to check or draft or other order unless such activity is specifically authorized by statute. Any person violating any provision of this section shall be guilty of a felony.

> *Id.* § 26-1201.

that Idaho acted because of concerns regarding EUB's integrity.[14] Shortly after Idaho's action, Antiguan banking authorities closed the institution.[15] Although Idaho's action was aimed at an offshore "rogue" institution, the statutes upon which Idaho relied do not expressly limit their potential applicability to a broader range of financial institutions.

Idaho's assertion of jurisdiction based on accessibility to, and apparent use by, Idaho residents of a foreign webpage raises potential issues for U.S.-sponsored websites that are accessed in foreign countries. For example, if a U.S. financial institution established a relationship with new customers in country X by virtue of X's residents downloading the financial institution's website and engaging in transactions, country X might contend that the interactive communications constituted the basis for exercise of jurisdiction over that U.S. institution. Thus, at a minimum, institutions utilizing websites should consider the various implications of doing Internet-initiated business with residents of other jurisdictions.[16] Foreign laws applicable to particular transactions may differ dramatically from those laws the institution assumes to be applicable. For example, Iranian law forbids the charging of interests on loans, although it does permit lending via discounted notes.[17]

[3]   WELLS FARGO BANK, N.A. AND THE MARKETING OF LOANS TO CANADA

A recent development regarding permissible U.S. financial institution lending activities "in" Canada illustrates some of the considerations raised by transnational banking activities. In what U.S. and Canadian banking institutions viewed as a significant development, Canadian banking authorities permitted Wells Fargo Bank to begin soliciting Canadian small businesses for loans.[18] Under its new program, Wells Fargo has not established a physical presence in Canada; it conducts all of its operations from its U.S. headquarters in California.[19] Wells Fargo solicits potential Canadian borrowers via direct mail and telemarketing. It may eventually use the Internet.[20] In order to satisfy the Canadian banking regulator, the Office of the Superintendent of Financial Institutions ("OFSI"), Well Fargo had to alter its business strategy to exclude any operations

---

[14]   These concerns were detailed in an article that discussed the escalating money laundering and connections to organized crime that off-shore banks in various Caribbean Islands have been experiencing, including concerns expressed by U.S. and British banking regulators. Douglas Farah, *Russian Crime Finds Haven in Caribbean; Colombian Drug Ties Suspected As Secretive Banks Proliferate*, WASH. POST, Oct. 7, 1996, at A15. In a response to the report by the Washington Post, the Bank of England issued a warning to its citizens concerning depositing their funds in the European Union Bank. Norma Cohen, *Investors Told to be Wary of Bank*, FIN. TIMES, Oct. 11, 1996, at 10.

[15]   *See* Mark Fineman, *Antigua's Loosely Regulated Internet Casinos Alarm Critics; After Collapse of Online Bank*, BUFFALO NEWS, Sept. 22, 1997, at 3A; Larry Rohter, *Failed Bank Puts Antigua in Hot Spot*, INT'L HERALD TRIB., Aug. 21, 1997, at 1; Emile Valere, *Fraud Feared as Antigua Net Bank Fails*, Aug. 6, 1997, *available at* (visited Jan. 6, 1998) <http://nytsyn.com/live/Latest/218_080697_110027_578.html>.

[16]   For example, foreign banks that have entered into written agreements with the U.S. bank regulators not to solicit deposits in the United States may find themselves prohibited from accepting deposits via the Internet.

[17]   *See generally* Kamran M. Dadkhah, *Foreign Investment in Iran and the Tehran Stock Exchange*, MIDDLE E. EXECUTIVE REP., June 1997, at 9.

[18]   *See* Richard Blackwell, *Under Siege: So What?: While Ottawa is Relaxing Barriers for Foreign Banks the Domestic Players' Hold on Retail Banking is not Likely to be Challenged*, FIN. POST, Oct. 4, 1997, at 12.

[19]   *See id.*; Sara Nathan, *Wells Blitzes Canada, Offering 100,000 Prequalified Loans*, AM. BANKER, Sept. 29, 1997, at 17; *Wells Fargo Offers $50 Million to Canadian Small Businesses; Launches First Phase of Direct Lending Program With Loans From $15,000 to $75,000*, BUS. WIRE, Sept. 22, 1997.

[20]   *See* Bertran Marotte, *Robbing the Banks: No-Frills Competitors are Stealing Customers Out From Under the Big Banks' Noses*, OTTAWA CITIZEN, Dec. 26, 1997, at E1.

within Canada, so as not to require a Canadian banking license. Rather than mailing loan applications from Canadian mailhouses, collecting payments in Canada, conducting telephone support in Canada, and allowing borrowers to access their lines of credit from Canadian Automated Teller Machines, Wells Fargo had to switch to a fully U.S.-based operation.[21]

In September 1997, the OFSI issued a consultation paper on foreign banks operating in Canada. In that paper, the OFSI raised the issue of cross-border banking and alluded to a range of potential changes to foreign bank operation, such as increased disclosure requirements, increased regulations on cross-border deposit solicitations, or even a complete ban on cross-border solicitations altogether.[22] Wells Fargo has reportedly taken the position that a ban on cross-border solicitation is without justification,[23] and would probably contravene the North American Free Trade Agreement.[24]

[4] NONBANK INTERNET ACTIVITIES AND FOREIGN REGULATION

Governments throughout the world are concerned about the potential impact of the Internet. In a number of instances, Governments have acted either to limit their citizens' use of the Internet, to restrict their website access, or to determine the type of content that they may access.

[a] **China.** China aggressively regulates the Internet,[25] by imposing strict conditions on citizens' rights to access to the Internet.[26] Prodigy, a U.S.-based Internet Service Provider ("ISP"), recently obtained permission to offer Internet service to subscribers within China. [27] In exchange for the right to operate within China, Prodigy installed software to "screen out" websites containing content that the Chinese government deems unfit.[28] The Chinese government requires all domestic organizations doing business via the Internet to apply for licenses from the government.[29] Applicants must provide information on the nature and scope of their networks

---

[21] *See* Richard Blackwell, *Wells Fargo Wants Ottawa to Clarify Banking Guidelines*, FIN. POST, Nov. 12, 1997, at 7. Also, in an apparent effort to satisfy Canadian banking regulators following informal discussions, Wells Fargo agreed not to pursue e-mail or Internet marketing of loans.

[22] *See id.* Although Canada may be seeking increased regulation of cross-border solicitations, proposals have been offered to amend the Canadian Bank Act to ease entry by foreign banks into Canada. Under the proposed modifications to the Bank Act, foreign banks would be allowed to set up branches directly owned by their parent banks, instead of having to set up a separately capitalized depository institution subsidiary. This will allow foreign banks the ability to package loans based on their parents' capital rather than based solely on the Canadian subsidiary's capital. The modifications do not propose, however, to allow foreign branches to take deposits, requiring instead that the deposit-taking business be conducted by separately capitalized subsidiaries. *See* Blackwell, *Under Siege, supra* note 18.

[23] *See* Blackwell, *Wells Fargo Wants Ottawa to Clarify Banking Guidelines, supra* note 21.

[24] *See* North American Free Trade Agreement Implementation Act, Pub. L. No. 103-182, 1993 U.S.C.C.A.N. (107 Stat.) 2057 (codified at 19 U.S.C. §§ 3301 *et seq.*). *See Proceedings of the Standing Senate Committee on Banking, Trade and Commerce* (Oct. 3, 1996) (Can.), *available at* (visited Jan. 30, 1998) <http://parl30.parl.gc.ca/english/senate/com-e/bank-e/11eva-e.htm> (hearing examining the state of the financial system in Canada, wherein counsel for Wells Fargo testified that it was her view that cross border marketing of loans would violate Chapter 14 of NAFTA).

[25] *See* Leonard R. Sussman, *The Hunt is On for Watchdogs Media: There Is A Frenzy Of New Anti-Press Law World-Wide, All Inching Closer To Censorship*, L.A. TIMES, June 2, 1997, at A5. Other Asian countries, such as Singapore and Indonesia, also aggressively regulate the Internet. *Id.*

[26] *See China Holds Centralized Control of Internet: Interview*, NIKKEI ENG. NEWS, Mar. 12, 1997.

[27] *See Prodigy Sets Up Shop In China*, INFO. & INTERACTIVE SERV. REP., May 2, 1997.

[28] *See id.*

[29] *See* Francesco Lao Xi Sisci, *Learning the Information Highway Code*, ASIA TIMES, June 2, 1997, at 4.

and the addresses of their computer hosts.[30] Offenders may be shut down and fined up to US $1,800.[31] In addition, all Internet users must register with the police.[32]

[b] Germany. Recently, German authorities indicted a CompuServe executive on criminal charges of "aiding" in the distribution of pornography.[33] The German government deems ISPs that fail to block pornography and other banned material from German subscribers to be aiding in the commission of criminal activities.[34] The CompuServe case represents the first instance in which an ISP, or its officers, have faced potential criminal liability for enabling subscribers to gain access to material banned under German law.[35] In 1995, CompuServe had agreed to block banned materials.[36] Critics suggest that CompuServe paved the way for enforcement of the censorship law, because it implied that it is feasible to block Internet content.[37]

[c] France. French law prohibits the use of the Internet for sexual exploitation of children or dissemination of racist propaganda.[38] It also bans encrypted communications under a 1990 law that reserves cryptography to military use.[39] In addition, it is illegal for a website operator to advertise, offer, or describe a service or product offered in France solely in English.[40] In January 1997, two French-language associations dedicated to the preservation of France's linguistic purity sued Georgia Tech Lorraine, a French university affiliated with the Georgia Institute of Technology, claiming that it violated the 1994 French law that prohibits advertising in any language other than French by operating English-language sites on the World Wide Web. The suit was dismissed on procedural grounds because the complaint should have first been filed with administrative authorities.[41]

[d] Comity of Nations. The ability to transcend national borders with communications, advertisements, and business transactions via the Internet may theoretically subject financial institutions, merchants, and other users to a myriad of national and local statutes, thus increasing the legal and financial uncertainty for all Internet commerce. One nation's desire to enforce its laws must be balanced against other nations' desires to enforce their own laws.[42] In the international context, when two applicable laws conflict, one country's

---

[30] *See id.*

[31] *See id.*

[32] *See The Cutting Edge, supra* note 10.

[33] *See CompuServe Executive Indicted,* INFO. & INTERACTIVE SERV. REP., Apr. 25, 1997.

[34] *See id.*

[35] *See* Louise Kehoe & Paul Taylor, *Long Arm of the Law Catches Up with the Internet,* FIN. POST, Apr. 25, 1997, at 53.

[36] *See id.*

[37] *See id.*

[38] *See The Cutting Edge, supra* note 10.

[39] *See id.*

[40] *See id.;* Wendy R. Leibowitz, *National Laws Entangle the Net: It's a Small, Small, Litigious Web,* NAT. L.J., June, 30, 1997, at B7.

[41] *See* Leibowitz, *supra* note 40; *see also Pataki,* 969 F. Supp. at 168 n.4.

[42] *See* VED P. NANDA & DAVID K PANSIUS, LITIGATION OF INTERNATIONAL DISPUTES IN U.S. COURTS, 5-1 to 5-2 (Release #9, 1996).

laws must yield to the other's.[43] Extraterritorial jurisdiction of the U.S. federal government recognizes the applicability of foreign laws and their potential conflict with U.S. statutes.[44] Generally, U.S. courts seek to balance application of U.S. laws to avoid undue intrusion into the affairs of other sovereign nations.[45] Though other nations may seek to apply their existing laws beyond their territory, "it is a long-standing principle of American law that legislation of Congress, unless a contrary intent appears, is meant to apply only within the territorial jurisdiction of the United States."[46] This legal principle, however, does not solve the problem. The Internet, by its very nature, transmits data worldwide into the territory of each and every nation that has access to the Internet, including the United States.

§ 19.04 THE FEDERAL GOVERNMENT AND THE COMMERCE CLAUSE

The United States Constitution grants express powers to a centralized government to represent the composite interests of the states that make up the Union. James Madison wrote over 200 years ago that if "we are to be one nation in any respect, it clearly ought to be in respect to other nations."[47] In that vein, the federal government was granted control over foreign relations, and specifically, Congress was granted the power to regulate commerce with foreign nations and among the states.[48] State and local governments, however, have increasingly interjected themselves into varying aspects of foreign affairs.[49] In a critique of local government's increasing involvement in foreign relations, one commentator states: "[t]he national interest demands that local interference in foreign and defense policy be curtailed before the federal government finds itself hamstrung by hundreds of would-be secretaries of state touting their own parochial agendas . . . . Foreign policy must be made in Washington and not in the citizens' backyards."[50]

---

[43] The *Restatement of Law of Foreign Relations* sets forth a reasonableness standard for determining which country must yield. After evaluating all relevant factors for determining reasonableness of jurisdiction, a country should defer to the other country if that country's interest is "clearly greater." RESTATEMENT (THIRD) OF THE FOREIGN RELATIONS LAW OF THE UNITED STATES § 403 (1987).

[44] *See* NANDA & PANSIUS, *supra* note 42, at 5-2.

[45] *See id.* Remedies should be tailored "to avoid undue interference with the domestic activities of other sovereign nations." *Republic of Philippines v. Westinghouse Elec. Corp.*, 43 F.3d 65, 75 (3d Cir. 1994).

[46] *EEOC v. Arabian American Oil Co.*, 499 U.S. 244, 248 (1991) (quoting *Foley Bros., Inc. v. Filardo*, 336 U.S. 281, 285 (1949)). *See also Smith v. United States*, 507 U.S. 197, 204 (1993).

[47] THE FEDERALIST NO. 42 (James Madison).

[48] U.S. CONST. art I, § 8, cl. 3.

[49] *See* Richard B. Bilder, *The United States Constitution in its Third Century: Foreign Affairs: Distribution of Constitutional Authority: The Role of States and Cities in Foreign Relations*, 83 AM. J. INT'L L. 821 (1989) (noting that over 1000 state and local governments participate in varying aspects of foreign affairs).

[50] *Id.* (quoting Peter J. Spiro, *Taking Foreign Policy Away From the Feds*, WASH. Q., No.1, 1988, at 191, 202-03).

Congressional statutes concerning foreign commerce prevail over any contrary state statutes.[51] The Commerce Clause is more than an affirmative grant of power to the U.S. Congress, it has a negative implication as well;[52] in the absence of federal law, state regulations or taxes are invalid if they unduly burden interstate or foreign commerce.[53] In a lawsuit involving a state's infringement of *foreign* commerce, rather than *interstate* commerce, a court will look to whether the state or local law prevents the federal government from speaking "with one voice when regulating commercial relations with foreign governments," among other factors.[54]

The Internet creates a conundrum because states seeking to regulate Internet commerce within their territories may be viewed as seeking to regulate the Internet worldwide. In this facet, the Commerce Clause restricts an individual state's interference with commerce. Section 19.04[1] examines New York's attempt to regulate the Internet and examines the difficulty of determining the geographic location of an Internet user. Section 19.04[2] discusses a line of cases involving situations where states have sought to extend the territorial effect of their statutes beyond their state borders. Section 19.04[3] reviews judicial precedent which recognizes that some state statutes enacted for legitimate purposes still violate the Commerce Clause under a balancing test weighing the state's interest against the burden on interstate commerce. Finally, Section 19.04[4] discusses various methods by which an Internet merchant or financial institution could attempt to limit the potential to be subject to multi-jurisdictional regimes.

[1]   THE INTERNET AS A RAILROAD OR "SUPERHIGHWAY"

As U.S. courts confront a state's application of its laws to the Internet, judges will naturally seek to determine the most appropriate analogy for the application of existing legal principles to activity on the Internet. In mid-1997, a federal court in New York, in the case of *American Library Association v. Pataki ("Pataki")*,

---

51 The Constitution provides that the laws and treaties of the United States are "the supreme law of the land" and preempt state law, international agreements, and federal determinations and interpretations of customary international law. U.S. CONST, art. VI, cl. 2. In determining whether a Congressional statute preempts state or local laws, courts determine whether the federal statute embodied the "clear and manifest purpose of Congress" to preempt the entire subject area covered by the state statute or whether by implicit legislative design, states were precluded from entering that field of law. *See Jones v. Rath Packing Co.,* 430 U.S. 519, 525 (1977); *Burbank v. Lockheed Air Terminal,* 411 U.S. 624, 633 (1973); *Rice v. Santa Fe Elevator Corp.,* 331 U.S. 218, 230 (1947). Though the Court has upheld a wide variety of statutes that regulate intrastate economic activity that substantially affect interstate commerce, the Supreme Court has struck down federal statutes that intrude upon intrastate matters that do not touch the economy or commerce amongst the states. *See United States v. Lopez,* 514 U.S. 549 (1995) (finding unconstitutional a federal statute regarding firearm possession in proximity to schools, on the basis that it was not a valid exercise of Congress' authority under the Commerce Clause because it did not regulate commercial activity or economic interests).

52 *Gibbons v. Ogden,* 22 U.S. (9 Wheat.) 1, 231-32 (1824) (Johnson, J., concurring). The negative implication of the Commerce Clause is also known as the "dormant" Commerce Clause.

53 For a discussion of the application of the Commerce Clause to the imposition of taxes on Internet commerce, see Chapter 10, Section 10.05[2][b][ii]. *See Philadelphia v. New Jersey,* 437 U.S. 617 (1978) (striking down a New Jersey statute that prohibited the importation into the state any wastes which originated outside the territorial limits of New Jersey). The Supreme Court noted that it not only looks to a state's purpose in whether or not the statute is discriminatory, but also whether the accomplishment of a valid purpose has the effect of discriminating against out-of-state articles of commerce. *Id.* at 626-27. *See also Kassel v. Consolidated Freightways Corp. of Del.,* 450 U.S. 662 (1981) (striking down an Iowa statute that prescribed a maximum length for tractor trailers, far shorter than the length used by many trucks in interstate commerce). In balancing the state's interest in the safety of its citizens against the burden on interstate commerce, the Court stated that "[r]egulations designed for [a] salutary purpose nevertheless may further the purpose so marginally, and interfere with commerce so substantially, as to be invalid under the Commerce Clause." *Id.* at 670.

54 *Japan Lines, Ltd. v. County of Los Angeles,* 441 U.S. 434, 449 (1979) (quoting *Michelin Tire Corp. v. Wages,* 423 U.S. 276, 285 (1976).

stated that "the phrase 'information superhighway' is more than a mere buzzword; it has legal significance."[55] The New York statute at issue in that case attempted to prohibit transmissions of sexually-related communications to minors via the Internet. The *Pataki* court issued an injunction preventing the statute's enforcement, finding it an unconstitutional infringement on interstate commerce.[56] In analogizing the Internet to a highway or railroad, the *Pataki* court stated that the Internet fits within the parameters of interests traditionally protected by the Commerce Clause.[57]

The *Pataki* court gave three grounds for its decision: (1) the New York Act represents an unconstitutional projection of New York law into conduct that occurs wholly outside New York;[58] (2) even if the New York Act is not a *per se* violation of the Commerce Clause, it is an invalid, indirect regulation of interstate commerce because it imposes on interstate commerce burdens that are excessive in relation to the benefits it confers;[59] and (3) the Internet is one of those areas of commerce that must be marked off as a *national preserve* to protect users from inconsistent legislation that, taken to its most extreme, could paralyze development of the Internet altogether.[60]

The *Pataki* court recognized that the "Internet is wholly insensitive to geographic distinctions."[61] Internet users generally do not know the location of the Internet resources that they access, and Internet service providers also cannot be certain from which jurisdiction the resources are accessed.

For example, a user may have four e-mail accounts with four different Internet service providers, each providing access to the World Wide Web. Two of the Internet service providers may be located in the District of Columbia while the other two are located in the State of Maryland. However, all are easily accessible from any computer located across the Potomac River in Northern Virginia by virtue of a local telephone call. In addition, the user could make a local telephone call from Northern Virginia for a remote login into one of the D.C. Internet service providers and then use a software application called Telnet to access another Internet service provider in Baltimore. From there, the user could access the worldwide resources of the Internet. The issue becomes: in which of the three jurisdictions, D.C., Maryland, or Virginia, may the user be sued or prosecuted for a violation of the law. The answer might be all three.

---

[55] *Pataki*, 969 F. Supp. at 161. Railroads, trucks, and highways have long been recognized under the law as "instruments of commerce," because they serve as conduits for the transportation of products and services. *See, e.g., Kassel*, 450 U.S. 662; *Southern Pacific Co. v. Arizona*, 325 U.S. 761 (1945).

[56] *Pataki*, 969 F. Supp. at 183-84. *But see New York v. Barrows*, 664 N.Y.S.2d 410 (N.Y. Sup. Ct. 1997) (upholding a similar N.Y. statute under the Commerce Clause because the statute forbids the transmission of sexually related communications via the Internet to minors, where such communications were intended to lure the child into sexual relations within the State of New York).

[57] *Pataki*, 969 F. Supp. at 161, 167.

[58] *Id*. at 169.

[59] *Id*.

[60] *Id*. (emphasis added).

[61] *Id*. at 170.

If a user accesses a website that distributes illegal materials such as pornography, then is the website owner subject to suit in any or all of the three jurisdictions discussed above?[62] If the website operator is subject to the jurisdiction in some or all of these sovereign territories, how might that operator curtail or limit its service to dispel this jurisdictional dilemma? According to one commentator, "[n]o aspect of the Internet can feasibly be closed off to users from another state,"[63] no more than a state may shut down its highways, railroads, or ports. The Internet is more than a communications system, it is the foundation for electronic commerce serving as the conduit for digital goods, including software, data, music, graphics, videos, literature, and economic information that can be downloaded from the provider's site or a mirror site to a user's computer anywhere in the United States and throughout the world.

The extraordinarily low cost of participation in worldwide commerce and communications is one of the most phenomenal developments in this Century. However, the emergence of a real threat of multi-jurisdictional liability and criminal prosecution may, in some instances, deter both business and individuals from using the Internet. Much of the democratization and liberalization of the barriers to the international marketplace created by the Internet may be lost if legislators, whether at the national, state, or local level, create a morass of jurisdictional entanglements on the World Wide Web. Merchants may be deterred by potentially conflicting content requirements, or the threat of potentially defending civil suits, or facing criminal prosecution in multiple jurisdictions. The expense and effort entailed in monitoring, and complying with, the regulatory requirements of every jurisdiction that an entrepreneur or user may electronically touch could be enormous.[64]

[2] EXTRATERRITORIAL ASSERTIONS OF STATE JURISDICTION THAT VIOLATE THE COMMERCE CLAUSE

States may not directly interfere with interstate commerce by establishing statutes or regulations that effectively dictate the manner in which commercial activities may occur beyond their borders. Put another way, the Commerce Clause precludes a state from exporting its regulatory policies into other states by legislative enactment.[65] State statutes that, on their face, directly regulate commercial transactions occurring wholly outside that state are *per se* violations of the Commerce Clause.[66] For example, a state's efforts to regulate the manner in which corporate takeovers are conducted, when the target corporation is an in-state corporation, violates the Commerce Clause if the state's attempt to prevent a takeover is based on considerations of fairness

---

[62] See Section 19.05[1] for a discussion of the exercise of personal jurisdiction over a foreign party.

[63] *Pataki*, 969 F. Supp. at 171. *See* Section 19.03[3][b] (discussing CompuServe's failure to block pornography websites from reaching German users, followed by an indictment of one of its corporate officers).

[64] *See* Burk, *supra* note 2, at 1126-28. California has enacted a criminal statute imposing consumer disclosure obligations for online vendors and explicitly regulating the manner in which those disclosures are presented to consumers on the vendors' web pages. The law applies to the sale of goods to any consumer who is a resident of California regardless of whether the vendor is from California, another state, or from another country. *See* CAL. BUS. & PROF. CODE § 17538 (Deering 1996); *see also California Applies Consumer Protections to Internet Commerce*, 21st CENTURY BANKING ALERT® No. 97-1-16, Jan. 16, 1997, *available at* <http://www.ffhsj.com/bancmail/21starch/970116.htm>. See Chapter 10 for a discussion of California's consumer protection disclosure statute.

[65] *See Pataki*, 969 F. Supp. at 174.

[66] *Healy v. The Beer Institute*, 491 U.S. 324, 336 (1989); *Brown-Forman Distillers Corp. v. New York State Liquor Authority*, 476 U.S. 573, 581-82 (1986).

to corporate shareholders, although not one of the shareholders is a resident of that state.[67] If one state were permitted to pass a statute that directly restrains interstate commerce on the Internet with sweeping extra-territorial effect, then any other state could do the same.[68] The Commerce Clause prevents such a regime of overlapping state regulations of commerce.

Regardless of the legitimate purpose of a statute, a statute that by its operation directly interferes with or burdens interstate commerce is invalid.[69] When the practical effect of a state statute is to control activities beyond its territorial borders, the statute will be struck down as violative of the Commerce Clause.[70] The courts will not only consider the consequences of the statute itself, but will determine how the statute interacts with "legitimate regulatory schemes of other States and what effect would arise if not one, but many or every, State adopted similar legislation."[71]

As discussed in Chapter 10, Sections 10.04 and 10.05, states may exert their power, to varying degrees, over several different aspects of Internet commerce. The worldwide interoperability of the Internet by necessity, however, requires uniform regulation. "The need to contain individual state overreaching thus arises not from any disrespect for the plenary authority of each [sovereign state] over its own internal affairs but out of a recognition that true protection of each state's respective authority is only possible when such limits are observed by all states."[72]

[3] INDIRECT REGULATION OF INTERSTATE COMMERCE THAT VIOLATES THE COMMERCE CLAUSE

Even if a statute withstands constitutional scrutiny because it does not directly affect interstate commerce through extraterritorial application, it may still be determined an impermissible indirect regulation of interstate commerce if the burdens it imposes on interstate commerce are excessive relative to the local benefits.[73] A court will first determine the legitimacy of the state's interest in prescribing the regulation. Then the court will determine the burden on interstate commerce in light of any benefit obtained in meeting the state's alleged

---

[67] *Edgar v. Mite*, 457 U.S. 624 (1982) (striking down an Illinois anti-takeover statute seeking to protect management of Illinois corporations). Only a plurality of the Court adhered to the extraterritoriality analysis, whereas a majority of the court struck down the statute under the balancing test discussed in Section 19.04[3]. *Id.* at 643. A majority of the Supreme Court has adopted the extraterritoriality rationale in later cases. *See Healy*, 491 U.S. at 336; *Brown-Forman Distillers*, 476 U.S. at 581-82.

[68] *See Edgar,* 457 U.S. at 642.

[69] *Shafer v. Farmers Grain Co.*, 268 U.S. 189, 199 (1925).

[70] *See Southern Pacific*, 325 U.S. at 775 (striking down a statute limiting the length of trains, and thereby preventing a state from imposing its regulatory policies on neighboring states).

[71] *Healy*, 491 U.S. at 336.

[72] *Pataki*, 969 F. Supp. at 176. *See also Huntington v. Attrill*, 146 U.S. 657, 669 (1892) ("Laws have no force of themselves beyond the jurisdiction of the State which enacts them, and can have extraterritorial effect only by the comity of other States.").

[73] *See Pike v. Bruce Church*, 397 U.S. 137, 142 (1970).

interest in enacting and enforcing the statute.[74] For example, the State of New York's interests in protecting minors from pedophiles, and the benefits associated with a statute to limit the transmission of pornography to minors, were found to be insufficient to outweigh the burdens on Internet commerce.[75]

[4]   AVOIDANCE OF INHOSPITABLE JURISDICTIONS

It is well-accepted that commercial parties may agree to have their contract governed in accordance with a particular state's laws, and agree that any disputes shall be resolved exclusively in that state's courts or by arbitration within that state. Choice of law and choice of forum provisions may increase legal certainty for commercial participants using the Internet. Such provisions, however, may not be enforceable if they are not reasonable or properly supported by consideration.[76] They also may not provide the legal certainty that Internet merchants seek when dealing with individual consumers worldwide.[77] Furthermore, although civil liability in commercial transactions may, as agreed by contract, be assessed in jurisdictions with more favorable laws, those same venue and choice of law provisions are not applicable to a sovereign's decision to impose its criminal laws.

Rather than relying solely upon choice of law provisions, an Internet merchant or financial institution may seek to conduct its activities on the Internet in a manner that avoids commercial transactions with citizens of a forum with unfavorable laws. This may be accomplished through several features incorporated into the merchant's or financial institution's website. The merchant or financial institute may prominently display either a list of jurisdictions to which it is directing its business, or list those jurisdictions in which it is not doing business, or both. It may also install filtering devices programmed to determine the location of any potential customers by requiring either zip code or other identifiable data to determine the customer's self-reported geographic location. Based on predetermined criteria, such software could reject attempts to transact business by customers of unfavorable states. If the merchant or financial institution subsequently becomes aware that a customer is a resident of a state in which it does not wish to conduct business, it may decide to return all funds received from, and cancel any orders made by, that customer. Of course, to the extent that a merchant or financial institution commits itself to not doing business with residents of particular jurisdictions, it must be prepared to experience a loss of potential revenue.

---

[74] "The distinction between direct regulations of interstate commerce, which are subject to a *per se* rule of invalidation, and indirect regulations subject to the less stringent balancing test has never been sharply defined. In either situation, however, the 'critical consideration is the overall effect of the statute on both local and interstate activity.'" *Pataki*, 969 F. Supp. at 177 n.8 (citing *Brown-Forman*, 476 U.S. at 579; *Raymond Motor Transportation, Inc. v. Rice*, 434 U.S. 429, 440-41 (1978)).

[75] *Pataki*, 969 F. Supp. at 178. *See also Hunt v. Washington Apple Advertising Comm'n*, 432 U.S. 333, 350 (1977) ("[A] finding that state legislation furthers matters of legitimate local concern, even in the health and consumer protection areas, does not end the inquiry.").

[76] *See* GEORGE B. DELTA & JEFFREY H. MATSUURA, LAW OF THE INTERNET § 3.04 (1998).

[77] *See id.*

§ 19.05   JURISDICTION OVER A FOREIGN PARTY

In the United States, federal and state governments have either already implemented legislation over Internet activities or are in the process of doing so.[78] Regulation may result in liability for proscribed online-activities.[79] The applicable scope of Internet legislation is not, however, without bounds.[80] As discussed above, Internet use may subject financial institutions and Internet merchants to multiple jurisdictions, theoretically requiring them to comply with the most restrictive laws created by a single state or nation. In this multijuris-dictional scenario, which entails the prospect for conflicting regulation, the potential for civil litigation may require electronic commerce participants to be concerned with which foreign courts they may be subject to suit in and the legal standards under which their conduct will be assessed.

[1]   PERSONAL JURISDICTION

Traditionally, a court may only hear disputes and render judgments in actions involving a foreign party if the court has personal jurisdiction over that party. Courts may assert personal jurisdiction over any party who is physically present within the territorial confines of the state in which that court sits.[81] Over the course of the 20th Century, as interstate travel and communication have become easier and more pervasive, the concept of "presence" has been expanded to include contacts between foreign parties outside the forum and persons in the forum.[82]

There are two types of personal jurisdiction: general and specific. General jurisdiction results when a party's ties to a certain forum are continuous, systematic, and ongoing.[83] A court with general jurisdiction over a party may exercise jurisdiction over disputes concerning matters unrelated to the party's contacts with the state.[84] Specific jurisdiction, often asserted when a party's contacts are not continuous, systematic, and ongoing, permits a court to assert jurisdiction over parties to a dispute arising from the party's contacts with a state.[85]

---

[78] Communications Decency Act ("CDA") of 1996, Pub. L. No. 104-104, § 507, 1996 U.S.C.C.A.N. (110 Stat.) 132 (codified at 18 U.S.C. § § 1462, 1465). *See also* GA. CODE ANN. § 16-9-93.1; Thomas P. Vartanian, Robert H. Ledig, Edward B. Whittemore, & James P. Baetzhold, *Georgia Internet Law Raises Jurisdictional Questions for Electronic Commerce*, ELECTRONIC BANKING L. & COM. REP., Feb. 1997, at 15.

[79] *See United States v. Thomas*, 74 F.3d 701, 706-07 (6th Cir. 1996) (applying the community decency standards of the forum state into which the nonresident defendants transmitted computer-generated images); *Playboy Enterprises, Inc. v. Chuckleberry Publishing, Inc.*, 939 F. Supp. 1032 (S.D.N.Y. 1996) (holding a nonresident in contempt for setting up an infringing website in violation of a previous injunctive order and finding jurisdiction based on the previous injunction).

[80] *See Reno v. ACLU*, __ U.S. __, 117 S.Ct. 2329 (1997) (finding two provisions of the CDA regarding "indecent" and "patently offensive" communi-cations on the Internet unconstitutional under the First Amendment); *ACLU v. Miller*, 977 F. Supp. 1228 (N.D. Ga. 1997) (enjoining enforcement of the Georgia Internet law); *Pataki*, 969 F. Supp. 160 (enjoining New York's effort to regulate Internet activity because of interference with the Commerce Clause).

[81] *Pennoyer v. Neff*, 95 U.S. 714 (1878).

[82] *International Shoe v. Washington*, 326 U.S. 310, 320 (1945).

[83] *See* STEVEN BAICKER-MCKEE, WILLIAM JANSSEN & JOHN B. CORR, FEDERAL CIVIL RULES HANDBOOK § 2.4 (1997) [hereinafter FEDERAL CIVIL RULES HANDBOOK].

[84] *Id.*

[85] *Helicopteros Nacionales de Columbia, S.A. v. Hall*, 466 U.S. 408, 414 (1984) (*quoting Shaffer v. Heitner*, 433 U.S. 186, 204 (1977)); *see also* FEDERAL CIVIL RULES HANDBOOK, *supra* note 83, § 2.5.

[2]   THE ASSERTION OF PERSONAL JURISDICTION BY FEDERAL AND STATE COURTS OVER FOREIGN PARTIES

In the United States, two general principles govern a court's assertion of personal jurisdiction over a foreign party: state long-arm statutes and the Due Process Clause of the Constitution.[86] This section will discuss state long-arm statutes and how these statutes have been applied by courts to disputes involving the Internet and related technology. This section will then examine the requirements imposed by federal Due Process when a court asserts personal jurisdiction.

[a] Long-Arm Statutes. Long-arm statutes provide state courts with the authority to hale foreign parties into court.[87] State long-arm powers cannot, however, exceed the constitutional limits of federal Due Process.[88] Long-arm statutes also affect a federal court's jurisdiction, for federal courts generally apply the state long-arm statute of the state in which the federal court sits to disputes involving foreign parties.[89]

Some long-arm statutes broadly define proper assertions of jurisdiction, permitting courts to interpret them as being coextensive with the limits of the 14th Amendment Due Process Clause.[90] Other long-arm statutes, however, do not reach to the fullest extent of federal Due Process, but only permit assertions of jurisdiction over foreign parties that operate within the state or cause tortious injury in the state.[91] Some long-arm statutes that reach to the extent of federal Due Process may nevertheless limit a state's assertion of jurisdiction to specific circumstances.[92]

---

[86]   FED. R. CIV. P. 4(k); *Wenz v. Memery Crystal*, 55 F.3d 1503 (10th Cir. 1995) (assertions of jurisdiction over nonresident defendants require an examination of both the state long-arm statute and issues of due process); FEDERAL CIVIL RULES HANDBOOK, *supra* note 83, § 2.3.

[87]   FEDERAL CIVIL RULES HANDBOOK, *supra* note 83, § 2.5.

[88]   *Id.* Federal Due Process, as used herein, refers to the protections offered under the due process clauses of the U.S. Constitutions, in particular the Fifth Amendment for federal actions and the Fourteenth Amendment for state actions. These protections have been interpreted to mean that the exercise of jurisdiction must not be fundamentally unfair to a defendant. *See id.* § 2.4.

[89]   *See, e.g., Reynolds v. International Amateur Athletic Fed'n*, 23 F.3d 1110, 1115 (6th Cir. 1994); *Aanestad v. Beech Aircraft Corp.*, 521 F. 2d 1298, 1300 (9th Cir. 1974); *Wilson v. Humphreys (Cayman) Ltd.*, 916 F.2d 1239, 1243 (7th Cir. 1990); FEDERAL CIVIL RULES HANDBOOK, *supra* note 83, § 2.5. However, certain federal causes of action, including suits under federal antitrust laws and securities laws, provide that courts can exercise nationwide personal jurisdiction. *Id.* § 2.7; *see, e.g.,* 15 U.S.C. § 22 (providing nationwide personal jurisdiction in antitrust claims). Additionally, Federal Rule of Civil Procedure 4(k)(2) permits the exercise of personal jurisdiction in federal causes of action where the defendant has sufficient minimum contacts with the United States as a whole, but not with any particular state. *See* FED. R. CIV. P. 4(k)(2).

[90]   *See Asahi Metal Industry Co. v. Superior Court*, 480 U.S. 102 (1987) (finding that California's long-arm statute authorizes jurisdiction "on any basis not inconsistent with the Constitution of this state or the United States"); *United States v. Ferrara*, 54 F.3d 825, 828 (D.C. Cir. 1995) (holding that the D.C. long-arm statute provides for the exercise of jurisdiction over any party to the extent permissible under the Due Process Clause, merging the statutory long-arm and constitutional jurisdictional questions into one inquiry); *Zippo Mfg. Co. v. Zippo Dot Com, Inc.*, 952 F. Supp. 1119 (W.D. Pa. 1997) (holding that the court was authorized to exercise jurisdiction to the limits of the federal Constitution); *see, e.g.,* D.C. CODE ANN. § 13-423; 42 PA. C.S.A. § 5322 (b). The California long-arm statute provides that "[a] court of this state may exercise jurisdiction on any basis not inconsistent with the Constitution of this state or that of the United States." 5 CAL. CIV. PROC. CODE § 410.10.

[91]   *See* FEDERAL CIVIL RULES HANDBOOK, *supra* note 83, § 2.5; *see, e.g.,* N.Y. C.P.L.R. § 302.

[92]   *See Alton v. Wang*, 941 F. Supp. 66, 67-68 (W.D. Va. 1996) (finding that the Virginia long-arm statute extends to the limits of federal Due Process, but that the statute limits jurisdiction by only providing jurisdiction in specific circumstances). For example, the statute may provide for jurisdiction over foreign parties because of their forum activities or based on the effect that their actions outside of a state have on the state or its residents.

[b] Long-Arm Statutes Applied to Disputes Involving the Internet and World Wide Web. Courts interpreting the reach of long-arm statutes in cases involving the World Wide Web have generally responded in one of three ways. Some courts have found that a foreign party's website falls within the specific provisions of the long-arm statute.[93] Other courts have found that a foreign party's website design did not satisfy the long-arm statute. They focused on the limited nature of the website, which they perceived as merely providing information to Internet users rather than selling products.[94] Those courts have held that even if foreign parties might reasonably expect their websites to have an effect in the forum, they could not reasonably expect to derive significant revenue from the forum, nor expect their websites to result in a significant injury in the forum.[95] Finally, a third group of courts dealing with such disputes have found that resolution of the federal Due Process question resolves any uncertainty about the state long-arm statute, because the reach of the statute is coextensive with Due Process.[96]

[c] Federal Due Process. Assertions of jurisdiction must comport with the strictures of federal Due Process.[97] An assertion of personal jurisdiction over a foreign party does not violate federal Due Process if the party has certain minimum contacts with the forum such that jurisdiction does not offend traditional notions of "fair play and substantial justice."[98] General jurisdiction is applicable where a party's ties to a state are continuous, systematic, and ongoing; rendering the assertion of jurisdiction, even for matters unrelated to the party's contacts with the state, compatible with federal Due Process.[99] Specific jurisdiction exists if a controversy relates to or "arises out of" a party's contacts with a forum and there is "a relationship among the defendant, the forum, and the litigation."[100]

[d] Applications of General Jurisdiction. In determining whether a court's assertion of general jurisdiction is proper, a court will analyze the nature of the defendant's contacts and business activities within the

---

[93] *See Maritz, Inc. v. Cybergold, Inc.*, 947 F. Supp. 1328 (E.D. Mo. 1996) (finding that a website produced an effect within the forum so that even if the website operator's actions were interpreted as occurring outside the forum, the contacts satisfied the long-arm statute); *Inset Systems, Inc. v. Instruction Set, Inc.*, 937 F. Supp. 161 (D. Conn. 1996) (finding that a foreign party's website constituted a continuous advertisement which could be accessed by forum residents, satisfying the "solicitation of business" provision of the Connecticut's long-arm statute).

[94] *See Bensusan Restaurant Corp. v. King*, 937 F. Supp. 295 (S.D.N.Y. 1996), *aff'd*, 126 F.3d 25 (2d Cir. 1997) (holding that the creation of a website with a telephone number to order an allegedly infringing product is not an offer to sell the product in the forum state within the meaning of the New York long-arm statute); *Hearst Corp. v. Goldberger*, No. 96 Civ. 3620, 1997 U.S. Dist. LEXIS 2065, *14, *26, *29 (S.D.N.Y. Feb. 26, 1997) (holding that the nonresident's website, e-mails with the media in the forum, and use of a disputed e-mail address did not constitute "transacting business" or "committing a tortious act" in New York under its long-arm statute).

[95] *Bensusan*, 937 F. Supp. at 300; *see Hearst*, 1997 U.S. Dist. LEXIS 2065, at *44-49.

[96] *Heroes Inc. v. Heroes Foundation*, 958 F. Supp. 1 (D.D.C. 1996) (finding that a nonresident's web page which solicited contributions and provided a toll-free telephone number for that purpose provided the court with jurisdiction within the ambit of federal Due Process); *Panavision Int'l., L.P. v. Toeppen*, 938 F. Supp. 616, 620 (C.D. Cal. 1996) (finding that because the California long-arm statute permits courts to assert jurisdiction to the extent of federal Due Process, the court need only examine whether jurisdiction meets the requirements of Due Process); *Zippo Mfg. Co. v. Zippo Dot Com, Inc.*, 952 F. Supp. 1119, 1122 (W.D. Pa. 1997) (finding that even if the situation does not satisfy a specific provision of the long-arm, the long-arm provides for jurisdiction to the extent of federal Due Process).

[97] *See Helicoptoros Nacionales De Columbia, S.A.*, 466 U.S. at 413-14 (1984).

[98] *See id.* at 414; *International Shoe Co. v. Washington*, 326 U.S. 310, 316 (1945) (*quoting Milliken v. Meyer*, 311 U.S. 457, 463 (1940)).

[99] *See* FEDERAL CIVIL RULES HANDBOOK, *supra* note 83, § 2.4.

[100] *See Helicopteros*, 466 U.S. at 414 (*quoting Shaffer v. Heitner*, 433 U.S. at 204); *see also* FEDERAL CIVIL RULES HANDBOOK, *supra* note 83, § 2.5.

forum.[101] Generally, if an entity maintains a corporate office in a forum from which it performs a variety of business activities, the entity will be subject to jurisdiction in that forum even if the office is temporary.[102] However, mere purchases of products from a state, even if regularly occurring, are insufficient for an assertion of general jurisdiction over the purchaser.[103]

[i] *Analysis.* Participants in Internet commerce may establish any of a number of contacts with a state through electronic banking and commerce. If financial institutions establish online accounts, transact business, advise customers, transfer money, conduct advertising or other business activities through a website, courts may deem these activities to be contacts within any state whose residents interact with the financial institution. The more substantial an activity, in terms of the interaction with the citizens of a forum, the more likely that courts will find each particular activity a contact with that state. The quality and quantity of these contacts in turn determine whether the contacts with the state qualify as continuous and systematic, subjecting a participant in Internet commerce to that state's jurisdiction for any lawsuit.

[ii] *General Jurisdiction Cases.* Only a handful of courts to date have conducted in depth examinations of the assertion of general jurisdiction based on a corporation's contacts with a state via the Internet.[104] In a 1996 case, *McDonough v. Fallon McElligott, Inc.,*[105] a federal district court in California considered four activities of a Minnesota advertising agency in determining the appropriateness of jurisdiction: (1) hiring in-state independent contractors; (2) purchasing advertising space from California-based entities; (3) placing advertisements in California; and (4) maintaining a website.[106] Recognizing the danger of asserting general jurisdiction over the advertising agency, because of its website and the possibility of failing to give reasonable effect to personal jurisdiction protections, the court held that use of the agency's website by citizens of the forum state cannot by itself establish jurisdiction.[107] The court focused on the agency's lack of significant forum clients and the fact that no residents of the forum state actually purchased the products placed into the stream of commerce by the nonresident.[108] The court found the purchase of advertisements, which were unrelated to the cause of action, insufficient to support an exercise of general jurisdiction.[109] Considering these contacts in

---

[101] *Perkins v. Benguet Consolidated Mining Co.,* 342 U.S. 437, 447 (1952). *See generally* JAMES WM. MOORE, MOORE'S FEDERAL PRACTICE (3d ed. 1997).

[102] *Perkins,* 342 U.S. at 447-48.

[103] *Helicopteros,* 466 U.S. at 418.

[104] *See California Software, Inc. v. Reliability Research, Inc.,* 631 F. Supp. 1356 (C.D. Cal. 1986) (finding that the use of a nationally-disseminated, computer-based information service and regular communications with forum residents through that service did not establish the minimum contacts necessary to support general jurisdiction). Another court found it unnecessary to consider the issue. *See Edias v. Basis,* 947 F. Supp. 413, 417 (D. Ariz. 1996) (finding that because all of the nonresident's contacts with the forum via the Internet gave rise to specific jurisdiction, it was unnecessary to consider whether the nonresident's ongoing business relationship with a forum resident, involving sales, visits, and communications into the forum, supported general jurisdiction).

[105] No. 95-4037, 1996 U.S. Dist. LEXIS 15139 (S.D. Cal. Aug. 5, 1996).

[106] *Id.* at *6-7.

[107] *Id.* at *7.

[108] *Id.* at *8.

[109] *Id.*

their entirety, the court found that they were not substantial, systematic, or continuous; and therefore did not support general jurisdiction over the agency.[110]

[e] Applications of Specific Jurisdiction. Participants in electronic commerce must be aware of the possibility of a court's assertion of specific jurisdiction over their activities. The assertion of specific jurisdiction does not violate the federal Due Process if (1) a party purposely avails itself of the privilege of conducting activities within the forum, rendering it reasonable for the party to anticipate being haled into court in the forum, and (2) the exercise of specific jurisdiction does not offend traditional notions of fair play and substantial justice.[111]

[i] Purposeful Availment. In determining whether a foreign party purposefully availed itself of the benefits bestowed by the laws of the forum, a court inquires as to whether the foreign party could reasonably have anticipated being haled into that forum's courts.[112] This anticipation is based on the extent that the foreign party's activities, sales, services, and business solicitations, or any manner in which they otherwise avail themselves of any of the benefits of the forum's laws, are calculated to reach the forum. The court will not only look to whether foreign parties regularly sell products to forum residents, but also to whether the parties indirectly, through others, serve or seek to serve the forum market.[113] A consumer's unilateral actions to take a foreign party's products to a distant forum, although foreseeable, does not render the subsequent suit foreseeable.[114]

However, by placing its products into the stream of commerce and expecting consumers in a forum to purchase those products, a corporation purposefully avails itself of that forum's laws.[115] For example, a magazine publisher is subject to suit in a forum in which it has "regular monthly sales of thousands of magazines."[116] Regular sales do not qualify as random, isolated, or fortuitous contacts such that personal jurisdiction may not be exercised.[117]

The Supreme Court has found a franchisee subject to the jurisdiction of a foreign forum because he deliberately reached out beyond his home state in negotiating with a Florida corporation to purchase a long-term franchise and its ongoing benefits.[118] The Court held that the franchise relationship, wherein the franchisee submitted to regulations issued by the franchiser from its Florida headquarters, did not constitute random,

[110] *Id.* at *11.

[111] *World-Wide Volkswagen Corp. v. Woodson*, 444 U.S. 286, 297 (1980); *Burger King Corp. v. Rudzewicz*, 471 U.S. 462, 475-77 (1985); *International Shoe Co.*, 326 U.S. at 316.

[112] *World-Wide Volkswagen*, 444 U.S. at 295 (holding that the New York distributor and retail dealer of an automobile is not subject to the jurisdiction of Oklahoma, the location of a collision involving an automobile purchased from the dealer).

[113] *Id.*

[114] *Id.* at 298.

[115] *Id.* at 297-298.

[116] *Keeton v. Hustler Mag.*, 465 U.S. 770, 774 (1984).

[117] *Id.*

[118] *Burger King*, 471 U.S. at 479-80.

fortuitous, or attenuated contacts with the forum.[119] A participant in electronic commerce or banking may use "pull technology"[120] for its contractual relationships with others and incorporate a choice of law and forum clause within the contract so as not to be haled into a foreign forum.

[ii] *Traditional Notions of Fair Play and Substantial Justice.* In examining whether an assertion of specific jurisdiction comports with traditional notions of fair play and substantial justice, a court will consider its forum's interest in adjudicating the dispute.[121] In particular, a court will focus on the foreign party's contacts and balance whether the forum's interest in deciding the dispute is greater than the interests of the foreign party's state.[122] Although resolution of a dispute in a foreign forum may be inconvenient and may burden the foreign party's ability to call witnesses, such inconvenience does not necessarily rise to a constitutional dimension.[123] Courts recognize that there are dangers accompanying assertions of jurisdiction based on contractual relationships with inequalities in bargaining power, but such concerns are generally unwarranted when both parties are commercial entities.[124]

[iii] *Analysis.* Whether a foreign party is subject to the specific jurisdiction of a court by virtue of its contacts via the Internet will have significant implications on the manner in which electronic banking and commerce disputes will be resolved.[125] Because electronic commercial activities create forum contacts not based on physical presence within a forum, the contacts are more attenuated. In evaluating the forum contacts created by electronic interaction with customers, courts could decide that the customers created the contacts by reaching out to commercial or banking websites; or they could decide that the banks purposely directed their activities into the particular forum. Regular advertisements or billing activity directed to forum consumers, the creation of special services appealing to forum residents, the absence of restrictions on electronic access, and efforts to comply with a forum's commercial regulations could be considered to be activities that may constitute purposeful availment of the benefits of that forum's laws.

[iv] *Internet and Technology Cases Interpreting Specific Jurisdiction.* Recently, courts have attempted to apply traditional jurisdiction principles to disputes involving the Internet and electronic technology. These cases leave unresolved many questions concerning how to classify cyberspace contacts. For instance, several courts have found websites sufficiently interactive in nature to provide a basis for jurisdiction, while one court examining this issue has refused to find jurisdiction based on what it characterizes as passive websites. Courts

---

[119] *Id.*

[120] "Pull" technology, such as a web browser, requires an Internet user to actively do something in order for the information to be transmitted from a foreign party's website to the user's computer. "Push" technology downloads data and other communications to a user's computer via the Internet without the user having requested the information, such as unsolicited e-mail communications and banner advertisements.

[121] *Burger King,* 471 U.S. at 482-86. *See also Asahi Metal Industry Co.,* 480 U.S. 102.

[122] *Burger King,* 471 U.S. at 482-83.

[123] *Id.*

[124] *Id.* at 484.

[125] *Kulco v. Superior Court,* 436 U.S. 84, at 96-98 (1978) (finding that commercial contacts with a forum are more likely to give rise to jurisdiction than personal and domestic relations).

examining this issue have faced a wide variety of technological contacts with forum states, including: use of online electronic database systems; creation of websites with varying interactive capabilities; registration of potentially infringing Internet domain names; and use of electronic mail between contracting parties. This section will analyze each of these contacts, revealing the manner in which courts have dealt and will deal with these emerging issues.

[A] *Online Electronic Database Systems.* Courts analyzing jurisdiction based upon electronic contacts between parties in one state and another have tended to find jurisdiction to exist where contacts are ongoing, are a part of a party's business operations, and involved clear recognition that their counterparty "is from another forum," and the formality of the relationship. To the extent that these elements are absent in whole or large part, courts have tended not to find jurisdiction present.

Reversing a lower court's decision, the Sixth Circuit in *CompuServe Inc. v. Patterson*[126] held that a federal district court in Ohio could assert jurisdiction over a nonresident of the forum state in a trademark and unfair competition claim arising from the nonresident's Internet contacts with the forum state. Patterson, the nonresident, created several contacts with the forum as a result of his computer activities by entering into a Shareware Registration Agreement ("SRA") with CompuServe and subscribing to CompuServe, an online electronic database system. He also sent e-mails and physical mail to CompuServe in Ohio, and posted a message on a CompuServe electronic forum. The SRA incorporated two other documents by reference. Collectively these documents created a relationship governed by Ohio law in which Patterson placed his software on the CompuServe system in exchange for CompuServe agreeing to provide its subscribers with access to Patterson's software for their use and possible purchase.

Focusing on Patterson's unique relationship with CompuServe, the court distinguished Patterson from a mere purchaser of services. Patterson chose to repeatedly transmit his software onto CompuServe's system located in the forum. Others gained access to Patterson's software via that system. Patterson advertised and sold his software through that system.[127] As the court stated, "Patterson deliberately set in motion an ongoing marketing relationship with CompuServe, and he should have reasonably foreseen that doing so would have consequences in Ohio."[128] The Sixth Circuit distinguished this from merely placing a product into the stream of commerce.[129] It also relied on the fact that Patterson had entered into the SRA. The court noted that either contact alone would be insufficient for jurisdiction, but taken together and analyzed along with other factors, the contacts rendered jurisdiction proper. These other factors included the SRA's choice of law provision, Patterson's sending of e-mail and physical mail to CompuServe in Ohio, and Patterson's posting a message on a CompuServe electronic forum. The court also considered Patterson's software sales through the CompuServe system, not only to consumers in the forum state, but also via the CompuServe system. Because the

---

[126] *CompuServe, Inc. v. Patterson*, 89 F.3d 1257 (6th Cir. 1996).

[127] *Id.*

[128] *Id.* at 1265.

[129] *Id.*

CompuServe system was located in the forum, the court considered the forum contacts created by Patterson in sending messages to consumers in other states. The court found the intangible and electronic nature of Patterson's contacts insignificant, applying a traditional analysis to this new medium. In holding Patterson subject to jurisdiction in the forum state of Ohio, where CompuServe's headquarters were located, the court declined to address whether Patterson's contacts were sufficient to subject him to jurisdiction in any other forum state in which CompuServe operated and via which Patterson's product might be available.[130]

In 1986, a California federal district court also considered the effect of the defendants nonresidents operation and use of an online electronic database in *California Software, Inc. v. Reliability Research, Inc.*[131] In *California Software,* the nonresident defendants, a Nevada corporation ("RRI") and its officers, made allegedly false statements in communications with customers of the plaintiffs, two California software firms. These communications were made with California residents as well as with individuals outside of California. The defendants communicated with these potential software purchasers, in three ways: by letters, telephone calls, and by a nationally disseminated computer based information service known as the Computer Reliability Forum ("CRF"), operated by the nonresident defendants.

The court found each contact sufficient to support specific jurisdiction. The court rejected the notion that, in this day of electronic communications, jurisdiction requires physical entrance into a forum state. The court found jurisdiction proper because the nonresident defendant, RRI, intended its message to affect the plaintiff, a California forum resident. The court considered the electronic nature of the contact irrelevant to the determination whether there was a basis for jurisdiction.[132] The defendants distributed their messages to a wider audience by placing them on the CRF system, and thus, correspondingly broadened the permissible scope of jurisdiction exercisable by courts. The court found jurisdiction proper due to the state's strong interest in protecting its citizens' rights and the reasonableness of the nonresident defending a suit in California.

In a 1992 case, *Plus System, Inc. v. New England Network, Inc.*,[133] a district court in Colorado considered whether to assert jurisdiction over a New England ATM network member. The defendant, New England Network, Inc. ("NENI"), consisted of approximately 700 financial institutions that marketed and promoted a regional shared ATM network in New England. The action arose out of a dispute over royalties on ATM transactions by customers of NENI members that do not use the "PLUS" network but in which the "PLUS" mark is the only mark that appears on both the customer's card and the ATM.

---

130 *Id.* Turning to the second factor in the minimum contacts analysis, the court also held that jurisdiction did not offend traditional notions of fair play and substantial justice. Although it may be burdensome for Patterson to defend a suit in Ohio, he was not a mere consumer but rather an entrepreneur who should have anticipated the possibility of being subject to jurisdiction when entering into the CompuServe relationship. The court held that Ohio and the plaintiff, CompuServe, both had a strong interest in adjudicating the dispute. *Id.* at 1267-68.

131 631 F. Supp. 1356 (C.D. Cal. 1986).

132 *Id.* Electronic messages sent from RRI in Vermont to corporations in Washington, New York, and Ontario, Canada via the forum Computer Reliability Forum provided one basis for jurisdiction.

133 804 F. Supp. 111 (D. Colo. 1992).

The court first analyzed whether NENI had purposely availed itself of the benefits of the forum state's (Colorado's) laws. The court found NENI's physical presence in Colorado unnecessary. The court considered two contacts in particular: (i) joining a Colorado-based national ATM network; and (ii) entering into a licensing contract signed, at least by the plaintiff, in Colorado. It also looked to the licensing contract's choice of law clause, the making of monthly payments to the plaintiff, a Colorado resident, NENI's sending of a representative to Colorado to initiate the PLUS relationship, and the frequent electronic communication of NENI's computers with PLUS. The court held that the above Colorado contacts, over the contract's life of five years, indicated that NENI purposely availed itself of Colorado.[134] It also found that the exercise of jurisdiction would not offend traditional notions of fair play and substantial justice because of the strong connection between Colorado and the dispute giving rise to the suit.

Also in 1992, a federal district court in California, in *Resolution Trust Corp. v. First of America Bank,*[135] analyzed whether it had jurisdiction over a defendant located in Michigan. At issue was whether the non-forum bank established minimum contacts in California by belonging to national clearing house service association and accepting wire transfers from a California bank. The court noted that the Michigan bank affirmatively entered the stream of commerce flowing to California by joining the clearing house association. However, the court recognized that entering the clearing house is a technological necessity in modern banking and that if this contact supported jurisdiction, all banks would be subject to jurisdiction in every state. The court stated that:

> [p]articipating in the national clearinghouse service seems analogous to having telephone service which allows people to call the bank from all parts of the country and world to perform banking transactions. Yet, such technology which makes banking services more accessible to customers does not commit the bank to national jurisdiction without some affirmative action to avail itself of a particular forum.[136]

The court thus held the assertion of jurisdiction would be inappropriate.[137]

In 1994, a Florida state court, in *Pres-Kap, Inc. v. System One, Direct Access, Inc.,*[138] examined the implications of the forum contacts created by a New York travel agency's use of an online electronic database located in Florida. Expressing concern about the far-reaching implications of basing jurisdiction on such contacts, the court held that maintenance of the suit offended traditional notions of fair play and substantial justice. The court found the notion of defending the suit "wildly beyond the reasonable expectations of such computer information users."[139] It compared the New York travel agency's situation to that of a nonresident

---

[134] *Id.* at 119.

[135] 796 F. Supp. 1333, 1334-35 (C.D. Cal. 1992).

[136] *Id.* at 1336.

[137] *Id.* at 1338.

[138] 636 So.2d 1351 (Fla. Dist. Ct. App. 1994).

[139] *Id.*

Lexis or Westlaw user and expressed concern about how many individuals would be subject to jurisdiction if it ruled otherwise.[140]

In 1997, in *Zippo Manufacturing. Co. v. Zippo Dot Com., Inc.*,[141] a federal district court in Pennsylvania considered whether a California corporation's operation of an Internet website and online Internet news service provides sufficient contacts to establish jurisdiction in Pennsylvania in a trademark domain dispute. The court summarized the applicable analysis under the established jurisdiction cases and Internet jurisdiction cases by stating:

> [T]he likelihood that personal jurisdiction can be constitutionally exercised is directly proportionate to the nature and quality of commercial activity that an entity conducts over the Internet. This sliding scale is consistent with well developed personal jurisdiction principles. At one end of the spectrum are situations where a defendant clearly does business over the Internet. If the defendant enters into contracts with residents of a foreign jurisdiction that involve the knowing and repeated transmission of computer files over the Internet, personal jurisdiction is proper. At the opposite end are situations where a defendant has simply posted information on an Internet website which is accessible to users in foreign jurisdictions. A passive website that does little more than make information available to those who are interested in it is not grounds for the exercise [of] personal jurisdiction. The middle ground is occupied by interactive websites where a user can exchange information with the host computer. In these cases, the exercise of jurisdiction is determined by examining the level of interactivity and commercial nature of the exchange of information that occurs on the website.[142]

In *Zippo,* the court held that Zippo Dot Com ("Dot Com"), a California corporation was subject to jurisdiction in the forum state of Pennsylvania because it engaged in Internet commerce with Pennsylvania residents. The court distinguished Dot Com's contacts with Pennsylvania from those discussed in other Internet cases. It found that Dot Com created an interactive website and had thereby engaged in active Internet commerce. The court focused on Dot Com's contracts with approximately 3,000 individuals and seven Internet access providers in the forum state. Dot Com's news service consisted of three levels of membership — public/free, "Original," and "Super." The "Original" and "Super" membership levels required the purchase of passwords and allowed Pennsylvania residents to download electronic information. The court refused to characterize Dot Com's contacts with Pennsylvania as merely fortuitous, finding that Dot Com's contacts with the forum would only be fortuitous if a consumer's unilateral action caused Dot Com's Pennsylvania contacts.

---

[140] Lexis and Westlaw are two popular computer research databases.

[141] 952 F. Supp. 1119 (W.D. Pa. 1997).

[142] *Id.* at 1124 (internal citations omitted).

[B] *Internet Websites.* Courts examining personal jurisdiction issues have scrutinized the manner in which a nonresident operated and maintained a website. Some of the factors these courts have consider include: the number of contacts with the forum; the nonresident's knowledge of forum users and access; the website's level of interactivity; and restrictions on access. A website's interactivity can be viewed as a broad spectrum of possibilities with the least interactive websites more closely resembling traditional advertising such as billboard advertising and the more interactive websites being equated to active conduct in the forum.

In *Cybersell, Inc. v. Cybersell, Inc.,*[143] the Court of Appeals for the Ninth Circuit held that a website that advertises a product or service without other activity or contact with the forum is not subject to personal jurisdiction in that forum's courts. In that case, a Florida corporation, Cybersell, Inc. was in the business of providing consulting services or strategic management and marketing for businesses on the World Wide Web. At the time Cybersell (Fla.) had commenced its operations, the U.S. Patent and Trademark Office had not granted the application of Cybersell, Inc., an Arizona corporation, for a service mark for the name of Cybersell. Cybersell (Az.) sued Cybersell (Fla.) for trademark infringement in a federal court in Arizona.

The Ninth Circuit noted that "it is essential that in each case that there be some act by which the defendant purposefully avails itself of the privilege of conducting activities within the forum State, thus invoking the benefits and protections of its laws."[144] The Ninth Circuit found that personal jurisdiction did not exist because the Florida website was passive; Cybersell (Fla.) did not encourage Arizona residents to access its site; there was no evidence that any part of its business, let alone a continuous part, was sought or accomplished in Arizona; there was no evidence that a resident of Arizona, besides Cybersell (Az.), had ever visited the Florida site. Furthermore, the court found that Cybersell (Fla.) had no contracts in Arizona, no telemarketing to Arizona, no income earned from Arizona, no toll free number permitting free phone calls from Arizona, nor any other factors that would have indicated that Cybersell (Fla.) availed itself of the privilege of conducting activities in Arizona, thereby acquiring the benefits and protections of Arizona law.

In *Maritz v. Cybergold, Inc.,*[145] a Missouri federal district court held that maintaining a website such that any Internet user, including those of the forum state, could access it, amounts to solicitation and promotional activities, providing the minimum contacts required to exercise personal jurisdiction. In *Maritz*, the plaintiff alleged that the defendant's Internet activities violated federal trademark laws.[146] Cybergold, the corporation maintaining the website, planned to act as a middleman for Internet advertisers and individuals desiring information via the Internet. Finding that Cybergold consciously transmitted advertising to all Internet users, knowing such information would be transmitted globally, the court rejected Cybergold's characterization of its website as passive. The court distinguished the website from more traditional forms of communication, finding that Cybergold automatically responded to each Internet user who accessed its site. The *Maritz* court also

---

[143] 130 F.3d 414 (9th Cir. 1997).

[144] *Id.* at 416-17 (quoting *Hanson v. Denckla,* 357 U.S. 235, 253 (1958)).

[145] 947 F. Supp. 1328 (E.D. Mo. 1996).

[146] Lanham Act, 15 U.S.C. § 1125(a). See Chapter 18 for a discussion of the Lanham Act and other intellectual property considerations.

considered the quantity of Cybergold's Missouri contacts. It noted that Cybergold had transmitted information to 131 forum residents and that it must be subject to jurisdiction in Missouri because it enjoyed the benefits of conducting business in Missouri via the Internet.

In 1996, a Connecticut federal district court in *Inset Systems, Inc. v. Instruction Set, Inc.*[147] decided whether to assert jurisdiction over the nonresident defendant, Instruction Set, Inc. ("ISI"), in a trademark dispute involving ISI's Internet domain name.[148] ISI's alleged contacts with the forum consisted of website advertising viewed by as many as 10,000 Connecticut residents. The court upheld jurisdiction, finding that ISI directed its Internet advertising to all states, including the forum of Connecticut, and satisfied federal Due Process by purposefully creating contacts with Connecticut.

In *Heroes Inc. v. Heroes Foundation*,[149] the Federal District Court for the District of Columbia considered whether to assert jurisdiction over the nonresident defendant, a New York charitable organization, in a trademark infringement claim involving a website. The court examined traditional forum contacts such as newspaper advertising as well as the nonresident's website in assessing the validity of asserting jurisdiction. The court appeared to reject the nonresident's argument that the website was passive and did not target the forum. Instead, the court found that the website design furthered jurisdiction. Significantly, the nonresident's web page solicited contributions and provided a toll-free telephone number for that purpose. The court held that the assertion of jurisdiction would not violate the federal Due Process under the circumstances.

In *Edias Software International, L.L.C. v. Basis International, Ltd.*,[150] a district court in Arizona examined whether a nonresident software distributor's contacts with Arizona residents provided a basis for jurisdiction. Edias Software alleged that Basis breached their contract and that Basis' website gave rise to claims for libel, defamation, tortious interference with contract, and violation of federal trademark laws. Basis' contacts with the state of Arizona included a contract with an Arizona resident, Arizona product sales, employee visits, phone calls, faxes, and e-mails. Furthermore, the nonresident's website was accessible in the forum. The *Edias* court determined that the website's ability to reach forum customers and e-mails to forum customers from nonresidents were sufficient contacts under the minimum contacts analysis to assert jurisdiction. The court asserted that nonresidents maintaining Internet web pages risk jurisdiction.[151]

In *Minnesota v. Granite Gate Resorts, Inc.*,[152] the Minnesota Attorney General alleged that a nonresident company and its president engaged in deceptive trade practices, false advertising, and consumer fraud under

---

[147] 937 F. Supp. 161 (D. Conn. 1996).

[148] ISI is a Massachusetts corporation that provides computer technology and support to organizations throughout the world.

[149] 958 F. Supp. 1 (D.D.C. 1996).

[150] 947 F. Supp. 413 (D. Ariz. 1996).

[151] *Id.* at 420.

[152] No. C6-95-7227, 1996 WL 767431 (Minn. Dist. Ct. Dec. 11, 1996), *aff'd* 568 N.W.2d 715 (Minn. Ct. App. 1997). *See also Banned in Kansas City — Missouri Residents Need Not Apply*, 21ST CENTURY BANKING ALERT NO. 97-7-11, July 11, 1997; *State of Minnesota Presses Jurisdiction Over Out-of-State Web Page*. 21ST CENTURY BANKING ALERT NO. 96-12-20.1, Dec. 20, 1996, *available at* <http://www.ffhsj.com/bancmail/bancpage.htm>.

Minnesota law when the nonresident included on its website an advertisement for its sports betting service based in Belize. In considering whether Granite Gate had established minimum contacts with the forum, the court noted that Granite Gate published a statement on its website asserting that it had the right to apply for injunctive or other relief with regard to a customer in the state where the customer resided. Discussing the nature of Granite Gate's website contacts with the forum, the court rejected the defendants' claim that it mailed nothing to Minnesota, sent nothing to Minnesota, and never advertised in Minnesota. The court stated that "[t]his argument is not sound in the age of cyberspace. Once the Defendants place an advertisement on the Internet, that advertisement is available 24 hours a day, seven days a week, 365 days a year to any Internet user until the Defendants take it off the Internet."[153] The court found that it would be inappropriate to view Granite Gate's website as a one-way contact. The court posited that if that were an accurate description, Minnesota residents would only receive a blank screen when clicking on Granite Gate website icons.[154] Instead, they received a plethora of information, including a Las Vegas phone number to Granite Gate's gambling service.

Examining the quantity of contacts with the forum, the Minnesota court found that Minnesota residents were regular visitors to the website and that Granite Gate's mailing list included Minnesota residents. During one two-week period, over 248 different locations in Minnesota accessed Granite Gate's website. In light of the detailed records kept by Granite Gate of website users, it could not reasonably claim that Minnesota residents were not accessing their website. Accordingly, the court held that jurisdiction was proper.

In *Digital Equipment Corp. v. AltaVista Technology, Inc.*,[155] a Massachusetts federal district court considered whether to assert jurisdiction over a nonresident defendant, a California corporation named AltaVista Technology, Inc.("ATI"), in a trademark dispute based on ATI's website. The defendant's website closely resembled the plaintiff's site, raising trademark infringement questions. ATI had several Massachusetts contacts: a contract with Digital Equipment Corporation ("Digital"), a Massachusetts corporation, solicitations of business via ATI's website, and three sales to Massachusetts residents. In its contract with Digital, ATI sold its rights to the trademark "AltaVista" and obtained a license to use "AltaVista" as part of its name and website address. The court held that ATI's "Web activities bring ATI 'over the line,' and render jurisdiction appropriate."[156]

A New York federal district court in a 1996 trademark infringement case, *Bensusan Restaurant Corp. v. King*,[157] rejected the proposition that the creation and maintenance of a website rendered a party subject to jurisdiction in a foreign forum. The court held that the nonresident, King, did not purposely avail itself of the benefits of New York. Stressing that King simply created a website, it characterized the website as a product placed in the stream of commerce rather than an activity purposely directed towards the forum. The court found King had not sought to solicit business in New York, encourage New York residents to access its website, or

---

[153] *Granite Gate Resorts*, 1996 WL 767431, at *6.

[154] *Id.* at *9.

[155] 960 F. Supp. 456 (D. Mass. 1997).

[156] *Id.* at 463.

[157] 937 F. Supp. 295 (S.D.N.Y. 1996), *aff'd*, 126 F.3d 25 (2d Cir. 1997).

conduct business in New York. It distinguished *CompuServe*, finding that the nonresident in *CompuServe* targeted, advertised, and conducted business in the forum. The Second Circuit affirmed the *Bensusan* decision in September 1997, noting that a nonresident must be physically present in the state for jurisdiction to attach.[158]

In *Telco Communications Group, Inc. v. An Apple a Day, Inc.*,[159] the court addressed the issue of personal jurisdiction over a defendant whose actions occurred over the Internet. In *Telco* the plaintiffs alleged that Apple a Day's press releases over the Internet defamed Telco. Apple a Day challenged the suit for lack of personal jurisdiction. The *Telco* court applied Virginia's long-arm statute to the Apple a Day's activities.[160] Under that statute a Virginia court may assert jurisdiction over a defendant who regularly does or conducts business in Virginia and causes tortious injury in Virginia by an act or omission outside Virginia.[161] Apple a Day did not challenge the fact that a tortious injury occurred as the result of an act or omission outside the state. The *Telco* Court therefore focused on the regular conduct of business prong and, agreeing with the Connecticut district court's decision in *Inset*, held that posting an advertisement or solicitation on a website constitutes a consistent course of conduct and that the press releases constituted doing or soliciting business. In doing so, the *Telco* court rejected the Second Circuit's holding in *Bensusan* that nonresidents must be physically present in the state for jurisdiction to attach. The court also found that jurisdiction existed based on a tortious injury resulting from an act or omission in Virginia.[162] It reasoned that the defendants were aware of the breadth of the distribution of the press releases, both from information they had received when contracting to post the press releases and from their knowledge of Telco's and an ISP's presence in Virginia. Finally, though the defendants did not challenge a finding of personal jurisdiction on federal Due Process grounds, the court held that the defendants could reasonably have anticipated being haled into court and thus no violation of federal Due Process would occur.

In *Hearst v. Goldberger*[163] the federal district court for the Southern District of New York faced the issue of whether, in a trademark infringement case, the court had personal jurisdiction over the defendant as a result of his website being accessible to and electronically visited by New York computer users. The court based its

---

[158] *Bensusan*, 126 F.3d at 28-29. The appellate court was following the precedent of the New York Court of Appeals, which has consistently held that long-arm jurisdiction based on a tortious act within the state under N.Y. C.P.L.R. § 302(a)(2) is only available if the actor or his agent was physically present in New York. *See, e.g., Platt Corp. v. Platt*, 217 N.E.2d 134 (N.Y. 1966); *Feathers v. McLucas*, 209 N.E.2d 68 (N.Y. 1965). *See also* N.Y. C.P.L.R. § 302(a)(2) & practice commentary C302:17 (stating that "if a New Jersey domicile were to lob a bazooka shell across the Hudson River at Grant's Tomb, *Feathers* would appear to bar the New York courts from asserting personal jurisdiction" in a resulting tort case). As a result, in 1966 the New York legislature added N.Y. C.P.L.R. § 302(a)(3), which applies to tortious acts committed outside the state by actors who should reasonably expect the tortious act to have consequences in the state, and who derive substantial revenue from interstate commerce. *See Bensusan*, 126 F.3d at 29; N.Y.C.P.L.R. practice commentary C302:17. This portion of the long-arm statute was not applicable in *Bensusan* because the defendant's business operations were purely local to Columbia, Missouri. *Bensusan*, 126 F.3d at 29.

[159] 977 F. Supp. 404 (E.D. Va. 1997).

[160] VA CODE ANN. §§ 8.01-328.1(A)(3), (4).

[161] *Id.* § 8.01-328.1(A)(4).

[162] *Id.* § 8.01-328.1(A)(3).

[163] No. 96 Civ. 3620, 1997 U.S. Dist. LEXIS 2065 (S.D.N.Y. Feb. 26, 1997).

analysis on one of New York's jurisdictional statutes, C.P.L.R. § 302.[164] It found that Goldberger's website, announcing the future availability of his services, amounted to the equivalent of an advertisement in a national magazine. Such advertisements do not provide a basis for personal jurisdiction under the transacted business or solicitation prongs of the statute. The *Hearst* court distinguished the case from *Bensusan*, stating that *Bensusan* addressed purposefully directed contact. It also distinguished *Maritz* and *Inset*, reasoning that in those instances defendants consciously decided to transmit advertising information to all Internet users.

In September 1997, the federal district court for the District of New Jersey had the opportunity to address whether Internet advertising could subject the defendant hotel chain, an Italian corporation, to personal jurisdiction in New Jersey. In *Weber v. Jolly Hotels*,[165] the court agreed with the *Hearst* court that advertising on the Internet "falls under the same rubric as advertising in a national magazine,"[166] an activity that fails to constitute "continuous and substantial" contacts with the forum state.[167] Further, the *Weber* court stated that exercising jurisdiction based on mere advertising activities would violate the federal Due Process.[168] The court also rejected plaintiff's assertion of specific jurisdiction, on the grounds that its relationship with a rival company in New Jersey did not rise to the level of purposeful availment of the benefits of New Jersey's laws.[169]

Finally, in *Smith v. Holly Lobby Store, Inc.*,[170] a district court decided whether the exercise of personal jurisdiction would be consistent with the Arkansas long-arm statute in the context of a wrongful death action.[171] The defendants were a Hong Kong corporation, BOTO, and the Arkansas retailer to which BOTO had sold the product blamed for causing a fatal fire. The court held that BOTO could not be subject to personal jurisdiction based on the sale of goods to the retailer, Hobby Lobby, nor could it be subject to jurisdiction based on an advertisement in a trade publication that appears over the Internet.[172]

[C] *Other Electronic Forum Contacts.* Courts examining jurisdiction have also based jurisdiction on non-website contacts such as e-mail[173] and registration of allegedly infringing Internet domain names.[174] Important

---

[164] N.Y. C.P.L.R. § 302. The court did note, however, that the defendants contacts with New York would not meet the requirements of "doing business" as set forth in N.Y. C.P.L.R. § 301. *Hearst*, 1997 U.S. Dist. LEXIS 2065, at *24.

[165] 977 F. Supp. 327 (D.N.J. 1997).

[166] *Weber*, 977 F. Supp. at 333.

[167] *See, e.g., Gehling v. St. George's School of Medicine*, 773 F.2d 539, 542 (3d Cir. 1985).

[168] *Weber*, 977 F. Supp. at 334.

[169] *Id.* at 332-33.

[170] 968 F. Supp. 1356 (W.D. Ark. 1997).

[171] *See* ARK. CODE ANN. § 16-4-101(B). In 1995 the Arkansas statute had been amended to provide that personal jurisdiction would be proper if consistent with the federal Due Process.

[172] *Holly Lobby*, 968 F. Supp. at 1365.

[173] *See Cody v. Ward*, 954 F. Supp. 43 (D. Conn. 1997) (holding that specific jurisdiction could be validly asserted based on the nonresident's frequent e-mails and phone calls to the forum, making it unnecessary to consider whether the nonresident's Prodigy messages counted as forum contacts).

[174] *See Porsche Cars N.AM. v. Chen*, No. 96-1006-A (E.D. Va. Mar. 27, 1997) (finding that a nonresident had transacted business and caused injury in the forum by registering an infringing domain name); *Panavision Int'l, L.P. v. Toeppen*, 938 F. Supp. 616, 621-22 (C.D. Cal. 1996) (finding in a trademark infringement and dilution action that the nonresident's registration of a domain name was a scam instead of a legitimate business enterprise, triggering the effects test approved by the Supreme Court in *Calder v. Jones*, 465 U.S. 783 (1984), in contrast to the minimum contacts analysis used in other Internet cases).

factors in these situations have been the number of contacts and whether they represented an attempt to conduct business or reply to an inquiry.[175]

In *Resuscitation Technologies Inc. v. Continental Health Care Corp.*,[176] the court discussed whether to assert jurisdiction over the nonresident defendants, who had planned to invest in a joint venture with the plaintiff corporation. The suit alleged a breach of contract arising from the failed business negotiations. Holding jurisdiction over the nonresident proper, the court found that the nonresident's 80 e-mail messages, sent to Indiana residents relating to the planned joint venture, amounted to sufficient minimum contacts.[177] The court asserted that applying traditional jurisdiction concepts to business over the Internet involves examining the transaction's level of interactivity, as well as the commercial nature of the information exchanged.[178] Here, the number of messages and the intent to create a long term business enterprise weighed in favor of jurisdiction.

[v] *Analysis.* The foregoing cases indicate that financial institutions and merchants must take into account the potential that the nature and scope of their Internet presence may be used as the basis for an assertion of jurisdiction over these entities in a foreign forum. Financial institutions and merchants should evaluate the trade-offs between an enhanced multi-jurisdictional marketing and transactional presence against the impact such presence may have on jurisdictional defenses. Participants in electronic commerce can take steps to minimize the risk of jurisdiction in a foreign forum by use of disclaimers or otherwise conveying intended geographic limitations of the entity's service area and by limiting the interactive nature of their electronic contacts with forum residents, limiting their non-Internet contacts with the forum, and as an extreme measure, restricting access via the forum or by forum residents.[179]

Even if sufficient minimum contacts exist to support jurisdiction, the assertion of jurisdiction must still comply with traditional notions of fair play and substantial justice. An entity's intentions and business plans may factor into this analysis. If an entity's business plan targets forum residents, jurisdiction is more likely than if that entity's business plan does not focus on the forum and its Internet presence makes random forum contacts possible. For example, the use of web page disclaimers may aid a claim that the assertion of jurisdiction is not appropriate.[180]

---

[175] *Id.*

[176] No. IP 96-1457-C-M/S, 1997 U.S. Dist. LEXIS (S.D. Ind. Mar. 24, 1997).

[177] *Id.* at *15-17.

[178] *Id.* at *13 (citing to *Zippo*, 952 F. Supp. 1119).

[179] *See* Robert A. Bourque & Kerry L. Konrad, *Avoiding Remote Jurisdiction Based on Internet Website*, N.Y.L.J., Dec. 10, 1996, at 4. The North American Securities Administrators Association ("NASAA") has adopted a resolution regarding initial public offerings on the Internet, exempting securities from states' securities registration provisions that include a disclaimer that securities are not being offered to the residents of a particular state and the offer is not otherwise specifically directed to any person in a state by or on behalf of the issuer of securities. *See Resolution Regarding Securities Offered on Internet*, NASAA Reports (CCH) ¶ 7040 (1996). To date, 31 states have adopted Internet exemptions. *See* Neal Sullivan, *Making a Case for Exemptive Authority*, WALLSTREETLAWYER.COM, June 1997, at 22.

[180] *See* Craig Peyton Gaumer, *The Minimum Cyber-Contacts Test: An Emerging Standard of Constitutional Personal Jurisdiction*, ILL. B. J., Feb. 1997, at 63.

New technologies have the potential to affect the jurisdictional equation. Financial institutions may soon begin using the new "push" technology, which allows networks to send information directly into the user's computer, in contrast to the more widespread Internet's "pull" system through the use of search engines, which requires consumer action to access Internet material. These "push" systems analytically resemble door to door salesman, raising the issue of whether companies employing "push" technology purposely avail themselves of the foreign forum.[181]

Financial institutions should monitor the development of Internet jurisdiction analysis resulting from either new legislation or court interpretations and be prepared to evaluate, on a continuing basis, whether to modify the nature and scope of their Internet presence.[182]

---

[181] They differ in that e-mail addresses unlike residences do not necessarily have a geographic component associated with them.

[182] *See Hearst*, 1997 U.S. Dist. LEXIS 2065 at *23 (*citing* Richard S. Zimbeck, *Jurisdiction and the Internet: Fundamental Fairness in the Networked World of Cyberspace*, 6 ALBANY L. J. SCIENCE & TECH. 339, 346 (1996)) (recognizing the possible need for a new body of law to deal with cyberspace personal jurisdiction but finding that in the absence of congressional or state actions, traditional laws should apply); Gaumer, *supra* note 180.

APPENDIX A

PREPARING THE RECORD FOR YEAR 2000 LITIGATION

UNDERSTANDING THE DYNAMICS OF THE PROBLEM AND THE REGULATORY CONCERNS

Banks and financial institutions face a daunting challenge in the remaining days before January 1, 2000 to ensure that the systems under their direct control and <u>all</u> interconnecting networks function properly. Concern over the scope of the task varies from moderate to severe. The October 4 issue of *The Economist* featured a cover story on what it designated "The Millennium Bug" and estimated the "costs" associated with the problem to be in the range of $52 billion to $3.6 trillion. The article offered simple advice to businesses: "Please panic early."

The Basle Committee on Banking Supervision issued a policy statement on the topic last month summarizing the problem for the world's banking industry in the following manner:

> The Year 2000 poses a significant challenge for financial institutions because many auto-mated applications will cease to function normally as a result of the way date fields have been handled historically. Failure to address this issue in a timely manner would cause banking institutions to experience operational problems or even bankruptcy and could cause the disruption of financial markets.

On September 25, Comptroller of the Currency Ludwig expressed concern that institutions may not adequately focus on the potential impact of the Year 2000 problem because they may believe it is not serious, will not adversely impact them, someone else will fix it, or there will be sufficient time to address the issue later rather than sooner.

For over a year, the federal bank regulatory agencies have been stressing the importance of undertaking a systematic review of the steps necessary to achieve Year 2000 compliance. Agency guidance includes FFIEC statements on: (1) The Effect of Year 2000 on Computer Systems, June 17, 1996; and (2) Year 2000 Project Management Awareness, May 5, 1997. The May 1997 statement divided the Year 2000 project management process into five categories.

Awareness Phase. Define the problem and obtain executive level support for the resources necessary to perform compliance work. Develop an overall strategy that covers in-house systems, service bureaus, vendors, auditors, customers and suppliers.

Assessment Phase. Assess the size and complexity of the problem, including identifying all systems that will be affected by the Year 2000. Management should also evaluate the effect of the problem on strategic initiatives, including mergers and acquisitions and corporate alliances.

Renovation Phase. Undertake code enhancements, hardware and software upgrades, system replacements, and vendor certifications.

Validation Phase. Testing and verification of changes to systems and coordination with outside parties.

Implementation Phase. Systems should be certified as Year 2000 compliant.

The magnitude and difficulty of this task will vary greatly among institutions based on factors such as the size of the institution, the complexity of its operations and the extent of its reliance on interconnecting networks.

Institutions should not underestimate the amount of effort, both internally and from third party consultants and service providers, that may be necessary to complete the Year 2000 compliance process. In some instances, it may be more practical to convert to a new system rather than modifying an existing one. Special attention should be paid to the efforts of third parties who operate systems that are not under the control of the institution, but upon which banks must rely to achieve Year 2000 compliance. The contractual agreements with such parties should be reviewed to determine the rights of the parties in the event a third-party-controlled system ultimately is not Year 2000 compliant. Written representations from third parties as to the status of and projections for Year 2000 compliance and the capacity of such systems to be modified should be obtained in written form. Institutions should also consider backup alternatives in the event compliance is not achieved and evaluate whether Year 2000 insurance may be a feasible or appropriate response.

Individual and systemic problems of various magnitudes are likely to occur in 2000, leading to errors, failures and information technology crashes which will cause financial loss and lead to litigation and regulatory enforcement actions. The way to reduce the likelihood of being a defendant in such litigation or administrative proceeding is to start preparing today the record of your institution's compliance with legal, regulatory and operational elements of the problem and management's attempt to exercise prudence in resolving the issues. Attached is our "Year 2000 Compliance Checklist," which should assist you in that process. We suggest that institutions initially consult with counsel regarding confidentiality considerations in regard to their Year 2000 compliance materials.

YEAR 2000 COMPLIANCE CHECKLIST

1. **Due Diligence Review and Assessment**

   Identify, catalog and review:

   1.1. Proprietary hardware, software systems and networks

   1.2. Leased, purchased, shared hardware, software systems and networks

   1.3. Interconnecting hardware, software systems and networks

   1.4. Environmental systems

   - vaults
   - alarm systems
   - elevators
   - telephones

   1.5. Applicable sales invoices, contracts, licensing agreements, operating agreements, warranties, representations for hardware, software systems and networks

   1.6. Vendor licensors, consultants, advisors and agents involved in acquisition, implementation and maintenance of hardware, software systems and networks

   1.7. Trademarks, patents and copyrights of hardware, software systems and networks

   1.8. Potential code enhancements, hardware and software replacements

   1.9. Data processing and information technology partnerships, investments, joint ventures and outsourcing

   1.10. Parties responsible for solutions

   - internal
   - external

   1.11. Leap year considerations

   1.12 Systems that are vulnerable prior to 2000

2. **Assign Responsibility for Compliance**

   2.1. Internal controls

   2.1.1. By departments, divisions or product

   2.1.2. By system, network or connectivity

   2.1.3. Determine and identify company spokespersons

   2.2. External parties (vendors, etc.)

   2.2.1. Written contact with all responsible third parties

   2.2.2. Written timelines and reports should be received from all third parties

   2.3. Consultants, advisors, counsel

   2.3.1. Determine expertise required

   2.3.2. Written engagement regarding scope of responsibility

3.   Identify Exposures, Issues and Concerns

3.1.   Regulatory

3.2.   Operational/Business

3.3.   Legal

3.4.   Accounting

3.5.   Financial

3.6.   Securities disclosure

3.7.   Conversion issues

3.8.   Tax

3.9.   Potential liabilities to others

3.10. Confidentiality of materials and findings

3.11   Remediation considerations

    3.11.1.   Authority to make modifications to software

    3.11.2.   Authority to allow third parties to have access to software

    3.11.3.   Ownership rights to modified software

3.12. Policies for acquisition of new systems

4.   Employee Considerations

4.1.   Identify critical employees

4.2.   Staff retention

4.3.   Confidentiality tools

4.4.   Codes of conduct

4.5.   Bonus compensation

5.   Document and Verify Compliance Efforts

5.1.   Initial letters to internal parties and third parties

    5.1.1.   Timelines

    5.1.2.   Identification of issues

    5.1.3.   Responses

    5.1.4.   Receipt of written certification of compliance procedures

    5.1.5.   Receipt of written certification of actual compliance

    5.1.6.   Verify compliance and document in writing

    5.1.7.   Review by management, consultants and counsel

    5.1.8.   Engagements and advisory contracts

5.2.   Internal documentation

    5.2.1.   Identification of designated officers and employees in communication tree

    5.2.2.   Audit procedures

    5.2.3.   Document compliance efforts

    5.2.4.   Document actual compliance and verification

    5.2.5.   Review by management, consultants and counsel

    5.2.6.   Board meeting minutes

    5.2.7.   Determination of privileged nature of documentation

5.3.   Communications with regulators

    5.3.1.   Proactive communications and reports

    5.3.2.   Response to exam criticisms

    5.3.3.   Involvement of specified officers

    5.3.4.   Review by consultants and counsel

5.4.   Follow-up letters and communications

5.5.   Reports to Board of Directors

    5.5.1.   Report status regularly

    5.5.2.   Presentation on final compliance and/or problems

6.   Testing

6.1.   Internal

6.2.   External

6.3.   Networks

6.4.   Service providers

6.5.   Vendors

6.6.   Intermediaries

6.7.   Documentation

6.8.   Determination of privileged nature of documentation

6.9.   Double and triple check by advisors and consultants

7.   State & Federal Law Considerations

7.1.   Likelihood that exculpatory laws will be enacted

7.2.   Compliance with regulatory directives

7.3.   Petition state and federal government agencies for relief

7.4.   "Act of God" categorization of Year 2000 problems

8.   Corporate Customer Compliance

8.1.   Assessment of issues

8.2.   Evaluation of exposure to credit outstanding

8.3.   Review credit agreements

8.4.   Remedial actions

9. Potential Institution Liabilities and Responsibilities of Third Parties

9.1. Contractual obligations of bank

9.2. Related theories of responsibility (*e.g.*, tort, vicarious, down-stream liability, etc.)

9.3. Contractual obligations of third parties

9.4. Risk analysis and loss calculation

9.5. Review by counsel

9.6. Determination of privileged nature of documentation

9.7. Director and officer liability

10. Additional Considerations

10.1. Insurance

10.2. Bonds

10.3. Codes of conduct

10.4. Securities disclosure, SEC Staff Legal Bulletin 5, October 5, 1997

10.5. Systems check

10.6. Impact of European monetary conversion

10.7. Development of disaster scenarios and procedures

10.8. Availability of back-up systems

10.9. Future acquisitions, purchases and systems

10.10. Public relations

10.11. Communications with customers

10.12. Impact on strategic decisions including mergers and acquisitions

APPENDIX B
UNIX CONTROL CHECKLIST

1. Is there a password policy? If so, does it include the following:

   • Password length minimum is established. (At least a length of six is acceptable.)

   • Passwords are required to be changed at least every ninety days.

   • Password syntax prevents users from using easy to guess passwords.

2. Proactive checking – Is password checking performed?

   • Is password or password+ used to proactively screen passwords as they are entered? (These programs run a series of checks on password when they are set and can help to screen out poor passwords. *They were not designed to work with shadow password systems.*)

   • Is CRACK executed to periodically check for weak passwords.

   • Is password aging utilized? If applicable.

3. Determine if there are adequate password controls. Review the **/etc/passwd** file to determine if there are adequate controls in place.

   • Do all ID's have passwords?

   • Are UID #'s unique? (The third, colon separated, field in **/etc/passwd** is the user ID number.) Unique UID's are important because UNIX identifies users by their UID #, not their ID. The system will identify duplicate UID numbers as the same user.

   • Are there any guest accounts? Any that exist should be disabled.

   • Are default vendor accounts (daemon, sys, bin, uucp, news, ingres and similar accounts) disabled?

4. Are the passwords encrypted or is the client using a shadow password file? (Beware of "*" in the password field. "*" disables the account on some UNIX systems, but it indicates "shadow" passwords are being used on others (AIX, for example). However, * does not always completely disable an account. The preferred way to disable an account is by changing the user's shell to /bin/false (a shell that does not exist) in /etc/passwd file. Ask the system administrator what the "*" indicates on the system.)

5.   Are shadow passwords implemented, and if so, review the **/etc/shadow** file to determine if there are adequate controls in place. Do adequate controls exist?

- Review that all ID's have an encrypted password.

- Ensure that the password was changed within ninety days. (To calculate this, use the following: Subtract 9125 from the last changed value. The difference is how many days from January 1, 1995 since the password was last changed. If this does not appear correct, contact the system administrator as this can vary between systems.)

- Review the minimum number of days before a user can change their password. Is the setting reasonable?

- Is the maximum number of days a password is valid reasonable?

- Review the number of days a login can remain unused before a password becomes inactive.

6.   Root Password

- Determine if access to superuser accounts (IDs with user number "0" in the third field of **/etc/passwd** are effectively superuser accounts) is limited on a business-need basis. NOTE: More than one user may share knowledge of the superuser password. Superuser access should be severely limited.

- Also, system administrators should be required to log in with their own non-superuser account and use the su command to become the superuser. This provides a better audit trail of superuser access.

7.   Is there a backup copy of the password file on the system? If so, is it adequately secure?

8.   Review the user groups listed in the **/etc/group** file. Ensure that end-users cannot become members of the root, bin, or admin groups. (See which user ID's are listed with the root, bin and admin groups.) Is this adequately restricted?

9.   Obtain the names of directories containing production programs and data. Are access to these files appropriately restricted?

10.   Obtain the names of the development directories. Is access to these directories appropriately restricted?

11.   Are all "r" commands (rlogin, rsh, etc.) disabled? To do this, comment out "r" commands in /etc/inetd.conf. To comment out a command, place the "#" at the beginning of the line. If these commands have not been disabled, explain why.

12. /etc/hosts/equiv

- Does this file exist in /etc? If so, why? This file allows other hosts to be trusted by your system. Programs like rlogin can then be used to log on to the same account name on a trusted machine without supplying a password.

If this file does exist:

a) Ensure there is only a small number of TRUSTED hosts listed. Verify the location of each host. Are any hosts located outside of the client?

b) Ensure that the client does <u>not</u> have a "+" by itself anywhere in the file. Is there a "+"? If so, why?

c) Ensure that first character is not "-". Is the first character "-"? If so, why?

d) Are permissions set to 600? If not, document the permission setting and explain why. (In Unix access reports permissions are listed "rwxrwxrwx". Each group of three characters adds up to 7, with r(ead)=4, w(rite)=2, and x(ecute)=1.)

e) Is the owner is set to root? If not, why?.

13. $HOME/.rhosts

a) Do users have an rhost file in their home directory? If so, why? (These pose a risk because an .rhost file can be created by each user.) If not, obtain a list of all users' home directory to ensure that hosts do not exist.

b) Does someone frequently check to ensure they do not exist?
  - If they do exist, are the following controls in place?:
  - The first character of the file is not "-".
  - The owner is the same person who owns the account.
  - Files do not contain the symbol "+" on any line.

14. Is write access to the following powerful files in the /etc file adequately restricted?

These files should not be world writable.

a. group – contains group definitions. Ensures that users cannot become members of root, sys, bin, or admin groups. If not adequately restricted users can gain unauthorized access through them.

b. password - contains user account definitions and passwords. A user could create an unauthorized ID if access to the password file is not adequately restricted.

c. profile – contains the system startup commands. A user could modify the system profile and add a line to perform a function granting unauthorized access.

d. shadow – contains the encrypted passwords and password related parameters and with time a user could decrypt the passwords.

If any of the above files have group write access, determine who is in the group and if access is granted on a business-need only basis.

15. Is write access to the following powerful files adequately restricted?

These files should not be world writable.

a. etc - this directory contains the critical files listed in question 3. This can be found in the /directory (root).

b. shells (csh, ksh, rsh, etc.) Shells can be used to gain unauthorized access. These can be found in the /bin or /usr/bin directory.

c. startup files (.profile, .exrc, .chsrc, and .mailrc). World writable startup files can be used to gain unauthorized access. These can be found in the / directory (root).

d. . and .. (directory index listings) - these control access within the current directory and the ability to navigate up a directory level. If they are world writable then a user can access any file on the system. These can be found in the / directory (root).

If any of the above files have group write access, determine who is in the group and if access is granted on a business-need only basis.

16. Determine if users can access the system prompt? Is access to the system prompt limited to MIS personnel?

17. Is dial-up access available in the environment?

18. Does the MIS function maintain control over all dial-up access devices?

19. Is the ability to dial into the system granted on a business-need-only basis?

If so, describe the security mechanism(s) that controls dial-up access.

20. If dial-up security software is in place, are dial-up access activity and violations regularly monitored by appropriate MIS personnel?

APPENDIX C
FIREWALL/WEB SERVER CHECKLIST

A. Background / Environment

1. List below the personnel interviewed.

2. Who is responsible for the installation and maintenance of the firewall?

3. Obtain an understanding of the network architecture including the location of the firewall and all routers. Provide a description of the set of components that make up the firewall and their functions with regard to network security.

4. Obtain the Acceptable Internet Use Policy. Ensure that the policy must be approved by users prior to being given an Internet account.

5. Obtain a list of accounts that can directly log into the servers that hold the Firewall, Oracle Web Server, and the Netscape Proxy Server.

B. Firewall

1. Does the vendor provide training and installation support?

2. Is the firewall source code provided as part of the purchase price?

3. What are the hours of customer support?

4. How many users will be passing through the firewall at peak usage?

5. What filtering does the firewall perform?

6. Which telnet standards (TN3270, TN5250, vt100) are required and which are supported (block mode vs. line mode)?

7. Does the firewall screen access through ftp by each ftp command (*i.e.,* get and put)?

8. Does the firewall screen access through http?

9. Is the SMTP proxy merely a forwarder program that forwards all messages to an internal SMTP gateway or is the proxy a modified, secured send mail program with additional controls?

10. If a SNMP proxy is provided, does it allow sets to be made through the firewall or up to the firewall?

11. Are there any applications that will be used in the future for which the firewall should provide proxy support (*e.g.,* Oracle, Sybase, etc.)?

12. Is a generic service needed? Can a generic proxy connection be initiated from the external network? Can generic proxies be configured to authenticate users with passwords?

13. What password controls can be implemented (formal, aging, etc.)?

14. Can users be put into access groups for the purpose of setting up access rules? Is this based on user names, source/destination IP network addresses, or both?

15. Is a DNS server running on the internal network or on a DMZ? Does the firewall provide a secure DNS proxy for the external network?

16. Can the firewall be managed locally at the console or will remote telnet access be necessary for remote maintenance?

17. How can remote maintenance be secured?

18. Does the firewall provide different levels of administrative access to the firewall for two levels of users (*e.g.,* systems administrator and assistant)?

19. What type of firewall management interface is used (*e.g.,* text-based or GUI)?

20. What are the firewall logging requirements? Are they by packet, bytes transferred, source and destination, or service used? Does the firewall support these requirements?

21. Does the firewall provide statistics functionality?

22. Is usage billing and accounting provided?

23. Can audit alarms (*e.g.,* e-mail, logging, SNMP traps, beepers) be configured for predetermined security events?

24. What encryption methods are supported (*e.g.,* DES, RSA)? Can encryption be supported from the workstation to the firewall only between network (firewalls—also known as virtual private networks (VPN's)—or between the firewall and other internal network systems?

C. Web Server

1. Does the vendor provide training and installation support?

2. Is the Web Server source code provided as part of the purchase price?

3. What are the hours of customer support?

4. How many users will be passing through the Web Server at peak usage?

5. What password controls can be implemented (formal, aging, etc.)?

6. Can users be put into access groups for the purpose of setting up access rules? Is this based on user names, source/destination IP network addresses, or both?

7. Can the Web Server be managed locally at the console or will remote telnet access be necessary for remote maintenance? How can remote maintenance be secured?

8. Does the Web Server provide different levels of administrative access to the Web Server for two levels of users (*e.g.*, systems administrator and assistant)?

9. What type of management interface is used (*e.g.*, text-based or GUI)?

10. Does the Web Server provide statistics functionality?

11. Is usage billing and accounting provided?

12. Can audit alarms (*e.g.*, e-mail, logging, SNMP traps, beepers) be configured for predetermined security events?

13. What encryption methods are supported (*e.g.*, DES, RSA)? Can encryption be supported from the workstation to the firewall only between network (firewalls—also known as virtual private networks (VPN's)—or between the firewall and other internal network systems?

D. Proxy Server

1. Does the vendor provide training and installation support?

2. Is the proxy server source code provided as part of the purchase price?

3. What are the hours of customer support?

4. How many users will be using the proxy server to access the Internet at peak usage?

5. Which proxy services have been allowed?

6. Which telnet standards (TN3270, TN5250, vt100) are required and which are supported (block mode vs. line mode)?

7. Does the http proxy authenticate outbound as well as inbound users? Is URL filtering supported?

8. Is the Proxy Server configured to authenticate users with passwords? If so, what are the password settings?

9. What password controls can be implemented (formal, aging, etc.)?

10. Can users be put into access groups for the purpose of setting up access rules? Is this based on user names, source/destination IP network addresses, or both?

11. Can the proxy server be managed locally at the console or will remote telnet access be necessary for remote maintenance?

12. How can remote maintenance be secured?

13. Does the proxy server provide different levels of administrative access to the proxy server for two levels of users (*e.g.,* systems administrator and assistant)?

14. What type of proxy server management interface is used (*e.g.,* text-based or GUI)?

15. What are the proxy server logging requirements? Are they by packet, bytes transferred, source and destination, or service used? Does the firewall support these requirements?

16. Does the proxy server provide statistics functionality?

17. Is usage billing and accounting provided?

18. Can audit alarms (*e.g.,* e-mail, logging, SNMP traps, beepers) be configured for predetermined security events?

19. What encryption methods are supported (*e.g.,* DES, RSA)? Can encryption be supported from the workstation to the firewall only between network (firewalls—also known as virtual private networks (VPN's)—or between the firewall and other internal network systems?

APPENDIX D

ENCRYPTION FOR ELECTRONIC BANKING AND COMMERCE

[1] ENCRYPTION SYSTEMS

Encryption is an esoteric and highly technical subject. Major encryption systems employ a level of mathematics that is not generally taught to college educated engineers or physicists. There is a good reason for those working in the field of electronic commerce, however, to develop a basic understanding of encryption.[1]

This discussion presents encryption at two different levels. Many of the major encryption components and algorithms will be explained by comparing them to physical objects. This is not hard because many of the algorithms were constructed because computer users wanted to simulate or duplicate some item from the real world. But these analogies only go so far and there are differences between the encryption system and its real world analog. For this reason, the discussion will also present simple versions of encryption systems that are insecure but designed to allow the reader to work through the process using basic arithmetic. These will provide the background for a better understanding of how the items work in the digital domain.

[a] **Private Key Encryption.** Secret or Private Key, or symmetric key, encryption is the classic form of encryption. In private key encryption both the encrypter and decrypter use the same secret key. The simplest analogy for private key encryption is a locked box. Everyone desiring access to the box must have a copy of the key. If the key is lost or surreptitiously copied, the security of the box is compromised.[2]

---

[1] For an extended discussion of encryption, see PETER WAYNER, DIGITAL CASH (1996) and PETER WAYNER, DISAPPEARING CRYPTOGRAPHY (1996).

[2] *See* BRUCE SCHNEIER, APPLIED CRYPTOGRAPHY, 4 (2d ed. 1996).

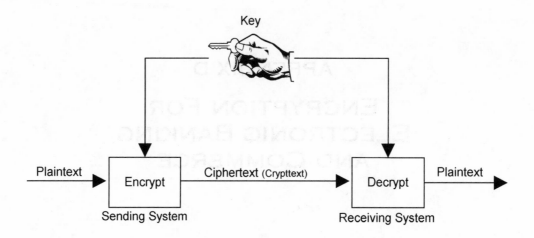

A simple example of a private key system is a letter shifting algorithm. Letter shifting algorithms encrypt each letter of a message by going n steps forward in the alphabet and renaming the original letter with that new letter. So the letter "H" encrypted using the key $n = 3$ becomes "K" and the letter "A" becomes "D." The end of the alphabet wraps around so that the letter "Z" would be encrypted with the Key 3 to be "C." Decryption is accomplished by the recipient who has received the value of n and applied it by stepping toward the beginning of the alphabet. Thus, an "L" decrypted with the $n = 3$ key reads as the letter "I."

Simple letter algorithms can encrypt words and sentences by repeating the same key for each letter, or by employing more numbers and patterns of numbers. For example, using the three number key pattern $n = 1$, $n = 2$, $n = 3$, the word 'Dogstar' would be encrypted to be 'EQJTVDS.' The more complex the pattern the harder it is to break the code. For example, breaking a code that uses a key that is only one number long can be accomplished by simply trying all possible values between 1 and 26, and working forward and backward until the answer appears.

The number of possible keys represents the outer limit of the difficulty a hacker will face in trying to break a code. Sometimes the underlying structure of an algorithm leaves patterns that hackers can use to their advantage. For instance, the classic system described here is relatively easy to break if you can guess something about the underlying test. For instance, the letter "D" is often followed by the letter "O" but rarely by the letter "Q." This information can be combined with some statistical calculations to quickly crack the code presented here.

[b] Key Management in Private Key Systems. One of the major problems with a private key system is arranging for all sides of a conversation or communication to have a copy of the key in their possession. Clearly the parties cannot merely transmit the key at the beginning of the conversation because any eavesdropper could grab a copy of the key. One solution is to distribute keys in advance on a computer readable disc through a trusted courier. This is commonly used for the most secure systems. A second solution is known as Diffie-Hellman Key Exchange. The Diffie-Hellman technique allows parties to agree upon a common key without giving this information to an eavesdropper. In Diffie-Hellman the two communicating systems A and B generate a secret value, y and z, respectively. Then from the secret value each system computes a corresponding public value, and it is then public values that the systems exchange. Using their own secret value and the received public value, each system will compute the same key. The Kerberos system presents a third solution. It uses a trusted computer on the network to maintain a secret key for each person that can be used to create a secure channel. For example, when two parties want to communicate, the Kerberos server generates a new key for the conversation and sends it to each party. The Kerberos system is widely used because it does not require licensing public key algorithms.

The description of simple private key systems illustrated how algorithms function to protect data. It is clear that a designer of digital key encryption system should pay particular attention to the length of the key and the design of the algorithm.

[c] Public Key Encryption. Public key encryption, created in the mid-1970's, offers an alternative to the private key systems described above. Its algorithms changed the approach to key management. Whereas private key encryption requires both parties to a communication to acquire a copy of the same key, public key algorithms use two keys. The first key encrypts the data. Only the second key can release and decrypt the data.

In public key encryption, the parties generate a pair of keys. One key is then placed in a public directory. The second key is stored in a secure location. To send a public key encrypted message to a party, one need only go to the public directory, find that party's published key, and use it to encrypt the message. Only the intended party will be able to decrypt the message, because only the second key of the pair, which has been securely tucked away, can open the message. For instance, if Tom wanted to send a message to Mom, he would find her public key in a directory and then use it to encrypt his message to her. Upon receipt of Tom's message, Mom will take her key from its secure location (*i.e.*, her computer or smart card) and use it to decrypt Tom's message. While she will not be able to verify who sent it unless Tom signs the message with his private key, she will know that the message was not altered during transmission if she can decrypt it.

Secret Unauthenticated Message

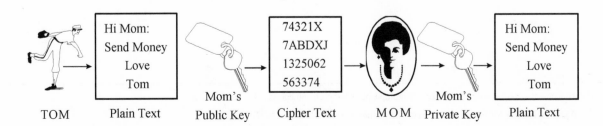

| TOM | Plain Text | Mom's Public Key | Cipher Text | MOM | Mom's Private Key | Plain Text |

An example of a simple system illustrates how a public-key system works. Assume two keys, $A = 18$ and $B = 82$. Notice that A and B add up to 100. A is the public part of the key pair. Everyone in the world can access it. B must be kept secret.

In a simplified example the document is a number, $D = 42$.[3] To send D to Mom in the encrypted form, Tom simply adds the public half of the key pair, $A = 18$, to the message. It becomes $42 + 18 = 60$. Tom can mail 60 to Mom.

Mom can decrypt the message by adding the private half of the key pair, $B = 82$, to 60 and removing the sum of the two keys, 100. That is $60 + 82 - 100 = 142 - 100 = 42$.

There are 99 possible key pairs in the system illustrated above. The number of possible pairs can be increased by increasing the size of the keys. Here, they are 2 digits long. If the keys are 8 digits long, then there are $10^8 - 1$ possible keys for the system. Popular public key encryption systems like RSA frequently use keys with 1024 bits which is equivalent to about 320 digits.[4]

This example is easy to break. A person who knows the public key, can easily recover the original message by simply subtracting the public key from 100. But real public key encryption systems use more complicated mathematics, such as logarithms, that cannot be inverted or reversed. Or at least there is no publicly known way to do so.

---

[3] If the document is long, it might be broken into multiple parts and each part encrypted in turn.

[4] *See* WARWICK FORD & MICHAEL S. BAUM, SECURE ELECTRONIC COMMERCE 110 (1997).

APPENDIX E

DIGITAL SIGNATURES AND RELATED TECHNOLOGY

[1] DIGITAL SIGNATURES — AN APPLICATION OF PUBLIC KEY ENCRYPTION.

An important use today of public key encryption is as the basis for electronic authentication and secure electronic communication through digital signatures.[1] Though similar to their namesake, the signature, they are not signatures, and digital signatures differ in the level of security they provide. Physical handwritten signatures can be forged by someone with manual dexterity and a copy of the person's signature. A digital signature cannot be copied by looking at another document that the party signed, because the signatures do not provide enough information. Forgery can occur, however, if the secret part of the public key pair falls into the wrong hands. This might be a result of bribery, theft, or computer espionage.

A document is digitally signed by first *hashing* the document using a cryptographically secure hash function. This produces a small number that is effectively unique for each document. This value is encrypted with the secret half of the key pair. The document recipient can check the signature's validity by computing the hash function and comparing it with the value obtained by decrypting the signature. If they match, the signature is considered valid.

---

[1] The best known public key algorithm is called RSA, named for its creators Ron Rivest, Adi Shamir and Len Adleman who were all at MIT when the work was done in the late 1970's. The RSA patent, as well as several other important cryptography patents, is now held by Public Key Partners which licenses the technology. One of the leading companies in this field is RSA Data Security. Most major computer companies like Apple, Sun and Microsoft license their encryption technology from RSA Data Security.

Another politically important implementation is called Pretty Good Privacy ("PGP"). This version is distributed free of charge and is often used by people for their personal protection. A commercial version of PGP which pays royalties to RSA Data Security is available.

There are many other public key encryption algorithms, but they have not been subject to either the same level of scrutiny or the same amount of economic development. Many mathematicians and scientists examined the RSA algorithm and RSA Data Security offers several cash incentives for reporting success at attacking it. This great focus of effort ensures that the algorithm has no easy to find holes.

The federal government created a Digital Signature Standard ("DSS"), which defines the Digital Signature Algorithm ("DSA") for use by all government agencies handling non-classified data. This system is a different type of public key system that can be used to create a digital signature for a document but not readily used to send secret information to someone. The government presumably hoped, perhaps, not to encourage people to send information that could not be accessed with wiretaps. Soon afterwards, Gus Simmons discovered a method for passing secrets through the choice of signatures. There are several other signature-only public key systems available and they also have this secret channel. *See* WARWICK FORD & MICHAEL S. BAUM, SECURE ELECTRONIC COMMERCE (1997).

For an extended discussion of digital signatures, see PETER WAYNER, DIGITAL CASH (1996).

[a] Blind Digital Signatures. One of the most surprising features of the digital signature technology is that it can be applied "blindly." A person can sign a computer file without having the information in the file revealed to them. A physical analogy can be constructed with carbon paper and an envelope. Place the carbon paper on the document at the location for the signature. Then place both inside an envelope and seal it. If a person signs the outside of the envelope, the pressure will place a signature on the document.

The simple insecure example of a digital signature system described in the previous Section can be extended to use blind digital signatures. In the simple example, a document $D = 42$ was signed by someone adding 18 to it. That person applying the signature would know the value of D because it was presented to them.

A blind digital signature could be created by adding a *blinding* factor before sending the document in for a signature. Let Mom create the document, D, and ask Tom for his signature upon it. In this example, another number $F = 31$ will act as Mom's blinding factor. She adds the value to D before hand forwarding it on to Tom. He gets $D + F = 73$ instead of 42. Tom looks at this value and adds the digital signature value, 18, producing 91. When Mom receives this, she removes the blinding factor $91 - F = 60$. This is the same signature that Tom would have generated, but Tom never had access to D at all.

This example works because addition is commutative. That is, you can rearrange the order of the operations and the answer still comes out the same. Many of the public key systems rely upon multiplication that is also commutative.

Key aspects of public key encryption include the following:

* Public-key encryption systems use two keys. One key is used for encrypting the message, and only the other key can be used to decrypt it.

* This removes the need for two people to establish a shared secret key through a trusted channel. Public-key systems "publish" one of the keys in a large directory.

* Digital signatures are produced when someone uses the secret half of their key pair to encrypt a message. Now anyone can decrypt the message by looking up the public half in the directory and be certain that only the person who knew the secret half could have generated the message.

* The public half of a key pair may be enclosed in a certificate. This includes at least one signature from some authority guaranteeing that the information is accurate. That is, the certificate can act like a photo identification.

* Anyone with a public key pair must guard the secrecy of one half of the pair while making the public half widely known. An institution must take great care to keep its secret half of the pair secret if it is going to be used to guarantee digital contracts or notes. However, it also must make sure that its public half is well-known and widely distributed in a way to prevent others from substituting their own version and masquerading as the institution.

[b] Key Management for Public Key Systems. Public key encryption solved an important problem faced by private key encryption systems. In a private key encryption system, each person needs a pair of keys, which means that two people need four keys altogether to hold a conversation. Tom encrypts his message to Mom using Mom's public key. When it arrives, Mom decrypts it with her private key and then encodes her response with Tom's public key. Tom uses his private key to read his mother's response.

Public key encryption removes the need for parties to exchange keys through secure channels by having the public portion of a key pair published in a public directory. It also allows multiple use of a bank's secret key with different customers. The problem of key management has not completely disappeared, however. It is important to verify that the public key in the directory is really the correct half of a key pair. For example, an attacker could substitute his own public key half for Mom's in the directory. Then Tom encrypts a message to Mom using what he thinks is her key. The result, however, is that Tom creates a message only the attacker can read.

One solution to this problem is the public-key certificate. This acts like a driver's license or any other identification document offered by a central agency. It is just the digital signature of some trusted agency applied to the public key half. So, when you look up the value of the public key half in the directory, it also comes with the signature of a trusted party that indicates that this is, in fact, the public key pair of a particular party.

The package of a public-key pair and a signature attesting to the pair's validity is known as a certificate. Sometimes a certificate might have several signatures from different groups who are often called certificate authorities.

Key management is the biggest component of system security. Digital signature systems require that the secret key be kept secret. Anyone able to access the secret key will be able to forge both documents and transactions without being detected. Traditionally, key management has proven to be the most difficult part of building secure data management systems and a bank must take every precaution to guard secret keys.

Banks should maintain separate keys for different uses. For instance, keys employing basic encryption technology with simple algorithms may be used for smaller transactions. The level of algorithm complexity can increase with the significance of the transaction. Naturally, the cost and inconvenience of assigning and changing keys should enter into the security equation. The security system design should encourage routine changes of the key material as a good technique for minimizing fraud.

Maintaining the physical security of the secret keys is an important element of the security equation. The computer that generates the keys should be located in a secure environment. Its connections with the outside world should be as minimal. Special tamper-resistant computers provide an additional level of security.

In order to isolate the secret keys from the general personal computing environment one solution is to employ tamperproof smart cards. These extra devices will generate the necessary signature without exposing the secret key to attack from arbitrary software. While the smart cards may still be vulnerable, they should be strong enough to prevent any widespread, automatic gathering of secret keys.

[2] CRYPTOGRAPHICALLY SECURE HASH FUNCTIONS

Public key-based digital signature applications have cost and efficiency implications. The encryption process nearly doubles the size of the original message. Communications and processing costs escalate as a result. Employing hash functions in the process reduces this effect.

A hash function takes a computer file and reduces it to a fixed length data item known as a message digest. The message digest, if altered or tampered with, will become a new and different digest.

It works as follows:

(1) hash function applied to file, digest created;

(2) digest encrypted with encryption key thus creating the signature;

(3) recipient recomputes digest and decrypts the signature;

(4) matching resultant values show that the originator knew the encryption key and that an unaltered message was received.

A good physical analogy for the hash function is the Vehicle Identification Number ("VIN") that is attached to all automobiles sold in the United States. This is designed to be unique for each car so you can use it as a shorthand representation of the car. There is no need to describe the paint, the interior colors, the various optional features or other facts about the car. The number is enough. This analogy is not perfect because hash functions are not guaranteed to be unique — they come as close as practically possible. Hash functions employed in the digital signature process should be hard to invert, *i.e.*, given some hash value, it is practically impossible to find a computer file that will hash to that value.[2]

---

[2] For more information about hash functions, see FORD & BAUM, *supra* note 1, at 115-16; BRUCE SCHNEIER, APPLIED CRYPTOGRAPHY, at 30-31, 351-54 (2d ed. 1996).

ABOUT THE AUTHORS
AND CONTRIBUTORS

AUTHORS

Thomas P. Vartanian is the Managing Partner of the Washington, D.C. office of Fried, Frank, Harris, Shriver & Jacobson, where he is Chairman of the Corporate Department and head of Financial Institutions Transactions and Technology (FIT²) Group. FIT² represents bank holding companies, commercial banks, savings institutions, mortgage bankers, investment banks, electronic money and technology firms, diversified financial services companies and other entities with respect to mergers and acquisitions, securities offerings, the development of innovative financial products; smart card, Internet and electronic commerce and currency products; on-line banking; regulatory/enforcement actions; litigation and a range of operating and regulatory issues.

Prior to joining Fried Frank, Mr. Vartanian was the General Counsel of the Federal Home Loan Bank Board and the Federal Savings and Loan Insurance Corporation, which also included responsibility for legal issues affecting the Federal Home Loan Bank System and the Federal Home Loan Mortgage Corporation ("Freddie Mac"). Prior to that, he was Special Assistant to the Chief Counsel of the Office of the Comptroller of the Currency and Senior Trial Litigator. He has been a Staff Counsel to the Depository Institutions Deregulation Committee, the Vice President's Task Group on Regulation of Financial Services, and the Administrative Conference of the United States.

Mr. Vartanian is an Adjunct Professor in the graduate law program at Georgetown University Law Center, where he teaches a course on 21st Century Banking Issues, and incoming Chairman of the American Bar Association's Committee on Cyberspace Law. He is a member of the Digital Signature Technical Advisory Committee of the Virginia Legislature's Joint Commission on Technology and Science, and serves on the Advisory Board of the *Electronic Banking Law and Commerce Report*. He is a member of the Information Security Exploratory Committee established by the National Information Infrastructure ("NII") Task Force of the President's National Security Telecommunications Advisory Committee ("NSTAC"). He was a legal reviewer of the Congressional Budget Office Study entitled "*Emerging Electronic Methods for Making Retail Payments*" (June 1996), and has testified before the FDIC concerning stored value cards and electronic payment systems. He is a co-author of *The Management of Risks Created by Internet-Initiated Value Transfers* a Report prepared for the Internet Council of the National Automated Clearing House Association. He is a co-author of *Survey of Selected Federal Regulatory and Legal Develoments in Electronic Financial Services,* 53 BUS. LAW. 1 (Nov. 1997). He is a regular contributor to the *American Banker* and a co-author of several books and publications, and has lectured throughout the nation on electronic financial services.

Robert H. Ledig is a partner in the Washington, D.C. office of Fried, Frank, Harris, Shriver & Jacobson and is a member of the Firm's Financial Institutions Transactions and Technology Group, specializing in financial institution-related matters. Prior to joining Fried Frank, he was an attorney in the Office of General Counsel of the Federal Home Loan Bank Board responsible for regulatory policy matters.

Mr. Ledig is co-author of *The Fair Lending Guide* and *Contracting With The RTC and FDIC*, as well as numerous articles on electronic financial products and services and financial institution matters. He has spoken widely on issues affecting financial institutions. He is a co-author of *The Management of Risks Created by Internet-Initiated Value Transfers* a Report prepared for the Internet Council of the National Automated Clearing House Association. He is a co-author of *Survey of Selected Federal Regulatory and Legal Develoments in Electronic Financial Services,* 53 BUS. LAW. 1 (Nov. 1997). He was a legal reviewer of the Congressional Budget Office Study entitled *Emerging Electronic Methods of Making Retail Payments* (June 1996). Mr. Ledig is a co-chair of the Electronic Financial Services Regulatory and Policy Forum of the American Bar Association's Joint Subcommittee on Electronic Financial Services. He is a member of the American Bar Association's Stored Value Task Force and contributed to the Task Force's report, *A Commercial Lawyer's Take on the Electronic Purse: An Analysis of Commercial Law Issues Associated with Stored Value and Electronic Money,* 52 BUS. LAW. 563 (Feb. 1997).

Mr. Ledig is a Lecturer-in-Law at George Mason University Law School. Mr. Ledig received his J.D. with honors from George Washington University Law School and his undergraduate degree with honors from Harpur College at the State University of New York at Binghamton.

Lynn Bruneau is the partner in charge of the Computer Risk Management (CRM) Group in Arthur Andersen's New York Metro region. Ms. Bruneau and her group are responsible for providing technology management and control-related support for the firm's financial audit and business advisory practice, and for its Contract Audit Services practice. The group also assists organizations in maximizing benefits from investments in information technology through cost-effective management and forensic reviews of business-related risks relating to enterprise-wide systems, information security, technology infrastructure management, electronic commerce, and Year 2000.

Prior to joining Arthur Andersen in 1996, Ms. Bruneau was a Vice President with Goldman Sachs & Co. She worked with a group of senior partners responsible for instituting an effective control program within the firm to identify and minimize reputational, operational, regulatory, and financial risks.

Before joining Goldman, Ms. Bruneau was an Information Technology Audit Partner with Coopers & Lybrand. While at C&L, she served as a member of the task force working with the Committee of Sponsoring Organizations of the Treadway Commission ("COSO") to draft and publish the *Internal Control-Integrated Framework* document. This document is used by many banks to comply with FDICIA requirements. Ms. Bruneau contributed to the *Handbook of EDP Audit* and she is a co-author of *The Management of Risks Created by Internet-Initiated Value Transfers* a Report prepared for the Internet Council of the National Automated Clearing House Association.

Ms. Bruneau frequently speaks at significant professional conferences and association gatherings, including those of the American Institute of Certified Public Accountants, Institute of Internal Auditors, and the Securities Industry Association. She received a Bachelor of Science degree in theoretical mathematics from Massachusetts Institute of Technology and has completed the coursework and thesis research for a Master of Science degree in geophysics at Pennsylvania State University. She is a charter member of the Certified Information Systems Auditor certification program and was elected in 1985 to the Academy of Women Achievers, an organization sponsored by the YWCA of New York City.

James P. Baetzhold is an associate in the Washington, D.C. office of Fried, Frank, Harris, Shriver & Jacobson. Mr. Baetzhold contributed the section of Chapter 10 discussing digital signatures and the section of Chapter 13 discussing cryptography policy. He received his undergraduate degree from the State University of New York at Buffalo (B.A., *summa cum laude*) and law degree from the University of Texas (J.D., with honors).

Nick Benvenuto is a partner in Arthur Andersen's Computer Risk Management (CRM) practice. Mr. Benvenuto is the leader of CRM's Financial Markets industry practice for the Metro New York Region. He has over 20 years of experience in technology, project management, internal and external auditing, and internal controls focused specifically in the Capital Markets, Banking, and Financial Products industries. His extensive internal audit experience includes technology audit leadership roles at a major money center bank (Chase Manhattan), an international investment bank (CS First Boston), and a major financial services institution (Prudential Investments). His experiences in these roles has included: directing and performing reviews over global systems development and implementation initiatives in the treasury, trading, and securities services, investment banking, and capital markets businesses; developing distributed computing control processes for asset management and investment management systems, and developing integrated audit approaches for front-office fixed income trading and portfolio accounting systems. Mr. Benvenuto contributed to Chapter 13.

Mr. Benvenuto was also a senior manager in the Information Technology Audit Services practice focused on Financial Services at another "Big 6" accounting firm. A selection of his experiences in external technology auditing and controls consulting includes: performing a review of the technical IT audit groups and the audit approaches in place at two merging New York money center institutions to identify best practices and skill sets; managing an integrated control assessment and security review of a major investment bank's compliance and surveillance systems required by the SEC, and; managing a security review of a major investment bank's internal and external treasury network links to its primary money center correspondent banks.

Mr. Benvenuto has a wide range of experience covering various technology environments including mainframes, distributed client/server environments, and Local Area Networks (LANs). He has given presentations on all aspects of technology auditing, the most notable of which was a presentation to the Securities Industry Association's Internal Auditors Division annual conference on "Managing your Technology Risks in a Distributed Processing Environment" and the American Institute of Certified Public Accountants Banking Industry Conference. He was a recognized contributor to the "Handbook of EDP Audit."

Mr. Benvenuto is a graduate of St. Bonaventure University. He is also a Certified Information Systems Auditor (CISA), Certified Data Processor (CDP), Certified Systems Professional (CSP) and a Series 7 Registered Representative.

Dan Carson is a consultant in the Computer Risk Management practice of Arthur Andersen's Metro New York Office. Mr. Carson's primary areas of practice include the banking and capital markets industries. He has assessed a variety of technology platforms including client-server, mainframes, networks, and internets. He contributed to Chapter 13.

Prior to joining Arthur Andersen, Mr. Carson worked at the White House, U.S. Congress, and a regional CPA firm. He holds a Bachelors of Arts degree in Economics from the University of Maryland and a Master of Science degree in Accounting from Strayer College of Washington, D.C.

Beth H. Colleye is an associate in the Washington, D.C. office of Fried, Frank, Harris, Shriver & Jacobson. Ms. Colleye contributed the securities discussion in Chapter 14. Before becoming an attorney, she worked for three years as a Legislative Assistant to Congressman Howard L. Berman (D-CA.) where she covered technology policy, among other issues. She received her undergraduate degree from Columbia University (B.A.) and her law degree from University of Chicago (J.D.).

Alison C. Conover is an associate in the Washington, D.C. office of Fried, Frank, Harris, Shriver & Jacobson. Ms. Conover served as the project coordinator and editor of *21st Century Money, Banking and Commerce*. She also contributed Chapters 5, 9 and 17 and substantial portions of Chapters 2, 4, and 6-8, 10-11. She is the co-author of *Survey of Selected Federal Regulatory and Legal Developments in Electronic Financial Services* 53 BUS. LAW. 1 (Nov. 1997). She received her undergraduate degree from Duke University (A.B.) and her law degree from Washington & Lee University School of Law (J.D.).

Paul H. Falon is a partner in the Washington, D.C. office of Fried, Frank, Harris, Shriver & Jacobson. Mr. Falon specializes in insurance industry regulatory and transactional work. He contributed to the insurance discussion in Chapter 14. He is an editorial reviewer for the *Journal of Insurance Regulation*, a co-author of *Insurer Insolvencies Interstate Cooperation*, and has lectured on reinsurance at the University of Connecticut School of Law's Annual Insurance Institute. He received his B.A., M.A., and J.D. from the University of Michigan.

Robert M. Fisher was an associate with Fried, Frank, Harris, Shriver & Jacobson. Mr. Fisher contributed Chapter 3. In addition to being a practicing corporate attorney, he is also an economist with a Ph.D. from Duke University.

Kevin Foley leads the Customer Satisfaction Group at Creative Solutions International, Inc., an international direct response advertising agency and consultancy. Creative Solution's clients range from the United Kingdom, Canada, the United States, and the Pacific Rim. Mr. Foley has over thirteen years experience in the direct response advertising, financial services, and telephony industries. He has held senior management positions for organizations such as NatWest Bank, US West Communications, First-Omni Bank — an Allied Irish subsidiary, and Mellon Bank. Kevin was a member of the Smart Card Forum and has served on MasterCard's Consumer Card Marketing Committee. He contributed portions of Chapters 3 and 16. Mr. Foley is a frequent speaker at various industry forums. He received his undergraduate degree from Mount Saint Mary's College.

Harry M. Gruber was as a summer associate in 1997 and will join the Washington, D.C. office of Fried, Frank, Harris, Shriver & Jacobson in the fall of 1998. Mr. Gruber has authored *Adding a Nondiverse Party Pursuant to Federal Rule of Civil Procedure 25(c),* 65 GEO. WASH. L. REV. 633 (1997) and *E-mail: The Attorney-Client Privilege Applied,* 66 GEO. WASH. L. REV. (forthcoming Spring 1998). He contributed portions of Chapter 19. He received his undergraduate degree from University of Michigan and will receive his law degree from the George Washington University Law School in 1998.

Anthony S. Higgins was a staff attorney in the Washington, D.C. office of Fried, Frank, Harris, Shriver & Jacobson. Mr. Higgins contributed portions of Chapters 14-16 and 19. He is the author of *Professional Responsibility-Attorney Client Privilege: Are Expectations of Privacy Reasonable for Communications Broadcast via Cordless or Cellular Telephones?* 24:2 U. BALT. L. REV. 273 (Spring 1995). He received his undergraduate degree from Michigan State University (B.S.), his law degree from the University of Baltimore School of Law (J.D., *cum laude*), and his masters degree in the Regulation of Securities and Financial Institutions from Georgetown University (LL.M., with distinction).

Jay R. Kraemer is a corporate partner in Fried, Frank, Harris, Shriver and Jacobson's Washington, D.C. office. Mr. Kraemer's practice is concentrated in nuclear, environmental, export control, and high technology licensing matters, with a national and international scope. He contributed to the discussion of U.S. cryptography in Chapter 13.

Mr. Kraemer's practice has included representing clients before the Nuclear Regulatory Commission in license transfers and decommissioning funding and rulemaking, and in the acquisition of U.S. companies engaged in various facets of nuclear supply. He has also assisted clients in understanding and obtaining requisite approvals for exports from the U.S. (and re-exports abroad) of dual-use equipment, materials, and technology. Since 1974, Mr. Kraemer has represented clients in adjudicatory hearings/NPDES permit hearings before Region 2 and 3 of the EPA. He has also been active in legislative activity to protect clients' interests under the Clean Water Act and the Export Administration Act.

Mr. Kraemer received his B.A., with Distinction, International Affairs, School of International Affairs, The George Washington University, and his J.D., with Highest Honors, from The George Washington University, National Law Center. Prior to joining the firm, he served as Law Clerk to the Honorable James R. Miller, Jr., U.S. District Judge, District of Maryland. Since 1996, he has been an Adjunct Professor of Law at the Georgetown University Law Center.

Joel Lanz is an Experienced Manager in Arthur Andersen's (AA) Computer Risk Management (CRM) Practice. Mr. Lanz is the lead CRM manager serving AA's Metro New York Financial Institution clients. His technology and audit consulting experience includes designing and assessing information reliability, effectiveness, and security strategies for a variety of financial service environments including community, regional, international, and money-center banks. He is a member of the firm's Global Electronic Commerce Assurance Action Team and leads the team's Payment Systems Solutions Task Force. He contributed to Chapter 13.

Mr. Lanz previously instructed technology and auditing contingency planning courses for New York University's graduate program in Performance and Information Systems Auditing. He was a contributor to *The Management of Risks Created by Internet-Initiated Value Transfers*, a report prepared for the Internet Council of the National Automated Clearing House Association (NACHA). Joel has spoken at significant professional conferences including the Information Systems Audit and Control Association's International Conference and the American Institute of Certified Public Accountants Security Industry Conference. Published contributions have appeared in professionally recognized journals such as the *IS Audit & Control Journal*.

Mr. Lanz joined AA from the Chase Manhattan Bank, N.A., where he was a Vice President and Audit Manager. Previously he was a Manager in the Management Consulting Services Division of another "Big" and a Senior EDP Auditor at The Equitable. He holds a Bachelor of Business Administration degree in Accounting and a Masters of Business Administration degree in Information Systems, both from Pace University. He maintains a certification as a Certified Public Accountant (CPA), Certified Information Systems Auditor (CISA), Chartered Financial Consultant (ChFC), and Certified Fraud Examiner (CFE).

Charles W. Lockyer, Jr. is an associate in the Washington, D.C. office of Fried, Frank, Harris, Shriver & Jacobson. He has extensive experience in commercial lending, having served as a senior executive officer at two banks. He is a past member of Robert Morris Associates, the national association of bank credit and lending officers, and has been a speaker at its national convention on the emerging role of thrifts in corporate lending. He contributed to Chapters 6 and 7.

Mr. Lockyer has served as an Adjunct Professor, teaching courses on accounting and law at Georgetown University Law Center and the George Washington University National Law Center. Mr. Lockyer received his A.B. with honors from Fordham University and a M.A. and Ph.D. from Princeton University. He is a graduate of the Georgetown University Law Center.

Eugene E. Mueller is an associate in the New York office of Fried, Frank, Harris, Shriver & Jacobson. Mr. Mueller has served as an alternate on the Insurance Law Committee of the Business Law Section of the California State Bar and is a member of California Insurance Counsel. Mr. Mueller is the author of *Speaking with One Voice: Constitutional Failure of State Insurance Government Ownership Statutes*, Nat'l. Ins. Law. Rev., vol. 6, no. 3 (*repr.* 26 Univ. of San Francisco L. Rev. 654). He received his undergraduate degree (B.A.) and graduate degrees (J.D./M.B.A.) from the University of Southern California.

Richard E. Salisbury is an associate in Washington, D.C. office of Fried, Frank, Harris, Shriver & Jacobson. He contributed the tax discussion in Chapter 10. He is a graduate of Brown University (A.B.) and the Columbia University School of Law (J.D.), where he was a Kent Scholar and a Harlan Stone Moot Court semi-finalist.

Peter H. Schwartz is an associate in the Washington D.C. office of Fried, Frank, Harris, Shriver & Jacobson, where he practices in the areas of banking and securities law. Mr. Schwartz is the co-author of a chapter entitled *Protecting the On-Line Investor and the Markets: SEC & SRO Activities*, contained in *Securities in the Electronic Age: A Practical Guide* (Glasser LegalWorks, forthcoming 1998) and has co-written articles on electronic commerce which have appeared in *The Journal of Electronic Commerce and Banking* and in *wallstreetlawyer.com*. He is a co-author of *The Management of Risks Created by Internet-Initiated Value Transfers,* a report prepared for the Internet Council of the National Automated Clearing House Association. He contributed the banking portions of Chapter 14. He received his undergraduate degree from Princeton University and graduate degree from the Massachusetts Institute of Technology (M.C.P/M.S.R.E), and Columbia University School of Law (J.D.).

Jeffrey D. Sullivan is an associate in the New York office of Fried, Frank, Harris, Shriver & Jacobson. Mr. Sullivan contributed the patent discussion in Chapter 18. He received his undergraduate degree in Physics from Georgetown University (B.S.) and law degree from the University of Texas School of Law (J.D.).

Jennifer Tipsord was an associate in the New York office of Fried, Frank, Harris, Shriver & Jacobson. Ms. Tipsord contributed the trademark and copyright discussions in Chapter 18. She received her undergraduate degree in Biomedical Engineering from Northwestern University (B.S.) and law degree from Hofstra University School of Law (J.D.).

Leila A. Tredemeyer was a project attorney in the Washington, D.C. office of Fried, Frank, Harris, Shriver & Jacobson. She served as an editor and marketing coordinator of *21st Century Money, Banking & Commerce*. Ms. Tredemeyer contributed to Chapters 2 and 5. She received her undergraduate degree from University of Rochester (B.A., *cum laude*) and her law degree from Georgetown University Law Center (J.D.).

Peter Wayner is a consultant living in Baltimore, Maryland who specializes in computer security and digital transaction systems. Mr. Wayner contributed to Chapter 13 and served as a consultant on the work. He has written seven books including *Digital Cash, Disappearing Cryptography*, and *Digital Copyright Protection*. He is a frequent contributor to BYTE magazine and the New York Times. His received his undergraduate degree in mathematics from Princeton University (A.B.) and doctorate in computer science from Cornell University (Ph.D.).

Maxim H. Waldbaum was a Partner in the New York office of Fried, Frank, Harris, Shriver & Jacobson. He contributed to Chapter 18. Mr. Waldbaum received a Bachelor of Science in Electrical Engineering from Rutgers University, a Master of Science in Engineering from the Moore School of Electrical Engineering, University of Pennsylvania, and a law degree, *cum laude*, Order of the Coif, from New York University School of Law.

Edward B. Whittemore is an associate in the Washington, D.C. office of Fried, Frank, Harris, Shriver & Jacobson Mr. Whittemore contributed Chapter 12 and portions of Chapters 10, 15 & 16. He is a member of the American Bar Association's Joint Subcommittee on Electronic Financial Services and its Task Force on Stored Value Cards. He contributed to the Task Force's report, *A Commercial Lawyer's Take on the Electronic Purse: An Analysis of Commercial Law Issues Associated with Stored Value Cards and Electronic Money,* 52 BUS. LAW. 653 (Feb. 1997). He is a co-author of *The Management of Risks Created by Internet-Initiated Value Transfers,* a report prepared for the Internet Council of the National Automated Clearing House Association. Mr. Whittemore is the co-author of *Beyond the Blue Horizon: Will the SEC be Able to Apply Its Principles of Extraterritorial Regulation to Securities Activities on the Global Internet?,* published in the L.A. LAWYER in September 1996, as well as a co-author of various articles on electronic commerce and banking in the *Electronic Banking Law and Commerce Report*. Mr. Whittemore received his undergraduate degree from Dartmouth (B.A.) and law degree from The National Law Center, George Washington University (J.D., with honors).